First presidential primary

ME. 4

French-Canadian Politics

N.H. 4

Governor Madeleine Kunin

VT. 3

First state to require literacy test

Anti-Abortion

MASS. 13

Shays's Rebellion

JFK born here

Concentration of educational institutions

BOSTON

N.Y. 36

ALBANY

POUGHKEEPSIE

First Written Constitution

R.I. 4

BUFFALO

FDR lived here

HARTFORD

I Support The President

Jack Kemp's District

West Point

CONN. 8

Stayed away from Constitutional Convention

Lower Taxes

NEW YORK CITY

George Washington inaugurated here

Has over 3 million voters Home of *The New York Times*

Let's Be Sensible

Job Safety Now

Coal Politics

Give A Hoot, Don't Pollute

PA. 25

Constitutional Convention 1787

N.J. 16

ERA

me of 7 ublican sidents

PHILADELPHIA

TRENTON

Bill Bradley, Tax Reform Leader

Atlantic Ocean

PITTSBURGH

Center for chemical industries

DEL. 3

Revenue –Sharing

Ban Strip– Mining

Curb The Bureaucracy

First presidential convention

Lower Taxes

Reduce Regulation!

W.VA. 6

Coal Politics

VA. 12

han ernor

RICHMOND

MD. 10

Strengthen The Congress

Birthplace of 8 Presidents, including George Washington

Annapolis Convention

Pro-Clean Air!

N.C. 13

Black majority here

onal Republican politics mountains here

Tobacco & Textile Politics

Granted vote for President by 23rd Amendment

Government By The People

D.C. 3

"Home Rule" granted for elections in 1974

S.C. 8

Jesse Jackson born here

Send a message to Washington

Decentralization!

No More Vietnams!

-yr-olds st given e here

Consumer Protection

ains, home of mmy Carter

A Guaranteed Income For All

No Nukes Is Good Nukes

Sunbelt country- rising Republican strength?

CAPE CANAVERAL

Statehood for Puerto Rico!

Stormy Politics

FLA. 21

Senior Citizen politics

No More "Nukes"

MIAMI

National Version

GOVERNMENT BY THE PEOPLE

Thirteenth Alternate Edition—1989 Printing

James MacGregor Burns
Williams College

J.W. Peltason
University of California, Irvine

Thomas E. Cronin
The Colorado College

Prentice Hall, Englewood Cliffs, New Jersey 07632

Library of Congress Cataloging-in-Publication Data

Burns, James MacGregor.
   Government by the people/James MacGregor Burns, J. W. Peltason,
Thomas E. Cronin. —13th alternate ed., national version.
     p. cm.
   Bibliography
   Includes index.
   ISBN 0-13-360876-X
   1. United States—Politics and government. I. Peltason, J. W.
(Jack Walter), (date). II. Cronin, Thomas E. III. Title.
JK274.B853 1989
320.973—dc19   88-39176
                                  CIP

Acquisitions editor: Karen Horton
Editorial/production supervision: Barbara DeVries
Interior and cover design: Judith A. Matz-Coniglio
Cover photos: Clockwise from top: Tommy Noonan/
Uniphoto; S. M. Wakefield; R. Maiman/
Sygma; background, S. M. Wakefield
Manufacturing buyer: Peter Havens
Page makeup: Meryl Poweski
Photo editor: Lorinda Morris-Nantz
Photo research: Caroline Anderson

Chapter opening photo credits: page 1, Independence National Historic Park, Philadelphia; page 41, Steve Harrison; page 66, Anne Ricigliano; page 94, UPI/Bettmann Newsphotos; page 124, Steve Northrup/Black Star; page 151, Dennis Brack/Black Star; page 171, Owen Franken/Stock, Boston; page 188, Jim Clark; page 216, Dennis Brack/Black Star; page 240, Robert Phillips; page 257, S.M. Wakefield; page 281, R. Lee, Uniphoto; page 313, Bill Fitz-Patrick/The White House; page 341, Arnie Sachs/Consolidated News Pictures; page 363, UPI/Bettmann Newsphotos; page 391, Linda Bartlett/Photo Researchers; page 422, Terry Ashe/Uniphoto; page 440, Dennis Brack/Black Star; page 464, Library of Congress; page 490, Internal Revenue Service; page 508, Stephen L. Feldman/Photo Researchers; page 535, Bill Gillette/Stock, Boston; page 555, New York Convention & Visitors Bureau.

Printed in the United States of America
10 9 8 7 6 5 4 3 2 1

ISBN   0-13-360876-X

Prentice-Hall International (UK) Limited, *London*
Prentice-Hall of Australia Pty. Limited, *Sydney*
Prentice-Hall Canada Inc., *Toronto*
Prentice-Hall Hispanoamericana, S. A., *Mexico*
Prentice-Hall of India Private Limited, *New Delhi*
Prentice-Hall of Japan, Inc., *Tokyo*
Simon & Schuster Asia Pte. Ltd., *Singapore*
Editora Prentice-Hall do Brasil, Ltda., *Rio de Janeiro*

Contents

5
Equal Rights under the Law   94

6
Rights to Life, Liberty, and Property   124

Part Three/The People in Politics

7
Interest Groups: The Politics of Faction   151

8
Movements: The Politics of Conflict   171

9
Parties: Decline and Renewal?   188

10
Beliefs and Ballots: Public Opinion and Voting   216

17

Bureaucrats: The Real Power? 391

Part Five/The Politics of National Policy

18

Making Public Policy 422

19

Making Foreign Policy 440

20

Providing for the Common Defense 464

21

The Politics of Taxing and Spending 490

Acknowledgments

We are pleased to acknowledge the help of several political scientists and colleagues who shared their ideas and suggestions with us. We thank Ted Craig, Harriett Speegle, and especially David Wagner who served as research assistants and made important suggestions throughout the book. We are in debt again to Ann B. Armstrong for her splendid proofreading, and to Doris Creakman for proofreading and assistance in helping us prepare this edition. A special thanks to William E. Sudduth and the Williams College Library staff for their valuable assistance, and to Johnny Tyler for his contributions.

Several scholars provided assistance, and although they bear no responsibility for our interpretation and writing, they have helped make this Thirteenth Alternate Edition a better book. We thank Gerald Benjamin, Elmer Cornwell, Louis Garinger, Donald S. Vaughn, and Jeff Weill, as well as the Prentice Hall reviewers:

Judith Best, *State University College at Cortland*
David Caputo, *Purdue University*
Rita Cooley, *New York University*
Robert DiClerico, *West Virginia University*
Pat Dunham, *Duquesne University*
James Foster, *Oregon State University*
John Geer, *Arizona State University*
Walter Giles, *Georgetown University*
George J. Gordon, *Illinois State University*
Kim Hunt, *University of Texas—Arlington*
Michael Johnston, *Colgate University*
Landis Jones, *University of Louisville*
David Kozak, *National War College*
Rosemary Allen Little, *Princeton University*
William Lunch, *Oregon State University*
J. N. Lybbert, *Tallahassee Community College*
Karen J. Maschke, *Oakland University*
Maureen Moakley, *Rutgers University*

Robert K. Peters III, *Tyler Junior College*
Mark Petracca, *University of California, Irvine*
Sue Tolleson Rinehart, *Texas Tech University*
Alan Rosenthal, *Rutgers University*
Stephen Schechter, *Russell Sage College*
William A. Schultze, *San Diego State University*
Jeffrey A. Segal, *State University of New York at Stony Brook*
John Shockley, *W. Illinois University*
Stephen A. Snyder, *University of Wisconsin—Stout*
Richard Tobin, *State University of New York at Buffalo*
Jerold Waltman, *University of Southern Mississippi*
Bruce A. Williams, *University of Kentucky*

Gifted professionals at Prentice Hall once again made this book possible and contributed greatly to its improvement. Production editor Barbara DeVries gave critical advice, assistance, and support at every stage of the process, and Colette Conboy provided continuing support. The professional guidance, advice, and encouragement of Susan Willig, Karen Horton, and Ann Marie McCarthy have been invaluable.

Barbara Heir coordinated supplemental materials; copy editors Louisa Hellegers and Martha Williams patiently and gently improved our prose; and Terri Peterson planned and coordinated marketing strategy. The talents of Judy Matz-Coniglio,

Lorinda Morris-Nantz, Mary Helen Fitzgerald, Peter Havens, and Meryl Poweski also played an important role in the production of this edition.

We call your attention to the expanded supplements package available with the Alternate Edition of *Government By The People*. Raymond L. Lee and Dorothy A. Palmer have written the *Study Guide to Government By The People*, designed to provide students an opportunity to participate more directly in the learning process. An *Interactive Study Guide* is also available for the IBM-PC and Apple-II series.

These authors have also prepared the *Instructor's Manual*, available from Prentice Hall to all teachers using this text. Also available is a revised and up-to-date *Test Item File* package, prepared by Barbara Feinberg. Test preparation is available both through the Prentice Hall phone-in testing service (800-526-0485) and on Diploma software for the IBM-PC and Apple-II. *Gradebook/Class Record File* is also available free to adopters. It allows the instructor to keep class records, compute class statistics, average grades, print graphs and sort by student name.

Professor Robert D. Loevy of The Colorado College has revised and expanded his series of educational microcomputer learning programs especially prepared for use with this Alternate Edition of *Government By The People*, designed as an additional way for students to explore and grasp the principles of our constitutional system. New to this Alternate Edition of *Government By The People* is a set of four color transparencies which is available free upon adoption. A set of 12 half hour audiocassettes funded by the Annenberg/Corporation for Public Broadcasting project is also available free to adopters. The tapes feature distinguished leaders and scholars who are actively engaged in national political life and provide students with exposure to varying approaches to political thought. There are also high quality, award winning videos available to qualified adopters of at least 100 copies of the book. In addition, a copy of the Constitution will be provided for every student who purchases a new copy of the text. Your Prentice Hall sales representative can provide information on all the material mentioned above.

JAMES MACGREGOR BURNS
Williams College
Williamstown, MA 01267

J. W. PELTASON
University of California, Irvine
Irvine, CA 92717

THOMAS E. CRONIN
The Colorado College
Colorado Springs, CO 80903

January 1989

P.S. Please point out errors and send comments, suggestions, and advice to us at our addresses above or addressed to us c/o Political Science Editor, Prentice Hall, Englewood Cliffs, New Jersey 07632.

Authors' Note

You will be reading this book after the 1988 elections when the American people "spoke" at the polls and elected a new president to lead them during the twentieth century's last decade. The legacy of the Reagan years is still very much with us as President George Bush and his cabinet and new officeholders in both elected branches tackle the problems confronting our nation and strive to make our government by the people work.

This special 1989 edition of *Government By The People* helps explain the 1988 elections and the key policies and processes of contemporary government. We have included new material on controversies over Supreme Court nominations, the Iran-contra affair, the Pentagon scandals, and the changing role of political parties in American elections. Now that we have celebrated the bicentennial of the drafting and ratification of the American Constitution, we are observing the bicentennials of the first presidency, the first session of Congress, the first session of the Supreme Court, and the drafting of the Bill of Rights.

We have placed the text of the Constitution of the United States of America itself near the start of this book (directly after Chapter 1) because that Constitution still governs us today. The framers of the Constitution were political and intellectual giants. Nonetheless, just as the Constitution's birthday cake may have sagged under the weight of its 200 candles, perhaps our constitutional system is sagging under the weight of its two centuries as well.

In short, we invite you to *celebrate* our constitutional system as citizens but at the same time to cerebrate the system—study it, understand it, evaluate it—as political scientists.

The authors are political scientists, or, more simply, students of politics. *Politics* is the method by which people live together, decide how to meet their basic needs, solve common problems, protect themselves against threats both foreign and domestic, even seek to realize the "good life." Briefly, politics is the process of "who gets what, when, and how." Clearly, this process involves conflict as people compete for what they can "get." *Government* seeks to resolve these conflicts in a way that enhances a nation's values and purposes.

In the broader sense *political science* is the study of politics and government. Political scientists seek to answer such questions as: What are the fundamental rules by which conflicts are settled? How are the rules changed? How do people think and behave politically? Who votes, who fails to vote, and why? What, if anything, do elections decide? Who has "clout" in government, and why? How does all this shape the final outcome—the policies that take money from us, give some of it back in a different form, shape our daily lives?

What can you learn from political science that you cannot learn from carefully reading the daily paper and news magazines? Political scientists seek to understand the *whole system* of government by analyzing how the interconnected elements relate to one another. We take up the Constitution in one chapter, Congress in another, the media in still another, and so on. But we are determined to understand how the parts interlock in a dynamic and changing system. Just as a skilled auto mechanic may understand how one part of a car works but perhaps not fully comprehend the physics and chemistry of the vehicle as a whole, so may a casual observer of American politics miss the ongoing interplay of the whole system. This kind of understanding is the job of the political scientist.

Political scientists, then, want to formulate theories about the why and the how of political life. They also want to ask, "So what?" Aristotle called the study of politics the "queen of sciences." Machiavelli, another political theorist, examined political systems and advised princes on how to secure and keep power, and on how to govern. Hobbes, Rousseau, Locke, and Montesquieu were grand political philosophers who also influenced the framers of the Constitution. So were Americans John Adams, Thomas Jefferson, and James Madison.

In this 1989 edition we invite you to undertake a great voyage of discovery of one of the supreme intellectual achievements in the history of the West—our Constitution. But as you study, keep in mind that not everything the founders invented or created was right. And certain parts of the Constitution worked less well than others. Today, as a result, we need students to become modern-day framers, persons who are committed to liberty but who also realize that after 200 years the problems and opportunities of government may have changed.

So, as we enter the 1990s, let us honor the framers of the United States Constitution and the Bill of Rights by doing what they would do if they were here today. For many, if not most, of the decisions they made then are still debated today. The electoral college, presidential and congressional war power, the veto power, terms of office, impeachment, the pardon power, federalism, freedom of speech, due process, cruel and unusual punishment, and many more of their actions were compromises that the original framers presumed future generations might alter or modify.

Thus, please accept our invitation to serve as a delegate or framer of the Constitutional Convention of 1787 and the first session of Congress—that are, in many ways, still in session. Then, as you read the following pages, seek to understand our political system and assess it from the viewpoint of a modern-day reframer. Raise tough questions and suggest ways to make our government by the people even more effective.

James MacGregor Burns

J. W. Peltason

Thomas E. Cronin

The Making of a Republic—1787

Late in 1786 messengers rode into George Washington's plantation at Mt. Vernon with alarming news. Some farmers in western Massachusetts, crushed by debts and taxes, were rebelling against foreclosures, forcing judges out of their courtrooms, and freeing debtors from their jails. Washington was appalled. Ten years before, he had been leading Americans in a patriots' war against British redcoats. Now Americans were fighting Americans!

"What, gracious God, is man!" Washington exclaimed, that he should be so fickle. "It is but the other day, that we were shedding our blood to obtain the Constitution of our choice." If government cannot check these disorders, he wrote to his friend James Madison, "what security has a man for life, liberty, or property?" It was obvious that without a stronger constitution, "thirteen Sovereignties pulling against each other, and all tugging at the federal head will soon bring ruin on the whole."

Not all Americans reacted as Washington did to the farmers' uprising, which came to be known as **Shays's Rebellion.*** Some sided with the rebels. When Abigail Adams, wife of the American minister in London, John Adams, sent the news to Thomas Jefferson, the minister in Paris, the Virginian replied: "I like a little rebellion now and then." Later Jefferson added, "The tree of liberty must be refreshed from time to time with the blood of patriots and tyrants. It is its natural manure."

At the time most informed Americans probably agreed much more with Washington than with Jefferson. They knew that their struggling little republic was surrounded by the big and hungry powers of Europe—Spanish to the south, in Florida; the French to the west, in the Mississippi Valley; and the British to the north, in Canada. These Americans remembered that in 1776 the Declaration of Independence had proclaimed the unalienable rights of life, liberty, and the pursuit of happiness. But how, they asked, could these rights be protected in a small nation vulnerable to attack from outside, divided into thirteen independent states, and wracked by internal disorder?

Shays's Rebellion petered out after the farmers attacked an arsenal and were

* Words in boldface type throughout this text are defined in the Glossary at the end of the book.

cut down by cannon fire. It was not much of a rebellion, but it sent a stab of fear into the established leadership. It also acted as a catalyst, precipitating the decision to call a convention to meet in Philadelphia in the summer of 1787. Its purpose: to build a stronger national government that would be truly able to protect "life, liberty, and property."

WHAT KIND OF CONSTITUTION?

In 1986 we celebrated a very special Fourth of July: The refurbished and glittering Statue of Liberty was re-presented to the American people and to lovers of liberty around the world. Once again we had a grand spectacle of fireworks over southern Manhattan, magnificent ships parading up and down the lower Hudson River, and fine television oratory by President Reagan and other notables. But did Americans learn anything about *liberty* itself—its slow development over the centuries, its many dimensions, its protection and enhancement, its relationship to government and politics, its applicability to the rest of the world, especially to the impoverished Third World?

Our current commemoration of the bicentennial era of the **Constitution** calls for hard thought and analysis, and not merely fireworks. The great charter of 1787 is a "living constitution" that centrally influences "who gets what, when, and how" in American society today; hence, it is still a subject of controversy. Too, the Constitution—and our whole constitutional system—is a most complex affair, and we ought to understand what we celebrate. It might also be helpful for younger persons today, who may live until the mid-twenty-first century, to evaluate how a great instrument of government invented for the eighteenth century can meet the enormous pressures and crises we can expect to arise in the future.

This, and virtually all the following chapters, deal with key aspects of these problems, because a constitutional system embraces the whole range of laws, institutions, politics, and procedures that make up our political universe today. But two elements of the Constitution of 1787 are so crucial that they need to be highlighted at the very start: the division of powers between the national and state governments, and the separation of powers among the legislative, executive, and judicial branches.

Division of powers means **federalism**. Virtually all nations divide power between the central and regional governments. Federalism is unique because power is not granted by the central government to the states, and hence cannot be withdrawn from them. Rather, a constitution divides the powers—delegating some to the national government and reserving others to the states. This arrangement seems to work most of the time. But will it hold up during the twenty-first century under intense pressures to centralize authority in the national government?

Separation of powers means more than allocating legislative powers to the Congress, executive powers to the president, and judicial powers to the Supreme Court and other federal courts. It also means giving each branch constitutional and political *independence*, and *checks and balances* that allow the various branches to delay or block the actions of the other branches. This was the supreme creation of the framers in 1787. Although the concept was not new, the framers built the idea into a system of government so ingeniously that it has become a lasting and central part of our system. But again the question arises: Can a governmental system so divided cope with the challenges that lie ahead?

Most other democracies operate on a principle quite different from checks and balances—that of majority rule, through a parliamentary system. Typically, if one party or a coalition of parties wins a majority of seats in parliament, that majority wins control of the government. This has been true, for example, of the

Under the leadership of Daniel Shays, a group of farmers forcibly restrained the Massachusetts courts from foreclosing their mortgages. The uprising was known as Shays's Rebellion. (*The Granger Collection*)

Constitutional Checks on Public Officials

Written Constitution
Regular elections
Separation of powers
Federalism
Judicial review
Minority rights
Right to petition for redress of grievances
Impeachment process
Rule of law, making public officials subject to criminal prosecution
Freedom of the press to criticize public officials

(conservative) Thatcher government in Britain and the (socialist) Mitterand government in France. The victorious party, the majority party in the parliament, the cabinet, and the prime minister are fused together for joint decision and action, though of course there are many variations in practice.

Contrast the American system. It was carefully designed to delay or block majority action, for even though the framers wanted energetic and competent government, they did not want the "masses"—people like those led by Daniel Shays—to take control of the government. Thus, they fixed it so that a majority **faction** cannot just win control of the House of Representatives. Rather, such a faction must, in a series of elections, win control of the Senate and of the presidency—and perhaps ultimately of the Supreme Court. Further, countless antimajoritarian devices have subsequently been built into the system—for example, the right to **filibuster** bills to death in the Senate.

Is this the "government of the people, by the people, and for the people" that Lincoln celebrated in his Gettysburg address? Some critics contend that our constitutional system is fundamentally undemocratic, antimajoritarian, and antipopular—that the framers were elitists who deliberately designed a system to protect their property. Defenders of the system reply that in the long run the people do control their government. Congress, the presidency, and even the judiciary—in fact all the checks and balances—merely cushion the impact of popular demands and passions; they cannot ultimately prevent the public will from being carried out. Moreover, they claim, the system protects minority rights—and minority rights are just as important as majority rule.[1]

Obviously some crucial questions are involved in celebrating the 200th birthday of the Constitution. As we note, these questions involve some of our most basic goals and values, including liberty, equality, and justice. We can hardly hope today to match the wisdom of the framers, one of the most talented groups in Western history. But perhaps we can match their commitment to rigorous study and reasoned analysis. The first step is to define relevant terms with care.

A Republic or a Democracy?

The American political system can be called either a constitutional republic or a constitutional democracy. Is there any real difference? The term *democracy* comes from two Greek roots: *demos*, the people, and *kratis*, authority. The word was used by the Athenians to mean government by the many, as contrasted with government by the few (**oligarchy**) or by one (**autocracy**). At one time democracy meant only the kind of *direct* or *pure* democracy used in some Greek city-states, or in New England town meetings today, in which all citizens may take part in making laws. Today democracy is more likely to mean a **representative democracy**—or, in Plato's term, a *republic*—in which all the people do not actually make the laws or administer them but choose the ones who do.

The framers preferred to use the term *republic* to avoid any confusion with pure democracy. For them democracy meant mob rule, and demagogues' appealing to the "masses."

Here we define **democracy** or **republic** to mean a system of government in which those who have the authority to make decisions (that have the force of law) acquire and retain this authority either directly or indirectly as the result of winning free elections in which the great majority of adult citizens are allowed to participate.

[1] For treatments of this question, see John Patrick Diggins, "Power and Authority in American History: The Case of Charles A. Beard and his Critics," *American Historical Review* (October 1981), pp. 701–30; James MacGregor Burns, *The Vineyard of Liberty* (Knopf, 1982), chaps. 1 and 2; and Robert A. Goldwin and William A. Schambra, eds., *How Democratic is the Constitution?* (American Enterprise Institute, 1981).

Constitutional Government

Ours is not only a democratic system; it is a *constitutional* one as well. Although these two concepts are related, they are also different. Democracy refers to how power is *acquired* and *retained*. Constitutionalism refers to how power is *granted*, *dispersed*, and *limited*. A government can be constitutional without being democratic, as it was in seventeenth-century England. It can also be democratic without being constitutional, as it was in Athens at the time of Pericles. All governments have constitutions in the sense of agreed-upon ways by which they proceed. But the term **constitutional government** now has a more restricted meaning: government which enforces clearly recognized and regularly applied limits on the powers of those who govern. By this definition Great Britain, Canada, and the United States are constitutional democracies, but the Soviet Union is not, for there are few popular checks on the powers of Soviet rulers.

Our founders created a system in which the first great safeguard against abuse of authority was to be reliance on the *people*—the democratic principle. But they also established a variety of checks on the power of officeholders, recognized and routinely enforced limits on what public officials—even those elected by the people—may do.

In the chapters that follow we look at our constitutional republic in greater detail. It is a complex system, difficult to describe and even harder to operate. Constitutional republics such as ours exist in only a few nations. Yet to democrats—or, if you prefer—to republicans, our system is precious because it is committed to protecting and expanding liberty. That commitment rests on certain fundamental convictions.

Basic Premises of Democracy

First, democrats recognize the fundamental dignity and importance of the *individual*. Individuals, democrats insist, have important rights, and, collectively, are the root source of legitimate governmental authority and power. These notions pervade all of democratic thought. They are woven into the writings of Thomas Jefferson, especially in the Declaration of Independence: *All men are endowed by their Creator with certain unalienable rights*. Individualism makes the person—rich or poor, black or white, male or female—the *central* measure of value. The state, the union, and the corporation are measured in terms of their usefulness to individuals. Not everyone, of course, believes in putting the individual first. Some believe in **statism**, considering the state supreme. Democrats, however, believe that the state, or even the community, is less important than the individuals who compose it.

Second, democrats recognize the right of each individual to be treated as a unique and inviolable human being. They do not insist that all are equal in talents or virtues; they do insist that one person's claim to life, liberty, and property must be recognized as much as another's. Although this right raises difficult questions about how equal rights can be secured, the *principle* of equality of right is clear.

Third, democrats are convinced that freedom is good in itself. *Liberty* or *freedom* (used interchangeably here) means that all individuals must have the opportunity to realize their own goals. The core of liberty is *self-determination*. Liberty is not simply the absence of external restraint on a person; it is the individual's power to act positively to reach his or her goals. Moreover, both history and reason suggest that individual liberty is the key to *social progress*. The greater people's freedom, the greater the chance of discovering better ways of life.

The basic values of democracy do not necessarily coexist happily in a particular society. The concept of individualism may conflict with the older tradition of public virtue and collective welfare—of the citizen as a participant in the general welfare. Freedom as the *liberation* of the individual may conflict with freedom as the *alienation*

Creating the Republic

April 1775	American Revolution begins at Lexington and Concord (Mass.)
June 1775	George Washington assumes command of Continental forces
July 1776	Declaration of Independence approved
Nov. 1777	Articles of Confederation adopted by Continental Congress
March 1781	Articles of Confederation ratified by the states
Oct. 1781	British defeated at Yorktown
Nov. 1782	Preliminary peace treaty signed
Late 1783	British forces leave; General Washington retires
April 1784	Congress ratifies Peace Treaty with British
Late 1786	Shays's Rebellion in western Massachusetts
May 1787	Constitutional Convention begins in Philadelphia
Sept. 1787	Constitution for United States adopted by Convention

of people from friends or communities. Individual self-determination may conflict with collective decision making for the national welfare or the public good. The right of mill owners to run their factories as they please, as compared to the right of millhands in those factories to join unions or even to share in the running of the plants, illustrates this type of conflict in everyday life.

Liberty and Equality: Democratic Goals

Probably the single most powerful idea in American history has been that of liberty. It was for life, liberty, and the pursuit of happiness that independence was declared; it was to secure the blessings of liberty that the Constitution was drawn up and adopted. Consider our patriotic anthems: It is to the "sweet land of liberty" that we sing. Or take a coin out of your pocket; that penny, nickel, dime, quarter, or half dollar proclaims not authority, security, or brotherhood, but *liberty*.

Liberty is a fuzzy as well as a compelling concept; much depends on how Americans define it as they make practical decisions. During the early decades of the republic, the American concept of liberty was essentially negative. The main aim of Jeffersonian democracy was to throw off the burdens of established governments, churches, and other institutions. These negative liberties were made explicit in the Bill of Rights of the Constitution, which granted free speech, free press, freedom of religion, and freedom of assembly. The main role of the Bill of Rights was to remove governmental constraints on individual liberties.

During most of the nineteenth century, liberty as "freedom *from*" meshed with the dominant economic and social doctrine of laissez faire. Under this doctrine individuals must be free of governments that might stop them from reaching maximum efficiency and productivity. The state, it was argued, must intervene no more than is absolutely necessary to protect life and property. Further intervention, in the form of minimum wages, health protection, or even compulsory vaccination, it was contended, is both immoral in theory and improper in fact. The idea is simple: The less governmental power, the more individual liberty.

The signing of the Declaration of Independence, 1776. (*CIGNA Museum and Art Collection*)

But what did liberty (or freedom) mean when not governments but other individuals—employers, lynch mobs, plantation owners—deprived persons of this right? Slavery forced Americans to rethink their ideas. "The world has never had a good definition of the word liberty," Abraham Lincoln said during the Civil War, "and the American people, just now, are in want of one. We all declare for liberty; but in using the same word we do not all mean the same thing. With some the word liberty may mean for each man to do as he pleases with himself, and the product of his labor; while with others the same word may mean for some men to do as they please with other men. . . ."[2]

With the coming of industrialization, urbanization, and agrarian and labor discontent; of unions, depressions, and social protest; and of leaders like William Jennings Bryan, Theodore Roosevelt, Robert La Follette, Eugene Debs, and Woodrow Wilson, liberty came to have far more positive meanings. Americans slowly came to understand that men and women, crowded more and more together, lived amid webs of all kinds: personal and private, institutional and psychological. To abolish one type of restraint (such as black slavery) might mean increasing another type of restraint (such as wage slavery). To cut down on governmental restraint of liberty might simply mean increasing private economic and social power. The question was not simply how to liberate people from *government*; it was how to use government to free people from *non*governmental curbs on liberty as well.

But what about the idea of *equality*, next to liberty probably the most vital concept in American thought. "All men are created equal and from that equal creation they derive rights inherent and unalienable, among which are the preservation of liberty and the pursuit of happiness." So read Jefferson's first draft of the Declaration, and the words indicate the primacy of the concept. Alexis de Tocqueville, James Bryce, Harold Laski, and other foreigners who investigated American democracy were struck by the strength of egalitarian thought and practice in both our political and social lives.

What did equality mean? What *kind* of equality? Economic, political, legal, social, or something else? Equality for *whom*? For blacks as well as whites? For children and teenagers as well as adults? Equality of *opportunity*—almost all Americans said they wanted that—but also of *condition*? This last question was the toughest. Did equality of opportunity simply mean that everyone should have the *same place at the starting line*? Or did it mean that an effort should be made to equalize most or all the factors that during the course of a person's life might determine how well he or she would fare socially or economically? (See also Chapter 5.)

Herbert Hoover posed the issue when he said: "We, through free and universal education, provide the training of the runners; we give to them an equal start; we provide in government the umpire of fairness in the race. . . ."[3] Franklin D. Roosevelt sought to answer the question when he proclaimed first the **Four Freedoms**— freedom from *want* and *fear* as well as freedom of speech and religion—and later a "second Bill of Rights." Under this second Bill of Rights, he said, Americans accepted the idea that a new basis of security and prosperity could be established for all, regardless of position, race, or creed. This meant good housing, health, jobs, and social security for all. The New Deal and its successor programs, in both their achievements and failures, have tried to advance the egalitarian intentions of the second Bill of Rights.

Thus, two concepts once considered opposites have coalesced into a philosophy that calls for government to help broaden people's *social* and *economic* liberties while it prevents other institutions (corporations or unions or landlords) from infring-

What Are Our Basic American Values?

Goals *

Liberty
Personal freedom
Dignity of the individual
Property rights
Equality before the law
Equality of opportunity
An open society
Justice

Means

Constitutionalism
Representative processes
Free and frequent elections
Majority rule, minority rights
Checks and balances
Bill of Rights
Federalism
Separation of powers
Due process
Judicial review

* Not everyone agrees on these goals, and people naturally weigh them differently according to their own values. How would you rank these goals? Would you elevate some of what we label as "means" to "goals"? A nation's values plainly have much to do with what kinds of processes, institutions, and political practices are encouraged and sustained.

[2] Speech at Sanitary Fair, 1864.
[3] Herbert Hoover, *American Individualism* (Doubleday, Page, 1922), p. 9. This ancient debate continues: See also John Rawls, *A Theory of Justice* (Harvard University Press, 1971), and Robert Nozick, *Anarchy, State and Utopia* (Basic Books, 1974). See also Michael Walzer, *Spheres of Justice* (Basic, 1983).

ing on those liberties. At the same time, the government must prevent *itself* from interfering with liberty. This is no small task, and it is not always performed well—but the idea is exciting. It means that Americans, perhaps without being wholly conscious of it, have brought together the values of liberty and equality. No longer can we say flatly: "The more government, the less liberty"; but neither can we say the opposite.

Liberty and equality interlock and stimulate each other at some points, and oppose each other at others. Sometimes they do not relate at all. Pushed too far, liberty could become license and unbridled individualism, and equality could mean leveling, a dull mediocrity, and even the erosion of liberty. Much of our political combat revolves around how to strike a balance.

Democracy as Political Means

Some favor democracy not only because they believe it stands for such goals as liberty and equality but also because they see it as the best way to govern a complex society. Those who admire democracy for the human ends it represents are called **principle democrats**; those who consider democracy a technique of self-government are called **process democrats**. Process democrats grant that democratic processes do not guarantee justice will be done, but they contend that the chances are better under "government by the people" than under any other system. Note what is *not* included in the concept of democracy as a process for making decisions: Process democrats do not judge a democracy by its policy output; their concern is with the *procedures* for making policy, and not with the rightness of the policy that is made.

Process democrats contend that government *by* the people usually produces government *for* the people. They reject the notion that it is possible to define the public interest "scientifically." If one believes, as did Plato, that decisions about public policy are of the same nature as, say, decisions about how to build a boat, then the best way to make policy is to turn everything over to a group of specialists or experts. Then, like Plato, one would favor a system that places authority in the hands of philosopher-kings or, in today's terms, in the hands of the "best and the brightest." Process democrats, on the other hand, take their stand with Aristotle, who argued that although an expert cook knows better than a nonexpert one how to bake a cake, the person who eats the cake is the better judge of how it tastes.

Most Americans do not trust experts very much. As President Dwight Eisenhower stated in his farewell address: "Yet in holding scientific research and discovery in respect, as we should, we must also be alert to the equal and opposite danger that public policy could itself become the captive of a scientific-technological elite." Few democrats—especially process democrats—wish to shift the control of our destinies from voters and their elected leaders to some new priesthood of systems analysts.

Fundamental Democratic Processes

The crucial mechanism in all genuinely popular governments is a system of free, fair, and open elections. Democratic governments take many different forms, but democratic elections have at least four essential elements:

1. *All citizens should have equal voting power.* This does not mean that all must or will have equal political influence. Some persons, because of wealth, talent, or position, have much more power than others. How much extra influence key figures should be allowed to exercise in a democracy is one of the questions that faces democrats. But a president or a pick-and-shovel laborer, a newspaper publisher or a lettuce picker, casts only one vote at the polls.

2. *Voters should have the right of access to facts, criticism, competing ideas,*

and the views of all candidates. Here again, the extent to which different ideas actually receive equal attention is a problem because of the nature of the mass media, the special access of the president to television and the press, and the inability of many lower-income people to make their ideas known. Still, the principle of free competition of ideas during an election is essential.

3. *Citizens must be free to organize for political purposes.* Obviously, individuals can be more effective when they join with others in a party, a pressure group, a protest movement, or a demonstration.

4. *Elections are decided by majorities (or at least pluralities).* Those who get the most votes win, even if the winning side seems to be made up of idiots. The persons chosen by the majority take office. How much power the winners may then have over the losing minority is another problem, but there is no question that the winners take office and assume formal authority.

The American System: Democratic and Constitutional

Our founders believed in democracy both as a *principle* and as a *process*. Their genius lay in how they related the *goals* of democracy to its *methods*. If the Declaration of Independence was more concerned with such *goals* as liberty and equality, the Constitution focused more on the *processes* that could help realize these goals without sacrificing such values as controlled power, stability, continuity, due process, and balanced decision making. For two centuries American politicians, jurists, and other leaders have been enormously influenced by the success of the revolutionaries of 1776 and 1787 in working out effective and durable political processes. The twentieth-century civil rights and women's rights violations, and the **Watergate** scandals, were dramatic warnings, process democrats remind us, that to abuse democratic processes is to threaten both the means and the ends of a free people.

"Remember, gentlemen, we aren't here just to draft a constitution. We're here to draft the best damned constitution in the world." (*Drawing by Steiner;* © *1982 The New Yorker Magazine, Inc.*)

THE ORIGINS OF THE AMERICAN REPUBLIC

The American Revolution was conservative in several respects. Certainly, it had constitutional goals. Those who declared our independence from England did so reluctantly, and in the name of the English Constitution. They sought not to establish a new order but to restore the rights taken from them by the king.[4] As Alexis de Tocqueville, the perceptive nineteenth-century French visitor to the New World, observed: "The great advantage of the Americans is that they have arrived at a state of democracy without having to endure a democratic revolution. . . ."[5] De Tocqueville had not forgotten our war period, 1775 to 1781. He meant that the American Revolution was primarily a rebellion of colonies against an empire. But even in this respect, "the Americans [other than blacks] were not an oppressed people; they had no crushing imperial shackles to throw off. In fact, the Americans knew they were probably freer and less burdened with cumbersome feudal and hierarchical restraints than any part of mankind in the eighteenth century."[6] In

---

[4] See Martin Diamond, "The Revolution of Sober Expectations," *The American Revolution: Three Views* (American Brands, 1975), p. 57.

[5] *Democracy in America*, vol. 2, ed., F. Bowen, (Sever and Francis, 1872), p. 13. For other statements of the same view, see Daniel J. Boorstin, *The Genius of American Politics* (University of Chicago Press, 1953), p. 68, and Louis Hartz, *The Liberal Tradition in America* (Harcourt, 1955).

[6] Gordon Wood, *The Creation of the American Republic, 1776–1787* (University of North Carolina Press, 1969), p. 3.

the modern sense it was hardly a revolution; there were no sharp breaks with the past and no great social, economic, or political upheavals. Contrast the colonists' demand for the "rights of Englishmen" with the French demand for the "rights of man" in 1789. "Even the fact that Americans jettisoned a monarch and suddenly and without much internal debate adopted a republican government marked no great upheaval." Thomas Jefferson observed in the summer of 1777 that Americans "seem to have deposited the monarchical and taken up the republican government with as much ease as would have attended their throwing off an old and putting on a new suit of clothes."[7] As a result, the American Revolution did not open class wounds. The political system based on such a revolution centered more on consensus than on conflict.

The New Governments

The destruction of English authority was the first step in establishing the American republic. The next was to create new state governments and to establish at least a limited central government under the Articles of Confederation.

Although the breaks with the past were not dramatic as compared to the French Revolution of a few years later (1789) or the Russian Revolution of this century (1917), the new governments were different from those they replaced. New state constitutions incorporated bills of rights, abolished most religious qualifications, and liberalized property and tax-paying requirements for voting.[8] There were no kings. Power was concentrated in the legislatures. The governors and judges—officials who reminded Americans of royalty—lost influence. Governors were made dependent on the legislatures for election, and the legislatures overrode judicial decisions and scolded judges whose rulings were unpopular. The legislative branch, later complained the writers of *The Federalist*, No. 48, was drawing all power into its impetuous vortex. What about the central government? Having just fought a war against one central government, Americans were reluctant to create another. The **Articles of Confederation,** when finally approved by all the state legislatures in 1781, more or less legalized the arrangements under which the Continental Congress had assumed power in 1776. The Articles established more of a fragile league of friendship than a national government.

From 1777 to 1788 Americans made some progress under this system. Yet as we know from our history, the practical difficulties confronting the new nation would have tested the strongest government. The end of the war reduced the sense of urgency that had helped to unite the states, and conflicts among them were frequent. Within the states economic differences between creditors and debtors grew intense. There were foreign threats as well. The English, French, and Spanish surrounded the new nation, which—internally divided and lacking a strong central government—made a tempting prize.

As the problems mounted, many leaders, especially in New York, Virginia, Massachusetts, and Pennsylvania, became convinced that it would not be enough merely to revise the Articles of Confederation. To create a union strong enough to resist external threats, they needed to create a stronger central government with

"You know, the idea of taxation with representation doesn't appeal to me very much either." (*Drawing by Handelsman;* © *1970 The New Yorker Magazine, Inc.*)

[7] Quoted by Wood, p. 92, Jefferson to Benjamin Franklin, August 2, 1777. In J. P. Boyd et al., eds., *Jefferson Papers*, vol. 2 (Princeton University Press, 1950), p. 26.

[8] Elisha P. Douglass, *Rebels and Democrats* (University of North Carolina Press, 1955). See also R. R. Palmer, *The Age of the Democratic Revolution* (Princeton University Press, 1959), pp. 217–35; Chilton Williamson, *American Suffrage: From Property to Democracy, 1760–1860* (Princeton University Press, 1960), p. 92; Robert A. Rutland, *The Birth of the Bill of Rights, 1776–1791* (University of North Carolina Press, 1955); Richard Ashcraft, "Locke's State of Nature: Historical Fact or Moral Fiction?" *American Political Science Review* (September 1968), pp. 898–915; Samuel Eliot Morison, *The Oxford History of the American People* (Oxford University Press, 1965), p. 276; Hannah Arendt, *On Revolution* (Viking, 1963), p. 139.

adequate powers. They therefore set out to establish a republican government that could be made to work by and for *ordinary people* .[9]

Although many Americans increasingly recognized the need to give Congress authority to regulate commerce and collect a few taxes, they were still suspicious of central government. But finally, in the late summer of 1786, under the leadership of Alexander Hamilton, those who favored a truly national government took advantage of a meeting in Annapolis, Maryland (on problems of trade and navigation, attended by delegates from five states) to issue a call for a "plenipotentiary Convention." Such a convention would have full authority to consider basic amendments to the Articles of Confederation. The delegates to the **Annapolis Convention** requested the legislatures of their states to appoint commissioners to meet in Philadelphia on the second Monday of May, 1787, "to devise such further provisions as shall appear to them necessary to render the Constitution of the Federal Government adequate to the exigencies of the Union." This convention, held in August of 1786, issued the call for what became the Constitutional Convention. The Annapolis Convention itself, attended by delegates from only five states, addressed mutual trade and navigation problems.

For a short time all was quiet. Then in Western Massachusetts that fall and winter, the farmers rebelled under Shays and other leaders. This seriously disturbed Washington and other political leaders. The message seemed clear: Some kind of action must be taken to strengthen the machinery of government. Spurred on by Shays's Rebellion, seven states appointed commissioners to attend the Philadelphia Convention. Congress, apathetic and suspicious, finally issued a cautiously worded call to the states to appoint delegates for the "sole and express purpose of revising the Articles of Confederation." The cautious legislators specified that no recommendation would be effective unless approved by Congress and confirmed by all the state legislatures, as provided by the Articles.

Eventually every state except Rhode Island appointed delegates. (The debtors and farmers who controlled the Rhode Island legislature rightly suspected that one of the major purposes of the proposed convention would be to limit the power of state legislatures to interfere with the rights of creditors.) Some of the delegates were bound by instructions only to consider amendments to the Articles of Confederation. Delaware went so far as to forbid its representatives to consider any proposal that would deny any state equal representation in Congress.

THE PHILADELPHIA CONVENTION, 1787

The delegates who assembled in Philadelphia that summer were presented with a condition, not a theory. They had to establish a national government powerful enough to prevent the nation from dissolving. What these men did continues to have a major impact on how we are governed. It also provides an outstanding lesson in political science.

The Delegates

Seventy-four delegates were appointed by the various states, but only fifty-five arrived in Philadelphia. Of these, approximately forty took a real part in the work of the convention. It was a distinguished gathering. Many of the most important men of the nation were there: successful merchants, planters, bankers and lawyers, and former and present governors and congressional representatives (thirty-nine of the

[9] Wood, *American Republic, 1776–1787*, pp. 122, 612. See also the essays in *This Constitution* (Congressional Quarterly Press, 1986).

No women ←
No Blacks.

John Hancock (1737–1793), Revolutionary patriot and signer of the Declaration of Independence. Hancock served as president of the Continental Congress (1775–1777) and later as governor of Massachusetts, both before and after the ratification of the Constitution. (*New York Public Library—Picture Collection*)

delegates had served in Congress). As theorists, most had read widely in the classics of political thought. As activists, most were interested in the practical task of constructing a national government.

The convention was as representative as most political gatherings at the time. Of course, there were no women or blacks. These well-read, well-fed, well-bred, and often well-wed delegates were mainly state or national leaders, for in the 1780s ordinary people were not likely to participate in politics. (Even today farm laborers, factory workers, and truck drivers are seldom found in Congress, although a self-styled peanut farmer and a movie actor have made their way to the White House.) Even though most of the leaders in attendance eventually supported the Constitution in the ratification debates, only eight of the fifty-six signers of the Declaration of Independence were present at the Constitutional Convention. Among those who did *not* come were Jefferson, Thomas Paine, Patrick Henry, Richard Henry Lee, Sam and John Adams, and John Hancock. Of the active participants at the convention, several men stand out as the prime movers.

Alexander Hamilton had been the engineer of the Annapolis Convention, and as early as 1778 he had been urging that the national government be made stronger. Hamilton had come to the United States from the West Indies and while still a student at Kings College (now Columbia University) had won national attention for his brilliant pamphlets in defense of the Revolutionary cause. During the war he served as General Washington's aide, and his experiences confirmed his distaste for a Congress so weak it could not even supply the Revolution's troops with enough food or arms.

From Virginia came two of the leading delegates: General George Washington and James Madison. Although active in the movement to revise the Articles of Confederation, Washington had been extremely reluctant to attend the convention. He accepted only when persuaded that his prestige was needed for its success. He was selected unanimously to preside over the meetings. According to the records, he spoke only twice during the deliberations, but his influence was felt in the informal gatherings as well as during the sessions. The assumption that Washington would become the first president under the new constitution inspired confidence in it. James Madison was only 36 years old at the time of the convention, but he was one of the most learned members present. He had helped frame Virginia's first constitution and had served both in the Virginia Assembly and in Congress. Madison was also a leader of those who favored the establishment of a strong national government.

The Pennsylvania delegation included Benjamin Franklin and Gouverneur Morris. Franklin, at 81, was the convention's oldest member and, as one of his fellow delegates said: "He is well known to be the greatest philosopher of the present age." Franklin enjoyed a world reputation unrivaled by that of any other American. Gouverneur Morris of Pennsylvania was more eloquent than brilliant. He addressed the convention more often than any other person. The elegance of the language of the Constitution is proof of his literary ability; he was responsible for the final draft.

Luther Martin of Maryland, John Dickinson of Delaware, and William Paterson of New Jersey did not agree with a majority of the delegates, but they ably defended the position that all states should have equal representation.

The proceedings of the convention were kept secret. Delegates were forbidden to discuss the debates with outsiders, in order to encourage everyone to speak freely. It was feared that if a member publicly took a firm stand on an issue, it would be harder for him to change his mind after debate and discussion. Also the members knew that if word of the inevitable disagreements got out, it would provide ammunition for the many enemies of the convention. There were critics of this secrecy rule, but without it agreement might have been impossible.

Benjamin Franklin (1706–1790), early American statesman, writer, printer, scientist. Franklin helped draft the Declaration of Independence and served as a delegate to the Continental Congress, postmaster general, a diplomat, and a delegate to the 1787 Constitutional Convention. He served his country with distinction in its early days. (*New York Public Library—Picture Collection*)

Consensus

The **Constitutional Convention** is usually discussed in terms of three famous compromises: the compromise between large and small states over representation in Congress, the compromise between North and South over the counting of slaves for taxation and representation, and the compromise between North and South over the regulation and taxation of foreign commerce. But this emphasis obscures the fact that there were many other important compromises and that on many of the more significant issues, most of the delegates were in agreement.

Although a few delegates might have personally favored a limited monarchy, all supported republican government—and this was the only form of government seriously considered. It was, indeed, the only form that would be acceptable to the nation. Equally important, all the delegates were constitutionalists who opposed arbitrary and unrestrained government, in whatever form.

The common philosophy accepted by most of the delegates was that of *balanced government*. They wanted to construct a national government in which no single interest would dominate. Because the delegates represented those alarmed by the tendencies of the farmers as an interest group to interfere with property, they were primarily concerned with balancing the government in the direction of protection for property and business. Most of them respected the remark of Elbridge Gerry (delegate from Massachusetts): "The evils we experience flow from the excess of democracy. The people do not want virtue, but are dupes of pretended patriots." Likewise, there was substantial agreement with Gouverneur Morris's statement that property was the "principal object of government."

Benjamin Franklin favored extending the right to vote to white male nonproperty owners, but most of the delegates agreed that owners of land were the best guardians of liberty. James Madison voiced the fear that those without property, if given the right to vote, either would combine to deprive property owners of their rights or would become the "tools of **demagogues**." The delegates agreed in principle on restricted suffrage, but differed over the kind and amount of property one must own in order to vote. Because the states were in the process of relaxing qualifications for the vote, the framers recognized they would jeopardize approval of the constitution if they made the federal **franchise** more restricted than the franchises within the states.[10] As a result, each state was left to determine the qualifications for electing members of the House of Representatives, the only branch of the national government in which the electorate was given a direct voice.

Within five days of its opening, the convention—with only Connecticut dissenting—voted to approve the Fourth Virginia Resolve, which stated that "a national government ought to be established consisting of a supreme legislative, executive, and judiciary." This decision to establish a national government resting on and exercising power over individuals profoundly altered the nature of the central government and changed it from a league of states to a national government.

Few dissented from proposals to give the new Congress all the powers of the old plus all other powers necessary to ensure that the harmony of the United States not be disrupted by the exercise of state legislation. The framers agreed a strong executive, which had been lacking under the Articles, was necessary to provide energy and direction. An independent judiciary was also accepted without much debate. Franklin favored a single-house national legislature, but most states had had two-chamber legislatures since colonial times, and the delegates were used to the system. **Bicameralism**—the principle of the two-house legislature—also expressed the delegates' belief in the need for balanced government. One chamber would represent the aristocracy and offset the more democratic House of Representatives.

[10] John P. Roche, "The Founding Fathers: A Reform Caucus in Action," *American Political Science Review* (December 1961), pp. 799–816, emphasizes the importance of such political considerations in the framers' deliberations.

U.S. Population Growth, 1790–1990

Year	Population
1790	3,929,214
1810	7,239,881
1830	12,860,692
1850	23,191,876
1870	38,558,371
1900	75,994,575
1920	105,710,620
1940	131,669,275
1960	179,323,175
1980	226,504,825
1990	250,000,000

Washington presiding over the Constitutional Convention. (*The Granger Collection*)

Conflict

There were serious differences among the various groups, especially between the representatives of the large states, who favored a strong national government (which they expected they could dominate), and the delegates from the small states, who were anxious to avoid being dominated. The Virginia delegation took the initiative. It had met during the delay before the convention and, as soon as the convention was organized, presented fifteen resolutions. These resolutions, the **Virginia Plan,** called for a strong central government. The legislature was to be composed of two chambers. The members of the more representative chamber were to be elected by the voters; those of the smaller and more aristocratic chamber were to be chosen by the larger chamber from nominees submitted by the state legislatures. Representation in both houses was to be on the basis of either wealth or numbers, which gave the more populous and wealthy states—Virginia, Massachusetts, and Pennsylvania—a majority in the legislature.

The Congress thus created was to be given all the legislative power of its predecessor under the Articles of Confederation as well as the right "to legislate in all cases in which the separate States are incompetent." Further, it was to have the authority to veto state legislation in conflict with the proposed constitution. The Virginia Plan also called for a national executive, to be chosen by the legislature, and a national judiciary with rather extensive jurisdiction. The national Supreme Court, along with the executive, was to have a qualified veto over acts of Congress.

For the first few weeks the Virginia Plan dominated the discussion. But by June 15 additional delegates from the small states had arrived, and they began to counterattack. They rallied around William Paterson of New Jersey, who presented a series of resolutions known as the **New Jersey Plan.** Paterson did not question the need for a greatly strengthened central government, but he was concerned about how this strength would be used. The New Jersey Plan would give Congress the right to tax and regulate commerce and to coerce states, but it would retain a single-house legislature in which all states, regardless of size, would have the same vote. The plan contained the germ of what eventually came to be a key provision of our Constitution: the *supremacy* clause. The national Supreme Court was to hear appeals from state judges, and the supremacy clause would require all the

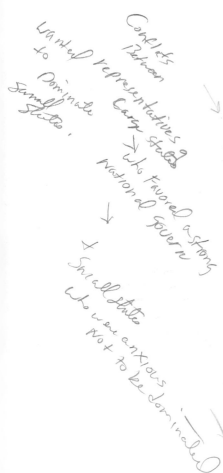

13

John Jay (1745–1829), a New York lawyer, diplomat, and author of five *Federalist* essays. He served at various times as president of the Continental Congress, peace negotiator with Britain, and secretary for foreign affairs during the last years of the Articles of Confederation; he was also the first chief justice of the United States. (*Bettman Archive*)

BlACK SLAVE
3/5 QUOTE.

"When my distinguished colleague refers to the will of the 'people,' does he mean his people or my 'people'?" (*Drawing by Richter*; © *1976 The New Yorker Magazine, Inc.*)

judges, state and national, to treat laws of the national government and the treaties of the United States as superior to the laws of each of the states.

Paterson maneuvered to force concessions from the larger states. He favored a strong central government, but not one the big states could control. Further, he raised the issue of practical politics: To adopt the Virginia Plan—which created a powerful national government dominated by Massachusetts, Virginia, and Pennsylvania and eliminated the states as important units of government—would guarantee defeat in the coming ratification struggle. But the large states resisted, and for a time the convention was deadlocked. The small states believed states should be represented equally in Congress, at least in the upper house. The large states insisted that representation in both houses be based on population or wealth, and that national legislators be elected by the voters rather than by state legislatures. Finally, a Committee of Eleven was elected to devise a compromise. On July 5 it presented its proposals.

Because of the prominent role of the Connecticut delegation, this plan has since been known as the **Connecticut Compromise**. It called for one house in which each state would have an equal vote, and a second house in which representation would be based on population and all bills for raising or appropriating money would originate. This was a setback to the large states, who agreed to it only when the smaller states made it clear that this was their price for union. After equality of representation in the Senate was accepted, most objections to establishing a strong national government dissolved.

Slavery was already an issue in 1787. The southern states wanted slaves to be counted in determining representation in the House of Representatives. It was finally agreed that a slave should count as three-fifths of a free person, both in determining representation in the House and apportioning direct taxes. Southerners were also fearful that a northern majority in Congress might discriminate against southern trade. They had some basis for this concern. John Jay, secretary of foreign affairs for the Confederation, had proposed a treaty with Great Britain that would have given advantages to northern merchants at the expense of southern exporters. To protect themselves the southern delegates insisted that a two-thirds majority be required in the Senate for ratification of treaties.

The delegates, of course, found other issues about which to argue. Should the national government have lower courts, or would one federal Supreme Court be enough? This issue was resolved by postponing the decision; the Constitution states that there *shall* be one Supreme Court and that Congress *may* establish inferior courts. How should the president be selected? For a long time the convention accepted the idea that the president should be elected by Congress. But it was feared either that Congress would dominate the president, or vice versa. Election by the state legislatures was rejected, because these bodies were distrusted. Finally, the electoral college system was devised. This was perhaps the most novel and contrived contribution of the delegates; today it is one of the most criticized provisions in the Constitution.[11]

After three months the delegates stopped debating. On September 17, 1787, they assembled for the impressive ceremony of signing the document they were recommending to the nation. All but three of those still present signed; others who opposed the general drift of the convention, had already left. Their work over, the delegates adjourned to the City Tavern to relax and celebrate a job well done.

[11] For studies on the early invention and establishment of the American presidency, see Charles Thach, *The Creation of the Presidency, 1775–1789* (Johns Hopkins Press, 1923), and Ralph Ketcham, *Presidents Above Party: The First American Presidency, 1789–1829* (University of North Carolina Press, 1984).

The Framers: What Manner of Men?

Were the delegates an inspired group of men who cast aside all thoughts of self-interest? Were they motivated by the desire to save the nation or by the desire to save themselves? Was the convention the inevitable result of the weaknesses of the Articles? Was it a carefully maneuvered coup on the part of certain elites? Was the difference between those who favored and those who opposed the Constitution mainly economic? Or was the difference mainly regional?

Students of history and government disagree on these and other questions. During the early part of our history, the members of the convention were the object of uncritical praise; the Constitution was the object of almost universal reverence. Early in the twentieth century a more critical attitude was inspired by J. Allen Smith and Charles A. Beard. Smith, in *The Spirit of American Government* (1911), painted the Constitution as the outgrowth of an antidemocratic reaction, almost a conspiracy, against the rule of majorities. Beard's thesis was that the Constitution represented the platform of the propertied groups who wanted to limit state legislatures and strengthen the national government as a means of protecting property. In his influential book, *An Economic Interpretation of the Constitution* (1913), Beard described the economic holdings of the delegates and argued that the latter's support or opposition to the Constitution could best be explained in terms of their financial interests. He explicitly denied he was charging the founders with writing the Constitution for their personal benefit. Rather, he contended that individuals' political behavior reflects their broad economic interests.

Many, but not all, recent historical works have questioned the soundness of Beard's scholarship and interpretation. Some historians have pointed out that in 1787 there was no great propertyless mass in the United States.[12] Even the poor were interested in protecting property. The founders, they argue, were too smart politically to think they could get away with a plan designed merely to protect their own wealth—even if that had been their motive.[13] Certainly, they were anxious to build a strong national government so that it could promote economic growth. Such a government would win the support of all classes of people.[14] These historians

[12] Robert E. Brown, *Charles Beard and the Constitution* (Princeton University Press, 1956), pp. 197–98, and Diggins, "Power and Authority in American History."

[13] Forrest McDonald, *We the People: The Economic Origins of the Constitution* (University of Chicago Press, 1958), pp. vii, 415; *Novus ordo seclurum: The Intellectual Origins of the Constitution* (University Press of Kansas, 1986).

[14] Gordon S. Wood, *The Convention and the Constitution* (St. Martin's Press, 1965), p. 31.

The signing of the Constitution in Independence Hall, Philadelphia. (*Culver Pictures*)

Following is a set of key questions about the constitutional system as it works today. You might want to refer to this checklist as you read through the following chapters, in which many of these questions are discussed.

1. Too much—or too little—national power. Are the limits on the powers of the federal government realistic and enforceable, given the intense pressures on the government?

2. Federalism: Does our form of it work? Does the Constitution provide for an efficient and realistic balance between national and state power?

3. Our individual liberties: Are they adequately protected in the Constitution?

4. Suspects' rights: Can representative government protect its citizens and yet uphold the rights of the criminally accused?

5. "All men are created equal": What kinds of equality are—and should be—protected by the Constitution, and by what means?

6. Women's rights: Are they adequately protected by the Constitution today?

7. Safeguarding minorities: Does the Constitution adequately protect the rights of blacks, native Americans, ethnics, and recent immigrants?

8. "Government by the people": Does the evolving constitutional system, including political parties and interest groups, strengthen fair and effective representation of the people?

9. The judicial branch: Is it too powerful? Are the federal courts exceeding their proper powers as interpreters of the Constitution?

10. Checks and balances: Are there too many? Does the constitutional separation of

contend that the political differences over the merits of the Constitution, just like political arguments today, cut through economic class divisions. The struggle, it is argued, was between differing ideologies.[15]

Political scientist Martin Diamond took issue with those who portray the Constitutional Convention as a reactionary attempt by aristocrats to curtail the brave democratic beginnings proclaimed in the Declaration of Independence. He calls this interpretation the "conventional wisdom of those who give academic and intellectual opinions to the nation." "The fact is," he wrote, "the Declaration . . . is neutral on the questions of forms of government; any form is legitimate, provided it secures equal freedom and is instituted by popular consent." The framers of our Constitution gave us a democratic form of government. "Of course, the Founders," Diamond comments, "criticized the defects and dangers of democracy and did not waste much breath on the defects and dangers of the other forms of government. For a very good reason. They were not founding any other kind of government; they were establishing a democratic form, and it was the dangers peculiar to it against which all their efforts had to be bent."[16]

The various interpretations of the American Revolution and of the framing of the Constitution reflect changing styles of thought; current political debates are read backward, into our past. But the various interpretations also reflect the fact that "the American Revolution . . . was so complex and contained so many diverse and seemingly contradictory currents that it can support a wide variety of interpretations and may never be comprehended in full."[17]

Beard himself recognized that people are motivated by a complex of factors, both conscious and unconscious. Self-interest, economic or otherwise, and principles are inextricably mixed in human behavior. The founders were neither gods for whom self-interest or economic considerations were of no importance, nor selfish elitists who thought only in terms of their own pocketbooks. They were, by and large, aristocrats fearful of the masses, but committed to an aristocracy of merit, education, and accomplishment—not of birth or wealth. The framers wanted to protect the nation from aggression abroad and dissension at home. Stability and strength were needed not only to protect their own interests, but also to secure the unity and order necessary for the operation of a democracy.

On one point almost all students of the founding era are agreed: The framers offered in the Constitution perhaps the most brilliant example of collective intellectual genius—of combining both theory and practice—in the history of the Western world. How could an America sixty-five times smaller in population than today produce several dozen men of genius in Philadelphia, and probably another hundred or so equally talented political thinkers who did not attend? The lives of the two main authors of *The Federalist*, Alexander Hamilton and James Madison, help explain the origins of that collective genius.

Like most of the other framers, Hamilton and Madison were superbly educated. Both had extensive private tutoring—a "one-to-one teacher–student ratio." As a young man Hamilton had free access to a patron's library. A graduate of the famed University of Edinburgh drilled the early-teenage Madison in Greek, Latin, logic, and the whole Edinburgh curriculum. Both young men attended leading institutions of higher education—Hamilton at what is now Columbia and Madison at what is now Princeton.[18]

[15] Wood, *American Republic, 1776–1787*, pp. 484–85.

[16] Martin Diamond, "The Declaration and the Constitution: Liberty, Democracy, and the Founders," *The Public Interest* (Fall 1975), pp. 40, 50, 52.

[17] Jack P. Greene, "The Reappraisal of the American Revolution in Recent Historical Literature," in Jack P. Greene, ed., *The Reinterpretation of the American Revolution, 1763–1789* (Harper & Row, 1968), p. 2.

[18] Richard B. Morris, *Witnesses at the Creation: Hamilton, Madison, Jay, and the Constitution* (Holt, Rinehart & Winston, 1985), pp. 28–30, 99–101.

Both men—again, like scores of other thinkers of the day—combined extensive practical experience with their schooling. Both were active in their political and religious groups; both took part in political contests and electoral struggles; both helped build political coalitions. Madison in particular saw much of the very political factions that he analyzed so brilliantly in *The Federalist*.

Both men were "moral philosophers" as well as political thinkers. They had strong views of the supreme value—liberty—as well as current issues. But instead of simply sermonizing about liberty, they *analyzed* it: They debated what *kind* of liberty, how to *protect* it, how to expand it. They also thought hard about other values enshrined in the Declaration of Independence, such as the virtues and dangers of equality and the nature of that "Happiness" Americans should pursue.

Finally, these men were "children of conflict." Because the stakes were so high—Hamilton and the others risked execution as traitors during the Revolution—every issue took on personal and passionate overtones. Thus their political and moral education was nourished by almost continuous controversy. After independence there was sharp conflict over state issues and elections. The question of *religious* liberty was also acute. In a neighboring county in Virginia the young Madison found some Baptists languishing in jail simply because they had opposed the estab-lished Church of England. "I shall not be silent," he promised the Baptists—and he was not.

TO ADOPT OR NOT TO ADOPT?

James Madison (1751–1836), a Virginian, was a key member of the Constitutional Convention of 1787, authored several impressive *Federalist* essays advocating ratification, served as speaker of the House of Representatives, and later became our fourth president. A political theorist who engaged in every form of practical political leadership, he is sometimes called the "father of the Constitution." (*National Portrait Gallery, Smithsonian Institution*)

The delegates had gone far. They had not hesitated to disregard Congress's instruc-tion about ratification or to ignore Article XIII of the Articles of Confederation. This article declared the Union to be perpetual and prohibited any alteration in the Articles unless agreed to by Congress and *by every one of the state legislatures*— a provision that had made it impossible to amend the Articles. But the convention delegates boldly declared that the Constitution should go into effect when ratified by *popularly elected conventions in nine states*. They had turned to this method of ratification for practical considerations and for reasons of principle. Not only were the delegates aware that there was little chance of securing approval of the new Constitution in all state legislatures, many also believed the Constitution should be ratified by an authority higher than a legislature. A constitution based on popular approval would have a higher legal and moral status. The Articles of Confederation had been a compact of state governments, but the Constitution was to be a "union of people."[19]

Nevertheless, even this method of ratification would not be easy. The nation was not ready to adopt the Constitution without a thorough debate. The supporters of the new government, by cleverly appropriating the name **Federalists,** took some of the sting out of the charges that they were trying to destroy the states and establish an all-powerful central government. By calling their opponents **Antifederal-ists,** they pointed up the negative character of the arguments of those who opposed ratification.

The split was in part geographical. The seaboard and city regions tended to be Federalist strongholds. The vast back-country regions from Maine through Geor-gia, inhabited by farmers and other relatively poor people, were generally Antifederal-ist. But, as in most political contests, no single factor completely accounted for the division between Federalists and Antifederalists. For example, in Virginia the leaders of both sides came from the same general social and economic class. New

[19] Max Farrand, ed., *The Records of the Federal Convention of 1787*, vol. 2 (Yale University Press, 1911), pp. 93, 476.

York City and Philadelphia strongly supported the Constitution, but so did predominantly rural New Jersey.

The great debate was conducted with pamphlets, papers, letters to the editor, and speeches. The issues were important, but the argument, in the main, was carried on in a quiet and calm manner. Out of the debate came a series of essays, known as *The Federalist*, written by Alexander Hamilton, James Madison, and John Jay to persuade the voters of New York to ratify the Constitution. *The Federalist* is still "widely regarded as the most profound single treatise on the Constitution ever written and as among the few masterly works in political science produced in all the centuries of history."[20] [Three of the most important *Federalist* essays, Numbers 10, 51, and 78 are found in the Appendix of this book] The great debate stands even today as an outstanding example of free people using the techniques of discussion and debate to determine the nature of their fundamental laws.

The Antifederalists' most telling criticism of the proposed Constitution was its failure to include a bill of rights.[21] The Federalists believed a bill of rights would be unnecessary. The general government had only delegated powers, and there was no need to specify that Congress could not, for example, abridge freedom of the press. It had no power to regulate the press. Moreover, the Federalists argued, to guarantee *some* rights might be dangerous, because it would then be thought that rights *not* listed could be denied. The Constitution already protected some important rights—trial by jury in federal criminal cases, for example. Hamilton and others also insisted that paper guarantees were weak reeds on which to depend for protection against governmental tyranny.

The Antifederalists were unconvinced. If some rights were protected, what could be the objection of providing constitutional protection for others? Without a bill of rights, what was to prevent Congress from using one of its delegated powers in such a manner that free speech would be abridged? If bills of rights were needed in state constitutions to limit state governments, why was one not needed in the national constitution to limit the national government? This was a government farther from the people and with a greater tendency, it was argued, to subvert natural rights. The Federalists, forced to concede, agreed to add a bill of rights if and when the new Constitution was approved.

The Politics of Ratification

The political strategy of the Federalists was to secure ratification in as many states as possible before the opposition had time to organize. The Antifederalists were handicapped. They lacked access to the newspapers, most of which supported ratification. Their main strength was in the rural areas, underrepresented in some state legislatures and difficult to arouse to political action. They needed time to perfect their organization and collect their strength. The Federalists, composed of a more closely knit group of leaders throughout the colonies, moved in a hurry.

In most of the small states, now satisfied by equal Senate representation, ratification was gained without difficulty. Delaware was the first state to ratify. The first large state to take action was Pennsylvania. The Federalists presented the Constitution to the state legislature immediately after the Philadelphia conven-

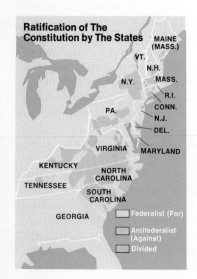

Ratification of The Constitution by The States

MAINE (MASS.)
VT.
N.H.
N.Y.
MASS.
R.I.
CONN.
PA.
N.J.
DEL.
VIRGINIA
MARYLAND
KENTUCKY
NORTH CAROLINA
TENNESSEE
SOUTH CAROLINA
GEORGIA

☐ Federalist (For)
☐ Antifederalist (Against)
☐ Divided

[20] Charles A. Beard and Mary R. Beard, *A Basic History of the United States* (New Home Library, 1944), p. 136. One of the most useful analyses of the arguments made in *The Federalist* papers can be found in David F. Epstein, *The Political Theory of The Federalist* (University of Chicago Press, 1984).

[21] See Herbert J. Storing, ed., abridgement by Murray Dry, *The Anti-Federalist: Writings by the Opponents of the Constitution* (University of Chicago Press, 1985).

Alexander Hamilton (1755–1804), Revolutionary leader, lawyer, aide to General Washington, delegate to the Constitutional Convention of 1787, author of many *Federalist* essays, and the leader of the Federalist party in its early years. Hamilton served for several years as President Washington's secretary of the treasury. (*National Portrait Gallery, Smithsonian Institution*)

Samuel Adams (1722–1803), Revolutionary leader, signer of the Declaration of Independence, and a major pamphleteer. Adams was the moving spirit behind the Boston Tea Party. Sometimes viewed as a radical, he nonetheless was elected governor of Massachusetts (1794–1797). (*Museum of Fine Arts, Boston*)

tion adjourned in September 1787. But the legislature was about to adjourn, and the Antifederalist minority felt that this was moving with too much haste (Congress had not even formally transmitted the document to the legislature for its consideration!). They wanted to postpone action until after the coming state elections, when they hoped to win a majority and so prevent calling a ratifying convention. When it became clear the Federalists were going to move ahead, the Antifederalists left the legislative chamber. Because the legislature was now two members short of a quorum, business was brought to a standstill. But Philadelphia, the seat of the legislature, was a Federalist stronghold. The next morning two Antifederalists were roused from their quarters, carried into the legislative chamber, and forced to remain. The resolution calling for election of delegates to a ratifying convention was adopted.[22] Under the generalship of James Wilson, the Pennsylvania convention ratified by a vote of 46 to 23 in December 1787.

By early 1788 New Jersey, Connecticut, and Georgia had also ratified. The scene of battle then shifted to Massachusetts, a key state as well as a doubtful one. John Hancock and Samuel Adams had not declared themselves, and these patriots of '76, with their great popular following, held the balance of power. The Federalists cleverly pointed out to Hancock that Washington would be the first president and that therefore the vice-president would undoubtedly be a New Englander. What citizen of New England was more distinguished than John Hancock? Whether or not this hint was effective, Hancock eventually came out for ratification. Adams was persuaded to vote for approval after securing a promise that a bill of rights would be forthcoming after adoption. Even so, Massachusetts ratified by a narrow margin (187 to 168).

By June 1788 Maryland, South Carolina, and New Hampshire had ratified; the nine states required to bring the Constitution into effect had been obtained. Still, neither Virginia nor New York had taken action, and without them the new Union would have little chance of success. Virginia was the most populous state and the home of many of the nation's outstanding leaders, and New York was important geographically.

The Virginia ratifying convention rivaled the Constitutional Convention in the caliber of its delegates. James Madison was the captain of the Federalist forces, and he had able lieutenants in Governor Randolph and in the young John Marshall. Patrick Henry, George Mason, and James Monroe within the convention, and Richard Henry Lee outside, led the opposition. Henry attacked the proposed government, point by point, with great eloquence; Madison turned back each attack quietly but cogently. At the critical juncture Washington sent a letter to the convention urging unqualified ratification. This tipped the scale, and Virginia ratified. News was rushed to New York.

The great landowners along the Hudson, unlike their southern planter friends, were opposed to the Constitution. They feared federal taxation of their holdings, and they did not want to abolish the profitable tax New York had been levying on the trade and commerce of other states. When the convention assembled, the Federalists were greatly outnumbered, but they were aided by the strategy and skill of Hamilton and by word of Virginia's ratification. New York approved by a margin of three votes. Although North Carolina and Rhode Island still remained outside the Union (the former ratified in November 1789, and the latter six months later), the new nation was created. In New York a few members of the old Congress assembled to issue the call for elections under the new Constitution. Then Congress adjourned without setting a day for reconvening.

[22] Julius Goebel, Jr., *Antecedents and Beginnings to 1801* (Macmillan, 1971), p. 267.

INTO THE THIRD CENTURY—AND SOME QUESTIONS

On September 17, 1787, after four months of heated debate, all but three of the delegates to the Constitutional Convention signed their names to the constitution they had prepared. While they were doing so Benjamin Franklin, pointing out the rising sun painted on the back of the president's chair, observed that painters had found it difficult to distinguish, in their art, a rising from a setting sun.

"I have," said he, "often and often in the course of the session, and the vicissitudes of my hopes and fears as to its issue, looked at that sun behind the president, without being able to tell whether it was a rising or setting; but now, at length, I have the happiness to know that it is rising and not a setting sun."

Two hundred years later the Constitution they wrote—amended significantly–yet only twenty-six times–remains the operating charter of our Republic. It is neither self-explanatory nor a comprehensive description of our constitutional rules. Still, it remains the starting point. Yet many Americans who swear by the Constitution have never read it. Copies can be found in the backs of most American government and American history textbooks, but who ever reads an appendix? (We hope, incidentally, that *you* will do so, for the appendix in this text contains, among other things, three great essays written to explain and defend the Constitution: *The Federalist*, Nos. 10, 51, and 78.)

Justice Hugo Black, who served on the Supreme Court for thirty-four years, kept a copy of the Constitution with him at all times. He read it often. We think that, especially in this Bicentennial era, reading the Constitution would be a good way for you to begin (and end) your study of the government of the United States. Thus, we have included a copy of it at the end of this chapter. It will not take long for you to read it carefully.

A constitution that is to endure must reflect the hard experiences and high hopes of the people for whom it is written. Those who framed our Constitution did not, of course, complete the task of constitution making. That process began long before the Constitutional Convention, and it continues still. Constitutions, even written ones, are growing and evolving organisms.

The completion of two centuries of self-government—a major accomplishment—*is* a time of national celebration. However, it is also appropriately a time of national questioning. The questions that are being asked have no easy answers. They are questions to which there is no single logical response, no answer that stems easily from an analysis of facts; they are basic questions that deal with value choices. The following questions may help stimulate your thinking as we proceed with a more detailed investigation of the operations of the American Republic:

1. Is the system sufficiently *open* to persons of all races, sexes, classes, and political views who wish to participate in making decisions?
2. Is the system sufficiently *responsive*? Is the leadership *accountable* to the voters?
3. Is the system sufficiently *representative*? This concept of "representation" is one of the most difficult in political science. Here we mean to focus not on whether those who govern precisely mirror divisions of class, race, interest, and region, but on whether those who govern are sensitive to the needs and opinions of differing groups.
4. Is the system sufficiently *responsible*? Does the leadership keep in mind the long-term needs of the entire nation and not merely respond to the short-term demands of the most vocal or most prosperous special interests?
5. Is the system *effective*? Does it permit us to solve our most pressing problems? Is it relevant to the challenges of the 1990s and the coming new century?

We must remember, as we consider these questions, that the framers did not favor a government in which the mass of people would participate directly, or one that would be representative of or responsive to the people at-large. Rather, they sought to control both the spirit of faction and the thrust of majorities. Their prime concern was how to fashion a viable, but limited, government. The framers had not seen a political party in the modern sense and would not have liked it if they had. They did not favor an arousing, mobilizing kind of leadership but preferred instead a stabilizing, balancing, magisterial leadership—the kind George Washington was expected to (and did) supply. Today we have *high-pressure politics* characterized by strongly organized groups and political-action committees, potent and volatile public opinion dominated by opinion-making agencies, parties vying to mobilize nationwide majorities, and celebrity-leaders intimately covered by the media. How responsive are our political agencies to fast-moving changes in public attitudes and moods? Will our Constitution and the system it created be able to deal with the problems of our third century?

According to an old story, Benjamin Franklin was confronted by a woman as he left the last session of the Constitutional Convention in Philadelphia in September 1787.

"What kind of government have you given us, Dr. Franklin?" she asked, "a Republic or a Monarchy?"

"A Republic, Madam," he answered, "—if you can keep it."

The Constitution of the United States of America

THE PREAMBLE

We the People of the United States, in Order to form a more perfect Union, establish Justice, insure domestic Tranquility, provide for the common defence, promote the general Welfare, and secure the Blessings of Liberty to ourselves and our Posterity, do ordain and establish this Constitution for the United States of America.

ARTICLE I—THE LEGISLATIVE ARTICLE

Legislative Power

Section 1   All legislative Powers herein granted shall be vested in a Congress of the United States, which shall consist of a Senate and House of Representatives.

House of Representatives: Composition; Qualifications; Apportionment; Impeachment Power

Section 2   The House of Representatives shall be composed of Members chosen every second Year by the People of the several States, and the Electors in each State shall have the Qualifications requisite for Electors of the most numerous Branch of the State Legislature.

No Person shall be a Representative who shall not have attained to the Age of twenty five Years, and been seven Years a Citizen of the United States, and who shall not, when elected, be an Inhabitant of that State in which he shall be chosen.

Representatives and direct Taxes[1] shall be apportioned among the several States which may be included within this Union, according to their respective Numbers, *which shall be determined by adding to the whole Number of free Persons, including those bound to Service for a Term of Years, and excluding Indians not taxed, three fifths of all other Persons.*[2] The actual Enumeration shall be made within three Years after the first Meeting of the Congress of the United States, and within every subsequent Term of ten Years, in such Manner as they shall by Law direct. The Number of Representatives shall not exceed one for every thirty Thousand, but each State shall have at least one Representative; and until each enumeration shall be made, the State of New Hampshire shall be entitled to chuse three, Massachusetts eight, Rhode-Island and Providence Plantations one, Connecticut five, New-York six, New Jersey four, Pennsylvania eight, Delaware one, Maryland six, Virginia ten, North Carolina five, South Carolina five, and Georgia three.

When vacancies happen in the Representation from any State, the Executive Authority thereof shall issue Writs of Election to fill such Vacancies.

The House of Representatives shall chuse their Speaker and other Officers; and shall have the sole Power of Impeachment.

Senate Composition: Qualifications, Impeachment Trials

Section 3   The Senate of the United States shall be composed of two Senators from each State, *chosen by the Legislature thereof,*[3] for six Years; and each Senator shall have one Vote.

Immediately after they shall be assembled in Consequence of the first Election, they shall be divided as equally as may be into three Classes. The Seats of the Senators of the first Class shall be vacated at the Expiration of the second Year, of the second Class at the Expiration of the fourth Year, and of the third Class at the Expiration of the sixth Year, so that one third may be chosen every second Year; *and if Vacancies happen by Resignation, or otherwise, during the Recess of the Legislature of any State, the Executive thereof may make temporary Appointments until the next Meeting of the Legislature, which shall then fill such Vacancies.*[4]

No person shall be a Senator who shall not have attained to the Age of thirty Years, and been nine Years a Citizen of the United States, and who shall not, when elected, be an inhabitant of that State for which he shall be chosen.

The Vice President of the United States shall be President of the Senate, but shall have no Vote, unless they be equally divided.

The Senate shall chuse their other Officers, and also a President pro tempore, in the Absence of the Vice President, or when he shall exercise the Office of President of the United States.

The Senate shall have the sole Power to try all Impeachments. When sitting for that Purpose, they shall be on Oath or Affirmation. When the President of the United States is tried, the Chief Justice shall preside: And no Person shall be convicted without the Concurrence of two thirds of the Members present.

Judgment in Cases of Impeachment shall not extend further than to removal from Office, and disqualification to hold and enjoy any Office of honor, Trust or Profit under the United States; but the Party convicted shall nevertheless be liable and

---

[1]Modified by the 16th Amendment
[2]"Other Persons" refers to black slaves. Replaced by Section 2, 14th Amendment

[3]Repealed by the 17th Amendment
[4]Modified by the 17th Amendment

subject to Indictment, Trial, Judgment and Punishment, according to law.

Congressional Elections: Times, Places, Manner

Section 4 The Times, Places and Manner of holding Elections for Senators and Representatives, shall be prescribed in each State by the Legislature thereof; but the Congress may at any time by Law make or alter such Regulations, except as to the Places of chusing Senators.

The Congress shall assemble at least once in every Year, *and such Meeting shall be on the first Monday in December, unless they shall by Law appoint a different Day.*[5]

Powers and Duties of the Houses

Section 5 Each House shall be the Judge of the Elections, Returns and Qualifications of its own Members, and a Majority of each shall constitute a Quorum to do Business; but a smaller Number may adjourn from day to day, and may be authorized to compel the Attendance of absent Members, in such Manner, and under the Penalties as each House may provide.

Each House may determine the Rules of its Proceedings, punish its Members for disorderly Behaviour, and, with the Concurrence of two thirds, expel a Member.

Each House shall keep a Journal of its Proceedings, and from time to time publish the same, excepting such Parts as may in their Judgment require Secrecy; and the yeas and Nays of the Members of either House on any question shall, at the Desire of one fifth of those Present, be entered on the Journal.

Neither House, during the Session of Congress, shall, without the Consent of the other, adjourn for more than three days, nor to any other place than that in which the two Houses shall be sitting.

Rights of Members

Section 6 The Senators and Representatives shall receive a Compensation for their Services, to be ascertained by Law, and paid out of the Treasury of the United States. They shall in all Cases, except Treason, Felony and Breach of the Peace, be privileged from Arrest during their Attendance at the Session of their respective Houses, and in going to and returning from the same; and for any Speech or Debate in either House, they shall not be questioned in any other Place.

No Senator or Representative, shall, during the time for which he was elected, be appointed to any civil Office under the authority of the United States, which shall have been created, or the Emoluments whereof shall have been encreased during such time; and no Person holding any Office under the United States, shall be a Member of either House during his Continuance in Office.

Legislative Powers: Bills and Resolutions

Section 7 All Bills for raising Revenue shall originate in the House of Representatives; but the Senate may propose or concur with Amendments as on other Bills.

Every Bill which shall have passed the House of Representatives and the Senate, shall, before it become a Law, be presented to the President of the United States; if he approve he shall sign it, but if not he shall return it, with his Objections to that House in which it shall have originated, who shall enter the Objections at large on their Journal, and proceed to reconsider

[5]Changed by the 20th Amendment

it. If after such Reconsideration two thirds of that House shall agree to pass the Bill, it shall be sent, together with the Objections, to the other House, by which it shall likewise be reconsidered, and if approved by two thirds of that House, it shall become a Law. But in all such Cases the Votes of both Houses shall be determined by yeas and Nays, and the Names of the Persons voting for and against the Bill shall be entered on the Journal of each House respectively. If any Bill shall not be returned by the President within ten Days (Sundays excepted) after it shall have been presented to him, the Same shall be a Law, in like Manner as if he had signed it, unless the Congress by their Adjournment prevent its Return, in which Case it shall not be a Law.

Every Order, Resolution, or Vote to which the Concurrence of the Senate and House of Representatives may be necessary (except on a question of Adjournment) shall be presented to the President of the United States; and before the Same shall take Effect, shall be approved by him, or being disapproved by him, shall be repassed by two thirds of the Senate and House of Representatives, according to the Rules and Limitations prescribed in the Case of a Bill.

Powers of Congress

Section 8 The Congress shall have Power To lay and collect Taxes, Duties, Imposts and Excises, to pay the Debts and provide for the common Defence and general Welfare of the United States; but all Duties, Imposts and Excises shall be uniform throughout the United States;

To borrow Money on the Credit of the United States;

To regulate Commerce with foreign Nations, and among the several States, and with the Indian Tribes;

To establish an uniform Rule of Naturalization, and uniform Laws on the subject of Bankruptcies throughout the United States;

To coin Money, regulate the Value thereof, and of foreign Coin, and fix the Standard of Weights and Measures;

To provide for the Punishment of counterfeiting the Securities and current Coin of the United States;

To establish Post Offices and post Roads;

To promote the Progress of Science and useful Arts, by securing for limited Times to Authors and Inventors the exclusive Right to their respective Writings and Discoveries,

To constitute Tribunals inferior to the supreme Court,

To define and punish Piracies and Felonies committed on the high Seas, and Offences against the Law of Nations;

To declare War, grant Letters of Marque and Reprisal, and make Rules concerning Captures on Land and Water;

To raise and support Armies, but no Appropriation of Money to that Use shall be for a longer Term than two Years;

To provide and maintain a Navy;

To make Rules for the Government and Regulation of the land and naval Forces;

To provide for calling for the Militia to execute the Laws of the Union, suppress Insurrections and repel Invasions;

To provide for organizing, arming, and disciplining, the Militia, and for governing such Part of them as may be employed in the Service of the United States, reserving to the States respectively, the Appointment of the Officers, and the Authority of training the Militia according to the discipline prescribed by Congress;

To exercise exclusive Legislation in all Cases whatsoever, over such District (not exceeding ten Miles square) as may, by

Cession of particular States, and the Acceptance of Congress, become the Seat of the Government of the United States, and to exercise like Authority over all Places purchased by the Consent of the Legislature of the State in which the Same shall be, for the Erection of Forts, Magazines, Arsenals, dock-Yards, and other needful Buildings;—And

To make all Laws which shall be necessary and proper for carrying into Execution the foregoing Powers, and all other Powers vested by this Constitution in the Government of the United States, or in any Department or Officer thereof.

Powers Denied to Congress

Section 9   The Migration or Importation of such Persons as any of the States now existing shall think proper to admit, shall not be prohibited by the Congress prior to the Year one thousand eight hundred and eight, but a Tax or Duty may be imposed on such Importation, not exceeding ten dollars for each Person.

The privilege of the Writ of Habeas Corpus shall not be suspended, unless when in Cases of Rebellion or Invasion the public Safety may require it.

No Bill of Attainder or ex post facto Laws shall be passed.

No Capitation, or other direct, Tax shall be laid, unless in Proportion to the Census or Enumeration herein before directed to be taken.[6]

No Tax or Duty shall be laid on Articles exported from any State.

No Preference shall be given by any Regulation of Commerce or Revenue to the Ports of one State over those of another; nor shall Vessels bound to, or from, one State, be obliged to enter, clear, or pay Duties in another.

No Money shall be drawn from the Treasury, but in Consequence of Appropriations made by Law; and a regular Statement and Account of the Receipts and Expenditures of all public Money shall be published from time to time.

No Title of Nobility shall be granted by the United States; And no Person holding any Office of Profit or Trust under them, shall, without the Consent of the Congress, accept of any present, Emolument, Office, or Title, of any kind whatever, from any King, Prince, or foreign State.

Powers Denied to the States

Section 10   No State shall enter into any Treaty, Alliance, or Confederation; grant Letters of Marque and Reprisal; coin Money; emit Bills of Credit; make any Thing but gold and silver Coin a Tender in Payment of Debts; pass any Bill of Attainder, ex post facto Law, or Law impairing the Obligation of Contracts, or grant any Title of Nobility.

No State shall, without the Consent of the Congress, lay any Imposts or Duties on Imports or Exports, except what may be absolutely necessary for executing it's inspection Laws: and the net Produce of all Duties and Imposts, laid by any State on Imports or Exports, shall be for the Use of the Treasury of the United States; and all such Laws shall be subject to the Revision and Controul of the Congress.

No State shall, without the Consent of Congress, lay any Duty of Tonnage, keep Troops, or Ships of War in time of Peace, enter into any Agreement or Compact with another State, or with a foreign Power, or engage in War, unless actually invaded, or in such imminent Danger as will not admit of Delay.

[6]Modified by the 16th Amendment

ARTICLE II—THE EXECUTIVE ARTICLE
Nature and Scope of Presidential Power

Section 1   The executive Power shall be vested in a President of the United States of America. He shall hold his Office during the Term of four Years and, together with the Vice President, chosen for the same Term, be elected as follows

Each State shall appoint, in such Manner as the Legislature thereof may direct, a Number of Electors, equal to the whole Number of Senators and Representatives to which the State may be entitled in the Congress: but no Senator or Representative, or Person holding an Office of Trust or Profit under the United States, shall be appointed an Elector.

The Electors shall meet in their respective States, and vote by Ballot for two Persons, of whom one at least shall not be an Inhabitant of the same State with themselves. And they shall make a List of all the Persons voted for, and of the Number of Votes for each; which List they shall sign and certify, and transmit sealed to the Seat of the Government of the United States, directed to the President of the Senate. The President of the Senate shall, in the Presence of the Senate and House of Representatives, open all the Certificates, and the Votes shall then be counted. The Person having the greatest Number of Votes shall be the President, if such Number be a Majority of the whole Number of Electors appointed; and if there be more than one who have such Majority and have an equal Number of Votes, then the House of Representatives shall immediately chuse by Ballot one of them for President; and if no person have a Majority, then from the five highest on the List the said House shall in like Manner chuse the President. But in chusing the President, the Votes shall be taken by States, the Representation from each State having one Vote; A quorum for this Purpose shall consist of a Member or Members from two thirds of the States, and a Majority of all the States shall be necessary to a Choice. In every Case, after the Choice of the President, the person having the greatest Number of Votes of the Electors shall be the Vice President. But if there should remain two or more who have equal Vote, the Senate shall chuse from them by Ballot the Vice President.[7]

The Congress may determine the Time of chusing the Electors, and the Day on which they shall give their Votes; which Day shall be the same throughout the United States.

No Person except a natural born Citizen, or a Citizen of the United States, at the time of the Adoption of this Constitution, shall be eligible to the Office of President; neither shall any Person be eligible to that Office who shall not have attained to the Age of thirty five Years, and been fourteen Years a Resident within the United States.

In Case of the Removal of the President from Office, or of his Death, Resignation, or Inability to discharge the Powers and Duties of the said Office, the same shall devolve on the Vice President, and the Congress may by Law provide for the Case of Removal, Death, Resignation, or Inability, both of the President and Vice President, declaring what Officer shall then act as President, and such Officer shall act accordingly, until the Disability be removed, or a President shall be elected.[8]

The President shall, at stated Times, receive for his Services, a Compensation, which shall neither be encreased nor diminished during the Period of which he shall have been elected, and he shall not receive within that Period any other Emolument from the United States, or any of them.

[7]Changed by the 12th and 20th Amendments
[8]Modified by the 25th Amendment

Before he enter on the Execution of his Office, he shall take the following Oath or Affirmation:—"I do solemnly swear (or affirm) that I will faithfully execute the Office of President of the United States, and will to the best of my Ability, preserve, protect and defend the Constitution of the United States."

Powers and Duties of the President

Section 2 The President shall be the Commander in Chief of the Army and Navy of the United States, and of the Militia of the several States, when called into the actual Service of the United States, he may require the Opinion, in writing, of the principal Officer in each of the executive Departments, upon any Subject relating to the Duties of their respective Offices, and he shall have the Power to grant Reprieves and Pardons for Offences against the United States, except in Cases of Impeachment.

He shall have Power, by and with the Advice and Consent of the Senate to make Treaties, provided two thirds of the Senators present concur; and he shall nominate, and by and with the Advice and Consent of the Senate, shall appoint Ambassadors, other public Ministers and Consuls, Judges of the supreme Court, and all other Officers of the United States, whose Appointments are not herein otherwise provided for, and which shall be established by Law: but the Congress may by Law vest the Appointment of such inferior Officers, as they think proper, in the President alone, in the Courts of Law, or in the Heads of Departments.

The President shall have Power to fill up all Vacancies that may happen during the Recess of the Senate, by granting Commissions which shall expire at the End of their next Session.

Section 3 He shall from time to time give to the Congress Information of the State of the Union, and recommend to their Consideration such Measures as he shall judge necessary and expedient; he may, on extraordinary Occasions, convene both Houses, or either of them, and in Case of Disagreement between them, with Respect to the Time of Adjournment, he may adjourn them to such Time as he shall think proper; he shall receive Ambassadors and other public Ministers; he shall take Care that the Laws be faithfully executed, and shall Commission all the Officers of the United States.

Section 4 The President, Vice President and all civil Officers of the United States, shall be removed from Office on Impeachment for, and Conviction of, Treason, Bribery, or other High Crimes and Misdemeanors.

ARTICLE III—THE JUDICIAL ARTICLE

Judicial Power, Courts, Judges

Section 1 The judicial Power of the United States, shall be vested in one supreme Court, and in such inferior Courts as the Congress may from time to time ordain and establish. The Judges, both of the supreme and inferior Courts, shall hold their Offices during good Behaviour, and shall, at stated Times, receive for their Services, a Compensation, which shall not be diminished during their Continuance in Office.

Jurisdiction

Section 2 The judicial Power shall extend to all Cases, in Law and Equity, arising under this Constitution, the Laws of the United States, and Treaties made, or which shall be made, under their Authority;—to all Cases affecting Ambassadors, other public Ministers and Consuls;—to all Cases of admiralty and maritime Jurisdiction;—to Controversies to which the United States shall be a Party;—to Controversies between two or more States; *between a State and Citizens of another State;*[9]—between Citizens of different States;—between Citizens of the same State claiming Lands under Grants of different States, and between a State, or the Citizens thereof, and foreign States, Citizens, or Subjects.

In all Cases affecting Ambassadors, other public Ministers and Consuls, and those in which a State shall be Party, the supreme Court shall have original Jurisdiction. In all the other Cases before mentioned, the supreme Court shall have appellate Jurisdiction, both as to Law and Fact, with such Exceptions, and under such Regulations as Congress shall make.

The Trial of all Crimes, except in Cases of Impeachment, shall be by Jury; and such Trial shall be held in the State where the said Crimes shall have been committed; but when not committed within any State, the Trial shall be at such Place or Places as the Congress may by Law have directed.

Treason

Section 3 Treason against the United States, shall consist only in levying War against them, or in adhering to their Enemies, giving them Aid and Comfort. No Person shall be convicted of Treason unless on the Testimony of two Witnesses to the same overt Act, or on Confession in open Court.

The Congress shall have Power to declare the Punishment of Treason, but no Attainder of Treason shall work Corruption of Blood, or Forfeiture except during the Life of the Person attainted.

ARTICLE IV—INTERSTATE RELATIONS

Full Faith and Credit Clause

Section 1 Full Faith and Credit shall be given in each State to the public Acts, Records, and judicial Proceedings of every other State. And the Congress may by general Laws prescribe the Manner in which such Acts, Records and Proceedings shall be proved, and the Effect thereof.

Privileges and Immunities; Interstate Extradition

Section 2 The Citizens of each State shall be entitled to all Privileges and Immunities of Citizens in the several States.

A person charged in any State with Treason, Felony or other Crime, who shall flee from Justice, and be found in another State, shall on Demand of the executive Authority of the State from which he fled, be delivered up to be removed to the State having jurisdiction of the Crime.

No person held to Service or Labour in one State, under the Laws thereof, escaping into another, shall, in Consequence of any Law or Regulation therein, be discharged from such Service or Labour, but shall be delivered up on on Claim of the Party to whom such Service or Labour may be due.[10]

Admission of States

Section 3 New States may be admitted by the Congress into this Union; but no new State shall be formed or erected within the Jurisdiction of any other State; nor any State be formed by

[9]Modified by the 11th Amendment
[10]Repealed by the 13th Amendment

the Junction of two or more States, or Parts of States, without the Consent of the Legislatures of the States concerned as well as of the Congress.

The Congress shall have Power to dispose of and make all needful Rules and Regulations respecting the Territory or other Property belonging to the United States; and nothing in this Constitution shall be so construed as to Prejudice any Claims of the United States, or of any particular State.

Republican Form of Government

Section 4 The United States shall guarantee to every State in this Union a Republican Form of Government, and shall protect each of them against Invasion; and on Application of the Legislature, or of the Executive (when the Legislature cannot be convened) against domestic Violence.

ARTICLE V—THE AMENDING POWER

The Congress, whenever two thirds of both Houses shall deem it necessary, shall propose Amendments to this Constitution, or, on the Application of the Legislatures of two thirds of several States, shall call a Convention for proposing Amendments, which, in either Case, shall be valid to all Intents and Purposes, as Part of this Constitution, when ratified by the Legislatures of three fourths of the several States, or by Conventions in three fourths thereof, as the one or the other Mode of Ratification may be proposed by the Congress; Provided that no Amendment which may be made prior to the Year One thousand eight hundred and eight shall in any Manner affect the first and fourth Clauses in the Ninth Section of the first Article; and that no State, without its Consent, shall be deprived of its equal Suffrage in the Senate.

ARTICLE VI—THE SUPREMACY ACT

All Debts contracted and Engagements entered into, before the Adoption of this Constitution, shall be as valid against the United States under the Constitution, as under the Confederation.

This Constitution, and the Laws of the United States which shall be made in Pursuance thereof; and all Treaties made, or which shall be made, under the Authority of the United States, shall be the supreme Law of the Land; and the Judges in every State shall be bound thereby, any Thing in the Constitution or Laws of any State to the Contrary notwithstanding.

The Senators and Representatives before mentioned, and the Members of the several State Legislatures, and all executive and judicial Officers, both of the United States and of the several States, shall be bound by Oath or Affirmation, to support this Constitution; but no religious Test shall ever be required as a Qualification to any Office or public Trust under the United States.

ARTICLE VII—RATIFICATION

The Ratification of the Conventions of nine States, shall be sufficient for the Establishment of this Constitution between the States so ratifying the Same.

done in Convention by the Unanimous Consent of the States present the Seventeenth Day of September in the Year of our Lord one thousand seven hundred and Eighty seven and of the Independence of the United States of America the Twelfth. *In Witness whereof We have hereunto subscribed our Names.*

THE BILL OF RIGHTS

[The first ten amendments were ratified on December 15, 1791, and form what is known as the "Bill of Rights"]

AMENDMENT 1—RELIGION, SPEECH, ASSEMBLY, AND POLITICS

Congress shall make no law respecting an establishment of religion, or prohibiting the free exercise thereof; or abridging the freedom of speech, or of the press; or the right of the people peaceably to assemble, and to petition the Government for a redress of grievances.

AMENDMENT 2—MILITIA AND THE RIGHT TO BEAR ARMS

A well regulated Militia, being necessary to the security of a free State, the right of the people to keep and bear Arms, shall not be infringed.

AMENDMENT 3—QUARTERING OF SOLDIERS

No Soldier shall, in time of peace be quartered in any house, without the consent of the Owner, nor in time of war, but in manner to be prescribed by law.

AMENDMENT 4—SEARCHES AND SEIZURES

The right of the people to be secure in their persons, houses, papers, and effects, against unreasonable searches and seizures, shall not be violated, and no Warrants shall issue, but upon probable cause, supported by Oath or affirmation, and particularly describing the place to be searched, and the persons or things to be seized.

AMENDMENT 5—GRAND JURIES, SELF-INCRIMINATION, DOUBLE JEOPARDY, DUE PROCESS, AND EMINENT DOMAIN

No person shall be held to answer for a capital, or otherwise infamous crime, unless on a presentment or indictment of a Grand jury, except in cases arising in the land or naval forces, or in the Militia, when in actual service in time of War or public danger; nor shall any person be subject for the same offence to be twice put in jeopardy of life or limb; nor shall be compelled in any criminal case to be a witness against himself, nor be deprived of life, liberty, or property, without due process of law; nor shall private property be taken for public use, without just compensation.

AMENDMENT 6—CRIMINAL COURT PROCEDURES

In all criminal prosecutions, the accused shall enjoy the right to a speedy and public trial, by an impartial jury of the State and district wherein the crime shall have been committed, which district shall have been previously ascertained by law, and to be informed of the nature and cause of the accusation; to be confronted with the witnesses against him; to have compulsory process for obtaining Witnesses in his favor, and to have the Assistance of Counsel for his defence.

AMENDMENT 7—TRIAL BY JURY IN COMMON LAW CASES

In Suits at common law, where the value in controversy shall exceed twenty dollars, the right of trial by jury shall be preserved, and no fact tried by a jury shall be otherwise re-examined in any Court of the United States, than according to the rules of the common law.

AMENDMENT 8—BAIL, CRUEL AND UNUSUAL PUNISHMENT

Excessive bail shall not be required, nor excessive fines imposed, nor cruel and unusual punishments inflicted.

AMENDMENT 9—RIGHTS RETAINED BY THE PEOPLE

The enumeration in the Constitution, of certain rights, shall not be construed to deny or disparage others retained by the people.

AMENDMENT 10—RESERVED POWERS OF THE STATES

The powers not delegated to the United States by the Constitution, nor prohibited by it to the States, are reserved to the States respectively, or to the people.

PRE-CIVIL WAR AMENDMENTS

AMENDMENT 11—SUITS AGAINST THE STATES

[Ratified February 7, 1795]

The Judicial power of the United States shall not be construed to extend to any suit in law or equity, commenced or prosecuted against one of the United States by Citizens of another State, or by Citizens or Subjects of any Foreign State.

AMENDMENT 12—ELECTION OF THE PRESIDENT

[Ratified July 27, 1804]

The Electors shall meet in their respective states, and vote by ballot for President and Vice-President, one of whom, at least, shall not be an inhabitant of the same state with themselves; they shall name in their ballots the person voted for as President, and in distinct ballots the person voted for as Vice-President, and they shall make distinct lists of all persons voted for as President, and of all persons voted for as Vice-President, and of the number of votes for each, which lists they shall sign and certify, and transmit sealed to the seat of the government of the United States, directed to the President of the Senate;—The President of the Senate shall, in presence of the Senate and House of Representatives, open all the certificates and the votes shall then be counted;—The person having the greatest number of votes for President, shall be the President, if such number be a majority of the whole number of Electors appointed; and if no person have such majority, then from the persons having the highest numbers not exceeding three on the list of those voted for as President, the House of Representatives shall choose immediately, by ballot, the President. But in choosing the President, the votes shall be taken by states, the representation from each state having one vote; a quorum for this purpose shall consist of a member or members from two-thirds of the states, and a majority of all states shall be necessary to a choice. And if the House of Representatives shall not choose a President whenever the right of choice shall devolve upon them, *before the fourth day of March next following*, then the Vice-President shall act as President, as in the case of the death or other constitutional disability of the President.[11] The person having the greatest number of votes as Vice-President, shall be the Vice-President, if such a number be a majority of the whole numbers of Electors appointed, and if no person have a majority, then from the two highest numbers on the list, the Senate shall choose the Vice-President; a quorum for the purpose shall consist of two-thirds of the whole number of Senators, and a majority of the whole number shall be necessary to a choice. But no person constitutionally ineligible to the office of President shall be eligible to that of Vice-President of the United States.

CIVIL WAR AMENDMENTS

AMENDMENT 13—PROHIBITION OF SLAVERY

[Ratified December 6, 1865]

Section 1   Neither slavery nor involuntary servitude, except as a punishment for crime whereof the party shall have been duly convicted, shall exist within the United States, or any place subject to their jurisdiction.

Section 2   Congress shall have power to enforce this article by appropriate legislation.

AMENDMENT 14—CITIZENSHIP, DUE PROCESS, AND EQUAL PROTECTION OF THE LAWS

[Ratified July 9, 1868]

Section 1   All persons born or naturalized in the United States, and subject to the jurisdiction thereof, are citizens of the United States and of the State wherein they reside. No State shall make or enforce any law which shall abridge the privileges or immunities of citizens of the United States; nor shall any State deprive any person of life, liberty, or property, without due process of law; nor deny to any person within its jurisdiction the equal protection of the laws.

Section 2   Representatives shall be apportioned among the several States according to their respective numbers, counting the whole number of persons in each State, excluding Indians not taxed. But when the right to vote at any election for the choice of electors for President and Vice President of the United States, Representatives in Congress, the Executive and Judicial officers of a State, or the members of the Legislature thereof, is denied to any of the male inhabitants of such State, being twenty-one[12] years of age, and citizens of the United States, or in any way abridged, except for participation in rebellion, or other crime, the basis of representation therein shall be reduced in the proportion which the number of such male citizens shall bear to the whole number of male citizens twenty-one years of age in such State.

Section 3   No person shall be a Senator or Representative in Congress, or elector of President and Vice President, or hold any office, civil or military, under the United States, or under any State, who, having previously taken an oath, as a member of Congress, or as an officer of the United States, or as a member of

---

[11]Changed by the 20th Amendment
[12]Changed by the 26th Amendment

any State legislature, or as an executive or judicial officer of any State, to support the Constitution of the United States, shall have engaged in insurrection or rebellion against the same, or given aid or comfort to the enemies thereof. But Congress may by a vote of two-thirds of each House, remove such disability.

Section 4 The validity of the public debt of the United States, authorized by law, including debts incurred for payment of pensions and bounties for services in suppressing insurrection or rebellion, shall not be questioned. But neither the United States nor any State shall assume or pay any debt or obligation incurred in aid of insurrection or rebellion against the United States, or any claim for the loss or emancipation of any slave; but all such debts, obligations and claims shall be held illegal and void.

Section 5 The Congress shall have power to enforce, by appropriate legislation, the provisions of this article.

AMENDMENT 15—THE RIGHT TO VOTE

[Ratified February 3, 1870]

Section 1 The right of citizens of the United States to vote shall not be denied or abridged by the United States or by any State on account of race, color, or previous condition of servitude.

Section 2 The Congress shall have power to enforce this article by appropriate legislation.

AMENDMENT 16—INCOME TAXES

[Ratified February 3, 1913]

The Congress shall have power to lay and collect taxes on incomes, from whatever source derived, without apportionment among the several States, and without regard to any census or enumeration.

AMENDMENT 17—DIRECT ELECTION OF SENATORS

[Ratified April 8, 1913]

The Senate of the United States shall be composed of two Senators from each State, elected by the people thereof, for six years; and each Senator shall have one vote. The electors in each State shall have the qualifications requisite for electors of the most numerous branch of the State legislatures.

When vacancies happen in the representation of any State in the Senate, the executive authority of such State shall issue writs of election to fill such vacancies: *Provided*, That the Legislature of any State may empower the executive thereof to make temporary appointment until the people fill the vacancies by election as the legislature may direct.

This amendment shall not be so construed as to affect the election or term of any Senator chosen before it becomes valid as part of the Constitution.

AMENDMENT 18—PROHIBITION

[Ratified January 16, 1919   Repealed December 5, 1933 by Amendment 21]

Section 1 After one year from the ratification of this article the manufacture, sale, or transportation of intoxicating liquors within, the importation thereof into, or the exportation thereof

from the United States and all territory subject to the jurisdiction thereof for beverage purposes is hereby prohibited.

Section 2 The Congress and the several states shall have concurrent power to enforce this article by appropriate legislation.

Section 3 This article shall be inoperative unless it shall have been ratified as an amendment to the Constitution by the legislatures of the several states, as provided in the Constitution, within seven years from the date of the submission hereof to the States by the Congress.[13]

AMENDMENT 19—FOR WOMEN'S SUFFRAGE

[Ratified August 18, 1920]

The right of the citizens of the United States to vote shall not be denied or abridged by the United States or by any State on account of sex.

Congress shall have power, by appropriate legislation, to enforce the provision of this article.

AMENDMENT 20—THE LAME DUCK AMENDMENT

[Ratified January 23, 1933]

Section 1 The terms of the President and Vice President shall end at noon on the 20th day of January, and the terms of the Senators and Representatives at noon on the 3rd day of January, of the years in which such terms would have ended if this article had not been ratified; and the terms of their successors shall then begin.

Section 2 The Congress shall assemble at least once in every year, and such meeting shall begin at noon on the 3rd day of January, unless they shall by law appoint a different day.

Section 3 If, at the time fixed for the beginning of the term of the President, the President elect shall have died, the Vice President elect shall become President. If a President shall not have been chosen before the time fixed for the beginning of his term, or if the President elect shall have failed to qualify, then the Vice President elect shall act as President until a President shall have qualified; and the Congress may by law provide for the case wherein neither a President elect nor a Vice President elect shall have qualified, declaring who shall then act as President, or the manner in which one who is to act shall be selected, and such person shall act accordingly until a President or Vice President shall have qualified.

Section 4 The Congress may by law provide for the case of the death of any of the persons from whom the House of Representatives may choose a President whenever the right of choice shall have developed upon them, and for the case of the death of any of the persons from whom the Senate may choose a Vice President whenever the right of choice shall have devolved upon them.

Section 5 Sections 1 and 2 shall take effect on the 15th day of October following the ratification of this article.

Section 6 This article shall be inoperative unless it shall have been ratified as an amendment to the Constitution by the legislatures of three-fourths of the several States within seven years from the date of its submission.

[13]Repealed by the 21st Amendment

AMENDMENT 21—REPEAL OF PROHIBITION

[Ratified December 5, 1933]

Section 1   The eighteenth article of amendment to the Constitution of the United States is hereby repealed.

Section 2   The transportation or importation into any State, Territory, or Possession of the United States for delivery or use therein of intoxicating liquors, in violation of the laws thereof, is hereby prohibited.

Section 3   This article shall be inoperative unless it shall have been ratified as an amendment to the Constitution by conventions in the several States, as provided in the Constitution, within seven years from the date of the submission hereof to the States by the Congress.

AMENDMENT 22—NUMBER OF PRESIDENTIAL TERMS

[Ratified February 27, 1951]

Section 1   No person shall be elected to the office of the President more than twice, and no person who has held the office of President, or acted as President, for more than two years of a term to which some other person was elected President shall be elected to the Office of the President more than once. But this Article shall not apply to any person holding the office of President when this article was proposed by the Congress, and shall not prevent any person who may be holding the office of President, or acting as President, during the term within which this Article becomes operative from holding the office of President or acting as President during the remainder of such term.

Section 2   This Article shall be inoperative unless it shall have been ratified as an amendment to the Constitution by the legislatures of three-fourths of the several states within seven years from the date of its submission to the States by the Congress.

AMENDMENT 23—PRESIDENTIAL ELECTORS FOR THE DISTRICT OF COLUMBIA

[Ratified March 29, 1961]

Section 1   The District constituting the seat of Government of the United States shall appoint in such manner as the Congress may direct:

A number of electors of President and Vice President equal to the whole number of Senators and Representatives in Congress to which the District would be entitled if it were a State, but in no event more than the least populous State; they shall be in addition to those appointed by the States, but they shall be considered, for the purposes of the election of President and Vice President, to be electors appointed by a State; and they shall meet in the District and perform such duties as provided by the twelfth article of amendment.

Section 2   The Congress shall have power to enforce this article by appropriate legislation.

AMENDMENT 24—THE ANTI-POLL TAX AMENDMENT

[Ratified January 23, 1964]

Section 1   The right of citizens of the United States to vote in any primary or other election for President or Vice President, for electors for President or Vice President, or for Senator or Representative in Congress, shall not be denied or abridged by the United States or any State by reason of failure to pay any poll tax or other tax.

Section 2   The Congress shall have power to enforce this article by appropriate legislation.

AMENDMENT 25—PRESIDENTIAL DISABILITY, VICE PRESIDENTIAL VACANCIES

[Ratified February 10, 1967]

Section 1   In case of the removal of the President from office or his death or resignation, the Vice President shall become President.

Section 2   Whenever there is a vacancy in the office of the Vice President, the President shall nominate a Vice President who shall take the office upon confirmation by a majority vote of both houses of Congress.

Section 3   Whenever the President transmits to the President pro tempore of the Senate and the Speaker of the House of Representatives his written declaration that he is unable to discharge the powers and duties of his office, and until he transmits to them a written declaration to the contrary, such powers and duties shall be discharged by the Vice President as Acting President.

Section 4   Whenever the Vice-President and a majority of either the principal officers of the executive departments, or of such other body as Congress may by law provide, transmit to the President pro tempore of the Senate and the Speaker of the House of Representatives their written declaration that the President is unable to discharge the powers and duties of his office, the Vice President shall immediately assume the powers and duties of the office as Acting President.

Thereafter, when the President transmits to the President pro tempore of the Senate and the Speaker of the House of Representatives his written declaration that no inability exists, he shall resume the powers and duties of his office unless the Vice President and a majority of either the principal officers of the executive departments, or of such other body as Congress may by law provide, transmit within four days to the President pro tempore of the Senate and the Speaker of the House of Representatives their written declaration that the President is unable to discharge the powers and duties of his office. Thereupon Congress shall decide the issue, assembling within 48 hours for that purpose if not in session. If the Congress, within 21 days after receipt of the latter written declaration, or, if Congress is not in session, within 21 days after Congress is required to assemble, determines by two-thirds vote of both houses that the President is unable to discharge the powers and duties of his office, the Vice President shall continue to discharge the same as Acting President; otherwise, the President shall resume the powers and duties of his office.

AMENDMENT 26—EIGHTEEN-YEAR-OLD VOTE

[Ratified July 1, 1971]

Section 1   The right of citizens of the United States, who are eighteen years of age, or older, to vote shall not be denied or abridged by the United States or by any State on account of age.

Section 2   The Congress shall have power to enforce this article by appropriate legislation.

2

The Living Constitution

Two hundred years after the event, it is hard to understand that at the time, some people were skeptical of the proposed constitution. After watching merchants and mechanics march side by side in a parade celebrating ratification, a Bostonian remarked sourly: "It may serve to please children, but freemen will not be so easily gulled out of their liberties." On the other hand, a Philadelphian said that the procession in his city had "made such an impression on the minds of our young people that 'federal' and 'union' have now become part of the household words of every family in the city." This effect on youth was significant, for it was on the younger generation that hopes for the new government depended.

Although only a few people liked all of the recently drafted constitution, most figured it was better than the one they had. It was a skinny document of only some 4550 words—you can carry it around in your coat pocket—but it packed a powerful constitutional punch. It was only intended to be a framework for governing; it was a document into which citizens could, if optimistic, read their hopes (or, if pessimistic, their fears). Our founding politicians had high hopes it would win adoption. Still, most of them would be surprised indeed to learn that 200 years later we have still not written another constitution, or two or three.

With the adoption of the Constitution, prosperity returned. Markets for American goods were opening in Europe, and business was pulling out of its postwar slump. Such events seemed to justify Federalist claims that adoption of the Constitution would correct the nation's problems. Within a surprisingly short time the Constitution lost its partisan character; both Antifederalists and Federalists honored it. Politicians differed less and less over whether the Constitution was good; they now began to argue over what it meant.

As the Constitution won the support of Americans, it began to take on the aura of natural law: "The Fathers grew ever larger in stature as they receded from view; the era in which they lived and fought became a Golden Age, in that age there had been a fresh dawn for the world, and its men were giants against the sky."[1]

A copy of the Constitution is located on the pages just before this chapter. If you have not already done so, please read it through to get a good idea of its content and structure. It won't take long. You will find it even more helpful to read the relevant parts as we move through the book.

The Constitution is a revered document. Yet too often those who revere it have never read it.

[1] Max Lerner, *Ideas for the Ice Age* (Viking, 1941), pp. 241–42.

Constitution
(National Loyalty)

This early Constitution worship helped bring unity to the diverse new nation. Like the Crown in Britain, the Constitution became a symbol of national loyalty evoking both emotional and intellectual support from all Americans, regardless of their differences. The framers' work became part of the American creed. It stood for liberty, equality before the law, limited government—indeed, for whatever anyone wanted to read into it.

The Constitution, however, is more than a *symbol*. It is also a *supreme* and *binding law* that both *grants* and *limits* powers. "In framing a government which is to be administered by men over men," wrote James Madison in *The Federalist*, No. 51, "the great difficulty lies in this: you must first enable the government to control the governed; and in the next place oblige it to control itself." (Take a look at *The Federalist*, No. 51, which appears at the back of this book in the Appendix.) The Constitution is both a *positive* instrument of government, which enables the governors to control the governed, and a *restraint* on government, which enables the ruled to check the rulers.

In what ways does the Constitution limit the power of the government? In what ways does it create governmental power? How has it managed to serve both as a great symbol of national unity and as a somewhat adaptable and changing instrument of government?

CHECKING POWER WITH POWER

Although it may seem strange to begin by stressing the ways in which the Constitution limits governmental power, we must keep in mind the dilemma the framers faced. They wanted a more *effective* national government, yet at the same time they were keenly aware that the people would not accept too much central control. Efficiency was not as overriding a concern as *liberty*. They wanted to ensure domestic tranquility and prevent future rebellions, but they also wanted to forestall the emergence of a home-grown George III. Accordingly, they allotted certain powers to the national government and reserved the rest for the states, thus establishing a system of federalism (the nature and problems of which we take up in Chapter 3). Even this was not enough. They believed they needed still other ways to limit the *national* government.

The most important way to make public officials observe the constitutional limits on their powers is through *free elections*: The voters have the ability to throw out of office those who abuse power. Yet the framers were not willing to depend solely on such *political* controls, because they did not fully trust the people's judgment. Thomas Jefferson, a firm democrat, put it this way: "Free government is founded on jealousy, and not in confidence . . . in questions of power, then, let no more be heard of confidence in man, but bind him down from mischief by the chains of the Constitution."[2] Even more important, the framers feared that a majority faction might use the new central government to deprive minorities of their rights. "A dependence on the people is, no doubt, the primary control on the government," Madison admitted, "but experience has taught mankind the necessity of auxiliary precautions." What were these "auxiliary precautions" against popular tyranny?

[2] Quoted in Alpheus T. Mason, *The Supreme Court: Palladium of Freedom* (University of Michigan Press, 1962), p. 10.

"And there are three branches of government, so that each branch has the other two to blame everything on." (*Dunagin's People by Ralph Dunagin © 1978, Field Newspaper Syndicate. By permission of News America Syndicate.*)

Congress enacts laws.
But Pres can veto.
Supreme court can declare unconstitutional laws passed by congress and signed by the Pres.
But the Pres appoints the justices with the senate approval

Separation of Powers

The first step was the separation of powers—that is, allocating constitutional authority to each of the three branches of the national government. In *The Federalist*, No. 47, James Madison wrote, "No political truth is certainly of greater intrinsic value, or is stamped with the authority of more enlightened patrons of liberty, than that . . . the accumulation of all powers, legislative, executive, and judiciary, in the same hands . . . may justly be pronounced the very definition of tyranny."

Logic alone, however, does not account for the inclusion of this principle in our Constitution. This doctrine had been the general practice in the colonies for over 100 years. Only during the Revolutionary period was authority concentrated in the hands of the legislature, and that unhappy experience confirmed the framers' belief in the merits of separation of powers. Many attributed the evils of state government and the lack of energy in the central government to the fact that there was no strong executive to both check legislative abuses and give energy and direction to administration.

Still, separating power was not enough. There was always the danger—from the framers' point of view—that different officials with different powers might pool their authority and act together. Separation of powers by itself would not prevent government branches and officials from responding to the same pressures—for example, an overwhelming majority of the voters. If separating power was not enough, what else could be done?

Checks and Balances: Ambition to Counteract Ambition

The framers' answer was a system of **checks and balances**. "The great security against a gradual concentration of the several powers in the same department," wrote Madison, "consists in giving to those who administer each department the necessary constitutional means and personal motives to resist encroachment on the others. . . . Ambition must be made to counteract ambition."[3]

Each branch is therefore given some role in the actions of the others. We have a "government of separated institutions sharing powers."[4] Thus, Congress enacts laws, but the president can veto them. The Supreme Court can declare unconstitutional laws passed by Congress and signed by the president, but the president appoints the justices with the Senate's approval. The president administers the laws, but Congress provides the money. Moreover, the Senate and the House of Representatives have an absolute veto over each other in the enactment of a law, because bills must be approved by both houses.

Not only does each branch have some authority over the actions of the others, but each is *politically independent of the others*. The president is selected by electors (now popularly elected). Senators are now chosen by the voters in each state, and the members of the House by voters in their districts. And although federal judges are appointed by the president with the consent of the Senate, once in office they virtually hold terms for life.

The framers also ensured that a majority of the voters could win control over only part of the government at one time. A popular majority might take control of the House of Representatives in an off-year (that is, a nonpresidential) election, but the president, representing a previous popular majority, would still have two

[3] *The Federalist*, No. 51, a copy of which can be found in the Appendix.
[4] Richard E. Neustadt, *Presidential Power*, rev. ed. (Wiley, 1976), p. 101.

years to go. Further, senators are chosen for six-year terms, but only one-third are selected every two years.

Finally, national courts were also provided. In fact, judges have become so important in our system of checks and balances that they deserve special attention.

JUDICIAL REVIEW
AND THE "GUARDIANS OF THE CONSTITUTION"

Judges did not claim the power of **judicial review**—the power of a court to refuse to enforce an act of the legislature that in the opinion of the judges is in conflict with the Constitution—until some years after the Constitution was in operation. From the beginning, however, judges were expected to restrain legislative majorities. "Independent judges," wrote Alexander Hamilton in *The Federalist*, No. 78 (which is also in the Appendix of this book), would be "an essential safeguard against the effects of occasional ill humors in society."

Judicial review is an American contribution to the art of government. If British or American citizens are thrown into prison without cause, they can appeal to the courts of their respective countries for protection. But no British judge may declare a law duly enacted by Parliament null and void because the judge believes it violates the British constitution: Parliament is the guardian of the British constitution. In the United States the courts, ultimately the Supreme Court, are the keepers of the constitutional conscience—not Congress and not the president. How did the judges get this tremendous responsibility?

Origins of Judicial Review

The Constitution itself says nothing about who should have the final word in disputes that might arise over its meaning. Whether the members of the Convention of 1787 intended to give the courts the power of judicial review is a question long since debated. The framers clearly intended the Supreme Court to have the power to declare *state* legislation unconstitutional, but whether they intended to give it the same power over *national* legislation is not clear. Edward S. Corwin, the outstanding authority on the American Constitution, concluded that unquestionably "the framers anticipated some sort of judicial review. . . . But it is equally without question that the ideas generally current in 1787 were far from presaging the present vast role of the court."[5] Why, then, did the framers not specifically provide for judicial review? Probably because they believed the power could readily be inferred from certain general provisions.

The Federalists—the men who wrote the Constitution and controlled the national government until 1801—generally supported a strong role for federal courts and favored judicial review. Their opponents, the Jeffersonian Republicans (called Democrats after 1832), were less enthusiastic. In 1798 and 1799 Jefferson and Madison (the latter by this time had left the Federalist party), with the Virginia and Kentucky Resolutions, came very close to the position that state legislatures—and not the Supreme Court—had the ultimate power to interpret the Constitution. These Resolutions even seemed to question whether the Supreme Court had the final authority to review state legislation, something about which there had been little doubt.

When the Jeffersonians defeated the Federalists in the elections of 1800, it was still undecided whether the Supreme Court would actually exercise the power

YOU DECIDE

Of the over 160 national constitutions in the world, the U.S. Constitution is the oldest and one of the most admired. A constitution cannot spell out everything, and every successful constitution has compromises. Some issues get left out; and some become less relevant over time—especially two centuries later. The Bicentennial of our Constitution's ratification has directed attention to how we might improve it. Can you point to topics you believe should be in our Constitution that were left out? And topics that would best be deleted or modified?

(Answer/Discussion is on page 26.)

[5] Edward S. Corwin, "The Constitution as Instrument and as Symbol," *American Political Science Review* (December 1936), p. 1078.

of judicial review. The idea was in the air, logical reasons to support a doctrine of judicial review were at hand, and some precedents could even be cited; nevertheless, judicial review was not an established power. Then in 1803 came *Marbury* v. *Madison*,[6] one of the most famous Supreme Court decisions of all time.

Marbury v. *Madison* (1803)

The elections of 1800 marked the rise to power of the Jeffersonian Republicans. President John Adams and his fellow Federalists did not take their defeat easily. Indeed, they were greatly alarmed at what they considered to be the "enthronement of the rabble." Yet there was nothing much they could do about it before leaving office—or was there? The Constitution gives the president, with the consent of the Senate, the power to appoint federal judges to hold office during "good behavior." If the judiciary were manned by good Federalists, thought Adams and his followers, they could stave off the worst consequences of Jefferson's victory.

The Federalist **lame-duck** Congress created dozens of new federal judicial posts. By March 3, 1801, Adams had appointed, and the Senate had confirmed, Federalists to all these new positions. Adams signed the commissions and turned them over to John Marshall, the secretary of state, to be sealed and delivered. Marshall had just received his own commission as chief justice of the United States, but he was continuing to serve as secretary of state until Adams's term expired. Working right up to 9 o'clock on the evening of March 3, Marshall sealed, but was unable to deliver, all the commissions. The important ones were taken care of, however, and only those for the justices of the peace for the District of Columbia were left undelivered. The newly appointed chief justice left the remaining commissions for his successor to deliver.

Jefferson was angered by this packing of the judiciary. When he discovered that some of the commissions had not been delivered, he told the new secretary of state, James Madison, to hold up seventeen of those still in his possession. Jefferson could see no reason why the District needed so many justices of the peace, especially Federalist justices.

Among the commissions not delivered was one for William Marbury. After waiting in vain, Marbury decided to seek action from the courts. Searching through the statute books, he came across Section 13 of the Judiciary Act of 1789, which authorized the Supreme Court "to issue writs of mandamus, in cases warranted by the principles and usages of law, to . . . persons holding office, under the authority of the United States." A **writ of mandamus** is a court order directing an official to perform a duty of an office. Delivering a commission is a ministerial act; the secretary of state is a person holding office under the authority of the United States. So, thought Marbury, why not ask the Supreme Court to issue a writ of mandamus to force Madison to deliver the commission? He and his companions went directly to the Supreme Court and, citing Section 13, they so asked.

What could Marshall do? If the Court issued the writ, Madison and Jefferson would probably ignore it. The Court would be powerless, and its prestige, already low, might suffer a fatal blow. On the other hand, by refusing to issue the writ, the judges would appear to support the Republican party's claim that the Court had no authority to interfere with the executive. Would Marshall issue the writ? Most people thought so; angry Republicans even talked of impeachment.

On February 24, 1803, the Supreme Court delivered its opinion. The first part was as expected. Marbury was entitled to his commission, said Marshall, and Madison should have delivered it to him; a writ of mandamus could be issued by the proper court against even so high an officer as the secretary of state.

Then came the surprise. Although Section 13 of the Judiciary Act seems to

Chief Justice John Marshall (1755–1835) is regarded as our most influential Supreme Court justice. Appointed in 1801, Marshall served as the fourth chief justice of the United States, he served until 1835. Earlier he had been a staunch defender of the U.S. Constitution at the Virginia ratifying convention, a member of Congress, and secretary of state. He was one of those rare people who served in all three branches of government. (*UPI/Bettman Newsphotos*)

[6] 1 Cranch 137 (1803).

Most scholars believe we should seldom change the Constitution, but a variety of proposals for amending it "are now at various levels on the nation's agenda. . . . Accordingly, while we may commit some sins in observing the Constitution's bicentenary, they are not likely to include smugness or mindlessness."* Some current proposals:

To require a balanced federal budget.

To reverse Supreme Court rulings disallowing state-sponsored prayers in public schools.

To reverse Supreme Court decisions limiting state governments' powers to make abortions illegal.

To provide for equal rights under the law for women.

To abolish the electoral college and provide for direct election of the president.

To alter the system for nominating presidential candidates.

To permit national legislation by initiative petitions and direct vote of the people.

To give the District of Columbia the powers of a state.

To provide for a single, nonrenewable, six-year term for the president.

To give the president an item veto over appropriations.

To bridge the separation of powers by giving cabinet members seats in Congress or requiring the president to choose cabinet members from members of Congress.

To move toward a more cohesive party system by electing the president, senators, and House members at the same time for terms of the same length.

Perhaps by the end of this course there will be other subjects you would like to see added or altered. Undoubtedly, however, you will appreciate that changing the Constitution, even in minor ways, is a complex task. It is also highly political.

* Austin Ranney, "What Constitutional Changes Do Americans Want?" in Donald L. Robinson, ed., *Reforming American Government* (Westview Press, 1985), p. 281. The ideas here are taken from this article.

give the Supreme Court original jurisdiction in cases such as that in question, this section, said Marshall, is contrary to Article III of the Constitution, which gives the Supreme Court original jurisdiction *only* when an ambassador or other foreign minister is affected or when a state is a party. Even though this is a case of original jurisdiction, Marbury is neither a state nor a foreign minister. If we follow Section 13, wrote Marshall, we have jurisdiction; if we follow the Constitution, we have no jurisdiction.

Marshall then stated the question in a more pointed way: Should the Supreme Court enforce an unconstitutional law? Of course not, he concluded. The Constitution is the supreme and binding law, and the courts cannot enforce any action of Congress that conflicts with it.

The real question remained unanswered. Congress and the president also had read the Constitution, and according to their interpretation, which was also reasonable, Section 13 was compatible with Article III. Where did the Supreme Court get the right to say they were wrong? Why should the Supreme Court's interpretation of the Constitution be preferred to that of Congress and the president?

Paralleling Hamilton's argument in *The Federalist*, No. 78, Marshall reasoned: The Constitution is law; judges—not legislators or executives—interpret law. Therefore, judges should interpret the Constitution. "If two laws conflict with each other, the courts must decide on the operation of each," he said. Case dismissed.

Jefferson fumed. For one thing, Marshall had said that a court with the proper jurisdiction could issue a writ of mandamus even against the secretary of state. Yet there was little Jefferson could do about what he thought was Marshall's arrogance. There was not even a court order he could refuse to obey. Thus, in a single stroke Marshall had lectured the Republicans for failing to perform their duties, and he had gone a long way toward acquiring for the Supreme Court the power to review acts of Congress. And he had done it in a manner that made it difficult for the Republicans to challenge.

Marbury v. *Madison* is a masterpiece of judicial strategy. Marshall went out of his way to declare Section 13 unconstitutional. He could have interpreted the section to mean that the Supreme Court could issue writs of mandamus in those cases in which it did have jurisdiction. He could have interpreted Article III to mean that Congress could add to, though not subtract from, the original jurisdiction the Constitution gives to the Supreme Court. He could have dismissed the case for want of jurisdiction without discussing Marbury's right to his commission. But none of these would have suited his purpose. Marshall was fearful for the Supreme Court's future; he reasoned that unless the Court spoke out, it would become subordinate to the president and Congress.

Marshall's decision, important as it was, did not by itself establish for the Supreme Court the power to review and declare acts of Congress unconstitutional. *Marbury* v. *Madison* could have been interpreted in a more limited way, so that the Supreme Court had the right to determine the scope of its *own* powers under Article III but that Congress and the president had the authority to interpret *their own powers* under Articles I and II, respectively. However, Marshall's decision has not been interpreted in this way (though it was not until the *Dred Scott* case in 1857 that another act of Congress was declared unconstitutional).[7] Had Marshall not spoken when he did, the Court might not have been able to assume the power of judicial review. The precedent had been created. Here we have a classic example of constitutional development through judicial interpretation. The Constitution gives no specific authorization for the Court to declare congressional enactments null and void; yet today this practice is a vital part of our constitutional system.

Several important consequences followed from the acceptance of Marshall's argument that judges are the official interpreters of the Constitution. The most

[7] *Dred Scott* v. *Sandford*, 19 Howard 393 (1857).

important is that even a law enacted by the Congress and approved by the president may, under many circumstances, be challenged by a single person. Simply by bringing a lawsuit, those who lack the clout to get a bill through Congress or who cannot influence a federal agency may often secure a judicial hearing. Litigation thus supplements, and at times takes precedence over, legislation as a way to make public policy.[8]

CHECKS AND BALANCES—DOES IT WORK?

What if a majority of the people should get control of all branches of government and force through radical measures? The framers knew that if the great majority of the voters wanted to take a certain step, nothing could stop them. Nothing, that is, except despotic government, and that they did not want. They reasoned that all they could do—and this is quite a lot—is to prevent, temporarily, full control by the popular majority.

It may seem surprising that most of the people did not object to these "auxiliary precautions," which often are barriers to action by a popular majority. But early Americans (and perhaps their descendants two centuries later) did not look on government as an instrument they could seize with their votes and use for their own purposes. Rather, it was something to be handcuffed, hemmed in, and rendered harmless. The separation of powers and the system of checks and balances were intended to make it difficult for a majority to gain control of the government. Equally important, they were intended to keep those who govern from exceeding their constitutional authority.

The framers, distrustful of both the elites and the masses, deliberately built *inefficiency* into our political system; and 200 years after the ratification of the Constitution, Americans continue to debate whether it is desirable to maintain these limits under the vastly different conditions of our times. Crucial questions remain: Are these checks necessary or sufficient to prevent abuses of political power? Is the greater danger that governments will not do the right things or that they will do the wrong things? Do these limitations work to prevent abuses, or do they make coherent governmental action for the general welfare difficult, if not impossible?

In 1857 the Supreme Court denied Dred Scott his freedom by ruling (*Dred Scott* v. *Sandford*) that slaves were property and protected as such by the Constitution, even in the territories. This decision declared the Missouri Compromise of 1820, an act of Congress, to be unconstitutional. It was overruled by the Fourteenth Amendment. (*Missouri Historical Society*)

Checks and Balances: Modifications

Even though fragmentation of political power remains, several developments have modified the way the system of checks and balances actually works.

1. *Rise of national political parties.* Parties serve to a limited extent as unifying factors—at times drawing together the president, senators, representatives, and sometimes even judges behind common programs. But the parties, in turn, have been splintered and weakened by having to work through a system of fragmented governmental power, so that we have never developed strong, cohesive parties.

2. *Changes in electoral methods.* The framers wanted the president to be chosen by wise, independent citizens free from popular passions and hero worship. Almost from the beginning, however, presidential electors have pledged prior to elections to cast their votes for their parties' presidential candidates. Further, senators, who were originally elected by state legislatures, are today chosen directly by the people.

[8] Karen Orren, "Standing to Sue: Interest Group Conflict in the Federal Courts," *American Political Science Review* (September 1976), pp. 723–41; J. W. Peltason, *Federal Courts in the Political Process* (Random House, 1955).

American System of Separation of Powers

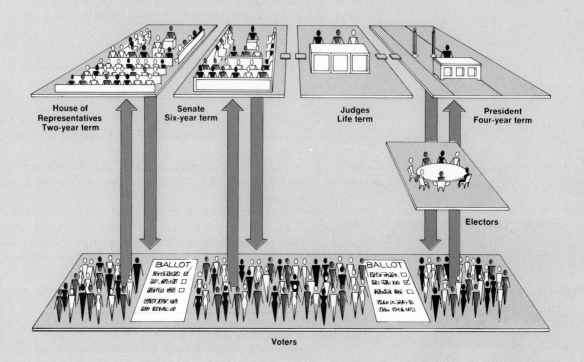

House of Representatives
Two-year term

Senate
Six-year term

Judges
Life term

President
Four-year term

Electors

Voters

3. *Establishment of agencies deliberately designed to exercise all three functions— legislative, executive, and judicial.* When the government began to regulate the economy, and detailed rules had to be made on such complex matters as policing business practices or preventing pollution of our air and water resources, it was difficult to assign responsibility to an agency without blending the powers to make and apply rules and to decide disputes.

4. *Changes in technology.* Nuclear bombs, television, computers, instant communications—these and other alterations in our environment create conditions very different from those of two centuries ago. In some ways, these new technologies have added to the powers of the president; in others, they have added leverage to organized interests working through Congress. They have also given greater independence and influence to nongovernmental agencies, such as the press. Governmental power remains fragmented, but the system of checks and balances operates differently from the way it did in 1789, when there were no televised congressional investigating committee hearings; no electronic listening devices or FBI; no *New York Times*, *Wall Street Journal*, *USA TODAY*, or nightly news programs with national constituencies; no presidential press conferences; and no live coverage of wars or of Americans being held hostage in foreign places.

5. *The emergence of the United States as a world power and the existence of recurrent crises.* Today crises and problems anywhere in the world become crises and problems for the United States, and vice versa. The need to deal with perpetual emergency has concentrated power in the hands of the chief executive and the presidential staff.

6. *The office of the president has sometimes served to impose some measure of national unity.* Drawing on constitutional, political, and emergency powers,

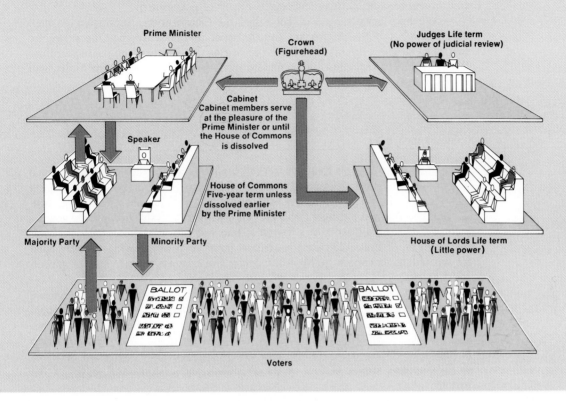

British Parliamentary System of Concentration of Responsibility

Prime Minister

Crown (Figurehead)

Judges Life term (No power of judicial review)

Cabinet
Cabinet members serve at the pleasure of the Prime Minister or until the House of Commons is dissolved

Speaker

House of Commons
Five-year term unless dissolved earlier by the Prime Minister

Majority Party   Minority Party

House of Lords Life term (Little power)

BALLOT   BALLOT

Voters

the president has sometimes been able to overcome some of the restraints imposed by the Constitution on the exercise of cohesive governmental power— to the applause of some, and the alarm of others.

A Study in Contrasts

Although many Americans question the usefulness and functions of our institutions, we tend to take the system of checks and balances for granted, considering it necessary for constitutional government. Like Madison (and especially since Watergate), we view the amassing of power by any one branch of government as leading to tyranny. Yet it is quite possible for a government to be constitutional without such an apparatus. Under the British system, voters elect members of Parliament from districts throughout the nation (much as we elect members of the House of Representatives). The members of the House of Commons have almost complete constitutional power: The leaders of the majority party serve as executive ministers, who collectively form the cabinet, with the prime minister as its head. When the executive officers lose the support of the majority in the Commons on a major issue, they must resign or call for new elections. Formerly the House of Lords could check the Commons, but now it is almost powerless. There is no high court with the power to declare acts of Parliament unconstitutional. The prime minister cannot veto them (though he or she may ask the Crown to dissolve Parliament and call new elections for members of the House of Commons). The British take their system as much for granted as we do our own.

The British system is based on *majority rule*—that is, a majority of the voters elects a majority of the legislators, who can put through the majority's program as long as the parliamentary majority stays together, at least until the next election.

Our system usually depends on the agreement of many elements of society. The British system *concentrates* control and responsibility in the legislature; ours *diffuses* control and responsibility among several organs of government.

We have a written document called the Constitution; Britain has no such document. Yet both systems are constitutional in the sense that the rulers are subject to regular restraints. The limits our written Constitution and the conventions the unwritten British constitution impose rest on underlying values, attitudes, and norms (rules).

THE CONSTITUTION AS AN INSTRUMENT OF GOVERNMENT

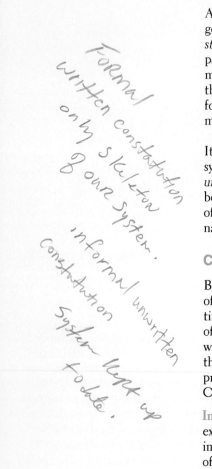

Formal written constitution only skeleton of our system.

informal unwritten Constitution System kept up to date.

As careful as our nation's founders were to limit the powers they gave the national government, the main reason they had assembled in Philadelphia was *to create a stronger national government*. They had learned that weak central government, incapable of governing, is a danger to liberty. They wished to establish a national government within the framework of a federal system and with enough authority to meet the needs of all times. They made general grants of power, leaving the way open for succeeding generations to fill in the details and organize the structure of government in accordance with experience.

Hence, our formal, written Constitution is only the skeleton of our system. It is filled in by numerous rules that must be considered part of our constitutional system in its larger sense. In fact, it is primarily through changes in our *informal unwritten Constitution* that our system is kept up to date. These changes are to be found in certain basic statutes and historical practices of Congress, decisions of the Supreme Court, actions of the president, and customs and usages of the nation.

Congressional Elaboration

Because the framers gave Congress authority over many of the structural details of the national government, it is not necessary to amend the Constitution every time a change is needed: Rather, Congress can act from year to year. Examples of congressional elaboration appear in such legislation as the Judiciary Act of 1789, which laid the foundations of our national judicial system; in the laws establishing the organization and functions of all federal executive officials subordinate to the president; and in the rules of procedure, internal organization, and practices of Congress itself. (All these are discussed in later chapters.)

Impeachment power—an example of congressional elaboration   A dramatic example of congressional elaboration of our constitutional system is the use of the impeachment power. Constitutional language is sparse. Take a look at your copy of the Constitution and note that according to Article I, the Legislative Article, it is up to Congress to give meaning to that language. Article I gives the House of Representatives the sole power of impeachment, and the Senate the sole power to try all impeachments. When sitting for that purpose, senators "shall be on oath or affirmation"; in the event the president is being tried, the chief justice of the United States presides. Article I also requires conviction on impeachment charges to have the agreement of two-thirds of the senators present. Judgments shall extend no further than removal from office and disqualification from holding any office under the United States, but a person convicted shall also be liable to indictment, trial, judgment, and punishment according to the law. In Article II—the Executive Article—the Constitution provides that the "President, Vice-President, and all civil officers of the United States, shall be removed from Office on Impeachment for, and Conviction of, Treason, Bribery, or other high Crimes and Misdemeanors." This Article also excepts cases of impeachment from the president's pardoning power. Article III—the Judicial Article—exempts cases of impeachment from the jury trial requirement. That is all the relevant constitutional language. We must look to history to answer most questions.

Fortunately, our experiences have triggered few acute constitutional disputes about the interpretation of impeachment procedures, and there is little history to go on. The House of Representatives has investigated about sixty-five persons for possible impeachment and has impeached fifteen; the Senate has convicted five (all federal judges). One judge resigned after being impeached, and the charges against him were dropped. One president, Andrew Johnson, was impeached in 1868, but the Senate failed by one vote to muster the two-thirds necessary to support the charges. Another president, Richard Nixon, resigned on August 9, 1974, to avoid impeachment after the House Judiciary Committee recommended three articles of impeachment against him. The House did not press the matter further, but the articles of impeachment were submitted by the committee and were "accepted" by the House.

Even though congressional precedents have rejected the *broadest* view—that the Constitution authorizes removal of officers by impeachment because of *political* objections to them or because of their unpopularity (a view that might have moved us more in the direction of a parliamentary type of government)—Congress has also rejected the *narrowest* construction—that impeachable offenses are only those that involve violations of the criminal laws. Rather, the firmly established position is that impeachment and conviction are justified if there have been serious violations of constitutional responsibilities and a clear dereliction of duty.[9]

Presidential Practice

Although the president's formal constitutional powers have not changed, the office is dramatically more important and more central today than it was in 1789. The more vigorous presidents—Washington, Jefferson, Jackson, Lincoln, Theodore Roosevelt, Wilson, Franklin Roosevelt, Truman, and Reagan—have boldly exercised their political and constitutional powers, especially during times of national crisis. Such presidential practices have become important precedents, building the power and influence of the office. Even John Tyler made his contribution to constitutional elaboration. Upon becoming president through vice-presidential succession, Tyler established the precedent that under such circumstances the vice-president becomes the president, not merely the acting president.

Nuclear-age realities add force to the president's role as the nation's "final arbiter." Political scientist Richard Neustadt says: "When it comes to action risking war, technology has modified the Constitution: the President, perforce, becomes the only such man in the system capable of exercising judgment under the extraordinary limits now imposed by secrecy, complexity, and time."[10]

The presidency has also become the pivotal office for regulating the economy and protecting the general welfare. Plainly, the president has become a key legislator as well as the nation's chief executive.

Custom and Usage

Customs and usages have rounded out our governmental system. Presidential nominating conventions and other party activities are examples of constitutional usages.

[9] John R. Labovitz, *Presidential Impeachment* (Yale University Press, 1978); Peter Charles Hoffer and N. E. H. Hull, *Impeachment in America, 1635–1805* (Yale University Press, 1984).

[10] Neustadt, *Presidential Power*, p. 280.

Although not specifically mentioned in the Constitution, these practices are fundamental to our system. In fact, it has been primarily through the development of national political parties and the extension of the suffrage within the states that our Constitution has become democratized. A broader electorate began to exercise control over the national government, and the presidential office was made more responsive to the people. In addition, the nature of the relations between Congress and the president was altered. Further, through the growth of political parties, some constitutional blocks to popular rule were overcome.

Judicial Interpretation

Judicial interpretation of the Constitution, especially by the Supreme Court, has played an important part in keeping the constitutional system up to date. As social and economic conditions have changed and new national demands have developed, the Supreme Court has changed its interpretation of the Constitution to reflect these trends. In the words of Woodrow Wilson, "The Supreme Court is a constitutional convention in continuous session." Because the Constitution adapts to changing times, it does not require frequent formal amendment.

The advantages of this flexibility may be appreciated when the national Constitution is compared with the rigid and often overly specific state constitutions. Many state constitutions, more like legal codes than basic charters, are so detailed that the hands of public officials are often tied. Such constitutions must be amended frequently or replaced every generation or so.

A Rigid or Flexible Constitution?

The idea of a constantly changing system disturbs many people. How, they argue, can you have a constitutional government when the Constitution is constantly being twisted by interpretation and changed by informal methods? This view fails to distinguish between two aspects of the Constitution. As an expression of *basic*

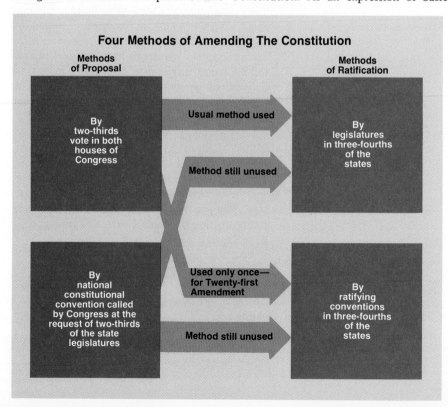

Four Methods of Amending The Constitution

Methods of Proposal

Methods of Ratification

By two-thirds vote in both houses of Congress

By legislatures in three-fourths of the states

Usual method used

Method still unused

By national constitutional convention called by Congress at the request of two-thirds of the state legislatures

By ratifying conventions in three-fourths of the states

Used only once— for Twenty-first Amendment

Method still unused

and timeless personal liberties, the Constitution does not and should not change. For example, a government cannot destroy free speech and still remain a constitutional government. In this sense the Constitution is unchanging. But when we consider the Constitution as an *instrument of government* and a *positive grant of power*, we realize that if it does not grow with the nation it serves, it will soon be pushed aside. The framers could not have conceived of the problems that the government of more than 240 million citizens in an industrial nation approaching the twenty-first century would have to face. Although the general purposes of government remain the same—to establish liberty, promote justice, ensure domestic tranquility, and provide for the common defense—the powers of government adequate to accomplish these purposes in 1787 are simply insufficient 200 years later.

"We the people"—the people of today and tomorrow, not just the people of 1787—ordain and establish the Constitution. "The Constitution," wrote Jefferson, "belongs to the living and not to the dead." So firmly did he believe this that he suggested there might be a new constitution for every generation. But new constitutions have not been necessary, because in a less formal way each generation has taken part in the process of developing and changing the original Constitution. In fact, because of its remarkable adaptability, the Constitution has survived democratic and industrial revolutions, the turmoil of civil war, the tensions of major depressions, and the dislocations of world wars.

CHANGING THE LETTER OF THE CONSTITUTION

The framers knew that future experiences would call for changes in the text of the Constitution and that some means of formal **amendment** was necessary. Take a look at Article V of the Constitution. Note that the framers gave this responsibility to Congress and to the states; the president has no formal authority over constitutional amendments. Presidential veto power does not extend to them, although presidential political influence is often crucial in getting amendments proposed by Congress and ratified by the states. Nor may governors veto ratification of amendments by their respective legislatures or ratifying conventions. The Constitution vests ratification in whichever body Congress designates—state *legislatures* or state ratifying *conventions*. The framers set up two ways to propose amendments and two ways to ratify them, and they saw to it that amendments could not be adopted by simple majorities. Each amendment must be both *proposed* and *ratified*.

(© 1982, *Field Newspaper Syndicate*. By permission of News America Syndicate.)

Proposing Amendments

The first method for proposing amendments—the only one that has been used so far—is by a two-thirds vote of both houses of Congress. Dozens of resolutions proposing amendments are introduced in every session. Thousands have been introduced since 1789, most of these during the last two decades. But few make any headway. Throughout our history Congress has proposed only thirty-three amendments (twenty-three, excluding the Bill of Rights).

Currently before Congress are resolutions guaranteeing equal rights for women, permitting states to encourage prayer in public schools, making abortions illegal, abolishing the electoral college, providing for a single six-year term for the president, balancing the federal budget, and restricting the powers of federal courts, to mention just a few. Why has amending the Constitution recently become such a "popular frenzy"?[11]

[11] Gary L. McDowell, "On Meddling with the Constitution," *Journal of Contemporary Studies*, Institute of Contemporary Studies (Fall 1982). See also Walter Dellinger, "The Process of Constitutional Amendment: Law, History, and Politics," *News for Teachers of Political Science* (Spring 1986), pp. 16–19.

"First thing to do is toss out a lot of this stuff adopted by the previous convention." (*Copyright © 1982 by Herblock in The Washington Post*)

How the Amendatory Power Has Been Used

1. Amendments whose chief importance is to *add to* or *subtract from* the power of the *national* government.

   □ The Eleventh took some jurisdiction away from the national courts.

   □ The Thirteenth abolished slavery and authorized Congress to legislate against it.

   □ The Sixteenth enables Congress to levy an income tax.

   □ The Eighteenth authorizes Congress to prohibit the manufacture, sale, or transportation of liquor.

   □ The Twenty-first repealed the Eighteenth and gives states the authority to regulate liquor sales.

2. Amendments whose main effect is to limit the power of state governments.

   □ The Thirteenth abolished slavery.

   □ The Fourteenth grants national citizenship and prohibits states from abridging privileges of national citizenship, from denying persons life, lib-

In part because interest groups unhappy with Supreme Court decisions seek to overturn them. In part because groups frustrated by their inability to get things done in Congress—balancing the budget, for example—seek an amendment, even if only for symbolic reasons. And in part because scholars or interest-group representatives (not necessarily mutually exclusive categories) and others seek to change the procedures and process of government to make the system more responsive.

The second method for proposing amendments—Congress's calling a constitutional convention whenever the legislatures in two-thirds of the states so petition—has never been used. "The Constitution's Other Method"[12] presents some difficult questions. How long do state petitions remain alive? How should delegates be chosen? How should a convention be run? Recently Congress has considered proposals on these questions. Most call on Congress to set the date and place for a convention whenever each chamber concludes that two-thirds of the state legislatures have petitioned about a particular subject closely enough in time to reflect a "contemporaneous national request" for action. Under most proposals, each state would have as many delegates to the convention as it has representatives and senators in Congress. Finally—a crucial point—the convention would be limited to considering only the subject specified in the state legislative petitions and described in the congressional call for the convention. (Scholars are divided on whether Congress has this authority to limit what a constitutional convention might propose.)[13]

Despite several organized efforts to force Congress to call a constitutional convention (or else to propose the amendment itself), so far Congress has not acted. The closest we came to a convention was in the spring of 1967 when the thirty-third state legislature—only one short of the required number—petitioned Congress to call a convention to propose an amendment that would set aside a Supreme Court ruling that both chambers of a state legislature must be apportioned on the basis of population. Congress, however, refused to propose an amendment. The thirty-fourth state never petitioned for a convention, and as the several state legislatures completed the process of reapportionment, pressures for such an amendment abated.

Recently, Congress has received petitions for a convention to propose amendments to permit states to encourage prayer in public schools, to reverse Supreme Court decisions relating to abortions, and to deal with school busing. The most active campaign is sponsored by the National Taxpayers Union in behalf of a Balanced Budget Amendment. Thirty-two state legislatures have petitioned Congress on this issue. (An American Bar Association committee concludes that twenty-four of these resolutions are of "questionable validity and the Alabama legislature has rescinded its call for such a convention.")[14]

Why has Congress been so reluctant to call a convention? Members of Congress, and many other concerned citizens, are fearful of a "runaway convention" in which delegates would ignore the restraints imposed upon them and propose amendments on a variety of topics—perhaps they would even call for a new form of government. They remember what happened 200 years ago when a reluctant Congress called into being a Constitutional Convention for the sole purpose of

[12] Ann Stuart Diamond, "A Convention for Proposing Amendments: The Constitution's Other Method," *Publius* (Summer 1981), pp. 113–46; Wilbur Edel, "Amending the Constitution by Convention: Myths and Realities," *State Government*, vol. 55 (1982), pp. 51–56.

[13] Frank J. Sorauf, "The Political Potential of an Amending Convention," in Kermit L. Hall, Harold M. Hyman, and Leon V. Sigal, eds., *The Constitutional Convention as an Amending Device*. For Project '87 (American Political Science Association, 1981), pp. 113–30. See also Bill Gaugush, "Principles Governing the Interpretation and Exercise of Article V Power," *Western Political Quarterly* (June 1982), pp. 212–21; and response by C. Herman Pritchett, "Congress and Article V, Conventions," *Western Political Quarterly* (June 1982), pp. 222–27.

[14] *The Wall Street Journal*, October 5, 1985, p. 1: *Congressional Quarterly Weekly Report*, Vol. 46, May 28, 1988, p. 1443.

erty, and property without due process, and from denying persons equal protection of the laws. This amendment has come to be interpreted as imposing restraints on state powers in every area of public life.

3. Amendments whose chief impact has been to expand the electorate and add to its power.

□ The Fifteenth extended the suffrage to black males in the North and South.

□ The Seventeenth took from state legislatures and gave to the voters in each state the right to elect their United States senators.

□ The Nineteenth extended the suffrage to women.

□ The Twenty-third gave voters of the District of Columbia the right to vote for president and vice-president.

□ The Twenty-fourth forbids any state to put a tax on the right to vote (the poll tax).

□ The Twenty-sixth extended the suffrage to otherwise qualified persons 18 years of age or older.

4. Amendments whose chief impact has been to subtract from the power of the electorate.

□ The Twenty-second took from the electorate the right to elect any person to the office of president for more than two full terms.

5. Amendments that have made structural changes in governmental machinery.

□ The Twelfth corrected deficiencies in the operation of the electoral college that were revealed by the development of a two-party national system.

□ The Twentieth altered the calendar for congressional sessions and shortened the time between the election of presidents and their assumption of office.

□ The Twenty-fifth provides procedures for filling vacancies in the vice-presidency and for determining whether presidents are unable to perform their duties.

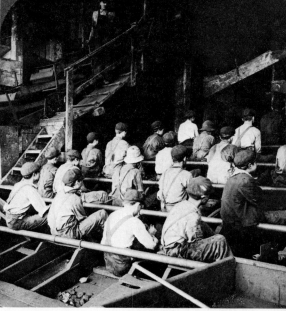

The Child Labor Amendment, proposed in 1924, was ratified by only twenty-eight state legislatures, the last in 1937. A reasonable time for ratification of the amendment has long since passed. But Supreme Court decisions since 1937 have provided Congress with other means to outlaw child labor. (*New York Public Library—Picture Collection*; *Culver Pictures*)

considering amendments to the Articles of Confederation, only to have that Convention ignore its instructions and disregard the procedures for amending the Articles. They also remember that in January 1789 James Madison expressed a strong preference that Congress propose a Bill of Rights in the form of amendments rather than call for a second convention. He wrote: "The Congress who will be appointed to execute as well as to amend the Government, will probably be careful not to destroy or endanger it. A convention, on the other hand, meeting in the present ferment of parties, and containing perhaps insidious characters from different parts of America, would at least spread a general alarm, and be but too likely to turn everything into confusion and uncertainty."[15]

Ratifying Amendments

After an amendment has been proposed, it must be ratified by the states. Again, two methods are provided—approval by the legislatures in three-fourths of the states or approval by specially called ratifying conventions in three-fourths of the states. Congress determines which method is used. All amendments except one—the Twenty-first (to repeal the Eighteenth, the Prohibition Amendment)—have been submitted to the state legislatures for ratification.

Seven state constitutions require for ratification an extraordinary majority of three-fifths or two-thirds of each chamber.[16] Although a state legislature may change its mind and ratify an amendment after it has voted against ratification, the weight of opinion is that once a state has ratified an amendment it cannot "unratify" it.[17]

Submitting amendments to legislatures rather than ratifying conventions allows changes to be made in the constitutions without any direct expressions by the

[15] Letter to George Eve, quoted in Walter E. Dellinger, "The Recurring Question," *Yale Law Journal* (October 1979), p. 1979.

[16] Clement E. Vose, "When District of Columbia Representation Collides with the Constitutional Amendment Institution," *Publius* (Winter 1979), p. 114.

[17] Samuel S. Freedman and Pamela J. Naughton, *ERA: May a State Change Its Vote* (Wayne State University Press, 1979).

YOU DECIDE !

Is 200 years a reasonable time?

In March 1982, Gregory Watson, a student at the University of Texas, was doing a paper on the Equal Rights Amendment. He came across an amendment proposed in 1789 as part of the Bill of Rights that would prohibit a raise for members of Congress until the intervention of an election for members of the House. He learned that only six of the original thirteen states had ratified it and that during the intervening years only three more states had done so.

Watson decided to start a ratification movement. He wrote around, got some publicity for his efforts and, with the help of a Republican state representative, Don Mielke, persuaded Maine, Colorado, South Dakota, New Hampshire, and Arizona to ratify this long forgotten proposed amendment. Resolutions are pending in other states. He and his colleagues aim to get the necessary three-fourths by 1989, the 200th anniversary of the inauguration of the Constitution. If they are successful, will this amendment become part of the Constitution?

Source: Bill Curry, "Pay Curb Move Gains Momentum, 1789 Amendment Comes Back to Haunt Congress," copyright © 1985, *The Los Angeles Times* (May 6, 1985), pp. 1, 11. Reprinted by permission.

(Answer/Discussion on page 37.)

The Fifteenth Amendment was ratified in 1870, yet blacks were kept from voting in many southern states until Congress implemented that amendment by the Voting Rights Act of 1965. Here, blacks lined up to register in Selma, Alabama, in January 1965 are stopped by local police officers at the main entrance. (*UPI/Bettman Newsphotos*)

voters: Legislators may have been elected before the proposed amendments were submitted to the states. In any event, state legislators are chosen because of their views on schools, taxation, or other matters, or because of their personal popularity. They are almost never elected because of their stands on proposed constitutional amendments, although the candidates' positions on the **Equal Rights Amendment (ERA)** did surface as a key issue in several state legislative elections.

Mechanics can make a difference. The decision to submit the Twenty-first Amendment to ratifying conventions came about because the "wets" rightly believed that repeal had a better chance of success with conventions than with the rural-dominated state legislatures. (For similar tactical reasons southern Democrats joined with eastern Republican conservatives in an unsuccessful effort to submit the Nineteenth Amendment, or Susan B. Anthony Amendment, as it was called, to ratifying conventions. Let the voters decide—the male voters, that is—they argued.)[18] Congress left it up to each state legislature to determine how the ratifying conventions would be organized and delegates elected. State delegates ran at-large on tickets that pledged they would vote for or against repeal. As a result, when a convention in a state was called to order, it quickly ratified the decision the voters had already made. In effect, ratification was submitted to the voters.

A state must ratify proposed amendments within (what Congress considers) a reasonable time. The modern practice is for Congress to stipulate that an amendment will not become part of the Constitution unless ratified by the necessary number of states within seven years from the date of its submission. (In fact, ratification ordinarily takes place rather quickly; see Table 2–1.)[19]

[18] Alan P. Grimes, *Democracy and Amendments to the Constitution* (Lexington Books, 1978), p. 95. See also Clement E. Vose, *Constitutional Change* (Lexington Books, 1972), pp. 342–44, which focuses on amendment politics in the case of women's suffrage, child labor, and prohibition.

[19] Gregory A. Caldeira, "Constitutional Change in America: Dynamics of Ratification under Article V," *Publius: The Journal of Federalism* (Fall 1985), p. 29.

2–1 The 26 Amendments: How Long They Had to Wait

Length of time between congressional approval and actual ratification of the amendments to the U.S. Constitution

Amendment	Time to Ratify	Ratified
1–10. Bill of Rights	1 year, 2½ months	1791
11. Lawsuits against states	3 years, 10 months	1798
12. Presidential elections	8½ months	1804
13. Abolition of slavery	10½ months	1865
14. Civil rights	2 years, 1½ months	1868
15. Suffrage for all races	1 year, 1 month	1870
16. Income tax	3 years, 7½ months	1913
17. Senatorial elections	1 year, ½ month	1913
18. Prohibition	1 year, 1½ months	1919
19. Women's suffrage	1 year, 2½ months	1920
20. Terms of office	11 months	1933
21. Repeal of prohibition	9½ months	1933
22. Limit on presidential terms	3 years, 11½ months	1951
23. Washington, D.C., vote	9 months	1961
24. Abolition of poll taxes	1 year, 5½ months	1964
25. Presidential succession	1 year, 6½ months	1967
26. 18-year-old suffrage	4 months	1971

Answer/Discussion

Not likely. Congress would have to decide that the amendment had been ratified within a "reasonable time." Two hundred years would seem not to be a "reasonable time expressing a contemporaneous national will." Nonetheless, Watson has effectively made a point about the national pastime of expressing its unhappiness with Congress.

Sometimes Congress places the seven-year limitation in the text of the proposed amendment, sometimes in the enabling legislation that accompanies it. The placement of the limitations can make a difference. For example, in the autumn of 1978 it appeared that the ERA would fall three short of the necessary number of ratifying states prior to the expiration of the seven-year limit—March 22, 1979. After an extended debate, and after voting down provisions that would have authorized state legislatures to change their minds and rescind prior ratification, Congress—by a simple majority vote—extended the time limit until June 30, 1982. It was argued that because the time limit was in the accompanying enabling legislation, not in the body of the proposed amendment, it was subject to congressional modification by simple majority. (The amendment failed, even with the extension, and made moot the pending court test of the extension's constitutionality.)

When Congress proposed an amendment to provide full congressional representation for the District of Columbia, it pointedly reverted to earlier practice and placed the seven-year limit in the text of the amendment. This suggests that: (1) Congress wanted to preclude any possibility of extending the time limit for ratification of this amendment by a simple majority of both houses; and (2) Congress sought to discourage proponents of unratified amendments from seeking extensions of time limits.

RATIFICATION POLITICS: ERA AND THE D.C. AMENDMENT

Until the submission of ERA and the D.C. Amendment, the Child Labor Amendment was the only formally proposed amendment since the Civil War that failed to be ratified. Ordinarily the existence of a political coalition sufficient to get an amendment proposed by Congress reflects enough support in the nation to ensure ratification. The failure of the ERA and the D.C. Amendment to get ratified makes it clear that this is not always the case.

Women from all political parties have been involved in the long struggle for women's rights: from Abigail Scott Duniway's battles in Oregon in the 1880s to achieve the vote for women (left) to rallies 100 years later in favor of the Equal Rights Amendment. (*Oregon Historical Society*; *Jim Anderson/Woodfin Camp & Associates*)

Politics of the Equal Rights Amendment

The ERA

Equal Rights Amendment (ERA)

Proposed March 22, 1972. Died June 30, 1982, three state legislatures shy of the thirty-eight needed for ratification.

Section 1. Equality of rights under the law shall not be denied or abridged by the United States or by any State on account of sex.

Section 2. The Congress shall have power to enforce by appropriate legislation the provisions of this article.

Section 3. This amendment shall take effect two years after date of ratification.

received overwhelming support in both houses of Congress. Both major political parties had repeatedly supported it in their national party platforms; not until 1980 did one party (the Republican) adopt a stance of neutrality. Every president from Truman until Reagan [and many of their wives] had endorsed the amendment. And, by the end of the campaign for ratification, more than 450 organizations with a total membership of over 50 million were on record in support of ERA.[20]

Soon after submission of the amendment in 1972, many legislatures quickly ratified—sometimes without hearings—and by overwhelming majorities. By the end of 1972 twenty-two states had ratified the amendment.[21] It appeared that the ERA would soon become part of the Constitution.

Then the opposition got organized under the articulate leadership of Phyllis Schlafly. The ERA became controversial. Opponents argued that "women would not only be subject to the military draft but also assigned to combat duty. Full-time housewives and mothers would be forced to join the labor force. Furthermore, women would no longer enjoy existing advantages under state domestic relations codes and under labor law."[22] The ERA also became embroiled in the controversy over abortion. Many opponents contended that its ratification would jeopardize the power of states and Congress to regulate abortion in any way, and would compel public funding of abortions.[23]

After the ERA became controversial, legislatures held lengthy hearings and floor debates became heated. Legislators hid behind parliamentary procedures and avoided for as long as possible having to make a decision. Opposition to ratification

[20] Janet K. Boles, "Building Support for the ERA: A Case of Too Much, Too Late," *P.S.* (Fall 1982), p. 572.

[21] Mark R. Daniels, Robert Darcy, and Joseph W. Westphal, "The ERA Won—At Least in the Opinion Polls," *P.S.* (Fall 1982), p. 583.

[22] Janet K. Boles, *The Politics of the Equal Rights Amendment* (Longmans, 1979), p. 4.

[23] Gilbert Y. Steiner, *Constitutional Inequality: The Political Fortunes of the Equal Rights Amendment* (The Brookings Institution, 1985), p. 64. See also Mary Francis Berry, *Why the ERA Failed: Politics, Women's Rights and the Amending Process of the Constitution* (Indiana University Press, 1985).

arose chiefly in the same cluster of southern states that had opposed ratification of the Nineteenth Amendment.

As the opposition grew more active, proponents redoubled their efforts. The National Organization for Women (NOW) called for an economic boycott of cities in nonratifying states, and many associations refused to hold their conventions in Chicago, Kansas City, Las Vegas, Miami, Atlanta, and New Orleans. Nonetheless, on March 22, 1982—the final deadline—the amendment was still three state legislatures short.

The framers intended that amending the Constitution should be difficult: The ERA ratification battle demonstrates how well they planned.[24]

Politics of the D.C. Amendment

Even though the D.C. Amendment passed both chambers of Congress by big margins and with impressive bipartisan support in 1978, it was ratified by only sixteen states. People who live in the District of Columbia (Washington, D.C.) pay federal (and D.C.) taxes and are subject to federal laws. Yet the District's only congressional voice is a nonvoting delegate who serves on committees, attends sessions, and participates (if desired) in all debates, but casts no vote. The 1978 amendment would have given the 640,000 people of the District of Columbia two senators and the same number of representatives in the House of Representatives as if it were a state (one, under current law). It would also have given the District three electoral votes with the possibility of more if its population grew to warrant it (it has three already, under the Twenty-third amendment), as well as a vote in the ratification of constitutional amendments. Finally, it would have repealed the Twenty-third amendment.

Proponents charged that the current situation is "taxation without representation." Initial hopes were high, but advocates of the amendment knew that ratification would be difficult. Many people view the District as being "too urban, too liberal, and too Democratic."

Nowadays proponents of the amendment have turned their attention to persuading Congress to admit the District to the Union as a state—except for a small portion that would provide the constitutionally required "seat of the Government of the United States." Such an action would accomplish all that the D.C. amendment could have done, and more. Moreover, admission of a new state requires only a simple majority vote of both houses of Congress with the concurrence of the president. Interest in the admission of the District as a state, possibly to be called Columbia or New Columbia, has been revived by the Democratic Party's pledge in its 1988 platform to bring this about and the expectation that Jesse Jackson would become one of the new state's first senators.

[24] Margery L. Elfin, "Learning from Failures Present and Past"; Marian L. Palley, "Beyond the Deadline," both in *PS* (Fall 1982), pp. 582–92. See also Mark R. Daniels and Robert E. Darcy, "As Time Goes By: Arrested Diffusion of the ERA," *Publius: The Journal of Federalism* (Fall 1985), p. 51.

Seat of Federal Government

1789–1790	New York City
1790–1800	Philadelphia
1800–present	Washington, D.C.

SUMMARY

1. Our Constitution both grants powers and limits them. The framers established a government to be operated by ordinary people; they did not anticipate that Americans would be so special that they could be trusted to operate without checks and balances. The framers were suspicious of people, especially of those having political power, so they separated and distributed the powers of the newly created national government in a variety of ways.

2. The framers were also concerned that the national government be strong enough to solve public problems.

They wanted it to be responsive to the wishes of the people and to carry out those wishes—that is, the matured and refined wishes of the people. Thus, they gave the national government substantial grants of power. But these grants were made with such broad strokes that it has been possible for the national government and the constitutional system to remain flexible and adapt to changing conditions.

3. Although the American governmental system has its roots in British traditions, our separation of powers and checks and balances system is different from the British system of concentrated responsibility. It is also different because our Supreme Court has the power of judicial review.

4. The system of checks and balances has been modified over time. The Constitution has been adapted to new conditions through congressional elaboration, modern presidential realities, custom and usage, and judicial interpretation.

5. Although adaptable, the Constitution itself needs to be altered from time to time, and the document provides for its own amendment. An amendment must be both proposed and ratified: proposed either by a two-thirds vote in each chamber of Congress or by a national convention called by Congress on petition of the legislatures in two-thirds of the states; ratified either by the legislatures in three-fourths of the states or by specially called ratifying conventions in three-fourths of the states. The Constitution has been formally amended twenty-six times.

FURTHER READING

WILBOURN E. BENTON, ed. *1787—Drafting the U.S. Constitution, Organized by Subject Matter*, 2 vol. (Texas A&M Press, 1986).

JAMES BRYCE. *The American Commonwealth*, vols. 1 and 2 (Macmillan, 1893).

JAMES MACGREGOR BURNS. *The Vineyard of Liberty* (Knopf, 1982).

CONGRESSIONAL RESEARCH SERVICE, LIBRARY OF CONGRESS. *The Constitution of the United States of America, Analysis and Interpretation* [Senate Document 99–16], (U.S. Government Printing Office, 1987). 1986 Supplement [Senate Document 100–9], 1987.

ALEXIS DE TOCQUEVILLE. *Democracy in America*, vols. 1 and 2 (Knopf, 1945, first published in 1835).

ROBERT A. GOLDWIN and WILLIAM A. SCHAMBRA, eds. *How Democratic Is the Constitution?* (American Enterprise Institute, 1980).

FORREST MCDONALD. *Novus Ordo Seclorum: The Intellectual Origins of the Constitution* (University Press of Kansas, 1985).

J. W. PELTASON. *Corwin & Peltason's Understanding the Constitution*, 11th ed. (Holt, Rinehart & Winston, 1988).

DONALD L. ROBINSON, ed. *Reforming American Government: The Bicentennial Papers of the Committee on the Constitutional System* (Westview Press, 1985).

SUBCOMMITTEE ON THE CONSTITUTION, COMMITTEE ON THE JUDICIARY, UNITED STATES SENATE. *Amendments to the Constitution: A Brief Legislative History* (U.S. Government Printing Office, 1985).

JAMES L. SUNDQUIST, *Constitutional Reform and Effective Government* (Brookings Institution, 1986).

This constitution, a collection of essays on the framing and early debates (Congressional Quarterly Press, 1986).

CLEMENT E. VOSE. *Constitutional Change* (Lexington Books, 1972).

American Federalism: Problems and Prospects

"Every president of the United States since the Second World War has had a plan for a new, revitalized federalism."[1] Most of these plans have not gotten very far, for as Charles Robb, former Governor of Virginia, has pointed out, "There are two ways to empty a room in Washington: Hold a fund raiser for a defeated candidate or a debate on federalism."[2] Outside of Washington as well, when you talk to people about federalism you are likely to see their eyes glaze over. Yet this has not always been the case.

Suppose you heard that Congress had sent a delegation to Ottawa to meet with representatives from Canada and Mexico to draft a constitution for a new government for the United Governments of North America. The situation is only roughly parallel to what happened in the summer of 1787, but it gives you some idea of the worries that citizens of Massachusetts and Virginia and the other states felt when they heard rumors about a constitution's being drafted in Philadelphia. According to these rumors, the new government was to have powers to tax and regulate the lives of the people. Citizens' apprehensions were heightened when the proposed constitution was published; they found out that most of the rumors were true. Yet again, in 1861, men and women fought and died for Virginia or Texas or for the Union (although it would be a mistake to think of the Civil War merely as a particularly heated debate over the principles of federalism).

Constitutionally speaking, our federal system consists only of the national government and the fifty states. "Cities are not," the Supreme Court recently reminded us, "sovereign entities." But in a practical sense we are a nation of nearly 83,000 governmental units—from the national government to the school board district. This does not make for a tidy, efficient, easy-to-understand system, but, as we shall see, it does have its virtues.

That ours is a federal system makes a lot of difference, even if we are not always aware that this is so. Almost everything is affected by several layers of government. Consider your college or university, public or independent. About half of the students are likely to be receiving some form of national or state financial

[1] Gordon L. Clark, *Judges and the Cities* (University of Chicago Press, 1985), p. 61.
[2] *The New York Times* (December 15, 1985), section A, p. 80.

assistance to help pay their tuition, fees, room, and board. The college itself is chartered by the state. Most of the funds that pay for the teachers, staff, and buildings come from state appropriations, state bonds, private gifts encouraged by national tax laws, or a combination of national, state, and private sources. The research your faculty is doing, especially in the sciences, and the public-service programs in which they are involved, are likely to be supported by some combination of national, state, and private—but tax-deductible—dollars. The conditions under which students are admitted, faculty and staff are appointed, faculty and staff are evaluated and promoted, and grades are posted and reported are issues that involve state and national regulations. Any experimental animals on your campus are subject to supervision by national government and state inspectors. How the laboratories dispose of the chemicals used in experiments are governed by national and state laws. Examples of such "intergovernmentalization" are innumerable; they even affect such vital matters as your intercollegiate and intramural sports programs.

What is a federal system? The mere existence of both national and state governments does not make our system federal. What is important is that a *constitution* divides governmental powers between the general, or national, government and the constituent governments (called states in the United States), giving substantial functions to each. Neither the central nor the constituent government receives its powers from the other; both derive them from a common source, a constitution. This constitutional distribution of powers cannot be changed by the ordinary process of legislation—for example, by an act of either a national or state legislature. Finally, both levels of government operate through their own agents and exercise power directly over individuals. Among the countries that have federal systems of government are the United States, Canada, Switzerland, Mexico, and Australia.[3]

A **unitary,** as opposed to a federal, system of government is one in which a constitution vests all governmental power in the central government. The central government, if it so chooses, may delegate authority to constituent units, but what it delegates it may also take away. Britain, France, Israel, and the Philippines have this form of government. In the United States the relation between states and their local governments, such as counties and cities, is usually of this sort.

A **confederation** is a government in which the constituent governments create a central government by constitutional compact but do not give it power to regulate the conduct of individuals. The central government makes regulations for the constituent governments, but it exists and operates only at their direction. The thirteen states under the Articles of Confederation operated in this manner, as did the Southern Confederacy during the Civil War.

It is unfortunate for our understanding of federalism that the founders of our Constitution used the term *federal* to describe what we now would call a confederate form of government. Moreover, today *federal* is frequently used as a synonym for national: People often refer to the government in Washington as "the federal government." But, in fact, the states and the national government together make up our federal system.

Number of Governments

States	50
Counties	3,042
Municipalities	19,205
Townships	16,691
School Districts	14,741
Special Districts	29,487
	83,216

Source: 1987 Census of Governments, U.S. Department of Commerce, Bureau of the Census.

WHY FEDERALISM?

In 1787 federalism was an obvious choice. Confederation had been tried and found unsuccessful, but a unitary system was out of the question. Most of the people were too deeply attached to their state governments to permit them to be subordinated to central rule. Even if a unitary state had been politically possible in 1787,

[3] See Ursula K. Hicks, *Federalism: Failure and Success, A Comparative Study* (Oxford University Press, 1979), for a discussion of federalism around the world.

Confederation: 1781—1788

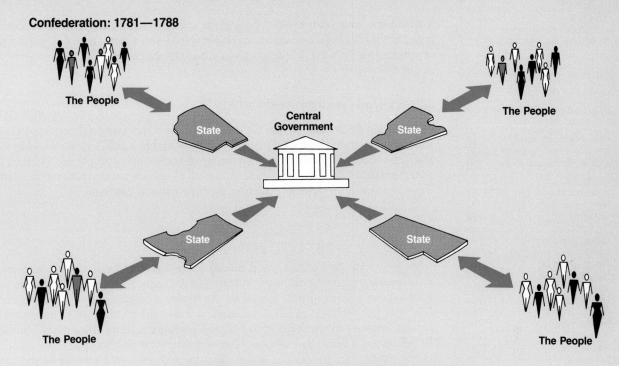

The Confederation was a union of states. The central government received power from the states and had no direct authority over the people.

—and Federation: 1789—

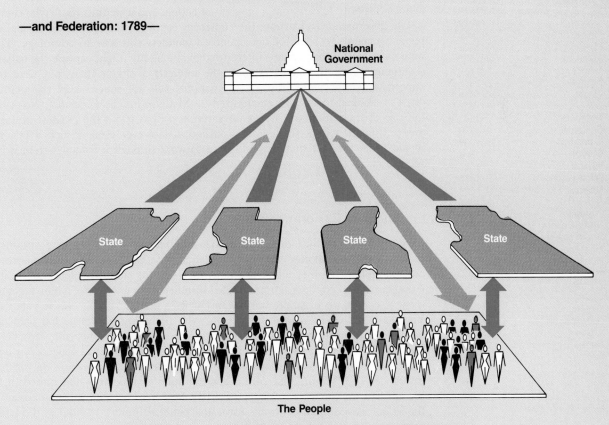

The Federal Union is a union of people. The national government and state governments receive power from the people and exercise authority directly over them.

it would not have been chosen. Federalism was, and still is, thought to be ideally suited to the needs of a heterogeneous people spread over a large continent, suspicious of concentrated power, and desiring unity but not uniformity.

Allows Unity without Uniformity

National politicians and parties do not have to iron out every difference on every issue in every state. Such issues as divorce, **comparable worth,** capital punishment, and the creation, operation, and financing of community colleges are debated in state legislatures and city halls; there is no need to enforce a single national standard. Thus, it is easier to develop consensus on truly national problems.

Checks the Growth of Tyranny

Although in the rest of the world federal forms have not been notably successful in preventing tyranny, and many unitary governments are democratic, Americans tend to equate freedom with federalism. As Madison pointed out in *The Federalist*, No. 10: "(If) factious leaders . . . kindle a flame within their particular states," national leaders can check the spread of the "conflagration into other states." Shays's Rebellion was a dramatic example. Moreover, when one political party loses control of the national government, it is still likely to hold office in a number of states. It can then regroup, develop new policies and new leaders, and continue to challenge the party in power at the national level.

Such diffusion of power creates its own problems. It makes it difficult for a national majority to carry out a program of action, and it permits those who control a state government to frustrate the consensus expressed through Congress and national agencies. To some of our country's founders this was an advantage. They were more fearful that a single-interest national majority might capture the national government and attempt to suppress the interests of others than they were that minority interests might frustrate the national will. Of course—and this point is often overlooked today (but emphasized by Madison in *The Federalist*, No. 10)—the size of the nation and the many interests within it are the greatest obstacles to the formation of a single-interest majority. However even if such a majority should form, the fact that it would have to work through a federal system would act as a check on it.

Encourages Experimentation

Justice Brandeis (on the Court from 1916 to 1939) pointed out that state governments provide great laboratories for experimentation with public policy. States serve as proving grounds. If they adopt programs that fail, the negative effects are limited; if programs succeed, they can be adopted by other states and by the national government. Georgia, for instance, was the first state to permit 18 year olds to vote; New York has been vigorous in its assault on water pollution; California has pioneered air pollution-control programs. Also, many states altered their abortion laws before the Supreme Court acted (whether this is progress or regression depends on one's values, as do so many questions of politics). Sunset laws, equal housing, no fault insurance, and "lemon" laws are a few examples of programs that started in the states. "The state role in policy experimentation may become more important as the federal government confronts fiscal and political limits . . . and as the nation confronts such matters as international economic competition . . . and the revolution

---

Statehood (1787–1987)

This is when states either ratified the U.S. Constitution or gained formal admittance to the Union.

Delaware	12/1787
Pennsylvania	12/1787
New Jersey	12/1787
Georgia	1/1788
Connecticut	1/1788
Massachusetts	2/1788
Maryland	4/1788
South Carolina	5/1788
New Hampshire	6/1788
Virginia	6/1788
New York	7/1788
North Carolina	11/1789
Rhode Island	5/1790
Vermont	3/1791
Kentucky	6/1792
Tennessee	6/1796
Ohio	3/1803
Louisiana	4/1812
Indiana	12/1816
Mississippi	12/1817
Illinois	12/1818
Alabama	12/1819
Maine	3/1820
Missouri	8/1821
Arkansas	6/1836
Michigan	1/1837
Florida	3/1845
Texas	12/1845
Iowa	12/1846
Wisconsin	5/1848
California	9/1850
Minnesota	5/1858
Oregon	2/1859
Kansas	1/1861
West Virginia	6/1863
Nevada	10/1864
Nebraska	3/1867
Colorado	8/1876
North Dakota	11/1889
South Dakota	11/1889
Montana	11/1889
Washington	11/1889
Idaho	7/1890
Wyoming	7/1890
Utah	1/1896
Oklahoma	11/1907
New Mexico	1/1912
Arizona	2/1912
Alaska	1/1959
Hawaii	8/1959

Note: This is provided not to be memorized (!) but to suggest the evolution and expansion of the nation in its first 200 years.

Although everybody is against pollution, deciding how to prevent it and establishing who should pay the costs of avoiding it arouse intense political controversy. (*Courtesy Aluminum Company of America; U.S. Coast Guard Official Photo*)

in family life, including, for example, surrogate motherhood, test-tube babies, adoption, and care of the elderly."[4]

Keeps Government Close to the People

Federalism, by providing numerous areas for decision making, involves many people and helps to keep government closer to the people. We have to be cautious, however, about the notion that state and local governments are necessarily "closer to the people" than the national government. True, more people are involved in local and state politics than in national affairs, and in recent years confidence in the ability of state governments has gone up. But national affairs are more on the minds of most people than are state or even local politics. Fewer voters participate in state elections than in congressional and presidential elections. Still, states and their local units remain very much a part of the political life of those concerned with public affairs.

CONSTITUTIONAL STRUCTURE OF AMERICAN FEDERALISM

Dividing powers and responsibilities among the national and state governments requires thousands of court decisions, hundreds of books, and a million speeches to explain—and even then the division lacks precise definition. The formal constitutional framework of our federal system, however, may be stated relatively simply: The national government has only those powers (with the one important exception of foreign affairs) *delegated* to it by the Constitution. The states have the powers not delegated to the central government except those *denied* to them by the Constitution and the constitutions of their states. Within the scope of its operations, the national government is *supreme*. Further, some powers are specifically denied to *both* the national and state governments; others are specifically denied *only* to the states; and still others are denied *only* to the national government.

[4] John Kincaid, "State Constitutions in the Federal System," *The Annals of the American Academy of Political and Social Sciences* (March 1988), p. 17.

3-1	The Most Popular Level of Government						

From which level of government do you feel you get the most for your money—federal, state, or local? (% U.S. public)

Level	1976	1978	1980	1982	1984	1986	1987
National	36%	35%	33%	35%	24%	32%	28%
Local	25	26	26	28	35	33	29
State	20	20	22	20	27	22	22
Don't know	19	19	19	17	14	13	21

Source: Advisory Commission on Intergovernmental Relations, *Changing Attitudes on Government & Taxes,* 1987.

"I wish I could help, Cinderella . . . but some clown has given all my powers back to the state . . ." (*Mike Peters, The Dayton Daily News. Reprinted by permission of UFS, Inc.*)

Powers of the National Government

The Constitution, chiefly in the first three articles, delegates legislative, executive, and judicial powers to the national government. In addition to these **express powers,** the Constitution delegates to Congress those **implied powers** that may be reasonably inferred from the express powers. The constitutional basis for the implied powers of Congress is the **necessary and proper clause** (Article I, Section 8), which gives Congress the right "to make all Laws which shall be necessary and proper for carrying into Execution the foregoing Powers, and all other Powers vested . . . in the Government of the United States."

In the field of foreign affairs, the national government has **inherent powers** that do not depend on specific constitutional grants. The national government has the same authority in dealing with other nations as if it were a unitary government. For example, the government of the United States may acquire territory by discovery and occupation, even though no specific clause in the Constitution allows such acquisition. Even if the Constitution were silent about foreign affairs—which it is not—the national government would have the right to declare war, make treaties, and appoint and receive ambassadors.[5]

Federal tax dollars often help state and local governments finance elementary school programs. (*Burk Uzzle/Woodfin Camp & Associates*)

National supremacy clause   Article VI states: "This Constitution, and the Laws of the United States which shall be made in Pursuance thereof; and all Treaties made . . . under the Authority of the United States, shall be the supreme Law of the Land; and the Judges in every State shall be bound thereby; any Thing in the Constitution or Laws of any State to the Contrary notwithstanding." All officials, state as well as national, are bound by constitutional oath to support the Constitution of the United States. States may not use their reserved powers to override national policies. (Local units of government are agents of the states. What states cannot constitutionally do, local units cannot do. In our discussion of the constitutional structure of federalism, local units are included in all references to states.)

Powers of the States

The Constitution reserves for the states all powers not granted to the national government, subject only to the limitations of the Constitution. Powers that are not given exclusively to the national government, by provision of the Constitution or by judicial interpretation, may be *concurrently* exercised by the states, as long as there is no conflict with national law. For example, each state has **concurrent powers** with the national government to levy taxes and to regulate commerce internal to each state. In practice this is not so simple. A state may levy a tax on the same item as the national government, for example. But a state cannot, by a tax,

[5] *United States* v. *Curtiss-Wright Export Corporation*, 299 U.S. 304 (1936).

"unduly burden" a function of the national government, interfere with the operation of a national law, or abridge the terms of a treaty of the United States. Who decides whether a state tax is an "undue burden" on a national function? Ultimately, the Supreme Court decides.

The issues are even more complicated regarding commerce. When Congress has not acted, the states may regulate those local aspects of interstate commerce that do not require uniform national treatment and unduly burden interstate commerce. But who decides what requires uniform national treatment and is an undue burden? If Congress is silent, ultimately the Supreme Court decides this too. The Court handles about four or so such cases every year.[6] It has upheld state laws imposing speed limits on trains within city limits and requiring the elimination of grade crossings, but it has invalidated laws requiring trains to stop at every crossing.

What of state regulations designed to protect consumers from fraud, guard the public health, or collect a fair share of taxes from those who use state facilities? Again, if there is no clear congressional direction, the Supreme Court must decide whether such regulations are within the reserved powers of the state; whether they are overridden by, or come into conflict with, superior federal regulations; or whether they unduly burden interstate commerce. As for state taxes on interstate commerce, recently the Supreme Court has tended to let Congress decide which, if any, state taxes on interstate commerce should be set aside because they are too much of a burden on interstate and foreign commerce.

Constitutional Limits and Obligations

To make federalism work, the Constitution imposes certain restraints on the national and state governments. States are prohibited from

1. Making treaties with foreign governments
2. Authorizing private persons to prey on the shipping and commerce of other nations—what the Constitution refers to as "granting letters of Marque and Reprisal"
3. Coining money, issuing bills of credit, or making anything but gold and silver coin a tender in payment of debts.

Nor may states, without the consent of Congress,

1. Tax imports or exports
2. Tax foreign ships
3. Keep troops or ships in time of peace (except for the state militia, now called the National Guard)
4. Enter into compacts with other states or foreign nations that "tend to increase the political power in the States, which may encroach upon or interfere" with the supremacy of the national government
5. Engage in war, unless invaded or in such imminent danger as will not admit of delay (of course, an invasion of one state would be an invasion of the United States itself).

The national government, in turn, is required by the Constitution to refrain from exercising its powers, especially its powers to tax and to regulate interstate commerce, in such a way as to interfere substantially with the ability of the states to perform their responsibilities. Making this generalization is easier than citing specific examples of national government actions that the Supreme Court has struck down in recent decades because of national interference with state sovereignty.

Interstate highways illustrate the need for federal coordination of state efforts. (*Jim Anderson/Woodfin Camp & Associates*)

---

[6] Steven G. Craig and Joel W. Sailors, "A Destructive Trade War between the States," *The Wall Street Journal* (February 5, 1985), p. 28.

CONSTITUTIONAL DISTRIBUTION OF POWERS

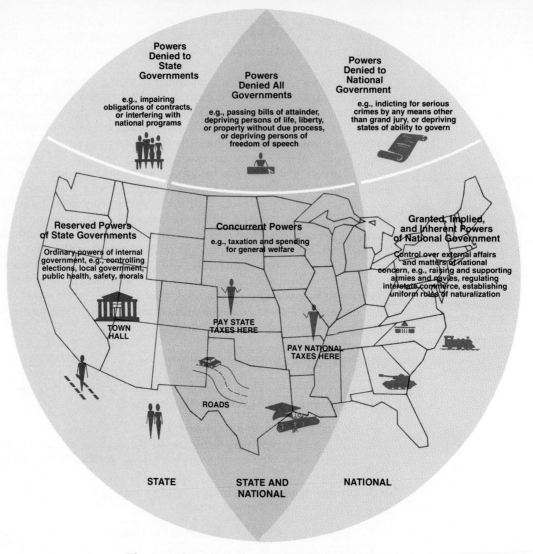

Powers Denied to State Governments

e.g., impairing obligations of contracts, or interfering with national programs

Powers Denied All Governments

e.g., passing bills of attainder, depriving persons of life, liberty, or property without due process, or depriving persons of freedom of speech

Powers Denied to National Government

e.g., indicting for serious crimes by any means other than grand jury, or depriving states of ability to govern

Reserved Powers of State Governments

Ordinary powers of internal government, e.g., controlling elections, local government, public health, safety, morals

TOWN HALL

Concurrent Powers

e.g., taxation and spending for general welfare

PAY STATE TAXES HERE

PAY NATIONAL TAXES HERE

ROADS

Granted, Implied, and Inherent Powers of National Government

Control over external affairs and matters of national concern, e.g., raising and supporting armies and navies, regulating interstate commerce, establishing uniform rules of naturalization

STATE

STATE AND NATIONAL

NATIONAL

The states have been protected by the political process—the built-in restraints that our system provides because persons elected from the states participate in the decisions of Congress—more than by any judicially created limitations.[7]

Until 1937 the Supreme Court, off and on, espoused the *doctrine of dual federalism*. Under this doctrine the national and state governments were viewed as equal sovereigns, each operating within its own restricted sphere, with the Supreme Court enforcing the boundary between the two. In 1976, echoes of this doctrine could be heard, in *National League of Cities* v. *Usery*, in which the Court by five to four held unconstitutional a 1974 amendment of the Fair Labor Standards Act extending federal minimum wages and maximum hours provisions to state and local government employees.[8]

Then, in 1985, again by a five to four vote, *National League of Cities* was overturned by *Garcia* v. *San Antonio Metro*. In *Garcia*, which has been reaffirmed and strengthened in 1988, the Court said, in essence, that Congress, not the courts,

[7] *Garcia* v. *San Antonio Metro*, 469 U.S. 528 (1985). James R. Alexander, "State Sovereignty in the Federal System" *Publius* (Spring 1986), pp. 1–15.
[8] 426 U.S. 833 (1976)

decides which actions of the states should and could be regulated by the national government. "Although Garcia left open the possibility that some extraordinary defects in the national political process might render congressional regulation of state activities invalid . . . nothing in Garcia or the Tenth Amendment authorizes courts to second-guess the substantive basis for congressional legislation" affecting state actions.[9] All the Reagan appointees except for Justice Kennedy, who has not spoken on this issue as yet, have dissented from the view that the political process is the states' only constitutional protection, and have predicted "this Court will in time again assume its constitutional responsibility" of defining the scope of state autonomy protected by federalism.[10] But even the dissenting justices acknowledged that the set of activities protected by state sovereignty from the reach of the national government "may well be negligible."

The Constitution also requires the national government to guarantee to each state a **republican form of government**. The framers used this term to distinguish a republic from a monarchy on the one side and from a pure, direct democracy on the other. Congress, not the courts, enforces this guarantee and determines what is or is not a republican form of government.[11] By permitting the congressional delegation of a state to take its seat in Congress, Congress is in effect deciding that the state has the republican form of government guaranteed by the Constitution.

In addition, the national government is obliged by the Constitution to protect the states against domestic insurrection. Congress has delegated authority to the president to send troops to put down insurrections at the request of the proper state authorities.[12] The president does not have to wait, however, for a request from state authorities to send federal troops into a state to enforce federal laws. It is hard to imagine a situation of domestic insurrection against a state today that would not also involve federal matters.

Horizontal Federalism: Interstate Constitutional Relations

Three clauses, taken from the Articles of Confederation, require the states to give full faith and credit to one another's public acts, records, and judicial proceedings; to extend to one another's citizens the privileges and immunities of their own citizens; and to return persons who are fleeing from justice.

Full faith and credit   The **full faith and credit clause** is one of the most technical provisions of the Constitution. In general, it requires each state court to enforce civil judgments of other state courts and to accept their public records and acts as valid documents. (It does not require states to enforce the criminal laws of other states; in most cases, for one state to enforce the criminal laws of another would be unconstitutional.) The clause applies especially to noncriminal judicial proceedings.

Interstate privileges and immunities   States must extend to citizens of other states the privileges and immunities granted to their own citizens, including the protection of the laws, the right to engage in peaceful occupations, access to the courts, and freedom from discriminatory taxes. Further, states may not impose unreasonable "durational residency" requirements to withhold such political rights as voting or such benefits as medical help from United States citizens who move into their states and thereby become state citizens. A day seems to be about as long as the Court will tolerate for welfare payments or medical care, fifty days or

Mario Cuomo, a popular two-term governor of New York, has consistently advocated more federal assistance for the states—often in opposition to the White House. (Don Pollard, New York State Executive Chamber)

[9] South Carolina v. Baker, 99 L Ed 2d 592 (1988).

[10] Justice Sandra O'Connor dissenting in Garcia v. San Antonio Metro.

[11] Luther v. Borden, 7 How. 1 (1849).

[12] Ibid.

so for voting privileges, and one year for payment of in-state tuition for state-supported colleges and universities. (Adults who move into a state just prior to enrolling in a state-supported university or college may be required to prove that they intend to remain after finishing their schooling; driver's licenses, car registrations, voter registrations, and continuous, year-round off-campus residence can serve as evidence.)

Extradition   The Constitution asserts that when criminals have fled from one state to another, the state to which they have fled is to deliver them to the proper officials upon request from the first state's governor. Congress has supplemented this constitutional provision for **extradition** by making the governor of the state to which fugitives have fled the agent responsible for returning them. Despite the use of the word *shall*, the federal courts will not order governors to surrender (extradite) persons wanted in other states. Normally, extradition is a routine matter. Further, Congress has made it a federal crime to flee from one state to another to avoid prosecution for a felony and has ordered the federal trial to take place in the state from which the person has fled.

Interstate compacts   In addition to these three obligations, the Constitution also requires states to settle disputes with one another without the use of force. States may carry their legal arguments to the Supreme Court, or they may negotiate **interstate compacts,** which they can also use to establish interstate agencies and to solve joint problems. Before most interstate compacts become effective, congressional approval is required. After a compact has been signed and approved by Congress, it becomes binding on all signatory states, and its terms are enforceable by the Supreme Court.

The Realities Today

This outline of the constitutional structure of federalism oversimplifies and—especially in terms of the division of powers between the national government and the states—even misleads. The basic law underlying the system has not changed, but the ways in which it is applied have altered greatly. As recently as the Great Depression of the 1930s, constitutional scholars and Supreme Court justices debated whether Congress had the authority to enact legislation dealing with agriculture, labor, education, housing, and welfare. Only two decades ago some questioned the constitutional authority of Congress to legislate against racial discrimination. And it remains technically correct that Congress lacks any general grant of authority to do whatever it thinks necessary and proper in order to promote the general welfare or to preserve domestic tranquility. But as a result of the rise of a national economy, the growth of national demands on Washington, and the emergence of a world in which war could destroy us in a matter of minutes, our constitutional system has so evolved that the national government has authority to deal with almost every issue.

Today, restraints on national power stem from constitutional provisions that protect the liberties of the people rather than from those relating to the powers of state governments. Still, despite the growth of national authority, states are vital and active governments backed by significant political forces.

TRIUMPH OF THE NATIONALIST INTERPRETATION

The preceding summary of the constitutional construction of our federal system jumps over 200 years of conflict and proclaims victory, at least for the moment, for the nationalist interpretation. (The debate between those who favor national action and those who favor state and local levels continues, but generally it does so outside the framework of constitutional principles.) This victory for the nationalists

Centralists v. Decentralists

Centralists' Arguments

1. State and local governments lack expertise.
2. State and local officials tend to be parochial.
3. State and local governments are unable or unwilling to raise enough money to meet demands.
4. State and local governments are more apt to reflect race and ethnic biases.
5. State and local governments are more likely to be dominated by conservative elites.
6. State and local governments are structurally incapable of dealing with problems of redistribution from the rich to the poor.
7. Given . . . the mobility of corporate and residential taxpayers, states and localities are not able to regulate business effectively.

Decentralists' Responses

1. Changes in population have made the states more competent and sensitive to urban needs.
2. Changes in tax structure have made states and local governments more flexible and progressive raisers of revenue.
3. Legal and political changes have made states and localities as sensitive to the needs of the poor and minorities as the national government.
4. Political reform movements have made state and local governments more effective governments.

Look closely at the operation of your state and city governments. Do the facts as you know them support the contentions of the centralists?

Source: Jeffrey R. Henig, *Public Policy and Federalism: Issues in State and Local Politics* (St. Martin's Press, 1985), pp. 34–41.

is recent. Throughout most of our history, powerful groups have favored states' rights; these days such states' righters prefer to be called decentralists.

The constitutional arguments revolving around federalism grew out of specific issues: whether the national government had the authority to outlaw slavery in the territories; whether states had the authority to operate racially segregated schools; whether Congress could regulate labor relations. The debates were frequently phrased in constitutional language and appeals were made to the great principles of federalism, but they were also arguments over who was to get what, where, and how, and who was to do what to whom.

Among those who favored the states' rights interpretation, with varying emphasis, were Thomas Jefferson, John C. Calhoun, the Supreme Court from the 1920s to 1937, and, more recently, Ronald Reagan. Their positions have been that the Constitution, an intergovernmental treaty among sovereign states, created the central government and gave it carefully limited authority. Because the national government is thus nothing more than an agent of the states, every one of its powers should be narrowly defined. Any doubt whether the states had given a particular function to the central government or had reserved it for themselves should be resolved in favor of the states.

The states' righters hold that the national government should not be permitted to exercise its delegated powers in a way that interferes with activities reserved for the states. The Tenth Amendment, they claim, makes this clear: "The powers not delegated to the United States by the Constitution, nor prohibited by it to the States, are reserved to the States respectively, or to the people." Decentralists insist that state governments are closer to the people and therefore reflect the people's wishes more accurately than does the national government. They maintain further that the national government is inherently heavy-handed and bureaucratic and that in order to preserve our federal system and our liberties, central authority must be kept under control.

The nationalist position, supported by Chief Justice John Marshall, Abraham Lincoln, Theodore Roosevelt, Franklin Roosevelt, and throughout most of our history by the Supreme Court, rejects the whole concept of the Constitution as an interstate compact. Rather, it views the Constitution as a supreme law established by the people. The national government is an agent of the people, not of the states, for it was the people who drew up the Constitution and created the national government. The sovereign people gave the national government sufficient power to accomplish the great objectives listed in the Preamble. They intended that the central government's powers should be liberally defined and that it be denied authority only when the Constitution clearly prohibits it from acting.

The nationalists contend that the national government is a government of all the people and that each state speaks for only some of the people. Although the Tenth Amendment clearly reserves powers for the states, as Chief Justice Stone said: "The Tenth Amendment states but a truism that all is retained which has not been surrendered" (*United States* v. *Darby*, 1941).[13] The amendment does not deny the national government the right to exercise to the fullest extent all the powers given to it by the Constitution. The supremacy of the national government, it is argued, does restrict the states; a government representing part of the people cannot be allowed to interfere with a government representing all of them.

McCulloch v. *Maryland*

In ***McCulloch v. Maryland*** (1819) the Supreme Court had the first of many chances to choose between these two interpretations of our federal system.[14] Maryland had levied a tax against the Baltimore branch of the Bank of the United

---

[13] 312 U.S. 100 (1941).

[14] 4 Wheaton 316 (1819).

States, a semipublic agency established by Congress. James William McCulloch, the cashier of the bank, refused to pay on the grounds that a state could not tax an instrument of the national government. Maryland's attorneys responded that, in the first place, the national government did not have the power to incorporate a bank—but even if it did, the state had the power to tax it.

Maryland was represented before the Court by some of the country's most distinguished lawyers, including Luther Martin, a delegate to the Constitutional Convention who had left early when it became apparent that a strong national government was in the making. Martin, basing his argument on the states' rights view of federalism, pointed out that the power to incorporate a bank is not expressly delegated to the national government. He contended that Article I, Section 8, Clause 18, which gives Congress the right to choose whatever means are necessary and proper to carry out its delegated powers, gives Congress only the power to choose those means and to pass those laws absolutely essential to the execution of its expressly granted powers. Because a bank is not absolutely necessary to the exercise of any of its delegated powers, Congress has no authority to establish it.

As for Maryland's right to tax the bank, Martin's position was clear: The power to tax is one of the powers reserved to the states, which they may use as they see fit.

The national government was represented by equally distinguished counsel, chief among whom was Daniel Webster. Webster conceded that the power to create a bank is not one of the express powers of the national government. However, the power to pass laws necessary and proper to carry out enumerated powers is expressly delegated to Congress, and this should be interpreted to mean that Congress has authority to enact any legislation convenient and useful in carrying out delegated national powers. Therefore, Congress may incorporate a bank as an appropriate, convenient, and useful means of exercising the granted powers of collecting taxes, borrowing money, and caring for the property of the United States.

Webster contended that though the power to tax is reserved to the states, states cannot use their reserved powers to interfere with the operations of the national government. The Constitution leaves no room for doubt: In case of conflict between the national and state governments, the former is supreme.

Speaking for a unanimous Court, Marshall rejected every one of Maryland's contentions. He wrote: "We must never forget that it is a constitution we are expounding . . . [a] constitution intended to endure for ages to come, and consequently, to be adapted to the various crises of human affairs." "The government of the Union," he continued, "is emphatically and truly a government of the people. In form and substance it emanates from them, its powers are granted to them, and are to be exercised directly on them. . . . It can never be to their interest and cannot be presumed to have been their intention, to clog and embarrass its execution, by withholding the most appropriate means." Marshall summarized his views on the powers of the national government in these now-famous words: "Let the end be legitimate, let it be within the scope of the Constitution, and all means which are appropriate, which are plainly adapted to that end, which are not prohibited, but consist with the letter and spirit of the Constitution, are constitutional."

Having thus established the doctrine of implied national powers, Marshall set forth the doctrine of **national supremacy.** No state, he said, can use its reserved taxing powers to tax a national instrument. "The power to tax involves the power to destroy. . . . If the right of the states to tax the means employed by the general government be conceded, the declaration that the Constitution, and the laws made in pursuance thereof, shall be the supreme law of the land, is empty and unmeaning declamation."

The long-range significance of *McCulloch* v. *Maryland* in providing support for the developing forces of nationalism can hardly be overstated. The arguments of the states' righters, if accepted, would have strapped the national government in a constitutional straitjacket and denied it powers needed to handle the problems of an expanding nation.

The Constitutional Basis of the Growth of the National Government

The formal constitutional powers of the national government are essentially the same today as they were in 1789. But the Supreme Court (building on Marshall's work in *McCulloch* v. *Maryland*), Congress, the president, and the people have taken advantage of the Constitution's flexibility to permit the national government to use whatever powers it needs to fight wars and depressions and to serve the needs of a modern industrial nation. The expansion of central government functions has rested on three major constitutional pillars.

The war power   The national government is responsible for protecting the nation from external aggression and, when necessary, for waging war. In today's world military strength depends not only on field troops but also on the ability to mobilize the nation's industry and to apply its scientific knowledge to the tasks of defense. The national government has the power to wage war and to do what is necessary and proper to wage it successfully. In these times this means that the government has the power to do almost anything that is not in direct conflict with constitutional guarantees.

The power to regulate interstate and foreign commerce   Congressional authority extends to all commerce that affects more than one state and to all those activities, wherever they exist or whatever their nature, whose control Congress decides is necessary and proper to regulate interstate and foreign commerce. The term *commerce* includes the production, buying, selling, renting, and transporting of goods, services, and properties.[15] The commerce clause—Article 1, Section 8, Clause 3— packs a tremendous constitutional punch. In these few words the national government has been able to find justification for regulating a wide range of human activity and property. Few aspects of our economy today affect commerce in only one state.

The commerce clause can also be used to sustain legislation that goes beyond commercial matters. When the Supreme Court upheld the 1964 Civil Rights Act forbidding discrimination because of race, religion, or national origin in places of public accommodation, it said: "Congress' action in removing the disruptive effect which it found racial discrimination has on interstate travel is not invalidated because Congress was also legislating against what it considers to be moral wrongs." Discrimination restricts the flow of interstate commerce; interstate commerce was being used to support discrimination; therefore, Congress could legislate against the discrimination. Moreover, the law could be applied even to local places of public accommodation because local incidents of discrimination have a substantial and harmful impact on interstate commerce. "If it is interstate commerce that feels the pinch, it does not matter how local the operation that applies the squeeze."[16]

The power to tax and spend   Congress lacks constitutional authority to pass laws solely on the ground that they will promote the general welfare, but it may raise taxes and spend money for this purpose. This distinction between legislating and appropriating makes little difference most of the time. Congress lacks constitutional power to regulate education or agriculture directly, but it does have the

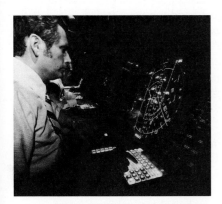

Federal air traffic controllers at work directing air commerce among the states. (*Courtesy Sperry Corporation*)

Territorial Expansion

Louisiana Purchase	1803
Florida	1819
Texas	1845
Oregon	1846
Mexican Cession	1848
Gadsden Purchase	1853
Alaska	1867
Hawaii	1898
The Philippines	1898–1946
Puerto Rico	1899
Guam	1899
American Samoa	1900
Canal Zone	1904
U.S. Virgin Islands	1917
Pacific Islands Trust Territory	1947

Note: Part of the genius and flexibility of our constitutional system has been the way in which we have acquired territory and later extended rights and guarantees by means of statehood, commonwealth, or territorial status.

[15] *Gibbons* v. *Ogden*, 9 Wheaton 1 (1824); see also *Russell* v. *United States*, 471 U.S. 858 (1985).
[16] *Heart of Atlanta Motel* v. *United States*, 379 U.S. 241 (1964).

power to appropriate money to support education or to pay farmers subsidies. By attaching conditions to its grants of money, Congress may regulate what it cannot directly control by law.

Because Congress puts up the money, it determines how the money will be spent. By withholding or threatening to withhold funds, the national government can influence—or control—state operations and regulate individual conduct. In 1964, for example, Congress stipulated that federal funds should be withdrawn from any program in which any person was denied benefits because of race, color, or national origin; subsequently the categories of sex and physical handicap were added.

These three constitutional powers—the *war* power, the power over *interstate commerce,* and, most especially, the power to *tax and spend* for the general welfare— have made possible a tremendous expansion of federal functions.

UMPIRES OF THE FEDERAL SYSTEM

Today there are few doubts about the national government's constitutional authority to deal with issues affecting the nation, whether they concern civil rights, speed limits on highways, or the sale of holiday lights. Nonetheless we still argue about (1) whether Congress intended to regulate a subject completely or to leave some regulation to state discretion and (2) whether, in the absence of congressional action, states may deal with subjects that affect commerce or people in other states.

Although couched in terms of federalism, such arguments reflect differences between various interests. The national and state governments are arenas in which and through which clashes take place between consumers and producers, workers and employers, airlines and railroads, and all the other contending groups that make up our political system. In these political battles judges, especially those on the Supreme Court, play a vital—but not exclusive—role.

The Role of the Federal Courts

Federal judges' authority to review the activities of state and local governments increased dramatically after the Civil War. The Thirteenth, Fourteenth, and Fifteenth amendments (especially the Fourteenth), the congressional legislation enacted to implement them, and the expansion of the habeas corpus jurisdiction of the federal district courts (see Chapter 6) ensure that almost every action by state and local officials can be challenged before a federal judge as a violation of the Constitution or of federal law. Federal judges have become major expounders of the principles of federalism, and federal courts have become major forums in which to challenge the actions of state and local authorities. In carrying out their judgments, federal judges have, in effect, taken over the supervision of state prison systems, public hospitals, public schools, and other public facilities.

Other recent Supreme Court decisions concerning intergovernmental relations have especially jolted city officials. First, the Supreme Court opened federal courts to suits for damages brought against municipalities by persons who believe city officials acting pursuant to governmental policy or custom have violated any of their federally protected rights—not just those guaranteed by the civil rights statutes.[17] As a result of these Section 1983 actions, as they are called, cities are now facing billions of dollars worth of damages. In 1982 the Court sent further "shock waves through the nation's localities" when it opened federal courts to

[17] *Oklahoma City* v. *Tuttle,* 471 U.S. 808 (1985); *Maine* v. *Thiboutot,* 448 U.S. 1 (1980); *Monell* v. *New York City Dept. of Social Welfare,* 436 U.S. 658 (1978). See Cynthia Cates Colella, "The United States Supreme Court and Intergovernmental Relations," in Robert J. Dilger, ed, *American Intergovernmental Relations Today: Perspectives and Controversies* (Prentice-Hall, 1985), p. 66.

damage suits against city ordinances alleged to violate federal antitrust laws, even those relating to public health, safety, and welfare.[18] Most city officials agreed with Justice Rehnquist, who wrote in dissent: "The Court's decision will impede local government's efforts to enact ordinances . . . aimed at protecting public health, safety, and welfare, for fear of subjecting the local government to liability under the Sherman Act." City officials appealed to Congress. Although Congress refused to exempt cities and their officials from the antitrust laws, it did exempt them from money damages when acting in their official capacities.

Stung by recent judicial defeats, state and local governments have formed a privately funded State and Local Legal Center. Although cities' attorneys are unlikely to have argued cases before the Supreme Court, lawyers representing those attacking the cities are probably specialists from the American Civil Liberties Union, the NAACP Legal Aid and Defense Fund, or the office of the solicitor general of the United States, who often appear before the High Court. As a result, according to Justice Powell, states and cities are often "outgunned." State and local officials hope that the new center will improve their records before the Court.[19]

Over the years the Court's decisions have favored national powers (including its own); nonetheless, few would deny the Supreme Court the power to review and set aside state actions. As Justice Holmes once remarked: "I do not think the United States would come to an end if we lost our power to declare an Act of Congress void. I do think the Union would be imperiled if we could not make that declaration as to the laws of the several States."[20]

Other Umpires (and Contestants) of the Federal System

Federal courts are not the only umpires of the federal system: Congress, too, has much to say about the distribution of functions and about whether federal or state standards will prevail. For example, since the Supreme Court upheld the right of states to use the so-called unitary method of taxation of multinational corporations, Congress has been trying to resolve the differences between the states and the multinationals, especially those headquartered in other nations.

The president and federal administrators also have their say about the operation of our federal system. After Congress authorizes federal grant programs, the president and federal administrators approve the guidelines for grants, decide which projects to approve, and largely determine how federal standards will be applied.

States and local governments are not passive partners in deciding how functions will be allocated. It is one thing to get a law through Congress; it is another to impose national standards on state and local officials and the people they represent. A national law may well be ambiguous. Also, powerful local and state political factions often persuade Congress to build safeguards into a law to protect their interests. In the implementation battles the greater political power may be with state and local officials rather than with national enforcers.

FEDERAL GRANTS

Today the "feds" are everywhere and into everything. Despite the federal government's expanding role, however, the number of people it employs is about the same today as it was two decades ago. Although state and local governments have

---

[18] *Community Communications Co.* v. *Boulder*, 455 U.S. 40 (1982). See George D. Brown, "The Courts and Grant Reform: A Time for Action," *Intergovernmental Perspective* (Fall 1981), pp. 6–14.
[19] Fred Barbash, *The Washington Post* (February 28, 1983), p. A4.
[20] Oliver Wendell Holmes, Jr., *Collected Legal Papers* (Harcourt, 1920), pp. 295–96.

gotten larger, the federal government has not. Congress has chosen to use the states, the cities, the counties, the universities—and at times even private agencies—to administer many new programs, deliver services, and carry out federal mandates.

Congress has done this by using federal grants, of which there are four general types: **categorical-formula grants, project grants, block grants, and revenue sharing.**

1. *Categorical-formula grants.* Under these grants (which were virtually the only kind of grant available before the 1960s) Congress appropriates funds for specific purposes—welfare, school lunches, the building of airports and highways. The funds are allocated by formula. Each eligible unit seeking a grant has to put up some of its own money, agree to establish an appropriate agency to spend the funds, submit plans for advance approval, permit national officials to inspect the completed work, and place employees who administer the grant under a merit system. Categorical-formula grants permit Congress to determine with great precision on what the funds will be spent. Still, they leave to governors, state legislators, and state and local officials an active role in determining how the programs are carried out.

2. *Project grants.* These came into great prominence in the 1960s. Congress appropriates a certain sum, but the dollars are allocated to state and local units—and in some instances to nongovernmental agencies—on the basis of applications from those who wish to participate.

3. *Block grants.* These grants have been promoted by the Advisory Commission on Intergovernmental Relations (see Box on page 52) and tend to be favored by presidents—especially Nixon and Reagan. They are broad grants to states for certain prescribed activities—elementary and secondary education, social services, preventive health, and health services—with only a few specific strings attached.

4. *Revenue sharing.* From 1972 to 1986 federal revenue funds were granted to state and local units of government to be used at their discretion, with only very general conditions set. The program initiated in 1972 provided $4.2 billion annually to states and local governments. In the 1980s, when federal budget deficits started to soar and, as Secretary of the Treasury James Baker said for the Reagan administration, "[there was] no revenue to share," state governments were ousted from the program. Local governments were ousted in 1986, with a one year reprieve until 1987.

The Politics of Federal Grants

Arguments about the forms of federal aid involve more than considerations of efficiency. They reflect differences about what constitutes desirable public policy, where power should be located, and who will gain or lose by the various types of grants. Republican presidents "have consistently favored fewer strings, less federal supervision, and the delegation of spending discretion to the state and local governments, whereas Democrats have advocated the opposite. Congress has divided similarly, with Democrats generally voting for centralization, and Republicans decentralization."[21]

Supporters of the more generalized kinds of federal aid, such as block grants and revenue sharing, hope that their use will bring about a "transfer not simply of money but power."[22] Opponents say Congress and federal administrators are more likely to put the money where it is most needed—that is, largely in the big cities.

Presidents and governors tend to urge that categorical-formula grants be consolidated into larger blocks. Congress and groups who benefit from existing programs are likely to resist, and most of the time they do so successfully. Consider the battle over libraries. " . . . [The] Administration proposed the consolidation of

Purposes of Federal Grants

1. To supply state and local governments with revenue.
2. To establish minimum national standards—for example, for giving aid to the blind.
3. To equalize resources among the states, on the "Robin Hood principle" of taking, through federal taxes, money from people with high incomes and spending it, through grants, in states where the poor live.
4. To improve the operations and levels of services of state and local governments.
5. To stimulate experimentation and new approaches.
6. To encourage the achievement of social objectives such as nondiscrimination.
7. To attack major problems but minimize the growth of federal agencies.

Source: Michael D. Reagan and John G. Sanzone, *The New Federalism*, 2nd ed. Copyright © 1981 by Oxford University Press, Inc. Reprinted by permission.

[21] John E. Chubb, "The Political Economy of Federalism," *The American Political Science Review*, vol. 79 (December 1985), p. 1005.

[22] Richard P. Nathan et al., *Monetary Revenue Sharing* (The Brookings Institution, 1975), p. 10.

several narrow library grants. The Congress resisted, and the reason is simple. It can be expressed quantitatively: 99.99% of the public is not interested in library grant reform. Of the .01 percent who are interested, all are librarians and oppose it."[23]

The debate about the form of grants is not just a dispute over whether state and local governments can be trusted to spend federal dollars wisely but a debate about which state and local officials should be given control over the spending. Specialists who work for state and local governments often have more in common with specialists working for the national government than they do with their own governors, mayors, or state legislators. These specialists (highway engineers, welfare administrators, educators) get together at meetings, read common journals, and jointly defend the independence of their programs from attempts by elected (national or state) officials to regulate them.[24]

The specialists may thus join forces with their counterparts among the interest groups to create powerful "guilds"[25] of closely connected people who are knowledgeable about the complexities of specific federal aid programs. When they combine forces with specialists working for congressional committees, they create "iron triangles"—of interest groups, congressional committee staffers, and federal bureaucrats (who in turn are connected to state and local bureaucrats)—of great effectiveness.

To counter the specialists' power, governors, mayors, county supervisors, state legislators, and other officeholders have stepped up their own lobbying activities. Over thirty state governments have offices in Washington, many located in the "Hall of the States," an office building near Capitol Hill that also serves as the Washington headquarters of the National Governors Association and the National Conference of State Legislatures. The National League of Cities has also become active. These "topcrats," as some call them, take an active interest in what goes on in Washington and are thus a political force with which specialists must also reckon.

The battle over "which piper calls the tune when one government raises the money and another spends it" tends to be cyclical. "Complaints about excessive federal control tend to be followed by proposals to shift more power to state and local governments. Then, when problems arise in state and local administration—and problems inevitably arise when any organization tries to administer anything—demands for closer federal supervision and tighter federal controls follow."[26] The cycle at the moment is toward fewer federal dollars, more block grants, and fewer program-specific national controls, but despite the decentralist rhetoric, new ways have been found to impose national controls.

FEDERAL REGULATIONS

Fewer federal grants have been given in recent years, but this has not resulted in fewer federal controls. On the contrary, federal policy makers "have turned . . . to new more intrusive, and more compulsory *regulatory* programs to work their will."[27] These new kinds of federal regulations of how states and local governments spend federal dollars, and in some instances even their own state and local dollars,

[23] Richard P. Nathan, *Special Revenue Sharing: Simple, Neat, and Correct*, unpublished manuscript.

[24] Deil S. Wright, *Understanding Intergovernmental Relations*, 2nd ed. (Brooks-Cole, 1982).

[25] Harold Seidman and Robert Gilmour, *Politics, Position and Power*, rev. ed. (Oxford University Press, 1985).

[26] Donald F. Kettl, *The Regulation of American Federalism* (Louisiana State University Press, 1983), pp. 154–55.

[27] Advisory Commission on Intergovernmental Relations, *Regulatory Federalism: Policy, Process, Impact and Reform* (ACIR, 1984), p. 1.

provide far more intrusive federal interventions into the affairs of states and local governments than the more obvious conditions of federal grants.[28]

There are four types of federal regulations:

1. *Direct orders.* In a few instances, federal regulation of state and local governments takes the form of direct orders that must be complied with under threat of criminal or civil sanction. Examples are the Equal Opportunity Act of 1982, barring job discrimination by state and local governments on the basis of race, color, religion, sex, and national origin and the Marine Protection Amendments of 1977, prohibiting cities from dumping sewage into the ocean. Because such direct orders raise mild constitutional concerns and more serious political ones, Congress favors other techniques to work the federal will on the states.

2. *Cross-cutting requirements.* The first and most famous of these—so-called because a condition on one federal grant is extended to all other federal funds—is Title VI of the 1964 Civil Rights Act, which holds that no person may be discriminated against in the use of federal funds because of race, color, national origin, sex, or handicapped status. Over sixty cross-cutting requirements concern the environment, historical preservation, contract wage rates, access to governmental information, the care of experimental animals, the treatment of human subjects in research projects, and so on.[29]

3. *Cross-over sanctions.* These sanctions permit the "feds" to use federal dollars in one program to influence state and local policy in another. One example is the Emergency Highway Energy Conservation Act of 1974, which prohibits the Secretary of Transportation from approving federal funding for highway construction projects in states having a speed limit in excess of 55 miles per hour. In 1986 the U.S. Department of Transportation said it would withhold federal highway aid to Arizona and Vermont because the two states were inadequately enforcing that speed limit. Another example is a 1984 act that reduces federal highway aid by up to 15 percent for any state that fails to adopt a minimum drinking age of 21 by 1987.

4. *Partial preemption.* This kind of control rests not upon the national government's power to spend but on its powers under the supremacy and commerce clauses to preempt conflicting state and local activities. Building on this constitutional authority, federal law in certain areas establishes basic policies but requires states to administer them. Some programs give states the option and funds to administer them, if they meet the nationally determined conditions or standards. However, if a state chooses not to participate then, the national government steps in and directly runs the programs. The Clean Air Act Amendments of 1970 called for *mandatory* partial preemption, in which the federal government set national air-quality standards but required states to devise plans for their implementation and enforcement. Examples of *voluntary* partial preemption are the Occupational Health and Safety Act of 1970 and the Surface Mining Control and Reclamation Act of 1977.[30]

At the other extreme from partial preemption are a few statutes that establish national programs but permit states to delay or even veto what the national government says it wants to do.[31] Under the Nuclear Waste Policy Act of 1982, for example, the Secretary of Energy is to nominate five sites as repositories for high-level radioactive waste and spent nuclear fuel to the president, who in turn is to submit to Congress a recommendation of one site. However, "the Governor or legislature of the State in which such site is located may disapprove the site designa-

---

[28] Kettl, *The Regulation of American Federalism*.

[29] Office of Management and Budget, *Managing Federal Assistance in the 1980's*, working papers, vol. 1 (Government Printing Office, 1980).

[30] Mel Dubnick and Alan Gitelson, "Nationalizing State Policies," in Jerome J. Hanus, ed., *The Nationalization of State Government* (D.C. Heath, 1981), pp. 56–57.

[31] Michael D. Reagan, *Intergovernmental Implementation of Partial Preemption Regulatory Programs*, paper presented at the Annual Meeting of the American Political Science Association, New Orleans, August 1985. The rest of the materials in this paragraph are taken from this source.

3–2 The 55 Miles per Hour Speed Limit

Do you favor or oppose keeping the 55 miles per hour speed limit?

	Favor	Oppose	Undecided
All people	**70%**	**28%**	**2%**
Those who drive 55 mph or slower	87	11	2
Those who drive 56–60 mph	70	29	1
Those who drive 61 mph or faster	34	64	2
Male	60	38	2
Female	79	19	2
East	77	21	2
Midwest	73	26	1
South	68	30	2
West	61	38	1
18–24	71	28	1
25–34	67	32	1
35–49	69	29	2
50–64	71	27	2
65 or older	83	14	3

Source: NBC–*Wall Street Journal* Poll, April 13–14, 1986. In 1987, Congress approved legislation permitting states to allow speeds up to 65 miles per hour on nonurban highways despite these poll results.

tion and submit to the Congress a notice of disapproval" within sixty days of the presidential recommendation. Such a site is then to be considered disapproved unless Congress passes a resolution approving it. "One can hardly imagine a better example of political buckpassing."

These new forms of federal regulation accelerated during the 1970s and abated only slightly during the 1980s despite the Reagan administration's emphasis on retrenchment of federal regulations. Pressures continue for national controls to force states to adopt drunk driving legislation, to cut off federal funds to cities that adopt rent controls, and to force on states and localities certain busing, abortion, and school prayer policies. Apparently liberals and conservatives alike favor fewer federal controls over state and local officials in the abstract, but they are still willing to make exceptions in policy areas when they feel strongly that something must be done to correct or prevent an injustice. And because there are plenty of injustices, federal regulation of state and local governments remains a continuing feature of our political system.

TWO LEVELS OR THREE?

During the urban crisis of the 1960s, the national government started in earnest to provide large-scale direct federal aid to cities, counties, school districts, flood-control districts, and other kinds of local units. In some ways Congress "became the city council of the nation," and the "president—acting very much like a Mayor"—started "taking on the meanest housekeeping concerns of daily existence."[32] As a result, there is "virtually no function of local government from police to community arts promotion, for which there isn't a counterpart federal aid program."[33]

[32] From H. F. Graff, "Presidents Are Now Mayors," *The New York Times* (July 18, 1979), section A, p. 23.
[33] Neal R. Peirce, "The State of American Federalism," *Civic Review* (January 1980), p. 32.

The combination of a strengthened national-city link and the corresponding state bypass resulted—at least in part—from the belief that Congress and federal authorities are more likely than state officials to ensure that the "poor and the black, especially the latter" will get their fair share from tax dollars.

Needless to say, governors and state legislators do not like to see federal funds go directly to city officials. As former Democratic Governor Bruce Babbitt of Arizona contended, Congress "ought to be worrying about arms control and defense instead of the potholes in the street. We just might have both an increased chance of survival and better streets."[34] On the other side are city officials, who of course favor such direct federal aid or any other means by which the federal government might provide money. (Some federal programs even attempted to bypass City Hall and to provide federal dollars directly to community agencies created especially to represent the poor. Because neither state nor city officials liked this approach, such programs did not last long.)

By the beginning of the 1980s the number and size of federal programs providing direct federal aid to cities started to be reduced. The Reagan administration's success in consolidating a few categorical-formula grants into block grants placed some of the funds in state rather than local hands, but Congress insisted on "pass-through" requirements that gave states no alternative but to deliver the federal funds to their cities.

Tensions between state and city officials are easing. Local authorities are finding that federal dollars bring federal controls that are often more burdensome than those imposed by their own states. Federal cutbacks make it clear that the national government is not necessarily a more reliable source of funds for cities than their own states. Moreover, political forces are making state officials more responsive to city issues. Pollution, crime, poverty, unemployment, and other problems once thought to belong exclusively to cities have become suburban problems as well.

Activities That Do Not Directly* Involve Both National and State Governments

National Government Only:

Making foreign policy

Operating the Postal Service

Taxing and regulating foreign commerce

Funding and managing the space program

State and Local Governments Only:

Regulating marriages and divorces

Probating wills

Issuing birth certificates

Issuing death certificates

*The operative word is *directly*. If it were deleted, these lists would be blank.

THE POLITICS OF FEDERALISM

Americans have long argued about the "proper" division of powers between central and local governments, and from time to time various governmental commissions and "experts" have tried to set definitive standards. But the experts discover, as did our country's founders, that few objective standards exist. Rather, the problems are largely *political*. At one time or another Northerners, Southerners, businesspeople, farmers, workers, Federalists, Democrats, Whigs, and Republicans have all championed "states' rights," but underlying their arguments have been such issues as slavery, labor-management relations, government regulation of business, civil rights, welfare politics, and so on. Until recent decades, for example, segregationists feared that national officials—responding to different political majorities—would work for racial integration. Thus they praised local governments, emphasized the dangers of overcentralization, and argued that the protection of civil rights was not a proper function of the national government.

Today the politics of federalism is more complicated than it was in the past. Even in the area of civil rights,[35] the choice of action by national or state governments is more difficult. It is no longer safe to predict that the national government will be more favorable to the claims of minorities than most state or city governments. State and local governments, for example, "have become the principal agents for advancing the cause of comparable worth. This role challenges the conventional

---

[34] Bruce Babbitt, "States Rights for Liberals," *The New Republic* (January 24, 1981), p. 23.

[35] Daniel J. Elazar, *American Federalism: A View from the States*, 3rd ed. (Harper & Row, 1984), p. 241.

Airports are built and operated through the combined efforts of the national, state, and local governments. (*George Hall/Woodfin Camp & Associates*)

"21 or Else" Mandate Angers States

Should the national government use its powers to force states to make 21 the minimum age to purchase beer, wine, or distilled spirits, or should the determination of the minimum age be left to the states? What are the constitutional issues? What are the questions relating to federalism?

Which of the following quotes sounds like Ronald Reagan and which would you guess is from a Democratic senator?

☐ "The problem is bigger than the individual States. It's a grave national problem, and touches all our lives. With the problem so clear-cut and the proven solution at hand, we have no misgivings about this judicious use of federal power."

☐ "The real issue is whether the Federal Government should intrude into an area that has traditionally and appropriately been left to the States and force them into accepting its solution to the problem of drunk driving."

What's your view?

Source: Elaine S. Knapp, "21 or Else Mandate Angers States," in Thad L. Beyle, ed., *State Government: CQ Guide to Current Issues and Activities, 1985–1986* (Congressional Quarterly, 1985), p. 184.

(Answer/Discussion on the next page.)

wisdom that only centrist alternatives can advance equal opportunity and civil rights for all citizens."[36]

On the whole, however, conservative ideology continues to favor state and local action, and liberal ideology to favor national action. Conservative theorists tend to champion local autonomy and decentralization as "means of protecting individual freedom," and local autonomy is often suspect by minorities, women, and the disadvantaged in general as "an exclusive haven for white privilege."[37] But these "solid" positions have begun to crumble. Much of the talk nowadays—from all political perspectives—is anti-Washington.

The Politics of National Growth

Over the past 200 years there has been a steady drift of power from other institutions—families, churches and synagogues, the marketplace—to all governments, especially the national government. "No one planned the growth . . . but everyone played a part in it."[38] How did this come about? First, many of our problems became national in scope. Much that was local in 1789, in 1860, or in 1930 is now national—even global. State governments could supervise the relations between small merchants and their few employees, but only the national government can supervise relations between an international industry and its thousands of employees, all organized in national unions. Big business, big agriculture, and big labor all add up to a big government.

As industrialization progressed, powerful interests made demands on the national government. First, business groups called on the government for aid in the form of tariffs, a national banking system, and subsidies to railroads and the merchant marine. Farmers learned that the national government could give more aid than the states, and they too began to demand help. By the beginning of this century, urban groups in general, and organized labor in particular, pressed their claims.

[36] Debra A. Stewart, "State Initiatives in the Federal System: The Politics and Policy of Comparable Worth in 1984," *Publius* (Summer 1985), p. 93.

[37] Gordon L. Clark, *Judges and the Cities: Interpreting Local Autonomy* (The University of Chicago Press, 1985), p. 8.

[38] Advisory Commission on Intergovernmental Relations, *Restoring Confidence and Competence* (ACIR, 1981), p. 30.

61

3–3 **Which of These Statements Comes Closest to Your View about Government Power Today?**

	1983		1984		1986	
	Whites	Non-whites	Whites	Non-whites	Whites	Non-whites
The federal government:						
1. Has too much power.	41%	21%	36%	29%	29%	22%
2. Has about the right amount of power.	18	15	25	20	25	18
3. Should use its power more vigorously.	28	45	33	41	40	52
4. Don't know/No answer.	13	19	6	10	6	8

Note: Figures represent percentage of U.S. public.

Source: Advisory Commission on Intergovernmental Relations.

Answer/Discussion

On July 17, 1984, President Reagan signed into law the National Minimum Drinking-Age Law, which gave the twenty-seven states with minimum drinking ages lower than 21 until October 1, 1986, to come into compliance or to face a gradually increasing loss, up to 15 percent, of their share of federal highway funds.

The first quote was made by the President when he signed the law. The second was made by Senator Max Baucus, Democrat of Montana, one of the sixteen senators who voted against the measure. The sentiment against teenage drivers in general and drinking drivers in general was building both at state and national levels in response to a very effective campaign by citizens' groups and members of the professional alcohol-treatment community. Between 1980 and 1984 twenty state legislatures increased the minimum drinking age.* Despite his commitment to states' rights and a limited role for the national government, President Reagan believed in this instance the dangers to the public safety were such that federal power should be asserted. All states have certified the 21 age. "We need our highway money desperately," said West Virginia Governor Arch Moore. "It was an easy matter to get us to go along with that blackmail."

* Sarah F. Liebschutz, "The National Minimum Drinking-Age Law," *Publius*, (Summer 1985), pp. 39–50. The quotes from President Reagan and Senator Baucus are also taken from this article.

The growth of a national economy and the creation of a national transportation and communications network altered people's attitudes toward the national government. Prior to the Civil War the national government was viewed as a distant, even foreign, government. Today, in part because of television, most people identify as closely with Washington as with their state capitals.

The Great Depression of the 1930s stimulated extensive national action on such issues as relief, unemployment, and agricultural surpluses. World War II brought federal regulation of wages, prices, and employment, as well as national efforts to allocate resources, train personnel, and support engineering and inventions. After the war the national government helped veterans and inaugurated a vast system of support for university research. Moreover, the United States became the most powerful member of the free world and had to maintain substantial military forces, even during times of peace.

With the advance of the Great Society in the 1960s, and "with a style and grandeur that transformed the fiscal foundations of the republic, the federal government for 20 years poured out grants-in-aid to states and localities until scarcely a function remains at those levels that Washington doesn't own a piece of."[39]

City dwellers, including blacks who had migrated from the rural South to northern cities, began to seek federal funds for—at the very least—housing, education, and mass transportation. In 1960 there were fifty federal grant programs. By 1980 there were more than 500, and they cost over $90 billion. (Note, however, that 90 percent of the dollar expenditures were accounted for by twenty programs.[40])

Although economic and social conditions account for many of the expanded functions of the national government, they do not explain them all. Members of Congress, presidents, federal judges, and federal administrators have actively promoted federal initiatives. Congress in particular has encouraged this trend. True, when there is widespread conflict about what to do—energy policy and social security reform are good examples—Congress waits for a national consensus and looks to presidents for leadership. But when an organized constituency wants something and there is no counterpressure, Congress, far "from being underresponsive . . . responds often to everyone, and with [great] vigour . . . ."[41]

Once established, federal programs generate groups with vested interests in promoting, defending, and expanding them. Associations are formed; alliances are

[39] Walter Guzzardi, Jr., "Who Will Care for the Poor?" *Fortune* (June 28, 1982), p. 34.

[40] Thomas J. Anton, "Decay and Reconstruction in the Study of American Intergovernmental Relations," *Publius: The Journal of Federalism* (Winter 1985), p. 71.

[41] Cynthia Cates Colella, "The Creation, Care and Feeding of the Leviathan: Who and What Makes Government Grow," *Intergovernmental Perspective* (Fall 1979), p. 9.

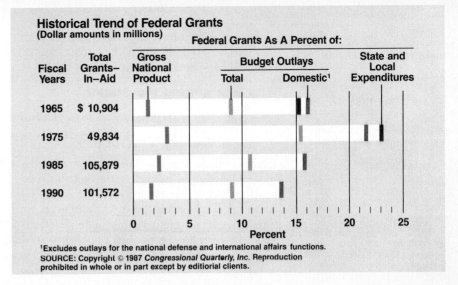

Historical Trend of Federal Grants
(Dollar amounts in millions)

Federal Grants As A Percent of:

Fiscal Years	Total Grants–In–Aid	Gross National Product	Budget Outlays		State and Local Expenditures
			Total	Domestic[1]	
1965	$ 10,904				
1975	49,834				
1985	105,879				
1990	101,572				

0   5   10   15   20   25
Percent

[1]Excludes outlays for the national defense and international affairs functions.
SOURCE: Copyright © 1987 *Congressional Quarterly, Inc.* Reproduction prohibited in whole or in part except by editiorial clients.

made. "In a word, the growth of government has created a constituency of, by, and for government."[42]

Yet the trend toward federal expansion, like most trends, has generated a reaction. By the beginning of the 1980s it encountered resistance from all points of the political spectrum. As national budget deficits mounted, liberals and conservatives, Republicans and Democrats agreed that the expansion of the national government had gone too far. First the Carter administration curtailed some federal programs. Then the Reagan administration proclaimed that its number one domestic priority was to reduce the role of the national government.

Regardless of which party controls Washington, federal grants are not likely to grow at the same rate in the next decade as they did during the 1960 to 1980 period. The high point of federal aid in terms of real dollars occurred in 1978.[43] By 1985 27 percent fewer categorical-formula grants were available for states and local governments than in 1980, and the number is dropping. Federal aid dropped from almost 32 percent of all state-local own-source revenues in 1980 to a little under 24 percent by 1984.[44] Recognizing that the national government cannot regulate everything or solve all problems, both parties want to limit federal expenditures.

This reversal in the trend toward the national government's taking on more and more responsibilities does not mean, however, that the national government will retreat to a pre-1930 posture or even a pre-1960 one. The underlying economic and social conditions that generated the demand for federal action have not substantially altered. On the contrary, in addition to such traditional issues as unemployment, inflation, and credit controls—which still require national action—countless new issues have been added with our transformation from an industrial economy to one based on high technology, service, and information. States have strengthened their governmental machinery during the last two decades and are more politically responsive than at any time in our history. But the states—at least most of them—still lack the jurisdiction by themselves to clean up the air, regulate the economy, and prevent pollution of our rivers. Workers displaced from our declining smokestack

"Not quite the building materials I was hoping for." (*Copyright © 1981 by Herblock in The Washington Post*)

[42] Aaron Wildavsky, "Bare Bones: Putting Flesh on the Skeleton of American Federalism," in Advisory Commission on Intergovernmental Relations, *The Future of Federalism in the 1980s*, report and papers from the Conference on the Future of Federalism, Alexandria, Virginia, July 25–26, 1980. (ACIR Publication M-126, 1981), p. 79.

[43] Richard P. Nathan and Fred C. Doolittle, "Federal Grants: Giving and Taking Away," *Political Science Quarterly*, (Spring 1985), p. 55.

[44] Kenneth T. Palmer and Alex N. Pattakos, "The State of American Federalism: 1984," *Publius* (Summer 1985), p. 6.

Tax Capacity Index

Economic ability to raise revenue—from most able to least
able—1983
U.S. average: 105

Alabama	74.8
Alaska	271.9
Arizona	97.0
Arkansas	77.7
California	118.7
Colorado	122.2
Connecticut	123.8
Delaware	118.1
Washington, DC	116.6
Florida	103.4
Georgia	86.9
Hawaii	113.7
Idaho	83.3
Illinois	98.1
Indiana	86.1
Iowa	90.8
Kansas	102.3
Kentucky	78.8
Louisiana	106.7
Maine	90.2
Maryland	99.0
Massachusetts	106.5
Michigan	90.2
Minnesota	97.0
Mississippi	68.2
Missouri	89.2
Montana	105.2
Nebraska	100.7
Nevada	147.2
New Hampshire	107.6
New Jersey	112.2
New Mexico	107.8
New York	95.4
North Carolina	86.8
North Dakota	110.8
Ohio	89.4
Oklahoma	114.9
Oregon	95.5
Pennsylvania	88.2
Rhode Island	85.8
South Carolina	75.5
South Dakota	87.4
Tennessee	80.3
Texas	123.6
Utah	82.1
Vermont	93.8
Virginia	95.6
Washington	100.7
West Virginia	87.1
Wisconsin	87.2
Wyoming	182.4

Source: *Tax Capacity of the States,
1983*, Advisory Commission on Intergovernmental Relations, April 1986,
p. 66.

industries and farmers no longer able to make a living from agriculture are not likely to be retrained, nor is the human capital to support the postindustrial society likely to be secured, without national action.

The War among the States

The politics of federalism differs from state to state. States vary tremendously in their economic abilities to raise taxes as well as in their political willingness to do so. Alaska, with few people and much wealth, has almost four times the taxing capacity of Mississippi, which has many people and few mineral resources (see Box).[45] Moreover, Sunbelt states with growing economies are more apt to elect "self-reliant" governors who do not want federal help than are those industrial states of the Northeast and Midwest who are facing industrial decline and who fear they are not getting a fair share of federal aid.[46]

In recent years Sunbelt-Frostbelt wars have become less intense. For one thing, there are fewer federal dollars over which to fight. Also the economic growth rates of the two regions have become more alike: Economic conditions in the Frost-belt, especially in New England, have improved with the growth of high-tech industries while those in the Sunbelt, dependent upon oil and other resources, have declined. Southern states are discovering that sunshine is no substitute for educational programs to develop human capital in the competition for high-tech industries. Regional differences persist and struggles for federal funds continue, but the battles are less intense, at least for the moment.[47] Yet considering how much federalism has changed in the last 200 years, what can be expected in the next 200?

The Future of the States

Predictions that states are about to disappear as meaningful governmental units are not new. In 1933, seeing state governments helpless during the Great Depression, one writer stated: "I do not predict that the states will go, but affirm that they have gone."[48] Thirty years later Senator Everett McKinley Dirkson from Illinois intoned that before too long, "the only people interested in state boundaries will be Rand-McNally."[49]

These prophets of doom were wrong. States are stronger than ever. "A revolution—albeit a quiet one—has transformed the states over the past quarter of a century."[50] "Almost unnoticed in Washington, there has been a revolution in state capitals from Albany to Santa Fe, from Olympia to Tallahassee, and from Richmond to St. Paul. No longer the province primarily of hangers-on and political hacks, most state governments today are remarkably sophisticated and professional, competent to address problems that only a decade ago seemed beyond their grasp."[51] "Far from being its 'fallen arches,' states are the 'arch supports' of the federal system."[52] Most have improved their governmental structures, taken on greater roles in funding education, launched programs to help distressed cities, and—despite

[45] Robert B. Lucke, "Rich States—Poor States; Inequalities in our Federal System," *Intergovernmental Perspective* (Spring 1982), pp. 22–28.

[46] James C. Smith, *Emerging Conflicts in the Doctrine of Federalism: The Intergovernmental Predicament* (University Press of America, 1984).

[47] Bernard L. Weinstein and Harold T. Gross, "The Frost Belt's Revenge," *The Wall Street Journal* (November 19, 1985), p. 30.

[48] Luther Gulick, "Reorganization of the States," *Civil Engineering* (August 1933), pp. 420–21.

[49] Quoted by Terry Sanford in *Storm over the States* (McGraw-Hill, 1967), p. 37.

[50] Carl Stenberg, in Mavis Mann Reeves, *The Question of State Government Capability: A Commission Report* (Advisory Commission on Intergovernmental Relations, 1985), p. 320. See also Ann O'M. Bowman and Richard C. Kearney, *The Resurgence of the States* (Prentice-Hall, 1986).

[51] Denis P. Doyle and Terry W. Hartle, "A Funny Thing Happened on the Way to New Federalism . . . ," *The Washington Post National Weekly Edition* (December 2, 1985), p. 23.

[52] Mavis Mann Reeves, *The Question of State Government Capability* (Advisory Commission in Intergovernmental Relations, 1985), p. 2.

new constitutional limitations—expanded their taxing bases. Outstanding men and women have been attracted to many governorships. "Today, states, in formal representational, policymaking and implementation terms at least, are more representative, more responsive, more activist, and more professional in their operations than they ever have been. They face their expanded roles better equipped to assume and fulfill them."[53] As the national government has started to retrench and cut its domestic spending, states had to take over some of its responsibilities. The constitutional and political durability of the states is secure.

[53] Ibid., p. 363.

SUMMARY

1. Our federal constitutional system has evolved into something only slightly different in form but significantly different in operation from the one with which we began. Whether or not we ever had a system in which it was possible to talk about neat divisions between the powers of the national and the state governments, we certainly can no longer do so accurately.

2. To recognize that the national government has the constitutional authority to do whatever Congress thinks may be necessary and proper to do is not the same as saying that federalism is dead. Although during the last two centuries constitutional power has moved toward the national center, political power remains dispersed. States remain active and significant political communities.

3. Ideological bias in favor of either national or state action is likely to reflect concrete political objectives. In recent years the conservatives' stand in favor of states' rights and the liberals' stand in favor of national action are no longer predictable. Shifting political issues continue to lead to shifting allegiances among the various levels of government.

4. The politics of federalism involves more than conflicts between the national government and the states. Recent conflicts among various regions of the nation over the distribution of federal dollars have begun to heat up.

5. The drift toward increasing federal action has been fueled more by underlying economic and social changes than by concerns about federalism, but we detect a vigorous trend toward the view that federalism as a political principle is worthy of being preserved.

6. The major instrument of federal intervention in recent decades has been various kinds of grants-in-aid, of which the most prominent are categorical-formula grants, project grants, block grants, and revenue sharing.

7. Additional forms of federal intervention to control the activities of state and local governments have become more important in recent decades; these include direct orders, cross-cutting requirements on federal funds, crossover sanctions in the use of federal funds, and partial preemption.

8. Today we no longer spend so much time debating the *law* of federalism. We have now moved to the *politics* of federalism. As now interpreted, the Constitution gives us the option to decide through the political process what we want to do, who is going to pay, and how we are going to get it done.

FURTHER READING

Advisory Commission on Intergovernmental Relations. *An Agenda for American Federalism: Restoring Confidence and Competence* (1981). Final volume of an 11-volume study under the general title, *The Federal Role in the Federal System: The Dynamics of Growth.*

Advisory Commission on Intergovernmental Relations. *Regulatory Federalism: Policy, Process, Impact and Reform* (1984).

Advisory Commission on Intergovernmental Relations. *Intergovernmental Perspective*. Published four times a year (U.S. Government Printing Office).

Raoul Berger. *Federalism: The Founders' Design* (University of Oklahoma Press, 1987).

Ann O'M. Bowman and Richard C. Kearney. *The Resurgence of the States* (Prentice-Hall, 1986).

The Center for the Study of Federalism. *Publius: The Journal of Federalism*. Published quarterly (Temple University).

Robert J. Dilger, ed. *American Intergovernmental Relations Today: Perspectives and Controversies* (Prentice-Hall, 1985).

Daniel J. Elazar. *American Federalism: A View from the States*, 3rd ed. (Harper & Row, 1984).

Parris N. Glendening and Mavis Mann Reeves. *Pragmatic Federalism: An Intergovernmental View of American Government*, 2nd ed. (Palisades Publishers, 1984).

George E. Hale and Marian L. Palley. *The Politics of Federal Grants* (Congressional Quarterly Press, 1981).

Jeffrey Henig. *Public Policy and Federalism* (St. Martin's, 1985).

Arnold M. Howitt. *Managing Federalism* (Congressional Quarterly Press, 1984).

Laurence J. O'Toole, Jr., ed. *American Intergovernmental Relations* (Congressional Quarterly Press, 1985).

Michael D. Reagan and John G. Sanzone. *The New Federalism*, 2nd ed. (Oxford University Press, 1981).

William H. Stewart, *Concepts of Federalism* (University Press of America 1984)

$\mathfrak{Congress}$ *shall make no law respecting an establishment of religion, or prohibiting the free exercise thereof; or abridging the freedom of speech, or of the press; or the right of the people peaceably to assemble, and to petition the Government for a redress of grievances.*

First Amendment Rights

"Congress shall make no law," declares the First amendment, "respecting an establishment of religion, or prohibiting the free exercise thereof; or abridging the freedom of speech, or of the press; or the right of the people peaceably to assemble, and to petition the Government for a redress of grievances." Stated here are the fundamental supports of a free society: freedom of conscience and freedom of expression.

Although the framers drafted the Constitution, in a sense the people drafted our basic charter of liberties. The Constitution drawn up in Philadelphia included no specific guarantee of the basic freedoms. The omission aroused suspicion and distrust among the people. In order to win ratification, the Federalists promised to correct this deficiency. And in its very first session, the new Congress proposed amendments that were ratified by the end of 1791 and became part of the Constitution. These ten amendments are known as the Bill of Rights.

Note that the Bill of Rights concerns the *national* government. As John Marshall held in *Barron* v. *Baltimore* (1833), the Bill of Rights limits the national but not the state governments.[1] Why not the states? In the 1790s the people were confident they could control their own state officials, and most of the state constitutions already had bills of rights. It was the new and distant central government the people feared.

As it turned out, those popular fears were largely misplaced. The national government, responsive to tens of millions of voters from a variety of races, creeds, religions, and economic groups, has shown less tendency to curtail civil liberties than have state and local governments. For the most part, state judges have not used the bills of rights in their respective state constitutions to protect civil liberties. Some state courts have, however, started to use their respective state constitutions to provide more protection for certain rights as current federal constitutional standards have been somewhat lowered.[2]

[1] 7 Peters 243 (1833).

[2] Stanley H. Friedelbaum, "Independent State Grounds: Contemporary Invitations to Judicial Activism," in Mary Cornelia Porter and G. Alan Tarr, eds., *State Supreme Courts: Policy Makers in the Federal System* (Greenwood Press 1982), p. 46. See also Justice William J. Brennan, "State Constitutions and the Protection of Individual Rights," *Harvard Law Review*, vol. 90 (1977), p. 489; and *Pruneyard Shopping Center* v. *Robins*, 447 U.S. 74 (1980).

When the Fourteenth amendment, which does apply to the states, was adopted in 1868, some contended that its due process clause required states to adhere to the Bill of Rights. At least, they argued, freedom of speech should be included in the Fourteenth amendment. For decades the Supreme Court refused to interpret the Fourteenth amendment in this way. Then in 1925, in *Gitlow* v. *New York*, the Court announced: "For present purposes we may and do assume that freedom of speech and of press—which are protected by the First Amendment from abridgment by Congress—are among the fundamental personal rights and 'liberties' protected by the due process clause of the Fourteenth Amendment from impairment by the States."[3]

Gitlow v. *New York* was a major, revolutionary decision. For the first time, the national Constitution protected freedom of speech and of the press from abridgment by state and local governments. In the 1940s the other provisions of the First amendment were brought within the scope of the Fourteenth amendment. Today the First amendment's restraints are applied to all those who exercise governmental authority—national, state, or local.

All this creates a paradox. Virtually all Americans agree that governmental power should not interfere with the freedoms of speech and conscience. Yet frequently we seem to be involved in quarrels about specific applications of these restraints (that certain ideas or practices, perhaps, should be restricted). The trouble starts when we move from generalities to specifics.

"All declare for liberty," wrote Justice Reed, "and proceed to disagree among themselves as to its true meaning."[4] In few areas have the problems been more difficult to resolve and the differences more intense than in the realm of religious freedoms. The controversy remains heated today.

A WALL OF SEPARATION

"The court reached a decision on silent prayer in school . . . They ruled that a moment of silence is impossible." (*Dunagins's People* by Ralph Dunagin © 1983, Field Enterprises, Inc. Courtesy of Field Newspaper Syndicate.)

The first words of the First amendment are emphatic and brief: "Congress shall make no law respecting an establishment of religion." But what do the words of this so-called **Establishment clause** mean? The Supreme Court has construed the Constitution to erect a high *wall of separation between church and state*, to prohibit any law or governmental action designed to confer any benefit on religion even if all sects are treated the same.[5] However, at times the Supreme Court gives an accommodationist twist to this doctrine: While there can be no governmental aid for religion, with or without preference for a particular one, sometimes the Court permits governmental accommodations to make religious activities possible or even allow some aid to flow indirectly to religious institutions.

According to the nonpreferentialist view, which is held by, among others, Chief Justice William Rehnquist, Justice Byron White[6] and perhaps Justices Antonin Scalia and Anthony Kennedy,[7] the Constitution simply prohibits favoritism toward

[3] *Gitlow* v. *New York*, 268 U.S. 652 (1925).

[4] *Breard* v. *Alexandria*, 341 U.S. 622 (1951).

[5] *Everson* v. *Board of Education*, 333 U.S. 203 (1947); R. Freeman Butts, *Religion, Education, and the First Amendment: The Appeals to History* (People for the American Way, 1986); Leonard W. Levy, *The Establishment Clause* (Macmillan, 1986).

[6] Daniel Patrick Moynihan, "What Do You Do When the Supreme Court Is Wrong?" *The Public Interest* (Fall 1979), pp. 3–24; Walter Berns, *The First Amendment and the Future of American Democracy* (Basic Books, 1976), pp. 1–76; Paul J. Weber and Dennis A. Gilbert, *Private Churches and Public Money* (Greenwood Press, 1981).

[7] *Bowen* v. *Kendrick*, 101 L Ed 2d 520 (1988).

a particular religion. It does not prohibit governmental encouragement of religious activities, even support for religious organizations.

Under prevailing doctrine, however, a law challenged for violating the Establishment clause must meet a three-part test put forward by the Court in *Lemon* v. *Kurtzman*. First, it must have a secular legislative *purpose*; second, its primary *effect* must neither advance nor inhibit religion; and finally, it must avoid "excessive government entanglement with religion." In other words, the Establishment clause is designed to prevent three main evils: "sponsorship, financial support, and active involvement of the sovereign in religious activity."[8]

When the *Lemon* test is given an accommodationist twist, a statute's purpose need not be *exclusively* secular. The statute must still have a primary effect that neither advances nor inhibits religion, but it is okay if the benefit to religion is slight or happens to harmonize with the tenets of some religion. An example of this accommodationist interpretation was a five to four vote by the Court upholding the right of Pawtucket, Rhode Island, to display the Nativity scene in the heart of its shopping district, along with Santa's house and other symbols of the Christmas season. The Court majority concluded that the city had a commercial, not religious, purpose, that the effect provided little or no benefit to religion in general or to the Christian faith in particular, and that there was no excessive entanglement between religion and government. The Constitution, said the majority, "[does not] require complete separation of church and state: it affirmatively mandates accommodation, not merely tolerance of all religions, and forbids hostility toward any."[9]

Because of the Establishment clause, states—and, of course, school districts—may not introduce any kind of devotional exercises into the public school curriculum. But the Supreme Court has not, as it is sometimes said, prohibited prayer in public schools: It is not unconstitutional for people to pray in a school building. What is unconstitutional is *sponsorship or encouragement of prayer by public school authorities*.[10] Thus, devotional reading of the Bible, recitation of the Lord's Prayer, and posting the Ten Commandments on the walls of classrooms are prohibited. Nor may a state forbid the teaching of evolution or condition the teaching of it on the simultaneous teaching of "creation science."[11]

The first case to reach the Supreme Court about states' providing for a moment of silence, as several have already done, involved an Alabama law authorizing public school teachers to hold a one-minute period of silence for "meditation or voluntary prayer." The law was struck down, because the clear intent of the Alabama legislature was to encourage the return of prayer to public schools. The statute had a religious purpose, which violates the first prong of the *Lemon* test.[12] The constitutionality of a more artfully drawn statute that does not endorse prayer but merely calls for a moment of silence remains open, but it probably would pass the Supreme Court's test.

On the other hand, the Constitution does not prevent the study of the Bible or of religion in public schools as part of a secular program of education. And Sunday closing laws—called "blue laws"—are constitutional. Although these laws originally had a religious purpose, they now have a secular goal—encouraging a day of rest, recreation, and family togetherness.

Tax exemption for church property, and for other nonprofit institutions, is constitutional. State legislatures and Congress may hire chaplains to open each day's legislative session, a practice that has continued without interruption ever

In this and the next several chapters, we talk at length about constitutional rules. As we have noted, to talk about the Constitution is to talk about Supreme Court decisions. Many of these decisions are cited in footnotes so that you can look them up if you wish. Two forms of citation are used here:

1. Official Supreme Court Reports. An example is *Gitlow* v. *New York*, 268 U.S. 652 (1925), which means that this case can be found in the 268th volume of the United States Supreme Court Reports, on page 652, and that it was decided in 1925. These reports are published by the United States Government Printing Office.

2. For more recent cases, the advance sheets of United States Supreme Court Reports, published by the Lawyers Cooperative Publishing Company of Rochester, New York. An example is *Hustler Magazine* v. *Falwell*, a case concerning the laws of libel and the First amendment. It is cited as 99 L Ed 2d 41 (1988), which means that it can be found in volume 99 of the Lawyers Edition, second series, on page 41, and that it was decided in 1988.

For additional information about citations, see For Further Research in the Appendix at the back of this book.

---

[8] *Walz* v. *Tax Commission*, 397 U.S. 664 (1970); and *Lemon* v. *Kurtzman*, 403 U.S. 602 (1971).

[9] *Lynch* v. *Donnelly*, 465 U.S. 668 (1984).

[10] *Engel* v. *Vitale*, 370 U.S. 421 (1962).

[11] *Edwards* v. *Aquillard*, 96 L Ed 2nd 510 (1987).

[12] *Wallace* v. *Jaffree*, 472 U.S. 38 (1985).

since the first session of Congress. If done in a public school, this practice would be unconstitutional. The difference, apparently, is that legislators as adults are not "susceptible to religious indoctrination or peer pressure."[13] Also, as the joke goes, the legislators need the prayer more.

One of the more troublesome areas involves attempts by many states to provide financial assistance to parochial schools. The Supreme Court has tried to draw a line between *permissible public aid to students*, including those in sectarian schools, and *impermissible public aid to religion*.

At the college level the problems are relatively simple. Tax funds may be used to construct buildings and operate educational programs at church-related schools, as long as the money is not directly spent on buildings used for religious purposes or used to teach religious subjects. Even if students chose to attend religious schools and become ministers, governmental aid is permissible: It has a secular purpose, its effect on religion is the result of individual choice, "and it does not confer any message of state endorsement of religion."[14]

At the elementary and secondary level, constitutional problems are more complicated. Here the secular and religious parts of institutions and instruction are much more closely interwoven. Students are younger and more susceptible to indoctrination, and chances are greater that aid given to church-operated schools might seep into aid for religion.

Despite these constitutional obstacles some states have attempted to provide tax credits or deductions for those who send their children to private, largely church-affiliated schools. As long as the deductions or credits were made available only to parents of children attending nonpublic schools, the Supreme Court—by split votes—declared them unconstitutional. Then, in 1983, by a vote of five to four, the Supreme Court (*Mueller* v. *Allen*) upheld a Minnesota provision allowing *all* taxpaying parents to deduct from their state income taxes what they paid, up to a certain amount, for tuition, textbooks, transportation, and other costs to send their children to school—public or private. Because parents who send their children to public schools pay no tuition, most of these deductions benefit those who send their children to private schools, 95 percent of which are sectarian. Nonetheless, the Court concluded that because Minnesota provided assistance to a broad spectrum of citizens, "no imprimatur of state approval can be deemed to have been conferred on any particular religion, or religion generally." The state was promoting a secular purpose: ensuring both a well-educated citizenry and the financial health of its private school system. No excessive government entanglement with religion was involved.[15]

The Supreme Court has also approved using tax funds to provide students attending elementary and secondary church-operated schools (except those that deny admission because of race or religion) with textbooks, standardized tests, lunches, transportation to and from schools, diagnostic services for speech and hearing problems, and other kinds of remedial help—provided such services take place away from the "pervasively sectarian atmosphere of the church-related schools."[16] These schools may also be reimbursed for scoring state-required standardized tests.

Tax funds, however, may *not* be used in religious schools to pay teachers' salaries, to provide equipment, to provide counseling for students, to produce teacher-prepared tests, to repair facilities, or to transport students to and from field trips. School authorities may not permit religious instructors to come into public school buildings during the school day to provide religious instruction on a voluntary basis. States may not send public school teachers to teach even secular subjects in sectarian schools, even after school hours, even in classrooms "leased" by the public schools.

"I disagree with what you say, sir, but, as you know, Congress shall make no law respecting an establishment of religion, or prohibiting the free exercise thereof; or abridging the freedom of speech, or of the press; or the right of the people peaceably to assemble, and to petition the Government for a redress of grievances, and far be it from me to do otherwise." (*Drawing by Barsotti, 1985. The New Yorker Magazine, Inc.*)

[13] *Marsh* v. *Chambers*, 463 U.S. 783 (1983).
[14] *Witters* v. *Wash. Dept. of Serv. for Blind*, 474 U.S. 481 (1986).
[15] 463 U.S. 388 (1983).
[16] *Wolman* v. *Walter*, 433 U.S. 229 (1977).

Similarly, states may not use public funds to provide remedial instruction and guidance services to parochial school students in parochial schools even if the schools are subject to supervision to ensure that there are no religious influences in these services.[17]

Why is it constitutional for state governments to pay for books but not for maps, for bus trips but not for field trips from schools, for standardized tests but not for tests prepared by teachers? The justices have argued that those on the "approved" side meet the three-part *Lemon* test, but those on the "forbidden" side fail one of the requirements. Transportation to and from school involves a routine trip that every student makes every day; it is unrelated to any aspect of the curriculum. Field trips, however, are controlled by teachers and are aids to instruction. Further, books and standardized tests can be evaluated much more easily than can maps or teacher-prepared tests, to ensure they are not designed to promote religion. And in cases involving teaching by public teachers in parochial schools, the supervision to ensure lack of religious influences created excessive entanglement of church and state.[18]

ALL PERSONS MAY WORSHIP AS THEY CHOOSE

The Constitution not only forbids the establishment of religion; it also forbids Congress and the states from passing any law "prohibiting the free exercise thereof." "The Court has struggled to find a neutral course between the two religion clauses, both of which are cast in absolute terms, and either of which, if expanded to a logical extreme, would tend to clash with the other."[19] A law that requires persons to do something that is contrary to the teachings of their religion interferes with their free exercise of religion. But to exempt them from the law because of their religious convictions may be to favor religion and offend the Establishment clause. The Court has tried to balance the claims of the two clauses: It has ruled, for example, that a state may not give employees an *absolute* right against their employers not to work on their chosen Sabbath, because this violates the Establishment clause. It confers a benefit in favor of Sabbath observers only. However, a state may require employers to make *reasonable* accommodations to employees because of religious needs.[20]

The right to hold any or no religious *belief* is one of our few absolute rights. No government has authority to compel the acceptance of or to censor any creed. A state may not compel a religious belief nor deny persons any right because of their beliefs or lack of them. Requiring religious oaths as a condition of public employment or as a prerequisite to running for public office is unconstitutional. In fact, the only time the Constitution mentions the word religion is to state: "No religious test shall ever be required as a Qualification to any Office of public Trust under the United States" (Article VI).

Although carefully protected, the right to *practice* one's religion has less protection than the right to hold particular beliefs: "It was never intended that the First Amendment . . . could be invoked as protection against the punishment of acts inimical to the peace, good order, and morals of society."[21] Religious convictions

YOU DECIDE

In the Adolescent Family Life Act of 1981 Congress provided for grants to charitable organizations, including religious organizations, to teach teenagers about "sexual prudence."

Does such a law violate the Establishment Clause? Do grants to religious organizations under the law violate the Establishment Clause?

Answer/Discussion on page 72.

[17] *Grand Rapids School District* v. *Ball*, 473 U.S. 373 (1985); and *Aguilar* v. *Felton*, 473 U.S. 402 (1985).

[18] *Committee for Public Education* v. *Regan*, 444 U.S. 646 (1980).

[19] *Walz* v. *Commission*, 397 U.S. 664 (1970).

[20] *Estate of Thornton* v. *Caldor, Inc.*, 472 U.S. 703 (1985); and *Trans World Airlines, Inc.* v. *Hardison*, 432 U.S. 63 (1977).

[21] *Reynolds* v. *United States*, 98 U.S. 145 (1879).

The right to practice one's religion covers many kinds of religious ceremonies." (*Larry Mulvehill/Photo Researchers*; *Dan Guravich/Photo Researchers*)

do not ordinarily exempt one from obeying otherwise valid and nondiscriminatory laws or government regulations. And the "incidental effects of government programs, which may make it more difficult to practice certain religions but which have no tendency to coerce individuals into acting contrary to their religious beliefs, . . . do not require government to bring forward a compelling justification for its otherwise lawful actions."[22] However, the courts will scrutinize laws that *directly* infringe on religious practices and insist upon some compelling public purpose.

The Supreme Court, for example, has upheld: the right of the federal government to build roads through a national forest, even through an area used for religious purposes by native Americans; laws forbidding the practice of polygamy; laws forbidding business activities on Sunday as applied to Orthodox Jews; military regulations forbidding the wearing of headgear while indoors as applied to an Orthodox Jew's wearing of a yarmulke (skullcap), a traditional religious obligation; and Internal Revenue Service regulations denying tax exemption to religious schools that admit only members of one race. In this last decision the Supreme Court pointedly wrote: "We deal only with religious schools, not with churches."[23]

On the other hand, a state may not require Jehovah's Witnesses (or anyone else, for that matter) to participate in public school flag ceremonies. A state may compel the attendance of children at schools, but parents have a constitutional right to send their children to church-sponsored schools. Furthermore, a state cannot compel the Amish to send their children to school *beyond* the eighth grade.

What is a church? What is a religion? The Constitution provides no definitions, and the Supreme Court has been reluctant—understandably—to get into these questions. "Far-out" religions are entitled to the same constitutional protections as are the more traditional ones, but only "beliefs rooted in religion are protected by the Free Exercise Clause."[24]

Disputes involving the two religion clauses promise to become even more complicated as governmental actions grow more pervasive and nontraditional religious groups grow in number. These are difficult disputes to resolve, because they involve matters about which people believe deeply.

FREE SPEECH AND FREE PEOPLE

Government by the people is based on every person's right to speak freely, to organize in groups, to question the decisions of the government, and to campaign openly against it. Only through free and uncensored expression of opinion can government be kept responsive to the electorate and political power be transferred peacefully. Elections, separation of powers, and constitutional guarantees are mean-

[22] *Lyng* v. *N.W. Indian Cemetery Prot. Asso.*, 99 L Ed 2d 534 (1988); *Wisconsin* v. *Yoder*, 406 U.S. 205 (1972).

[23] *Bob Jones University* v. *United States*, 461 U.S. 574 (1983).

[24] Ibid. See also Charles M. Whelan, "Governmental Attempts to Define Church and Religion," in Dean M. Kelley, ed., *The Uneasy Boundary: Church and State*, *The Annals* (November 1979), p. 37.

ingless unless all citizens have the right to speak frankly and to hear and judge for themselves the worth of what others have to say.

Despite the fundamental importance of free speech to a democracy, some people seem to believe that speech should be free only for those who agree with them. Americans overwhelmingly support principles of tolerance when such principles are presented in general, abstract fashion (e.g., "Do you believe in freedom of speech?"). But once questions or conflicts become more specific, Americans exhibit a discouragingly low level of support for free speech.[25] Not only do three Americans in four "draw a blank when asked if they know what the First Amendment . . . is or with what it deals," but almost 40 percent of the public would like to see strict curbs placed on newspapers.[26]

Free speech is not simply the personal right of individuals to have their say; it is also the right of the rest of us to hear them. John Stuart Mill, whose *Essay on Liberty* (1859) is the classic defense of free speech, put it this way: "The peculiar evil of silencing the expression of opinion, is that it is robbing the human race. . . . If the opinion is right, they are deprived of the opportunity of exchanging error for truth; if wrong, they lose, what is almost as great a benefit, the clearer perception and livelier impression of truth, produced by its collision with error."[27]

Freedom of speech is not merely freedom to express ideas that differ slightly from ours. It is, as the late Justice Jackson said, "freedom to differ as to things that touch the heart of the existing order."[28] Yet some who say they believe in free speech draw the line at ideas they consider dangerous. What is a dangerous idea? Who decides? In the realm of political ideas, who can find an objective, eternally valid standard of right? The search for truth involves the possibility—even the inevitability—of error. The search cannot go on unless it proceeds freely in the minds and speech of all. This means, in the words of Justice Holmes, not only freedom of expression for those who agree with us "but freedom for the thought we hate."[29]

Even though the First amendment denies Congress the power to pass *any* law abridging freedom of speech, the amendment has never been interpreted in such sweeping terms. Like almost all rights, the right to freedom of speech and of the press is limited. In discussing the constitutional power of government to regulate speech, it is useful to distinguish among *belief*, *speech*, and *action*. At one extreme is the right to believe as one wishes, a right as absolute as any can be for people living in organized societies. Despite occasional deviations in practice, the traditional American view is that *thoughts* are inviolable. No government has the right to punish a person for beliefs or to interfere in any way with freedom of conscience.

At the other extreme is *action*, which is constantly restrained. We may believe it is all right to drive an automobile 75 miles an hour, but if we do so, we may be punished. Because one person's action directly affects the liberty and property of others, "the right to swing your arm ends where the other person's nose begins."

Speech stands somewhere between belief and action. It is not an absolute right, as is belief, but neither is it as exposed to governmental restraint as is action. Speech that is obscene, libelous, or **seditious** or speech that constitutes fighting words, is not entitled to constitutional protection, although many problems arise

[25] Michael Corbett, *Political Tolerance in America: Freedom and Equality in Public Attitudes* (Longman, 1982), p. 44. Herbert McClosky and Ada Brill, *Dimensions of Tolerance* (Russell Sage, 1983).

[26] Results of Gallup Opinion Index reported in *Today* (April 25, 1980).

[27] John Stuart Mill, "Essay on Liberty," in E. A. Burtt, *The English Philosophers from Bacon to Mill* (Modern Library, 1939), p. 961.

[28] *West Virginia State Board of Education* v. *Barnette*, 319 U.S. 624 (1943).

[29] For a thoughtful statement of a somewhat contrary point of view, see Berns, *The First Amendment and the Future of American Democracy*.

in distinguishing between what does and does not fit into these categories. (We discuss these problems shortly.) All other speech is entitled to constitutional protection. But are there any limits?

Historical Constitutional Tests

Although the Supreme Court today uses other language, the three great constitutional tests developed earlier in this century continue to reflect basic attitudes toward governmental regulation of speech. These are the **bad tendency doctrine**, the **clear and present danger doctrine**, and the **preferred position doctrine**.

The bad tendency doctrine   This doctrine, which stems from the common law, has not had the support of the Supreme Court since *Gitlow* v. *New York* in 1925. Many, however, including (as late as 1982) some state courts,[30] continue to hold this position. According to the adherents of the bad tendency doctrine, legislatures and not courts have the primary responsibility to determine when speech should be outlawed. The Constitution, they argue, authorizes legislatures to forbid speech that has a tendency to lead to illegal action. Moreover, "the legislature cannot reasonably be required to measure the danger from every . . . utterance in the nice balance of a jeweler's scale. . . . It may, in the exercise of its judgment, suppress the threatened danger in its incipiency."[31]

Suppose a legislature decides that public utterances of abusive racial remarks are dangerous because they often lead to violence and makes such remarks illegal. Those who hold to the bad tendency test argue that, because it is not totally unreasonable that abusive racial remarks could cause violence, such a law is constitutional.

The clear and present danger doctrine   Justice Holmes announced this celebrated doctrine in *Schenck* v. *United States*. He wrote: "The question in every case is whether the words are used in circumstances and are of such a nature as to create a clear and present danger that they will bring about substantive evils that Congress has a right to prevent."[32] Furthermore, "no danger flowing from speech can be deemed clear and present," concurred Justice Brandeis in *Whitney* v. *California*, "unless the incidence of the evil is so imminent that it may befall before there is opportunity for full discussion."[33]

Supporters of the clear and present danger doctrine concede that speech is not an absolute right. But they believe free speech to be so fundamental that no government should be allowed to restrict it unless it can demonstrate that there is such a close connection between a speech and illegal action that the speech itself takes on the character of the action. (To shout "Fire" falsely in a crowded theater is Justice Holmes's famous example.) A government should not be allowed to interfere with speech unless it can prove, ultimately to a skeptical judiciary, that the particular speech in question presented an immediate danger of a major evil—for example, that it clearly would have led to a riot, the destruction of property, the corruption of an election, or direct interference with recruiting of soldiers. Consider our previous example. Advocates of the clear and present danger doctrine would argue that even though a legislature had made it illegal to use abusive racial remarks in public, judges should not permit the law to be applied in any specific incident unless the government presents convincing evidence that the particular remarks made by a particular individual clearly and presently might lead to a riot or to some other serious evil.

[30] *Brown* v. *Hartlage*, 456 U.S. 45 (1982), in which the Supreme Court reversed a decision of the Kentucky Court of Appeals based on the bad tendency doctrine.

[31] *Gitlow* v. *New York*, 268 U.S. 652 (1925).

[32] 249 U.S. 47 (1919).

[33] 274 U.S. 357 (1927).

Freedom of speech is a fundamental right guaranteed by the First amendment. *(Ken Karp)*

The Best Test of Truth

Justice Oliver Wendell Holmes, dissenting in *Abrams* v. *United States*,* wrote:
Persecution for the expression of opinion seems to me perfectly logical. If you have no doubt of your premises or your power and want a certain result with all your heart you naturally express your wishes in law and sweep away all opposition. . . . But when men have realized that time has upset many fighting faiths, they may come to believe even more than they believe the very foundations of their own conduct that the ultimate good desired is better reached by free trade in ideas—that the best test of truth is the power of the thought to get itself accepted in the competition of the market, and that truth is the only ground upon which their wishes safely can be carried out. That at any rate is the theory of our Constitution. It is an experiment, as all life is an experiment.

* 250 U.S. 616 (1919).

Members of the Supreme Court Since 1946

Justice	Years On Court	President Who Appointed
Hugo L. Black	1937–1971	Roosevelt
Stanley F. Reed	1938–1957	Roosevelt
Felix Frankfurter	1939–1975	Roosevelt
William O. Douglas	1939–1975	Roosevelt
Francis W. Murphy	1940–1949	Roosevelt
Robert H. Jackson	1941–1954	Roosevelt
Wiley B. Rutledge	1943–1949	Roosevelt
Harold H. Burton	1945–1958	Truman
Frederick M. Vinson*	1946–1953	Truman
Tom C. Clark	1949–1967	Truman
Sherman Minton	1949–1956	Truman
Earl Warren*	1953–1969	Eisenhower
John Marshall Harlan	1953–1971	Eisenhower
William J. Brennan, Jr.	1956–	Eisenhower
Charles E. Wittaker	1957–1962	Eisenhower
Potter Stewart	1958–1981	Eisenhower
Byron R. White	1962–	Kennedy
Arthur J. Goldberg	1962–1965	Kennedy
Abe Fortas	1965–1969	Johnson
Thurgood Marshall	1967–	Johnson
Warren E. Burger*	1969–1986	Nixon
Harry A. Blackmun	1970–	Nixon
Lewis F. Powell, Jr.	1971–1987	Nixon
William H. Rehnquist*#	1971–	Nixon
John Paul Stevens	1975–	Ford
Sandra Day O'Connor	1981–	Reagan
Antonin Scalia	1986–	Reagan
Anthony Kennedy	1988–	Reagan

* Chief Justices. # Elevated from Associate to Chief in 1986.

The preferred position doctrine   This was the official view of the Supreme Court for a brief time during the 1940s; it still represents pretty much the present Court position on speech about *political matters*. Those who take this view, such as the late Justice Hugo Black, come close to the position that freedom of expression—that is, the use of words and pictures—may *never* be curtailed. (This does not mean that there is nothing left for judges to decide, for a line must still be drawn between speech and nonspeech.)

The preferred position interpretation of the First amendment is that these freedoms have the highest priority in our constitutional hierarchy. Judges have a special duty to protect these freedoms and should be most skeptical about laws trespassing on them. Legislative majorities are free to experiment with and to adopt various schemes regulating our economic lives. But when they tamper with freedom of speech, they interfere with the channels of the political process. Only if the government can show that limitations on speech are absolutely necessary to avoid imminent and serious substantive evils are such limitations to be allowed.

If we apply the preferred position doctrine to our example of a law against abusive racial remarks, we would declare the law itself unconstitutional. Restraints on such abusive speech are not absolutely necessary to prevent riots. Whatever danger may come from such remarks does not justify restricting free comment. Moreover, supporters of the preferred position doctrine contend that the law, and not merely its application, violates the Constitution.

Justice Hugo Black, a member of the Court from 1937 to 1971, was a noted champion of First Amendment rights. (*UPI/Bettman Newsphotos*)

Current Constitutional Tests

The three historic doctrines just discussed still provide the background for debates on freedom of speech. Today, however, the Supreme Court is more apt to use the following doctrines to measure the limits of governmental power:

Prior restraint   Of all the forms of governmental interference with expression, judges are most suspicious of those that impose restraints prior to publication; these include licensing requirements before a speech can be made, a motion picture shown, or a newspaper published. The Supreme Court has refused to declare all forms of prior censorship unconstitutional, but a "prior restraint on expression comes to this court with a 'heavy presumption' against its constitutionality. . . . The Government thus carries a heavy burden of showing justification for the enforcement of such a restraint."[34]

One of the more celebrated examples of the Court's hostility to prior restraints is *The New York Times Company* v. *United States* (1971). The attorney general had secured from a lower court an injunction against the publication by several newspapers of the *Pentagon Papers*, a classified study of the government's decision-making process on Vietnam policy. Justices Black and Douglas took the view that the First amendment forbids a court to impose, however briefly and for whatever reason, any prior restraint on a newspaper. The prevailing view, however, was that in this particular instance, especially without any congressional authorization, the attorney general had failed to show that the publication of these documents would cause immediate and specific damage to national security.[35]

Except as applied to motion pictures, the only examples in modern times of the Court's approval of prior restraints relate to the power of military commanders to regulate what is distributed in military bases and to the screening by the CIA of what its agents and ex-agents publish.

Editors of the Hazelwood (MO) East High School student newspaper, *Spectrum*, lost their battle against censorship by the principal when the Supreme Court ruled in 1988 that school officials have broad powers of censorship over student newspapers. (*AP/Wide World Photos*)

Vagueness   A law is unconstitutional if it "either forbids or requires the doing of an act in terms so vague that men of common intelligence must necessarily guess at its meaning and differ as to its application. . . ."[36] Laws touching First amendment freedoms are required to pass even more rigid standards. These laws must not allow those who administer them so much discretion that they could discriminate against those whose views they dislike. The laws must also not be so vague that people are afraid to exercise protected freedoms. Such vague and overbroad laws have a "chilling effect" on freedom of speech. The Supreme Court has struck down laws that condemn "sacrilegious" movies or publications of "criminal deeds of bloodshed or lust . . . so massed as to become vehicles for inciting violent and depraved crimes."[37]

Overbreadth   Closely related to the vagueness doctrine is the requirement that a statute relating to First amendment freedoms cannot be so broad that it sweeps within its prohibitions protected speech as well as nonprotected activities—for example, a loyalty oath that endangers protected forms of association along with illegal activities. Because the very existence of overbroad statutes tends to repress protected speech, such statutes may be declared unconstitutional on their face—that is, entirely and not in some particular application of the law.[38]

Least Drastic Means   Even for an important purpose, a legislature may not choose a law that impinges on First amendment freedoms if there are other ways to handle the problem. To illustrate, a state may protect the public from unscrupulous lawyers, but it may not do so by forbidding organizations to make legal services

[34] *Nebraska Press Assn.* v. *Stuart*, 427 U.S. 539 (1976). See also Fred W. Friendly, *Minnesota Rag: The Dramatic Story of the Landmark Supreme Court Cast that Gave New Meaning to Freedom of the Press* (Random House, 1981).
[35] 403 U.S. 713 (1971).
[36] *Lanzetta* v. *New Jersey*, 306 U.S. 451 (1939).
[37] *Winters* v. *New York*, 333 U.S. 507 (1948); and *Burstyn* v. *Wilson*, 343 U.S. 495 (1952).
[38] *Secretary of State of Md.* v. *J.H. Munson, Co.*, 467 U.S. 947 (1984). *Brockett* v. *Spokane Arcades, Inc.*, 472 U.S. 491 (1985).

available to their members, or by forbidding attorneys from advertising their fees for simple services. Other ways to protect the public do not impinge on freedom of association or speech.

Content neutral   Content neutral laws are much less likely to be struck down than those that restrict speech because of its content. For example, a law forbidding posting of handbills on telephone polls was sustained. But a law prohibiting posting of handbills advocating racism or sexism would in all probability be declared unconstitutional, because it would relate to what is being said rather than where and how it is being said. (Justice Stevens believes the content neutral standard is of little help. He quipped: "Any student of history who has been reprimanded for talking about the World Series during a class discussion of the First Amendment knows that it is incorrect to state that a time, place, or manner restriction may not be based upon either the content or subject matter of speech.")[39]

Centrality of political speech   The Court gives much greater constitutional protection to speech relating to public policy and politics than to speech relating to other matters. "Not all speech is of equal First amendment importance," it has said. "It is speech on 'matters of public concern that is at the heart of the First amendment's protection.' "[40]

There is some contradiction between content neutrality and centrality of political speech. Legislatures and city councils are supposed to pass laws that are content neutral, but in determining whether or not those laws violate the Constitution judges may take into account what kind of speech is involved.

Plainly, doctrines and judicially elaborated constitutional tests do not decide cases: Judges do. Doctrines are judges' starting points; each case requires a judge to weigh a variety of factors. *What* was said? *Where* was it said? *How* was it said? What was the *intent* of the person who said it? What were the *circumstances* in which it was said? *Which government* is attempting to regulate the speech—the city council that speaks for a few people, or the Congress that speaks for many? (Few congressional enactments have ever been struck down because of conflict with the First amendment.) *How* is the government attempting to regulate the speech? By prior censorship? By punishment after the speech? *Why* is the government attempting to protect the rights of unpopular religious minorities? To prevent criticism of those in power? These and scores of other considerations are involved in the never-ending process of determining what the Constitution permits and what it forbids.

FREEDOM OF THE PRESS

Although we still utilize street-corner meetings and public rallies to communicate ideas and influence public policies, most of us today rely on television, newspapers, radio, movies—the mass media—to tell us what is happening in the world. The Constitution, not surprisingly, also speaks of freedom of the press.

Until recently few people questioned whether the press has freedoms beyond those of other persons. It was assumed that freedom of speech is the same as freedom of the press—except that the clause relating to speech protects oral communications, and the phrase relating to the press embraces written ones. This remains the prevailing view. However, former Chief Justice Burger acknowledged that media representatives have a valid claim to function as "surrogates for the public and

[39] *Consolidated Edison Company v. Public Service Commission of N.Y.*, 447 U.S. 530 (1980).
[40] *Dun & Bradstreet v. Greenmoss Builders*, 472 U.S. 749 (1985).

thus may be provided special seating and priority of entry [at trials] so that they may report what people in attendance have seen and heard."[41]

Further, although the First amendment does not prohibit the application of general economic regulations to newspapers, the Supreme Court has been very careful to protect the press from special tax burdens, even when there is no evidence of any evil intent on the part of the taxing authorities. Finally, Justices O'Connor, Marshall, and Powell have hinted that "media defendants" might have more protection against libel suits than "nonmedia defendants."[42]

Still, the prevailing view is: "The First Amendment does not 'belong' to any definable category of persons or entities; it belongs to all who exercise its freedoms."[43] Representatives of the press continue to argue otherwise. Moreover, they claim not merely the constitutional right to publish but also a right of access, the right to protect their sources, and the right to secure their files against search warrants. If the press should prevail, the Court will have to determine who qualifies for whatever such special benefits.

Does the Press Have a Right to Know?

Courts have carefully protected reporters' rights to publish information—no matter how they got it. But reporters, editors, and others have argued this is not enough. If the press is excluded from places where public business is being done, or denied access to information the government controls, it will not be able to perform its historic function of keeping the public informed.

The Supreme Court has refused to acknowledge a right to know, or a right of access. However, in 1980, in *Richmond Newspapers, Inc.* v. *Virginia*—which Justice Stevens called "a water-shed case"—the Supreme Court ruled that the press, along with the public, does have a First amendment right to attend criminal trials, more because such trials are public forums than because of a constitutional right to know.[44] Nonetheless, if the Court expands this right to other areas, *Richmond Newspapers* will, as the lawyer representing the American Society of Editors said, "rank right up there with some of the most significant First Amendment cases of the century."[45]

Although they have no constitutional obligation to do so, many states have adopted **sunshine laws** requiring public agencies to open their meetings to the public and the press. Congress, too, requires many federal executive agencies to open various types of hearings and meetings of advisory groups to the public. Congress, in fact, holds most of its committee meetings in public. Federal and state courtroom trials are open, but judicial conferences are not.

Congress has authorized the president to establish a classification system to keep public documents and governmental files secret, and it is a crime for any person to divulge such classified information. So far, however, no newspapers have been prosecuted for doing so, although they have been threatened.

During the 1940s and 1950s public officials began to classify more and more information. Then from the mid-1950s until the Reagan administration the trend was reversed; the presumption was established that information should not be classified. Executives who wished to classify information had to prove it was necessary.

Myron Farber (in dark shirt), *The New York Times* reporter who refused to turn over his notes during a murder trial, leaves the Bergen County jail after the New Jersey Supreme Court stayed his indefinite sentence pending an appeal of his contempt conviction. He was jailed on August 4, 1978. In January 1982 he was pardoned by Governor Byrne, and the fines he and *The Times* had paid were remitted. (*AP/Wide World Photos*)

---

[41] *Richmond Newspapers, Inc.* v. *Virginia*, 448 U.S. 555 (1980). For a comprehensive history, see David A. Anderson, "The Origins of the Press Clause," *UCLA Law Review* (February 1983), pp. 455–537.

[42] *Philadelphia Newspapers* v. *Hepps*, 475 U.S. 767 (1986).

[43] *Dun & Bradstreet* v. *Greenmoss Builders*, 472 U.S. 749 (1985). See also William W. Van Alstyne, *Interpretations of the First Amendment* (Duke University Press, 1984), pp. 50–67.

[44] 448 U.S. 555 (1980), and David M. O'Brien, *The Public's Right to Know: The Supreme Court and the First Amendment* (Praeger, 1981).

[45] Richard M. Schmidt, Jr., *The New York Times* (July 3, 1980).

The Reagan administration, however, reversed this trend again, and lowered the threshold requirements for classifying information.

By the Freedom of Information Act (1966, and amended in 1974), Congress has liberalized access to *nonclassified* government records. This act makes the records of federal agencies available on request, subject to certain exceptions, such as private financial transactions, personnel records, criminal investigation files, interoffice memoranda, and letters used in the internal decision-making process of the executive branches. The act requires federal agencies to move promptly on requests, and it gives persons speedy judicial hearings if they are denied the information they seek. The burden is on the agency to explain any refusal to supply materials. Moreover, if the judge decides the government is wrong, the government has to pay the legal fees.

Executive Privilege

Most presidents have claimed a constitutional right of **executive privilege,** which allows them to withhold information not only from the press but even from Congress and the courts if, in their judgment, its release would jeopardize national security or interfere with the confidentiality of advice given to them. In the celebrated case of *United States* v. *Nixon* (1974), however, the Supreme Court ruled that a president is subject to judicial subpoena for material relevant to a criminal prosecution.[46] This historic decision—which marked the first time the Supreme Court decided a matter directly involving the president as a party to a case—rejected the president's claim of *absolute* executive privilege and the idea that the president, rather than the judges, has the final say about what information to release and what to withhold. The Court did, however, fully recognize that a president's "singularly unique role" gives the office a *limited* executive privilege to which judges should show the "utmost deference."

Does the Press Have a Right to Withhold Information?

Although many reporters have challenged the right of the government to withhold information, they claim a right to do so themselves, including the right to keep information from grand juries and legislative committees. Without this right, they argue, they cannot assure their sources of confidentiality, and they will not be able to get the information they need to keep the public informed. But the Supreme Court has declared that reporters, and presumably scholars, have no constitutional right to withhold information from juries.[47] Speaking for the Court, Justice White quoted from Jeremy Bentham: "Were the Prince of Wales, the Archbishop of Canterbury, and the Lord High Chancellor, to be passing by in the same coach, while a chimney sweeper and a barrow woman were in dispute about a halfpennyworth of apples, and the chimney sweeper or the barrow woman were to think proper to call upon them for their evidence, could they refuse it? No, most certainly." The Court concluded: " 'The public has a right to every man's evidence,' except for those persons protected by a constitutional, common-law, or statutory privilege." If any privilege is to be given to newspeople, said the Court, it should be done by act of Congress and of the states. The dissenting justices argued: "When neither the reporter nor his source can rely on the shield of confidentiality against unrestrained use of the grand jury's subpoena power, valuable information will not be published and the public dialogue will inevitably be impoverished." [48]

Following a nationwide television speech, President Nixon sits in his office with his subpoenaed transcripts. (*UPI/Bettman Newsphotos*)

[46] 418 U.S. 683 (1974). See also Daniel N. Hoffman, *Governmental Secrecy and the Founding Fathers: A Study in Constitutional Controls* (Greenwood Press, 1981).

[47] *Branzburg* v. *Hayes*, 408 U.S. 665 (1972).

[48] Ibid.

Congress has not yet responded to the Supreme Court's suggestion that it should adopt a **shield law,** which would establish the conditions under which newspaper people would be protected from having to respond to federal investigatory and judicial agencies. The attorney general has, however, issued guidelines limiting federal prosecutors' discretion in issuing subpoenas to newspersons. Most states, too, have shield laws limiting state officials.

The Press and Police Searches

The press has not fared any better in its claim that the Constitution gives it special protection against police searches. Officers of the Santa Clara (California) County district attorney's office obtained a warrant to search through the files of the *Stanford Daily* for pictures of persons involved in a student takeover of the Stanford University Hospital. The newspaper argued that such searches jeopardized the ability of the press to gather, analyze, and disseminate news. It contended that materials could constitutionally be obtained from its files only by a subpoena issued by a judge after a hearing, not by a surprise search based on a warrant. A majority of the Supreme Court ruled otherwise.[49]

Following the *Stanford Daily* decision, Congress prohibited the issuance of search warrants to federal, state, and local police for searches of the "work products" of news organizations and others engaged in First amendment activities, unless (1) the persons involved are suspected of crimes related to the materials they are holding, or (2) there is reason to believe that the immediate seizure of the materials is necessary to prevent death or serious bodily injury. Those searched in violation of this act may sue for damages, but evidence otherwise admissible at a trial is not to be excluded from federal courts because it has been gathered in violation of the law.

"I hope you're not going to make a big issue of this." (*Drawing by Modell*; © 1986. *The New Yorker Magazine, Inc.*)

Freedom of the Press versus Fair Trials

When newspapers and television report in vivid details the facts of a crime, interview prosecutors and police, question witnesses, and hold press conferences for defendants and their attorneys, they may so inflame the public that conducting a fair trial is difficult.

In England, strict rules determine what the media may report, and judges do not hesitate to punish newspapers that comment on pending criminal proceedings. In the United States, in contrast, free comment is emphasized. The Supreme Court has even set aside contempt citations against editors who threatened judges with political reprisals unless the judges imposed severe punishments on certain named defendants. Yet the Supreme Court has not been indifferent to protecting persons on trial from inflammatory publicity. Its remedies have been to order new trials or to instruct judges to impose sanctions on prosecutors and police, not on reporters.

Although defendants have a right to public trials, they have no right to private ones. On the contrary, even if defendants want their judges to exclude the press and public from their trials, the judges themselves must have weighty reasons for doing so. However, despite the First amendment protections for trials, which we noted earlier, states have no obligation to permit trials to be photographed or televised. They may do so if they wish, and forty-three states now do permit television coverage of courtroom proceedings. Defendants, however, always have the right to present evidence that televising their particular trials interfered, prevented fair hearings, and deprived them of due process.

[49] *Zurcher* v. *Stanford Daily*, 436 U.S. 547 (1978).

When the Constitution was written, "the press" referred to leaflets, newspapers, and books. Today the Constitution also protects speech that comes from such other media as the mails, motion pictures, radio, television, picketing, and certain kinds of symbolic conduct. Because each form of communication entails special problems, each needs a different degree of protection.

The Mails

Sixty years ago, Justice Holmes wrote in dissent: "The United States may give up the Post Office when it sees fit, but while it carries it on, the use of the mails is almost as much a part of free speech as is the right to use our tongues." [50] In 1965 the Court adopted Holmes's views by striking down the first congressional act ever held to conflict with the First amendment. That act directed the postmaster general to detain foreign mailings of "communist political propaganda" and to deliver these materials only upon the addressee's request. The Court has also set aside federal laws authorizing postal authorities to make administrative determinations of obscenity and to exclude such material from the mails, as well as a law prohibiting the mailing of unsolicited advertisements for contraceptives. "The level of discourse reaching a mailbox," said Justice Thurgood Marshall for the Court, "simply cannot be limited to that which would be suitable for a sandbox." [51]

Although government censorship of the mails is unconstitutional, household censorship is not. The Court has sustained a law giving any householder the absolute right to ask the postmaster to order mailers to delete their names from all mailing lists and to refrain from sending any advertisements that householders in their sole discretion believe to be "erotically arousing or sexually provocative." It makes no constitutional difference if the householder includes a dry-goods catalogue in such a category. Moreover, Congress may forbid—and has forbidden—the use of mailboxes for any materials except those sent through the United States mails.

Motion Pictures

Films may be treated differently from books or newspapers. Prior censorship of films is not necessarily unconstitutional under all circumstances. However, laws calling for submission of films to a review board, or authorizing judges to issue restraining orders against showing motion pictures, are constitutional only if there is a prompt judicial hearing. The burden is on the government to prove to the court that the particular film in question is in fact obscene.

Today, classification of films by the motion picture industry has largely replaced prior censorship. The Dallas Motion Picture Classification Board is the only local reviewing agency still in operation.[52]

Radio and Television

Television is the most important means of distributing news as well as the primary forum for appealing for votes. But "of all the forms of communication, it is broadcasting that has received the most limited First Amendment protection." [53] Congress

[50] *Milwaukee Pub. Co. v. Burleson*, 255 U.S. 407 (1921).
[51] *Bolger v. Youngs Drug Product Corp*, 463 U.S. 60 (1983).
[52] Edward de Grazia and Roger K. Newman, *Movies, Censors and the First Amendment* (R. R. Bowker, 1983).
[53] *Federal Communications Commission v. Pacific Foundation*, 438 U.S. 726 (1978).

has established a system of commercial broadcasting, supplemented by the Corporation for Public Broadcasting, which provides funds for public radio and television. The entire system is regulated by the Federal Communications Commission (FCC). Broadcasters use publicly owned airwaves, but they have no constitutional right to use these facilities without licenses. The FCC grants licenses for limited periods and regulates their use.

The major argument for greater regulation of broadcasters than newspaper and magazine publishers is that the public owns the limited number of airwaves and those who have access to these airwaves have control over a limited resource. This rationale for treating broadcasting differently from the print media is under increasing attack. In a footnote to a 1984 decision the Court majority noted, "the prevailing rationale for broadcast regulation has come under increasing criticism in recent years" because such technological changes as cable, direct beam broadcast, and videotapes may be undermining the assumption that the scarcity of channels justifies substantial government regulation. "We are not prepared, however," wrote Justice Brennan for the majority, "to reconsider our long-standing approach without some signal from Congress or the FCC that technological developments have advanced so far that some revision of the system of broadcast regulation may be required."[54] Here we have another example of the constitutional consequences of technological changes.

The First amendment does not, under prevailing interpretations, prevent the FCC from adopting, as it did from 1949 to 1987, what came to be known as the **fairness doctrine,** requiring broadcasters to cover issues of public significance and to reflect differing viewpoints. Thus, if licensees made editorial statements or endorsed candidates, they had to give persons representing a different point of view an opportunity to respond. Congress imposed an **equal-time requirement** requiring licensees to be sure that all candidates for public office had equal air time. (Congress has modified this requirement to make possible presidential debates between only candidates of the two major parties.)

In response to the Supreme Court's recent invitations to Congress and the FCC to "signal" whether technological changes have altered the approach to governmental regulation of broadcasting, in 1987 the FCC, with the enthusiastic support of the Reagan Administration and commercial broadcasters, repealed the fairness doctrine. Congress angrily tried to reimpose it, but backed down, at least temporarily, when faced with a presidential veto. Clearly the debate over the fairness doctrine is not over. Democratic congressional leaders have made plain their intent to restore the fairness doctrine. There are also new constitutional challenges by commercial broadcasters to the equal-time requirement. Thus, courts and Congress are revising First amendment doctrines as they apply to the evolving technical media.[55]

Do political parties, candidates for office, or interest groups have a right to radio or television time if they are willing to pay for it? The answer to this difficult question divides champions of free speech: It is hard to tell the good guys from the bad ones. Although a unanimous Supreme Court concluded that governments could not force newspapers to accept advertisements or print replies from those they have criticized, judges have had a much harder time finding the "right answer" to questions about broadcasting. Without too much trouble the justices concluded that Congress may impose on broadcast licensees an obligation to sell time to legally qualified federal candidates, and that the FCC may supervise how they do so. On the other hand, seven justices concluded (*Red Lion Broadcasting Co.* v. *Federal Communications Commission*) that neither the First amendment nor the Federal

"And here with us this evening, to skirt the issues, are Senator Tom Kirkland and Congressman Alan Sullivan." (*Drawing by Martin*; © 1971. *The New Yorker Magazine, Inc.*)

---

[54] *FCC* v. *League of Women Voters of California*, 468 U.S. 364 (1984).
[55] Ibid.

One form of protest and "speech" is this farmers' tractorcade to Washington. (*Chuck Fishman/Contact Press Images*, *Woodfin Camp & Associates*)

Communications Act gives anybody the right to buy air time. The Court, however, could not muster a majority behind any single opinion. Chief Justice Burger noted that if broadcasters had to accept the offers of all who wished to buy air time, those with the most money would monopolize radio and television. He argued that although the First amendment gives no one a right of access to broadcasting facilities, Congress or the FCC could provide such access. Justice William O. Douglas, a long-time advocate of an expansive interpretation of the First amendment, argued that refusal by broadcasters—with the sanction of the FCC—to accept paid political advertisements violates the First amendment rights of those who are denied access to television audiences.[56]

Handbills, Sound Trucks, and Billboards

Religious and political pamphlets, leaflets, and handbills have been historic weapons in the defense of liberty, and their distribution is constitutionally protected. So, too, is the use of their more contemporary counterparts, sound trucks and billboards. A state, for example, cannot restrain the passing out of leaflets merely to keep its streets clean; nor can it ban handbills that do not carry the name and address of the author. However, reasonable, content neutral regulations specifying where publications may be sold are permissible. As for sound trucks, those that emit loud and raucous noises may be banned. Further, content neutral regulations detailing the time, place, and manner in which amplification devices may be used are also acceptable. Billboards, too, are entitled to constitutional protection. Those used for noncommercial purposes, however, are more protected than those used for commercial reasons.

Picketing

A state law forbidding all peaceful picketing would be an unconstitutional invasion of speech. However, "picketing involves elements of both speech and conduct, i.e., patrolling," and "because of this intermingling of protected and unprotected elements, picketing can be subject to controls that would not be constitutionally permissible in the case of pure speech.[57]

Even peaceful picketing can be restricted if it is conducted for an illegal purpose, such as to press an employer to practice racial or sex discrimination in hiring workers. Federal regulations are so comprehensive for trade union picketing, however, that the power of states to interfere is much narrower than it might appear from First amendment decisions.

Commercial Speech

Even though commercial speech is constitutionally protected, common-sense differences do exist between commercial and other kinds of speech. Commercial speech is, therefore, subject to much more regulation than other speech: Overbreadth analysis does not apply, nor perhaps does the prohibition against prior restraint.

Advertising the sale of anything illegal may be forbidden, as can false and misleading *commercial* advertising. (A law forbidding false and misleading political speech or political advertising is clearly unconstitutional. In political debate, no

---

[56] *Red Lion Broadcasting Co.* v. *Federal Communications Commission*, 395 U.S. 367 (1969). See also Fred W. Friendly, *The Good Guys, the Bad Guys, and the First Amendment* (Random House, 1976), for a discusson of the fairness doctrine, its evolution, and its application; Steven J. Simmons, *The Fairness Doctrine and the Media* (University of California Press, 1979); and Irving R. Kaufman, "Reassessing the Fairness Doctrine: Should the First Amendment Apply Equally to the Print and Broadcast Media?" *The New York Times Magazine* (June 19, 1983), pp 18–20, for the views of a judge of the Court of Appeals for the Second Circuit.

[57] *Amalgamated Food Employees* v. *Logan Plaza*, 391 U.S. 308 (1968).

one can say what is false and misleading.) Moreover, if government has a "substantial reason" it may even regulate nonfalse and nonmisleading commercial advertising about legal activities. For example, by a five to four vote the Supreme Court ruled that Puerto Rico could ban local advertising for gambling casinos, which are legal in Puerto Rico, but still allow such advertising outside the island. In this way, Puerto Rico can attract tourists from elsewhere—but not encourage locals—to come to gamble.[58] Advertising on radio and television is subject to even greater regulation than advertising transmitted in print.

Symbolic Speech

"We cannot accept the view," wrote Chief Justice Earl Warren, "that an apparently limitless variety of conduct can be labeled speech whenever the person engaged in the conduct intends thereby to express an idea." [59] Similarly, Chief Justice Warren Burger wrote: "Conduct that the State police power can prohibit on a public street does not become automatically protected by the Constitution merely because the conduct is moved to . . . a 'live theatre' stage, any more than a 'live' performance of a man and woman locked in a sexual embrace at high noon in Times Square is protected by the constitution merely because they simultaneously engaged in a political dialogue." [60]

The burden is on those who engage in expressive conduct to show that the First amendment applies. Even if it does, however, government may forbid or regulate symbolic expressive conduct: (1) if the conduct itself may be regulated; (2) if the regulation is content neutral; (3) if the regulation is narrowly drawn to further a substantial governmental interest; (4) if this interest is unrelated to the suppression of free speech; and (5) if ample alternative channels for communication of the information are left open.[61]

Of course, the line between speech and conduct is not always clear. Deliberately burning a draft card in violation of a congressional regulation is not, for example, a constitutionally protected form of speech; nor is the right of municipal police officers to have long hair while serving on the police force. But, in contrast, even though public school authorities can impose reasonable dress codes, they cannot—without evidence that the conduct would lead to disruption—forbid students to wear black armbands to school to protest such political events as the war in Vietnam.

LIBEL, OBSCENITY, AND FIGHTING WORDS

As we have already noted, some kinds of speech are not entitled to constitutional protection. This does not mean that the constitutional issues relating to these kinds of speech are simple. On the contrary. How we prove **libel**, how we define **obscenity**, and how we determine which words are **fighting words** are hotly contested issues.

Libel

At one time newspaper publishers and editors had to take considerable care about what they wrote, for fear they might be prosecuted for libel by the government or sued for money damages by individuals. Nowadays, through a progressive raising

[58] *Posados de Puerto Rico Associates, Condado Holiday Inn v. Tourism Company of Puerto Rico*, 92 Led 2d 266 (1986).
[59] *United States v. O'Brien*, 391 U.S. 367 (1968).
[60] *Paris Adult Theatre I v. Slaton*, 413 U.S. 49 (1973).
[61] *Clark v. Community for Creative NonViolence*, 468 U.S. 228 221 (1984).

of constitutional standards, it has become more difficult to win a libel suit against a newspaper or magazine.

In *The New York Times* v. *Sullivan*, and its subsequent cases, the Supreme Court has established the guidelines: Neither *public officials nor public figures* can collect damages for any comments made about them unless they can prove the comments were made with knowledge of their falsity or with reckless disregard for whether the comments were true or false—that is, unless they can prove the comments were made with "actual malice." [62]

Constitutional standards for libel charges that are brought by *private persons* or that do not involve "matters of public concern" are not so rigid. States may permit private persons to collect damages if they can prove that the charges made against them were false and negligently published. Moreover, one does not lose status as a private person and become a public figure, and thus become subject to more rigid requirements for collecting libel damages, merely because of newspaper publicity—for example, for getting a divorce, for being accused of being a spy, or for receiving a federal grant and being accused by a senator of wasting taxpayers' money.

Obscenity

Today, fears about obscenity and pornography (see the next section) appear to have replaced the seventeenth-century fears about heresy and the 1950s fears about sedition. In 1970 a Presidential Commission on Obscenity and Pornography funded studies that, to the disappointment of the Nixon administration, found no evidence that exposure to obscenity plays a significant role in causing delinquent or criminal behavior. In 1986 an Attorney General's Commission on Pornography argued that evidence does exist that "some forms of sexually explicit material bear a causal relationship . . . to sexual violence" and called for an all-out war on "smut." The Commission made over ninety recommendations for tighter regulation and tougher punishments, especially of cable television.[63] Two dissenting commissioners declared, however, that " 'no self-respecting investigator' would accept the panel's findings as scientific." [64]

In the past, pressure for regulating obscenity came primarily from political conservatives and religious fundamentalists concerned that obscenity undermines moral standards. More recently, some feminists have joined them, arguing that "pornography is central in creating and maintaining sex as a basis for discrimination" and that it "is a systematic practice of exploitation and subordination based on sex which differentially harms women." [65]

Obscene publications are not entitled to constitutional protection, but the members of the Supreme Court, like everybody else, have had great difficulty in defining what is obscene. Since 1957 almost 100 separate opinions have been written on the matter by Supreme Court justices. In *Miller* v. *California* (1973) the Court was finally able to assemble a majority opinion. Speaking for five members of the Court, Warren Burger again stated that obscenity is not entitled to constitutional protection, and once again tried to clarify a constitutional definition of obscenity. A work may be considered legally obscene provided: (1) the average person, applying contemporary standards of the particular community, would find that the work, taken as a whole, appeals to a prurient interest in sex. (The Court has never been

"I like Senator Goniff. Heck, I think he's one great guy. Right now, as I write this story, feeling great warmth and affection for the senator, it seems impossible that he bilked the people of his district out of $3 million." (*Ed Stein. Reprinted by courtesy of Rocky Mountain News.*)

[62] 376 U.S. 254 (1964).

[63] *Los Angeles Times* (May 1, 1986).

[64] "An-X Rated Report that Has the Capital Buzzing," *U.S. News & World Report* (June 9, 1986), p. 20.

[65] "From Preamble to Indianapolis City-County Ordinance," cited by Joel B. Grossman in "The First Amendment and the New Anti-Pornography Statutes, *News for Teachers of Political Science* (American Political Science Association, 1985), p. 18.

very clear about what the difference is between something that appeals to a prurient interest in sex and something that appeals to a normal interest—but see the next paragraph); [66] (2) it depicts or describes in a patently offensive way sexual conduct specifically defined by the applicable law or authoritatively construed; and (3) the work, taken as a whole, lacks serious literary, artistic, political, or scientific value.[67] Chief Justice Burger specifically rejected part of the previous test—the so-called *Memoirs* v. *Massachusetts* (1966) formula: No work should be judged obscene unless it is "utterly without redeeming social value." [68] He argued that such a test made it impossible for a state to outlaw hard-core pornography.

Currently, to test for obscenity a jury must determine whether or not a work appeals to prurient interests in sex—that is, patently offensive interests "over and beyond those that would be characterized as normal." [69] The standards applied are those of the community from which the jury comes, which leaves open the possibility that a particular book or movie might be considered legally obscene in one community but not in another. The literary, artistic, political, or scientific merit of a work, on the other hand, is not limited by the values of a community, but is open to review by judges as well.

Did the *Miller* decision mean that local communities could ban whatever a prosecutor could persuade a jury was obscene? Many hoped this was so; many others feared this was so. They read *Miller* to mean that the Supreme Court would no longer review each book or movie in order to second-guess a decision of local authorities. But how far could the local community go? Could it decide to ban "Little Red Riding Hood"? After all, who really knows what went on in that bedroom?

A year after the *Miller* decision, the Supreme Court warned: "It would be a serious misreading of *Miller* to conclude that juries have unbridled discretion in determining what is patently offensive." [70] Appellate courts, said then Justice Rehnquist speaking for the Court, should review jury determinations to ensure compliance with constitutional standards. And the Supreme Court itself, after such review, ruled that the movie *Carnal Knowledge* was not patently offensive, contrary to the conclusion of a jury in Albany, Georgia.

Obscenity, then, is not entitled to constitutional protection. But governments must proceed under laws that specifically define the kinds of sexual conduct forbidden in word or picture. Moreover, it is not a crime for booksellers to offer obscene books for sale; they must be shown to have done so *knowingly*. Otherwise, booksellers would tend to avoid placing on their shelves materials that some authorities might consider objectionable, and the public would be deprived of an opportunity to purchase anything except some person's determination of the "safe and sanitary." The mere private possession of obscene materials is not a crime either.

States are primarily responsible for regulating obscene literature. Yet ever since Anthony Comstock started a national crusade against "smut" in the 1880s, Congress has been concerned with the subject. It has adopted, and the Supreme Court has upheld, laws forbidding the importing into the United States of obscene materials or the sending of such materials through the mails or interstate commerce—even to willing adults, even transported for private use in a briefcase in an airline.

What about "dirty books" and "X-rated movies" that fall short of the constitutional definition of obscenity? They are entitled to constitutional protection, but less protection than political speech; and they are subject to greater government regulation. "[Society's] interest in protecting this type of expression is of a wholly different, and lesser, magnitude than the interest in untrammeled political debate.

[66] *Brockett* v. *Spokane Arcades, Inc.*, 472 U.S. 491 (1985).
[67] 413 U.S. 15 (1973).
[68] *Memoirs* v. *Massachusetts*, 383 U.S. 413 (1966).
[69] *Brockett* v. *Spokane Arcades, Inc.* See citation above.
[70] *Jenkins* v. *Georgia*, 418 U.S. 153 (1974).

. . . The state may legitimately use the content of these materials as the basis for placing them in a different classification from other motion pictures." [71] Cities may also regulate, by zoning laws, where "adult motion picture theaters" may be located. Yet the small Borough of Mount Ephraim, New Jersey, went too far when it applied its zoning ban on live entertainment to prevent nude dancing in an adult book store. Said the Supreme Court: "Entertainment, as well as political and ideological speech, is protected by the Constitution," and "nude dancing is not without its First Amendment protections from official regulation." [72]

Sexually explicit materials either *about minors or aimed at them* are not protected by the First amendment. Provided they act under narrowly drawn statutes, state and local governments can, for example, ban the knowing sale of "girly" magazines to minors, even if such materials would not be considered legally obscene if sold to adults. And they can make it a crime to depict sexual conduct by children, even if the depicted behavior would not be considered obscene if done by adults.

Pornography

Pornography used to be merely a synonym for obscenity. In recent years, however, some feminists have defined pornographic materials as sexually explicit pictures or words that depict women as sexual objects who enjoy pain and humiliation or that present abuse of women as a sexual stimulus for men. They argue that just as sexually explicit materials about minors are not entitled to First amendment protection, so there should be no such protection for pornographic materials. Advocates of antipornography laws contend that pornography promotes sexual abuse of individual women and perpetuates social subordination of women as a class. They propose that civil penalties be imposed on pornographers and that women—and others who have had pornography forced upon them—be given the right to file complaints.

Not all feminists favor antipornographic ordinances, but those who do have been joined by social conservatives, and this new chapter in the battle over pornography has just begun. Women and men have differed significantly in their attitudes about pornography. Men, by a two to one ratio, do not think pornography damages adults who read it, and they are about equally divided on whether newsstands should be permitted to sell pornographic material. In contrast, women, by about a three to one ratio, say newsstands should not be allowed to sell pornographic magazines and that laws against pornography are not strict enough.[73]

For this new antipornography coalition to be successful, however, a substantial alteration in constitutional doctrine will be required.[74] Although several cities have been considering adopting antipornography ordinances, only Indianapolis has done so, and that law was declared unconstitutional in a decision affirmed by the Supreme Court without opinion.[75]

Censorship of films and books may be imposed by a variety of means other than formal action. In some cities such local groups as the Legion of Decency may pressure the authorities. Feminists have threatened boycotts of bookstores that sell magazines they believe to depict women in a demeaning and pornographic manner. Local police have been known to threaten booksellers with criminal prosecution if they persist in showing films or selling books of which some local people

A small business cleverly uses "First Amendment" in its name. Local opponents of pornography protested its presence, and in 1986 arsonists burned the store to the ground. (*Stan Wakefield*)

[71] *Young* v. *American Mini Theatres*, 427 U.S. 51 (1976). See also *Renton* v. *Playtime Theatres, Inc.*, 89 L Ed 2d 29 (1986).

[72] *Schad* v. *Borough of Mount Ephraim*, 452 U.S. 61 (1981).

[73] Barry Sussman, "With Pornography, It All Depends on Who's Doing the Looking: Washington Post-ABC News Poll," *The Washington Post National Weekly Edition* (March 24, 1986), p. 37.

[74] "Anti-Pornography Laws and First Amendment Values," *Harvard Law Review*, vol 98 (1984), pp. 460 ff.

[75] *Hudnut* v. *American Booksellers*, 89 L Ed 2d 291 (1986).

disapprove. In the spring of 1986 the Attorney General's Commission Against Pornography wrote letters to various retail companies saying that the commission had received testimony alleging that they were supplying pornography because they sold *Playboy* or *Penthouse* magazines or adult video cassettes. The retailers were given a chance to respond to the allegations, but they were also told that "failure to respond will necessarily be accepted as an indication of no objection to the allegation." [76] Some of the stores did stop selling the magazines, but the matter is now before the federal courts. Of course, anyone is free to stay away from pictures or books he or she dislikes, and even to try to persuade others to stay away. What the Constitution forbids is the use of coercive powers of government to keep adults from seeing or reading what they wish to see or read.

Fighting Words

Certain well-defined and narrowly limited classes of speech "by their very utterance inflict injury or tend to incite an immediate breach of peace that governments may constitutionally punish." [77] Fighting words are those that "have a direct tendency to cause acts of violence by the person to whom, individually, the remarks are addressed." [78] The mere fact that the words are abusive, harsh, or insulting is not sufficient. For example, a four-letter word used in relation to the draft and worn on a sweater is not a fighting word, at least when it is not directed to any specific person.

RIGHT OF THE PEOPLE PEACEABLY TO ASSEMBLE, TO PETITION THE GOVERNMENT, AND TO ASSOCIATE

Freedom of Assembly

"The right to assemble peaceably applies not only to meetings in private homes and meeting halls, but to gatherings held in public streets and parks, which since . . . time out of mind have been used for purposes of assembly . . . and discussing public questions."[79] In the winter of 1977, Frank Collins, "a racist and a fascist, a bigoted totalitarian, a self-avowed Nazi," [80] threatened to lead his small band, dressed in brown shirts and carrying swastika regalia, in a jack-booted march through the streets of Skokie, Illinois, a half-Jewish Chicago suburb. Some of these citizens are themselves survivors of Hitler's extermination camps; many of them had relatives who lost their lives in the Holocaust. Many people, including the officials of Skokie and a local judge, argued that Collins and his followers should not be allowed to march. They argued that this would be like shouting "Fire!" in a crowded theater, and that to permit such a use of the streets presented a clear and present danger of inciting people to violence. These same arguments were put forward to contend that Iranian followers of the Ayatollah Khomeini should not be allowed to protest publicly in Washington at a time when most Americans were angry about Khomeini's illegal and brutal treatment of innocent American hostages in Tehran. The right

[76] Robert L. Jackson, "Pornography Case Judge Rebukes Panel," *Los Angeles Times* (July 4, 1986), p. 1.

[77] *Chaplinsky* v. *New Hamsphire*, 315 U.S. 568 (1942).

[78] *Cohen* v. *California*, 403 U.S. 15 (1971). See also *NAACP* v. *Claiborne Hardware Co.*, 458 U.S. 886 (1982).

[79] *Hague* v. *C.I.O.*, 307 U.S. 496 (1939).

[80] David M. Hamlin, "Swastikas & Survivors: Inside the Skokie Nazi Free Speech Case," *The Civil Liberties Review* (March–April 1978).

to assemble peaceably, they said, should not be extended to Iranian aliens who were abusing this right to provoke Americans to violence. In both cases judicial authorities defended the rights of these unpopular minorities. But it is not always the "bad guys" whose rights have to be protected by the courts: It also took occasional judicial intervention in the 1960s to preserve for Martin Luther King, Jr., and those who marched with him, their right to demonstrate in the streets of southern cities in behalf of blacks' rights.

Such incidents present the classic free speech problem of the "heckler's veto." It is almost always easier, and certainly politically more prudent, to maintain order by curbing public demonstrations of unpopular groups than by moving against those who are threatening them. On the other hand, if police did not have the right to order groups to disperse, public order would be at the mercy of those who resort to demonstrations to create tension and provoke street battles.

Does the Constitution require police officers always to protect unpopular groups whose public demonstrations arouse others to violence or threats of it? In 1951, in *Feiner* v. *New York*, the Court upheld the conviction for unlawful assembly of a sidewalk speaker who, against the orders of the only two police officers present, refused to move on after his provocative remarks aroused a crowd to anger.[81] The Feiner case has not been overruled, but since that decision the Court has refused to sustain convictions of persons whose only offenses have been to engage in peaceful but unpopular demonstrations.

It is clear, however, that the Constitution does not give a person the right to communicate "one's views at all times and places or in any manner that may be desired." No one has the right to deliberately incite others to violence, to block traffic, or to hold parades or make speeches in public streets or on public sidewalks whenever he or she wishes. Governments may make reasonable *time, place,* and *manner* regulations, provided they are content neutral. Thus the Supreme Court, after striking down a District of Columbia prohibition against the display of banners and signs critical of a foreign country within 500 feet of that country's embassy, nonetheless unanimously sustained a provision making it unlawful for a congregation of three or more persons to refuse to disperse within 500 feet of an embassy "when the police reasonably believe that a threat to the security or peace of the embassy is present."[82]

The Supreme Court has divided public property into three categories—public forums, limited public forums, and nonpublic forums—and the extent to which governments may limit access depends on the nature of the forum. "Public places historically associated with the free exercise of expressive activities, such as streets, sidewalks, and parks, are considered, without more, to be 'public forums.' " Courts look at time, place, and manner regulations as applied to traditional public forums to ensure they are applied evenhandedly and that action is not taken "because of what is being said."[83] In traditional public forums, no restrictive laws are permitted unless they are viewpoint neutral and the government can prove they are necessary for a compelling governmental interest.

Some public property, designated as "limited public forums," is open for assembly and speech. Limited public forums may be open for limited purposes, a limited amount of time, and even for a limited class of speakers, provided the distinctions between those allowed and those not allowed access are viewpoint neutral.

What of public facilities, such as airports, libraries, courthouses, schools, swimming pools, and government offices, designed to serve as other than public forums? As long as persons assemble to use such facilities within the normal bounds of conduct, they may not be constitutionally restrained from doing so. However,

Here, police protect a pro-Iran demonstrator in Los Angeles in November 1979. (*UPI/Bettman Newsphotos*)

[81] 340 U.S. 315 (1951).

[82] *Boos* v. *Barry*, 99 L Ed 2d 333 (1988); *Heffron* v. *International Society for Krishna Consciousness*, 452 U.S. 640 (1981).

[83] *United States* v. *Grace*, 461 U.S. 171 (1983).

if they attempt to interfere with programs or try to appropriate facilities—such as a *university chancellor's office*—for their own use, governments have authority to punish such activities. "Control over access to a nonpublic forum can be based on subject matter and speaker identity so long as the distinctions are reasonable in light of the purpose served by the forum and are viewpoint neutral." [84] Speakers may be excluded from such forums if they want to talk on subjects or engage in activities for which the forum was not created.

What of private property? The right to assemble does not include a right to trespass on private property. A state may protect property owners against those who attempt to convert property to their own uses, even if they are doing so to express ideas. The spread of large, privately owned shopping malls, which may cover many acres and which are larger than some towns, presents some difficult constitutional issues. The Supreme Court has set the following guidelines (*Pruneyard Shopping Center* v. *Robins*): Privately owned shopping malls are neither public streets nor places of public assembly; no one has a constitutional right to use such a mall to hand out political leaflets, to picket for political purposes, or otherwise to exercise First amendment freedoms. On the other hand, states and cities, if they wish, and to an extent still to be defined, may legally obligate the owners of such centers to permit their use for peaceful political purposes such as distributing handbills or getting people to sign petitions. In other words, although people have no constitutional right to engage in political action in a nonpublic shopping center, neither do the owners of such centers have a constitutional right to close them to political action in the face of reasonable state or local regulations providing access that does not interfere with their primary commercial purposes.[85]

Does the right of peaceful assembly and petition include the right to violate a law nonviolently but deliberately? We have no precise answer. But in general, civil disobedience—even if peaceful—is not a protected right. When Dr. Martin Luther King, Jr., and his followers refused to comply with a state court's injunction forbidding them to parade in Birmingham without first securing a permit, the Supreme Court sustained their conviction, even though there was serious doubt about the constitutionality of the injunction and the ordinance on which it was based. Justice Stewart, speaking for the five-member majority, said: "No man can be judge in his own case, however exalted his station, however righteous his motive, and irrespective of his race, color, politics, or religion." Persons are not "constitutionally free to ignore all the procedures of the law and carry their battles to the streets." [86] The four dissenting justices insisted that one does have a right to defy peacefully an obviously unconstitutional statute or injunction.

Freedom to Petition

The *right to petition the government for redress of grievances* is guaranteed by the Constitution, but "the right to commit libel with impunity is not." Anyone who with actual malice expresses libelous falsehoods in such petitions may therefore be held accountable in damage suits.[87]

Freedom of Association

The right to organize to peacefully promote political and other causes is not specifically mentioned in the Constitution, but "it is beyond debate that freedom to engage in association for the advancement of beliefs and ideas is an inseparable

---

[84] *Cornelius* v. *NAACP Legal Defense & Educational Fund*, 473 U.S. 788 (1985).

[85] 447 U.S. 74 (1980).

[86] *Walker* v. *Birmingham*, 388 U.S. 307 (1967).

[87] *McDonald* v. *Smith*, 472 U.S. 479 (1985).

aspect of the 'liberty' assured by the Due Process clause of the Fourteenth Amendment which embraces freedom of speech." [88] The Supreme Court has written of the freedom to associate in two distinct senses: In one line of decisions it has protected people's right to enter into and maintain "certain intimate human relationships" against "undue intrusion by the State. . . . In this respect, freedom of association receives protection as a fundamental element of personal liberty." [89] In this sense freedom of association sometimes comes into conflict with the government's action to protect people against discrimination. We discuss this aspect of the freedom of association in Chapter 6. The other aspect of freedom of association relates to activities protected by the First amendment: speech, assembly, petition and the redress of grievances, and the free exercise of religion.

Many troublesome constitutional questions grow out of the conflict between the constitutional right to join political parties and the right of governments to regulate the conditions of public employment. Federal **Hatch Acts** (most states have similar laws) forbid nearly all federal employees from actively campaigning or taking leadership roles in political parties; these acts have been upheld as reasonable measures to ensure a neutral civil service and to free government employees from coercion in behalf of the party in power (see discussion in Chapter 17). The Supreme Court has even declared that under most circumstances the patronage system itself is unconstitutional.

Congress, and many states, have regulated the amount of money that candidates, parties, and interest groups can raise and spend for political purposes. But many of these regulations have come into conflict with people's constitutional right to associate to promote political and social causes. In *Buckley* v. *Valeo* the Court sustained limits on the amount of money people may *contribute* to candidates and their campaign committees on the grounds that such limits only marginally restrict contributors' abilities to express political views.[90] But it has struck down limits on the amounts that may be contributed to associations formed to support or oppose ballot measures submitted to popular vote.

Limits on what people can *spend*, in contrast to what they can contribute, have fared even less well. Governments may not set limits on the amounts that people—including candidates—can spend on political matters. However, presidential candidates who accept federal funds for their campaigns may be limited in what they spend as a condition of receiving these public funds. Constitutionally, these limitations on what presidential candidates can spend apply only to expenditures by the candidates' party organizations and "coordinated" groups, not to "independent groups or committees," who have a constitutional right to spend as much as they wish to further the candidates' elections.[91]

SUBVERSIVE CONDUCT AND SEDITIOUS SPEECH

"If there is any fixed star in our constitutional constellation," Justice Robert Jackson said, "it is that no official, high or petty, can prescribe what shall be orthodox in politics, nationalism, religion, or other matters of opinion. . . ." [92] Any group can champion whatever position it wishes: vegetarianism, feminism, sexism, communism, fascism, black nationalism, white supremacy, Zionism, anti-Semitism, Americanism.

[88] *NAACP* v. *Alabama*, 357 U.S. 449 (1958).
[89] *Roberts* v. *United States Jaycees*, 465 U.S. 609 (1984).
[90] 424 U.S. 1 (1976).
[91] *FEC* v. *National Conservative Political Action Committee*, 470 U.S. 480 (1985).
[92] *West Virginia State Board of Education* v. *Barnette*, 319 U.S. 624 (1943).

But what about people who are unwilling to abide by democratic methods, and who attempt through force or violence to impose their views on others? How can democratic government protect itself against antidemocrats working to destroy the democratic system and preserve constitutional freedoms and democratic procedures at the same time?

Traitors, Spies, Saboteurs, Revolutionaries

Laws aimed at acts of violence, espionage, sabotage, or treason in themselves raise no constitutional questions, nor do they infringe on protected constitutional liberties. However, they can be used to intimidate if they are loosely drawn or indiscriminately administered. The framers of the Constitution, themselves considered traitors of the English Crown, knew the dangers of defining **treason** loosely. Accordingly, they carefully inserted a constitutional definition: Treason consists only of the overt acts of giving aid and comfort to the enemies of the United States or levying war against it. Further, in order to convict a person of treason, two witnesses to the overt treasonable acts must testify, or the defendant must confess, in open court.

The national government may also move against other conduct designed to subvert the democratic system. Congress, for example, has made it a crime to engage in espionage or sabotage, or to cross interstate boundaries or use the mails or interstate facilities to bomb buildings and schools. (This law, passed in 1960, was aimed at the white segregationists who were alleged to have blown up black churches and to have used force to intimidate black leaders and their white allies.) It is also a crime to cross state lines or use interstate facilities with the intent to incite a riot (the so-called Rap Brown law passed in 1968, aimed at black militants who were alleged to foment riots), or to conspire to do any of the just-described activities.

More often than not, when the government prosecutes under such laws, the charge is **conspiracy**. It is easier to prove conspiracy than to sustain a charge against named defendants that they have thrown a brick, planted a bomb, engaged in a riot, or committed an act of violence. However, conspiracy charges, although long known to Anglo-American jurisprudence, are especially threatening to civil liberties; they can be abused by prosecutors to intimidate the politically unpopular.

For the most part, the highly charged prosecutions of the late 1960s and the early 1970s against political radicals and black militants for allegedly engaging in, or conspiring to engage in, violent acts led to verdicts of not guilty, or reversals on appeal. To some this is evidence that our court system is strong and can be counted on to protect the innocent. To others it is evidence of the inability of the government to bring to justice those who should have been punished for their deeds. To still others it is evidence that governments can use legal procedures to intimidate adherents of unpopular causes: Even if defendants are finally acquitted, the effort and expense of defending themselves in court have an intimidating impact on political dissenters. Historians, journalists, political scientists, and others will be debating the lessons of these trials for many years.

Seditious Speech

It is one thing to punish persons for what they *do*; it is quite another to punish them for what they *say*. The story of the development of free government is in large measure the story of making this distinction clear. Until recent centuries seditious speech was so broadly defined that all criticism of those in power was considered criminal. As late as the eighteenth century in England, seditious speech was said to cover any publication intended to incite disaffection against the king or the government, or to raise discontent among the people, or to promote feelings of ill will between different classes.[93] And it made no difference if what was said was true. On the contrary: "The greater the truth the greater the libel." If one charged the king's ministers with being corrupt, and in fact they were corrupt, such a charge would more likely cause discontent among the people than if it were false.

The adoption of the Constitution and the Bill of Rights did not result in a quick, easy victory for those who wished to establish free speech in the United States.[94] In 1798, only seven years after the First amendment had been ratified, Congress passed the first national **sedition** law. Those were perilous times for the young republic, for war with France seemed imminent. The Federalists, in control of both Congress and the presidency, persuaded themselves that national safety required some suppression of speech. The Sedition Act made it a crime to utter false, scandalous, or malicious statements intended to bring the government or any of its officers into disrepute or "to incite against them the hatred of the good people of the United States." [95] Popular reaction to the Sedition Act helped defeat the Federalists in the elections of 1800. They had failed to grasp the democratic idea that a person may criticize the government of the day, work for its downfall, and oppose its policies, but still be loyal to the union.

The Smith Act of 1940

During World War I and the "Red scare" that followed it, a flurry of legislation and prosecutions was aimed at seditious speech. Hundreds of people who expressed mildly radical ideas found themselves in trouble. Some went to jail.[96] But the first peacetime sedition law since the Sedition Act of 1798 was the Smith Act of 1940. The Smith Act forbids persons to advocate overthrow of the government with the intent to bring it about; to distribute, with disloyal intent, matter teaching or advising the overthrow of government by violence; and to organize knowingly or to help organize any group having such purposes.

In *Dennis* v. *United States* (1951) the Court agreed that the Smith Act could be applied to the leaders of the Communist party, who had been charged with conspiring to advocate the violent overthrow of the government.[97] Since then the court has substantially modified its holding. Congress may not outlaw the mere advocacy of the abstract doctrine of violent overthrow: "The essential distinction is that those to whom the advocacy is addressed must be urged to do something now or in the future, rather than merely to believe in something." [98] Moreover, advocacy of the use of force may not be forbidden "except where such advocacy is directed to inciting or producing imminent lawless action and is likely to incite or produce such action." [99]

In short, seditious speech, if narrowly defined to cover only the advocacy of immediate and concrete acts of violence, is not constitutionally protected. Such narrow interpretation of the sedition laws means people are free to work for their political objectives as long as they abandon the use of force—or its specific and immediate advocacy—as a means of bringing it about.

[93] Zechariah Chafee, Jr., "The Great Liberty: Freedom of Speech and Press," in Alfred H. Kelly, ed., *Foundations of Freedom in the American Constitution* (Harper & Row, 1958).

[94] See two works by Leonard Levy, *Legacy of Suppression* (Harvard University Press, 1960), and *Freedom of the Press from Zenger to Jefferson* (Bobbs-Merrill, 1966).

[95] See James Morton Smith, *Freedom's Fetters: The Alien and Sedition Laws and American Civil Liberties* (Cornell University Press, 1956).

[96] The classic coverage of this episode is Zechariah Chafee, Jr., *Free Speech in the United States* (Harvard University Press, 1941).

[97] 341 U.S. 494.

[98] *Yates* v. *United States*, 354 U.S. 298 (1957).

[99] *Brandenburg* v. *Ohio*, 395 U.S. 444 (1969).

SUMMARY

1. First amendment freedoms—freedom of religion, freedom from the establishment of religion, freedom of speech, freedom of press, freedom of assembly and petition, and freedom of association—are at the very heart of the democratic process.

2. Roughly since World War I, the Supreme Court has become the primary agency for giving meaning to these constitutional restraints. And since 1925 these constitutional limits have been applied not only to Congress but to all governmental agencies—national, state, and local.

3. Clashes about First amendment freedoms are not profitably thought of as battles between the "good guys" and the "bad guys," or as dramas in which judges rush to the rescue of liberty. Rather, these are arguments over conflicting notions of what is good. Those who argue for restraint on First amendment freedoms do so for a variety of reasons.

4. Over the years, the Supreme Court has taken a practical approach to First amendment freedoms. It has refused to make them absolute rights above any kind of governmental regulation, direct or indirect, or to say that they must be preserved at whatever price. But the justices have recognized that a democratic society tampers with these freedoms at great peril. They have insisted upon compelling justification before permitting these rights to be limited. How compelling the justification is, in a free society, will always remain an open question.

FURTHER READING

T. BARTON CARTER, MARC A. FRANKLIN, and JAY B. WRIGHT. *The First Amendment and the Fourth Estate*, 3d ed. (Foundation Press, 1985).

ZECHARIAH CHAFEE, JR. *Free Speech in the United States* (Harvard University Press, 1941).

EDWARD DE GRAZIA and ROGER K. NEWMAN. *Banned Films: Movies, Censors and the First Amendment* (R. R. Bowker, 1982).

ITHIEL DE SOLA POOL. *Technologies of Freedom* (Belnap Press, 1983).

FRANKLYN S. HAIMAN. *Speech and Law in a Free Society* (University of Chicago, 1981).

NAT HENTOFF. *The First Freedom: The Tumultuous History of Free Speech in America* (Delacorte, 1980).

LEONARD W. LEVY. *The Establishment Clause: Religion and the First Amendment* (Macmillan, 1986).

MARTHA M. MCCARTHY. *A Delicate Balance: Church, State, and the Schools* (Phi Delta Kappan Educational Foundation, 1983).

JOHN STUART MILL. *Essay on Liberty*. First published in 1859, it is available in many editions, one of which is Arthur Burtt, ed., *The English Philosophers from Bacon to Mill* (Random House, 1939).

WILLIAM LEE MILLER. *The First Liberty: Religion and the American Republic* (Knopf, 1986).

DAVID M. O'BRIEN. *The Public's Right to Know: The Supreme Court and the First Amendment* (Praeger, 1981).

J. W. PELTASON. *Understanding the Constitution* 11th ed. (Holt, Rinehart & Winston, 1988).

BERNARD SCHWARTZ. *The Great Rights of Mankind: A History of the American Bill of Rights* (Oxford University Press, 1977).

WILLIAM W. VAN ALSTYNE. *Interpretations of the First Amendment* (Duke University Press, 1984).

CHAPTER 5

Equal Rights Under The Law

Consider again the ringing words of the Declaration of Independence: "We hold these truths to be self-evident, that all men are created equal, that they are endowed by their Creator with certain unalienable Rights, that among these are Life, Liberty, and the pursuit of Happiness. . . ." The Declaration does not talk about equality of white, Christian, or Anglo-Saxon men, but of all men. (Undoubtedly, if the Declaration were to be written today, the framers would speak of persons rather than men.) This creed of individual dignity and equality is older than our Declaration of Independence; its roots go back at least as far as the teachings of Judaism and Christianity.

Certain liberties are essential to the operation of democratic government. But these liberties are not merely means of attaining self-government; they are ends in themselves. They do not exist to protect the government; the government exists to protect them. Long ago they were called natural rights; today we speak of human rights—but the belief is still the same: the primacy of people over government and the dignity and worth of each individual.

Denial of equal rights not only negates the equality the Declaration of Independence asserts, but it is also contrary to the guarantees of the Constitution. The Constitution provides two ways of protecting civil rights: It ensures that government itself imposes no discriminatory barriers; and it grants the national and state governments authority to protect civil rights against interference by private individuals. This chapter is concerned with both problems.

EQUALITY AND EQUAL RIGHTS

Americans are committed to equality. Equality, however, is an elusive term and "few issues have sparked more controversy or held more sway over the course of history."[1] Part of the difficulty is that equality lacks precise meaning. The concept

[1] From Sidney Verba and Gary R. Orren, *Equality in America: The View from the Top* (Harvard University Press, 1985), p. 1, on which this section is based. See also Jennifer L. Hochschild, *What's Fair? American Beliefs about Distributive Justice* (Harvard University Press, 1981).

Women's History is Half of History

Lucretia Mott, Elizabeth Cady Stanton barred from this convention	Declaration of Sentiments, Seneca Falls	Sewing machine invented	Women's Rights Convention	Sojourner Truth	Women's Loyal League	Clara Barton, Mother Bickerdyke, nurses — Harriet Tubman leads raid
		Harriet Beecher Stowe, *Uncle Tom's Cabin*				

1840 ————————————————————————— **1860** —————

World Anti-slavery Convention	Irish immigration begins	Gold Rush		Dred Scott decision	Lincoln elected	Emancipation Proclamation
	Texas admitted to the Union			Harper's Ferry	Fort Sumter	

for which there is the greatest consensus, and that is most clearly written into the Constitution, is that everybody should have an *equality of opportunity* regardless of race, ethnic origin, religion, and, in recent years, sex. Ensuring this equality of opportunity is what we mean by the struggle for civil rights.

Another variation of the concept of equal opportunity is *equality of starting conditions*. There is not much of an equal opportunity if one person starting the race is born into a well-to-do family, lives in a quiet suburb, has good food, and gets a good education while another is born into a poor, broken family, lives in a slum neighborhood, and attends inferior schools. Thus, it is argued, if we are to have equality of opportunity in a meaningful sense we must compensate the disadvantaged to ensure that they have equality of opportunity.

Compensating persons so they may have equality of conditions can be, and is most often, accomplished in the United States by ensuring that individuals are not placed at a disadvantage because of prejudice or poverty. But such action sometimes shades into a concept of *equality among groups*. Traditional emphasis has been upon individual achievement. When large disparities in wealth and advantage exist among groups, as between blacks and whites or women and men, equality becomes a highly divisive political issue. The disadvantaged tend to emphasize those common traits that exclude them from the "mainstream." Under such conditions programs are likely to provide special help to people based upon their group memberships. These are among the most controversial current debates.

Finally, equality sometimes means *equality of results*. One perennial debate, especially among college students, is whether social justice and "genuine" equality can coexist in a nation in which some people have so much money and so many good things in life and others have so little. Socialists and some others argue that they cannot. Yet such a view has had little support in the United States. There is some consensus for guaranteeing a minimum floor below which no one should be allowed to fall, but our insisting on equality of results would greatly restrict or undermine equality of opportunity. The "American Dream" is not that everybody should have the same amount of material goods, but that all people should be able to hope, yearn, and strive to improve their lot and, especially, the opportunities for their children. Thus, whatever a person's economic status for the moment, that person should be able to think that things will get better and that hard work and risk taking will be rewarded.

It is within the context of these concerns for equality that we need to look at the struggle for civil rights. The first phase took up the first 200 years of our nation's existence. The struggle is not over yet, but we have largely achieved equality under the law. The basic ground rules provide equality of formal opportunity. Whether this is enough is a major issue of current domestic politics.

To put into perspective the court decisions, laws, and other kinds of governmental actions relating to civil rights for women, blacks, Hispanics, and native Americans, we review next the political and social contexts in which these constitutional issues

(Bennett for the St. Petersburg Times, State Legislatures, April 1984)

95

				Clara Barton, Red Cross		
"Battle Hymn of the Republic," Julia Ward Howe	Equal Rights Association		Frances Willard, Women's Christian Temperance Movement	Evaporated milk available	Radcliffe, Bryn Mawr	Mother Mary Jones, labor organizer

Emily
Dickinson

1880

| Lee surrenders
to Grant | 14th Amendments
makes blacks citizens
and adds the word
"male" to the
Constitution | 15th
Amendment—
black male
suffrage | Reconstruction | | | Civil Service
reform |

Lincoln
assassinated

Custer,
Little Big Horn

Transcontinental
railroad
completed

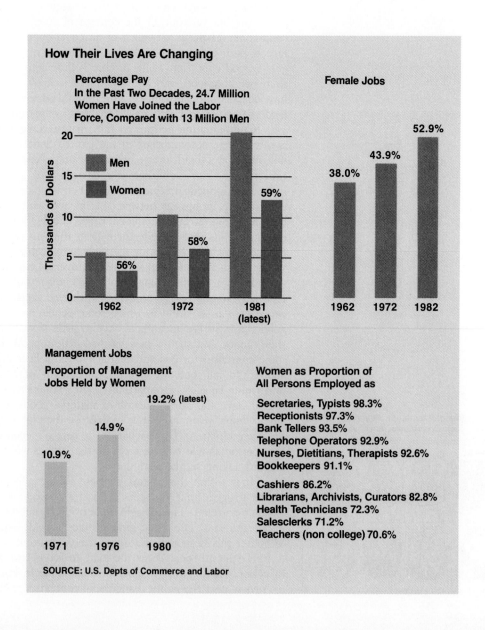

How Their Lives Are Changing

Percentage Pay
In the Past Two Decades, 24.7 Million
Women Have Joined the Labor
Force, Compared with 13 Million Men

Female Jobs

Men

Women

56%
58%
59%

1962
1972
1981
(latest)

Thousands of Dollars

38.0%
43.9%
52.9%

1962
1972
1982

Management Jobs

**Proportion of Management
Jobs Held by Women**

10.9%
14.9%
19.2% (latest)

1971
1976
1980

**Women as Proportion of
All Persons Employed as**

Secretaries, Typists 98.3%
Receptionists 97.3%
Bank Tellers 93.5%
Telephone Operators 92.9%
Nurses, Dietitians, Therapists 92.6%
Bookkeepers 91.1%

Cashiers 86.2%
Librarians, Archivists, Curators 82.8%
Health Technicians 72.3%
Salesclerks 71.2%
Teachers (non college) 70.6%

SOURCE: U.S. Depts of Commerce and Labor

International Council of Women   *Ladies Home Journal*

General Federation of Women's Clubs

National American Woman Suffrage Association

Susan B. Anthony

Jane Addams— Hull House

Florence Kelly, reformer

Charlotte Perkins Gilman, *Women and Economics*

Women's Trade Union League

Brandeis brief— protective legislation

1900

Samuel Gompers, American Federation of Labor

Populists

Immigration from Southern Europe

Battle of Wounded Knee

Progressive Era

Theodore Roosevelt

Panama Canal begun

are raised. Constitutional questions do not involve just a series of court decisions, laws, and constitutional amendments; they encompass the entire social, economic, and political system. Although the struggles of all groups are interwoven, they are not identical, so we comment briefly and separately on each of them. (Chapter 8 includes more detail on the movements behind these battles for legal equality.)

Women's Rights

The struggle for equal rights for women has long been intertwined with the battle to secure such rights for blacks (remember the obvious fact that half of black Americans are women). The Seneca Falls Women's Rights Convention (1848), which launched the women's movement, involved men and women who had long been active in the campaign to abolish slavery.

As the Civil War approached, women were urged to abandon their cause, at least temporarily, and devote all their energies to getting rid of slavery.[2] The Civil War brought the women's movement to a halt. The Fourteenth amendment even introduced into the Constitution a provision that overtly allowed discrimination against women: It provided that any state that kept *males* over 21 from voting should suffer a reduction of its representation in the House of Representatives. Women were no better served by the Fifteenth amendment. For a time, the Temperance Movement diverted attention away from women's rights as well.

By the turn of the century, however, a vigorous campaign was under way for women's suffrage within the states. The first victories came in western states. Wyoming led the way. As a territory, Wyoming had given women the right to vote: It is said that when members of Congress in Washington grumbled about this "petticoat provision," the Wyoming legislators replied that they would stay out of the Union 100 years rather than come in without women's suffrage. Congress gave in and admitted Wyoming to the Union, women's suffrage and all. By the end of World War I, over half the states had granted women the right to vote in some or all elections.

To suffragists this state-by-state approach seemed slow and uncertain. They wanted a decisive victory—a constitutional amendment that would, with one blow, force all states to allow qualified women to vote. Finally in 1920 Congress proposed the Nineteenth amendment. Opposition to its adoption and ratification was intertwined with opposition to the rights of blacks. Many southerners opposed the amendment: Not only would it extend the franchise to black women, but it might also bring federal officials to investigate elections to ensure that the amendment was

Women's suffrage parades and similar protest and promotion activities took place for years before the Nineteenth Amendment was finally ratified in 1920. (*AP/Wide World Photos*)

---

[2] Judith Hole and Ellen Levine, *Rebirth of Feminism* (Quadrangle, 1971). See also Ellen Carol DuBois, *Feminism and Suffrage: The Emergence of an Independent Women's Movement in America, 1848–1869* (Cornell University Press, 1978); and Joan Hoff-Wilson, "Women and the Constitution," *News for Teachers of Political Science* (American Political Science Association, Summer 1985), pp. 10–15.

| National Women's Party | Suffragists jailed for White House demonstration | Woman's Committee, National Council of Defense | Women get the vote | League of Women Voters | Alice Paul introduces Equal Rights Amendment (ERA) | Margaret Mead, *Coming of Age in Samoa* | The Flapper | Frances Perkins, Secretary of Labor | Frozen foods Introduced | Clare Booth Luce, *The Women* | Eleanor Roosevelt |

1920

| Woodrow Wilson | U.S. enters World War I | Treaty of Versailles | 19th Amendment ratified | Prohibition | Herbert Hoover | Depression | Stock market crash | FDR— New Deal |

being obeyed, which would thereby call attention to how blacks were being kept from voting.[3]

Senator James Vardman, Democrat from Mississippi, opposed the Nineteenth amendment and called for "repeal of the Fifteenth, the modification of the Fourteenth . . . , making this a government by white men, of white men, for all men."[4] But opposition to women's suffrage was not limited to southerners. Senator William Borah, a noted liberal Republican from Idaho, also opposed it, again on racial grounds: "There are 100,000 Japanese and Chinese women [in the Pacific states], and I have no particular desire to bestow suffrage upon them," he stated.[5]

With the ratification of the Nineteenth amendment in 1920, women won the right to vote. Still, women were denied equal pay and equal rights, and they suffered numerous legal disabilities imposed by both national and state laws. During the last several decades the struggle to secure the adoption of the Equal Rights Amendment has occupied much of the attention of the women's movement.[6] But there are other goals, and the political clout of women is being mobilized increasingly behind issues that range from pay, through pensions, to peace.

The Struggle for Racial Justice

Americans have had a special confrontation with the problems of race—before, during, and after the Civil War. As a result of the northern victory, the Thirteenth, Fourteenth, and Fifteenth amendments became part of the Constitution. Congress also passed a series of civil rights laws to implement these constitutional provisions and established such special programs as the Freedmen's Bureau to provide educational and social services for the freed slaves.

Before these programs had a significant effect, the southern white male political community was restored to power. By 1877 Reconstruction was ending. Northern political leaders abandoned blacks to their fate at the hands of their former white masters. The president no longer concerned himself with the enforcement of civil rights laws, and Congress enacted no new ones. The Supreme Court either declared old laws unconstitutional or interpreted them so narrowly that they were ineffective. The Court also gave such a limited construction to the Thirteenth, Fourteenth, and Fifteenth amendments that they failed to accomplish their intended purpose of protecting the rights of blacks.

[3] Alan P. Grimes, *Democracy and the Amendments to the Constitution* (D. C. Heath, 1979), pp. 90–91.

[4] Ibid.

[5] Ibid.

[6] See the National Commission on the Observance of International Women's Year, *An Official Report to the President, the Congress, and the People of the United States, The Spirit of Houston* (U.S. Government Printing Office, 1978).

WACS, WAVES, WASPS—Women's Service Corps	**800,000 women fired by aircraft companies**		**Dr. Spock**		**Title VII prohibits sex discrimination in employment**	**Executive Order mandates affirmative action**
Rosie the Riveter		**Suburbia**	**Mary McCarthy, The Group**	**Betty Friedan, The Feminine Mystique**		**The "Pill"**

1940   **1960**

Pearl Harbor	**Atomic bomb**	**Television**		**The New Frontier**	**Kennedy assassinated**	**Civil Rights Act**	**Vietnam**
			Korea	**March on Washington—**			**Peace movement**
	War ends		**Eisenhower**	**Martin Luther King**	**The Great Society**		

By 1900 white supremacy was unchallenged in the South, where most blacks lived. Blacks were kept from voting; they were forced to accept menial jobs; and they were denied educational opportunities. In 1896, in *Plessy* v. *Ferguson*, the Supreme Court gave constitutional sanction to government-imposed racial segregation.[7] Even if the Court had declared segregation unconstitutional, a decision so contrary to popular feeling and political realities would have had little impact. In 1896 blacks were lynched an average of one every four days, and few whites raised a voice in protest.

During World War I blacks began to migrate to northern cities to seek educational opportunities and jobs. These trends were accelerated by the New Deal and World War II, and the South, through urbanization and industrialization, became more like the rest of the nation. As migration of blacks out of the rural South into southern and northern cities shifted the racial composition of cities, the black vote became important in national elections. Although discrimination continued, there were more jobs and more social gains. Above all, these changes created a black middle class opposed to segregation as a symbol of servitude and a cause of inequality. By the middle of the twentieth century, urban blacks were active and politically powerful citizens. There was a growing, persistent, and insistent demand for the abolition of color barriers.

The national government begins to respond   Because of the special nature of the electoral college and the pattern of our political system, by the 1930s it became more difficult for a person living in the white House—or anyone hoping to live there—to ignore the aspirations of blacks. The commitment of our presidents to the cause of equal protection became translated into the appointment of federal judges more sympathetic to a broad construction of the Thirteenth, Fourteenth, and Fifteenth amendments.

In the 1930s blacks began resorting to lawsuits to secure their rights, and especially to challenge the doctrine of segregation. They emphasized litigation because they had no alternative; they lacked sufficient political power to make their demands effective before either state legislatures or Congress. By the 1950s civil rights litigation began to have an impact. Under the leadership of the Supreme Court, federal judges started to use the Fourteenth amendment to reverse earlier decisions that rendered it and federal legislation ineffective. The Court outlawed all forms of government-imposed segregation and struck down most of the devices that had been used by state and local authorities to keep blacks from voting.[8]

Rosa Parks, a black Montgomery seamstress, was arrested on February 22, 1956, on charges of boycotting buses in a mass protest against bus segregation. Indictments were returned against 115 defendants accused of taking an active part in the eleven-week boycott. Thousands of blacks had refused to ride the buses since December 5, 1955, when Mrs. Parks was fined $14 for refusing to move to the "Negro Section" of the bus. Mrs. Parks was sentenced to fourteen days in jail in lieu of the fine. (*UPI/Bettmann Newsphotos*)

[7] 163 U.S. 537.

[8] For a general history of Supreme Court decisions affecting the constitutional rights of blacks, see Loren Miller, *The Petitioners* (Meridian Books, 1967). For a history of the political role of blacks, see Robert P. Turner, *Up to the Front Line: Blacks in the American Political System* (Kennikat Press, 1975).

International
Women's Year

National Women's
Strike

National Women's
Conference, Houston

National
Organization
for Women
(NOW)

Gloria Steinem,
Ms. Magazine

ERA passed
by Congress

Title IX
prohibits sex
discrimination
in education

Women's Educational
Equity Act Passed

Supreme Court
legalizes abortion

Episcopalians
ordain women

Kassebaum elected
to Senate

ERA ratification
deadline extended

1980

Student
unrest

Resurrection
City

Cambodia

Watergate

Carter

Iran

Nixon

Moon
landing

Mid-East peace talks

Adapted from COMMENT, A Research/Action Report on Wo/Men, June 1980

Presidents used their executive authority to fight segregation in the armed services and the federal bureaucracy, and they directed the Department of Justice to enforce whatever civil rights laws were available.

As the 1950s came to a close, the emerging national consensus in favor of governmental action to protect civil rights, and the growing political voice of blacks, began to have some impact on Congress. In 1957 Congress overrode a southern filibuster in the Senate and enacted the first federal civil rights laws since Reconstruction. During the 1950s the conflict was primarily an attempt by the national government to compel southern state governments to stop segregating blacks into inferior schools, parks, libraries, houses, and jobs. Then came the summer of 1963.

A turning point   A decade after the Supreme Court declared public school segregation unconstitutional, most black children in the South still attended segregated schools. In Northern cities segregation in housing and education remained the established pattern as well. Most legal barriers in the path of equal rights had fallen. Yet most black Americans still could not buy houses where they wanted, secure the jobs they needed, find educational opportunities for their children, or walk on the streets without being insulted. What had once been thought of as a southern problem was recognized as a national problem. By 1963 the struggles in the courtrooms were being supplemented by a massive social, economic, and political movement.

The black revolt of 1963 did not come unannounced, and its immediate background was not the struggle to desegregate the schools. In one sense it began when the first black slave was educated 300 years ago. Its more recent origin was in Montgomery, Alabama, when seamstress Rosa Parks, who refused to give up a seat in the front of a bus, was taken from the bus. The black community of Montgomery responded by boycotting city buses. The boycott worked. And Montgomery produced a charismatic national civil rights leader: Reverend Martin Luther King, Jr. Through his Southern Christian Leadership Conference and his doctrine of nonviolent resistance, Dr. King gave a new dimension to the struggle. By the early 1960s new organizational resources came into existence in almost every city to support and sponsor sit-ins, freedom rides, live-ins, and nonviolent demonstrations.

The forces of social discontent exploded in the summer of 1963. The explosion started with a demonstration in Birmingham, Alabama, which was countered by the use of fire hoses, police dogs, and mass arrests. It ended in a march in Washington, D.C., where at least 250,000 people heard Dr. King speak in person and countless millions of others listened and watched him over television. By the time the summer was over, there was hardly a city, North or South, that had not had demonstrations, protests, or sit-ins; some also had violence. This direct action had some effect: Civil rights ordinances were enacted in many cities, and more schools were desegregated that fall than in any year since 1956. At the national level, President John

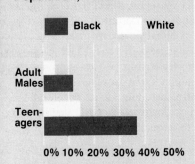

Unemployment in the Civilian Population, 1988

Black   White

Adult Males

Teen-agers

0% 10% 20% 30% 40% 50%

SOURCE: *Employment and Earnings*, U.S. Department of Labor Bureau of Statistics, March, 1988.

First Woman Supreme Court justice appointed

ERA Deadline passed without ratification

ERA reintroduced in Congress

First woman Geraldine Ferraro, nominated as vice-presidential candidate of a major political party (the Democrats)

State of Washington adopts comparable worth for some state employees

Congress reverses impact of Grove Supreme Court decision that had limited scope of major federal civil rights laws

Reagan

Challenger tragedy

Reagan-Gorbachev talks-INF Treaty

Bush

1990

Kennedy urged Congress to enact a comprehensive civil rights bill. Late in 1963, the nation's grief over the assassination of President Kennedy, who had become identified with civil rights goals, added political fuel to the drive for federal action.[9] President Lyndon Johnson gave civil rights legislation the highest priority. On July 2, 1964, after months of debate, he signed into law the Civil Rights Act of 1964.[10]

Two societies?   At the close of the 1960s the legal phases of the civil rights movement had about come to a close. As "things got better," discontent grew. When blacks had been completely subjugated, they had lacked resources to defend themselves. Then, as is true of almost all social revolutions, as conditions began to improve, demands became more and more insistent. Millions of impoverished black Americans, like white Americans before them, demonstrated growing impatience with the discrimination that remained. This volatile situation gave way to racial violence and disorders. By 1965, the year of the Watts riots in Los Angeles, racial disorders were clearly becoming a part of the American scene. In 1966 and 1967 the disorders increased in scope and intensity. The Detroit riot in July 1967 was the worst such disturbance in modern American history.[11]

President Johnson appointed a special Advisory Commission on Civil Disorders to investigate the origins of the disorders and to recommend measures to prevent or contain such disasters in the future. When the commission (called the Kerner Commission after its chair, then Governor Otto Kerner of Illinois) issued its report, it said in stark, clear language: "What white Americans have never fully understood— but what the Negro can never forget—is that white society is deeply implicated in the ghetto. *White institutions created it, white institutions maintain it, and white society condones it.*" The basic conclusion of the commission was that "our nation is moving toward two societies, one black, one white—separate and unequal" and that "only a commitment to national action on an unprecedented scale" could change this trend.

The commission made sweeping recommendations on jobs, education, housing, and improving the welfare system. But the Vietnam War, the partial calming of racial tensions, and a growing skepticism about the effectiveness of governmental action diverted attention from these recommendations, at least temporarily.

[9] For treatments of John F. Kennedy and civil rights policy, see Carl M. Brauer, *John F. Kennedy and the Second Reconstruction* (Columbia University Press, 1977). See also Joel D. Aberbach and Jack L. Walker, "The Meanings of Black Power," *American Political Science Review* (June 1970), pp. 367–88, and Harris Wofford, *Of Kennedys & Kings: Making Sense of the Sixties* (Farrar, Straus & Giroux, 1980).

[10] Charles and Barbara Whalen, *The Longest Debate: A Legislative History of the 1964 Civil Rights Act* (Sevenlocks Press, 1985).

[11] Aldon D. Morris, *The Origins of the Civil Rights Movement: Black Communities Organizing for Change* (The Free Press/Macmillan, 1985), and James Farmer, *Laying Bare the Heart: An Autobiography of the Civil Rights Movement* (Arbor House, 1985).

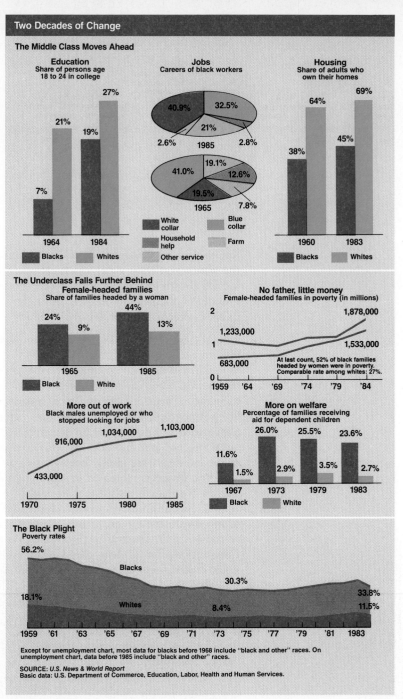

Two Decades of Change

The Middle Class Moves Ahead

Education
Share of persons age 18 to 24 in college

- 1964: Blacks 7%, Whites 21%
- 1984: Blacks 19%, Whites 27%

Blacks / Whites

Jobs
Careers of black workers

1985:
- White collar 32.5%
- Blue collar 21%
- Farm 2.8%
- Other service 2.6%
- Household help 40.9%

1965:
- White collar 19.1%
- Blue collar 12.6%
- Farm 7.8%
- Other service 19.5%
- Household help 41.0%

White collar / Blue collar / Household help / Farm / Other service

Housing
Share of adults who own their homes

- 1960: Blacks 38%, Whites 64%
- 1983: Blacks 45%, Whites 69%

Blacks / Whites

The Underclass Falls Further Behind

Female-headed families
Share of families headed by a woman

- 1965: Black 24%, White 9%
- 1985: Black 44%, White 13%

Black / White

No father, little money
Female-headed families in poverty (in millions)

- 1959: 683,000
- 1984: 1,878,000 and 1,533,000
- 1,233,000

At last count, 52% of black families headed by women were in poverty. Comparable rate among whites: 27%.

1959 '64 '69 '74 '79 '84

More out of work
Black males unemployed or who stopped looking for jobs

- 1970: 433,000
- 1975: 916,000
- 1980: 1,034,000
- 1985: 1,103,000

More on welfare
Percentage of families receiving aid for dependent children

- 1967: Black 11.6%, White 1.5%
- 1973: Black 26.0%, White 2.9%
- 1979: Black 25.5%, White 3.5%
- 1983: Black 23.6%, White 2.7%

Black / White

The Black Plight
Poverty rates

- Blacks: 1959 56.2%, 30.3%, 1983 33.8%
- Whites: 1959 18.1%, 8.4%, 1983 11.5%

1959 '61 '63 '65 '67 '69 '71 '73 '75 '77 '79 '81 1983

Except for unemployment chart, most data for blacks before 1968 include "black and other" races. On unemployment chart, data before 1985 include "black and other" races.

SOURCE: *U.S. News & World Report*
Basic data: U.S. Department of Commerce, Education, Labor, Health and Human Services.

From U.S. News & World Report, Inc., Jan. 31, 1983.

Today, legal barriers have been lowered, if not removed, by civil rights legislation, executive orders, and judicial decisions. Blacks can vote, get a meal where they want, and stay at hotels. And hundreds of thousands of them have entered the middle class. Although some still find ways to circumvent or obstruct the force of certain civil rights laws, especially those that apply to housing, by and large the actions by governments in the 1960s did open the legal system and provide blacks with equal rights under the laws. Yet, said James Farmer, a civil rights activist: "They were victories largely for the middle class—those who could travel, entertain in restaurants and stay in hotels. Those victories did not change life conditions

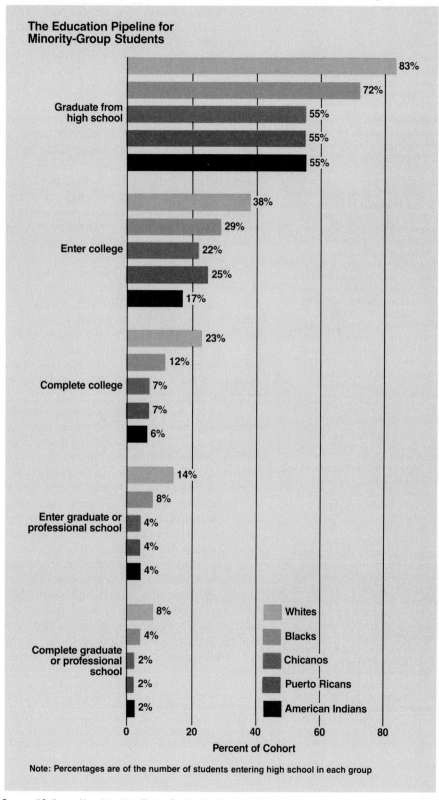

The Education Pipeline for Minority-Group Students

Graduate from high school
- 83%
- 72%
- 55%
- 55%
- 55%

Enter college
- 38%
- 29%
- 22%
- 25%
- 17%

Complete college
- 23%
- 12%
- 7%
- 7%
- 6%

Enter graduate or professional school
- 14%
- 8%
- 4%
- 4%
- 4%

Complete graduate or professional school
- 8%
- 4%
- 2%
- 2%
- 2%

Whites
Blacks
Chicanos
Puerto Ricans
American Indians

Percent of Cohort

Note: Percentages are of the number of students entering high school in each group

Source: "Colleges Urged to Alter Tests, Grading for Benefit of Minority-Group Students," *Chronicle of High School Education*, February 3, 1982, p. 11.

for the mass of blacks who are still poor."[12] A third of all black families still live below the poverty level—cut off from white society and alienated from the black middle class.

"I Have a Dream . . ."

Five score years ago, a great American in whose symbolic shadow we stand, signed the Emancipation Proclamation. This momentous decree came as a great beacon light of hope to millions of Negro slaves who had been seared in the flames of withering injustice. It came as a joyous daybreak to end the long night of captivity. But one hundred years later, we must face the tragic fact that the Negro is still not free. One hundred years later, the life of the Negro is still sadly crippled by the manacles of segregation and the chains of discrimination. One hundred years later, the Negro lives on a lonely island of poverty in the midst of a vast ocean of material prosperity. One hundred years later, the Negro is still languished in the corners of American society and finds himself an exile in his own land. So we have come here today to dramatize an appalling condition. . . .

I have a dream that one day this nation will rise up and live out the true meaning of its creed: "We hold these truths to be self-evident; that all men are created equal."

I have a dream that one day on the red hills of Georgia the sons of former slaves and the sons of former slaveowners will be able to sit down together at the table of brotherhood.

I have a dream that one day even the state of Mississippi, a desert state sweltering with the heat of injustice and oppression, will be transformed into an oasis of freedom and justice.

I have a dream that my four little children will one day live in a nation where they will not be judged by the color of their skin but by the content of their character. . . .

Martin Luther King, Jr., August 28, 1963, at the Lincoln Memorial, Washington, D.C., speaking to 250,000 persons who participated in a "march for jobs and freedom."

Native Americans

Of the 1,418,195 people who designated themselves as Indians (or native Americans, as many prefer to be called) in the 1980 census, 680,000 live on or near a reservation and are enrolled as members of one of the 280 tribes within the continental United States or one of the 200 native Alaskan communities served by the Bureau of Indian Affairs. Indian tribes within the United States are wards of the nation. They are not states; nor are they nations possessed of the full attributes of sovereignty. Rather, they are a separate people with power to regulate their own internal affairs, subject to congressional supervision. Congress has special responsibilities to American Indians. States are precluded from regulating or taxing the tribes unless authorized to do so by Congress.[13]

By act of Congress, Indians are American citizens, and by act of the states in which they live, they have the right to vote. Off reservations they have the same rights as any other Americans. If they are enrolled members of a recognized tribe, they are entitled to certain benefits created by law and by treaty. These benefits are administered by the Bureau of Indian Affairs of the Department of the Interior. Moreover, Indians who belong to these federally recognized tribes have preference in employment within the Bureau, a preference the Supreme Court upheld as a grant not to a "discrete racial group, but, rather, as members of quasi-sovereign tribal entities. . . .[14]

As a result of the growing militancy of native Americans and a greater national awareness of the concerns of minorities, more Americans are aware that most Indians live in poverty. Congress's Office of Technology Assessment reports that American Indians "are in far worse health than the rest of the population, dying earlier and suffering disproportionately from alcoholism, accidents, diabetes and pneumonia."[15] Some reservations lack adequate health care facilities, educational opportunities, decent housing, and jobs. Congress has started to compensate native Americans for past injustices and to provide more opportunities for the development of tribal economic independence. Judges are also showing a greater vigilance in the enforcement of Indian treaty rights.

The struggle for civil rights has by no means been limited to women, blacks, and native Americans. As each new wave of immigrants arrived, it was considered suspect by those who arrived earlier—all the more so if its members were not white or English speaking. Formal barriers of law and informal ones of custom have combined to deny equal rights. But as groups have established themselves, first economically, then politically, most of these barriers have been swept away and constitutionally guaranteed rights asserted. We discuss some of these groups next.

[12] James Farmer in Rochelle L. Stanfield, "Black Complaints Haven't Translated into Political Organization and Power," *National Journal* (June 14, 1980), p. 465. Alphonso Pinkey, *The Myth of Black Progress* (Cambridge University Press, 1984), argues that the failure of blacks to make greater progress is due to white racism; Julius Wilson, *The Declining Significance of Race*, 2nd ed. (University of Chicago Press, 1984), argues to the contrary that the problems are those of class, not of race.

[13] Vine Deloria, Jr. and Clifford M. Lytle, *The Past and Future of American Indian Sovereignty* (Pantheon Books, 1984).

[14] *Morton v. Mancari*, 417 U.S. 535 (1974). See also Theodore W. Taylor, *The Bureau of Indian Affairs* (Westview Press, 1984).

[15] Spencer Rich, "Native Americans, They Can Still Get Free Health Care If They're Indian Enough," *The Washington Post National Weekly Edition* (July 14, 1986), p. 34.

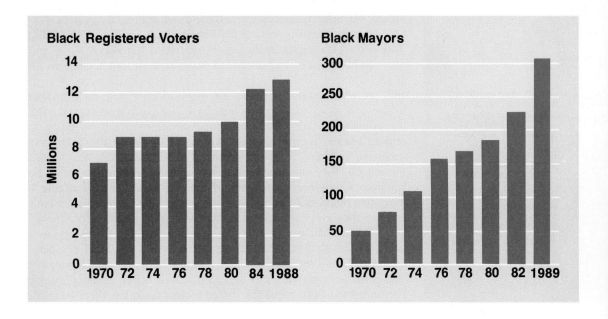

Black Registered Voters

Millions

14
12
10
8
6
4
2
0

1970 72 74 76 78 80 84 1988

Black Mayors

300
250
200
150
100
50
0

1970 72 74 76 78 80 82 1989

Martin Luther King, Jr., at the Lincoln Memorial on August 28, 1963. (*UPI/Bettmann Newsphotos*)

Hispanics

Hispanics "are among the world's most complex groupings of human beings. Most . . . are white, millions . . . are mestizos, nearly half a million in the United States are black or mulatto."[16] The largest group consists of 8 million Mexican-Americans, often called Chicanos. A third of them are descended from citizens living in Mexican territory annexed to the United States in 1848. The rest have come to the United States in increasing numbers since 1920. Most live in Arizona, Texas, New Mexico, and California, but many now live in other parts of the nation as well. They are being joined by millions of "undocumented aliens" who cross our southern borders in search of jobs.

The second largest group of Hispanics consists of the 2 million Puerto Ricans who reside on the mainland, primarily in the "barrios" of New York, Chicago, and other northern cities. Puerto Ricans are in worse economic shape than any other Hispanic group. They retain close ties with Puerto Rico and move back and forth from the island to the mainland. The politics of the Commonwealth of Puerto Rico as it debates whether to retain its special relationship with the United States, become a state, or become an independent nation are of great interest to Puerto Ricans living on the mainland.

The third subgroup consists of about 800,000 persons who fled from Castro's Cuba early in the 1960s, and a second wave of refugees who fled in the 1980s. These Cubans, who live mainly in south Florida, include a substantial number of well-educated, successful businesspeople and professionals. The fourth group includes a rapidly growing number of refugees from other nations in Central and South America who presently number around 2 million. This number is likely to grow as economic turmoil and political repression in that part of the world increase.

Hispanics are our fastest-growing minority: Seventeen million Hispanics live in our country today, as compared with about 27 million blacks. By the end of this century more than 40 million Hispanics could well be living in the United

[16] Valdes Y. Tapia, "Hispanics Need to Unite to End Their Exile at Home," *The Denver Post* (July 19, 1980), p. 7.

A few years ago over 2000 Indians paraded past the White House on their way to the Washington Monument. This climaxed a five-month trek, called the "Longest Walk," to protest discrimination. (*UPI/Bettmann Newsphotos*)

States; Martinez is already one of our most common surnames.[17] We have the fourth largest Spanish-speaking population of any country in this hemisphere. New York is the fifth largest Spanish-speaking city in the world.

To black power has been added brown power—sometimes as an ally, sometimes as an opponent. Yet not only do many Hispanics lack even the patronizing ties with the white power structure that provided some help for blacks—at least prior to the civil rights movement—they have also been handicapped because English, the primary language of mainstream America, is not their native tongue. Until recent decades "no provision whatsoever was made for the education of Mexican-American children" in the Southwest. "When eventually they were allowed into the schools, they were segregated from Anglo children because of their language handicap. Considered by school authorities to be children of an inferior race, they were often punished for speaking Spanish, heard their names involuntarily Anglicized, and saw their cultural background systematically ignored in textbooks."[18]

Taking their cue from blacks, Hispanics are becoming increasingly active in politics, although they do not yet register or vote in significant numbers as compared to blacks.[19] In Los Angeles County, home of 2 million Hispanics, there is not one Hispanic supervisor and only one school board member. And even though Hispanics total 7 percent of the United States population, there are only ten Hispanic members of the 435 member U.S. House of Representatives. However, this situation is beginning to change: Hispanic mayors preside in San Antonio, Denver, Miami, and Tampa; New Mexico had an Hispanic governor recently; and the number of Hispanics in other leadership positions is growing. The Mexican-American Legal Defense and Education Fund, the Puerto Rican Legal Defense and Education Fund, and the League of United Latin American Citizens (LULAC) are becoming increasingly active.

High on the Hispanic agenda is support for bilingual and bicultural education. In 1974, in *Lau* v. *Nichols*, a case involving Chinese students in San Francisco, the Supreme Court ruled that Title VI of the 1964 Civil Rights Act requires a school district to take steps to open instructional programs and overcome language difficulties whenever it has a substantial number of non-English-speaking students.[20] Many Hispanics actively support these programs, especially those providing for instruction in Spanish. Such programs, they argue, not only assist Hispanic children in gaining an education, but help preserve their heritage. (Opponents of bilingual education argue that fluency in English is essential for success in American society, and that many bilingual programs retard the learning of English.) Hispanics have also worked to amend civil rights laws to protect the rights of language minorities. Clearly, as the political position of Hispanics becomes more important in the years ahead, governments will be even more responsive to their claims.

Asian Americans

The term "Asian" describes individuals from many different countries and many different ethnic backgrounds. Moreover, most people from Asian backgrounds do not think of themselves as "Asians" but rather as Americans of Chinese, Japanese, Vietnamese, Cambodian, and so on, ancestry.

The Chinese were the first Asians to come to the United States. Beginning in 1847, when young male peasants came to get away from poverty and to work in our mines, on our railroads, and in our agricultural fields, the Chinese ran into

[17] Ibid.

[18] Alan Pifer, *Annual Report of the Carnegie Corporation of New York* (1979), p. 16.

[19] Jesus Rangel, "U.S. Puerto Rican Need Debated in Island Parley," *The New York Times* (June 3, 1985), p. 11

[20] 414 U.S. 563 (1974).

economic and cultural fears of the white majority who did not understand them or their culture. Facing this, and considering their intentions to return home, the Chinese did not try to assimilate but instead gravitated to "Chinatowns."

Discriminatory immigration and naturalization restrictions, imposed beginning in 1882, were strengthened in the following years and were not removed until the end of World War II. Since that time the Chinese have moved into the mainstream of American society, and they are beginning to move into politics.

The Japanese first migrated to Hawaii in the 1860s and then into California in the 1880s. Most remained in the west coast states. By the beginning of the twentieth century they faced overt public hostility. In 1905 labor leaders organized the Japanese and Korean Exclusion League and in 1906 the San Francisco Board of Education excluded all Chinese, Japanese, and Korean children from neighborhood schools. Some western states passed laws denying aliens ineligible to become citizens, that is persons of Asian ancestry, the right to own land. During World War II anti-Japanese hysteria provoked the incarceration of west coast Japanese, most of whom were American citizens guilty of no crimes, into prison camps, the largest of which was Manzanar, at Tule Lake, California. Japanese property was confiscated or sold at confiscatory rates. Following the war, the exclusionary acts were repealed, and, by Congressional, presidential, and court action, laws designed to keep Japanese-Americans from participating fully in American economic and political life were set aside. In 1988 President Reagan signed a law providing $20,000 restitution to each of the approximately 60,000 surviving internees.

Koreans are concentrated in southern California, Honolulu, and New York City. Until recently, like other Asian-Americans, they faced discrimination in jobs and housing. A Korean middle class is growing: Many Koreans are entering the learned professions, while many others continue operating their small family businesses such as dry cleaners, florists, and small grocers.[21]

When Filipinos first came to the United States they were considered nationals, because the United States then owned their native country. Nonetheless, they were denied their rights to full citizenship and faced discrimination, including Anti-Filipino riots in the state of Washington in 1928 and later in California, where one-third of the approximately 750,000 Filipinos live.[22] Their economic status has improved, but their influence in politics remains as small as their numbers.

The newest Asian group consists of IndoChinese refugees from Vietnam, Laos, and Cambodia, who first came to the United States in April and May 1975 and settled in California's Los Angeles, Orange, and San Diego counties. Although this group includes middle-class people who left during the fall of Saigon, it also consists of large numbers of "boat people," mostly peasants in their homelands, who came to our shores without any financial resources. In a relatively short time most have established themselves economically. Although they are starting to have political influence—most of them have apparently registered as Republicans—they remain socially and economically segregated and have not been in the United States long enough to become an effective part of the political process.

In January 1983 three Japanese-Americans who were jailed during World War II for resisting internment on the West Coast successfully sued the United States for damages and the overturn of their 1942 convictions. They claimed that the army lied about possible security threats. Minoru Yasui of Denver (center) said at a press conference, "I remember rattling in a stinking cell in Multnomah County Jail, Portland, Oregon. It could be justified if we can correct the injustices." Fred Korematsu of Oakland, California, is at left, and Gordon Hirabayashi of Seattle is at right. (*UPI/Bettmann Newsphotos*)

EQUAL PROTECTION UNDER THE LAWS—WHAT DOES IT MEAN?

The Fourteenth amendment declares: "No state [including any subdivision thereof] shall . . . deny to any person within its jurisdiction the equal protection of the laws." Although there is no **equal protection clause** limiting the national government,

[21] Won Moo Hurh, *Korean Immigrants in America* (Fairleigh Dickinson University Press, 1984).

[22] Antonio J. A. Pido, *The Filipinos in America: Macro/Micro Dimensions of Immigration and Integration* (Center for Migration Studies of New York, 1986).

the Fifth amendment's due process clause has been understood to impose the same restraints on the national government.

The Constitution does not prevent the government from making distinctions among people, because it could not legislate without doing so. What the Constitution forbids is *unreasonable* classifications. In general, a classification is unreasonable when there is no relation between the classes it creates and permissible governmental goals. A law prohibiting redheads from voting, for example, would be unreasonable. On the other hand, laws denying to persons under 18 the right to vote, to marry without the permission of their parents, or to apply for a license to drive a car seem to have some rationale (at least to most persons over 18).

One of the most troublesome constitutional issues is how to distinguish between a reasonable and an unreasonable classification. The Supreme Court has developed a variety of tests: rational basis, suspect classifications, quasisuspect classifications, and fundamental rights.

The Rational Basis Test

The traditional test to determine whether a law complies with the equal protection requirement places the burden of proof on those attacking it. If any facts justify a classification, it will be sustained: "It's enough that the state action be rationally based and free from invidious discrimination. . . . It does not offend the Constitution because the classification is not made with mathematical nicety or because in practice it results in some inequality."[23] For example, it was held that Illinois could exempt individuals from personal property taxes but impose such taxes on corporations.

Usually if the Supreme Court chooses to apply this **rational basis test,** the law in question will be sustained. Occasionally, however, a state law fails to meet even the minimal standards of this test—as when Alaska was told it could not give more from its surplus revenues to old-time citizens of the state than it gives to newcomers, and when a city was told it could not require a special use permit for group homes for mentally retarded people when it did not require such a permit for other multiple-dwelling facilities.[24]

The Supreme Court applies a more stringent standard than the rational basis test when a law is challenged under the equal protection clause in three situations: when a suspect classification is involved, when a quasisuspect classification is involved, and when a fundamental right is involved.

Suspect Classifications

A suspect class is a class historically suffering disabilities, subjected to purposeful unequal treatment in the past, or relegated by society to a position of such political powerlessness as to require extraordinary judicial protection.[25] Race and national origin are **suspect classifications.** So is religion, although there is no specific Supreme Court decision to this effect, probably because states have seldom classified people according to religion. Alienage is another suspect classification with respect to state (not national) laws' imposing *political* disabilities upon aliens.

When a law involves a suspect classification, the normal presumption of constitutionality is reversed. It is not sufficient that the law be a reasonable means to handle a particular problem. Such laws are subject to strict scrutiny. The Supreme Court must be persuaded both that there is a "compelling public interest" to justify such a classification and that there is no other, less restrictive way to accomplish this compelling public purpose.

Some Recent Governmental Actions Declared Unconstitutional by the Supreme Court Because of Sex Discrimination*

Provisions of social security laws providing benefits to families with unemployed fathers but not unemployed mothers.

A state law giving sons child support from their fathers until they are 21, but daughters only until they are 18.

A state law prohibiting the sale of beer to males under 21, but to females under 18.

A state law providing that husbands, but not wives, may be required to pay alimony.

A state law excluding males from enrolling in a professional nursing program, designed for women, offered by a public university.

* The Constitution protects men as well as women from discrimination because of sex.

[23] *Dandridge* v. *Williams*, 397 U.S. 471 (1970).
[24] *Zobel* v. *Williams*, 457 U.S. 55 (1982), and *Cleburne* v. *Cleburne Living Center*, 473 U.S. 432 (1985).
[25] *San Antonio School District* v. *Rodriguez*, 411 U.S. 1 (1973).

Quasisuspect Classifications: Illegitimacy and Sex

Some have argued that laws imposing disabilities on illegitimate children should be subject to the same severe tests as laws based on race. The Supreme Court has been unwilling to go that far. However, in view of the long history of treating illegitimate children less favorably than legitimate ones, the Court has subjected laws dealing with illegitimate children to a "heightened level" of scrutiny only slightly less exacting than those applied to suspect classifications such as race.

What of classifications based on sex? Not until 1971 was any classification based on sex declared unconstitutional. Prior to that time many laws that purported to provide special protection for women—such as one in Michigan forbidding any woman other than the wife or daughter of a tavern owner to serve as barmaid— were upheld. As Justice William Brennan wrote for the Court in 1973: "There can be no doubt that our nation has had a long and unfortunate history of sex discrimination. Traditionally such discrimination was rationalized by an attitude of 'romantic paternalism' which, in practical effect put women, not on a pedestal, but in a cage."[26]

Today the Court's view is that sex classifications, although not as suspect as those based on race, are subject to "heightened scrutiny." To sustain a classification based on sex, the burden is on the government to show that it serves "important governmental objectives" and is substantially related to these objectives. Treating women differently from men (or vice versa) is forbidden when supported by no more substantial justification than "archaic and overbroad generalizations," "old notions," and "the role-typing society has long imposed upon women."[27] If the government's objective is "to protect members of one sex because they are presumed to suffer from an inherent handicap or to be innately inferior," that object itself is illegitimate.[28]

In recent years the Supreme Court has struck down most, but not all, laws brought before it alleged to discriminate against women. (Those the Court has refused to strike down include the all-male draft and veterans' preference in civil service jobs.) The Court has also sustained some legislation said to discriminate against men. Overall, "Except for the right to vote, U.S. women have experienced more improvement in their legal status in the last twenty years than in the last two hundred."[29]

In summary classifications based on sex, although not suspect, require considerable justification before the Court will sustain them.

Is poverty a suspect classification?   The Supreme Court has been pressed to treat poverty as a suspect class, but it "has never held that financial need alone identifies a suspect class for purposes of equal protection analysis."[30] Thus, a state may rely on property taxes for funds for schools even if this means that schools in "rich" districts spend more per pupil than those in poor districts.

One recent and controversial case involved the so-called Hyde Amendment to the Medicaid program, which Congress has adopted every year since 1976. Medicaid is a joint national-state program that reimburses the poor for certain medical costs. The Hyde Amendment, in the form considered by the Court, prohibited the use of any federal funds to pay for abortions except when the life of the mother would be endangered or for victims of rape or incest. As a result, poor women could get reimbursed for the costs of having children, but not for abortions, except

---

Some Recent Governmental Actions Alleged to be Unconstitutional Discriminations Against Persons Because of Sex, but Sustained by the Supreme Court

A state law granting a property tax exemption to widows but not to widowers.

A naval regulation giving women thirteen years to be promoted or discharged, but giving male officers only nine years.

A provision giving larger social security retirement benefits to women than to men.

A federal law requiring registration for a possible draft for males but not for females.

---

[26] *Frontiero* v. *Richardson*, 411 U.S. 677 (1973).

[27] *Califano* v. *Webster*, 430 U.S. 313 (1977).

[28] *Mississippi* v. *University of Women* v. *Hogan*, 458 U.S. 718 (1982).

[29] Joan Hoff-Wilson, "Women and the Constitution," *News for Teachers of Political Science* (American Political Science Association, Summer 1985, p. 14). (Italics deleted from the original.)

[30] *San Antonio School District* v. *Rodriguez*, 411 U.S. 1 (1973).

in limited circumstances. In *Maher* v. *Roe* the Court ruled (by a vote of five to four) that because poverty is not a suspect classification, the appropriate constitutional test is whether the legislation is rationally related to a legitimate governmental objective. The majority concluded that the congressional provision bears a rational relationship to the government's legitimate interest in protecting the fetus.[31]

Is age a suspect or quasisuspect classification?   Age is not a suspect or quasisuspect class. Historically our laws and practices have commonly made distinctions based on age: to get a driver's license, to get married without parental consent, to attend schools, to buy alcoholic drinks, and so on. Many governmental institutions have age-specific programs: for senior citizens, for adult students, for midcareer persons. Although the Supreme Court has not made age a classification requiring extra judicial scrutiny under the equal protection clause, Congress is responding to "Gray Power," by treating age more and more as a protected category. The Congress has made it illegal for governments or interstate employers to discriminate on the basis of old age unless they can convincingly demonstrate that age is related to proper job performance. As the law presently stands, there can be no mandatory retirement age for federal civil servants, and no requirement less than 70 years of age for others. Congress has also provided that no federal funds can be given to any program or activity that denies benefits to persons because of age, except where age is a factor in the normal operations of the program or activity, such as a program created specifically for children.

Fundamental Rights

In addition to subjecting state regulations to strict close scrutiny when they touch upon suspect classifications, the Court also does so when the laws impinge on "fundamental rights." However, the justices are not too clear about what makes a right fundamental. As Justice Lewis Powell explained in *San Antonio School District* v. *Rodriguez* (1973), it is not the social importance of the right nor the justices' conclusions about the significance of the right that determines whether or not it is fundamental, but whether it *is* explicitly or *implicitly guaranteed by the Constitution*. Under this test the right to travel has been held to be fundamental, along with the right to vote and such First amendment rights as the right to associate for the advancement of political beliefs. However, the right to get an education, or to receive housing or welfare benefits, or to have an abortion have not been held to be fundamental. Important as many feel these rights to be, they are not guaranteed by the Constitution. Nor do any specific constitutional provisions protect these rights from governmental regulation.

HOW TO PROVE DISCRIMINATION

Does the fact that a law or a regulation has a differential impact on persons of different races by itself establish that it is unconstitutional? In one of its more important decisions of recent years, *Washington* v. *Davis* (1976), the Supreme Court stated: "The invidious quality of a law claimed to be racially discriminatory must ultimately be traced to a racially discriminatory *purpose*."[32] Or, as the Court said in a later case: "The Fourteenth Amendment guarantees equal laws, not equal results."[33]

[31] *Maher* v. *Roe*, 432 U.S. 464 (1977).

[32] *Washington* v. *Davis*, 426 U.S. 229 (1976), and *Hunter* v. *Underwood*, 471 U.S. 222 (1985).

[33] *Personnel Administrator of Massachusetts* v. *Feeney*, 442 U.S. 256 (1979).

What does this mean in practical terms? It means city ordinances that permit only single-family residences and thus make low-cost housing projects impossible are not unconstitutional—even if their effect is to keep minorities from moving into the city—unless it can be shown that they were adopted with the intent to discriminate against minorities. It means that a preference for veterans in public employment does not violate the equal protection clause, even though its effect is to keep many women from getting jobs: The distinction between veterans and nonveterans was not adopted deliberately to create a sex barrier.

Still, the fact that a law or governmental practice has a differential impact is not irrelevant. In a community that has a large number of blacks or Hispanics, it would be considered suspicious if only a few of them were called for jury duty. Under such circumstances the burden of proof shifts to the state or city to demonstrate that it has not engaged in unconstitutional discriminatory conduct. Similarly, if a community with a past history of discrimination against black voters adopts new regulations that reduce the number of blacks eligible to vote, the burden of proof shifts to the state or city to demonstrate that it is not willfully discriminating.

But note what is constitutional can nonetheless be made illegal. (Things that are unconstitutional are always illegal, but that which is illegal may not always be unconstitutional.) Congress has made illegal, in many circumstances, the use of tests unrelated to job performance, if in fact such tests screen out members of one race or sex to a greater extent than another, regardless of the motives of the employers.

THE LIFE AND DEATH OF JIM CROW EDUCATION

Laws requiring that blacks be segregated into separate public facilities date only from the end of the nineteenth century. Prior to that time social custom and economic conditions, rather than the law, kept the two races apart.[34] But from the end of that century until the Supreme Court struck down such laws in the 1950s, southern states and cities made it illegal for whites and blacks to ride in the same train cars, attend the same theaters, go to the same schools, be born in the same hospitals, or be buried in the same cemeteries. **Jim Crow laws**, as they came to be called, blanketed southern life. How could these laws stand in the face of the equal protection clause?

Is Segregation Discrimination? *Plessy* v. *Ferguson*

In 1896, in *Plessy* v. *Ferguson*, the Supreme Court endorsed the view that racial segregation did not constitute discrimination if equal accommodations were provided for the members of both races.[35] Even equal accommodations were not required except for public facilities and for a limited category of public utilities, such as trains and buses. Under this separate-but-equal formula, southern states, and some places in the North, enforced segregation in transportation, places of public accommodation, educational facilities, swimming pools, and parks. Although the Plessy decision required equality as the price for compulsory segregation, the "equal" part of the formula was meaningless. States segregated blacks into unequal facilities, and blacks lacked the political power to protest.

The passage of time did not lessen the inequalities. In 1950, all the segregated states had a total of fourteen medical schools for whites, none for blacks; sixteen law schools for whites, five for blacks; fifteen engineering schools for whites, none

"Treat people as equals and the first thing you know they believe they are." (*Drawing by Mulligan*, © 1982. The New Yorker Magazine, Inc.)

[34] C. Vann Woodward, *The Strange Career of Jim Crow* (Oxford University Press, 1968).
[35] 163 U.S. 537.

The 101st Division protects students in Little Rock Central High after a Court order to integrate in 1957. (UPI/Bettmann Newsphotos)

for blacks; five dentistry schools for whites, none for blacks. Beginning in the late 1930s blacks started to file lawsuits challenging the doctrine. They cited facts to show that in practice, separate but equal always resulted in discrimination against blacks. However, the Supreme Court was not yet willing to upset the doctrine directly. Rather, it began to undermine it. The Court scrutinized each situation and, in case after case, ordered facilities to be equalized.

The End of Separate but Equal: *Brown* v. *Board of Education*

Finally, in the spring of 1954, in *Brown* v. *Board of Education*, the Supreme Court reversed its 1896 holding as applied to public schools. It ruled that "separate but equal" is a contradiction in terms. Segregation is itself discrimination.[36] A year later the Court ordered school boards to proceed with "all deliberate speed to desegregate public schools at the earliest practical date."[37] In the years following the *Brown* decision, federal judges struck down a whole battery of schemes designed to evade the Court's ruling.

Beginning in 1963 the Supreme Court gradually reversed its second *Brown* decision granting school districts time to prepare for desegregation. In 1969 the Court completed that reversal, stating: "Continued operation of racially segregated schools under the standard of 'all deliberate speed' is no longer constitutionally permissible. School districts must immediately terminate dual school systems based on race and operate only unitary school systems."[38]

Title VI of the Civil Rights Act of 1964 stipulates that federal dollars must be withdrawn from an entire school or institution of higher education that discriminates "on the ground of race, color, or national origin in any program or activity receiving federal financial assistance." (Sex, the handicapped, the aged, Vietnam veterans, and disabled veterans have since been added.)

In 1984 the Supreme Court in *Grove City College* v. *Bell*, limited Title VI's, and in effect similar federal laws', coverage to only those programs and activities that directly received federal funds rather than the entire institution of which they were a part.[39] Then in 1988 Congress, overriding a presidential veto, set aside the impact of *Grove* and made it clear that if any part of an institution receives federal funds, the entire entity is covered. For example, if a department of computer sciences receives federal funds, then no program or activity of that college is exempt from the requirements of these acts.

Busing and Federal Courts

Half of all American students are bused to schools. Of these, less than 7 percent are bused to achieve school desegregation. Still, busing is one of the most hotly debated questions of our time.[40]

[36] 347 U.S. 483 (1954). See also J. W. Peltason, *Fifty-eight Lonely Men: Southern Federal Judges and School Desegregation* (University of Illinois Press, 1971), p. 248.

[37] *Brown* v. *Board of Education*, 349 U.S. 294 (1955). For a comprehensive history of the events leading up to *Brown* v. *Board of Education*, see Richard Kluger, *Simple Justice* (Knopf, 1976). Earl Black, *Southern Governors and Civil Rights: Racial Segregation as a Campaign Issue in the Second Reconstruction* (Harvard University Press, 1977), shows response, reaction, and eventually neutralization of race as a political issue following the *Brown* decision.

[38] *Alexander* v. *Board of Education*, 396 U.S. 19 (1969).

[39] *Grove City* v. *Bell* 465 U.S. 555 (1984).

[40] K. Arrington, *With All Deliberate Speed: 1954–19??* (U.S. Commission on Civil Rights, 1981); Gary Orfield, *Must We Bus? Segregated Schools and National Policy* (Brookings Institution, 1979); James Bolner and Robert Shanley, *Busing: The Political and Judicial Process* (Praeger, 1974); Jennifer L. Hochschild, *The New American Dilemma: Liberal Democracy and School Desegregation* (Yale University Press, 1984).

The Supreme Court, however, has endorsed busing as one of the tools a federal judge may use to remedy the consequences of officially sanctioned—that is, **de jure segregation,** or segregation by law.[41] On the other hand, it has refused to permit busing to overcome the effects of **de facto segregation.** In other words, if judges find that authorities have operated segregated schools in the past or by systematic and purposeful actions have caused segregation, they may order a school district to bus pupils. But judges may not order busing to overcome racial imbalances in schools not caused by official actions.[42]

In large metropolitan areas—partly as the result of white flight to the suburbs and private schools to escape court-ordered busing—many school districts in central cities are predominantly black. Under such circumstances it is difficult to integrate schools by judicial decree without interdistrict busing. But judges may not order cross-district busing unless they can establish that school district lines were drawn for the purpose of maintaining segregation, and that the suburban districts are also being operated in a discriminatory fashion. (Justice Thurgood Marshall, who dissented from the Supreme Court decision imposing this restrictive view of the power of federal judges to order cross-district busing, commented: "Unless our children begin to learn together, there is little hope that our people will ever learn to live together.")[43]

BARRIERS TO VOTING

States determine suffrage qualifications for all elections, but they do so subject to a variety of constitutional restraints. Article I, Section 4, gives Congress the power to supersede state regulations as to the "times, places, and manner" of elections for federal officers—that is, for members of the House of Representatives, senators, and presidential electors. Congress has used this authority to set age qualifications and residency requirements to vote in national elections, a uniform day for all states to hold elections for members of Congress and presidential electors, and to give American citizens who reside outside the United States the right to vote for members of Congress and presidential electors in the states in which they previously lived.

The major limitations on the state's power to set suffrage qualifications, however, are contained in the Fourteenth and Fifteenth amendments (forbidding unreasonable qualifications and those based on race), the Nineteenth amendment (forbidding qualifications based on sex), and the Twenty-sixth amendment (forbidding states to deny citizens 18 years of age or older the right to vote on account of age). These amendments also empower Congress to enact the laws necessary to enforce their provisions.

Getting Around the Fourteenth and Fifteenth Amendments

Despite fierce opposition to the Nineteenth amendment, no organized resistance surfaced after its ratification to allowing all women in the North and white women in the South to exercise the rights secured for them. Not so in the case of the

---

[41] Bernard Schwartz, *The School Busing Case and the Supreme Court* (Oxford University Press, 1986).

[42] *Swann* v. *Charlotte-Mecklenburg Board of Education*, 402 U.S. 1 (1971).

[43] *Milliken* v. *Bradley*, 418 U.S. 717 (1974). See also David L. Kirp, *Just Schools: The Idea of Racial Equality in American Education* (University of California Press, 1982), and Jeffrey A. Raffel, *The Politics of School Desegregation: The Metropolitan Remedy in Delaware* (Temple University Press, 1980).

Ku Klux Klansmen walk the streets of downtown Houston in 1985 to protest a gay-rights measure on a city referendum. (*AP/Wide World Photos*)

Fourteenth and Fifteenth amendments. Following their adoption, blacks were allowed to participate in the political life of the southern states only because the federal government insisted upon it. As soon as federal troops were withdrawn from the South in 1877, southern Democrats regained control of state governments and set out to keep blacks from voting. They used social pressure and threats of violence, and they organized secret societies like the Ku Klux Klan that engaged in such terrorist activities as threats, midnight shootings, burnings, and whippings.

These measures "worked." But toward the end of the nineteenth century, and for the first time since the Civil War, parts of the South had two strong political parties: the Democrats and the Populists. White supremacists were fearful that the parties might compete for the black vote and that the blacks might come to hold the balance of power. White supremacists also feared that the continued use of excessive force and fraud to disenfranchise blacks might cause the president and Congress to intervene.

Southern leaders reasoned that if they could pass laws depriving blacks of the vote on grounds other than race, blacks would find it difficult to challenge the laws in the courts. Some whites protested that laws could be used against whites as well as blacks. But keeping poor whites from voting did not disturb the conservative leaders of the Democratic party, for they were often just as anxious to undermine white support for the Populist party as they were to disenfranchise blacks: "The disenfranchisement movement of the 'nineties' gave the Southern states the most impressive system of obstacles between the voter and the ballot box known to the democratic world."[44]

In the 1940s the Supreme Court began to strike down one after another of the devices used to keep blacks from voting. In 1944 (*Smith* v. *Allwright*) the Court declared the **white primary** unconstitutional.[45] In 1960 it held that racial gerrymandering was contrary to the Fifteenth amendment. The Twenty-fourth amendment had eliminated the **poll tax** in federal elections, and in 1966 the Court held that the Fourteenth amendment forbade the tax as a condition in any election.

Those wishing to deny blacks the right to vote were forced to rely on registration requirements. On the surface these requirements appeared to be perfectly proper: It was the way they were administered that kept blacks from the polls. They were often applied by white election officers while white police stood guard, with white judges' hearing appeals from decisions of registration officials. These officials often seized on the smallest error in an application blank as an excuse to disqualify a voter. In one parish in the state of Louisiana, after four white voters filed affidavits in which they challenged the legality of the registration of black voters on the grounds that these voters had made an "error in spilling" [sic] in their applications, registration officials struck 1300 out of approximately 1500 black voters from the polls.[46] In many southern areas literacy tests were administered by registration officials to discriminate against blacks. Some states, either as an additional requirement or as a substitute, required applicants to demonstrate to the satisfaction of election officials that they understood the national and state constitutions and, further, that they were persons of good character. Whites were often asked simple questions; blacks were asked questions that would baffle a Supreme Court justice. In Louisiana, 49,603 illiterate white voters were able to persuade election officials they could understand the Constitution, but only two illiterate black voters were able to do so.

[44] V. O. Key, Jr., *Southern Politics* (Knopf, 1949), p. 555. For a history of the rise and fall of black disenfranchisement, see Steven F. Lawson, *Black Ballots: Voting Rights in the South, 1944–1969* (Columbia University Press, 1976).

[45] 321 U.S. 649 (1944).

[46] *Report of the United States Commission on Civil Rights* (U.S. Government Printing Office, 1959), pp. 103–4.

Action by the National Government

For over twenty years federal courts, under the leadership of the Supreme Court, carefully scrutinized voting laws and procedures in cases brought before them. But this approach did not open the voting booth to blacks, especially those living in rural areas of the Deep South. Finally Congress began to act. At first Congress left the major responsibility with the courts: Civil rights statutes protecting the right to vote were strengthened. The Civil Rights Act of 1964 had hardly been enacted when events in Selma, Alabama, dramatized the inadequacy of depending on the courts to prevent racial barriers in polling places. A voter-registration drive in that city, led by Martin Luther King, Jr., produced arrests, marches on the state capitol, and the murder of two civil rights workers but no major dent in the color bar at the polls.

Responding to events in Selma, President Lyndon Johnson made a dramatic address to the nation and to Congress calling for federal action to ensure that no person would be deprived of the right to vote in any election for any office because of color or race. Congress responded with the Voting Rights Act of 1965.[47]

The Voting Rights Act of 1965 The adoption of this act—almost a century after the Fifteenth amendment was ratified—finally made it possible for blacks to register and vote in every district in the United States.[48] The act has been extended and strengthened three times, most recently in 1982. This law marks a major departure from earlier civil rights acts. Instead of depending solely on lawsuits brought by private citizens whose rights have been abridged, and upon local officials, the Voting Rights Act of 1965 authorizes federal officials to register voters when local ones fail to do so, and instructs those federal officials to ensure that those individuals they register are allowed to vote and that their ballots are honestly counted.

This act concentrates on states and political subdivisions, mostly but not exclusively in the South, that had a long history of discrimination against blacks. It also covers areas in which more than 10 percent of voting-age citizens belong to language minorities—persons of Spanish heritage, Asian-Americans, American Indians, and Alaskan natives. In areas covered because of the presence of language minorities, bilingual election materials must be provided.

As a result of the act, literacy tests are, in effect, set aside *everywhere*. In areas covered by the law, except those that are included only because of the presence of language minorities, the attorney general may call upon the Office of Personnel Management to appoint federal examiners to observe elections and if necessary to register voters. If local election officials turn away any voter federal examiners find entitled to vote, the examiners may secure an order from a federal district court impounding all ballots until all persons entitled to vote are allowed to do so. In practice, it has been unnecessary to appoint examiners in most areas, because the mere threat of sending them has been enough. Nonetheless, as late as 1983 federal observers were still being sent into some places to ensure that blacks were being allowed to vote. The attorney general may also appoint poll watchers to ensure that the votes of all qualified persons are properly counted.

The act contains some unusual provisions designed to keep states from minimizing the effect of the voting power of blacks. No state or political subdivision covered by the act may make any change in its voting practices or laws, such as reapportioning a legislative body or changing from single-member districts to a multimember at-large election system—or even altering its boundaries—without prior clearance from the attorney general or from the United States District Court for the District of Columbia. Over the last decade, the preclearance provisions of Section 5 have

Black Americans are registering and voting in record numbers in the 1980s. (*Roger Clark, Jr./Photo Researchers*)

[47] David J. Garrow, *Protest at Selma: Martin Luther King and the Voting Rights Act of 1965* (Yale University Press, 1978).

[48] *South Carolina* v. *Katzenbach* 383 U.S. 301 (1966).

been used to push more and more jurisdictions to replace at-large elections with single membership districts in order to maximize minority office holding.

Section 2 of the act, as amended in 1982, forbids governments from using procedures, regardless of intent, that result in the dilution of black voting power. The act does not guarantee that "members of a protected class" have a "right to have members . . . elected in numbers equal to their proportion in the population." However, in any state in which blacks make up a substantial proportion of the population, the fact that few or none of them get elected because of some practice or procedure is part of the "totality of circumstances" judges must consider to determine if the act has been violated.[49]

The Voting Rights Act of 1965 has been effective. True, "race, unlike ethnicity, is so distinct as to make the process of political integration considerably more difficult and different for Afro-Americans than it was for European immigrants."[50] Yet, millions of blacks now participate in our political life. More than 6500 blacks hold national, state, or local office.[51] More than 300 blacks are mayors including those of such key cities as Atlanta, Birmingham, Chicago, Detroit, Los Angeles, New Orleans, Philadelphia, and Washington, D.C.[52] There are blacks in all southern legislatures, and there are more blacks in the U.S. House of Representatives than at any time since Reconstruction.

The influence of black voting, moreover, is to be measured by means other than the number of black office holders. In fact, although single membership districts may increase the number of black voters, "a ward plan may sacrifice influence for guaranteed seats."[53] When black voters can provide the margin of victory, they may have great political influence, even if they are unable to elect a black office holder. Since the passage of the Voting Rights Act of 1965, governors and senators, especially in areas where there are large numbers of black voters, have become much more sympathetic to the concerns of black voters.

The black constituency must also be taken into account by those who appoint and confirm federal judges. This political fact was demonstrated when Judge Robert Bork's nomination to the Supreme Court was rejected by the Senate in 1987, in large part because of objections to his constitutional views by leaders of civil rights and women's groups. The role of Jessie Jackson in the 1988 presidential election is another clear signal that black voters have become an influential part of the American electorate.

BARRIERS TO PUBLIC ACCOMMODATIONS, JOBS, AND HOMES

The Fourteenth amendment applies only to *governmental* action, not to private discriminatory conduct. Moreover, our Constitution creates:

> a zone of privacy which precludes government from interfering with private clubs or groups. The associational rights which our system honors permit all-white, all-black, all-brown, and all-yellow clubs to be established. They also permit all-Catholic, all-Jewish, or all-agnostic clubs . . .[54]

However, families, churches, or private groups organized for political, religious,

[49] *Thornburg* v. *Gingles*, 478 U.S. 30 (1986).

[50] Dianne M. Pinderhughes, *Race and Ethnicity in Chicago Politics, A Reexamination of Pluralist Theory* (University of Illinois Press, 1987), p. xvi.

[51] *The Washington Post National Weekly Edition* (October 5, 1987), p. 14; Leonard A. Cole, *Blacks in Power: A Comparative Study of Black and White Elected Officials* (Princeton University Press, 1976).

[52] "Outlook Bright For More Black Mayors," *The Orange County Register*, July 3, 1986, p. A12.

[53] Thernstrom, *op. cit.*, p. 243.

[54] Justice Douglas dissenting in *Moose Lodge No. 107* v. *Irvis*, 407 U.S. 163 (1972).

cultural, or social purposes are constitutionally different from large associations organized along other lines, such as the United States Jaycees or a large law partnership. The Supreme Court, to illustrate, has upheld the application of the Minnesota Human Rights Act to compel the Jaycees, the Junior Chamber of Commerce, to admit women. That association is not a small intimate group; nor did it demonstrate that allowing women to become members would change the content or impact of the organization's purposes.[55] Similarly, the Court was unpersuaded that the rights of law partners to associate permitted the partnership to ignore federal laws forbidding discrimination in employment.[56]

Until recent decades serious constitutional constraints hindered Congress's authority to regulate against discriminatory conduct by *private individuals*. In 1883 the Supreme Court declared unconstitutional an act of Congress that made it a federal offense for any operator of a public conveyance, hotel, or theater to deny accommodations to any person because of race or color on the grounds that the Fourteenth amendment does not give Congress authority to legislate against discrimination by private individuals.[57] In addition, for 100 years the Court so narrowly construed the Thirteenth amendment's grant of power to Congress to legislate against slavery and involuntary servitude that Congress could act only against physical compulsion or peonage (a condition of compulsory servitude based on indebtedness of the worker to the employer).

Since the 1960s, however, the constitutional authority of Congress to legislate against discrimination by private individuals is no longer an issue. The Court has so broadly construed the **commerce clause** (see the next two sections) that it alone justifies almost any action that Congress might want to take against discriminatory conduct by individuals. In addition the Court has reinterpreted the Thirteenth amendment, at least as far as racial discrimination is concerned, to sustain congressional legislation against discrimination. Speaking for the Court, Justice Potter Stewart concluded:

> When racial discrimination herds men into ghettos and makes their ability to buy property turn on the color of their skin, then it too is a relic of slavery. . . . At the very least, the freedom that Congress is empowered to secure under the Thirteenth Amendment includes the freedom to buy whatever a white man can buy, the right to live wherever a white man can live. If Congress cannot say that being a free man means at least this much, then the Thirteenth Amendment made a promise that the Nation cannot keep.[58]

The Thirteenth amendment (and the Fourteenth) are not the only sources of national power to legislate against discrimination. The government may use (and has used) the power to tax and spend to prevent not merely racial discrimination but discrimination based on ethnic origin, sex, disability, and age. It may also use the power to regulate interstate commerce to do so, as it did in the most important and sweeping Civil Rights Act—that of 1964.

The Civil Rights Act of 1964, Title II: Places of Public Accommodation

For the first time since Reconstruction, Congress authorized the massive use of federal authority to combat privately imposed racial discrimination. Title II forbids discrimination in places of accommodation and makes it a federal offense to discriminate against any customer or patron because of race, color, religion, or national

[55] *Roberts* v. *United States Jaycees*, 468 U.S. 609 (1984).
[56] *Hishon* v. *King & Spalding*, 467 U.S. 69 (1984).
[57] *The Civil Rights Cases*, 109 U.S. 3 (1883).
[58] 393 U.S. 409 (1968).

origin. It applies to any inn, hotel, motel, or lodging establishment (except establishments with fewer than five rooms and occupied by the proprietor—in other words, small boardinghouses); to any restaurant or gasoline station that services interstate travelers or serves food or products of which a substantial portion have moved in interstate commerce; and to any movie house, theater, concert hall, sports arena, or other place of entertainment that customarily presents films, performances, athletic teams, or other sources of entertainment that are moved in interstate commerce.

Title II has been vigorously enforced. Blacks organized programs to test it; the Department of Justice filed more than 400 lawsuits; and within a few months after its adoption, the Supreme Court (in *Heart of Atlanta Motel* v. *United States*) unanimously sustained its constitutionality.[59] As a result, most establishments, including those in the South, opened their doors to all customers.

The Civil Rights Act of 1964, Title VII: Employment

The Constitution forbids *governments* to deny persons employment because of race, color, religion, or sex. In addition, under Title VII of the Civil Rights Act, Congress has now made it illegal for any employer or trade union in any industry that affects interstate commerce and employs fifteen or more people (and, since 1972, any state or local agency such as a school or university) to discriminate in employment practices against any person because of race, color, national origin, religion, or sex.[60] Other legislation makes it illegal to engage in these activities against those with physical handicaps, veterans, or persons between the ages of 40 and 70.

There are a few exceptions. Religious institutions such as parochial schools may use religious standards. Further, age, sex, or handicap may be considered where bona fide occupational qualifications are necessary to the normal operation of a particular business or enterprise. The bona fide occupational qualification exception has been construed narrowly: Airlines may not specify that one must be a female or unmarried to serve as a flight attendant. Also, minimum height and weight requirements for prison guards are not permissible, although a state was allowed to deny women the right to serve as guards in a maximum security prison for males. States have also been allowed to compel the retirement of state police officers prior to age 70.

Recent problems involve the use of employment tests or prior-experience requirements that work to the disadvantage of blacks, Hispanics, women, and other protected groups. Title VII goes beyond constitutional standards. It forbids tests or practices, even if neutral on their face and adopted without intent to discriminate, that have a greater negative effect on persons of one race or sex. The only exceptions are for practices directly related to on-the-job performance and for seniority systems that give advantages to employees based on their length of employment.

Title VII was passed to protect minorities and women. Nonetheless, employers who discriminate against white males also violate its provisions. Moreover, when Congress adopted Title VII it stated that it should not be used to require any employer to grant preferential treatment to any individual or to any group on account of racial or sexual imbalance that might exist in the employer's workforce.

Title VII, however, does not preclude employers, public or private, from adopting race-sensitive *affirmative action* programs designed to overcome *past discrimination* against minorities and women. Affirmative action programs may *temporarily* set *goals*, but not quotas, and may give minorities certain preferences in training, initial employment, or promotion, but not in protection against layoffs—provided they do not unnecessarily trammel the interests of white employees.

"Thanks for coming in. It's such a relief to be able to deny someone a loan when there's no possibility of being charged with sex, race, age, or ethnic bias." (*Drawing by Ed Fisher,* © *1976. The New Yorker Magazine, Inc.*)

[59] 379 U.S. 421 (1964).

[60] Paul Burstein, *Discrimination, Jobs, and Politics; The Struggle for Equal Employment Opportunity in the United States since the New Deal* (The University of Chicago Press, 1985).

Title VII has several special features. Not only do aggrieved persons have a right of private action to sue for damages for themselves, but they can do so for other persons similarly situated—in a so-called **class action.** In addition, Congress created the Equal Employment Opportunity Commission, known as the EEOC, to enforce its provisions. The commission, which consists of five members appointed by the president with the consent of the Senate, works together with state authorities to try to bring about compliance with the act. It has authority to seek judicial enforcement of complaints against private employers: The attorney general prosecutes Title VII violations by public agencies.

Title VII is supplemented, indeed in some instances even supplanted, by a 1965 presidential executive order requiring all contractors of the federal government, including universities, to adopt and implement affirmative action programs to correct for "underutilization" of women and minorities. Such programs may not establish racial or ethnic quotas for minorities or women, but they do call on contractors to establish timetables and goals; to follow open-recruitment procedures; to keep records of applicants by race, sex, and national origin; and to explain why their labor force does not reflect the same proportion of persons in the covered categories as are found within the labor market pools. Failure of contractors to file and implement an approved affirmative action plan may lead to loss of federal contracts or grants. The Reagan administration was, however, less vigorous than its predecessors in enforcing this executive order.

Housing: The Civil Rights Acts of 1866 and 1968

Fair housing is the last frontier of the civil rights crusade, the area in which progress is slowest and genuine change most remote:

> Segregated housing contributes mightily to a vicious circle that also includes educational and employment discrimination. . . . Because of poor schools for many minorities, they cannot find well-paying jobs. Without such jobs they often cannot afford to live in nicer neighborhoods with decent housing. And because of their location in less desirable communities, good educational systems are less likely to be available.[61]

As former Senator Birch Bayh pointed out, we face a "sordid endless chain of inequality. That interlocking system of education, employment, and housing has been used to enslave a people by keeping them undereducated, jobless, and poor, as well as separately and substandardly housed."[62]

In 1948, in *Shelley* v. *Kraemer*, the Supreme Court held that judges could no longer enforce racially restrictive covenants (a provision in a deed to real property restricting its sale).[63] In 1962 President Kennedy ordered federal housing authorities to cease making federal funds available to any project operating on a segregated basis. And, in 1968 the Supreme Court interpreted the Civil Rights Act of 1866 to open federal courts to damage suits by those who are denied the right to buy homes because of race. In 1968 Congress passed a Civil Rights Act relating directly to housing.

This Civil Rights Act covers all housing offered for rent or sale except that owned by private individuals who own no more than three houses, who sell or rent these houses without the services of an agent, and who do not indicate any preference or discrimination in their advertising; dwellings that have no more than four separate living units, in which the owner maintains a residence ("Mrs. Murphy boardinghouses"); and religious organizations and private clubs housing their own members on a noncommercial basis.

For all other housing the Act forbids owners to refuse to sell or rent to any

[61] Charles M. Lamb, "Housing Discrimination and Segregation," *Catholic University Law Review*, (Spring 1981), p. 370.
[62] Quoted in ibid, pp. 391–392.
[63] 334 U.S. 1 (1948).

person because of race, color, religion, national origin, and—since 1974—sex. No discriminatory advertising is permitted. So-called blockbusting techniques—that is, attempts to persuade persons to sell or rent a dwelling by representing that blacks or other racial or religious groups are about to come into the neighborhood—are outlawed. Real estate brokers and lending institutions are also prohibited from discriminatory practices.

"The weakest links" in the act turned out to be the sections dealing with administration and enforcement. The act created no enforcement agency: Primary responsibility for enforcement falls upon those injured by discriminatory housing practices. The injured party had to file a complaint with the Secretary of the Department of Housing and Urban Development (HUD) or initiate a suit in a federal court. HUD could pursue a complaint only by "informal methods of conference, conciliation, and persuasion," and if all else failed, HUD could do nothing but refer the matter to the Department of Justice.

In 1988 Congress strengthened the enforcement procedures. Complainants may now bring their allegations of discrimination before administrative law judges within HUD. This should provide a quicker and less expensive enforcement.

Because purposeful discrimination must be proved, it is hard to attack tactics such as "steering," in which realtors direct black prospects to black neighborhoods and white prospects to white neighborhoods. Black leaders have given housing a lower priority than employment or education.[64] Twenty years after the adoption of the Housing Act of 1968, many, if not most, blacks still meet discrimination when they seek to rent a home or buy a house.[65] In most large cities, "While blacks and other minorities have made strides in voting rights, education and jobs, the homes they return to each night are in communities still largely defined by race."[66]

But some progress has been made. The courts have built up such "a formidable body of precedent that almost anyone who can prove discrimination, and has the determination and money to do so, can get the house he wants and even substantial damage awards."[67] And the 1988 enforcement procedures provide considerably greater teeth to the federal law.

Allan Bakke, who led a landmark U.S. Supreme Court decision striking down minority admissions quotas, chats with fellow graduates at the University of California at Davis. (*AP/Wide World Photos*)

AFFIRMATIVE ACTION—IS IT CONSTITUTIONAL?

Some Supreme Court Affirmative Action Decisions under Title VII of the Civil Rights Act and the Equal Protection Clause

Public universities may not create separate racial admission, but they may consider race as one factor in order to secure a diversified student body. From *Regents of the University of California* v. *Bakke*, 438 U.S. 265 (1978). Chief attention to equal protection clause.

Prior to 1954, when white majorities were using state power to segregate blacks and impose disabilities upon them, civil rights advocates cited with approval the words of the first Justice Harlan dissenting in *Plessy* v. *Ferguson*: "Our Constitution is color-blind and neither knows nor tolerates class among citizens."[68] Even though the Supreme Court itself seemed to be moving closer to Justice Harlan's view, it nevertheless sustained during World War II a national program forcing persons of Japanese ancestry, including American citizens, to move into what were called "relocation camps," but that were in fact prisons. (In 1983 a national commission

[64] Robert Reinhold, "Race Barriers in Housing Still High 11 Years after the Civil Rights Act," *The New York Times* (June 8, 1979).

[65] Jonathan Kaufman, "Black Mood," *The Wall Street Journal* (May 23, 1980).

[66] "The Racism Next Door: Segregated Housing Is Still a Blight in Most Neighborhoods," *Time Magazine* (June 30, 1986), p. 40.

[67] Reinhold, "Race Barriers."

[68] 163 U.S. 537 (1896).

Supreme Court Decisions *cont.*

In order to overcome lack of blacks in the skilled labor force a private employer may voluntarily adopt an affirmative action training program which temporarily reserves certain openings for blacks. From *Steelworkers* v. *Weber*, 443 U.S. 193 (1979). Chief attention to Title VII.

Congress may require that at least 10 percent of federal funds granted to local public works projects be used to procure services or supplies from minority business enterprises. From *Fullilove* v. *Klutznick*, 448 U.S. 448 (1980). Chief attention to equal protection requirements of the due process clause.

A city forced to cut back its firefighters may *not* ignore a valid seniority system and layoff some white firefighters more senior to some recently hired black firefighters in order to preserve the ratio of minority firefighters only recently gained in its workforce as the result of a legitimate affirmative action program. From *Firefighters* v. *Stotts*, 467 U.S. 561 (1984). Chief attention to Title VII.

In order to protect its affirmative action hiring program when it has to cut back, a school board may *not* lay off some white teachers more senior to some black ones. From *Wygant* v. *Jackson Board of Education*, 476 U.S. 267 (1986). Chief attention to equal protection clause.

Federal courts may approve consent orders in which private employers settle discrimination suits under Title VII of the Civil Rights Act by agreeing to preferential hiring and promotion of minority-group members. From *Firefighters* v. *City of Cleveland*, 92 L Ed 2d 405 (1986). Chief attention to Title VII.

Federal courts may order the establishment of a numerical "hiring" goal for minority apprentice memberships in a union with a long history of deliberate discrimination, and until that goal has been met require the union to give some preferences in admitting minorities. From *Sheet Metal Workers* v. *EEOC*, 92 L Ed 2d 344 (1986). Chief attention to Title VII.

characterized these actions as a "grave injustice" motivated by "race prejudice, war hysteria and a failure of political leadership."[69]

Then, in 1954 Justice Harlan's views triumphed. In *Brown* v. *Board of Education* the Court called racial classifications "odious to our system" and made race a suspect class—probably an outlawed one. In the years immediately following, the Court also established that although the Fourteenth amendment was adopted to protect blacks, its provisions extend to other minorities, women, and white males. The Court emphasized that the rights protected belong to each and every individual, not to the group to which he or she may belong.

Then, in the 1960s, came a new series of constitutional and national public policy debates. Many asserted that government neutrality is not enough: If governments and universities and employers merely stop discriminating against blacks, Hispanics, and women, but change nothing else, those previously discriminated against are still kept from equal participation in American life. They have been so handicapped by past discrimination that in the competition for openings in medical schools, or for skilled jobs, or for their share of government grants, they suffer disabilities not shared by white males.

What if governments, heeding these arguments, adopt, and require private employers and others to adopt, race-ethnic-sex-conscious remedies—popularly known as affirmative action programs by those who support them but as reverse discrimination by those who oppose them—that provide special help for minorities and women? Are these kinds of classifications also suspect? Are they unconstitutional? No constitutional issue has been more hotly debated.[70]

The issue has been raised most directly with respect to affirmative action programs for blacks. Supreme Court justices are divided—as is the nation—whether race may properly be taken into account to overcome past discrimination, and, if so, how and to what extent. As Justice White has written, "Agreement upon a means for applying the Equal Protection Clause to an affirmative-action program has eluded this Court every time the issue has come before us."[71]

The first major statement of the Court on these perplexing issues came in a very celebrated recent case that relates to university admissions rather than to employment. Allan Bakke, a white male and a top student at Minnesota and Stanford Universities, as well as a Vietnam War veteran, applied in both 1973 and 1974 to the medical school of the University of California at Davis. In each of those years the school admitted 100 new students, eighty-four in a general admissions program and sixteen in a special admissions program created for blacks, Chicanos, Asian-Americans, and American Indians—groups who had been totally underrepresented there until the special admissions program was established.

Bakke's application was rejected in each year; but both times students with lower grade-point averages, test scores, and interview ratings were admitted under the special admissions program. After his second rejection Bakke brought a suit in federal court claiming he had been excluded because of his race, contrary to the requirements of the Constitution and of Title VI of the Civil Rights Act of 1964.

[69] Commission on Wartime Relocation and Internment of Civilians, quoted in *The New York Times* (June 17, 1983) p. 6.

[70] See Robert M. O'Neil, *Discrimination against Discrimination* (Indiana University Press, 1975); John C. Livingston, *Fair Game? Inequality and Affirmative Action* (W. H. Freeman, 1979); and Joel Dreyfus and Charles Lawrence, *The Bakke Case* (Harcourt Brace Jovanovich, 1979), in favor of such programs. See Nathan Glazer, *Affirmative Discrimination* (Basic Books, 1976); Alan H. Goldman, *Justice and Reverse Discrimination* (Princeton University Press, 1979); and Gary L. McDowell, *Equity and the Constitution* (University of Chicago Press, 1982) against. See also Allan P. Sindler, *Bakke, DeFunis, and Minority Admissions* (Longman, 1978) and Timothy J. O'Neill, *Bakke and the Politics of Equality* (Wesleyan University Press, 1984).

[71] Concurring in *Wygant* v. *Jackson Board of Education*, 476 U.S. 267 (1986).

In *University of California Regents* v. *Bakke* (1978), the Supreme Court declared unconstitutional the Davis plan.[72] But in an opinion by Justice Powell, which no other member of the Court completely shared, the Court also declared that affirmative action programs are not necessarily unconstitutional. In order to get a diversified student body, a state university may properly take race and ethnic background into account as one of several factors in choosing students. (However, the university's goal may not be to redress past misconduct by the society or to ensure that more minority members become doctors.) The problem with the California plan was that it created a category of admissions from which whites were excluded solely because of their race.

Where Do We Stand?

Since the Bakke case, the Supreme Court has dealt with the issue of affirmative action a half dozen times (see box) and it will continue to do so. Although the Court has not been able to muster clear majorities behind a definitive set of statements most of the justices agree:

1. The goal of achieving racial balance in a workforce is *not* constitutionally permissible as a justification for an affirmative action program.
2. However, in a *remedial context* there is no requirement that governments "act in a wholly color-blind fashion."
3. Societal discrimination alone is *insufficient* to justify an affirmative action program.
4. On the other hand, an individual finding by a court that the "particular entity" seeking to institute an affirmative action program has committed discriminatory acts in the past is not necessary.
5. The means to overcome past discrimination may *not* impose disproportionate harm on the interests of innocent individuals adversely affected by a plan's racial preference. Thus, *temporary* hiring goals for minorities may be permissible whereas layoffs of nonminorities would not be. "While hiring goals impose a diffuse burden, often foreclosing only one of several opportunities, layoffs impose the entire burden of achieving racial equality on particular individuals. . . . The burden is too intrusive."[73] On the other hand, there is no definitive ruling that layoffs as remedies are always precluded.
6. *Goals* that measure achievement and set forth objectives for hiring or promoting particular numbers of minorities are permissible, but *quotas* that require an employer to hire a particular number of minorities or else automatically suffer penalties are not.
7. Preferences in training, hiring, or promoting must be *temporary* and can be in place only as long as necessary to overcome past discrimination.
8. "As part of this Nation's dedication to eradicating racial discrimination, innocent persons may be called upon to bear some of the burden of the remedy,"[74] and race-conscious relief may benefit individuals who are not identified victims of unlawful discrimination. "The purpose of affirmative action is not to make identified victims whole, but rather to dismantle prior patterns of employment discrimination and to prevent discrimination in the future."[75]

---

[72] 438 U.S. 265 (1978).

[73] Justice Powell in *Wygant* v. *Jackson Board of Education.*

[74] Ibid.

[75] Justice Brennan, *Sheet Metal Workers* v. *EEOC.*

In summary, the Court still firmly and unanimously adheres "to the traditional view that racial classifications that stigmatize—because they are drawn on the presumption that one race is inferior to another or because they put the weight of government behind racial hatred and separatism"—are not only suspect, but outlawed. However, a carefully crafted affirmative action program "which is designed to further a legitimate remedial purpose and which implements that purpose by means that do not . . . unnecessarily trammel the rights of innocent individuals . . . adversely affected by a plan's racial preference" are consistent with the Constitution.[76] There are more decisions to come as the Court—and the nation—engage in the never-ending business of clarifying constitutional guidelines.

[76] Justice O'Connor, in *Wygant v. Jackson Board of Education.*

SUMMARY

1. The crusade for women's rights was born out of the struggle to abolish slavery. The fate of these two social movements has long been intertwined. Recently the struggle for equal rights under the law has been expanded to cover concerns for the rights of native Americans, Hispanics, and Asians.

2. Progress in securing civil rights for blacks was a long time in coming. After the Civil War the national government briefly tried to secure for the freed slaves some measure of protection and to enforce the Thirteenth, Fourteenth, and Fifteenth amendments and the civil rights laws passed to implement them. But when the national government withdrew from the field in 1877, blacks were left to their own resources, and the rights granted by the Constitution became meaningless. The Supreme Court reversed an 1896 decision and, in *Brown* v. *Board of Education*, announced that enforced racial segregation in public education was unconstitutional. Eventually Congress and the president threw their weight behind a major effort to prevent racial segregation and discrimination against blacks.

3. The Supreme Court uses a three-tiered approach to evaluate the constitutionality of laws challenged as violating the equal protection clause. Laws touching economic concerns are sustained if they are rationally related to the accomplishment of a legitimate government goal. Laws that classify people because of sex or illegitimacy are sustained only if they meet the more rigorous test of serving important governmental objectives and if they are substantially related to achieving those objectives. The top or most stringent tier is used to review laws that touch fundamental rights or classify people because of race or ethnic origin. Such laws will be sustained only if the government can show a "compelling public interest."

4. After a long struggle women achieved the right to vote with the adoption of the Nineteenth amendment in 1920. With the rebirth of the women's movement in the 1960s, federal courts began to interpret constitutional provisions to protect women against sex discrimination.

5. Most recently older Americans have joined with Hispanics, native Americans, and Asian Americans to secure legislative protection for their special concerns.

6. The desirability and constitutionality of affirmative action programs that provide special benefits to those who have been subjected to past discrimination divide the nation and the Supreme Court. Remedial programs, especially those designed by Congress, closely tailored to overcome specific instances of disadvantage due to past discrimination are likely to pass the Supreme Court's suspicion of race, national origin, and sex classifications.

FURTHER READING

HARRY S. ASHMORE. *Hearts and Minds: The Anatomy of Racism from Roosevelt to Reagan* (McGraw-Hill, 1982).

RUSSEL LAWRENCE BARSH and JAMES YOUNGBLOOD HENDERSON. *The Road: Indian Tribes and Political Liberty* (University of California Press, 1980).

GEORGE H. BROWN, NAN L. ROSEN, and SUSAN T. HILL. *The Condition of Education for Hispanic Americans* (U.S. Government Printing Office, 1980).

PAUL BURSTEIN. *Discrimination, Jobs, and Politics: The Struggle for Equal Employment Opportunity in the United States since the New Deal* (University of Chicago Press, 1985).

FIRST NATIONAL WOMEN'S CONFERENCE. *The Spirit of Houston* (U.S. Government Printing Office, 1978).

RICHARD KLUGER. *Simple Justice* (Knopf, 1976).

REPORT ON INDIAN EDUCATION. *Final Report to the American Policy Review Commission* (U.S. Government Printing Office, 1976).

ALLAN P. SINDLER. *Bakke, DeFunis, and Minority Admissions* (Longman, 1978).

We Mutually Pledge: A Report on the National Hispanic Leadership Conference, July 20–22, 1977 (The Dallas-Ft. Worth Spanish-Speaking Program Coordinators Council, 1977).

J. HARVIE WILKINSON, III. *From Brown to Bakke: The Supreme Court and School Integration: 1954–1978* (Oxford University Press, 1979).

6

Rights to Life, Liberty, and Property

Public officials have great power. Under certain conditions they can seize our property, throw us in jail, and—in extreme circumstances—even take our lives. It is necessary to give great power to those who govern; it is also dangerous. It is so dangerous that to keep officials from becoming tyrants, we are unwilling to depend on the ballot box alone. We know that political controls mean little when a majority uses its power to deprive unpopular minorities of their rights. Because public power can be dangerous, we parcel it out in small chunks and surround it with restraints. No single official can decide to take our lives, liberty, or property: Officials must act according to the rules. If they act outside the scope of their authority or contrary to the law, they have no claim to our obedience.

These are the precious rights of all who live under the American flag—rich or poor, young or old, black or white, man or woman, alien or citizen. The Constitution also confers some special rights on citizens and protects our right to become and to remain American citizens. Who belongs to the body politic? Who is an American?

Every nation has rules that determine nationality—that is, who is a member of, owes allegiance to, and is the subject of the nation-state. But in a democracy citizenship is more than nationality, more than merely being a subject.[1] Citizenship is an office and, like other offices, it carries with it certain powers and responsibilities. How citizenship is acquired and retained should therefore be a matter of considerable importance to everyone.

HOW CITIZENSHIP IS ACQUIRED AND LOST

Not until 1868, when the Fourteenth amendment was adopted, was this basic right of membership in the body politic given constitutional protection. The Fourteenth amendment makes "all persons born or naturalized in the United States and subject to the jurisdiction thereof . . . citizens of the United States and of

[1] Martin Edelman, *Democratic Theories and the Constitution* (State University of New York Press, 1984), p. 304.

Dual Citizenship

Because each nation has complete authority to decide for itself the question of nationality, it is possible for a person to be considered a citizen by two or more nations. Dual citizenship is not unusual, especially for persons from nations that do not recognize the right of the individual to choose his or her own nationality, called the right of *expatriation*. (One of the issues of the War of 1812 was that England did not recognize that sailors born in England had abandoned their English citizenship on becoming naturalized American citizens.) Persons born abroad to American citizens may also be citizens of the nation in which they were born. Persons born in the United States of parents from a foreign nation may also be citizens of their parents' country.

Dual nationality carries negative as well as positive consequences; for example, such an individual may be subject to national service obligations and taxes in both countries.

Ellis Island in New York harbor, where immigrants were examined for diseases before being allowed to enter the United States. (*Library of Congress*)

the State wherein they reside." All persons born in the United States, except children born to foreign ambassadors and ministers, are citizens of this country regardless of the citizenship of their parents. (Congress has defined the United States to include Puerto Rico, Guam, the Northern Marianas, and the Virgin Islands.) Although the Fourteenth amendment alone does not make members of Indian tribes citizens of the United States or of the states in which they live, Indians have been declared American citizens by act of Congress.

The Fourteenth amendment confers citizenship according to the principle of **jus soli**—by place of birth. In addition, Congress has granted, under certain conditions, citizenship at birth according to the principle of **jus sanguinis**—by blood. A child born after 1952 of an American living abroad becomes an American citizen at birth as long as the American parent has been present in the United States for five years, including two years after age 14.

Citizenship may also be acquired by **naturalization**, either collective or individual. The granting of citizenship to the people of the Northern Marianas in 1977 by an act of Congress is an example of collective naturalization. Individual naturalization requirements are determined by Congress. Today, with minor exceptions, non-enemy aliens over age 18 who have been lawfully admitted for permanent residence and who have resided in the United States for at least five years and in a state for at least six months are eligible for naturalization.

Any court of record (state or federal) in the United States can grant citizenship. The Immigration and Naturalization Service (INS) makes the necessary investigations and a report to a judge. The final step is a hearing in open court. If the judge is satisfied that the applicant has met all the requirements, the applicant renounces allegiance to his or her former country, and swears to support and defend the Constitution and laws of the United States against all enemies and to bear arms in behalf of the United States when required to do so by law. Those whose religious beliefs prevent them from bearing arms are allowed to take an oath that, if called to duty, they will serve in the armed forces as noncombatants, or that they will perform work of national importance under civilian direction. The court then grants a certificate of naturalization.

Naturalized citizenship may be revoked by court order if the government can prove that it was secured by deception. In addition, citizenship, however acquired, may be voluntarily renounced. But Congress cannot order that citizenship be taken away from persons because of what they have done—for example, committed certain crimes, voted in foreign elections, or served in foreign armies. However, some actions, such as taking out citizenship in another country or swearing allegiance to another nation, may be taken into account as "highly persuasive evidence of a purpose to abandon citizenship." Even so, the government must prove by a predominance of the evidence that the citizen "not only voluntarily committed the expatriating act prescribed in the statute, but also intended to relinquish his citizenship."[2]

Rights of American Citizenship

An American citizen becomes a citizen of one of our states merely by residing in that state. (Residence, as used in the Fourteenth amendment, means domicile, the place one calls home. The legal status of domicile should not be confused with the fact of physical presence. A person may be living in Washington, D.C., but be a citizen of California—that is, consider California home. Residence is primarily a question of intent.)

Many of our most important rights flow from state citizenship rather than from United States citizenship. In the *Slaughter House Cases* (1873) the Supreme Court carefully distinguished between the privileges of United States citizens and

[2] *Vance v. Terrazas*, 444 U.S. 252 (1980).

those of state citizens. It held that the only privileges attaching to national citizenship are those that "owe their existence to the Federal Government, its National Character, its Constitution, or its laws."[3] These privileges have never been completely specified, but they include the right to use the navigable waters of the United States; to assemble peacefully; to petition the national government for redress of grievances; to be protected by the national government on the high seas; to vote, if qualified to do so under state laws, and to have one's vote counted properly; and to travel throughout the United States.

The right to travel abroad Although the right of interstate travel is virtually unqualified, the right to international travel can be regulated within the bounds of due process. Under current law it is unlawful (except as otherwise provided by the president, as has been done for travel to Mexico and Canada) for citizens to leave or enter the United States without a valid passport. The president, acting through the secretary of state, may refuse to grant or may revoke a passport if the government judges that a holder's activities in foreign countries are causing or are likely to cause serious damage to our national security or to the foreign policy of the United States.

The right to live in the United States This right, which is not subject to any congressional limitation, is perhaps the most precious aspect of American citizenship. Aliens have no such right.

RIGHTS OF ALIENS—ADMISSION TO THE UNITED STATES

Albert Einstein (1879–1955), his daughter (right), and his secretary (left) take the oath of citizenship in 1940. A theoretical physicist known for formulating the theory of relativity, Einstein is regarded as one of the wisest scientists of all time. Born in Germany, he later became a Swiss citizen before again becoming a German citizen. In 1934, however, the Nazi government confiscated his property and revoked his German citizenship. At this time he immigrated to the United States. (*UPI/Bettmann Newsphotos*)

Some Americans want the United States to live up to its heritage as a haven for people fleeing religious and political persecution. (President Franklin Roosevelt is reputed to have opened his address to a Daughters of the American Revolution convention with the salutation, "Fellow immigrants and revolutionaries.") Others, however, question the wisdom of admitting refugees while many Americans do not have jobs. Throughout our history there have been intense debates among those wishing to open our borders and those wishing to close them.

Congress decides how many and which aliens shall be admitted to the United States and under what conditions. By 1875 it began to restrict the entry of persons alleged to be "undesirable," such as prostitutes and revolutionaries. During World War I, Congress for the first time set limits on the number of aliens who could be admitted each year. The Immigration Act of 1924 did the same, by creating a national origin system that discriminated against immigrants from southern and southeastern Europe and Asia.

In 1965, after years of debate, a new immigration law was adopted. It remains the basic legislation, although it has often been amended. The law sets the annual ceiling of persons allowed to come here as permanent residents at 270,000—plus immediate relatives of permanent resident immigrants. Preference is given to family members of U.S. residents.

The 270,000 cap, however, is of little significance because of the many allowable exceptions, of which the family exception is the most important. Moreover, it has been supplemented by a series of ad hoc congressional measures to allow the admission of large numbers of political refugees.

In the Refugee Act of 1980, Congress established policies and procedures to deal with the increasing numbers of political refugees seeking admission. The base number allowed is 50,000 annually, but each year, after consultations with Congress,

[3] 16 *Wallace* 36 (1873).

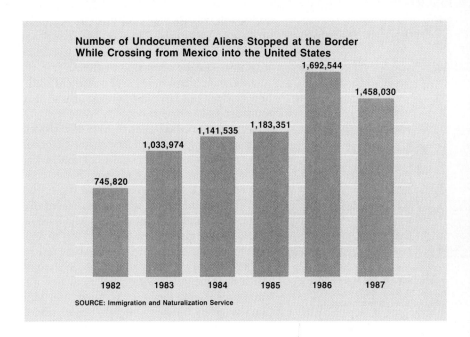

Number of Undocumented Aliens Stopped at the Border While Crossing from Mexico into the United States

1,692,544

1,458,030

1,183,351

1,141,535

1,033,974

745,820

| 1982 | 1983 | 1984 | 1985 | 1986 | 1987 |

SOURCE: Immigration and Naturalization Service

Naturalization Requirements

An applicant for naturalization must:

1. Be over 18.
2. Be lawfully admitted to the United States for permanent residence, and have resided in the United States for at least five years and in a state for at least six months.
3. File a petition of naturalization with a clerk of a court of record (federal or state) verified by two witnesses.
4. Be able to read, write, and speak English.
5. Possess a good moral character.
6. Understand and demonstrate an attachment to the history, principles, and form of government of the United States.
7. Demonstrate that he or she is well disposed toward the good order and happiness of the country.
8. Demonstrate that he or she does not now believe in, nor within the last ten years has ever believed in, advocated, or belonged to an organization that supports opposition to organized government, overthrow of government by violence, or the doctrines of world communism or any other form of totalitarianism.

the president may set a higher number. Since the act was adopted, the annual flow has been in excess of 75,000, and in some years over twice that.

In addition, the attorney general, acting through the Immigration and Naturalization Service, may grant asylum to persons already in the United States, at ports of entry, or in countries other than their own if they have well-founded fears of persecution in their own countries based on race, religion, nationality, social class, or political opinion. It is not enough, however, that applicants for asylum face the same conditions, no matter how terrible, that all other citizens of their countries face or that they wish to escape from economically or politically bad conditions. They must show individual danger of persecution. Because there is an elaborate system of review for those who request asylum once in the United States, it is time consuming and in fact, difficult to expel any who claim this status.[4] For this reason many persons risk great danger getting here and possible detention once they arrive just to have the possibility of seeking asylum status. In recent years, more than 600,000 immigrant visas have been granted annually, most under the 1954 Act, but many to refugees or persons granted asylum.

Prior to World War II most immigrants to the United States came from European nations; today most immigrants come from Latin and Central American nations and from Asia. Pressures are building in Congress for another major overhaul of the basic immigration legislation. Many believe that the present law, giving preference to family members, including not only spouses, parents, and minor children but also brothers and sisters and even in-laws, should be amended to give a higher priority to persons who have useful job skills and educational backgrounds. And there are differences as to whether the numbers allowed into the United States should be increased or decreased. As always, immigration policy is highly contentious.

Undocumented Aliens

Even more controversial than who to admit and under what conditions is the question of how to deal with the variously estimated 2 to 12 million aliens who have illegally crossed our borders, most from Mexico but many from other nations in Central

[4] Arnold H. Leibowitz, "The Refugee Act of 1980: Problems and Congressional Concerns," *The Annals*, (May 1983), pp. 163–71. See also Robert Pear, "Q.A. on Asylum: Some of the Ins and Outs of Who Gets In," *The New York Times* (May 25, 1985), section E, p. 5. See also Gil Loescher and John Scanlan, *Calculated Kindness: Refugees and America's Half-Open Door, 1945 to Present* (Free Press, 1986).

These Mexican farm laborers are wading across the Rio Grande at Juarez to seek farm jobs in Texas. (*UPI/Bettmann Newsphotos*)

Andres Martinez hugs his nephew Raimundo Martinez, who arrived with his family at Miami International Airport. Raimundo's father, Raimundo Martinez, was one of eleven political prisoners arriving from Cuba with their families under a U.S.–Cuba immigration pact. (*UPI/Bettmann Newsphotos*)

and South America because they are escaping from poverty.[5] There is no question about the constitutional power of national authorities to expel such illegal aliens: "Over no conceivable subject is the legislative power of Congress more complete than it is over the admission of aliens."[6]

The problems here are of a different kind. The Immigration and Naturalization Service does not have the money or staff to patrol the thousands of miles of our southern and northern borders. Moreover, it is even more difficult to track down these undocumented aliens inside the United States, round them up, and expel them in a fashion consistent with the practices and policies of a free society. Once here, undocumented aliens do not find it hard to become invisible, especially in our larger cities, or to find jobs. Some employers prefer to hire them, because they often work for less money than those who are here lawfully.

The Immigration Reform and Control Act of 1986 deals with three major topics. First, undocumented aliens who have been in the United States since January 1, 1982, were given until May 4, 1988 to apply for "amnesty," for legal status that gives them time to qualify for permanent residence status and to become naturalized. Second, it imposes new obligations on employers to make a good faith effort to check documents showing legal residency for their employees. If they knowingly hire illegal aliens, they may be fined from $250 to $5000 per alien; repeat offenders may be given up to six-month prison terms. But employers are also subject to penalty if they discriminate against foreign-born legal residents. Third, the act allows a certain number of aliens into the United States as temporary farm workers.

The act's provisions are the outcome of bargains designed to assuage the fears of various groups: Hispanic groups', that employers will hesitate to hire Hispanics or persons who look or sound foreign; employers', that they will be required to keep costly records and be subject to harassment by the INS; farm workers employers', that they will not have enough labor to pick seasonal crops; workers', that itinerant low-paid workers from outside the United States will be used.

More than 2 million persons were eligible for amnesty under the act but only 1.5 million applied. These applicants came from ninety countries, most from Mexico. Asians represented less than 5 percent. Many undocumented aliens failed to apply for amnesty because of the cost for processing the applications, the inability to document their status, and the fear that they might expose family members to deportation. The Act is silent on how to deal with the family of a worker who qualifies for amnesty. The service's policy is not to deport family members who are listed in an application, but to grant legal status only if the service finds "certain compelling or humanitarian factors" in addition to family membership to nonqualified persons.[7]

Rights of Aliens Inside the United States

While in the United States—no matter how they get here—aliens enjoy considerable constitutional protection. Most of the provisions of the Constitution speak of the rights of persons, not just of citizens. Congress and the states, for example, have no greater authority to interfere with an alien's freedom of religion than with a citizen's. State and local regulation of aliens is subject to "heightened" judicial scrutiny. In fact, the Supreme Court has ruled that states cannot keep children of undocumented aliens living within their boundaries from attending public schools free of charge. All aliens, it should also be noted, are "subject to the full range of

[5] The National Research Council concluded that the number is between 2 to 4 million; other studies have estimated it to be as high as 12 million. Many cite 6 million as the correct number. See Gaylord Shaw, "Number of Illegal Aliens in U.S. May Be as Low as 2 Million, New Study Contends," *Los Angeles Times* (June 25, 1985), and George C. Kiser and Martha Woody Kiser, eds., *Mexican Workers in the United States: Historical and Political Perspectives* (University of New Mexico Press, 1979).

[6] *Kleindienst v. Mandel*, 408 U.S. 753 (1972).

[7] *Congressional Quarterly*, vol. 45, October 31, 1987, p. 2673.

obligations, including the payment of taxes, imposed by the states' civil and criminal laws."[8]

The rules under which aliens come and stay here are determined by Congress. Congress has wide discretion in setting the terms and conditions for staying, even to making retroactive conditions. Present laws make aliens deportable, for example, for such things as conviction of two crimes involving moral turpitude, for joining organizations that advocate revolution, or for engaging in activities that the attorney general believes to be "subversive to national security."

CONSTITUTIONAL PROTECTION OF PROPERTY

Property does not have rights: People do. *Property rights* are the rights of an individual to own, use, rent, invest, or contract for property. Historically, the close connection between liberty and ownership of property, between property and power, has been emphasized in American political thinking and American political institutions.

A major purpose of the framers of the Constitution was to establish a government strong enough to protect all persons' rights to use and enjoy their own property. At the same time the framers wanted a government so limited that it could not endanger that right. They were disturbed by the efforts of some state legislatures in behalf of debtors at the expense of creditors. As a result, they ensured that the Constitution forbade states to make anything except gold or silver legal tender for the payment of debts or to pass any law "impairing the obligation of contracts."

The Contract Clause

The contract clause was designed to prevent states from extending the period during which debtors could meet their payments or otherwise get out of their contractual obligations. The framers had in mind an ordinary contract between private persons. However, beginning with Chief Justice John Marshall, the Supreme Court expanded the coverage of the clause to prevent states from altering in any way privileges previously conferred on a corporation.

In effect, the contract clause was used to protect vested property at the expense of the power of the states to guard the public welfare. In the 1880s, however, the Court began to restrict gradually the coverage of the contract clause and to subject contracts to what in constitutional law is known as **police powers**—the power to protect the public health, safety, welfare, and morals. By 1934 the Supreme Court actually held that even contracts between individuals—the very ones the contract clause was intended to protect—could be modified by state law in order to avert social and economic catastrophe.[9] Although the contract clause is still invoked occasionally to challenge a state regulation of property, it is no longer a significant limitation on governmental power.

Eminent Domain—What Happens When the Government Takes Our Property?

Both the national and the state governments have the power of **eminent domain**— that is, the power to take private property for public use—but the owner must be fairly compensated. This limitation was the first provision of the Bill of Rights to be incorporated within the Fourteenth amendment and thus to be made applicable to the states.

[8] Justice Brennan in *Plyler* v. *Doe*, 457 U.S. 202 (1982).
[9] *Home Building & Loan Assn.* v. *Blaisdell*, 290 U.S. 398 (1934).

What constitutes a "taking" for purposes of the eminent domain clause? Ordinarily, but not always, the taking must be direct and a person must lose title and control over the property. The clause does not require compensation merely because governmental action may result in property loss—for example, if a zoning regulation restricts an area to single-family residential use and thus lowers the value of a particular property.

Sometimes the courts find that the government has "taken" property and owes compensation to its owners even when title is left in the hands of the owners. For example, if a government creates landing and take-off paths for airplanes over property adjacent to airports such that the land is no longer suitable for its prior use (say, raising chickens), compensation is warranted.

"Just compensation" is not always easy to define. In case of dispute, the final decision is made by the courts.

Due Process

Perhaps the most difficult parts of the Constitution to understand are the clauses in the Fifth and Fourteenth amendments that forbid national and state governments to deny any person life, liberty, or property without due process of law. These **due process clauses** have resulted in more Supreme Court decisions than any other provisions in the Constitution, although the equal protection clause runs a close second. Even so, it is impossible to explain due process precisely. The Supreme Court itself has refused to give "due process" a precise definition.

There are two kinds of due process: procedural and substantive. **Procedural due process** generally refers to the methods by which a law is enforced. But a law itself, as enacted, may violate the procedural due process requirement, in several ways.

First, the statute may be too vague: "A statute which either forbids or requires the doing of an act in terms so vague that men of common intelligence must necessarily guess at its meaning and differ as to its application, violates the first essential of due process."[10] A vague statute fails to provide adequate warning and does not contain sufficient guidelines for law enforcement officials, juries, and courts (see accompanying box).

A second way in which a law itself may violate procedural due process is by creating an improper presumption of guilt. Persons are presumed innocent; due process places the burden on the government to prove guilt beyond a reasonable doubt. This burden cannot be shifted, nor the standard of proof diminished by a statutory presumption of guilt. Laws presuming, for example, that all marijuana or cocaine in one's possession must have been obtained illegally have been declared unconstitutional. Still, the Court did uphold such a presumption with respect to heroin, because little, if any, heroin is made in this country, and virtually all of it is illegally imported. It is therefore not unreasonable to presume that a person who possesses heroin obtained it illegally.

Traditionally, however, procedural due process refers to the way in which a law is applied. To paraphrase Daniel Webster's famous definition, it requires a procedure that hears before it condemns, proceeds upon inquiry, and renders judgment only after a trial or some kind of hearing. Originally procedural due process was limited to criminal prosecutions, but it now applies to many different kinds of governmental proceedings. It is required, for instance, in juvenile hearings, disbarment proceedings, proceedings to determine eligibility for welfare payments, revocation of drivers' licenses, disciplinary proceedings in state universities and public schools, and even applications by parents to admit their minor children to state mental hospitals.

[10] *Connally* v. *General Construction Co.*, 269 U.S. 385 (1926).

Some Statutes Declared Void for Vagueness

A statute making it a crime to treat "contemptuously" the American flag.

A vagrancy ordinance classifying vagrants as "rogues and vagabonds," "dissolute persons who go about begging," "common night walkers," and so on.

An ordinance requiring persons who loiter or wander the streets to provide "credible and reliable" identification and to account for their presence when required by a police officer.

"What's so great about due process? Due process got me ten years."
Drawing by Lorenz; © 1972. *The New Yorker Magazine, Inc.*

A Statute Not Considered Vague

An ordinance requiring a license for businesses selling any items "designed or marketed for use with illegal cannabis or drugs"— what are commonly known as "headshops."

The controversy over the Supreme Court's ruling on abortions is demonstrated by these two groups of marchers. Fifteen years after the ruling, protest rallies by both sides of this controversy are still a regular part of the Washington landscape. (*UPI/Bettman Newsphotos*)

Procedural due process has taken on new importance with the expanded interpretation of the words "liberty" and "property." The liberty that is protected is more than freedom from being thrown into jail; and the property that is secured goes beyond mere ownership of real estate, things, or money. Rather, liberty includes "the right of the individual to contract, to engage in any of the common occupations of life, to acquire useful knowledge, to marry, to establish a home and bring up children, to worship God according to the dictates of his own conscience, and generally to enjoy those common law privileges long recognized as essential to the orderly pursuit of happiness of free men."[11]

The property interests that are protected are not created by the Constitution; they are created by state law. They include variety of rights, such as people's jobs, various kinds of licenses, and many other items of value conferred by state laws.

This expansion of the meanings of liberty and property has blurred the distinctions between liberty rights and property rights. Moreover, it has lessened the difference between a right and a privilege. Today public welfare, housing, education, employment, professional licenses, and so on, are increasingly becoming matters of entitlement. Their denial thus involves some form of due process.

Nevertheless, "the range of interests protected by procedural due process is not indefinite." Not every "grievous loss visited upon a person by the State is sufficient to invoke the procedural protections of the due process clause."[12] Whether or not an interest is protected by due process depends on the nature of the interest, not its importance to the individual. Faculty members in public institutions, for instance, are not entitled to procedural due process before being denied tenure, because they have no constitutional right to teaching jobs. (However, public employees who are given tenure rights by law or institutional policies are entitled to due process before they may be deprived of their property rights to their jobs.[13])

"Once it is determined that due process applies, the question remains what process is due." What is due varies with the kind of interest involved, the reliability of the procedures used, and the governmental purposes to be served.[14] In a federal courtroom, due process requires the careful observance of the provisions of the Bill of Rights as outlined in amendments Four through Eight.

The question in other kinds of proceedings is what must be done to ensure fundamental fairness. It is hard to generalize because many kinds of proceedings are involved, but at a minimum the person involved must have *adequate notice* and an *opportunity to be heard*. The hearing required must be appropriate to the interest involved, and it usually has to be held prior to an adverse governmental action. For example, tenured public employees are entitled before termination to notice, oral or written, an explanation of the reasons and an opportunity to present their side of the case. Juveniles cannot be declared delinquent without a hearing in which they have the right to confront and cross-examine hostile witnesses, to present evidence, and to be represented by counsel, but they are not entitled to have the decision made by a jury. Children are entitled to due process when their parents seek to send them to mental hospitals, but adversary proceedings that pit children against parents are not necessary: Personal interviews and reviews of the decisions by neutral health professionals are sufficient.

Substantive Due Process

Procedural due process places limits on *how* governmental power may be exercised; **substantive due process** places limits on *what* that power may be used to do, no matter how it is done. Procedural due process has to do with the *procedures* of

[11] *Meyer* v. *Nebraska*, 262 U.S. 390 (1923).
[12] *Meachum* v. *Fano*, 427 U.S. 215 (1976).
[13] *Cleveland Bd. of Education* v. *Loudermill*, 470 U.S. 532 (1985).
[14] *Morrissey* v. *Brewer*, 408 U.S. 471 (1972).

the law; substantive due process has to do with the *content* of the law. Procedural due process mainly limits the executive and judicial branches; substantive due process mainly limits the legislative branch. Substantive due process means that an "unreasonable" law, even if properly passed and properly applied, is unconstitutional. It means that there are certain things governments should not be allowed to do, no matter how they do it.

Perhaps the most celebrated—certainly the most controversial—illustration of the Court's recent use of substantive due process is *Roe* v. *Wade* (1973). The Court ruled:

1. During the first trimester of a woman's pregnancy (about the first three months), it is unreasonable interference with her liberty and privacy rights, and unconstitutional, for a state to interfere with her right to choose an abortion or with her doctor's medical judgments about how to carry it out.
2. During the second trimester the state's interest in protecting the health of women who undergo abortions becomes compelling, and a state may make reasonable regulations about how, where, and when abortions may be performed.
3. During the third trimester the state's interest in protecting the unborn child is so important that the state can proscribe abortions altogether, except when necessary to preserve the life or health of the mother.[15]

The Supreme Court has also concluded that although a woman has the constitutional right to have an abortion during the early months of pregnancy, if she wishes, she has no right to have the state pay for it. A state may, therefore, refuse to pay the nontherapeutic abortion-related medical expenses of poor women, even though it does pay for such expenses related to childbirth.[16]

Before 1937 substantive due process was used primarily to protect "liberty of contract"—that is, business liberty. Indeed, the adoption of the doctrine of substantive due process and the simultaneous expansion of the meaning of liberty and property made the Supreme Court, for a time, the final judge of our economic and industrial life. During this period the Supreme Court was dominated by conservative jurists who considered almost all social welfare legislation unreasonable. They used the due process clause to strike down laws regulating hours of labor, establishing minimum wages, regulating prices, and forbidding employers to fire workers for union membership. The Supreme Court vetoed laws adversely affecting property rights unless the judges could be persuaded that such laws were necessary to protect the public health or safety.

The trouble with substantive interpretation of due process is that people's determination of the reasonableness of a law depends on their economic, social, and political views. In democracies, elected officials are supposed to accommodate opposing notions of reasonableness and to decide what regulations of liberty and property are needed to promote the public welfare. When the Supreme Court substitutes its own ideas of reasonableness for those of the legislature, it acts like a superlegislature. But how competent are judges to say what the nation's economic (or other) policies should be?

In response to this criticism, since 1937 the Supreme Court has largely refused to apply the doctrine of substantive due process to review laws regulating the economy. The Court now believes that deciding what constitutes reasonable regulations of our business and commercial life is a legislative, not a judicial, responsibility. As long as the justices see some connection between a law and the promotion of the public welfare, the Supreme Court will not interfere.

YOU DECIDE

Scott E. Ewing was dismissed by the University of Michigan from a six-year combined undergraduate and medical educational program after failing an examination required to qualify for the final two years. His request to retake the examination was denied. He brought an action in a federal district court, alleging that because every other medical student who had failed the examination had routinely been given at least a second chance to take the test that he had a property interest in his continued enrollment in the program. He contended that his dismissal was arbitrary and capricious and was thus in violation of his substantive due process rights guaranteed by the Fourteenth amendment. The university answered that he had been dismissed for proper academic reasons, that no one has a constitutional right to a second examination, and that what it had done was perfectly reasonable.

Did Ewing have a due process property interest to continued enrollment free from arbitrary state action?

Did the state of Michigan violate his substantive property right in this instance?

(Answer/Discussion on page 134)

[15] 410 U.S. 113 (1973).

[16] *Akron* v. *Akron Center for Reproductive Health*, 462 U.S. 416 (1983).

The abandonment of the doctrine of substantive due process as a limit on the government's power to regulate business has not meant an abandonment of substantive due process. Quite the contrary. Since 1937 the word liberty in the Fifth and Fourteenth amendments has been expanded to include the basic civil liberties. Substantive due process has been given new life as a limitation on governmental power regarding these liberties. Further, since the 1950s the Supreme Court has developed a substantive interpretation of the equal protection clause to supplement the substantive interpretation of due process.

Prior to 1937 liberal justices (in dissent) and liberal commentators accused conservative justices of using substantive due process to impose their own ideas upon the nation. Today conservative judges are contending that once again the Supreme Court is going beyond the bounds of its responsibilities (see Chapter 16). Justices who support the current application of substantive due process, of course, deny they are merely substituting their own values for those of the legislature. They argue that there is a fundamental difference between what they are doing in protecting civil liberties and what the pre-1937 conservative justices did to protect property rights. The earlier justices were writing into the Constitution the principles of laissez-faire economics, whereas the present justices are extracting from the Constitution its principles of civil liberties. Justice Powell, in behalf of the Court, conceded:

> Substantive due process has at times been a treacherous field for this Court. There are risks when the judicial branch gives enhanced protection to certain substantive liberties without the guidance of the more specific provisions of the Bill of Rights. . . . There is reason for concern lest the only limits to such judicial intervention become the predilections of those who happen at the time to be Members of this Court. . . . That history counsels caution and restraint. But it does not counsel abandonment [of substantive due process].[17]

The notion that laws must be reasonable has deep roots in natural law concepts and a long history in the American constitutional tradition. For most Americans most of the time, it is not enough merely to say that a law reflects the wishes of the popular or legislative majority. We also want our laws to be just, and we continue to rely heavily on judges to decide what is just. In Chapter 16 we look again at the tensions between democratic procedures and judicial activism.

FREEDOM FROM ARBITRARY ARREST, QUESTIONING, AND IMPRISONMENT

Some Laws Declared To Deny Substantive Due Process

A school board regulation requiring teachers to cease teaching past the fourth month of pregnancy and barring them from returning to the classroom until three months after the birth of a child.

A state law permitting confinement of nondangerous mentally ill persons against their wishes.

James Otis's address in 1761 protesting arbitrary searches and seizures by English customs officials was the signal for the American Revolution. As John Adams later said of that speech: "American independence was then and there born." The Fourth amendment states: "The right of the people to be secure in their persons, houses, papers, and effects, against unreasonable searches and seizures, shall not be violated, and no Warrants shall issue, but upon probable cause, supported by Oath or affirmation, and particularly describing the place to be searched, and the persons or things to be seized."

What Is Unreasonable Search and Seizure?

Despite what we sometimes see in television police dramas and read about in the news, law-enforcement officers have no general right to invade homes and break down doors. They are not supposed to search people except under certain conditions,

[17] *Moore v. City of East Cleveland*, 431 U.S. 494 (1977).

Edward Lawson, known as the California Walkman, brought a suit for damages against San Diego police after they had arrested him fifteen times. Lawson frequently walked late at night, and often in neighborhoods other than his own. He won his case. (UPI/Bettmann Newsphotos)

Answer/Discussion

Eight members of the United States Supreme Court said that even if it is assumed that Ewing had such a right, the responsibility for determining academic matters belongs to the faculty, and judges should interfere only if there is "a substantial departure from accepted academic norms as to demonstrate that the faculty did not exercise professional judgment and acted clearly in an arbitrary and capricious manner." Justice Lewis Powell concurred, but would not even concede that Ewing might, for purposes of the decision, have a substantive due process property right not to be dismissed by a state university in an arbitrary manner.

You might want to read this short opinion. Most libraries have it listed under the name of *Regents of the University of Michigan* v. *Ewing*, 88 L Ed 2d 523 (1985). Eventually it will be issued by the U.S. Government Printing Office under the citation 474 U.S. ___ (1985).

and they have no right to arrest them except under certain circumstances. This is a highly technical area, and one in which the Supreme Court has had great difficulty in determining what the Constitution means.[18]

Arrests   The Constitution does not forbid all searches and seizures, only "unreasonable" ones.[19] "Seizures," or what we now call police detentions and arrests, are in fact given less protection than searches. Most arrests take place without arrest warrants. Police may arrest persons *in public places* without warrants, provided they have *probable cause* to believe the persons have committed or are about to commit crimes. Immediately after making an arrest, especially one made without a warrant, the police must take the person arrested to a magistrate so that the latter—not just the police—can decide whether probable cause existed to justify the warrantless arrest.

Generally, arrests without warrants can take place only in public places. Except in emergencies—for example, when somebody's life is at stake or when police are in hot pursuit of a person they have seen commit a felony—police may not force their way into a suspect's home without a warrant to make an arrest. Even with a warrant, police may not break into a third party's home to arrest a suspect.

Not every encounter between police and citizens is a seizure. A person is seized in a constitutional sense only when police—by means of physical force or a show of authority—restrain that person's freedom of movement such that a "reasonable person would have believed that he was not free to leave."[20]

Deadly Force   Under the common law police officers who have to apprehend a fleeing felon could use weapons that might result in a suspect's serious injury, even death. But the Fourth amendment places substantial limits on the use of "deadly force." It is unconstitutional to shoot an apparently unarmed suspected fleeing felon unless the officer has probable cause to believe that the suspect poses a significant threat of death or serious injury to the officer or others. Also, when feasible, the officer must first warn the suspect—"Halt or I'll shoot."[21]

Searches   For the most part (see accompanying box for exceptions), a police search without proper consent is constitutionally unreasonable, unless it has been authorized by a valid search warrant, issued by a magistrate after the police indicate under oath that they have "probable cause" to justify its issuance. Magistrates must perform this function in a neutral and detached manner and not serve merely as rubber stamps for the police.[22]

General search warrants are outlawed by the Constitution. When a magistrate issues a warrant, the warrant must describe what places are to be searched and what things are to be seized. Also, a warrant to search a public place, such as a tavern, does not authorize the search of persons who happen to be in that place.

Any place a person has a reasonable, legitimate "expectation of privacy"—for example, in a hotel room, in a rented home, in a friend's apartment, or even in a telephone booth—is protected against a warrantless search. Observation of an individual's backyard by police in low flying airplanes is not so protected.[23] In short, the Fourth amendment protects people, not places, from unreasonable governmental intrusions. However, once police have a valid search warrant, they may intrude into places of privacy. They may even break and enter if such entry is the only means by which they may execute the warrant.

[18] The most comprehensive analysis of these complicated issues is Wayne R. LaFave, *Search and Seizure: A Treatise on the Fourth Amendment* (West Publishing, 1978, and 1984 supplement).

[19] Jeffrey A. Segal, "Predicting Supreme Court Cases Probabilistically: The Search and Seizure Cases, 1962–1981," *The American Political Science Review* (December 1984), pp. 891–900.

[20] *United States* v. *Mendenhall*, 446 U.S. 544 (1980).

[21] *Tennessee* v. *Garner*, 471 U.S. 1 (1985).

[22] *Lo-Ji Sales, Inc.* v. *New York*, 442 U.S. 319 (1979).

[23] *California* v. *Ciraolo*, 476 U.S. 207 (1986).

The Fourth amendment protects against searches by government officers other than the police, such as public school teachers and officials, internal revenue agents, health inspectors, and occupational and safety inspectors. However, less stringent conditions apply to nonpolice searches. Although covered by the Fourth amendment, public school officials, for example, may search a student when there are "reasonable grounds for suspecting that the search will turn up evidence that the student has violated or is violating either the law or the rules of the school." Such a search is constitutionally permissible in its scope, according to the national Constitution, when it is "not excessively intrusive in light of the age and sex of the student and the nature of the offense."[24]

The inventions of science have confronted judges with new problems in applying the Fourth amendment. Obviously, the writers of the Fourth amendment intended such physical objects as books, papers, letters, and other kinds of documents to be unseizable by police except on the basis of limited search warrants issued by magistrates. But what of tapping phone wires, using electronic devices to eavesdrop, or using secret television cameras to make videotapes? In *Olmstead* v. *United States* (1928) a bare majority of the Supreme Court held that there was no unconstitutional search unless seizure of physical objects or actual physical entry into a premise was involved. Justices Holmes and Brandeis, in dissent, argued that the Constitution should keep up with the times; the "dirty business" of wiretapping produced the same evil invasions of privacy the framers had in mind when they wrote the Fourteenth amendment.[25]

Forty years later, in *Katz* v. *United States* (1967), the Supreme Court adopted the Holmes-Brandeis position: "The Fourth Amendment protects people—and not simply 'areas'—against unreasonable searches and seizures." The use by police officers of electronic devices to overhear a conversation in a public telephone booth is a search and seizure within the meaning of the Constitution. "Wherever a man may be" (subsequently modified and limited to those places where one has a "legitimate expectation of privacy"),[26] "he is entitled to know that he will remain free from unreasonable searches and seizures."[27]

Because conversations are now constitutionally protected, legislatures and judges have had to develop rules to govern when and which conversations may be intercepted. The basic federal legislation is contained in a section of the Crime Control and Safe Streets Act of 1968. This act makes it a crime for any unauthorized person to tap telephone wires or use or sell in interstate commerce electronic bugging devices. However, it empowers the attorney general to secure a warrant from a federal judge authorizing federal agents to engage in bugging in order to track down persons suspected of certain federal crimes. As amended in 1984, the act permits wiretaps without prior court approval for forty-eight hours in emergency situations involving certain crimes, such as child pornography, illegal currency transactions, offenses against crime witnesses, or immediate danger of death or serious injury. At the state level the act authorizes the principal prosecuting attorney of any state or political subdivision to apply to a state judge for a warrant approving wiretapping or oral intercepts for felonies. (Most state and local jurisdictions allow such intercepts.) Judges may issue warrants only if they decide probable cause exists that a crime is being, has been, or is about to be committed, and that information relating to that crime may be obtained only by the intercept. (Congress is likely to extend the act to cover electronic mail and computer transactions, and to make it clear that it also protects cellular phone conversations from automobiles.)

Although the act left unresolved the question of whether the president has

"I TAKE THE IRAN-CONTRA DEFENSE—I WOULDN'T HAVE HAD TO BREAK ANY LAWS IF YOUR STUPID LAWS HAD FIT IN WITH WHAT I WANTED TO DO"

(From HERBLOCK AT LARGE, Pantheon Books, 1987)

"The Court finds itself on the horns of a dilemma. On the one hand, wiretap evidence is inadmissible, and on the other hand I'm dying to hear it." (Drawing by Handelsman; © 1972. The New Yorker Magazine, Inc.)

[24] *New Jersey* v. *T.L.O*, 469 U.S. 365 (1985).

[25] 277 U.S. 438 (1928).

[26] *Rakas* v. *Illinois*, 439 U.S. 128 (1978).

[27] 389 U.S. 347 (1967).

the inherent constitutional authority to order electronic surveillance, without warrant, of agents of foreign powers or of persons suspected of subversion, the Supreme Court has ruled that the president has no such power regarding surveillance of persons suspected of domestic subversion: "The danger to political dissent is acute where the government attempts to act under so vague a concept as the power to protect domestic security."[28] The Court pointedly did not decide on the scope of presidential authority to order surveillance of foreign agents.

By 1978, with the adoption of the Foreign Intelligence Surveillance Act, "Congress sent a message that it no longer recognized executive branch 'inherent power' " to order warrantless electronic surveillance of *anybody* for *any purpose*.[29] Congress itself, however, has authorized such searches by officials of the National Security Agency—the agency in charge of making and breaking codes. No other agency may "bug" foreign agents, unless it first secures a warrant from the United States Foreign Intelligence Surveillance Court, which consists of seven designated federal district judges, who meet twice each month, in secret. The Court grants warrants for "bugging" agents of foreign powers, whether or not they are American citizens. It has refused, however, to authorize "black-bag" jobs—that is, surreptitious entry for the purpose of physical surveillance.[30]

Note that as long as police officers do not make illegal entries or improper searches and seizures, nothing either in the Constitution or in any federal law prevents them from resorting to undercover tactics in their pursuit of wrongdoers. For example, they may use secret cameras or recording devices on their own persons; they may use trained dogs to sniff luggage located in public places (to locate narcotics or bombs); and they can listen in to telephone conversations via extension phones, provided they have the consent of one of the parties to the conversation and are in a place where they have a right to be. (Some official eavesdropping, however, may violate other constitutional rights, such as the right to a privileged conversation with one's attorney, for example.)

A specially trained dog is used to sniff for narcotics. (*Judy Porter/Photo Researchers*)

The Exclusionary Rule

Combining the Fourth amendment prohibition against unreasonable searches with the Fifth amendment injunction that persons shall not be compelled to be witnesses against themselves, the Supreme Court ruled, in *Mapp* v. *Ohio*, that evidence unconstitutionally obtained cannot be used in a criminal trial as part of the government's main case against persons from whom it was seized.[31] This exclusionary rule was adopted in large part to prevent police misconduct. Because police are seldom prosecuted for making illegal searches and are often unable to pay civil damages, the justices felt that the exclusionary rule was the best—and maybe the only—sanction.

Critics of the exclusionary rule, including Chief Justice Rehnquist and Attorney General Meese, question why criminals should go free just because of police misconduct.[32] So far the Supreme Court has refused to abandon the rule, but it has started making some exceptions to it.

The Court has also narrowed the exclusionary rule to cover only trials of those from whom the evidence was unconstitutionally seized, as one citizen, Jack Payner, found out. Internal Revenue Service agents, aided by a private investigator,

Search Warrants Are Not Required for Police Searches

1. When searches are based on consent.
2. Under certain conditions involving automobiles, including mobile motor homes.
3. To stop briefly and to frisk quickly possibly armed and dangerous persons, to remove weapons from them and to search areas under their immediate control, such as the passenger compartment of an automobile. (Such a search is known as a *Terry* search because it was first sanctioned by the Supreme Court in *Terry* v. *Ohio*.*)

[28] *U.S.* v. *U.S. District Court*, 407 U.S. 297 (1972).

[29] *Congressional Quarterly* (October 15, 1978), p. 2966.

[30] *The Washington Post* (June 24, 1981).

[31] 367 U.S. 643 (1961).

[32] See arguments of Chief Justice Burger and Justice Rehnquist in *California* v. *Minjares*, 443 U.S. 916 (1979); of Justice White in *Illinois* v. *Gates*, 462 U.S. 213 (1983); and of Attorney General Meese, "Square Miranda with Reason," *The Wall Street Journal* (June 13, 1986), p. 18.

4. When police officers have a reasonable suspicion that the person in question was involved in or is wanted in connection with a felony (This must be a *Terry* search.)

5. When police have an arrest warrant or probable cause to make an arrest, which allows them to make a complete search of the persons being arrested and the area under such persons' immediate control.

6. When incriminating evidence or contraband is in "plain view."

7. As part of the routine procedure incident to incarcerating an arrested person, to search articles in the possession of the person being arrested.

8. At international border crossings. This includes opening mail entering the country if officials have "reasonable cause" to suspect it contains merchandise imported contrary to the law. It also includes detention and bodily searches if customs officials have a reasonable ground to suspect smuggling of drugs or other contraband in bodily cavities.

9. On ships on the waterways of the United States, including inland waterways that provide access to the open seas.

10. When officers do not have time to secure a warrant before evidence is destroyed or when there is a need "to protect or preserve life and avoid serious injury"—for example, when firefighters and police need to break into a burning building.

* *Terry* v. *Ohio*, 392 U.S. 1 (1968).

operating in the best tradition of television police dramas, broke into Payner's banker's hotel room while a female undercover agent lured the banker out to dinner. The agents "borrowed" the banker's briefcase, photographed documents, put the original documents back, and returned the briefcase. This "caper" was clearly a deliberate intrusion into the banker's privacy and a violation of his Fourth amendment rights. Nonetheless, the evidence was allowed to be used to convict Payner, one of the banker's customers, of income tax evasion. Payner could expect neither privacy in his banker's briefcase nor any ownership of the documents taken from it.[33]

The Right to Remain Silent

During the seventeenth century certain special courts in England forced confessions of heresy and sedition from religious dissenters. The British privilege against self-incrimination developed in response to these practices. Because they were familiar with this history, the framers of our Bill of Rights included in the Fifth amendment the provision that persons shall not be compelled to testify against themselves in criminal prosecutions. This protection against self-incrimination is designed to strengthen a fundamental principle of Anglo-American justice: that no person has an obligation to prove innocence. Rather, the burden is on the government to prove guilt.

The privilege against self-incrimination applies literally only in criminal prosecutions, but it has always been interpreted to protect any person subject to questioning by any agency of government. A witness before a congressional committee, for example, may refuse to answer incriminating questions. However, to invoke the privilege, the witness must not only prove that his or her answers might be embarrassing or might lead to loss of a job or even to civil suits; he or she must also have a reasonable fear that the answers might support a criminal prosecution or "furnish a link in the chain of evidence needed to prosecute" a crime.[34] Sometimes authorities would rather have answers from a witness than prosecute him or her. Congress has established procedures so that prosecutors and congressional committees may secure from a federal judge a grant of immunity for such a witness. After immunity has been granted, a witness may no longer claim a right to refuse to testify. However, the only immunity that Congress presently provides is that, except for perjury prosecution, the government cannot use the information directly derived from the testimony.

The Third Degree

Police questioning of suspects is a key procedure for solving crimes. It can, however, be easily abused. Police officers sometimes forget or ignore the constitutional rights of suspects, especially of those who are frightened and ignorant. Torture, detention, and sustained interrogation to wring confessions from suspects, common practices in police states, are not unknown in the United States.

What good is the presumption of innocence if, long before the accused are brought before the court, they are detained and forced to prove their innocence to the police? Judges have done much to stamp out police brutality. The Supreme Court has ruled that even though there may be sufficient evidence to support a conviction apart from a confession, the admission into evidence of a coerced confession violates the self-incrimination clause, deprives a person of the assistance of counsel guaranteed by the Sixth and Fourteenth amendments, deprives a person of due process, and undermines the entire proceeding.

The federal rules of criminal procedure and the laws of all our states require officers to promptly take those whom they have arrested before magistrates. The

[33] *United States* v. *Payner*, 447 U.S. 727 (1980).
[34] *Blau* v. *United States*, 340 U.S. 332 (1951).

magistrates must inform persons in custody of their constitutional rights and allow them to get in touch with friends and to seek legal advice. Although the police have no right to hold persons for questioning prior to hearings before the magistrates, they are often tempted to do so. Police may believe that if they can quiz suspects before the suspects know their constitutional rights to remain silent, they can get them to confess.

In *Miranda* v. *Arizona* in 1966, the Supreme Court announced that no conviction—federal or state—could stand if evidence introduced at the trial had been obtained by the police as the result of "custodial interrogation," unless the following conditions were met: Suspects have been (1) notified that they are free to remain silent; (2) warned that what they say may be used against them in court; (3) told that they have a right to have attorneys present during the questioning; (4) informed that if they cannot afford to hire their own lawyers, attorneys will be provided for them; and (5) permitted at any stage of the police interrogation to terminate it. If suspects answer questions in the absence of an attorney, the burden is still on the prosecution to demonstrate that the suspects knowingly and intelligently gave up their rights to remain silent and to have their own lawyers present. Failure to comply with these requirements will lead to reversal of a conviction even if other evidence is sufficient to establish guilt.[35]

Many critics of the *Miranda* decision believe the Court has unnecessarily and severely limited the ability of the police to bring criminals to justice. The importance of pretrial interrogations is underscored by the fact that roughly 90 percent of all criminal convictions result from pleas of guilty and never reach full trials. Nevertheless, the Supreme Court has upheld *Miranda*, modified to some extent: Evidence obtained contrary to the *Miranda* guidelines may be used to attack the credibility of statements defendants make at their trials if what the defendants say is contrary to what they have previously told the police.

The Right of Privacy

Although there is no mention of the right of privacy in the Constitution, the Supreme Court has put together some elements from the First, Fourth, Fifth, Ninth, and Fourteenth amendments to recognize that personal privacy is one of the rights protected by the Constitution. There are three aspects of this right: (1) the right to be free from governmental surveillance and intrusion, especially in marital matters; (2) the right not to have private affairs made public by the government; and (3) the right to be free in thought and belief from governmental compulsion.[36]

Congress showed some concern about privacy with the adoption of the Family Educational Rights Act of 1974 and the Privacy Act of 1974. These laws limit the record-keeping and record-disclosing activities of schools and universities that receive federal funds; place restraints on files kept by federal agencies; and, under certain conditions, give individuals access to government files in order to correct information about themselves. But privacy, although highly valued in the abstract, has often run afoul of other rights—for example, the rights of the press. When in conflict with these other rights, it has not fared well before either Congress or

[35] 384 U.S. 436 (1966). Liva Baker, *Miranda: Crime, Law and Politics* (Atheneum, 1983), explores every aspect of the decision, including subsequent controversy about its effects.
[36] Philip B. Kurland, *Some Reflections on Privacy and the Constitution* (The University of Chicago Center for Policy Study, 1976), p. 9. A classic and influential article about privacy is S. D. Warren and L. D. Brandeis, "The Right to Privacy," *Harvard Law Review* (December 15, 1890), pp. 193–220. David M. O'Brien, *Privacy, Law, and Public Policy* (Praeger, 1979), is a comprehensive discussion of the privacy doctrine.

the courts. (The exception is the Supreme Court's protection of marital privacy from state regulation.)

The Writ of Habeas Corpus

Even though the framers did not think a Bill of Rights was necessary, they considered certain rights important enough to be included in the original Constitution. Foremost is the guarantee that the **writ of habeas corpus** will be available unless suspended in time of rebellion or invasion. Permission to suspend the writ is found in the article setting forth the powers of Congress, so, presumably, only Congress has the right to suspend it.

As originally used, the writ was merely an inquiry by a court to determine whether or not a person was being held in custody as the result of an act of a court with proper jurisdiction. But over the years it has developed into a remedy "available to effect discharge from any confinement contrary to the Constitution or fundamental law."[37] Simply stated, the writ is a court order to any person having another in custody directing the official to produce the prisoner in court and to explain to the judge why the prisoner is being held. The person being held in custody, or subject to restraint, applies under oath, usually through an attorney, and states why he or she believes he or she is being unlawfully held. The judge then orders the jailer to show cause why the writ should not be issued. If a judge finds that a petitioner is being unlawfully detained, the judge may order the prisoner's immediate release.

The case of Messrs. Duncan and White is a good example of one use of the writ. Two years after Pearl Harbor Duncan, a civilian shipfitter, had been convicted by military authorities for assaulting two marine sentries. Eight months after Pearl Harbor White, a stockbroker, had been convicted by military authorities for embezzling stock from another civilian. Duncan and White both filed petitions for writs of habeas corpus in the district court of Hawaii, citing both statutory and constitutional reasons why the military had no right to try them and to keep them in prison. The court then asked the military to show cause why the petition should not be granted. The military replied that Hawaii had become part of an active theater of war; that the writ of habeas corpus had been suspended; that martial law had been established; and that, consequently, the district court had no jurisdiction to issue the writs. Moreover, the writ of habeas corpus should not be issued in this case because the military trials of Duncan and White were valid. The district court, in an action eventually approved by the Supreme Court, agreed with Duncan and White and issued writs ordering their release.[38]

State judges may not issue writs of habeas corpus to find out why persons are being held by national authorities, but federal judges may do so to find out why persons are being restrained by state and local officials. Sometimes a single federal judge will set aside a conviction even after it has been reviewed by the state supreme court. Partly because of criticism by state judges, partly because of concern for the principles of federalism, and partly because of a growing overload on the federal courts, the Supreme Court has begun to restrict the use of habeas corpus by federal judges.[39] For example, if a state court has already provided an opportunity for persons to present the argument that the evidence used against

YOU DECIDE

At 1 a.m. on July 18, 1982, Ralph E. Watkinson was closing his shop for the night, when someone pointing a gun came toward him. Watkinson drew his own gun and fired, the fire was returned, and Watkinson was hit in the leg. He watched his assailant flee, apparently wounded on the left side. Later that night Rudolph Lee, Jr., suffering from a gunshot wound to his left chest, was identified by Watkinson as the man who shot him. Lee was charged with the crime. Shortly thereafter the Commonwealth of Virginia moved in a state court for an order directing Lee to undergo surgery to remove (in effect, search for) an object thought to be a bullet lodged under his left collarbone.

Does such a search violate the Fourth amendment?

(Answer/Discussion on next page.)

[37] *Presier* v. *Rodriguez*, 411 U.S. 475 (1973).

[38] *Duncan* v. *Kahanamoku*, 327 U.S. 304 (1946).

[39] See Neil D. McFeeley, "The Supreme Court and the Federal System: Federalism from Warren to Burger," *Publius* (Fall 1978), p. 13, and William F. Duker, *A Constitutional History of Habeas Corpus* (Greenwood Press, 1980).

them was unconstitutionally obtained, a federal district judge may no longer review the matter in a habeas corpus hearing.

EX POST FACTO LAWS AND BILLS OF ATTAINDER

The Constitution forbids both the national and the state governments to pass ex post facto laws or enact bills of attainder (Article I, Sections 9 and 10).

An **ex post facto law** is a retroactive criminal law that works to the disadvantage of an individual. For example, an ex post facto law can make a particular act a crime that was not a crime when committed. Or it can increase punishment for a crime after the crime was committed. The prohibition does not prevent the passage of retroactive penal laws that work to the benefit of an accused—a law decreasing punishment, for example. Nor does the prohibition against ex post facto laws prevent the passage of retroactive civil laws: Income tax rates as applied to income already earned may be increased.

A **bill of attainder** is a legislative act inflicting punishment without judicial trial on named individuals or members of a specified group. Although a law working to the disadvantage of an individual does not necessarily make it a bill of attainder, such bills are not limited to those imposing criminal sanctions. They also include laws depriving people of property or jobs. Although laws are not infrequently challenged as a bill of attainder, only a few have ever been so held, and two of those were in the last four decades. One denied three named federal employees the right to be paid by the federal government, and the other denied members of the Communist party the right to serve as trade union officers.

President Richard Nixon alleged that Congress enacted a bill of attainder when it stripped him of control over his presidential papers and instructed the administrator of the General Services Administration to take custody of the papers and tapes, to return to Nixon his personal and private papers but to preserve in government custody—and eventually make public—those papers having historical value. Because every previous president had been given custody of his own papers, Nixon contended that Congress had singled him out. The Supreme Court majority agreed that legislation subjecting a named individual to such humiliating treatment raises serious questions under the bill of attainder clause. Still, seven members of the Court held that Nixon was a "legitimate class of one" and that Congress was not motivated by a desire to punish.[40]

In another example, some college students charged that Congress imposed a bill of attainder on them when application of what came to be known as the Solomon Amendment made ineligible for federal student financial aid men who refused to state that they had complied with the registration requirements of the Military Selective Service Act. A federal district judge sided with the students, but the Supreme Court did not. Rather, Chief Justice Burger, speaking for the Court, pointed out that any student who wishes to apply for aid may become eligible for it at any time by registering. In addition to not singling out an identifiable group, the Solomon Amendment was also said "not to impose a disability approaching the kinds . . . historically associated with punishment."[41]

Rupert K. Murdoch, the publishing magnate, charged that because his newspapers, especially the *Boston Herald*, had been critical of Senator Kennedy, Congress had imposed a bill of attainder on him. Congress had allowed into a 1000-page appropriation bill, a provision aimed solely at Murdoch which would keep the FCC from waiving its regulations relating to the cross-ownership of television stations

[40] *Nixon* v. *Administrator of General Services, James M. Burns et al.*, 433 U.S. 425 (1977).

[41] *Selective Service System et al.* v. *Minnesota Public Interest Research Group et al.*, 468 U.S. 841 (1984).

and newspapers, even if it wished to do so. As a consequence of the provision, co-sponsored by Senator Kennedy, Murdoch, and only Murdoch, would be forced to sell a newspaper and a television station. A resolution of the issues is pending before the courts.[42]

The Short and Not Too Happy Life of John F. (Federal) Crook

The rights of persons accused of crime by the national government can be found in the Fourth, Fifth, Sixth, and Eighth amendments. In order to gain some idea of how these constitutional safeguards are applied, let us follow the fortunes and misfortunes of John F. Crook (a fictitious name).

Federal courts   John Crook sent circulars through the mails soliciting purchases of stock in a nonexistent gold mine, an action contrary to at least three federal laws. When postal officers uncovered these activities, they went to the district court and secured from a United States magistrate a warrant to arrest Crook and another warrant to search his home for copies of the circulars. They found Crook at home and read the *Miranda warning* to him, emphasizing especially his *right to remain silent* and *to have the assistance of counsel.* They showed him the warrants, arrested him for using the mails to defraud, and found and seized some of the circulars.

Crook was promptly brought before a federal district judge. (He could have had his preliminaries handled by a United States magistrate; see Chapter 16.) The judge again emphasized that Crook had a constitutional right to assistance of counsel. (Judges have a positive obligation to ensure that all persons subject to any kind of custodial interrogation are represented by lawyers.[43] Unless the record clearly shows that the accused were fully aware of what they were doing and gave up the right to counsel or intelligently exercised the right to represent themselves, the absence of such counsel will render criminal proceedings unconstitutional. The right extends to all trials, for all offenses for which an accused was in fact deprived of liberty, whether or not a jury trial is required. Trials in which fines are the only penalty are exempt from the assistance-of-counsel requirement. This assistance is required at every stage of a criminal proceeding after the initiation of formal charges—preliminary hearings, bail hearings, trial, sentence, and first appeal.[44]) When Crook told the judge he could not afford to hire his own counsel, the judge appointed an attorney to represent him, paid for by the federal government. The judge set bail at $2500, and Crook was held over until the convening of the next federal grand jury. After hiring a professional bondsman who posted the bail and collected a 10 percent fee, Crook was free, as long as he remained within the judicial district.

Note that the Eighth amendment does not require that bail be set at all, but forbids *imposition of "excessive" bail.* Prior to the Supreme Court's decision in *United States* v. *Salerno* in 1987, it was generally thought that the Constitution did require bail for all except for capital crimes and that bail higher than might reasonably be calculated to ensure the presence of a defendant at trial would be considered "excessive." Since persons are considered innocent until their guilt has been determined by a trial, the sole constitutional justification for bail was thought to be to prevent flight before trial. But in the *Salerno* case, the Court upheld the preventive detention provision of the Bail Reform Act of 1984—there are similar laws in thirty

"Paul Harrison, Colorado v. Harrison, meet Joe McFarland, Illinois v. McFarland."

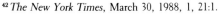

[42] *The New York Times*, March 30, 1988, 1, 21:1.

[43] *Johnson* v. *Zerbst*, 304 U.S. 458 (1938), and *Gideon* v. *Wainwright*, 372 U.S. 335 (1963). Anthony Lewis, *Gideon's Trumpet* (Random House, 1964 and 1972), has become a classic on this issue.

[44] *Moran* v. *Burbine*, 475 U.S. 412 (1986).

or so states—that authorizes federal judges to deny bail to "dangerous persons" charged with certain felonies. Suspects are entitled to a hearing on the matter within five days, and the judge or magistrate must explain in writing the clear and convincing evidence that no condition of pretrial release can reasonably ensure the safety of other persons and the community. In sustaining the law, Chief Justice Rehnquist stated for the Court, "We believe that when Congress has mandated detention on the basis of a compelling interest other than prevention of flight, as it has here, the Eighth amendment does not require release on bail."[45] Crook's crime was not one, however, covered by the Preventive Detention Act.

When the next grand jury was convened, the United States district attorney brought before the twenty-three jurors evidence that Crook had committed a federal crime. Grand jurors are concerned not with a person's guilt or innocence but merely with whether there is enough evidence to warrant a trial. No person has a right to appear before a grand jury, but one may be invited or ordered to do so. If a majority of the grand jurors agree that a trial is justified, they return what is known as a *true bill*, or *indictment*. Except for members of the armed forces, the national government cannot require anyone to stand trial for a serious crime except *on grand jury indictment*. In Crook's case the grand jury returned a true bill against Crook.

After a copy of the indictment was served, Crook was again ordered to appear before a federal district judge. The Constitution guarantees the accused *the right to be informed of the nature and cause of the accusation* so that he or she can prepare a defense. Consequently, the federal prosecutor had ensured that the indictment clearly stated the nature of the offense and that copies had been properly served on Crook and his lawyer.

Actually, prior to the hearing, Crook's attorney had discussed with the United States attorney's office the possibility of Crook's pleading guilty to a lesser offense. **Plea bargaining** is used often. Faced with more cases than they can handle, prosecutors often prefer to accept a guilty plea to a reduced charge rather than to prosecute for the more serious offense. Likewise, defendants are often willing to "cop a plea."

When defendants plead guilty, they are usually forever prevented from raising objections to their convictions. That is why, before accepting guilty pleas, judges question defendants to be sure that their attorneys have explained the alternatives and that they know what they are doing. It never came to this in Crook's case, however. After discussing the matter with his attorney, Crook elected to stand trial on the charge and entered a plea of not guilty.

After indictment Crook's bail was raised to $5000. Now the federal government was obliged to give him *a speedy* and *public trial*. Do not, however, take the word "speedy" too literally. Crook had to be given time to prepare his defense. Defendants often ask for delays which work to their advantage. If, in contrast, the government denies the accused a speedy trial in a constitutional sense, the remedy is drastic: Not only is the conviction reversed, but the case must be dismissed outright.

Crook's lawyer pointed out that under the Sixth amendment, Crook had a right to *trial before an impartial jury* selected from the state and district in which the alleged crime was committed, because he was being tried for a crime punishable by more than six months in prison or a $500 fine. Although federal law requires juries of twelve, the Constitution requires only that juries consist of at least six persons. Conviction in federal courts must be by unanimous vote. (The Constitution permits state courts to render guilty verdicts by nonunanimous juries, provided such juries consist of six or more persons.) An impartial jury, and one that meets the requirements of due process and equal protection, consists of persons who represent a fair cross-section of the community. Although persons are not entitled to juries

---

[45] *United States* v. *Salerno*, 95 L Ed 2d 6907 (1987).

on which there are necessarily members of their own races, sexes, religions, or national origins, they are entitled to be tried by juries from which persons have not been excluded for having these characteristics.

In preparation for his defense, Crook told his lawyer that he had dinner with George Witness on the night on which he was charged with sending the damaging circulars. The attorney took advantage of Crook's constitutional *right to obtain witnesses in his favor* and had the judge subpoena Witness to appear at the trial and testify. Although Witness could have refused to testify on the grounds that his testimony would tend *to incriminate* him, he agreed to do so. Crook himself, however, chose to use his constitutional right *not to be a witness against himself* and refused to take the stand. He knew that if he did so, the prosecution would have a right to cross-examination, and he was fearful of what might be uncovered. The judge conducting the trial cautioned the jury against drawing any conclusions from Crook's reluctance to testify. All prosecution witnesses appeared in court and were available for defense cross-examination; the Constitution insists that accused persons have *the right to be confronted with the witnesses against them*.

At the conclusion of the trial, the jury brought in a verdict of guilty. The judge then raised Crook's bail to $7500 and announced that she would hand down a sentence on the following Monday. The Eighth amendment forbids the levying of *excessive fines* and the inflicting *of cruel and unusual punishments*. Furthermore, in the Sentencing Reform Act of 1984 Congress created a United States Sentencing Commission—whose members include three federal judges, appointed by the president with the consent of the Senate—to set sentencing guidelines to be used by all federal judges. The judge, in accordance with these guidelines, gave Crook the maximum punishment of $7500 and three years in the penitentiary. Such a sentence could not be considered cruel and unusual. Crook could have appealed both his sentence, and his conviction to the Court of Appeals (see Chapter 16), but he chose not to do so.

The ban against cruel and unusual punishments limits government in three ways:

"Considering the overwhelming case load in our nation's judiciary, Your Honor, may I suggest you dismiss the charges against me?" (*Drawing by Stevenson,* © *The New Yorker Magazine, Inc.*)

1. It limits the kinds of punishment that may be imposed—for example, it prohibits using torture, intentionally denying medical care to prisoners, holding prisoners in inhumane conditions, or unnecessarily or wantonly inflicting pain.

2. It prohibits punishments that are grossly disproportionate to the severity of the crime. However, "outside the context of capital punishment"—where the Court has limited the death penalty to crimes in which a life has been taken—the Court has been "reluctant to review legislatively mandated terms of imprisonment,"[46] and "successful challenges to the proportionality of particular sentences will be exceedingly rare."[47] The only noncapital punishment the Court has set aside for being cruel and unusual—and that by a vote of five to four—was a South Dakota court's sentence of life in prison, without the possibility of parole, after conviction for passing a bad $100 bill following conviction for six previous nonviolent felonies. The Court found that the defendant's crimes were relatively minor; that he was being treated more severely by South Dakota than were criminals who had committed far more serious crimes, and more severely than he would have been in any other state; and that therefore his punishment was "significantly disproportionate."

3. It limits the power of the government to decide what can be made a criminal offense. For example, the mere act of being a chronic alcoholic may not be

[46] *Hutto* v. *Davis*, 454 U.S. 370 (1982).
[47] *Solem* v. *Helm*, 463 U.S. 277 (1983).

made a crime, because it is an illness. However, being drunk in public may be made a criminal offense.

Crook's case did not involve a capital offense. But what of capital punishment in other cases? After much soul searching, and many cases, the Supreme Court has ruled that the death penalty is not necessarily cruel and unusual punishment for the *crime of murder*. (Such decisions are of more than passing interest to the well over 1000 persons now under death sentences in thirty-two states. For many years after 1972, when the Supreme Court held in *Furman* v. *Georgia* that most death penalty statutes were unconstitutional, because they left juries with undirected discretion, no persons were executed in the United States.[48] Now most states have revised their statutes, and executions have begun again.) The death penalty may, however, be imposed only on those convicted of crimes resulting in a death but no longer does the Court insist that only the "triggerman" be subject to such a penalty.[49]

A state must ensure that whoever imposes the death penalty—judge or jury—does so only after careful consideration of the character and record of the person and the circumstances of the particular crime. The automatic use of the death sentence for every person convicted of a specified capital offense is not acceptable: "It is essential that the capital sentencing decision allow for consideration of whatever mitigating circumstances may be relevant to either the particular offender or the particular offense."[50] The Court has suggested that the best procedure is first to have a jury determine guilt, and then, in a subsequent proceeding, to focus attention on whether the circumstances justify the death penalty.

The nationalization of the Bill of Rights

While still in the federal penitentiary, Crook was taken by federal authorities before the state courts to answer charges that he had also committed a state crime. Because Crook was entitled to a speedy trial on these state charges, the state could not wait until he had been released by federal authorities before bringing him to justice.

Through his state-appointed attorney, Crook protested that he had already been tried by the federal government for using the mails to defraud. He pointed to the Fifth amendment provision that no person shall be "subject for the same offense to be twice put in jeopardy of life or limb." This **double jeopardy** limitation, Crook's attorney pointed out, has been interpreted by the Supreme Court (*Benton* v. *Maryland*) to be part of the Fourteenth amendment and therefore to be a limit on the power of a state.[51] The judge answered: "The Supreme Court has said that double jeopardy prevents two criminal trials by the *same* government for the *same* criminal offense." (Trial by a state and one of its municipalities is trial by the same government; trial in a juvenile proceeding precludes another trial for the same offense by the state in its regular courts.) It does not prevent punishment by the national and the state governments for the same offense or for successive prosecutions for the same crime by two states, including even conviction by one government after acquital for the same offense by another sovereign.

What constitutional rights can Crook claim in the state courts? First, every state constitution contains a bill of rights listing practically the same guarantees as found in the national Bill of Rights. But, at least until recently, most state

---

On The Death Penalty

Do you favor or oppose the death penalty for persons convicted of murder?

	Favor	Op-pose	No Opin-ion
1972	57%	32%	11%
1976	65	28	7
1978	62	27	11
1981	66	25	9
1985	75	17	8
1986	70	22	8

Source: Gallup Poll.

The Fourteenth Amendment and the Nationalization of the Bill of Rights

A process of selective incorporation:

1925 Freedom of Speech (*Gitlow* v. *New York*)

1931 Freedom of press (*Near* v. *Minnesota*)

1932 Fair trial (*Powell* v. *Alabama*)

1934 Free exercise of religion (*Hamilton* v. *Regents of California*, confirmed in 1940 by *Cantwell* v. *Connecticut*)

1937 Freedom of assembly (*De Jonge* v. *Oregon*)

1942 Right to counsel in capital cases (*Betts* v. *Brady*)

1947 Separation of church and state; establishment of religion (*Everson* v. *Board of Education*)

1948 Public trial (*In re Oliver*)

1949 Right against unreasonable searches and seizures (*Wolf* v. *Colorado*)

---

[48] 408 U.S. 238. See Raoul Berger, *Death Penalties: The Supreme Court's Obstacle Course* (Harvard University Press, 1982), for an attack on the Court for interfering with states' rights to impose the death penalty. See also Hugo Adam Bedau, *The Death Penalty in America*, 3rd ed. (Oxford University Press, 1982), for a more balanced collection of readings by an opponent of the death penalty.

[49] *Tison* v. *Arizona*, 95 L Ed 2d 127 (1987).

[50] *Roberts* v. *Louisiana*, 431 U.S. 633 (1977).

[51] 395 U.S. 784 (1969).

Source: David M. O'Brien.

judges have been less inclined than federal judges to interpret the constitutional guarantees of their own state constitutions liberally in favor of those accused of crime.

To what extent does the national Constitution protect courtroom procedures from state actions? The Bill of Rights does not apply to the states, but the Fourteenth amendment does. For some time a persistent minority on the Supreme Court argued that the due process clause of the Fourteenth amendment should be interpreted to impose on states exactly the same limitations the Bill of Rights imposes on the national government: They favored "total incorporation" of the Bill of Rights into the Fourteenth amendment.

Other justices argued that the due process clause does not prescribe any set procedures, but only requires states to provide "fundamental fairness." State actions contrary to a provision of the Bill of Rights should not be declared unconstitutional unless they deprive persons of fundamental fairness.

Still other justices argued that some provisions of the Bill of Rights should be incorporated into the due process clause, but not all of them. In fact, this doctrine of selective incorporation has prevailed.

In Palko v. Connecticut Justice Benjamin Cardozo formulated the test for distinguishing between those provisions of the Bill of Rights that are incorporated into the Fourteenth amendment and those that are not. The rights to be incorporated are those "implicit in the concept of ordered liberty" and so important that neither "liberty nor justice would exist if they were sacrificed."[52] The rights not incorporated are those that though congenial to our system of justice, could be replaced by other procedures without necessarily resulting in a denial of justice or liberty.

Beginning in the 1930s, and at an accelerating pace after 1960, the Supreme Court selectively incorporated provision after provision of the Bill of Rights into the due process clause.[53] Today the Fourteenth amendment imposes on the states all the provisions of the Bill of Rights except those of the Second, Third, Seventh, and Tenth amendments, and the grand jury requirements of the Fifth amendment. (No specific Supreme Court decision applies the excessive bail and fine limitation to the states. However, almost by definition, if a bail or fine is excessive, its imposition is likely to be considered a denial of due process.)

The Supreme Court will probably not incorporate additional provisions; most lawyers, political scientists, and other observers believe states should be allowed to continue to indict persons for serious crimes by means other than grand juries. Eighteen states no longer require grand juries for any crimes; twenty-one require them only for felonies; and only eight require them for all except minor offenses. Other provisions not yet incorporated are really not applicable to the states.

Seeking to incorporate the whole Bill of Rights into the Fourteenth amendment, the late Justice Hugo Black argued that "the first section of the Fourteenth amendment not only incorporates the specifics of the first eight amendments, but it is confined to them."[54] Justice Black would not have allowed members of the Court to impose on the country their own notions of fundamental rights, but only those specified in the Constitution. He quoted approvingly from Judge Learned Hand: "For myself it would be most irksome to be ruled by a bevy of Platonic Guardians, even if I knew how to choose them, which I assuredly do not."[55]

Justice Black has lost the argument to those who believe that in addition to

[52] 302 U.S. 319 (1937).

[53] Richard C. Cortner, The Supreme Court and the Second Bill of Rights: The Fourteenth Amendment and the Nationalization of Civil Liberties (University of Wisconsin Press, 1981), carefully traces these developments.

[54] Henry J. Abraham, Freedom and the Court: Civil Rights and Liberties in the United States (Oxford University Press, 1967), p. 75. See also James J. Magee, Mr. Justice Black: Absolutist on the Court (Virginia Legal Studies, 1980).

[55] Griswold v. Connecticut, 381 U.S. 479 (1965).

incorporating most of the specific provisions of the Bill of Rights, the due process clause protects other fundamental rights, too. "For example, the rights of association and of privacy, the right to be presumed innocent and the right to be judged by a standard of proof beyond a reasonable doubt in a criminal trial, as well as the right to travel, appear nowhere in the Constitution or Bill of Rights. Yet these important but unarticulated rights have nonetheless been found to share constitutional protection in common with explicit guarantees.[56] This view, now adhered to by a majority on the Supreme Court, sees the role of the Supreme Court in the words, quoted approvingly by Justice Douglas, of the late Edmond Cahn: "Be not reasonable with inquisitions, anonymous informers, and secret files that mock American justice. . . . Exercise the full judicial power of the United States; nullify them, forbid them, and make us proud again."[57]

HOW JUST IS OUR SYSTEM OF JUSTICE?

What are the major criticisms of the American system of justice? How have they been answered?

Too Many Loopholes

Some observers argue that by protecting the innocent and placing the burden of proof on the government, we delay justice, encourage disrespect for the law, and allow guilty persons to go unpunished. Justice should be swift and sure without being arbitrary. But under our procedures criminals may go unpunished because (1) the police decide not to arrest them; (2) the judge decides not to hold them; (3) the prosecutor decides not to prosecute them; (4) the grand jury decides not to indict them; (5) the jury decides not to convict them; (6) the judge decides not to sentence them; (7) an appeals court decides to reverse the conviction; (8) a judge decides to release them on a habeas corpus writ; or (9) if retried and convicted, the executive decides to pardon, reprieve, or parole them. As a result, the public never knows whom to hold responsible when laws are not enforced. The police can blame the prosecutor, the prosecutor can blame the police, and they can all blame the judges.

Others argue that in our impossible pursuit of perfect justice, we are not achieving effective justice.[58] Many critics blame the Supreme Court for imposing its own notions of justice on the country and for placing so many disabilities on police and prosecutors that these officials are finding it increasingly difficult to bring any cases to conclusion. Others take a different view. They point out that there is more to justice than simply securing convictions. All the steps in the administration of criminal laws have been developed out of centuries of trial and error, and each has been constructed to provide protection against particular abuses. History warns against entrusting the instruments of criminal law enforcement to a single officer. For this reason, responsibility is vested in many officials.

Too Unreliable

Critics who complain that our system of justice is unreliable often point to trial by jury as the chief source of trouble. Trial by jury, they argue, leads to a theatrical combat between lawyers who base their appeals on the prejudices and sentiments of the jurors. "Mr. Prejudice and Miss Sympathy are the names of witnesses whose

Police officers being briefed by supervisor. Progress has been made in most areas to integrate police departments in terms of race, gender, and ethnic background. (*Sybil Shelton*)

[56] *Richmond Newspapers Inc.* v. *Virginia*, 448 U.S. 555 (1980).
[57] As quoted in Abraham, *Freedom and the Court*.
[58] Macklin Fleming, *The Price of Perfect Justice* (Basic Books, 1974).

testimony is never recorded, but must nevertheless be reckoned with in trials by jury."[59] No other country relies as heavily on trial by jury as does the United States. Jury trials are also time consuming and costly.

Defenders of the jury system reply that trial by jury provides a check by nonprofessionals on the actions of judges and prosecutors. Also, no evidence supports the charge that juries are unreliable. On the contrary, decisions of juries do not systematically differ from those of judges.[60] Moreover, the jury system helps to educate citizens and enables them to participate in the application of their own law.

The grand jury system has also come under attack. In theory, the grand jury has two functions: to protect the innocent from having to stand trial by requiring prosecutors to demonstrate behind closed doors that they have evidence to justify trial; and to provide an independent agency, uncontrolled by those in power, to investigate wrongdoing. Critics charge, however, that the grand jury has become a tool of the prosecutor. Said Justice Douglas: "It is, indeed, common knowledge that the grand jury, having been conceived as a bulwark between the citizen and the Government, is now a tool of the Executive."[61]

During the 1960s critics from the left side of the political spectrum charged that grand juries had become instruments to intimidate radicals, blacks, and antiwar militants. However, by 1973 grand juries were being used to investigate the executive branch. It was through the use of the grand jury that the special prosecutor was able to get before the courts his contention that the president had no constitutional right to withhold information about wrongdoing. As the editors of the *Congressional Quarterly* have pointed out: "Liberals can applaud grand juries for investigating Watergate and denounce them for intimidating militants. Conservatives might just as easily reprove them for the former and commend them for the latter. The important question about grand juries is whether they are an effective instrument for protecting the innocent and bringing the guilty to trial. . . . On these questions, the jury is still out."[62]

Discrimination

The Supreme Court has worked particularly hard during the last several decades to give reality to the ideal of equal justice under the law. At the trial level persons accused of crime who cannot afford attorneys must be furnished them at government expense. If transcripts are required for appeals, such transcripts must be made available to those who cannot afford to purchase them. If appeals are permitted, the government must also provide attorneys for at least one legal appeal of the decision of the trial court. Poor people cannot be imprisoned because of inability to pay a fine. Nor, once sentenced, can poor persons be kept in jail beyond the term of the sentence because they cannot afford to pay a fine. Even for civil proceedings—divorce proceedings, for example—fees cannot be imposed that deny poor persons their fundamental rights, such as the right to obtain a divorce. (A state has no obligation, however, to waive fees for those seeking to be declared bankrupt. The Court apparently believes that people have a constitutional right to be absolved of the ties that bind but not of their debts.)

[59] Jerome Frank, *Courts on Trial* (Princeton University Press, 1949), p. 122. See Harry Kalven, Jr., and Hans Zeisel, *The American Jury* (University of Chicago Press, 1971), for findings of the University of Chicago's massive study of the jury system. See also Rita James Simon, ed., *The Jury System in America: A Critical Overview* (Sage Publications, 1975).

[60] Kalven and Zeisel, *The American Jury*, pp. 57 ff.

[61] *United States* v. *Mara*, dissenting, 410 U.S. 19 (1973).

[62] "The Supreme Court; Justice and the Law," *Congressional Quarterly* (1973), p. 93. See also Leroy D. Clark, *The Grand Jury: The Use and Abuse of Political Power* (Quadrangle, 1975), a critical account calling for reform of the grand jury.

Major difficulty arises outside the courtroom, however, because one of the most acute problems of our society is the tension between the police and the black and Hispanic communities congregated in the ghettos and barrios of our large cities. Many members of minorities do not believe we have equal protection under the law: "Whether the stated belief is well founded or not is at least partly beside the point. The existence of the belief is damaging enough."[63] Blacks consider the police to be enforcers of white law. Studies proving prejudice on the part of some white police officers and examples of rough—if not brutal—police treatment of blacks are ample evidence to support their point of view.

Still, if we explain the behavior of those who break the law sociologically—they are victims of poverty, prejudice, and other social factors—we cannot simply moralize about the misbehavior of those who enforce the law—they are brutal and without proper moral standards. In fact, "the policeman," wrote one former attorney general, "is the most important American. He works in a highly flammable environment. A spark can cause an explosion. He must maintain order without provocation which will cause combustion."[64]

Police officers have a vital role in preserving (or restricting) civil liberties. They determine who shall be arrested; they give daily reality to the protections of our Constitution; and, as events in our large cities in the 1960s and in Miami in 1980 made clear, they are central in preventing or causing civil disorders. Yet these persons on whom we depend for so much, the only persons in our civil society whom we legally arm with deadly weapons, often discover that the public is indifferent, or hostile.

In the late 1960s, for a variety of reasons, a sustained drive was begun to improve the quality of police services. Action was taken to recruit more blacks, Hispanics, and women. Community relations programs were established. Considerable progress was made, and tensions between police and minority communities appeared to be improving. However, after disorders in Miami in 1980 (sparked by the acquittal of white police officers who killed a black civilian during a high-speed chase for a minor traffic violation), tensions between police and minority communities once again began to rise. Many blacks continue to feel that "the police force is racist whether officers are black or white," an attitude that makes recruiting black officers difficult.[65] "Within minority communities the perception that police abuse of authority is discriminatory is reinforced by national statistics that show that disproportionally large numbers of minority civilians are victims of brutality and use of deadly force. This remains a potentially explosive issue which not only inhibits effective policing but in fact undermines the public security."[66] According to a member of the United States Commission on Civil Rights: "Although it would be cynical to conclude that there has been no progress in the last 20 years, serious problems persist in many cities."[67]

The Supreme Court and Civil Liberties

Plainly, judges—especially those on the Supreme Court—play a major role in enforcing constitutional guarantees. In fact, this combination of judicial enforcement and written guarantees of enumerated liberties is one of the basic features of the American

---

[63] George Edwards, *The Police on the Urban Frontier* (Institute of Human Relations Press and The American Jewish Committee, 1968), p. 28.

[64] Ramsey Clark, Foreword to Edwards, *The Police on the Urban Frontier*, p. viii.

[65] John Herbers, "Minority Groups' Distrust of Police Force Said to Be on the Rise around the Country," *The New York Times* (May 25, 1980), p. 16.

[66] United States Commission on Civil Rights, "Police Practices and the Preservation of Civil Rights" (statement issued July 9, 1980), p. 3.

[67] *The Washington Post* (July 10, 1980), p. A7.

system of government. As Justice Jackson wrote, "The very purpose of a Bill of Rights was to withdraw certain subjects from the vicissitudes of political controversy, to place them beyond the reach of majorities and officials and to establish them as legal principles to be applied by the courts. One's right to life, liberty, and property, to free speech, a free press, freedom of worship and assembly, and other fundamental rights may not be submitted to vote: they depend on the outcome of no elections."[68]

This emphasis on constitutional limitations and judicial enforcement is an example of the "auxiliary precautions" James Madison believed were necessary to prevent arbitrary governmental action. In other free nations citizens rely more on elections and political checks to protect their rights; in the United States we appeal to judges when we fear our freedoms are in danger.

Such reliance on judicial protection of our civil liberties focuses attention on the Supreme Court. Yet only a small number of controversies are actually carried to the Court, and a Supreme Court decision is not the end of the policy-making process. Compliance with its rulings "does not necessarily, universally, or automatically follow. . . ."[69] Lower court judges as well as police, superintendents of schools, and local prosecutors give reality to Court's doctrines.

The Supreme Court can do little unless its decisions reflect a national consensus. Judges by themselves cannot guarantee anything: Neither can the First amendment. As Justice Robert Jackson once asked:

> Must we first maintain a system of free political government to assure a free judiciary to guarantee free government? . . . [It] is my belief that the attitude of a society and of its organized political forces, rather than its legal machinery, is the controlling force in the character of free institutions. . . . [Any] court which undertakes by its legal processes to enforce civil liberties needs the support of an enlightened and vigorous public opinion . . . .[70]

[68] *West Virginia State Board of Education* v. *Barnette*, 319 U.S. 624 (1943).

[69] See Richard M. Johnson, *The Dynamics of Compliance: Supreme Court Decision-Making from a New Perspective* (Northwestern University Press, 1967), p. 3.

[70] Robert H. Jackson, *The Supreme Court in the American System of Government* (Harvard University Press, 1955), pp. 81–82. See also Jonathan D. Casper, *The Politics of Civil Liberties* (Harper & Row, 1973).

SUMMARY

1. One of the basic distinctions between a free society and a police state is that there are effective restraints in a free society on the way public officials, especially law-enforcement officials, perform their duties. In the United States these constitutional restraints are judicially enforceable.

2. The Constitution protects the acquisition and retention of citizenship. It protects the basic liberties of citizens as well as aliens. It protects our property from arbitrary governmental interference, although debates about which interferences are reasonable and which are arbitrary are not easily settled.

3. The Constitution imposes limits not only on the procedures government must follow but also on the ends it may pursue. Some actions are out of bounds no matter what

procedures are followed. Legislatures have the primary role in determining what is reasonable and what is unreasonable. However, the Supreme Court continues to exercise its own independent and final review of legislative determinations of reasonableness, especially on matters affecting civil liberties and civil rights.

4. The framers knew from their own experiences that in their zeal to maintain power and to enforce the laws, public officials are often tempted to infringe on the rights of those accused of crimes. To prevent such abuse, the Constitution imposes detailed procedures national officials must follow in order to make searches and arrests and to bring people to trial.

5. The Supreme Court interprets the Constitution, especially the Fourteenth amendment, to impose on state and

local governments almost the same restraints in the administration of justice as it imposes on the national government.

6. The Supreme Court continues to play a prominent role in developing public policy to protect the rights of the accused, to ensure that the innocent are not punished, and to guarantee that the public is protected against those who break the laws. The Court's decisions influence what the public believes and how police officers and others involved in the administration of justice behave. But the Court alone cannot—and should not—ensure fairness in the administration of justice.

FURTHER READING

VINCENT BLASI, ed. *The Burger Court: The Counter Revolution that Wasn't* (Yale University Press, 1983).

ABRAHAM S. BLUMBERG. *Criminal Justice: Issues and Ironies*, 2nd ed. (New Viewpoints, 1979).

ALAN M. DERSHOWITZ. *The Best Defense* (Random House, 1982).

MACKLIN FLEMING. *The Price of Perfect Justice* (Basic Books, 1974).

NATHAN GLAZER, ed. *Clamor at the Gates: The New American Immigration* (ICS Press, 1985).

J. DAVID HIRCHEL. *Fourth Amendment Rights* (Lexington Books, 1979).

MARY M. KRITZ, ed. *U.S. Immigration and Refugee Policy* (Heath, 1982).

JAMES S. KUNEN. *How Can You Defend Those People? The Making of a Criminal Lawyer* (Random House, 1983).

STUART NAGEL, ERIKA FAIRCHILD, and ANTHONY CHAMPAGNE. *The Political Science of Criminal Justice* (Charles C Thomas, 1983).

DAVID M. O'BRIEN. *Privacy, Law and Public Policy* (Praeger, 1979).

CHARLES E. SILBERMAN. *Criminal Violence and Criminal Justice* (Random House, 1978).

LLOYD WEINREB. *Denial of Justice: Criminal Process in the United States*, 2nd ed. (Free Press, 1979).

CHAPTER

Interest Groups: The Politics of Faction

Where should we start our study of American *politics*? With the political *attitudes* people hold? With their actual *behavior* in politics—how they vote or fail to vote, and why? With political *processes*—elections, primaries, conventions? With political *leaders*—men and women who dominate the world of politics? All these aspects of politics are crucial, and we deal with them in later chapters. But we choose to start with the nature and role of political *interest groups*.

Why groups? Because our political attitudes are largely formed by the groups we grew up in or now belong to. Ask yourself what family grouping, neighborhood circle, religious association, income or occupational group you grew up in—then ask yourself what political attitudes these groups held. This should give you a pretty good indication of your own political views. Of course, students sometimes rebel against their families and other group origins, but such rebellion will still be a result of their group affiliations.[1]

For centuries Americans have been busy joining their own groups and fearing the other guys'. A dozen years before the Revolution, John Adams complained that a group was meeting in Tom Dawes's house, where they "smoke tobacco till you cannot see from one end" of the house to the other, drank flip, and chose selectmen and assessors before the town could vote on them.[2] The framers of the Constitution were so concerned about the power of groups that they tried to devise ways of controlling them, as we note in the next section. In later years financier Jay Gould, representing the Erie Railroad interests, boasted, "In a Republican district I was Republican; in a Democratic district I was a Democrat; and in a doubtful district I was doubtful—but I was always Erie." In his book *Babbitt*, novelist Sinclair Lewis satirized Americans' tendencies to join any and all kinds of groups, including odd ones.

As a student you may belong to a variety of groups: your dorm, an athletic team, a sorority, a debate club, the Young Democrats or Young Republicans. Your

[1] Nelson W. Polsby, "Prospects for Pluralism," *Society* (November/December 1984), pp. 30–34, discusses the impact of television and other media on traditional group loyalties.
[2] L. H. Butterfield, ed., *Diary and Autobiography of John Adams*, vol. 1 (Harvard University Press, 1961), p. 238.

experience with these groups—with the coalitions and rivalries within them and among them—trains you well for "real-life" political activities. Does this sound fanciful? Some years ago a first-year student entered the Southwest Texas State Teachers College at San Marcos, sized up the faculty and students ("who got what, when and where"), and decided to overthrow an elite group of athletes—the Black Stars—who ran the campus. He formed a group called the White Stars and then recruited support from other groups: "the YMCA group, the townies, the debating society, the music and art group."[3] He mobilized support from poor undergraduates by promising to distribute the student activities funds more equitably. After extensive campus politicking, he and his group defeated the Black Stars. It is said that his campaigning and group coalition building forecast much of his later political career. His name was Lyndon B. Johnson.

THE MAZE OF GROUP INTERESTS

Whether we see the economy in material or moral terms, issues and factions are at the heart of government and politics. In *The Federalist*, No. 10, James Madison argued that such factions are inherent in society. Persons by nature have diverse faculties, "from which the rights of property originate," and "the protection of these faculties is the first object of government. From the protection of different and unequal faculties of acquiring property, the possession of different degrees and kinds of property immediately results"—hence the "division of the society into different interests and parties." The principal task of government is to regulate the "various and interfering interests": landed, manufacturing, mercantile, moneyed, creditor, and debtor.

Factions involved in *interest-group politics* focus on concerns that are most often already well enmeshed in governmental institutions. We call this the politics of vested interests; throughout our history certain groups have written their concerns—principles, policies, or programs—into both the Constitution and statutory or case law through a process of bargaining and compromise.

Factions also take part in *movement politics* by focusing on concerns that have either been excluded from the government's agenda or insufficiently addressed. In one sense movements act for interests that have not yet found a niche in government. But movements also arise from group actions to change the structure of government itself—to change the arrangement of the niches themselves, so to speak. (We examine movement politics in the next chapter.)

Madison's Fear of Factions

What does this kind of factional struggle mean for government by the people? When the young Virginian, James Madison, was writing what would become *The Federalist*, No. 10 (see Appendix) for the *New York Packet*, Dan Shays's desperate farmers were still on his mind. Madison had been almost as disturbed by the tumult and bloodshed as had his mentor, George Washington. In his small, precise handwriting Madison warned of the tendency of popular government toward the "vice" of faction, toward "instability, injustice, and confusion" in the "public councils."

Madison favored the proposed new federal constitution because he believed it would control the effects of factionalism without suppressing liberty. He would have been disturbed by the violence surrounding women's struggle for the vote, and appalled by the many eruptions of violence in the nation's history: Northerners

Groups: Straightening Out the Terms

Groupings: persons with certain characteristics in common—country music lovers, 16 year olds, women, blacks, the aged.

Groups: persons who share common goals and who interact with one another—union leaders, a particular family, the senior class of your college.

Interest groups: persons who share common goals, interact with one another, and press claims on government—veterans, soy bean growers, bankers.

Associations: formal associations created by interest groups—the NAACP, National Organization for Women (NOW), AFL-CIO, National Rifle Association.

Factions: term used by James Madison and others of our country's founders to refer to what we now call interests or interest groups.

---

[3] Doris Kearns, *Lyndon Johnson and the American Dream* (Harper & Row, 1976), chap. 2; Robert A. Caro, *The Years of Lyndon Johnson: The Path to Power* (Knopf, 1982), part 2.

Organizations such as the Girl Scouts are an important part of the socialization process of the young. They instill a sense of pride in the American political culture. (*Courtesy Girl Scouts of the U.S.A.*)

Richard Viguerie, a noted leader behind several right-wing conservative groups. A businessman and conservative political activist, Viguerie is a king of direct-mail fundraising. (*UPI/Bettman Newsphotos*)

and Southerners slaughtering each other, whites brutalizing and lynching blacks, employers shooting strikers and strikers beating "scabs," protesting farmers seizing other farmers' milk and dumping it into the ditches. But Madison would also have noticed an enormous amount of peaceful conflict among factions, as interest groups bargained and compromised with one another within the federal system.

In the late eighteenth century Madison was concerned about religious, political, and economic factions. What are the key groups and issues today? What are the sources of the groups' strengths and weaknesses? How do they seek to influence government? Are they as dangerous to the public interest now as Madison feared they were in his time? And, if so, what has been done about it, and what else could be done?

Group Interests Today

The United States has often been called a nation of joiners. Europeans sometimes make fun of us for setting up all sorts of organizations, and we ourselves are often amused by the behavior of our groups—the noisy conventions of veterans' associations, the solemn rites of great fraternal organizations, the oratory of patriotic societies. Yet most of these groups are serious in their aims, and they play an enormous role in politics.

How many groups are there in America? There is no way of knowing accurately. Families are the most basic and important groups of all, and there are over 60 million families in the United States. We have a quarter of a million religious congregations; diverse farm groups and trade unions; and over 2000 trade associations. And all these are groups in the broadest sense of the term—that is, their members share some common outlook or attitude, and they interact with one another in some way.[4] Also, we cannot measure the variety of groups in America, although we know it is tremendous; ranging from such well-known groups as the local Elks or the PTA or the controversial Moral Majority, to such exotic species as the Blizzard Men of 1888 (who commemorate a devastating storm) or Friends of the Snail Darter.

One person may belong to a great variety of groups and organizations. At home he or she belongs to a family, a neighborhood, and so on. But such a person may also be a member of a religious congregation, the Rotary Club, the Masons, a law firm, the American Automobile Association, a taxpayers' association, the Republican party, a bowling league, the American Bar Association, or the state bar association. A person may be a member of all these groups but not *equally* so. Loyalty to family or law firm may greatly outweigh loyalty to all the other groups. Do an individual's allegiances to a wide variety of groups ever come into conflict with one another? Indeed yes. The AAA may demand better roads, while the taxpayers' association wants less governmental spending. The neighborhood may be largely Democratic, while the individual in question is a Republican.

Organized **interest groups** raise questions very close to the central problem addressed in this book. Do the organized groups fairly represent the great range and variety of interests in the United States? Do the leaders of specific associations—union presidents, for example—fairly represent the various interests of their own members?

Interest groups are of many types: Some are formal associations or organizations; others have no formal organization at all. Several interest groups may even exist within a single formal organization. Inside the American Bar Association, for example, two or three interest groups may be in conflict over a particular issue. An interest

[4] David B. Truman, *The Governmental Process* (Greenwood, 1981), chap. 2. The basic approach of this chapter is drawn largely from Truman's 1951 book and from A. F. Bentley's pioneer work, *The Process of Government* (University of Chicago Press, 1908).

group may be either broader or narrower than a particular organization. The American Federation of Labor and Congress of Industrial Organizations (AFL-CIO), for example, may be opposed to a specific labor reform measure. But not all members of the AFL-CIO are likely to oppose the bill, and some people who are not members will oppose it. The interest group working to oppose this measure, then, is composed of most members of the AFL-CIO, but not all, along with some people outside the formal labor organization.

Politics is largely a conflict among competing groups with different ideas of what constitutes the general interest. In political arguments we inevitably talk about special interests versus the general welfare. But in political analysis it is better to talk about *this* group's idea of the general welfare as compared with *that* group's. We are all committed to particular values as persons, but as social scientists we cannot pretend to set up a clearly defined national interest. But how can we discover more general interests? Let us begin by examining some of the major interests at work in our society today.

MAJOR INTERESTS: SIZE AND SCOPE

The vast majority of gainfully employed Americans are members of at least one of the big occupational associations, which have much to say about income and working conditions for employers and professional people as well as for farmers and union workers. The typical large association is a mosaic of local and state bodies, and the product of slow and painful growth over a period of decades.

Major Economic Interests

Probably the oldest "unions" in America are farm organizations. The earliest farm group—the South Carolina Agricultural Society—was founded even before the Constitution was written. In the late nineteenth century the National Grange, or Patrons of Husbandry, led farm rebellions against low farm prices, railroad monopolies, and middlemen. The Grange, once a fighting organization with over a million members, is today smaller and more conservative than other big farm groups. The largest farm group now is the American Farm Bureau Federation, which is especially strong in the corn belt. Originally organized around government agents who helped farmers in rural counties, the Federation today is almost a semigovernmental agency, but it retains full freedom to fight for such goals as price supports and expanded credit facilities. The most liberal (or radical) farm organization today is the Farmers Union, founded in 1902, which represents Plains States farmers to a marked extent and works for legislation that will protect the small farmer. A number of other farm organizations are based on the interests of those who produce specific commodities, such as the American Soybean Association.

Workers, too, have long been organized: The earliest trade union locals were founded during Washington's first administration. Throughout the nineteenth century workers organized political parties and local unions. Their most ambitious effort at national organization, the Knights of Labor, claimed 700,000 members. By the beginning of this century, the American Federation of Labor, a confederation of strong and independent-minded national unions mainly representing craftworkers, was the dominant organization. During the ferment of the 1930s, unions more responsive to industrial workers broke away from the AFL and formed a rival national organization, the Congress of Industrial Organizations. Later the AFL and CIO reunited in the organization that exists today, but some industrial union leaders contend that the AFL-CIO has become too conservative, and some large unions, including the United Auto Workers, remain outside the AFL-CIO.

Business associations are the most varied and numerous of all. The several thousand national trade associations and local groups are as diverse as the products and services they sell. The main general agency for business is the Chamber of Commerce of the United States, organized in 1912. The chamber is a federation of federations, composed of several thousand local chambers of commerce representing tens of thousands of business firms. Loosely allied with the chamber on most issues is the National Association of Manufacturers, which, since its founding in the wake of the depression of 1893, has tended to speak for the more conservative elements of American business.

Some of the smaller and less well-known business groups nevertheless have considerable influence. The Conference Board, founded in 1916, conducts research on practical problems and seeks to inform the public on the role of business in the economy. It does not take public stands on issues but emphasizes economic and policy analysis developed through a large staff. Frequently it also holds conferences, briefings, and seminars. The Business Roundtable, organized in 1972, is an association of the heads of major corporations, banks, and utilities. Founded in the belief that top business executives need to take unified public stands on such issues as taxation, government regulation, and energy, the Roundtable seeks to ensure that the views of big business are heard in public policy debates. It was reported to have had a major role in defeating a 1977 picketing bill strongly backed by the AFL-CIO.

Professional people have organized some of the strongest "unions" in the nation. Some are well known, such as the American Medical Association and the American Bar Association. Others are divided into many subgroups: Teachers are organized in the National Education Association, the American Federation of Teachers, the American Association of University Professors, and also in particular subject groups, such as the Modern Language Association. Many professions are closely tied in with government, especially on the state level. Lawyers, for example, are licensed by the states, which have set up, often as a result of pressure from lawyers themselves, certain standards of admission to the state bar.

The Crisscross of Interests

Cutting across associations based on economic interest or occupation are other groups based on sex or national origin, or on religious, racial, ideological, recreational, and other ties. Few Americans are members of more than one occupational group, but because they have endless nonoccupational interests, they are often emotionally and financially involved in various other groups, such as the American Legion, Veterans of Foreign Wars, or Amvets; nationality groups, such as the multitude of Irish, German, Polish, Scandinavian, Hispanic, and other organizations; or religious organizations, such as the Knights of Columbus. The variety of such groups is remarkable; more than 150 nationwide organizations are based on national origin alone.

Cutting across both economic and ethnic groups are interest-group associations focused on issues and ideology. Virtually all interest groups convince themselves that they are devoted to the public welfare and not merely to their own self-interests; issue and ideological groups usually present their cases in terms of their value to the "public interest." The Americans for Democratic Action (ADA), for example, campaigns for liberal candidates and issues while the Young Americans for Freedom (YAF) works for conservative ones. The YAF is active on university and college campuses, where it supported Ronald Reagan and George Bush in recent campaigns; the ADA endorsed Senator Edward M. Kennedy for the Democratic nomination in 1980. Countless groups have organized around specific issues, such as civil liberties, birth control, abortion, opposition to the Panama Canal treaty, environmental protection, nuclear energy, and nuclear arms. Some highly ideological groups are thriving in the otherwise pragmatic, pluralistic politics of the 1980s, but the

Voting Blocks— Can a Candidate Pile Them Up?

Persons Age 18 or Older

2.5 mil.	Asians
3.1 mil.	Farmers (20 or older)
4.7 mil.	Jews
9.0 mil.	Hispanics
17.0 mil.	Homosexuals
18.0 mil.	Union members
19.0 mil.	Blacks
28.2 mil.	Elderly (65 or older)
29.0 mil.	Young (18-24)
40.0 mil.	Evangelical Christians
91.0 mil.	Women

NOTE: People may belong to more than one group. Basic data: U.S. Departments of Commerce and Labor, American Jewish Committee, American Coalition for Traditional Values, National Gay Task Force.

SOURCE: Reprinted from *U.S. News & World Report* (July 16, 1984). Copyright 1984, U.S. News & World Report, Inc.

Interest-group publicity event protesting apartheid (a system of racial segregation peculiar to the Republic of South Africa). (*AP/Wide World Photos*)

Police drag away a demonstrator protesting United States involvement in Nicaragua. (*UPI/Bettman Newsphotos*)

John Birch Society, on the extreme Right, has survived with only a hard-core membership in the tens of thousands. The Libertarian party, more an interest group than a party, has also attracted a small but provocative following on the Right. The Moral Majority, on the other hand, has large numbers and apparently had a significant impact in recent elections.

Large associations themselves are often made up of alliances of many small associations. As Tocqueville observed long ago, Americans form and reform associations for every conceivable purpose and function. And as government has become more central to Americans' lives, these associations have turned their attention more and more to government. In Washington today the associations rival the federal bureaucracy itself in number, size, complexity, and resources.

Of special importance in recent years have been the "public-action" groups that arose out of the political ferment of the 1960s. Common Cause, founded in 1970 by independent Republican John W. Gardner and later led by noted Watergate prosecutor Archibald Cox, campaigned effectively for electoral reform and for making the political process more open. Its Washington staff raises money through direct mail campaigns, oversees state chapters, issues a flood of research reports and press releases on current issues, and lobbies on Capitol Hill and in major government departments. Ralph Nader started a conglomerate of consumer organizations that investigate and report on governmental and corporate action—or inaction—relating to consumer interests. These groups have had a direct impact on legislation—for example, on the passage of the National Traffic and Motor Vehicle Safety Act and the Highway Safety Act.

More and more, groups are organizing to promote or oppose certain foreign policies. For years, one of the most powerful associations in Washington, the China Lobby, carried on an intensive campaign against United States recognition of "Red China." Perhaps the most prestigious—and most controversial—foreign affairs group is the Council on Foreign Relations in New York. Long denounced by critics as the center of conservative and corporate power, the Council is in fact a relatively tame association of mainly aging Establishment types who gather to hear speakers and to make use of an unusually good library of international affairs. The Trilateral

Commission is a newer but equally prestigious and controversial organization concerned with the economic problems of industrialized nations. Both the Right and the Left consider the commission to be a conspiracy: The extreme Right believes it will bring universal communism, and the extreme Left believes it will bring worldwide monopoly capitalism.

Although political factions are not a new phenomenon, in recent years there has been a virtual explosion in the number and variety of interests and associations. This is especially true of "single-cause" groups. (Again, this is not new: The Anti-Saloon League of the 1890s was single-mindedly devoted to barring the sale and manufacture of alcoholic beverages. It was said that the League did not care whether a legislator was drunk or sober as long as he voted dry.) Today single-cause groups crusade tirelessly for or against highly specialized, but politically "hot" questions—such as the National Rifle Association's opposition to regulation of the sale of firearms, or the Nuclear Freeze movement's dedication to the peace issue.

The number, intensity, and specialized nature of these single-cause groups raise a basic question about our "government by the people": Can it represent some kind of general or majority interest at the same time as it responds to a welter of narrow and particular interests?

WEAPONS OF GROUP POWER

Some Americans tend to overreact to organized groups—especially to ones they oppose. They consider such groups to be vast, well organized, well financed, and all but irresistible in political action. They should remember, however, that large and relatively well-organized groups have weaknesses as well as strengths. The larger the group, the greater the likelihood of crisscrossing interests that drain it of unity, energy, money, and singleness of purpose.

Strengths and Weaknesses

Obviously size is still a central test of political power; an organization representing 5 million voters will have more influence than one speaking for 50,000. Obviously, too, the unity of the membership is a key element. Unity, however, is easier to achieve in a small group that focuses on a relatively specific and concrete concern that does not noticeably affect others—for example, a tariff on steel pins. But we need to look at these and other bases of group power more closely.

A fundamental factor in group impact is the attitude and makeup of the membership. Many people join an organization for reasons that have little to do with its political objectives. They may join to secure group insurance, to take advantage of travel benefits, to participate in professional meetings, or to get a job. When organizational leaders can depend on the political backing of their followers, the organization is able to put its full strength into pursuing its aims, and it will have an enormous advantage in the political arena. If they cannot, the organization will not be nearly so effective.

Most Americans are members of many groups; their loyalties are divided. It is this fact of *overlapping membership* that largely determines the cohesiveness of a group. Organization leaders run up against the problem time after time. Suppose a union official, for example, asks a dozen members to come to a meeting. Several may say they will come. But two others may have to be with their bowling club that night; two others may have to stay home with their families; and another may have to attend a church supper. Even those who finally do show up may not be 100 percent supporters. Perhaps they are asked to vote for a particular candidate in a coming election. Some will. But one may decide to vote for the other candidate because they are neighbors or because they are both Italian-Americans, or Republicans, or Legionnaires. Or perhaps one will not know what to do and will not vote at all.

Usually a mass-membership organization is made up of three types of members.[5] The first is a relatively small number of formal leaders who may hold full-time, paid positions or at least devote much of their extra time, effort, and money to the group's activities. The second is a hard core of those involved in the group organizationally and psychologically: They identify with the group's aims, show up at meetings, cheerfully pay dues, and do a lot of the legwork. The third type comprises people who are members in name only: They do not participate actively; they do not look on themselves as Teamsters or Rotarians or Legionnaires; and they cannot be depended on to vote in elections or otherwise act as the leadership wants. In a typical organization, for every top leader there might be a few hundred hard core activists and 10,000 more or less inactive members.

A second factor in the cohesion of a group is its organizational structure. Some groups have no formal organization. Others consist of local organizations that have joined together in some sort of loose state or national federation. The local organizations retain a measure of separate power and independence, just as the states did when they entered the Union. A sort of separation of powers may be found as well. The national assembly of an organization establishes—or at least ratifies—policy. An executive committee meets more frequently. A president or director is elected to head and speak for the group. And permanent, paid officials form the organization's bureaucracy. Power may be further divided between the organization's main headquarters and its Washington office. An organization of this sort tends to be far less cohesive than a centralized, disciplined group such as the Army or some trade unions.

Closely related to cohesion is a third factor: the nature of the leadership. In a group that embraces many attitudes and interests, leaders may either weld the various elements together or sharpen their disunity. The leader of a national business association, for example, must tread cautiously between big business and little business, between exporters and importers, between chain stores and corner grocery stores, between the makers and the sellers of competing products. Yet leaders must not be mere punching bags for different interests, for above all they must lead. They must show how to achieve whatever goals can be agreed on. The group leader is in the same position as a president or a member of Congress: He or she must know when to lead followers and when to follow them.

We have been talking about the characteristics of groups; but the power of a group is also affected by the nature of the political and governmental system in which it operates. Because of our federal system, a group consisting of 3 million supporters concentrated in a few states will usually have less influence than another group consisting of the same number of supporters spread out in a large number of states. A group whose goals are contrary to widely accepted values will have a more difficult time than another group that can clothe its demands in acceptable ideology. And, as we see in later chapters, governmental structures are significant, because they allow some groups more direct access to decision makers, and other groups much less.

Our typical image of interest groups in action is that of powerful, hard-nosed lobbyists skillfully employing a combination of knowledge, persuasiveness, personal influence, charm, and money to influence legislators and bureaucrats. Interest-group representatives seeking to wield influence can often choose from a variety of political weapons and targets. These include persuasion, litigation, rule making, election activities, and lobbying.

"I would guess, sir, by the look on your face, that you are a single-issue person." (Drawing by Dana Fradon; © 1981 The New Yorker Magazine, Inc.)

[5] V. O. Key, Jr., *Public Opinion and American Democracy* (Knopf, 1961), pp. 504–7.

Techniques

Persuasion   All interest groups exploit the communications media—television, radio, newspapers, leaflets, signs, direct mail, and word of mouth—to influence voters during elections and to motivate constituents to contact their representatives between elections. Business enjoys a special advantage in this arena, and businesspeople have the money to utilize propaganda machinery. Being advertisers on a large scale, they know how to deliver their message effectively. Most important, they generally have easy access to the means of disseminating propaganda, such as the press. Other groups have also become aware of the uses of propaganda. When a business organization places full-page messages in newspapers across the nation, unions often find the funds to hire similar spaces for answers. Although labor has not yet matched the propaganda skills of business, it is devoting a good deal of money and attention to this technique. Other interest groups, such as doctors and teachers, are also making use of publicity methods.

How effective is group propaganda? It is impossible to measure precisely the impact of propaganda campaigns, for too many other factors are involved. But we know enough to be skeptical of some of the extravagant claims made for them. For example, organized labor strongly denounced the **Taft-Hartley Act** (which banned the closed shop, slightly limited the right to strike, and restricted union activities in other ways) for years after its passage, but surveys have shown that the great majority of the public and of *union members* either wanted to keep the new law or had no opinion about it. Also, the more a group publicizes its position, the more it risks arousing the opposition and stimulating *its* propaganda potential.

Litigation   When groups find the usual political channels closed to them, they may seek other ways to influence public policy.[6] The courts have increasingly become the center of such efforts. The NAACP, for example, has instituted and won numerous cases in its efforts to improve legal protection for blacks. The technique is not new, of course,[7] but in recent decades urban interests and environmental groups, feeling underrepresented in state and national legislatures, have turned to the courts. Also, women's groups—such as the National Organization for Women and the American Civil Liberties Union Women's Rights Project—have used the courts as one arena for pursuing their objectives.[8] Ralph Nader, too, has exploited this device.

Groups can gain a forum for presenting their points of view by seeking permission to file **amicus curiae (friend of the court) briefs** even in cases in which they are not direct parties. The American Civil Liberties Union, for example, files many such briefs with the Supreme Court in cases that question constitutional liberties.

Rule making   Groups have ready access to the rule-making process, in which executive and regulatory agencies write the rules that implement laws. Agencies publish proposed regulations in the *Federal Register* and invite responses and reactions from all interested persons before the rules are finalized. The *Federal Register* is published daily on weekdays. Well-staffed associations and corporations peruse the *Register*, ever alert for proposed agency actions that will affect their interests. You can find the publication in your school or public libraries.

Election activities   Although nearly all large organizations say they are nonpolitical, almost all organized groups are involved in politics in one way or another.

An estimated 2500 teachers, parents, and children demonstrate in downtown Los Angeles to protest Proposition 13 and cuts in schooling. (*UPI/Bettman Newsphotos*)

Activists in AIDS demonstration. (*Paul Conklin/Uniphoto*)

---

[6] Lucius J. Barker, "Third Parties in Litigation: A Systemic View of the Judicial Function," *Journal of Politics* (February 1967), pp. 41–69; Jethro K. Lieberman, *Litigious Society*, rev. ed. (Basic, 1983); Clement E. Vose, "Litigation as a Form of Pressure Group Activity," *The Annals of the American Academy of Political and Social Science* (September, 1958), pp. 20–31.

[7] See, for example, C. Peter Magrath, *Yazoo: Law and Politics in the New Republic* (Brown University Press, 1966).

[8] Karen O'Connor, *Women's Organizations' Use of the Courts* (Lexington Books, 1980).

The League of Women Voters sponsors candidate debates or forums such as this every two years for federal and statewide elections. (*UPI/Bettman Newsphotos*)

What group leaders usually mean when they say they are nonpolitical is that they are *nonpartisan*. A distinguishing feature of organized interest groups is that they try to work through one or both parties. Usually this means working for individual candidates in either party. The policy labor has followed for years—helping friends and defeating enemies—is the policy of almost all interest groups.

This policy is put into action in different ways. Occasionally an organization openly endorses a candidate and actively works for that person's election. In 1924, for instance, many labor unions endorsed "Fighting Bob" La Follette for president; the CIO officially backed Roosevelt in 1944; and the AFL-CIO supported Humphrey Carter, Mondale, and, in 1988, Dukakis. Some labor organizations formally stay neutral, but prominent officials take a partisan stand. Because of such factors as overlapping membership, an organization may set up a front organization to carry on its political activities; the Committee on Political Education (COPE) of the AFL-CIO is a case in point.

Individual labor unions, which have somewhat homogeneous memberships, can sometimes afford to take rather firm positions. Other organizations are handicapped by the diversity of their members. A local retailers group, for example, might be composed equally of Republicans and Democrats, and many of its members might refuse to take an open position on a candidate for fear of losing business. In such cases more subtle means may be equally effective: At meetings word may be passed around that candidate X is sound from the organization's point of view; perhaps the hat is passed around, too.

Ideological groups, on the other hand, may "target" candidates, seeking to change the candidates' positions or to influence voters. The Christian Voter's Victory Fund, for example, publicizes congressional candidates' "scores"—based on their roll call votes—on abortion, sex education, school busing, school prayer, and the Equal Rights Amendment. Americans for Democratic Action and Americans for Constitutional Action publish ratings of incumbents on a number of liberal and conservative issues, respectively.

How effective is electioneering by interest groups? No generalization is possible, because everything depends on the kinds of factors we have been discussing: the group's size, unity, objectives, political resources, and leadership, and the political context in which it is operating. In general, though, the power of the mass-membership organizations to mobilize their full strength in elections has been exaggerated in the press. Too many cross-pressures are operating in the pluralistic politics of America for any one group to assume a really commanding role. Some groups reach their maximum influence only by allying closely with one of the two major parties. They have placed their members on local, state, and national party committees and have helped send them to party conventions as delegates. But this means losing some of their independence and singleness of purpose.

Another interest-group strategy is to form a political party with the intent less of winning *elections* than of publicizing a *cause*. The Free Soil party was formed in 1848 to propagandize against the spread of slavery, and the Prohibition party was organized twenty years later to ban the sale of liquor. Farmers have formed a variety of such parties.

PACS: INTEREST GROUPS IN COMBAT

In the last few years the number and impact of **political action committees (PACs)** has exploded. Technically, a PAC is simply the political arm of a business, labor, professional, or other interest group, legally entitled to raise funds on a voluntary basis from members, stockholders, or employees in order to contribute funds to favored candidates or political parties.[9] Because PACs link two vital techniques of influence—giving money and other political aid to politicians and persuading office-holders to act or vote "the right way" on issues—we look at PACs more broadly as the means by which interest groups seek to control "who gets what, when, and how" through electoral activity and lobbying.

Let's look at some specific cases. Between January 1987 and October 1988, Congressman Charles Rangel of New York City raised a war chest of just under half a million dollars, $301,400 of which came from PACs; Congressman John Dingell of Michigan raised just over half a million, $379,852 of which came from PACs; and Congressman Martin Frost of Texas raised $524,000, about half of which came from PACs. While this was nothing new—Rangel had raised $74,150 of PAC money in the first six months of 1985—PAC contributions escalated during the 1980s. But the most significant aspect of these donations was that *none of the above congressmen was facing opposition in 1988.* The PACs in 1988 made a total donation of almost $15 million to 59 congressmen facing token opposition, or none at all. Why such interest in these men? Some were on tax-writing or other financial committees. Senate Finance Committee Chairperson Bob Packwood, the top PAC recipient, alone received $691,015 from what the President of Common Cause (representing a "special interest," too) characterized as "special interest groups intent on preserving their tax breaks, providing a sea of PAC dollars to the Congressional tax writers."[10] With crucial financial issues bound to arise in the 1989–1990 Congress as President Bush confronts a Democratic House and Senate, PAC money can be expected to have an even greater influence.

Ironically, considering that the explosion of PACs has occurred mainly in the business world, it was organized labor that invented this device. In the 1930s John L. Lewis, president of the United Mine Workers, set up the Non-Partisan Political League as the political arm of the newly formed CIO. When the CIO merged with the American Federation of Labor, the new labor group established the Committee on Political Education (COPE). This unit came to be the model for most political-action committees: "From the outset, national, state, and local units of COPE have not only raised and distributed funds, but have also served as the mechanism for organized and widespread union activity in the electoral process,

[9] Herbert E. Alexander, *PACs: What They Are, How They Are Changing Political Campaign Financing Patterns* (Grass Roots Guides, 1979), p.3.

[10] *Congressional Quarterly Weekly Reports* (September 14, 1985), p. 1806.

for example, in voter registration, political education, and get-out-the-vote drives."[11] Some years later manufacturers formed the Business-Industry Political Action Committee, but this committee, and the small number of other PACs in the 1960s, had a limited role.

The 1970s brought a near-revolution in the role and influence of PACs. The number of PACs increased dramatically from about 150 to over 4000 today. Corporations and trade associations contributed most to this growth; today their PACs comprise the majority of all PACs. Labor PACs, on the other hand, increased only slightly in number, representing less than 10 percent of all PACs. But the increase in the number of PACs is less important than the intensity of recent PAC participation in elections and in lobbying.

PAC Money in Elections

"Talking with politicians is a fine thing, but with a little money they hear you better," comments Justin Dart, Chairperson of Dart Industries.[12] PACs take part in the entire election process, but their main influence lies in their capacity to contribute money to candidates. Candidates today need big money to wage their election or reelection campaigns. It is no longer uncommon for House candidates to spend over a million dollars, and many Senators or would-be Senators have already spent ten times that amount.[13] The Federal Election Commission reported that 28 percent of the funding for congressional campaigns in 1986 came from PACs. The vast majority of these funds go to incumbents; sitting House members received 68 percent of the PAC money in that year, while their opponents received only 13 percent. The remainder went to candidates for open seats.[14] The $132.2 million donated by PACs in 1986 represents a 26 percent increase from 1984. Democrats received 56 percent of PAC dollars, and Republicans, 44 percent.[15]

As corporate and industrial PACs increase rapidly in number, their influence grows accordingly. What counts is not so much the amounts they give but rather to whom they give: the more influential incumbents. House members receiving the greatest amount of PAC contributions in 1986 included majority leader Jim Wright (D–Texas), Ways and Means Trade Subcommittee chairman Sam Gibbons (D–Florida), Budget Committee chairman William Gray (D–Pennsylvania), and minority leader Robert Michel (R–Illinois).[16]

Despite lurid reports of freewheeling spending by big corporations, most business PACs proceed rather cautiously.[17] In deciding which candidates to help and

[11] Edwin M. Epstein, "Business and Labor under the Federal Election Campaign Act of 1971," in Michael J. Malbin, ed., *Parties, Interest Groups, and Campaign Finance Laws* (American Enterprise Institute for Public Policy Research, 1980), p. 112. See also Gary Jacobson, *Money in Congressional Elections* (Yale University Press, 1980).

[12] Quoted in *The Wall Street Journal* (August 15, 1978), p. 1.

[13] Senator Charles C. Mathias, *The New York Times* (February 27, 1986), p. A31.

[14] *Congressional Quarterly Weekly Report* (May 16, 1987), p. 991. See also *Congressional Quarterly Weekly Report* (May 23, 1987), p. 1062.

[15] *Statistical Abstract of the United States: 1988* (U.S. Government Printing Office, 1988), p. 254.

[16] *Congressional Quarterly Weekly Report* (May 16, 1987), p. 993.

[17] Gary J. Andres, "Business Involvement in Campaign Finance: Factors Influencing the Decision to Form a Corporate PAC," *PS* (Spring 1985), p. 213.

7–1   Score Card: Endorsements and Claimed Outcomes

Interest Group	House Endorsements	Percentage Victories	Senate Endorsements	Percentage Victories
Americans for Democratic Action (Liberal)	138	73%	18	44%
AFL-CIO/COPE (Labor)	374	64	31	65
Business-Industry Political Action Committee (Business)	103	37	17	47
Americans for Constitutional Action (Conservative)	144	78	15	47
National Conservative Political Action Committee (Conservative)	86	81	3	0

Source: *Congressional Quarterly Weekly Report* (November 6, 1982), pp. 2811–16.

YOU DECIDE

In 1984, 3006 Political Action Committees donated $104.9 million to candidates, almost 80 percent of it to incumbents. The President of anti-PAC organization Common Cause has declared that "PACs are at the center of stopping people from changing the system." If you were a member of Congress, would you vote to limit PAC spending? And if you were on the Supreme Court, would you rule such limitations constitutional?

(Answer/Discussion on the next page.)

with how much, PACs first consider the candidate's record and the likelihood of his or her voting as the PAC wishes. But other factors must be considered too: the likelihood that the candidate will win; how much difference the money would make in the campaign; whether the candidate is an incumbent (and hence would reasonably have more chance of winning); and the PAC's access to the candidate if elected. Party is not a major criterion for corporate-related PACs, though they do contribute somewhat more to Republican candidates than to Democratic ones. Labor PACs, on the other hand, give overwhelmingly to Democrats.

How much influence does PAC money, especially corporate PAC money, have on election outcomes, legislation, and representation? One critic has written that "Members of Congress are growing more and more dependent on PAC money and less and less free to respond to the needs of their constituents." An organization called Citizens Against PACs publishes attacks on members who, in their opinion, accept too many out-of-state PAC contributions. Obviously, in this area, as in others, "money talks." But it is easy to exaggerate that influence. Corporations find that raising political money from a diverse group of stockholders and/or executives is a slow venture. In fact, corporations usually do not wish to raise a great deal of political money for fear that they will be attacked in the press for their "huge slush funds." In addition, it is not clear that campaign contributions have much effect on election outcomes, that winning candidates will feel willing and able to "remember" their financial angels or that the money in the end produces a real payoff in legislation. So even big corporate PACs have learned to be patient. Bernadette A. Budde, political education director of the Business-Industry PAC, declared: "You know you're not going to make 10 yards on the first down, so you try to make 2 or 3 or 4 yards at a time."[18]

Much depends, however, on the context within which money is given and received.[19] Many campaigns—especially congressional and state and local campaigns—are "low-voltage" undertakings in which a sizable amount of money seems to make a difference. Amid all the "murk" of campaigning, a candidate may feel grateful for so tangible and convertible a contribution as money. But much depends on whether PACs can protect their financial investment with the exercise of influence *within* government—that is, whether they can lobby effectively.

[18] Quoted in *National Journal* (November 24, 1979), p. 1983.

[19] Sandra Davis, "PACs in the American Political System" (unpublished manuscript).

LOBBYING, OLD AND NEW

Lobbying, one of the best-known weapons of group influence, is probably also the oldest; it is certainly one of the most criticized. Generations of Americans have been stirred by exposés of an "invisible government." From the time of the Yazoo land frauds 185 years ago, when a whole legislature was bribed and the postmaster general was put on a private payroll as a lobbyist, to the latest logrolling scandal in Congress, Americans have enjoyed denouncing lobbyists. Some truly powerful lobbies flourished in the last century. One of these was the Anti-Saloon League which after years of warring against "demon rum" actually managed to win passage of a constitutional amendment—the highest and most difficult achievement in American politics. These so-called "drys" included such famous women as Frances Willard and Carry Nation, as well as the Women's Christian Temperance Union. An equally powerful lobby of "wets," all male except for Pauline Morton ("When It Rains It Pours") Sabin and her Women's Organization for National Prohibition Reform, won repeal of the Prohibition Amendment, which of course required another constitutional amendment.[20]

Today lobbying is far more extensive and sophisticated, though not necessarily more effective. Thousands of lobbyists are active in Washington today, but few of them are as glamorous or as unscrupulous as the media suggest, nor are they necessarily very influential. Most lobbying is a rather routine affair conducted by spokespersons for such organizations as the National Fertilizer Association, the Retired Officer Association, or the Institute of Shortening and Edible Oils. Lobbyists for these associations are usually Washington attorneys who have long experience in the agencies and on "the Hill"; they are retained to keep an eye on a handful of bills and to keep in touch with a few administrative officials and members of Congress. Because lawmaking today is highly technical, these lobbyists—or legislative counsels, as they prefer to be called—play a large role in modern government.

Lobbyists await decision on date of revenue bill in 1982. (*Dennis Brack/Black Star*)

Busy administrators or legislators, threading their way through mountains of paper and among conflicting interests, often turn to them gladly for their views and information.

All this is the traditional "stuff" of government, but with the rise of Big Government and the huge stakes of business and other organizations in governmental decisions, lobbying has taken on far greater importance. Lobbyists know that influence in Washington depends on influence in the "precincts" and that they must use techniques of public persuasion in order to create the right political "climate" for the governmental actions they want. Hence, they must also know how to mobilize their organizations back home so that a blizzard of letters, telegrams, and petitions descends on Washington. Lobbyists have to be experts in the arts of political influence and legislative technique, as they take part in drafting laws, testifying before committees, and helping to speed some bills through while slowing up others.

Legal and political skills, along with specialized knowledge, have become so crucial in executive and legislative policy making as to be a form of power in themselves. Elected representatives in particular increasingly depend on their staffs for guidance. These staffs in turn are linked with the staffs of executive departments and of the interest-group associations. Issue specialists will know more about Section 504 or Title IX or the amendment of 1972, and who wrote that amendment and why, than the political and administrative leaders, who are usually generalists. It is in this gray area of policy making that many interest groups play a vital role, as

[20] See Ruth Bordin, *Woman and Temperance: The Quest for Power and Liberty, 1873–1900* (Temple University Press, 1981); David E. Kyvig, *Repealing National Prohibition* (University of Chicago Press, 1979); Carol S. Greenwald, *Group Power: Lobbying and Public Policy* (Praeger, 1977); Norman J. Ornstein and Shirley Elder, *Interest Groups, Lobbying and Policymaking* (Congressional Quarterly Press, 1978).

Answer/Discussion

Congress *did* pass such a law, and the Supreme Court struck it down as unconstitutional (see Chapter 16 for a discussion of that case). Despite the Court's ruling, both sides of the PAC debate continue to agitate over limitations on PAC expenditures.

people move freely from congressional or agency staff to association staff and perhaps back again.

The recent growth of PACs has immensely expanded these traditional activities and sharpened the issue of their rightful place in the battle of interest groups. More than ever before, interest groups, through PACs, can organize a "triple-threat" offensive: skillful mobilization of public opinion through large, well-financed public relations campaigns; direct assistance to candidates in the form of money, campaign propaganda, "education" of voters by mailings, advertisements, and the like; and direct influence on officeholders through lobbying. The National Rifle Association (NRA), one of the most powerful medium-sized interest groups, with a membership of more than a million and a staff of 300, "has become a master at mobilizing citizens who support its cause. . . . The NRA boasts that it can flood Congress with 500,000 pieces of mail virtually overnight in opposition to any gun control proposals."[21]

Labor's Political "Machine"

For some years labor's COPE has been one of the most respected—and most feared—political organizations in the country.[22] In the Kennedy-Johnson years it won a reputation as the strongest national political "machine"—the word the late George Meany, AFL-CIO chief, used to describe his political arm. In many respects COPE could boast of its political effectiveness: It encouraged and supervised grass-roots political activity on the part of the tens of thousands of union locals at the base of the AFL-CIO. The national organization adopted a detailed, explicit "platform," fifty or sixty pages long, which spelled out labor's position on the issues. Labor contributed money to candidates, ran registration and get-out-the-vote campaigns, and supported its favorites with leaflets, picnics, motorcades, and television and radio programs. COPE granted, or withheld, endorsements of candidates. Finally, in Washington, and in many of the state capitals, organized labor marshaled one of the largest, most experienced, and most knowledgeable lobbies of all the interest groups.

Yet this political "machine" often sputtered and faltered. Because the AFL-CIO is a federation of powerful and independent national unions, state and local groups or federations of unions were often politically divided. Also, the aging national leadership of the AFL-CIO had been in office so long that it lacked vigor and freshness of approach. When George Meany retired in 1979, he had been president of the national organization for twenty-seven years; William Green had headed it for twenty-eight years before Meany, and Samuel Gompers had been in control off and on for thirty-eight years before Green. Moreover, the AFL-CIO by no means spoke for all labor: Union labor represented about 60 percent of the nation's work force, and AFL-CIO membership amounted to about 60 percent of the total number of those organized.[23] In 1982, 64 percent of the COPE-endorsed candidates for United States representative won their elections—only a fair record. In 1984, under President Lane Kirkland, the AFL-CIO took the unusual step of endorsing a Democratic presidential candidate, Walter F. Mondale, even before the primary season began. When Mondale won the nomination but lost the general election, many pundits concluded that labor's endorsement had become a liability. Nevertheless, Kirkland insisted that the AFL-CIO would once again offer an early endorsement in the 1988 presidential election. However, they did not.

Labor's political and lobbying muscle is obviously limited, and the prospects

United Auto Workers rally in Dallas, Texas. (*Black Star*)

---

[21] Dennis S. Ippolito and Thomas G. Walker, *Political Parties, Interest Groups, and Public Policy: Group Influence in American Politics* (Prentice-Hall, 1980), p. 335.

[22] Harry Holloway, "Interest Groups in the Postpartisan Era: The Political Machine of the AFL-CIO," *Political Science Quarterly* (Spring 1979), pp. 117–33.

[23] Ibid., p. 120.

for increasing influence in the future are dim. Organized labor's membership is dwindling relative to the increase in the national work force; it has failed to unionize a large part of industry in the South and the Sunbelt generally; and the number of corporate PACs has increased greatly while the number of labor PACs has remained almost the same. Knowing that it must look for political allies, labor is working increasingly closely with the Democratic party. Still, labor is jealous of its political independence and hesitates to join a party that has its own problems and weaknesses. Another possibility is for labor to form temporary coalitions with other groups that have certain interests similar to its own. Labor often follows this tactic, working closely with consumer, public-interest, liberal, and sometimes—especially when faced with the issue of foreign imports—even with industry groups. But labor pays a price for such collaboration: watering down or even giving up some of its own goals. "We do our best when we're part of a coalition" says a top labor lobbyist, "and you don't have a coalition on a pure issue."[24]

Cooperative Lobbying

Other groups besides labor need to work with like interests without sacrificing their own goals. Business groups have worked out day-to-day, informal, flexible alliances, and some of these have developed into organizations in their own right. The Food Group, a thirty-year-old informal conference group in Washington, has, for example, represented more than sixty business and trade associations. In addition, it spawned an Information Committee on Federal Food Regulations to fight "truth-in-packaging" legislation. Although the Food Group has been fairly effective, it does run into the usual problem of differences over goals and priorities and has found it difficult to put strong and unified pressure on Congress and government agencies.[25]

Other like-minded groups have also worked out cooperative arrangements. The Leadership Conference on Civil Rights brought together many black and other group interests in this area. Different types of environmentalists work together, as do consumers and ideological groups on the Right and on the Left. Women continue to be represented by a large variety of groups that reflect their diverse interests; many of these banded together as ERAmerica to support passage of the ERA. But the larger the coalition, the greater the chance that women, like other groups, may divide over issues such as abortion and equal rights.

Temporary, flexible coalitions have often been viewed as relatively ineffective, given the American political process. A recent study of women's organizations, however, challenges this view. In this case issue coalitions seem to be both the most realistic and the most common way to organize diverse interests. Cooperative lobbying allows "a great deal of diversity of opinion among cooperating groups while still combining lobbying capabilities. This is very important for an interest as varied as that of American women. Groups only need to agree on a single issue to join an ad hoc issue coalition."[26] Analysts of other common group interests might, of course, reach a different conclusion.

CONTROLLING FACTIONS—200 YEARS LATER

If James Madison were to return today, nearly 200 years after writing *The Federalist*, he would not be surprised by the existence of interest groups. Nor would he be surprised by the variety of interest groups. He *would* be surprised, however, by

[24] *Congressional Quarterly Weekly Report* (July 19, 1975), p. 1533.
[25] Donald R. Hall, *Cooperative Lobbying: The Power of Pressure* (University of Arizona Press, 1969).
[26] Anne N. Costain, "The Struggle for a National Women's Lobby: Organizing a Diffuse Interest," *Western Political Quarterly* (December 1980), p. 490.

the intense modern expression of factionalism—the varied weapons of group influence, the deep involvement of interest groups in the electoral process, and the vast number of lobbyists in Washington and the state capitals. And doubtless Madison, if he were alive today, would be more concerned than ever about the power of faction, especially its tendency toward instability and injustice.

Certainly, Americans today are worried about the power of faction, and for somewhat the same reasons. Specifically, they fear that (1) the struggle among factions is not a fair fight; narrower, more highly organized and better-financed "single-issue" or "single-cause" groups hold a decided advantage over more general groups; (2) the interest-group battle leads to great inequities, because lower-income people are grossly underrepresented among interest groups as compared to richer, more highly organized people, many of whom are represented by a multitude of organizations and lobbyists; (3) the organization of hundreds of single-issue groups has reinforced the diffusion of power and fragmentation in government so desired by our nation's founders. The result is incoherent policies, waste and inefficiency, endless delays, and inability to plan ahead and anticipate crises.

"*Single-issue* groups," which are intensively organized for or against particular policies—abortion, handgun control, tobacco subsidies, intervention in Nicaragua, for example—have aroused much concern in recent years. "It is said that citizen groups organizing in ever greater numbers to push single issues ruin the careers of otherwise fine politicians who disagree with them on one emotional issue, paralyze the traditional process of governmental compromise, and ignore the common good in their selfish insistence on getting their own way," notes Sylvia Tesh.[27] But which "single issues" reflect narrow, selfish interests? Women's rights—even a specific issue such as the Equal Rights Amendment—are hardly "selfish," women's rights leaders argue, because they would help over half the population. Peace groups, too, claim that they are representing the *whole* population, as do those supporting prayer in schools. These issues would seem quite different from those concerned with subsidies to dairy farmers, for example. But some doubt the feasibility of distinguishing between narrower and broader issues.

What to do, if anything? For decades Americans have been trying to find ways to keep interest groups in check. They have agreed with Madison that the "remedy" of suppressing factions would be worse than the disease—it would be absurd to abolish liberty simply because it nourished faction. Today the existence and activity of interest groups and lobbies are solidly protected by the Constitution. By safeguarding the value of *liberty*, Americans have allowed interest groups to threaten *equality*, the second great value in our national heritage. So we are left with the question: How can interest groups be regulated in a way that (1) does not threaten their constitutional liberties but (2) curbs their tendencies toward inequity?

Regulation of Interest-Group Lobbying

On the whole, Americans have responded to this question by seeking to regulate lobbying in general and political money in particular. Concern over the use of money—especially corporate funds—to influence politicians goes back well over a century, to the Crédit Mobilier scandals. In 1877 Georgia simply wrote into its constitution the provision that lobbying is a crime—but that provision violated the federal constitution. By the turn of the century the liberal press was charging that corporations were pouring millions into the presidential campaigns of candidates like Benjamin Harrison and William McKinley. During the "Progressive" first decade of this century, Congress passed legislation outlawing corporate contributions in federal elections and requiring disclosure as to the use of money. In 1925 Congress passed the Federal Corrupt Practices Act, requiring disclosure reports, both before

[27] Sylvia Tesh, "In Support of 'Single-Interest' Politics," *Political Science Quarterly* (Spring 1984), pp. 27–44. See also the references to other literature in this article.

and after elections, of receipts and expenditures by Senate and House candidates and by political committees seeking to influence federal elections in more than one state. Note that these were *federal* laws applying to *federal* elections; regulation of state lobbying and elections was left to the states, which often failed to act effectively or at all.

Federal legislation, including the 1946 Federal Regulation of Lobbying Act, was not very effective either. It was, in fact, largely unenforced. Many candidates filed incomplete reports or none at all. The reform mood of the 1960s brought basic changes, "nurtured by the ever-increasing costs of campaigning, the incidence of millionaire candidates, the large disparities in campaign spending between various candidates and political parties, some clear cases of undue influence on the decision-making process by large contributors and special interests, and the apparent disadvantages of incumbency in an age of mass communications with a constant focus on the lives and activities of office-holders."[28] The upshot was the Federal Election Campaign Act (FECA) of 1971, which supplanted the earlier legislation.

Because the main significance of recent laws has been their impact on elections, we discuss them later, in Chapter 12. Here we must note the major impact of the 1971 act on interest groups themselves, especially on their political arms. Ironically, that impact was not to decrease or restrict them, but to enlarge their number and importance. The main reason for this was the new strategy of the 1971 law: to authorize direct and open participation by both labor and corporate organizations in elections and lobbying, with the hope that allowing a proper role for interest-group activity, in the clear light of day, with effective enforcement, would be constitutional under the First Amendment and effective in the world of practical politics. The 1971 act allowed unions and corporations to communicate on political matters to members or stockholders; to conduct registration and get-out-the-vote drives; and to spend union and company funds to set up "separated segregated funds" to be used for political purposes.

At last corporations could be sure that their open and regulated political activities were wholly legal—and they made the most of it. The explosion of corporate PACs followed. But organized labor, which had previously enjoyed the right to set up its PACs, had less need of the act (except to legitimate what it was already doing). There was little increase in the number of labor PACs. The result, labor leaders contend, is a greater imbalance than ever between the political action and organization of a relatively small number of corporation executives and stockholders, and the large membership, and potential membership, of labor unions.

In 1976 the Supreme Court ruled unconstitutional all limitations on individual or candidate campaign spending (*Buckley* v. *Valeo*), and in 1985, it extended that ruling to include PACs. In a series of suits initiated by Democrats who had hoped to prevent powerful right-wing PACs from avoiding federal campaign laws, the Court vetoed regulation of independent PAC spending. Over $15 million of the $16.7 million in independent expenditures in 1984 was devoted to Ronald Reagan's reelection, but the Supreme Court nevertheless decided that Congress may not constitutionally limit independent PAC spending for publicly funded presidential candidates. The decision, grounded in First Amendment guarantees of freedom of speech, did not affect separate congressional provisions limiting the amount PACs may contribute directly to candidates.[29]

Lobbyists: Defense and Attack

Lobbyists have been defended as providing a kind of "third house" of Congress. Whereas the Senate and House are set up on a geographical basis, lobbyists represent

[28] Alexander, *PACs: What They Are*, p. 5.
[29] *Congressional Quarterly Weekly Report* (March 23, 1985), p. 532.

people on the basis of their main interests: their jobs or other economic interests, their issue positions, and their ideological leanings. Small but important groups, such as professional associations, can sometimes get representation in the "third house" that they might be unable to gain in the other two. In a nation of vast and important interests, this kind of functional representation, if not abused, is most useful as a supplement to geographical representation. Should the former kind of representation supplant the latter? Most analysts say no, because legislative institutions are needed to represent people in the totality of their lives and needs.

There are other arguments for "hands off the lobbyists." PACs support both Democratic and Republican candidates and hence do not favor just one party; ideological groups, especially those of a conservative cast, usually contribute more money than either business or labor, but that money does not have as direct or marked an effect on actual policy making as many outsiders suppose.[30] Another argument is that the increase in PAC corporate spending is not as great as it appears, that, in fact, much of the PAC money may be "old wine in new bottles"— that is, money given earlier in the form of legal or illegal personal campaign contributions by business chiefs.[31] Finally, we are reminded, in the spirit of Jeffersonian and Madisonian libertarianism, that whatever the evils, no action should be taken that even remotely threatens the liberties and autonomy of corporations or interest groups in general.

The usual response to this problem depends on the interest group to which one belongs. Union leaders believe that business PACs are allowed too much financial power, and business leaders hold that labor is allowed too much electoral power. Groups with insufficiently vested interests—those defined in terms of race and sex— argue that a system so grounded in economic interests discriminates against those with little access to economic power. Is a more objective position possible?

Scholars analyzing PACs and campaign financing have concluded that, on balance, the situation is serious, though not desperate. As summarized by one participant, a Harvard study group concluded that "PAC money is 'interested money'— that is, linked to a legislative lobby agenda; that reliance on PAC funds had led to a nationalization of the sources of money available to candidates, bringing in funds from outside a candidate's state or district (particularly Washington); and that the growing role of PACs has resulted in political money becoming bureaucratically organized—that is, detached from their source and aggregated in a fashion which renders them unaccountable."[32] Others argue that PAC money helps candidates challenge incumbents, which leads to much-needed "new blood" in Congress— though, in fact, PACs overwhelmingly favor incumbents.[33]

To Reform or Not Reform?

Some observers favor wider regulation of political money and publicly financed congressional elections. Others call for "deregulation" of the political arms of interest

[30] Some of these arguments are summarized in Edwin M. Epstein, "Business and Labor under the Federal Election Campaign Act of 1971," in Michael J. Malbin, ed., *Parties, Interest Groups, and Campaign Finance Laws* (American Enterprise Institute for Public Policy Research, 1980), pp. 107–51.

[31] Michael J. Malbin, "Campaign Financing and the 'Special Interest,'" *The Public Interest* (Summer 1979), pp. 21–42. But for a somewhat different view, see David Cohen and Wendy Wolff, "Freeing Congress from the Special Interest State: A Public Interest Agenda for the 1980s," *Harvard Journal of Legislation*, vol. 17, no. 2 (1980), pp. 253–93.

[32] The Institute of Politics, John F. Kennedy School of Government, Harvard University, *An Analysis of the Impact of the Federal Election Campaign Act, 1972–78: A Report by the Campaign Finance Study Group to the Committee on House Administration of the U.S. House of Representatives*, May 1979, based in part on analysis by Xandra Kayden; summarized by Epstein in Malbin, ed., *Parties, Interest Groups*, p. 142.

[33] Gary C. Jacobson and Samuel Kernell, *Strategy and Choice in Congressional Elections* (Yale University Press, 1983).

groups, assuming that the groups will find a natural and proper balance. Still others believe that the balance must be righted between the present wide and intensive activity of corporate PACs, and the far less influential role of PACs for consumer groups, women's groups, environmental groups, and civil rights groups.[34]

A quite different school of thought holds that none of these "solutions" will work; the problem lies more outside interest groups and PACs than within them or among them. This school notes that James Madison set a good example in concluding that the *causes* of faction could not be removed and that the *effects* could be controlled only by fundamental changes in the whole political system. His solutions (extending the sphere of government to take in "a greater variety of parties and interests" [establishing a stronger national government]; creating federal-state-local tiers of government [federalism]; and fragmenting the power of government so no majority or minority could control it [checks and balances]) worked to some degree but also aggravated the problems. Today the main proposal for controlling interest groups by reshaping the external political system is that of proponents of stronger political parties (see Chapter 9).

Finally, there are those who believe that the main problem lies not in interest groups but in the way public opinion is made, managed, and manipulated—above all, by the rise of the barons of the electronic media, in a new age of communications politics. These observers are urging Congress to limit what commercial television stations can charge for political advertising and to discourage so-called "negative targeting" of candidates in political advertising. We turn to this subject in Chapter 11.

[34] See David Jessup, "Can Political Influence Be Democratized? A Labor Perspective," in Malbin, ed., *Parties, Interest Groups*, pp. 26–55.

SUMMARY

1. The dominant interest groups are economic or occupational, but a variety of other groups—religious, racial, ideological, ethnic—have memberships that cut across the big economic groupings and both reduce and stabilize their influence.

2. The sources of group power are size, unity, singleness of purpose, organization, and leadership, but the actual power of an interest group stems from the manner in which these elements relate to the political and governmental environment in which the interest group is operating.

3. For many decades interest groups have engaged in lobbying, but these efforts have become far more pervasive

and significant with the deep involvement of groups in the electoral process, especially through the expanded use of political-action committees (PACs).

4. Concern about PACs centers on their ability to raise money and spend it on elections, in behalf of endorsed candidates. This concern has led to extensive regulation of interest-group political spending.

5. The key issue today in "controlling factions" is whether to allow groups to find some kind of balance of their own, to try to regulate groups, or to seek reforms outside the groups by building up balancing power in political parties or elsewhere.

FURTHER READING

JEFFREY BERRY. *The Interest Group Society* (Little, Brown and Company, 1984).

ALLAN J. CIGLER and BURDETT A. LOOMIS, eds. *Interest Group Politics*, 2nd ed. (Congressional Quarterly Press, 1986).

CAROL S. GREENWALD. *Group Power: Lobbying and Public Policy* (Praeger, 1977).

MILDA K. HEDBLOM. *Women and American Politics: A Perspective on Organizations and Institutions*, test ed. (American Political Science Association, 1983).

MICHAEL J. MALBIN, ed. *Parties, Interest Groups, and Campaign Finance Laws* (American Enterprise Institute for Public Policy Research, 1980).

JEFFREY BERRY. *The Interest Group Society* (Little, Brown and Company, 1984).

ANDREW S. MCFARLAND. *Common Cause: Lobbying in the Public Interest* (Chatham House, 1984).

NORMAN J. ORNSTEIN and SHIRLEY ELDER. *Interest Groups, Lobbying and Policymaking* (Congressional Quarterly Press, 1978).

LARRY J. SABATO. *PAC Power: Inside the World of Political Action Committees* (Norton, 1984).

KAY LEHMAN SCHLOZMAN and JOHN T. TIERNEY. *Organized Interests and American Democracy* (Harper & Row, 1986).

PHILIP M. STERN. *The Best Congress Money Can Buy* (Pantheon, 1988).

8

Movements: The Politics of Conflict

It was a strange sight, that January day in 1917 at the gates of the White House. A group of women—society ladies from the Washington area, eminent professionals, young college graduates, workers from a munitions plant—marched up and down, carrying banners: "MR. PRESIDENT! WHAT WILL YOU DO FOR WOMAN SUFFRAGE?" "HOW LONG MUST WOMEN WAIT FOR LIBERTY?" As the days passed, the banners became more militant. Hoodlums and self-styled patriots began to harass the picketers, heckling them and tearing down their banners. Then the police began to arrest the women. Over 200 were taken into custody; almost 100 were jailed. The picketers dramatized their plight by going on hunger strikes; prison authorities responded with brutal efforts at forced feeding. By now the whole country was aware of the women's ordeal; a small band of leaders had aroused the consciousness of a nation.

Clearly, suffragists comprised an "interest group" as described in the last chapter; yet they were much more than a group. Indeed, they can best be described as a political *movement*. They were heavily politicized and looked toward political action as the chief means of reaching their goals. They also had a sense of being excluded by law and society from full political participation on the basis of their sex. Even more, they perceived themselves as subject to a more powerful group—men—and as confined to the "private sphere" of the home while being excluded from the "public sphere."[1]

Despite its tremendous gains, the women's movement is still struggling to achieve equal rights. Other groups as well, both on the left and on the right, are seeking their versions of liberty and justice within the American value system.[2] In all these movements, the central role of leadership in raising movement consciousness is apparent. Note also the role of conflict as the "outsiders" in movements confront

[1] For a discussion of women as a sex-class, see Zillah Eisenstein, *The Radical Future of Liberal Feminism* (Longman, 1981). On the suffragists see Ellen Carol DuBois, *Feminism and Suffrage: The Emergence of an Independent Women's Movement in America 1848–1869* (Cornell University Press, 1978).

[2] For a discussion of the differences between women of the right and the left, see Kristin Luker, *Abortion and the Politics of Motherhood* (University of California Press, 1984). See also Laura L. Vertz, "The New Feminist Politics," in Benjamin Ginsberg and Alan Stone, eds., *Do Elections Matter?* (M. E. Sharpe, 1986), pp. 134–47.

the "insiders" in authority—conflict that in turn solidifies movement consciousness and enhances the role of movement leaders.

MOVEMENTS: THE WHY AND HOW

Interest groups such as Greenpeace work on behalf of ecological concerns. (*UPI/Bettmann Newsphotos*)

A movement is a large body of people, united around a central idea of continuing significance, which has varying degrees of centralized leadership and organized membership.

Interest-group politics and movement politics may overlap or resemble each other. Labor, for example, may at times act as a movement but at other times more as a pressure group.

Interest groups, as we use the term, operate within the political system. For them, the system generally works, and the pressures they can exert, the bargains they can strike, and the **transactional** relationships they can establish with government officials and agencies usually serve their ends. Movements, however, are unwilling or unable to engage in ordinary political activity. Often the groups that form movements feel alienated, disenfranchised and ignored by those in power. In addition, movements are frequently more "moral" than political in tone; they have a confidence and determination far less conducive to compromise. Their goals—unlike those of interest groups—are **transformational.** So movements bypass regular lobbying channels in favor of the streets and the airwaves.

The following brief histories of some political movements illustrate how groups organize and act as they attempt to bring about major changes in the political system. Other types of groups also form to challenge or regain basic values—philosophical, moral, or material—that cut across race, sex, and economic lines. A classic example is peace movements. Certain religious groups have long rejected the notion of a *state* possessed of the ultimate authority to use violence for its formation or preservation. Historically nonviolent groups did not actively oppose or confront the state's use of violence; rather, they withdrew from society and were allowed to pay fines for noncompliance. Other groups, rejecting the military aspects of government, sought through elections or through movements to prevent the use of armed force to settle disputes. These *pacifists*, practitioners of what some call "active nonviolence," had visions of a peaceful society guided by individual and collective conscience. In matters of conscience concerning the use of violence, they refused to cooperate with the State; they even refused to pay fines for noncompliance. Rather, they engaged in acts of civil disobedience for which they were arrested and often sent to jail.

For as long as the United States has drafted armed forces and engaged in wars, even defensive wars, organized groups—religious as well as secular—have resisted such governmental actions. These groups include the Women's Peace Party, Women's International League for Peace and Freedom, Women's Strike for Peace, Fellowship of Reconciliation, War Resisters League, American Friends Service Committee, War Tax Resistance, and New Mobilization Committee to End the War in Vietnam, to name just a few.[3] The peace movement today manifests itself in the nuclear arms race and anti-Star Wars protests. Pacifists and believers in active nonviolence have also brought their writings and tactics—mass civil disobedience, marches, demonstrations—to the abolitionist, civil rights, and women's movements.

Movements v. Groups

Groups in American politics tend to operate within the framework of government and the existing two-party system, to use the political tactics of lobbying, to build policy coalitions within the legislature and executive, to strive for consensus outside of government, and to advance their goals as beneficial to all groups—not just their own.

Movements tend to feel "left out" of government, to conduct political action at the grass-roots level, to put pressure on government from the outside, to build coalitions among mobilized publics, to see their causes as morally right and the opposition as wrong—even evil—and to thrive on social and political conflict.

[3] See Helen Michalowski, "The Roots of American Nonviolence 1650–1915," in Robert Cooney and Helen Michalowski, eds., *The Power of the People: Active Nonviolence in the United States* (Peace Press, 1977), pp. 14–37.

The Antitaxers

The antitax movement—not to be confused with the war tax resistance—is an attempt to restore the basic conservative principle: "That government is best which governs—and taxes—least." Sparked by the "crusty charisma of Howard Jarvis," the tax revolt started in California in 1978. Jarvis was responsible for placing Proposition 13—to cut property taxes by more than half—on a California ballot in order to reduce "unneeded" government services and bureaucratic waste. The proposition received 65 percent of the vote in California and attracted nationwide media attention. More than half the states soon followed California's example with similar tax-cut or spending-limitation referenda.

The antitax movement—which in most of its manifestations operates within the system like pressure groups—rises in part from a general feeling of impotence in political decision making and distrust of political leadership.[4] The efforts of President Reagan and conservative senators and representatives to bring down federal spending in the nonmilitary sector of the federal budget and to institute income tax cuts were part of a continuing tax revolt, even after the conservative leaders themselves came to the helm of government. The governor of Georgia, Joe Frank Harris, running on a simple platform of "No New Taxes," won handily in 1982. Tax limitation or spending curbs were again on the ballot in many cities and states in 1986. San Antonio, Texas and California regularly face these movement-initiated issues at the ballot box.

What of the large numbers of people who do not own property, or who do not earn large enough incomes to benefit from lower taxes? Will they turn to electoral politics or party politics to stem the tide of decreasing governmental services? Or will they be unable to find a party or candidates to run against the tax revolt? Movements provoke countermovements—yet not necessarily of equal strength.

California tax fighter, the late Howard Jarvis, stands in front of the Internal Revenue Service Headquarters and announces formation of the "American Tax Reduction Movement" to cut federal spending. (*UPI/Bettmann Newsphotos*)

THUNDER ON THE RIGHT

One of the more prominent movements in the 1970s and 1980s emerged on the far right. Large numbers of Americans, inspired by George Wallace and Barry Goldwater, faulted the national government for its busing policies, for affirmative action, for banning prayer in schools and for court-approved abortion. Many Americans resented the national government's failure to curb the rise in violent crime and the proliferation of pornography. Partisans of the New Right believed the national government was wasting far too much money on welfare and antipoverty programs—money that they believed merely created dependency and encouraged laziness.

Countless thousands of Americans rallied to these causes, as much out of frustration as from any positive support for specific policies or candidates. Yet one common denominator was a bitter frustration with the Supreme Court of the Earl Warren years (1953–1969). The Court, these people thought, was too problack and procriminal and had lost its balance. A vague but growing mood favoring more "law and order," propolice and prodeath penalty gradually developed.

In many instances, traditional interest groups such as the National Rifle Associa-

Movements in America (some examples)

Abolitionist
Suffragist
Prohibitionist
Populist
Progressives
Civil Rights
Anti-Vietnam War
Tax Cutters
Moral Majority
Nuclear Freeze
Animal Liberationists

[4] David Lowery and Lee Sigelman, "Understanding the Tax Revolt: Eight Explanations," *American Political Science Review* (December 1981), pp. 963–74. See also Howard Jarvis, *I'm Mad as Hell!* (Times Books, 1979).

tion or the conservative factions of the Republican party played a key role in mobilizing people to enlist in the cause. Radio talk shows and religious leaders also aroused people to join in the crusade. Political candidates, in both political parties, wooed voters who expressed these sentiments. Perhaps the Reverend Jerry Falwell and his "Moral Majority," especially active in the late 1970s and early 1980s, served to symbolize this movement. Senator Jesse Helms of North Carolina, Reagan Interior Secretary James Watt, and other U.S. Senators such as Orrin Hatch of Utah and Jeremiah Denton of Alabama also became prominent spokespersons for the New Right. Congressman Jack Kemp from the Buffalo, N.Y. area became identified with this movement as well, although he generally stressed economic conservatism more than the social concerns of those within the "religious Right."

The proliferation of probusiness organizations, along with allied groups favoring "law and order" and bigger defense programs, rendered the New Right movement in need of political coordination. Some of this coordination was provided by Howard Phillips and Richard A. Viguerie, founders of the Conservative Caucus. Viguerie pioneered the massive and skillful use of computerized direct mail. By the election of 1980 he had amassed the names of 4.5 million conservatives, drawn from single-issue and multiissue groups, including the National Right to Work Committee and the National Rifle Association. Operating apart from the major party organizations, Viguerie helped both Democrats and Republicans—if they were solid conservatives.

The right-wing movement attracted intense support from "social" and "moral" conservatives concerned less with economic issues than with abortion, prayer in the classroom, busing, and sexual freedom. One of the most effective efforts in the "profamily" movement was STOP ERA, led by Phyllis Schlafly, a mother of six children and an author of nine books who earned a law degree at the age of 54. Schlafly took on the battle against the Equal Rights Amendment when it seemed almost certain to pass. In *The Power of the Positive Woman*, Schlafly urged women to "reject socialism" and defend "our Judeo-Christian civilization." Her national 50,000-member movement against ERA, which viewed the amendment as communist-inspired at worst and unnecessary at best, had a central role in defeating it.[5]

How has the New Right movement related to presidential and party politics? Although Reagan, Bush, and the movement have shared opinions on such issues as busing and school prayer, each side has viewed the other with some suspicion. When Reagan told a friendly meeting of evangelicals in Florida, "Let our children pray," New Right leader Richard Viguerie praised the President's statement but added: "The President has always been very good at giving conservatives their rhetoric. It remains to be seen if the White House staff will stay the President's course and fight for these issues."[6] When the Republican party platform called for a "religious test" requiring all federal judicial nominees to subscribe to an antiabortion perspective, the Reverend Jerry Falwell, a television and evangelical leader of the Moral Majority, triumphantly cried, "Now we'll get to appoint three justices."[7] And in the 1980 and 1984 elections, evangelicals and self-described born-again Christians accounted for almost 10 percent of Reagan's landslide.

The right-wing message, once thought discredited as recently as 1964 when

The Reverend Jerry Falwell, one of the leaders of the "Moral Majority" movement, and one of the most effective television preachers. (*Dennis Brack/Black Star*)

[5] On right-wing movements and their leaders see Alan Crawford, *Thunder on the Right* (Pantheon, 1980); Kevin P. Phillips, *Post-Conservative America: People, Politics and Ideology in a Time of Crisis* (Random House, 1982); Carol Felsenthal, *The Sweetheart of the Silent Majority: The Biography of Phyllis Schlafly* (Doubleday, 1981); Richard A. Viguerie, *The New Right: We're Ready to Lead* (Carolina House, 1981).

[6] David E. Rosenbaum, "Poll Shows Many Choose Reagan Even if They Disagree With Him," *The New York Times* (September 19, 1984), p. 1.

[7] Mary McGrory, "Falwell tries a new tactic," *Boston Globe* (January 8, 1986), p. 7.

U.S. Senator Barry Goldwater (R-Arizona) went down in devastating defeat, has enjoyed a stunning comeback in the 1980s. Although familiarity took much of the sting out of the far-right's agenda, and the Reagan presidency helped to make its politics socially and politically acceptable—particularly on such issues as affirmative action, busing, and the death penalty.

This new receptivity to the New Right's call led to surprising results in Illinois' 1986 Democratic gubernatorial primary. Former U.S. Senator Adlai Stevenson III, and the rest of the nation were shocked when his preferred candidates for lieutenant governor and secretary of state were unexpectedly defeated by disciples of the elusively right-wing maverick Lyndon B. Larouche. Running under the banner of the "National Democratic Policy Council," these candidates asserted the Larouche doctrine that the Queen of England, Henry Kissinger, Nelson Rockefeller, the International Monetary Fund, the Red Cross, the Ku Klux Klan, and the B'Nai B'rith's Anti-Defamation League are involved in a peculiar conspiracy to distribute narcotics, are responsible for AIDS, and are supporters of international terrorism. Larouche's stunning success in Illinois was mainly due to voter apathy and a badly weakened Illinois Democratic party. But some observers think it may have also been partly due to demagoguery and prejudice in a climate in which the message of the far right, though distorted by Larouche, had nonetheless gained credibility.

BLACKS: FREEDOM NOW

"Ain't gonna let nobody, Lawdy, turn me 'round, turn me 'round, turn me 'round. Ain't gonna let nobody turn me 'round, gonna keep on a-walkin', keep on a-talkin,' marchin' up to Freedom Land. . . .[8]

Throughout our history, black African-Americans have struggled to rise from chattel slavery to full participation in American society. African-American movements have followed several paths of development, from slave rebellions and underground escapes, to the more recent freedom rides, sit-ins, marches, and boycotts. As with other movements, intragroup disagreements over goals and strategies have always existed. Within the black community the central question has been whether to strive for equality of opportunity inside the present federal system or outside of it.

Free black men and women lived, worked, and voted in small numbers in the northern colonies, and in smaller numbers in the southern colonies, by the nineteenth century. The majority of black Africans and succeeding generations of African-Americans, though, lived in slavery mainly on southern farms and plantations. Europeans wrenched these African peoples from complex and sophisticated societies in West Africa—Ghana, Mali, Hausa—herded them into slave trading posts along the West African coast, and branded and packed them into the holds of ships for the treacherous six- to ten-week Atlantic crossing. Trade in humans supplied the workers and "breeders" of workers required by the whites to develop the economic staples of tobacco and cotton in the South and the textile industry in the North and in England.[9]

[8] Adaptation of traditional song by members of the Albany Movement, 1961–1962, which Bernice Reagon, then an Albany State College student, called the "Singing Movement." See Clayborne Carson, *In Struggle: SNCC and the Black Awakening of the 1960s* (Harvard University Press, 1981), especially pp. 56–65. The song is recorded on *Sing for Freedom: Lest We Forget,* vol. 3, produced by Guy and Candie Carawan of the Highlander Center, Newmarket, Tennessee, for Folkways Records, 1980. Printed in *We Shall Overcome,* songs of the Southern Freedom Movement, compiled by Guy and Candie Carawan (Oak Publications, 1963).

[9] See August Meier and Elliott M. Rudwick, *From Plantation to Ghetto* (Hill and Wang, 1966); and Lerone Bennett, Jr., *Before the Mayflower: A History of the Negro in America 1619–1964,* rev. ed. (Penguin, 1966).

Resistance and Revolt

Coming from communal societies in which both men and women exercised recognized and important functions, the Africans held their own well-developed conceptions of life, liberty, and property. In the New World Africans and their descendants began to construct their own cultures and relations anew.[10] Strategies used by slaves to overcome suppression ranged from what their owners took to be docility and ignorance to outright revolt. Many times rebellions were individual and spontaneous; at other times small groups defied their masters. Others escaped, sometimes via the Underground Railroad, engineered by people such as Harriet Tubman and Frederick Douglass. At the northern ends of the lines, greeting the escapees as they emerged from southern forests under cover of night, were Vigilance Committees—groups of free blacks who helped the escapees start new lives.

A series of slave uprisings—desperate, isolated, and abortive—broke out during the eighteenth and early nineteenth centuries, headed most notably by Gabriel Prosser in Richmond in 1800; Denmark Vesey in Charleston in 1822; and Nat Turner in Virginia in 1831. These uprisings revealed communication networks and leaders who were able to calculate opportunities and organize human and material resources.[11] The white authorities harshly put down all these revolts. Still, knowledge of the uprisings has provided black citizens with the courage and historical perspective needed to overcome continuing discrimination.

While black slaves in the South continued to resist their oppression, their brothers and sisters in the North were joined by white men and women convinced that slavery must somehow be ended. At first antislavery activists aimed to free the slaves and colonize them outside the United States—as evidenced by the formation of the American Colonization Society. But this movement soon flagged. William Lloyd Garrison later reinvigorated the movement by calling for a new direction and goal: Emancipate the slaves and grant equal rights to blacks as citizens of the United States. Such publications as Garrison's newspaper *Liberator* and Lydia Maria Child's *An Appeal in Favor of that Class of Americans Called Africans*, along with meetings of local and state antislavery societies, culminated in the formation of the American Anti-Slavery Society in 1833. By 1838 a quarter of a million persons belonged to the 1350 individual societies that made up the national organization.

Dissension grew within this organization because of Garrisons's radical views. Not only did he castigate church ministers who did not support abolition, but he also advocated the "right" of women to speak in public. Garrison and his group became convinced, ironically, that secession of the *nonslave* states from the Union was a necessity. They argued that to continue union with the South was to support a Constitution that legitimized slavery.[12] The American and Foreign Anti-Slavery Society formed in opposition to Garrison, to pursue a more gradualist approach to ending slavery. The abolition movement continued up to the Civil War, and helped spawn the Liberty and Free Soil parties. Abolitionist agitation was centrally responsible for the formation of the Republican party, which emerged out of the split among the Whigs over the issue of slavery. It was finally the proslavery rather than the antislavery states that seceded from the Union; the Civil War accomplished in part what the Abolitionists began.

---

[10] Herbert G. Gutman, *The Black Family in Slavery and Freedom 1750–1925* (Vintage Books, 1977).

[11] Eugene D. Genovese, *From Rebellion to Revolution: Afro-American Slave Revolts in the Making of the New World* (Vintage Books, 1981), pp. 4, 27.

[12] Louis Ruchames, *The Abolitionists: A Collection of Their Writings* (Capricorn Books, 1964), pp. 13–24.

KKK: Countermovement

Following the Civil War many movements arose supporting or opposing reform. Two movements in particular concerned newly "freed" black people directly: the Ku Klux Klan (KKK), who lynched people and burned homes to keep blacks "in their place"; and the antilynching movement, led by one black woman, Ida Bell Wells-Barnett, who was joined by others in forming antilynching societies.

The KKK sought to preserve their version of the white southern way of life. On the one hand, Klan leaders wanted to maintain the cheap black labor pool and prevent black ownership of property. On the other, they wanted to protect the symbol of the pure white woman, whose value would be greatly diminished if women were "violated" through any kind of contact with black men. They gave no regard to black women, who literally and regularly had been violated by their white owners and masters,[13] nor to white women who might not wish to be so used and protected by being confined to a "pedestal."[14] A more complex intertwining of race, sex, and class issues can hardly be found. Black scholar and activist W. E. B. Du Bois pinpointed the very human basis of the Klan fear: "The method of force, which hides itself in secrecy, is a method as old as humanity. The kind of thing that men are afraid or ashamed to do openly, and by day, they accomplish secretly, masked, and at night."[15] Many small and often violent Klan groups are still active today.

After writing antilynching editorials in her own Memphis weekly, Ida Bell Wells-Barnett went on to launch a national, even international, crusade against lynching. Her investigations into lynching incidents took her into the forbidden and murky heart of sex-race relations. She found that though the rape of white women was popularly thought to be the reason for lynching, rape was actually charged in only a third of the over 700 lynchings reported for the ten-year period she studied. Her last *Free Speech* editorial hinted at a truth on which she later elaborated in a study of lynching entitled *A Red Record.*[16] Black men lynched for "rape" often were involved in mutually affectionate, though necessarily clandestine, relationships with white women.

Continued lynchings spurred the formation of other antilynching societies and the antilynching committee of the National Association for the Advancement of Colored People (NAACP). The Anti-Lynching Crusaders, led by Mary B. Talbert, was organized in 1922 as a national effort to draw women into the NAACP efforts. Finally, in 1930 white women formed the Association of Southern Women for the Prevention of Lynching and brought home their own "revolt against chivalry."[17] This group chose to work for state laws against lynching. Though President Truman's 1947 Committee on Civil Rights called for federal antilynching legislation—the goal of the movement—it was never passed.

The Black Movement Today

The contemporary black freedom movement began to surface quietly during World War I in New York City with an NAACP-sponsored Silent Parade protesting racial

[13] Gerda Lerner, ed., *Black Women in White America: A Documentary History* (Vintage Books, 1973), especially pp., 150–93.

[14] Anne Firor Scott, *The Southern Lady: From Pedestal to Politics 1830–1930* (University of Chicago Press, 1970).

[15] W. E. B. Du Bois, *Black Reconstruction in America 1860–1880* (Meridian Books, 1964, first published by Harcourt, Brace and Company, 1935), pp. 677–78.

[16] Ida B. Wells, *A Red Record* (Donohue & Henneberry, n.d.; reprinted by Arno Press, 1969).

[17] Jacquelyn D. Hall, *Revolt against Chivalry: Jessie Daniel Ames and the Women's Campaign against Lynching* (Columbia University Press, 1979).

segregation. The movement grew slowly as first one organization and then another formed, their leaders inspired by news of the nonviolent marches and other actions of Gandhi in India. By the 1950s the movement against racial segregation was becoming more and more public. To combat segregated public transportation, the Congress of Racial Equality (CORE) and later the Student Nonviolent Coordinating Committee (SNCC) went freedom riding through the South on Greyhound and Trailways buses. In Montgomery, Alabama, Mrs. Rosa Parks refused to give up her seat on a city bus to a white person. Her arrest sparked the formation of the Southern Christian Leadership Conference (SCLC) by the Reverends E. D. Nixon, Ralph Abernathy, and Martin Luther King, Jr. Black students and their parents challenged segregated schools and universities by enrolling in Little Rock High School, the University of Mississippi, and the University of Alabama, among other institutions. Federal troops had to be called in to ensure the black students' safety. (See Chapter 5 for more details on the fight for equal rights.)

Beginning in the 1960s the movement accelerated. Black college students challenged segregated public accommodations by sitting in at lunch counters in the South. As more and more people sat in or went on freedom rides, an increasing number were arrested and jailed for their nonviolent civil disobedience. SNCC advocated "jail, not bond," and these jail-ins brought many people into contact with racism and poor conditions in numerous southern jails. Activists challenged the white electoral process through the Voter Education Project (VEP), sponsored by the NAACP, CORE, SCLC, and SNCC. Black voter registration was a revolutionary action in the deep South and drew countless violent reactions by white mobs and police.[18] Throughout the nation there were other violent reverberations, including assassination of leaders in or associated with ideas of the movement: Medgar Evers in June 1963; President John F. Kennedy in November 1963; Malcolm X in February 1965; Martin Luther King, Jr., in April 1968; and Robert Kennedy in June 1968.

Through direct actions—both spontaneous and organized—labor leaders, workers, ministers, students, blacks and whites, and countless others brought about comprehensive changes in the laws of the United States. But laws do not operate in a vacuum. Their implementation tends to be slow, complicated by bureaucratic politics. By the 1960s many blacks were living in poverty in large cities, without the economic and social resources to take advantage of the opportunities held out by the laws. Police incidents in black ghettoes in Los Angeles (Watts), Detroit, and Newark set off riots—or what many came to consider rebellions against continuing racism.[19]

The legacy of the African-American movement is one of continuing activism, even though (or more likely because) racism and critical socioeconomic obstacles remain. More and more blacks are organizing and are winning elections. However, critical socioeconomic obstacles remain: Racism still exists; the KKK is still active. Black movements continue. Witness, for example, the landmark mayoral victories of Chicago's Harold Washington and Philadelphia's Wilson Goode in 1983, and of black leaders in scores of major cities. Moreover, the blacks' electoral strength is seen in their increased mobilization and voter registration stimulated by Jesse Jackson's 1984 and 1988 presidential campaigns. Nonetheless, growing distinctions between the black middle class and the black lower class threaten to divide the contemporary black movement. But new issues are cutting across such class cleavages. The antiapartheid struggle in South Africa, for one, is drawing together forces today, similar to the 1960s Black Freedom movement, and it is raising the consciousness of many contemporary black youths.

Jesse Jackson, activist Democrat and spokesman for various minority interests. (UPI/Bettmann Newsphotos)

[18] Carson, *In Struggle.* See also Cooney and Michalowski, *The Power of the People. Active Nonviolence in the United States.*

[19] *Report of the National Advisory Commission on Civil Disorders* (Kerner Commission) (Bantam, 1968).

WOMEN: THE CONTINUING STRUGGLE

The story of women's movements in the United States is the story of a group of persons—large in numbers but otherwise lacking in political power—who developed a sense of group consciousness, moved into politics despite countless frustrations and setbacks, and, after long struggles, achieved some of their major political goals.

Independence for America in the 1770s brought little independence for its women, who—like their sisters in western Europe—were still dependents of fathers and husbands. Women could not make legal arrangements or contracts, earn wages separate from those of their husbands, or vote. By marrying, they forfeited to their husbands legal custody of themselves as well as custody of all property and children.[20] "A wife is dead in law" was a commonly accepted doctrine. And lacking the right to vote, women could not turn to electoral politics to overcome this kind of discrimination. Rather, they "determined to foment a rebellion," in Abigail Adams's words, for "we would not hold ourselves bound by any laws in which we have no voice or representation."[21]

Women needed to become conscious of themselves as a group and to learn their rights. During the Revolution, and later during the War of 1812, many wives had to take over their husbands' work. Later, tens of thousands of women flocked to New England and other textile mill areas to work in factories.[22] This experience, along with that encountered on farms and on the expanding western frontier, made women more conscious of their abilities and resources, both as individuals and as a group. It also made them more aware of their legal and political powerlessness.

Initially, political activity among women was confined mainly to three areas: for literacy, and against slavery and liquor. Formal education for women was restricted to female academies in which daughters of the wealthy were taught social graces and other "female arts." Early reformers encouraged education for men and women alike. And although women were involved in the earliest campaigns against slavery, even like-minded males tried to distance themselves from the "female agitators." Seeing the effects of "demon rum" on their families further encouraged women to form temperance societies to combat its effects.

Such forays into the world of politics helped lay the groundwork for the movements to come, and numerous leaders emerged to organize their sisters. Sarah Bagley, a young Lowell mill worker, organized women workers in the Massachusetts and New Hampshire textile mills and founded the Female Labor Reform Association. The FLRA, together with other labor groups, submitted a petition, in favor of the ten-hour day and signed by 10,000 workers, to the Massachusetts legislature. Lucretia Mott, a Philadelphia Quaker, toured meetings of the Friends to speak on temperance, peace, antislavery, and women's rights. Elizabeth Cady Stanton, who as a child in her father's law office had heard women pour out their grievances about discrimination and oppression, devoted her life to denouncing discrimination against women. In 1821 Emma Willard founded Troy Seminary for Women, a college that offered higher mathematics as well as the more conventional arts. Most controversial of all was Frances Wright, advocate of more liberal divorce laws, birth control, equal rights, and free public education. "Fanny" was denounced for her belief in the equality of all, regardless of sex, color, and class. It was even rumored that she favored "free love."

The women's suffrage movement was a long and celebrated example of focused political action. (*Culver Pictures*)

[20] Eleanor Flexner, *Century of Struggle* (Harvard University Press, 1975), pp. 7–8, 63–65.

[21] Letter of Abigail Adams to John Adams, March 31, 1776, in Miriam Schneir, *Feminism: The Essential Historical Writings* (Vintage Books, 1972), p. 3.

[22] Milton Cantor and Bruce Laurie, eds., *Class, Sex, and the Woman Worker* (Greenwood Press, 1977).

At an international antislavery meeting in London in 1840, delegates Lucretia Mott and Elizabeth Cady Stanton suffered the humiliation of being refused seats as delegates; rather, they were sent off to the gallery to watch. Then and there they resolved to hold a women's rights convention on their return home. Eight years later such a convention was held in Seneca Falls, New York, to discuss the "social, civil, and religious conditions and rights of woman." The convention was a curious "mixture of womanly modesty and feminist militancy."[23] Because no woman would chair the meeting, Lucretia Mott's husband was asked to do so. The women's demands were radical for the times. The convention adopted resolutions calling for equal rights in marriage, property, contracts, trades, professions, and universities. Even more radical was a resolution to secure women's suffrage. Pushed by Elizabeth Cady Stanton and supported by Frederick Douglass, the measure barely passed.[24] Other conventions followed, in the East and as far west as Akron, Ohio. Women were on the march.

A Century of Struggle

Between the 1850s and the 1950s, leaders of the women's movement fought their political campaigns on many fronts. They took part in the antislavery movement, organized women's suffrage associations, won the right to vote in several western states, collaborated with temperance and other reform movements, helped found the National Association of Colored Women in 1896, fought against sexist discrimination on a state-by-state basis, established their right to higher education and professional positions, cooperated with women trade union workers, encountered defeat after defeat in their efforts to win the vote state by state, and finally won the national suffrage in August 1920, after a hard campaign for the enactment of the Nineteenth amendment.

Many believe the women's movement died after this victory. But in fact, women's organizations continued to work on "women's issues"—that is, issues directly affecting women's status as women—and on other concerns, such as voter education, prison reform, antilynching measures, child welfare, and peace. Two organizations in particular continued the fight on women's issues: the National Woman's Party (NWP) and the National Federation of Business and Professional Women (NFBPW). Founded by Alice Paul, the NWP believed the vote alone would not get rid of economic inequality in the workplace. They held instead that only a constitutional amendment could establish the *principle* of sex equality. The NWP was responsible for introducing the Equal Rights Amendment in Congress in 1923 and for keeping it alive there session after session until it was embraced by the "second wave" of the women's movement in the 1960s. The NFBPW supported the Equal Rights Amendment during this period and worked generally to improve employed women's educational and employment opportunities.[25]

In contrast, during this period the Women's Bureau of the Department of Labor worked against the Equal Rights Amendment. Because working conditions associated with so many women's jobs were harsh and unhealthy, the Women's Bureau instead supported protective legislation for employed women.[26]

This century of struggle raised a number of questions of ends and means, of strategy and tactics—questions that also confront other major groups. What is the *goal* of the women's movement—to secure rights only for women, or to win them

"ERA YES" and "STOP ERA" buttons were in evidence as pro and anti-ERA proponents listened to opening speeches at the Republican platform committee hearings in 1980. Supporters and opponents battled for their views to be written into the Republican platform. (*UPI/ Bettmann Newsphotos*)

[23] DuBois, *Feminism and Suffrage*, p. 23.

[24] Ibid., pp. 40–41.

[25] Ethel Klein, *Gender Politics: From Consciousness to Mass Politics* (Harvard University Press, 1984), and Susan J. Carroll, *Women as Candidates in American Politics* (Indiana University, 1985).

[26] Judith Hole and Ellen Levine, *Rebirth of Feminism* (Quadrangle/The New York Times Book Company, 1971), especially pp. 77–81.

also for other disadvantaged groups, such as blacks, low-paid labor, immigrants, and Indians? If women's rights is the essential goal, *which* rights—to vote, to have a good education, to enjoy legal protection, to have a decent job, or to receive equal pay? To what extent should women work with *other groups*, at the expense possibly of having to dilute their own efforts? Should women form their own *party*, work within the existing two-party system, emphasize nonparty action (such as education and lobbying), or build a mass protest movement, march, and demonstrate for their demands? Should the movement concentrate on influencing the *federal* government, focus more on *state* action, or stress *local*, day-to-day concerns, such as education or neighborhood improvement?

Like most groups, women experimented by shifting tactics to meet new goals and circumstances. The national leaders of the past century actually split over whether to fight for suffrage alone or for a broader program, whether men should be allowed in the movement and on what basis, and what specific tactics should be adopted.

The National Organization for Women (NOW), often thought of as the premier group of the women's movement, has been criticized for gaining legal and political reforms that help white middle-class women but not poor and other minority women. Many feminists contend, moreover, that political and legal reforms are not enough to restructure gender roles that limit women's economic and educational opportunities, and constrain the lives of both women and men.[27] Women's groups have met problems in mobilizing women for collective action; and even though women have become more politically conscious in the last decade, they have not identified as a group in the same way as blacks, whose group consciousness has fostered collective action for social change. Further, there is a growing distinction between *women* and *feminists* as the goals and methods of the movement change. Women are a majority of the population in the United States, but on issues such as "equal pay for equal worth," pornography, civil rights, and the ERA, there is little unanimity.

In the end, using a variety of political tactics and operating at all governmental levels paid off in securing the right to vote. Because conventional political action had not worked without the right to vote, it took the arrests of picketers and the forced feeding of society women in jails to dramatize the issues. The fact that many women were organized for both national and state politics paid off when they pushed the suffrage amendment through the House and Senate, and then through three-quarters of the state legislatures. In fact, the Senate passed the amendment by exactly the two-thirds required, and the last legislature to ratify (Tennessee's) did so by a majority of one!

A New Consciousness: ERA

Armed with the right to vote, many American women entered the 1920s with heightened self-confidence and political influence. Congress acted favorably on maternity and infancy legislation, consumer bills, and other issues of special interest to women. By the end of 1921 twenty states had granted women the right to serve on juries. A few states passed equal pay and equal rights laws. Soon came the first woman governor, woman senator, and woman cabinet member; and others followed. A new organization, the League of Women Voters, educated its members on issues and urged them to exercise their hard-won right to vote.

But if women had new political clout, they also faced new handicaps. A reaction to feminist successes set in. The child-labor constitutional amendment failed to make any headway, and conservative groups put down feminist groups and women leaders, calling them communists, antifamily, and deviant lesbians. Some

YOU DECIDE

As a leader in the women's movement today, you are serving on a planning group considering new political strategies, in light of the failure of the Equal Rights Amendment to pass. A rank-and-file activist tells your group that movement politics has failed, that a *party* strategy is necessary—and that women must form their own party. What is your response?

(Answer/Discussion on the next page.)

[27] Eisenstein, *The Radical Future of Liberal Feminism.*

This button of the mid-1980s was worn to dramatize the fact that women are commonly paid 60 cents for every $1 men get for the same or similar work.

Answer/Discussion

You might note that women outnumber men and that this would help a party strategy. But you should also note that most women cast their vote influenced more by economic, social, religious, and even some ethnic concerns than because of gender factors. Historically third parties have often been self-defeating. They have rarely gained power because our electoral system is biased against third parties. In this case a women's party might siphon women activists away from a major party that spoke for feminists concerns for other goals, such as peace and education. You might propose a somewhat different party strategy—that women focus their efforts in one of the existing major parties and hence benefit from that party's broader electoral support. But which major party would you select? Why?

women who had been active in or influenced by the women's movement veered off in other directions. Most pursued "lifestyle feminism," using the opportunities opened up by the women's movement for their own personal self-development, and leaving behind the group effort that made the opportunities possible. Although fewer continued to pursue the political aspects of feminism, they kept the fire burning until it burst out again in the 1960s.[28]

Women's goals expanded immensely following World War II, during which women had taken on heavy responsibilities, including military service. In the late 1950s and early 1960s, the struggle for black rights involved hundreds of women leaders and precipitated a more militant political effort. In the course of the struggle for "freedom now," it began to occur to more and more women, black and white, that sex as well as race was a source of oppression. Women in the anti-Vietnam War and draft resistance movements began to realize they were being relegated to nonpolicy-making roles in those efforts. Whether black, socialist, or radical feminist, many broke off and joined the women's movement.[29] Women in the labor movement likewise recognized sexism in the movement as well as in the workplace and formed the Coalition of Labor Union Women (CLUW). To many women—especially middle-class housewives or those destined for that role—the appeals of Betty Friedan and other feminist writers came like fire sirens in the night.[30]

In expanding women's consciousness of their real needs and aspirations, literary and political leaders also expanded women's political and legislative goals. No longer would women be content working for a small number of legislative enactments; now they took positions, lobbied, marched, demonstrated, or "boycotted" for bills cutting across all their concerns: equal pay, discrimination on the job, legal equality, divorce and child care, welfare rights, health care, protection against brutality and rape, equal credit opportunities, and educational equity. This range of interests required women to create new general organizations such as NOW, as well as multitudes of women's liberation groups backing specific proposals or providing particular services.[31]

The women's movement of the late 1970s became more and more conscious of its own diversity; it was not just a white middle-class phenomenon. Many began to work on coalition building within the movement as well as with other groups—consumers, trade unions, blacks, religious and educational groups—in order to push bills in Congress and the state legislatures. As in any movement, women were internally divided: Some women deserted NOW because it was too radical, others because it was too conservative.

As we saw in Chapter 2, the efforts of many groups came to a focus in the battle for the Equal Rights Amendment (ERA) in the 1970s. To this struggle pro-ERA leaders brought not only moral claims and raised consciousness but also potentially vast numbers of voters and a large coalition of organizations. By the mid-1970s an alliance of younger organizations such as NOW and older groups such as the League of Women Voters and the BPW had set up a national lobby, ERAmerica, with headquarters in Washington. Yet the battle for the ERA, like that for the vote a century before, proceeded slowly. Even though women constituted a majority of the American people, they faced opposition from well-organized minorities. Many women flatly opposed the ERA, and they formed their own organization: STOP ERA. Others favored the ERA but feared that concentrating so much on this one general issue would divert efforts from more specific and practical goals.

[28] Rayna Rapp and Ellen Ross, " 'It Seems We've Stood and Talked Like This Before': Wisdom from the 1920s," *Ms.* (April 1983), pp. 54–56.

[29] Sara Evans, *Personal Politics: The Roots of Women's Liberation in the Civil Rights Movement and the New Left* (Vintage Books, 1980).

[30] Betty Friedan, *The Feminine Mystique* (Norton, 1963).

[31] Jo Freeman, *The Politics of Women's Liberation* (David McKay, 1975).

Moreover, even though many men supported the ERA, others assailed it. And millions of Americans, both women and men, were apathetic.

By the mid-1980s supporters of the ERA were still unable to win majorities in both houses of enough of the thirty-eight states needed to pass the amendment.[32] But a striking symbolic victory occurred in 1984 when the Democrats chose Congresswoman Geraldine A. Ferraro of New York as their vice-presidential candidate. Although she proved to be a vigorous campaigner, there is no indication she helped to win votes for the Democratic ticket that November.

The 1980s strikingly parallel the 1920s in reacting to feminism. A conservative Republican occupied the White House, and many conservatives have viewed the women's movement as radical and antifamily. Yet women in the movement during the 1980s have learned from the past. They are more politically conscious and capable of organizing around controversial issues, and they have more political and economic resources and experiences upon which to draw. Women activists are aware that their struggle will be difficult and that history will not repeat itself if they remain active and organized.

AMERICAN INDIANS: THE OLDEST MOVEMENT?

Indian leaders seek change in U.S. policy. (*George Tames/NYT Pictures*)

Centuries ago colonists sailed west looking for another India. Often holding grants of land from their own governments, they believed the land in the New World "belonged" to them. However, the land belonged by long usage to "Indians," tribal peoples who had long inhabited its mountains and valleys, meadows and plains. As settlers moved west, colonial leaders dealt with Indian representatives to obtain land for colonists, to reserve certain lands to Indians, and to gain access for Indian hunters in the ceded areas. Much was settled by negotiation and agreement; in North America the British made treaties with the Creek Confederacy, the Cherokee Nation, Wyandot, the Iroquois Confederacy, and the Seneca Nation.[33] But as the white people aggressively pressed into Indian lands, conflicts arose—and the red people resisted through both violent and nonviolent means.

Background of the Movement

The early Indian resistance movements reflected a deep division between cultures. Early in this century a congressional committee chairperson reflected the white cultural bias: "As a race of people, the Indian is not much inclined to continuous work; he is not very ambitious; he specially enjoys fishing, hunting, racing and other sports rather than any kind of hard labor; governmentally he is naturally tribalist; he is more inclined to tribalism than to individualism. . . ."[34] White leaders, reflecting their own patriarchal society, assumed Indian tribes were patriarchal as well and hence dealt only with Indian men. But in some tribes the braves lacked full authority.[35] Thus, the political cultures of the white and red peoples clashed, especially with regard to patriarchy, private property, individualism, capitalism versus communalism, tribalism, nonprivate lands, and a nonprofit economy.

Historically the federal government has followed a dual policy toward native Americans. On the one hand, Congress did not propose to rule the tribes but

[32] Janet K. Boles, *The Politics of the Equal Rights Amendment* (Longman, 1979).

[33] Dorothy V. Jones, *License for Empire: Colonialism by Treaty in Early America* (University of Chicago Press, 1982).

[34] Quoted in Russel Lawrence Barsh and James Youngblood Henderson, *The Road: Indian Tribes and Political Liberty* (University of California Press, 1980).

[35] On the roles of American Indian women, see Rayna Green, "Native American Women," *Signs: Journal of Women in Culture and Society* (Winter 1980), pp. 248–67.

1831 *Cherokee Nation* v. *Georgia*: Indian tribes are "wards" of the United States.

1832 *Worcester* v. *Georgia*: Treaties between Indian tribes and the United States assume tribal sovereignty, and the state of Georgia cannot interfere with internal tribal affairs.

1830–1836 Act of May 28, 1830, Act of July 2 1836, and United States treaties with various tribes: Indian tribes east of the Mississippi River must move to territories west of the Mississippi River.

1884 *Elk* v. *Wilkins*: Indians are not citizens, the Fourteenth amendment notwithstanding.

1887 Dawes Indian General Allotment Act: United States subdivides tribal territories and allots plots of land to individual Indians, confers U.S. citizenship to Indians who left reservations.

1924 Act of June 2, 1924: United States confers citizenship on Indians; includes Indian women who marry non-Indians.

1934 Indian Reorganization Act: Indian tribes on reservations may adopt constitutions, which must be approved by the Secretary of the Interior.

1953 Public Law 83-280 and various subsequent acts: United States terminates relations with and services to Indian tribes.

1968 Indian Civil Rights Act: United States provides a Bill of Rights for individual Indians in relation to their tribes.

1983 *Arizona* v. *California*: Five southwestern Indian tribes cannot relitigate an original 1952 case to increase tribal water rights, even though the United States failed to claim all the tribes' rights for them in the original case.

simply to regulate trade with them. In fact, white settlers continued to move into tribal lands, often with backing from their local and state governments—in defiance of treaties made in Washington. According to Chief Justice Marshall, Indians were "domestic dependent nations." "They occupy a territory to which we assert a title independent of their will, which must take effect in point of possession when their right of possession ceases. Meanwhile they are in a state of pupilage. Their relationship to the United States resembles that of a ward to his guardian."[36] Many native Americans, however, preferred their own culture.

In 1944 some Indian leaders formed the National Congress of American Indians (NCAI), with Ruth Muskrat Bronson as its first director. In some respects the NCAI operated as a typical interest group, working on legislation affecting Indian tribes and conducting litigation in behalf of Indian voting rights, welfare, and civil rights. But the NCAI was also militant in defense of Indian culture. "Tribalism is not an association of interest but a form of consciousness," according to two authorities; it is a feeling of being born "into a family, a territory, a spiritual world . . . the mental experience" of "a warm, deep and lasting communal bond among all things in nature in a common vision of their proper relationship."[37]

This sense of "movement militance" erupted in charges that the United States government had practiced genocide in the Indian wars from 1790 to 1915—beginning with wars against the Indian tribes in the Old Northwest Territory and ending with wars against the Paiute in Colorado. Indian leaders also charged that the government had destroyed rights supposedly guaranteed by treaties, such as rights to fishing and hunting, as well as to timber and other natural resources. Such charges coincided with movements for national liberation that were surfacing in the 1960s around the world, especially in third-world nations in Asia and Africa. American Indian leaders even claimed a kind of fourth-world status, as a "colony within a nation."

More Recent Movement Militance

In the summer of 1961 ten young college-educated Indians, five men and five women—a Paiute, a Mohawk, a Ute, a Shoshone-Bannock, a Ponca, a Potawatomi, a Tuscarora, two Navajos, and a Crow—met in the Gallup, New Mexico, Indian Community Center. They came to decide how to carry out a Declaration of Indian Purpose adopted at a national gathering of Indian tribal leaders earlier in the summer. They formed the National Indian Youth Council (NIYC). "In the Indian way," they elected one another members of the council and chose Paiute Mel Thom as their first president. Their membership grew large in the following years. In Mel Thom's words: "The movement grew in the Indian way. We had decided what we needed was a movement. Not an organization, but a movement. *Organizations rearrange history. Movements make history . . . .* Long ago the Indians knew how to use direct action. You might say that was the traditional way that Indians got things done. We were concerned with direct action: Indians moving out and doing something."[38]

NIYC's first venture was to challenge their alleged denial of the Indians' tribal fishing rights by the state of Washington. Beginning in 1964 the NIYC and the Northwest Indian tribes held "fish-ins" on the Quillayute, Puyallup, Yakima, Nisqually, Columbia, and Green Rivers. Men, women, and children participated, and the police arrested and jailed many of them. The NIYC actions sparked a surge of Indian activism. Indians of All Tribes, first organized in the San Francisco Bay area, retook Alcatraz Island. The American Indian Movement (AIM) occupation

[36] *Cherokee Nation* v. *Georgia*, 5 Peters 25, 17 (1831).
[37] Barsh and Henderson, *The Road*, pp. vii–viii.
[38] Stan Steiner, *The New Indians* (Harper & Row, 1968), p. 40. (Emphasis added.)

of Wounded Knee mobilized the Indians of many tribes and focused attention on recovering sovereignty in Indian lands.

Though differences do exist between the more traditional Indian tribal leaders and the more militant advocates of Indian rights, such as Russell Means of AIM, the tribe still seems to be a focal point of concern. And as long as native Indians cherish their culture, it can be expected that their movement—militant but nonviolent—will continue.

THE POLITICS OF PEACE

Peace movements—or at least antiwar campaigns—began early in American history. The Civil War and other major conflicts aroused strong opposition on a local, and sometimes on a national, basis. The Women's Peace Party and the Fellowship of Reconciliation were formed in the United States during World War I. The bloodbaths of that war brought a powerful revulsion against militarism, interventionism, and the "merchants of death" who were said to profit from wars they helped bring about. The antiwar movement of the 1930s, headed by such diverse figures as the popular heroic pilot Charles A. Lindbergh and socialist Norman Thomas, caused President Franklin Roosevelt to move warily against the gathering forces of fascism.

Concern over peace rose to a new intensity with the advent of nuclear weapons and the onset of the Korean and Vietnam Wars. Students and other activists took to the streets, disrupted classrooms, occupied administration buildings, and took part in (usually) nonviolent action against the authorities. As the superpowers stepped up their nuclear arsenals, new organizations arose—most notably the liberal Committee for a Sane Nuclear Policy (SANE) and the more activist Committee for Non-Violent Action (CNVA), and later a host of religious groups and professional organizations such as Physicians for Social Responsibility.[39] In 1980 peace leaders joined with environmentalists behind the Citizens Party and nominated noted biologist Barry Commoner for president, but this third-party effort failed, as have a number of others throughout history.[40]

The election of Ronald Reagan in that year, and perhaps more importantly, his reelection in 1984, left the peace movement divided and frustrated. Campaigns continued to "ban the bomb" and to ensure a mutually verifiable nuclear "freeze," but the peace movement lacked unified leadership, a coherent policy program, and a realistic political strategy. Arguments broke out as to the proper course of action, and the peace leaders sometimes appeared unable to keep peace among themselves. A 1986 peace march across the United States faltered, somewhere on the Great Plains. The old questions that had dogged all American movements stared these leaders in the face: Should the peace activists link themselves more closely with the two major parties or with one of the major third-party groups, in which case the smaller party might be engulfed by the larger one? Or should they link with one existing major party, presumably the Democrats, who were looking for allies? Or should they be content to serve as the junior partner in some multiparty coalition in Congress, without any hope of gaining the presidency?

With the passing of the 1988 election and a new administration in 1989, peace leaders sought to enlarge their ranks and fashion a more effective movement. But Ronald Reagan, instead of galvanizing the peace movement, appears to have

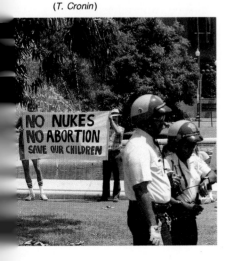

(T. Cronin)

NO NUKES
NO ABORTION
SAVE OUR CHILDREN

[39] Ulrike C. Wasmuht, "A Sociological Survey of American Peace Movements," *Alternatives IX* (Spring 1984), pp. 581–91.

[40] Alan Wolfe, "Why Is There No Green Party in the United States?" *World Policy Journal* (Fall 1983), pp. 161–80, quoted on p. 172.

diffused it—especially with arms negotiations with Soviet leader Mikhail Gorbachev. Peace leaders remained divided over strategy and tactics. Whether the peace effort would remain a loosely connected cluster of peace *campaigns* for specific goals, such as the nuclear freeze, or become a strong movement that could directly influence parties and candidates—or something in between—remained unresolved. Some peace leaders wondered if a dramatic or even tragic event might be necessary to stimulate the movement and Americans generally—but who wished for such an event in an era of superpower nuclear rivalry?

MOVEMENTS AND THE CONSTITUTION

Our Constitution—still relevant and effective after 200 years—protects movements. In other countries movements are viewed as a threat to government. Indeed, they may be—to a government in South Africa or Poland, for example, which is unable to deal peaceably with movements. But the Constitution, and specifically the Bill of Rights, guarantees the rights of Americans to free assembly, free speech, due process, and to all the liberties that allow movement politics—majority or minority forces—to thrive. Movements polarize opinion, but they also can persuade many people to change some of their attitudes and raise public consciousness about critical issues when the forces of government would otherwise ignore those same issues.

But obstacles, constitutional or otherwise, do exist for movements. Leaders of movements throughout history have faced and overcome these obstacles to their political involvement. For example, the Constitution barred Congress from stopping the slave trade prior to 1808 and allowed a tax of $10 on each slave so imported. It not only prohibited any amendment of this clause but provided for the return of fugitive persons "held to service or labor"—slaves—to their owners. In fact, until the Thirteenth Amendment was ratified, the Constitution made any major movement against slavery appear to be unconstitutional.

The Constitution is all but silent concerning women. It speaks of "we the people" and "persons" but also refers to "a President . . . He." The fourteenth Amendment specifically mentions *male* voting rights. Thus, the basic law of the land excluded women from the public sphere of government until the ratification of the Nineteenth Amendment.[41]

Indians cannot complain of being ignored in the Constitution, for the charter specifically acknowledged the existence of Indian tribes. The population to be counted in determining representation in the House of Representatives was to exclude "Indians not taxed"; and Congress was to regulate commerce "with foreign nations . . . and with the Indian tribes." Politically, however, the Indians had scant hope of operating within the constitutional system: Their scattered numbers, their divisions, and the overwhelming military weight of incoming settlers effectively precluded their participation.

However, defenders of the Constitution contend that even though the constitutional system as it operated in the eighteenth and nineteenth centuries excluded women and slaves from the political process, these "outside" groups worked their way into the Constitution during this century. Blacks and Indians, they assert, have won more through litigation and lobbying than through movement politics. The Constitution was not written for women, admittedly; but for an eighteenth-century charter it is alleged to be rather advanced. This is a vital question for discussion during the present bicentennial era of "rethinking our Constitution."

[41] From Diane L. Fowlkes, *How Gender Politics Reconstructs American Government and Politics* (American Political Science Association, 1983). See also Sarah Slavin, *Women and the Politics of Constitutional Principles* (American Political Science Association, 1983).

Centrist Movements?

Why is it that nearly all political movements come from either the left or right? By definition, a movement emerges not from within the mainstream of the political system, but from the fringes or from "the outside". Thus populists, moralists, and anti-Establishment activism periodically arises from the left and the right.

Centrists or mainstream political activists may temporarily lend their allegiance to a proconsumer campaign or to a short-lived cause such as the John B. Anderson independent candidacy for President in 1980. Invariably, however, such activism either dissipates or is quickly channeled back through regular political parties or existing interest groups. This is why this chapter has focused primarily on the crusades and causes of the far right and the left. Movements seldom if ever erupt from the center. Are movements futile, lost causes? Centrists would often say yes. Movement leaders insist that their causes are the "causes yet to be won!"

SUMMARY

1. Movements of large numbers of people who are frustrated with government policies have always been with us in the U.S. Blacks, women, native Americans, and the economic have-less underdogs have at various times organized themselves into movements. This so-called "New Right" and "religious Right" are a mix of movement and traditional interest group politics.

2. The key components of movements are negative perceptions of the political system; group consciousness of mistreatment, organization, and leadership; and direct actions involving large numbers of group members and supporters.

3. Individuals gain group consciousness through movements. They may experience direct action itself or participate in alternative educational experiences, or they may be encouraged by families or movement leaders.

4. Movement politics involves groups outside the political system who are in conflict with and confront the system in public, direct actions intended to achieve comprehensive change. In contrast, interest-group politics involves groups inside the political system who bargain privately within a framework of consensus to bring about incremental change.

5. The "latest movement" is the New Right headed by television evangelist Jerry Falwell, and inspired and supported by Ronald Reagan.

6. The focal point of the black movements is to change the original slave status of black Africans to freedom as persons and full-fledged citizens of the United States.

7. The focal point of women's movements is to transcend the artificially imposed dichotomy of the public and private spheres.

8. The focal point of American Indian movements is to recover tribal sovereignty, which was first established by treaties and then abrogated continuously as settlers violated the treaties.

9. The peace movement is fractured at a time when a cohesive strategy is most critical. Different goals, clashing methods, and conflicting priorities threaten to negate the potentially potent effect of peace activists.

FURTHER READING

SAUL ALINSKY. *Rules for Radicals* (Random House, 1972).

RUSSEL LAWRENCE BARSH and JAMES YOUNGBLOOD HENDERSON. *The Road: Indian Tribes and Political Liberty* (University of California Press, 1980).

DEE BROWN. *Bury My Heart at Wounded Knee* (Holt, Rinehart & Winston, 1971).

RUFUS P. BROWNING, DALE ROGERS MARSHALL, and DAVID H. TABB. *Protest Is Not Enough: The Struggle of Blacks and Hispanics in Urban Politics* (University of California Press, 1984).

CLAYBORNE CARSON. *In Struggle: SNCC and the Black Awakening of the 1960s* (Harvard University Press, 1981).

JEAN L. COHEN, ed. "Social Movements," *Social Research*. (Winter 1985).

ROBERT COONEY and HELEN MICHALOWSKI. *The Power of the People: Active Nonviolence in the United States* (Peace Press, 1977).

ALAN CRAWFORD. *Thunder on the Right* (Pantheon, 1980).

GLORIA T. HULL, PATRICIA BELL SCOTT, and BARBARA SMITH, eds. *All the Women Are White, All the Blacks Are Men, but Some of Us Are Brave: Black Women's Studies* (Feminist Press, 1982).

HOWARD JARVIS. *I'm Mad as Hell!* (Times Books, 1979).

ALDON D. MORRIS. *The Origins of The Civil Rights Movement: Black Communities Organizing for Change* (Free Press/ Macmillan, 1985).

BARBARA DECKARD SINCLAIR. *The Women's Movement* (Harper & Row, 1983).

U.S. COMMISSION ON CIVIL RIGHTS. *Indian Tribes: A Continuing Quest for Survival* (U.S. Government Printing Office, 1981).

RICHARD VIGUERIE. *The New Right* (Carolina House, 1981).

CHAPTER 9

Parties: Decline and Renewal?

In the early pages of this book we noted how our Constitution divides government by setting the legislative, executive, and judicial branches at odds with one another. The framers of 1787 did this by making the president, Senate, House, and even the judiciary (indirectly) responsive to different alignments of voters (see Chapter 2). The purpose, you will recall, was to keep government limited in its power and impact so it would not "gang up" against the people's liberties. Most early Americans favored this idea. Like many of us today, they wanted to keep government—especially the federal government—"off their backs."

But there was a flip side to this idea. Americans then also wanted efficient, orderly, and effective government—just as we do today. They wanted teamwork in government: a group of officials who could work together and be held collectively responsible for what they did or failed to do. So Americans in effect invented a "second constitution"—political parties. Two or more parties would compete for office. The winning party, or coalition of parties, would put its leaders in office, both legislative and executive. These leaders would form a team able to unite government to carry out its party principles. The losing party would serve as a loyal—but forceful—opposition. It may seem paradoxical to call a party system a constitution. Yet in the most basic sense, political parties organize power, grant and withhold authority, and try to keep officeholders accountable, as written constitutions do.

Note the contrasts between the "first constitution" of 1787 and the "second—the party—constitution" of the 1830s and 1840s. The first Constitution was written in a single summer by the elite of the day: by the "well bred, the well read, the well fed, and the well wed." The second constitution was shaped over a long period of time, by many men and women—often "common people"—meeting in taverns and caucuses and town halls. The first Constitution went into effect as soon as it was ratified by state constitutions; the "party constitution" took decades to take root in people's minds and acts, and to grow into a full-bodied system with party leaders, whips, activists, and supporters. The Constitution of 1787 was framed by the nation's heroes—men like Washington and Franklin and Madison. The party constitution was slowly shaped by local leaders and by a few national ones—notably Martin Van Buren, a young man of low social status who had absorbed politics

The winning ticket. George Bush and Dan Quayle after their 1988 nomination as Republican presidential and vice-presidential candidates. (R. Maiman/Sygma)

Seven Realities about American Parties

1. Parties began as soon as people began taking sides in the debate over ratifying the U.S. Constitution—although it took a few years for them to organize into formal bodies.

2. Political parties, and especially our two-party system, have persisted over the course of our history.

3. Ours is, and just about always has been, a two-party system, making us stand out from most nations that have a one-party or multi-party system.

4. Since 1830 we have witnessed reasonably effective competition in our national party system.

5. Our parties have historically been highly decentralized and fragmented, but there has been a marked increase in the importance of the national committees in recent years.

6. Winning office and power have been more important to party leaders than specific issues or platforms; political parties in the United States are primarily organized to win or obtain political power.

7. Our parties can be characterized as moderate, centrist, and pragmatic, with only modest ideological cohesion and voting discipline—especially when compared to European political parties.

by listening to great talkers in his father's tavern and who went on to become Democratic party leader and president. The first Constitution was a comprehensive plan, the second developed slowly, by trial and error.

The greatest contrast between the two constitutions, however, lay in their impact on government. The party constitution was an instrument of majority rule—of "rule by the people"—whereas the 1787 Constitution protected rule by a minority, or coalition of minorities. By making presidents, senators, and representatives responsive to different constituencies, the 1787 Constitution impeded teamwork in government; by making presidents and members of Congress responsive to one organized party majority, the party constitution encouraged teamwork. The 1787 Constitution was accepted early on; the very idea of parties was attacked from the start by Washington and others as divisive, fractious, turbulent, and overly democratic. The 1787 Constitution depended on checks and balances to protect the people's liberties; the party constitution relied on regular, open, and democratic elections.

You might expect that the paper Constitution, the framers' constitution of 1787, would become antiquated and feeble, and that the dynamic "people's constitution" would endure. On the contrary: The formal Constitution endures, as you can see every time the House of Representatives and the Senate fail to agree, or the president vetoes a bill passed by both chambers. Meanwhile, the party system may be in decline, as we discuss later. And this raises a very urgent question: If the health of our whole system depends on a balance between a Constitution that divides leaders and a party system that unites them, what will happen if one of these constitutions declines and even disappears?

But are the parties in fact declining? Further on in this chapter we discuss this question in detail. Perhaps part of the question can be answered by you, the reader. How partisan are you? Your parents? Your friends and neighbors? If there is a Young Democrats or Young Republicans or some other party club in your school, are you a member of it? Chances are—statistically—that you are not strongly partisan, nor are most of the people you know.

Contrast this with the "grand old days" of American parties. A century ago you and many of your friends would have been fiercely partisan. The party was part of your way of life, part of the eternal order of things, like the family and religion. It was part of your inheritance. Belonging to the "other" party was not quite respectable. *Which* party you belonged to was often a regional matter. If you were white and grew up in the South, Republicans were alien beings who opposed all you stood for. If you were black and grew up in the South, Republicans were the emancipators (except that they pulled their federal troops out too soon and you lost your rights to vote and hold office). If you were raised in Kansas, Democrats were people who frequented saloons and lived off a few patronage crumbs from Washington.

Things are different today. For thirty years or so parties have been declining in popular support and organizational strength. "Strong" Republicans and "strong" Democrats have dropped by about a third in the past quarter century, and the number of unaffiliated has grown during the same period. Party organization is feeble in most states. Where the party is strong locally, it is often ruled by a small group of "old timers." Americans have been losing faith—or interest—in parties, as they have in most other institutions.[1]

The party as an organization no longer makes the single most crucial decision in national politics—the choice of the presidential nominee. The two winning candidates are formally chosen in the parties' national conventions; but in most cases, as in 1988, they are *actually* chosen in a string of state presidential primaries.

---

[1] On party decline and other aspects of party, see Gerald M. Pomper, ed., *Party Renewal in America* (Praeger, 1980). For the argument that people have grown neutral, not hostile, to parties, see Martin P. Wattenberg, *The Decline of American Political Parties, 1952–80* (Harvard University Press, 1984).

Independents as well as partisans vote their candidate preferences at the polls, while the party organizations stand by almost inactive. In 1976 Jimmy Carter won the nomination, even though he had little influence with the national Democratic party, and Ronald Reagan almost defeated President Ford, a long-time leader in the GOP. In 1984 Gary Hart almost toppled the consensus choice of the senior party regulars, because voters responded to his television appeal, while in 1988 Governor Michael Dukakis of Massachusetts won the nomination with few close links to the national party.

Perhaps the most dramatic—and most tragic—example of party weakness was **Watergate.** In his 1972 reelection campaign President Nixon largely bypassed the Republican party organization and depended on his personal organization, the Committee for the Re-election of the President—the infamous CREEP. Watergate grew in part out of CREEP: its illegal actions, its secrecy, its financing, its excessive personal loyalty to Mr. Nixon. In the 1980s Ronald Reagan, like earlier presidents, converted his party's national committee into his own campaign vehicle, despite efforts of party leaders to work for all the party's nominees. Governors and mayors, whether Democratic or Republican, often control state and city party organizations, as did the late Mayor Richard Daley of Chicago.

Most Americans have mixed feelings about the parties. Critics charge that the parties evade the issues; that they fail to deliver on their promises; that they have no new ideas; that they are sources of corruption and misgovernment; that they follow public opinion rather than lead it; or that they are just one more special interest. Others favor our party system and take part in it. Most Americans believe in voting for individual candidates regardless of party label, but even this group wants party labels kept on the ballot.[2]

Our parties are in deep trouble. Does it matter? Are parties relevant to "government by the people"? If so, can we breathe new life into them?

PARTIES: THEIR RISE AND THEIR ROLE

Before we begin, we need to make a crucial distinction between the *factions* we discussed in earlier chapters and the *parties* we now consider. If you find this question a bit baffling, you are in good company—it baffled our country's founders too. In fact, they confused the issue; we must try to clarify it.

The founders did understand the nature of faction; Madison's definition of it in *The Federalist*, No. 10 (see Appendix) is still the best we have. Madison and others called the factions they opposed "cliques," or "juntos," or even "parties" (by which they meant factions). Fearing the excesses of economic, social, and other highly organized groups, they devised a federal constitution that would moderate the power of faction, as we saw in Part One of this text. And because they did not want to extinguish the freedom that stimulated faction, they provided for the fundamental liberties we examined in Chapters 4, 5, and 6.

To the leaders of the young Republic, parties usually meant bigger, better organized, and fiercer factions—and they did not want them. Benjamin Franklin worried about the "infinite mutual abuse of parties, tearing to pieces the best of characters." In his farewell address, George Washington warned against the "baneful effects of the Spirit of Party." And Thomas Jefferson said: "If I could not go to heaven but with a party, I would not go there at all."[3]

How, then, did parties get started? Largely out of practical necessity. To get its measures passed through Congress and administered by the new government,

---

[2] These mixed attitudes toward parties are summarized in Austin Ranney, *Curing the Mischiefs of Faction* (University of California Press, 1975), pp. 53–56.

[3] Washington, Franklin, and Jefferson, as quoted in Richard Hofstadter, *The Idea of a Party System* (University of California Press, 1969), pp. 2, 123.

Although the symbols of our major parties have remained the same, their positions and bases of support have shifted, making them fundamentally different from the parties of a century ago. (*Courtesy of the Democratic and Republican National Committees*)

the first administration (under Washington) had to build a kind of coalition among factions—that is, a rudimentary party. This job fell to Treasury Secretary Alexander Hamilton, who built an informal Federalist "team" while Washington stayed "above politics." Secretary of State Jefferson and other officials who hated Hamilton's aristocratic ways gravitated into their own political orbit, revolving around a more republican point of view. When Jefferson left Washington's cabinet at the end of 1793, his fellow Virginians remained in Congress, where they built a rudimentary party in opposition to Federalist fiscal and foreign policies. In 1800 Jefferson returned to the political wars and pieced together a coalition of groups and regions strong enough to defeat President John Adams and put himself into the newly built White House. Aaron Burr helped Jefferson in Manhattan by setting up a "party ticket" of Anti-Federalist candidates, organizing rallies, and establishing get-out-the-vote committees in the wards. (Anti-Federalists were later known as Republicans, then as Democratic-Republicans, then as Democrats.)

Soon President Thomas Jefferson, the man who had denounced parties, became for a time one of the most successful party leaders the nation has known. Again, this was a matter of practical necessity. Jefferson wanted to get the Louisiana Purchase and other big bills and appropriations through Congress. He wanted to carry on the debate against the Federalists. And he wanted to win reelection and keep the Republicans in power. So he had to maintain a coalition of group interests—southerners and northerners; farmers, laborers, and other economic interests; and religious groups—and thus, in effect, he created a party.

But Jefferson as party leader turned out to be something of a flash in the pan. On the whole, the first Republicans never built a grass-roots organization. Jefferson did not seem very clear about his party role, nor did he understand the role of the minority party as the loyal opposition. As a strong national force his party hardly outlived him. His successor, James Madison, tried to act more as a broker among factions than as a national party leader. This resulted in a weak presidency. Following a period of partyless government, another great leader arose to knit together a winning combination of regions, group interests, and political doctrines. This was Andrew Jackson, brilliantly seconded by Martin Van Buren, who had had experience in party building in New York State. The Federalists, who never felt really comfortable appealing to the grass roots, faded as a party during the long period of Republican supremacy. They were succeeded by the Whigs, who developed as an opposition party to Jackson. By the time Van Buren followed Jackson in the White House in 1837, the Democrats had become a large, nationwide movement with national and state leadership, a clear party doctrine, and grass-roots organization. The Whigs were almost as strong; in 1840 they put their own man, General William Henry Harrison—"old Tippecanoe"—into the White House. A two-party system had been born.

We have had that two-party system ever since. The party system flowered in the 1830s and 1840s. Whigs and Democrats competed strenuously. They reached out for supporters and helped broaden the franchise by gradually lifting property qualifications on voting. They fostered cooperation between presidents and other partisans in Congress. They developed the national convention, party platforms, and strong party leadership in the House and Senate. Still, the Whigs never achieved as broad and durable a coalition as the Democrats. And neither party was strong enough to cope with the issue of slavery in the 1860s; Abraham Lincoln was elected in 1860 amid party disruption.

Out of the crisis evolved a new major party: the second Republican party—ultimately the "Grand Old Party." As the party of the Union, the Republicans won the support not only of financiers, industrialists, and merchants but also of large numbers of white and newly freed black male workers and farmers. For fifty years after 1860 this Republican coalition won every presidential race, except for

Grover Cleveland's victories in 1884 and 1892. The Democratic party survived with its durable white male base in the South. For all their noisy battles during the century, both parties remained true to the idea that under a two-party system neither side can afford to be extremist. However, both parties contained liberal and conservative elements, and both appealed for support to all major economic interests, including business and labor. But the Democrats were less effective than the Republicans in building broad coalitions. They won (with Woodrow Wilson as their candidate) only in 1912 and 1916, when the Bull Moosers under Theodore Roosevelt rebelled against Republican party regulars. After 1920, the GOP was again dominant.

The Democrats were unable to build a durable winning coalition until the early 1930s, when the Hoover administration was overwhelmed by the Great Depression. Franklin Roosevelt strengthened the farm-labor-southern alliance that Woodrow Wilson had begun to build. He also put together a "grand coalition" of these groups plus unemployed middle-class persons, intellectuals, and national and racial minorities. This coalition reelected Roosevelt three times and brought presidential victories to the Democrats (except when Eisenhower ran) for two decades after Roosevelt died.

Still, the "Roosevelt coalition" was vulnerable to Dwight Eisenhower's personal popularity and to Richard Nixon's own coalition building. In 1968 Nixon brought together an alliance of predominantly white middle-class voters, "hard-hat" workers, southern conservatives, suburbanites, and business elements. Neither Hubert Humphrey in 1968 nor George McGovern in 1972 was able to overcome the Nixon organization, though the Democrats retained large majorities in Congress. In 1976 Jimmy Carter brought together just enough of the old coalition of union members, blacks, party regulars, and new liberals to produce a razor-thin majority at the polls.[4] The key question facing Carter was whether he could convert his electoral coalition into a governing coalition. By 1980 his critics charged that he had failed to do so, and the way was open for the Grand Old Party to build a countercoalition big enough to vote the Democrats out of power.

This was what President Reagan accomplished in the 1980s. On the one hand he succeeded in winning and holding the support of millions of conservatives while converting the "Grand Old Party" into the nation's right-wing party. On the other hand, through such tactics as choosing and keeping George Bush as his running mate and making occasional concessions to moderates in the party, he maintained a broad electoral coalition. While Reagan helped win the election in 1988, the Democrats increased their numbers in Congress, indicating that Reagan had not been able to convert his personal popularity into wide and stable *party* support.[5]

Key Aspects of the Parties Today

Both parties are now middle-aged: The GOP has celebrated its centennial, and in a few years the Democrats will mark their bicentennial (they claim the present Democratic party grew directly out of the first Republican party, born when Jefferson departed from Washington's cabinet in 1793). The longevity of the two parties is remarkable, considering the depressions, wars, social changes, and political crises they have survived. But if the names and the symbols have stayed the same, what they represent has clearly changed. Extensive shifts have occurred in the positions of the major parties and in their social bases and electoral support.

[4] Warren E. Miller and Teresa E. Levitin, *Leadership and Change*, 2nd ed. (Winthrop, 1977), chap. 7. See also Gerald M. Pomper et al., *The Election of 1976* (McKay, 1977).
[5] Charles Jones, ed. *The Reagan Legacy* (Chatham House, 1988).

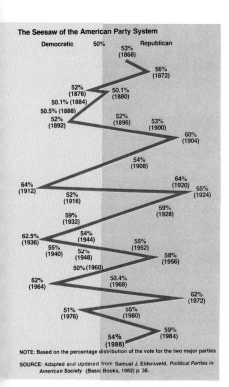

The Seesaw of the American Party System

Democratic   50%   53% (1868)   Republican

56% (1872)
52% (1876)   50.1% (1880)
50.1% (1884)
50.5% (1888)
52% (1892)   52% (1896)   53% (1900)
60% (1904)
54% (1908)
64% (1912)   64% (1920)   65% (1924)
52% (1916)   59% (1928)
59% (1932)
62.5% (1936)   54% (1944)   55% (1952)
55% (1940)   52% (1948)   58% (1956)
50% (1960)
62% (1964)   50.4% (1968)
62% (1972)
51% (1976)   55% (1980)
54% (1988)   59% (1984)

NOTE: Based on the percentage distribution of the vote for the two major parties

SOURCE: Adapted and updated from Samuel J. Eldersveld, *Political Parties in American Society* (Basic Books, 1982) p. 38.

YOU DECIDE

These days we are celebrating the birthdays of the formal Constitution—of its drafting in 1787, its adoption in 1788, and its taking effect in 1789. What about the "people's" constitution: Will we be celebrating its bicentennial, and, if so, when? (Answer/ Discussion on the next page.)

Both parties are moderate in their policies and leadership, although the GOP has shifted to the right in the past decade.[6] Successful party leaders must be group diplomats; to win presidential elections, they must find a middle ground among more or less hostile groups so that they can reach agreement on general principles. Each party takes its extremist supporters more or less for granted and seeks out the voters in the middle. This is one reason college students on the far Left or far Right are impatient with the leadership of the major parties. Both parties seem to such students to operate in the center—and in fact they do. (Some party analysts believe the major parties have become so weak and disorganized that they are not capable of following *any* strategy—Left, Right, or Center.)

The major parties are more complex today than they were in the last century. Like the government itself, they have national, state, and local organizations, and each level has executive, legislative, and other elements. Each party includes (1) a pyramid of national, state, and local organizations; (2) inner circles of leaders holding or seeking public office; (3) networks of leaders (sometimes called "bosses") who tend the organizational machinery continually; (4) party activists who give money, time, and enthusiasm to the party's candidates; and (5) voters who identify strongly with the party, almost always support its nominees, and desert it only as a result of such disasters as an unpopular war, a scandal like Watergate, or the soaring inflation and unemployment of the late 1970s.

Long after George Washington many Americans still feared parties: There was deep apprehension that a great popular majority—the kind led by a Jefferson or Jackson or Roosevelt—might be radical or extremist and thus threaten the liberties of free Americans. Before the Civil War the great South Carolina constitutional philosopher, John Calhoun, advanced the doctrine of "concurrent majority rule"— the idea that any large and significant region or interest should have the right to veto the actions of a numerical majority. Calhoun, of course, had a particular region and interest in mind—the South and its plantation slaveholders—but his reasoning has been used by countless minority leaders ever since.

These fears, however, were largely unrealized: In their own way, parties act as a check on governmental power. To win a party nomination, a candidate has to appear to be fairly moderate in order to appeal to a broad range of party interests. And to win the presidency itself, a candidate must appeal to an even broader and more varied range of interests across the country. Such a process tends to squeeze out the dogmatic or extremist group, although Ronald Reagan seemed to defy this trend, and candidate George Bush actively sought far-right support for his presidential bid. More typically, "extremist" candidates are seen as losers—witness Barry Goldwater in 1964, George McGovern in 1972, and Jesse Jackson in 1984.

Parties are a potential vehicle for large masses of people to use for gaining power in government. Farmers in the nineteenth century, workers during the past century, women and blacks during recent decades, Sunbelt conservatives during the 1980s—these and other movements and groups have tried to work through the major parties, with varying degrees of success. In all cases, however, they have had to work with other groups in the major parties, thus enhancing the role of the party as a balancing, mediating, stabilizing force.[7]

Third Parties: Persistence and Frustration

Although we have been focusing on major parties, we must not lose sight of all the exotic third parties in American history: abolitionists, populists, antiliquor, Bull Moose, Communist, the Citizens' Party of 1980, and John Anderson's Independent party. Third parties are described by some scholars as "a response to major party

[6] See John Chubb and Paul Peterson, eds., *The New Direction in American Politics* (Brookings, 1985).
[7] James MacGregor Burns, in Pomper, *Party Renewal in America*, pp. 194–96.

9–1 Third Parties in Presidential Elections

Year	Party	Presidential Candidate	Percentage of Vote	Electoral Vote
1832	Anti-Masonic	William Wirt	7.8	7
1856	American (Know Nothing)	Millard Fillmore	21.5	8
1860	Democratic (Secessionist)	J. C. Breckinridge	18.1	72
1860	Constitutional Union	John Bell	12.6	39
1892	People's (Populist)	James B. Weaver	8.6	22
1912	Progressive	Theodore Roosevelt	27.4	88
1924	Progressive	Robert M. La Follette	16.6	13
1948	States' Rights	Strom Thurmond	2.4	39
1968	American Independent	George C. Wallace	13.5	46
1980	National Unity Ticket	John B. Anderson	6.6	0

failure," but the crucial aspect about third parties is how often they charge into the national party arena and how they never win.[8] To be sure, they have had a significant indirect influence. They have drawn attention to controversial issues the major parties wished to duck. And they have organized special-interest or "cause" groups such as the antislavery and anti-civil rights movements. They boast, sometimes correctly, that they are champions not of lost causes, but of causes yet to be won. But they have never won the presidency or more than a handful of congressional seats, unless one calls the Republican party of 1860 a third party. They have never shaped national policy from inside the government. And their influence on policy in general, and on the platforms of the two major parties, has been limited.[9]

Third parties have taken two forms. One type has been the *doctrinal* party, such as the small labor and socialist parties on the left and even the smaller conservative movements on the Right. Most of these parties have lived on for decades publicizing their ideas but not expecting to win elections. The other type is the *issue* party that arises (or splinters from a major party) over a particular issue and then dies as the issue is resolved or fades away. Several such third parties, such as the Free Soilers, rose and fell before the Civil War. The Progressive parties of Theodore Roosevelt in 1912 and of Robert La Follette in 1924 challenged the political power of big business. Most recently, in 1968, George Wallace's American Independent party (AIP) won about 13 million votes over desegregation and other race issues. But the AIP was evidently fading even before Wallace was badly wounded in an assassination attempt in May 1972.

Why this pattern of failure? Why do we stick to a two-party system when most democracies have multiparty systems? The major reason is our electoral system.[10] Most of our election districts have a single incumbent, and the candidate with the most votes wins. Because only one candidate can win, the largest and second-largest parties have a near-monopoly. The system of electing the president operates in this way on a national scale. The presidency is the supreme prize in American politics: A party that cannot attain it, or show promise of attaining it, simply does not operate in the major league.[11]

Congressman John Anderson's 1980 candidacy, which aroused much enthusi-

Answer/Discussion

You can answer this yourself by looking at the brief party history in the preceding section. Would you perhaps choose to start counting in 1790, when Hamilton began to build a Federalist party team under President Washington? Or in 1793, when Jefferson quit Washington's Cabinet team to go eventually into opposition? Or in 1800, when Jefferson and his "campaign manager" James Madison led the opposition party into power? Or in 1828, when we began to rely on national conventions to nominate our national candidates? Or in some other year?

[8] Steven J. Rosenstone, Roy L. Behr, and Edward H. Lazarus, *Third Parties in America: Citizen Response to Major Party Failure* (Princeton University Press, 1984).

[9] On the impact of third parties, see Howard R. Penniman, "Presidential Third Parties and the Modern American Two-Party System," in William Crotty, ed., *The Party Symbol* (W. H. Freeman, 1980), pp. 101–17. See also Frank Smallwood, *The Other Candidates: Third Parties in Presidential Elections* (University Press of New England, 1983).

[10] William H. Riker, "The Two-Party System and Duverger's Law: An Essay on the History of Political Science," *American Political Science Review* (December 1982), pp. 753–66. For a classic analysis, see E. E. Schattschneider, *Party Government* (Rinehart, 1942).

[11] Timothy Conlon, Ann Martino, and Robert Dilger, "State Parties in the 1980s: Adaptation, Resurgence, and Continuing Restraints," *National Civic Review* (July–August 1985).

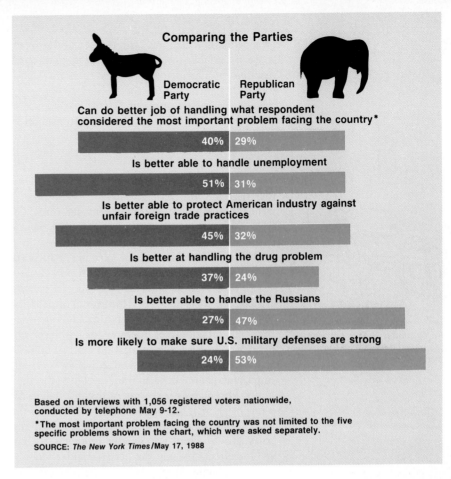

Comparing the Parties

Democratic Party

Republican Party

Can do better job of handling what respondent considered the most important problem facing the country*

40%	29%

Is better able to handle unemployment

51%	31%

Is better able to protect American industry against unfair foreign trade practices

45%	32%

Is better at handling the drug problem

37%	24%

Is better able to handle the Russians

27%	47%

Is more likely to make sure U.S. military defenses are strong

24%	53%

Based on interviews with 1,056 registered voters nationwide, conducted by telephone May 9-12.

*The most important problem facing the country was not limited to the five specific problems shown in the chart, which were asked separately.

SOURCE: *The New York Times*/May 17, 1988

asm on many college campuses, illustrates the handicaps third parties face. Anderson first tried to win the Republican presidential nomination and then decided to run as an independent. Significantly, both John Anderson and Barry Commoner, of the Citizens Party, returned to two-party politics in 1984; Anderson rejected the Republicans entirely by endorsing Democrat Walter Mondale and Commoner worked with the Reverend Jesse Jackson. In 1988 some blacks were tempted to break away from the Democratic party and form a party of their own, and some evangelicals talked about splitting away from the GOP, but in the end Jesse Jackson ran for president in the Democratic primaries and television evangelist Pat Robertson ran in the Republican contests. Once again the vast majority of American politicians operated within the two-party system, even though some of them complain that the two parties often fail to represent the interests and attitudes of large numbers of people.

PARTY TASKS: THE HEAVY BURDEN

Our major parties are expected to take on many heavy tasks. As indicated, one of the key functions of our two-party system has been to unify the electorate and bring together groups, sections, and ideologies. The parties failed to bring the sections together in 1860 and broke up under the pressure of the North-South rupture. For over a century since that great break, however, the parties have managed to please various power groups and continue in operation.

The functions of the parties have also changed over time. Party activity used to be an important source of public welfare. To win votes, local party organizations provided jobs, loans, free coal, picnics, and recreation for the needy; they also helped those in trouble over pensions, taxes, and licenses. The boss of the Republican machine in Philadelphia bragged that his organization was "one of the greatest welfare organizations in the United States . . . without red tape, without class, religion, or color distinction." The takeover of welfare by the government during the New Deal removed this function from most city organizations, but not entirely.

Party Functions Today

To gain votes, parties simplify the choices. Usually they present the voters with two relatively different alternatives. But some people argue that parties confuse rather than simplify alternatives to get votes. On a popular issue the parties may try to appeal to such a wide electorate that there seems to be no difference between them. Parties also help to stimulate interest in public affairs. An election contest is exciting: It makes politics look like a big prizefight, or the World Series, and draws millions of people into controversy.

After a polite interval following an election, the opposition party begins to criticize the party in power. However, it often fails to perform this role very effectively. It tends to break up into opposing factions that take potshots at the government from all directions, or to mute its criticism on the grounds that some issues— foreign policy, religion, education, and so on—should be above politics.

Parties may recruit political leaders. In the past, in fact, the parties were important channels of upward mobility for those "on the outside" of American public life (such as Irish Americans and Italian Americans). During the last century, a few black men rose to leadership positions in the Republican party; in this century some black men and women have attained high offices within the Democratic party. Today there is a greater tendency for political leaders to be recruited—or self-recruited—outside the party organization.

For some Americans local parties are not only a ladder but a home. Local clubs provide a place to meet, talk about community and political affairs, have a social drink, work together on voting lists, and enjoy a sense of belonging. It is in part because the bosses of the big cities maintained these local associations—along with their glee clubs and athletic teams—that "bossism" flourished for so long. Because the parties are also nationally organized, local associations help build personal and political bonds between local communities and the national government.[12]

Parties, especially at the local level, have served as a kind of employment agency through their control of **patronage**. Leaders have long used their influence over government officials to obtain jobs for friends and party workers. They defended this practice on the grounds that when a party wins an election, it should be able to put its own supporters into office in order to carry out the mandate of the election. Patronage has dwindled in importance in recent decades due to the rise of the civil service; moreover, government salaries have not maintained parity with those of the private sector. It is estimated that of 2.8 million federal jobs, only a few thousand are patronage positions. The patronage system was delivered a heavy blow in 1980, when the Supreme Court ruled that public employees cannot ordinarily be fired solely on the basis of party affiliation.[13] The question, said Justice Stevens, speaking for the Court, "is not whether the label 'policy maker' or 'confidential' fits a particular position; rather the question is whether the hiring authority can demonstrate that party affiliation is an appropriate requirement for the effective performance of the public office involved." Justice Powell, speaking in part for a minority of three, pointed out that many people consider that patronage helps

"I'm registered, but I'm not a voter."
(Copyright © 1988, USA TODAY. Reprinted by permission)

Functions of Major Parties*

Recruit candidates
Nominate candidates
Raise campaign funds
Register voters
Clarify issues
Unify diverse interests
Mobilize voters
Help run elections
Simplify voting choices
Provide some patronage
Write platforms
Oppose the incumbent party's policies
Help leaders to bridge the separation of powers
Help in the peaceful management of conflicts
Link popular wishes and government action

* Parties are expected to perform most of these functions. Some are performed well, some not so well, and some hardly at all.

---

[12] See Wilson Carey McWilliams, "Parties as Civic Associations," in Pomper, *Party Renewal in America*, pp. 51–68.

[13] *Branti* v. *Finkel* 445 U.S. 507 (1980).

Formal and Actual Party Organization

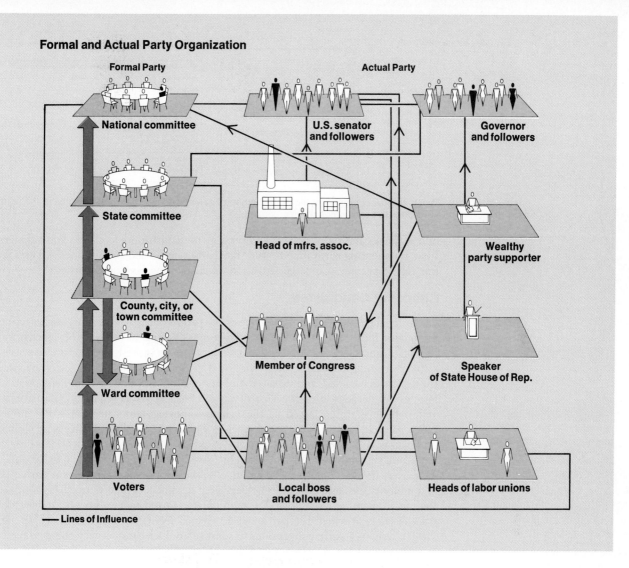

Formal Party

- National committee
- State committee
- County, city, or town committee
- Ward committee
- Voters

Actual Party

- U.S. senator and followers
- Governor and followers
- Head of mfrs. assoc.
- Wealthy party supporter
- Member of Congress
- Speaker of State House of Rep.
- Local boss and followers
- Heads of labor unions

—— Lines of Influence

build strong political parties and helps keep the government responsive to the voters—and that, in any case, the issue of patronage versus civil service is one for the legislature, not the judiciary, to decide.

Parties sometimes serve as key instruments for uniting persons of different races, religions, and classes. Parties have an interest in playing down social conflict. Even though more Americans are white Protestants, party leaders and candidates for public office seek to appeal to Hispanics, blacks, and Jews, if only because they represent a large number of votes. Of course, parties can be divisive as well: The Democrats sometimes play up issues, like civil rights or social welfare, in order to win support; and the GOP sometimes takes controversial positions, as it did in 1984, on the ERA, abortion, and military aid to Nicaraguan rebels. Just when parties should unite people and when they should divide them is a major tactical, strategic, and moral question for party leaders.

Parties can serve as the link between the wishes of the people and the action government finally takes. By choosing candidates in an open and democratic way, parties help legitimize our elected policy makers. They help organize the machinery of government and influence the men and women they have helped put into office. The president serves as party leader; Congress is organized on party lines; even bureaucrats are supposed to respond to new party leadership. Thus, parties partly

FOR PRESIDENTIAL ELECTORS

VOTE FOR ONE PAIR OF CANDIDATES

POR ELECTORES PRESIDENCIALES

VOTE POR UN PAR DE CANDIDATOS

GEORGE BUSH DAN QUAYLE	REPUBLICAN	4
MICHAEL S. DUKAKIS LLOYD BENTSEN	DEMOCRAT	7
EARL F. DODGE GEORGE D. ORMSBY	COLORADO PROHIBITION PARTY	10
LENORA B. FULANI JOYCE DATTNER	NEW ALLIANCE PARTY	13
RON PAUL ANDRE MARROU	COLORADO LIBERTARIAN PARTY	16

FOR UNITED STATES CONGRESS, DISTRICT 5 VOTE FOR ONE

POR CONGRESO DE LOS ESTADOS UNIDOS, DISTRITO 5 VOTE POR UNO

JOHN J. MITCHELL	DEMOCRAT	21
JOEL HEFLEY	REPUBLICAN	22

FOR STATE BOARD OF EDUCATION, AT LARGE VOTE FOR ONE

POR JUNTA DE EDUCACION DEL ESTADO, SIN LIMITACION VOTE POR UNO

FRANK J RICOTTA	DEMOCRAT	24
SYBIL DOWNING	REPUBLICAN	25
ELSI J. DODGE	COLO. PROHIBITION PARTY	26

FOR REGENT OF THE UNIVERSITY OF COLORADO, AT LARGE VOTE FOR ONE

POR REGENTE DE LA UNIVERSIDAD DE COLORADO, SIN LIMITACION VOTE POR UNO

KATHY ARNOLD	REPUBLICAN	28
MIKE DINO	DEMOCRAT	29
CALVIN G. DODGE	COLO. PROHIBITION PARTY	30

FOR REGENT OF THE UNIVERSITY OF COLORADO, DISTRICT 5 VOTE FOR ONE

Today, the direct primary is the main method of selecting candidates. Members have the right to vote for the candidates of their choice.

bridge the separation of powers and prevent the constitutional checks and balances from fragmenting government. But the parties have had only limited success in this role, especially compared with traditionally strong European parties.[14]

Choosing Candidates

Certainly, the function that takes most of the party's energy is recruiting and selecting candidates for office. From the very beginning, parties have been the mechanism by which candidates for public office are chosen. The earliest method, the **caucus**— a closed meeting of local leaders—was used in Massachusetts only a few years after the *Mayflower* landed, and it played an important part in pre-Revolutionary politics. For several decades after the Union was established, party groups in the national and state legislatures served as the caucus. The legislators in each party simply met separately to nominate candidates. Our first presidential candidates were chosen by senators and representatives meeting as party delegates.

But the legislative caucus brought "secret deals" and "smoke-filled rooms." Moreover, it could not be representative of the people in areas where a party was in a minority, because only officeholders were members. There were efforts to make the caucus more representative: For example, the mixed caucus brought in delegates from districts in which the party had no elected legislators. During the 1830s and 1840s a system of **party conventions** was instituted. Delegates, usually chosen directly by party members in towns and cities, chose the party standardbearers, debated and adopted a platform, and provided a chance to whip up party spirit and perhaps to celebrate a bit. But the convention method in turn came under criticism. It was charged that the convention was subject to control by the party bosses and their machines. Delegates were freely bought and sold, instructions from rank-and-file party members were ignored, and meetings got completely out of control.

To make party selections fairer and more democratic, and to cut down the power of party "bosses," the **direct primary** was used by Wisconsin on a statewide basis in 1903. It was adopted by state after state during the next fifteen years. This system gives every member of a party the right to vote on candidates in a primary election. The state supplies the ballots and supervises the election, which takes place sometime before the general election in November. The direct primary was promoted as a major cure for party corruption. But it did not cure all the evils; in fact, it actually led to some new ones. The rise of primaries has nevertheless been an important development in American politics; we return to this subject in the next chapter. Today the primary is the main method of picking party candidates, but in a few states the nominating convention is available in one form or another. The convention has also been retained nationally for picking presidential candidates.

(Democratic presidential hopefuls during 1988 primary debate. Wally McNamee/ Woodfin Camp)

[14] See, for example, David W. Brady and Charles S. Bullock, IV, "Party and Faction Within Legislatures," in G. Loewenberg, S. Patterson, and M. Jewell, eds., *Handbook of Legislative Research* (Harvard University Press, 1985), chap. 4.

Nor has the caucus disappeared from party life; it has been reborn in some states, but in a much more open, democratic, and participatory form. In these states party caucuses—open to all persons who profess themselves to be members of the party—choose delegates to higher party committees or conventions, which in turn select delegates to state and national conventions. The caucus system today is one of the most dynamic elements of party organization. In 1984 and 1988 the Iowa caucuses were the opening gun of the presidential nomination race. College students found they could enter these caucuses with no hassles such as absentee registration. Also, they had equal voice and vote with any of the local VIPs.[15]

HOW THE PARTIES ARE ORGANIZED

Republican candidates at 1988 primary debate. From left: Bush, Kemp, Robertson, Dole. (*AP/Wide World Photos*)

If you look at an organizational chart of the Democratic or Republican party, everything seems neat and tidy. At the top is the presidential convention, which meets every four years and sets policy for the party. Below it is the national committee, and then the pyramid widens out to state committees, hundreds of county and city committees, and thousands of ward, town, and precinct committees. But such a chart is deceptive. In fact, the national organizations have limited power over the state and local bodies; power typically flows up rather than down. Our parties have been essentially loose coalitions of state and local committees, with little national machinery, cohesion, or discipline. In this respect, too, the parties are a "second constitution."

Why have our parties been so decentralized? The main reason is the *federal* basis of our government. The Constitution has shaped our political system, just as the political system has shaped our government structure. Parties are a prime example of this circular relation. They tend to be structured around elections and officeholders. Because our federal system sets up elections and offices on a national-state-local basis, our parties are organized on a similar basis.

National Party Leadership

The supreme authority in both major parties is the *national presidential convention*. The convention meets every four years to nominate candidates for president and vice-president, to ratify the party platform, and to elect officers and adopt rules. But the convention in fact has limited power. The delegates have only three or four days in which to accomplish their business, and many key decisions have been made ahead of time. As stated above, the convention usually simply ratifies the presidential aspirant already chosen in the presidential primaries and caucuses during the preceding months.

Jesse Jackson, following his 1988 Democratic Convention speech in Atlanta. (*Jim Clark*)

More directly in charge of the national party—at least on paper—is the *national committee*. In the past the national committee gave large states only a little more representation than small ones. Committee members were usually influential in their states but had little national standing, and the committees rarely met. Recently the Republicans made their national committee more representative, and the Democrats, largely as a result of the reform spirit of 1968, enlarged their national committee to make it more responsive to areas that tended to be more populous and more Democratic. Such changes, however, have not necessarily brought stronger leadership.

The main job of the national party committee *chairperson* is to manage the presidential campaign. Although this top officer is elected by the national committee, he or she is actually chosen by the party's presidential candidate at the close of the convention. Once that candidate enters the White House, the power of the

[15] For an appraisal of key electoral criteria in another caucus state, Minnesota, in comparison with those in primary states, see Thomas R. Marshall, "Turnout and Representation: Caucuses Versus Primaries," *American Journal of Political Science* (February 1978), pp. 169–82.

chairperson dwindles. Even though he or she is often described as a liaison person for the White House, he or she usually serves at the pleasure of the president. A *defeated* presidential candidate, on the other hand, may have little control over the national chairperson; moreover, the national committee may elect a new head to respond to the balance of forces within the committee. The basic tasks of the national chairperson have been well summarized as image maker, fundraiser, campaign manager, administrator, and hell raiser.

A retiring national chairperson of the Republican party summed up the problems of running the party in competition with a Republican president:

> It is a tough, tough job to be National Chairman when you have the White House. . . . The unique thing that always will exist—Democrats or Republicans—is that every clerk and secretary in the White House thinks that they can do your job better than you can, and they don't even know what you do. . . . Last year, you know why they wanted my job. Very simple. I had 40-million bucks and we could spend it any way we wanted to spend it.[16]

The White House, of course, wanted to control that spending.

The national chairperson, backed by the president, gives the party a little measure of unity and direction when it is in power. When the party loses a presidential race, it often has no real central leadership. The defeated nominee is the **titular leader,** who usually has little power over the organization without jobs or other rewards to hand out. As a result, the party out of power has no one who can really compete with congressional leaders in calling the signals. Who should speak for the "loyal opposition"—the party's leaders in the House and Senate or the national chairperson? There is no agreement about this within either party. While Congressional leaders have rarely been willing to take a back seat, party leaders have tried at times to assert themselves as well. Former U.S. Senator William Brock was an aggressive and effective leader when he took charge of the Republican party during the late 1970s. He was an enormously successful fundraiser, and he harnessed direct-mail technologies and polling strategy to rebuild the national Republican party.[17] But other Republican leaders on Capitol Hill, such as Senator Howard Baker, also competed for the limelight.

The *congressional* and *senatorial campaign committees* help members of Congress in their reelection campaigns. Today both the Republican and Democratic senatorial campaign committees are composed of senators chosen for two-year terms by party members in the Senate. The House campaign committees are chosen in the same way. After candidates who appear to have a good chance of winning have been nominated, the committees send them money, provide speakers, and supply campaign material. The Republican committees in recent years have been able to offer their candidates four or five times as much financial and technical assistance as they had in the 1960s.[18]

Both a cause and a result of party disorganization is the manner in which candidates are nominated. Ordinarily politicians seeking nomination run on their own; the party remains "neutral." Lacking organized party support, each candidate builds a personal organization. And because several candidates are sometimes running to become the party's nominee, the party becomes a confused arena. Rivalries developing at this time may carry over into the general election, even though the party

1988 national political conventions.
(*Jim Clark; S. M. Wakefield*)

---

[16] Richard Richards, interviewed in *Party Line* (February 1983), quoted on p. 7.

[17] This story is well told by James Reichley, "The Rise of National Parties," in Chubb and Peterson, eds., *The New Direction in American Politics*, chap. 7.

[18] This is well documented in Thomas B. Edsall, *The New Politics of Inequality* (Norton, 1984), and in Gary C. Jacobson, "The Republican Advantage in Campaign Finance," in Chubb and Peterson, eds., *The New Direction in American Politics*, p. 6.

Levels of Party Involvement

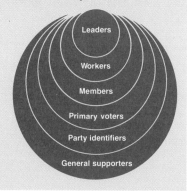

Leaders

Workers

Members

Primary voters

Party identifiers

General supporters

should be unified in order to put up a strong fight. Thus, although a heated primary contest may seem democratic, it can also be damaging to party unity.[19]

Parties at the Grass Roots

At the next lower level in the hierarchy are the *state committees*. These are similar to the national committees but are filled by members chosen locally. Most state committees are dominated by governors, senators, or coalitions of local elected, business, and ethnic leaders. State chairpersons are sometimes chosen by governors or senators; occasionally, however, they are the party bosses on the state level and are able to influence the nomination of governors, senators, and other key officials.

Below the state committees are *congressional district* and *county committees*. These vary tremendously in functions and power. A few county chairpersons are powerful bosses, as was the late Mayor Richard J. Daley.[20] Many county chairpersons decide the party slates for such offices as county commissioner, sheriff, and treasurer. Some, however, are just figureheads.

It is at the base of the party pyramid—at the city, town, ward, and precinct level—that we find the grass roots of the party in all their richness and variety. In a few places party politics is a round-the-clock, round-the-year occupation. The local ward and precinct leaders do countless favors for constituents, from fixing parking tickets to organizing clambakes, to obtaining racing passes in a state such as Arkansas. But such strong local organization is rare. Most local committees are poorly financed and inactive except during the few weeks before election day.[21]

Our party systems are complex. For example, a state party organization may include a state committee, congressional district committees, county committees, state senatorial district committees, state judicial district committees, and precinct committees. Contemporary politics tends to be individualistic and personalized; in fact, it would be more nearly correct to say that we have *candidate* or *officeholder* politics rather than party politics. Also, our constitutional arrangements provide for many officeholders at many levels of government. And the diversity of our country and the absence of strong national direction and control mean that party systems vary a good deal from state to state but in general are organizationally weak.

This complex situation opens a great gulf between national party headquarters and state and local parties. Deepening this gulf is the fact that elections—the main activity of parties—are actually regulated and run by the *states*, not by the national government. Some states hold their state and local elections in different years from national elections (mostly in an effort to insulate state politics from national). New York state, for example, elects its governors for four-year terms in even-numbered years between presidential elections, and New York City elects its mayors every four years in odd-numbered years. Most town and city elections are "nonpartisan" and often do not involve the parties as such.

PARTIES ON TRIAL

Clearly, there is a big gap between what American parties *might* do and what they *actually* do. Ideally, parties build a bridge between the people and their government. They strengthen national unity by bringing conflicting groups together. They

[19] Robert A. Bernstein, "Divisive Primaries Do Hurt," *American Political Science Review* (June 1977), pp. 540–45.

[20] For a fascinating account of Daley's chairmanship in Cook County, Illinois, see Milton Rakove, *Don't Make No Waves, Don't Back No Losers* (Indiana University Press, 1975).

[21] Local party effort is hard to measure, but it does have some influence. See Xandra Kayden and Eddie Mahe, Jr., *The Party Goes On* (Basic Books, 1985).

soften the impact of extremists at both ends of the political spectrum. They stimulate and channel public discussion. They find candidates for the voters and voters for the candidates. They help run elections. They both stimulate and moderate conflict. In short, parties should do much of the hard, day-to-day work of democracy. But, in fact, parties do not perform these tasks very well. In many cases candidates' personal campaign organizations do a better job of raising money and electioneering than do the party organizations.

There are two main charges against the American party system: (1) The parties do not take meaningful and contrasting positions on issues, especially the issues of the 1980s. (2) Organizationally, they are in such a mess that they could not achieve their goals even if they wanted to, so they are not vehicles for popular expression and social progress. How valid are these charges?

Tweedledum and Tweedledee?

The typical party platform, it is said, seems designed to pick up every stray vote rather than to speak out in a convincing manner on the vital questions of the day. Platforms are so vague, and candidates' statements so ambiguous, that voters have no basis on which to choose. This charge may once have been valid, but recent scholarship indicates that today it overstates the problem. By the 1960s, at least, many voters *knew* that their own party or the opposition party stood for something. Thus, most business and professional people consider that the Republican party best serves their interests. Workers tend to look on the Democrats as the party most helpful to them. It is likely that the proportion of voters discerning important differences increased sharply in recent years, when parties seemed to become more polarized. Of course, there may be some *mis*perception involved: People who are strong Democrats or strong Republicans tend to look at events through the eyes of their party. This tendency is called selective perception or perceptual distortion.

After studying recent party platforms to see how similar they were, one scholar concluded: "Democrats and Republicans are not 'Tweedledee' and 'Tweedledum.' "[22] In 1984 the differences between the two parties were sharper than usual. Parties share a consensus on many matters, but their policies and supporters are hardly identical, as a reading of the 1984 Democratic and Republican platforms makes clear.[23]

Weak Party Membership

Some critics believe the root of all this trouble lies in the absence of solid, rank-and-file memberships. They note that anyone 18 or over can "join" a party simply by registering as a party member, or (in some states) by voting in a primary and asking for the ballot of a particular party (which automatically registers a person in that party), or by voting in a caucus. Critics point out that such party "members" pay no dues, do not work for the party, and rarely take part in discussions or activities.

Some local party organizations do have active memberships. Involved workers may be in the party mainly for personal and material reasons: jobs, favors, or access to government officials. Others belong mainly for social reasons: The local committee or club gives them a chance to meet other people. Still others use the party to advance public policies or candidates they support. The former types are the professionals or regulars; they stick with their party through thick and thin, support all

A humorous slogan which appeared on college and university campuses in 1988, posed by a student who very much believes in the other, real, two party system. (*Joan Burns*)

ADVOCATE
OF TWO PARTY
SYSTEM.

(ONE ON
FRIDAY NIGHT,
ONE ON
SATURDAY NIGHT.)

Answer/Discussion

Is there a Democratic or Republican committee in your ward or town? Do you know any of the members? Who is the chairperson? Is either committee listed in the telephone directory? Does it have a headquarters? Does it meet regularly? Is it active at campaign time, or do the candidates themselves run the whole campaign effort?

[22] Gerald M. Pomper, *Elections in America*, rev. ed. (Longman, 1980). See also Alan D. Monroe, "American Party Platforms and Public Opinions," *American Journal of Political Science* (February 1983), pp. 27–42.

[23] Students can address this question for themselves by consulting Donald Bruce Johnson, ed., *National Party Platforms* (University of Illinois Press, 1978), vol. 1, 1840–1956; vol. 2, 1960–1976.

its candidates, keep the organization going between elections. The latter are the volunteers, who may be "issue purists" or "candidate loyalists." They consider party activity not as an end in itself but as a means to a greater good, such as changed governmental policies or new social programs.[24]

Tension and hostility sometimes develop between the two types of party members. The party veterans often come from middle-income backgrounds. The volunteers may be better educated and more ideological. Over a period of time, however, volunteers may gradually assume the political style and motive patterns of the professionals, with the result that the party becomes less concerned with ideology and programs. Some fear that the "defection" of the volunteers to the professional style may make the party less active as an agent of the public as a whole. But this view assumes that the well-educated, issue-oriented volunteer is more representative of the general population than is the professional.

All this reminds us that there are different kinds of party membership. The professional and the volunteer each offer certain strengths and weaknesses. The party base will have splits in it as long as the party appeals to a great range of people with very different motives. But different kinds of membership may also provide greater strength and durability.[25]

Parties versus Progress?

American parties, some charge, are not vehicles for social reform. The fact that both major parties must be such inclusive and moderate organizations means that neither one can act boldly for the great mass of lower-class, lower-income, and politically vulnerable people. Over the course of American history, some feel, this "party passiveness" has probably had a good effect: helping the parties to perform a peace-making or reconciling function. But in a period of exceptionally rapid and extensive change, it may enfeeble the political system.[26] Because rapid social change seems continuous these days, it can be argued that parties were useful only in the past and are now outdated and should be scrapped.

According to this view, weak parties simply end up strengthening the status quo. The rich and powerful have plenty of political weapons of their own, such as lobbyists, money, and influence over the media; the political party, meanwhile, could be the vehicle of collective popular action. Ideally, it could be the "people's lobby." If the party is insipid in doctrine, ineffective both when in power and when in opposition, and disorganized from top to bottom, it blights the people's hopes instead of realizing them. Others contend that parties are more effective than critics admit—that pluralistic, decentralized parties are appropriate for a pluralistic, individualistic society.

Democrats versus Republicans—But What's the Difference?

Perhaps because they have not experienced the great party battles that their parents and teachers have, students often ask, "How do these parties really differ?" The question is an important one. The answer, as in so many other aspects of the

"I'm not worried. The Democrats are always in disarray." (*Drawing by Lorenz;* © *1975 The New Yorker Magazine, Inc.*)

[24] For further distinctions between volunteers and professionals, see Jeane Kirkpatrick, *The New Presidential Elite* (Russell Sage Foundation—Twentieth Century Fund, 1976); and Robert T. Nakamura, "Beyond Purism and Professionalism: Styles of Convention Delegate Followership," *American Journal of Political Science* (May 1980), pp. 207–32.

[25] See Douglas I. Hodgkin, "Presidential Primaries, Caucuses, and the Recruitment of 1984 State Convention Delegates." Paper delivered at the New England Political Science Association Annual Meeting, Hartford, Connecticut, April 5, 1986.

[26] Everett Carll Ladd, Jr., *American Political Parties: Social Change and Political Response* (Norton, 1970), pp. 307–8. For the contention that mass-membership organizations impede rather than facilitate political action by the poor, see Frances Fox Piven and Richard A. Cloward, *Poor People's Movements* (Pantheon, 1977).

confusing American political system, is complex. Much depends on which aspect of the parties we are looking at—their policies and platforms, their leadership, their rank-and-file membership, or their national, state, or local organizations. And much depends on our own perceptions—on what we see from where we sit.

Certainly the party leaders and activists see a great gap between the two parties. "A fundamental choice awaits America," proclaimed the Democratic party platform of 1984—"a choice between two futures."

"It is a choice between solving our problems, and pretending they don't exist; between the spirit of community, and the corrosion of selfishness; between justice for all, and advantage for some; between social decency and Social Darwinism; between expanding opportunity and contracting horizons; between diplomacy and conflict; between arms control and an arms race; between leadership and alibis." The Republican platform proclaimed an equally big gap.

Democrats and Republicans also hold sharply contrasting images of one another. In the late 1980s Democrats consider "Reagan's party" to be a John Wayne/Rambo/ tough-guy party that talks a hard line against communists and terrorists in foreign affairs and against criminals, welfare cheats, and "draft dodgers" at home. Republicans consider the Democratic party to be the party of "the losers, the lame, and the lazy"—the party that will not meet the nation's responsibilities in the world arena, the party that is too soft toward the communists abroad and too tolerant of fringe groups at home: feminists, peaceniks, gays, and "troublemakers" in general.

Some in both parties scoff at the alleged "gap." For years conservative Republicans attacked top GOP leaders like Dwight Eisenhower and Nelson Rockefeller as being "me-too Republicans" cuddling up to Democratic party principles and policies. These critics have been far happier under Reagan's leadership. Today a host of Democrats attack their national party and congressional leadership as being too moderate—or at least as being too responsive to the conservative wing or enclaves in the party. Jim Hightower, the (elected) Texas agricultural commissioner, spoke for many of these critics when he assailed fellow Democrats who urged a "go along—get along" strategy and a "cautious middle path." Hightower quoted a farmer friend of his: "Hell, Hightower, there's nothing in the middle of the road but yellow stripes and dead armadillos."[27]

What then *is* the difference between the parties? Let us consider several criteria, beginning with the rank-and-file attitudes.

Rank-and-file Democrats and Republicans do differ sharply on a number of general principles, such as the proper role of government and liberalism versus conservatism. Most Democrats believe the federal government should help people in need of housing, medical care, and the like, while most Republicans believe that government should be involved with people's lives as little as possible. On some highly sensitive issues such as abortion voters do not divide sharply along party lines. On many routine, day-to-day issues party rank-and-file differences are only moderate, though even a moderate difference may have significant policy results in Washington. Here is how Democrats and Republicans lined up *in favor of* the following issues less than a year before the 1988 elections, according to a *New York Times*/CBS News Poll (Democratic support listed first): limiting imports of foreign goods, 72 percent and 68 percent; passing a balanced budget amendment to the Constitution, 73 percent and 80 percent; government working to uphold "traditional moral values," 54 percent and 58 percent; decreasing defense spending, 45 percent and 28 percent.

Nor can one discern sharp differences between the party memberships in their economic or social circumstances, with a few important exceptions. Republicans may seem to some the "party of the rich," but there are high-income Democrats

"I'm not speaking to you as a Republican or as an American. I'm speaking to you as your grandfather."
(*Drawing by Dana Fradon*; © 1987. The New Yorker Magazine, Inc.)

[27] Jim Hightower, "A Texan's Rx for What Ails the Democratic Party" (address to the National Press Club), *Boston Globe* (June 5, 1985).

as well. Of respondents earning over $50,000 a year 45 percent identified themselves as Republicans, 25 percent as Democrats. And even if the Democrats call themselves the "party of the poor," 18 percent of those earning less than $10,000 a year considered themselves Republicans. Of a total 1984 sample, white women divided between the Democratic and Republican parties, in that order, 37 percent to 27 percent; Protestants, 37 percent to 31 percent; businesspersons, 29 percent to 35 percent; farm people, 42 percent to 38 percent; high school graduates, 38 percent to 25 percent. Democrats did enjoy a decided advantage in certain categories: black females, 64 percent to 7 percent; black males, 63 percent to 3 percent; Catholics, 45 percent to 19 percent; Jews, 52 percent to 18 percent; less-than-high-school educated, 49 percent to 17 percent; skilled workers, 40 percent to 20 percent. But these Democrats do not necessarily *vote* Democratic; moreover, these percentages, collected by the National Opinion Research Center in 1983 and 1984, may quickly change.

If the two party memberships are not sharply divided in policy and in socioeconomic makeup, what about in their leadership? Here we find a sharper set of differences. This is due in part to the strong move of the Republican party leadership in the past decade or so toward the right and toward a more unified conservative leadership. It was not always thus in the GOP. For years centrist or moderately liberal leaders like Governors Thomas E. Dewey and Nelson Rockefeller were engaged in open warfare with Republican senators like Robert A. Taft and Barry Goldwater. In winning the presidency in 1980 Ronald Reagan drew into the GOP millions of religious fundamentalists; prolife, proprayer, and prodefense activists; and integration, busing, and racial-quotas opponents.

Broadly united around their neoconservative creed, Republican leaders have been able to take a clear stand in opposition to their ancient party adversary. What about the Democratic party leaders? Here the story is quite different. The Democratic party is a huge holding company for liberal senators like Edward Kennedy, Alan Cranston, and Howard Metzenbaum, conservatives like David Boren, moderates like Senators Albert Gore and Charles Robb, strong defense advocates like Senator Sam Nunn and Populists like Jesse Jackson, up-and-coming progressive governors such as James Blanchard of Michigan and Mario Cuomo of New York, as well as such enigmatic personalities as Senators Bill Bradley and Tim Wirth, and leaders of labor, women, blacks, gays, Hispanics, and other active groups. Democratic party leaders, moreover, are organized in rival groups within the party: the moderate Democratic Leadership Council, dominated by a mainly southern array of governors and senators; the conservative Coalition for a Democratic Majority; and such liberal or left organizations as Americans for Democratic Action, the United Automobile Workers, and the Democratic Socialists of America.

Riven by such disparate groups, it has been hard for Democrats to pull together and bring about the unity and coherence necessary to offer effective opposition to the GOP. The 1988 National Democratic Party Convention in Atlanta appeared to have been a turning point, as Democrats temporarily reconciled major differences.

Are the Parties Dying?

Some party experts fear that the parties are so weak that they are mortally ill—or at least in a long decline. They point first to the long-run impact of the progressive reforms early in this century—reforms that robbed party organizations of their control of the nomination process by allowing masses of independents and "uninformed" voters to enter the primaries and vote for candidates who might not be acceptable to party leaders. They also point to a long series of "reforms," such as nonpartisan elections in cities and towns and the staggering of national, state, and local elections, that made it harder for parties to influence the election process.

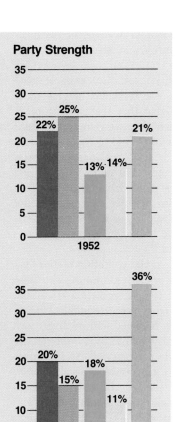

Party Strength

1952: Strong Democrats 22%, Weak Democrats 25%, Strong Republicans 13%, Weak Republicans 14%, Independents 21%

1984: Strong Democrats 20%, Weak Democrats 15%, Strong Republicans 18%, Weak Republicans 11%, Independents 36%

■ Strong Democrats
■ Weak Democrats
■ Strong Republicans
▫ Weak Republicans
▫ Independents

SOURCE: Xandra Kayden and Eddie Mahe, Jr., *The Party Goes On* (Basic Books, 1985), p. 160.

This was bad enough, say the party pessimists, but parties suffer from further ills today. The rise of television and VCR cassette campaigns, and the parallel rise in campaign, media, and direct-mail consultants, have denied parties their historic role of educating, mobilizing, and channeling the electorate. In addition, partly as a result of media influence, the most powerful electoral forces today are officeseeker or officeholder organizations, not party organizations. Officeseekers, supported by money and media, organize their personal followings to win nominations (while the party leaders are supposed to stand by neutrally); if they win office, they are far more responsive to their personal followings than to the party leadership. All this means that the party lacks clout over politicians and policy.

According to this view, the very foundations of parties are eroding away. There has been a virtual collapse of local party organizations during the past quarter century, they fear. Party membership is weaker and scarcer at the grass roots, as noted earlier. Voters identify less with their parties: They talk more about "voting the person rather than the party." Harry Truman now appears to have symbolized an earlier era: Truman "always voted for the best man," he said, "and that man is always the Democrat." Today television plays up the man or woman, the personality, the celebrity, the candidate who can buy media attention and advertising through colossal spending.[28]

The "party optimists" concede some of this diagnosis: the decay of local organization, the decline in strong partisan attitudes, the weakness of grass-roots party membership. But they see signs of party revival that they feel the pessimists ignore. The national parties are far better funded than they were in earlier days; they even have big modern headquarters in Washington, D.C. In fact, the two major parties are so strong nationally that for decades no third party has been able to mount a major threat; today there is no serious third party (that is, one capable of tipping a presidential election one way or the other) even on the horizon. Most important, the parties, because of their powerful fundraising capacities, are able more than ever before to help finance national campaigns and congressional candidates. This should give the national parties some leverage over the positions that officeseekers and officeholders take on party issues.[29]

How can these "party doctors" differ so widely on the condition of the "patient"? For two reasons, mainly: Party pessimists are usually examining the state of the Democratic party, which most observers agree is in a weakened condition, whereas party optimists are more likely to be focusing on the Republican party, which under President Reagan has come to be heavily financed and relatively well organized on the national level. Moreover, the contrasting interpretations rest on differing notions of what makes for a strong and enduring party. Party pessimists tend to have an "old-fashioned" view of the party as a pyramid of local, county, and state committees culminating in the national leadership; as a broad-membership, grass-roots organization at the bottom; as an organization, both democratic and disciplined, that can put forth a meaningful platform, nominate and elect politicians committed to that platform, and exercise considerable influence over the legislative and executive roles of its elected members in government.

Other party analysts consider parties essentially as organizations devoted to helping candidates get elected. Because most top leaders are elected through the efforts of their own personal organizations, raise their own money, earn their own attention from the media, and vote with or against their party as they wish in

[28] For the "pessimistic view" of the party condition, see Wattenberg, *The Decline of American Political Parties*, and Alan Ware, *The Breakdown of Democratic Party Organization 1940–1980* (Clarendon Press, 1985).

[29] For the "optimistic view" of the party condition, see Goldman, *Search for Consensus*, pp. 366–373; Kayden and Mahe, *The Party Goes On*; Joseph A. Schlesinger, "The New American Political Party," *American Political Science Review* (December 1985), pp. 1152–69; and David E. Price, *Bringing the Parties Back* (Congressional Quarterly Press, 1984).

Congress, some party optimists consider the modern party to be more a "pro-candidate" organization than a party organization. "Although it is still true that neither party completely controls its own destiny, and both have minimal influence on the nomination of their presidential candidates," according to at least two of the optimists, "they are beginning to emerge as the *single most effective participant in electoral politics* outside the campaign organization."[30]

Again, however, these experts seem to be talking more about the Republicans than the Democrats. It is the GOP today that commands the most money, the best campaign technology, and at least somewhat more party discipline (this was especially true during Reagan's first term).

SAVING THE PARTIES:
REFORM, RENEWAL, REALIGNMENT

From the start, the very idea of political parties upset some Americans. George Washington's indictment of parties in his farewell address was remarkably broad and bitter for this man of rather moderate opinion. The spirit of party, he said, "serves always to distract the Public Councils and enfeeble the Public administration. It agitates the Community with ill-founded jealousies and false alarms, kindles the animosities of one part against another, foments occasionally riot and insurrection. It opens the door to foreign influence and corruption . . . through the channels of party passions."[31] Most of the other political leaders of Washington's day strongly agreed.

These critics were really attacking big and powerful *factions*, because the party in the modern sense had not yet been born. But when sophisticated political parties developed during the Jacksonian era, they were equally controversial. Critics attacked them for granting the spoils of office to party henchmen, for exercising too much influence over the press (most of the newspapers of the day were violently partisan), and for turning lawmakers and other officials into robots hewing to the party line. But behind these criticisms was a deeper fear: that one party might become the instrument for the great mass of people to take over the government and convert it to their own purposes. This was the fear of majority rule—or majority tyranny. Whigs accused the Democratic party under Jackson and Van Buren of truckling to the ignorant and unwashed. The "second" or "people's" constitution of the 1830s, in short, was even more controversial than the Constitution of 1787.

Much of this distrust has persisted into the present era. A politician is suspect if he or she is excessively partisan. And public officials are constantly urged by editorial writers to rise above party. On the other hand, most Americans think of themselves as Democrats or Republicans. They contribute a fair amount of money to parties. They look for the "R" or the "D" on the ballot. So far, at least, they have not given much support to presidential candidates who try to run as independents, outside of the party system. They believe, at least vaguely, that you cannot run a big democracy without parties.

Americans, in short, have a love-hate attitude toward parties. The practical result of this has been curious. On the one hand, we want to maintain our parties—we even subsidize them a bit through our taxes. On the other hand, we keep trying to change and improve them. First we tried to reform our parties. Then we tried to reorganize or renew them. Currently some people are trying to realign them. Let us look at each of these efforts in turn.

[30] Kayden and Mahe, *The Party Goes On*, p. 11 (emphasis added).
[31] John C. Fitzpatrick, ed., *Writings of Washington*, vol. 35 (United States George Washington Bicentennial Commission, 1940), p. 227.

Party Reform

By 1900 party organizations had fastened their grip on countless American cities. These were not called organizations, however, but "machines" in the grip of party "bosses." Boss Tweed of New York City was long since dethroned and jailed, but his image lived on—the image of a crooked power wielder, in the midst of a vast web of influence, buying and selling legislators and councilors by the job lot, handing out spoils to party henchmen, bribing officials when he could not control them outright, making corrupt deals with business interests, living off kickbacks from contractors, and commanding a following of "toughs" and strong-arm men. The essence of the boss's power lay in his control of nominations. The party machine controlled nominations by packing conventions with its own people. By the dawn of the twentieth century, middle-class, white-collar people were becoming increasingly indignant. These reformers struck at the heart of bossism by taking the nominating process back to "the people" by means of the party primary. But many party experts hold the primary responsible for the downfall not only of the "bosses" but of parties as responsible and efficient organizations: The conventions were not just a means of picking candidates; they were also the grass-roots leadership corps of the party. In most cities and some states, the convention—and with it much of the leadership corps—simply disappeared.

The national party convention survived the onslaught, even though many reformers preferred a nationwide direct primary for choosing presidential candidates. The next great wave of reform came in the 1960s, with a dramatic effort to change the way in which conventions were managed, convention delegates chosen, and other party affairs conducted. This was particularly the case in the Democratic party, but the GOP, too, was influenced by the political reforms of the 1960s and 1970s.

The critical year was 1968—and what a year that was! Amid rising tumult over Vietnam, Senator Eugene McCarthy of Minnesota challenged President Johnson for renomination, and soon Senator Robert Kennedy of New York plunged into the fray. After suffering an image (though not an electoral) defeat in the New Hampshire Democratic primary, Johnson suddenly announced he would not run again. As the temper of the country became more and more ugly, Martin Luther King, Jr., was assassinated, as was Robert Kennedy, shortly after he won the California primary. The 1968 Democratic convention scene in Chicago dissolved into near-chaos, as outside the hall Yippies conducted love-ins, anti-Vietnam protestors demonstrated, thousands of outraged people ringed the Chicago hotels, and the police responded with clubbings and tear gas. Within the convention hall insurgents and regulars fought bitterly over the nomination, which had been made almost worthless as millions of television viewers watched the Democratic party bleed.

Hardly noticed in all the commotion was the appointment of a commission to study and improve the way in which convention delegates were chosen, for many years a bone of contention at Democratic conventions. Chaired by Senator George McGovern of South Dakota, the commission proposed a series of reforms.[32] A number of these guidelines, as they were called, were mainly procedural. State parties were to ensure that party meetings were held with proper advance notice, in public places, and at set times. Voting by proxy was to be forbidden. Under the O'Hara Commission, the **unit rule**, by which the vote of a whole delegation was cast as the majority voted, was prohibited. Although such reforms might seem rather elementary, they were in fact a response to frequent violations of fair play.

[32] These proposals are drawn mainly from the report of the McGovern Commission, *Mandate for Reform: A Report of the Commission on Party Structure and Delegate Selection to the Democratic National Committee* (Commission on Party Structure and Delegate Selection, Democratic National Committee, 1970).

Other guidelines were more substantive and involved efforts to broaden participation.[33] Just as proponents of party primaries at the turn of the century had charged that bosses restricted participation in conventions, the reformers of the 1960s held that countless Democrats were being excluded from party functions and decision making. Here the commission proposed three changes. One was not controversial: It ensured that party rules barred discrimination on the basis of race, color, creed, sex, or national origin. Another was a bit controversial: It allowed and encouraged all those 18 or older to take part in party affairs (the Twenty-sixth Amendment had not yet been ratified). A third was *very* controversial: It proposed that specific steps must be taken to provide representation in party affairs (and especially in nomination decisions) of young people, women, and minorities "in reasonable relation to their presence in the state's population"—that is, it proposed enforced proportional representation. But despite heated debate over so-called quotas, the most lasting effect of the McGovern-Fraser Commission has been that party primaries now dominate the process by which delegates are elected. Recently, commissions such as that led by former North Carolina Governor James Hunt have undone many of the McGovern-Fraser "reforms," in an attempt to bring party professionals back into the nominating process with the creation of "superdelegates" and other devices. Nevertheless, most people sent to party conventions are candidate and issue enthusiasts, not party activists.

The commission's proposals were hotly opposed by some Democrats. Although they favored broadening the party, "centrists" feared that too much effort would be made to bring in young people and women, but not enough to recruit working-class people, labor unionists, the elderly, and others. The emphasis on a participatory rank-and-file party, they declared, was really undemocratic: Those who would attend open grass-roots caucuses were the more educated and affluent—people who had the time, the stamina, and the interest to debate all night. Working and poor people lacked the leisure, energy, or self-confidence to express their interests at meetings or even to attend them. Critics especially opposed the quota system—"democracy by demography"—as arbitrary and basically unrepresentative. So heavy was the opposition to the quota system that it has been substantially eliminated.[34] However, it was clear that most of the essential reforms were here to stay. Party rules require nondiscrimination on the basis of "sex, race, age, religion, economic status, sexual orientation, ethnic identity, national origin, or color."[35]

In 1986, the Democratic party's Fairness Commission resisted any major changes in party rules. It did, however, lower the threshold—from 20 to 15 percent—that a presidential candidate needs to qualify for a proportional share of national convention delegates. Iowa will continue to hold the first caucus, and New Hampshire the first primary, although South Dakota and Michigan challenged that status. Wisconsin and Montana were also exempted from a previous rule limiting participation in a Democratic presidential primary or caucus only to those voters who expressly declare themselves to be Democrats. Also in 1986, Democrats agreed to a Southern "regional primary," a "Super Tuesday," on which fourteen Southern and border states, twenty states in all, conducted 1988 presidential primaries.

How to Tell 'em Apart: Another View

Republicans usually wear hats. Democrats usually don't.

Democrats buy banned books. Republicans form censorship committees and read them.

Republicans employ exterminators. Democrats step on the bugs.

Democrats eat the fish they catch. Republicans hang them on the wall.

Republicans sleep in twin beds—some even in separate rooms. That is why there are more Democrats.

Source: Adapted from National Republican Congressional Committee, *Newsletter*, October 7, 1974.

---

[33] William J. Crotty, *Political Reform and the American Experiment* (Crowell, 1977), pp. 241–47, offers a full listing of the resolutions of the Democratic Charter conference. See also Crotty's *Party Reform* (Longman, 1983); and Ranney, *Curing the Mischiefs of Faction*. For a general discussion of party reform and its consequences, see Byron E. Shafer, *Quiet Revolution* (Russell Sage Foundation, 1983); and Nelson W. Polsby, *Consequences of Party Reform* (Oxford University Press, 1983).

[34] Coalition for a Democratic Majority, Task Force on Democratic Party Rules and Structure, "Toward Fairness and Unity for '76," mimeographed (1974).

[35] *Delegate Selection Rules for the 1984 Democratic National Convention* (Democratic National Committee, 1982), p. 6. For a history of majority and minority women at the Democratic national conventions, see *Democratic Women Are Wonderful: A History of Women at Democratic National Conventions* (National Women's Political Caucus, 1980).

The Republicans have been more relaxed over the issue of party reform than the Democrats. For one thing, the pressure of minority elements in the GOP for recognition has not been as intense as within the Democratic party; for another, Republicans are reluctant to give the national party too much authority over state and local parties. Still, Republican party rules prohibit discriminatory practices, and state committees are urged—though not required—to take positive action and to encourage broad participation in the delegate-selection process by young people, women, minority and ethnic groups, and senior persons.[36]

Party Renewal

Some politicians and scholars, both Republican and Democrat, are far more concerned about party *renewal* than party reform. In their view—or at least in the view of the "party pessimists"—the party system needs to be saved and strengthened, not reformed. They may accept some of the proposed changes—especially those that fortify the party as an organization—but they would nurse both the elephant and the donkey back to health and vitality before they would teach either animal how to improve its ways.

So, while some Democrats at the 1968 and 1972 conventions were stressing the need for more participation, proper procedures, and fairer representation, other Democrats were focusing on the need to turn the party into a better-structured, more active, more effective, and more policy-oriented organization. This feeling came to a head at the 1972 convention in a successful movement to call a charter conference—a meeting that might revamp the Democratic party (just as a state constitutional convention might reorganize a state governmental system). Two years later more than 2000 delegates assembled in Kansas City for long sessions of debate on a proposed charter. Once again battles erupted between reformers and renewers, but most of the delegates were convinced that revitalization was crucial. In drawing up the first written "constitution" in American major-party history, the charter convention took the following steps:

1. It recognized the national convention as the supreme governing body of the party and required state parties to adapt their rules and practices to national party standards.
2. It enlarged the Democratic National Committee to make it stronger and more representative.
3. It strengthened the national and financial agencies in the party.
4. It authorized midterm national party conferences for the discussion of national public policy, at a point halfway through the presidential term.

The most important—and most fleeting—of these changes was the creation of the **midterm party conference.** Following Jimmy Carter's election some doubted that the conference would even be called for 1978, because the White House might fear that the delegates would "get out of hand" and criticize the administration for not living up to its 1976 campaign promises. But the conference was held, and Senator Edward Kennedy and other delegates did criticize the administration. Further, the conference voted to divide nominating convention delegate spots equally between men and women, and to remove all vestiges of "winner take all" from presidential primaries, thereby settling two fights that have raged in the party for more than a decade.[37]

U.S. Senator Bill Bradley (D-NJ), a highly respected member of the Senate Finance Committee, helped to shape the 1986 tax reform. (*Art Stein*, *Photo Researchers*, *Inc.*)

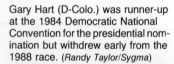

Gary Hart (D-Colo.) was runner-up at the 1984 Democratic National Convention for the presidential nomination but withdrew early from the 1988 race. (*Randy Taylor/Sygma*)

[36] Delegates and Organizations (DO) Committee, *The Delegate Selection Procedures for the Republican Party*, Part II of the DO Committee Progress Report (Republican National Committee, 1971). For a history of majority and minority women at the Republican national conventions, see *Republican Women Are Wonderful: A History of Women at Republican National Conventions* (National Women's Political Caucus, 1980).

[37] Ken Bode, "Miniconvention," *The New Republic* (December 23 and 30, 1978), p. 14.

Governor Mario Cuomo (D-NY) speaking at the 1984 Democratic nomination convention. He chose not to run for the Democratic presidential nomination in 1988. (*Chris Brown/Stock Boston*)

U.S. Representative Richard Gephardt (D-Missouri) is a broker in the House and is a spokesman for moderate Democrats. He was an early leader in the 1988 Democratic presidential race. (*Courtesy Congressman Richard Gephardt*)

But in 1982 the midterm conference faced a greater challenge: Without a president to mediate disputes, the Democratic party turned to its chairperson to guide the conference. Plans were formulated for the upcoming 1982 Congressional elections and the strategic and financial groundwork was laid for the 1984 Presidential contest.[38]

Then in 1985, after only two such conferences, the Democratic National Committee moved quickly and quietly to eliminate the midterm convention. Out of fear that the conference would spawn divisiveness and destroy the unity necessary to regain the Senate in 1986 and the Presidency in 1988 (and to save $1 million), newly elected Chairperson Paul G. Kirk canceled what many Democrats conceived as an effective tool for shaping a vision and a strategy for Democratic success.

Republicans, concerned about the health of their own party, were not idle during this period. The GOP, however, faced somewhat different problems. The national party had long been better organized and funded than the Democratic one, and it had a larger, more professional staff in Washington. At the same time Republicans believed in a decentralized system and had no strong wish to nationalize the party. As a result, they have followed a middle road in efforts at reform and renewal. Committees have proposed giving the national committee more control over presidential campaigns in an effort to avoid Watergate-type excesses. Also, state parties have been urged to encourage broader participation by all groups, including women, minorities, youth, and the poor. As a result of its strenuous efforts at self-renewal, the Republican party entered the 1980s with a party organization far superior to that of Democrats. With Bill Brock as chairperson, the GOP emphasized grass-roots organization and membership recruitment. Seminars were held to teach Republican candidates how to make speeches and hold press conferences, and weekend conferences were organized for training young professionals. Candidates were taught how to "draw up a campaign plan, write and buy advertising, raise money, set up phone banks, recruit volunteers, and schedule [their] time.[39]

A number of other forces may be strengthening the leadership of both parties. In this day of complex campaign laws, finance legislation, and election technology, it is likely that state and local parties, and candidates at every level, will increasingly turn to the national party for technical advice or assistance. Although the GOP may remain just a federation of state parties, national headquarters will gain more visibility and perhaps influence from its expanded services. In the Democratic party as well, the influence of federal campaign finance laws, expanded campaign advisory services, and bigger and more professional staffs may well favor centralization. One analyst predicts that both national parties "will become national bureaucracies with hierarchies, divisions of labor," and specialized experts.[40]

Must reform or renewal be alternatives, or even conflict with each other? Some party experts believe that parties can be open, representative, participatory, and fair in their procedures, *and* at the same time well organized, competently led, politically effective, and highly competitive. The key to such a fusion, they feel, may lie at the base of the party, in the local caucus. Properly conducted, caucuses are open to all local-area persons. All present have the same vote, and the same right to speak. Decisions are made by majority vote, but minorities may still have the right to some representation—for example, in the selection of delegates to higher party meetings. Caucuses can actively recruit and involve new members

[38] Democrats Meet to Pump Life into Tired Ideas," *Congressional Quarterly Weekly Report* (June 19, 1982), pp. 1467–69; and "Democrats Develop Tactics; Laying Groundwork for 1984," *Congressional Quarterly Weekly Report* (July 3, 1982), pp. 1591–95.

[39] Morton Kondracke, "The G.O.P. Gets Its Act Together," *The New York Times Magazine* (July 13, 1980), p. 44.

[40] Xandra Kayden, "The Nationalizing of the Party System," in Michael J. Malbin, ed., *Parties, Interest Groups, and Campaign Finance Laws* (American Enterprise Institute for Public Policy Research, 1980), pp. 257–82, quoted on p. 276.

of the party; they can help finance party activities through the collection of dues; they can train people in party issues and administration; they can be an active party presence in the community; and they can identify talented persons and supply leadership to the higher echelons. In short, caucuses can be the building blocks of both participation and organization. Other state parties may adopt the caucus-based model of Iowa and Minnesota. In 1979 Massachusetts Democrats, for example, adopted a party charter that requires local ward and town committees to convene open caucuses whenever candidates or public issues are voted on.

The Politics of Realignment

What did Reagan accomplish? In his two terms as president he transformed the Republican party from the more moderate and reactive GOP to a distinctively activist party of the right wing. Reagan accomplished in the 1980s what Barry Goldwater was unable to do in the 1960s: He narrowed his party's program without condemning the GOP to the status of a perpetual minority. And what of the Democrats? While Reagan was polarizing (and expanding) his party, the Democrats were struggling to maintain the "Grand Coalition" of labor, the unemployed, minorities, the middle class, small business, intellectuals, big cities, and the South, which for five decades had defined the party and brought it consistent victory. But, with such a strong leader as Reagan, the Republicans were more successful in their task than the Democrats were in preserving the coalition and ideology pioneered fifty years earlier by President Franklin Roosevelt.

Ronald Reagan, most of his supporters, and many of his Democratic opponents were united in the belief that neither reform nor renewal adequately addresses the problem of party decline. They turned to the third R of **party** discourse—**realignment.** A party is more than an ideology; it is also a confederation of factions, a coalition drawn to a leader or to a party philosophy. So too is realignment more than political centrism or polarization; it is also the reshuffling of coalitions within parties. Coalitions may reconstitute themselves—or be reconstituted by a party leader—because of new issues dominating their attention, or because of new positions taken by a party or party leaders on those issues, or because the electorate itself has changed its politics. Add to this formulation election victories and losses for parties and candidates, and you have all the tools you need for examining one of the most fascinating and perplexing aspects of electoral politics, realignment.

In the 1930s, the United States faced a devastating economic collapse. After a century of sporadic government action, the New Dealers stepped in and fundamentally altered the relationship between government and society. In an unprecedented response to the unprecedented crises of massive depression, political deadlock, social disorder, urban blight, and other twentieth-century ailments, Franklin Roosevelt assumed both power and responsibility over the welfare of the citizenry, and in so doing led the way toward transforming his party into the resourceful—and victorious—majority party it would be for the next generation. The realigned configuration of coalition and ideology acted as a safety valve, and it rewarded the party that responded positively to crisis with electoral success. For two decades the Republican opposition could do nothing but watch—and oppose.

Under the popular General Dwight Eisenhower the Republicans temporarily regained the White House, but it was the legacy of Roosevelt and Truman that shaped the political landscape.[41] When in 1964 Senator Barry Goldwater of Arizona challenged the assumptions of the New and Fair Deals, he was resoundingly defeated. Even under the presidency of Richard M. Nixon, the Republicans could rarely

---

Party Preferences, 1988

Several polling companies regularly ask people their party preferences. As of 1988, Democrats enjoyed a small edge over Republicans in these loyalties. But Republicans have gained in recent years, and many in the South who say they are Democrats sometimes vote Republican in national elections.

When asked with which party they identified, this was the nationwide response:

Democrats	35%
Republicans	30
Independents	30
Don't Know/ No Ans.	5%

In addition, Republicans typically are more likely to register to vote and are also somewhat more likely to vote than are those identified as Democrats.

---

[41] William E. Leuchtenberg, *In the Shadow of FDR: From Truman to Reagan* (Cornell University Press, 1982).

9–2 Party Identification among Floridians Registered to Vote in the 1980s

	1980	1983	1986
Republicans	21%	27%	38%
Independents	29	27	26
Democrats	50	45	38

Source: Suzanne L. Parker, "Shifting Party Identification In Florida." Paper presented at Florida Political Science Association Annual Meeting, Sarasota, Florida, April 11, 1986.

break out of the mold of moderate opposition, or of minority party, not only in Congress but in voter identification and registration as well. That would wait for the leadership of Ronald Reagan, who through his electoral challenge in 1976, and victories in 1980 and 1984, successfully transformed the ideology of the Republican party. At times it appeared in the 1980s that Reagan had placed the Republican Party on the road to majority status. But this was not to be.

And where are the Democrats? Although the values and objectives of the New Deal are as challenging as ever, its original coalition is nearly impossible to preserve. With each success of the Democratic–Great Society agenda, many argue, Roosevelt's "Grand Coalition" was fractured; and with every stopgap measure to preserve the aged coalition, the progressive politics of the next generation stagnated in the name of compromise. North and South, once united over FDR's attempts to heal a nation, began to drift apart as the liberalism the 1930s had hastened to extend to poverty and unemployment was applied to federal civil rights measures in the 1950s and 1960s. Today, the ties between the politics of the national, northern Democratic party and southern Democratic supporters are tenuous, but both sides are hesitant to make a clean break. Further, the Democrats suffer from their past victories: A generation that matured in union households, amidst immigrant workers, and through the distresses of the Great Depression now join other beneficiaries of the New Deal who seek to preserve their economic gains—through the Republican party! Social Security, Medicaid, GI Bills, and student loans helped to expand the middle and upper classes, but they also diminished the natural constituency that gave the Democrats their victories and allowed them to govern.

Those pundits and party professionals who would renew the Democratic party through a polarizing realignment find inspiration in a strange place—in the actions of their Republican opponents. The "realigners" would guide the Democrats as swiftly and confidently toward a progressive posture as the GOP has been led to a conservative one. Rather than fearing the future, the proponents of polarization assert that Democrats should embrace it and reject "centrist schizophrenia." Then, perhaps, they may inspire those who are now alienated, apathetic, disempowered, and disenfranchised to aid in rejuvenating the Democratic party. Be courageous, as Reagan and the Republicans have been, they proclaim, and you too shall be victorious.

But realignment is more than a change in party ideology, or an exchange of voters or voting blocs. Reagan claimed that the 1980s were a period of Republican realignment, and that long-term GOP domination is just over the horizon. Democrats retort that this is just a swing of the political pendulum, a temporary aberration failing to influence the composition or ideology of the electorate. For answers, and for evidence of a contemporary realignment, we must examine election results and the party preference of the populace.

Voters today describe themselves as more conservative than they did twenty years ago. Although they liked Reagan's tax cuts and his strengthened defense policy, and the favorable economic indicators during his administration, only 4 percent of the electorate in 1984 reported that they voted for Ronald Reagan because he

9–3 The 1988 Election: Characteristics of Party Supporters, January 1988

	DEM	REP	OTHER	UN-SURE		DEM	REP	OTHER	UN-SURE
Total	46%	48	1	5	**Education**				
Region					Less than high school	54%	37	1	8
East	47%	46	1	6	High school graduate	46%	48	1	5
Midwest	51%	43	—	6	Some college	44%	52	—	4
South	44%	52	1	3	College graduate	35%	60	1	4
West	44%	50	—	6	Post-graduate	46%	49	—	5
Age					**Sex**				
18–24	42%	54	—	4	Men	43%	52	1	4
25–29	44%	49	2	5	Women	50%	44	1	5
30–39	50%	46	—	4					
40–49	40%	50	3	7					
50–64	48%	48	1	3					
65 and over	49%	42	—	9					

Source: *World Opinion Update* 12, no 2 (February 1988), p. 19; data from Harris Poll (national adult sample of 1,101 voters).

was conservative. In that election, a clear electoral and popular landslide, the Republican party nevertheless lost two seats in the Senate and gained a scant eighteen in the House.[42] During the New Deal, the Democrats wrested control of the House of Representatives away from the Republicans; the Republicans have not come close to capturing the House while in control of the presidency.[43] Yet when questioned in exit polls during the 1984 presidential election, more than twice as many voters described themselves as conservative than as liberal.[44] This conservatism translated into a victory for Ronald Reagan in 1984, but not for most Republican challengers.

Why has realignment moved so slowly? Why aren't good conservatives now happily ensconced in the Republican party, and all stout liberals gladly lodged in the Democratic? In part because Americans do not blithely cross party lines. If you have grown up in a conservative New Hampshire family whose forebears have voted Republican for a century, you are pretty much conditioned to stay with the GOP. Even if that party took a direction you disliked, you might continue to be registered as a Republican but quietly vote Democratic to avoid friction in the family. Or if you come from a "Yellow Dog" Democratic family in Texas (meaning a family that would vote for anyone as long as he or she ran as a Democrat), you might continue to vote Democratic locally even though you disliked various Democratic candidates for president.

The other reason for slow realignment is the *federal* nature of the party. For decades conservative Democrats in the South have been voting for Republican candidates for president, such as Reagan and Bush, without "crossing the aisle" from the Democratic party to the Republican. Why? Partly because of family attitudes, as noted above. But also because such voters may wish to stay in their party so that they can vote in primaries for candidates for state and local office, or perhaps for candidates for Congress.

All in all, prospects for realignment are mixed. Although the rise of the media has undermined party strength (see Chapter 11), the public is not hostile to parties:

[41] William E. Leuchtenburg, *In the Shadow of FDR: From Harry Truman to Ronald Reagan* (Cornell University Press, 1983).

[42] Nelson Polsby, "Did the 1984 Election Signal Major Party Realignment?" *Key Reporter* (1985).

[43] David W. Brady and Patricia A. Hurley, "The Prospects for Contemporary Partisan Realignment," *PS* (Winter 1985), p. 64.

[44] *The New York Times–CBS News Election Day Exit Poll* (November 7, 1984), pp. A1, A20.

It is neutral, and increasingly apolitical.[45] This phenomenon of neutrality may be **dealignment**: On both sides of the political fence, partisanship is declining, although the Democrats are suffering slightly more than are the Republicans.

[45] Arthur H. Miller and Martin R. Wattenberg, "Measuring Party Identification: Independent or No Partisan Preference?" *American Journal of Political Science* (February 1983), p. 106, and Everett Carll Ladd, Jr., "On Mandates, Realignments, and the 1984 Presidential Election," *Political Science Quarterly* (Spring 1985), p. 1.

SUMMARY

1. Over the past generation, American political parties have declined both in organizational strength and in the estimation of many Americans. The current Republican National Committee is an exception to this generalization.

2. The major parties maintained their ascendancy in the past by bringing factions and interests together in coalitions broad enough to win the presidency and congressional elections.

3. Today some people believe that the parties are moderate and middle-aged, and that they rest on weak foundations. Others contend that we are in the midst of a party renaissance, with another "golden age" for parties lying just over the horizon.

4. Throughout our history third parties—whether doctrinal or forming around current issues or personalities—have been notably unsuccessful.

5. Parties have many functions, which they often perform inadequately: recruiting and nominating candidates, raising money, clarifying issues, mobilizing voters, providing patronage, uniting diverse interests, and serving as a link between government and the grass roots.

6. The two major parties have been criticized as being too much alike, yet this criticism is overstated. They are also said to be poorly organized and financed, a criticism that has been true, but much more so for the Democrats.

7. Whether the major parties—or any parties—can survive depends on their capacity for effective reform, renewal, and realignment.

FURTHER READING

ROBERT H. BLANK. *Political Parties: An Introduction* (Prentice-Hall, 1980).

JOHN E. CHUBB and PAUL E. PETERSON, eds. *The New Direction in American Politics* (Brookings Institution, 1985).

THOMAS B. EDSALL. *The New Politics of Inequality* (Norton, 1984).

SAMUEL J. ELDERSVELD. *Political Parties in American Society* (Basic Books, 1982).

LEON EPSTEIN, *Political Parties in the American Mold* (University of Wisconsin Press, 1986).

XANDRA KAYDEN and EDDIE MAHE, JR. *The Party Goes On* (Basic Books, 1985).

WILLIAM J. KEEFE, *Parties, Politics, and Public Policy in America*, 5th ed. (Congressional Quarterly Press, 1988).

DAVID MAYHEW. *Placing the Parties in American Politics* (Princeton University Press, 1986).

NELSON W. POLSBY. *Consequences of Party Reform* (Oxford University Press, 1983).

GERALD M. POMPER, ed. *Party Renewal in America* (Praeger, 1980).

DAVID E. PRICE. *Bringing Back the Parties* (Congressional Quarterly Press, 1984).

STEVEN J. ROSENSTONE, ROY L. BEHR and EDWARD H. LAZARUS. *Third Parties in America* (Princeton University Press, 1984).

LARRY J. SABATO. *The Party's Just Begun: Shaping Political Parties for America's Future* (Scott, Foresman, 1988).

FRANK SMALLWOOD. *The Other Candidates: Third Parties in Presidential Elections* (University Press of New England, 1983).

JAMES SUNDQUIST. *Dynamics of the Party System*, rev. ed. (Brookings Institution, 1983).

10

Beliefs and Ballots: Public Opinion and Voting

The most dynamic aspect of politics involves the political opinions people hold and how they convert these opinions into votes on election day. When does this process start? The answer is now clear: in childhood. For centuries some philosophers held that childhood was a time of innocence, even of ignorance, about the great world of politics outside the home. But now we know that—at least for Americans— politics starts *in* the home, that children are not cut off from the world outside, and that we begin to form opinions at an early stage.

The noted child psychologist Robert Coles spoke with youngsters in American homes and elsewhere. "Children are not empty vessels into which the content of culture is poured," Coles concluded. "They are as much makers as receivers."[1]

In this chapter, we examine the process of opinion formation in greater detail.

HOW WE LEARN OUR POLITICAL BELIEFS

No one is *born* with political views. We *learn* them, and we have many teachers. American children typically show political interest by the age of 10, or even earlier, and by the early teens their interest may be fairly high. The process by which we develop our political attitudes and values is called **political socialization.** Learning experiences gradually shape the values and beliefs we acquire in childhood. As children and teenagers we begin not only to influence other persons' attitudes but to be influenced by them as well.

Political beliefs often stem from religious, racial, gender, ethnic, and economic attitudes. The sources of these and other views are, of course, immensely varied in the pluralistic political culture of America. But we can make one generalization quite safely: We form our attitudes in groups—not only in the major groups described in Chapter 7, but even more in close-knit groups. When we identify closely with

[1] Robert Coles, *The Moral Life of Children* (Atlantic Monthly Press, 1986); and Robert Coles, *The Political Life of Children* (Atlantic Monthly Press, 1986).

the attitudes and interests of a particular group, we tend to see politics through the "eyes" of that group.[2]

Does this mean that an active member of a strong group, such as a family, is a captive or even a "slave" to that group? Not necessarily. Each member of a group—even a child, as noted earlier—influences the group and is influenced by it. More important, group members usually bring their own emotions, feelings, memories, and resistances to their groups. The extent to which persons are captive to groups is indeed a running argument among scholars from different disciplines. Sociologists tend to emphasize the pervasive influence of groups over their members. Certain schools of psychology focus more on the developmental influences within individuals that preserve their independence and individualism. Political scientists traditionally have tended to agree with the sociological approach.[3] Political psychologists seek to combine both approaches.

The Influence of the Family

Consider your own political socialization. You probably formed your picture of the world listening to your parents at breakfast or absorbing the tales your older brothers and sisters brought home from school. Perhaps you heard about the family past from grandparents, aunts, and uncles. Increasingly you influenced the family in turn, if only by bringing some of your own school hopes and problems back home. What we first learn in the family are not so much specific political opinions but rather basic attitudes that will shape our opinions—attitudes toward our neighbors, other classes or types of people, and society in general. Some of us may rebel against the ways of the close little group in which we live, but most of us conform. The family is a link between the past and the present. It translates the world to us, but it does so on its own terms. And the terms are many and varied: Families may be extended or nuclear, two headed, female single headed, male single headed, or communal.

Studies of high school students indicate a high correlation between parents and children in the political parties they support. And this relatively high degree of correspondence continues throughout life. Such a finding raises some interesting questions: Does the *direct* influence of parents create the correspondence? Or are parents and children equally influenced by living in the same social environment? The answer is *both*—and one influence often strengthens the other. A daughter of Democratic parents growing up in a small southern town of strong Democratic leanings will be affected by friends, by other parents, and perhaps by youngsters in a Sunday school group, all of whom may reinforce the attitudes of her parents.[4]

Who has greater influence—the mother or the father—over children's political opinions? It used to be assumed that the father had the dominant impact, perhaps because it was assumed that "politics is a man's business." But the balance of influence between the two parents seems to be surprisingly level; it may even be tipped in the mother's favor. What happens when mother and father disagree politically? Children are likely to favor the party of the parent with whom they have had closer ties.

"Before I tell you who I'm for, perhaps you'd be interested to hear a little something about how my political thinking has evolved over the years." (*Drawing by Stevenson*; © *1980 The New Yorker Magazine, Inc.*)

---

[2] Pamela Johnston Conover, "The Influence of Group Identifications on Political Perception and Evaluation," *Journal of Politics* (August 1984), pp. 760–85; and Henry E. Brady and Paul M. Sniderman, "Attitude Attribution: A Group Basis for Political Reasoning," *American Political Science Review* (December 1985), pp. 1061–78.

[3] Shawn W. Rosenberg, "Sociology, Psychology, and the Study of Political Behavior: The Case of the Research on Political Socialization," *Journal of Politics* (May 1985), pp. 715–31.

[4] See Russell J. Dalton, "Reassessing Parental Socialization: Indicator Unreliability Versus Generational Transfer," *American Political Science Review* (June 1980), pp. 421–31.

Still, older children sometimes do not share the views of their parents. Parental influence over their offsprings' party choices has been declining. What other forces are at work?

Political Impact of the Schools

Schools also mold young citizens' values and attitudes. At an early age schoolchildren begin to pick up specific political values and acquire basic attitudes toward our system of government. Even very small schoolchildren know the name of the president and the president's party affiliation, and they have strong feelings about the chief executive. Children as young as 9 or 10 begin to have fairly precise knowledge of what a president stands for, though this will vary with the personality of the president. For example, one researcher found that "the Kennedy image was rich, specific, and considerably more politicized than we had anticipated. He was particularly well remembered for his efforts on behalf of peace and civil rights."[5]

Do school influences give young people greater faith in political institutions? Yes and no. A classic study examined relationships between community leaders' attitudes, civics texts, and students' attitudes in three Boston communities—one upper middle class, one lower middle class, and one working class. The school texts in all communities stressed the right of citizens to try to influence government, but the texts used in the upper-middle-class community were the only ones to stress politics as a *conflict* process for settling differing group demands. And only the upper-class community leaders underscored politics as a conflict process, and thus reinforced the lessons in the texts. Edgar Litt concluded that the lower-class students were being brought up to view government as a process carried out by institutions in the students' behalf, while the upper-class students were learning to understand the political process in realistic terms and to take part in that process on their own behalf.[6]

Another study found no evidence that the civics curriculum has a significant effect on the political orientations of the great majority of American high school students. Of course, students differed in their interest in politics, but this resulted not from taking (or not taking) civics or government courses, but from the students' backgrounds and life plans.

How does *college* influence political opinions? One study suggested that students planning to attend college are more likely to be knowledgeable about politics, more in favor of free speech, and more likely to talk and read about politics. Perhaps reflecting national trends, campus moderation, conservatism, and Republicanism have increased in recent years.[7] Is this the influence of the professors, the curriculum, or the students? It is difficult to generalize. Parents sometimes fear that professors have too much influence on their offspring in school; professors are likely to be skeptical about this.

But why talk in generalities when students reading this book can make their own judgments? What has influenced *you* the most—a teacher, a book (possibly even a *textbook?*), movies such as "Rambo" or "Wargames," a particular course, a political campaign, discussions with other students, "60 Minutes"? And *how* have you been influenced?

Voter registration. (*Bruce Roberts/ Rapho-Photo Researchers*)

A voter registration drive in Ohio. One of the most important functions of a political party is to register voters affiliated with their party. (*AP/ Wide World Photos*)

[5] Roberta S. Sigel, "Image of a President: Some Insights into the Political Views of School Children," *American Political Science Review* (March 1968), pp. 216–26.

[6] Elizabeth Léonie Simpson, *Democracy's Stepchildren* (Jossey-Bass, 1971); M. Kent Jennings and Richard G. Niemi, *The Political Character of Adolescence* (Princeton University Press, 1974); Stanley Allen Renshon, "Personality and Family Dynamics in the Political Socialization Process," *American Journal of Political Science* (February 1975), pp. 63–80; and Frances FitzGerald, *America Revised* (Atlantic-Little, Brown, 1979).

[7] Alexander W. Astin et al., *The American Freshman: National Norms for Fall 1984* (UCLA Graduate School of Education, 1984), pp. 3–4.

10–1 Evangelicals versus Nonevangelicals on Key Social Issues		
Issue	Evangelicals	Nonevangelicals
Favor ban on all abortions	43%	31%
Oppose ERA	44	30
Oppose homosexual teachers in the schools	84	67
Favor prayer in schools	84	56

Source: Survey by the Gallup Organization, August 1980, in *Public Opinion* (April–May 1981), p. 25. Reprinted by permission of Elsevier Science Publishing Co., Inc. Copyright © 1981 by The Trustees of Columbia University.

"He's trustworthy, loyal, obedient, cheerful, and all that, but he leans to the left." (*Drawing by Dedini,* © *1988. The New Yorker Magazine, Inc.*)

Other Influences

Family and school are not the only sources of influence on children and adolescents. Religious and ethnic attitudes may also be important, both within and outside the family. On the whole, Protestant families tend to be more conservative than Catholics on economic and welfare issues, whereas Jewish families tend to be more liberal on both economic and noneconomic issues than either Catholics or Protestants. But Protestants are quite variable on certain social issues, and all persons are subject to "cross pressures." Evangelicals, who include a small percentage of Catholics but who are mainly made up of Protestants and many of the more fundamentalist sects, tend to be more socially conservative than nonevangelicals (see Table 10–1). Children in ethnic families learn of the heritage and customs of other countries; they may also learn of historical or current struggles so vividly that their attitudes toward current American foreign policy are affected.

What happens when a young person's parents and friends disagree? One study revealed that when high school students were "cross-pressured" in this way, they tended to go along with parents rather than friends on party affiliations; with friends rather than parents on the issue of the vote for 18 year olds; and somewhere in between on their actual votes in presidential elections.[8]

Adults are not simply the sum of all these early experiences. Analysts are becoming more and more interested in the ways in which adults keep modifying their views *after* completing school or college. A major factor may be a harsh experience, such as a war or depression, that shocks people out of their existing attitudes. Most people, however, keep on growing as they move into new social situations and become exposed to new newspapers, television programs, and political leaders. Democrats or Republicans, for example, may shift their party affiliations in their adult years simply because the "party of their family and forebears" no longer responds to their attitudes and interests.[9]

THE FABRIC OF PUBLIC OPINION

Perhaps even now, years later, you can recall a Sunday evening in November 1983. You might well have been watching one of the most dramatically heralded and widely watched programs in television history: "The Day After," a dramatization of the horror and desolation caused by a nuclear war between the United States and the Soviet Union. Many viewers would long remember the increasingly devastating scenes: a university student paying little attention to a radio report about trouble abroad; the rapid escalation of hostility and crisis; the trails left by American nuclear

[8] Suzanne Koprince Sebert, M. Kent Jennings, and Richard G. Niemi, "The Political Texture of Peer Groups," in Jennings and Niemi, *The Political Character of Adolescence*, p. 246.

[9] Charles H. Franklin, "Issue Preferences, Socialization, and the Evolution of Party Identification," *American Journal of Political Science* (August 1984), pp. 459–78.

rockets over the peaceful Kansas terrain; the mushrooming clouds after the Soviet attack; the overburdened hospitals; people dying from radiation sickness amid the rubble of their homes.

The program raised much controversy and high expectations. Supporters of President Reagan's defense program charged that it was designed to undermine confidence in the administration. Some labeled it "blatant political propaganda" that would stimulate pacifist efforts. Some nuclear-freeze advocates, on the other hand, expected the program to make many more people worry about their prospects of surviving a nuclear war, stimulate grass-roots participation in antiwar movements, make voters more dubious about Reagan's ability to stay out of a nuclear war, and perhaps even cause people to feel more "politically efficacious" in preventing war. At the very least, these observers expected the program to trigger a vast flood of antiwar mail to the White House and Capitol Hill.

What happened? None of these fears or hopes was realized. Confidence in President Reagan actually increased, in a kind of "rally-around-the-flag" phenomenon. The program did not increase expectations of a nuclear war or people's ability to survive it; did not stimulate grass-roots peace activity; did not make people feel more politically efficacious; did not produce a torrent of mail to Washington. A team of George Washington University researchers concluded that, after years of discussion and controversy, Americans' political opinions about nuclear issues and policy were so intense and stable that no television program, no matter how graphic, could markedly change those opinions.[10]

(*From private collection of Bruce Adams/Photo by Eugene Gordon*)

Beneath the Surface

This episode reminds us that to understand public opinion we must look beneath the surface features—beneath the little waves and eddies—and study the more basic tides and currents that continuously shape people's attitudes and opinions. Because journalists and pollsters so often look only at the surface manifestations, their analyses and predictions often go awry. They speak, for example, of "public opinion," when in fact there are many publics, with differing sets of opinions.

(*From private collection of Bruce Adams/Photo by Eugene Gordon*)

Suppose a group of students at your school invites a notorious criminal to speak on crime and punishment. Think of the public opinion this incident creates. The "public" is actually made up of a number of publics—the rest of the student body (itself divided into subpublics), the administration, the faculty, the local towns-people, parents, and taxpayers. And all react in different ways. Some don't react at all; others shake their heads and promptly forget about it; others write to the governor or their state legislator. Many approve the invitation, but for conflicting reasons.

Translate the student episode into a national issue. A president's speech about labor legislation falls differently on the ears of union leaders and members, business-people, farmers, Democrats, and Republicans. When a senator calls for the end of government "handouts," many businesspeople applaud because they want lower taxes, but businesspeople *receiving* subsidies are critical. They may cry out that "the American public" wants a strong (that is, subsidized) merchant marine. Instead of one public opinion, we must think in terms of the diversity of opinion within a particular population. We must ask: What portion of the people is on one side of an issue, what portion on the other? Who feels strongly, who does not? What, in short, makes up the fabric of public opinion?

(*From private collection of Bruce Adams/Photo by Eugene Gordon*

[10] William C. Adams et al., "Before and After 'The Day After': A Nationwide Survey of a Movie's Political Impact." Paper presented at the Annual Meeting of the International Communication Association, San Francisco, May 27, 1984.

10–2　Gallup Poll Public Opinion Referendum

What if we had a national referendum at the same time we elected the American president? This is what might have resulted in 1984 when Ronald Reagan won by a landslide.

Survey participants were handed a card listing ten key voter issues and asked this question: "This card lists various proposals being discussed in this country today. Would you tell me whether you generally favor or generally oppose each of these proposals?"

Ten Issues	PERCENTAGE		
	Favor	Oppose	No Opinion
Tax increases to reduce federal deficit	34%	62%	4%
Prayer in public schools	69	28	3
Reduce defense spending	50	46	4
Tuition tax credits for children attending private or parochial schools	50	45	5
A ban on all abortions except in cases of rape, incest, or when the mother's life is in danger	50	45	5
Passage of Equal Rights Amendment to the Constitution	63	31	6
Increased spending for social programs such as education and Medicare	74	24	2
An agreement between the U.S. and Soviet Union for an immediate, verifiable freeze on the testing and production of nuclear weapons	78	18	4
Relaxing pollution controls to reduce cost to industry	33	64	3
Maintaining cost-of-living increases on Social Security benefits	88	10	2

Source: Gallup Poll, November 18, 1984. Based on in-person interviews with 1590 adults, 18 and older. Note that some people might well tell a pollster one thing yet vote differently if they had the right to vote and their votes were binding in an issues referendum election.

(From private collection of Bruce Adams/Photo by Eugene Gordon)

(From private collection of Bruce Adams/Photo by Eugene Gordon)

(From private collection of Bruce Adams/Photo by Eugene Gordon)

Stability and Fluidity

Some of our opinions change very little; they are part of our personalities, and we hang onto them all our lives. Other opinions may change slowly, even though the world is changing rapidly. This is especially true of loyalty toward our own groups and hostility toward competing groups. In general, people who remain in the same place, in the same occupation, and in the same income group throughout their lives tend to have more stable opinions. But people can carry their attitudes with them. Families who move from cities to suburbs often retain their big-city attitudes long after they have made their moves.

Still other kinds of public opinion can change dramatically, and almost overnight. Opposition to Roosevelt's foreign policies in 1941, for example, practically disappeared following Japan's attack on Pearl Harbor. Change often comes about as a result of *events*—a depression, the nomination by a major party of a southerner for the first time in over 100 years, a sharp increase in the crime rate, a natural event like a long drought in the Southeast, the taking of hostages by Iran, or a tragic disaster, such as the explosion of the space shuttle *Challenger.*

Sometimes even the strongest and most stable opinions are subject to change. One of the "sacred cows" of American politics twenty-five years ago was nonrecognition of the People's Republic of China. A powerful lobby, composed of leaders of both major parties, carried on a militant campaign against admitting "mainland

China" to the United Nations. Then President Nixon, who had earlier been against the recognition of Peking, made his dramatic trip to the People's Republic. Soon he was following a policy of detente toward Peking. Many Americans, responding to Nixon's leadership, shifted their own position toward friendlier relations with China.

Other Aspects of Public Opinion

Intensity   This factor produces the brightest and deepest hues in the fabric of public opinion. People vary greatly in the fervor of their beliefs. For example, some are mildly in favor of gun-control legislation while others are mildly opposed; still others are fanatically for or against. Some people may have no interest in the matter at all, still others may not even have heard of the issue.

Latency   Political opinions may exist merely as a *potential*—they may not have crystallized. But they can still be important, for they can be evoked by leaders and converted into action. Latent opinions set rough boundaries for leaders, who know that if they take certain actions, they will trigger the opposition or support of millions of persons. But latent opinions are also a great opportunity for leaders. If they have some understanding of people's real wants, needs, and hopes, they will know how to activate those motives, mobilize people in groups or parties, and draw them to the polls on election day.

Salience   What causes opinions to be stable or fluid, intense or latent? A major factor is salience. Some people are deeply involved in certain issues and care little or nothing about others. By salience we mean the extent to which people feel issues relate to their own lives and *connect* with them. Your next-door neighbor may feel intensely about abortion or gun control, whereas you may get excited

PEANUTS

AND THAT'S THE WAY I SEE IT! ABSOLUTELY, FOR SURE!

ACTUALLY, YOU HAVE YOUR FACTS MIXED UP, CHARLIE BROWN...

I DO? I GUESS MAYBE YOU'RE RIGHT

I HAVE VERY STRONG OPINIONS, BUT THEY DON'T LAST LONG!

(© 1984 United Feature Syndicate, Inc.)

10–3   Public Remains Closely Divided on 1973 Court Abortion Ruling

The U.S. Supreme Court has ruled that a woman may go to a doctor to end pregnancy at any time during the first three months of pregnancy. Do you favor or oppose this ruling?

	Favor	Oppose	No Opinion
National	45%	45%	10%
Men	45	43	12
Women	45	46	9
18–29 years	49	41	10
30–49 years	49	44	7
50 & older	38	48	14
College grads.	59	35	6
College inc.	47	43	10
High school grads.	43	47	10
High school inc.	42	46	12
Grade school	27	57	16
Catholics	40	48	12
Protestants: total	42	50	8
Southern Baptists	31	60	9
Methodists	53	40	7
Republicans	42	49	9
Democrats	48	44	8
Independents	45	42	13

Source: Gallup Poll, February 20, 1986. Based on in-person interviews of 1570 adults, 18 years of age and older.

about drug abuse or unemployment. Most people are more concerned about personal issues like health and jobs and families than about national issues. But connect their personal concerns with national issues, and salience rises sharply.

Salience may change over time. During the depression of the 1930s, Americans were mainly concerned about jobs, wages, and economic security. In the late 1930s and early 1940s, foreign issues came to the fore. In the 1960s, problems of race, poverty, and drugs aroused intense feeling. These were followed by Vietnam and then Watergate. Recently jobs and prices as well as nuclear arms seem to top the agenda, along with continuing crises in Central America.

Consensus and polarization   Considering the electorate as a whole, we may find some opinions on which most people agree or most people disagree. When at least 75 percent of a sample agree on an issue—for example, that schools should be racially integrated—a consensus exists on that issue. But on most issues, people are more evenly divided—and in various proportions. When a large portion of each side feels very intensely about the issue, the voters are polarized on that issue. Vietnam a few years ago, and abortion today, are examples of polarizing issues.

What is the impact of these forces of public opinion on how Americans behave at the polling booths? How, in other words, are attitudes translated into votes?

(From private collection of Bruce Adams/Photo by Eugene Gordon)

WHO VOTES? AND WHO DOES NOT?

The most striking aspect of voting in America is the huge number of citizens who vote on election day; an equally striking fact is the huge number of Americans who do *not* vote. A presidential election in particular seems to be a glorious rally of the citizenry. From a few minutes after midnight—when voters in some mountain hamlet will trudge to a polling place in the darkness in order to be the first to vote—to very late in the evening—when polls on the West Coast close long after Eastern television pundits may already have "called the election"—over 90 million Americans flock to the polls in this mighty demonstration of democracy in action.

But on the other side of the coin, almost 90 million adult Americans do *not* flock to the polls—even for a presidential election that has been the focus of television and other media for months. And they flock even less to statewide, congressional, county, and local elections. Lumping all elections together at all levels, we have to face the fact that in the aggregate, more eligible Americans do not vote in election contests than do.

Why do we begin our study of voting by looking at *non*voters rather than voters?

- ☐ Because the extent of nonvoting is so large that it mightily affects the nature and impact of those who do vote.
- ☐ Because the social makeup and attitudes of the nonvoters are significantly different from those of voters, and hence greatly distort the representative system.
- ☐ Because Americans, who like to consider their country as something of a democratic model, have one of the poorest voter-turnout records of all the industrial democracies.[11] A few years ago, when 100 nations were ranked on turnout, America was twelfth from the *bottom*.

Political Participation/ Awareness in America in the Late 1980s

Vote in presidential elections	53%
Vote in congressional elections	35–40
Know name of congressional representative	36
Know names of both U.S. senators	29
Occasionally contact local officials	28
Vote in local elections	10–30
Occasionally attend public meetings	19
Occasionally contact federal or state officials	16
Know name of state senator	13
Give money to candidate or party	13
Know name of state representative	12

Source: Selected polls, including Gallup, *Denver Post* Poll, University of Michigan.

[11] G. Bingham Powell, Jr., "American Voter Turnout in Comparative Perspective," *American Political Science Review* (March 1986), pp. 17–43.

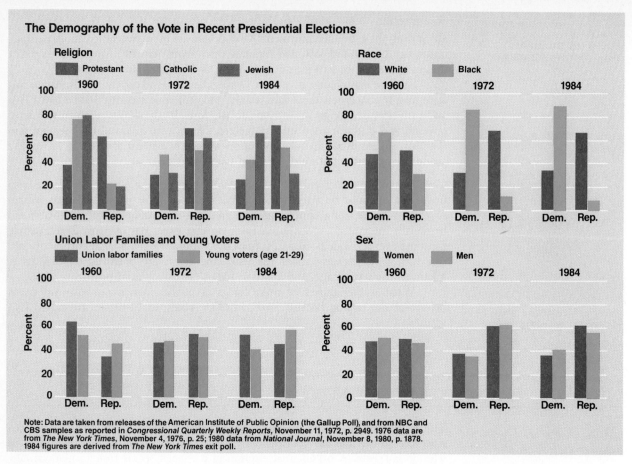

The Demography of the Vote in Recent Presidential Elections

Note: Data are taken from releases of the American Institute of Public Opinion (the Gallup Poll), and from NBC and CBS samples as reported in *Congressional Quarterly Weekly Reports*, November 11, 1972, p. 2949. 1976 data are from *The New York Times*, November 4, 1976, p. 25; 1980 data from *National Journal*, November 8, 1980, p. 1878. 1984 figures are derived from *The New York Times* exit poll.

□ Because voter turnout in the United States has been *falling* over the past quarter century—from almost 63 percent in 1960 to about 56 percent in 1972 to about 53 percent in 1980 and 1984 to barely 50 percent in 1988.

Who fails to vote? Why? Is low voter turnout a serious problem in a democracy? If so, what could be done about it?

Why Is Turnout So Low?

The simplest explanation of low voter turnout is sheer apathy. It is easy to criticize people as "just too lazy to vote." If people do not want to vote, a columnist wrote, "to hell with them—serves them right." The problem is not that simple. Of course some people just do not care: They would not go to the polls if King Kong were running against Snow White. But the vast majority of Americans are not like that. Paradoxically, we compare favorably with other nations in political interest and awareness.[12] But we fail to convert these qualities into votes, mainly for *institutional* and *political* reasons. Let us consider both.

The main institutional block is voter-registration requirements, along with absentee ballot complications. People may forget to register in time, especially if the cutoff date is early. They may have failed to register—or reregister—because they were bedridden or away on long trips. Registration itself can be slow and burdensome. And—as many a student has found—getting and casting an absentee ballot can also be a hassle.

What effect do registration laws have on actual turnout? If registration could be eliminated as a block to voting, it is estimated that turnout would rise by at

[12] Ibid., pp. 18–22.

Why People Don't Vote

Did not register	38%
Do not like the candidates	14
Are not interested in politics	10
Have no particular reason	10
Are sick or disabled	7
Are not U.S. citizens	4
Are new residents in area	4
Are away from home	3
Cannot leave job	2
Have no way to get to polls	2
Other reasons	6

Source: *U.S. News & World Report* Charts. Basic data from U.S. Department of Commerce, the Gallup Poll, 1980.

least 10 percent.[13] Such a boost, however, would still leave America with low voter turnout. Other explanations besides registration must be relevant as well.

Two key explanations are political and even psychological factors. In other large industrialized democracies the political parties shoulder much of the burden of persuading people to vote. American parties are too weak to take on this task; with well-known incumbents, in particular, the Democratic party, which has an enormous stake in a heavy voter turnout from lower-income Americans, talks big about its registration plans but very rarely does the job. Another key factor is the absence of real competition in many election contests. Americans like a good close fight in politics, just as they do in sports, but in the one-party districts election outcomes are known far in advance. Finally, there is a strong *psychological* factor: Some Americans believe it makes no difference who wins. They perceive that there is no real choice between candidates or parties; that winning candidates and parties fail to carry out their promises; and that the same people run the government no matter who wins. Many of these persons are not apathetic toward politics; on the contrary, they contend that American politics and government are apathetic toward *them*.[14]

Who Fails to Vote?

Nonvoting might not be a serious problem if those who *do* vote were a cross-section of those who do not. But this is not the case. The extent of voting varies widely among different types of *voters* and *elections* (see figure "Group Characteristics of Voters," next page). Race and ethnicity help produce different levels of voting. Note the dropoff from whites to blacks to Hispanics, whatever the other characteristics being examined. Also note that lack of citizenship still accounts for some of the low Hispanic turnout.

Education seems by far the most important influence on voting, regardless of race and ethnicity: "Education increases one's capacity for understanding complex and intangible subjects such as politics," according to one study, "as well as encouraging the ethic of civic responsibility. Moreover, schools provide experience with a variety of bureaucratic problems, such as coping with requirements, filling out forms, and meeting deadlines."[15] The data are convincing: Those who finish elementary school are more likely to vote than those who do not; those who graduate from high school tend to turn out more than those who finish elementary school; and those who graduate from college turn out more than those who graduate from high school. Only black men and women with less than eighth-grade educations seem to contradict this finding. Also, the effects of college education are not so clear-cut for Hispanics.

Income and age are also important factors. Those with higher family incomes are more likely to vote than those with lower incomes. Income, of course, corresponds to type of occupation, and those with higher-status careers are more likely to vote than those with lower-status jobs. The older you are (unless you are *very* old and perhaps infirm), the more likely you are to vote. Persons 18 to 24 years of age have a poor voting record; so do persons over 70. Women's increased turnout generally is attributed to higher levels of education and employment; black women in

Xavier L. Suarez, first Cuban-born mayor of Miami, Florida. The Cuban-American community in south Florida is a major influence in Florida politics. This community has voted solidly for Republican candidates in recent presidential elections. (*Courtesy of Mayor's office, Miami.*)

[13] Frances Fox Piven and Richard A. Cloward, "Prospects for Voter Registration Reform: A Report on the Experiences of the Human *Serve* Campaign," *PS* (published quarterly by the American Political Science Association) (Summer 1985), pp. 582–92.

[14] See Paul R. Abramson and John H. Aldrich, "The Decline of Electoral Participation in America," *American Political Science Review* (September 1982), pp. 502–21; and Norman R. Luttbeg, "Attitudinal Components of Turnout Decline: Where Have Some States' Voters Gone?" *Social Science Quarterly* (June 1985), pp. 435–43.

[15] Raymond E. Wolfinger and Steven J. Rosenstone, *Who Votes?* (Yale University Press, 1980), p. 102. See also Sandra Baxter and Marjorie Lansing, *Women and Politics: The Invisible Majority* (University of Michigan Press, 1980), pp. 35–37.

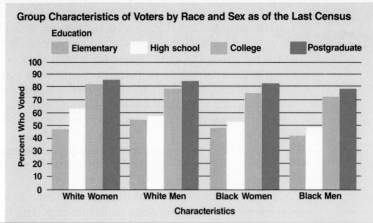

Group Characteristics of Voters by Race and Sex as of the Last Census

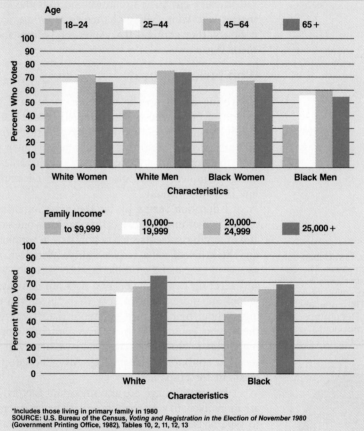

*Includes those living in primary family in 1980
SOURCE: U.S. Bureau of the Census, *Voting and Registration in the Election of November 1980*
(Government Printing Office, 1982), Tables 10, 2, 11, 12, 13

particular are influenced by their party identification and by feminism.[16] Also, voting varies geographically from state to state.

But the most important fact remains: The poor, the uneducated, and the members of racial minorities are still seriously underrepresented in the voting booth. More specifically, according to the conclusions of a study based on a wide sample, the "least educated, the very poor, Puerto Ricans, Chicanos, and people who moved in the year before the 1974 election are all underrepresented by between one-third

[16] See Baxter and Lansing, *Women and Politics*. See also Claire Knoche Fulenwider, *Feminism in American Politics: A Study of Ideological Influence* (Praeger, 1980). On age as a key correlation with high turnout, see Lee Sigelman, Philip W. Roeder, Malcolm E. Jewell, and Michael A. Baer, "Voting and Nonvoting: A Multi-Election Perspective," *American Journal of Political Science* (November 1985), pp. 749–65.

and one-half. In addition, people without a high school diploma or below the median income, those who live in the South, the young, the elderly, the unemployed, the unmarried, and blacks show voting strength reduced by at least 15 percent. On the other hand, college graduates are overrepresented by nearly one-third, as are people who earn more than $25,000."[17] The study added that the strength at the polls of government employees was 24 percent *greater* than their share of the population.

Why do low-income people vote in fewer numbers than the wealthy, especially when the poor would seem to have such a stake in government? For several reasons: They have less sense of involvement and confidence; they feel less of a sense of control over their political environment; they feel at a disadvantage in social contacts; and their social norms tend to deemphasize politics. Thus, nonvoting is not accidental—it is part of a larger political and psychological environment that discourages political activity.[18]

Black voting patterns, especially in the South, show another aspect of the voting–nonvoting equation. Since 1965 southern black voters have been turning out at higher and higher rates; but they are still not voting at the same rates as whites. Apathy accounts for only a small part of nonvoting. In fact, strong black political organization increases black voter turnout, and perception of black electoral gain probably boosts turnout.[19] But a primary factor in the South is the weakness of black political organizations. In the North the election of Mayor Harold Washington of Chicago, Wilson Goode of Philadelphia, and Tom Bradley of Los Angeles seem to be examples of the effects of organization and perceived stake on black voter turnout.

[17] Wolfinger and Rosenstone, *Who Votes?*

[18] See Angus Campbell, Philip E. Converse, Warren E. Miller, and Donald E. Stokes, *The American Voter* (Wiley, 1960). This volume remains a foundation of modern voting analysis despite much new evidence and reinterpretation. See also Norman H. Nie, Sidney Verba, and John R. Petrocik, *The Changing American Voter* (Harvard University Press, 1976); and Warren E. Miller and Teresa E. Levitin, *Leadership and Change* (Winthrop, 1976).

[19] Douglas St. Angelo and Paul Puryear, "Fear, Apathy, and Other Dimensions of Black Voting," in Michael B. Preston, Lenneal J. Henderson, Jr., and Paul Puryear, eds., *The New Black Politics: The Search for Political Power* (Longman, 1982), pp. 109–30; and Philip L. Miller, "The Impact of Organizational Activity on Black Political Participation," *Social Science Quarterly* (March 1982), pp. 83–98.

Highest and Lowest Voter Turnout—1988

Highest Voter Turnout

Minnesota	65%
Wisconsin	62
Montana	62
Maine	62
South Dakota	61

Lowest Voter Turnout

District of Columbia	37%
Georgia	38
South Carolina	38
Florida	43
Texas	43

On May 25, 1986, 5 million Americans joined hands in the "Hands Across America" rally to raise funds for the poor and hungry in our society. (*T. Cronin*)

Nonvoting—How Serious Is It?

Some political scientists contend that nonvoting is not a critical problem. "Nonvoting is not a social disease," contends a noted student of politics. He points out that legal and extralegal denial of the vote to blacks, women, Hispanics, persons over 18, and other groups has now been outlawed, so nonvoting is *voluntary*.[20] He quotes the late Senator Sam Ervin as saying: "I don't believe in making it easy for apathetic, lazy people" to vote.

Those who argue that nonvoting *is* a critical problem cite above all the "class bias" of those who do vote. Nonvoters tend to be the low-income, blue-collar, less educated, "less white" Americans, as noted earlier. The "very poor, those with incomes below $5,000 a year, have about two-thirds the representation among voters that their numbers would suggest." Thus the people who most need help from government lack their fair share of electoral power to obtain it. And, it is argued, this situation is growing worse.[21]

Some reject this "class bias" argument. They admit that nonvoters tend to be much poorer, less educated, and "less white" than voters, but they cite polls that show nonvoters' attitudes are not much different from voters', so that attracting 10 or 20 million poor people to the polls would not result in a change in policy for the benefit of the poor. Those who see a class bias reject this argument. Such polls, they say, reflect "the underdevelopment of political attitudes resulting from the historic exclusion of low-income groups from active electoral participation."[22] In short, part of the poverty of low-income, less educated people is their failure to be conscious of their real interests. Dynamic leadership or strong party organization—or both—would not only attract the poor to the polls but make clear their "class grievances and aspirations."

How can we overcome the barriers to voting? The main target is the registration hurdle. Representatives from such organizations as the League of Women Voters and the National Association for the Advancement of Colored People have joined to challenge archaic registration laws and procedures. They have urged the use of government offices as registration places. They also favor registration by post card. If government offices can be used to register young people for the *draft*, they say, why cannot they be used to register people to *vote*? But registration simplifiers have run into countless obstacles. Even some Democratic party officials and office holders, who would appear to have a profound interest in broadening the vote, have been resistant. Some moderate Democrats, it is alleged, fear an influx of poor voters who might "radicalize" the party.[23] The Republican party, on the other hand, appears not to fear an "influx from the right." The GOP cooperated with efforts of the Moral Majority, the Assemblies of God, and thousands of church groups to register people, bring voters to the polls, and help Ronald Reagan retain the presidency in 1984.

We now know about those who do not vote. What about those who *do*?

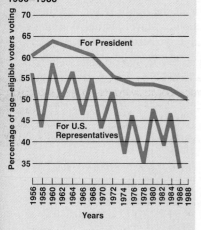

Voting Turnout for President and U.S. House of Representatives, 1956–1988

Percentage of age-eligible voters voting

For President

For U.S. Representatives

Years

1956 1958 1960 1962 1964 1966 1968 1970 1972 1974 1976 1978 1980 1982 1984 1986 1988

HOW WE VOTE: ELECTORAL PATTERNS

Sometimes Americans are called fickle voters because they switch from party to party. Actually a majority of Americans stay with one party year after year, and their sons or granddaughters vote for the same party long after that. Politically,

---

[20] Austin Ranney, "Nonvoting Is Not a Social Disease," *Public Opinion* (October/November 1983), pp. 16–19.

[21] Thomas Byrne Edsall, *The New Politics of Inequality* (W. W. Norton, 1984), p. 181.

[22] Piven and Cloward, "Prospects for Voter Registration Reform," p. 589.

[23] Richard A. Cloward and Frances Fox Piven, "Trying to Break Down the Barriers," *The Nation* (November 2, 1985), pp. 433–36.

these voters are "set in their ways." Of course, there are still millions of so-called independent voters. They help make our elections the unpredictable affairs they so often are. Still, even within the year-to-year variations, there are certain persistent elements:

1. A pattern of *sectional* voting. The South is the most famous example. The Democratic solidarity of the states that formed the Confederacy lasted over eighty years in presidential elections, and continues today in state and local elections. Republican sectionalism was not so clear-cut, but northern New England and parts of the Midwest used to be dependable areas for the GOP. Vermont has given its electoral votes to the Democrats only once since the Civil War, and Maine only twice since 1912. More recently the South has become more Republican and the Northeast more Democratic. Ronald Reagan won all of the South in 1984. Today the Republican "solid West" almost rivals the Democrats' "solid South" of old—at least for presidential elections.[24]

Sectional patterns tend to be fuzzy and sometimes brief. Lately there has been much talk about the Sunbelt, the area from the southeastern states to California, which was considered to be the base of a rising American conservatism. But in many recent elections the divisions have tended to lie between the East and the West, and this pattern may not last long either. Sectional patterns often reflect very close election results within states, and those patterns can easily be changed by other influences.

2. A pattern of *national* voting. Traditional sectional alignments also give way to national trends. The Franklin Roosevelt administration, for example, ushered in a new age of Democratic popularity that affected even the most traditionally Republican areas, and Eisenhower's popularity accelerated the breakup of the solid South. States and sections are subject to a variety of local influences, but they cannot resist the great political tides that sweep the nation.

3. A pattern of *similar* voting for *different* offices. Sectional and national forces affect voting for different candidates and offices in the same election. A considerable number of voters usually vote a straight ticket—that is, they throw their support to every one of their party's candidates. If one candidate is an especially good vote getter, the party's whole slate may gain. This is the famous **coattail effect,** whose precise nature is one of the challenging problems in the study of political behavior. Evidently, popular presidential candidates like Roosevelt or Reagan have long coattails that help elect many other candidates on their party tickets. But congressional and state candidates may have helpful coattails too, and it is not easy to tell which candidates ride on whose coattails or just how important the relation is.[25]

4. A pattern of voting over *time*. Great political tides seem to flow back and forth across the generations. Most presidential elections are **maintaining elections**, in which the existing pattern of partisan support persists. Long periods of maintaining elections are occasionally interrupted by **deviating elections**, which the "out" party wins because it has an especially attractive presidential candidate or because the existing administration has lost the nation's confidence. In such elections the underlying division of party support is not long disturbed, and the next election result

Boston Mayor Raymond Flynn flashes the victory sign after winning the mayor's race. Flynn has been a popular mayor. A star basketball player in college, he once tried out for but was cut from the legendary Boston Celtics team. (*AP/ Wide World Photos*)

[24] Important works on southern politics are Jack Bass and Walter DeVries *The Transformation of Southern Politics* (Basic Books, 1976), and Louis Seagull, *Southern Republicanism* (Wiley, 1975). A provocative sectional theme is found in Kirkpatrick Sale, *Power Shift: The Rise of the Southern Rim and Its Challenge to the Eastern Establishment* (Vintage, 1976).

[25] For an example of some of the complex factors at work, see Barbara Hinckley, "Incumbency and the Presidential Vote in Senate Elections: Defining Parameters of Subpresidential Voting," *American Political Science Review* (September 1970), pp. 36–42. See also Gary C. Jacobson, "Presidential Coattails in 1972," *Public Opinion Quarterly* (Sumner 1976), pp. 194–200; and Frank B. Feigert, "Illusions of Ticket-Splitting," *American Politics Quarterly* (October 1979), pp. 470–88. See also Raymond E. Wolfinger, Steven J. Rosenstone, and Richard A. McIntosh, "Presidential and Congressional Voters Compared," *American Politics Quarterly* (April 1981), pp. 245–56.

**Political Tides:
Eleven Presidential
Elections, 1932–1988**
(First figure, popular vote
second figure, electoral vote)

1932

Roosevelt (D)
22,809,638
472

Hoover (R)
15,758,901
59

Other
1,153,297
0

1940

Roosevelt (D)
27,243,466
449

Willkie (R)
22,304,755
82

Other
267,091
0

1948

Truman (D)
24,105,812
303

Dewey (R)
21,970,065
189

Other
2,611,730
39

1956

Stevenson (D)
26,022,752
73

Eisenhower (R)
35,590,472
457

Other
194,166
1

1960

Kennedy (D)
34,227,000
303

Nixon (R)
34,109,000
219

Other
500,000
15

Alaska

Hawaii

1964

Johnson (D)
43,126,506
486

Goldwater (R)
27,176,799
52

Other
320,000
0

Alaska

Hawaii

1968

Humphrey (D)
31,271,839
191

Nixon (R)
31,783,783
301

Other
10,142,601
46

Alaska

Hawaii

1976

Carter (D)
40,800,000
297

Ford (R)
39,100,000
241

Other
960,000
0

Alaska

Hawaii

1980

Carter (D)
34,910,000
49

Reagan (R)
43,220,000
489

Anderson (Ind.)
5,580,000
0

Alaska

Hawaii

1984

Mondale (D)
36,930,923
13

Reagan (R)
53,428,357
525

Alaska

Hawaii

1988

Dukakis (D)
41,000,000
112

Bush (R)
47,900,000
426

Alaska

Hawaii

Popular Preferences and Convention Nominations

Usually the presidential candidate nominated by a party's convention is the person who has the most support in opinion polls of the party rank and file. There are exceptions, however. In 1952 and 1972, the Democrats nominated someone other than the most popular Democrat, and in 1964 the Republicans nominated a man who was tied with his rival in voter popularity.

	Democrats			Republicans	
Election year	Candidate preferred by party voters	Candidate nominated by party convention	Election year	Candidate preferred by party voters	Candidate nominated by party convention
1944	Roosevelt	Roosevelt	1944	Dewey	Dewey
1948	Truman	Truman	1948	Dewey	Dewey
1952	Kefauver	Stevenson	1952	Eisenhower	Eisenhower
1956	Stevenson	Stevenson	1956	Eisenhower	Eisenhower
1960	Kennedy	Kennedy	1960	Nixon	Nixon
1964	Johnson	Johnson	1964	Goldwater or Nixon (tie)	Goldwater
1968	Humphrey	Humphrey	1968	Nixon	Nixon
1972	Humphrey or Wallace (tie)	McGovern	1972	Nixon	Nixon
1976	Carter	Carter	1976	Ford	Ford
1980	Carter	Carter	1980	Reagan	Reagan
1984	Mondale	Mondale	1984	Reagan	Reagan
1988	Dukakis	Dukakis	1988	Bush	Bush

SOURCE: Reprinted by permission of Elsevier North Holland, Inc., from "Winning the Presidential Nomination: National Polls and State Primary Elections, 1936–1972" by James R. Beniger, *Public Opinion Quarterly*, Vol. 40, p. 27. Copyright 1976 by The Trustees of Columbia University. 1976, 1980, 1984, and 1988 entries based on Gallup poll data. NOTE: Data are from last poll taken before convention.

returns to the old pattern. Very occasionally, however, a **realigning election** brings a basic and long-lasting transformation of party loyalties. A whole new balance of parties comes into being, as it did in the 1930s.[26] Some have predicted that we are on the eve of another series of realigning elections and a historic realignment of the parties. (See Chapter 9.) Others see mainly a pattern of confusion and dislocation.

Why do some voters stick with one party while others shift back and forth from election to election, and still others vote a split-party ticket in every election? In recent decades a vast amount of effort has been devoted to answering these questions.

A traditional explanation for the great political tides is that they reflect economic conditions. A drop in business activity has often preceded a loss of congressional seats and then a presidential defeat for the party in power. But we cannot be sure that business cycles *cause* political cycles. Psychological, political, traditional, sectional, international, and other forces may muddle the effect of economic factors.[27] It was not primarily economic issues but rather the sharply rising concern over slavery that precipitated the breakup of the Democratic-Whig party system in the 1850s. On the other hand, the Great Depression in the early 1930s was the main reason the GOP was toppled after its long period of supremacy. The Democrats won the elections of 1974 and 1976 in part because of public reaction against Watergate—a noneconomic issue. But the GOP won in 1980 on high inflation

[26] These three types of elections are defined and discussed in Angus Campbell, Philip F. Converse, Warren E. Miller, and Donald E. Stokes. *Elections and the Political Order* (Wiley, 1966). See also Walter Dean Burnham, *Critical Elections and the Mainsprings of American Politics* (Norton, 1970).

[27] For a noneconomic cyclical theory of presidential elections, see James David Barber, *The Pulse of Politics* (Norton, 1980).

and interest rates, and in 1984 on having "whipped inflation" and revived the economy.

Any patterns that do exist in American politics are rough and often blurred by unexplained variations. Indeed, patterns may exist for years and then disappear. Before the 1948 election a change in party control of Congress in an off-year election had regularly preceded a change in party fortunes in the following presidential election. But the Democrats, who lost control of Congress in 1946, won both houses and—to everyone's surprise, especially Thomas Dewey's and perhaps even Harry Truman's—the presidency in 1948. And despite a 1954 congressional victory for the Democrats, the GOP won the presidential election of 1956.

Group Factors in Voting

Republicans won the White House again in 1984 after some setbacks in the 1982 congressional elections. Despite the murkiness of voting tendencies, analysis of massive amounts of voting data has uncovered some basic patterns:

1. Voting as members of *family groups*. Most Americans vote the same way their families or friends or workmates vote. Although on election day they mark their ballots or check off their voting machine levers in private, voting is largely a group experience. The most homogeneous of all groups in terms of molding party identification and ultimately the voting behavior of its members is the family. Members of the family shape one another's attitudes (often unintentionally); and members of the same family are naturally exposed to similar economic, religious, class, and geographical influences.[28]

As young adults move away from their families, they become members of many different groups. Some of their group memberships may mutually *reinforce* voting decisions. A young engineer who has grown up in a Democratically inclined family may marry a more conservatively inclined man, associate on her job with Republican executives, socialize a good deal with other members of a country club, and join a taxpayer's organization. The engineer will probably become a Republican, though she may long feel a Democratic tug from family years. Group memberships, however, may have conflicting impacts on a person's vote. A factory worker, for example, may associate with Democrats in his local union but with Republicans in his social group or ethnic organization. Such persons are said to be "cross-pressured" and sometimes take the easiest way out by not voting at all.

Group influences on voting may change over time. Blue-collar workers, blacks, and some urban ethnic groups tended to rally round FDR and the New Deal in the 1930s in part because they felt the Republican party had failed them and, in part because the New Deal Democrats recognized them and gave them concrete social and economic benefits. Business and professional men and women tended to oppose New Deal "experimentation" and "waste." In the 1960s and 1970s newer issues—Vietnam, racial equality, law and order, Watergate—cut across group alignments, created new group allegiances to Republican candidates, and caused severe splits within the Democratic party coalition. Now, in the 1980s, such economic, military, and social issues as sexual equality, abortion, and gay/lesbian rights have come to the fore, with different impacts on groups.

2. Voting as members of *parties*. In this century most voters have identified with one or the other of the major parties. Many support their party almost automatically, no matter who the candidate or what the issues.[29]

IF YOU'RE GOING TO BE OUT OF TOWN ON ELECTION DAY...

VOTE BY ABSENTEE BALLOT

FEEL THE POWER
VOTE AMERICA
AMERICA'S FUTURE DEPENDS ON AMERICA'S VOTERS

Find out how convenient it is to vote by absentee ballot this November. Call your local Board of Elections now for more information. A non-partisan project of the Vote America Foundation

(Vote America Foundation)

---

[28] See Richard E. Dawson and Kenneth Prewitt, *Political Socialization* (Little, Brown, 1969); and for a specific example of an intrafamily relationship, M. Kent Jennings and Richard O. Niemi, "The Division of Political Labor between Mothers and Fathers," *American Political Science Review* (March 1971), pp. 69–82.

[29] The Center for Political Studies, University of Michigan, periodically measures dimensions of party support.. See also Philip E. Converse, *The Dynamics of Party Support: Cohort-Analyzing Party Identification* (Sage Library of Social Research, 1976).

"I'm an Episcopalian on my mother's side and a supply-sider on my father's." (*Drawing by Dana Fradon*; © *1981 The New Yorker Magazine, Inc.*)

Women have become a majority of the American electorate. Registration drives like this stress the importance of becoming qualified to vote. (*Bettye Lane/Photo Researchers*)

Is party loyalty declining? A large number of Democrats ignored their long-time party identification in 1984, as did many Republicans in 1976. Democratic and Republican party self-identifiers (that is, persons who state that they are to some degree "Democrats" or "Republicans" when asked by pollsters) have dropped in recent years. Many voters identify with one of the major parties but vote for the opposition candidates. People usually do not openly and suddenly give up their party memberships; rather, they talk more about voting "for the person and not the party." Whether the drop in party identification is a short-term or long-term development remains to be seen, but party feeling is still the best indicator of a person's vote.

3. Voting in terms of *class*, *occupation*, and *income*. For the last several decades a strong relationship has existed among those three influences. However we define social class—by occupation, income, or social-identification—the higher the class, the stronger the tendency toward Republicanism.

4. Voting by *religion* and *race*. In the 1960s "religion remained a potent source of political cleavage in the United States . . . the single most important of four predictors of political party identification, and was comparable to, if not more important than, the *combined* effects of education, occupation, and income." [30] John Kennedy's campaign for the presidency tended to align Catholics even more with the Democrats, and Protestants with the GOP. In 1984 religious issues experienced a political resurgence; emphasis on issues such as abortion and prayer in the classroom led Catholics and Protestants to vote Republican, by substantial margins. These results, heavily favoring Reagan, came despite opposition from minister's son Walter Mondale and from Geraldine Ferraro, a Catholic.

Racial voting has been a polarizing force. During the late nineteenth century northern blacks voted heavily Republican, and southern whites almost exclusively Democratic—a carry-over from the Civil War. During Roosevelt's New Deal and Truman's Fair Deal, blacks began shifting over to the Democratic party and to the civil rights policies that party was supporting. For the same reason, southern whites began to move toward the Republican party. Blacks today are probably the most strongly Democratic of all groups: They stuck with George McGovern in 1972 when other groups deserted him, and they were crucial to Carter's victory in 1976. This, in part, influenced Jesse Jackson's decisions to run for the Democratic nomination in 1984 and 1988. He hoped to highlight the particular concerns of the black community and to prevent the party from taking for granted the black vote. The support Jackson received earned black Americans an enhanced voice with the party leadership.

5. Voting by *sex* or *gender*. [31] Women as a whole voted differently from men as a whole in 1980; women were more likely to vote for Carter, men for Reagan. Still, in absolute numbers more women *and* men voted for Reagan. The last time such a "gender gap" occurred was in the 1950s, when women voted for Ike at higher rates than men. In terms of values, women evaluate President Reagan more negatively than do men on issues of war and peace; and these negative evaluations are related to women's greater tendency to vote against Republicans and for Democrats.[32]

The "gender gap" illustrates how peoples' political *behavior* can differ from their political *attitudes*. During 1984 polls reported that fewer women than men approved of Reagan's stands on economic, social and defense issues. Especially with the *first* woman nominee for vice-president on the Democratic party ticket, it was expected that women would tilt heavily toward Mondale in the election. In the

[30] David Knoke, "Religion, Stratification and Politics: America in the 1960s," *American Journal of Political Science* (May 1974), p. 344.

[31] On the difference between sex and gender, see Reesa M. Vaughter, "Review Essay: Psychology," *Signs: Journal of Women in Culture and Society* (Autumn 1976), pp. 122–23, note 14.

[32] Kathleen A. Frankovic, "Sex and Politics—New Alignments, Old Issues," *PS* (Summer 1982), pp. 439–48.

voting, however, Reagan gained 56 percent of the votes cast by women—an increase of seven percentage points over 1980.[33] These results suggest the women's vote will not be won merely by having a woman on the national ticket.[34]

6. Voting by *age*. From 1936 until recently, the younger you were the less chance there was you would vote Republican; young voters who came to maturity after the Depression and the New Deal identified with Democrats. But youth, unlike race or religion, is fleeting, and as such is a less reliable voting indicator. Prior to 1980, new voters tended to be Democratic; in 1984, however, they were Ronald Reagan's strongest age group.[35] Whether youth's commitment will survive a popular president's departure will be tested in 1988.

Partisans and Independents

Plainly, party affiliation is a key factor in how people vote, yet voting is also heavily influenced by opinions on major issues, evaluations of the candidates, and the impact of events at home and abroad. The stronger people's party feeling, however, the more likely they will look at issues and candidates through their "party lens"— that is, fit those factors into the overriding party factor. Those who are worried about party influence, however, can relax, because that influence seems to be declining. Moreover, parties do not reflect totally basic social, economic, geographical, or religious differences; thus there is no "party of the poor."

Is this "party fuzziness" desirable? Some favor a situation in which neither major party can claim a monopoly of any group, because this keeps the parties from reinforcing and exaggerating differences.[36] Some party activists disagree. Parties with more clear-cut electoral support might supply national leaders with the kind of mandate they need to offer a firmer sense of direction to the American people.

In any event, although partisans are still important, independents are on the rise. Both groups are worth further examination.

Who are the partisans?   We measure party identification by asking people, "Generally speaking, do you usually think of yourself as a Republican, a Democrat, an Independent, or what?" Those who name one of the two major parties are then asked, "Would you call yourself a strong Republican/Democrat or a not very strong Republican/Democrat?" By 1987, strong and weak Democrats comprised less than 40 percent of the adult population, Republican identifiers accounted for about 30%, and independents comprised about 31%.[37]

Who are the independents?   More than a third of the voters can be classified as unaffiliated or independent—but "independent" is a tricky term. Some persons are called independent because they are party switchers; they cross and recross party lines from election to election. Some are ticket splitters; at the same election they vote for candidates of different parties.[38] Some are independents because they *feel* independent. Some call themselves independents because they think it is socially more respectable, but actually they vote for one party. One study indicates that younger voters with above-average incomes and college educations tend to be more

Source: (*Bruce Beattie, News-Journal (Daytona Beach, Fla.) Copley News Service.*)

[33] Jane J. Mansbridge, "Myth and Reality: The ERA and the Gender Gap in the 1980 Election," *Public Opinion Quarterly* (Spring 1985), pp. 164–78.

[34] Ethel Klein, "The Gender Gap: Different Issues, Different Answers," *The Brookings Review* (Winter, 1985), pp. 33–37.

[35] *The New York Times* (October 16, 1984), p. 1.

[36] S. M. Lipset, *Political Man* (Doubleday, 1960), p. 31.

[37] Updated and adapted from Warren E. Miller, Arthur H. Miller, and Edward J. Schneider, *American National Election Studies Data Sourcebook, 1952–1978* (Harvard University Press, 1980), p. 81. See also Ellis Sandoz and Cecil V. Crabb, Jr., eds., *Election 84* (Mentor, 1985).

[38] Walter De Vries and V. Lance Tarrance, *The Ticket-Splitter: A New Force in American Politics* (Erdmans, 1972). See also Feigert, "Illusions of Ticket-Splitting."

independent than other voters, but that the independent vote otherwise is rather evenly distributed throughout the population.

Many who identify themselves as independents have made a conscious decision to be independent of either party; they are not merely apathetic. This category grew from almost 21 percent in 1964 to a peak of almost 29 percent in 1976, and dropped to about 24 percent in 1980. By 1988 the percentage was up a bit to 26 percent. On the other hand, some independents have no partisan preference. Although they are aware of the party system, they are much more attuned to *individual candidates*. These nonpartisans have grown from 2 percent to almost 10 percent of the electorate.[39]

Is the independent voter the more informed voter? There has been heated debate over this question, but much of it is fruitless—the answer depends on what kind of independent we are talking about. If independents are defined as those who fail to express a preference between parties, the independent voter tends to be less well informed and less likely to vote. But if we mean those who switch parties between elections, we find some who are highly informed and who carefully pick and choose at the polls. The independent is really not all that different from the partisan. Independents seem to be neither more nor less cynical about the "system" than party supporters. Most independents seem to vote as regularly for one or the other party as do those who identify with a party. Still, in a nation in which parties seem to be losing many of their old-time supporters, candidates seek to appeal to the "independent" voter, however defined.

TAKING THE PULSE OF THE PEOPLE

A Philadelphia woman being interviewed for a Gallup Poll survey. Scores of public opinion companies regularly ask Americans their views on policies, candidates, the parties, and the general processes of government. (*AP/Wide World Photos*)

"What I want," Abraham Lincoln once said, "is to get done what the people desire to have done, and the question for me is how to find that out exactly." This question faces every politician, in office or out. Another president, Woodrow Wilson, once complained to the newspapers that they had no business saying that all the people out their way thought so and so: "You do not know, and the worst of it is, since the responsibility is mine, I do not know, what they are thinking about. I have the most imperfect means of finding out, and yet I have got to act as if I knew. . . ."

How can a politician find out what the people are thinking? The usual way, of course, is to look at election results. If Jane Brown wins over James Smith, presumably the people want what Jane Brown stands for. If Brown is an advocate of gun regulation and Smith is 100 percent against any form of control, evidently the majority of the people support some kind of firearms regulation. But we know that in practice things do not work this way. Elections are rarely fought on single issues, and candidates rarely take clear-cut stands. It is impossible, moreover, to separate issues from candidates. Did Reagan win in 1984 because of economic conditions, his personality, opposition to Mondale, or shifts in party support? The answer is that he won for some of these reasons, and for many others. Which brings us back to the question—what do the people want?

This is where public opinion polls come in. In this country public opinion polls are over a century old, but their main development has taken place in the last three decades. Today there are hundreds of polling organizations. We are usually aware of them because they constantly measure and report presidential popularity.

If a politician or a social scientist wants to measure opinion precisely, the

[39] See Arthur H. Miller and Martin P. Wattenberg, "Measuring Party Identification: Independent or No Partisan Preference?" *American Journal of Political Science* (February 1983), pp. 106–21.

first thing to be determined is the **universe**, the whole group whose opinion is being sought—every adult, all students on this campus, all students in the United States, all voters in city X. If the universe consists of only thirty units, the most precise way to find out what they think on a particular issue is to poll every one of them. But for most politically significant problems, this is impossible; so pollsters *sample* the universe in which they are interested. The accuracy of the results depends largely on securing a sample representative of the total universe. If drawn properly, so that each unit in a universe has an equal chance to be included, a relatively small sample can provide accurate results. Beyond a certain point an increase in the size of the sample reduces only slightly the **sampling error**, the difference between the divisions found in the sample and those of the universe.

One way to develop a representative sample is to draw the sample completely at random. But this type of **random sampling** is impossible for most political surveys. Instead, we use census tracts (when these are available), which give the number of residences and their locations. By shuffling census tracts, drawing out at random the required number, and then sending interviewers to every fifth or tenth or twentieth house, we get a random sample. A less complicated, but less reliable, method is **quota sampling**. Here an attempt is made to secure a sample which reflects those variables among the population that might affect opinion. In testing opinion thought to be affected by income status (for example, views on the income tax), a polling organization makes up a sample based on two wealthy persons, fourteen members of the upper-income class, fifty-two from the middle-income groups, and thirty-two from the poor. Interviewers are instructed to question people in each group until they have reached the quota for that group.

People are often suspicious of results based on what appears to be a small sample. Is it really possible to generalize about the opinions of 250 million persons on the basis of a few thousand interviews? The answer is yes. In comparisons of demographic characteristics based on census results and those based on a carefully drawn sample, the differences in an exemplary study were very small. The census reported that 18.8 percent of the population were between the ages of 21 and 29, 23.5 percent were between 30 and 39, and 20.9 percent were between 40 and 49. The sample results were 18.4, 23.8, and 21.5, respectively.[40] Social scientists assume that if a sample chosen by modern techniques reproduces such characteristics of the population so precisely, it will reproduce the attitudes and opinions of the total population equally well.

Asking the Right Questions in the Right Way

Pollsters have a lot of leeway in choosing questions. The average person may be concerned with problems that pollsters and political leaders know little about or have trouble defining. Another major difficulty is in phrasing questions. If you ask a question in a certain way, you can get the answer you want. Ask people if they favor labor unions and they may say no. But ask them if they favor organized efforts by workers to improve their well-being, and chances are more will answer yes. Also, trouble may arise in the alternatives a question presents. Clearly, asking a person "Do you favor the United States' entering a world government, or do you prefer our traditional independence in determining our own affairs?" is loading the dice. Polling organizations go to great efforts to make their questions fair; some conduct trial runs with differently worded questions.[41]

One way to avoid this difficulty is to ask a multiple-choice question. For example, a Gallup poll asked, "How far do you, yourself, think the federal government

How You Ask It Shapes How You Answer It

Q. Do you agree or disagree with this statement? The Federal government should see to it that all people have adequate housing.

Agree: 55.1%

Disagree: 44.9%

Q. Some people feel the federal government should see to it that all people have adequate housing, while others feel each person should provide his own housing. Which comes closest to how you feel about this?

Government responsible: 44.6%

Government not responsible: 55.4%

Q. Some people feel each person should provide his own housing, while others feel the federal government should see to it that all people have adequate housing. Which comes closest to how you feel about this?

Government responsible: 29.5%

Government not responsible: 70.5%

Source: Adapted from Howard Schuman, *Questions and Answers in Attitude Surveys: Experiments on Question Form, Wording, and Context* (New York: Academic Press, 1981), pp. 70–71.

[40] Samuel A. Stouffer, *Communism, Conformity, and Civil Liberties* (Doubleday, 1955), p. 238.
[41] See Donald J. Devine, "The Problem of Question Form in Describing Public Opinion," *Polity* (Spring 1980), pp. 522–34.

should go in requiring employers to hire people without regard to race, religion, color, or nationality?" The respondent could answer: all the way; none of the way; depends on type of work; should be left to state governments; or don't know. A variation of this type—the open-ended question—allows respondents to supply their own answers. They may be asked simply, "How do you think we should deal with the problem of air pollution by automobiles?" (The answers to this type of question are, of course, hard to tabulate accurately.)

Interviewing is a delicate task. Most interviews today are done by telephone and the sincerity of a person's voice is important. For in-person interviews the interviewer's appearance, clothes, language, and way of asking questions may influence the replies. Inaccurate findings may result from the bias of the interviewer or from failure to do the job fully and carefully. And the persons interviewed may be the source of error. Respondents suspicious of the interviewer's motives may give false or confused answers. Their memories may be poor. To cover up ignorance they may give neutral answers or appear undecided. Or they may give the answers they think the interviewer would like them to give.

Polls may give a false impression of the firmness and intensity of opinion; as we have seen, opinions may be volatile and fleeting. Moreover, polls do not differentiate among people. They give equal weight to a follower and to an opinion leader who may in the end influence other voters. Studies suggest that public opinion is not like an iceberg: The movement of the top does not necessarily indicate the movement of the great mass underneath. The visible opinion among leaders and activists or among the more outspoken may be moving in a different direction—indeed, it may even be differently located—from that of the great mass of less-visible opinion. In short, it is far easier to measure the surface of public opinion than to gauge its depth and intensity.

Interpreting the Results

Election forecasting intrigues the average American; everyone likes to know in advance how an election will turn out. During the campaign pollsters submit regular "returns" on the standings of the candidates. On the whole, the record of the leading forecasters in "day-before" polling has been good, as Table 10–4 shows. The most sensational slip came in 1948, during the presidential battle between President Truman and Governor Dewey. The polls repeatedly indicated that Truman was running far behind. The President denounced the polls as unreliable, but the pollsters stood pat on their statistics. Early in September one of them actually announced that the race was over. Gallup gave the president 44.5 percent of the popular vote in his final forecast, and Roper predicted 37.1 percent. Actually, Truman won 49.4 percent of the popular vote, and the pollsters were subjected to general ridicule. Since then they have been more cautious in making predictions, and more careful in their methods.[42]

Political polls have taken on increasingly significant functions in our political system. Candidates use polls to determine where to campaign, how to campaign, and even whether to campaign. In the years and months preceding a national convention, politicians watch the polls to determine who among the hopefuls has political appeal.

Surely the polls are no substitute for elections. Faced with a ballot, voters must translate opinions into concrete decisions between personalities and parties. They must decide what is important and what is not. Democracy is more than the expression of views, more than a simple mirror of opinion; it is also *choosing* among leaders taking sides on certain issues, and among the governmental actions

"Would you say Attila is doing an excellent job, a good job, a fair job, or a poor job?" (*Drawing by Chas. Addams*; © 1982 The New Yorker Magazine, Inc.)

[42] See Harold Mendelsohn and Irving Crespi, *Polls, Television, and the New Politics* (Chandler, 1970), chap. 2.

10–4 Presidential Forecasts by the Pollsters (by percentage)

Year	Actual Dem. Vote	Roper Poll	Gallup Poll	Harris Poll
1944	53.8	53.6	53.3	—
1948	49.4	37.1	44.5	—
1952	45.+	43.0	46.0	—
1956	42.0	40.0	40.5	—
1960	49.4	47.0	49.0	—
1964	61.4	—	61.0	—
1968	42.7	—	40.0	43.0
1972	37.7	—	35.0	34.8
1976	51.0	51.0	46.0*	46.0*
1980	41.0	—	44.0*	41.0
1984	41.0	45.0	41.0	44.0
1988	46	—	44.5	48

* In 1976 both Gallup and Harris said it was a "tossup" and refused to make a prediction. They also reported that more people than usual had not made up their minds. In 1988, the *Washington Post/ ABC* poll predicted a 54% to 44% Bush win; *USA Today*/CNN predicted in its last poll a 55% to 44% Bush win.

that may follow. Democracy is the thoughtful participation of people in the political process; it means using heads as well as counting them. Elections, with all their failings, at least establish the link between the many voices of "We the People" and the decisions of their leaders.

From Opinions to Votes

What about those who *do* vote? How does public opinion translate into individual votes, which translate into elected office holders? Let us look first at voting for presidents. Even the most sophisticated studies have concluded that the opinion most directly related to that decision is *which candidate the voter likes best*. The sophistication comes in explaining *how* voters come to like one candidate better than another. As we have noted, the main influences are three-fold: party identification, attitudes on issues, and candidates' perceived integrity or competence as well as their past performance.

One's party identification has a lot to do with one's evaluation of the candidates—unless the favored party's candidate is assessed negatively on performance or on personal qualities. For example, in the 1980 election President Carter's loss appears to have resulted from the voters' negative assessments of his general competence as a leader. In the 1972 election Democratic voters defected in large numbers because they viewed George McGovern negatively both on the issues and on performance during the campaign. Generally we can say that voters tend to rely on their partisan identification when they see little or no difference between the candidates in terms of personal qualities or performance. When the voters have no party identification and/or when they do see differences between the candidates, they tend to vote for the candidate who comes out best in their assessment of personal qualities and/or issues.[43]

Several studies have found a relationship between "out" party gains (and "in" party losses) in congressional seats and the state of the economy,[44] but only

Although the "election forecasting" of the opinion polls has been generally good, it has been known to miss the mark. This now-classic 1948 presidential election forecast is an unquestionable example. (*UPI/Bettmann Newsphotos*)

[43] See Samuel Popkin, John W. Gorman, Charles Phillips, and Jeffrey A. Smith, "Comment: What Have You Done for Me Lately? Toward An Investment Theory of Voting," *American Political Science Review* (September 1976), pp. 779–805; and further exchanges on this subject in ibid., pp. 806–49. Also of interest is Gregory B. Markus, "Political Attitudes during an Election Year: A Report on the 1980 NES Panel Study," *American Political Science Review* (September 1982), pp. 538–60.

[44] See, for example, Gerald H. Kramer, "Short-Term Fluctuations in U.S. Voting Behavior, 1896–1964," *American Political Science Review* (March 1971), pp. 131–43, and the revision reprinted by Bobbs-Merrill (PS-498). See also Edward R. Tufte, "Determinants of the Outcomes of Midterm Congressional Elections," *American Political Science Review* (September 1975), pp. 812–26.

recently have political scientists been able to locate the sources of this effect in individual voters' decision making. Voters tend to vote against candidates of the "in" party, including even incumbents (according to some studies), if the voters perceive that they themselves have experienced a decline or standstill in their own personal financial situations.[45] But a more recent study finds that this relationship is based on the voters' socioeconomic status. Lower-status voters tend to judge candidates on the basis of the voters' personal financial condition. Upper-status voters, who personally tend to suffer less when economic conditions decline, are more likely to watch the national performance of the economy through the newspapers and to judge candidates on that basis.[46]

Analysts of voting behavior have engaged in heated debates about the role of *issues* and *opinions* in voters' decisions. Whatever the outcome of these debates, we do have some idea from a recent survey about the status of issue voting—especially single-issue voting. Asked "Is there any *one* issue that is so important to you that you would change your vote because you disagreed with a candidate's position on that single issue?", 51 percent of the registered voters in a representative sample replied yes. Of these, 33 percent cited economic issues, including inflation and unemployment; 15 percent named abortion; and 13 percent mentioned social security. Four percent each were concerned most about nuclear war and the nuclear freeze, defense spending, foreign policy, or social programs.[47] In 1984, President Reagan was reelected even though some of his supporters preferred Walter Mondale's issue positions. Reagan's mandate was a mixture of support for his economic and defense initiatives and his reassuring personality. It was also, in part, a vote of no confidence in Mondale and the national Democratic Party.

[45] John R. Hibbing and John R. Alford. "The Educational Impact of Economic Conditions: Who is Held Responsible?" *American Journal of Political Science* (August 1981), pp. 423–39; and Morris P. Fiorina. "Who is Held Responsible? Further Evidence on the Hibbing-Alford Thesis," *American Journal of Political Science* (February 1983), pp. 158–64.

[46] M. Stephen Weatherford, "Economic Voting and the 'Symbolic Politics' Argument: A Reinterpretation and Synthesis," *American Political Science Review* (March 1983), pp. 158–74.

[47] See "Election, '82," *Public Opinion* (December/January 1983), p. 21.

SUMMARY

1. Public opinion is not a solid unit but a loose and complex combination of views and attitudes individuals acquire through various influences from childhood on. It takes on qualities of stability, fluidity, intensity, latency, consensus, or polarization—all closely affected by a person's feelings about salience of opinions to themselves.

2. Better-educated, middle-aged, and more party- and group-involved people tend to vote more; the poor tend to vote the least.

3. Voting tends to be higher in national elections than in state and local ones, and higher in executive than legislative elections.

4. Sectional, cyclical, party, economic, and other patterns can be found in American voting behavior, but these patterns are cloudy and subject to change.

5. We have fairly reliable methods for roughly measuring people's opinions at a given time, provided the polling is done carefully and responsibly using tested procedures and safeguards.

6. People decide how to vote on the basis of complex calculations involving their party identifications, as well as comparative assessments of the candidates on the issues, the candidates' past performances, and their personal qualities.

FURTHER READING

HERBERT ASHER, *Polling and the Public* (Congressional Quarterly Press, 1988).

SANDRA BAXTER and MARJORIE LANSING. *Women and Politics: The Invisible Majority* (University of Michigan Press, 1980).

THOMAS BYRNE EDSALL. *The New Politics of Inequality* (Norton, 1984).

HERBERT McCLOSKY and JOHN ZALLER. *The American Ethos: Public Attitudes toward Capitalism and Democracy* (Harvard University Press, 1984).

MICHAEL B. PRESTON, LENNEAL J. HENDERSON, JR., and PAUL PURYEAR, eds. *The New Black Politics: The Search for Political Power* (Longman, 1982).

See also *Public Opinion* and *Public Opinion Quarterly*.

11

Media Politics: The Blurred Lens?

1984 vice-presidential candidate, Geraldine Ferraro, faces the media during the investigation of her husband's tax irregularities. (*Tannenbaum/Sygma*)

When Walter Mondale telephoned Geraldine Ferraro in July 1984 and asked, "Will you be my running mate?" Ferraro did not pause for a moment. "That would be terrific," she said. But later she had misgivings. Even though she was a three-term Democratic Congresswoman from Queens she had never run a big campaign. Leading Democrats were saying that the women's vote would be the key to the 1984 election; could she help mobilize that vote without overdoing it? The Mondale campaign headquarters was dominated by men; could she and her many women aides and advisers cooperate with the Mondale camp without being unduly submissive?

Ferraro, morever, had worries that no male candidate could have. She insisted on wearing dresses rather than professional-looking suits—but then she had to remind herself not to trip as she walked to podiums. The press was speculating whether she would or would not kiss Mondale when they met publicly for the first time after her nomination (she did not). She and her aides also learned to demand that they be *consulted* by the Mondale staff and not simply told what to do.

"They're not used to dealing with a woman," she told Mondale at one point about his staff, "but they're going to have to learn." She went on, "To help them along, let me suggest that until they get used to recognizing I'm a partner in this thing, they should pretend every time they talk to me or even look at me that I'm a gray-haired Southern gentlemen, a senator from Texas." Mondale got the point.

All such items were important, because they involved Ferraro's image in the media. And that was her biggest worry: the "male-dominated media." For a time she seemed to be the "darling of the press" as the reporters made much of her being the first woman to run on the presidential ticket of the two major parties. Later, however, when Ferraro's husband was found to have been involved in financial irregularities as a lawyer, she found what it was like to have the media pressing her for statements, camping outside her door, seizing on any slip. And she did make a slip, when she tried to explain why her husband had declined to release his tax returns. Her husband, she said, had told her, "Gerry, I'm not going to tell you how to run the country. Don't tell me how to run my business." Then she went on: "You people who are married to Italian men, you know what it's like."

Soon this quip was blown up to monstrous proportions. Combined with the financial scandal, she felt, it struck an almost fatal blow to her candidacy.[1]

Geraldine Ferraro survived this crisis, and many others. She proved herself to be a tough, resolute campaigner who could take defeat as well as victory. She learned a lot about the media: the volatility of media attention, the constant hunt for an "angle" or a headline, the emphasis on personalities, sometimes distorted. She felt, indeed, that her image was often distorted in the media. In short, she learned about the "power of the press."

THE POWER OF THE MASS MEDIA

Whereas your parents and grandparents tended to look at politics through a Democratic or Republican "party lens," today we filter politics through a very different and a very real lens—that of a television camera. The mass media—newspapers, magazines, radio, television, satellite broadcasts, and audio and video tapes—are powerful institutions whose strength is greater than their size (in comparison with other industries), and whose influence is growing as our society becomes more involved in creating, processing, managing, and disseminating information. The media, and the press in particular, have been called the "other government," "the fourth estate," and "the fourth branch of government," with equal amounts of anger and appreciation.[2] Certainly the media are big business. They live off high audience ratings and substantial advertising traffic, essential to their "bottom line" of big profits.

The media seem to be very powerful indeed. They envelop us in information, music, symbols, and images; they provide vicarious experiences that contribute to our socialization; and they serve as surrogate companions. Through advertising, the major part of their revenue, they suggest one product after another for our consumption. And yet combined, they have less revenue than IBM; indeed, Exxon receives more revenue in a week than *The New York Times* receives in a year.[3]

Why are these private, relatively small companies and corporations nonetheless called "media giants"? And how does their existence relate to politics? The media permeate our environment. They have caused campaign costs to skyrocket, and they have placed a premium on a candidate's ability to communicate through a television camera. Media are called "the fourth branch," yet they are politically unaccountable within government's ordinary structures. Who controls them: their reporters, editors, producers, anchors, or stockholders? And what have the mass media done to political parties?

As mediating devices, parties allowed leaders to communicate with their constituents. Today, television and the press serve that role. But the press and TV alone no longer dominate the mass media as they once did, just as the three networks no longer have sole command of television as they once did. CNN, C-SPAN, TBS, and a host of similar abbreviations beam their messages across the country via satellite or generate them through coaxial cable. And though once the focus of media politics was on editorials, today the emphasis is more on whether the press picks up a story or whether a network chooses a thirty-second spot for the evening news, and, if it does, the manner in which it uses and projects it. The power of

"I am old and tired, so I am stepping aside. From now on, television will rule your lives." (*Drawing by Levin*; © 1984. The New Yorker Magazine, Inc.)

[1] Geraldine A. Ferraro, with Linda Bird Francke, *Ferraro: My Story* (Bantam Books, 1985).

[2] William Rivers, *The Other Government* (Universe Books, 1982); Douglas Cater, *The Fourth Branch of Government* (Houghton Mifflin, 1959); Dom Bonafede, "The Washington Press—An Interpreter or a Participant in Policy Making?" *National Journal* (April 24, 1982), pp. 716–721; and Michael Ledeen, "Learning to Say No to the Press," *Public Interest* (Fall 1983), p. 113.

[3] Benjamin M. Compaine, ed., *Who Owns the Media? Concentration of Ownership in the Mass Communications Industry* (Knowledge Industry Publications, 1979), p. 1.

Presidential candidates Michael Dukakis and George Bush meet for a 1988 debate at Wake Forest University. (*AP/Wide World Photos*)

reporters is diminishing as viewers can *see* and interpret images and events themselves—particularly since senators joined representatives on TV, and took their cases directly to the people.

The presidency has also been altered by its relationship with the media.[4] Presidential events and "photo opportunities" are held with the evening news and its format in mind. And the media in turn respond to such manipulation: White House news releases are frequently exposed directly to national audiences. How does the press use government officials, how do government officials use the press, and to what extent can and should the press and television be regulated are critical questions for study.

A political system must have freedom of thought and speech—in other words, competition of ideas and symbols—if it is to be considered a democracy. In America, that freedom is guaranteed by the First Amendment. Can a few media conglomerates support competition of ideas?[5] But without them, can the local populations scattered around the country find out what is happening in the nation's capital, if they depend only on local media companies? Why not have government-owned media carry out educational and information functions, as well as entertainment functions, as they do in Great Britain and France?[6] Americans are too suspicious of the government and too jealous of their rights ever to accept this.

In this country the media are privately owned, and even though the media and their practices are often criticized, this is unlikely to change. The mass media include almost 1800 daily newspapers and almost 10,000 other newspapers, about 18,000 radio and television stations, over 9000 magazines or serial publications, over 4300 film producers and distributors, over 10,000 movie theaters, and about 1300 book publishers.[7] Many are owned singly. Some are owned by groups who in turn own, for example, more than one newspaper or more than one television station or combinations of media types. Some are owned by conglomerates (such as Gulf and Western or General Tire and Rubber) who deal in products other than the media. Twenty newspaper chains control more than half the daily newspaper sales in the United States; twenty corporations command just over half the annual magazine sales; and only 2 percent of the newspapers face competition from other newspapers in their communities.[8]

An estimated 60 million Americans watch some part of the weekday evening news programs on the three major networks. Americans buy about 65 million newspapers a day, and countless foreign-language newspapers, thousands of weeklies, and many publications of a free-wheeling alternative press. Walter Lippmann called the newspaper the "bible of democracy, the book out of which a people determines its conduct." And radio continues to reach tens of millions of persons. What, then, is the ultimate impact of the media on public opinion? For many years observers of the media have been debating this issue, which is really two issues: How great is the influence, and is it beneficial or not?

For a long time analysts tended to play down the influence of the news media in American politics. Franklin D. Roosevelt's use of radio for his "fireside chats" seemed to symbolize the power of the politician as against that of the news

FDR made effective use of the radio; his "fireside chats" reached millions of homes. (*UPI Bettmann Newsphotos*)

[4] Harvey G. Zeidenstein, "New Media Perceptions of White House News Management," *Presidential Studies Quarterly* (Summer 1984).

[5] Ben H. Bagdikian, *The Media Monopoly* (Beacon Press, 1983).

[6] On these media functions see Doris A. Graber, *Mass Media and American Politics* (Congressional Quarterly Press, 1980). On socialization see M. Margaret Conway, Mikel L. Wyckoff, Eleanor Feldbaum, and David Ahern, "The News Media in Children's Political Socialization," *Public Opinion Quarterly* (Summer 1981), pp. 164–78; and U.S. Department of Health and Human Services, *Television and Behavior: Ten Years of Scientific Progress and Implications for the Eighties* (National Institute of Mental Health, 1982).

[7] Compaine, *Who Owns the Media?*

[8] Bagdikian, *The Media Monopoly*; Graber, *Mass Media and American Politics*.

Jesse Jackson with the media.
(*AP/Wide World Photos*)

editor. FDR spoke directly to his listeners over the radio in a way—and at a time—of his own choosing. No network official was able to block or influence that direct connection. President John Kennedy's use of the televised press conference represented the same kind of direct contact with the public. Most studies concluded that exposure to the media rarely changed people's minds, or that the media's effects were at best of secondary importance.[9] However, analysts were working from the false assumption that the media had "hypodermic" effects—that is, that the content sent through the various channels—newspapers, radio, television—was received at the other end by people who accepted it whole.

If the news media are relatively unimportant, what influences people's opinion? First, the basic perceptions and ideas of the public. People are not empty vessels to be filled up with torrents of television talk or acres of newsprint. Rather, they tend to focus on those speeches and news stories that meet their interests or fit their bias; they buy the newspapers and magazines that tend to support their prejudices. The news media may present "new facts," but we have an enormous capacity to filter those "facts" and see what we want to see. This difference between exposure and effect is largely caused by *selective perception*.

A second powerful opinion-making force, and thus a check on the direct influence of the news media, is group affiliation. Authoritative members of groups who *do* consume the media act as *opinion leaders* in channeling and interpreting media content for others in the group.[10] In this way family and other primary groups that heavily influence growing children also intervene between adults and the direct impact of the media. Direct face-to-face contacts often have far more impact on people than the more impersonal tube or newspaper. Belonging to a party also acts as a powerful filter.[11] A conservative Reagan Republican may watch the "liberal Eastern networks" night after night and year after year and stick to his or her own opinions—perhaps even strengthen them.

More recent studies have found somewhat greater influence by the news media on public opinion in general. Also, analysts have begun to look at the different reasons people have for using the media. One study of television viewers found that people use the media to have something to talk about, to gain information with which to influence others, to get ideas for their own creative activities, to escape from problems and boredom, to lift their own spirits and feel better about themselves, to foster intellectual stimulation and growth, and to be with their families.[12]

YOU DECIDE

Do the mass media have a heavy impact on public opinion? Some years ago experts—especially people in the media—considered the media to be very influential. Recent and more systematic research indicated that the power of the media has been exaggerated, and throws new and different light on the question. But what about your own experience? How deeply do you believe your political views have been influenced by the mass media, as compared with your parents, teachers in high school or college, siblings and friends, religious instructors?

[9] See the classic works Paul Lazarsfeld, Bernard Berelson, and Hazel Gaudet, *The People's Choice*, 3rd ed. (Columbia University Press, 1968); and Bernard Berelson, Paul Lazarsfeld, and William McPhee, *Voting* (University of Chicago Press, 1954).

[10] Elihu Katz and Paul Lazarsfeld, *Personal Influence: The Part Played by People in the Flow of Mass Communications* (Free Press, 1955).

[11] See another classic, Angus Campbell et al., *The American Voter* (Wiley, 1960).

[12] Ronald E. Frank and Marshall G. Greenbury, *The Public's Use of Television* (Sage Publications, 1980).

Top Newspapers in Circulation*

1. Wall Street Journal	2,026,276
2. USA Today	1,311,792
3. New York Daily News	1,278,118
4. Los Angeles Times	1,117,952
5. New York Times	1,056,924
6. Washington Post	796,659
7. Chicago Tribune	758,464
8. New York Post	740,123
9. Detroit News	678,399
10. Detroit Free Press	639,720

* Total average weekday paid circulation for a six-month period ending March 31, 1987.
Source: *Information Please Almanac* (© 1987 by Houghton Mifflin Company. Reprinted by permission of Houghton Mifflin Company).

Answer/Discussion

Media *do* make a significant difference. How much, of course, depends on the type of person or group being influenced, the nature of the issue, and the nature of the medium, especially newspapers versus television. "Reading a newspaper increases the ability to discriminate between the candidates in a presidential election." This study reminds us that we must deal with such questions in terms of specific influences and "targets," and media influence on rational or intelligent public opinion, including the ability to discriminate.

How about yourself—what media not only influence you more but help make you a more thoughtful observer of events?

Source: Joseph Wagner, "Media Do Make a Difference: The Differential Impact of Mass Media in the 1976 Presidential Race," *American Journal of Political Science* (August 1983), pp. 407–30, quoted on p. 426.

Political messages may be found in all types of programming. Every sports event begins with the national anthem, which exhorts people to be proud of their country. Many entertainment programs include jokes about political figures. Most media content, including ever-present advertising, still portrays mostly white men and women. And, the token black, Hispanic, and Asian men and women who *are* portrayed are often shown in stereotypic gender and race roles, which subtly reinforce the cultural values of sex and race inequality.[13]

A major part of the mass media's influence is their agenda-setting function: The media ultimately filter the events that become "the news." At the least, the mass media news determines to a large degree what issues people will be discussing during a particular period of time.[14]

Newspapers: What Kind of Impact?

As the coils of Watergate tightened around him, Richard Nixon said, "Basically, they're ultra-liberal and I am conservative. . . . The reasons for their attitudes toward the president go back many years, but they're basically ideological, and I respect that. If I would pander to their liberal views, I could be infinitely popular with some of our friends out there, and a lot of the heat would go out of Watergate." Nixon had long been battling with the press, and a year after entering the White House, had launched a campaign against the television networks. Now he was trying to shift responsibility for Watergate to the news media.

This was by no means the first time politicians had attacked the news media, or at least tried to turn them to their own uses. Jefferson was so upset by the influence of the Federalist press that he founded a Republican newspaper. During the nineteenth century most newspapers were proudly and openly partisan. In recent decades liberals contended that the newspapers were overwhelmingly biased toward conservative policies and candidates. And because they felt that the press was mainly Republican or conservative Franklin Roosevelt turned to radio and John Kennedy to television.

Newspapers today do still tend, sometimes by overwhelming margins, to endorse Republican over Democratic presidential candidates. Nixon had the support of 83 percent of the daily circulation in 1960, and of 78 percent in 1968; Ronald Reagan garnered similar editorial support in 1980 and 1984. But the issue today is not so much partisanship (few newspapers support a party as such) as ideology or general point of view. President Lyndon B. Johnson believed the "big" media were controlled by a handful of persons in the Northeast who hated him because he was a Texan and an outlander. Moderates and conservatives like Irving Kristol and Kevin Phillips fear that the big newspapers, television networks, wire services, and many magazines are controlled by members of the "liberal establishment." Long before he became senator from New York, Daniel P. Moynihan saw a growing tendency for journalists to be recruited from among college graduates, especially those graduates with hostile attitudes toward middle-class Americans.[15] Others contend that although reporters may tend to be liberal, publishers take conservative positions; like other businesspeople, they worry about sales and profits. According to a recent study, although journalists as a group are liberal and Democratic in

[13] Matilda Butler and William Paisley, *Women and the Mass Media* (Human Sciences Press, 1980). See also Paula M. Poindexter and Carolyn A. Stroman, "Blacks and Television: A Review of the Research Literature," *Journal of Broadcasting* (Spring 1981), pp. 103–22.

[14] Shanto Iyengar, Mark D. Peters, and Donald R. Kinder, "Experimental Demonstrations of the 'Not-So-Minimal' Consequences of Television News Programs," *American Political Science Review* (December 1982), pp. 848–58.

[15] "The Presidency and the Press," *Commentary* (March 1971), p. 43.

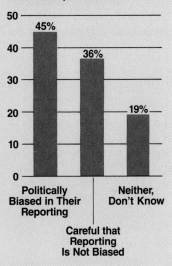

Is Reporting Biased?
Percentage of people who think that reporters are:

- 45% — Politically Biased in Their Reporting
- 36% — Careful that Reporting Is Not Biased
- 19% — Neither, Don't Know

SOURCE: *The People and The Press* (Times Mirror, 1986), p. 28.

opinion, their professional behavior as news reporters does not reflect their personal opinions and partisan identification (see table, page 254).[16]

Certain newspapers, such as *The New York Times*, *The Washington Post*, and *The Wall Street Journal*, have special influence because of the leaders they reach at home and abroad. They even serve as communications links among such leaders. Readers of these newspapers tend to be more affluent and more liberal than the rest of the nation, though the business-oriented *Journal* attracts a more conservative readership. Moynihan contends that, as a result, our most influential newspapers tend "to set a tone of pervasive dissatisfaction with the performance of the national government, whoever the presidential incumbent may be and whatever the substance of the policies."[17]

Some people feel, in contrast, that the editorial columns of newspapers do not affect opinion very much, because editors think one way and people vote the opposite. Franklin D. Roosevelt's four presidential victories in a row, against heavy editoral opposition, are cases in point; so, to a lesser degree, is Kennedy's victory in 1960. Although it is significant that Roosevelt and Kennedy won despite heavy press opposition, we should also question the extent to which they had to modify their political views in order to minimize the effect of that opposition.

In discussing media influence we tend to focus attention on the national news—to talk about a Dan Rather versus a Ronald Reagan. But, as former Speaker Tip O'Neill pointed out, politics in the final sense is mainly local. Indeed, it is at the local level that the media may be more influential. Let us consider the case of a member of Congress from a district in which there is one key newspaper and one important radio station. If the newspaper editor or station manager asks the member to vote a certain way on a bill, the member will think twice before offending that person, who is a "big media frog in a small puddle."

Not only do editorials directly influence our political attitudes and voting decisions, but the press also shapes our political opinions through its overall news and editorial posture. Through its use of headlines and pictures, and by its playing up some items while downplaying others, the press influences the "picture in our heads," the basic attitudes that predispose us to interpret news one way or another. The press has a long-term, continuous influence on opinions that may not be obvious in a particular election.

[16] Michael Jay Robinson, "Just How Liberal Is the News? 1980 Revisited," *Public Opinion* (February/March 1983), pp. 55–60.
[17] "The Presidency and the Press," p. 44.

11–1 Presidential News Conferences with White House Correspondents, 1929–1984

President	Average per Month	Total Number
Hoover (1929–1933)	5.6	268
Roosevelt (1933–1945)	6.9	998
Truman (1945–1953)	3.4	334
Eisenhower (1953–1961)	2.0	193
Kennedy (1961–1963)	1.9	64
Johnson (1963–1969)	2.2	135
Nixon (1969–1974)	0.5	37
Ford (1974–1977)	1.3	39
Carter (1977–1981)	0.8	59
Reagan (1981–1986)	0.5	39

Source: Samuel Kernell, *Going Public* (Congressional Quarterly Press, 1986), p. 69; and "News Conferences" *Weekly Compilation of Presidential Documents*, 21:1 (Jan. 7, 1985)–22:53 (Jan. 5, 1987) pp. 1–1685, Washington: U.S. Government Printing Office.

Criticism of newspapers has been abundant; practical remedies have been few. Some suggest that newspaper chains be broken up through antimonopoly legislation. Others propose that the government subsidize competing newspapers. Such proposals have received little support; many Americans oppose any action that might, in their view, threaten the freedom of the press. Better a biased, commercially oriented press, they feel, than a government-controlled one. As a result, the press has been allowed to "police" its own practices.

Television news anchors often command a great deal of trust among the viewers.

Peter Jennings, ABC
(UPI/Bettmann Newsphotos)

Dan Rather, CBS
(Courtesy CBS News)

Tom Brokaw, NBC
(S. M. Wakefield)

Television News: Electronic Throne?

Some observers believe television in general, and TV news in particular, is a much greater threat to popular government than all other media. Numerous newspapers that cross state lines provide considerable choice for the reader, but only a few networks dominate the American television scene; each of these has about 200 local affiliates. And people seem exceptionally vulnerable to the tube. They *trust* television far more than they do newspapers (see table, page 255). Television news exposure cuts across age groups, educational levels, social classes, and races to an astonishing degree. Moreover, the TV audience is often captive, compared to newspaper subscribers who can read selectively. And video, with all its concreteness, vividness, and drama, has an emotional impact print cannot hope to match.[18]

Some observers believe television is a threat to *representative* government. Direct television coverage of White House news reports or of conflict in South Africa bypasses the government structures through which information was traditionally passed and political conflict organized. Today, the public is more likely to tune in to a debate on ABC's "Nightline." Also, television now covers congressional committee exercises, in which much dealing, swapping, and compromising occurs. How will this "brokerage" play on television? Will viewers expect the committee members to be more principled and high-minded? And if the brokers hear of such reactions, will they be less willing to bargain and barter—processes at the heart of the legislative process?

Some fear "big television" will become allied with "big government." Presidents can command television networks at prime time, virtually at will. They can speak directly to the nation. They do not need to answer questions, and they can minimize their press conferences, as Reagan did. Thus, television has been called an "electronic throne." According to one observer: "No mighty king, no ambitious emperor, no pope, or prophet ever dreamt of such an awesome pulpit. . . ."[19] In the age of Reagan, many of these fears became more pronounced. Reagan was more adept at manipulating and exploiting television than any president before him. Politically, television provided an invaluable aid in his dealings with Congress and the public; personally it helped him become one of the most liked presidents this nation has ever had.

Other observers have been less extravagant but still concerned. A close study of a controversial and much-touted CBS special evening news program, "The Selling of the Pentagon," found that the show led viewers to believe the American military had taken part in national politics, and misled the public about Vietnam. Television journalism has a special importance, this study concluded, because it "disseminates news and information far more widely than does any other news source, bringing political information to people in the society who might never have bothered to obtain this information before television arrived, and who might still not bother, were it not for TV news." More broadly the study suggested that reliance on

[18] Gary L. Wamsley and Richard A. Pride, "Television Network News: Re-Thinking the Iceberg Problem," *Western Political Quarterly* (September 1972), pp. 434–50.

[19] Fred W. Friendly, foreword to Newton M. Minow, John Bartlow Martin, and Lee M. Mitchell, *Presidential Television* (Basic Books, 1973), pp. vii–viii.

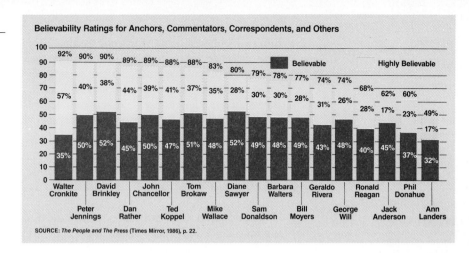

television news fostered political cynicism, distrust, and negativism.[20] (The cynicism, however, may be caused by the unhappy reality investigative reporters often reveal.)

Another study—of the CBS and NBC evening news, and of the two newsmagazines *Time* and *Newsweek*—focused on the kind of people who control the news media. According to this study, the national news organizations are dominated by persons of privileged background and standing. Because the producers believe in individualism, moderation, social order, and strong national leadership, these ideas tend to be reflected in the news. In the long run the news media cater to, and uphold the actions of, "elite individuals and elite institutions." News, in short, has a major class bias that favors the status quo.[21] This view has been extensively rebutted, of course, especially by the media.

Are these problems serious enough to warrant any action? Diverse proposals have been offered to deal with such problems as news media sensationalism, overemphasis on "theater" and spectacles, obsession with violence, lack of self-criticism within the media, lack of objectivity, superficial reporting, and so on. The news media have been urged to conduct more in-depth reporting, to deal effectively with complex issues like energy and ecology, to develop better staffs in local stations, and to try to educate readers, listeners, and viewers—not merely entertain them.[22]

Critics hesitate to propose harsh or sweeping remedies for the failures of press, television, and radio, because they fear any threat to First amendment liberties. But they are also uncertain about how serious the problem really is and how improvement can best be accomplished.[23] Further, the seriousness of the problem varies widely with the situation. For example, in closely balanced election races, where media influence or bias might be large enough to tilt the outcome one way or the other, the opinions put forth by major press and networks might be crucial. Still, in our pluralistic nation, which is comprised of the enormous variety of groups and movements mentioned in Chapters 7 and 8, Americans have so many "filters" through which to observe events that it is extremely difficult to influence public opinion—as many a propagandist has discovered.

Our decentralized governmental system may also serve as a partial defense against undue media influence. Members of Congress may be far more concerned about what the local anchorperson reports about them than whether or not Tom

(Dana Summers. © 1988, Washington Post Writers Group. Reprinted with permission.)

[20] Michael J. Robinson, "Public Affairs Television and the Growth of Political Malaise: The Case of 'The Selling of the Pentagon,'" *American Political Science Review* (June 1976), pp. 409–32, quoted on p. 430.

[21] Herbert J. Gans, *Deciding What's News: A Study of CBS Evening News, NBC Nightly News, Newsweek, and Time* (Pantheon, 1979), p. 61,

[22] For some of these proposals see Bernard Rubin, *Media, Politics, and Democracy* (Oxford University Press, 1977).

[23] Norman E. Isaacs, *Untended Gates: The Mismanaged Press* (Columbia University Press, 1985).

Brokaw mentions them. Most congressional candidates are more dependent on local press coverage than on television, because even local channels, covering perhaps half a dozen congressional districts, cannot pay much attention to any one race. Thus, although the overall combined influence of the media is enormous, how it affects the president and several hundred members of Congress in their own political habitats is a matter for analysis, not overgeneralization.

"IMAGE CAMPAIGN": THE MASS MEDIA ELECTION

"I must admit to a real frustration today," the usually cheerful George Bush admitted one morning a few weeks before the Republican presidential convention of 1980. Candidate Bush had just won a resounding victory in Michigan over Ronald Reagan, but when he watched the television news, all he heard were reports of how Reagan had sewn up the Republican presidential nomination. "If this kind of thing keeps up," Bush told reporters, "by 1984 Howard Cosell will be deciding the nomination during a commercial break on the 'Laverne and Shirley' show."[24] When 1984 arrived, however, Bush, Cosell, and "Laverne and Shirley" had all lost some of their luster. Nonetheless, the media's impact on elections is still a contentious topic.[25]

Late in 1979, about the time Edward Kennedy announced his candidacy for the Democratic presidential nomination, CBS aired an interview of the Massachusetts senator by Roger Mudd. Kennedy seemed strangely ambiguous about why he was running for the presidency—so much so that the interview became a political event in itself, as people compared this vague Kennedy with the heroic figure they thought they knew. Actually, relatively few persons saw the Roger Mudd interview: Most were watching *Jaws* on another network. The interview nevertheless got Kennedy's campaign off to a poor start, from which he never seemed to recover. Viewers did not know that Roger Mudd had actually conducted the interview much earlier, and that Kennedy was evasive about the presidency in part because he did not want to reveal his political plans prematurely.

It was clear to most Americans long before Ronald Reagan's 1980 campaign for the presidency that the former California governor was in his late 60s. But as the campaign began, the media kept beating this point to death. Even though his vigor was evident in his indefatigable campaigning, when it came time for Reagan to choose a running mate we were once again told that he was choosing a likely "next president of the United States." The "issue" of Reagan's health was nonetheless almost nonexistent for the next four years, until an embarrassing performance in debate with Walter Mondale temporarily renewed discussion of Reagan's age. The media found other things to occupy its attention, though, and soon dropped the matter entirely.

"Today, in a surprise move, everyone in the media veered slightly to the right." (*Drawing by Joe Mirachi*; © 1988. The New Yorker Magazine, Inc.)

To describe the modern presidential campaign as just a matter of rules and strategies would be like portraying the Kentucky Derby as just a collection of riders racing around a track in accordance with certain rules. Both events are dominated by celebrities, crowds of spectators, big money, and endless coverage by television, radio, and the "print media."[26] The "mass media campaign" aims to create certain images about the candidates. This campaign has two aspects: One is the intentional and unintentional impact of the mass media on the voters, especially in the primaries. The other is the effort of candidates to exploit the media in their own behalf.

[24] *The New York Times* (May 22, 1980), section B, p. 11.
[25] Ronald Barkman and Laura W. Kitch, *Politics in the Media Age* (McGraw-Hill, 1986).
[26] Richard Stout, "The Pre-Pre-Campaign-Campaign," *Public Opinion* (December/January 1983), pp. 17–20, 60.

The News Media: Election Impact

Long ago there was much more concern about the way candidates exploited the media than about the electronic and print media themselves. But in recent decades network television, big-circulation newspapers and magazines, and large radio chains have become huge industries with their own identities, interests, internal politics, and political biases. Even when the media try to be neutral, some critics say, they bias the outcome of campaigns. They do this by focusing public attention on certain candidates or controversies rather than others, by playing up certain issues and ignoring or playing down others, and by openly editorializing about candidates and campaign issues. A key criticism of the media—especially television—is that it often treats campaigns more as games than as serious encounters over issues. Presidential primaries are treated as "horse races," with the news media awarding attention to the most photogenic or provocative candidate, rather than to the candidate who—like Michael Dukakis in 1988—is slowly rolling up delegate votes.[27]

"Many stories focus on who is ahead, who is behind, who is going to win, and who is going to lose, rather than examining how and why the race is as it is," according to one analysis.[28] The press "sees the electorate as a people influenced mostly by tactics and strategy," and "thus exaggerates seemingly dramatic forces such as 'momentum.' "[29] The media seem to alternate between a kind of "gee whiz" attitude toward their current hero and a tendency to pounce on a candidate's ill chosen or witty remarks and exploit them for days, as they did with Jimmy Carter's comment about lust in his heart in the 1976 *Playboy* interview, George Bush's 1980 attack on Ronald Reagan's "voodoo economics," or Senator Lloyd Bentsen's "you're no Jack Kennedy" retort to Dan Quayle in a 1988 debate.

Sensationalizing or trivializing campaigns is serious enough, but even more serious is playing down the *substance* of the campaign, especially issues. A media advertising expert says the press spends too much time reporting why a candidate chooses a speech for a particular day and place, what the candidate's staff argued about in writing the speech, and so on: "What tends to get lost is what he *said*."[30]

Criticism of the news media increased during the 1970s and 1980s. In May 1987, several *Miami Herald* newsmen staked out the townhouse of Democratic presidential candidate, Gary Hart. A team of reporters then wrote a front-page news story claiming that Hart was linked to model Donna Rice. Other charges of Hart's "womanizing" followed, and ultimately the front runner for the Democratic presidential nomination was forced to give up the race. The disclosure in the Miami newspaper resulted in such backlash from the public about Hart's "character" that he was forced to withdraw from the campaign. [31]

A study of television coverage of the 1972 Nixon-McGovern race concluded:

> First, most election issues are mentioned so infrequently that viewers could not possibly learn about them. . . . Second, most issue references are so fleeting that they could not be expected to leave an impression on viewers. . . . Third, the candidates' issue positions generally were reported in ways guaranteed to make them elusive. Often, issue references were only part of the audio while the news film pictured the candidate getting off an airplane, wading through a crowd, or riding in a motorcade. . . .

"Finally, let me put to rest the so-called 'character' issue." (*Drawing by Weber*, © *1987. The New Yorker Magazine, Inc.*)

Households Viewing Network Evening News
(in millions)

1965	22.2
1970	24.0
1975	28.9
1980	34.0
1985	39.5

SOURCE: *U.S. News & World Report*, June 9, 1980, p. 60; "The Network News Anchors," *New York Times Sunday Magazine*, July 27, 1986, p. 41.

[27] Thomas R. Marshall, "Issues, Personalities, and Presidential Primary Voters," *Social Science Quarterly* (September 1984), p. 750.

[28] See John H. Aldrich, *Before the Convention* (University of Chicago Press, 1980), p. 65, a study of candidates' choices and strategies. See also Thomas E. Patterson, *The Mass Media Election* (Praeger, 1980).

[29] John Foley et al., *Nominating a President: The Process and the Press* (Praeger, 1980), p. 39. For the press's treatment of incumbents see James Glen Stovall, "Incumbency and News Coverage of the 1980 Presidential Election Campaign," *Western Political Quarterly* (December 1984), p. 621.

[30] Ibid., p. 78. Emphasis added.

[31] See in general Hendrick Hertzberg, "Sluicegate," *The New Republic* (June 1, 1987) pp. 11–12; and M. C. Stein "Miami Herald Newsmen Defend Their Coverage," *Editor and Publisher* (July 4, 1987) pp. 17 and 19.

Other recent presidential races have brought a turning point in our understanding of the media and elections. According to Michael J. Robinson, though the media "dominate candidate schedules and campaign decisions,"[32] they may not affect the outcome as much as is commonly believed. Or, at least, the media—especially news coverage—may have different influences on different subgroups of the electorate. Robinson's analysis suggests that while the news reporters and commentators were covering the "horse race," the voters were focusing on the perceived differences between the candidates' stands on the economic situation and national defense.[33]

Probably it is the early deciders—often strong party identifiers and activists—who most enjoy watching exciting campaign coverage. Swing voters—mainly independents and weak party identifiers—tend to vote on the issues important to them, not on whom the media report as winning.

Paid campaign advertising in congressional elections may have more influence than presidential campaign advertising. But again conditions determine the greatest effectiveness. For example, advertising—especially negative advertising—is more effective if left unanswered. A rule of thumb in the "old politics" was to ignore the charges of the opposition, thus according one's rival no importance or standing; that practice may be changing.

Advertising is particularly effective for the candidate whose public image is vague, and who is taking on an incumbent thought to be on the "wrong" side of issues that are salient to the electorate during the time of the campaign.[34] But even if paid political advertising (sometimes known as "polispots") lacks great influence on the voting public in general, it does significantly affect potential campaign workers, contributors, and the reporters and analysts who cover the election.[35]

Building the Candidate's Image: Campaign Technology

There is nothing new in office seekers' trying to improve their standing with the voters through various techniques of advertising and promotion. What is new is the rapidly expanding technology of image building, and the escalating financial costs of doing it. So complex and elaborate is this technology that candidates regularly hire media advisers and campaign consultants. These are typically experts in mass-mail promotion, "thirty-second spots" and other television advertising devices, intensive fundraising methods, improving relations with the press, "targeting" special audiences, staging campaign activities for maximum media impact, and much more.[36]

Polling is also a key weapon in the arsenal of campaign technology. Candidates and their political consultants use polls to assess the strengths and weaknesses in the present "images" of clients and opposing candidates, to learn how voters feel about policy issues and "character" issues, and to discover where candidates should make their main efforts. When and where polls should be taken, when and how the results should be released, and whether or not to release disappointing poll results in order to "lower expectations" and thus make the final election outcome look better are some of the choices that make campaign polling both an art and a science. Patrick Caddell, Jimmy Carter's pollster in both 1976 and 1980, and

"The pleasantries having been dispensed with, we now go right for the jugular." (*Drawing by Maslin,* © *1987. The New York Magazine, Inc.*)

---

[32] Michael J. Robinson, "The Media in 1980: Was the Message the Message?" in Austin Ranney, ed., *The American Elections of 1980* (American Enterprise Institute for Public Policy Research, 1981), p. 178.

[33] See also Jeff Greenfield, *The Real Campaign: The Media and the Battle for the White House* (Summit Books, 1982).

[34] Robinson, "The Media in 1980."

[35] Edwin Diamond and Stephen Bates, *The Spot: The Rise of Political Advertising on TV* (MIT Press, 1984). For a historical look at political advertising see Kathleen Hall Jamieson, *Packaging the Presidency* (Oxford University Press, 1984).

[36] See Larry J. Sabato, *The Rise of Political Consultants* (Basic Books, 1981).

A media reporter conducts an interview at the 1988 Democratic Convention. (*T. Cronin*)

Gary Hart's in 1984, illustrates the influence such campaign technicians may have.[37] Like other major pollsters, he advised his clients on major questions of strategy, the state of public opinion and the mood of the voters, and the relation between popular expectations and desires and government policy. Caddell advised Carter on the existence of the "national malaise" the President thought he found in the summer of 1979. He also advanced another idea that Carter seemed to adopt— "governing with public approval requires a continuing political campaign."[38]

Some critics charge that the consultants have taken the place of the old-time party leaders. Such leaders made their judgments about possible candidates on the basis of long observation of the candidates' performances under fire, decisiveness, conviction, political skill, and other "presidential" qualities (in addition to their chances of victory). The consultants, according to the critics, think more in terms of the candidates' images, television techniques, flexibility, "salability," and the like. Some critics allege that political consultants have become a new "political elite" that can virtually choose candidates by determing in advance what men and women have the right images—or at least images that can be restyled for the widest popularity.[39]

Political consultants say they are simply modernizing election techniques and adapting them to the electronic age. They also warn against exaggerating the impact of television advertising: In 1984 John Glenn (D-Ohio) built his campaign around a heavily financed television advertising effort, but he ran well behind other candidates in the presidential primaries. However, the advertising consultant for Republican Howard H. Baker, Jr., sees the issue differently: "Television is more and more a dominant part of politics," he notes. "There's been an enormously dramatic increase in that dominance from 1976 to 1980."[40] Critics of television advertising fear this tendency will intensify in the 1990s.

HOW POWERFUL ARE THE MEDIA? A SUMMING UP

Ted Koppel, popular ABC anchorman. (*Courtesy ABC News*)

The debate over the power of the press has raged for centuries in America, for Americans have had a special concern about the role of a free press in a democracy. Two hundred years ago the framers returned from Philadelphia, in the fall of 1787, without having included a bill of rights in the new Constitution. But in 1788 the delegates to the state ratifying conventions agreed to accept the new charter only if the framers agreed to add a bill of rights through the amending process. Thus the people from the grass roots proved *their* devotion to protecting the freedom of the press, among other bill of rights liberties. But they also wanted to protect their freedom *from* the press—from its bias or undue influence.

As communication technologies have expanded over recent decades, so too has the debate over the political impact of the media on our lives. This debate includes the central questions raised in this chapter: What is the media's role in our democracy? Which media do we mean: television or newspapers? What, if any, are their biases: Are they liberal or conservative, or something else altogether? And whose bias is most crucial—that of journalists, the editors, or the owners? With what type of ideas do the media deal, and upon which targets—which viewers,

[37] Sidney Blumenthal, *Boston Globe Magazine* (April 20, 1980), p. 9.

[38] Ibid., p. 56.

[39] See in general Bernard Rubin, *Media, Politics, and Democracy* (Oxford University Press, 1977); and James David Barber, *The Pulse of Politics: Electing Presidents in the Media Age* (Norton, 1980). See also Fred Barnes, "The Myth of Political Consultants," *The New Republic* (June 16, 1986), p. 16.

[40] Douglas Bailey, quoted in William J. Lanouette, "You Can't Be Elected with TV Alone, But You Can't Win Without It Either," *National Journal* (March 1, 1980), pp. 344–48.

which voters, which candidates—do they have the greatest influence? What are the goals of the media? And how much effect do they actually have on people's politics? Finally, do these questions affect the news that eventually emerges from television and newspapers, or the politics of the viewers and readers?

Some commentators believe the power of the press has been vastly overstated in political discussion. They argue that parties, interest groups, and the personalities of politicians are far more important. City, state, and federal governments, they assert, have far more impact on a person's politics than television or the press. Religion, friends, family, teachers, wars, depressions and assassinations are all more important than the media—which can only reflect the nation's wants, cater to its needs, and sometimes, perhaps, illuminate its troubles or successes. Political scientists asked people to rank the impact of various institutions on their lives; those listed as possessing "a great deal of power" appear in the marginal box.[41]

Others consider the media to be far more powerful than this popular perception. To them, the media are "an integral part of the daily functioning of government."[42] They note that 67 percent of the adult public watches some television news and reads at least one newspaper daily.[43] They argue that the media define the issues we discuss, set the boundaries of political debate, and serve as both player and referee in the game of politics: They even call foul when a participant exceeds the parameters of the press. Michael K. Deaver, Ronald Reagan's onetime Chief of Staff and White House communications director, has talked candidly about how he tailored the "news" to media's needs: "The majority of people get their news from television, so you have to pay attention to them. You're aware of how we construct events and craft photos that are designed for 30 seconds to a minute so that it can fit into that "bite" on the evening news. We'd be crazy if we didn't think in those terms."[44]

"Since the 1960s," asserts one critic of media power, "the press has taken on all the trappings of other elite institutions: high salaries, luxurious perks, status, top billing on the society pages."[45] And when questioned about its power, even the press agrees; it lists itself as the second most powerful American political institution after business and before the federal government.[46]

Not all those who think the media are powerful agree that their power is bad. After all, they argue, people get 45 percent of their information about issues that concern them from television, 30 percent from newspapers—the media perform a vital educative function.[47] Further, they continue, almost 70 percent of the public think the press is a watchdog of government and that it keeps leaders from doing bad things.[48]

However, those people who are most susceptible to television and print media's impact are also those least likely to view these messages with a critical or skeptical set of eyes and ears. And some insist that the media's treatment of politics, particularly television's, "tends to suppress the ability to perceive significant differences between candidates," and thereby decreases election interest and turnout among the public that is exposed.[49]

SOURCE: *The People and The Press*, (Times Mirror, 1986), p.41.

[41] Leo Bogart, "The Public's Use and Perception of Newspapers," *Public Opinion Quarterly* (Winter 1984), p. 711.

[42] Michael A. Ledeen, "Learning to Say "No" to the Press," *Public Interest* (Fall 1983), p. 117.

[43] Bogart, "The Public's Use and Perception of Newspapers," p. 710.

[44] "Michael Deaver Rates the President's Press," *Washington Journalism Review* (April 1984), p. 25.

[45] Ledeen, "Learning to Say "No" to the Press," p. 114.

[46] Ibid., p. 116.

[47] Bogart, "The Public's Use and Perception of Newspapers," p. 712.

[48] *The People and the Press* (Times Mirror, 1986).

[49] Joseph Wagner, "Media Do Make a Difference," *American Journal of Political Science* (August 1983).

Peter Jennings (ABC) broadcasts
from Moscow during the Reagan/
Gorbachev summit meeting in 1988.
(*Peter Turnley/Black Star*)

Media Endorsements—Do They Matter?

A survey of most of the nation's major newspapers by *Editor and Publisher* found that in 1988 most papers did not endorse a presidential candidate:

No endorsement	428
Endorsed Bush	243
Endorsed Dukakis	103

Influential papers, such as the *Wall Street Journal, Washington Post, Los Angeles Times,* and *USA Today,* endorsed no one. The *New York Times* endorsed Dukakis and the *New York Daily News* endorsed George Bush. Any support and recognition is sought by the candidates and doubtless a strong endorsement can be of assistance, but most voters make up their minds based on economic, partisan, and character considerations.

Presidential candidates remain unconvinced. Every four years they dutifully allocate at least half their budgets to television advertising.[50] On a congressional level, Democrat Robert C. Byrd of West Virginia was challenged by his colleagues for his Senate leadership position in 1985 and 1987, not because he was a poor party leader, but in large part because he was not perceived as telegenic enough. At the very least, the media have the power to mold the agenda of the day, and at most, in the words of the late Theodore White, to "determine what people will talk and think about—an authority that in other nations is reserved for tyrants, priests, parties, and mandarins."[51]

The Rise of the National Media

Many of those who are otherwise unconcerned with the power of the media have lately expressed some serious reservations about a different trend: the modern emergence of a centralized, national media that is described as a diluting, homogenizing, and moderating influence on American press and television. *USA Today*, *The Wall Street Journal*, the three networks, and C-SPAN are the stars of the new national media, which bridge gaps in local coverage and absorb smaller stations and papers as they grow from coast to coast.

Ten business and financial corporations control the three major television and radio networks, thirty-four subsidiary television and radio stations, 201 cable television systems, sixty-two radio stations, twenty record companies, fifty-nine magazines, including *Newsweek*, and *Time*, fifty-eight newspapers, including *The New York Times*, *The Washington Post*, *The Wall Street Journal*, and the *Los Angeles Times*, forty-one book publishers, and various motion picture companies such as Columbia and Twentieth Century Fox. In addition, 75 percent of the major stockholders of ABC, CBS, and NBC are banks, such as Chase Manhattan, Morgan Guaranty Trust, Citibank, and Bank of America.[52]

There is a countertrend, though, in the rise of such alternative media as cable television, the highly successful CNN channels, satellite communication, public broadcasting, the Christian press and television, video cassettes and talking books. However, it is questionable whether these combined forces are a match for the consolidated power of the national media.

Institutional and Political Biases

"Television networks are large corporations whose first and foremost concern is profit."[53] To many critics of the media this observation defines the peculiar nature of the press: It is dedicated, on the one hand, to the impartial and unadulterated reporting of "fact," and, on the other, to a search to please ratings analysts, circulation managers, advertisers, sponsors, and, ultimately, stockholders. Somewhere along the line, some say, the search for truth gets lost.[54]

Equally disturbing to some observers is the media's political bias, whether liberal or conservative. But to whom are these critics referring? To reporters, writers, editors, producers, or owners of TV and newspapers? Do they assume a journalists's personal politics will be translated into biased reporting? And does the public think so?

[50] C. Don Livingston, "The Televised Presidency," *Presidential Studies Quarterly* (Winter 1986), p. 22.

[51] Ibid., p. 25.

[52] Michael Parenti, *Inventing Reality* (St. Martin's Press, 1986), p. 27.

[53] Fred Smoller, "The Six O'Clock Presidency: Patterns of Network News Coverage of the President," *Presidential Studies Quarterly* (Winter 1986), p. 34.

[54] See Nelson Polsby, "The Subculture of News Media," *Consequences of Party Reform* (Oxford, 1983), pp. 142–46. See also "Media and Business Elites: Two Classes in Conflict!" *The Public Interest* (Fall 1982).

	Public	Journalists	College Educated Professionals
Consider self			
Liberal	23%	55%	38%
Conservative	29	17	30
President Reagan			
Favor	56	30	57
Oppose	27	60	33
Economic issues			
Sympathize with			
Business	33	27	52
Labor	32	31	27
Government regulation of business			
Favor	22	49	26
Oppose	50	41	57
Government aid to those unable to support themselves			
Favor	83	95	81
Oppose	11	3	12
Government should reduce income inequality			
Favor	55	50	56
Oppose	23	39	24
Foreign affairs			
U.S. withdraw investments from South Africa			
Favor	31	62	48
Oppose	27	29	27
Verifiable nuclear freeze			
Favor	66	84	79
Oppose	22	13	17
CIA aid to Nicaraguan contras			
Favor	19	17	27
Oppose	44	76	53
Increase defense budget			
Favor	38	15	32
Oppose	51	80	63
Social issues			
Allowing women to have abortions			
Favor	49	82	68
Oppose	44	14	28
Prayer in public schools			
Favor	74	25	58
Oppose	19	67	36
Affirmative action			
Favor	56	81	67
Oppose	21	14	20
Death penalty for murder			
Favor	75	47	67
Oppose	17	47	26
Hiring homosexuals			
Favor	55	89	68
Oppose	31	7	24
Stricter handgun controls			
Favor	50	78	63
Oppose	41	19	34

Source: *Public Opinion* (August/September 1985), p. 7.

Journalists by and large are more liberal than the population as a whole, although editors tend to be a bit more conservative than their reporters, and media stockholders more conservative still. Twenty-three percent of the public describe themselves as liberal, compared to 38 percent of college-educated professionals, from whose ranks most journalists are drawn. But even among these professionals, journalists' liberalism stands out—55 percent describe themselves as such (see Table

	Public	Journalists
Highest standards of honesty and integrity:		
News media	43%	83%
Business	13	3
Organized labor	9	1
Government	15	2
Highest standards of fairness and impartiality:		
News media	44	88
Business	13	2
Organized labor	11	1
Government	17	4
Has done most to promote the public good:		
News media	38	55
Business	16	6
Organized labor	12	4
Government	22	22

Source: *Public Opinion* (August/September 1985), p. 11.

11–4 **Recognition Levels of Famous Journalists and Political Leaders**

Barbara Walters	77%
Geraldine Ferraro	70
George Bush	68
Dan Rather	47
Ted Koppel	37
Mike Wallace	36
Tom Brokaw	35
Caspar Weinberger	24
George Will	12

Source: *The People and the Press* (Times Mirror, 1986), p. 14.

11–2). The public *and* college-educated professionals voted for Ronald Reagan in 1984 by a two-to-one margin; journalists distinguished themselves both from their readers and their demographic grouping by voting for Walter Mondale, two-to-one.[55] Nevertheless, 40 percent of the public describe the papers they commonly read as middle-of-the road, 24 percent as conservative, and only 16 percent as liberal.[56] Further, the public believes that the media on the whole has made Ronald Reagan look better than he actually is, and that in the 1970s they made Jimmy Carter look worse.[57] One columnist attributes this to "media realignment," and argues that contemporary journalists—like contemporary America—have become less liberal.[58]

Why do newspapers get viewed as moderate or even conservative if most journalists persist in describing themselves as liberal? Other factors must be at work. William A. Henry, III, an editor of *Time* magazine, ascribes this to journalists' preoccupation with the inner machinations of the power structure, to which they aspire to belong, identify with, and ultimately defend.[59] In general, Henry and his associates argue, the media and the government are mutually supportive; the press dutifully reports the central transactions among democracy's institutions, presumed to be good, and reserves criticism for the transient personalities that run those institutions, usually presumed to be bad.[60]

Despite all the criticism—the view of the press as elitist, leftish, self-righteous, vindictive, power- and profit-hungry, and unduly concerned with its ratings or sales—public confidence in the media remains surprisingly favorable (as indicated by Table 11–3). The media are perceived as more trustworthy than business, state and local governments, or the presidency; representatives of the press are more widely recognized than corporate, political, or sports personalities.[61]

---

[55] William Schneider and I. A. Lewis, "Views on the News," p. 6.

[56] Bogart, "The Public's Use and Perception of Newspapers," p. 715.

[57] William Schneider and I. A. Lewis, "Views on the News," p. 11.

[58] Fred Barnes, "Media Realignment," *The New Republic* (May 6, 1985), p. 12.

[59] "Roundtable: The Press and the Election," *The Brookings Review* (Winter 1985), p. 38.

[60] Walter Guzzardi, "Press and Government," *Public Opinion* (August/September 1985).

[61] *The People and the Press* (Times Mirror, 1986).

SUMMARY

1. The president is the focal point of much mass media news coverage. The relationship between the press and the president sometimes breaks down in time of severe crisis, but otherwise the routine is a predictable combination of consensus and conflict, a process of honeymoon, competition, and detachment.

2. The power of the mass media over public opinion is significant but not overwhelming. People may not pay much attention to the media, or believe what they read or see or hear. They may be critical or suspicious of the media and hence resistant to it. They live in groups or homes or neighborhoods that "filter" opinions coming in through the media.

3. A major effect of mass media news is agenda setting—that is, determining what problems will become salient issues for people to form opinions about and to discuss.

4. The mass media are big business, but their product is information, which is protected under the First amendment.

5. The media are under attack for sensationalism, superficial reporting, biased coverage, and overemphasis on "theater." Any efforts at comprehensive reform will be frustrated, however, by at least two factors: Reformers are not agreed on what course to follow; and they, and virtually all other Americans, fear taking any action that might threaten the freedom of the press.

6. Presidential campaigns are dominated by the media during both the pre- and postconvention stages. One effect of media influence is that most people seem more interested in the contest as a "game" or "horse race" than as an occasion for serious discussion of issues and candidates.

FURTHER READING

Jeffrey Abrahamson, Christopher Arterton, and Gary Orren. *The Electronic Commonwealth: The Impact of New Media Technologies on Democratic Politics* (Basic Books, 1988).

W. Lance Bennett. *The Politics of Illusion* (Longman, 1988).

David S. Broder. *Behind the Front Page: A Candid Look at How the News Is Made* (Simon & Schuster, 1987).

James Deakin. *Straight Stuff: The Reporters, The White House, and the Truth* (William Morrow, 1984).

Edwin Diamond and Stephen Bates. *The Spot: The Rise of Political Advertising on Television* (MIT Press, 1984).

Doris A. Graber. *Processing the News: How People Tame the Information Tide* (Longman's, 1984).

Michael B. Grossman and Martha J. Kumar. *Portraying the President: The White House and the News Media* (Johns Hopkins University Press, 1981).

David Halberstam. *The Powers That Be* (Knopf, 1979).

Stephen Hess. *The Ultimate Insiders: U.S. Senators in the National Media* (Brookings Institution, 1986).

Stephen Hess. *The Washington Reporters* (Brookings Institution, 1981).

Thomas C. Leonard. *Power of the Press* (Oxford University Press, 1986).

M. J. MacKuen and S. L. Coombs. *More Than News: Media Power in Public Affairs* (Sage Publications, 1981).

Dorothy D. Nesbit. *Videostyle in Senate Campaigns* (University of Tennessee Press, 1988).

David L. Paletz and Robert M. Entman. *Media Power Politics* (Free Press, 1981).

Thomas E. Patterson. *The Mass Media Election* (Praeger, 1980).

Charles Press and Kenneth Verburg. *American Politicians and Journalists* (Scott, Foresman, 1988).

Austin Ranney. *Channels of Power: The Impact of Television on American Politics* (Basic Books, 1983).

Michael J. Robinson and Margaret A. Sheehan. *Over the Wire and on TV: CBS and UPI in Campaign '80* (Russell Sage Foundation, 1983).

Larry Speakes, *Speaking Out: Inside the Reagan White House* (Scribner's, 1988).

CHAPTER 12

Elections: The Democratic Struggle

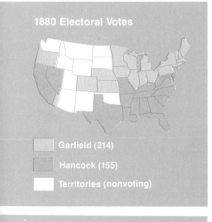

1880 Electoral Votes

Garfield (214)

Hancock (155)

Territories (nonvoting)

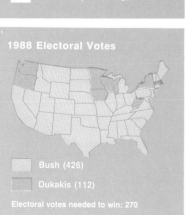

1988 Electoral Votes

Bush (426)

Dukakis (112)

Electoral votes needed to win: 270

Nothing concerned the framers in 1787 more than the manner in which elections would be conducted in the new republic. Eighteenth-century English citizens had little to say about who governed them. Elections for members of the House of Commons were still tightly controlled affairs in which "rotten boroughs" and districts were bought and sold by aristocrats and landed gentry. And even though the colonists did elect their own legislators, the American colonies were governed by royal appointed governors.

Thus, it is not surprising that the framers devoted so much attention to the electoral system. Because they represented many states with diverse interests, they were forced to adopt a variety of compromises. The framers were well aware that many republics had foundered because their leaders had manipulated their election systems, tampered with terms of office, or simply abolished elections altogether.

If you turn back to the text of the Constitution between Chapters 1 and 2, you will note that the framers dealt at length with some of the basic aspects of elections, especially in the long Article I—"The Legislative Article." They gave us the foundations of elections that still exist today: They specified what federal officials will be chosen, how the voters will "chose" them, when they will be elected, how many Representatives and Senators each state would be entitled to, and more. However, the new Constitution left it to the states to decide the suffrage requirements and subject to a congressional override, "the Times, Places and Manner of holding elections," which in effect paved the way for the exclusion of blacks, Native Americans, women, and the landless from the electoral process.

It did not take long—only sixteen years—before the people started to choose the president, and before long the suffrage was expanded, but it did take another 100 years before blacks and women were effectively brought into their country's political life. Despite this indefensible delay, elections today lie at the very heart of "government by the people."

At first office seeking tended to be rather genteel in the new republic; likely candidates who were "co-opted" by local elites might run for office (or ride—on horseback or by carriage) in a friendly way, as did James Madison and his congressional rival James Monroe (see Chapter 13). But electioneering was already changing in the 1790s, particularly in the cities. By the end of the century a Jeffersonian Republican in New York City—Aaron Burr—was organizing his campaign aides on a ward-by-ward basis, card-indexing voters' names and attitudes, setting up house-to-house fundraising teams, and arranging transportation for voters on election day.

The nature of election struggles has, of course, changed immensely in the past two centuries, largely as the result of the influence of the modern media and new technologies, as described in the previous chapter. But the election struggle still lies at the heart of democratic politics. In this chapter we look more closely at modern campaigns for Congress and the presidency. We note three problems in particular—the *lack of competition* for some offices, the danger and distortion inherent in the *electoral college*, and the influence of *money*—that appear to be entrenched in our electoral system.

RUNNING FOR CONGRESS

How candidates run for Congress obviously depends largely on the nature of their district or state. Much also depends on who they are: a first-term senator or representative running for reelection, a veteran with a strong personal organization, or a novice who has never run for Congress before. We can, however, note certain similarities between and among Senate and House elections.

First, we find a relative lack of competitiveness in elections, as defined by closeness of the vote between the two major parties.[1] Although competition has increased slightly beginning with the 1966 midterm elections, in large part the strength of incumbency explains the lack of competition.[2] Once a person has gained a seat in the House or Senate, that office holder can use the powers and privileges of office to maintain the support of the constituency.[3] If the recent trend toward more competitive elections continues, however, it may be due to two factors: (1) the efforts of first the Republicans and then the Democrats to recruit strong candidates to challenge incumbents; and (2) the availability of larger and larger amounts of PAC money for the campaigns of strong candidates to run against incumbents as well as for open seats.[4]

Less competition means more safe seats. The existence of such seats affects the number and kinds of persons willing to compete for the House, as well as affecting that body's policy-making process and output. Even though many Senate seats tend to be noncompetitive, the situation is less pronounced there than in the House. The population of a whole state is much more diverse than that of the usual congressional district, and diversity of population enhances competitiveness of elections.

Presidential performance also affects both House and Senate elections. We have noted the coattail effect: Some presidential candidates modify voters' attitudes in ways that help determine who wins congressional races as well. There is some evidence that presidents affect congressional races even in midterm elections. To

Congressional candidate campaigning in a rural community.

[1] Jon R. Bond, Cary Covington, and Richard Fleisher, "Explaining Challenger Quality in Congressional Elections," *Journal of Politics* (May 1985), p. 510.

[2] James C. Garand and Donald A. Gross, "Changes in the Vote Margins for Congressional Candidates: A Specification of Historical Trends," *American Political Science Review* (1984).

[3] See, for example, Keith Drehbiel and John R. Wright, "The Incumbency Effect in Congressional Elections: A Test of Two Explanations," *American Journal of Political Science* (February 1983), p. 140. See also James E. Campbell, "The Return of Incumbents: The Nature of the Incumbency Advantage," *Western Political Quarterly* (1984).

[4] Larry J. Sabato, *PAC Power* (Norton, 1985).

a considerable degree the votes cast in these elections seem to be a judgment or referendum on the performance of the president and especially on the latter's management of the economy. Although the nationwide congressional vote of the party controlling the White House almost always declines in the midterm elections two years into a presidential term, "the magnitude of that loss is substantially smaller if the President has a high level of popular approval, or if the economy is performing well, or both."[5]

Most campaigns for the House and Senate are increasingly influenced by the new technology of politics: computers, the use of campaign agencies, opinion polling, consultants, fundraising, direct mail, the media, "political packaging," basic information systems, and so on. Some fear this new technology emphasizes *personality* at the expense of issues and party. And consultants are often criticized for running "negative campaigns" that focus primarily on opponents' alleged failings.

Campaigning for the House

For a person contemplating running for the U.S. House of Representatives, the first question is one of timing. Does the year look good for the candidate and the party? Is there any kind of groundswell against the incumbent? If it is a presidential election year, will the party's ticket be headed by attractive national or state candidates? If so, can the would-be representative get a firm hold on their coattails? Should the candidate wait two or four years in order to broaden his or her own range of acquaintances? Or will it be too late by then?

After deciding to run, the candidate must first plan a primary race, unless there are no opponents for the party's nomination. (This piece of luck is more likely when a party has little chance of carrying the district.) The first step is to build a *personal* organization, because the *party* organization usually stays neutral until the nomination is decided. A candidate can build an organization while holding a lesser office, such as a seat in the state legislature, or by deliberately getting to know people, serving in civic causes, helping other candidates, and being conspicuous without being overly controversial. The next step is to raise funds to hire campaign managers and technicians, to buy television and other advertising, to conduct polls, and so on.

Although in recent years parties, especially the Republican party, provide candidates with considerable financial help, the party inheritance is worth less today than it was several decades ago. In fact, the party provides them with far less financial support than they need. The 1980 elections, however, seem to have been a turning point, and 1984 confirmed the more recent trend: The Republicans led the way in supplying more "in kind" contributions and money for coordinated expenditures than in the past.[6] Still, candidates find they must depend on a personal organization and contributions from individuals to provide the bulk of their financial support. Most congressional campaigns cost under $500,000, but in recent years the top ten spenders laid out over $1 million for the House (see Table 12–1).

The main problem for a congressional candidate usually is one of *visibility*. Candidates do get some attention from the press and from state and national party leaders. In a large metropolitan area, however, it is hard to get attention in the press and on television, and in rural areas the press may even play down political news. As a result, congressional candidates often stress advertising and promotion. Especially for nonincumbents, candidates' spending on radio and television has a

House of Representatives' Seats Gained or Lost by White House Party in National Midterm Elections

1930	−49
1934	+9
1938	−71
1942	−45
1946	−55
1950	−29
1954	−18
1958	−48
1962	−4
1966	−47
1970	−12
1974	−48
1978	−12
1982	−26
1986	−5

[5] See Gary C. Jacobson, *The Politics of Congressional Elections* (Little, Brown, 1983), pp. 131–37; and Randall L. Calvert and John A. Ferejohn, "Coattail Voting in Recent Presidential Elections," *American Political Science Review* (June 1983), pp. 407–19.

[6] Jacobson, *The Politics of Congressional Elections*, pp. 51–59.

12–1 "Big Spenders" in 1984 House and Senate Elections—And How They Fared

House		
Andrew Stein (D-New York)	$1,762,120	Lost
Jim Jones (D-Oklahoma)	1,423,193	Won
Bill Green (R-New York)	1,104,348	Won
Bob Dornan (R-California)	1,003,583	Won
Ron Dellums (D-California)	951,668	Won
Senate		
Jesse Helms (R-North Carolina)	16,244,642	Won
Jay Rockefeller (D-West Virginia)	12,044,988	Won
Phil Gramm (R-Texas)	9,379,957	Won
James Hunt (D-North Carolina)	9,194,298	Lost
Rudy Boschwitz (D-Minnesota)	5,849,855	Won

Source: Federal Election Commission

positive effect on the margin of victory.[7] But in congressional campaigning there is no substitute for personal contact—shaking hands, canvassing homes, emphasizing local problems, remembering peoples' names. A congressional election is usually a combination of national politics, congressional policy making, and grass-roots politicking. "All politics is local," says former U.S. House of Representatives Speaker Thomas (Tip) O'Neill.

Keeping a House seat is usually much easier than gaining it. Representatives over the years have provided themselves with a host of perquisites that help them gain reelection. These "perks" include patronage (for example, census jobs), free mailings to constituents (franking), free tapings that can be played over local radio stations, and much else, along with a large staff that can do countless favors, or "casework," in the members' name, and send a stream of press reports back to the district. Astute representatives also try to win committee posts that relate especially to the needs of their districts, even if these are on relatively minor committees.[8] A high percentage of representatives who run for reelection retain office, if they work at it. Representatives seeking reelection typically run on their own and rely on their own staffs and campaign organizations. Ironically, when presidents need stable congressional support, congressional candidates sometimes distance themselves from the presidential candidates and adopt the role of political long-distance "lonely runners."[9]

Running for Senator

Because state populations vary so widely, generalizing about Senate campaigns is difficult. But running for the Senate is big-time politics. The six-year term and the national exposure make a Senate seat a glittering prize, so competition is usually intense. The race may easily cost a million dollars. In 1984 two candidates spent over $10 million each (see Table 12–1). Candidates for the Senate are far more visible than those for the House. They find it more important to take positions on national problems, and they cannot duck tough issues very easily.

Otherwise, Senate races tend to be much like those for the House. The essential tactics are to get others involved, use as much personal contact as possible, be brief in statements to the public, not publicize the opposition if possible, and have a simple campaign theme. Candidates for the Senate, like other candidates, must persuade people by *reinforcing* their present feelings, *activating* their latent attitudes, and *converting* their opposing views to the extent possible. Facts do not speak for

Important Factors in Winning a Contested Election

Uncontrollable factors:

Incumbent rerunning or open seat
Strength of party organization
National tides or landslide possibility
Socioeconomic makeup of district

Organizational factors:

Registration drives
Fundraising machinery
Campaign organization
Volunteers
Effective media campaign
Direct mail campaign efforts
Get-out-the-vote effort

Personal leadership factors:

Candidate's personal appeal
Candidate's knowledge of issues
Candidate's speaking and debating ability
Candidate's commitment and determination
Candidate's ability to earn unpaid, positive media coverage

[7] Ibid.

[8] David R. Mayhew, *Congress: The Electoral Connection* (Yale University Press, 1975).

[9] Charles M. Tidmarch and Douglas Carpenter, "Congressmen and the Electorate, 1968 and 1972," *Journal of Politics* (May 1978), p. 487. See also George C. Edwards, III, "Presidential Electoral Performance as a Source of Presidential Power," *American Journal of Political Science* (February 1978), pp. 152–68.

"And, unlike my opponent, I don't owe a thing to special interests . . . In fact, they still owe me two installments!" (*Dunagin's People by Ralph Dunagin, © News Group Chicago, Inc. Courtesy of News America Syndicate*)

themselves: Candidates must provide an intellectual and psychological framework. And Senate races usually call for even more campaign technology than those for the House.

Other things being equal, incumbency is also an advantage for a U.S. Senator though not quite as much as for a U.S. Representative. The reason is not wholly clear. "It may simply be," says Barbara Hinckley, "that an incumbent is more widely known than his opponent—due to the publicity available as a member of the Senate, the franking privilege, etc.—and that with generally low levels of voter interest and information about Congress, voters will tend to vote for the more familiar (less unfamiliar) name."[10] But even though 76 percent win reelection, incumbents are not unbeatable.[11] In 1974, for example, Senator William Fulbright, a thirty-year veteran of the Senate, and probably its most distinguished spokesperson on foreign policy, was beaten in the primary in Arkansas by a young, vigorous, and popular governor, Dale Bumpers. In 1980 Jacob Javits of New York faced a similar threat from a much younger Republican opponent, Alphonse D'Amato; the veteran senator lost. In 1984 Charles Percy (R-Illinois), Chair of the Senate Foreign Relations Committee, was defeated by Democratic House member Paul Simon. And in 1986 Republican Paula Hawkins, running without Ronald Reagan on the national ticket, lost to popular Florida Governor Bob Graham.

Is there any place for rational planning in all this? Or is being elected simply a matter of following a few obvious rules of thumb like those just listed? Most politicians would argue that victory is nine-tenths perspiration and one-tenth inspiration. But careful calculation may pay off, especially in the tricky business of picking a good year to run and a good presidential candidate to run with or against.

In 1964 Republican candidates faced the difficult decision of whether to cling to the coattails of Barry Goldwater or conduct independent campaigns. Those who thought Goldwater a sure winner and climbed aboard his bandwagon fared worse at the polls than those who ran somewhat separate campaigns. A decade later, Republican candidates in most districts did their best to separate themselves from President Nixon, Watergate, and inflation, as did many Democrats from Walter Mondale in 1984. But most election results are also affected by factors over which candidates have little control. These include ballots that emphasize the link between presidential and congressional candidates, national trends, party registration, and the influence of local candidates.

We may be entering a period in which campaign effectiveness will become even more significant in determining election outcomes. This may happen not merely because of the greater effectiveness of new political techniques but also because a growing number of young voters are not loyal to any one party. They enter the campaign periods ready to be persuaded. Although party loyalties will not disappear altogether, there are likely to be fewer voters to whom candidates can appeal in terms of party loyalty alone.

RUNNING FOR PRESIDENT: RULES AND STRATEGIES

There are really two campaigns for the presidency. One is the "mass media election,"[12] which we examined in Chapter 11. The other is the day-to-day efforts of campaigners to win delegates in a series of primaries and caucuses, gain a majority

[10] Barbara Hinckley, "Incumbency and the Presidential Vote in Senate Elections: Defining Parameters of Subpresidential Voting," *American Political Science Review* (September 1970), pp. 841–42.

[11] Peter Tuckel, "The Initial Re-election Chances of Appointed and Elected U.S. Senators," *Polity* (Fall 1983), p. 138.

[12] Thomas E. Patterson, *The Mass Media Election: How Americans Choose their President* (Praeger, 1980).

Michael Dukakis on campaign trail, 1988. (*UPI/Bettmann Newsphoto*)

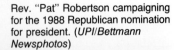

Rev. "Pat" Robertson campaigning for the 1988 Republican nomination for president. (*UPI/Bettmann Newsphotos*)

at the national convention, and win a majority in the electoral college on the first Tuesday after the first Monday in November. The "formal" campaign has three stages.

Stage One: Winning Delegates

Presidential hopefuls must make a series of tactical decisions, any one of which might be critical. The first is when to start campaigning. Some candidates begin almost two years before election day, as several Democratic and Republican hopefuls did in 1986. "Inactive" candidates are not really inactive; they can concentrate on quietly lining up key governmental and party leaders who might deliver delegate support at the convention. In either case, presidential nominating campaigns now begin so early that some analysts fear nominations are decided even before the first primary is held. The hardest job for the candidate, however, is calculating how to deal with the crazy-quilt system of presidential primaries and caucuses that makes up the delegate-choosing system. This complex system varies from state to state and often between the two parties in the same state. Although the process is influenced somewhat by federal regulation and national party rules, within broad limits the states can set up the systems they prefer. The result has been a smörgasbord.

Presidential primaries   State **presidential primaries** for choosing convention delegates (unknown before this century) have become by far the main method of choosing such delegates. Today about thirty states, including most of the larger states and hence the vast majority of voters, use presidential primaries. The rest use "old-fashioned" caucuses or conventions (see the next section). Presidential primaries have two main features: the "beauty contest," in which voters indicate their choice for president, usually from a list; and the actual selection of delegates to the convention. Different combinations of these two features have produced the following main systems:

1. *Proportional representation* of voters' presidential preference. Delegates to the national convention are allocated on the basis of the votes candidates win in the "beauty contest." This system has been used in most of the states, including several of the largest ones.[13]

2. *Winner take all.* The results of the presidential preference poll bind all the delegates, so that whoever wins the "popularity contest" wins *all* the delegates in that state or district. To win all the delegates of a state like California, of course, is an enormous bonus to a candidate. (George Bush won all of California's delegates in 1988.) Only the Republicans use this system; the Democrats banned it in 1976.

3. *Delegate selection*, no preference poll. In several states, large and small, voters choose delegate candidates who may or may not have indicated how they will vote in the presidential convention. The names of the presidential hopefuls do not appear separately on the ballot; there is no presidential preference poll or "beauty contest." Under this arrangement delegates chosen are more likely to feel free to exercise their independent judgment at the convention.

4. *Delegate selection and separate presidential poll*. In several states, including New Hampshire (where in recent years the first primary has been held), voters decide twice: once to state their choice for president and once to choose delegates shown on the ballot to be pledged, or at least favorable, to a presidential candidate. This is one of the oldest types of presidential primary.[14]

[13] Paul T. David and James W. Ceaser, *Proportional Representation in Presidential Nominating Politics* (University of Virginia Press, 1980), assess the influence of proportional representation on candidate support and convention balloting.

[14] These types are drawn from James W. Davis, *Presidential Primaries*, rev. ed. (Greenwood Press, 1984), chap. 3. See pp. 56–63 for specifics on each state (and Puerto Rico). This material is used with the permission of the publisher.

Dukakis at podium, 1988 Democratic Convention. (*Jim Clark*)

George Bush addresses the 1988
Republican National Convention.
(*Jim Clark*)

Caucuses and conventions   About twenty states do not use the presidential primary at all; they use a caucus and convention system for choosing delegates. This is the oldest method of choosing delegates and is fundamentally different from the primary system because it centers on the *party organization*. In principle the caucus and convention system is far simpler than the primary method. Delegates to national conventions are chosen by delegates to state or district conventions, who themselves are chosen earlier in county and precinct caucuses or at other local meetings. The process starts with precinct meetings open to all party members, who discuss and take positions on candidates and issues and elect delegates to the next higher caucus. This process is repeated until presidential convention delegates are chosen at the higher levels.

There are many varieties of the caucus and convention system, because they are regulated by different state parties and legislatures. The most important and significant type may be that of Iowa, because Iowa has held the first caucuses. Early in 1988, on a Monday evening, Iowa held hundreds of Democratic and Republican precinct meetings. A large number of persons showed up at these small "party town meetings." Although an even larger number of Iowans would doubtless have voted in a primary had there been one, the thousands attending these caucuses at least had a chance to meet and to exchange views about issues and candidates and then be the first in the nation officially to name their choices for president. A special feature of the Iowa meetings was that college students could attend local caucuses in their college or home towns, as they preferred, with a minimum of hassle.

Stage Two: Capturing the Convention

Presidential conventions compress into three or four days all the excitement of the preceding six or seven months of preconvention politics. The first convention probably was held in 1808, when a few Federalist leaders met secretly in New York to nominate candidates for president and vice-president. In the early 1830s, under the leadership of Democrats Andrew Jackson and Martin Van Buren, the first real "open" convention was held by a major party. Today the national convention is a famous and unique political institution. For about four days every four years, each party enjoys world attention; covered by batteries of cameras and battalions of newspersons, selected incidents in the convention hall are carried to millions in this country and abroad. This is very much a *party* affair; even though nominating or confirming the nomination of a president is the main event, the party has a chance to come together as a national institution, parade its leaders, adopt a platform, and indulge in oratory, hoopla, and high jinks.

For the presidential hopeful the object in either major party convention is simple: to win a straight majority of votes on the earliest ballot possible, preferably the first. A key factor is the makeup, as well as the presidential preferences, of the state delegations. Each party convention represents the states roughly in proportion to the number of voters in the state, but there is a bonus for states in which the party is especially strong. The two parties have often changed their rules for dividing the votes among the states in an attempt to satisfy both criteria.

Historically delegates have arrived at national conventions with all degrees of commitment, semicommitment, and noncommitment to presidential candidates. Some delegates were pledged to no candidate at all; others to a specific candidate for one or two ballots; others to their favorite "until hell freezes over." Recent conventions have seen two changes. Because of the adoption of "reforms" requiring delegates to pledge themselves to a definite presidential hopeful, and because a Reagan or a Bush, a Carter or a Dukakis has been able to amass the necessary amount of delegate support in advance, recent conventions have merely ratified decisions already made in the primaries and caucuses. And because of "reforms" encouraging delegates to stick to the person to whom they are pledged, there has been less room for maneuver at conventions.

encouraging delegates to stick to the person to whom they are pledged, there has been less room for maneuver at conventions.

How tightly should delegates be bound in the convention to presidential candidates to whom they were pledged in the primaries? This question dominated the first day of proceedings at the 1980 Democratic convention. Delegates supporting President Carter, who had won most of the primaries, argued that primaries would be a farce, and conventions undemocratic and unrepresentative, if delegates could violate their "pledges." Delegates backing Senator Edward Kennedy contended that such a rule would make delegates into "pawns" and conventions into "rubber stamps." Why have a convention at all, they asked, if delegates could not act in a deliberative—rather than merely a representative—capacity, especially because months had gone by since many delegates had been selected, and conditions had changed. A majority of the convention supported the president's position, and party rules appeared to require that "delegates elected to the national convention pledged to a presidential candidate shall in all good conscience reflect the sentiments of those who elected them."[15]

Conventions have their own rules, routines, and rituals. Usually the first day is devoted to a keynote address as well as to other speeches touting the party and denouncing the opposition; the second day to committee reports; the third day for presidential balloting; and the fourth to choosing a vice-presidential nominee.[16] Balloting for president is, of course, the highlight of the proceedings, but dramatic struggles can occur over the adoption of the rules and the platform, if one or more candidates see some advantage in challenging a convention rule or a party plank. Not long ago sharp encounters occurred over credentials—that is, over which delegates should be seated when the matter was in dispute—but recently these have dwindled because of more nearly certain procedures in choosing delegates.

Conventions usually spend many hours debating their platforms. Why? Critics have long pointed out that the party platform is binding on no one. It has been compared to a train platform—something to get in on, not to stand on. But presidential politicians take the platform seriously. It gives a good indication of the general direction a party wants to take and provides rival candidates with a test of their convention strength. Most presidents also make considerable efforts to implement their parties' platforms.[17]

The choice of the vice-presidential nominee has become increasingly important. For many years the just-elected presidential nominee has dictated the choice of a running mate; this practice is now taken for granted. Rarely does a person actually "run" for the vice-presidential nomination, because only one vote counts. But there is a good deal of maneuvering in order to capture that one vote.

Traditionally the presidential nominee has chosen a running mate who would "balance the ticket." George Bush's appointment of Indiana Senator Dan Quayle as his running mate in late 1988 surprised nearly everyone and evoked considerable criticism. Quayle, however, may have helped solidify conservative support for Bush even if his selection raised widespread doubts about the wisdom of this choice.

In 1986, both major parties in Nebraska nominated women as gubernatorial candidates. At top, Republican Kay Orr, who won and is the current governor. Below is Democrat Helen Boosalis, former Mayor of Lincoln, who lost this race.

(Courtesy of the Governor's Office)

(Courtesy Boosalis for Governor)

Stage Three: The Fall Campaign

The convention adjourns immediately after the presidential and vice-presidential candidates deliver their acceptance speeches to the delegates. The presidential nominee may choose a new party chair, who usually serves as presidential campaign

[15] *Delegate Selection Rules for the 1984 Democratic National Convention* (Democratic National Committee, 1982), p. 13.

[16] Stephen J. Wayne, *The Road to the White House*, 2nd ed. (St. Martin's Press, 1984).

[17] Jeff Fishel, *Presidents and Promises* (Congressional Quarterly Press, 1984).

manager. After a rest the candidate spends the final days of the summer binding up party wounds, gearing the party for action, and planning campaign strategy. By early fall the presidential race is on.

Strategy differs from one election to another, but politicians, pollsters, and political scientists have collected enough information in recent decades to agree broadly that a number of basic factors affect election outcomes. The great bulk of the electorate votes on the basis of party, candidate appeal, and issues. Much depends on voter turnout as well as on party disposition. Nationally the Democrats have an advantage in party registration (see Chapter 9). But the Republicans also have an advantage, because their partisans are more likely to turn out on election day, and they have better access to money and usually a somewhat more favorable press (at least in terms of editorial endorsements). Pledges on policy and program may not arouse the mass of the electorate, but they do help activate interest groups and party organizations, which in turn help get out a favorable vote.

The course of the presidential campaign has become familiar over time. First there is a postconvention breathing spell, which allows the candidates and their entourages to plan strategy. For example, they must decide where to stump: Building group support calls for a major effort. Each candidate sets up veterans, farmers, and other campaign groups to operate within such big interest-group organizations as the American Legion, the AFL-CIO, and the American Medical Association. The question of offensive or defensive strategies plagues the tacticians: Do Americans vote for or against candidates? Should the opposition be attacked or ignored? Should the candidate campaign aggressively? And work always needs to be done on the image of the candidate. This was a major, and evidently highly effective, effort of the 1968 Nixon campaigners, who knew the Republican nominee had to shed his old image of divisive campaigning and, indeed, of failure as a campaigner.[18]

No one has captured the spirit of presidential campaigning better than Adlai E. Stevenson, the unsuccessful Democratic candidate in 1952 and 1956:

> You must emerge, bright and bubbling with wisdom and well-being, every morning at 8 o'clock, just in time for a charming and profound breakfast talk, shake hands with hundreds, often literally thousands, of people, make several inspiring, "newsworthy" speeches during the day, confer with political leaders along the way and with your staff all the time, write at every chance, think if possible, read mail and newspapers, talk on the telephone, talk to everybody, dictate, receive delegations, eat, with decorum—and discretion!—and ride through city after city on the back of an open car, smiling until your mouth is dehydrated by the wind, waving until the blood runs out of your arm, and then bounce gaily, confidently, masterfully into great howling halls, shaved and all made up for television with the right color shirt and tie—I always forgot—and a manuscript so defaced with chicken tracks and last-minute jottings that you couldn't follow it, even if the spotlights weren't blinding and even if the still photographers didn't shoot you in the eye every time you looked at them. (I've often wondered what happened to all those pictures!) Then all you have to do is make a great, imperishable speech, get out through the pressing crowds with a few score autographs, your clothes intact, your hands bruised, and back to the hotel—in time to see a few important people.
>
> But the real work has just commenced—two or three, sometimes four hours of frenzied writing and editing of the next day's immortal mouthings so you can get something to the stenographers, so they can get something to the mimeograph machines, so they can get something to the reporters, so they can get something to their papers by deadline time. (And I quickly concluded that all deadlines were yesterday!) Finally sleep, sweet sleep, steals you away, unless you worry—which I do. . . .[19]

Senator Lloyd Bentsen, left, and Senator Dan Quayle shake hands after a 1988 vice presidential debate. (*AP Laser Photo/Ron Edmonds*)

Bush supporters in Colorado. (*Curtis Cook*)

[18] On the key factor of personality in presidential campaigning, see Richard W. Boyd, "Presidential Elections: An Explanation of Voting Defection," *American Political Science Review* (June 1969), pp. 498–514. See also Herbert Asher, *Presidential Elections and American Politics*, rev. ed. (Dorsey Press, 1980), especially pp. 235–37.

[19] Adlai E. Stevenson, *Major Campaign Speeches, 1952* (Random House, 1953), pp. xi–xii. Copyright 1953 by Random House, Inc.

Presidential debates   In recent years presidential debates have enlivened—or at least focused—the campaigns. In 1960 John Kennedy and Richard Nixon challenged each other to a series of debates. Kennedy's apparent "victory" in the first debate greatly boosted his campaign. In the following elections incumbent Presidents Johnson and Nixon did not deign to give their opponents equal billing in debates, but in 1976 President Ford had the courage to do so. A new feature in the 1976 campaign was a debate between the vice-presidential candidates. Again, both showed their debating skill, but—according to many observers—Walter Mondale gained some votes for his national ticket.[20] The Bush-Dukakis debates in October 1988 stirred interest yet left most viewers lukewarm toward the candidates. Dukakis scored quite well on content but fared less well on warmth and likeability. Lloyd Bentsen out-debated Dan Quayle in the vice-presidential debates, but voters were mainly concerned with their presidential choice, and Dukakis apparently failed to win over most viewers.

Other campaign considerations   Even more enlivening are the inevitable mistakes that occur in presidential campaigns. In speaking for the "absolute and total separation of church and state," Jimmy Carter warned in a *Playboy* interview against the sin of pride. To illustrate his point, he went on: "I've looked on a lot of women with lust. I've committed adultery in my heart many times." This comment became a "nine-days' wonder" at the height of the campaign. President Ford matched this blunder by stating, in defending his record of negotiating with Russia over Eastern Europe, that each of these countries "is independent, autonomous, it has its own territorial integrity, and none was under Soviet domination." The Democrats exploited this for a full week.[21] Such blunders probably have only a little effect on the final vote. The major influences on election outcome are party affiliation, interest-group membership, attitudes on issues, the candidates' personalities, and the nominees' exploitation of these various factors.

One standard feature of presidential campaigns almost disappeared in 1976: the desperate search for money. President Harry Truman ran so short in 1948 that he had to raise funds from day to day to keep his campaign train moving. Presidential candidates have found the task of raising money a demeaning business, and an ever-present worry that donors are trying to buy special influence, or at least access. In 1976, for the first time, government funding was available for the fall campaign. Since 1976 the major party presidential candidates have each received a flat grant of about $30 million (that amount will increase with inflation every four years). By accepting these funds, the candidates become ineligible to receive private donations, although groups sympathetic but independent of these candidates are allowed to raise and spend funds to help elect them. For election expenses each major party is allowed to raise about $3 million more from private donations. Aside from the federal grants to the parties for their conventions, the big subsidies go directly to the candidates' campaigns.

George Bush (top) and Michael Dukakis (bottom) presented their views to the electorate in a 1988 debate. (*AP/Wide World Photos*)

The electoral college system: Mechanics   To win the presidency, candidates must put together a combination of electoral votes that will give them a majority in the **electoral college**. This unique institution never meets and serves only a limited electoral function. Yet it has an importance of its own. The framers of the Constitution devised the electoral college system because they wanted the president chosen by electors exercising independent judgment. Subsequent political

[20] See generally Austin Ranney, ed., *The Past and Future of Presidential Debates* (American Enterprise Institute for Public Policy, 1979). See also Joel L. Swerdlow, *Beyond Debate: A Paper on Televised Presidential Debates* (A Twentieth Century Fund Paper, 1984).

[21] Gerald Pomper et al., *The Election of 1976* (David McKay, 1977), deals with this and other aspects of the Carter-Ford contest that have implications for the future. See also Jules Witcover, *Marathon, 1972–1976* (Viking, 1977).

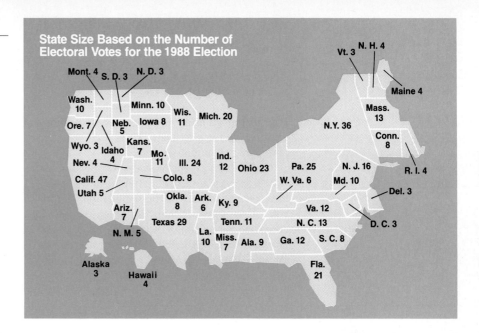

State Size Based on the Number of Electoral Votes for the 1988 Election

1988 Democratic presidential candidate Michael Dukakis and his vice-presidential running mate, Lloyd Bentsen. (*Daemmrich/Uniphoto*)

changes have transformed the electors into straight party representatives who simply register the voters' decision.

In making a presidential choice on election day, the voter technically does not vote directly for a candidate but chooses between slates of presidential electors. Each slate is made up of persons selected by the state party (in most states in party conventions) to serve in this essentially honorary role. The slate that wins the most popular votes throughout the state gets to cast all the electoral votes for the state (a state has one electoral vote for every senator and representative).

The electors on the winning slate travel to their state capital the first Monday after the second Wednesday in December; go through the ceremony of casting their ballots for their party's candidates; perhaps hear some speeches; and go home. The ballots are sent from the state capitals to Washington, where they are formally counted by the House and Senate early in January. The name of the next president is then announced.

The House must also act when no presidential candidate secures a majority of the electoral votes. This is not likely as long as there are only two serious contending parties. Nevertheless, it has happened twice in the case of president and once in the case of vice-president. When this situation occurs, the House chooses the president from among the top three candidates. Each *state delegation has one vote*, and a majority is necessary for election. (A tied delegation has no vote.) If no person receives a majority of the electoral vote in the vice-presidential contest, the Senate picks from between the top two candidates. Each senator has one vote, and again a majority is required.

The electoral college system: Politics   The operation of the electoral college, with its statewide electoral slates, sharply influences the presidency and presidential politics. In order to win a presidential election, a candidate must appeal successfully to urban and suburban groups in such states as New York, California, Pennsylvania, and Illinois. Under the electoral college system, as we have seen, a candidate wins either *all* a state's electoral votes or *none*. So presidential candidates ordinarily do not waste time campaigning in states unless they have at least a fighting chance of carrying those states; nor do they waste time in states in which their parties are sure winners. The fight usually narrows down to the medium-sized and big states where the balance between the parties tends to be fairly even.

Both the mechanics and politics of the electoral college can be unpredictable.

In 1976 an elector in the state of Washington chosen on the Republican ticket refused to cast his vote for Ford and gave it to Ronald Reagan. Such departures from custom are rare and have never affected the outcome of an election. But many people agree it is dangerous to have a system that allows individual electors to vote for whomever they wish despite the results of the popular vote in their state. Although under the present system some states attempt by law to bind electors to vote for the presidential and vice-presidential candidates of their party, these laws may not be enforceable.

All states except Maine now provide for the selection of electors on a general, statewide, winner-take-all, straight-ticket basis. This makes it possible for a person to receive a majority of the national popular vote but not a majority of the electoral vote. This happened in 1824, when Andrew Jackson won 12 percent more of the vote than John Quincy Adams; in 1876, when Samuel Tilden received more popular votes than Rutherford Hayes; and again in 1888, when, despite his large popular vote, Grover Cleveland got fewer electoral votes than Benjamin Harrison.

CAMPAIGN MONEY

Big, long campaigns—especially presidential campaigns—require big money. Compare elections in the United States to those in Great Britain, where each candidate for Parliament in the 1983 general election—including the prime minister—was limited to spending $6633.72 in a three-week campaign.[22] (They did, however, get free TV time.) **Watergate**, the resignations of President Nixon and Vice-President Agnew, "laundering" of money through secret bank accounts outside the country, heavy presidential primary spending in 1980—these and much else have fueled American worries over the use of money in campaigns to buy influence in politics and government. But the world of political money still remains shadowy. How much does campaigning cost? Should it cost that much? Who gives the money? Why? Where does it go? Is campaign money a serious problem? If so, what has been done about it? What can be done about it?

Presidential campaigns are expensive, and the cost is going up. In the last two decades the costs of primary and general elections have grown enormously, although there are limits to what presidential aspirants may spend. No such limits exist, however, for independent expenditures—and foundations, PACs, and other privately run organizations have exploited these loopholes. Big-time Senate campaigns can cost a lot, too, as we have already seen. In the decade of 1976 to 1986, costs for all national campaigns have gone from $175 million to more than $500 million.

These are big sums, but they must be put into perspective. The $500 million spent on national races is but a fraction of a percent of the total cost of government. One Trident submarine, for example, costs hundreds of millions of dollars. Consider, too, the money spent on commercial advertising: One big soap company will budget in 1988 almost as much as the cost of all campaigning for that presidential year. Political expenditure per voter in the United States is also lower than political spending in other countries. Americans spent $1.12 per capita in a recent year, much less than that spent in most countries. In Israel, for contrast, the cost per voter was $21.

People give political money for many reasons. Most givers want something specific. Business, labor, and other groups want certain laws passed or repealed,

**Typical Congressional
Campaign Budget**

Entertainment	$ 7,500
Travel	12,000
Hotels	1,500
Hq. equipment, furniture	10,000
Rent	13,000
Media consultant	35,000
Printing	46,000
Research	1,500
Television and radio advertising	180,000
Stamps	6,000
Telephone charges	14,000
Tickets for dinners, etc.	3,000
Staff payroll	80,000
Direct-mail campaign	55,000
Polls	17,000
Voter surveys	20,000
Mail and vote list computerization	12,000
Videotape machines	2,000

[22] R. W. Apple, Jr., "Campaigning in Britain: No Frills and No Glamour, Just $6,633.72," *The New York Times* (June 4, 1983), p. 3.

"MY NAME IS JOE CANDIDATE. MY OPPONENT IS A CROOK AND A SLEAZEBAG AND WOULD SELL YOUR DAUGHTERS INTO PROSTITUTION. THANK YOU." "PAID FOR BY THE JOE CANDIDATE COMMITTEE FOR CLEAN POLITICS."

(From HERBLOCK AT LARGE, Pantheon Books, 1987)

certain funds appropriated, or certain administrative decisions rendered. Those holding government jobs want to stay in office (and in certain cities pay the party an assessment to do so). Occasional big donors want ambassadorships or other important posts. Some want recognition—an invitation to a White House dinner, a low license plate number, an honorific appointment. Many simply want *access* to office holders. They neither expect nor get specific governmental rewards for their "cash on the barrelhead"; what they *do* expect, and usually get, is the opportunity to see the office holder after the election and to present their cases. Many givers are moved by higher motives. They believe their candidates or parties will govern best for them and their country. Their motives might range from the vaguest idealism to the most hardheaded calculation.[23]

Is giving worthwhile? Is there a payoff? This question is unanswerable because the relation between giving money and getting an act passed, for example, is extremely obscure. Too many other factors are involved (including the giving of money by people on the other side of an issue). Perhaps it is enough to say that most politicians and most donors *think* that giving money brings results.

Regulating Campaign Money

For many years the national and state governments have been trying to "sanitize" campaign finance, with mixed results. Reformers have tried three basic strategies to prevent abuse: imposing *limitations* on the giving, receiving, and spending of political money; requiring *disclosure* of the sources and uses of political money; and giving governmental *subsidies* for campaigns, including incentive arrangements. Recent campaign finance laws have tended to use all three in attempts to deal with a problem that sometimes seems insoluble.

Limiting campaign spending is one of the older methods. Under the 1925 Corrupt Practices Act, a candidate for the United States House of Representatives could not spend more than certain set sums. The act was utterly unrealistic and easily evaded. Reporting was inadequate; often reports were filed after the election was over. Policing was almost nonexistent. And much of the corrupt practices legislation did not even cover primary elections. The 1925 act was "more loophole than law."

In 1971 Congress decided to emphasize disclosure. All political committees that anticipated receiving or spending more than $1000 on behalf of federal candidates in any year were required to register with the government; periodic reports had to be filed including full data on all major contributions and expenditures; and one person was not allowed to contribute in the name of another person. The amounts candidates for federal office could spend on campaign advertising were also limited. The main thrust of the act was to throw the "pitiless light" of full publicity onto the sources and uses of political money. Its impact was limited.

In another act in 1971 Congress turned to a different strategy: subsidy tax incentives. The purpose was to draw into politics more money with no strings attached. The law provided that political donors might claim tax credit against their federal income taxes for part of their contributions. This 1971 law also provided a tax checkoff that allowed taxpayers to direct $1 of general revenue to a fund to subsidize presidential campaigns.

Watergate gave a sharp push to further regulation of political money. Late in 1974, after prolonged debate, Congress passed and President Ford signed the most sweeping campaign reform measure in American history. The new act established more realistic limits on contributions and spending. For example, there would

---

[23] Clifford W. Brown, Jr., Roman B. Hedges, and Lynda W. Powell, "Modes of Elite Political Participation: Contributors to the 1972 Presidential Candidates," *American Journal of Political Science* (May 1980), pp. 259–90.

be a spending limit of $30 million for each presidential candidate in the general election. The act tightened disclosure, reporting, and accountability. But what made the new measure a breakthrough was a new set of provisions for public financing of presidential campaigns. Under the 1974 law:

□ The Federal Election Commission appointed by the president with the consent of the Senate regulates the campaign financing of candidates for president, senator, and representative.

□ All candidates must report contributions and expenditures. Originally personal spending of congressional candidates was also limited, but a Supreme Court decision overturned that restriction.[24]

□ Presidential candidates who wish to receive federal subsidies (most of which come out of the tax checkoff) are limited as to what they may spend. They are not required to accept federal subsidies, *but if they do*: In the preconvention stage they may spend about $15 million, half of which may be federal matching funds; as party nominees they may spend $40 million in the general election campaign, all of it provided by the federal treasury.

□ A national political party may receive a subsidy federal of $6 million for its national convention expenses.

□ Each party may spend about $7 million in presidential and congressional elections, without federal subsidies.

□ Any minor party that polled 5 percent of the total vote in the previous presidential election is also eligible for subsidy, which it can receive after the current election if it polls at least 5 percent.

□ Individuals and organizations can spend as much as they choose on independent activities—that is, activities not coordinated with a candidate's campaign.

□ A person can give up to $1000 to a candidate in each primary and general election and no more than a total of $25,000 in all federal campaigns. Organizations can give up to $5000 per candidate per election.[25]

The Impact of Campaign Finance Laws

How has all this supervising, regulating, and subsidizing worked out? The 1974 law had a marked impact on all subsequent elections. For the first time in American history, over half the costs of a presidential campaign were covered by public subsidy. The amount of private money invested in the national election dropped from $127 million in 1972 to less than half of that.[26] A number of presidential campaign committees, including that of Jimmy Carter, were fined by the Federal Election Commission for various violations. Carter's committee was fined $11,200 for use in campaign trips of a plane owned and operated by a Georgia bank. Reports on the 1984 presidential campaign, however, indicate that campaign spending has soared, especially through the independent expenditure loophole.[27]

Campaign finance legislation has been defended as having largely met the original goals of broadening the base of public support, reducing dependence on large donors, curtailing contributions, and equalizing the financial support of the Democratic and Republican parties. It has reduced the role of large contributors and boosted the role of small ones. Through stringent reporting requirements it

YOU DECIDE

As a member of Congress who almost lost out to a heavily PAC-financed candidate in the last election, you are urged by constituents to take a bold and simple step: Vote to abolish all PACs. A bill is introduced that would simply abolish all such committees on the grounds that through financial contributions to candidates they are gaining excessive influence over politics and policy. How do you vote?

(Answer/Discussion on p. 272.)

---

[24] *Buckley* v. *Valeo*, 424 U.S. 1 (1976).

[25] For an extensive discussion of recent legislation, see Herbert E. Alexander, *Financing Politics: Money, Elections and Political Reform*, 2nd ed. (Congressional Quarterly Press, 1980).

[26] Report of the Federal Election Commission, June 4, 1977, *The New York Times* (June 5, 1977), p. 25.

[27] Campaign Finance Study Group, *Financing Presidential Campaigns*.

(*Cartoon by Herblock*, © 1988. *The Washington Post*)

has brought the whole world of political money out of the shadows and into the light of public scrutiny and debate.

The legislation has, however, been soundly criticized as well. Some say it plays into the hands of rich candidates—such as Kennedy and Bush. These critics say big money makes a big difference, and wealthy candidates can afford to spend the amounts of money required to get a decisive head start especially in the period before the primaries. Further, the act does little to curb the growing power and heavy spending of PACs (see Chapter 7). Independent expenditures by groups or individuals do not face the same limits as do expenditures by candidates and their organizations, and this loophole has been legitimated by the Supreme Court on free speech grounds. Some also criticize the law for giving vast sums to candidates and relatively little—mainly for convention costs—to the national parties. Helping candidates at the expense of parties, it is said, intensifies the growing trend toward more personalistic, fragmented, and individualistic politics. Some would favor greater subsidies to parties, until they can get on their feet and be self-supporting.

The severest criticism comes from those who support independent candidates, such as John B. Anderson in the 1980 presidential election. It is bad enough, they say, that some states make it difficult for candidates to get on the ballot. It is even worse, though, because independent candidates often receive only a fraction of the subsidy that major party candidates receive. Another major criticism is that the independent-expenditures loophole provides a channel for increasingly large contributions and expenditures for which there is no accountability.[28] Also, many contend that the 1974 legislation has prompted a shift of private money from presidential to congressional races, which in turn encourages big spending on a local level.

Many Democrats, Republicans, and independents also agree on a gaping hole in the subsidy law—its inapplicability to congressional campaigns. Money is considered a serious problem in the legislative branch, especially as the number of PACs and the amount of their contributions have skyrocketed. Although President Carter urged Congress to extend public financing to campaigns for the House and Senate, Congress has refused to "subsidize" itself. The result is that wealthier Senate and House candidates have a big advantage over poorer ones.

There is skepticism that Congress will ever reform itself in this area. Members would fear that subsidies might encourage opponents to run against them, and equalize the battle of the "outs" versus the "ins." On the other hand, opposition might be discouraged because potential rivals might not accept subsidies if they also had to accept ceilings on their campaign spending—which they would have to do if they accepted public money. Some supporters of public funding of congressional races have urged that, if such a law is passed, government money be channeled to candidates through party organizations—not directly—in order to strengthen the role of the party. But most members of Congress operate quite independently of parties and would be little tempted by this proposal.

There is little doubt that PACs will continue to be the key financial contributors to congressional campaigns—and that they will continue to be controversial. In a "Declaration of War" on PACs, Common Cause declared that "unless we change our system for financing Congressional campaigns and change it soon, our representative system of government will be gone. We will be left with a government of, by and for the PACs." Common Cause would like to see rigid limits on PAC contributions. In response, the Mobil Corporation ran magazine ads that called PACs "truly the voice of the people—people who band together to make their electoral choices more emphatic by pooling their funds in support of one or more

[28] Xandra Kayden, "Independent Spending," in *Financing Presidential Campaigns*, pp. 7–31.

candidates." The alternative, Mobil said, might be public campaign financing, causing inequities and taxing voters without giving them the chance to name the candidate for whom their dollars were intended.[29]

IS THIS THE WAY TO PICK PRESIDENTS?

Concern over how we choose presidents now centers on two main issues: the rise in the number and power of presidential primaries, which now dominate the whole presidential selection process, and the continued threat that a presidential election might be thrown into Congress, with possibly dire results. Although the American people have "lucked out" in the electoral college gamble in recent years, the threat remains.[30]

Presidential Primaries: Pros and Cons

The main argument for presidential primaries is that they open up the nominating process to a larger number of voters than was previously the case. Today the media play up the primary in every important state, and voters follow the race in other states as well as their own. In doing so they can judge the candidates' political qualities—their abilities to organize campaigns, to communicate through the media, to stand up under pressure, to avoid making mistakes (or to recover if they do make them), to adjust their appeals to shifting events and to different regions of the country, to control their staffs as well as to utilize them, to be decisive, articulate, resilient, informed, and ultimately successful in winning votes. In short, the primaries, it is said, test candidates on the very qualities they must exhibit in the presidency.[31]

Presidential primaries, it is argued, are also open in another way: They are open to candidates who are rich or poor, from big states or small, from North or South. A candidate from a small state, such as George McGovern of South Dakota, or a candidate from a southern state, such as Jimmy Carter of Georgia, now has a reasonable chance to win the big prize. Candidates with little money—and with few moneyed friends—can now run with some hope of success, in part because they can pick a limited number of states in which to "show their stuff," and in part because of federal campaign subsidies.

Finally, it is said, the primaries are not only the most participatory but also the most *representative* methods for choosing our presidents. With millions of voters participating in over thirty state primaries,[32] the public gets a good picture of the popular support for each candidate. As the primaries take place, some aspirants drop out. The number of entrants is thus narrowed down, and the public learns who are the most popular remaining candidates—for example Republicans Ronald Reagan and George Bush and Democrats Jimmy Carter and Michael Dukakis. The primary results are then converted into delegate votes at the presidential conventions, which in turn become more representative of party rank-and-file feeling than before.

Critics of primaries rebut these arguments and add some criticisms of their own. They grant that more voters take part in primaries than in the caucus and

[29] See Herbert E. Alexander, "Public Financing of Congressional Campaigns," *Regulation* (January–February 1980), pp. 27–32. See, in general, Gary C. Jacobson, *Money in Congressional Elections* (Yale University Press, 1980). On the PAC controversy see *Campaign Practices Reports* (February 28, 1983), pp. 5–6, and an advertisement by Mobil, "PACs—Consider the Alternatives," *Time* (May 9, 1983), p. 4.

[30] Edward N. Kearney, "Presidential Nominations and Representative Democracy: Proposals for Change," *Presidential Studies Quarterly* (Summer 1984).

[31] Barbara Norrander and Gregg W. Smith, "Type of Contest, Candidate Strategy, and Turnout in Presidential Primaries," *American Politics Quarterly* (January 1985), p. 28.

[32] Estimate of Austin Ranney. *The New York Times* (June 8, 1980), section E, p. 5.

committee methods of choosing delegates, but they question the *quality* of the participation. For one thing, there is no chance for supporters of the different candidates to deliberate together in public. Voters in primaries, therefore, must depend largely on the news media and advertising for their information and basis for judgment. Voters in presidential primaries tend to be more interested in or influenced by candidates' personalities and media skills than in their positions on vital issues.[33]

Second, the primaries are badly scheduled and last too long.[34] The first primary takes place in New Hampshire, a small, untypical state. Most of the southern states held their primaries on the same day, March 8, 1988, a Super Tuesday for presidential aspirants that year. Primaries in some of the larger states, such as Pennsylvania, are held later in the spring. In 1984 California, New Jersey, and five other states did not hold their primaries until June 5—when the contests in both parties had been virtually decided, most of the people had become somewhat bored with the process, and the voters of those seven states felt rather miffed that the fight was over before they were able to participate. The length of the primary campaign exhausts the candidates and tries the patience of the voters. Victory may go to the candidates with the stronger physiques rather than the stronger brains.[35]

The main criticism directed against primaries is that they test candidates for their ability to compete in the media "game" rather than for the qualities needed in the presidency. Players in this "game" must demonstrate flexibility, resourcefulness, attractiveness, and articulateness; are these the key qualities required of a *president?* Thomas Jefferson, Abraham Lincoln, and Harry Truman were great presidents, critics say, but they would never have gained or retained their posts if they had had to pass the test of "media appeal." Critics point to Jimmy Carter as a candidate who was generally effective with the media but less so in governing the country. This gap between the qualities required to carry primary contests and the qualities needed to organize an administration, get support on issues, and deal with congressional leaders, governors, and mayors worries critics of the primary system.

Proposed Reforms

What would the critics substitute for state presidential primaries? Some argue in favor of a *national presidential primary*. This would take the form of a single nationwide election, probably held in May or September, or of separate state primaries held in all the states on the same day. Supporters contend that a one-shot national presidential primary (though a runoff might be necessary) would be simple, direct, and representative; would cut down the wear and tear on candidates; and would attract a large turnout because of intensive media coverage. Opponents argue that this "reform" would make the present system even worse, would enhance the role of media showmanship and candidate gamesmanship, and would be enormously expensive and hence hurt the chances of candidates lacking strong financial backing.[36]

A more modest proposal—tried by the Democrats in 1988—is to hold *regional primaries*, possibly at two- or three-week intervals across the country. At present, however, only the South has committed itself to such an idea. Regional primaries

(From private collection of Bruce Adams/Photo by Eugene Gordon)

[33] See John G. Geer, "Voting in Presidential Primaries." Paper prepared for delivery at the annual meeting of the American Political Science Association, Washington, D.C., September 1984. See also Thomas R. Marshall, "Evaluating Presidential Nominees: Opinion Polls, Issues and Personalities," *Western Political Quarterly* (December 1983), p. 650.

[34] George S. McGovern, "Considerations on our Political Processes," *Presidential Studies Quarterly* (September 1983).

[35] American Enterprise Institute Memorandum (Spring 1986), p. 10.

[36] Compare "A National Agenda for the Eighties," *Report of the President's Commission for National Agenda for the Eighties* (Washington, D.C.: U.S. Government Printing Office, 1980), p. 97, which proposes holding only four presidential primaries, scheduled about one month apart.

might bring more coherence to the process, encourage more emphasis on issues of regional concern, and cut down a bit on wear and tear. But they would retain most of the disadvantages of the present system—especially the emphasis on money and media. And they might encourage regional candidates and polarization among sections of the country.

A quite different proposal is to cut down drastically on the number of state presidential primaries and to make more use of the *caucus* system. The huge turnout of voters in the Iowa caucuses of 1984, it is said, demonstrates that participation can be high; the fact that participants had to spend some hours discussing candidates and issues proves that such participation can be thoughtful and informed. In caucus states candidates are less dependent on the media and more dependent on their abilities to reach political activists. By centering delegate selection in *party* meetings, the caucus system would also enhance the role of the party.[37]

Still another idea, used by Colorado to make *state* nominations since 1910, would turn the process around so that beginning in May, local caucuses and then state conventions would precede a national convention in July, which would precede a national primary in September, which would choose the party nominee to run in the November general election. In this *Colorado plan* or *national preprimary convention plan*, all over the country participants in local party caucuses scheduled in early May would choose delegates to state conventions, which in turn would choose delegates to a national convention in which 25 percent of all delegates would be required to be unpledged. Deliberations at the national convention would result in the selection of two or three candidates who would appear on a September primary ballot. Voters registered by party would be allowed to vote in their respective party primaries, and the winners of the primaries would be the parties' candidates in the November general election.

Reforming the Electoral College

Americans have long been concerned about the nature and workings of the electoral college. Critics argue that (1) small states and large "swing" states are overrepresented; (2) the winner-take-all aspect distorts equal representation of all voters and can elect a candidate who receives fewer popular votes than an opponent; (3) electors can (and do) vote for a person other than the candidate for whom they were pledged to vote; (4) if no candidate wins a majority, the issue is thrown into the House of Representatives, where each state delegation, no matter how large or small, has one vote, which thus distorts the representative process even more. The electoral college has been compared to the human appendix: useless, unpredictable, and possibly dangerous.

Defenders of the system say opponents exaggerate the possible dangers; the system has not broken down so far, and probably never will. And if the electoral college is antipopular or antimajoritarian—so what? "The electoral college promotes unity and legitimacy by helping to generate majorities that are not narrow, geographically or ideologically, and by magnifying (as in 1960, 1968, 1976) narrow margins of victories in the popular vote," says George F. Will.[38]

The simplest and least drastic reform would be to abolish the individual electors but retain the winner-take-all method of counting the electoral vote. This proposal has never gotten far, mainly because it does not deal with the main issue of "misrepresentation." Another reform proposal is the proportional plan, under which each candidate would receive the same proportion of the electoral vote of a state as he or she had won of its popular vote; actual electors would be abolished. Thus, a candidate who got one-third of the popular vote in a state having twelve electoral votes

Who Voted For Bush? (Figures are Percent Republican Vote)	
Men	57%
Women	50
Whites	59%
Blacks	12
Hispanics	30
Liberals	18%
Moderates	49
Conservatives	80
East	50%
Midwest	52
South	58
West	52
Family Income	
Under $12,500	37%
$12,500–$24,999	49
$25,000–$34,999	56
$35,000–$49,999	56
$50,000 and over	62

Source: The *New York Times*–CBS News Exit Poll; N = 11,645 voters.

[37] Nelson W. Polsby, *Consequences of Party Reform* (Oxford University Press, 1983), p. 118.

[38] George F. Will, "Don't Fool with the Electoral College," *Newsweek* (April 4, 1977), p. 96.

would win four electoral votes. Liberal Democrats fear this proposal would increase the influence of rural, small-town conservatives. Because the present system forces presidential candidates to fight especially hard for the big, urban states, many liberals feel the president must be especially responsive to the needs and hopes of working-class, black, ethnic, and lower-income groups who make up the urban electorate.

The most controversial reform proposed is *direct popular election of the president*. Presidents would be elected directly by the voters just as governors are; the electoral college and individual electors would be abolished. This kind of plan usually provides that if no candidate receives at least 40 percent of the total popular vote, a **runoff election** be held between the two contenders with the most votes. Supporters argue that this plan would give every voter the same weight in the presidential balloting, in accordance with the one person, one vote doctrine. Winners would take on more credibility or "legitimacy" because of their clear-cut popular victories. And, of course, the dangers and complications of the present electoral system would be replaced by a simple, visible, and decisive method. Opponents argue that the plan would require a national election system, which would further undermine federalism; that it would encourage naked, unrestrained majority rule and hence political extremism; and that it would submerge the smaller states, who would lose some of their present influence. Some also fear that the plan would make presidential campaigns more remote from the voters; candidates might stress television and give up their present forays into shopping centers and city malls.[39]

From time to time Congress considers proposals for an amendment to elect presidents directly. Such proposals, however, seldom get very far because of the strong opposition of various interests who believe they may be disadvantaged by such a change—for example, such "minorities" as blacks and farmers who fear they might lose their "swing" vote power.

An ingenious proposal for a "national bonus plan" has been worked out by a group of scholars and politicians. Under this plan the electoral college would be retained, but it would be heavily weighted toward the winner of the popular vote. The plan would work like this: A pool of 102 electoral votes (two for each state and the District of Columbia) would automatically be granted to the candidate who gained the most popular votes. These bonus votes would be added to that candidate's electoral college vote gained in the election. He or she would be elected if these totaled a majority in the electoral college. If not, a runoff would be held between the two candidates' winning the most popular votes. The position of elector would be eliminated. Proponents contend the plan would ensure that the popular vote winner would also be the electoral vote winner; reduce the chances of deadlock in the electoral college; encourage two-party competition in one-party states; and do away with the elector who votes against the decision in his or her state. Opponents say minor parties and independent candidates would be discouraged by such a system. This and similar plans have not garnered much public support. Only a major electoral college crisis will bring about any significant reform.

INTERPRETING THE 1988 ELECTIONS

George Bush handily won the 1988 elections, winning comfortably by a 54 percent to 46 percent margin in the popular vote and by an even more impressive 426 to 112 margin in the electoral college. His victory was the fifth for Republicans in six

[39] Neal R. Peirce and Lawrence Longley, *The People's President*, 2nd ed. (Yale University Press, 1981), describes and advocates the direct-vote alternative. Nelson W. Polsby and Aaron B. Wildavsky, *Presidential Elections*, 6th ed. (Scribners, 1984), essentially favors the present system. Lawrence D. Longley and Alan G. Braun, *The Politics of Electoral College Reform* (Yale University Press, 1972), is a comprehensive treatment.

presidential races. It was also the first time Republicans have won three elections in a row since 1928. Yet Bush failed to bring along with him a Democratic Congress. In fact, Democrats picked up several seats in the U.S. Congress and also gained another governorship, making the margin of state chief executives 28 Democrats to 22 Republicans. As the Bush presidency began, it faced a Congress with its two houses both solidly controlled by the opposition party.

Key factors in the 1988 elections   How did the Bush Republicans win the 1988 elections and what did it mean? What kind of "mandate" if any arose out of the Bush victory? And what are the key questions raised by the 1988 national elections?

More than anything else, Bush benefited from the presumed good economic conditions in 1988. Most voters most of the time are influenced in how they vote by how they think the economy is doing. In 1988 voters believed that the Reagan-Bush policies deserved credit for relatively low unemployment and good economic times in general. Many people were doubtless apprehensive about the growing national debt and budget deficits and the loss of trade to other nations, yet on balance they thought that the economy had improved during the 1980s. Bush campaigned on the theme of continuing Reagan's policies and improving the economic opportunity for Americans. He also kept saying he would not raise taxes. His opponent, Governor Michael Dukakis of Massachusetts, pointed to those areas in the country where the economy was not booming and also focused attention on the millions of Americans who were struggling to make ends meet. But he was generally unable to persuade the vast bulk of those in the middle and upper classes that Bush should be faulted for deficits or any unevenness in the performance of the American economy. Thus prosperity, at least for most of those who vote, was a decisive factor in Bush's victory.

A second key factor was peace. Not only was America at peace, but the Reagan administration had recently successfully negotiated a widely acclaimed arms reduction treaty with the Soviet Union. Reagan, moreover, had held several summits with the Soviet leader Gorbachev. The Soviets were, at election time, withdrawing troops from Afghanistan. Iran and Iraq were ending their war, and concerns about war in the Persian Gulf were easing. Chad, Angola, and other nations were ending small wars in their respective regions of Africa. On balance, the Reagan-Bush foreign policy record appeared positive, especially since both Reagan and Bush were deemphasizing their previously unpopular positions about military aid for the contras in Nicaragua.

And if "prosperity and peace" were not enough, Bush also gained strength because of his ties and "understudy" association with the then popular President Ronald Reagan. Reagan had lost popularity in 1987 when his Iran-contra scandal had been exposed and investigated. But by late 1988 his popularity was back to nearly 60 percent. That is, almost 60 percent of Americans approved of the way he was handling the job of being president. Reagan campaigned actively for Bush and in the last weeks of the campaign made several important campaign trips to close states such as California, Illinois, Ohio, and Texas.

A fourth factor that contributed to Bush's success in 1988 was his, and his campaign's, ability to portray Michael Dukakis as an out-of-the-mainstream liberal. Polls consistently showed in 1988 that there were only 17 percent or 18 percent of the electorate who considered themselves as liberals whereas about twice as many people, thirty-four percent, considered themselves to be conservatives. The others, perhaps about 49 percent, called themselves moderates. It was therefore an effective strategy to paint Dukakis as a liberal, which in many respects he is and was. Bush staffers created several hard-hitting negative ads—some were even sleazy—all with the intent of raising questions about Dukakis's competence and leadership ability. Initially, Dukakis ignored the charges. He was not, he said, "a label." He preferred

Democratic presidential nominee Michael Dukakis campaigning in New York. (*David Burnett/Contact Press Images*)

President George Bush and wife Barbara admiring a Super Tuesday shirt during his successful 1988 presidental campaign. (*David Valdez/ The White House*)

Cuomo and Dole compare notes on 1988 campaign. (*UPI/Bettmann Newsphotos*)

to talk about issues and what he would do when he became president. Yet the ads worked. Increasing numbers of voters began to have doubts about Dukakis.

Bush also reminded voters of his many years of experience in top positions in the national government, Congress, diplomatic posts, the cabinet and as vice-president. His experience was an asset and he understandably and convincingly turned it to his advantage.

Meanwhile, Dukakis ran an uninspiring campaign. As one writer aptly put it, he let the charges of the Bush campaign splatter against him and stick like glue. He looked weak and, at times, foolish. After the campaign ended Dukakis acknowledged that he should have responded and responded quickly to the often unfair negative attacks made against his crime and environmental records and his patriotism. He and his aides also admitted that he was often too wooden and mechanical. *Time* magazine accused him at one point of running for accountant-in-chief instead of commander-in-chief.

Dukakis said the negative advertising against him plainly worked and that he did not respond in kind because he is basically a positive person who had tried all his life to provide positive leadership. The Dukakis campaign staff also shares in the blame for the poorly run Dukakis effort; there were considerable strife and feuding in his inner circle and this took its obvious toll on Dukakis.

Overall, however, Dukakis lost because most voters viewed Bush as more likely to continue the Reagan record of peace and prosperity. Voters also expressed concern about Dukakis's liberalism and his lack of experience at the national level. The Dukakis attempt to rally people to a "It's time for a Change" campaign theme never really worked. Liberals and Democrats stuck with him, and about half of those who had been called Reagan Democrats returned to the Democratic candidate, but upper-income groups, Southerners, white males, and white Protestants continued their drift toward the Republican Party. Eighteen percent of those who call themselves Democrats did not vote for Dukakis. Fifty-five percent of the Independents gave their vote to Bush and Quayle; only 43 percent voted for Dukakis and Bentsen.

Still it was a lukewarm victory for Bush. Large numbers of those who voted for him did so more because they disliked Dukakis than because they liked Bush. Bush voters also would have preferred Lloyd Bentsen to Dan Quayle as their vice-presidential choice. Further, many Bush supporters were critical of Bush's emphasis in the campaign on attacking Dukakis rather than emphasizing what he would do to help solve major problems such as deficits, trade imbalances, and environmental pollution. Americans nonetheless voted for Bush because a vote for Bush was a vote for the status quo, a vote for continuity.

Many observers believed that Bush's relatively content-less campaign meant that his victory, despite its impressive eight point margin, was without any clear mandate. Much would depend on his ability in his first year to speak to key issues, build alliances with the Democratic leaders in Congress, and rally the American people around a sensible policy agenda.

Congressional election results   One of Bush's difficulties was that voters all across the country exhibited a kind of split personality when they voted in the November 1988 elections. They may have voted for Bush, yet at the same time many voted to send large Democratic majorities back to Congress. Were voters saying that they want no party in total charge? Voters sent a Republican back to the White House yet at the same time made it nearly impossible for President Bush to whip Congress into line with any regularity. Perhaps the voters want neither party to exercise unbridled power in shaping national policies. They like the checks and balances built into our Constitution, yet just in case one branch should be inclined to overreach, the voters appear to have created an additional check or constraint— this one from the voting booth.

George Bush on the presidential campaign trail, 1988. (*David Valdez/ The White House*)

Still, much of the confusion over the meaning and mandates of the 1988 campaign arise because the American people were not especially excited about the appeals from either candidate or either party. Rightly or wrongly, many voters thought the best candidates were not running, and those who were running too often ducked or danced around the important issues. In the end, Bush won not so much because of who he is or what he stands for, but because of peace and prosperity, Reagan's popularity, and Dukakis's inability to attract majority support for his woefully vague vision of a better America.

Beyond the 1988 Elections: What About the 1990s?

The 1988 presidential election once again confirmed that the solid South now generally votes Republican in presidential elections and is likely to for the near future. But the 1988 elections also suggest that if the Republicans have had a lock on the electoral college, the Democrats appear to have a stronger hold on the U.S. Congress. Neither of these trends is irreversible, yet they have surely become patterns.

Republicans believe they have regularly won the White House because they, better than the Democrats, appeal to the conservative values of family, patriotism, strong defense, and a tough stance against criminals. Republicans believe the family is the foundation of our social order and that it is important that we reflect upon and consider carefully the impact of government upon family life. Bush and the Republicans strive to cut out excessive regulations and decentralize the federal government and return power and policy discretion to the state and local levels.

Critics of George Bush's campaign in 1988 agree that he appealed to "traditional" American values—but these were bigotry, envy, greed, chauvinism, and fear. They also think he was unrealistic, if not dead wrong, in saying that he would not raise taxes. Many critics say the 1988 election was one of the worst in recent memory—with too much mud-slinging on both sides and too little direct and thoughtful discussion of cutting-edge national issues. Political scientist Walter Dean Burnham of the University of Texas says that, at the very least, there ought to be a major congressional inquest about the role of negative advertising and the failure of the Federal Election Commission to do anything about it. Others say, however, that this was a perfectly acceptable election and that hard-hitting comparative advertising is now a standard feature in modern elections. Further, they add, the candidates did speak to the issues; it was the media that emphasized the occasional negative or personal attacks and blew these out of proportion.

Jesse Jackson in Iowa during the 1988 primary campaign. Jackson was a strong contender in Democratic presidential primaries. (*AP/Wide World Photos*)

Whatever the case, partisanship is likely to color many of the relations between Congress and the presidency in the next few years. A certain bitterness remains well after the 1988 elections.

The Democrats are already in prolonged debate about the future of their party and its chances to win back the White House in the 1990s. Jesse Jackson and liberal Democrats say the Democrats have failed because they have lost their soul and been unwilling to become the programmatic party that people would respect. Moderate Democrats such as Senator Sam Nunn, Senator Charles Robb, and Senator Lloyd Bentsen insist the Democrats have to move away from the issues and programs of the 1930s and 1960s and focus on the issues of the 1990s. They say, too, that Democrats have to move more to the center, noting that Lyndon Johnson and Jimmy Carter, both Southerners and moderate Democrats, have been the only Democrats to make it to the White House in the last 25 years. This Democratic debate is not new, yet it is more sharply expressed these days.

Several Democrats either have their eye on the White House or have supporters who would like them to run in 1992. Liberal Democrats, such as Jesse Jackson and New York Governor Mario Cuomo, are regularly mentioned. Senators Nunn,

A jubilant George Bush with his family, celebrating his election to the presidency. (*AP/WideWorld Photos*)

Robb, Gore, Biden, and Bradley are also prominently mentioned. Senator Lloyd Bentsen, who won such widespread bipartisan respect in his vice-presidential quest in 1988, also is mentioned although his age might be a handicap.

Republicans are expected to rally around President Bush in 1992 unless he suffers major political setbacks during the early 1990s. Still there are other Republicans, such as former Congressman Jack Kemp and Senator Robert Dole, who might reenter presidential politics if Bush falters. Television evangelist Pat Robertson would also very likely make himself available if George Bush were for some reason not to be a candidate in 1992.

Meanwhile, Republican President Bush and the Democratic Congress have to tackle the major issues of the deficit, the national debt, trade, drugs, AIDS, environmental pollution, the quality of education and basic research, and continued negotiations with the Soviets. Much depends on the willingness of both institutions and both parties to reconcile their differences and work for the broad longer-term interests of the American people. The American people want innovative leadership that will rise above partisan bickering; they want problems to be solved and the creative energies of the nation to be unlocked and empowered. Voters in 1990 and again in 1992 will judge our national leaders not on their ability to blame their opponents but on their records of performance.

SUMMARY

1. Candidates for the Senate and the House tend to campaign more on the basis of their personal organizations and access to the media than of party affiliation.

2. The race for the presidency actually consists of three campaigns: winning delegate support in presidential primaries and caucuses, gaining the actual party nomination at the presidential convention, and winning a majority of the electoral college.

3. Even though presidential nominations today are usually decided weeks or months before the conventions, these conventions still have an important role in setting the parties' direction, unifying their ranks, and adopting their platforms.

4. Because large campaign contributions are suspected of improperly influencing public officials, Congress has long sought to regulate political money. Its main approaches have been: (1) imposing limitations on receiving and spending money; (2) requiring public disclosure of the sources and uses of political money; and (3) giving government subsidies to candidates, campaigns, and parties. Present regulation includes all three approaches.

5. The electoral college lends extra influence to the small and large states. It could also throw a presidential election into the House of Representatives, where the influence of small states would be enhanced.

6. The present presidential selection system is under criticism because of its length and expense, and because it seems to test candidates for qualities that are less needed in the White House than certain others, such as the ability to form coalitions of diverse interest groups and to govern. In short, many accuse our present system of failing to recruit presidential leadership.

FURTHER READING

LARRY M. BARTELS. *Presidential Primaries and the Dynamics of Public Choice* (Princeton University Press, 1988).

GARY C. JACOBSON. *The Politics of Congressional Elections* (Little, Brown, 1983).

MALCOLM JEWELL and DAVID OLSEN. *American State Political Parties and Elections,* 3rd ed. (Dorsey Press, 1988).

JOHN KESSEL. *Presidential Parties* (Dorsey, 1984).

MICHAEL NELSON, ed. *The Elections of 1988* (Congressional Quarterly, 1989).

NEAL R. PEIRCE and LAWRENCE LONGLEY. *The People's President: The Electoral College in American History and the Direct-Vote Alternative,* 2nd ed. (Yale University Press, 1981).

KEVIN PHILLIPS. *The Post Conservative Majority* (Vintage, 1984).

NELSON POLSBY and AARON WILDAVSKY. *Presidential Elections,* 7th ed. (Free Press, 1988).

GERALD POMPER et al. *The Election of 1988* (Chatham House, 1989).

LARRY J. SABATO. *The Rise of Political Consultants* (Basic Books, 1981).

FRANK J. SORAUF. *Money in American Elections* (Scott, Foresman, 1988).

STEPHEN J. WAYNE. *The Road to the White House,* rev. ed. (St. Martin's, 1988).

13

Congress: The People's Branch?

In January, 1789 James Madison ran for a Congress that did not yet exist. The "Father of the Constitution," having led the great effort to draft a new Constitution in Philadelphia two years before, wanted to represent his section of Virginia in the new House of Representatives. It was not an easy contest for the young Virginian. For one thing, it was so cold that after one meeting, held outdoors in the snow, Madison had to ride twelve miles to find a place to stay overnight and suffered severe frostbite during the journey. For another, his opponent was James Monroe, another popular young Virginian. But his real enemy was the famous Patrick Henry, who feared that under the new Constitution the national government would have too much power. Using his influence in the Virginia legislature, Henry had rigged congressional districts in such a way that Madison was thrown into competition with Monroe.

Things went well for Madison. He and Monroe were personally friendly, and they agreed to journey from county to county in a series of friendly debates. Of course, Madison supported the new Constitution and Monroe opposed it, but Madison made clear he favored adding a bill of rights. Madison won by what his friend George Washington called a "respectable majority."[1]

Madison visited Mount Vernon, then hastened to New York, where the first Congress was due to meet March 4. Held up by snow, floods, and impassable roads, he did not arrive in Manhattan until much later in the month but no matter—the other congressmen-elect were delayed too. Nearly a month passed before both chambers in this newly fashioned **bicameral** body had enough members (a quorum) to begin business.

Madison and his fellow politicians were about to set up a brand new government in an old town. Long before, the young Virginian had become used to the sights of lower Manhattan—cows wandering up and down Broadway, hogs rooting through the garbage-clogged gutters, milkmaids carrying buckets of milk hanging from a yoke, chimney sweeps calling out "Sweep ho! Sweep ho!"—all amid a bedlam of knife grinders, ragmen, and lamp menders calling out their special cries. These

[1] George Washington to James Madison, Feb. 16, 1789, Robert A. Rutland and Charles F. Hobson, eds., *The Papers of James Madison* (University Press of Virginia, 1977), vol. 11, p. 446.

The Many Meanings of Representation

Representation is one of the more troublesome concepts in political science, and one of the most important. These definitions may be helpful:

1. Formal representation is the authority to act in another's behalf, gained through an institutional process or arrangement such as free and open elections. The *formal* arrangement of selection, not the behavior of the representative, defines representation in this usage.

2. Descriptive or demographic representation is the extent to which a representative mirrors the characteristics of the people he or she formally represents. According to this usage of the term, a representative legislature should be an exact portrait, in miniature, of the people.

3. Symbolic representation is the extent to which a legislator is accepted as believable and as "one of their own" by the folks back home. This usage has a lot to do with a legislator's style and nonverbal signals.

4. Substantive representation is a legislator's responsiveness to constituents. Do the policy and voting views of a legislator match those of constituents, or does the legislator rely primarily on his or her own judgment? This second approach is that of a guardian or trustee, as opposed to a direct delegate of the citizens.

familiar scenes contrasted markedly with the spacious remodeled room in City Hall that would house the new representatives.

At sunset on March 3, 1789, the struggling and now repudiated government created by the Articles of Confederation came to an end. Eighteen months had elapsed between the signing of the Constitution in Philadelphia and the first working day of the new Congress. Eleven states had ratified the Constitution, and the newly elected or selected members of Congress (senators were appointed by state legislatures) began straggling into New York City (population 30,000), the temporary seat of the new republic.

Problems of enormous importance awaited Congress, but this first branch of government got off to an uncertain start. It was nearly a month before each chamber had a quorum; the house managed to obtain the proper number on April 1, 1789; it took the Senate until April 6.

Soon Congress moved to select its leaders and set in motion the constitutional provisions for establishing the rest of government. As you will recall from reading the Constitution, Congress was to count the ballots of the first electoral college and arrange to swear in the first president and vice-president. Congress began this task, although a few more weeks passed before it actually inaugurated the president. Even more time and more delays followed before it enacted the enabling legislation and the judiciary came into being.

This first Congress, not unlike the 101st Congress (1989 to 1991), was made up of talented, experienced, and generally well-to-do elites. Eighteen of twenty-six senators and thirty-six of the sixty-five members of the House of Representatives had served in previous Congresses under the Articles of Confederation. Eleven senators and nine representatives had served as delegates in Philadelphia at the Constitutional Convention. Many others had served in the Revolutionary army and in their state legislatures. Still others had participated in ratifying conventions and as local jurists. Although some of them had not been ardent supporters of the Constitution, once it was adopted they were willing to try to make it work. They were especially eager to ensure that the first Congress take up the matter of a bill of rights.

Of the many policy matters that awaited them, the most pressing was the need to raise revenue to pay the country's bills. Sound familiar? This seems to be the ever-present matter before Congress. The Continental Congress had lacked the power to raise needed funds. The new Constitution changed all that. After just one week Congress was debating how best to impose import fees and tariffs, and Madison took part. In a sense, this new Congress picked up precisely where the Confederation's Congress had displayed its greatest incapacity.[2]

Two hundred years later, the 101st Congress is a much larger and different kind of institution, located in the midst of a sprawling federal government in Washington, D.C., yet most of its major functions remain the same. We still look to Congress to make the laws, raise revenues, represent the citizens, confirm top administrative and judicial appointees, investigate the abuse of power, and oversee the executive branch. Congress is still a bicameral organization and its chambers, as we shall discuss, serve to check one another as together they check the other two major branches of government.

In its first years Congress met for several months a year. Nowadays Congress regularly meets all year. Senators are directly elected by the people, and members of the House represent nearly twenty times as many constituents as they originally did. Most members engage in continual electioneering to stay in office. Relative to the 1790s, many of the members appear driven by their desire to win reelection—so much so that, much of what takes place in Congress—such as the angling over

[2] On the early history of Congress, see Alvin M. Josephy, Jr., *On the Hill: A History of the American Congress from 1789 to the Present* (Touchstone, 1980), chap. 1.

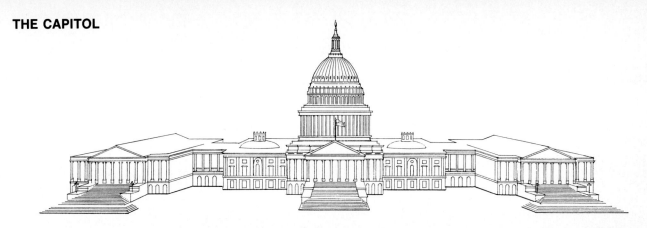

Congress is the seat of legislative authority, the center of public debate, a carry-over of folksy political traditions from earlier days—and a collection of several hundred relatively independent politicians with separate but overlapping constituencies. The architecture of the capitol bespeaks its ways: two chambers, endless corridors, ornate rotundas and galleries, and a rabbit warren of grand rooms, tiny offices, and winding passageways. There is no culminating point of authority but a multiplicity of decision centers.

what committees to serve on—seems mainly designed to promote reelection. These efforts work. Most incumbents most of the time win reelection in both chambers. But these efforts, combined with the absence of strong party discipline, have also encouraged internal fragmentation and diffusion of power. More and more of the work these days is done in committees or subcommittees. Multiple, successive decision points make it much easier to prevent than to pass legislation.

How does such a Congress make any progress? In an institution where all members act as individual entrepreneurs and consider themselves leaders, the task of providing *institutional* leadership is big. This is particularly true in the U.S. Senate, which prides itself on extended debate and deliberation. With only limited and constrained resources, and only sometimes aided by the president, congressional leaders are asked to bring together a fragmented, nonhierarchical institution. The congressional system requires majority action and acts only when majorities can be achieved. Congress functions as an effective collective body only to the extent that leadership emerges in both parties and in both houses of Congress. The framers can well be proud that their original objective of having a Congress that would not move with undue haste has been generally well, and sometimes too well, satisfied over the years.

Most Americans realize Congress is not a perfect institution, and we often characterize it as a bickering, timid, ignorant, selfish, or narrow-minded body. Yet we also often admire the stamina and civic responsibility of members of Congress whom we know. And incumbent members of Congress keep getting reelected— presumably because people like them and their work.

Members of Congress are popular, but Congress is not. This is because we expect Congress to solve most of our national ills, yet judge members of Congress primarily on how well they serve the interests of their states and districts, and on their personal appeal. Much of the criticism of Congress is unjustified. Critics usually forget that our national legislature is particularly exposed. First, Congress does nearly all its work directly in the public eye. Unfortunate incidents—quarrels, name calling, evasive actions, inaccurate statements—that might be hushed up in the executive or judicial branches are almost always observed by journalists. Second, Congress by its nature is controversial and argumentative. Its 535 members are found on both sides, sometimes on half a dozen sides, of every important question. The average citizen who holds one opinion is likely to be intolerant of other views and

HOUSE OF REPRESENTATIVES

Washington, D.C. 20515

1 Speakers' Offices
2 Committee on Ways and Means
3 Parliamentarian
4 House Floor Library
5 Cloakrooms
6 Members' Retiring Room and Lobby
7 House Chamber
8 Committee on Appropriations
9 Minority Whip

10 House Reception Room
11 House Minority Conference Room
12 House Majority Conference Room
13 House Document Room
14 Committee Meeting Room
15 Representatives' Offices
16 Prayer Room
17 Minority Leader

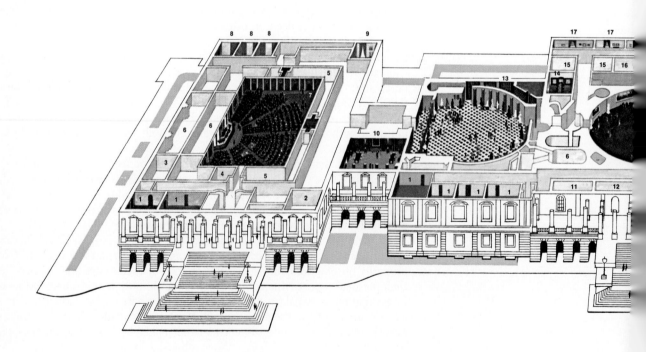

PUBLIC AREAS

18 Statuary Room
19 Rotunda
20 Senate Rotunda
21 Old Senate Chamber

SENATE

Washington, D.C. 20510

22 Senators' Offices
23 Executive Clerk
24 Senate Conference Room
25 Majority Leader
26 Majority Leader
27 Minority Leader
28 Office of the Vice-President
29 Senators' Reception Room

30 Cloakrooms
31 Senate Chamber
32 Marble Room
33 President's Room
34 Offices of the Secretaries
35 Chief Clerk
36 Bill Clerk and Journal Clerk
37 Official Reporters of Debates

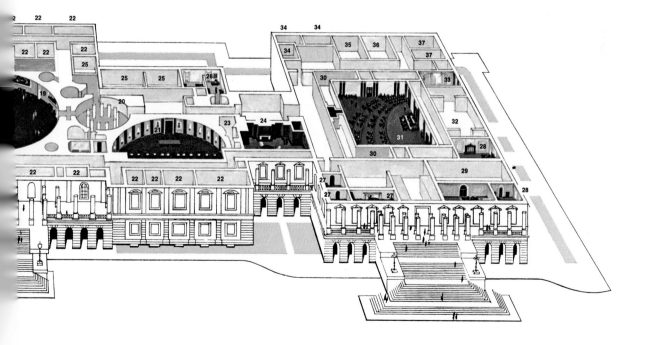

of the legislators holding them. Also, there is a considerable difference between holding an opinion and writing legislation.

The chief complaints about Congress are that it is inefficient, unrepresentative, and not accountable enough. Further, critics say it is paralyzed by personal bickering and interest-group favoritism. Some contend that many members of Congress are too beholden to special interests. Legislators are described as being obsessed with staying elected—indeed, as concentrating solely on winning reelection—often at the expense of critical national issues such as the arms race, unemployment, foreign policy, and trade. Former House Republican leader John Rhodes was especially harsh when he wrote that "the majority of congressional actions are not aimed at producing results for the American people as much as perpetuating the longevity and comfort of the men who run Congress."[3]

Some of the paralysis in Congress is caused by the proliferation of subcommittees, the overlapping jurisdictions of these committees, and the great increase of congressional staff. A complicated budget process, recently made even more complicated, has also caused problems. Better-educated and more independent-minded persons are coming to Congress, often with loose or weak ties to political parties. This has made it difficult for party leaders to build coalitions and to stick to an efficient agenda for Congress.

Many people allege that special interests and single-issue groups are stronger than ever, and that they are able to fragment and often delay or block proceedings in Congress. The current system of financing congressional elections has been called a scandal. It forces members of Congress to beg for money from Washington-based special-interest, political-action committees whose primary purpose is to seek support for their pet legislation.

Others wonder if the problems of Congress, especially encouraging cooperation between Congress and the presidency, arise because some of our constitutional arrangements are outmoded. Certain scholars and practitioners suggest, for example, that we might be better served by having four-year terms for members of the House, by having some members of Congress serve simultaneously in the president's cabinet, and by having some members of the cabinet serve in Congress. These reformers also seek means to strengthen partisan ties and cooperative efforts to better link the two chambers with the executive branch. In short, these observers say many of Congress's flaws are the result of too much reverence for the Constitution and unwillingness to consider constitutional reform.[4]

But would a Congress that "leads" more be what everyone wants? As it is, Congress sometimes acts too quickly. Interest groups don't always have enough power to block Congress. We have to ask ourselves, too, what would happen to the presidency and the courts if Congress "leads" more. Also, not everyone wants greater cooperation between president and Congress. For example, certain educators and nuclear freeze advocates wish Congress had cooperated less with Reagan in the 1980s.

Criticism of Congress—its alleged incompetence, its overresponsiveness, its inefficiencies—are not issues that can be dealt with outside the context of policy preferences and democratic procedures. Sometimes criticism tells us more about the critic than it does about the effectiveness of Congress. Democracy is not supposed to be efficient. Congress was never intended to act "swiftly"; it was not created to be a rubber stamp or even a cooperative partner for presidents. Congress is supposed to reflect geographical and special interests—to register the diverseness

[3] John Rhodes, *The Futile System* (EPM Publications, 1976), p. 15. See also Gregg Easterbrook, "What's Wrong with Congress?" *The Atlantic Monthly* (December 1984), pp. 57–84.

[4] See James L. Sundquist, *Constitutional Reform and Effective Government* (Brookings Institution, 1986); James MacGregor Burns, *The Power to Lead* (Simon & Schuster, 1984); and Donald L. Robinson, ed., *Reforming American Government* (Westview Press, 1985).

of America. The real question is whether Congress is operating effectively enough to deal most of the time with those broad national issues the general public feels require national action.

Some suggest that Congress has such a split personality that there are at least two Congresses. The first Congress is a *law-making institution*. It is asked to write laws and make policy for the entire nation. In this capacity all the members are expected to set aside their personal ambitions and perhaps even their concerns about their own constituencies. But Congress is also a *representative assembly*, made up of 535 elected officials who serve as links between their constituents and the national government. The dual roles of *making laws* and *responding to constituents' demands* were very much bound together in the minds of the framers of the Constitution when they designed a legislature elected from states and geographical districts. Since the first Congress formed, these two functions have forced members to balance national issues with the personal concerns of their constituents.

In fact, pressures mount continuously on members of Congress to help constituents deal with an increasingly complicated government. Indeed, members must spend considerable time and effort helping constituents, especially if they want to stay elected. This notion of the "two Congresses" has important implications for how Congress works and how it is organized—a subject we consider later.

WHO ARE THE LEGISLATORS?

Congresswoman Patricia Schroeder of Denver, Colorado (elected in 1972) is currently the woman with greatest seniority in the U.S. Congress. Schroeder ran a brief but unsuccessful campaign for the Democratic nomination for president in early 1988. (*Courtesy Congresswoman Patricia Schroeder*)

All members of Congress are successful politicians, mostly between the ages of 35 and 70 who have risen to national office through local processes in their home communities and states. The entire membership of the House of Representatives (435) is elected every second year. Elections for the six-year Senate terms are staggered, so that one-third of the Senate's 100 members are chosen every two years. The Constitution sets up no major barriers to holding office except age and citizenship. Members of the House of Representatives must be 25 years old and must have been citizens for seven years. Senators must be at least 30 and must have been citizens for nine years. Yet the composition of Congress does not reflect the socioeconomic makeup of the people as a whole. The overwhelming number of national legislators are male (95 percent), well educated, middle-aged, and from middle- or upper-middle-income backgrounds. Until recently members were also mainly white Anglo-Saxon Protestants (WASPs). The greater numbers of Roman Catholics and Jews in recent Congresses—about 140 Catholics and thirty-eight Jews—now bring the religious makeup of Congress closer in line with that of the general population. But there are far fewer blacks and women in Congress than in the general public (see Table 13–1.)[5] In the 101st Congress (1989–1991) there are also a handful of members of Asian descent and about a dozen with Spanish heritage.

About 40 percent of national legislators are lawyers. The Congress also includes one veterinarian, two former judges, a retired admiral, two members of the clergy, about two dozen farmers, and a large number of teachers, professors, and business people. Plainly, Congress does not mirror the nation as a whole from an occupational standpoint. Rarely does a member of Congress emerge out of trade unions or from the so-called blue-collar occupations, although a dozen or so members of the House of Representatives in the early 1980s briefly formed a "blue-collar caucus" composed of members with working-class backgrounds. Among these were a former longshoreman, a pipefitter, a warehouse worker, and an ex-riverboat captain. How important

[5] For a study of female members of Congress, see Irwin N. Gertzog, *Congressional Women: Their Recruitment, Treatment, and Behavior* (Praeger, 1984). See also Robert A. Bernstein, "Why Are There So Few Women in the House?" *Western Political Quarterly* (March 1, 1986), pp. 155–64.

13–1   Profile of the 101st Congress (1989–1991)

	House		Senate	
Party				
Democrats	262	Democrats		55
Republicans	173	Republicans		45
Age				
U.S. House	52	Senate		55
Sex				
Male	441	Male		98
Female	24	Female		2
Religion (in recent Congresses)				
Protestant	59%	Protestant		69%
Catholic	29	Catholic		20
Other	12	Other		11
Number of blacks	23			0
Lawyers (by percentage)				
Lawyers	32%	Lawyers		60%

Note: Numbers reflect actual number of people within each category unless otherwise specified.

is this "misrepresentation"? Critics say it offers just one more instance of government of the elite by the elite and for the elite. Defenders point out that we would hardly expect to find the national percentage of high school dropouts mirrored in Congress. Whatever its makeup, an important question is whether a Congress composed of legislators drawn from a restricted segment of the population is biased in favor of certain points of view. The present makeup of Congress doubtless means that such specific questions as women's rights and antipoverty measures get somewhat less support than they would if Congress were representative in a literal sense. Still, just because most members are the products of middle- and upper-class families does not necessarily mean they are interested only in improving the position of that portion of the population.

GETTING TO AND REMAINING IN CONGRESS

Getting elected to Congress depends on a number of factors—as noted in Chapter 12: party strength in the area, personal character and appeal, first-term or incumbent status, occasional national tides (such as in the 1964, 1974, or 1980 elections), and campaign strategies and fundraising abilities. An overriding factor, however, is the type of district or state in which a candidate runs. Is it a safe seat—one that is predictably won by one party or the other—or a highly competitive one? Congress has left control over the drawing of congressional districts to the state legislatures. Senators, of course, represent entire states, but House seats are distributed among the states according to population; each state receives at least one seat.

In many states the party in control of the state legislature openly engages in **gerrymandering**—that is, it tries to draw district boundaries in such a way as to secure for its party as many representatives as possible. This is why congressional districts take on weird shapes. The once rural-dominated legislatures used to arrange the districts so as to overrepresent rural areas. But this was modified both by the population shift to the cities and suburbs and by a 1964 Supreme Court decision. The Court ruled the Constitution requires all congressional districts in a state to have precisely the same number of people (as nearly as possible), so that one person's vote is equal to that of every other person. How much difference did this and subsequent Supreme Court rulings make? Population inequalities have ended. The

The Capitol. (*T. Cronin*)

voice of suburban populations has been strengthened. But a certain amount of gerrymandering continues: State politicians still draw boundary lines—usually to protect incumbents.

The Incumbency Advantage

Incumbents in Congress have an excellent chance of remaining in Congress: About 80 percent of Senate incumbents and at least 95 percent of House members who run again are reelected. Most House seats are "safe" in the sense that incumbents win by such majorities that the chances of challengers' defeating them are minimal. Yet, as most House members know, they can be challenged twice every two years and defeat may be as near as a good opponent with lots of money in either their own party's primary or at the next general election.

As long as the members can keep "the folks and the interests back home" happy, they can remain reasonably independent from the president and from their party leadership. Of course, an incumbent can be voted out of office, especially if a legislator loses touch with constituents or national needs. But how would the voters know if this were the case? Few people know the names of their representatives. Senators are better known, but one-third to one-half the public do not know their names. Still fewer citizens evaluate legislators on their stands or votes on issues. Unhappily (or happily, depending on your view), members of Congress are judged on service to their constituents, communications with the district, attendance records, "small favors done over the years," and other such nonlegislative matters.

Not surprisingly, most members of Congress pursue policies and assignments, and allocate their time and energy, in ways that increase their chances of getting reelected. A safe seat, however, permits a legislator to serve as a national leader without having to worry too much about constantly returning home. Senator Edward Kennedy, for example—as long as he does not take issue with sensitive domestic concerns of the people of Massachusetts—can count on the base from which he has become a national spokesperson for certain economic and foreign policy points of view. Representatives from competitive states or districts, on the other hand, find it somewhat more difficult to ignore local concerns, and tend to concentrate their time and energies on narrower issues. Doubtless the rise in the number of safe seats has increased in large part because members of Congress have skillfully organized their staffs and their own schedules to serve constituent interests.[6]

"Yes, I did promise to take care of the people in the district. Similarly, I'm sure that each of you has at one time or another said something rash in the heat of the moment."
(*Reprinted by permission.*)

THE POWERS OF CONGRESS

The Constitution is generous in its grant of powers to Congress. In the very first article the framers outlined the structure, powers, and responsibilities of Congress, giving it "all legislative powers herein granted." Among these powers are the power to spend and tax in order to "provide for the common defense and general welfare of the United States"; the power to borrow money; the power to regulate commerce with foreign nations and among the states; the power to declare war, raise and support armies, and provide and maintain a navy; the power to establish post offices and postroads; and the power to set up the federal courts under the Supreme Court. As a final catch-all, the Constitution gave the Congress the right "to make all

[6] See John R. Johannes, *To Serve the People: Congress and Constituency Service* (University of Nebraska Press, 1984); Morris Fiorina, *Congress: Keystone to the Washington Establishment* (Yale, 1977); Richard Fenno, *Home Style: House Members in Their Districts* (Little, Brown, 1978); and Bruce Cain, John Ferejohn, and Morris Fiorina, "Constituency Service in the United States and Great Britain," in Lawrence C. Dodd and Bruce I. Oppenheimer, *Congress Reconsidered*, 3rd ed. (Congressional Quarterly Press, 1985), pp. 109–30.

laws which shall be necessary and proper for carrying into execution" the powers set out. Several nonlegislative functions were also granted, such as participating in the process of constitutional amendment and impeachment (given to the House), and trying an impeached federal officer (given to the Senate).

The Constitution confers special additional responsibilities on the Senate. The Senate has the power to confirm presidential nominations—sometimes as many as 500 key executive and judicial nominees a year. (In Chapter 15 we discuss how the Senate meets this responsibility.) The Senate must also give its consent, by a two-thirds vote of the senators present, before a president may ratify a treaty. This gives the Senate a special role in foreign policy.

The House also has some special responsibilities, but these have not proved to be as important as those given to the Senate. For example, all revenue bills must originate in the House. In fact, this has made little practical difference, because the Senate has freely amended bills that originate in the House, and has changed everything except the title.

The framers had no intention of making Congress all-powerful: They reserved certain authority to the states and to the people and gave other powers to the executive and judicial branches of the national government. As time passed, Congress gained power in some respects and lost it in others. The power of Congress also changes depending on the times and the president. As the role and authority of the national government have expanded, so too have the policy-making and oversight responsibilities of Congress. Still, Congress has not kept pace with its great rival, the presidency, which in many respects today holds the place in our national government that most of the founders apparently desired for Congress. The president's national security responsibilities, media visibility, and agenda-setting authority have all enhanced the position of the presidency in the past generations. This may be part of a worldwide trend. Legislative bodies almost everywhere have become subordinate to the executive at all levels of government.

Despite its secondary role in recent decades, Congress still performs at least these six important functions: *representation*, *lawmaking*, *consensus building*, *overseeing*, *policy clarification*, and *legitimizing*. Representation is expressing the diversity and conflicting views of the regional, economic, social, racial, religious, and other interests making up the United States. Law making is enacting measures to help solve substantive problems. Consensus building is the bargaining process by which these interests are reconciled. Overseeing the bureaucracy means seeing that laws and policies approved by Congress are faithfully carried out and that they accomplish what was intended. Policy clarification, or "policy incubation," as it is sometimes called, is the identification and publicizing of issues. Legitimizing is the formal ratifying of policies through proper channels.

THE JOB OF THE LEGISLATOR

National legislators lead a hectic life. Congress now meets year round, whereas 200 years ago and even 100 years ago it often met for just a few months each year. There is never enough time to digest all the information, letters, complaints, reports, and advice that pour in. Staying elected is a chief priority; some members seem to have few other interests. But most keep on top of their committee responsibilities, stay in touch with key leaders and activists back home, and strive to understand national problems. Most legislators work extremely hard. They drive themselves at a pace far more strenuous than that of typical professional or business persons. Their travel commitments are as demanding as those of airline pilots or cross-country truck drivers. The average member remains in Congress for about twelve years.

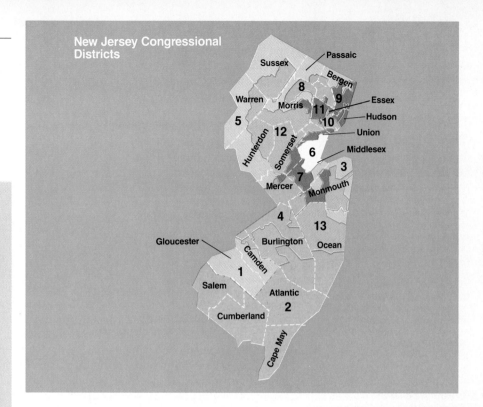

New Jersey Congressional Districts

Depending on the kind of district, the personality of the member, and the issues of the day, members of Congress emphasize representation, lawmaking and committee work, constituency casework, external relations with interest groups or the White House, or reelection tasks.

Legislators as Representatives

For whom does the representative speak? The geographical district and its immediate interests? The party? The nation? Some special clientele? His or her conscience? How legislators define their representative roles has been one of the major questions in political science—and for good reason. Congress was intended to serve as a forum for registering the interests and values that make up the nation. It was never intended that the legislative branch represent views identical with those of the executive. But to whom does the individual representative listen?

Although certain patterns are evident, their meaning is far from clear. For one thing, members of Congress perceive their roles differently. Some believe they should serve as **delegates** from their districts; they should find out what the "folks back home" need or want and serve those needs as effectively as possible. In a sense they would primarily *re-present* the views of the voters who sent them to Washington. This orientation, studies find, is often assumed by Republicans, nonleaders, non-southerners, or members with low seniority.

But most members see their role as that of **trustee**. Their constituents, they contend, did not send them to Congress to serve as mere agents or robots. They are to vote independently, on the basis of their own, more complete information and greater experience, for the welfare of the whole nation. As one member once put it: "This means that we must on occasion lead, inform, correct, and sometimes even ignore constituent opinion, if we are to exercise fully that judgment for which we were elected." This view echoes the stand once championed by famed English legislator Edmund Burke, who said his judgment and conscience ought not to be sacrificed to the opinions of others. In his view a legislature was a place for deliberation

Congressman Phil Gramm (R-Texas) made news in 1983 by resigning from Congress as a Democrat and running again as a Republican in a special election. Then in 1984 he won an impressive victory to become a U.S. Senator from Texas—also as a Republican. In 1986, this ex-economics professor at Texas A&M added to his fame by cosponsoring the much-talked about Gramm-Rudman-Hollings deficit-reduction policy. (*Courtesy Senator Phil Gramm*)

Whom and What Do the Representatives Represent?

Survey of House Members: Do you feel that you should be primarily concerned with looking after the needs and interests of your own district, or do you feel that you should be primarily concerned with looking after the needs and aspirations of the nation as a whole?

Whole nation	45%
Both nation and district	28
District	24
Not sure	3
	100%

When there is a conflict between what you feel is best and what you think the people in your district want, do you think you should follow your own conscience or follow what the people in your district want?

Follow own conscience	65%
Depends on the issue	25
Follow district	5
Not sure	3
	98%

Source: "Sample Survey of over 140 House Members," *Final Report, Commission on Administrative Review, U.S. House of Representatives,* vol. 2 (December 31, 1977), pp. 887, 890.

and learning. It was not a mere gathering of ambassadors from localities. Interviews with members of the House of Representatives suggest that the trustee, or national, focus is more common among Democrats, House leaders, Southerners, and high-seniority members.

Although the question of delegate versus trustee is an old one, it is somewhat misleading. Representatives cannot follow detailed instructions from their constituents because such instructions seldom exist. On many important policy questions, members hear nothing from their constituents. And they hear most often from those who agree with them. On the other hand, it is rather unrealistic to expect a legislator to be able to define the national interest if this means understanding the needs and aspirations of millions of people. Most legislators shift back and forth in their role, depending on their perception of the public interest, the electoral facts of life, and the pressures of the moment.

Legislators as Law Makers

In their major role as law makers, the members of Congress are influenced by how they perceive the nation's key problems and what can be done about them; how they respond to their constituents' interests; and how they follow suggestions from colleagues, staff, the White House, and lobbies.

How a member of Congress makes up his or her mind varies according to issues and to the contexts of decision making. No single factor determines how a member votes most of the time. Members cast more than 1200 votes on a wide variety of subjects in the span of a single Congress. Some issues are controversial and directly affect a member's district or state. On such occasions a national legislator will more often than not heed the interests of the folks back home. On complicated issues that have little or no bearing on the home district, most members of Congress tend to rely on their own convictions and on the advice of colleagues and friends. Sometimes the president will single out an issue as crucial to the success of the administration, and this factor plus party considerations may weigh more heavily. Obviously, how a member decides to vote depends on many factors and contexts.[7]

The influence of a member's policy and philosophical convictions   Ideological or issue orientation is the best predictor of how members will vote on a variety of issues. A liberal on social issues is also likely to be a liberal on tax and national security issues. The policy convictions of a Senator Bill Bradley (D-New Jersey) are reasonably consistent, as are those of a Representative Jack Kemp (R-New York). Thus, on controversial issues such as national health insurance, gas and oil decontrol, or defense spending and the strategic defense initiative (Star Wars), knowing the general philosophical leanings of individual members provides a helpful guide both to how they make up their minds and how they will vote. One study finds that an increasing and continuing ideological split has developed in Congress: A social and economic justice coalition is pitted against a growing coalition of free market economic conservatives.[8] In a watered down sense it is a Walter Mondale versus Ronald Reagan split; in economic terms it pits John Kenneth Galbraith "progressives" versus a Milton Friedman "free-market" coalition. Other scholars detect flexible majorities of the moment and say ideology plays a less constant role.

The influence of the voters   Much of the time a major influence on legislators is their perception of how their constituents feel. Party and executive branch pressures also play a role, but when all is said and done, the members' political future depends on how a majority of voters feel about their performance. Rarely does a person consistently and deliberately vote against the wishes of the people back home.

[7] See David C. Kozak, *Contexts of Congressional Decision Behavior* (University Press of America, 1984).
[8] Jerrold E. Schneider, *Ideological Coalitions in Congress* (Greenwood Press, 1979).

This commonsense observation is supported by several studies. On such domestic issues as social welfare and civil rights, there is usually a great deal of agreement between legislators and their districts. Junior members from competitive seats, in particular, often vote their constituencies' attitudes as they perceive them. But even members who win by substantial margins are not necessarily free to ignore the concerns of the voters. They may, in fact, have won precisely because people know they will follow voters' wishes on issues important to them.[9] Of course, the extent to which members try to respond to their constituents' views also depends on the measure under consideration. Legislators might pay more attention to voter attitudes when social and economic matters are involved than when mass opinion is not so well informed.

A paradox is evident here. Members of Congress sometimes think their individual law-making actions may have considerable impact on constituents. Yet the constituents' general ignorance of how their representatives vote implies that the impact can be small. Members may think their constituents like (or dislike) what they are doing, when actually the voters have little idea of what is going on in Congress. This is explained in part by the tendency of legislators to overestimate their visibility; most citizens don't even know the names of their senators and representatives. Also, members must constantly be concerned about how they will explain their votes. And some members are worried about small shifts in the vote on election day. Even if only a few voters are aware of their stands on a given issue, this group might make the difference between victory and defeat.

A Retiring Congressman's Liberated Letter to a Constituent

Representative Mendel Davis, Democrat of South Carolina, retired from Congress in early 1980. After he had announced he was going to retire, he took off the kid gloves with one constituent.

In a letter to a town councilman back home who was also a member of the John Birch Society, Congressman Davis wrote:

"One of the small but gratifying benefits of leaving Congress is that I no longer have to put up with your unending drivel. I have instructed my staff to properly dispose of any future mail from you in the only manner appropriate to its content."

"Had any of your correspondence ever shown the common sense of a gnat, or the simple courtesy one expects even of a small child, I would have been more impressed by your reasoning."

Mr. Robert Payne, the constituent, said Congressman Davis probably was provoked by a postcard he had sent Davis calling him a "rotten skunk" and "liar" because of his voting record on the Panama Canal treaties.

The influence of colleagues   Voting decisions are also affected by the advice members obtain from other representatives. Severe time limitations and the frequent necessity to make decisions with only a few hours or even a few minutes notice force legislators to depend on others. Most members develop friendships with people who think as they do. They often ask one another what they think of a piece of pending legislation. In particular, they look to respected members of the committee working on the bill.

Unlike most of the voters back home, other members usually have detailed knowledge about many of the issues before Congress. Their views are often public. They may have voted on the matter in previous sessions or in committee, and their public statements may have been placed in the *Congressional Record.* Sometimes members are influenced to vote one way merely because they know a colleague is on the other side of the issue. More often legislators find out how their friends stand on an issue, listen to the party leadership's advice, and take into account the various committee reports. If they are still in doubt, they consult additional friends and staff. The members most often consulted by their colleagues are those who represent similar districts or the same region or state, or like-minded members of the same party or faction—especially those who serve on the committee from which the legislation has come.

A member may also go along and vote with a colleague in the expectation that the colleague will later vote for a measure about which the member is highly concerned. Thus, some vote trading takes place to build coalitions so that members can "bring home the bacon" to their constituencies. This is as much a case of reciprocity in congressional relations as it is of deference to colleagues' superior information or expertise.

The influence of congressional staff   Perhaps the fastest-growing bureaucracy in Washington is that attached to Congress. For years political scientists urged Congress to strengthen its staff. Without additional help, they said, representatives and senators were at a disadvantage in dealing with the executive branch and were overly dependent on information supplied them by the White House or lobbyists.

[9] John W. Kingdon, *Congressmen's Voting Decisions*, 2nd ed. (Harper & Row, 1981).

U.S. Representative Norman Mineta (D-California) of San Jose, a highly respected member of the House of Representatives. (*Courtesy U.S. House of Representatives*)

Congressman Newt Gingrich (R-Georgia) known for his effective oratory and populist-conservative philosophy. (*Courtesy Congressman Gingrich*)

Congress has responded—some would say with a vengeance. Every committee and subcommittee is now elaborately staffed. In addition, members of Congress have all enlarged the number of personal staff working for them in both their Washington and home district offices. Congress in recent years also added a Congressional Budget Office, and an Office of Technology Assessment to its already existing Library of Congress and General Accounting Office staffs.

Congress is the only legislature in the world with a vast staff. This is one of its chief sources of power; without its staffs Congress would doubtless become too much the prisoner of the executive branch and interest groups. Complexity of issues and increasingly demanding schedules have led to an explosion in congressional staffs. About 38,000 staff members, researchers, budget analysts, and others now work for Congress (this figure includes the U.S. Government Printing Office, which is nominally part of the legislative branch). This number has grown at least fourfold in the last twenty-five years. But numbers tell only part of the story of staff influence. Members of Congress have to delegate all kinds of tasks to their staffs. Some members, in fact, now ask whether they or their staffs are in charge.

Increasing numbers of congressional staff members now work in the home district or state offices. About one-third of all staff of the House of Representatives, and one-fourth of the Senate, are home-based. In part this is due to the increased attention focused on constituency services and casework. Doubtless, too, it helps members stay in close communication with the voters back home. Much of the work done in these district offices is akin to a continuous campaign effort—generating favorable publicity, arranging for local appearances and newspaper interviews, scheduling and general contact with important civic and business leaders in the region.[10]

One consequence both of the increasing congressional staff and of growing demands on members of Congress is that the latter sometimes become very dependent on staff. This is especially true of senators, who tend to have a wider range of subject matter specialties than do representatives. At congressional hearings it is often the staff member who tells the legislator what to ask. Congressional staff become knowledgeable about the special policy areas and deal on a day-to-day basis with their counterparts in the executive departments and interest groups. Indeed, many close observers say some of the most powerful people in Washington are congressional "staffers," as they are called. They draft bills, do the research, and often do much of the parliamentary negotiating and coalition building. No wonder an increasing number of lobbyists concentrate on influencing staffers.[11]

Yet we should not exaggerate the independent power base of staffers, who can be summarily fired at the whims of the people they serve. Staffers lack civil service protection—although they cannot be dismissed because of their race, sex, or national origin. And they know that if they wander too far from the views of the one person who can hire and fire them, they will quickly be called back into line.

The influence of the party   Another source of influence on legislative behavior is the *political party*. Friendships tend to develop within the party. Of course, there is a fair amount of natural agreement among party colleagues. On some issues the pressure to conform to a party position is immediate and direct. Sometimes there is pressure to go along with the party even when a member does not believe in the party position.

[10] For a comparison of how different members serve their districts' needs, see John Johannes, *To Serve the People: Congress and Constituency Service* (University of Nebraska Press, 1984). See also Steven H. Schiff and Steven B. Smith, "Generational Change and the Allocation of Congressional Staff," *Legislative Studies Quarterly* (August 1985), pp. 457–67.

[11] Michael J. Malbin, *Unelected Representatives* (Basic Books, 1980). See also Robert H. Salisbury and Kenneth A. Shepsle, "Congressional Staff Turnover and the Ties-that-Bind," *American Political Science Association*, vol. 75 (1981), pp. 381–96.

13–2 Senate Roll-Call Vote on Amending the Constitution to Require a Balanced Budget*

FOR AMENDMENT—66

Democrats—23

Bentsen, Tex.	Gore, Tenn.	Pell, R.I.
Bingaman, N.M.	Harkin, Iowa	Proxmire, Wis.
Boren, Okla.	Heflin, Ala.	Pryor, Ark.
Chiles, Fla.	Hollings, S.C.	Sasser, Tenn.
DeConcini, Ariz.	Johnston, La.	Simon, Ill.
Dixon, Ill.	Long, La.	Stennis, Miss.
Exon, Neb.	Melcher, Mont.	Zorinsky, Neb.
Ford, Ky.	Nunn, Ga.	

Republicans—43

Abdnor, S.D.	Grassley, Iowa	Pressier, S.D.
Andrews, N.D.	Hatch, Utah	Quayle, Ind.
Armstrong, Colo.	Hawkins, Fla.	Roth, Del.
Boschwitz, Minn.	Hecht, Nev.	Rudman, N.H.
Cochran, Miss.	Helms, N.C.	Simpson, Wyo.
D'Amato, N.Y.	Humphrey, N.H.	Specter, Pa.
Danforth, Mo.	Kasten, Wis.	Stevens, Alaska
Denton, Ala.	Laxalt, Nev.	Symms, Idaho
Dole, Kan.	Lugar, Ind.	Thurmond, S.C.
Domenici, N.M.	Mattingly, Ga.	Trible, Va.
Durenberger, Minn.	McClure, Idaho	Wallop, Wyo.
East, N.C.	McConnell, Ky.	Warner, Va.
Garn, Utah	Murkowski, Alaska	Wilson, Calif.
Goldwater, Ariz.	Nickles, Okla.	
Gramm, Tex.	Packwood, Ore.	

AGAINST AMENDMENT—34

Democrats—24

Baucus, Mont.	Eagleton, Mo.	Levin, Mich.
Biden, Del.	Glenn, Ohio	Matsunaga, Hawaii
Bradley, N.J.	Hart, Colo.	Metzenbaum, Ohio
Bumpers, Ark.	Inouye, Hawaii	Mitchell, Me.
Burdick, N.D.	Kennedy, Mass.	Moynihan, N.Y.
Byrd, W.Va.	Kerry, Mass.	Riegle, Mich.
Cranston, Calif.	Lautenberg, N.J.	Rockefeller, W.Va.
Dodd, Conn.	Leahy, Vt.	Sarbanes, Md.

Republicans—10

Chafee, R.I.	Hatfield, Ore.	Mathias, Md.
Cohen, Me.	Heinz, Pa.	Stafford, Vt.
Evans, Wash.	Kassebaum, Kan.	Weicker, Conn.
Gorton, Wash.		

* It takes a two-thirds vote to amend the Constitution, and this proposal lost in the Senate by just one vote. A vote "for" was a vote in favor of the proposed change—a change President Reagan repeatedly advocated. Also, as is usually the case, the vote was not a pure party vote, yet party members tended to go along with their colleagues. Liberal and moderate Republicans defected, and conservative and southern Democrats were more likely than liberal Democrats to vote in favor.

Source: *Congressional Record* (March 25, 1986).

The result of party pressure is a tendency, on major bills, for *most* Democrats to be arrayed against *most* Republicans. Members of Congress typically vote with their party majority about two-thirds of the time. However, senators are slightly more independent than representatives. Party influence also varies over time. It was stronger during the nineteenth century than it has been in this century, and it is somewhat stronger in recent years than it was in the post-World War II era.

Party influence varies by issue. Party differences have been stronger over domestic, regulatory, and welfare measures than over foreign policy and civil liberty issues.

In the past few years party leaders in both chambers and parties have tried to encourage more cohesive and loyal party voting. Proponents of increased party cohesion (when partisans stick together and vote with greater unity) say this is the only realistic way to achieve collective responsibility in Congress. They claim that increased partisan unity in voting would help Congress solve problems and the wheeling and dealing of ad hoc and shifting coalitions would decline. Early in Reagan's first term, Republicans in both chambers did vote in somewhat greater unison, but this pattern faded in Reagan's later years. The tendency for members of Congress to "go their own way" or "rise above party" is still far more characteristic of U.S. national legislators than of European parliamentarians. Despite some innovative strategies to encourage stronger partisan voting patterns, it appears to be declining.[12]

Presidential and other influences   Many forces—regional, local, ties of friendship—can override party influence. Members are sometimes influenced by informal groups (state delegations, ideological groups, ethnic caucuses, regional groupings, and even the class of colleagues with whom they were elected—for example, "the class of 1986").[13] Also, they are influenced by the more important interest groups and lobbyists—especially those who can help pay off past and future campaign debts.[14]

One voting pattern in Congress reflects a conservative coalition of Republicans and southern Democrats. In the 1950s and 1960s a majority of southern Democrats and a majority of Republicans voted against the majority of northern Democrats on about a quarter of the important roll-call votes. Although this was less the case in the 1970s, it reappeared in the Reagan years. The conservative coalition is most likely to appear on domestic issues, especially on social welfare legislation. But its strength in Congress cannot be measured by voting decisions alone, because the many committee leaders who are members of this group are often able to prevent legislation they oppose from ever being voted on. The pattern is now changing, because Democrats elected from the South in recent years are more "national" than "sectional" in their voting patterns; and members of both parties in the House, have strengthened party discipline.

Presidents and executive-branch officials can also influence how legislators vote.[15] Some critics say Congress has yielded extensive policy initiation and budgetary planning to the administrative branch: They say no matter how hard Congress may struggle on one issue, it is overwhelmed by the vastly greater forces of the presidency. Even today a fair number of legislators complain (as they have throughout our history) that, as now organized and staffed, Congress cannot really come to grips with the enormously complex questions involved in making national policy.

Even if Congress were better organized or its members more expert, the growing significance of foreign policy and complicated economic issues would still make the role of the president vital. Presidents have the tools of foreign policy in

---

Influences on a Member of Congress's Vote

- Member's policy and philosophical convictions
- Member's perception of the state's or district's needs
- Constituent opinion and mail
- Committee leaders
- Other committee members
- Members of his or her delegation
- Other members of Congress
- Informal caucuses
- Congressional staff members
- Interest groups and lobbyists
- Ideological or ethnic caucuses
- President's position
- Party leaders
- Campaign contributors
- Political-action committees
- Congressional research publications

---

[12] Melissa P. Collie and David W. Brady, "The Decline of Partisan Coalitions in the House of Representatives," in Lawrence C. Dodd and Bruce I. Oppenheimer, eds., *The Congress Reconsidered*, 3rd ed. (Congressional Quarterly Press, 1985), pp. 272–87. See also David Price, *Bringing Back the Parties* (Congressional Quarterly Press, 1984), and David Brady, "Congressional Parties and Clusters of Policy Change," *British Journal of Political Science* (1978), pp. 79–99.

[13] On the growing role and influence of informal or ad hoc caucuses, see Susan Webb Hammond, Daniel P. Mulhollan, and Arthur Stevens, *Informal Congressional Groups in National Policymaking* (forthcoming).

[14] See Kay Lehman Schlozman and John T. Tierney, *Organized Interests and American Democracy* (Harper & Row, 1986), especially chaps. 10 to 12.

[15] For vivid examples of Reagan administration efforts to influence Congress on budget, tax, and deficit matters, see David A. Stockman, *The Triumph of Politics* (Harper & Row, 1986).

their hands, and even those they share with Congress, such as the treaty-making power, are usually less significant than their overall negotiating and agenda-setting roles. Through the full use of their constitutional and political powers, presidents like Lyndon Johnson and Ronald Reagan have become serious, full-time partners in legislation; nonetheless, members of Congress are reluctant to admit they are influenced by pressures from the White House. Some studies suggest, moreover, that presidential influence on congressional voting decisions may not be as significant as commonly believed.[16] Although a president has more impact on votes in the area of national security policy than in other areas, even on these questions power is very much a shared responsibility.[17] On key domestic issues legislators are more likely to be influenced by what the constituents want (or what they think they want) and by their own policy convictions than by what the White House wants.

The Legislative Obstacle Course

From the beginning Congress has been a system of multiple vetoes. This was in part the intent of the framers, who wanted to disperse powers so they could not be accumulated by any would-be tyrant. In addition, Congress has developed an elaborate set of customs that distributes political influence in different ways to different people. To follow a bill through Congress is to see this *dispersion of power*. Procedures and rules in the two houses are somewhat different, but the basic distribution of power, in its effect on shaping legislation, is roughly the same.

Every bill, including those drawn up in the executive branch, must be introduced in either house by a member of that body. The vast bulk (more than 95 percent) of the 10,000 to 15,000 or so bills introduced every two years die in a subcommittee for lack of support. On major legislation that has significant backing, the committee or one of its subcommittees holds hearing to receive opinions. It then meets to "mark up" (discuss and revise) and vote on the bill. If the subcommittee and then the parent committee vote in favor of the bill, it is reported—or sent— to the full house, where it is debated and voted on. If passed, it goes to the other house, where the whole process is repeated. If there are differences between the bills as passed by the House and the Senate—and there often are—the two versions must go to a conference committee for reconciliation.

In 1789 through 1790, 142 bills were introduced in the House of Representatives, and only eighty-five reports were filed from committees. Nowadays 10,000 to 15,000 bills are introduced in each Congress; of these less than 1000 are enacted into law. These figures are lower than they were ten and twenty years ago because Congress has had to focus more on budget, tax, and deficit concerns than on new programs.

Opportunities for Delay

The complexity of the congressional system provides a tremendous built-in advantage for the opponents of any measure. Those who sponsor a bill must win at every step; opponents need to win only once. Multiple opportunities for vetoes exist because of the dispersion of influence and because at a dozen points in committee or in the House, a bill may be killed or allowed to die. Whether good or bad, a proposal can be delayed by any one of the following: (1) the chairperson of the House substantive committee; (2) the House substantive committee; (3) the House Rules

---

[16] George G. Edwards, III, *Presidential Influence in Congress* (Freeman, 1980), chaps. 5, 6, and 7.

[17] See Cecil V. Crabb, Jr., and Pat M. Holt, *Invitation to Struggle*, 3rd ed. (Congressional Quarterly Press, 1988), and Thomas M. Franck and Edward Weisband, *Foreign Policy by Congress* (Oxford University Press, 1979).

13–3 Comparison of House and Senate Activity and Workload, 83rd and 98th Congresses

Category	83rd Congress (1953–1954) Senate	83rd Congress (1953–1954) House	98th Congress (1983–1984) Senate	98th Congress (1983–1984) House
Standing committees	15	19	16	22
Subcommittees	63	81	102	139
Hearings	—	—	2471	5661
Days in session	294	240	281	266
Messages from president	—	5	235	179
Messages from executive departments	—	1855	3642	4164
Resolutions passed	321	519	380	397
Bills passed	2231	2129	936	978

Source: Adapted from Roger H. Davidson and Thomas Kephart, "Indicators of Senate Activity and Workload," and by the same authors, "Indicators of House of Representatives Workload and Activity," Congressional Research Service, Library of Congress (June 1985).

Committee; (4) the House; (5) the chairperson of the Senate subcommittee; (6) the Senate committee; (7) the majority of the Senate; (8) the floor leaders in both chambers; (9) a few members of the Senate in the case of a filibuster; (10) the House-Senate conference committee if the chambers disagree; and (11) the president. If the agreement of still other committees is required—appropriations, for example—the points of possible veto are multiplied.

Clearly, a controversial bill cannot get through without good legislative leadership and compromise. One tactical question at the start is whether to push for initial action in the Senate or in the House. If a bill is expected to have a rough time in the Senate, for example, its sponsors may seek passage in the House and hope that a sizable victory will spur the Senate into action. Another question concerns the committee to which the bill should be assigned. Normally referral to a committee is automatic. Sometimes, however, a bill cuts across more than one jurisdiction, but it can be written in such a way that it is bound to go to one committee rather than another.

Getting a bill through Congress requires more than a majority at any one time or place. Majorities must be mobilized over and over again—in subcommittee, in committee, and in chamber. These majorities shift and change, and they involve different legislators in different situations at different points in time. New coalitions must be built again and again.

These days, almost everything Congress wants to do by legislation requires dollars. So even if a bill passes, it must go through the process again to secure appropriations. Congress may go through the entire process of authorizing a program, and then fail to appropriate money to implement it; or it may appropriate so little money that what was authorized cannot be carried out.

THE HOUSES OF CONGRESS

The single most important fact about Congress is the dispersion of power between its two houses. The Senate and the House each had an absolute veto over the other's law making. Each house runs its own affairs, sets its own rules, and conducts its own investigations. The law-making role, however, is shared. Each house must be seen as a separate institution, even though both houses reflect somewhat similar political forces and share organizational patterns.

How a Bill Becomes Law

This graphic shows the most typical way in which proposed legislation is enacted into law. There are more complicated, as well as simpler, routes, and most bills fall by the wayside and never become law.

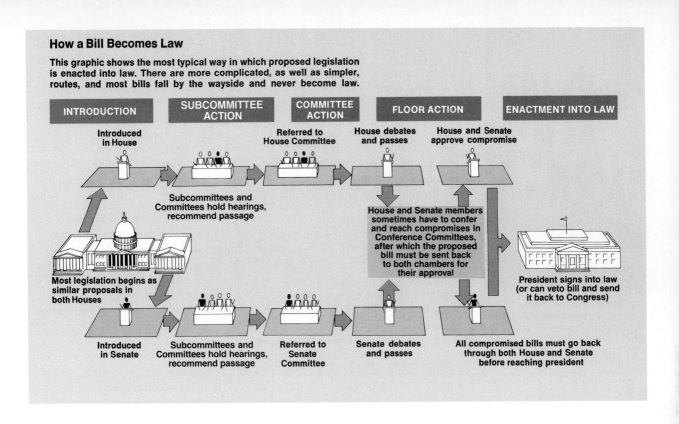

| INTRODUCTION | SUBCOMMITTEE ACTION | COMMITTEE ACTION | FLOOR ACTION | ENACTMENT INTO LAW |

Introduced in House

Referred to House Committee

House debates and passes

House and Senate approve compromise

Subcommittees and Committees hold hearings, recommend passage

House and Senate members sometimes have to confer and reach compromises in Conference Committees, after which the proposed bill must be sent back to both chambers for their approval

Most legislation begins as similar proposals in both Houses

President signs into law (or can veto bill and send it back to Congress)

Introduced in Senate

Subcommittees and Committees hold hearings, recommend passage

Referred to Senate Committee

Senate debates and passes

All compromised bills must go back through both House and Senate before reaching president

---

The Constitution's framers intended the national legislature to be divided so as to perform different functions. As Madison says in *The Federalist*, No. 51 (see Appendix), the protection against giving too much power to the legislature "is to divide the legislature into different branches; and to render them by different modes of election and different principles of action, as little connected with each other, as the nature or their common functions, and their common dependence on the society will admit." The House of Representatives was expected to reflect the popular will of the average citizen, whereas the Senate was to provide for stability, continuity, and lengthy policy deliberation. In fact, many of the framers hoped the Senate would stem rash populist impulses of the other chamber.

Although the Seventeenth amendment to the Constitution, which provides for direct election of U.S. Senators, has altered the character of the Senate's membership, the two chambers still organize themselves differently, approach issues differently, and structure their actions differently. Two hundred years later the two houses of Congress are still composed of different institutions, which have, in Madison's terms, "different principles of action." Plainly, however, the two houses are more similar today in their membership and operations than they were 200 or even 100 years ago—and this blurring will doubtless continue during the next 100 years.[18]

The House of Representatives

Organization and procedure in the House are somewhat different than in the Senate, if only because the House is over four times as large as the Senate. In recent years these two bodies have grown more similar. Still, *how* things are done usually affects *what* is done. The House assigns different types of bills to different calendars.

[18] See David C. Kozak, "House-Senate Differences: A Test among Interview Data," in David C. Kozak and John D. Macartney, eds., *Congress and Public Policy*, 2nd ed. (Dorsey Press, 1987), chap. 3.

Presidents give their State of the Union addresses before joint sessions of both houses of Congress. (*Pete Souza/The White House*)

For example, finance measures—tax or appropriations bills—are put on a special calendar for quicker action. The House has worked out other ways of speeding up law making, including an electronic voting device. Ordinary rules may be suspended by a two-thirds vote, or immediate action may be taken by unanimous consent of the members on the floor. By sitting as the *committee of the whole*, the House is able to operate more informally and more quickly than under its regular rules. A quorum in this committee is only 100 members, rather than a majority of the whole chamber, and voting is quicker and simpler. Members are limited in how long they can speak. In contrast to the Senate, debate may be cut off simply by majority vote.

The speaker   The **speaker** is the presiding officer in the House of Representatives. This officer is formally elected by the House but actually selected by the majority party. Throughout most of this century House members were unwilling to vest power in their party leaders. Revolts in 1910 by the rank-and-file progressives stripped speakers of most of their authority, which included control over who served on congressional committees. In the mid-1970s, however, several changes strengthened the speakership. The 1910 changes, designed to reduce the power of the speaker, were introduced as progressive reforms: Sixty years later, progressive reforms gave back to the speaker some of these powers.

The routine powers of the speaker include recognizing members who wish to speak, ruling on questions of parliamentary procedure, and appointing members to select and conference committees—that is, temporary committees, not standing committees. In general, the speaker directs the business on the floor of the House. More significant, of course, is a speaker's political and behind-the-scenes influence. (When Democrats are in the majority, the speaker chairs the influential Democratic Steering and Policy Committee. This committee consists of about twenty-four members: the speaker's lieutenants, four others appointed by the speaker, and twelve elected by regional caucuses within the House Democratic party. It devises and directs party strategy.) The speaker has the authority to refer legislation to the relevant committee and to select most members and the chair of the House Rules Committee.

The job of speaker goes to a member of the majority party, usually someone with substantial seniority.[19] The speaker is assisted by a **majority floor leader,** who helps plan party strategy, confers with other party leaders, and tries to keep members of the party in line. The minority party elects a **minority floor leader** who usually steps into the speakership when his or her party gains a majority in the House. Assisting each floor leader are the party **whips.** (The term comes from the whipper-in, who in fox hunts keeps the hounds bunched in the pack.) The whips serve as liaisons between the House leadership of each party and the rank and file. They inform members when important bills will come up for a vote, and prepare summaries of the bills' contents; do nose counts for the leadership; exert mild pressure on members to support the leadership; and try to ensure maximum attendance on the floor for critical votes.

At the beginning of the session and occasionally afterward, each party holds a **caucus** of all its members (called a conference by Republicans) to elect party officers, approve committee assignments, elect committee leaders, discuss important legislation, and perhaps try to agree on party policy.

Speaker of the House James C. Wright of Texas. (*Courtesy Congressman James C. Wright, Jr.*)

The house rules committee   One way in which the House differs from the Senate is in the procedure for deciding the flow of business. In the House this power is vested in the Rules Committee, one of the regular House standing commit-

[19] For an analysis of how congressional leaders get selected, see Robert L. Peabody, "House Party Leadership: Stability and Change," in Lawrence C. Dodd and Bruce I. Oppenheimer, *Congress Reconsidered*, 3rd ed. (Congressional Quarterly Press, 1985), pp. 253–71.

tees. In the normal course of events, a bill does not come up for action on the floor without a rule from the Rules Committee. By failing to act or refusing to grant a rule, the committee can hold up a bill. The rule granted gives the conditions under which the bill will be discussed, and these conditions may seriously affect the bill's chance of passage. The Rules Committee may grant a rule that makes it easy for a bill to be amended to death on the floor. A special rule may prohibit amendments altogether or provide that only members of the committee reporting the bill may offer amendments. The rule also sets the length of debate and specifies what can and cannot be amended.

Up to about the mid-1960s the Rules Committee was dominated by a coalition of Republicans and conservative Democrats. Liberals denounced it as unrepresentative, unfair, and dictatorial. Today it seldom blocks legislation unless the House leadership prefers measures to be held up. Meanwhile the Rules Committee membership—due to deaths and new appointments—has come to reflect the views of the total membership of the majority party. Because the speaker can control its membership, the Rules Committee today is usually an arm of the leadership. And rather than block legislation, it offers a "dress rehearsal" opportunity to those who are trying to press for new initiatives.

The Senate

In many respects the Senate resembles the House. It has the same basic committee structure, elected party leadership, and dispersion of power. But because the Senate is a smaller body, its procedures are more informal, and it has more time for debate.

The president of the Senate (the vice-president of the United States) has little influence. Such an official can vote only in case of a tie and is seldom consulted when important decisions are made. The Senate also elects from among the majority party a **president pro tempore,** who is the official chairperson in the absence of the vice-president. But presiding over the Senate is a thankless chore and is rotated among junior members of the chamber.

Party machinery in the Senate is somewhat similar to that in the House. There are party conferences (caucuses), majority and minority floor leaders, and party whips. Each party has a *policy committee*, composed of the leaders of the party, which is theoretically responsible for the party's overall legislative program. (In the Senate the party steering committees handle only committee assignments.) Unlike the House political party steering committees, the Senate's party policy committees are formally provided for by law, and each has a regular staff and a budget. Although the Senate policy committees have some influence on legislation, they have not asserted strong legislative leadership or managed to coordinate policy.

The **Senate majority leader,** however, is usually a person of influence within the Senate and sometimes nationally. As the Senate's major power broker, the majority leader has the right to be the first senator heard on the floor. In consultation with the minority floor leader, the majority leader determines the Senate's agenda and has much to say about committee assignments for members of the majority party. But the position confers somewhat less authority than the speakership in the House, and its influence depends on the person's political and parliamentary skills and on the national political situation.[20]

Political environment   Senators are a somewhat different breed from most House members, and some people believe the Senate has a character all its own. Senators have more political elbow room than representatives, if only because of their six-

Senator Bill Bradley (D-New Jersey)
(Tannenbaum/Sygma)

[20] For a lively account of Howard Baker as majority leader in the early and mid-1980s, as well as a general account of Senate life, see James A. Miller, *Running in Place: Inside the Senate* (Simon & Schuster, 1986).

Differences between House and Senate

House

- Two-year term
- 435 members
- Smaller constituencies
- Less staff
- Equal populations represented
- Less flexible rules
- Limited debate
- More policy specialists
- Less media coverage
- Less prestige
- Less reliance on staff
- Important Rules Committee
- More powerful committee leaders
- Very important committees
- 22 major committees
- Nongermaine amendments ("riders") not allowed

Senate

- Six-year term
- 100 members
- Larger constituencies
- More staff
- States represented
- More flexible rules
- Unlimited debate
- Policy generalists
- More media coverage
- More prestige
- More reliance on staff
- More equal distribution of power
- Less important committees
- 16 major committees
- Less important Rules Committee
- Special treaty ratification power
- Special confirmation power
- Nongermaine amendments ("riders") allowed

year-terms. In addition, senators are more likely to wield power in their state parties. Average senators become visible and politically significant earlier in their careers. This is due partly to the relative smallness of the Senate and to its easier access to the media, and partly, no doubt, to the larger staffs that senators have.[21]

To a degree the Senate is a mutual-protection society. Members tend to guard the rights and privileges of other senators—so that their own rights and privileges will be protected in turn. Like many close-knit social or professional groups, the Senate has developed a set of informal folkways—standards of behavior to which new members are expected to conform. Courtesy in debate is a cardinal rule, for example, and debate takes place in the third person. By far the most important folkway is *reciprocity*. A senator requests and receives many favors and courtesies from colleagues, always with the understanding that he or she will repay the kindness. A senator may be out of town and request that the vote on a particular bill be delayed. Or a senator may ask a committee chair how a given bill will affect constituents, and rely on the colleague's judgment. Reciprocity may involve trivial pleasantries—or millions of dollars in traded votes for public works appropriations.

In times past liberal and new senators used to complain of a conservative "Establishment" or "club" that dominated the Senate through the power of these folkways and through control of key committees and processes. But the Senate has changed. An activist and attractive senator can sometimes become a national political figure in less than a few years, and can soon thereafter be talked about as a possible candidate for the presidency. Indeed, presidential ambition in the Senate has also led to the decline of the Senate Establishment. What is notable about the Senate today is the dispersion of power among party leaders, sixteen committee leaders, several dozen subcommittee chairs, senators from the larger states, and issue experts or activists, such as Senator Sam Nunn, Democrat of Georgia on defense issues, or Senator Phil Gramm, Republican of Texas on budget issues. The contemporary Senate is individualistic. Committee leaders have more power than regular members, but with the expanding role of subcommittee chairs and expanding staff, their influence has lessened. More and more key decisions are made on the Senate floor. The Senate is a more open, fluid, and decentralized body now than it was a generation or two ago. Indeed, it is often said that the Senate has 100 separate power centers and is so splintered that the party leaders have difficulty arranging the day-to-day schedule. "It's pretty hard to set the agenda over here," said Senator Robert Dole. "The leadership is powerless unless the senators are willing to give them authority."[22]

The filibuster rule   A major difference between the Senate and the House is that debate is almost unlimited in the Senate. A senator who gains the floor has the right to go on talking until relinquishing it voluntarily or through exhaustion. This right to unlimited debate may be used by a small group of senators to **filibuster**—or delay the proceedings of the Senate in order to prevent a vote.

At one time the filibuster was a favorite weapon used by southern senators to block civil rights legislation. More recently the filibuster has been used less frequently. But at the end of any Senate session, when there is a fixed date for adjournment, threat of filibuster is a real danger for controversial legislation. The knowledge that a bill might be subject to a filibuster is often just enough to force a compromise satisfactory to its opponents. Of course, if there are enough votes, the objections can be overcome—if there is enough time. But at the end of a session, senators are anxious to go home and campaign. Sometimes the leadership, knowing that a filibuster would tie up the Senate and keep it from enacting other needed legislation, does not bother to bring a bill to the floor.

[21] See Stephen Hess, *The Ultimate Insiders: U.S. Senators and the Media* (Brookings Institution, 1986).
[22] Steven V. Roberts, "Wheels Are Spinning over the Senate Rules," *The New York Times* (February 26, 1986), p. 8.

Can a filibuster be defeated? The majority can keep the Senate in continuous session so that a filibustering senator will have to give up the floor. But if two or more senators cooperate, they can keep on talking almost indefinitely. They merely ask one another long questions that permit their partners to take lengthy rests.

Until 1917 the Senate could terminate debate or a filibuster only if every member agreed. That same year, however, the Senate adopted its first debate-ending or **cloture** rule. Now, as long as the senators who are doing the talking stay on their feet, debate can be shut off only by a cloture vote. The rule of cloture specifies that, two days after only sixteen members sign a petition, the question of curtailing debate must be put to a vote. If three-fifths of the total number of elected senators (60 of the 100 members) vote for cloture, no senator may speak for more than one hour. Nowadays, too, a final vote must be taken after no more than 100 hours of debate—including all delaying tactics such as quorum calls, roll call votes on procedure, and the like. After the 100 hours debate the motion before the Senate must be brought to a vote.

Filibusters are rare. Still, the filibuster, and the threat of it, remain a delaying device available to Senate minorities that forces the majority to compromise and water down their preferences. Not surprisingly, cloture votes are relatively rare as well, yet they are more common today than in earlier years. As many as twenty attempted cloture votes (over a two-year session) have been typical in recent years, with cloture votes to end filibusters successful at least half of the time. Sponsors sometimes invoke a cloture vote hoping to expedite floor business before debate has even been seriously begun.

"Well, we've seen the U.S. Senate in action on TV . . . Bill Cosby can relax." (*Dunagin's People by Ralph Dunagin. Copyright News America Syndicate, 1986. By permission of North America Syndicate, Inc.*)

COMMITTEES: THE LITTLE LEGISLATURES

Senate Watergate Committee Chairperson Sam Ervin was a very strong force throughout those difficult but important hearings. (*Don Carl Steffen/Photo Researchers*)

It is sometimes said that Congress is a collection of committees that come together in a chamber every once in a while to approve one another's actions. There is much truth in this. Almost from the beginning Congress has relied on committees to get much of its work done.[23] The main struggle over legislation takes place in committees and especially in subcommittees, for this is where the basic work of Congress is done.[24] The House of Representatives has twenty-two standing committees, each with an average membership of about thirty-five representatives. These committees have a total of about 140 subcommittees. The committees are "the eye, the ear, the hand, and very often the brain of the House."

Standing committees have great power, for all bills introduced in the House are referred to them. They can defeat bills, pigeonhole them for weeks, amend them beyond recognition, or speed them on their way. A committee reports out favorably only a small fraction of all the bills that come to it. Although a bill can be forced to the floor of the House through a **discharge petition** signed by a majority of the membership, legislators are reluctant to bypass committees: They regard committee members as experts in their fields. Sometimes, too, they are reluctant to risk the anger of committee leaders. And there is a strong sense of reciprocity— "You respect my committee's jurisdiction, and I will respect yours." Not surprisingly, few discharge petitions gain the necessary number of signatures.

The Senate has sixteen standing committees, each composed of twelve to twenty-nine members. Whereas members of the House hold relatively few committee

[23] See, for example, Thomas W. Skladony, "The House Goes to Work: Select and Standing Committees in the U.S. House of Representatives, 1789–1828," *Congress & the Presidency* (Autumn 1985), pp. 166–87.

[24] The best books on congressional committees, their staffs, and their influential roles are: Steven S. Smith and Christopher J. Deering, *Committees in Congress* (Congressional Quarterly Press, 1984), and Joseph Unekis and Leroy N. Rieselbach, *Congressional Committee Politics* (Praeger, 1984).

assignments, each senator normally serves on three committees and an average of seven subcommittees. Among the important Senate committees are foreign relations, budget, finance, and appropriations. Senate committees have the same powers over the framing of legislation as do those of the House, but they have somewhat less power to keep bills from reaching the floor.

Choosing Committee Members

Partisanship shapes the control and staffing of standing committees. The chair and a majority of the members are elected from the majority party. The minority party is represented roughly in proportion to its membership in the entire chamber. Getting on a politically advantageous committee is important to members of Congress. A representative from Kansas, for example, would much rather serve on the agriculture committee than on the merchant marine and fisheries committee. Members usually stay on the same committees from one Congress to the next, although younger members who have had undesirable assignments often bid for better committees when places become available.

How are committee members chosen? In the House of Representatives a Committee on Committees of the Republican membership allots places to new Republican members. This committee is composed of one member from each state having Republican representation in the House; the member is almost always the senior member of the state's delegation. Because each member has as many votes in the committee as there are Republicans in the delegation, the group is dominated by senior members from the large-state delegations. On the Democratic side assignment to committees is handled by the Steering Committee of the Democratic caucus in negotiation with senior Democrats from the state delegations. In the Senate veterans also dominate the assignment process; each party has a small steering committee for that purpose. In making assignments, leaders are guided by various considerations: how talented and cooperative a member is, whether his or her region is already well represented on a committee, and whether the assignment will aid in reelecting the member.

One reason Congress can cope with its huge workload is that its committees and subcommittees are organized around subject-matter specialties. This allows members to develop technical expertise in specific areas and to recruit skilled staffs, so that Congress is often able to criticize and challenge experts from the bureaucracy. Interest groups and lobbyists realize the great power a specific committee has in certain areas and focus their attention on its members. Similarly, members of executive departments are careful to cultivate the committee and subcommittee chairs and members of "their" committees. One powerful Senate committee chairperson reminded his constituents of the amount of federal tax money being spent in their state: "This does not happen by accident," the senator's campaign pamphlet said. "It takes power and influence in Congress."

Committee Diversity and Persistence

Most committees are separate little centers of power, with rules, patterns of action, and internal processes of their own. Analyzing the House appropriations committee, students of Congress discovered it is characterized by remarkable agreement among its members on key issues and on the role the committee should play. Leadership is stable, and members tend to remain a long time. They have worked out a way of life emphasizing conformity, give-and-take, and hard work. The subcommittee chairpersons of the House Appropriations Committee become specialists on the budgets and programs of the agencies within their jurisdiction, and often exercise more influence over administrative policy than any other single representative. For example, the chair of the Appropriations Subcommittee on Foreign Aid has more

What Do Committees Do?

- Study legislative proposals
- Consider communications from the executive branch
- Confirm or reject federal appointees
- Conduct hearings and investigations
- Review ongoing executive operations
- Prepare reports and surveys, and make recommendations about corrective legislation
- Review reports, documents, and research related to committee policy
- Meet informally with public- and private-sector leaders about their committee domain
- Conduct on-site visits/inspections
- Hold hearings that send messages about preferred policies, priorities, and personnel nominees

Congressional committee meeting.
(*Terry Ashe / Uniphoto*)

influence over that program than the chair of the House Committee on Foreign Affairs. The various appropriations subcommittees defer to one another's recommendations and back up the decisions of the parent committee.

Committees, however, differ. Whereas some are powerful, others are much less important. Because of the Senate's special role in foreign policy, for example, the Senate Foreign Relations Committee is usually more influential than the House Committee on Foreign Affairs. For the two appropriations committees, however, the reverse is true: The House committee sometimes plays a more significant role than the Senate committee. However, these differences are less than they used to be. We should also note that committees differ not only for institutional reasons but also according to the goals and abilities of their members.[25]

How Congress uses committees is critical in its role as a partner in national policy making. In recent years progress has been made to open hearings to the public and to improve the quality of committee staffs. But it is difficult to modernize jurisdictions, and jurisdictional overlap is common. For example, a dozen different committees deal with energy and education. Efforts to make the committee system more rational are often considered as a threat to the delicate balance of power within the chamber. In 1977, however, the Senate did streamline its committee structure. It prohibited any senator from chairing more than three committees and subcommittees, reduces the number of Senate committees, provided for somewhat more coherent committee jurisdiction, and established a computer system to schedule committee and subcommittee meetings, to avoid conflicts.

The Importance of Committee and Subcommittee Chairs

Committee and subcommittee leaders exercise influence over both the operations of their committees and the final output of Congress. Until the mid-1970s leaders determined the total workload of committees; hired and fired staff; and formed subcommittees and assigned them jurisdictions, members, and aides. Chairs also managed the most important bills assigned to their committees. In recent years, however, younger members have insisted they be given more authority. Subcommittee chairs have also tended to be more independent from the parent committees. It is not uncommon these days for a member of Congress of only one or two terms to be the chair of an important subcommittee, and indeed this is the tradition in the Senate.

Chairs are still usually awarded on the basis of *seniority*. The member of the majority party who has had the longest continuous service on the committee

U.S. Senator Richard Lugar (R-Indiana), a former Rhodes Scholar and Mayor of Indianapolis, Lugar has been a key force in the Senate Foreign Relations Committee. (*Courtesy Senator Richard Lugar*)

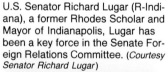

[25] Richard F. Fenno, Jr., *Congressmen in Committees* (Little, Brown, 1972).

ordinarily becomes its head. The chair may be at odds with other members of the party, may oppose the party's national program, and may even be incompetent; still, he or she usually wins the chair position because of seniority.

Modifying Seniority

Committee chair as well as assignments are the responsibility of the party caucuses in both chambers. The custom of seniority still prevails, but it is not a written rule, and other factors are beginning to be taken into account. In 1971, for example, the House Republican Conference decided that ranking Republicans on committees would henceforth be elected by the conference by a secret ballot. Soon afterwards Democrats authorized a secret ballot vote on chair positions if 20 percent of the caucus demanded it. In 1975 rank-and-file House Democrats, their ranks swollen and resolve stiffened by seventy-five mostly liberal newcomers, removed from their membership three elderly committee chairpersons. In early 1985 Les Aspin of Wisconsin was elected chair of the House Armed Services Committee by a coalition of junior and older members who respected him as the best choice and believed he was right on some major issues, even though he was not next in the line of seniority.

When Republicans control the Senate, Republican members of the major committees choose each committee's chair. When their party loses control over the Senate, these same persons become the ranking minority members. As a regular practice, Republican members almost always elect the senior member to serve as their leader on a committee.

The Senate Democrats choose their nominees for ranking minority members or for chair positions by a secret ballot of the Democratic Conference whenever requested to do so by 20 percent of the Senate Democratic membership. The Senate Democrats almost always do elect the senior Democratic member of the Senate committee to serve as the ranking committee member, but the fact that the Democratic Conference could by secret ballot do otherwise has forced senior members to make concessions to ensure their reelection.

The system of seniority tends to give the most influence in Congress to those constituencies that are politically stable or even stagnant. These are the areas where party competition is low or where a particular interest group or machine influence may be greatest. It stacks the cards against areas where the two parties are more evenly matched, where interest in politics is high, and where competition is keen.

Seniority is defended on the gounds that elevating the most experienced members to leadership positions is automatic and impersonal and prevents disputes. Seniority is also one of the important conflict-reducing norms practiced in both chambers of Congress. It facilitates the organization of Congress.

The argument over seniority is in large part over policy and political influence. Rural interests used to favor the system. And historically, it was opposed by such groups as organized labor, civil rights advocates, and other urban-based interests, who believed it gave rural interests and their conservative representatives too much power in Congress. Yet liberal groups may also profit from the system. The passage of time may cause the seniority custom to increase the influence of suburban and urban-based northern interests. As time passes, and more women and minorities win election to Congress, they too will likely attain chairships under the seniority custom that might be denied to them under more free-wheeling selection rules.

The system of seniority remains because it supports the interests of congressional leaders. Many legislators conclude: "The longer I'm here, the better I like the system." Further, those who are most anxious to change the system have the

U.S. Senator Alan Simpson (R-Wyoming) has served recently as Deputy Majority Leader. A tall former college basketball player and long-time state legislator, Simpson is widely admired for his wit and effectiveness as a legislator. (*Courtesy Senator Alan Simpson*)

U.S. Senator "Pete" Domenici (R-New Mexico) has headed the Senate Budget Committee and won widespread publicity for urging Reagan to cut more spending and raise revenues to balance the budget. (*Courtesy Senator Peter Domenici*)

least power to produce such changes. But as power has become dispersed, and as subcommittees have become increasingly important, the issue of seniority has diminished in importance. Subcommittee chairs tend to be members with less seniority, and they are likely to be more moderate than the committee chairs. In the Senate all but a handful of the majority party chair their own subcommittees; in the House more than 100 Democrats are subcommittee chairs. In recent years there have also been moves to strengthen the powers of the party leaders and caucuses—again at the expense of the committee chairs.

Committee Investigations

One of the most controversial activities of Congress is its investigations, especially such well-publicized open hearings as those of the Senate Foreign Relations Committee during the Vietnam War or those of various committees that have investigated the Iran-contra affair in 1987. Why does Congress investigate? Hearings by standing committees, their subcommittees, or special select committees are an important source of information and opinion. They provide an arena in which experts can submit their views and statements and statistics can be entered in the record.

Public hearings are an important channel of communication and influence. Senator Albert Gore of Tennessee, for example, held hearings to investigate the record industry and allegations that many radio stations play music based on money slipped under the table, not on the record's merits. Saying a " 'new payola' is alive and well and worse than ever," Gore sought to focus public attention on these corrupt and illegal bribery practices.[26] A committee or its chair may use a hearing to address Congress. Committee hearings may also be used to communicate with the public at-large. The Senate's Watergate Committee's televised investigations into election practices and campaign finance abuses in 1973, for example, were intended less to obtain new information than to arouse citizens and to promote public support for election reforms.[27] Some investigations by regular committees involve overseeing the current administration: A committee can summon administration officials to testify in hearings. Some officials fear these inquiries; they dread the loaded questions of hostile members and the likelihood that some administrative error in their agency may be uncovered and publicized.[28]

A legislative inquiry is a two-edged sword: It can spur Congress and the public to support needed laws or corrective legislation, or it can debase First amendment principles, invade the privacy of citizens, and afford a platform for grandstanding demagogues. Congressional investigations can also diminish executive branch morale. In the mid-1970s the Senate Select Committee on Intelligence Activities publicized such questionable practices by the CIA and FBI as plans to assassinate foreign leaders, dubious covert operations in foreign nations, and activities at home that probably undermined the basic rights of American citizens. Their goal as an investigatory committee was to raise important questions, to encourage greater executive branch accountability to the public, and to impress on Congress the need for legislation to prevent the abuse of power in the intelligence agencies.[29] Such hearings

[26] David T. Cook, "Congress to Investigate Record Industry," *Christian Science Monitor* (April 3, 1986), p. 7.

[27] For a study of the role of congressional investigations, see James Hamilton, *The Power to Probe: A Study of Congressional Investigations* (Vintage, 1976).

[28] See Lawrence C. Dodd and Richard Schott, *Congress and the Administrative State* (Wiley, 1979), chaps. 3, 5, and 6; and Morris S. Ogul, *Congress Oversees the Bureaucracy* (University of Pittsburgh Press, 1976).

[29] Loch Johnson, *A Season of Inquiry: The Senate Intelligence Investigation* (University of Kentucky Press, 1985).

can also help set the political agenda and send messages to the executive regarding personnel and policy preferences.[30]

GETTING IT TOGETHER: CONFERENCE COMMITTEES AND SENATE-HOUSE COORDINATION

When the framers created a two-house national legislature, they anticipated that the two chambers would represent sharply different interests. The Senate was to be a small chamber of persons elected indirectly by the people and holding long, overlapping terms. As noted, it would have the sole power to confirm nominations. Proposed treaties required the approval of a two-thirds vote in the Senate. The Senate was to be a chamber of scrutiny, a gathering of wise leaders who would counsel and sanction a president—whether that president liked it or not.

The House of Representatives, elected anew every two years, was to be a more direct instrument of the people. The Senate was a conservative check on the House, especially in the late nineteenth and early twentieth centuries, when it was extremely conservative and something of a rich man's club. But some factors—chiefly political—have altered the character of both the House and the Senate. Sometimes now the House serves as a conservative check on the Senate. Executive departments and agencies sometimes consider the Senate to be a court of appeals for appropriations that have been shot down by the House—although this was somewhat less the case in the Reagan years, when the Senate was controlled by Republicans.

How has this come about? A senator's constituency nearly always consists of a wider variety of interests than does that of a member of the House. But the Senate's behavior is also partly a result of the appropriations process and institutionalized rules. In the appropriations area the House completes its work before the Senate—and this has its consequences. Senate committee decisions often take the form of reactions to prior House decisions: adjustments of the appropriation figures upwards or downwards, depending on the issue.

Given the differences between the House and the Senate, it is not surprising that the version of a bill passed by one chamber may differ substantially from the version passed by the other. Only if both houses pass an absolutely identical measure can it become law. As a general rule, one house accepts the language of the other, but about 10 percent of all bills passed (usually major ones) must be referred to a **conference committee**.[31]

If neither house will accept the other's bill, a conference committee—a special committee of members from each chamber—settles the differences. Both parties are represented, but the majority party has more members. The proceedings of this committee are usually an elaborate bargaining process. When it is brought back to the two houses, the conference report can be accepted or rejected (often with further negotiations ordered), but it cannot be amended. Each set of conference members must convince its colleagues that any concessions made to the other house were on unimportant points and that nothing basic in their own version of the bill was surrendered.

How much leeway does a conference committee have? Ordinarily the members are expected to stay somewhere between the different versions. On matters for which there is no clear middle ground, members are sometimes accused of exceeding their instructions and producing a new bill. The conference committee has even

[30] John W. Kingdon, *Agendas, Alternatives and Public Policies* (Little, Brown, 1984).

[31] See John Ferejohn, "Who Wins in Conference Committees," *Journal of Politics*, vol. 3 (1975), pp. 1033–46; and Gerald S. Strom and Barry Rundquist, "A Revised Theory of Winning in House-Senate Conferences," *American Political Science Review*, vol. 71 (1977), pp. 448–53.

been called a "third house" of Congress, one that arbitrarily revises policy. Conference committees are also criticized on the ground that they are not representative, even of the committees approving the bill, and that they disproportionately represent senior committee leaders. Critics also complain that little can be done about biases that may creep into the bill in the conference committee, because the houses are usually confronted with a take-it or leave-it situation. Despite such criticism, some kind of conference committee is needed for a two-house legislature to work. Conference committees integrate the houses, help resolve disputes, and make compromises.

CONGRESSIONAL REFORM

There is so much criticism of Congress that we can only briefly review the main charges against it here.

1. Congress is *inefficient*. The House and Senate are simply not suited to the needs of an industrial nation. An endless amount of time is required to get bills through the complicated legislative process, and bills are often buried or defeated by procedural devices. Members are not as well informed as they should be. The dispersion of power guarantees slowness, if not inertia.

Some of this criticism is exaggerated. Evaluating procedure and structure is difficult to separate from evaluating policy, about which everyone has an individual preference. For example, from the White House vantage point, Congress is inefficient when it does not process the president's bills quickly.

Congress deals with an enormous number of complex measures. Many procedures in both houses expedite handling of bills, and the committee and subcommittee system is a reasonable device for hearing arguments and compiling information. Still, the question of efficiency remains. Many members themselves feel defeated by the system. Study groups inside and outside Congress have urged the houses to reduce the number of committee assignments, establish better information systems, centralize a bit more power in their leadership positions, and strengthen majority rule. Congress has done many of these things—but the pace is not much improved.

2. Congress is *unrepresentative*. The complaint is often made that Congress represents constituents' interests over the national interest. It is also said that the committee system often responds to organized regional or special interests. The seniority system, even with its modifications, biases both houses toward conservatism. Defenders of Congress contend there should be a strong institution to guarantee minority rights and to act as a check on mindless majority rule. Critics answer by arguing that minorities should have a right to publicize and delay what the majority proposes to do, but not to defeat it.

Both houses, critics hold, overrepresent well-organized economic power structures at the expense of the average citizen. Can the members of Congress, who are so much the products of upper- or upper-middle-class backgrounds, really speak for the needs of low-income groups? Can a Congress that has only 4 percent women and 3 or 4 percent black membership truly represent our female and minority population?

In fact, we have a system of dual representation in which both Congress and the president can and do claim to speak for the people. But because "the people" seldom, if ever, speak with a single voice, the structure and character of the two systems tend to give us a Congress that speaks for one majority and a president who often speaks for another. Between the two, we sometimes get a kind of balance—and sometimes a deadlock.

3. Congress is *unethical*. Many critics complain that some members of Congress are too tied to the economic interests they are asked to regulate. Others charge

Answer/Discussion

Normally you vote Republican and support the president, who is, after all, the leader of your party. But you may also decide on the basis of the following factors. First, you would consider the merits or demerits of the Department of Education. Perhaps you would ask for some studies of its effectiveness and efficiency. You might examine alternatives—a subcabinet agency, for example. You might also determine how the vote is likely to go. Does the president really need your support? If the measure is going to win easily or lose decisively, you might reason that your vote is rather unimportant. A close vote, however, is another matter. Also, you are likely to consider the will of the people—especially the voters back home—on the issue. Are the teachers who wrote you a small minority voice, or are they representative? And how important are they to your next election? These and other considerations—the views of your staff, the opinions of your best friends in Congress, and any lobbying efforts toward you on the issue by the president—may determine how you decide.

that members of Congress get too many personal privileges and that there have been too many abuses of these so-called fringe benefits. To be sure, the misbehavior of members of Congress is more frequently played up in the press than the misbehavior of others.

In response to occasional scandals, both houses have passed reasonably strong ethics codes and have created ethics committees. These changes require public disclosure of income and property holdings by legislators, key aides, and spouses. They also bar gifts of over $100 to a legislator, a staff member, or a legislator's family from a registered lobbyist, an organization with a political-action committee, a foreign government, or a business with an interest in legislation before Congress.

4. Congress *lacks collective responsibility*. The main problem in Congress is the dispersion of power among committee and subcommittee leaders, elected party officials, factional leaders, informal caucus leaders, and other legislators. It is a "nobody's in charge" system. This dispersion of power means that to get things done, congressional leaders must bargain and negotiate. The result of this "brokerage" system is that laws may be watered down, defeated, delayed, or written in vague language. Also, according to some critics, too much leeway is given to unknown bureaucrats. Accountability is confused, responsibility is eroded, and well-organized special interests who know how to work the system are given an unfair advantage.

Critics worry that if Congress responds to so many single interests, it cannot speak for the great majority or for the nation as a whole. It cannot anticipate problems, plan ahead, and put together political coalitions to deal with critical problems. Those concerned about congressional irresponsibility do not blame a few conservative interests or elite elements. They recognize that brokerage is mainly the result of a constitutional system that divides authority, checks power with power, and disperses political leadership. Yet other factors making it difficult for Congress to act as a unified branch arise from the fact that each house may be controlled by a different political party. Also, we are now electing brighter and more independent-minded individuals who are less inclined to go along with party leaders.

5. Congress *delegates too much to the executive branch*. Another charge is that Congress fails to do its job, and tends to delegate too much authority to the executive branch. Because of the complexity of modern problems and an inability to work out coalitions and compromises, there is a tendency for Congress to say to the executive branch: "Do something" about affirmative action; or "Do something" about consumer product safety. If Congress turns a matter over to an administrative agency, the result may be that the rules and regulations issued by the administrators effectively become the law.

These critics often disagree with the policy initiatives in question. Still, the complaint is valid, for we expect our *elected* officials to hammer out public policies. Congress is aware of this criticism, but sometimes escaping responsibility is a major consideration. If Congress passed specific legislation, affected persons or groups might then blame Congress rather than the administrative agencies—and perhaps even particular members of Congress, who then might lose their seats.

6. Congress is *too responsive to organized interests that through their political-action committees make large campaign contributions*. This final charge suggests that even though few members of Congress can be bought by campaign contributions, the way Congress conducts its business—and who gets heard at its hearings and in its corridors—is influenced to too great an extent by those who can raise and disburse large sums of money. Former Senator S. I. Hayakawa put it this way: "I'm not saying my colleagues are corrupted by the system. But it isn't hard for the recipient of a generous contribution from, let us say, the dairy industry to convince himself that what is in the interest of the dairy industry is indeed in the public interest."[32] Congressional campaign costs have skyrocketed in recent years; typical campaigns

[32] Quoted in *U.S. News & World Report* (December 20, 1982), p. 24. See also The Twentieth Century Fund Task Force on Political Action Committees, *What Price PACs?* (Twentieth Century Fund, 1984), and Gary C. Jacobson, *Money in Congressional Elections* (Yale University Press, 1980).

How to "Reform" Congress

The list of what should be done to save, rescue, or "cure" Congress never ends. Perhaps you can discuss these suggestions in class or with your professor.

□ Move to a European-style parliamentary system

□ Extend House terms to four years

□ Limit House and Senate tenure to twelve years

□ Provide for public financing of campaigns, and ban campaign contributions

□ Radically reduce the number of committees and subcommittees

□ Strengthen the power and resources of the party leaders

□ Reduce the size of congressional staffs, or enlarge them

□ Set and abide by an agenda agreed to at the beginning of each session

□ Have shorter sessions for Congress, so members can live in their districts and be "from somewhere" rather than be "Washingtonians"

□ Elect a senior senator rather than the vice-president to preside permanently over the Senate

□ No "reform" is neutral in terms of effects: Some groups will benefit more than others from the passage of a reform proposal. Also, most reforms have unanticipated consequences that often create more problems than they solve. Still, the search goes on for practical ways to improve Congress's ability to do the people's work.

cost over $400,000 for the House, and often several million dollars for the Senate. Money buys access, so it is claimed. The 1979 ABSCAM scandals, in which FBI agents posing as Arab sheiks successfully bought several promises of influence and favors from a handful of members of Congress, provide evidence for this criticism. It is small consolation that these members subsequently indicted and convicted by the federal courts. Former representative, senator and Reagan cabinet member Richard S. Schweiker said, "We've reached the point where a member has to be either a millionaire or a continual fundraiser, and that's a tragic commentary on where we are going."[33]

Defenders of Congress say these charges are overstated. They say money would hardly influence the three dozen or more millionaires who are members of the Senate and the 100 or so members of the House who are well off financially. Defenders of Congress also point out that many members of Congress regularly turn down certain types of campaign contributions. Because of various campaign reform laws, candidates for Congress must now report all major campaign contributions to the Federal Elections Commission. Thus, who gives what to whom is at least part of the public record. Still, the criticism is valid, and a large number of Americans are perplexed or disturbed about the degree of influence seemingly associated with campaign contributions.

In *The Federalist*, No. 57, James Madison wrote: "Who are to be the electors of the Federal Representatives? Not the rich more than the poor; not the learned more than the ignorant; not the haughty heirs of distinguished names, more than the humble sons of obscure and unpropitious fortune." Yet as the access and influence-buying increase, and as the body of elected officials continues to come from essentially the upper or upper-middle class, one must question whether ours is the open, representative system once envisioned by the drafters of the Constitution.

As we celebrate the bicentennial of the ratification of the Constitution and the first Congress, the following questions have to be raised: Can Congress create majorities? Can it have a long-range view, staying power, span of attention, and the ability to make sensible laws for the whole nation? Although answers would differ, all would agree that a vital, responsive, and effective Congress is a must if we would make government by the people work.

[33] David S. Broder, "Who Took the Fun out of Congress?" *The Washington Post National Weekly Edition* (February 17, 1986), p. 10. For an overview of congressional reform efforts, see Burton D. Sheppard, *Rethinking Congressional Reform: The Reform Roots of the Special Interest Congress* (Schenkman Books, 1985).

SUMMARY

1. Senators and representatives come primarily from upper- and middle-class backgrounds. They are far better educated than Americans as a whole. The typical member of the 101st Congress is a middle-aged, white, male lawyer.

2. Most of the work in Congress gets done in committees and subcommittees. Congress has attempted in recent years to streamline its committee system and modify its methods of selecting committee chairs. Seniority practices are still generally followed, but the threat of removal forces committee chairs to consult with younger members of the majority party. Subcommittees are now more important in an increasingly decentralized Congress.

3. Congress performs these functions: representation, law making, consensus building, overseeing, policy clarification, and legitimizing. Congress as a collective body must attempt to perform these tasks even as most of its members serve as ombudsmen for their constituents and work for their own reelections.

4. The workload for Congress is considerable. Much could be done to make our national legislature perform its functions more effectively. Some improvements have been made in recent years: Redistricting and reapportionment have shaped a Congress that more accurately reflects the population. The filibuster in the Senate and the Rules Committee in the House are less obstructive than they once were. The role of the speaker and of party steering committees has been enhanced, and Congress is better staffed.

5. The negative image of Congress as a ponderous or sluggish institution is still common. Its greatest strengths—

its diversity and deliberative character—also weaken against the executive branch. Its members will rarely be fast on their 1070 feet. The 535 members, divided into two houses, two parties, dozens of committees, and hundreds of subcommittees, will always have a difficult time arriving at a common strategy to combat a president determined to use executive powers to the full. How effectively can Congress assert itself, especially with respect to the presidency? How can it deal with budget deficits and national security? We return to a consideration of these questions in Chapter 15, after we have examined the modern presidency and its responsibilities.

FURTHER READING

WILLIAM S. COHEN and GEORGE J. MITCHELL. *Men of Zeal: A Candid Inside Story of the Iran-Contra Hearings* (Viking, 1988).

JOSEPH COOPER and G. CALVIN MacKENZIE, eds. *The House at Work* (University of Texas Press, 1981).

ROGER H. DAVIDSON and WALTER J. OLESZEK. *Congress and its Members*, 2nd ed. (Congressional Quarterly Press, 1985).

CHRISTOPHER J. DEERING, ed. *Congressional Politics* (Dorsey, 1989).

LAWRENCE C. DODD and BRUCE I. OPPENHEIMER, eds. *Congress Reconsidered*, 4th ed. (Congressional Quarterly Press, 1989).

RICHARD F. FENNO, JR. *Home Style: House Members in their Districts* (Little, Brown, 1978).

MORRIS FIORINA. *Congress—The Keystone of the American Establishment* (Yale University Press, 1977).

ALVIN M. JOSEPHY, JR. *On the Hill: A History of the American Congress* (Simon & Schuster, 1979).

GERHARD LOEWENBERG, SAMUEL C. PATTERSON, and MALCOLM JEWELL, eds. *Handbook of Legislative Research* (Harvard University Press, 1985).

MICHAEL MALBIN. *Unelected Representatives: Congressional Staff and the Future of Representation* (Basic Books, 1980).

DAVID R. MAYHEW. *Congress: The Electoral Connection* (Yale University Press, 1974).

JAMES A. MILLER. *Running in Place: Inside the Senate* (Simon & Schuster, 1986).

WALTER J. OLESZEK. *Congressional Procedures and the Policy Process*, 2nd ed. (Congressional Quarterly Press, 1983).

STEVEN S. SMITH and CHRISTOPHER J. DEERING. *Committees in Congress* (Congressional Quarterly Press, 1984).

DARRELL M. WEST. *Congress and Economic Policymaking* (University of Pittsburgh, 1987).

14

The Presidency: Leadership Branch?

It is well known that the framers in 1787 perceived the presidency in the image of George Washington, the man they expected would first occupy the office. The American chief executive, like Washington, was to be a wise, moderate, dignified, nonpartisan "president of all the people." But should the future presidency be "above politics" or should it be a frankly political institution? Should the president *lead* the people, or wait upon a consensus? Should he be essentially a "republican monarch" or a democratic politician, a man of the people?

This last question provoked a quarrel among the politicians establishing the new government in New York. Some believed that the president should be addressed as "His Highness" or even "His Elective Highness." John Adams said that "President" wasn't dignified enough—one could be president of *any* little organization. But good Republicans were shocked. "His Highness" was the title used for monarchs! The Republicans won out—"President" or "Mr. President" it would be.

No one in 1789 commanded the trust and respect that George Washington did. He had served his country in a variety of ways, most notably as commander in chief of the Continental army for eight years and as an instigator of, and later presiding officer at, the Constitutional Convention of 1787. In early 1789 he was unanimously elected the first president of the new Republic.

Washington knew the country needed more continuity and more foreign policy and emergency leadership from its fledgling government. Yet, as he set out in April 1789 for New York (the temporary seat of government), his feelings about the role of the presidency in American society were mixed. If he had doubts about his qualifications for this new post, they must have magnified as he traveled slowly up the East Coast from Mt. Vernon to New York. A series of parades and fireworks greeted him as he went. His whole trip was one long ovation, a celebration of and yearning for leadership. Just as they would do in other periods of crisis or major transition, Americans turned to one strong individual to provide unity and to symbolize the best in the nation.

Washington and his compatriots were of two minds about executive power for good reasons. Today we would call this attitude an ambivalence toward power. To put it simply, the framers and their supporters admired yet feared leadership.

14–1 Qualities Desired in a Presidential Candidate:	
Honesty	94%
Intelligence	87
Ability to communicate	74
Political experience	52
Political philosophy	33
Political party	23

Source: US News and World Report—CNN poll of 1000 adults, 1986.

Three presidents—Harry S Truman, Dwight D. Eisenhower, and John F. Kennedy—are shown together in this picture. They were attending the 1962 funeral of Speaker of the House, Sam Rayburn, in Texas. (*UPI/Bettmann Newsphotos*)

They realized the country needed more effective, centralized governance mechanisms, yet they were suspicious of the potential abuses of power, and especially of great power vested in a single individual. They had every right to these fears after what they had lived through in the 1760s and 1770s. Moreover, people like Washington hardly wanted to jeopardize the rights and liberties they had fought so hard to win in the recent revolution.

Although Constitutional Convention delegates James Wilson and Gouverneur Morris are credited with writing many of the constitutional provisions for the presidency, George Washington also played an important role in shaping the American presidency.[1] Since at least 1780 he had been calling for the strengthening of the leadership capacities of the new government. His experience and many of his functions as commander in chief were incorporated into the new job of the president. Other key aspects of the new invention were modifications of the office of governor in New York and Massachusetts, or variations of powers exercised by the Crown, and lessons learned from the ineffectual attempts by the Continental Congress to provide ad hoc executive leadership. But just as important, the debates in Philadelphia about what kind of presidency we would have were also debates over what powers the delegates were willing to grant to George Washington, because most of the delegates there hoped he would serve as the first national executive.

On April 30, 1789, after the first Congress had been in session for several weeks, George Washington was sworn in at Federal Hall in the downtown financial district of New York. Standing along side him were Vice-President John Adams and several Revolutionary generals. A crowd of artisans as well as society and business types watched as the Chancellor of New York administrated the oath of office to Washington. As Washington concluded the oath, the American flag was raised on the staff above the balcony and the crowd shouted, "Long live George Washington, President of the United States!", while the guns of the battery roared their salute. After this brief ceremony, Washington stepped inside to the Senate's chamber and delivered the first presidential inaugural address.

Washington's misgivings about his qualifications and about the scope of presidential power faded as he set precedents and fulfilled the hopes of the people. He was sensitive to the fine line between providing stronger leadership and infringing on the individual rights and liberties of the people. He knew then, as every president after him has either known or learned, that Americans have a strong streak of anti-government and even anti-authority sentiment. We want strong presidential leadership when the times demand or when it serves our favorite causes, yet we also insist that no elected official or governmental agency dare infringe on our rights.

We have never been wholly pleased by the reality of strong governments and centralized leadership institutions such as the presidency. Nonetheless, most Americans today accept these as necessities in our complex and highly developed modern world. We still worry about the abuses of power, the diminution of our rights and liberties, and the extent to which we have concentrated power in Washington, D.C.; yet, paradoxically, we also revere our successful presidents, and we often hunger for compelling, creative, dynamic leadership.

AN EFFECTIVE PRESIDENCY?

What does it take to be an effective president? Are the constitutional powers of the presidency adequate for carrying out modern presidential responsibilities? Can the modern presidency meet our high expectations? And can it survive the grinding pressures of crises abroad and human demands at home?

[1] Glenn A. Phelps, "George Washington and the Building of the Constitution: Presidential Interpretation and Constitutional Development," *Congress & the Presidency* (Autumn 1985), pp. 95–109.

Who Were the Best Presidents?

A. Surveys of *historians* (including a 1983 survey of 970 historians) have consistently obtained these results:

1. Lincoln
2. Washington
3. F. D. Roosevelt
4. Jackson
   Jefferson
   Theodore Roosevelt
   Wilson

B. But surveys of the public turn out differently: The Gallup Poll (1975) asked the American people: "What three presidents do you regard as the greatest?"

1. Kennedy   52%
2. Lincoln   49%
3. F. D. Roosevelt   45%
4. Truman   37%
5. Washington   25%
6. Eisenhower   24%

C. The Gallup Poll (1983) asked the American people: "Of all the Presidents we have ever had, who do you wish were President today?"

1. Kennedy   30%
2. F. D. Roosevelt   10%
3. Truman   9%
4. Reagan   8%
5. Lincoln   5%
6. Carter   5%
7. Eisenhower   4%

Our Constitution establishes only three qualifications for the office: A president must be at least 35 years of age, have lived in the United States for fourteen years, and be a natural-born citizen. Our "unwritten presidential job description"— the one we carry around as images in our heads—says that a president has to be many things to many people. Every four years Americans search the national landscape for a new superstar who is blessed with the judgment of a Washington, the mind of a Jefferson, the steadfastness of a Lincoln, the calm of an Eisenhower, and the grace of a John F. Kennedy. Although the American presidency may not have been designed in 1787 as a leadership institution (certainly not as a party, legislative, or economic leadership post), the situation has certainly changed.

Presidents are expected to provide strong, able, and popular leadership. Americans want leaders who can grasp the real needs and higher aspirations of the American people and who can make our huge, fragmented system of government serve those needs and aspirations. In periods of crisis our so-called three-branch system seems to have worked best as a presidential system—that is, as a system in which the presidency has been dominant. Only strong presidents have been able to overcome the tendency toward inertia inherent in a nation so beset with checks and balances and separated powers.

But exactly what do the American people want of their president? They want leadership—but what kind of leadership?—an ability to work with Congress, to solve economic problems, to keep the peace, to gain the people's confidence, and to get things done. They also want someone who can provide a sense of purpose— someone who can remind us of our basic aspirations as a democratic and generous nation, and as an innovative and experimenting people.

Voters often place more emphasis on a candidate's character and integrity than they do on the candidate's *policy* preferences. This is not misguided. Presidents have enormous power, especially in emergencies. They also play an important role in making appointments, which in turn reflects their interest in upholding ethical standards of governmental performance. Thus, it is important to assess their characters. Will they become rigid or dogmatic in dealing with crises, or with Congress, the press, advisers, and critics? Will they display vision, judgment, a grasp of history, a sense of proportion, and a sense of humor? To be sure, people prefer candidates whose views on issues accord with their own; if they like a person's personality, they trust that individual's policy ideas to be acceptable. Hence, a candidate's character and policy preferences sometimes get blurred—if not reversed—in the voter's mind.

In addition, the public also wants a president to be tough, decisive, and competent. Voters recognize the need, *even in a democracy*, for strong leadership. They yearn for a leader with foresight and personal strength. Moreover, people want someone who will simplify politics, symbolize the protective role of the state, and yet seem to be concerned with *them*. We want *effectiveness*, but also *fairness*. Do we ask too much? Novelist John Steinbeck thought so: "We give the President more work than a man can do, more responsibility than a man should take, more pressure than a man can bear. We abuse him often and rarely praise him. We wear him out, use him up, eat him up. . . . he is ours and we exercise the right to destroy him."[2]

Americans applaud presidents when things go well and blame them when things go wrong. Disasters as well as triumphs are credited to presidents—Wilson's League of Nation's, Hoover's Depression, Roosevelt's New Deal, Johnson's Vietnam War, Nixon's Watergate, Carter's Iranian crisis, Reagan's tax cuts. An exaggerated sense of presidential wisdom and power has caused us to forget that there are limits to what presidents can accomplish. Although the tragedies of American involvement in Vietnam and of presidential involvement in the Watergate scandals de-

[2] John Steinbeck, *America and Americans* (Bonanza Books, 1966), p. 46.

The White House

1600 Pennsylvania Ave., N.W.
Washington, D.C. 20500

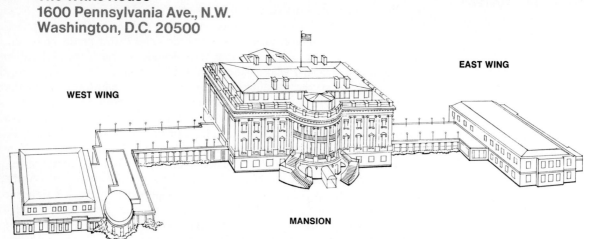

WEST WING

EAST WING

MANSION

The White House is an executive office, a ceremonial mansion, and a home. Several presidents have viewed it almost as a jail, preferring to spend as much time as possible at other presidential retreats outside of Washington. But most Americans view the rather elegant White House as the center of political and social activity in the nation's capital. It is also something of a national shrine as millions of people from America as well as around the world visit and inspect it each year.

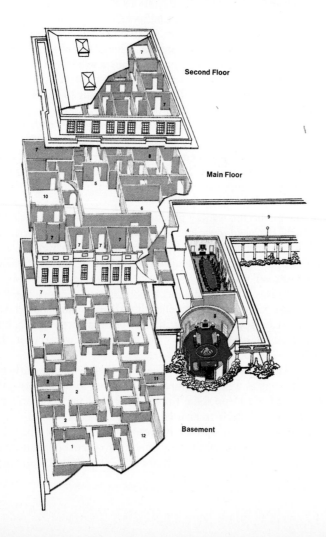

Second Floor

Main Floor

Basement

WEST WING

1 Situation Room
2 National Security Council Staff
3 Oval Office
4 Cabinet Room
5 West Lobby
6 Roosevelt Room (Conference Room)
7 Assistants to the President
8 Presidential Press Secretary
9 Press Briefing Room and Filing Center
10 Vice-President's Office
11 Photo Office
12 White House Staff Dining Room

glamorized the presidency, the vitality of our democracy still depends in large measure on creative presidential leadership.

IS THE PRESIDENCY TOO STRONG—OR NOT STRONG ENOUGH?

Some critics see the presidency as fast becoming inconsistent with democratic ideals. They view it as an often remote and autocratic institution, as the citadel of the status quo, as the center of the industrial-military-political complex—and as the very heart of the Establishment. They charge that presidents are less accountable today than ever before, and that they have the power to get around the formal checks and balances designed by the Constitution's framers. Critics complain too that presidents now manipulate the public's sense of reality by relying on secrecy, emergency powers, and the "electronic throne" of television.

Many people care more about the purposes of presidential authority than about the extent or uses of it: Only when the president appears to represent interests that these people approve do they say the power should be left unchecked. Other critics are more concerned about *process*. If the president's actions reflect the wishes of the majority of the people most of the time, the process is assumed to be working properly.

Activists in both parties, on the other hand, look to the president as the potential spokesperson for the common person. Throughout the twentieth century active presidents have tended to bring about changes that have pleased the progressive forces. The New Deal and the Kennedy-Johnson initiatives on civil rights are examples. There is no guarantee, of course, that an activist president will please the progressives. Vietnam provides an example to the contrary. The Reagan tax and budget cuts are another example.

Historically the great presidents have been strong presidents who have moved outside elite power structures to reach and serve the masses. That was how Jefferson and Jackson overcame the established elites of their day; that is how the two Roosevelts overcame the "economic royalists" of their day. Although presidents often have to compromise with existing elites, sometimes the chief executive has the power to defy the "Establishment." Presidents like to quote Franklin Roosevelt who, after some businesspeople had cursed him for his "radical" New Deal policies, cried out at the height of his 1936 reelection campaign: "I should like to have it said of my first Administration that in it the forces of selfishness and of lust for power met their match. I should like to have it said of my second Administration that in it their forces met their master!"

After the Watergate scandals of the Nixon administration, many argued persuasively that our system of checks and balances needed to be strengthened. But once Watergate had faded into the past and the nation was faced with inflation, unemployment, huge federal deficits, severe trade imbalances, and countless other problems that nobody seemed able to solve—including Presidents Ford and Carter—the public seemed to demand stronger national leadership.

Ronald Reagan came to office after two short and some would say failed presidencies. He rallied "middle class" and conservative interests against the congressional establishment and enjoyed several successes during his first term. But his second term witnessed soaring budget deficits, several legislative defeats and a number of celebrated scandals including indictments and convictions of some of his White House aides and advisors. Congress thwarted nominations and used its investigation powers to counter some of Reagan's less valued initiatives.

Perhaps there is something, after all, to the check and balance system, which forces a president to work through the elites and build political–popular pressures via the media.

Public attitudes, as well as those of scholars who study the presidency, are difficult to pin down, and they change often. Everyone seems to favor strong leadership; yet this does not necessarily mean strong executive leadership. We want, apparently, strong presidents, provided they do what we want them to do. Otherwise, we want them to be limited by checks and balances. Indeed, all our checks and balances make the prospects for positive presidential leadership difficult.[3]

THE JOB OF THE PRESIDENT

The nation's founders created a presidency of somewhat limited powers. They wanted a presidential office that would stay clear of parties and factions, enforce the laws passed by Congress, deal with foreign governments, and help states put down disorders. They wanted a presidency strong enough to match Congress, but not so strong that it would overpower Congress. They seemed to have in mind that the president should be an elected king, with substantial personal authority, who served the common good and minimized the baleful influence of the worst factions. The framers of the Constitution rejected a *plural* or *collegial* executive; there would be no ceremonial head separate from an administrative one. The term of office would be four years, and presidents would be indefinitely reeligible to succeed themselves. Although independent from the legislature, presidents would still share considerable power with Congress. The essence of the arrangement would be an *intermingling* of powers with Congress. To achieve change, the separate branches would have to work in cooperation and consult with one another. A president's major appointments would have to be approved by the Senate; Congress could override the chief executive's veto by a two-thirds vote of each chamber; and the president could make treaties only with the advice and consent of two-thirds of the senators. All appropriations (the power of the purse), of course, would be legislated by Congress, not the president.

Even a presidency with such limited powers, hemmed in by the system of checks and balances, worried some Americans in 1787. The framers deliberately gave to the president broadly outlined, as well as vaguely defined, powers. The president, they thought, should have discretionary power, so that this official could act when other governmental branches failed to meet their responsibilities or to respond to the urgencies of the day. But they were reassured by the fact that George Washington was to be the first chief executive. And they recognized that, at least on paper, Congress was truly the first branch. A relatively unified Congress could make life pretty miserable for a president. It could, for example, refuse to confirm a president's vital nominations, refuse to pass legislation suggested by a president, refuse funds for key programs, and refuse to ratify treaties. It could also **override** the chief executive's vetoes. But the historical record suggests most presidents have enjoyed far greater cooperation with Congress than this implies. Nonetheless, modern-day presidents are much more powerful than those of the last century, even though their constitutional powers have not changed.

After nearly two centuries our presidential "track record" is good. Perhaps in no other nation have persons with such power at their command so carefully followed the restraints imposed on them by a written Constitution. But to describe presidential power is inadequate. The exact dimensions of executive power at any given moment are partly the consequence of the incumbent's character and energy,

Constitutional Responsibilities of a President

- Act as commander in chief
- Conduct foreign policy
- Negotiate treaties
- Nominate top federal officials, including federal judges
- Veto bills
- Faithfully administer federal laws
- Pardon for federal offenses
- Address Congress and nation

[3] See Bert A. Rockman, *The Leadership Question* (Preager, 1984), and James MacGregor Burns, *The Power to Lead* (Simon & Schuster, 1984).

Additional Presidential Responsibilities and Informal Roles

- Morale builder
- Party leader
- Legislative leader
- Coalition builder
- Crisis manager
- Personnel recruiter
- World leader
- Budget setter
- Priority setter
- Bargainer and persuader
- Conflict resolver

combined with the needs of the time and the challenges to our nation's survival.[4] By and large, the history of presidential power is one of steady but uneven growth. Of the forty one individuals who have filled the office, about a third have enlarged its powers. Jackson, Lincoln, and both Roosevelts, for example, strengthened both the institution and its powers by the way they responded to crises and set priorities.

In this extension of the executive power Congress and the courts have often been willing partners. In emergencies Congress often rushes to delegate discretion to the executive branch; and the legislature sometimes seems incapable of dealing with matters that are highly technical or that require constant management or consistent judgment. Some people think what Congress lacks most is the will to use the powers it already has. But this hardly seems to be a satisfactory explanation, because Congress is not unique among legislative bodies. During the last two centuries in all democracies, and at all levels, power has drifted from legislators to executives. The English prime minister, the French president, the governors of our states, and the mayors of our cities all play more dominant roles than they did, generally speaking, 100 years ago.

The danger of war plainly increases a president's impact on the nation's affairs. The Cold War shattered most of the remaining nostalgia for **isolationism.** The combination of an enormous standing army, nuclear weapons, and the Cold War invited presidential dominance in national security matters. Television has also contributed to the growth of presidential influence. With access to prime time, presidents can take their cases directly to the people. This invitation to bypass and sometimes to ignore Congress, the Washington press, and even party leaders weakens the checks once imposed on the presidency.

The great growth of the federal role in domestic and economic matters has also enlarged presidential responsibility and contributed to the swollen presidential establishment. Problems not easily delegated to any one department often get pulled into the White House. When new programs concern several federal agencies, someone near the president is asked to set a consistent policy and reconcile conflicts. White House aides, with some justification, claim the presidency is the only place in government where it is possible to establish and coordinate national priorities. And presidents constantly set up central review and coordination units. These help formulate new policies, settle jurisdictional disputes among departments, and provide access for the well-organized interest groups who want their views to be given weight in decision making.

The swelling of the presidency has also been encouraged by the public's expectations. Although we may dislike or condemn individual presidents, popular attitudes toward the institution of the presidency remain positive. We want very much to believe in and trust our presidents. Perhaps this is because we have no royal family, no established religion, and no common ceremonial leadership divorced from executive responsibilities. In an effort to live up to unrealistic expectations, some presidents overextend themselves. Maintaining presidential popularity encourages them to make frequent appeals to the general public. This may help presidents temporarily improve their public images and even win occasional fights in Congress, but they may gamble too often that they can use public support as a chip to secure bargains in their favor.[5] They may also undermine their relations with Congress and help render the parties less important in supplying policy ideas and keeping presidents and other elected officials accountable.[6]

Nowadays a president is asked to play countless roles that are not carefully

The White House. (*T. Cronin*)

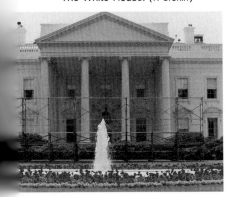

[4] For a different point of view, see Benjamin I. Page and Mark P. Petracca, *The American Presidency* (McGraw-Hill, 1983), chap. 1.

[5] See Lyn Ragsdale, "Presidents and Publics." Paper presented at annual meeting of the American Political Science Association, New Orleans, August 29–September 1, 1985.

[6] See Theodore J. Lowi, *The Personal President* (Cornell University Press, 1985).

FUNCTIONAL LEADERSHIP	EXAMPLES OF POLICY RESPONSIBILITIES		
	Foreign Policy	*Economics*	*Domestic Policy*
Crisis management	Dealing with Iranian crisis, U.S. troops in Lebanon	FDR's handling of the Depression, 1930s	Controlling immigration and drug flow
Symbolic and morale-building leadership	Reagan's visit to Normandy Beach	Being bullish on American productivity	Visiting flood and disaster victims
Recruitment of top officials	Selecting chairpersons of the Joint Chiefs of Staff	Hiring wise economic advisers	Appointing a chief justice
Priority setting and problem clarification	Defining our relations with the USSR—INF Treaty	Outlining a tax-cut program	Setting priorities in environmental protection
Legislative and political coalition building	Reagan's fighting for aid for El Salvador and Contras	Reagan's campaigning for tax reform	Fighting over domestic spending
Program implementation and administration	Making Middle East peace accords work	Shoring up the social security program	Seeing that the laws are faithfully executed
Oversight of government performance and early detection of possible problems	Evaluating our relations with Japan and Mexico	Monitoring internal revenue service performance	Appraising the impact of federal social programs

Presidential Age and Turnover

- Oldest when elected: Reagan, 69 (first term), 73 (second term)
- Youngest when elected: Kennedy, 43
- Average age at inauguration: 54
- Average service: 4.9 years
- One-term presidents: 25
- Two-term presidents: 13
- Three terms + : 1 (FDR)

spelled out in the Constitution. We want the chief executive to be an international peace maker as well as a national morale builder, a politician-in-chief, and a unifying representative of all the people. We want every new president to be virtually everything all our great presidents have been. Rightly or wrongly, we believe our greatest presidents were models of talent, tenacity, and optimism: persons who could clarify the vital issues of the day and mobilize the nation for action. We like to think of our great presidents as leaders who could not only symbolize the best in the nation and move the enterprise forward, but who could summon the highest kinds of moral commitment from the American people. These storybook images of our great presidents often make it tough for modern presidents to do their job.

In addition to the obvious leadership responsibilities a president has in foreign policy, economics, and domestic policy, seven broad functional kinds of leadership are expected of a president. These policy areas and functions, when examined together, permit us to develop a job profile of an American president (see Table 14–2).

PRESIDENTS AS CRISIS MANAGERS

"The President shall be Commander in Chief of the Army and the Navy of the United States," reads Section 2 of Article II of the Constitution. Even though this is the first of the president's powers listed in the Constitution, the framers intended the military role to be a limited one—far less than a king's. It was as if the president would be a sort of first general and first admiral. As it turns out, the military role has become much more important: The president has a finger on the nuclear button and appears to have sole authority over limited wars as well.

When crises and national emergencies occur, Americans instinctively turn to the chief executive, who is expected to provide not only executive and political leadership but also the appearance of a confident, "take-charge" leader who has a steady hand at the helm. Public necessity forces presidents to do what Lincoln

YOU DECIDE !

Before he left office, President Reagan called for the repeal of the Twenty-second amendment to the Constitution, the one that limits a president to two terms. He said he wanted it, not to go into effect for him, but for future presidents. Why do you think he favored it? What additional reasons could be put forth to persuade people to repeal this relatively new (1951) provision in the Constitution? What are the best reasons for retaining the Twenty-second? How would you decide if you were asked to vote on a proposed amendment to repeal this amendment?

(Answer/Discussion on the next page.)

and Franklin Roosevelt once did during the national emergencies of their day—namely, to protect the union and to safeguard vital American interests.

Nearly two centuries of national expansion and recurrent crises have increased the powers of the president beyond those specified by the Constitution. The complexity of Congress's decision-making procedures, its unwieldy numbers, and its constitutional tasks make it a more public, deliberative, and divided organization than the presidency. When major crises occur, Congress traditionally holds debates—but just as predictably delegates authority to a president, charging that official to take whatever actions are necessary.

The primary factor underlying this transformation in the president's function as commander in chief has been the changed role of the United States in the world, especially since World War II. In the postwar years every president argued for and won widespread support for the position that military strength, especially military superiority over the Soviet Union, was the primary route to national security. Nations willingly grew dependent on our assistance, which rapidly became translated into a multitude of treaties, pacts, and **executive agreements.** From then on, nearly every threat to the political stability of our far-flung network of allies became a test of whether we would honor our commitments in good faith. These commitments, plus the fear of nuclear war and the importance of deterrence, prompted Congress to give great flexibility to presidents in this area.

Presidents are expected to be crisis managers in the domestic sphere as well. Whenever things go wrong, we demand presidential-level planning and problem solving. When both New York City and the Chrysler Corporation were on the verge of bankruptcy, people turned to the White House for help. When terrorists attacked U.S. citizens on an airplane, people assumed that the president would retaliate (as Reagan did against Libya). In many crises, however, a president is often little more than a victim of fast-breaking events and environmental forces. Presidents are sometimes surprised, overtaken by developments beyond their control, and placed on the defensive.

PRESIDENTS AS MORALE-BUILDING LEADERS

Presidents are the nation's number-one celebrity; almost anything they do is news. Merely by going to church or to a sports event, presidents command attention. By their actions presidents can arouse a sense of hope or despair, honor or dishonor.

The framers of the Constitution did not fully anticipate the symbolic and morale-building functions a president must perform. Certain magisterial functions, such as receiving ambassadors and granting pardons, were conferred. But over time the presidency has acquired enormous symbolic significance. No matter how enlightened or rational we consider ourselves, all of us respond in some way to symbols and rituals. The president often affects our images of authority, legitimacy, and confidence in our political system.

Although Americans like to view themselves as hardheaded pragmatists, they—like humans everywhere—cannot stand too much reality. Humans do not live by reason alone. Myths and dreams are an age-old form of escape. And people turn to national leaders just as tribespeople turn to shamans—for meaning, healing, empowerment, assurance, and a sense of purpose.

Americans expect many things from their presidents: honesty, credibility, crisis leadership, agenda-setting and administrative abilities, and also certain tribal-leader or priestly functions. Many people find comfort in an oversimplified image of the president as a warrior-captain at the helm of the great ship of state, as a liberator, prophet, defender of liberty and democracy, and spokesperson for the American Dream.

George Washington and his advisors recognized from the beginning, in 1789, that the job of the presidency demanded symbolic leadership. They knew that effective leadership must symbolize the best in the community, the best in our traditions, values, and purposes. Effective leadership infuses vision and a sense of meaning into the enterprise of a nation.

The Popular Need for Leadership

A president's personal conduct affects how millions of Americans view their political loyalties and civic responsibilities. Of course, the symbolic influence of presidents is not always evoked in favor of worthy causes, and sometimes presidents do not live up to our expectations of moral leadership.

"The Presidency is the focus for the most intense and persistent emotions. . . . The President is . . . the one figure who draws together the people's hopes and fears for the political future. On top of all his routine duties, he has to carry that off—or fail."[7]

It would be much easier for everyone, some say, if our president were a prime minister, called on merely to manage the affairs of government in as efficient and practical a way as possible and not also our chief of state. But this is not the case.[8] Americans are not about to invent a head-of-state position separate from the presidency. That would be too much like England. Moreover, it would weaken an already fragile institution.

Presidential head-of-state duties often seem trivial and unimportant. For example, pitching out the first baseball of the season, buying Christmas or Easter seals, pressing buttons that start big power projects, and consoling the survivors of American victims of terrorist attacks do not require executive talents. Yet our president is continuously asked to champion our common heritage, to help unify the nation, and also to create an improved climate within which the diverse interests of the nation can work together.

A Presidential Dilemma

Under ordinary conditions the presidential claim to be "leader of all the people," or symbolic leader of the nation, conflicts with the reality of a president who tries to act as party leader. Some expectations for presidents are fundamentally inconsistent with one another. On the one hand, the president is a party leader: the spokesperson and representative of a segment of the population that is loosely identified with a particular party. As such the chief executive not only directs the national party organization but—as chief legislator—also takes specific positions on issues for or against some groups. On the other hand, as ceremonial leader and chief of state, the president attempts to act for all the people. A chief executive must faithfully administer the laws, whether passed by Democratic or Republican majorities in Congress. Yet in choosing subordinates and in applying the law, presidents often understandably think first of the interests of those who elected them.

The relationship between these presidential roles is uneasy. For example, the president may wish to address the nation about a problem—and usually the chief executive is granted free time on radio and TV. But if an election is close, the opposition often charges the president is really acting as party chief and that the party should pay for the radio or TV time. The same question comes up in connection with a president's inspection trips, especially when they are used as occasions for

[7] James David Barber, *The Presidential Character*, 3rd ed. (Prentice-Hall, 1985). See also George Edwards, *The Public Presidency* (St. Martin's Press, 1983).

[8] For a more extensive treatment of the symbolic implications of the presidency, see Michael Novak, *Choosing our King* (Macmillan, 1974).

political talks and general politicking. Ronald Reagan's visit to the People's Republic of China in 1984, or his Liberty Weekend 1986 talks and activities in New York harbor, or his ceremonial visit to the Normandy beaches and cemeteries to commemorate D-Day are classic examples of this dilemma.

Most of the time a president manages to combine the offices of chief of state and party leader without much difficulty. Most people accept that a president holds both roles and moves from one to the other as conditions demand. There is nothing wrong with the symbolic powers that come with the job. They become a problem only when they lead the public to believe symbolism equals accomplishment, or when ceremonial responsibilities keep presidents from performing their other demanding duties.

The morale-building job of the president involves much more than just ceremonial, cheerleading, or quasichaplain duties. Presidential leadership, at its finest, radiates confidence and empowers people to give their best, to unleash the vast energies for good that are at-large in the nation. Our best leaders have been able to provide this special and often intangible element. Although it may defy easy definition, we judge a president's success and popularity by it. Still, we know all too well that it is not something that the Constitution confers or something conveniently closeted in the White House for the use of each new occupant.

PRESIDENTS AS CHIEF RECRUITERS

Often a single appointment may achieve more than scores of presidential policy initiatives. President Eisenhower's nomination and appointment of Earl Warren to be Chief Justice of the United States may have been the single most significant decision of that administration in the area of domestic policy. Warren served in that post for over fifteen years and presided over vast changes in civil rights and civil liberties. President Reagan's Supreme Court appointees, William Rehnquist, Sandra O'Connor, Antonin Scalia and Anthony Kennedy, will also have long-term effects. In a similar way selection of a secretary of state, of top economic advisers, of the secretary of the interior, or of top White House aides can have an enormous impact on long-term national policy.

George Washington. (*New York Public Library–Picture Collection*)

Effective presidents shrewdly use their appointment powers—presidents have control over 5000 appointments, including hundreds of federal judgeships and top positions in the military and diplomatic service—not only to reward campaign supporters and enhance ties to Congress but also to communicate priorities and policy directions. (Note, however, that many appointments must be made with the approval of the Senate. This limits the appointment powers to some extent.) Because a president's top appointees are also a major link between the White House and the millions of people who serve in the career federal and military services, the chief executive needs the best possible managers and motivators in these crucial positions. Besides identifying and recruiting them, the president must also try to keep the most talented of these officials in government as long as possible.[9]

The turnover problem is acute. Many able people come to top positions—say in the cabinet or subcabinet—and stay for only eighteen months or two years. Less than a third stay for more than three years. These top federal posts do not pay as much as comparable positions in the private sector. Also, living in Washington can be expensive.

Various financial-disclosure and conflict-of-interest requirements, imposed on presidential appointees as a result of the Ethics in Government Act of 1978, discourage some potential appointees from accepting government jobs. They must fill out

[9] See G. Calvin MacKenzie, *The Politics of Presidential Appointments* (Free Press, 1981).

Abraham Lincoln. (*New York Public Library–Picture Collection*)

different forms, and they must testify at complicated, time-consuming, and confusing congressional hearings. Critics of these laws say they have raised the risks of personal embarrassment and subjected appointees' private lives to much greater scrutiny.[10] Media scrutiny of these citizen leaders called to government service has also become more intensive. Recruiters for recent presidents report they often go to their second or third choice before they find someone willing to accept an appointment. "No other nation relies so heavily on noncareer personnel for the management of its government. . . . If talented Americans decline the opportunity for public service, if they endure it only for brief periods, or if they are ill-prepared for the challenges they will face in the public sector, the system will not deliver on its promise."[11] This system puts another heavy burden on presidents.

A president must strengthen the hand of the ablest people working in the bureaucracy and often also promote these people to higher positions at the senior reaches of the executive branch. In short, the personnel responsibilities of a president are greater and require more time than anyone, including presidents, expects.

PRESIDENTS AS PRIORITY SETTERS

Presidents, by custom, have become responsible for proposing new initiatives in the areas of foreign policy, economic growth and stability, and the quality of life in America. This was not always the case. But beginning with Woodrow Wilson, and especially since the New Deal, a president is expected to promote peace, prevent depressions, and propose reforms to ensure domestic progress. The trend in national policy making is toward greater centralization: Federal program ideas are seized upon by a president searching for campaign issues or legislative program material, and they are refined by the executive office staff and by special presidential task forces and commissions, as well as by the Congress.

Theodore Roosevelt. (*Brown Brothers*)

National Security Policy

Presidents generally have more leeway in foreign policy and military affairs than they have in domestic matters. This is due partly to grants of authority stipulated in the Constitution, and partly to the character of diplomatic and military activity. The framers foresaw a special need for speed and unity in our dealings with other nations. The Constitution vests in a president command of the two major instruments of foreign policy—the diplomatic corps and the armed services. It also gives the chief executive responsibility for negotiating treaties and commitments with other nations, although Congress, of course, also gets to vote on these matters.

Congress has granted presidents wide discretion in initiating foreign policies, for diplomacy frequently requires quick action. A president can act swiftly; Congress usually does not. The Supreme Court has upheld strong presidential authority in this area. In the **Curtiss-Wright** case in 1936, the Court referred to the "exclusive power of the president as the sole organ of the federal government in the field of international relations—a power which does not require as a basis for its exercise an act of Congress, but which, of course, like every other governmental power, must be exercised in subordination to the applicable provisions of the Constitution."[12] These are sweeping words. Yet a determined Congress *that knows what it wants to do*, and can agree on it, does not lack power in foreign relations. It must authorize

---

[10] See G. Calvin MacKenzie, ed., *The In and Outers: Presidential Appointees and the Problems of Transient Government in Washington* (Johns Hopkins Press, 1987), chap. 1.

[11] "Leadership in Jeopardy: The Fraying of the Presidential Appointments System," *National Academy of Public Administration Report* (November 1985), p. 3.

[12] *United States* v. *Curtiss-Wright Export Corp.*, 299 U.S. 304 (1936).

and appropriate the funds that back up our policies abroad. It is a forum for debate and criticism. And, as it at least tried to do after the Vietnam War, it can specify the conditions of war making (more on this in Chapter 15).

Economic Policy

Ever since the New Deal, presidents have been expected to prevent unemployment, fight inflation, keep taxes down, ensure economic growth and prosperity, and to do whatever they think necessary and proper to prevent recession. The Constitution does not place these duties on the White House, but presidents know that if they fail to act, they will suffer the fate of Herbert Hoover, who was denounced for years by the Democrats for his alleged inaction during the Great Depression. Recent elections have turned largely on economics.

The chief advisers to the president on economic policy are the secretary of the treasury, the three members of the Council of Economic Advisers, and the director of the Office of Management and Budget. Indirectly the chairperson of the Federal Reserve Board of Governors is often also a key White House adviser on the economy. Although presidents sometimes get their economic advice elsewhere, they often get advice on what actions to take from these persons. The growth and complexity of economic problems have placed even more initiative in the hands of the president. The delicate balancing required to keep a modern economy operating means that the presidency must regularly make key fiscal and budgetary policy decisions.

Domestic Policy

A leader is one who knows where the followers are. Lincoln did not invent the antislavery movement. Kennedy and Johnson did not begin the civil rights movement. Reagan did not initiate the "cut the taxes" crusade. But they all, in their respective times, became embroiled in these controversies, for a president cannot ignore for long what divides or inspires a nation.

The essence of the modern presidency lies in its potential capability to resolve societal conflicts. To be sure, much of the time a president will avoid conflict when possible, and will seek instead to defer, delegate, or otherwise delay controversial decisions. An effective president, however, will clarify the major issues of the day, define what is possible, and organize the governmental structure so that important goals can be realized.

A president—with the cooperation of Congress—can set national goals and propose legislation.[13] Close inspection indicates, however, that in most instances a president's "new initiatives" in domestic policy are measures that have been under consideration in previous sessions of Congress. Just as the celebrated New Deal legislation had a fairly well-defined history extending back several years before its embrace by Franklin Roosevelt, many of Reagan's initiatives were the fruits of long campaigns by congressional activists and special interests.

PRESIDENTS AS LEGISLATIVE AND POLITICAL COALITION BUILDERS

The president "shall from time to time give to the Congress information on the State of the Union, and recommend to their Consideration such Measures as he shall judge necessary and expedient," the Constitution provides. From the start

[13] See Paul Light, *The President's Agenda: Domestic Policy Choice from Kennedy to Carter* (Johns Hopkins University Press, 1982).

"I used to be swayed by the media's analysis of every move the President made . . . but not any more. Now I wait for the polls!" (*Reprinted by permission Tribune Media Services*)

strong presidents have exploited this power. Washington and Adams came in person to Congress to deliver information and recommendations. Jefferson and many presidents after him sent written messages, but Wilson restored the practice of delivering a personal, and often dramatic, message. Franklin Roosevelt used personal appearances (as have most presidents since then) to draw the attention of the whole nation to his program. Reagan visited Congress the very week after he was elected—and went back on several additional occasions to give major reports to the nation.

Less obvious, but perhaps equally important, are the frequent written messages dispatched from the White House to Capitol Hill on a vast range of public problems. These messages may not create much stir, but they are important in defining the administration's position and in giving a lead to friendly legislators. Moreover, these messages are often accompanied by detailed drafts of legislation that members of Congress may sponsor with little or no change. These White House proposals, the products of bill-drafting experts on the president's own staff or in the executive departments and agencies, may be strengthened or diluted by Congress, but many of the original provisions survive.

An effective president is an effective politician—the most visible and potentially the strongest mobilizer of influence in the American system of power. *Politician* is a nasty word to many Americans; it denotes a scheming, evasive fixer person out for his or her own self-interest. Little wonder many politicians claim they are "above politics." There is, however, a more constructive definition of *politician*: one who helps manage conflict; one who knows how to negotiate, bargain, and help reconcile different views in order to make the difficult and desirable become a reality. Presidents cannot escape political coalition-building tasks. As candidates, they have made promises to the people. To get things done and to be reelected, a president must work with many people and countless interest groups who have differing loyalties and responsibilities. Inevitably, a president becomes embroiled in legislative politics, bureaucratic politics, and lobbying politics.

Presidents make good on more of their promises than the general public appreciates. Most presidents enjoy at least partial success on most of the initiatives they favored during their campaigns or soon after they came to the White House.[14] Although presidents control most of what they decide to recommend to Congress, other institutions, especially the Congress, control what presidents can achieve. Presidents may control what and how they initiate, at least within reason, but other political leaders determine the fate, shape, and funding of these presidential initiatives.

Despite the available formal powers, presidents can rarely command; they spend most of their time *persuading* people. Potentially, presidents have enormous persuasive powers, but in the long run people think of their own self-interests, and presidential wishes often go unheeded. In a government of separated institutions that share powers, some congressional, bureaucratic, and even military leaders are beyond the political reach of the president. They have their own constituencies—a House committee, for example, or a powerful interest group. Presidents cannot simply give orders like a first sergeant. Before Dwight Eisenhower became president, Harry Truman said of him: "He'll sit here, and he'll say, 'Do this! Do that!' And nothing will happen, Poor Ike—it won't be a bit like the Army. He'll find it very frustrating."[15] *All* presidents have found it frustrating.

Many students of the presidency think the power to persuade is the chief resource of a president and that such power comes through bargaining. Bargaining, in turn, comes primarily through getting others to feel that it is in their own self-interests to cooperate. Hence, the skill of a president in communicating and in

[14] Jeff Fishel, *Presidents and Promises* (Congressional Quarterly Press, 1984).
[15] Richard E. Neustadt, *Presidential Power* (Wiley, 1980), p. 9.

winning others over is the necessary energizing factor in moving the institutions of the national government to action. This school of thought also holds that a president cannot be shy and above the battle, or above politics. Rather, a president must enjoy the give and take of congressional-presidential relations, and the give and take between the parties and between the White House and the press. Classic examples of effective presidential political coalition building are Franklin Roosevelt's building of public support around his New Deal programs, Lyndon Johnson's successfully passing his "Great Society" legislation, and Ronald Reagan's mobilizing public and congressional support for his programs.

The Prime-Time Presidency

No other politician (and few television or film stars) can achieve a closer contact with the people than can the president. Typically, the chief executive has been a prominent senator, a vice-president, or a governor, and has built up a host of followers. Having won nominations and elections, most presidents have been in the public eye for years. But the White House is the finest platform of all. A television studio that can be used for a direct appeal to the people exists right in the White House. Presidents can meet the press when they wish, arrange fireside chats or radio call-in shows, choose sympathetic audiences, or undertake "nonpolitical" speaking tours. And they can time all these moves for maximum advantage.[16]

The press conference is an example of how the president can employ the machinery of communication in a systematic manner. Years ago press conferences were rather casual affairs. Franklin Roosevelt ran his get-togethers informally and was a master at withholding information as well as giving it. Under Truman the conference became an institutionalized part of the presidential communications apparatus. Kennedy authorized the first live telecast of a press conference and used it frequently for direct communication with the people. Ronald Reagan regularly and effectively used five-minute Saturday afternoon radio chats to communicate his views, ask for support, and win Sunday morning media coverage.

Presidents commission private polls to gauge public opinion; they want to be able to distinguish the public's petty whims, estimate the strength and direction of its opinions, and respond to its impatience—and they must anticipate its potential impact. Presidents must know not only what to do but when to do it. Public opinion can be unstable and unpredictable. The public generally rejects government by public opinion; they do not want a president to fall captive to the polls. President Johnson recognized that his wide popular support of the mid-1960s had melted away by 1968, when he decided not to run again. President Nixon's dramatic drop of nearly 45 percentage points in public-opinion polls, a result of the Watergate scandals, helped force his resignation. Most presidents lose support the longer they are in office. (Eisenhower and Reagan are exceptions to this rule.) Dissatisfaction sets in; interest groups grow impatient; unkept promises must be accounted for; and the president gets blamed for many of the things that go wrong.

George Bush after winning 1988 presidential election. (*AP PhotoColor*)

Party Leadership

Another potential source of influence for the president is the political party. Most presidents since Jefferson have been party leaders, and generally the more effective the presidents, the more use they have made of party support. Wilson, the two Roosevelts, and Reagan fortified their executive and legislative influence by mobilizing support within their party. Yet no president has ever fully led a party.

[16] Samual Kernell, *Going Public* (Congressional Quarterly Press, 1986), and George Edwards, *The Public Presidency* (St. Martin's Press, 1983).

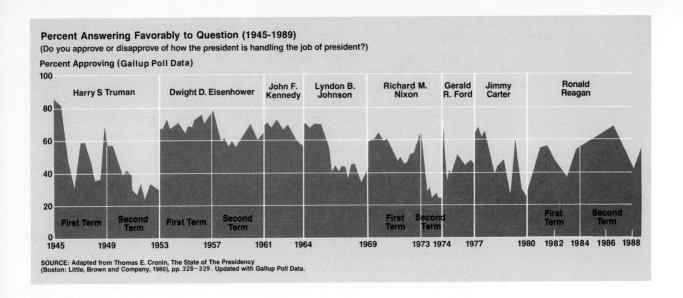

Percent Answering Favorably to Question (1945–1989)
(Do you approve or disapprove of how the president is handling the job of president?)

Percent Approving (Gallup Poll Data)

SOURCE: Adapted from Thomas E. Cronin, The State of The Presidency
(Boston: Little, Brown and Company, 1980), pp. 328–329. Updated with Gallup Poll Data.

The president has no formal position in the party structure, but the chief executive's influence over national policies and over thousands of appointments commands respect from party leaders. Both president and party need each other. The president needs the party's backing in order to enact a legislative program. The party needs the president's direction and prestige—and the political "gravy" that flows from the White House.

The strings of the national organization all lie in a president's hands. Formally, the national party committee picks the national party chair; actually, the president lets the committee know the desired candidate and the members choose that person. Today presidents can hire or fire national party chairs much as they shift department heads or even their own staff. The president's pronouncements on national party policy are more authoritative than those of any party committee or the party platform itself. Presidents can give a candidate a good deal of recognition and publicity in Washington. They can grant—or deny—campaign assistance and even financial assistance.

Limits on Party Leadership

Yet the president's practical power over the party is limited and often comes to an end precisely when it is needed most. Presidents rarely have influence over the selection of party candidates for Congress and for state and local office. Presidents also sometimes have trouble getting crucial votes from individuals in their own parties in Congress. This is due in part to the chief executive's limited control of state and local organizations. But also, party organizations themselves do not control their candidates in office: Most candidates win office less through the efforts of the organized party than through their own individual campaigning. Of course, the situation varies from place to place, but in most instances *personalized politics* emphasizing the candidate is more successful than *programmatic politics* emphasizing party and issues.

Presidents must *bargain* and *negotiate* with the party leaders in Congress and in the states just as they do with other independent power centers. Lacking full support from the whole party, presidents usually fall back on the personal organizations that enabled them to be nominated in the first place.[17]

PRESIDENTS AS ADMINISTRATORS

The Constitution charges the president to "take care that the laws be faithfully executed." Presidents, however, must delegate much of their administrative authority, because they are forever overscheduled and other responsibilities demand most of their attention. They are, then, dependent on their subordinates. Theoretically, at least, orders flow down an administrative *line*, from president to department heads, to bureau chiefs, and down to smaller offices. The president, like all top executives, is assisted by a *staff*, who advise the chief executive. This line and staff organization is inherent in any large administrative entity, whether it be the Army, General Motors, or the United Nations.

Presidents have come to rely heavily on their personal staffs. Nowhere else—not in Congress, not in the cabinet, not in the party—can presidents find the loyalty, and single-mindedness that often develops among their closest aides.[18] Moreover, presidents come to view most cabinet heads as advocates, who advance ideas that benefit the particular friends and interest groups associated with their departments. Presidents apparently think their own aides will provide them with more neutral and objective advice. But there are substantial costs to listening only to one's closest aides. The White House can usefully be thought of as a palace court in which strong presidents create an environment that weeds out any assistant who persists in presenting irritating thoughts. "Palace-guard survivors learn early to camouflage themselves with a coating of battleship grey. . . . Inevitably in a battle between courtiers and advisers, the courtiers will win out. This represents the greatest of all barriers to presidential access to reality . . ."[19] And an astute British writer notes: ". . . if a president needs to be protected by his White House staff against the departments, he also needs to be kept on guard by the departments against his White House staff, who may all too easily begin to think only they know the purposes and the needs and the mind of their president, until *he* becomes *their* creature and believes that his interests are safe with them."[20]

The number of employees in the presidential entourage has grown steadily since the early 1900s, when only a few dozen people served a president at a cost of less than a few hundred thousand dollars annually. Today a White House staff of over 500 operates at the cost of several million dollars a year. The Executive Office of the President, approved by Congress in 1939, was the recommendation of President Franklin Roosevelt's Committee on Administrative Management. The Executive Office was to provide presidents the help they obviously needed to carry

Growth of White House Staff

Year	President	Staff
1943	FDR	50
1949	Truman	240
1953	Ike	250
1962	JFK	340
1965	LBJ	300
1971	Nixon	580
1975	Ford	525
1988	Reagan	550*

* estimate

[17] For a more detailed treatment see Thomas E. Cronin, "The Presidency and the Parties," in Thomas E. Cronin, ed., *Rethinking the Presidency* (Little, Brown, 1982), chap. 21, and Robert Harmel, ed., *The President as Party Leader* (Praeger, 1984).

[18] This is not to suggest that all White House aides and advisors necessarily like one another or that a team spirit always emerges. For discussion of the disarray and backbiting in the Reagan White House, see David Stockman, *The Triumph of Politics* (Harper & Row, 1986).

[19] George Reedy, *The Twilight of the Presidency* (World, 1970), p. 98. For different points of view see Henry Kissinger, *The White House Years* (Little, Brown, 1979), and Zbigniew Brzezinski, *Power and Principle* (Farrar, Straus & Giroux, 1983).

[20] Henry Fairlie, *The Kennedy Promise* (Doubleday, 1973), pp. 167–68. See also Stephen Hess, *Organizing the Presidency* (Brookings Institution, 1976), and Edward Weisband and Thomas M. Franck, *Resignation as Protest* (Penguin, 1975).

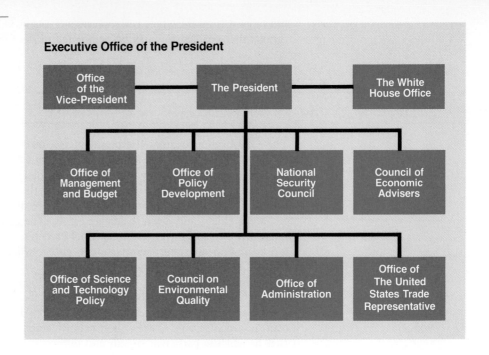

Executive Office of the President

- Office of the Vice-President
- The President
- The White House Office

- Office of Management and Budget
- Office of Policy Development
- National Security Council
- Council of Economic Advisers

- Office of Science and Technology Policy
- Council on Environmental Quality
- Office of Administration
- Office of The United States Trade Representative

out the growing responsibilities imposed by the Depression and by the enlarged role of government.[21]

The Institutionalized Executive Office

The **Executive Office of the President** consists of the Office of Management and Budget, the Council of Economic Advisers, and several other staff units. The most prominent and controversial presidential staff, of course, is the White House Office. A president's immediate staff, working out of the White House itself, does not have fixed form; indeed, part of its value lies in its flexibility and adaptability. Most presidents, however, have an appointments secretary, a press secretary, a correspondence secretary, a legal counsel, a national security adviser, military aides, and several other legislative, administrative, and political assistants. The staff of the White House office can be categorized by functions: (1) domestic policy; (2) economic policy; (3) national security or foreign policy; (4) administration and personnel matters (as well as personal paper work and scheduling for the president); (5) congressional relations; and (6) public relations.

Presidential aides sometimes insist they are simply the eyes and ears of the president, that they make few important decisions, and that they never insert themselves between the chief executive and the heads of departments. But the burgeoning White House staff and the inevitability of a strong chief of staff have made this traditional picture nearly obsolete. Some White House aides, impatient with bureaucratic and congressional bottlenecks or even political sabotage, come to view the presidency as if it alone were the whole government. Separation of powers means little to them, and they lose sight of their location within the larger constitutional

(T. Cronin)

[21] See Fred I. Greenstein, "Nine Presidents In Search of a Modern Presidency," in Anthony King, ed., *The New American Political System*, 2nd ed. (American Enterprise Institute, 1987). See also John Kessel, "The Structure of the Carter White House," *American Journal of Political Science* (August 1983), pp. 431–63, and "The Structure of the Reagan White House," *American Journal of Political Science* (May 1984), pp. 231–58.

system. Listen to a Nixon aide: "There shouldn't be a lot of leeway in following the President's policies. It should be like a corporation, where the executive vice-presidents [the cabinet officers] are tied closely to the Chief Executive, or to put it in extreme terms, when he says jump, they only ask how high."[22] And a Carter aide told one of the authors that giving so much power to the cabinet members "was probably President Carter's biggest mistake."

The **Office of Management and Budget (OMB)** continues to be the central presidential staff agency. Its director advises the president in detail about the hundreds of government agencies—how much money they should be allotted in the budget, and what kind of job they are doing. The OMB seeks to improve the planning, management, and statistical work of the agencies. It makes a special effort to see that each agency conforms to presidential policies in its dealings with Congress; each agency has to clear its policy recommendations to Congress through the OMB first.

A budget is not just a financial plan, because it reflects power struggles and indicates policy directions (and wishful thinking).[23] To the president the budget is a means of control over administrators who may be trying to join ranks with politicians or interest groups to thwart presidential priorities. Through the long budget-preparing process, presidents use the OMB as a way of conserving and centralizing their own influence.

[22] John Erlichman, interview published in *The Washington Post* (August 24, 1972). See also Jeb Stuart Magruder's account of White House life in the Nixon administration, *An American Life: One Man's Road to Watergate* (Atheneum, 1974), and Donald Regan's account of the Reagan White House, *For the Record* (Harcourt, Brace, Jovanovich, 1988).

[23] See David Stockman, *The Triumph of Politics* (Harper & Row, 1986); Howard E. Shuman, *Politics and the Budget,* 2nd ed. (Prentice-Hall, 1988); Aaron Wildavsky, *The Politics of the Budgetary Process,* 4th ed. (Little, Brown, 1983).

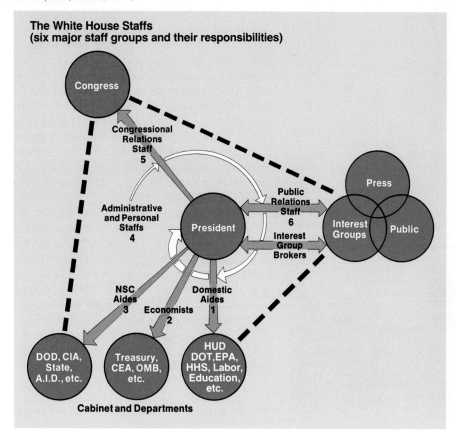

The White House Staffs
(six major staff groups and their responsibilities)

Congress

Congressional
Relations
Staff
5

Administrative
and Personal
Staffs
4

President

Public
Relations
Staff
6

Interest
Group
Brokers

Press

Interest
Groups

Public

NSC
Aides
3

Economists
2

Domestic
Aides
1

DOD, CIA,
State,
A.I.D., etc.

Treasury,
CEA, OMB,
etc.

HUD
DOT, EPA,
HHS, Labor,
Education,
etc.

Cabinet and Departments

The Cabinet

It is hard to find a more unusual institution than the cabinet. It is not specifically mentioned by name in the Constitution. Yet since George Washington's administration, every president has had a cabinet. Washington's consisted of his secretaries of state, treasury, and war, plus his attorney general. Today the selection of cabinet members is just about the first major job for the president-elect. The cabinet consists of the president, the vice-president, the officers who head the thirteen executive departments, and a few others (See the accompanying box). The cabinet has always been a loosely designated body, and it is not always clear who belongs to it. In recent years, for example, certain executive-branch administrators and White House counselors have been accorded cabinet rank.

Cabinet government as practiced in parliamentary systems simply does not exist in America. In fact, a president is not required by law to form a cabinet or to hold regular meetings. Kennedy, Johnson, and Nixon all preferred small conferences with those specifically involved in a problem. Kennedy saw no reason to discuss defense department matters with his secretaries of agriculture and labor, and he thought cabinet meetings wasted valuable time for too many already busy people. During his administration crucial decisions were often reached in informal conferences between the president, the heads of two or three major departments, and senior White House staff members. Both Carter and Reagan tried to revive the cabinet, and both met often with their cabinets during their first two years. But the longer they remained in office, the less frequently they met with their cabinets as a whole. And, one of Reagan's top aides actually admitted that Reagan often "dozed off" during cabinet meetings.

Personal presidential advisers and the heads of various White House based cabinet councils or review units such as the **National Security Council** and the Office of Management and Budget have gained superior status over many of the department and cabinet secretaries. This has occurred in part because these people are located physically in or next door to the White House. Further, presidents believe their department heads adopt narrow "advocate" views: the agriculture cabinet officer as a strident advocate for the farmers; the Housing and Urban Development cabinet officer as an ambassador for the housing industry and to some extent also for the mayors; and so on through much of the cabinet—especially those preoccupied with domestic policy matters. As good relations between presidents and these cabinet members weaken, the former, in frustration, turn more often to trusted senior White House staff aides to settle conflicts and coordinate policy. As a result, tension almost always builds between senior White House aides and their counterparts in the cabinet. Personal staff remains close to the president's ear, and more influential as a result.

Some presidents form various cabinet councils in an attempt to integrate key departmental and White House advisers around major policy matters. President Ford was pleased with this system. President Reagan, who had a notable penchant for delegating responsibility, also relied on these cabinet councils: He usually had a cabinet member or senior White House aide in charge of the council. Such councils are patterned after the National Security Council, which was established by law in 1947. The Reagan efforts were aimed at decentralizing policy discussions and collaborative efforts while giving the various cabinet members a genuine feeling they were being consulted and involved in important policy developments.[24] However, they worked less well in practice than Reagan had hoped. Designed to give more regard to the counsel of cabinet members, these councils generally end up

Ronald Reagan meets with cabinet members Secretary of State George Schultz (left) and Secretary of Defense Caspar Weinberger. (*Pete Sousa / The White House*)

[24] Fred I. Greenstein, ed., *Leadership in the Modern Presidency* (Harvard University Press, 1988).

centralizing more decision making in the White House or in a small select group of "inner cabinet" members.[25]

Cabinet members, as individuals, are often important advisers and administrators. But the cabinet as a decision-making body is not as important as press accounts would have us believe. At present it would take a leap of imagination to think of cabinet meetings as a place where the large outlines of policy are hammered out in common, or where essential strategy is decided upon.

THE VICE-PRESIDENCY

Woodrow Wilson was one of the first presidents to set trends in national policy making. (*UPI/Bettmann Newsphotos*)

Though the vice-presidency is now a part of the presidential establishment, it has not been that way for long. Most vice-presidents served mainly as president of the Senate. In most administrations the vice-president was at best a kind of fifth wheel and at worst a political rival who sometimes connived against the president. The office was often dismissed as a joke. The main reason for the vice-president's posture as an outsider was that presidential nominees usually chose as running mates candidates who were geographically, ideologically, and in other ways likely to "balance the ticket."

In recent decades, however, presidential candidates have selected somewhat more like-minded persons for their running mates and have made more use of them. Vice-president George Bush did his best to avoid upstaging the President, as did Walter Mondale before him, but these days the vice-presidency brings both virtues and liabilities to a vice-president who aspires to the presidency. The job surely provides exposure to the issues and challenges of the office, but it is hard to appear "presidential" while at the same time not being disloyal to or upstaging the president—as George Bush found out.[26]

Ideally, a vice-president serves several roles in addition to the largely ceremonial function of acting as president of the Senate. A vice-president gets to cast the tie-breaking vote if the Senate has a tie vote—but this usually occurs less than once a year. As successor to the president should the latter die, resign, or become incapacitated, the vice-president works as an understudy who assumes some of the president's party and ceremonial duties, and thereby eases some of the president's burden. A vice-president can also perform specialized assignments, such as chairing advisory councils, cabinet-level committees, or a White House conference, or undertaking good-will missions abroad.

Tensions usually develop between top presidential aides and vice-presidents and their staffs. Part of the problem arises because presidents seldom wish to give up any ceremonial duties for which they themselves can win credit. Neither do cabinet members like to share their responsibilities with vice-presidents, which makes it very hard for vice-presidents to gain administrative experience. Then too, presidents often delegate unpleasant political chores to their vice-presidents.

The importance of the way in which we select and use vice-presidents is underscored by the fact that eight presidents have died in office—four by assassination, four by natural death—and one president has resigned. One-third of our presi-

[25] The notion of an "inner cabinet" is developed in Thomas E. Cronin, *The State of the Presidency*, 2nd ed. (Little, Brown, 1980). See also Kevin Mulcahy and Margaret Jane Wyszomirski, *White House Government* (Brooks/Cole, 1987); and Ronald Brownstein and Dick Kirschten, "Cabinet Power" *National Journal* (June 28, 1986), pp. 1582–89.

[26] For an analysis of the recent growth of the role of the vice-president as a potential adviser to the president, see Thomas E. Cronin, "Rethinking the Vice Presidency," in T. E. Cronin, ed., *Rethinking the Presidency* (Little, Brown, 1982), and Report of the Twentieth Century Fund Task Force on the Vice Presidency, *A Heartbeat Away* (Priority Press, 1988).

dents were once vice-presidents, including four of our last eight presidents. Support exists for devising better ways to pick vice-presidential nominees as well as for making the vice-presidency a more significant office. Both major parties have considered practical means of making the selection procedure for the vice-presidency more democratic. Under the existing system presidential nominees have a free hand in choosing their running mates. Although there are some notable advantages to the present system—especially the possibility that the ticket will be ideologically compatible—drawbacks are also clear. Disadvantages of the present methods include the pressure of time, the lack of formalized consultation within the party, the rubber-stamp role for convention delegates, and the absence of public scrutiny of prospective vice-presidential candidates before the nomination.

The vice-presidency has been significantly affected by two post-World War II constitutional amendments. The *Twenty-second amendment*, ratified in 1951, imposes a two-term limit on presidents, so that vice-presidents have a better chance of moving up to the Oval Office. The *Twenty-fifth amendment*, ratified in 1967, confirms the prior practice of making the vice-president not acting president but president, in the event of the death of a president. Of greater significance, this amendment provides a procedure to determine whether an incumbent president is unable to discharge the powers and duties of the office, and it establishes procedures to fill a vacancy in the vice-presidency. For a few hours in 1985, George Bush became the first "acting president" when the first of these provisions was invoked while President Reagan underwent a minor cancer operation. In the event of a vacancy in the office of the vice-president, the president nominates a vice-president, who takes office upon confirmation by a majority vote of both houses of Congress. This procedure generally ensures the appointment of a vice-president in whom the president has confidence. Thus, vice-presidents who have to take over the presidency can be expected to reflect most of their predecessors' policies.

The vice-presidency will remain attractive to aspiring politicians if only because it is one of the major paths to the presidency. The policy-advising role of the vice-president was enhanced under Carter and Reagan. However, the tensions between a president and a vice-president are natural (after all, everybody else who works closely with presidents can be fired by them). It is almost certain the vice-president will continue to have an undefined role, subject more to the good will and moods of the president than to any fixed job description.[27]

CAN THE MODERN PRESIDENCY SURVIVE THE MODERN MEDIA?

Ronald Reagan once walked away from one of his news conferences, and turning to an aide, "cussed out" his press adversaries, not realizing a microphone was picking up his very words. John F. Kennedy once canceled over fifty White House subscriptions to the *New York Herald Tribune* because he was furious about how the paper was treating his decision making. Lyndon Johnson regularly planted "softball questions" (questions he could easily answer) among friendly reporters at presidential press conferences. All recent presidents have complained both that the modern media have misrepresented them and that the media report only the bad news.

Enjoying enormous First amendment rights in this country, reporters go about their business of analyzing and criticizing presidents with striking gusto. Scores of media representatives are regularly stationed at the White House, and they travel

[27] Three books on the vice-presidency worth consulting are: Paul Light, *Vice Presidential Power* (Johns Hopkins University Press, 1984); Joel Goldstein, *The Modern Vice Presidency* (Princeton University Press, 1982); and Marie Natoli, *American Prince, American Pauper* (Greenwood Press, 1985).

DUNAGIN'S PEOPLE

"Look on the bright side . . . you're becoming obscure enough to be Vice-President." (*Dunagin's People by Ralph Dunagin, Copyright, 1984, The Orlando Sentinel, Field Newspaper Syndicate. By permission of North American Syndicate, Inc.*)

President Jimmy Carter conducts a press conference. (*National Archives*)

everywhere the president goes, reporting on the president's every move. Presidential statements—even on the most trivial matter—get sent back to the newsrooms and usually get printed or aired. Major statements and policy initiatives are reported and subjected to interpretative analysis. The media, at the White House and elsewhere, also force to the forefront of national attention issues that might never have been discussed publicly in earlier times—and never do get discussed in many other countries. Presidents, of course, want all their intiatives printed and praised as much as possible.

But the press and the media believe they should provide a context in which presidential statements can be understood. Hence, they not only tell people what a president said but often try to explain what the statement means. This is done primarily by columnists, editorial writers, and commentators—who are expected to agree with or to criticize a president and to provide their reasons for doing so. Further, the management of most newspapers and radio and television stations in the country want to balance their stories about what presidents say—especially in presidential speeches—with an equal amount of time for the spokespersons of the opposition party or at least for persons who hold different points of view. Thus, when President Reagan spoke in support of aid to the Nicaraguan Contras or in favor of his Strategic Defense Initiative (Star Wars), the media frequently gave an almost equal amount of attention to the views of various senators who opposed him on these issues.

In recent years this kind of adversarial media coverage has often left the impression that a president's influence is more divisive than unifying. Except when a president attends a baseball game or welcomes to the White House some noted sports or arts hero, media coverage always seems to be—at best—ambivalent. No reporter has ever won a Pulitzer or any other media prize for writing a story favorable to the administration. The journalism profession honors those who uncover wrongdoing.

What have presidents done about this? Typically they have been patient and respected the critical dialogue so essential in a democracy. However, presidents and their aides have also engaged in extensive public relations efforts. Reagan, for example, frequently invited friendly newspaper reporters for extensive interviews. Out-of-town editors were invited in for special briefings, and special efforts were made to get the President out of Washington for meetings with local and regional media representatives, who were generally viewed as less critical than Washington-based media. Special White House media experts regularly met to devise better ways to get the president's point of view out to the public, to get the President on prime-time television, or to arrange for flattering action photos.

Reagan's efforts were not novel; every recent president has tried similar public relations strategems. Presidents and their aides often conclude that unifying national leadership is almost impossible to achieve in a country that encourages such critical—even cynical—media. Some White House aides go so far as to say the media are badly hurting the nation. "They destroy every hero," said a Reagan deputy. "We don't have heros anymore, we don't have anyone to believe in because they strip them naked."[28]

The modern media are perhaps the primary adversary of the modern presidency. Some complain the American presidency is being brutally wounded and its capacity for leadership sapped—if not paralyzed—because of excess of media criticism. Although media admit occasional abuses by the press, they rally to cherished "free press" traditions. Defenders of the press also like to quote from Thomas Jefferson,

[28] Juan Williams, "Presidential Newsmaking: How Reagan's Staff Spreads His Message," *The Washington Post* (February 13, 1983), p. 18. Two books that examine Washington reporters and the White House press office are Stephen Hess, *The Washington Reporters* (Brookings Institution, 1981), and Michael B. Grossman and Martha J. Kumar, *Portraying the President* (Johns Hopkins University Press, 1981).

who although angered by the press when he was president, once said: "Were it left to me to decide whether we should have a government without newspapers or newspapers without a government, I should not hesitate to prefer the latter." Finally, defenders of the media say that presidents have too often lied or manipulated the public's understanding of the issues. The media, they contend, are obligated to stand up and speak out—especially when they think a president is wrong.

No matter who is in the White House, presidents and the media will often be in conflict. This ongoing struggle is inherent in a democracy. The Watergate scandals fortified the media in their independence—and many people credited the media with playing an important role in bringing these scandals to the public's attention. Further, because the media—especially television—are viewed as more trustworthy and believable than most other American institutions, most Americans, most of the time, believe what they hear on television is as true as what presidents say. The goal of a president and of the media are often in conflict; and as long as this continues to be the case, presidents and the media will be adversaries. But the resources of the White House, especially in the hands of communicators such as FDR, John Kennedy, and Ronald Reagan, seem worthy combatants in taking on the so-called fourth branch of government.

MAKING THE PRESIDENCY SAFE FOR DEMOCRACY

The startling series of events of the **Watergate** and Iran-Contra scandals sharpened the old question: How much executive power can a democracy afford? New questions were also raised: Was a bigger presidency necessarily better? Did presidential powers grow because they were usurped by presidents or handed over by Congress? Would we be better served by a six-year presidential term? Would some form of parliamentary government be better than our three-branch "presidential" system?

During the past two decades, presidents have been criticized for impounding billions of congressionally approved funds, obstructing justice, abusing the doctrine of executive privilege, lying about the conduct of the Vietnam War, and acting with excessive secrecy. People lost confidence first in Johnson's and then in Nixon's brand of leadership, and then, for different reasons, in Ford, Carter, and Reagan. The credibility if not legitimacy of the presidency itself was often tested.

How much formal authority does and should a president have? The Constitution grants broad executive authority without defining boundaries. Scholars hold that in emergencies the president has wide powers to protect the public interest, even at the cost of overriding existing laws or acting before the Congress has the chance to do so. There seems to be a kind of *inherent* power in the presidency, vast but undefined, that an aggressive president can exploit in times of crisis. Unfortunately, crisis is now the rule rather than the exception.

Presidents Ford, Reagan, Nixon, and Carter came together in 1981. The three pre-Reagan presidents joined the U.S. delegation going to the funeral of Egyptian President Anwar Sadat. (*UPI/Bettmann Newsphotos*)

Franklin Roosevelt's conception of his power, in the Jefferson and Lincoln tradition—sometimes called the *prerogative theory*—was that in the face of emergencies a president had the same power once claimed by kings: the power to act according to discretion for the public good, without the prescription of the law and sometimes even against it. The World War II destroyer-bases agreement, for example, in which Roosevelt on his own initiative traded naval destroyers to England in return for some military bases, conflicted with several laws and set what some believe was a dangerous precedent that others (like Nixon) seem to have followed.

Presidential Character

What about presidential personality? If the presidency has too much power for the safety of the country (and the world), and yet not enough to solve some of the nation's toughest problems, what kind of person do we need in this office?

14–3 **Barber's Classification of American Presidents**

ENERGY LEVEL IN THEIR POLITICAL JOB

		ACTIVE:	PASSIVE:
Emotional attitude toward politics and the job of the presidency	POSITIVE:	Franklin Roosevelt Harry Truman John F. Kennedy Gerald Ford Jimmy Carter	William H. Taft Warren Harding Ronald Reagan
	NEGATIVE:	Richard Nixon Lyndon Johnson Herbert Hoover Woodrow Wilson	Dwight Eisenhower Calvin Coolidge

Should We Have a Six-Year Nonrenewable Term for Presidents?

Pro:

It might help take the politics out of the presidency, and thereby lessen the likelihood of scandals like Watergate.

Four years is too short a time to get the job done.

Presidents could concentrate on the job rather than on reelection.

During wartime a president wouldn't waste time campaigning.

Budgets are already cast for about two years ahead when a president gets into office.

Six years is enough even for the healthiest of presidents.

Con:

A six-year term would give us two more years of the "clunkers" and two fewer years of the great ones.

Four years is long enough to tell whether a president is doing the job.

The best way to be reelected is to do the job well, maintain majority support, and be an effective leader.

The four-year term forces presidents to be accountable for their promises and platforms.

Many of our great presidents served ably for more than six years: Washington, Jefferson, Wilson, FDR, and Ike.

A healthy, democratic country needs a politician in the White House: one who can bargain, persuade, build crucial political coalitions, and get diverse political factions to work together.

We should not surrender a hard-won democratic right: to kick a leader *out* of office.

Political scientist James David Barber writes that because the issues are always changing, we should be concerned somewhat less with the stands a candidate takes than with the candidate's *character*. The character, Barber claims, will stay pretty much the same.[29]

Barber claims we can classify presidents and would-be presidents according to their *activism* (how active and assertive they are) on the one hand and their *enjoyment* of politics and public service on the other. With these two dimensions, he contends, we can pretty well predict presidential performance. Table 14–3 shows Barber's classification scheme and how he assesses most twentieth-century presidents.

Barber holds that the people best suited for the presidency are politicians who creatively shape their environment and savor the give-and-take exchanges of political life. He calls them "active-positives." Beware, he tells us, of the active-negative types. They are the driven personalities, compelled to feverish activity, yet doomed by rigidity and personal frustration in the way they approach their jobs. Wilson, Hoover, Johnson, and Nixon are illustrative cases. Barber said Ford was an active-positive type, but others think of Ford as somewhat more of a passive-positive. Some observers thought Carter was as much in the negative category as in the positive. Still others thought that the contradictory conclusions about where to put them merely demonstrated that this scheme was more confusing than helpful—and more likely to tell us about the classifiers than the classified. Barber calls Reagan a passive-positive. He worries that Reagan would be tempted to let things drift and that he will be overly deferential to his friends.

Our understanding of personality and character, however, is not yet so developed that we can make accurate predictions about suitable presidential candidates. Moreover, critics doubt that Barber's generalizations are based on sufficient evidence.[30] Then, too, many people judge Reagan to be an "active" and not a "passive," at least in Barber's terms. Still others, who are at least partially persuaded by Barber's analysis, doubt that we can really put it to work during most elections. What happens, for example, if most of the candidates are "active-positive"? Further, using strict character criteria to screen candidates probably would have prevented the moody and often depressed Abraham Lincoln from winning office. Nor can we be sure that a president's character will stay the same throughout an entire

[29] James David Barber, *The Presidential Character*, 3rd ed. (Prentice-Hall, 1985). See evaluations of this study by Alexander L. George, "Assessing Presidential Character," *World Politics* (January 1974), pp. 234–82, and by Alan C. Elms, *Personality in Politics* (Harcourt Brace Jovanovich, 1976), chap. 4. See also Michael Nelson, "James David Barber and the Psychological Presidency," *Virginia Quarterly Review* (Autumn 1980).

[30] See, for example, Fred F. Greenstein, *The Hidden-Hand Presidency* (Basic Books, 1982), which suggests Barber is wrong on Eisenhower, and Betty Glad, *Jimmy Carter in Search of the Great White House* (Norton, 1980), for a somewhat different view on Carter. For a different analysis of recent presidents, see also Hedley Donovan, *Roosevelt to Reagan* (Harper & Row, 1985).

The Reagan Legacy

No one doubts that Reagan made the presidency work after it had been a troubled institution for several years. He possessed both the mind of an ideologue and the skill of a politician. He proved to be a natural horse-trader who often seemed to relish fashioning compromises as he moved the political system toward his political ends. He proved also to be a genius at American pomp and pagentry. Americans had heard that the presidency had grown too complex for one person to manage, but Reagan seemed to reassert the force of individual leadership and make the office function with ease.

Critics say he was lucky. It's hard to tell whether he was an effective president or an average one who got lucky. But he did help to restore self-assurance to the American people and to the presidency. His presidency marked a watershed in domestic policy and signaled a fundamental shift in attitude with the federal government assuming a much smaller responsibility for social and urban issues. If the Roosevelt New Deal served as a period of ascendancy in identifying and dealing with social concerns, the Reagan presidency marked a turning away from that agenda. He had a clear idea of what he wanted to do—cut the budget on the domestic side, raise it on the military side, and cut inflation and interest rates—and often he succeeded. He was far less successful at balancing the budget and lessening our trade imbalances. And his administration will always be known for scandals—at the White House, in the Justice Department, and in Defense procurement.

Reagan will be judged on the effect of his national security policies and especially on how the economy performs in the next

term or even over the life span of an issue. In addition to a presidential candidate's character, voters want and deserve to know the issue positions of the candidates. It would also help to know the kind of people a candidate seeks out as advisers.

Perhaps too much emphasis is placed on presidential personality and character. Psychologists, of course, tend to emphasize the personal more than the institutional. But the personality of the president is but one factor, and Barber's classifications lack so much precision that they predict little and explain less. If institutions and constitutional and political arrangements matter, as we have suggested they do, then it may be a mistake to suggest that changing the personality of the individual president will have a major impact on presidential effectiveness. The causes of presidential ineffectiveness are probably due more to the shape of our political system than to the personality of our presidents. This is not to say that the president's character, integrity, and leadership or management styles are unimportant. But these considerations are only one set of concerns, and they may be less important than our institutional structures and processes. Political scientists debate these differing emphases, and we encourage you to do so as well.

New Checks and Balances

Presidential power is greater today than ever before. It is misleading, however, to infer from a president's capacity to begin a nuclear war that the chief executive has similar power to bring about positive change and solutions in policy-making areas. Seldom are presidents free agents in bringing about basic social change. As priority setter, politician, and executive, a president shares power with members of Congress, bureaucrats, and interest-group elites. The ability to set priorities, and pass laws, is not the same as the ability to enforce and administer them properly. Presidents who want to be effective in implementing policy changes must know what they want to achieve and how to motivate and strengthen the bureaucracy to that end.

This is a tough assignment in a political system held together in such large measure by compromise and contradictory goals. Not only must presidents deal with key congressional leaders, cabinet members, important bureaucrats, a vice-president, party chiefs, and even leaders of the opposition party, but they must also cope with the political forces operating around the White House: public opinion, pressures from organized interests, demands from their own party. They must negotiate endlessly among individuals and among interests. They will constantly struggle with investigative reporters and muckrakers. And they must respond to public sentiment at the same time as they educate it. The fierce light of public opinion, magnified by the press and the electronic media, beats down upon the White House.

A New Attitude toward the Presidency?

Unrealistic expectations of the presidency have helped to weaken it. Part of the reason presidents have turned to secrecy and subordinated substance to style has been that we have overburdened the office with exaggerated expectations. We elect a politician and then insist on a superhuman performance. As currently designed, the presidency is an institution that manipulates its occupants, and accentuates their *shortcomings* as well as their virtues.[31]

In one sense the best safeguard and restraint on presidential powers rest with the attitudes of the American people. Citizens have far more power than they generally realize. Presidents usually hear when they are "sending a message." Citizens can also "vote" between elections in innumerable ways—by changing parties, by organizing protests, by voting for the opposition party in off-year elections, by voting for or against issues in state referendums.

We need a healthy skepticism toward presidential decisions. A lesson learned from the Watergate period is not that the powers of the presidency should be

[31] See Bruce Buchanan, *The Presidential Experience* (Prentice-Hall, 1978).

Reagan *cont.*

few years. He will also be evaluated in retrospect on whether he truly represented the nation as a whole or just one stratum within it. Experts say that a great or near-great president has to show that he wants the blessings of this country shared by all the people. A great president has to contribute to the soundness of our economy and to the security of the nation—both physical and psychological.

But, however the historians treat and assess the Reagan legacy, he modified the presidential job description and made a large mark on the institution of the presidency.

Factors that Constrain Presidents

- The Constitution
- Federalism
- Separation of powers
- Congress
- Federal courts
- Investigative press and media
- Public opinion
- Opposing party
- Opposing factions in president's party
- Interest groups
- Editorial opinion (and cartoonists)
- Bureaucratic resistance
- Opposing world powers
- World public opinion and UN policies
- Regularly fixed elections
- Unrealistic expectations
- Party platforms
- Independent counsels
- The shape of the economy and the imperatives of economic development
- Fear of losing next election for self or party

lessened, but that other institutions—parties, Congress, the courts—should grow in stature. Unless we can find ways to revitalize our political parties, to achieve some measure of responsiveness to the electorate and party control over public policy, we may well be destined to continue the march toward an American version of the De Gaulle model of leadership in France—a highly personalized and centralized system.[32]

A few presidential advisers and scholars believe we need to rethink our constitutional system and our doctrine of a separation of powers. Our old constitutional restraints, they fear, too severely constrain presidential leadership, especially the ability of a president to get a program enacted. To make the presidency more effective, these "reformers" would amend the Constitution so that Congress and the president would be elected at the same time, and perhaps on some type of ticket, the voter would choose a package or unified party ticket rather than opt for a representative and senator from one party and a president from another. It has also been suggested that presidents serve a single, six-year term, and that they be able to ask a member of Congress to serve in the cabinet—as is done in parliamentary systems. Other reformers would repeal the two-term limitation imposed by the Twenty-second amendment. Still bolder is the suggestion that presidents—failing to get support for their programs in Congress—be empowered to dissolve Congress and call for new elections as a test of strength and as a kind of referendum or vote of confidence for their programs.[33] These are radical steps, and they are not likely to win approval; yet students and scholars should at least think about them.

One of the persisting paradoxes of the American presidency is that on the one hand, it is always too powerful, and on the other, it is too weak: It is always too strong, because in many ways it is contrary to our ideals of government by the people and decentralization of power; yet the office seems to have inadequate powers, because presidents seldom are able to keep the promises they make. Of course, the presidency is always too strong when we dislike the incumbent. And the presidency is always too constrained when we believe a president is striving to serve the public interest as we define it.

The ultimate dilemma for concerned Americans is that curbing the powers of a president who abuses public trust will usually undermine the capacity of fair-minded presidents who would dedicate themselves to serving the public interest. In the nearly two centuries since Washington took office, we have multiplied the requirements for presidential leadership and yet made it increasingly difficult for presidents to lead.

The presidency will surely remain one of our nation's best sources for creative policy change. Americans will expect presidents to do more, not less, in the future. The presidency will almost certainly continue to be a hard-pressed office, laden with the cumulative weight of contradictory expectations. Americans' mixed views of the job of the president often put our presidents in "no-win" situations.[34] Thus, we want our president to be:

1. Gentle and decent but also forceful, cunning, and decisive;
2. A common person who can give an uncommon performance;
3. Above politics, yet a skilled political coalition builder;
4. An inspirational leader who never promises more than can be achieved;

[32] See the analysis in Theodore J. Lowi, *The Personal President* (Cornell University Press, 1985).

[33] See Lloyd Cutler, "To Form a Government—On the Defects of Separation of Powers," in Cronin, *Rethinking the Presidency*. See also James MacGregor Burns, *The Power to Lead* (Simon & Schuster, 1984); Donald Robinson, ed., *Reforming American Government* (Westview, 1985); and James L. Sundquist, *Constitutional Reform* (Brookings Institution, 1986).

[34] These and related paradoxes are discussed in Thomas E. Cronin, *The State of the Presidency*, 2nd ed. (Little, Brown, 1980), chap. 1. See also Godfrey Hodgson, *All Things to All Men* (Simon & Schuster, 1980).

5. A programmatic but also pragmatic and flexible leader;
6. Innovative and inventive, ahead of the times, yet always responsive to popular majorities;
7. A moral leader, yet not too preachy or moralizing;
8. A leader of all the people, but also a leader of one political party.

History suggests there is no foolproof way to guarantee that our presidents will possess the appropriate functional skills as well as the moral character the office requires. Yet after 200 years and 50 presidential elections, the voters have chosen remarkably well. Still, James Madison's advice remains useful: "A dependence on the people is, no doubt, the primary control of the government; but experience has taught mankind the necessity of auxiliary precautions."[35] We must maintain the effectiveness of these "auxiliary precautions"—Congress, parties, the courts, the press, and concerned citizens' groups—if we are to ensure a properly balanced and constitutional presidency.

[35] James Madison, *The Federalist*, No. 51 (Modern Library, 1937), p. 337.

SUMMARY

1. Presidents must act as crisis-managing, morale-building, recruiting, priority-setting, coalition-building, and managerial leaders. No president can divide the job into tidy compartments. Ultimately, all the responsibilities mix with one another.

2. The office of the president is a combination of the huge presidential establishment, a president's personality and character, and the heavy demands and expectations on the chief executive. It is still being reshaped as new presidents with ideas and styles of their own move into the White House.

3. The expansion of presidential powers has been a continuous development during the past several decades. Crises, both foreign and economic, have enlarged the powers of the president. When there is a need for decisive action, presidents are asked to supply it. Congress, of course, is traditionally expected to share in the formulation of national policy. Yet Congress is often so fragmented that it has been a willing partner in the growth of the presidency—at the same time that it is constantly setting boundaries on how far presidents can extend their influence. Every president must learn anew the need to work closely with the members of Congress and to enlist their support before major policy changes can be made.

4. The overriding task of American citizens is to bind presidents to the majority will without shackling them. To expect too much of our presidents may be to weaken them in the leadership tasks we need them to perform. To require immediate accountability might paralyze the presidency. Presidential leadership, properly defined, must be more than the power to persuade and less than the power to coerce: It must be the power to achieve by democratic means results acceptable to the people.

FURTHER READING

Peri Arnold. *Making the Managerial Presidency: Comprehensive Reorganization Planning, 1905–1980* (Princeton University Press, 1986).

James David Barber. *The Presidential Character*, 3rd ed. (Prentice-Hall, 1985).

Bruce Buchanan. *The Citizen's Presidency* (Congressional Quarterly Press, 1986).

James MacGregor Burns. *The Power to Lead: The Crisis of the American Presidency* (Simon & Schuster, 1984).

Thomas E. Cronin, ed. *Inventing the American Presidency* (University Press of Kansas, 1989).

Thomas E. Cronin. *The State of the Presidency*, 2nd ed. (Little, Brown, 1980).

Robert E. DiClerico, ed. *Analyzing the Presidency* (Dushkin, 1985).

George C. Edwards, Steven A. Shull, and Norman C. Thomas, eds. *The Presidency and Public Policy Making* (University of Pittsburgh, 1985).

Charles O. Jones, ed. *The Reagan Legacy* (Chatham House, 1988).

Samuel Kernell. *Going Public: New Strategies of Presidential Leadership* (Congressional Quarterly Press, 1986).

Samuel Kernell and Samuel Popkin, eds. *Chief of Staff: Twenty-Five Years of Managing the Presidency* (University of California Press, 1986).

Gary King and Lyn Ragsdale. *The Elusive Executive* (Congressional Quarterly Press, 1988).

Theodore J. Lowi. *The Personal President* (Cornell University Press, 1985).

Benjamin I. Page and Mark P. Petracca. *The American Presidency* (McGraw-Hill, 1983).

Bert A. Rockman. *The Leadership Question: The Presidency and the American System* (Praeger, 1984).

15

Congress v. President: The Politics of Shared Powers

Clearly, the framers anticipated that the president and the Congress would on occasion disagree over policy, for they gave the president a veto power over legislation and they gave Congress the power to override that veto. The framers actually made such disagreement inevitable by providing that the president, Senate, and House would be elected or selected by different constitutencies acting through different electoral mechanisms. Indeed, the framers *wanted* such disagreement, because checks and balances within the government would prevent president and Congress from "ganging up" against the people's liberties.

Oddly, however, in 1789, the first few weeks and months of the new government—run by many of the framers themselves—were a time of remarkable harmony among the branches. The reasons were severalfold: Although Congress started legislating weeks before Washington, the great Revolutionary War general, even took the oath of office, it was made up largely of his admirers and was thus not disposed to challenge him. And Washington in turn respected the leaders of Congress—especially his fellow Virginian James Madison—and had no intention of using his veto power often, if at all, or of wielding undue influence in the national legislature.

Today, the high point of cooperation between the two branches in 1789 seems almost amusing—and certainly extraordinary. At Washington's request, Madison "ghost-wrote"—as we would say today—Washington's inaugural address. He then wrote the formal reply of the House of Representatives. Then President Washington asked Madison to compose his reply to the House—and also his reply to the Senate. For a week or so Madison was a man "in dialogue with himself."[1]

This early harmony was short-lived. Soon Congress and the president shifted to their historic posture of differing over legislation and other matters, and the dominant influence shifted back and forth between the White House and "the Hill." A century later conflict seemed normal. "Oh, if I could only be president and Congress too, for just ten minutes!" President Theodore Roosevelt once re-

---

[1] Charles F. Hobson and Robert A. Rutland, eds., *The Papers of James Madison*, vol. 12 (University Press of Virginia, 1979), pp. 120–21.

marked. Although most presidents share the same wish, our Constitution rules this out—and for good reason.

The United States is unique among major world powers because it is neither a parliamentary democracy nor a wholly executive-dominated government. Our Constitution invites both Congress and the president to set policy and govern the nation. Much of the time during the twentieth century, the main role of Congress has been to respond to executive branch leadership; the president serves as policy promoter and the Congress as a policy adapter. But this has not always been the case, and in recent years Congress has often yearned to be an equal partner in national policy formulation.

Article I of the Constitution grants to Congress "all legislative powers" but limits them to those "herein granted." It then sets forth in some detail the powers vested in Congress. Article II, in contrast, grants to the president "the executive power," but describes these powers only in vague terms. Is this difference significant? Some scholars and most presidents have argued that a president has additional undefined power to act to promote the well-being of the United States. Therefore, they contend, a president is not limited to the powers spelled out in the Constitution, as is Congress. Other scholars and most members of Congress have argued that the president has no such inherent power.

Whatever the language of the Constitution, the president has often exercised powers not expressly defined in it. These powers have a variety of names: implied or inherent powers or moral, residual, and emergency powers. Implied powers are often considered more restricted in scope than inherent or emergency powers. Clear distinctions, however, are hard to establish.[2]

The framers did expect presidents to be a major influence in foreign policy. In the eighteenth century foreign affairs were generally thought to be an executive matter. But our framers did not want the president to be the only agent. Indeed, some of the powers specified in the Constitution as being vested in Congress were designed to bring Congress into foreign policy.

The framers never intended the president to be the dominant agent in domestic policy making either. For much of the twentieth century, however, scholars have held that we needed a strong, dynamic presidency to overcome the tremendous fragmentation of power in America. The creaky machinery of our government, they contend, can be made to work only if we give a president the proper amount of help and authority. The American people generally favored the expansion of presidential powers. With the development of radio and television, the visibility of the president increased. Indeed, considering the publicity given presidents, it is hardly surprising that citizens look to them to solve the nation's problems.

As the roles of Congress and the presidency have changed, tensions between the branches have been inevitable. They were, as we have noted, not only anticipated but planned: The branches were designed with different constituencies, different-length terms, and different responsibilities. The branches are also organized differently, and they are jealous of their powers. Members of both branches are often suspicious of the other.

Still, even though the Constitution disperses power and invites a continuing struggle between these two branches, it also requires the two branches to integrate the fragmented parts of the system into a workable government. And usually these two branches do work together. Even when the relationship "is guarded or hostile, bills get passed and signed into law. Presidential appointments are approved by the Senate. Budgets are enacted and the government is kept afloat. This necessary

---

Gerald Ford on Congress Versus the Presidency

"When I was in the House for 25 years I almost always looked down Pennsylvania Avenue at the White House, regardless of whether Democrats or Republicans were there, and wondered why they were so arrogant. Then, when I was in the White House myself, I looked up at the Congress and wondered how there could be 535 irresponsible members of Congress."

Source: Talk at Hinckley Institute of Politics, University of Utah, February 1982.

---

[2] Louis Fisher, *Constitutional Conflicts between Congress and the President* (Princeton University Press, 1985), and Christopher H. Pyle and Richard Pious, *The President, Congress, and the Constitution* (Free Press, 1984).

cooperation goes on even when the White House and the Capitol are controlled by different parties.''[3]

What are the sources of conflict and cooperation between these two branches? In dealing with this central question we look first at the legislative role of presidents and the efforts of Congress to fulfill its constitutional responsibilities.

PRESIDENTIAL INFLUENCE IN CONGRESS

The presidential record of dealing with Congress in recent years is a mixed one. Presidents enjoy considerable success in getting most of their nominations confirmed by the Senate. Also, few presidential vetoes have been overturned by Congress, and the vast bulk of presidential budget requests eventually win approval. On the other hand, often only 50 percent of presidents' major policy initiatives are passed.[4] Even though President Reagan won more of his major legislative struggles with Congress than did his three immediate predecessors, he, like several before him, fared less well with Congress the longer he was in office. Many actions that he would have liked, such as weakening the Clean Air Act or abolishing the Departments of Energy and Education, were either defeated or shelved because they lacked support.

Why are presidents in conflict with Congress so often? In part, because the whole process was designed to maximize checks and balances and deliberation—rather than cooperation and speedy action. And Americans by and large want it that way. They do not want presidents' dictating policies and laws (see Table 15–1).

Another reason for conflict is that the presidency and Congress represent different constituencies. Not only do members of Congress represent state and local citizenry—and hence reflect somewhat different geographical interests than a president—but some are elected two years earlier than a president, and some two years later; this no doubt makes them responsible to somewhat different moods and points of view. Moreover, many members of Congress may have been there

"Kingsley says if he were President he'd tell Congress to either put up or shut up." (*Drawing by Stan Hunt;* © *1978 The New Yorker Magazine, Inc.*)

15–1 **Public Expectations of the Role of Congress and the President in Policy Making**

Question: Now I would like to ask you some questions about the president and Congress. Some people think that the president ought to have the major responsibility for making policy, while other people think that Congress ought to have the major responsibility. In general, which do you think should have the major responsibility for setting policy?

Who Should Have the Major Responsibility?	Economic Policy	Foreign Policy	General Responsibility
Congress	40%	27%	36%
Equal	20	18	22
President	34	49	37
Don't know	6	6	5
	100	100	100

Source: Gallup poll, nationwide survey of over 1500 adults conducted by WHYY, Inc., Philadelphia–Wilmington (Fall 1979).

[3] Roger H. Davidson and Walter J. Oleszek, *Congress and Its Members* (Congressional Quarterly Press, 1981), p. 282.

[4] See George C. Edwards, III, *Presidential Influence in Congress* (W. H. Freeman, 1980). See also his "Measuring Presidential Success in Congress: Alternative Approaches," *Journal of Politics* (Summer 1985), pp. 667–85.

Sources of Congress-Presidency Conflict

- Diverse geographical constituencies
- Staggered terms of election
- Conflicting responsibilities
- Different partisan ties (often)
- Constitutional provisions requiring extensive sharing of power
- Presidents' seeing Congress as disorganized and inefficient
- Congress's viewing the White House as arbitrary and insensitive
- Each wanting the credit for successes, and each seeking to blame the other when things go wrong

Factors That Sometimes Help a President Win Support in Congress

- Publicity power (press conferences, addresses)
- Popularity (when it is high)
- Patronage powers (appointments, public-works project support)
- Party leader role (sometimes)
- Personal lobbying and persuasiveness
- Informal social ties
- Political bargaining
- Threat of a presidential veto
- National emergencies

for ten or twenty years, and look forward to serving perhaps another ten. Presidents, however, think mainly about the present.

Still other factors are at work. The opposition party in Congress often tries to mount its own programs. It will, when possible, defeat a president's policy initiatives and substitute its own. Sometimes it will merely defeat White House measures. This becomes especially troublesome for a president if Congress is controlled by a majority of the opposition—as has been the case for ten years of the past generation (1953–1954 and 1969–1977). President Reagan was forced to deal with a Democratically controlled House throughout his two terms.

What can and does a president do in working with Congress? What are the chief sources of influence? The greatest asset for presidents working with Congress is to have both houses populated by large numbers from their own political parties. Presidents often try to enlarge their parties' representation in Congress during the midterm elections, but they are seldom successful in this effort.[5] Indeed, they almost always lose support as a result of midterm elections. Nowadays most members of Congress prefer to run their own campaigns quite independent of the president. Even when they do seek a president's help, it is not clear whether this aid is effective. Presidential coattails, once thought to be a significant factor in helping to elect members of a president's party to Congress, have had little effect in recent years. Members of Congress usually get reelected because of the quality of their constituency services and because they can take advantage of incumbency.

From the president's vantage point it is seldom helpful to punish party mavericks. With power dispersed and decentralized in Congress it is just too risky for a president to single out a few party "disloyalists" for retribution. White House congressional relations aides abide by the motto of "no permanent allies, no permanent enemies." Someone whose vote is lost today may cast the crucial vote on some other measure next week.

A president who wins widespread backing in the country—and in the states and congressional districts—can use this popularity to try to influence certain members of Congress. In addition, presidents are now expected to build coalitions with key interest groups. Lyndon Johnson and Ronald Reagan were effective in this regard. Presidents today are expected to meet regularly not only with the leadership within Congress but also with the members of key committees and subcommittees.

Members of Congress take it for granted that a president will meet with them socially, arrange visits to their districts by cabinet officers (or even by the president personally), and send them autographed photos, and so on. The White House now employs a staff just to "service" these requests and favors. The granting or withholding of these favors, however, probably does not help a president in dealings with Congress, because members of Congress have come to expect these favors from the White House.

On balance, a president's position in dealing with Congress is relatively fragile. President Nixon misused and abused many presidential powers, but he was no more able to influence Congress than other presidents. In fact, he won passage of fewer key policy initiatives than did most recent presidents. To say a president is in a relatively weak position in dealing with Congress is to say the White House does not have a large number of resources with which to influence most members of Congress. Presidents can make stirring appeals for party unity—if their parties enjoy majorities in Congress. They can also try to educate and rally the public around their major programs. They can—as President Reagan did with his tax-cut and tax-reform proposals—build effective public coalitions in support of a key measure.

But much of the time a president must deal with a Congress that moves according to its own pace and that responds to a variety of interests above and

---

[5] See Randall L. Calvert and John A. Ferejohn, "Coattail Voting in Recent Presidential Elections," *American Political Science Review* (June 1983), pp. 407–19.

Rarely does a president come before a congressional committee. Here, however, President Ford faces the House Judiciary Subcommittee on Criminal Justice to explain why he pardoned former President Richard M. Nixon. (*UPI/Bettmann Newsphotos*)

beyond those coming from the White House. As we noted in Chapter 13, members of Congress are influenced more by their own philosophical and ideological convictions, by their colleagues in Congress, and by the interests of their districts back home than they are by instructions or pleas from the White House. These realities will remain central factors in presidential-congressional relations.

Watergate—and the first forced resignation of a president in our history—aroused public concern about the role of Congress. Most people wished Congress to be a more coequal branch of government, to be more assertive and alert, and to be more jealous of its own powers. The change in public attitudes is documented by polls taken before and after Vietnam and Watergate. Support for Congress soared in the mid-1970s, although public support for the two branches became more balanced by about 1980. But Congress was put on notice by the American people: Shape up and assert yourself!

What form did congressional reassertion take? Did a new array of checks and balances cripple the presidency and undermine its potential for creative leadership? Did Congress overreact to Vietnam and Watergate? We examine these questions in the rest of this chapter. We explore how Congress tried to reclaim its policy-making powers and the impact of this on the presidency.

THE IMPERIAL PRESIDENCY ARGUMENT

Many critics held that, because of abuse of power by presidents, especially abuse of the war powers and secrecy, during the 1960s and early 1970s the presidency became an imperial institution. In his book *The Imperial Presidency*, historian and former John Kennedy adviser Arthur M. Schlesinger, Jr., argued that presidential power was so expanded and misused by 1972 that it threatened our constitutional system.[6] Schlesinger claimed that an imperial presidency was created as a result of America's wartime experiences, particularly Vietman.

Proponents of the "imperial presidency" view contend that the difficulty stems in part from ambiguity concerning the president's power as commander in chief: It is an undefined *office*, not a *function*. Schlesinger and others acknowledge that Nixon and Johnson did not create the imperial presidency; they merely built on some of the more questionable practices of their predecessors. But observers contend there is a distinction between the *abuse* and the *usurpation* of power. Abraham Lincoln, FDR, and Harry Truman temporarily usurped power in wartime. Johnson and Nixon abused power, even in peacetime, by claiming absolute powers to be a part of their office.

Secrecy has often been used to protect and preserve a president's national security power. It is argued that Nixon pushed the doctrine beyond acceptable limits. Before Eisenhower Congress expected to get the information it sought from the executive branch. Instances of secrecy and executive privilege were the rare exceptions. By the early 1970s they had become the rule. And a Congress that knows only what the president wants it to know is not an independent body.

Those who are critical of Nixon contend that he made the presidency not only fully imperial but also revolutionary. For example, in authorizing members of his own White House staff to retaliate against his political opponents, Nixon became the first president in our history to establish an extralegal investigative force, paid for by the taxpayers but unknown to Congress and accountable to no one but himself. Because Nixon also misused intelligence agencies and authorized breaking and entering, he became the only American president to have supervised lawless actions in peacetime.

[6] Arthur M. Schlesinger, Jr., *The Imperial Presidency* (Houghton Mifflin, 1973).

President Franklin D. Roosevelt, surrounded by congressional leaders, signs Declaration of War against Japan on December 8, 1941. This was the last time the United States declared war. (AP/Wide World Photos)

Political scientist Theodore Lowi contends that presidents have little choice but to be imperial given the relationship between the development of the American national state and the significant practical role of the executive in that development. He suggests that Schlesinger's interpretation exaggerates the case of personal abuse of power by Nixon and others and underestimates the fact that the modern presidency is largely the construction of the Congress with the cooperation of the federal courts. He suggests that the vast growth of presidential power began with the coming of New Deal domestic programs and cannot be linked solely or even primarily with the expansion of the president's foreign policy powers. Although "there may be many specific cases of usurpation by modern presidents, these are extreme actions in pursuit of powers and responsibilities by and large willingly and voluntarily delegated to the president by Congress."[7]

Still Schlesinger's book is a useful point of departure for discussing the alleged too-powerful presidency. The chief complaints involve such presidential privileges as war making, emergency powers, diplomacy by executive agreement, and government by veto.

Presidential War Making

The Constitution delegates to Congress the authority to *declare* the legal state of war (with the consent of the president), but in practice the commander in chief often starts or initiates war (or actions that lead to war). This power has been used by the chief executive time and time again. In 1846 Polk ordered American forces to advance into disputed territory; when Mexico resisted, Polk informed Congress that war existed by act of Mexico, and a formal declaration of war was soon forthcoming. McKinley's dispatch of a battleship to Havana, where it was blown up, helped precipitate war with Spain in 1898. The United States was not formally at war with Germany until late 1941, but prior to Pearl Harbor Roosevelt ordered the Navy to guard convoys to Great Britain and to open fire on submarines threatening the convoys. Since World War II every president, from Truman through Reagan, has sent forces into combat without specific congressional authorization— to Korea, Berlin, Vietnam, Lebanon, Grenada, Cuba, Libya—in fact, around the world.[8]

Thus, from Washington's time on, by ordering troops into battle, the president has often decided when Americans will fight, and when they will not. When the cause has had political support, the president's use of this authority has been approved. Abraham Lincoln called up troops, spent money, set up a blockade, and fought the first few months of the Civil War without even calling Congress into session. More recently it became obvious that the president needed the power to respond to sudden attacks and to protect the rights and property of American citizens. The State Department described this enlarged mandate as follows:

> In the twentieth century the world has grown much smaller. An attack on a country far from its shores can impinge directly on the nation's security. . . . The Constitution leaves to the President the judgment to determine whether the circumstances of a particular armed attack are so urgent and the potential consequences so threatening to the security of the U.S. that he should act without formally consulting the Congress.[9]

But Congress became upset when it learned (several years after the fact) that in 1964 President Johnson won approval of his Vietnam initiatives on the basis of misleading information. In 1969 and 1970 a secret air war was waged in Cambodia with no formal congressional knowledge or authorization. The military

[7] Theodore Lowi, *The Personal President* (Cornell University Press, 1985), p. 179.

[8] See Thomas A. Bailey, *The Pugnacious Presidents: War Presidents on Parade* (Free Press, 1980.)

[9] Leonard C. Meeker, "The Legality of U.S. Participation in the Defense of Vietnam, *Department of State Bulletin* (March 28, 1966), pp. 484–85.

also operated in Laos without formally notifying Congress. It was to prevent just such acts as these that the framers of the Constitution gave Congress the power to declare war; and many members of Congress believe that what happened in Indochina was the result of the White House's bypassing the constitutional requirements. But they also agree that presidential excesses came about because Congress either agreed with presidents or did nothing to stop them.

What the Johnson and Nixon war experiences also show is that at the beginning of hostilities, the country and Congress rally behind a president. As casualties mount and fighting continues, support usually falls off. In both Korea and Vietnam presidential failure to end the use of American ground forces led to increased political trouble. Eisenhower swept into power in 1952 saying, "I shall go to Korea" and thus arousing hope among voters that he would bring about an end to the Korean War. Nixon won in 1968 when Johnson was forced out over Vietnam. But even though Congress may have been misled during the Vietnam War, it enthusiastically supported the president and went along with his actions. Not until the war turned sour did senators and representatives begin to charge misrepresentation. Why, then, were they so easily talked into approving funds for the war? They continued to pass appropriations for it right up to April 1975. The more general lesson appears to be that the country and Congress (and the courts) tend to go along with a president's judgments about military action overseas.

There are additional reasons why no formal congressional declarations of war have been issued in recent times. During a state of war the president assumes certain legal prerogatives that Congress might not always be willing to grant. There are also international legal consequences of a formal declaration of war regarding foreign assets, the rights of neutrals, and so on, which our allies would not always be willing to recognize and which would be difficult to insist upon. Moreover, there is the psychological consequence of declaring war, compounded by the fact that—according to Article 2, Section 2, of the United Nations Charter—war is illegal except in self-defense.

Emergency Powers

From the early 1930s to the mid-1970s, Congress passed about 500 federal statutes collectively giving a president extraordinary powers. Once a state of emergency is declared, for example, a president can seize property, organize and control the means of production, seize commodities, assign military forces abroad, declare martial law, and control all transportation and communications. A president might, in fact, control almost all aspects of citizens' lives. Abuses of presidential power under these emergency laws include detention of American citizens of Japanese ancestry during World War II, coverup of bombings in Cambodia, and directives to the FBI for illegal domestic surveillance and intelligence work.[10]

Diplomacy by Executive Agreement

The growing use of **executive agreements,** as indicated in Table 15–2, shows their popularity with recent presidents. Before a president can ratify a treaty, two-thirds of the Senate must consent. But a president can enter into formal agreements with a foreign nation, by executive agreements, without senatorial approval. These agreements have been recognized as distinct from treaties since George Washington's day, and their use by the executive has been upheld by the courts. What irked Congress in the 1960s and 1970s was that the Senate was being asked to ratify

President Lyndon Johnson giving his State of the Union address in 1964. (*UPI/Bettmann Newsphotos*)

[10] For a discussion of abuses of power in U.S. intelligence agencies during the Cold War years, see Morton H. Halperin, Jerry J. Berman, Robert L. Borosage, and Christine M. Marwick, *The Lawless State* (Penguin, 1976), and David Wise, *The American Police State: The Government against the People* (Random House, 1976).

15–2 Treaties and Executive Agreements, 1789–1985

PERIOD	TREATIES	EXECUTIVE AGREEMENTS	TOTALS
1789–1839	60	27	87
1840–1889	215	238	453
1890–1939	524	917	1441
1940–1973	364	6395	6759
1974–1979	102	2233	2335
1980–1985	101	1940	2041
	1366	11,750	13,116

Source: Congressional Research Service, Library of Congress.

international accords only on trivial matters. Critically important mutual-aid and military agreements were being arranged by the White House without its even informing Congress.

For example, while the Senate was ratifying treaties to preserve archeological artifacts in Mexico and maintain certain lights in the Red Sea, the president was using executive agreements to make vital decisions about United States presence in Vietnam, Laos, Korea, and Thailand. Several senators and others argued that these practices violated the Constitution's intent that Congress share in making foreign policy. And so the members of Congress began to look for ways to limit a president's executive agreement authority.

Ironically, during the 1940s and 1950s conservative members of Congress tried to check the president's power to make executive agreements. In 1953 Senator John Bricker (R-Ohio) introduced a constitutional amendment that would have required Congress to approve all executive agreements. He was opposed by liberals, especially liberal political scientists and historians, who feared the Bricker amendment would reintroduce mindless **isolationism.** Bricker was opposed too by Eisenhower's secretary of state who called the amendment dangerous to our peace and security. In the wake of Vietnam and especially during the Nixon administration, the shoe was on the other foot: The liberals, fearing an interventionist foreign policy, now wanted to limit executive agreements.[11]

President Nixon resigning from office. (*UPI/Bettmann Newsphotos*)

Government by Presidential Veto?

A president can veto a bill by returning it, together with specific objections, to the house in which it originated. Congress, by a two-thirds vote in each chamber, may then override the president's veto. Another variation of the veto is known as the **pocket veto.** In the ordinary course of events, if the president does not sign or veto a bill within ten weekdays after receiving it, it becomes law without the chief executive's signature. But if Congress adjourns within the ten days, the president—by taking no action—can kill the bill.

The veto's strength lies in the ordinary failure of Congress to get a two-thirds majority of both houses. Historically Congress has overridden only about 3 percent of presidents' vetoes. Yet a Congress that can repeatedly mobilize such a majority against a president can almost take command of the government. Such was the fate of Andrew Johnson in the late 1860s.

In ordinary times Congress will manipulate legislation to reduce the chance of a presidential veto. It can attach irrelevant but controversial provisions, called

[11] On executive agreements and treaties see Lawrence Margolis, *Executive Agreements and Presidential Power in Foreign Policy* (Praeger, 1986), and William L. Furlong and Margaret E. Scranton, *The Dynamics of Foreign Policymaking: The President, The Congress and the Panama Canal Treaties* (Westview Press, 1984).

PRESIDENT	VETOES	VETOES OVER-RIDDEN	PRESIDENT	VETOES	VETOES OVER-RIDDEN	PRESIDENT	VETOES	VETOES OVER-RIDDEN
George Washington	2	—	James Buchanan	7	—	Warren G. Harding	6	—
John Adams	0	—	Abraham Lincoln	7	—	Calvin Coolidge	50	4
Thomas Jefferson	0	—	Andrew Johnson	29	15	Herbert Hoover	37	3
James Madison	7	—	Ulysses S. Grant	93	4	Franklin D. Roosevelt	635	9
James Monroe	1	—	Rutherford B. Hayes	13	1	Harry S. Truman	250	12
John Q. Adams	0	—	James A. Garfield	0	—	Dwight D. Eisenhower	181	2
Andrew Jackson	12	—	Chester A. Arthur	12	1	John F. Kennedy	21	—
Martin Van Buren	1	—	Grover Cleveland	414	2	Lyndon B. Johnson	30	—
W. H. Harrison	0	—	Benjamin Harrison	44	1	Richard M. Nixon	43	7
John Tyler	10	1	Grover Cleveland	170	5	Gerald R. Ford	66	12
James K. Polk	3	—	William McKinley	42	—	Jimmy Carter	31	2
Zachary Taylor	0	—	Theodore Roosevelt	82	1	Ronald Reagan	76	8
Millard Fillmore	0	—	William H. Taft	39	1	Total	2467	102
Franklin Pierce	9	5	Woodrow Wilson	44	6			

Source: Library of Congress and *Congressional Quarterly*.

riders, to legislation the president considers vital. Presidents must either accept or reject the whole bill, for they do not have the power to delete individual items—that is, they do not have the item veto. In one appropriations bill, for example, law makers may combine badly needed funds for the armed forces with costly pork-barrel items. The president must take the bill as it is or not at all.

For their part, presidents can also use the veto power in a positive way. They can announce that bills under consideration by Congress will be turned back unless certain changes are made. They can use the threat of vetoes against some bills Congress wants badly in exchange for other bills that they want. A presidential veto can also protect a national minority from hasty, unfair legislation passed in the heat of the moment. But the veto is essentially a negative weapon of limited use to a president who has a positive program. For it is the *president* who is usually pressing for action.

The presidential veto power has stirred less controversy than the other changes we have discussed. Carter vetoed only thirty-one bills, Nixon vetoed forty-three, Ford sixty-six, and Reagan as of late 1986 forty-seven. Still, the occasional use of the pocket veto has stirred some criticism. Some members of Congress said our founders envisioned a more limited use of the veto. Other members of Congress, led by Senator Edward Kennedy, objected to Nixon's use of the pocket veto during short holiday recesses. The courts upheld Kennedy's contention that the pocket veto did not apply while Congress was in recess, but only when it had adjourned.

In fact, there is little that Congress can do when confronted with a presidential veto. It must either get enough votes to override the veto or modify the legislation and try again.

THE PRESIDENT BLAMES CONGRESS AND CONGRESS BLAMES THE PRESIDENT! WHAT'S GOING ON HERE?

NO-FAULT GOVERNMENT—

(© 1980, King Features Syndicate, Inc. World rights reserved)

CONGRESS REASSERTS ITSELF?

The end of the war in Vietnam, the 1974 impeachment hearings, and the resignation of President Nixon gave Congress new life.[12] It set about to recover lost authority and discover new ways to participate more fully in making national policy. Some of Congress's more notable efforts to reassert itself are outlined next.

[12] See James Sundquist, *The Decline and Resurgence of Congress* (Brookings Institution, 1981).

The War over the War Powers

In 1973 Congress overrode a presidential veto and enacted the War Powers Resolution. Congress declared that henceforth the president can commit the armed forces of the United States only (1) after a declaration of war by Congress; (2) by specific statutory authorization; or (3) in a national emergency created by an attack on the United States or its armed forces. After committing the armed forces under the third circumstance, the president is required to report to Congress within forty-eight hours. Unless Congress has declared war, the troop commitment will be ended within sixty days. The president is allowed another thirty days if the chief executive claims the safety of United States forces requires their continued use. A president is also obligated by this resolution to consult Congress "in every possible instance" before committing troops to battle. Moreover, at any time, by concurrent resolution *not subject to presidential veto*, Congress may direct the president to disengage such troops. Because of a 1983 court ruling, the question of whether Congress can remove the troops by concurrent resolution or legislative veto is now in doubt (see the discussion of the legislative veto later in this chapter).

Not everyone was pleased by the passage of the War Powers Resolution.[13] But many experts believed the War Powers legislation to be of symbolic and institutional significance, because it reflected a new determination in Congress. Presidents now know that commitment of American troops is subject to congressional approval. They will have to persuade the nation that their actions are justified by the gravest of national emergencies.

All our recent presidents have opposed the War Powers Resolution as unwise and overly restrictive. They claim it gives to Congress the right to force them to do what the Constitution says they do not have to do—to withdraw American forces at some arbitrary moment. The War Powers Resolution has not been tested in the courts, and probably will not be, because it raises political questions with which judges are unwilling to be involved.

How has the Resolution worked? Since its adoption in 1973 the process spelled out in the War Powers Resolution has been used several times. It was used, for example, when Marines were sent in 1975 to free the merchant cargo ship *Mayaquez*, which had been captured by the Cambodians. In 1982 President Reagan reported to Congress, along the lines of the Resolution, after he sent troops into Lebanon. Yet he made clear in a written statement that his compliance did not "cede any of the authority vested in me under the Constitution as President and as commander in chief. . . . Nor should my signing be viewed as any acknowledgement that the President's constitutional authority can be impermissibly infringed by statute."[14] Then, in the 1983 United States invasion, or rescue mission, in Grenada, Reagan acted completely on his own until after the troops had already landed. Furthermore, he acted as though he did not need any sort of authorization. What did Congress do? Virtually nothing. A few members grumbled.

Nor did President Reagan invoke the War Powers Resolution provisions for military operations in Honduras. He also employed military power against Libya twice in 1986 and in neither case did he seek prior advice from Congress. Although he sent reports about these actions to Congress after the incidents, he went out of his way to make it clear that he was not acting in accordance with the War Powers Resolution. Both military actions against Libya won widespread support in Congress and in the country, although Congressman Dante Fascall (D-Florida), chair of the House Foreign Affairs Committee, complained that the President was waltzing around the War Powers Resolution and was developing "a new way of

U.S. Marines at work.
(*Courtesy U.S. Marine Corps.*)

[13] Ann Van Wynen Thomas and A. J. Thomas, Jr., *The War-Making Powers of the President* (Southern Methodist Press, 1982).

[14] Quoted in Christopher Madison, "Despite His Complaints Reagan Going Along with Spirit of War Powers Law," *National Journal* (May 19, 1984), p. 990.

The Troubled Life of the War Powers Resolution

When Congress passed the War Powers Resolution in 1973 it hoped the Resolution would pave the way for improved White House-Congressional cooperation when U.S. troops had to be used in emergency situations. In the years that followed, however, conflict and strain characterized these relations more than cooperation. Congress seldom believes it is properly consulted. Presidents Nixon, Ford, Carter, and Reagan all believed the War Powers Resolution was unconstitutional, impractical, or undesirable. All three branches have weakened the spirit of the War Powers Resolution. Presidents often ignored it or complied with it in a minimal way. The Burger Court ruled on another measure that implicitly suggested a major provision of the Resolution was unconstitutional. Congress sometimes failed to follow through and use the Resolution. After a long struggle, for example, Congress ruled the president could keep troops in Lebanon for up to eighteen months. And Congress seemed overwhelmed both by the president and public opinion and never even put the War Powers Resolution into effect in the Grenada case.

going to war which totally bypasses the Constitution" and its requirements that only Congress can declare war."[15] Reagan responded that he was acting in self-defense against terrorism. His State Department spokesperson said, "the deployment of anti-terrorist units . . . would seem to fall completely outside the scope of the (War Powers) Resolution."[16]

For the most part, then, the War Powers Resolution has not hindered presidential military and war-making action. Nor has it, as Nixon had argued, weakened the presidency in any visible way. Even its chief sponsor in the Senate recognized its inadequacies.[17]

What is the future of the War Powers Resolution? It will remain, as will the considerable disputes over its effectiveness and constitutionality. Someday Congress is likely to improve it by defining a group of congressional leaders with whom the president should consult prior to commitment of American forces abroad.

Curbing the Emergency Powers

The National Emergencies Act of 1976 terminated, as of 1978, the extensive powers and authorities possessed by the president as a result of the continuing state of emergency in which the nation had been since the mid-1930s. It also established authority for the declaration of future emergencies in a manner that will clearly define the powers of the president and provide for regular congressional review.

The act also calls upon presidents to inform Congress in advance and to identify those laws they plan to use when declaring a national emergency. A state of emergency so declared would automatically end after six months. But Congress must review the declaration of emergency powers at least every six months.

Congress hopes this legislation will ensure that emergency powers can be utilized only when legitimate emergencies actually exist, and then only with the safeguard of legislative review. As one senator reported to Congress: "Reliance on emergency authority, intended for use in crisis situations, would no longer be available in non-crisis situations. At a time when governments throughout the world are turning with increasing desperation to an all-powerful executive, this legislation is designed to insure that the United States travels a road marked by carefully constructed legal safeguards."[18]

Congress and the Intelligence Agencies

Presidents have also been charged with abusing the intelligence and spying agencies. The Central Intelligence Agency (CIA) was established in 1947, when the threat of "world communism" led to a vast number of national security efforts. When the CIA was established, Congress recognized the dangers to a free society inherent in such a secret organization. Hence, it was stipulated that the CIA *was not to engage in any police work or to perform operations within the United States.*

From 1947 to the mid-1970s, no area of national policy making was more removed from Congress than CIA operations. In many instances Congress acted as if it really did not want to know what was going on. Said one senator: "It is not a question of reluctance on the part of CIA officials to speak to us. Instead it is a question of our reluctance, if you will, to seek information and knowledge on

---

[15] Quoted in "In Wake of Libya, Skirmishing over War Powers," *Congressional Quarterly* (May 10, 1986), p. 1021.

[16] Abraham D. Sofaer, "The War Powers Resolution and Antiterrorist Operations." Statement before the Subcommittee on Arms Control, International Security and Science, House Foreign Affairs Committee, April 29, 1986.

[17] Jacob K. Javits, "War Powers Reconsidered," *Foreign Affairs* (Fall 1985), pp. 130–40.

[18] Abraham Ribicoff, quoted in *National Emergencies Act*, *Report of the Committee on Government Operations*, *United States Senate* (U.S. Government Printing Office, 1976), p. 2.

subjects which I personally, as a Member of Congress and as a citizen, would rather not have."[19] There is much evidence that both Congress and the White House were lax in supervising intelligence activities. By 1973, the CIA was accused of plotting assassinations, experimenting with mind-altering drugs, carrying out extensive foreign paramilitary operations, and, most important, spying on American citizens during the Watergate era.

Congress has tried to reassert control over the CIA. It now requires the Agency to report to two committees—the House and the Senate oversight committees—any plans for clandestine operations. In 1976, in an unprecedented exercise of power, Congress amended the Defense Appropriations Bill to terminate American covert intervention in Angola. But skeptics doubt whether Congress will be able to maintain control over the CIA.

Presidents have criticized Congress for weakening the CIA—for going too far in making covert operations too difficult. President Carter especially pressed this case during the Iranian and Afghanistan crises of 1980. The Reagan administration gave to the CIA a new era of prominence and enhanced powers, of which its coordinating role in providing American assistance to the Nicaraguan contras is perhaps the most striking example.

Former CIA Director Stansfield Turner argues that congressional oversight has been useful. It forces, he contends, intelligence officers to exercise greater judiciousness and to maintain a healthy sense of the national temper. He also believes that congressional oversight strengthens the hand of the CIA director in controlling what has always been a notoriously independent agency.[20] On balance we have to conclude that for all the talk of greater congressional control, the CIA and the president have not been seriously hampered in carrying out what they deem necessary.

The 1974 Congressional Budget and Impoundment Control Act

During the Nixon administration, some members of Congress used to joke that ours was a system of checks and balances all right: Congress wrote the checks and the White House kept the balance. They were referring to President Nixon's frequent use of the powers to impound funds appropriated by Congress.

By *impounding* funds a president forbids an executive branch agency to spend money even though it has been appropriated by Congress. **Impoundment** can take many forms. It may be necessary to accommodate a change in events (if a war ends) or to alter a managerial approach (to carry out a project more efficiently). Before Nixon, impoundments were infrequent and usually temporary; generally they involved small amounts of money. Nixon stretched the use of impoundment to new lengths. He claimed that the Democratic Congress was spending too much and causing huge deficits. Congress responded that Nixon was using impoundment to set policy and that he was violating the Constitution, which states: "No money shall be drawn from the Treasury, but in consequence of appropriations made by law." Congress took this to mean it had the final say in fiscal policy making. But Congress not only complained; it acted as well: It passed the 1974 Congressional Budget and Impoundment Control Act.

By this act Congress was trying to prevent presidential impoundments. It was also responding to the fact that since the days of FDR its influence over federal spending had diminished, while that of the Office of Management and Budget in the executive office of the president had increased. With no budget

YOU DECIDE

You are president. The director of the CIA and the chair of the Joint Chiefs of Staff at the Pentagon advise you that a country in North Africa headed by an anti-American dictator has, with the help of the Soviet Union, assembled a team of scientists who are about to build an atomic bomb.

They also advise you that within that country a group of persons who oppose the head of state believe that if they are given some weapons they can overthrow the government and establish one that would be friendly to the United States, would be more democratic, and would pledge not to introduce atomic weapons into the Middle East.

Many members of Congress oppose covert actions by the CIA. Should you, would you, authorize the CIA to assist the rebels in a covert way?

(Answer/Discussion on page 354.)

[19] Statement of Senator Leverett Saltonstall (R-Massachusetts), quoted in Henry Howe Ransom, *The Intelligence Establishment* (Harvard University Press, 1970), p. 169.
[20] Stansfield Turner, *Secrecy and Democracy: The CIA in Transition* (Houghton Mifflin, 1985).

system of its own—only many separate actions and decisions—Congress has become dependent on the president's budget proposals. Members of Congress grew to appreciate, if not respect, the old saying: The one who controls the purse has the power.

The 1974 act created a permanent budget committee for each chamber of Congress, and a Congressional Budget Office (CBO). It provided budgetary and fiscal experts and computer services and gives Congress technical assistance in dealing with the president's proposals. Some members of Congress hoped the CBO would provide hard, practical data to guide the drafting of spending legislation. Others saw it as a potential "think tank" that might propose standards for spending and national priorities. In fact, the CBO is most frequently used to provide routine cost estimates of spending and tax bills and to keep track of the overall budget level.

Optimists hoped this budget reform act would force Congress into more systematic and timely action on budgetary legislation. They hoped, too, it would tie separate spending decisions in with fiscal policy objectives. Its budgetary timetable gave Congress three additional months to consider the president's recommendations. By May 15 of each year, Congress adopts a tentative budget that sets target totals for spending and taxes. This target serves as a guide for the committees considering detailed appropriations measures. By September 15 Congress adopts a second resolution that either affirms or revises the earlier targets. If necessary to meet the final budget totals, this resolution must also dictate any changes in expenditures and revenues.[21]

How has the "reformed" budget process worked? The quality of information produced by the CBO improved congressional deliberation on the budget; the new budget committees in each house worked reasonably well and the budget resolutions provided a vehicle for certain helpful debates on key economic issues. But overall the new budgetary process did not diminish the budgetary powers of the president. In fact, President Reagan dramatically used the "reconciliation" aspect of the process to push through major budget cuts. Although it was perfectly legal this presidential use of the act was unanticipated by those who wrote it. The effect was to give Reagan, backed by majorities in both houses of Congress, an influence over the budget process that no president had exercised before. And it was contrary to what the writers of the act intended; indeed it was the very kind of presidential assertiveness Congress had hoped to limit. Reagan, however, enjoyed less success in controlling the budget after this remarkable first-year experience. Budget process politics became highly partisan in both houses of Congress, and legislative-executive budget relations often became strained.

The budgetary reforms of the 1970s did not do the job. Some progress was made, but surely the fondest hopes of the reformers have not been achieved. Congress still fails to apply intelligent cuts to the "sacred cows" of welfare, subsidy, and defense spending. Far too much confusion still surrounds the budgetary process. The whole point of this new budget process was to force Congress to make choices, to put together in one place the spending claims and the revenues, and to decide what it wants. Many people believe the problem is structural and not the result of personal faults of members of Congress. Congress reflects local pressures, presidents reflect national pressures. All this gets reflected in the budget process. Congress may well have to restructure itself to strengthen places where overall consensus can be built. But this would mean weakening subcommittees and curbing the recent tendencies to disperse power—something Congress is unlikely to do. If it cannot

Item Veto

Recent presidents have called for an amendment to the Constitution that would permit the president to veto, or in effect to delete, any subsection of an appropriations bill passed by Congress. They argued it would give the president a major tool to reduce deficits. Nearly 70 percent of the American people favor the idea of an item veto. Nevertheless, Congress has so far been unwilling to approve such an amendment for fear that it would "provide more power than an effective president needs and more than a misguided president should have."

Source: Thomas E. Cronin and Jeffrey J. Weill, "An Item Veto for the President?" Congress and the Presidency (Autumn 1985), pp. 127–51.

---

[21] Three books describing the origins and early years of the 1974 Congressional Budget and Impoundment Control Act are Lance T. LeLoup, *The Fiscal Congress: Legislative Control of the Budget* (Greenwood Press, 1980); Allen Schick, *Congress and Money: Budgeting, Spending and Taxing* (Urban Institute, 1980); and Howard Shuman, *Politics and the Budget*, 2nd ed. (Prentice-Hall, 1989).

do this, Congress will very likely have to respond to the choices and priorities set by presidents.[22]

The impoundment control provisions of this new 1974 law worked only slightly better than the budgetary process provisions. The 1974 Congressional Budget and Impoundment Act repealed the 1921 language used by Nixon to justify his impoundments. It also stipulated two new procedures—*rescissions* and *deferrals*—by which a president, at least temporarily, can override appropriations decisions or delay spending. A president may propose to cancel, or rescind, enacted appropriations or subsections of a larger appropriations bill, but unless Congress agrees (with a majority vote in both houses) to the rescission within forty-five days, the money must be spent by the executive branch.

All our recent presidents have used this provision, which has cut several billions from the budget, and Congress has usually gone along with the presidential suggestions for rescission. Some have complained, however, that this provision creates too much paperwork. Reports need to be sent to Congress even when a few thousand dollars are not spent for simple managerial and efficiency purposes. Others complain about the vagueness of the law. Still, this part of the law did reclaim some of the diminished power of the purse for Congress.

The second provision, permitting the deferral of spending by the executive, has caused considerable confusion. According to the law, the president may propose to defer spending of funds already appropriated for up to a year. The law only required that the executive notify Congress of these deferrals and that new notifications be filed with Congress to continue a deferral into a second year. The law permitted either the Senate or the House to overturn a deferral. But in 1983 the Supreme Court invalidated what are called "legislative vetoes" and in effect said, although in a broader ruling, that the only way to counter a president's deferral of funds was to pass a law doing so.

Until 1986 President Reagan, the only president to be affected by the 1983 Supreme Court ruling, was able to defer some spending and work out informal agreements with Congress to make the system work in an acceptable manner. At this point, however, Reagan and his new budget director began using the deferral more frequently and for larger spending projects. Both Congress and the federal courts protested that this was a violation of the law. When a federal district court ruled that the White House was wrong to halt an expenditure of more than $5 billion for housing and other matters, it in effect affirmed Congress's authority to shape federal spending. Meanwhile, members of Congress proposed to repeal the entire deferral provision. There clearly will be further debate on this idea, and further court rulings. As some members of Congress observed, the whole deferral process "is a mess."[23]

Budget Reform Revisited— Gramm–Rudman–Hollings

After several years in which virtually no one believed the budget process had worked well, Congress, with President Reagan's support, voted to approve the Balanced Budget and Emergency Deficit Reduction Act of 1985 (popularly known by the names of its sponsors, Gramm, Rudman, and Hollings). After years of being unable to cure the problem of deficit spending, Congress opted for what many call radical

Answer/Discussion

The case for covert operations is that they are deemed necessary in order to protect America's vital national security interests. Defenders of covert operations say that the Soviet Union does not hesitate to operate in the "back alleys" of the world and that the United States puts itself at a serious disadvantage by ruling out all covert operations.

The case against covert action is that such actions have caused us trouble rather than helped us. Critics say the era of superpower interventionism has passed; its discovery causes an uproar in the third world. Further, covert operations are basically at odds with American democracy.

It turns out, of course, that Congress as a whole does not want to eliminate all covert actions. It does want to support those covert actions that can be kept truly secret but requires they be reported to congressional leaders. Reagan supported covert operations. Many leading Democrats have opposed them. You get to decide again!

[22] See Louis Fisher, *Constitutional Conflicts between Congress and the President* (Princeton University Press, 1985); Allen Schick, *Crisis in the Budgetary Process* (American Enterprise Institute, 1986); and David A. Stockman, *The Triumph of Politics* (Harper & Row, 1986).

[23] See "President's Deferral Powers Threatened," *Congressional Quarterly* (April 12, 1986), p. 792; see also, "Court Strikes Deferral Power over Loss of Legislative Veto," *Congressional Quarterly* (May 17, 1986), p. 1092, and "A Budget Sideshow: Fighting over Deferrals," *Congressional Quarterly* (April 5, 1986), pp. 737–38.

Judge Robert Bork and supporters at his 1987 Senate confirmation hearing: Congressman Hamilton Fish, former president Gerald Ford, Bork, Robert Dole, and Senator John Danforth. Supporters claimed he was one of the most qualified persons ever to be nominated to the Supreme Court. Critics faulted him for being too far out of the mainstream of legal thinking; some accused him of being an extremist. The Senate, by a vote of 58 to 42, rejected Reagan's nomination of Bork, the largest margin of defeat for any Supreme Court nominee in history. (*UPI/Bettmann Newsphotos*)

surgery. This new legislation sets maximum allowable deficit levels on a declining basis from 1986 to 1991, when the deficit must be at zero. The reduction of deficits is to be achieved through cancellation of budget authority and actual spending. An initial version of the bill had given the comptroller general of the General Accounting Office the final word in ordering the president to trim spending and reduce deficits. But a 1986 Supreme Court ruling said that would violate the separation of powers doctrine because the comptroller general was in effect an officer of the Congress (because a vote of Congress could terminate or remove that official). Congress then reverted to a fall back position that required it to pass a resolution in both houses and send it to the president to order spending cuts. Certain spending, such as for Social Security or interest on the national debt, was exempt from this process but almost all domestic and military spending would be subject to these cuts.

Even the sponsors of this budget-balancing measure called it a "bad idea whose time had come." But they insisted that it was needed to bring a dose of reality that would force hard choices about domestic spending, military spending, and taxes. It is far preferable, proponents argued, than the processes of the previous decade, during which no choices were made and annual deficits rose to over $200 billion and the national debt to over $1 trillion.

Critics of the Gramm–Rudman–Hollings act called it the worst form of congressional posturing and feared that it would bring about an unprecedented shift of power from the legislative to the executive branch. "With this additional power," wrote Senator Bill Bradley (D-New Jersey), "Ronald Reagan, if he plays hard ball, could dismantle the nondefense portion of the budget and wreak havoc with America's poor."[24] Others have noted other aspects of this measure that transfer power to the executive. For example, the proposal requires the president to bring future federal budgets into line with the deficit-reduction schedule by reducing, or even eliminating, cost-of-living allowances and similar automatic spending increases previously enacted in entitlement programs. But to allow a president to suspend such automatic increases or withhold other already appropriated funds is to grant to the White House the unilateral authority to limit or even extinguish whatever legal rights the recipients had to these increased payments.

It will obviously take a few years to weigh the pros and cons of this controversial legislation. Yet there is reason to believe that whatever its merits, it renders Congress unable to perform some of its critical functions and once again forces Congress to yield some of its authority to the executive in hopes of resolving our debt and deficit problems.

Confirmation Politics

The framers of the Constitution regarded the confirmation process and its advice and consent by the Senate as a check on executive power. Alexander Hamilton viewed it as a way for Congress to prevent the appointment of "unfit characters." Even today, the Senate and the president often struggle over control of top personnel in the executive and judicial branches. The Constitution leaves the question somewhat ambiguous: "The President . . . shall nominate, and by and with the advice and consent of the Senate, shall appoint Ambassadors, other public Ministers and Consuls, Judges of the Supreme Court, all other officers of the United States. . . ." Presidents, however, have never enjoyed exclusive control over hiring and firing in the executive branch. The Senate jealously guards its right to confirm or reject major appointments; during the period of congressional government after the Civil War, presidents had to struggle to keep their power to appoint and dismiss. But

[24] Bill Bradley, "Congress at Its Worst," *The Washington Post National Weekly Edition* (October 28, 1985), p. 29.

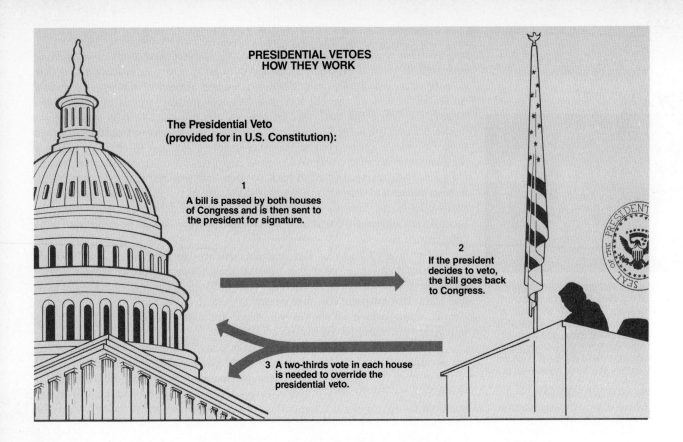

**PRESIDENTIAL VETOES
HOW THEY WORK**

**The Presidential Veto
(provided for in U.S. Constitution):**

1
A bill is passed by both houses
of Congress and is then sent to
the president for signature.

2
If the president
decides to veto,
the bill goes back
to Congress.

3 A two-thirds vote in each house
is needed to override the
presidential veto.

for most of the twentieth century, presidents have gained a reasonable amount of control over top appointments. This has happened in part because public administration experts warned that a chief executive cannot otherwise be held accountable.

In recent years, however, the Senate has taken a somewhat tougher stand on presidential appointments. Senators are especially concerned about potential conflicts of interest. Time spent evaluating and screening presidential nominations has increased. "Our tolerance for mediocrity and lack of independence from economic interests is rapidly coming to an end," said one senator. Another summed it up this way: "Surely, we have learned that one item the government is short on is credibility." Screening became somewhat tighter; Presidents Ford and Carter had several high-level appointees turned down. Reagan lost several potential nominees, such as Judge Robert Bork, because of conflict-of-interests problems, and others were denied confirmation because of their policy views. During one session of Congress today, presidents regularly submit as many as 8000 civilian and over 100,000 military nominations that require Senate confirmation.

The confirmation provisions in the Constitution have fulfilled most of the intentions of the founders. The Senate has been able to use its power to reject unqualified nominees. It has sometimes also been able to prevent those with conflicts of interest from taking office. In addition, senators have been able to use the confirmation process to make their views known to prospective executive officials. Indeed, the very existence of the confirmation process deters presidents from appointing weak, questionable, or "unfit characters." Yet by and large presidents have still been able to appoint the people they want to important positions.

The Senate's role in the confirmation process was never intended to eliminate politics but rather to use politics as a safeguard. Some conservatives in the Reagan years objected that the Senate rejected occasional nominees because of their political beliefs and thus interfered with the executive power of presidents. In such instances, so this complaint goes, the Senate's decision is not a reflection of the fitness of a nominee but rather of the political strength of the president.

Despite the importance of this constitutional power, the Senate has never established clear guidelines or a systematic process for screening presidential nominees. The Senate's participation during the past twenty-five years has become more thorough, more independent, and even somewhat more consistent. "Unfortunately, the process has also become more tedious, time-consuming, and intrusive for the nominees," according to one recent study. "For some, this price is too high, particularly in conjunction with the requirements of the Ethics in Government Act. For others, the process is annoying and distasteful but not enough of a roadblock to prevent them from going forward."[25]

To appoint someone to a *federal* position in a *state* (a U.S. attorney, for example), a president needs the approval of the senators from the state, especially if these senators are members of the president's party and that party controls the Senate. They need that approval because of a practice known as **senatorial courtesy:** the willingness of the Senate to confirm presidential appointments only if they are not "personally obnoxious"—that is, politically objectionable—to the senators from the state. Thus, for nearly all district court judgeships, many appellate court judgeships, and a variety of other positions, senators exercise what is in fact a veto. This veto can be overriden only with great difficulty. Further, it is usually exercised in secret and is subject to little accountability. But the patronage is so important to senators that senatorial courtesy is likely to continue.

The Legislative Veto

As yet another means of trying to strengthen itself as it struggled with the presidency, Congress in the 1970s and early 1980s turned often to the **legislative veto.** Using this device Congress would draft a law broadly but incorporate a provision allowing it to review the executive branch's implementation of the law. The legislative veto could be put into effect by a majority vote of one house, by both houses, or sometimes even by a single congressional committee, depending on how the law was written.

Whatever the form, the legislative veto allowed Congress to delegate general power and then take it away without having to secure presidential approval. In effect, it permitted Congress to legislate without exposing its handiwork to a presidential veto, as the framers intended. The Constitution stipulates that every bill, resolution, or vote for which the agreement of the Senate and the House of Representatives may be necessary shall be presented to the president for approval or veto. "Joint resolutions" were regularly submitted to the president; not so "concurrent resolutions." In the past this made little difference, because concurrent or simple one-house resolutions were mainly used to express congressional opinion and had no force of law.

Then in 1932, Congress passed a resolution allowing President Herbert Hoover limited authority to reorganize the executive branch agencies. The resolution stipulated that the president's proposals would not be put into effect for ninety days, during which time either house of Congress, by a simple resolution, could veto the proposal. For the next fifty-one years, the legislative veto became a standard practice.[26] Congress usually required sixty to ninety days in which to consider a

Constraints on the President: Post-Watergate Congressional Assertiveness

- War Powers Resolution of 1973
- Redefinition of national emergency powers
- Curbs on CIA and FBI
- 1974 Congressional Budget and Impoundment Act
- Slightly better use of the confirmation hearing process
- Frequent use of legislative vetoes (until Supreme Court ruled them unconstitutional in 1983)
- Growth of congressional staffs and research agencies
- Curbs on executive agreements
- Somewhat better oversight of executive branch program implementation
- Greater congressional involvement in national security policy and arms trade deals
- Establishment of independent counsels to investigate illegal or unethical behavior among top executive branch officials.

[25] Christopher J. Deering, "Damned If You Do and Damned If You Don't: The Senate's Role in the Appointment Process," in G. Calvin Mackensie, ed., *The In-and-Outers: Presidential Appointees and the Problems of Transient Government in Washington* (Johns Hopkins Press, 1987), chap. 5.

[26] Joseph Cooper and Patricia Hurley, "The Legislative Veto: A Policy Analysis," *Congress and the Presidency* (Spring 1983), pp. 25–46. See also Barbara Hinkson Craig, *The Legislative Veto* (Westview Press, 1983).

Independent Prosecutors

After President Nixon fired a special prosecutor who had been appointed by the attorney general to look into charges against the White House, Congress provided for the selection of independent prosecutors to look into allegations of misbehavior by the president and presidential staff. Such independent prosecutors are appointed by a special three-judge court acting at the request of the attorney general. The special court sets the scope of the investigation and the independent prosecutor is removable by the attorney general only for good cause or incapacity.

The Justice Department in the Reagan administration, supported by attorneys general from previous administrations, challenged the law on the grounds that it violates the separation of powers principle by taking from the president the executive power to control those who are exercising an executive function, interferes with the presidential responsibilities to see to it that the laws are faithfully executed, and violates the appointments clause by vesting the appointment of a major executive officer in a court and unconstitutionally restricts executive removal authority. The speaker of the House and the Senate legal counsel filed amicus curie briefs on the other side.

In *Morrison* v. *Olson* 101 L Ed 2d 569 (1988), the Supreme Court, by a surprisingly unanimous vote—seven to one with Justice Kennedy not participating—in an opinion delivered by Chief Justice Rehnquist, supported Congress and almost without debate held that the presidential objections lacked merit. Justice Scalia argued in a bitter dissent that the Court majority had seriously undermined the secure structure of separate powers, which he described as the bulwark of a meaningful Bill of Rights.

proposed regulation. During that time either house could veto the regulation by passing a resolution. However, Congress sometimes simply required legislative approval *before* a regulation took effect.

Between 1932 and mid-1983 at least 210 pieces of legislation carried some form of legislative veto. About half of these were enacted between 1973 and 1983. The device was used to ensure that bureaucratic regulations conformed to congressional intentions. This was important to Congress because of the rapid increase of such regulations, which often have the same or nearly the same force as laws. In any given year in the late 1970s or early 1980s, Congress might have passed a few hundred public laws; but the administrators in about seventy executive branch agencies were responsible for twenty times as many regulations.

But the legislative veto was also used to keep presidents in check. Arms sales had to be submitted to Congress for its scrutiny. Presidential use of military troops abroad had to be reported to Congress and was subject to recall by unilateral congressional action. In short, upset by presidents who had either lied to or ignored Congress, a reassertive legislature attempted to use the legislative veto to recapture some of its authority.

Then in June 1983 Chief Justice Warren Burger—speaking for a Supreme Court majority in a 7 to 2 decision (*INS* v. *Chadha*)—said that to maintain the separation of powers, the carefully defined limits on the power of each branch must not be eroded: The legislative veto was found unconstitutional. Said Burger: "With all the obvious flaws . . . we have not yet found a better way to preserve freedom than by making the exercise of power subject to the carefully crafted restraints spelled out in the Constitution."[27] In effect, the Court told Congress that to obtain more influence over an agency or the presidency, Congress should pass a law that accomplished this explicitly. In the words of dissenting Justice Byron White, the Court's decision "strikes down in one fell swoop provisions in more laws enacted by Congress than the Court has cumulatively invalidated in its history."

In this historic decision, the Court tried to curb a weapon that Congress had sometimes used effectively to intimidate executive branch officials. Clearly, the existence of the legislative veto stimulated compromise between executive and legislative officials. Some observers viewed the decision as just one in a long series of Supreme Court rulings that generally approve of and encourage an assertive and increasingly powerful presidency.

What the long-range effect of the decision will be is yet to be determined. Congress has been a little more explicit about the policy directions it sets. It is also exercising some options that make it clear to executive departments that if congressional committees are displeased by the actions of the departmental officials, congressional retribution in the form of reduced appropriations is likely. Congress appears to have found ways to exercise the functional equivalent of a legislative veto.[28]

Other Actions

Congress has also become more involved in general foreign policy. Shaking off years of inertia, Congress imposed a cutoff of aid to Vietnam and a bombing halt in Cambodia. As of 1972 it required the secretary of state to submit to Congress the final texts of executive agreements. It also restrained the Ford administration from getting involved in Portugal and Angola. This was clearly a case of Congress's imposing its goals on the executive. Congress has also demanded, and won, a greater

[27] 77 L Ed 2d 317 (1983).

[28] Daniel P. Franklin, "Why the Legislative Veto Isn't Dead," *Presidential Studies Quarterly* (Summer 1986), p. 499.

role in arms sales abroad and in determining U.S. involvement in Lebanon, Central America, and the Caribbean.

In addition, individual members of Congress are likely to travel around the world to international trouble spots, to conduct their own investigations and sometimes even their own negotiations. Presidents Ford, Carter, and Reagan became increasingly bothered by such second-guessing and attempts by Congress to interfere with presidential foreign policy making. These and myriad other actions were all an effort by Congress to reclaim its lost authority and to respond to a public that seemed to want power shared in a way that placed Congress on a more equal footing than had been the case under Presidents Johnson and Nixon.

Not every effort by Congress in the 1970s succeeded; nor did every effort guarantee that Congress was playing a better or more creative role. Indeed, many well-intentioned reforms that sought to reclaim authority for the national legislature were merely congressional victories that stopped or inhibited presidents from carrying out their policy plans. Rarely did the reforms of the 1970s ensure that Congress would formulate better policy alternatives; more typically it meant that Congress could delay or modify what a president sought to achieve. And sometimes, it merely brought about a deadlock or stalemate.

THE PRESIDENT AND CONGRESS; THE CONTINUING STRUGGLE

Most informed observers now believe that Congress did not really gain back many of its alleged lost powers, and they are skeptical of Congress's ability to match the advantages of the presidency for setting the long-term policy direction of the nation. At least in his first term, Ronald Reagan demonstrated that a popular president who knew what he wanted to do could not only tremendously influence the national policy agenda but could also win considerable cooperation from the Congress.

Even before Reagan won the 1980 presidential election, support for a re-strengthened presidency was gaining public support. Some people believed Congress (and the press) had overreacted to both Vietnam and Nixon's antics and abuses of power. Others believed Congress was correct to try to win back some of its powers, but felt it had gone a bit too far. Others could understand what Congress was doing, but soon realized that our system functions best when a strong positive president is willing to play a key role initiating legislative and budgetary proposals.

The American public may have lost confidence in its leaders, but it had not lost hope in the efficacy of strong, purposive leadership. Whether or not people believed in Ronald Reagan's policy priorities, many supported his view that the country needed a strong president who would strengthen the presidency and make the office a more vital center of national policy than it had been in the years immediately following the Watergate scandals.

A central question during this period of the late 1970s and early 1980s was whether, in the wake of a somewhat diminished presidency, the Congress could furnish the necessary leadership to govern the country. Most people, including many members of Congress, did not think Congress could play that role. The routine answer as we approach the 1990s is that the United States will need a presidency of substantial power if we are to solve the trade, deficit, productivity, and other economic and national security problems we currently face. We live in a continuous state of emergency: Instant terrorism and especially nuclear warfare can destroy our country. In addition, global competition of almost every sort highlights the need for swift and sure leadership, and a certain amount of efficiency and unity, in our government. Many people realize too that weakening the presidency may,

Lt. Col. Oliver North and his lawyer appear before the House Foreign Affairs Committee in connection with the Iran-contra investigations held by Congress. (*UPI/Bettmann Newsphotos*)

as often as not, strengthen the vast federal bureaucracy more than strengthen Congress.

It is clear today, far more than it was in 1978 or 1979, that the congressional reassertion efforts of the 1970s were more a groping and often unsystematic, if well-intentioned, attempt by Congress to be taken seriously than an effort to weaken the presidency. It did not take long for close observers to appreciate that when a president is unable to exercise authority and leadership, no one else is able to supply comparable purpose and initiative. Not only did we reaffirm the pre-Watergate view that history has shown the presidency to be the most effective instrument for innovation, experimentation, and progress, but a majority of Americans concurred that to the extent the country is governable on a national basis, it is governed from the White House by a president and his top advisers in cooperation with the Congress.

How did Reagan infuse the presidency with more energy and effectiveness? First, he came to office with enormous self-confidence and optimism and a personal style that celebrated the promise of American success and achievements. He much more fully appreciated the symbolic and morale-building functions of the modern presidency than had his predecessors. Second, he knew the power of ideas and themes, and he cleverly focused both his own energies and the attention of the nation on four or five fresh policy initiatives (such as tax cuts and tax reform, increased military spending, and reductions in what he claimed were unnecessary federal regulations). He also capitalized on his perceived landslide victory and claimed he had a mandate to alter national priorities. He used his appointment powers wisely as well.

Perhaps his most important successes came in clarifying and redefining for the average American some basic values about the role of government. Time and again he stressed that we should turn to the federal government mainly for national defense needs but that we should return more of the domestic activities of the national government back to state and local governments and, if possible, even back to the private sector and individual responsibility. His consistent trumpeting of these views and his effective use of the media soon enabled him to score impressive victories in Congress. Reagan was also almost always ready to accept 70 or 80 percent of his legislative programs; in so doing, he often appeared to be a conciliating legislative leader.

Reagan's last years in office were less effective. It was as if he had run out of steam, and of ideas. Further, the scandals surrounding Iran-contra events, his attorney general, Edwin Meese, and Pentagon procurement procedures made him look ineffective, not to mention the soaring debt trade imbalances, the country's increasing drug problems, and the U.S.'s becoming a major debtor rather than creditor nation.

George Bush's election was in many ways a vote for continuing existing foreign and national security policies. His selection of James Baker as his secretary of state signaled his intention of emphasizing a strong defense while trying to reach further accords with the Soviets. His friends expect he will work closely with Congress and will negotiate with strength. Bush will need help from Congress; he knows this and the leaders in Congress do too.

The Future?

However much the public may want Congress to be a major partner with the president and a major check on the president, the public's support for Congress is always subject to deterioration. Power is dispersed in Congress. Its deliberations and quarrels are public. After a while, the public begins to view Congress as "the bickering branch," especially if a persuasive activist is in the White House.

Polls show that people think Congress pays more attention to public views than does the president. Assuredly, Congress is a splendid forum that represents and registers the diversity of America. But that very virtue makes it difficult for Congress to provide leadership and difficult for it to challenge and bargain effectively with presidents. Not surprisingly, a wary public—dissatisfied with programs that do not work and policies that do not measure up to the urgencies of the moment—will look elsewhere, often to the president or to an aspiring presidential candidate.

Reagan exploited the growing sentiment in favor of a stronger presidency. And he exploited some of the new opportunities presented by the so-called "reforms" of the 1970s. Political scientist Norman Ornstein puts it well:

> Future Presidents will find Congress frustrating, confusing, capricious and challenging. Past Presidents found Congress frustrating, confusing, capricious and challenging. Enough has changed in the past decade or so to make the confusion different and the challenge more formidable, perhaps, but the changes also offer a President new opportunities and openings for influence in Congress. A combination of old political skills applied in new ways can make a future President at least as pleased with his relations with Congress as were past giants [such] as FDR and LBJ.[29]

A theory of cyclical relations between the president and Congress has long been fashionable. It holds that there will be periods of presidential ascendancy followed by periods of congressional ascendancy. Usually these periods last a decade or more, and sometimes they are a generation in length. Analysis suggests that a moderate but real congressional resurgence did take place in the immediate post-Watergate years. But the responsibilities of the presidency these days, coupled with the complexities of foreign and economic policy, do not really permit any serious weakening of the office. Congress has regained some of its own lost power, and it has tried to curb the misuse and abuse of power—but it has not really weakened the presidency.

Many will continue to worry about future imperial presidents and about the possible alienation of the people from their leaders as complex issues continue to centralize responsibilities in the hands of the national government and the executive. Those who are concerned about these matters will not content themselves, nor should they, with the existing safeguards against the future misuse of presidential powers. It is not easy, however, to contrive devices that will check the president who would misuse powers without hamstringing the president who would use those same powers for purposive and democratically acceptable ends.

Both the president and Congress have to recognize they are not supposed to be two sides out to "win" but two parts of the same government, both elected to pursue together the interests of the American people. Too much has been made by too many presidents and by too many scholars of that ancient but partial truth that only the president is the representative of all the people. Members of Congress do not represent the people exactly as a president does, but its two houses collectively represent them in ways a president cannot and does not.

In the end, the issue is not so much whether the presidency should be stronger than Congress, or vice versa. The real issue is that Congress and the presidency must both be strengthened to do the pressing work required for the well-being of the nation.

---

[29] Norman Ornstein, "Something Old, Something New: Lessons for a President about Congress in the Eighties," in James S. Young, *Problems and Prospects of Presidential Leadership in the Nineteen Eighties*, vol. 2 (University Press of America, 1983), p. 29.

SUMMARY

1. Congressional-presidential relations are not merely *constitutional* questions; they are also *political* struggles for the support of public opinion, as well as attempts to influence public policy. People may be far more attentive to presidents than to the operations of Congress, yet most Americans believe that Congress should also have a major role in forming public policy.

2. During the 1970s Congress made notable efforts to reassert itself as a coequal policy-making branch. Congressional self-confidence increased as Congress reformed some of its practices and redefined certain presidential practices. During the 1980s the Reagan presidency was characterized by equally notable efforts to reassert old and gain additional presidential authority.

3. We have a system of checks and balances that is designed to be strong enough for effective leadership, but in which power is dispersed enough to ensure liberty. This delicate balance is constantly being readjusted.

4. Congressional reassertion took place in the immediate post-Watergate years. But the responsibilities of the presidency today, coupled with the complexities of foreign and economic policy, have not really permitted any serious weakening of the office. Congress has its work cut out for itself just strengthening and organizing itself to stay involved in national policy making. And presidents, as always, have their work cut out for them just trying to win influence in Congress and in the nation for the priorities and policies they think are best for the nation.

FURTHER READING

CECIL V. CRABB, Jr., and PAT M. HOLT. *Invitation to Struggle: Congress, the President and Foreign Policy* (Congressional Quarterly Press, 1980).

GEORGE C. EDWARDS, III. *Presidential Influence in Congress* (W. H. Freeman, 1980).

LOUIS FISHER. *Constitutional Conflicts between Congress and the President* (Princeton University Press, 1985).

LOUIS FISHER. *The Politics of Shared Power: Congress and the Executive* (Congressional Quarterly Press, 1981).

LAWRENCE MARGOLIS. *Executive Agreements and Presidential Power in Foreign Policy* (Praeger, 1986).

CHRISTOPHER H. PYLE and RICHARD M. PIOUS. *The President, Congress, and the Constitution* (Free Press, 1984).

ALLEN SCHICK, and others. *Crisis in the Budget Process* (American Enterprise Institute, 1986).

ARTHUR M. SCHLESINGER, JR. *The Imperial Presidency* (Houghton Mifflin, 1973).

DAVID A. STOCKMAN. *The Triumph of Politics* (Harper & Row, 1986).

JAMES SUNDQUIST. *The Decline and Resurgence of Congress* (Brookings Institution, 1981).

See also *Congress and the Presidency*, published twice a year at American University.

CHAPTER 16

Judges: The Balancing Branch

It was not a very inspiring occasion. The few people present could hardly know that they were witnessing the first meeting of what was to become the most important court in the world, the Supreme Court of the United States. It began on February 2, 1790. Chief Justice John Jay of New York, Justice James Wilson of Pennsylvania, and Justice William Cushing of Massachusetts were the only three of the original six appointees who made it through the muddy roads to New York City. They met in the Royal Exchange Building, an open air market for butchers, which was the seat of the new federal government. The term lasted ten days, but there were no cases to hear, there was no quorum. The time was devoted to the admission of lawyers to practice before the Court.[1]

Four years later, Chief Justice John Jay resigned in part because the federal court system lacked "energy, weight, and dignity," and in part to become governor of New York. But by the time of Chief Justice John Marshall (1801–1835) the Supreme Court had taken its place as a coequal third branch of the federal government. In fact, foreigners are often amazed at the power Americans give their judges, especially federal judges. In 1834, after his visit to America, French aristocrat Alexis de Tocqueville wrote: "If I were asked where I place the American aristocracy, I should reply without hesitation . . . that it occupies the judicial bench and bar. . . . Scarcely any political question arises in the United States that is not resolved, sooner or later, into a judicial question."[2] A century later English laborite Harold Laski observed: "The respect in which federal courts and, above all, the Supreme Court are held is hardly surpassed by the influence they exert on the life of the United States."[3]

Should our judges play such a central role in our political life? Before answering, we must first understand *why* they do have such great influence. One reason, as we saw in Chapter 2, is that in *Marbury* v. *Madison* John Marshall successfully claimed for judges the power of **judicial review**—that is, the power to interpret authoritatively of the Constitution. Only a constitutional **amendment** or a later

[1] Henry J. Abraham, *The Judicial Process*, 5th ed. (Oxford University Press, 1986), p. 197.
[2] Phillips Bradley, ed., *Democracy in America*, vol. 1 (Knopf, 1944), pp. 278–80.
[3] Harold J. Laski, *The American Democracy* (Viking, 1948), p. 110.

Just because judges make policy, however, does not mean they are free to make it as they wish. They are subject to a variety of limits on what they decide—some imposed by the political system of which they are a part, some by their own professional obligations as lawyers. Among these constraints is the rule of stare decisis, the rule of precedent.

Adherence to Precedent

Stare decisis pervades our judicial system. Judges are expected to abide by all previous decisions of their own courts and all rulings of superior courts. Although adherence to precedent is normal, the doctrine of stare decisis is not nearly so restrictive as some people think.[12]

Consider, for example, the father who, removing his hat as he enters a church, says to his son: "This is the way to behave on such occasions. Do as I do."[13] The son, like the judge trying to follow a precedent, has a wide range of possibilities open to him: How much of the performance must be imitated? Does it matter if the hat is removed slowly or quickly? If the hat is put under the seat? If it is not replaced on the head inside the church? The judge can distinguish precedents by stating that a previous case does not control the immediate one because of differences in context. In addition, many areas of law have conflicting precedents, one of which can be chosen to support a decision for either party.

The doctrine of stare decisis is even less controlling in the field of constitutional law. Because the Constitution itself, rather than any one interpretation of it, is binding, the Court can reverse a previous decision it no longer wishes to follow, as it has done dozens of times. Supreme Court justices are therefore not seriously restricted by stare decisis. As the first Justice Harlan told a group of law students: "I want to say to you young gentlemen that if we don't like an act of Congress, we don't have too much trouble to find grounds for declaring it unconstitutional."[14]

"It's nothing personal, Prescott. It's just that a higher court gets a kick out of overruling a lower court." (Copyright © 1967 by Sidney Harris. Reprinted from Saturday Review.)

FEDERAL JUSTICE

"The judicial Power of the United States," says Article III of the Constitution, "shall be vested in one supreme Court, and in such inferior Courts as the Congress may from time to time ordain and establish." Courts created to carry out this judicial power are called *Article III* or *constitutional courts*. Congress may also establish *Article I* or *legislative courts* to carry out the legislative powers the Constitution has granted to it. The main difference between a legislative and a constitutional court is that the judges of the former need not be appointed "to hold their Offices during good Behavior" and may be assigned other than purely judicial duties.

The Constitution requires a Supreme Court. It is a necessity if the national government is to have the power to frame and enforce laws superior to those of the states. The lack of such an agency to maintain national supremacy, to ensure uniform interpretation of national legislation, and to resolve conflicts among the states was one of the glaring deficiencies of the central government under the Articles of Confederation.

Federal systems, however, can and do operate without lower national courts: that business could be left to the state courts. Congress decides whether there will be national courts in addition to the one Supreme Court ordained by the

Benjamin Cardozo, *The Nature of the Judicial Process* (Yale University Press, 1921).

This discussion is based on Hart, *The Concept of Law*, pp. 121, 122.

Quoted by E. S. Corwin, *Constitutional Revolution* (Claremont and Associated Colleges, 1941), p.

Constitution. (The Constitution also allows Congress to determine the size of the Supreme Court.) The first Congress divided the nation into districts and created lower national courts for each district. That decision, though often supplemented, has never been seriously questioned.

Federal Courts of General Jurisdiction

Today the hierarchy of national courts of general jurisdiction consists of *district courts*, *courts of appeals*, and *one Supreme Court*. The workhorses of the federal judiciary are the district courts within the states, in the District of Columbia, and in the territories. Each state has at least one district court. Larger states have as many as the demands of judicial business and the pressure of politics require (though no state has more than four).

Each district court is composed of at least one judge, but it may have as many as twenty-seven. District judges normally sit separately and hold court by themselves. There are presently eighty-nine district courts in the fifty states, plus one in the District of Columbia and one in the Commonwealth of Puerto Rico. All district judges are nominated by the president and confirmed by the Senate. District judges hold office for life.

District courts are trial courts of *original jurisdiction*. They are the only federal courts that regularly employ **grand** (indicting) and **petit** (trial) **juries.** Many cases tried before district judges involve citizens of different states, and the judges apply the appropriate state laws. Otherwise, district judges are concerned with federal laws. For example, they hear and decide cases involving crimes against the United States—suits under the national revenue, postal, patent, copyright, trademark, bankruptcy, and civil rights laws. District judges are assisted by clerks, bailiffs, stenographers, law clerks, court reporters, probation officers, and United States magistrates. All these persons are appointed by the judges.

The 260 full-time and 250 part-time federal magistrates are becoming increasingly important. After being screened by panels composed of residents of the judicial districts, these magistrates are appointed for eight-year terms. Magistrates issue warrants for arrest, hold hearings to determine whether arrested persons should be held for action by the grand jury, and, if so, set bail. They hear motions subject to varying kinds of review by their district judges. They preside over civil trials—jury and nonjury—with the consent of both parties, and over nonjury trials for petty offenses with the consent of the defendants.[15]

United States marshals, appointed by the president and operating under the supervision of the attorney general, are assigned to each district court.

> Although their most dramatic exploits may be called to mind by references to names like Bat Masterson, Wyatt Earp, and David Neagle, or to events like the enforcement of civil rights legislation in the 1960's, the primary assistance to the federal judiciary provided by the marshals has been in the area of protection of the trial process, including the courtroom itself, and the service of writs issued by the judges.[16]

Except for cases that may be taken directly to the Supreme Court, a final decision of a district court is reviewable by a court of appeals. The United States is divided into twelve judicial circuits, one of which is the District of Columbia. Each has a court of appeals consisting of from six to twenty-eight permanent judgeships. Each court of appeals normally hears cases in panels of three but for especially

---

Special Article III Courts

In addition to Article III courts of general jurisdiction, Congress has created constitutional courts with special jurisdiction:

United States Court of Claims: Consists of sixteen judges, who have jurisdiction over all property and contract damage suits against the United States.

United States Court of International Trade (formerly U.S. Customs Court): Consists of nine judges—but no more than five from the same political party—who review rulings of customs collectors and conflicts arising under various tariff and trade laws.

Foreign Intelligence Surveillance Court: Consists of seven district judges who serve part time, to review government applications for electronic surveillance of foreign agents.

United States Court of Appeals for the Federal Circuit: Consists of twelve judges who sit in panels of three to hear appeals of cases from all federal courts relating to patents, as well as to review decisions of the Patent Office and of the Court of International Trade.

Temporary Emergency Court of Appeals: Consists of eight district and circuit judges, designated by the chief justice, who sit in panels of three and have exclusive jurisdiction of all appeals from the district courts in cases arising under economic stabilization laws.

---

[15] Steven Puro and Roger Goldman, "U.S. Magistrates: Changing Dimensions of First-Echelon Federal Judicial Officers," in Philip L. Dubois, ed., *The Politics of Judicial Reform* (Heath, 1982). See also Caroll Seron, "Magistrates and the Work of Federal Courts: A New Division of Labor, *Judicature* (April–May 1986), pp. 353–59.

[16] Justice Stevens dissenting in *Pennsylvania Bureau of Correction* v. *United States Marshals Service*, 474 U.S. 34 (1985).

important and controversial cases all judges may be present—that is, they may sit *en banc*. A Court of Appeals for the Federal Circuit has national jurisdiction.[17]

Circuit judges are appointed for life by the president with the consent of the Senate. The United States courts of appeals have only **appellate jurisdiction**. They review decisions of the district courts within their circuits and also some of the actions of the independent regulatory agencies, such as the Federal Trade Commission. These courts are powerful policy makers. Less than 1 percent of the cases from these courts are looked at carefully by the Supreme Court.

State and Federal Courts

In addition to this complex structure of federal courts, each state maintains a complete judicial system of its own. (And many large municipalities have judicial systems as complex as those of the states.) State courts have sole jurisdiction to try all cases not within the judicial power the Constitution grants to the United States.

This dual system of courts is not common—even among nations with federal systems of government. The two court systems are related, but they do not exist in a superior–inferior relationship. Except for the limited **habeas corpus** jurisdiction of the district courts—the power to order state officers who are holding persons in custody to explain by what authority they are doing so, and ordering the release of the prisoners if the federal judge is not legally satisfied with the answer—the Supreme Court is the only federal court that may review state court decisions. And it may do so only under special conditions.

Except for the original jurisdiction that the Constitution vests directly in the Supreme Court, no federal court has any jurisdiction except that granted to it by act of Congress. Congress also determines whether this judicial power of the United States will be exercised exclusively by federal courts or concurrently by both federal and state courts.

Major Article I or Legislative Courts

United States Court of Military Appeals: Consists of three civilian judges appointed for fifteen years each by the president with the consent of the Senate. This court, created by Congress under its grant of authority to make the rules and regulations for "land and naval Forces," applies military law, which is separate from the body of law that governs the rest of the federal court system.

Bankruptcy judges: Consists of almost 300 judges appointed by the courts of appeals to serve as adjuncts to the federal district courts for terms of fourteen years each. These judges handle bankruptcy matters subject to review by federal district judges.

OVERLOADED CIRCUITS: IMPROVING THE SYSTEM

In the past forty years the caseload for each district judge has doubled. The courts of appeals and the Supreme Court are also being overwhelmed. "We are," says former Chief Justice Burger, "approaching a disaster area." If nothing is done and the caseload continues to increase at the same rate, by the 1990s each justice will have to consider more than 6500 cases.[18] The former Chief Justice's concern is shared by some, but not all, members of the Court, most of whom have gone to the unusual extreme of making public speeches about the need for some changes if justice is to be properly served.

What should be done? The justices, the legal profession, and Congress—although generally in agreement that there are problems—do not agree as to solutions.

Some things have already been done. The number of federal judges has been substantially increased. Judges have been assigned more help in the form of law clerks and administrative assistants. (This may serve to undermine the judges' unique function of being the only major actors of government who do their own work.)[19]

[17] J. Woodward Howard, Jr., *Courts of Appeals in the Federal Judicial System: A Study of the Second, Fifth, and District of Columbia Circuits* (Princeton University Press, 1981).

[18] *The New York Times* (February 13, 1983).

[19] Philip B. Kurland, *Watergate and the Constitution* (University of Chicago Press, 1978), p. 35. See also Richard B. Hoffman, "The Bureaucratic Specter; Newest Challenge to the Courts," *Judicature* (August 1982), pp. 60–72.

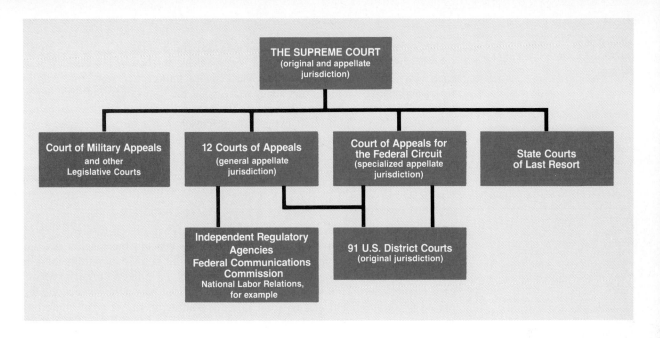

```
                        THE SUPREME COURT
                      (original and appellate
                            jurisdiction)


  Court of Military Appeals    12 Courts of Appeals    Court of Appeals for      State Courts
      and other                (general appellate      the Federal Circuit      of Last Resort
  Legislative Courts              jurisdiction)       (specialized appellate
                                                          jurisdiction)


            Independent Regulatory          91 U.S. District Courts
                 Agencies                    (original jurisdiction)
            Federal Communications
                 Commission
            National Labor Relations,
                for example
```

A Court of Appeals for the Federal Circuit has been created to hear the highly technical and time-consuming cases having to do with patents. Six-person juries are being used more often in civil trials. Laws and rules have been adopted to speed the hearing of criminal trials.

Despite these changes, the workload has not diminished. What else might be done? Suggestions include:

Learned Hand, distinguished member of the U.S. Court of Appeals, Second Circuit, 1924–1951. (*Wide World*)

1. Abolish diversity jurisdiction of the federal courts (cases between citizens of different states), which would thereby eliminate about 25 percent of their civil caseload.

2. Refer more conflicts to arbitration or mediation.

3. Reform the system of worker's compensation for railroad and maritime workers, which would thus eliminate another 7 percent of the civil caseload.

4. Give the newly created Court of Appeals for the Federal Circuit jurisdiction to take on antitrust and tax cases.

5. Persuade judges, especially those on the Supreme Court, to write fewer concurring and dissenting opinions.

6. Persuade Congress to stop enacting legislation that imposes greater burdens on the courts.

7. Persuade the justices to make it more difficult for persons to bring lawsuits.

The proposal that has generated the most attention and the most controversy is that of former Chief Justice Burger. With the support of five of his colleagues on the Supreme Court, Burger suggested creating, at least on an experimental basis, a new court of appeals composed of nine federal appellate judges. This new court would review conflicting rulings of the courts of appeals to assure that "all Americans are living under the same Constitution and laws." "Unless some relief is given," the Chief Justice said, "it is not unreasonable to think that there may be some judges in some courts who will exploit the reality that, since the chance of being reviewed by the Supreme Court is swiftly diminishing, they need not pay very much attention to what the Supreme Court decides."[20] But many in Congress and on the bench, including some appeals court judges, Justices Stevens, Brennan,

[20] Philip Hager, "Overburdening of High Court May Lead Judges to Ignore Its Rulings, Burger Says," *Los Angeles Times* (May 8, 1985), section A, p. 50.

and Marshall, are skeptical. They point out that the Supreme Court has virtually total control over its own docket and is responsible for how many cases it hears each year. They contend that the Court creates unnecessary work for itself by reviewing relatively minor issues about which what the justices say is of little importance. Chief Justice Rehnquist supports the recommendation for this new court. If he gives the recommendation the same attention as did his predecessor, it will enhance the probability that Congress will act favorably upon it.

PROSECUTION AND DEFENSE: FEDERAL LAWYERS

Judges decide cases; they do not prosecute persons. That job, on the federal level, falls to the Department of Justice: to the attorney general, the solicitor general, the ninety-one United States attorneys, and some 1200 assistant attorneys. The president, with the consent of the Senate, appoints a United States attorney for each district court. United States attorneys serve a four-year term but may be dismissed by the president at any time. These appointments are of great interest to senators, who, through **senatorial courtesy** exercise significant influence over the selection process. Because the U.S. attorneys are almost always members of the president's political party, it is customary for them to resign if the opposition party wins the White House.[21]

The attorney general, in consultation with the U.S. attorney in each district, appoints assistant attorneys. Some districts have only one. The Southern District of New York has over sixty-five and is the largest. Working with the U.S. attorney, assisted by the Federal Bureau of Investigation and other federal law-enforcement agencies, these attorneys begin proceedings against those alleged to have broken federal laws. They also represent the United States in civil suits. In criminal cases the U.S. attorney or one of the assistants presents evidence to a grand jury that a national law has been violated by a particular person. If the grand jury agrees, it indicts, and the U.S. attorney's office prosecutes.

The Key Role of Prosecutors

Prosecutors decide whether to charge an offense and which offense to charge. They have largely unreviewable discretion. "So long as the prosecutor has probable cause to believe that the accused committed an offense defined by statute, the decision whether or not to prosecute, and what charge to file or bring before a grand jury, generally rests entirely in his discretion."[22]

Prosecutors negotiate with **defendants** (usually through their lawyers) and often work out *plea bargains*: Defendants agree to plead guilty to one offense to avoid having to stand trial for another, more serious one. Prosecutors make recommendations to judges about what sentences to impose.

Attorneys from the Department of Justice and from other federal agencies participate in well over half the cases on the Supreme Court's docket. Within the Department of Justice special divisions—such as the criminal division, civil division, antitrust division, and civil rights division—coordinate the work of the attorneys in the field, develop cases, and send out specialists to assist the attorneys. Of special importance is the solicitor general, who appears for and represents the government before the Supreme Court. When the solicitor general petitions the

The Judicial Power of the United States

To hear and decide cases or controversies in law and equity if

1. They arise under the Constitution, a federal law, or a treaty.

2. They arise under admiralty and maritime laws.

3. They arise because of a dispute involving land claimed under titles granted by two or more states.

4. The United States is a party to the case.

5. A state is a party to the case (but not if a suit was begun or prosecuted against a state by an individual or a foreign nation).

6. They are between citizens of different states.

7. They affect the accredited representatives of a foreign nation.

---

[21] James Eisenstein, *Counsel for the United States: U.S.* Attorneys in the Political and Legal Systems (The Johns Hopkins Press, 1978).

[22] *Bordenkircher* v. *Hayes*, 434 U.S. 357 (1978). See also *Wayte* v. *United States*, 470 U.S. 598 (1985).

Supreme Court and asks it to review an opinion of a lower court, the Court is likely to do so.[23] Moreover, no appeal may be taken by the United States to any appellate court without the approval of the solicitor general.[24]

Federal Defense Lawyers

Federal prosecutors are not the only lawyers provided by the national government. The Criminal Justice Act of 1970 provides funds for attorneys for poor defendants. Each district court has some discretion as to how to provide this assistance. Most districts use the traditional system of assigning a private attorney to defend such people, paying the attorney from public funds. Over forty districts have opted to use the public defender system—most through a Federal Public Defender Organization, some through community defender organizations that receive federal grants. These salaried public defenders operate under the general supervision of the Administrative Office of the United States Courts.

Congress has created a private nonprofit organization—The Legal Services Corporation—to financially support legal assistance to the poor in noncriminal proceedings. The Board of Directors is appointed by the president with the advice and consent of the Senate. The Corporation receives funds from Congress, which it in turn uses to provide financial assistance to organizations that furnish legal help to the poor.

Original

In all cases affecting ambassadors, other public ministers, and consuls.
In cases in which a state is a party.

Appellate

In all other cases arising under the judicial power of the United States. The Supreme Court has appellate jurisdiction—power to review decisions of other courts—except when Congress determines otherwise.

THE JUDGES

The Constitution empowers the president to select federal judges with the advice and consent of the Senate. But political reality imposes constraints on the president's power. The selection of a federal judge is actually a complex bargaining process. The principal figures involved are the candidates, the president, United States senators, the Department of Justice, the Standing Committee on the Federal Judiciary of the American Bar Association, and political-party leaders.[25]

The Politics of Selection

The practice of **senatorial courtesy** gives a senator veto power over the appointment of a judge who is to sit in his or her state, if that senator is a member of the president's party. Even a senator from the opposition party must be consulted. When the Senate is controlled by political opponents of the president, the chief executive must negotiate with both senators from the state, regardless of party affiliation. If negotiations between the senators and then between the senators and the Department of Justice deadlock, a seat may stay vacant for years.[26] The rule of senatorial courtesy no longer applies to Supreme Court appointments and is less often applied to selection of judges for the courts of appeals, because these judges do not serve in any one senator's domain. This difference in selection politics

Anthony Kennedy is given the constitutional oath by Chief Justice William Rehnquist as Mary Kennedy holds Bible (February, 1988). (*UPI/ Bettmann Newsphotos*)

[23] Gerald F. Uelmen, "The Influence of the Solicitor General upon Supreme Court Disposition of Federal Circuit Court Decisions: A Closer Look at the Ninth Circuit Record," *Judicature* (April–May 1986), p. 362.

[24] Karen O'Connor, "The Amicus Curiae Role of the U.S. Solicitor General in Supreme Court Litigation," *Judicature* (December–January 1983), pp. 256–64.

[25] Harold W. Chase, *Federal Judges: The Appointing Process* (University of Minnesota Press, 1972), pp. 3–47; and Paul Simon, "The Senate's Role in Judicial Appointments," *Judicature* (June–July 1986), pp. 55–58.

[26] See Chase, *Federal Judges*, and the more provocative journalistic account of Joseph C. Goulden, *The Benchwarmers: The Private World of the Powerful Federal Judges* (Ballantine, 1976), chap. 1.

16–1 Party Affiliation of Judges Appointed by Presidents from FDR to Reagan

President	Party	Appointees from Same Party
Roosevelt	Democrat	97%
Truman	Democrat	92%
Eisenhower	Republican	95%
Kennedy	Democrat	92%
Johnson	Democrat	94%
Nixon	Republican	93%
Ford	Republican	81%
Carter	Democrat	90%
Reagan	Republican	97%

Source: David M. O'Brien, *Judicial Roulette: Report of the Twentieth Century Fund Task Force on Judicial Selection* (Priority Press, 1988) p. 37.

means that district court judges often reflect values different from those of persons appointed to the courts of appeals or the Supreme Court.

The American Bar Association's Committee on the Federal Judiciary plays an important role in the appointment process. Federal appointments are sent to the Committee for evaluation. Although its critical ratings do not bind a president, any president is hesitant to submit for Senate confirmation a candidate rated unqualified by this group.

The selection process focuses on evaluating nominees' legal competence, integrity, and judicial temperaments. These qualities are essential but not sufficient. Federal judges have too much power and too much discretion to be appointed without inquiry into and concern about their political views and basic values.

The Role of Party

Presidents seldom nominate judges from the opposing party, and the use of judgeships as a form of political reward was, until recently, openly acknowledged by those involved. While disavowing the significance of partisan considerations, President Carter—like all presidents—appointed to the bench (with few exceptions) persons from his own party. President Reagan has been more open about the importance of partisan affiliation, and his nominees have come overwhelmingly from his own party. (See Table 16–1.)

Race and Sex

Although partisan considerations remain as significant as ever, newspeople are paying less attention to the party score cards and more to race and sex. President Carter appointed forty women, thirty-eight blacks, and sixteen Hispanics to the federal bench—more minority members and women than all other presidents combined. President Reagan, although the first to appoint a woman to the Supreme Court, appointed decidedly fewer minority members or women than did Carter, perhaps in part because far fewer minorities and women could pass the Reagan administration's ideological screening (see the next section).

The Role of Ideology

Finding a party member is not enough. Presidents want to pick the "right" kind of Republican or "our" kind of Democrat. By and large they have been successful in getting the kind of judges they want. At the district court level, "most conservative judges are Republicans appointed by GOP presidents, . . . the most liberal are Democrats appointed by Democrats, and the voting of opposite-party appointees falls almost exactly between these two extremes."[27]

When the appointment is to the Supreme Court, the policy orientation of the nominee is especially important. As President Abraham Lincoln told Congressman Boutewell when he appointed Salmon P. Chase to the Court: "We wish for a Chief Justice who will sustain what has been done in regard to emancipation and legal tender."[28] (Lincoln guessed wrong on Chase and legal tender.) Chief Justice William Rehnquist says presidents are likely to be disappointed because the people they pick are not likely to carry out presidential intentions. Harvard Law Professor Laurence Tribe argues to the contrary. Historical analysis suggests that at the Supreme Court level, presidents guess right 75 percent of the time—that is, the judges they appoint do conform to their expectations.[29]

Theodore Roosevelt voiced the same concern to appoint the "correct" person in a letter to Senator Lodge about Judge Oliver Wendell Holmes of the Massachusetts Supreme Judicial Court, whom he was considering for the Supreme Court: "Now I should like to know that Judge Holmes was in entire sympathy with our views, that is with your views and mine. I should hold myself guilty of an irreparable wrong to the nation if I should [appoint] any man who was not absolutely sane and sound on the great national policies for which we stand in public life."[30]

President Carter was one of the few presidents who did not have a chance to appoint a single Supreme Court justice, but he did select 202 district judges and fifty-six judges to the courts of appeals—almost 40 percent of the federal judiciary. He left the initial screening of candidates to bipartisan panels selected by senators from each state, but his appointments, by and large, reflected his ideological persuasion. Because of Carter's willingness to defer to the recommendations of minority and women's organizations, the lower federal branch threatened or promised, depending upon your views, to become more liberal than the Supreme Court.

President Ronald Reagan's two terms made it possible for him to join Presidents Franklin D. Roosevelt and Dwight D. Eisenhower as the only presidents in modern times to appoint a majority of the federal bench. Like his predecessors, he has been concerned about the ideologies of those he has nominated, but his administration has acted more carefully and systematically to nominate only those whose views about the role of the courts and constitutional issues are consistent with his own.[31] Each prospective nominee received a ten-page questionnaire and was interviewed by a special Department of Justice committee. Not only have a large number

Number of Black Judges Appointed by Presidents from FDR to Reagan*

Court	Number of Judges	Appointing President
Supreme Court	1	Johnson
Courts of Appeals	1	Truman
	1	Kennedy
	2	Johnson
	9	Carter
	1	Reagan
District Courts	3	Kennedy
	5	Johnson
	6	Nixon
	3	Ford
	28	Carter
	4	Reagan
Special Courts	1	Johnson
	1	Eisenhower
Total:	66	

*Nine of these black judges were women. One was appointed by Johnson, seven by Carter, and one by Reagan.

Number of Women Judges Appointed to the Federal Bench

Court	Number of Judges	Appointing President
Supreme Court	1	Reagan
Court of Appeals	1	Roosevelt
	1	Johnson
	11	Carter
	6	Reagan*
District Courts	1	Truman
	1	Kennedy
	2	Johnson
	1	Nixon
	1	Ford
	29	Carter
	22	Reagan*
Special Courts	1	Coolidge
	1	Eisenhower
	1	Carter
	1	Reagan
Total:	81	

*Reagan appointed two women to the district courts and subsequently elevated them to the appellate bench. They are counted here only as appointments to the court of appeals.

SOURCE: David M. O'Brian *Judicial Roulette: Report of the Twentieth Century Fund Task Force on Judicial Selection* (Priority Press, 1989) pp. 40, 41.

[27] Robert A. Carp and C. K. Rowland, *Policymaking and Politics in the Federal District Courts* (University of Tennessee Press, 1983), p. 82.

[28] Quotation from Lincoln in J. W. Peltason, *Federal Courts in the Political Process* (Doubleday, 1955). See also Robert Scigliano, *The Supreme Court and the Presidency* (Free Press, 1971), pp. 146–47. William Rehnquist's quotation from *The New York Times* (October 20, 1984), section 1, p. 1.

[29] Laurence H. Tribe, *God Save this Honorable Court: How the Choice of Supreme Court Justices Shapes Our History* (Random House, 1985). See also Henry J. Abraham, *Justices and Presidents: A Political History of Appointments to the Supreme Court*, 2nd ed. (Oxford University Press, 1985).

[30] Henry Cabot Lodge, *Selections from the Correspondence of Theodore Roosevelt and Henry Cabot Lodge*, vol. 1 (Scribner's, 1925), pp. 518–19.

[31] Nadine Cohodas, "Reagan's Judicial Selections Draw Differing Assessments," *Congressional Quarterly* (January 15, 1983), p. 83. See also "Reagan's Legacy," editorial in *Los Angeles Times* (October 6, 1985); and Robert Friedman and Stephen Wermiel, "Stacked Bench? Reagan Appointments to the Federal Bench Worry U.S. Liberals," *The Wall Street Journal* (September 6, 1985), p. 1.

of judicial conservatives been appointed, but many of them—because they are comparatively young—will have a longlasting effect on judicial policy making well into the next century.

Judicial Philosophy: Restraint v. Activism

What about the candidates' "judicial philosophies"? Do the prospective candidates believe, it is asked, in **judicial restraint**, or in **judicial activism**? Are the candidates what we now call "interpretivists," who believe that judges should try to interpret the Constitution to reflect what the framers intended and what its words literally say? Or are they "noninterpretivists," who believe the Constitution cannot and should not be literally interpreted but rather adapted to reflect current conditions and philosophies.

Judicial *philosophy* is closely related to political *ideology*. Prior to 1937 judicial self-restraint was the battle cry of liberals, and for decades federal courts were more conservative than Congress, the White House, or the state legislatures. The judicial conservatives in these courts struck down many laws regulating the economy. They were often attacked by liberal presidents, most notably Franklin D. Roosevelt, who accused the "Nine Old Men" of the Supreme Court of imposing their own views and values on the country. In the name of judicial reform President Roosevelt proposed a scheme (see below) that would have allowed him to appoint judges reflecting the views and values of the New Deal.

By the time of Richard Nixon and Ronald Reagan, the judicial shoe was on the other foot. Nowadays a believer in judicial self-restraint, or what we now call "interpretivism," is likely to be a conservative. In a speech before the American Bar Association in late 1985, Reagan's attorney general, Edwin Meese, III, called for "a Jurisprudence of Original Intention." He suggested that the Reagan administration would only appoint judges who would apply the Constitution to reflect the intentions of the framers. He even went so far as to suggest that the accepted view that the Fourteenth amendment incorporates most provisions of the Bill of Rights is "constitutionally suspect." "We are committed to finding," said a Department of Justice official in charge of the judicial nomination process, "what President Reagan wants: Judges who won't use the Constitution as a hook to hang their hat on while they are making social policy from the bench."[32] What is wanted is judges who will let Congress, the president, and the state legislatures do what they want unless it clearly contravenes the precise words of the Constitution—for example, regulate or forbid abortions, adopt prayers for public schools, impose capital punishment, authorize police to engage in wire tapping, and so on.

Democrats and liberals attacked this contention—that judges should interpret the Constitution as the framers wrote it—as nothing but a veiled attack on judicial independence. Justice William Brennan said, "It is a little more than arrogance" to believe that it is possible to "gauge accurately the intent of the framers. We current Justices read the Constitution in the only way that we can: as 20th century Americans."[33] Other critics of the Reagan administration accused it of wanting "extremists who would undo everything that happened in civil rights over the last three to four decades."[34]

It would be wrong to argue that judicial philosophy is nothing more than another way to argue about political ideology. Some conservatives, for example, favor judicial activism because they want current judges to reverse the last half

---

Justice William Brennan, On Constitutional Interpretation

There are those who find legitimacy in fidelity to what they call "the intention of the Framers." In its most doctrinaire incarnation, this view demands that Justices discern exactly what the Framers thought about the question under consideration and simply follow that intention in resolving the case before them. It is a view that feigns self-effacing deference to the specific judgments of those who forged our original social compact.

But in truth it is little more than arrogance cloaked in humility. It is arrogant to pretend that from our vantage we can gauge accurately the intent of the Framers on application of principle to specific, contemporary questions. Apart from the problematic nature of the sources, our distance of two centuries cannot but work as a prism refracting all we perceive.

One cannot help but speculate that the chorus of lamentations calling for interpretation faithfully to "original intention"—and proposing nullification of intepretations that fail this quick litmus test—must inevitably come from persons who have no familiarity with the historical record. . . .

We current Justices read the Constitution in the only way we can: as 20th century Americans. We look to the history of the time of framing and to the intervening history of interpretation. But the ultimate question must be, what do the words of the text mean in our time?

For the genius of the Constitution rests not in any static meaning it might have in a world that is dead and gone, but in the adaptability of its great principles to cope with current problems and current needs.

Source: Speech at Georgetown University, October 12, 1985. Reprinted in *The New York Times* (October 13, 1985), p. 36.

---

[32] Philip Hager and Ronald J. Ostrow, "Warn of Right-Wing Litmus Test, Critics Stepping Up Fight on Reagan Court Choices," *Los Angeles Times* (December 25, 1985), p. 13.

[33] Justice Brennan stated that he wrote his comments long before Attorney General Meese made his comments, and that his talk was not in response to Meese. *The New York Times* (October 13, 1985), p. 13.

[34] Ibid.

Attorney General Edwin Meese, III, On the Theory of a Jurisprudence of Original Intention

. . . a drift back toward the radical egalitarianism and expansive civil libertarianism of the Warren Court would once again be a threat to the notion of limited but energetic government.

What, then, should a constitutional jurisprudence actually be? It should be a Jurisprudence of Original Intention. By seeking to judge policies in light of principles, the Court could avoid both the charge of incoherence *and* the charge of being either too conservative or too liberal.

A jurisprudence seriously aimed at the explication of original intention would produce defensible principles of government that would not be tainted by judicial predilection.

This belief in a Jurisprudence of Original Intention also reflects a deeply rooted commitment to the idea of democracy. The Constitution represents the consent of the governed to the structures and powers of the government. The Constitution is the fundamental will of the people; that is why it is the fundamental law. To allow the Court to govern simply by what it views at the time as fair and decent, is a scheme of government no longer popular; the idea of democracy has suffered. The permanence of the Constitution has been weakened. A Constitution that is viewed as only what the judges say it is, is no longer a constitution in the true sense.

Those who framed the Constitution chose their words carefully; they debated at great length the most minute points. The language they chose meant something. It is incumbent upon the Court to determine what that meaning was.

Source: Address to the American Bar Association, July 9, 1985.

century of precedents and actively seek to protect property rights from government regulation. Some liberals favor judicial restraint because they believe that democracy will flourish best when judges stay out of policy debates. Nonetheless, most of the country understands enough about the role of judges in policy making to recognize that the debates about the proper role of the courts and about how to interpret the Constitution reflect different ideas of what is in the public interest.

The debate over the Supreme Court's role these days is less about activism and restraint than it is about competing conceptions of the proper balance between government authority and individual rights.

Reagan's Judicial Activism?

"The Reagan Administration has gotten a good deal of political mileage from assailing the Federal courts for entering into social and political controversies. Its campaign to reshape the Federal judiciary serves the avowed purpose of seating judges who will not be 'activists,' who will exercise 'restraint.' Yet the positions that the Administration has been urging on the courts ever since it took office show that when it comes to furthering the Reagan social and political agenda, it is itself rather eager for activism. [Voting rights, affirmative action, abortion are good examples.] To further our own [visions of the good society], all of us welcome a dose of judicial activism. This may not be such a bad thing, but nobody should hide the fact that this is what is going on." (Herman Schwartz, "What About Mr. Reagan's Own Judicial Activism?" *The New York Times* July 28, 1986, p. V 15.)

Ideology and judicial philosophy affect not only presidents' nominations for the federal courts but also the time that sitting judges choose to retire. Because federal judges serve for life, they may be able to schedule their retirements to allow a president whose views they approve of to nominate their successors. Chief Justice Taney stayed on the bench long after his health began to fail in order to prevent Lincoln from nominating a Republican. In 1929, Chief Justice Taft wrote: "I am older and slower and less acute and more confused. However, as long as things continue as they are, and I am able to answer in my place, I must stay on the court in order to prevent the Bolsheviki [Hoover—a Republican—was in the White House] from getting control."[35]

Ronald Reagan's presidency brought constant speculation whether the elderly justices, most especially those of the liberal wing of the Court—William J. Brennan, Jr. and Thurgood Marshall—and the equally elderly centrist judges—Lewis F. Powell, Jr., Harry A. Blackmun, and Byron R. White—could outlast the Reagan presidency and prevent him from transforming the court.

When Chief Justice Burger decided to retire in 1986, he denied that his decision had been influenced by a desire to permit President Reagan to replace him with a constitutional conservative of similar persuasion. But his retirement did give Reagan an opportunity to rejuvenate the conservative wing of the Court: He promoted a then 61-year old Associate Justice William Rehnquist, an articulate constitutional conservative, to replace the 78-year old Burger, and he picked another constitutional conservative, the 50-year old Antonin Scalia, from the Court of Appeals for the District of Columbia to take the seat vacated by Rehnquist.[36] They were both confirmed by the Senate, but Rehnquist was put through some tough questioning by the Democratic members of the Senate Judiciary Committee.

These two appointments did not change the ideological balance of the Court. But, in July of 1987, at the end of the term, Justice Powell surprised most court watchers by announcing his retirement. Justice Powell had become the critical swing

[35] Letter to Horace Taft, November 14, 1929, quoted in H. Pringle, *The Life and Times of William Howard Taft*, vol. 2 (Farrar, 1939), p. 967.
[36] Sue Davis, "Federalism and Property Rights: An Examination of Justice Rehnquist's Legal Positivism," *The Western Political Quarterly* (June 1986), pp. 250–64.

Reagan announces new nominees, 1986. *(UPI/Bettmann Newsphotos)*

Former Attorney General Edwin Meese III shares a laugh with two Reagan nominees to the Supreme Court, Robert Bork (left) and Douglas Ginsberg (right). Bork failed to win Senate confirmation, and Ginsberg withdrew his name from nomination when questions arose about his experience, ideology, and alleged use of marijuana in the 1960s and 1970s. *(AP/Wide World Photos)*

vote on such controversial issues as the scope of affirmative action and the extent of governmental power to regulate abortions. President Reagan quickly nominated Robert Bork, a member of the Court of Appeals for the District of Columbia, a jurist and legal scholar of note who for decades had attacked the Warren and Burger Courts for their judicial activism. Despite his controversial writings and the fact that the Democrats had gained control of the Senate as a result of the 1986 elections, initially it appeared that, because of his eminence and constitutional knowledge, Judge Bork would be confirmed. However, his nomination aroused many people, especially women's organizations and black organizations; their opposition was so intense that they organized a campaign to block the Bork nomination.

After almost four months of national debate, twelve days of extensive questioning by the members of the Senate Judiciary Committee, and 23 hours of debate on the Senate floor, the Senate voted 58 to 42 against Bork's confirmation. An angry President Reagan quickly sent to the Senate the name of Douglas H. Ginsburg, another judge from the Court of Appeals of the District of Columbia. Judge Ginsburg, a purported judicial conservative, had written very little outside of his relatively few judicial opinions, and his votes on major constitutional issues were unknown. Although the Democratic members of the Senate Judiciary Committee made clear that they would carefully evaluate Judge Ginsburg's qualifications, it was again anticipated that Judge Ginsburg would be confirmed, in part because of the political exhaustion of those who were fearful of the Reagan appointees, in part because of a lack of record with which to attack him. But after a storm of public protest over Judge Ginsburg's acknowledgment that he had used marijuana in the past, he withdrew his candidacy. The third time, Reagan nominated a more mainstream conservative, Judge Anthony M. Kennedy from the Court of Appeals of the Ninth Circuit, who, after considerable searching through his judicial record, was unanimously recommended by the Senate Judiciary Committee and unanimously confirmed by the Senate. He took his seat on the Court a half year after Justice Powell's retirement.

Senate Judiciary Committee

The normal presumption is that the president should be allowed considerable discretion in the selection of federal judges, especially those who are to sit on the Supreme Court. Yet despite this presumption in favor of presidential nominees, the Senate takes seriously its responsibility to confirm presidential nominations, most especially if the party that controls the Senate is different from that of the president's.

Nominations are processed through the Judiciary Committee. Although it always seeks an evaluation of each nominee from the ABA Standing Committee on the Federal Judiciary, the Committee makes its own investigations. Most senators consider it improper to ask a prospective judge directly about how he or she would decide a specific case. And candidates ordinarily refuse to respond if asked. Nonetheless, there is no longer any pretense that questions about "judicial philosophy" or "constitutional orientation" are merely technical concerns about legalities.

The modern practice is to require each candidate to fill out an elaborate questionnaire about views, finances, and activities. When the Democrats control the Senate, candidates are likely to be asked whether they belong to clubs that have discriminated against persons because of race or sex and, if so, whether they have worked to change the rules. When the Republicans control the Senate, the questionnaire is likely to delete questions about equal justice and club memberships, and substitute a set of questions having to do with judicial activism. Nominees have been asked to write essays not unlike those required of law and political science students—for example, "Please discuss your views on judicial activism."[37]

[37] Sheldon Goldman, "Judicial Selection and the Qualities That Make a Good Judge," *The Annals* (July 1982), p. 117–18. See also Elliot E. Slotnick, "The ABA Standing Committee on Federal Judiciary: A Contemporary Assessment," *Judicature* (March–April 1983), pp. 348ff and 385ff.

The Senate Judiciary Committee, and sometimes the full Senate, have rejected or refused to act on twenty-nine of the 138 presidential nominations for Supreme Court justices, including seven in this century.[38]

16–2 Supreme Court Nominations Rejected, Postponed, or Withdrawn Due to Senate Opposition			
Nominee	Year Nominated	Nominated By	Actions[1]
William Paterson[2]	1793	Washington	Withdrawn (for technical reasons)
John Rutledge[3]	1795	Washington	Rejected
Alexander Wolcott	1811	Madison	Rejected
John J. Crittenden	1828	J. Q. Adams	Postponed, 1829
Roger B. Taney[4]	1835	Jackson	Postponed
John C. Spencer	1844	Tyler	Rejected
Reuben H. Walworth	1844	Tyler	Withdrawn
Edward King	1844	Tyler	Postponed
Edward King[5]	1844	Tyler	Withdrawn, 1845
John M. Read	1845	Tyler	No action
George W. Woodward	1845	Polk	Rejected, 1846
Edward A. Bradford	1852	Fillmore	No action
George E. Badger	1853	Fillmore	Postponed
William C. Micou	1853	Fillmore	No action
Jeremiah S. Black	1861	Buchanan	Rejected
Henry Stanbery	1866	Johnson	No action
Ebenezer R. Hoar	1869	Grant	Rejected, 1870
George H. Williams[3]	1873	Grant	Withdrawn, 1874
Caleb Cushing[3]	1874	Grant	Withdrawn
Stanley Matthews[2]	1881	Hayes	No action
William B. Hornblower	1893	Cleveland	Rejected, 1894
Wheeler H. Peckham	1894	Cleveland	Rejected
John J. Parker	1930	Hoover	Rejected
Abe Fortas[6]	1968	Johnson	Withdrawn
Homer Thornberry	1968	Johnson	No action
Clement F. Haynsworth, Jr.	1969	Nixon	Rejected
G. Harrold Carswell	1970	Nixon	Rejected
Robert H. Bork	1987	Reagan	Rejected
Douglas H. Ginsburg	1987	Reagan	Withdrawn

[1] A year is given if different from the year of nomination.

[3] Nominated for chief justice.

[5] Second appointment.

[2] Reappointed and confirmed.

[4] Taney was reappointed and confirmed as chief justice.

[6] Associate justice nominated for chief justice.

Source: David M. O'Brien, *Judicial Roulette: Report of the Twentieth Century Fund Task Force on Judicial Selection* (Priority Press, 1988), p. 67. Data from Library of Congress, Congressional Research Service.

Furthermore, the importance the Senate's role is not to be measured merely by its rejection of presidential nominations. For "outcome is not the only relevant question for hearings . . . Senators pursue [other] important goals . . . Not the least of these goals is to influence the next nomination even before it is made."[39]

Although the Senate often confirms without debate—or much debate—what the Judiciary Committee recommends, floor debates over judicial nominees are not rare, especially in the case of Supreme Court nominations.

[38] Tribe, *God Save this Honorable Court.* See also Abraham, *Justices and Presidents,* and O'Brien, *Judicial Roulette.*

[39] George Watson and John Stookey, "Supreme Court confirmation hearings: a view from the Senate," *Judicature* (December–January 1988), p. 193.

The politics of judicial selection may shock those who like to think judges are picked strictly in terms of legal merits and without regard for party, race, sex, or ideology. But as a former Justice Department official has said: "When courts cease being an instrument for political change, then maybe the judges will stop being politically selected."[40]

Changing the Numbers

Partisan politics also affects decisions about the number of federal judges. One of the first actions of a political party after gaining control of the White House and Congress is to increase the number of federal judgeships. However, when one party controls Congress and the other holds the White House, a stalemate is likely—relatively few new judicial positions will be created. During Andrew Johnson's administration, Congress went so far as to reduce the size of the Supreme Court to prevent the President from filling two vacancies. After Johnson left the White House, Congress returned the Court to its prior size to permit Grant to fill the vacancies.

In 1937 President Roosevelt proposed an increase in the size of the Supreme Court of one additional justice for every member of the Court over 70, up to a total of fifteen members. Ostensibly, the proposal aimed to make the Court more efficient. In fact, Roosevelt and his followers were frustrated because the Court had declared much of the New Deal unconstitutional. Despite Roosevelt's popularity, the "court-packing scheme" aroused intense opposition. In the midst of the congressional debate, Justice Roberts, who had previously voted with the conservative members of the Court against the New Deal, began to vote with the more liberal justices to sustain some important New Deal legislation. Because the Court was no longer an obstacle, Roosevelt's proposals to change its size failed. He lost the battle, but he won the war.

Changing Jurisdiction

Congressional control over the structure and jurisdiction of federal courts has been used to influence the course of judicial policy making. Although unable to get rid of Federalist judges by impeachment, the Jeffersonians abolished the circuit courts the Federalist Congress had created just prior to leaving office. In 1869 radical Republicans in Congress altered the Supreme Court's appellate jurisdiction in order to snatch from the Court a case it was about to review involving the constitutionality of some reconstruction legislation (*Ex parte McCardle*).[41]

During the early years of the Reagan administration, a dramatic increase occurred in the number of bills introduced in Congress either to take from all federal courts their jurisdiction to deal with cases relating to abortion, school prayer, and school busing, or to eliminate the appellate jurisdiction of the Supreme Court over such matters. These bills sparked a major debate about whether the Constitution gives Congress authority to take these actions and whether Congress ought to do so. So far, persons angered by a particular line of decisions have not persuaded a majority of Congress to make what could amount to a fundamental shift in the nature of the relationship between Congress and the Supreme Court.

[40] Donald Santarelli, as quoted in Jerry Landauer, "Shaping the Bench," *The Wall Street Journal* (December 10, 1970), p. 1. See also Peltason, *Federal Courts in the Political Process*, p. 32.

[41] Wallace 506 (1869).

Supreme Court justices are in session from the first Monday in October through the end of June. They listen to oral arguments for two weeks and then adjourn for two weeks to consider the cases and write their opinions. Six justices must participate in each decision. Cases are decided by a majority. In the event of a tie vote, the decision of the lower court is sustained, although the case may be reargued.

At 10 A.M. on the days when the Supreme Court sits, the eight associate justices and the Chief Justice, dressed in their robes, file into the Court. As they take their seats—arranged according to seniority, with the chief justice in the center—the clerk of the Court introduces them as the "Honorable Chief Justice and Associate Justices of the Supreme Court of the United States." Those present in the courtroom are seated; and counsel take their places along tables in front of the bench. The attorneys for the Department of Justice, dressed in formal morning clothes, are at the right. The other attorneys are dressed conservatively; sport coats are not considered proper. This is all part of the high ritual of the Court:

> the majesty of its courtroom; the black robes of the justices; the ritual of its proceedings at oral argument and on decision day; the secrecy and isolation of its decision-making conferences; the formal opinions invoking the symbols of Constitution, precedent, and framers' intent; and all the other elements of setting and conduct that distinguish the Supreme Court, a body of constitutional guardians, from all other officials.[42]

What Cases Reach the Supreme Court?

When citizens vow they will take their cases to the highest court of the land, even if it costs their last penny, they perhaps underestimate the difficulty of securing Supreme Court review, overestimate the cost (although it costs plenty), and reveal a basic misunderstanding of the Court's role. The rules for taking cases **on appeal** to the Supreme Court are established by act of Congress. Nowadays all appellate cases come before the Court by means of a discretionary **writ of certiorari.** (Until

[42] Richard Johnson, *The Dynamics of Compliance* (Wiley, 1967), pp. 33–41. This summary of Johnson's comment is taken from David Adamany, "Legitimacy, Realigning Elections, and the Supreme Court," *Wisconsin Law Review* (1973), p. 792.

The Supreme Court

"We are very quiet there but it is the Quiet of a storm center. . . ."
—Oliver Wendell Holmes, Jr.

1988 there were a few types of cases the Supreme Court was obliged to review.[43])
In addition, the Constitution stipulates that the Supreme Court has original jurisdiction in a few specified situations. But the fact is that the Supreme Court has control of its agenda and decides which cases it wants to consider. The justices closely review around 200 of the thousands of cases annually presented to them.

It is not enough, for example, that Jones thinks he should have won his case against Smith. There probably has already been at least one appellate review of the trial, either in a federal court of appeals or in a state supreme court. The Supreme Court will review Jones's case only if his claim has broad public significance. For instance, the rulings of two courts of appeals may conflict. By deciding Jones's case, the Supreme Court can establish which rule is to be followed throughout the judicial system. Jones's case may instead raise a constitutional issue on which a state supreme court has presented an interpretation with which the Court disagrees. The crucial factor in determining whether the Supreme Court will hear a case is its importance not to Jones, but to the operation of the governmental system as a whole.

The Court accepts cases under the "rule of four." If four justices are sufficiently interested in a petition for a writ of certiorari, the petition will be granted and the case brought forward for review. Denial of a writ of certiorari does not mean that the justices agree with the decision of the lower court, nor does it necessarily establish precedents. Refusal to grant such a writ may indicate all kinds of possibilities—the justices may not wish to become involved in a political "hot potato," or the Court may be so divided on an issue that it is not yet prepared to take a stand.[44]

Most cases presented to the court on appeal—that is, under its mandatory obligation to review—are also disposed of without full opinion either "for want of a substantial federal question," or "for want of jurisdiction."[45]

The Briefs and Oral Argument

Before a case is heard in open court, the justices receive printed briefs, perhaps hundreds of pages long, in which each side presents legal arguments, historical materials, and relevant precedents. In addition, the Supreme Court may receive briefs from **amici curiae**—friends of the court. These may be individuals, organizations, or government agencies who have an interest in the case and claim they have information of value to the Court. This procedure guarantees that the Department of Justice is represented if a suit between two private parties calls the constitutionality of an act of Congress into question. The friend of the court brief is also used by presidents, via the Department of Justice—the Reagan administration has done so more often than any other—to try to persuade the Supreme Court to change its mind about established constitutional doctrine.[46] A brief brought by a private party or interest group may help the justices by presenting an argument or point of law that the parties to the case have not raised. Often the briefs are filed as a means of "pressuring" the Court to reach a particular decision. In the 1954 school desegregation cases, twenty-four amicus briefs were filed. In the Bakke case, in which the Supreme Court first dealt substantively with questions about the constitutionality of affirmative action, thirty-seven amicus briefs were filed for the university, sixteen for Bakke, and five which did not take sides.

Attorney General William French Smith, President Reagan, and Sandra Day O'Connor. O'Connor, first woman on the Supreme Court, was formerly state legislator and state judge in Arizona. She advises law school students not to despair if they begin their careers in seemingly unimportant positions. "If your career path is at all like mine, you won't be starting at the top of the ladder," she says. O'Connor graduated third in her class at Stanford Law School, but "The only job offer I received upon graduating from my law school was as legal secretary," she recalls. She refused that offer and began her career by opening her own small law firm. (*Michael Evans/The White House*)

[43] Stuart Taylor, Jr., "High Court Expected to Gain Freedom in Selecting Its Cases," *The New York Times*, June 9, 1988, p. 11.

[44] Sidney Ulmer, "The Supreme Court's Certiorari Decisions: Conflict as a Predictive Variable," *American Political Science Review* (December 1984), pp. 901–11.

[45] *Hopfmann v. Connolly*, 471 U.S. 459 (1985).

[46] Elder Witt, "Reagan Crusade before Court Unprecedented in Intensity," *Congressional Quarterly* (March 15, 1986), p. 616.

Formal oratory before the Supreme Court, perhaps lasting for several days, is a thing of the past. As a rule, counsel for each side is limited to a thirty-minute argument—sometimes less, sometimes more. Lawyers use a lectern to which two lights are attached. A white light flashes five minutes before time is up and when the red light goes on, the lawyer must stop, even in the middle of an "if."[47]

The entire procedure is formally informal. Sometimes, to the annoyance of the attorneys, the justices talk among themselves or consult briefs or legal volumes during the oral presentation. Sometimes, if justices find a presentation particularly bad, they frequently and ostentatiously consult their watches.

The justices freely interrupt the lawyers to ask questions and to request additional information. If a lawyer seems to be having a difficult time, the justices may try to help him or her present a better case. Occasionally, the justices bounce arguments off a hapless attorney, and at one another. During oral argument in the school desegregation cases, for example, Justice Frankfurter was grilling an NAACP lawyer: "Are you saying that we can say that 'separate but equal' is not a doctrine that is relevant at the primary school level? Is that what you are saying?" he demanded.

Justice Douglas tried to help the lawyer out. "I think you are saying," he ventured, "that segregation may be all right in streetcars and railroad cars and restaurants, but . . . education is different from that."

The lawyer found the Douglas paraphrase to his liking. "Yes, sir," he replied. Douglas continued, "That is your argument, is it not? Isn't that your argument in this case?" Again a grateful "yes" from counsel.

Frankfurter, however, was not even moderately impressed. "But how can that be your argument . . . ?" he cried, and the lawyer was once again on his own.[48]

Behind the Curtains—The Conference

Wednesday afternoons and all day Friday the justices meet in conference. They have heard the oral arguments, read and studied the briefs, and examined the petitions. Before every conference each justice receives a list of the cases to be discussed. Each brings to the meeting a red leather book in which the cases and the votes of the justices are recorded. These conferences are secret affairs, although in recent years the secrecy has been penetrated. They are marked by informality and vigorous give-and-take. The chief justice presides. He usually opens the discussion by stating the facts, summarizing the questions of law, and making suggestions for disposing of the case. Each member of the Court is then asked, in order of seniority, to give his or her views and conclusions. Recently the justices have not bothered with formal votes—because they have already expressed their views at the discussion stage—but if they do vote, they do so in order of seniority.

The dynamics of the conference are illustrated by the maneuvering in the case of *National League of Cities* v. *Usery*, taken up by the Court at its Friday, March 5, 1976, session.[49] (This case was reversed nine years later in *Garcia* v. *San Antonio Metro.*)[50] The chief justice opened the discussion. The question was whether the federal minimum wage law should be applied to municipal police and firefighters and other workers. In 1968, in *Maryland* v. *Wirtz*, the Court had upheld the application of this same law to state hospital workers and school employees.

The Supreme Court of The United States

1. Chief Justice Rehnquist
2. Justice Brennan   3. Justice White
4. Justice Marshall   5. Justice Blackmun
6. Justice Stevens   7. Justice O'Connor
8. Justice Scalia   9. Justice Kennedy
10. Clerk of the Court   11. Marshall of the Court
12. Counsel

[47] Edwin McElwain, "The Business of the Supreme Court." *Harvard Law Review*, vol. 69 (1949), pp. 5–26; David M. O'Brien, *Storm Center: The Supreme Court in American Politics* (Norton & Co, 1986), p. 227.

[48] Daniel M. Berman, *It Is So Ordered: The Supreme Court Rules on School Segregation* (Norton, 1966), p. 69.

[49] Bob Woodward and Scott Armstrong, *The Brethren* (Simon & Schuster, 1979), p. 406. These materials are taken from pp. 406–10.

[50] *Garcia* v. *San Antonio Metropolitan Transit Authority*, 105 S.Ct. 1005 (1985).

This would appear to be a binding precedent. Chief Justice Burger said for the time being he would pass, although the justice knew he really would like to see *Wirtz* overruled. Justice Brennan, next in seniority, argued that the Court was bound by the *Wirtz* precedent. Justice Potter Stewart told his colleagues that although he had dissented in *Wirtz*, he would not vote to overrule it unless five other justices wanted to do so. In other words, he did not want to be the one to cause a reversal. Justices White and Marshall agreed that the *Wirtz* precedent controlled. As the discussion went around the table, the vote was three for applying the federal law to city workers, Justice Stewart prepared to go along, and the chief justice on the fence.

Justice Blackmun "wondered if there was some way to distinguish the case from Wirtz so that they could avoid the precedent."[51] Justices Powell and Rehnquist agreed with Blackmun that there was a way to make a distinction between the two types of employees, although they were quite ready to overrule *Wirtz* and hold that the federal law should not be applied to either state hospital workers or to city police and firefighters, if the rest of the justices would go along. Justice Stevens, the junior justice, said he thought *Wirtz* should prevail. Thus, there were five votes to uphold the law as applied to the additional state and municipal employees and to reinforce the *Wirtz* decision. But the discussion was not over. Justice White chided Justice Stewart for refusing to become the fifth vote to overturn a prior decision they both thought was wrong. Justice Stewart responded: "I think you are right, I'll vote the other way." But he said he was not going to vote for some underhanded formula: He wanted a clear ruling that *Wirtz* was being overruled. The chief justice now declared he would vote to overrule, so the vote became five to four to do so. He assigned Justice Rehnquist the responsibility for drafting an opinion for the Court.

The Opinion

Opinion assigning is important. The justices want to work on opinions that deal with significant issues, and the justice to whom the opinion is assigned can influence the outcome. When voting with the majority, the chief justice decides who writes the first draft opinion. When the chief justice is in the minority, the senior justice among the majority makes the assignment, often to himself or herself. Justices are free to write dissenting opinions if they wish. If a justice agrees with the majority on how the case should be decided but differs on the reasoning, that justice may write a **concurring opinion**.

Circulating Drafts

The justice selected to write the Court's opinion is faced with an exacting task. The document must win the support of at least four—even more, if possible—intelligent, strong-willed persons, all of whom may have voted the same way but perhaps for very different reasons. In recent years law clerks have taken a more prominent role in opinion writing as the pressure of court business reduced the justices' time (see later discussion). Assisted by the law clerks, the assigned justice writes a draft and sends it to colleagues for their comments. If the justice is lucky, the majority will accept the version, perhaps with only minor changes. But the draft may not be satisfactory to the other justices. In that case the justice must redraft and recirculate the opinion until a majority can reach agreement.

If the initial version is not acceptable to a majority, an elaborate bargaining

Justice Antonin Scalia, Associate Justice nominated and confirmed, 1986. (*J. L. Atlan/Sygma*)

[51] Woodward and Armstrong, *The Brethren*, p. 407.

William Hubbs Rehnquist. Former Supreme Court law clerk, Assistant Attorney General, Associate Justice (1971–1986) Chief Justice of the United States, 1986. (*The Supreme Court Historical Society*)

process occurs. The opinion ultimately published is not necessarily the opinion the author would have liked to write. Like a committee report, it represents the common denominator. Holmes bitterly complained to Laski that he had written an opinion "in terms to suit the majority of the brethren, although they didn't suit me. Years ago I did the same thing in the interest of getting a job done. I let the brethren put in a reason that I thought bad and cut out all that I thought good and I have squirmed ever since, and swore that never again—but again I yield and now comes a petition for rehearing pointing out all the horrors that will ensue from just what I didn't want to say."[52]

The two major weapons justices can use against their colleagues are their votes and their willingness to write separate opinions attacking a doctrine the majority wishes to see adopted. A dissenting opinion is often written and circulated for the stated purpose of convincing the majority. If the opinion writer is persuaded by the logic of the dissenter, the dissenting opinion may never be published. Even if this is not done, and it seldom is, the justice writing for the majority may be forced to give in to the demands of a colleague on his or her side as a price of keeping the majority together. Especially if the Court is closely divided, one justice may be in a position to demand that a given argument be included in—or removed from—the opinion as the price of his or her vote. Sometimes this can happen even if the Court is not closely divided. An opinion writer who anticipates that a decision will bring critical public reaction may very much wish to have it presented as the view of a unanimous Court and may be prepared to compromise to achieve unanimity. (See Table 16–3 for a comparison of dissent rates in various Courts.)

The Internal Politics of Opinion Writing

The internal battling over the opinion in *National League of Cities* v. *Usery* is typical of what happens in many cases. After the first round of voting, it appeared that Justice Brennan would assign the opinion, because he was the senior justice in what appeared to be the majority. But when Justice Stewart switched his vote, the chief justice was with the majority, so it now fell to him to assign the opinion, which he did—to Justice Rehnquist. As Justice Rehnquist circulated his draft, Justices Stevens and Brennan each sent around strong dissents. Justice Stewart's clerks hoped that they might be able to persuade him to change his mind, so they presented him with their own critical analysis of the Rehnquist draft. Despite the pressures, Justice Stewart stood fast with Rehnquist. Justice Blackmun was wavering, and how he would go would determine the outcome. Justice Rehnquist modified his draft to take Blackmun's views into account, to be sure that he kept Blackmun's vote. Justice Brennan was also working on Blackmun. In his dissent he had written: "I cannot recall another instance in the Court's history when the reasoning of so many decisions covering so long a span of time has been discarded in such a roughshod manner."[53] On the draft he sent to Justice Blackmun he wrote a personal note, "asking if there was anything that he could do to get his vote."[54]

Although Justice Blackmun was disturbed by the sarcastic tone of Brennan's opinion, he still had not made up his mind to stay with Rehnquist. He "toyed with concurring in the result only,"[55] which would have meant that Rehnquist would have been denied the fifth vote for his opinion, which was necessary to make it a controlling precedent. Finally, he decided merely to write a single-paragraph

[52] Mark De Wolfe Howe, ed., *Holmes-Laski Letters*, vol. 2 (Atheneum, 1963), pp. 124, 125.

[53] 426 U.S. 833 (1976).

[54] Woodward and Armstrong, *The Brethren*, p. 409.

[55] Ibid., p. 410.

16–3 Comparison of Dissent Rates

Justice	Number of Dissenting Opinions	Average per Term
"The Great Dissenters"		
W. Johnson, 1804–1834	30	1.0
J. Catron, 1837–1865	26	0.9
N. Clifford, 1858–1881	60	2.6
J. Harlan, 1877–1911	119	3.5
O. Holmes, 1902–1932	72	2.4
L. Brandeis, 1916–1939	65	2.9
H. Stone, 1925–1946	93	4.6
H. Black, 1937–1971	310	9.1
F. Frankfurter, 1939–1962	251	10.9
J. Harlan, 1955–1971	242	15.5
The Burger Court		
W. Douglas, 1969–1974	231	38.5
J. Stevens, 1975–1984	205	20.5
W. Brennan, Jr., 1969–1984	281	17.5
W. Rehnquist, 1971–1984	219	15.6
T. Marshall, 1967–1984	241	15.0
P. Stewart, 1969–1980	130	10.8
B. White, 1969–1984	171	10.6
H. Blackmun, 1971–1984	145	10.3
L. Powell, Jr., 1971–1984	144	10.2
S. O'Connor, 1981–1984	31	7.7
W. Burger, 1969–1984	106	6.6

Source: David M. O'Brien, *Storm Center: The Supreme Court in American Politics* (Norton, 1986).

Thurgood Marshall, Associate Justice of the Supreme Court since 1967, served earlier as a federal district judge and Solicitor General of the U.S. He was the first black appointed to the nation's highest court. (*The Supreme Court Historical Society*)

concurring opinion explaining that in different situations where the federal government has a greater interest than it did in this particular case, federal intervention into the affairs of state and local governments might be justified. But because his concurrence endorsed the Rehnquist opinion, that opinion became the opinion of the Court and thus a controlling precedent. (It was Justice Blackmun who nine years later wrote the opinion for the Court in *Garcia* v. *San Antonio Metro*, which overturned *National League of Cities* v. *Usery*.)

As a general rule, Supreme Court opinions state the facts, present the issues, announce the decision, and, most importantly, explain the reasoning of the Court. These opinions are the Court's principal method of expressing itself to the world, and the justices address these opinions to various audiences. Perhaps the most important function of opinions is to instruct the judges of all other courts in the United States, state and federal, how to decide similar cases in the future.

Judicial opinions may be directed at Congress or at the president. If the Court regrets that "in the absence of action by Congress, we have no choice but to . . ." or insists that "relief of the sort that petitioner demands can only come from the political branches of government," it is clearly asking Congress to act.[56]

Finally, the justices use published opinions to communicate with the public. A well-handled opinion may increase support among specialized publics—especially lawyers and judges—and among the general population for a policy the Court is stressing. For this reason, the Court delayed declaring school segregation unconstitutional until unanimity could be secured. The justices understood that any sign of dissension on the bench on this major social issue would be an invitation to evade the Court's ruling.

[56] Berman, *It Is So Ordered*, p. 114; Walter F. Murphy, *Elements of Judicial Strategy* (University of Chicago Press, 1964), p. 66; O'Brien, *Storm Center*, pp. 262–72.

The Powers of the Chief Justice

The ability of the chief justice to influence the Court has varied considerably. Chief Justice Hughes ran the conferences like a stern schoolmaster, keeping the justices talking to the point, moving the discussion along, and doing his best to work out compromises. He tried to achieve unanimous votes in order to give decisions greater weight. Chief Justice Stone, on the other hand, encouraged justices to state their own points of view and let the discussions wander. Chief Justice Burger devoted much of his time to judicial reform, speaking to bar and lay groups and trying to build political support for modernizing the judicial process. Chief Justice Rehnquist brings fifteen years prior Court experience and demonstrated personal warmth as he begins his new job as "The Chief." What kind of Chief Justice he will be remains to be seen. For as one scholar warns us, "The Chief Justiceship does not guarantee leadership. It only offers its incumbent an opportunity to lead. Optimum leadership inheres in the combination of the office and an able, persuasive, personable judge."[57]

The Rise of the Law Clerks

Beginning in the 1930s federal judges began the practice of hiring the best recent graduates of law schools to serve as clerks for a year or two. As the judicial work load has increased, more law clerks have been apointed. Today each Supreme Court justice is entitled to four clerks. (Circuit judges have three, and each court of appeals has "staff attorneys.") Clerks draft opinions and screen writs of certiorari, which determine the cases the Court will review.

Law clerks are young and energetic, and they know how to use computers to do research and prepare drafts of opinions. As the number of law clerks and computers has increased, so has the number of concurring and dissenting opinions. Further, opinions are longer, and they have more substantive footnotes and elaborate citations of cases and law review articles.[58]

After the Lawsuit Is Over

Victory in the Supreme Court does not necessarily mean that winning parties get what they want. As a rule, the Court does not implement its own decision, but "remands" the case to the lower court with instructions to act in accordance with the Supreme Court's opinion. The lower court often has considerable leeway in interpreting the Court's mandate as it disposes of the case.

The impact of a particular ruling announced by the Supreme Court on the behavior of those who are not immediate parties to a lawsuit is even more uncertain. Many of the more important decisions require further action by administrative and elected officials before they become the effective law of the land. Sometimes Supreme Court decisions are simply ignored. Despite the Supreme Court's holding that it is unconstitutional for school boards to require prayers within schools, for example, some school boards continue their previous practices.[59] And, for years after the Supreme Court held public school segregation unconstitutional, many school districts remained segregated. The Constitution may be what the Supreme

[57] David Danelski, "The Influence of the Chief Justice in the Decisional Process of the Supreme Court," in Thomas P. Jahnige and Sheldon Goldman, eds., *The Federal Judicial System: Readings in Process and Behavior* (Holt, Rinehart & Winston, 1968), p. 148. See also The White Burkett Miller Center of Public Affairs, *The Office of Chief Justice* (University of Virginia, 1984).

[58] Richard A. Posner, *The Federal Courts: Crisis and Reform* (Harvard University Press, 1985), pp. 102–30.

[59] Stephen L. Wasby, *The Impact of the United States Supreme Court* (Dorsey Press, 1970), and the literature cited therein.

Court says it is, but a Supreme Court opinion, for the moment at least, is what a trial judge or police officer or a prosecutor says it is.

The most difficult Supreme Court decisions to implement are those that require the cooperation of large numbers of officials. For example, a Supreme Court decision announcing a new standard for police arrest procedures is not likely to have an impact on the way police make arrests for some time. Not many police officers subscribe to the *United States Supreme Court Reports*. The process is more complex: Local prosecutors, state attorneys general, chiefs of police, and state and federal trial court judges must all participate to give "meaning" to Supreme Court decisions.

Although Congress or a president has occasionally "ignored" or "construed" a Supreme Court ruling to avoid its impact, decisions whose enforcement requires only the action of a central governmental agency usually become effective immediately. Thus, when the Supreme Court held that President Truman lacked constitutional authority to seize steel companies temporarily to avoid a shutdown during the Korean War, the President promptly complied. Of course, subsequent presidents have great discretion in determining how that particular precedent should be applied to their own behavior.

JUDICIAL POWER IN A DEMOCRACY

An independent judiciary is one of the hallmarks of a free society. As impartial dispensers of equal justice under the law, judges should not be dependent on the executive, the legislature, the parties to the case, the electorate, or a mob outside the courtroom. But this very independence, essential to protect judges in their roles as legal umpires, raises basic problems when a democratic society decides—as has ours—also to make judges key policy makers. Perhaps in no other society do interests and individuals resort to litigation as much as they do here as a means of making public policy.

The involvement of our courts, especially the Supreme Court, in choosing among competing values has historically exposed the judiciary to political criticism. Throughout our history the Supreme Court has been attacked for engaging in "judicial legislation." This is nothing new. Yet the more active role of the federal courts in recent years and the Reagan administration's frontal attack on that role have returned these issues to the forefront of public debate.

Since the end of World War II, federal courts under the Supreme Court's leadership have removed most of the constitutional restraints on government regulation of business. At the same time, they have imposed many more restraints in order to protect civil liberties and civil rights, especially for the poor and the black. Since 1943 the Supreme Court has declared unconstitutional more than fifty provisions of acts of Congress as well as more than 400 acts of state legislatures and city councils. (Overall, the Supreme Court has struck down 135 acts of Congress and almost 1000 pieces of state legislation and state constitutional provisions. In one 1983 decision, *INS* v. *Chadha*, it called into question 200 provisions of various federal laws.)

Whereas in earlier times the judges occasionally told other parts of government what they could not do, today they often tell the other agencies of government what they must do. For example, federal judges have told Congress and state legislatures they must provide attorneys for the poor, ensure adequate care for mental patients, modernize prisons, and even break up the telephone system (although in this last case the courts responded to the initiative of the Department of Justice).

Judges have always been policy makers; it is not a matter of choice but of role. But nowadays they also govern. The causes of this explosion are complex and imperfectly understood, but the effects are plain. "Both in volume of litigation and in tasks undertaken there have been quantum leaps of judicial power. . . . Courts have become surrogate lawmakers . . . (and) administrators of greater enterprises. . . . Courts have become ombudsmen of bureaucratic mistakes."[60]

The Great Debate over the Proper Role of the Courts

Naturally, those who like what the judges have done tend to defend their right to do it. Judges should do what is right, they say, even if such actions are not politically popular. They contend that courts have a duty to protect the long-range interests of the public, even against the short-range wishes of the voters. Defenders of this kind of judicial role argue that if Congress, the White House, and the state legislatures are unable to resolve pressing problems, the courts should do so. The Supreme Court, they argue, should be "a leader in a vital national seminar that leads to the formulation of values for the American people."[61]

Critics of *judicial activism*, on the other side, contend that in recent years, in their zeal to protect the people, especially the poor, the federal courts have become unhinged from their political moorings in the political system. It was wrong for conservative justices prior to 1937 to strike down laws that did not conflict with the literal terms of the Constitution, they argue, so it is wrong for today's more liberal justices to do so. These critics contend that even if courts make the "right" decisions, it is not right for courts to take over the legislative responsibilities of the people's elected representatives.

Others contend that the debate between those who favor "interpretivism" or judicial restraint and those who favor "noninterpretivism" or judicial activism, oversimplifies the choices. They argue that judges should take a leadership role in some areas but a restrained role in others. They stand with Justice Harlan Stone, who, in his famous Footnote Four in his opinion in *Carolene Products*, argued that courts have a special duty to intervene (1) whenever legislation restricts the political process by which decisions are made or (2) whenever legislation restricts the rights of "discrete and insular minorities." In all other areas the political process should be allowed to work, and judges should not set aside legislation or interfere with administrative agencies merely because they would prefer some other policy or even some other interpretation of the Constitution.[62]

The People and the Court

Whether judges are liberal or conservative, defer to legislatures or not, try to apply the Constitution as the framers intended or interpret it to conform to current values, there are linkages between what the judges do and what the people want done. The linkages are not direct, and the people never speak with one mind, but these linkages are the heart of the matter.

We no longer find acceptable the explanation that it is right to give the power of judicial review to independent judges because their own policy views are irrelevant to the decisions they make. The absurdity of the assumption that they are merely carrying out the clear commands of the Constitution is indicated by

YOU DECIDE

A few years ago the Texas state legislature decided Texas taxpayers should no longer provide a *free* public education for the children of undocumented aliens—that is, persons illegally in the United States and subject to deportation by the Federal government. The legislature acted after it estimated that tens of thousands of such children were attending Texas public schools at no cost.

Setting aside for a moment whether or not you think such a policy is desirable, in your judgment is there anything in the United States Constitution, especially in the equal protection clause (see Chapter 5), that should prevent the Texas legislature from making such a choice?

(Answer/Discussion on the next page.)

[60] J. Woodford Howard, Jr., "Are Heavy Caseloads Changing the Nature of Appellate Justice?" *Judicature* (August 1982), p. 57.

[61] Arthur S. Miller, "In Defense of Judicial Activism," in Stephen C. Halpern and Charles M. Lamb, eds., *Supreme Court Activism and Restraint* (Heath, 1982), p. 177. See also, by the Chief Justice of the West Virginia Supreme Court, Richard Neely, *How Courts Govern America* (Yale University Press, 1981).

[62] *United States* v. *Carolene Products*, 304 U.S. 144 (1938). Variations on this basic position have been restated in dozens of recent books. Halpern and Lamb, *Supreme Court Activism and Restraint*, is a comprehensive treatment from all perspectives. For another analysis of this great debate, see also Lief H. Carter, *Contemporary Constitutional Lawmaking* (Pergamon Press, 1985).

the fact that the justices divide so frequently over what the Constitution means. More acceptable is the explanation that although judges do choose between competing values, they are not free to adopt whatever policies they wish. They are restricted by a variety of limitations, the most significant of which come from the political system of which the judges are a part.

In the first place, the president and the Senate are likely to appoint justices whose decisions reflect contemporary values. When the people elected Carter, they also got judges who reflected Carter's perspectives. When they elected Reagan, they got judges who reflected Reagan's values. Although his views about the Supreme Court probably had little to do with his victory, Reagan made it clear in his campaigns in both 1980 and 1984 that, if elected, he would select judges of a more conservative bent than those who were chosen by Carter or Mondale. And Carter and Mondale made an issue of whether the voters wanted Ronald Reagan to be the man who, if elected, might well have the chance to pick several Supreme Court justices and pack the lower federal courts with conservatives. As noted, President Reagan did what he said he would do, although on various occasions the Democrats and the liberal Republicans in the Senate restrained his ability to pick whomever he chose.

Even without a change in judicial personnel, changing currents of public opinion influence what the judges decide. This connection between the public and the Supreme Court does not come about because of Mr. Dooley's celebrated charge, "The Supreme Court follows the illiction returns."[63] On the contrary, after major realigning elections, when a new political coalition takes over the White House and/or Congress, the old regime stays on in the federal courts. Or, as one unknown wit put it: "The good presidents do dies with them, the bad lives on after them on the Supreme Court." But despite initial clashes, the new electoral coalitions eventually also "take over" the federal courts. Before too long, new interpretations of the Constitution reflect the dominant political ideology.

Judges have neither armies nor police to execute their rulings. Although Congress cannot reverse Supreme Court decisions and only four decisions have been reversed by formal constitutional amendment, the political system can alter the course of judicial policy making in other, only slightly more subtle ways. Decisions are binding on the parties to a particular case, but the policies involved in judicial decisions are effective and durable only to the extent that they are supported by a considerable portion of the electorate. To win a favorable Supreme Court decision is to win something of considerable political value, but the policies reflected by that decision may or may not alter the way people behave. If the Court's policies are too far out of step with the values of the country, the Court is likely to get "reversed."

The policy-making process is complex. What Congress and the White House and the state legislatures and police officers do has an effect on what the Supreme Court does, and what the Supreme Court does has an effect on what Congress and the White House and the state legislatures and the police do. Most important, what all these agencies do is related to what the various segments of "the people" want done. Consider, for example, the chain of developments that made the Constitution more reflective of the values of equal rights under the law. Changing economic and social conditions led to the growth of a black leadership, which in turn generated political power for blacks, which led presidents to care about what blacks wanted, which resulted in their appointing judges who reflected the values of civil rights advocates. And this action led to action and reaction in city councils, school boards, and state legislatures. The judges certainly played a leadership role in the development

[63] Finley Peter Dunne, "Mr. Dooley's Opinions," in Bartlett's *Familiar Quotations*, 14th ed. (Little, Brown, 1968), p. 890.

16–4 U.S. Supreme Court Declarations of Unconstitutionality of Federal Statutes (in Whole or in Part)

Time Span	Chief Justice	Number of Declarations of Unconstitutionality	Commentary
1798–1801	Jay	0	
	J. Rutledge	0	Weak, placid Court
	Ellsworth	0	
1801–1835	Marshall	1	1803: *Marbury* v. *Madison*
1836–1864	Taney	1	1857: *Dred Scott* v. *Sandford*
1864–1873	Chase	10	1870: *Legal Tender cases*
1874–1888	Waite	9	1833: *Civil Rights cases*[1]
1888–1910	Fuller	14 (15)	1895: *Income Tax cases*
1910–1921	White	12	1918: *Child Labor case*
1921–1930	Taft	12	1923: *Minimum Wage case*
1930–1936	Hughes	14	Of these, 13 came in 1934–36!
1936–1941	Hughes	0	The New Deal Court emerges following the "switch-in-time that saved nine" in 1937
1941–1946	Stone	2	New Libertarian emphasis
1946–1953	Vinson	1	Abstemious Court
1953–1969	Warren	25	High-water mark of Liberal-activism
1969–1986	Burger	34	First Amendment, Equal Protection, and Separation of Powers concerns
1986–present	Rehnquist	?	?
Total		135	

Note: Table is arranged chronologically in accordance with tenure of chief justices; as of July 1986.
[1] Consolidated five different cases in one opinion (here counted as one).

Source: Adapted from Henry J. Abraham, *The Judicial Process,* 5th ed. (Oxford University Press, 1986), p. 294.

Factors Constraining Federal Judges

The Constitution

Precedent—*stare decisis*

Statutory law

Legal thought as found in books and law reviews

Opinions of other courts

Interest groups

Public opinion

Media opinion

Views of colleagues

Views of law clerks

Contemporary events and general social environment

Traditions of the law

Actions of the legislature, past and future

Actions of executives, past and future

Note: These factors are not listed in any particular order. Some weigh more heavily at one time than at another, and on some judges more than on others.

of a national "civil rights" consensus, but where they led the people followed. What the Constitution "means" about affirmative action is being decided only in part by what the judges say it means.

"The people" speak in many ways and with many voices. The Supreme Court— and the other courts— represent and reflect the values of some of these people. Although the Court is not the defenseless institution portrayed by some commentators, and its decisions are as much shapers of public opinion as reflections of it, ultimately the power of the Court rests on retaining the support of most of the people most of the time. No better standard for determining the legitimacy of a governmental institution has been discovered.

The Supreme Court, 1989. (*UPI/Bettmann Newsphotos*)

SUMMARY

1. Judges in the United States play a more active role in political life than they do in other democracies. Federal courts receive their jurisdiction directly from Congress, which must decide the constitutional division of responsibilities among federal and state courts.

2. Federal judges apply statutory law, common law, equity, admiralty and maritime law, and administrative law. They apply federal, criminal, and civil law. Although bound by procedural requirements, including *stare decisis*, they have to exercise discretion.

3. Improvement in the administration of federal courts has become a major political issue.

4. Partisanship and ideology are important factors in the selection of federal judges at all levels, and they ensure a linkage between the courts and the rest of the political system.

5. The Supreme Court, which has almost complete control over the cases it reviews as they come up from the state courts and from the courts of appeals and district courts, is a revered but somewhat mysterious branch of our government. Annually its nine justices dispose of thousands of cases, but most of their time is concentrated on the less than 200 cases per year that establish guidelines for lower courts and the country.

6. A continuing concern of major importance is the reconciliation of the role of judges—especially those on the Supreme Court—as independent and fair dispensers of justice for the parties before them with their vital role as interpreters of the Constitution. This is an especially complex problem in our democracy because of the power of judicial review and the significant role courts play making public policy.

7. The debate about how judges should interpret the Constitution is almost as old as the Republic. Two hundred years after the Constitution was inaugurated the argument between those who contend judges should interpret the document literally and those who believe they cannot and should not has returned to the headlines.

FURTHER READING

HENRY J. ABRAHAM. *The Judiciary: The Supreme Court in the Governmental Process*, 6th ed. (Allyn and Bacon, 1983).

HENRY J. ABRAHAM. *Justices and Presidents: A Political History of Appointments to the Supreme Court*, 2nd ed. (Oxford University Press, 1985).

MARK W. CANNON and DAVID M. O'BRIEN, eds. *Views from the Bench: The Judiciary and Constitutional Politics* (Chatham House, 1985).

BENJAMIN N. CARDOZO. *The Nature of the Judicial Process* (Yale University Press, 1921).

JESSE H. CHOPER. *The Supreme Court and Its Justices: The Best of the ABA Journal* (The American Bar Association, 1987).

JOHN HART ELY. *Democracy and Distrust: A Theory of Judicial Review* (Harvard University Press, 1980).

STEPHEN C. HALPERN and CHARLES M. LAMB, eds. *Supreme Court Activism and Restraint* (Heath, 1982).

WALTER F. MURPHY and C. HERMAN PRICHETT. *Courts, Judges and Politics: An Introduction to the Judicial Process*, 4th ed. (Random House, 1986).

DAVID M. O'BRIEN. *Judicial Roulette* (Priority Press, 1988).

DAVID M. O'BRIEN. *Storm Center: The Supreme Court in American Politics* (W. W. Norton, 1986).

JACK W. PELTASON. *Federal Courts in the Political Process* (Doubleday, 1955).

RICHARD A. POSNER. *The Federal Courts* (Harvard University Press, 1985).

BERNARD SCHWARTZ. *Super Chief: Earl Warren and His Supreme Court—A Judicial Biography* (New York University Press, 1983).

LAURENCE H. TRIBE. *God Save this Honorable Court: How the Choices of Supreme Court Justices Shape Our History* (Random House, 1985).

ELDER WITT, ed. *Congressional Quarterly's Guide to the United States Supreme Court* (Congressional Quarterly, 1979).

CHAPTER **17**

Bureaucrats: The Real Power?

The framers of the Constitution could hardly have anticipated the large and diverse national bureaucracy that exists today. Current federal employment (civilian and military) is considerably larger than the population of the entire thirteen states in 1789.

Nor did the framers provide explicit guidance on the proper place of the federal bureaucracy in the American political system. The design of our political system makes it difficult for presidents to win control and cooperation from those who staff the executive branch departments:

> Constitutional design, coupled with a multiplicity of interests in the country, guarantees that the interests of the White House, an agency's political leadership, and members of Congress rarely converge. With a constitutionally based fuzzing of hierarchical control in the public sector, and contradictory orders coming from various legitimate sources, the job of the public manager is especially challenging.[1]

Former President Reagan came to Washington justifiably suspecting that many of the federal bureaucrats were more loyal to New Deal and Great Society programs than they would be to his notions of retrenchment and greater reliance on the private sector or local governments. Hence, he came to Washington vowing to tame the federal bureaucracy. He didn't mince words: "We need to get the bureaucracy off of our backs and out of our pocketbooks." Reagan put it very simply: "Government is not the solution to our problem, government *is* the problem." And Reagan followed through on this pledge: The single largest budget cut early in his administration was federal civilian workers' pay and fringe benefits.

During the Reagan years, as a result, it has been argued, the career workforce of government has been demoralized, the institutional capacity of bureaucracy to perform well is suffering from a variety of factors, and, it is alleged, White House efforts to "overcontrol" administrative agencies has led to a politicization and manage-

[1] Edie N. Goldenberg, "The Grace Commission and Civil Service Reform: Seeking a Common Understanding," in Charles H. Levine, ed., *The Unfinished Agenda for Civil Service Reform* (Brookings Institution, 1985), p. 90.

Bureaucracy entails endless filing of huge quantities of records. (*Mike Kagan/Monkmeyer Press*)

rial rigidity in some federal agencies.[2] This has been less a result of an intentional campaign to harm the bureaucracy than of the fact that Reagan is a politician responding both to popular attitudes toward the bureaucracy and to a new set of policy initiatives that often seek to bypass or undercut New Deal and Great Society programs and bureaucracies.

Reagan's complaint and strategies are familiar ones. Attacking the bureaucracy is as traditional as kissing babies and marching in Fourth of July parades. Candidates for public office frequently take aim at the federal bureaucracy and speak about it as an alien force or a foreign power. "Our government . . . is a horrible bureaucratic mess," said Jimmy Carter. "It is disorganized, wasteful, has no purpose and its policies are incomprehensible or devised by special interest groups with little regard for the welfare of the average citizen."

Members of Congress like to joke with the folks back home that there is a parlor game played in the nation's capital. "It's called 'Bureaucracy,'" they say. "And there is only one rule. The first one to move loses."

The public at-large also dislikes or fears bureaucracy. Liberals say the federal bureaucracy is an overzealous guardian of the status quo and is too lazy or unimaginative to innovate or experiment. Conservatives fear a powerful national bureaucracy is too liberal and could bring about a social revolution. They also think the federal bureaucracy is too large, too powerful, and too unaccountable. People in the ideological center often fear the bureaucracy is not working at all. And nearly everyone is suspicious that there is too much waste and fat in government—especially having heard of $400 hammers, Defense Department procurement cost overruns, and general inefficiencies.

Such stereotypes may be as old as the nation (and probably a lot older, for bureaucracies have never been popular), but the skepticism and hostility toward public bureaucracies seems greater today than before.[3]

The federal bureaucracy is an inviting target: There is hardly a citizen who has not been irritated, defeated, or offended at one time or another in dealing with the Internal Revenue Service, the Postal Service, the U.S. Army, the Department of Health and Human Services, or one of the dozens of national regulatory agencies such as the Food and Drug Administration or the Occupational Health and Safety Administration. Moreover, career public servants really have no press secretary who can tell their side of the story. But, as with much of the oversimplified campaign talk in American politics, the "bureaucrats-are-bums" speeches are often misleading. Of course, we have a lot of **red tape** and overlap in our public administration processes—too much. And it is quite proper to ask whether bureaucracy and its methods have in some way stifled productivity. The real question is less the

[2] See Charles T. Goodsell, *The Case for Bureaucracy*, 2nd ed. (Chatham House, 1985), chap. 8; Charles H. Levine, "The Federal Government in the Year 2000: Administrative Legacy of the Reagan Years," *Public Administration Review* (May/June 1986), pp. 195–206; and Howard Rosen, *Servants of the People: The Uncertain Future of The Federal Civil Service* (Olympus, 1985).

[3] See Herbert Kaufman, "Fear of Bureaucracy: A Raging Pandemic," *Public Administration Review* (January–February 1981), pp. 1–9; and Goodsell, *The Case for Bureaucracy*.

size or the existence of bureaucracy than whether the bureaucracy is responsive to the real needs and best interests of the country. We want to know whether the bureaucracy is accountable to the president, to Congress, and ultimately to the citizens. Finally, we wonder if the various bureaucratic entities perform their assigned functions in an efficient and timely manner.

WHO ARE THE BUREAUCRATS?

In this chapter we are mainly interested in the nearly 5 million people (2.85 million civilians and about 2.1 million in uniform) who make up the executive branch of the federal government. Certain facts about these people need to be emphasized:

1. Only about 12 percent of the career civilian employees work in the Washington area. The vast majority are employed in regional, field, and local offices scattered throughout the country and around the world. California alone has about 300,000 federal employees.
2. About 37 percent of the civilian employees work for the Army, the Navy, the Air Force, or for some other defense agency.
3. The welfare state may consume a sizable portion of our budget, but the size of the federal bureaucracy that administers it is relatively small. Only about 15 percent of the bureaucracy works for welfare agencies (such as the Social Security Administration or the Rural Electrification Administration), and about half of these work for the Veterans Administration. A still smaller proportion of government employees work in regulatory agencies.
4. Federal employees are not of one type. Indeed, in terms of social origin, education, religion, and other background factors, bureaucrats are more broadly representative of the nation than are legislators or politically appointed executives.[4]
5. Federal employment per 1000 people in the United States' population has decreased steadily over the past generation.
6. Bureaucrats work at an endless variety of jobs. Over 15,000 different personnel skills are represented in the federal government. Unlike Americans as a whole, however, most federal employees are white-collar workers: secretaries, clerks, lawyers, inspectors.

The vast number of **bureaucrats** are honest professionals, experts at their business. Bureaucrats are often criticized, but presidents and Congress ignore their advice at considerable risk. A compelling example is provided by the CIA's perceptive memos (many of them later published in the celebrated *Pentagon Papers*) arguing that the Vietnam War as President Johnson was intending to conduct it would be a disastrous failure. This was good advice, from an expert bureaucracy, that Johnson simply disregarded. The Nixon White House similarly chose to ignore or bypass the advice of the bureaucracy on matters of civil liberties—a move Nixon and his aides later regretted.

Bureaucrats, or career government employees, work in the executive branch, in the thirteen cabinet-level departments and more than fifty independent agencies embracing about 2000 bureaus, divisions, branches, offices, services, and other sub-units. In size, five big agencies—the Departments of the Army, Navy, and Air Force, the Postal Service, and the Veterans Administration—tower over all the others. Most of the agencies are responsible to the president, but some are partly independent. Virtually all the agencies exist by act of Congress; legislators could abolish them either by passing a new law or by withholding funds.

[4] For discussions of the representative character of the federal bureaucracy, see Samuel Krislov and David H. Rosenbloom, *Representative Bureaucracy and the American Political System* (Praeger, 1981).

YOU DECIDE !

To Whom Should Bureaucrats Be Accountable?

To the Constitution

To the laws and statutes

To Congress

To the president

To their administrative superiors: bureau chiefs, cabinet officers, and so on

To their own view of "the public interest"

To court rulings

To public opinion

To interest groups

To the media

To their profession

To public-employee unions

To political parties and their platforms

To intellectual opinion

To their coworkers and colleagues

(Answer/Discussion on the next page.)

Formal and Informal Lines of a Bureaucratic Organization

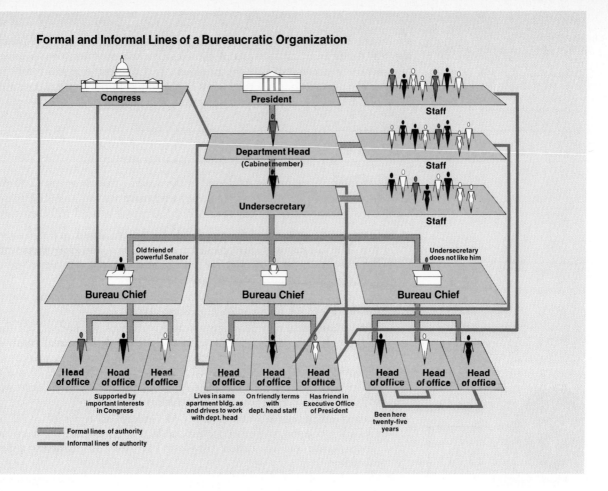

Congress

President

Staff

Department Head
(Cabinet member)

Staff

Undersecretary

Staff

Old friend of powerful Senator

Undersecretary does not like him

Bureau Chief

Bureau Chief

Bureau Chief

Head of office | Head of office | Head of office

Supported by important interests in Congress

Head of office | Head of office | Head of office

Lives in same apartment bldg. as and drives to work with dept. head

On friendly terms with dept. head staff

Has friend in Executive Office of President

Head of office | Head of office | Head of office

Been here twenty-five years

Formal lines of authority
Informal lines of authority

Formal Organization

The executive branch departments are headed by cabinet members called secretaries (except Justice, which is headed by the attorney general). The secretaries are directly responsible to the president. Although the departments vary greatly in size, they have certain features in common: A deputy or an undersecretary takes part of the administrative load off the secretary's shoulders, and several assistant secretaries direct major programs. Like the president, the secretaries have various assistants who help them in planning, budget, personnel, legal services, public relations, and other staff functions. The departments are, of course, subdivided into bureaus and smaller units, but the basis for their division may differ. The most common basis is function. For example, the Commerce Department is divided into the Bureau of the Census, the Patent and Trademark Office, and so on. The basis may also be clientele (for example, the Bureau of Indian Affairs of the Interior Department), or work processes (for example, the Economic Research Service of the Agriculture Department), or geography (for example, the Alaskan Air Command of the Department of the Air Force).

The score or more of **government corporations,** such as the Tennessee Valley Authority and the Federal Deposit Insurance Corporation, may be described as a sort of cross between business corporations and regular government agencies. Government corporations were designed to make possible a freedom of action and flexibility not always found in the regular agencies. These corporations have been freed from certain regulations of the Office of Management and Budget and the comptroller general. They have also had more leeway in using their own earnings as they please.

Answer/Discussion

Most bureaucrats, most of the time, follow guidelines provided either in the law or by their administrative superiors—but at times many of the factors listed on the previous page come into play as bureaucrats have to exercise judgment and discretion. Many of the considerations listed there shape bureaucratic behavior implicitly rather than explicitly. Much of this chapter analyzes the question of bureaucratic accountability. Perhaps you will revise your "answer" by the time you have finished this chapter.

Executive Departments*

1. State
2. Treasury
3. Defense
4. Interior
5. Justice
6. Agriculture
7. Commerce
8. Labor
9. Health and Human Services
10. Housing and Urban Development
11. Transportation
12. Energy
13. Education
14. Veterans Affairs

* In order of age.

Bureaucrats at work, at U.S. Bureau of Census (top) and Internal Revenue Service (bottom). One group is storing data; the other is disposing of excess mailing debris. (*AP/Wide World Photos*)

Still, because the government owns the corporations it retains basic control over their activities.

The **independent agencies** have many types of organization and many degrees of independence. Broadly speaking, all agencies that are not corporations and that do not fall under the departments are called independent agencies. Many of these agencies, however, are no more independent of the president and Congress than the departments themselves. The huge General Services Administration is not represented in the cabinet, for example, but its director is responsible to the White House and its actions are closely watched by Congress.[5]

Another type of independent agency is the independent **regulatory board** or **commission**—agencies like the Securities and Exchange Commission, the National Labor Relations Board, and the Federal Reserve Board. Congress deliberately set up these boards to keep them somewhat free from White House influence; they exercise **quasilegislative and quasijudicial** functions. Congress has protected their independence in several ways: The boards are headed by three or more commissioners with overlapping terms; they often have to be bipartisan in membership; and the president's power to remove members is curbed.

Within the departments, corporations, and independent agencies are many subordinate units. The standard name for the largest subunit is the **bureau**, although it is sometimes called an office, administration, or service. Bureaus are the working agencies of the federal government. In contrast to the big departments, which are often holding companies for a variety of agencies, the bureaus usually have fairly definite and clear-cut duties, as their names show: the Bureau of the Census in the Commerce Department, the Bureau of the Mint in the Treasury Department, the Bureau of Indian Affairs in the Interior Department, and the Bureau of Prisons in the Justice Department. Note that the U.S. Forest Service in Agriculture, the Social Security Administration in the Department of Health and Human Services, the Drug Enforcement Administration in Justice, and the National Park Service in Interior are also examples of what we here call a "bureau."

All this elaborate organization gives order to the business of administration. It assigns certain functions to certain units, places officials at the head of each unit and makes them responsible for performance, allows both specialization and coordination, permits ready communication, and in general makes our far-flung administration somewhat controllable and manageable. But this formal organization can be somewhat misleading. Informal ties are sometimes equally important.

Informal Organization

Bureaucrats, like all people, differ—in attitude, motive, ability, experience, and political influence. Their very diversity leads to all kinds of complications. Relationships among officials in an agency may be based on influence rather than on formal authority, on expertise, or on political clout with constituency interest groups. Leadership may be lodged not at the top but in a variety of places. A certain group of officials may have considerable influence, whereas another group, with the same formal status, may have much less. Further, the loyalties of some officials may cut across the formal aims of the agency.

Informal organization can have a substantial effect on administration. A subordinate official in an agency might be especially close to the chief simply because they went to the same college or played poker together, or because the subordinate knows how to ingratiate himself with the chief. A staff official may have tremendous

[5] For a discussion of these and the whole range of administrative agencies, see Harold Seidman and Robert Gilmour, *Politics, Position and Power: From the Positive to the Regulatory State*, 4th ed. (Oxford University Press, 1986), chap. 11. On government corporations, see John T. Tierney, "Government Corporations and Managing the Public's Business," *Political Science Quarterly* (Spring 1984), pp. 73–94.

influence not because of formal authority but because experience, fairness, common sense, and personality make people turn to him or her for advice. In an agency headed by a chief who is weak or unimaginative, a vacuum may develop that encourages others to try to take over. Such informal organization and communication, cutting across regular channels, is inevitable in any organization—public or private, civilian or military.

THE UNITED STATES CIVIL SERVICE: A BRIEF HISTORY

Until the middle of the nineteenth century, the federal civil service was based mainly on the spoils system. To ensure responsive government, it was believed new presidents should be free to put their own followers into office. This view was summarized in the famous American political expression "To the victor belongs the spoils." Besides, it was thought government should not be that complicated—almost anybody should be able to do the job. Later in the nineteenth century, however, a sharp reaction set in against this system. In response to a series of events, including the assassination of President James Garfield in 1881 by a disappointed office seeker, Congress passed the Pendelton Act. This set up a merit system under a three-person bipartisan board called the Civil Service Commission (which functioned from 1893 to 1978).[6]

The Civil Service Reform Act of 1978 abolished the Civil Service Commission and split its functions between two new agencies. The Office of Personnel Management (OPM) administers and enforces the civil service laws, rules, and regulations. An independent Merit Systems Protection Board and its staff is supposed to protect the integrity of the federal merit system and the rights of federal employees. It conducts special studies of the merit system, hears and decides charges of wrongdoing, considers employee appeals against adverse agency actions, and orders corrective and disciplinary actions against an executive agency or employee when appropriate. The independent special counsel of this Merit Systems Protection Board investigates prohibited personnel practices and prosecutes officials who violate civil service rules and regulations.

Senior government administrators work with the Office of Personnel Management in staffing their agencies. OPM acts as a central clearing house for recruiting, examining, and appointing government workers. It advertises for new employees, prepares and administers oral and written examinations throughout the country, and makes up a register of names of those who pass the tests. OPM has a policy of delegating to individual agencies the responsibility for hiring new personnel, subject to its standards. Individual agencies may promote people from within or transfer a civil servant already in the government. If, however, they wish to consider an "outsider," they request OPM to certify possible candidates from its roster of applicants. OPM typically certifies the top three applicants who have applied for the departmental or agency opening. Normally the agency then selects one of these. However, the agency can decide to make no appointment or to request other applicants if it thinks none of the three is qualified. These procedures are intended to protect the merit principle and to meet agencies' needs for qualified personnel. But "in practice, the two objectives are not the same. Tradeoffs have to be made, particularly between central control by OPM and delegation of discretionary author-

---

[6] For a thoughtful analysis of the use and abuse of the civil service system in the early twentieth century, see Stephen Skowronek, *Building a New American State* (Cambridge University Press, 1982).

Hatch Act Rules: What Federal Employees May and May Not Do

- **May** register and vote as they choose
- **May** assist in voter-registration drives
- **May** express opinions about candidates and issues
- **May** participate in campaigns in which none of the candidates represents a political party
- **May** contribute money to political organizations or attend political fundraising functions
- **May** wear or display political badges, buttons, or stickers
- **May** attend political rallies and meetings
- **May** join political clubs or parties
- **May** sign nominating petitions
- **May** campaign for or against referendum questions, constitutional amendments, municipal ordinances

- **May not** be candidates for public office in partisan elections
- **May not** campaign for or against a candidate or slate of candidates in partisan elections
- **May not** make campaign speeches or engage in other campaign activities to elect partisan candidates
- **May not** collect contributions or sell tickets to political fundraising functions
- **May not** distribute campaign material in partisan elections
- **May not** organize or manage political rallies or meetings
- **May not** hold office in political clubs or parties
- **May not** circulate nominating petitions
- **May not** work to register voters for one party only

Note: Applies to nearly all federal civil servants. Rules are stricter still for military personnel. An election is partisan if any candidate for an office is running as a representative of a political party whose candidate received electoral votes in the last presidential election.

Source: Adapted from *Political Activity and The Federal Employee* (U.S. Merit Systems Protection Board, 1984).

ity to the agencies. Furthermore, pursuit of both objectives is enfeebled by introduction of yet additional and often incompatible objectives"—for example, the veteran preference system.[7]

The Hatch Act

In 1939 Congress passed an "Act to Prevent Pernicious Political Activities," usually called the **Hatch Act** after its chief sponsor, Senator Carl Hatch of New Mexico. In essence, this law bars federal civil service employees from getting overly involved in elections. Because an increasing portion of the nation's workforce was on the government payroll, some people in the late 1930s saw a danger that civil servants would be able to shape, if not dictate, the election of presidents and members of Congress. The Hatch Act was designed to neutralize the federal civil service. Federal employees may vote, but they may not take an active part in partisan politics. The Supreme Court has ruled that such limitations are constitutional. The Hatch Act also makes it illegal to dismiss nonpolicy-making federal officials (those below cabinet and subcabinet rank) for partisan reasons.

The Hatch Act, say detractors, is an outmoded ban that denies millions of federal employees the political rights all other Americans enjoy, and discourages political participation among the kinds of people who would otherwise be vigorous activists in party and election activities. Supporters of the Hatch Act like to quote Thomas Jefferson, who said the best way to achieve an impartial government and protect the rights of all federal workers is through a politically neutral civil service. Jefferson held that a government employee's attempts to influence the votes of others is inconsistent with the spirit of the Constitution. Supporters say the Hatch Act was passed to ensure impartiality and integrity, and to protect federal workers from coercion or threats by superiors. Other defenders, fearing the growing influence of government employee unions, contend that a weakened Hatch Act could encourage these unions to extort from Congress both the right to strike and ever greater pay raises and fringe benefits.[8]

Thus far efforts to modify the Hatch Act have failed.

BUREAUCRACY IN ACTION: THE CLASSICAL OR TEXTBOOK MODEL

Early in this century, several scholars developed a formal model of administration from which they derived certain principles:

1. *Unity of command*. Every officer should have a superior to whom to report and from whom to take orders.
2. *Chain of command*. There should be a firm line of authority running from the top down, and responsibility running from the bottom up.
3. *Line and staff*. The staff advises the executive but gives no commands, whereas the line has operating duties.
4. *Span of control*. A hierarchical structure should be established so that no individuals supervise more agencies directly than they can effectively handle.

---

[7] James Fesler, *Public Administration: Theory and Practice* (Prentice-Hall, 1980), p. 100.

[8] On the general subject of federal pay, see Robert W. Hartman and Arnold R. Weber, eds., *The Rewards of Public Service: Compensating Top Federal Officials* (Brookings Institution, 1980). See also Robert Hartman, *Pay and Pensions for Federal Workers* (Brookings Institution, 1983).

Professor Woodrow Wilson of Princeton University. (*The Bettmann Archive*)

5. *Decentralization*. Administrators when possible should delegate decisions and responsibilities to lower levels.

Woodrow Wilson, while still a professor, adopted many of these views. He also argued that *politics* and *policy administration* should be carefully separated: Leave politics to Congress and management to administrators who adhere to the laws as passed by Congress. Followers of the noted German sociologist Max Weber argued that a properly run bureaucracy could be a model of efficiency. Together with Weber's idea, various textbook principles of public administration were thought to promote rational and impartial management.

According to the textbook model, bureaucrats should not have much discretion in making independent judgments. They should be closely controlled by established rules and regulations. Although this is not always true in practice, it is generally the case: Administrators are not free to make any rules they wish or to decide disputes any way they please. Several kinds of limitations exist:

1. The basic legislative power of Congress compels the agencies to identify the will of Congress and to interpret and apply laws as Congress would wish. Congress can amend a law to make its intent clearer, conduct oversight hearings and investigations, or restrict appropriations.

2. Congress has closely regulated the procedures to be followed by regulatory agencies. Under the Administrative Procedure Act of 1946, agencies must publicize their machinery and organization, must give advance information of proposed rules to interested persons, must allow such persons to present information and arguments, and must allow parties appearing before the agency to be accompanied by counsel and to cross-examine witnesses.

3. Under certain conditions final actions of agencies may be appealed to the courts.

4. Other federal agencies place limits on the administrators' activities—for example, the Office of Management and Budget (OMB) and the General Accounting Office (GAO). In addition to reviewing an agency's budget requests annually in the name of the president, the OMB has a management section to review management, organization, and administrative practices on a more or less continuous basis. The GAO conducts audits of agency spending, and it also investigates the effectiveness of alternative programs designed for similar ends.

Max Weber (1864–1920) was a noted German sociologist who was a leading student of bureaucracy and organizational behavior. (*Culver Pictures*)

5. Administrators are also surrounded by informal political checks. They must keep in mind the demands of professional ethics, the advice and criticism of experts, and the attitudes of Congress, the president, interest groups, political parties, private persons, and so on. In the long run, these safeguards are the most important of all.

The textbook or classical model (sometimes also called "the rational person" approach) remains an influential ideal for those engaged in government administration. It describes a part of the reality of bureaucracy—*but only a part*. We need to emphasize here, however, that laws passed by Congress are not just important: They are central. Most scholars and practitioners agree that the more they see of the bureaucracy, the more impressed they become with the fact that the agencies and the career public servants are very much the creatures of the enabling laws under which they work. So this textbook model is also, in part, the reality.

BUREAUCRATS AS ADMINISTRATORS—SOME REALITIES

Today we know we cannot separate the administration of policy from political conflicts over what the policy should be. Congress cannot possibly spell out exactly what needs to be done in every instance. Our political system is, as we have noted in earlier chapters, always marked by a fair amount of compromise and ambiguity. Put another way, often we can agree on something only by leaving the matter a little vague. Because this is so frequently the case, a considerable amount of discretion is usually left to the thousands of senior bureaucrats who administer federal programs and enforce government regulations.

Bureaucrats are heavily involved in the politics of national policy. Public employees are called upon for advice and policy judgments during the policy-making process. Suppose Congress passes a law setting federal standards for automobile safety and designates the Department of Transportation to carry out the program. Conflicts over standards—or politics—do not stop with the adoption of the law. Or suppose a president announces that we are about to become "energy self-sufficient," and Congress designates the Department of Energy to carry out certain programs and appropriates funds. Politics—conflicts over who is to get what and who is to do what—still need to be considered as the policy is applied to changing economic or environmental conditions. Hence, certain political decisions are merely transferred or delegated from the legislators to the bureaucrats.

Pressures and Problems

Federal administrators must anticipate and understand what is expected by their superiors, by fellow professionals, by Congress, by the courts, and by the dictates of conscience. Career administrators are in a good position to know when a program is not operating properly and what action is needed. But one of the major complaints about bureaucrats is that they do not go out of their way to make things better. The problem is that many bureaucrats often learn by hard experience that they are more likely to get into trouble by attempting to improve or change programs than they are if they just do nothing. Hardening of administrative arteries is more likely than administrative aggressiveness.

In those cases in which administrators *are* aggressive, they usually seek to increase the size and scope of their agencies. Often the fiercest battles in Washington are not over principles or programs but over territorial boundaries, personnel cuts, and fringe benefits: Career employees come to believe the health of their organization is vital to the public interest. Administrators sometimes become more skillful at building political alliances to protect their own organization than at building the alliances that may be needed to ensure the effectiveness of the programs their organization is supposed to administer.

Career government workers, like all those who work in complex organizations, tend to use the resources at their command on flashy programs, and to give priority to issues that help focus attention on their activities. For example, a few years ago we heard much of the Defense Department's efforts to "sell the Pentagon," but except for the sheer size of its efforts, the Pentagon is not exceptional. All organizations, public and private, work to promote a favorable image.

Organizations, again both public and private, also tend to resist change and to resent "outside" direction whether by a president or by other external supervisors or boards. A department head in the government, in a large corporation, or in a university is likely to consider the president to be an outsider whose authority in matters affecting his or her bureau is always suspect.

Administrators as Political Alliance Builders

In the real bureaucracy career administrators often become intricately involved in politics. They sometimes have more bargaining and alliance-building skills than the elected and appointed officials to whom they report. In one sense, agency leaders are at the center of action in Washington. Over time many administrative agencies

Applicants lined up to apply for Civil Service jobs. (*UPI/Bettmann Newsphotos*)

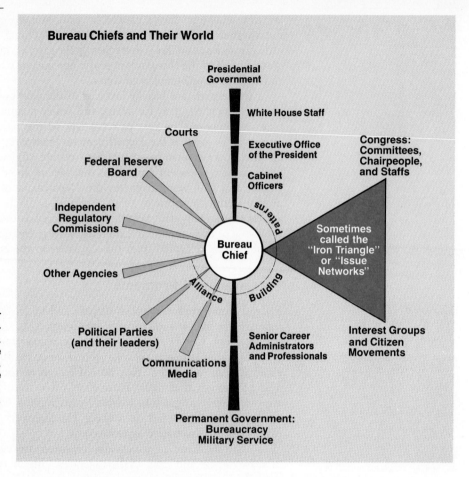

Bureau Chiefs and Their World

As this diagram suggests, bureau chiefs have to respond to a number of power centers in addition to cabinet members and the White House. Bureau chiefs are very much in the center of the action in Washington. Nearly everyone seeks to influence them, especially their strategies of policy and program implementation. Note especially the "iron-triangle," sometimes called "issue networks," linking senior bureaucrats with interest groups and congressional officials.

come to resemble entrenched pressure groups in that they continually operate to advance *their own* interests.

Most career bureaucrats develop a keen sensitivity to the political pressures on their bureaus. It is impossible for them not to get caught up in a network of issue specialists and policy politicians that make up the thousand and one policy subgovernments in Washington. With the growth of federal programs has come an explosion in the number of policy aides on Capitol Hill, of Washington law firms that specialize in assisting clients who are interested in policy developments, and of the lobbyists (some say at least 30,000) who work with Congress and the federal bureaucracy to advance various economic and professional interests.[9] Groups that perceive real or potential harm to their interests cultivate the bureau chiefs and agency staffs of concern to their programs. They also work closely with the specific committees or subcommittees of Congress that authorize, appropriate, and oversee programs run by these key bureaucracies. One former cabinet member, testifying before a congressional committee, described the process this way:

> It is a fact, unknown to the general public, that some elements in Congress and some special interest lobbies have never really wanted the departmental Secretaries [cabinet members] to be strong. As everyone in this room knows but few people outside of Washington understand, questions of public policy nominally lodged with the Secretary are often decided far beyond the Secretary's reach by a trinity—not

[9] See the useful discussion of this in Hugo Heclo, "Issue Networks and the Executive Establishment," in Anthony King, ed., *The New American Political System* (American Enterprise Institute, 1978), pp. 87–124.

exactly a holy trinity—consisting of (1) representatives of an outside lobby, (2) middle-level bureaucrats, and (3) selected Members of Congress, particularly concerned with appropriations.

In a given field these people may have collaborated for years. They may have formed deep personal and family friendships. They have traded innumerable favors. They have seen Secretaries come and go. . . . They have a durable alliance that cranks out legislation and appropriations in behalf of their special interest.[10]

Some bureaucrats become more entangled than others with these external coalitions. Bureau chiefs in particular become logical targets for the efforts of concerned interest groups. On the other hand, bureau chiefs, often recognizing the power of interest groups, frequently recruit them as allies in pursuing common goals. Sometimes bureau chiefs try to coopt potential adversaries among the interest groups by getting them appointed to governmental advisory committees or by arranging for certain contracts for that particular interest. The main point is that bureau leaders seldom ignore powerful interest groups. Pragmatic alliances are usually sought and established.

What are the consequences of all this? First, it illustrates once again that the political system is composed of a wide variety of power centers. More specifically, it suggests that the executive branch of government is a many-splintered branch of government. Cabinet members and the White House have their work cut out for them, because such alliances cause the bureaucracy to resist change and direction from their appointed or elected political "superiors." Some view these external relations as a kind of administrative guerrilla warfare—and as a serious roadblock in the way of fulfilling electoral or party responsibility or of holding elected leaders to account. Others anticipate merely an inevitable clash over values in a system that should provide ample opportunities for such clashes. After all, the bureaus themselves are merely one more forum for registering the many demands that make up the people's will.

Members of Congress pressure and cultivate bureau officials just as special interests nurture close ties with both Congress and bureau heads. Congress controls agency budgets and has the power to approve or deny requests for needed legislation. A bureau is especially careful to develop good relations with the members of the congressional committees and subcommittees handling its legislation and appropriations. The following exchanges at hearings illustrate this point:

Official of the Fish and Wildlife Service: Last year at the hearings . . . you were quite interested in the aquarium there [the Senator's state], particularly in view of the centennial coming up. . . .

Senator: That is right.

Official: Rest assured we will try our best to have everything in order for the opening of that centennial.

Subcommittee Chairman: I wrote you gentlemen . . . a polite letter about it . . . and no action was taken. . . . Now, Savannah may be unimportant to the Weather Bureau but it is important to me. . . .

Weather Bureau Official: I can almost commit ourselves to seeing to it that the Savannah weather report gets distribution in the northeastern United States [source of tourists for the subcommittee chairman's district].[11]

(T. Cronin)

(T. Cronin)

[10] John W. Gardner, testimony before the U.S. Senate Committee on Government Operations, *Executive Reorganization Proposals*, *Hearings* (U.S. Government Printing Office, 1971), pp. 57–58. See also R. Douglas Arnold, *Congress and the Bureaucracy* (Yale University Press, 1979).

[11] Quoted in Aaron Wildavsky, *The Politics of the Budgetary Process*, 4th ed. (Little, Brown, 1984), pp. 80, 81. See also Lawrence Dodd and Richard Schott, *Congress and the Administrative State* (Wiley, 1979).

We have discussed the pressures and loyalties amid which bureaucrats must work. We have seen how bureaucrats build alliances; sometimes they become so powerful that they defy presidents and Congress and seem to be little empires unto themselves.

The late J. Edgar Hoover, as chief of the FBI, was nominally subject to direction from the attorney general and the president of the United States. In fact, he was so popular with Congress and the public that he was practically immune from control. That immunity served the country poorly at times, such as when Hoover was able to wiretap Dr. Martin Luther King, Jr., or others he disliked, but it served the country well when Hoover was able to thwart President Nixon and his aides in certain of their illegal efforts to undermine political opponents. But how safe is a democracy when the administrative head of a major agency can defy even the elected president?

Of course, bureaucrats come in all shapes and sizes, with all kinds of political clout and alliances. Let us look at two case studies. One is real; the other is fictionalized but realistic.

Rickover of the Navy

The career of the late Admiral Hyman G. Rickover points up the sharp limits on the authority of presidents and cabinet members over some bureaucrats. Rickover served as an officer for 63 years, longer than any other naval officer in American history. Hailed for supervising the production of the nuclear-powered submarine, he often ignored red tape, bullied subordinates, intimidated superiors, and in general attacked the naval bureaucracy. For over thirty years Admiral Rickover worked with powerful members of Congress to build a nuclear-powered navy, often in complete and open defiance of the chief of naval operations, the secretary of defense, and the president. In fact, he outlasted fourteen secretaries of defense, fourteen secretaries of the navy, and at least ten chiefs of naval operations. Time and again Congress chose to listen to Rickover rather than to Rickover's bureaucratic superiors, even when they had vigorous backing from various presidents. Yet Rickover was an admiral in the U.S. Navy and as such was presumably subject to the authority of many of those whom he defied:

President Jimmy Carter and the late Admiral Rickover. (*National Archives*)

> On the face of it, there is something extraordinary about an engineer who is essentially an expert in nuclear propulsion playing such an important role in defense policy. Rickover, who has never held a major Navy command, has risen from captain to four-star admiral in two decades of doing exactly what he does now. On paper he is a bureaucrat whose two offices are so obscure that they are hard to find on government organization tables. As deputy commander of the nuclear power directorate in the Naval Sea Systems Command, and director of naval reactors in the Energy Research and Development Administration, Rickover has only about 250 employees in Washington plus another 100 or so in the field.
>
> Through these two posts, Rickover, backed by a loyal band of powerful congressmen, has wrought an astounding transformation of our naval forces. Since the *Nautilus* sent its epic message ("Under way on nuclear power") . . . Congress has entrusted Rickover with $27 billion to build what some Senators like to call "Rickover's Navy."[12]

One reason for Rickover's success was that his ships worked better than promised. Another reason was that he had unwavering support from the members of the Armed Services Committees of both the House and the Senate and from members of the Joint Committee on Atomic Energy. "Rickover's skill at cultivating Congress—he works the hallways of congressional office buildings as assiduously as

[12] Juan Cameron, "Admiral Rickover's Final Battle," *Fortune*, © 1976 Time Inc. For a critical view of Rickover's defiance of his superiors and his cozy relations with well-placed members of Congress, see Elmo R. Zumwalt, Jr., *On Watch: A Memoir* (Quadrangle, 1976), chap. 5.

any lobbyist for a cause—has given his supporters on the Hill a sense that they also played a key role in creating the nuclear fleet."[13] He was a frequent expert witness at congressional hearings and a notoriously tough manager with his employees.

Bureau Chief George Brown

The following case is fictional but based on actual experiences of a typical bureaucrat. (Note that not only is our main character, George Brown, fictitious, but so are the Bureau of Erosion and the Department of Conservation. Other agencies mentioned do exist.) It illustrates some of the painful choices bureaucrats have to make, whether they are in Washington or in the field.

George Brown is chief of the Bureau of Erosion in the Department of Conservation. He is in his mid-40s; his appointment to the post was a result of both ability and luck. When the old bureau chief retired, the president wanted to bring in an erosion expert from Illinois, but influential members of Congress pressed for the selection of a former member of the U.S. House of Representatives from a farm state. After deadlock and delay, and as a compromise, Brown, then a division head in the Bureau of Erosion, was promoted to bureau chief. A graduate of a midwestern agricultural college, Brown is a career official in the federal service and a member of the Senior Executive Service.

Early in March of Brown's second year in his new post, his boss, the secretary of conservation, summoned him and the other bureau heads to an important conference. The secretary informed the group that he had just attended a cabinet meeting in which the president had called on each department to make at least a 10 percent cut in spending in the coming fiscal year. The president, the secretary reported, was convinced that there was a great popular demand for federal fiscal restraint.

Brown quickly calculated what this cutback would mean for his agency. For several years the Bureau of Erosion had been spending about $600 million a year to help farmers protect their farmland. Could it get along on about $540 million, and where could savings be made? Returning to his office, Brown called a meeting of his personnel, budget, and management officials, and his four division chiefs. After several hours of discussion it was agreed that savings could be effected only by decreasing the scope of the program—which would involve ending the jobs of about 1500 of the bureau's employees. Brown asked his subordinates to prepare a list of employees who were the least useful to the bureau. He would decide which to drop after checking with the affected members of Congress.

A few weeks later Brown presented a $540 million budget to Secretary Jones, who approved it and passed it along to the White House. The president then went over the figures in a conference with the director of the Office of Management and Budget, and a few weeks later the White House transmitted the budget for the whole executive department, incorporating the Erosion Bureau's $540 million, to Congress.

Meanwhile Brown was running into trouble. News of the proposed budget cut had leaked immediately to the bureau's personnel in the field. Nobody knew who would be dropped if the cut went through, and some officials were already looking around for other positions. Morale fell. Hearing of the cut, farmers' representatives in Washington notified local farm organizations throughout the country. Soon Brown began to receive letters asking that certain services be maintained. Members of the farm bloc in Congress were also becoming restless.

Shortly after the president's budget went to Congress, Representative Smith of Kansas asked Brown to meet with him. Smith was chairperson of the Subcommittee on Agriculture and related agencies of the House Appropriations Committee and thus was a powerful factor in congressional treatment of the budget. Brown immedi-

(T. Cronin)

[13] Ibid., p. 200.

ately went up to the Hill. Smith began talking in an urgent tone. He said he had consulted his fellow subcommittee members, both Democratic and Republican, and they all agreed that the Erosion Bureau's cut must not go through. The farmers needed the usual $600 million and even more. They would practically rise up in arms if the program were reduced. Members of Congress from agricultural areas, Smith went on, were under tremendous pressure. Leaders of farm groups in Washington were mobilizing the farmers everywhere. Besides, Smith said, the president was unfair in cracking down on the farm program; he did not understand agricultural problems, and he failed to understand that programs designed to increase agricultural output were the best way to reduce our trade imbalance. Besides, the cuts in federal programs should be made elsewhere.

Then Smith came to the point. Brown, he said, must vigorously oppose the budget cut. Hearings on appropriations would begin in a few days, and Brown as bureau chief would of course testify. At that time he must state that the cut would hurt the bureau and undermine its whole program. Brown would not have to volunteer this statement, Smith said. He could just respond to leading questions put by committee members. Brown's testimony, Smith thought, would help clinch the argument against the cut, because the committee would respect the judgment of the administrator closest to the problem.

Smith informed Brown that other bureaucrats were fighting to save their appropriations. Obviously, said Smith, they are counting on public reaction to get them exemptions from the 10 percent cutback. Brown would be foolish not to do the same.

Brown was in an embarrassing position. He had submitted his estimates to the secretary of conservation and to the president and it was his duty to back them up. The rules of the game demanded, moreover, that agency heads defend budget estimates submitted to Congress, whatever their personal feelings might be. The president had appointed him to his position, and had a right to expect loyalty. On the other hand, he was on the spot with his own agency. The employees all expected their chief to look out for them. Brown had developed happy relations with "the field," and he squirmed at the thought of having to let more than a thousand employees go. What would they think when they heard him defend the cut? More important, he wanted to maintain friendly relations with the farmers, the farm organizations, and the farm bloc in Congress. Finally, Brown was committed to his program. He grasped its true importance, whereas the president's budget advisers were less likely to understand it. And he knew that his pet project—aid to rural poverty areas in Appalachia—would probably be sacrificed, because it was not supported by a powerful constituency.

Brown turned for advice to an old friend in the Office of Management and Budget. This friend urged him to defend the president's budget. He appealed to Brown's professional pride as an administrator and career public servant. He reminded him that the chief executive must have control of the budget, and that agency heads must subordinate their own interests to the executive program. He said the only way to balance the budget would be for all agencies to make program cuts. As for the employees to be dropped—well, that was part of the game. A lot of them could get jobs in defense agencies; civil service would protect their status. Anyway, they would understand Brown's position. In a parting shot he mentioned the president had Brown in mind for bigger things.

The next day Brown had lunch with the senator, wise and experienced in Washington ways, who had helped him get his start in government. The senator was sympathetic. But there was no doubt about what Brown should do, the senator said. He should follow Representative Smith's plan, of course, being as diplomatic as possible about it. This way he would protect his position with those who would be most important in the long run.

"After all," the senator said, "presidents come and go, parties rise and fall, but Smith and those other members of Congress will be here a long time, and so will these farm organizations. They can do a lot for you in future years. And remember one other thing: These people are elected representatives of the people. Constitutionally, Congress has the power to spend money as it sees fit. Why should you object if they want to spend an extra 30 or 50 million?"

Leaving the Dirksen Senate Office Building, Brown realized that his dilemma was worse than ever. The arguments on both sides were persuasive. He felt hopelessly divided in his loyalties and responsibilities. The president expected one thing of him. Congress (he was sure Smith reflected widespread sentiment on Capitol Hill) expected another. As a career man and professional administrator, he sided with the president; as head of an agency, however, he wanted to protect his team and his programs. His future? Whatever decision he made, he was bound to upset important people and interests.

After much soul searching, Brown decided the issue involved more than loyalties, ambitions, and programs. Ultimately it boiled down to two questions: First, to whom was he, Brown, legally and administratively responsible? Formally, of course, to the chief executive who appointed him and who was accountable to the people for the actions of the administration. And second, which course of action did he think was better for the welfare of all the people? Looking at the question this way, he believed the president was right in asking for fiscal restraint. As a taxpayer and consumer himself, Brown knew of the strong sentiment for doing something about the federal budget deficits. To be sure, Congress must make the final decision. Yet to make the decision, Brown reflected, Congress had to know the attitude of the administration, and the administration should speak with one voice for the majority of the people, or it should not be speaking out at all. With mixed feelings Brown decided to support the president. Being a seasoned alliance builder, however, he hedged his bets somewhat. He came out strongly for the president's budget, but at the same time he sent to friendly members of Congress some questions to be asked of himself in future hearings, so that he might be able to give some hints of the impact of the cutbacks. He also circulated to some of these same members of Congress an analysis of the impact of personnel and funding cuts in their states and districts. The case studies just considered lead to three important generalizations:

1. Bureaucrats are people, not robots, and as people they are subject to many influences.
2. Bureaucrats do not respond merely to orders from the top but to a variety of motives stemming from their own personalities, formal and informal organization and communication, their political attitudes, their educational and professional backgrounds, and the political context in which they operate.
3. Bureaucrats are important in government. Some of them have considerable discretion and make decisions of great significance. The cumulative effect of all their policies and actions on our daily lives is enormous.

WHAT THE PUBLIC THINKS OF BUREAUCRATS

Cynical citizens think "government employees have got it made, and they know it." In general, the American people think federal bureaucrats are paid too much to do too little and that too many people are on the payroll. More than two-thirds believe government wastes a lot of their tax money. Further, a survey of the public

HOW THE PUBLIC JUDGES FEDERAL BUREAUCRATS (1983)

Q. Overall, who do you think works harder—people in federal government jobs, or people in similar jobs outside the government?

Government Workers	14%
Non-Government Workers	60
No Difference	17
No Opinion	9

Q. How about the number of people employed by the federal government: In general, do you think the federal government employs too many people or too few people to do the work that must be done?

Far Too Many	29%
Somewhat Too Many	28
About The Right Number	11
Too Few	16
Too Many In Some Areas, Not Enough In Others	5
No Opinion	11

Q. Do you believe that federal employees are paid more, less or about the same as people in similar jobs outside the government?

Paid More	55%
Paid Less	10
Paid About The Same	22
No Opinion	13

Q. (*Asked of people who say they have had at least some dealings with a federal government agency in the past year*) Overall, would you say you were pleased with the conduct of the government worker or workers you dealt with, or not? . . . Would you say you were very pleased/displeased, or just pleased/displeased?

Very Pleased	14%
Pleased	57
Displeased	14
Very Displeased	4
No Opinion	11

SOURCE: Figures are from a national telephone poll of 1167 people taken by the *Washington Post*, January 16, 1983, section A, p. 80.

The Public View of Whether Government Wastes Money

	1964	1968	1972	1984
A Lot	47%	59%	66%	65%
Some	44	34	30	29
Not Very Much	6	4	2	4
No Opinion	3	3	2	2

SOURCE: Survey Research Center
University of Michigan

---

at-large indicates that most Americans believe federal employees do not work as hard as those who hold similar nongovernmental jobs.

These findings are not too surprising. Big bureaucracy in the abstract—especially when it is out of sight in some remote capital—is unpopular; it engages in so many activities that most people find something it does offensive (like taxing them, inspecting them, conscripting them, and so on). Big bureaucracy has been defined as that part of the government people dislike. If someone is not directly concerned about a program one way or the other, it is easy for that person to say the national government should stay in Washington and mind its own business!

But a poll by the The Washington Post had some good news for bureaucrats: The public actually likes and approves of the general conduct of most of the federal employees with whom it comes in contact.[14] An impressive 71 percent of the public who have had dealings with the government said they were pleased or very pleased by the performance of those federal employees they actually met and dealt with on a face-to-face basis. Relatively few people said they were just *displeased* by

[14] See *The Washington Post* (July 16, 1983), section A, p. 8. Similar positive findings are discussed in Goodsell, *The Case for Bureaucracy*, chap. 2.

17–1 Contrasting Criticisms of Federal Workers

Americans simultaneously condemn our nation's civil servants for being ineffective clerks and for being too powerful. Following are two lists of time-honored criticisms or stereotypes aimed at the federal bureaucracy:

Bureaucrats as Paper-Shuffling Clerks Are:	Bureaucrats as the Real Power in Washington Are:
1. Timid and indecisive	1. A self-anointed elite in our nation's capital
2. Flabby, overpaid, and lazy	2. An oppressive foreign power
3. Ruled by inertia	3. The fourth branch of government
4. Unimaginative	4. Intolerably meddlesome
5. Devoted to rigid procedures	5. A demanding giant
6. Slow to accept new ideas	6. The permanent government
7. Slow to abandon unsuccessful policies	7. Super-Bureaucrats who wield vast power
8. Impersonal and lacking individuality	8. Enormously powerful to do great injury
9. Red-tape artists	9. Intrusive, arrogant empire builders
10. On "one long coffee break"	

What Top Federal Career Employees Like Least and Most About Their Work

Like Least:

- Inability to take personnel actions that should be a manager's prerogative (e.g., hiring and discipline) — 49%
- Inadequate resources (e.g., personnel, budget) — 40
- Personal financial sacrifice — 38
- "Red tape" — 36
- Frustrations in dealing with interest groups, Congress, etc. . . . — 30

Like Most:

- Challenging assignments — 75%
- Opportunity to have an impact on policy or management of a particular program — 66
- Opportunity for public service — 53
- Opportunity to use and expand one's knowledge and occupational skills — 42
- Caliber of person worked with — 35

Source: Government survey of 300 recently retired federal career executives from Annette Gaul, "Why Do Executives Leave the Federal Service?" *Managment* (Fall 1981) and the Office of Personnel Management.

their contact with federal workers. This suggests that in contrast to public scorn for bureaucrats and bureaucracy in the abstract, the typical American actually appreciates and approves of the conduct of such people as postal service delivery persons, forest rangers they met on camping trips, Veterans Administration officials who helped their ailing uncles, or the U.S. Department of Agriculture county field agents who help with the local 4-H programs. They also admire astronauts, marines, and FBI agents, all of whom are also federal employees.

One of the paradoxes of public attitudes toward bureaucrats is that some of the time we criticize federal employees for working too little, for being lazy, or for lacking initiative—for failing to abide by the so-called work ethic. But at the same time we view federal workers as too powerful, and we accuse them of intervening in or regulating our lives far too much.

Can bureaucrats in reality be both timid and empire builders? In fact, there are enough bureaucrats to fulfill all kinds of contrasting stereotypes—so perhaps it is possible to hold both views about them, despite the seeming contradiction.

Even federal employees themselves gripe about the system. Although top federal employees say they *like* the challenge of their work, the opportunity to participate in forming and managing important policies, and the quality of people with whom they work, as indicated in the margin box, these workers *dislike* the rigidity, the red tape, and many of the frustrations of dealing with interest groups and politicians. Since 1962, federal employees have had the right to form unions or associations that represent them in seeking to improve government personnel policies, and about a third of them have joined such unions. Some of the more important unions representing federal employees today are the American Federation of Government Employees, the National Treasury Employees Union, the National Association of Government Employees, and the National Federation of Federal Employees. Unlike unions in the private sector, these groups lack the right to strike and are not able to bargain militantly over pay and benefits. What can they do? They attempt to negotiate better personnel policies and practices for federal workers, and they also represent federal bureaucrats during grievance and disciplinary proceedings. Further, they testify before Congress on measures affecting personnel changes.

Federal bureaucrats are aware that the public is not fond of them. However, this situation might change if more people took the time to learn about what the federal bureaucracy does, and if more politicians resist giving those "bureaucrats-are-bums" talks that win such ready applause. Still, the public will probably go on blaming the bureaucracy for rising taxes and for all the waste or crazy regulations about which they read in the newspapers.

Since 1789, Americans have always been skeptical of big government. We still like to think of ourselves as a nation of rugged individualists, and we cherish the dream of a self-reliant, self-help society in which government looms small. Bureaucrats—especially Washington bureaucrats—are an emblem or symbol of losing that dream—of what Thomas Paine once called "a badge of innocence lost." To think of the bureaucracy is to think of our dependence on others, our inability to solve things at the neighborhood or family levels, and our impersonal way of trying to solve so many of today's complicated problems.

Finally, bureaucrats have become the favorite punching bag—a credible and convenient scapegoat—for members of Congress or for reporters who have to place the blame on someone for things that go wrong in government. An irreverent and influential journal in the nation's capital, *The Washington Monthly*, rails against clumsy bureaucracy in every issue. *Fortune* magazine and the *Wall Street Journal* often feature banner stories critical of the federal bureaucracy. Senator William Proxmire (D-Wisconsin) gives a monthly "Golden Fleece" award to some governmental entity that has wasted money or deceived the American taxpayer—and federal bureaucrats are the most frequent recipients of these unwelcome public awards.

Plainly, the "organization man" or the "bureaucratic man" has never been a hero in America. The lone cowboy or rugged individualist remains the cultural hero for most of us.

THE CASE AGAINST BIG BUREAUCRACY AND ITS WASTE

Americans generally view big government as bad. We equate bigness with remoteness, injustice, incompetence, and unresponsiveness. We also assume that the bigger government gets, the more it wastes.

Perhaps the most criticized aspect of the federal bureaucracy is that career public employees seem to enjoy the closest thing to permanent tenure; they are almost as secure in their jobs as if they were confirmed for the Supreme Court. Critics say that for all practical purposes, federal workers can neither be fairly punished nor justly rewarded for performing well. Hence, most of them perform the bare minimum.

Few ever get fired. The government's rate of discharge for inefficiency is said to be less than one-seventh of 1 percent. And of that one-seventh of 1 percent, a substantial number are reinstated after appeals in the federal courts. Even the occasional reductions-in-force (known as RIFs) during the Reagan years involved few people: mostly those encouraged to retire a bit earlier than they otherwise would have.

When Jefferson was president, the federal government employed 2120 persons: Indian commissioners, postmasters, collectors of customs, tax collectors, marshals, lighthouse keepers, and clerks. Today the president heads an executive branch of, as noted earlier, about 2.85 million civilians and over 2 million military employees, who work in at least 2000 units of federal administration. Critics say the federal bureaucracy is growing at an alarming rate and that by the year 2000 it will control nearly every aspect of our lives. Figures can indeed be presented that make the federal establishment look like a mushrooming giant. For example:

1. In 1929 federal spending amounted to about 2.5 percent of the gross national product (GNP). Today the federal share is over 24 percent of the GNP.
2. The estimated annual cost of federally mandated paperwork is at least $40 billion.
3. In the last fifteen years or so, nearly 250 new federal agencies or bureaus have sprung into being; less than two dozen have been disbanded.

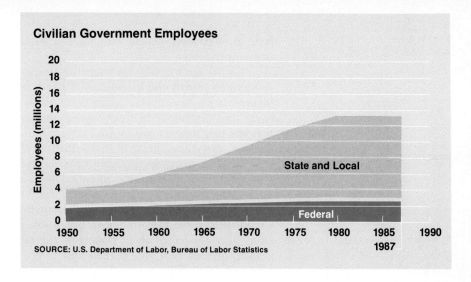

Civilian Government Employees

SOURCE: U.S. Department of Labor, Bureau of Labor Statistics

4. The national government owns one-third of the nation's land—and nearly 50 percent of the land west of Denver, Colorado. The Department of Defense alone owns land equivalent to the size of the state of Virginia. The government holds title to more than 400,000 buildings that cost well over $100 billion. It pays well over $800 million a year for rent for another 54,000 buildings.

5. President Kennedy, in 1961, was the first president to have a budget of over $100 billion. It is now over $1000 billion.

6. Several studies today find that for every worker on the federal civilian payroll as many as three or four wokers may earn their livings indirectly from the federal government (as consultants and contractors). In other words, there may be about 8 to 10 million "invisible federal employees" as the government contracts out more of its work in order to keep its employment levels steady.

7. Another way the federal government conceals its growth is by shifting its work to the state and local governments. The federal government provides for about one-fourth of total spending at the state and local levels. Although no one knows exactly how many jobs this creates at those levels, estimates run as high as 5 million (of the 12 million state and local government jobs).

No wonder people often conclude the government is trying to do too many things and make too many decisions, in too great detail, on too many subjects, for too many separate purposes. Some have advocated "birth control" for bureaucracy and federal programs. One person even suggested that before Congress can enact a new law, it should be required to repeal two existing ones. The central problem with the bureaucracy, critics add, is not that it exists, but that we have failed to subject it to the control and discipline alleged to operate in the private sector. In private business "the workings of self-interest are tempered and channeled by market disciplines, such as competition and consumer choice, and by public restraints, such as antitrust laws."[15] A corporation president who served as secretary of the treasury said one of the lessons he learned about working in government was "that the tests of efficiency and cost-effectiveness which are the basic standards of business, are in government not the only—and frequently not even the major—criteria."[16] President Ford put it this way: "One of the enduring truths of the nation's capital is that bureaucrats *survive*. Agencies don't fold their tents and quietly fade away after their work is done. They find Something New to Do. Invariably, that Something

[15] Tom Alexander, "Why Bureaucracy Keeps Growing," *Fortune* (May 7, 1979), p. 164. See also Frederic V. Malek, *Washington's Hidden Tragedy: The Failure to Make Government Work* (Free Press, 1978).
[16] W. Michael Blumenthal, "Candid Reflections of a Businessman in Washington," *Fortune* (January 29, 1979), p. 41.

New involves more people with more power and more paperwork—all involving more expenditures."[17]

Critics say too that the incentive system in the national bureaucracy seems to promote growth and inefficiency. Growth improves chances for promotion and higher salaries. After a while a significant portion of time in a bureaucracy is devoted to its own expansion. In short, one of the most common complaints is that our national civil servants seldom have any incentive to save taxpayers money. On the contrary, everything seems to tempt them in the opposite direction.

Another charge leveled against the bureaucrats is that they extend the authority granted to them beyond the intention of Congress. However, they often do so not because they are "hungry for power," but because once a program is established, the people assigned to it tend to be committed to the "cause." In the Office of Civil Rights in the Department of Education, for example, appointments generally go to those concerned about protecting the rights of women and minorities. That is their assigned task, and in their zeal to get those things done, they strengthen their authority. Those assigned to the Bureau of Narcotics are likely to be persons convinced that enforcement of the federal laws against narcotics is of supreme importance; in carrying out their duties, they sometimes go beyond their vested authority. Further, and perhaps most to the point, those groups outside the government who want the laws to be enforced and their programs carried forward will place pressure on the agencies. Women's groups and minority advocacy groups carefully watch the Office of Civil Rights, for instance.

Herbert Kaufman, a noted student of bureaucracies, set out a few years ago to study whether any old government agencies ever die. He began by looking at 175 agencies in selected areas of the national government that existed in 1923, and then traced them for the next fifty years. All but twenty-seven were alive and well in 1973. In the meantime 246 new agencies had been created to work in these same areas, for a new total of 394. Kaufman found that death of a bureaucracy is the exception rather than the rule. Further, he discovered that the birth of new units continued regardless of whether a Democrat or a Republican occupied the White House. New bureaucracies seem to be encouraged either by sudden shifts in economic conditions or international tensions or by a "built-in thrust that . . . assists the even finer division of labor in organizations."[18] Excessive workloads in existing agencies, pressure by groups who believe a new agency will be more sympathetic to their point of view, and a variety of societal change factors all work in the direction of creating more units of government.

Grace Commission and Bureaucratic Waste

How wasteful is the federal government? A Reagan-appointed commission, composed mainly of corporate leaders, concluded that $424 billion could be saved in just three years. To do this, the Grace Commission (formally, the President's Private Sector Survey on Cost Control) made 2478 recommendations that called for, among other things, strengthening presidential veto powers to cut programs, introducing common-sense private-sector business and accounting practices into federal procurement and management procedures, and ending countless programs and policies that lead to expensive fringe benefits and subsidy programs. The Grace Commission would end military commissaries, sell off the National and Dulles, Washington, D.C. area, airports, get the Veterans Administration out of the hospital-construction

"This is brief, clear, concise and to the point. Try again and remember this is a U.S. government office."
(*Reprinted from Federal Times, with permission*)

Privatization—One View

"British Prime Minister Margaret Thatcher has successfully privatized more than a dozen nationalized industries, including British Aerospace, Jaguar, and British Telecom, generating over £7 billion for the treasury.

In this country, state and local governments have taken the lead in contracting out such public services as garbage collection, street cleaning, and even prison services to the private sector. Not surprisingly, the result has been reduced costs and better service. . . . Our government can follow Britain's example and responsibly ask the private sector to do a better job."

Ronald Reagan,
January 23, 1986

---

[17] Gerald R. Ford, *A Time to Heal: The Autobiography of Gerald R. Ford* (Harper & Row/Reader's Digest, 1979), p. 272.

[18] Herbert Kaufman, *Are Government Organizations Immortal?* (Brookings Institution, 1976), p. 67. See also Carl Grafton, "The Creation of Federal Agencies," *Administration and Society* (November 1975), pp. 328–65.

business, impose much higher user fees for Coast Guard and national park services, and sharply reduce most of the fringe benefits and early-retirement arrangements for government employees.

This same commission found that the federal government is the nation's largest borrower, lender, employer, insurer, landowner, tenant, and landlord. It is responsible, they said, for the medical care received by 47 million people per year, and it provides 95 million subsidized meals each day. In an effort to arouse the nation's 82 million taxpayers, "the true victims of government waste," their report concluded that the federal government was both big and poorly run. Waste and inefficiency abound in virtually every governmental program.

The Grace Commission alleged, among other things, that the Veterans Administration spends twice as much per hospital bed as the private sector, that half the government's computers are obsolete, that the General Services Administration employs seventeen times as many people to manage its facilities as comparable private-sector firms, and that military and civil service retirees received from three to six times the total lifetime pension benefits compared to their private-sector counterparts.

Commission chairperson J. Peter Grace, chief executive officer of a large American corporation, says the commission did not come up with easy solutions, "but the solutions don't get any easier by ignoring the problem." He especially faults Congress for most of the waste. His report's general conclusions are twofold: Strengthen presidential control over the bureaucracy, and move much of what the government is now doing back to the private sector. "Remember that Congressional instinct is to spend, never to save. We need to administer shock treatment to our elected representatives and let them know that their continued fiscal irresponsibility can no longer be tolerated. Much like the character in the movie *Network*, we're asking you to join with us in telling them that 'We're mad as hell, and we're not going to take it anymore!'"[19]

The Grace Commission was welcomed enthusiastically by President Reagan, who proceeded to use it effectively as an election year tool in 1984. However, Reagan implemented probably less than 15 percent of the Grace Commission suggestions. He did, however, pick up on the themes of privatization by raising or imposing for the first time various user fees. He also continued to appeal for public suppport for an item veto for the president.

The Grace Commission allegations of waste and cost overruns were less warmly greeted by Congress, the bureaucrats, and various students of government. Both the General Accounting Office and the Congressional Budget Office said the horror stories exaggerated the problems of the federal government. Moreover, many of the recommendations were politically unfeasible.

Nearly everyone agrees that the government should charge a fair (meaning higher) price for the electricity it generates, the crop irrigation it provides, the inland waterways it operates, and the grazing rights and firewood it almost gives away. "A citizens' campaign urging Congress to resist pork-barrel pressures and other wasteful tendencies could be a very useful thing—if it were built on realistic expectations of both savings and consequences," observes an editorial writer for *The Washington Post*. "But a campaign built on a false perception—the belief that better government management could make a big dent in the deficit—will only frustrate honest efforts in Congress and the administration to come to grips with the problem."[20]

One critic took the Grace Commission to task for grossly exaggerating and

"Bureaucrat"

The terms "bureaucrat" and "bureaucracy" are of recent origin. Initially referring to a cloth covering the desks or flat writing tables of French government officials in the eighteenth century, the term "bureau" came to be linked with a suffix signifying rule of government (as in "democracy" or "aristocracy").

Bureaucracy today can refer to a professional corps of officials organized in a pyramidal hierarchy and functioning under impersonal, uniform rules and procedures. In the social sciences the term usually does not carry the negative or pejorative associations of popular usage. It typically refers to the whole body of non-elective and non-presidentially appointed government officials.

We use the term in this chapter in a neutral and not a negative sense. However, many people use the word bureaucrat to describe an officious, blundering official engaged in slow operations, buck-passing, and wasteful redundancy. Roget's *Thesaurus* goes even further, linking bureaucracy to "officialism, red-tapism, red-tapery, red-tapedom, and Bumbledom."

---

[19] J. Peter Grace, *Burning Money: The Waste of Your Tax Dollars* (Macmillan, 1984), p. 172.

[20] Jodie T. Allen, "The Grace Book," *The Washington Post National Weekly Edition* (January 7, 1985), p. 28.

wildly misleading the general public. Steven Kelman of Harvard University's John F. Kennedy School of Government agreed that the government does produce a given output less efficiently than the private sector, yet "If I had to hazard a guess, I would say that the government might typically use, not four times or 17 times as many resources as the private sector to produce a given output, but perhaps 1.2 times."[21] Those responsible for the activities in question, Kelman adds, generally pay attention to costs and ways to keep them down. Critics like Grace, he says, are too quick to conclude that policies and programs are wasteful when they believe the programs are not worthwhile. In these cases, the real disagreement is over policies, not administration.[22]

Even the critics of the Grace Commission concede that considerable saving could be realized with improved accounting methods, increased user fees, and continued contracting of noncore government functions out to private organizations, especially if the same products can be produced more cheaply that way.

What is the long-run impact of reports like the Grace findings? Efforts to "combat waste" by introducing additional rules and additional layers of control are likely to hinder good performance—and may, as the example of the procurement system suggests, not even reduce costs. Yet it is exactly the headline-grabbing horror stories, such as the ones in which the Grace Commission specialized, that lead more than anything to the development of ever-newer rules and clearance points. In this sense, the Grace Commission may have betrayed the "war on waste" it set out to wage.[23]

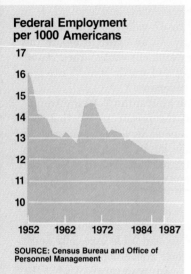

Federal Employment per 1000 Americans

17
16
15
14
13
12
11
10

1952   1962   1972   1984 1987

SOURCE: Census Bureau and Office of Personnel Management

THE CASE FOR BUREAUCRACY

Perhaps we often ask too much of our government; sometimes we probably give it problems that are impossible to solve. Former Senator Gary Hart once said our problem with big bureaucracy was not simply size or spending or taxes: "The central problem of big government springs from our attitudes and expectations. The problem of big government is big promises that cannot be backed up by performance. The problem of big government is inflated expectations that generate disillusionment rather than hope and progress. The problem of big government is the myth that it can solve every problem and meet every challenge. The problem of big government, frankly, is the demand placed upon it by every interest group in our society."[24]

Bureaucracy is not a function only of governments, but also of corporations and universities: They are a fact of life. The size of the federal bureaucracy has remained fairly stable for at least the past generation despite population growth and the expansion of federal programs.

What about red tape? One person's red tape is another's proper procedures. Red tape may be viewed as a hopeless tangle of rules and regulations that keep public servants from doing anything but stamping and shuffling papers. Or these same rules and regulations may be said to ensure that public servants act impartially. A student who is told by her dean that she cannot drop a course after eight weeks without a penalty may complain about "red tape" and unfeeling bureaucrats. But the rule was adopted so that all students would be treated alike, so the dean would

YOU DECIDE !

How can private and public organizations' employees learn from one another? Can management and leadership strategies used by IBM, Hewlett-Packard, or Prentice-Hall be as easily used in the public sector? You decide!

(Answer/Discussion on page 415.)

---

[21] Steven Kelman, "The Grace Commission: How Much Waste in Government?" *The Public Interest* (Winter 1985), p. 78.

[22] Ibid., p. 78.

[23] Ibid., p. 82.

[24] Gary Hart, "Big Government: Real or Imaginary?" *Civil Service Journal* (July–September 1976), p. 19.

not be able to allow only students he or she likes to drop the course. In other words, red tape stems in large part from our desire not to give public servants too much discretion, and to hold them accountable. After all, they are spending other people's money.

A comparison of our bureaucracy with most bureaucracies in the world suggests we should be grateful for the service we do get from our public employees. The U.S. Postal Service provides a good example. Although it is criticized as being the last dinosaur, it is faster, more efficient, and less costly than any comparable service in the world. Another example is the United States tax system: It is the most effective such system in the world.

Further, not all bureaucracies keep getting bigger. Some get bigger, some remain stable, and others actually shrink. The growth that does occur is often due to population or workload expansion rather than Parkinson's Law or bureaucratic "empire building."[25] Little evidence is available to support contentions that bigness necessarily creates inefficiency and rigidity. Some studies even come to the opposite conclusion. Surely the success of IBM and General Electric in the private sector and the Universities of California and Michigan in the public sector suggest some virtues of bigness.

Finally, compared to most other nations U.S. government employment has not grown much at all. Government employment in Sweden grew by more than 20 percent in the past generation, and by over 11 percent in Italy and Germany during the same period. Even England, with a stagnant economy, had a 5 percent growth in government employment. Growth in U.S. government employment since 1950 has been at the 1 to 1.5 percent level, depending on which figures and years are used.[26] Moreover, government employment as a percentage of total employment in the U.S. is 20 to 50 percent lower than in these western European democracies. Forty years ago, there were about nineteen federal civil servants for every 1000 Americans; now there are less than twelve per 1000. Defenders of the size of government also note that the proportion of our economic output consumed or distributed by the national government has increased only a few percentage points during the past two generations.

Still, what is probably the best-equipped, highly trained, and, possibly, the most efficient national bureaucracy in the world, operating in one of the most technologically advanced societies, remains the target of public criticism. And perhaps the skepticism is healthy. In a way, it is yet another check and balance in our system of constraints on those who wield public power.

BIG BUREAUCRACY—HOW RESPONSIVE IS IT?

One of the most complex questions concerning public bureaucracies is whether they are responsive enough to the citizens. Being *responsive* means being answerable as well as being quick to respond to treating someone sympathetically. How responsive an agency is depends on the perceptions of the person involved. A person who has to stand in a long line, whether at the post office or at a welfare agency, often complains about unresponsive bureaucrats. Or someone who has a new or novel problem that a federal bureaucrat treats "by the book" rather than by providing personalized service, also develops a critical view.

Bureaucracies necessarily have to develop routines and standard operating procedures. They do so in order to increase efficiency and productivity. They also do so because they are striving to achieve fairness and evenhandedness. But on occasion

[25] Goodsell, *The Case for Bureaucracy*.

[26] Richard Rose, *Understanding Big Government* (Sage, 1984), pp. 143–44.

such "red tape" reduces flexibility. Just about everyone has at one time or another been turned away from the local post office because a package to be mailed was too large, or too small, or in the wrong kind of container. It is hard on such occasions to hold in our anger. Why can't they be flexible? Why can't they be reasonable? Why can't they be helpful and deal with me in a personal way?

The procedures that allow the post office, the army, the IRS, or the Veterans Administration to perform efficiently for large numbers sometimes also diminish the ability of these organizations to respond to the personalized needs of individuals. Routines help to prevent chaos and allow government behavior to be consistent, uniform, and just. The inevitable and necessary result of big bureaucracy is often a tradeoff: Responsiveness—quick, personalized, individualized, and sympathetic service—often must be sacrificed for the sake of orderly and impersonal routines.

A related question is whether certain problems ought to be handled by mechanisms other than bureaucracies. Political leaders of all persuasions now recognize that we sometimes turn problems over to government bureaucracies when perhaps there is a more effective way to solve them. For example, can the government effectively regulate health-care costs through bureaucracies, or should we allow the economic market mechanism to handle such policy matters? Perhaps something inherent in bureaucratic procedures makes public bureaucracy less appropriate for certain types of activities. Perhaps some programs or policies are best left to the private sector, or to state and local governments, or to the market system. This may be especially true of international trade policies, the government role in high-technology industries, and various energy policies. However, the "privatization" of public programs can sometimes mean only shifting from one bureaucracy (public) to another (private).

In the final analysis, the question of *bureaucratic responsiveness* is extremely difficult to disentangle from the question of *bureaucratic accountability*. In determining the responsiveness of the Navy, or of the FBI, we must also ask to whom they should be most responsive—which is very similar to asking who should oversee and control them. Let us consider now who controls, and who should control, the federal bureaucrats.

"Think of it! Presidents come and go, but WE go on forever!" (© 1976 by NEA, Inc. Reprinted by permission)

CONTROLLING THE BUREAUCRATS: WHO AND HOW?

To whom *should* the bureaucrats (sometimes called the "powercrats") be accountable: themselves, organized interest groups, the majority who elected the president, or the majority as reflected by Congress? Plainly, most Americans would like the bureaucracy to be responsive to the public interest. *But defining the public interest is the crucial problem.* Both the president and Congress claim to speak in behalf of the public interest. Following are some of the realities and some of the recent suggestions for making bureaucrats more responsive and accountable.

Presidents and Bureaucrats

One school of thought says the president should clearly be in charge, for the chief executive is responsive to the broadest constituency. The president, it is argued, must see that popular needs and expectations are converted into administrative action. When the nation elects a conservative president, such as Ronald Reagan, who favors major cutbacks in federal programs and restricted governmental intervention in the economy, these policies can be carried out only if the bureaucracy responds. The majority's wishes can be translated into action only if the bureaucrats support presidential policies.

Answer/Discussion

Many similarities exist between private and public organizations. Middle-level managers in a bank and in the Internal Revenue Service, for example, have similar managerial tasks and define and implement similar organizational goals. Personnel in welfare organizations can learn from the United Way or a well-run private hospital how to deliver their services. The Postal Service has obviously begun to learn some effectiveness strategies from Federal Express. Important morale-building and organizational renewal efforts have to take place in public as well as private enterprises.

Yet differences exist too. Demands for accountability, and equity are greater in the public sector than in the private corporation. Efficiency is only one of the goals of a government agency, not its primary goal. Unable to be single-minded in pursuing efficiency, a public-sector organization will seldom be as efficient as a private sector business. "Those who focus on the similarities of public and private sectors tend to have an image of a civil service that is hierarchically subordinate to, and solely responsive to, the president and his priorities. That image is unrealistic given the structure and design of this country's government."*

* Edie N. Goldenberg, "The Grace Commission and Civil Service Reform," in Charles H. Levine, ed., *The Unfinished Agenda for Civil Service Reform* (Brookings Institution, 1985), p. 90. But see also Martha M. Weinberg, "Public Management and Private Management: A Diminishing Gap?" *Journal of Public Policy Analysis and Management* (Fall 1983), pp. 107–15.

Yet, as we have seen, under the American system of checks and balances a single political majority winning a presidential election does not acquire control of the national government, or even of the executive branch itself. Under our Constitution the president is not the undisputed master of the executive structure. Congress sets up the agencies, broadly determines their organization, provides money, and establishes the ground rules under which they operate. Congress constantly reviews the activities of the bureaucrats in appropriation hearings, special investigations, or informal inquiries. And, as we have also seen, the Senate must confirm most of the important cabinet-level leaders. In fact, presidents come into an ongoing system over which they have relatively little control—or relatively little leeway to shape the bureaucracy and make it responsive to their view of the public interest. Still, some presidential control over the bureaucracy may be exercised through the powers of *appointment*, *reorganization*, and *budgeting*. More specifically, a president can attempt to control the bureaucracy by appointing or promoting sympathetic personnel, mobilizing public opinion and congressional pressure to foster responsiveness, structurally changing the administrative apparatus, controlling the budget, using extensive personal persuasion, and, if the preceding fail, shifting a bureaucracy's assignment to another department or agency (although this usually requires congressional approval).

Presidents are allowed about 5000 political appointments to top positions within the executive branch. However, many of these apply to confidential assistants or highly specialized aides to cabinet officers. Moreover, many require confirmation by the Senate and thus are not exclusively a president's choice. Some reformers suggest that a president's hand could be strengthened if the chief executive were able to make two or three times as many political appointments.

Assistant secretaries—a weak link   But there is more to control than having the president appoint more people. The question is: Do those who are appointed have much to say once they are in office? Although presidents can usually recruit to their cabinets persons of prominence and influence, they find it much harder to hire outstanding persons at the assistant secretary level. Presidents depend in part on the assistant secretaries to infuse into the federal bureaucracy the views and values of the White House. These citizen-leaders are also expected to serve as links between the people who elect the presidents and the civil servants. Many people, however, are not willing to give up or interrupt their professional or business careers to become assistant secretaries: Over the last several years the position has become one of relatively low pay, little prestige in Washington, short tenure, and high cost to one's family. As a result presidents often fill these slots with relatively young people who, from the day they arrive in Washington, are looking for their next jobs. As a result, these assistant secretaries, or people in comparable appointed posts, are forced to wear "kid gloves" with those they are supposed to regulate, because it is from them that their next jobs are most likely to come. Others who tend to become assistant secretaries have strong ideological convictions, but little experience in administration and congressional politics. Still others use the position as a transition to retirement.

Once in Washington these presidential appointees have to deal with civil servants who know their "bosses" will not be there long. Most civil servants have virtually secure jobs, and all they have to do to ignore presidentially selected assistant secretaries is to wait them out for a year or two. Moreover, in and around Washington government workers comprise a powerful political group; assistant secretaries who try to significantly alter the policy directions of those who are supposedly under their supervision may do so at considerable political and legal peril.

President Carter did succeed in making some alterations in the higher reaches of the civil service. One of the changes brought about by the Civil Service Reform Act of 1978 was the creation of a Senior Executive Service. This service, or pool of about 7000 career (plus some noncareer) officials, can be filled without senatorial confirmation, and its individual members are subject to transfer from one agency to another according to an administration's wishes. The creation of the Senior Executive Service was intended to alleviate the feeling on the part of several recent presidents that the senior career bureaucrats—especially those enmeshed in outside networks—are not responsive to the goals and policy preferences of the White House. With this new service presidents and their political appointees can have greater flexibility in selecting, promoting, and rewarding with financial bonuses those in the top career service who are productive and responsive. Up to half of the senior career executives in an agency could, in theory, get bonuses each year of up to 20 percent of their base salaries. Other financial incentives are also available; for example, 5 percent of the executives in the service could be named to special ranks in which they could each earn a bonus of $10,000 for distinguished work in a given year. On the other hand, nonproductive executives could be put back into the ranks of the regular civil service, with severe reductions in pay and responsibilities.

The Civil Service Reform Act of 1978 was viewed with skepticism and even some alarm as it was first being implemented.[27] Some observers feared it would create an executive service that would be put to political use. Others worried that without strong White House support, the noble intentions of the act would not be achieved. President Carter was enthusiastic about the new plan, but President Reagan was noticeably less interested. Reagan was more preoccupied with cutting budgets and, where possible, cutting personnel. For a variety of reasons, the Senior Executive Service has not lived up to its creators' expectations. Many analysts now say it has had no significant impact on the federal workers it was supposed to help. Because of federal budgetary problems, most of the financial bonuses and related incentives have been held back. Morale in the senior ranks of the federal bureaucracy is the same or worse than it was before it was adopted. The White House, however, has enjoyed an increase in flexibility of assignments, and Reagan used this to his advantage.

Should We Return to a Patronage System?

Some writers call for a more radical overhaul of the civil service system. One observer, for example, would end career-long tenure in federal positions and allow for appointments of only six to twelve years, depending on a person's specialty. Tenure creates dead wood, they say, and periodic reexamination of a person's qualifications would greatly increase productivity and responsiveness. Although specialization is vital to modern organization, rotation (either from outside government or within government) might loosen up stiffened joints, bring new blood to agencies, and encourage a sense of breadth rather than fixed routines. It might even break up the "iron triangle"—alliances among senior civil servants, members of Congress, and outside client interest groups.

A related proposal deals with the heart of the democratic process. It is concerned not with making bureaucrats more effective but with ensuring that they are responsive to the electorate that elects the president. The emphasis here is on a vastly increased number of patronage positions, and much less reliance on the so-called merit system. One veteran observer of the Washington bureaucracy has complained that the greatest obstacle to reform of the civil service is that most people think it is better to have a system based on merit hiring than one based on political patronage. "But the fact is that getting a government job has only

---

Why Presidents Reorganize the Bureaucracy

Shake up an organization to increase managerial control

Simplify or streamline the bureaucracy or a specific agency

Reduce costs by lessening overlap, duplication, inefficiencies

Symbolize priorities by signaling new responsibilities in new agencies

Improve program effectiveness by bringing separate but logically related programs to the same agency

Improve policy integration by placing competitive or conflicting interests within a single organization

Source: Adapted from Peter Szanton, "So You Want to Reorganize the Government?" in Peter Szanton, ed., *Federal Reorganization* (Chatham House, 1981), p. 2.

---

[27] Mark Huddleston, "The Carter Civil Service Reforms: Some Implications for Political Theory and Public Administration," *Political Science Quarterly* (Winter 1981–82), pp. 607–21; and Bruce Buchanan, "The Senior Executive Service: How Can We Tell If It Works?" *Public Administration Review* (May–June 1981), pp. 349–58.

the most modest relation to merit." He adds, "Veterans get five free points added to their civil service exam score; disabled veterans get an extra ten. For nonveterans the trick is to get their names requested [from the Office of Personnel Management] by the agency filling the job, and the way to do that is to know someone inside the agency. People already in the system are the first to know about a job opening, and knowing both the applicant and the job, they can tailor the job description to fit the person they want to hire. So the civil service is a patronage ring based not on politics but on friendship."[28] Thus, he calls the existing system a buddy system, and urges this unorthodox but intriguing proposal:

> It is widely assumed that a patronage system will result in a government run by unqualified people. Let's take a look at that assumption. Why do political employees *have* to be unqualified? A politically appointed typist could be required to type the same number of words per minute as the civil service typist. Remember that merit appointment and promotion are not the reality in the present civil service, it's only make believe. Friendship and a military background have a lot more to do with hiring and advancement.
>
> Isn't it possible that government jobs might best be filled by politicians who are interested in putting together an administration that will do a good enough job to get them re-elected? The same principle applies to most of the decisions government employees make. Why shouldn't they be made on a partisan basis if the motive behind them is doing a good enough job to be re-elected?[29]

Not surprisingly, neither Congress nor most career bureaucrats look with favor on this proposal. With the Watergate scandals of just a decade ago, and with the general indifference, if not contempt, most people have for our political parties, it is probable that most Americans would oppose this proposal as well. Plainly, however, it holds considerable appeal for those who have to work directly on behalf of a president.

Presidents as chief executives also have the power to reorganize the executive branch.[30] Recent presidents tried to employ these powers, but they achieved few of their aims. President Nixon wanted to abolish six departments (Labor, Commerce, Transportation, Agriculture, Housing and Urban Development, and Health, Education and Welfare) and replace them with four new departments organized in broader categories, such as natural resources, human resources, and economic development. Nixon said this restructured national bureaucracy could provide coherent planning, resolve interdepartmental conflicts, and deliver services more efficiently. Congress and major interest groups disagreed. So did various department heads and career officials within the existing departments. Congressional committee leaders are always aware that if they restructure the federal administration, they may have to reorganize their own committee system. This would upset the balance of power in Congress. In short, changing the shape of administration is more than a matter of efficiency and economy. It also involves *policy outcomes*: Who gets what, how, and why.

President Carter learned these same realities. His ambitious plans for reshaping and reorganizing the federal bureaucracy came to little. Most of his ideas for sweeping organizational change, including the idea of a natural resources cabinet department, fell victim to the same political forces that had dealt the death blow to Nixon's reorganization efforts.

Ronald Reagan came to the White House pledging to abolish both the Education and Energy departments, but failed to do so. He also proposed changing the Commerce Department into a Department of Trade. Reagan found out what most of his predecessors learned: Although everybody favors sensible reorganization, diffi-

Chief Executive versus The White House Mouse

Students sometimes think presidents sit high atop the executive branch pyramid, barking out commands. Occasionally this is the case, but the degree to which a president can win cooperation or compliance varies enormously. And presidents can often be just as frustrated as parents are with their teenage offspring. Listen to the sad story of the White House mouse who had climbed inside a wall of the Oval Office and died there. The odor became offensive just as President Carter was about to greet a visiting diplomat.

An emergency call went out to the General Services Administration (the agency that maintains and oversees federal property), but the GSA refused to respond. The dead mouse, GSA officials said, had obviously come in from outside the building and was therefore the responsibility of the Department of the Interior. Interior officials, however, objected; they contended the mouse was not their concern because it was now inside the White House and their jurisdiction was merely the outside grounds.

Well, an exasperated Carter finally ordered officials from both agencies to his office where he angrily told them, "I can't even get a damn mouse out of my office. . . ." So how was the problem solved? By a two-agency White House supervised task force, of course.

[28] Charles Peters, *How Washington Really Works* (Addison-Wesley, 1980), pp. 47–48.

[29] Ibid., pp. 48–49.

[30] Szanton, *Federal Reorganization*.

culties and controversies arise when you get specific because the specifics may upset the already-established balance of power in the Washington power system. Nonetheless Reagan did effectively use the civil service reforms passed under Carter, and his appointment and speech clearance prerogatives, to discipline the upper reaches of the executive branch.[31]

Office of Management and Budget

Ever since Franklin Roosevelt strengthened the staffs of the presidency, the president's budget bureau, currently called the Office of Management and Budget, has been a key resource in helping to manage the executive branch. The OMB's primary task is to prepare the president's annual budget. A budget usually becomes the major vehicle for shaping a president's policy priorities. It is the place (and the process) that determines which programs will get more funds, which will be cut, and which will remain the same. Departments and agencies all over Washington fight to win larger chunks of the president's budget projections. The OMB supervises the preparation of the budget and hence assists very directly in the formulation of policy. The OMB is the closest thing a president has to an interest-free perspective on weighing and evaluating the merits of the countless proposals and pleas that constantly pour in upon the White House.

Ninety-six percent of the OMB's staff are career officials trained to evaluate ongoing projects and new spending requests. The OMB's top officials, of course, are presidential appointees, and they are often among a president's most important advisers. Together the OMB officials help a president make critical decisions not only about the budget but also about management practices, collaborative efforts among government agencies, and legislative planning. The OMB and its predecessor organization (the old Bureau of the Budget) have been actively involved in making sure that both the departments and Congress are informed of the president's legislative preferences.[32] All in all, the OMB plays an important role in expanding the policy and administrative options open to a president.[33]

Congressional Control over the Bureaucracy

Congress has a number of means of exercising control over the bureaucracy: by participating in the budget process, appropriating funds, confirming personnel, authorizing new programs or new shifts in direction, conducting investigations and hearings, reorganizing authority, and publicly rebuking the officials in a particular agency.

The foundation of bureaucratic power is, of course, a bureaucrat's information and expertise. Ordinarily, bureaucrats know much more than anyone else about their programs and the consequences of what they are doing. Recognizing this, Congress may request agency heads to make initial proposals and to provide cost and price estimates. It has imposed stiff penalties for providing misleading information—as a means of reducing bureaucratic deception.[34]

Still, Congress is under fire, at least in some quarters, for encouraging the growth of bureaucracy and for deliberately allowing it to remain somewhat out of

[31] See, for example, Richard Nathan, *The Administrative Presidency* (Wiley, 1983), chaps. 6 and 7.

[32] For useful studies of these functions of the OMB, see Larry Berman, *The Office of Budget and Management and the Presidency, 1921–1979* (Princeton University Press, 1979); and Howard Shuman, *Politics and the Budget* (Prentice-Hall, 1984).

[33] Of course, the OMB does not always win, nor is it always right. See David Stockman, *The Triumph of Politics* (Harper & Row, 1986).

[34] Jonathan Bender, Serge Taylor, and Roland Van Gaalen, "Bureaucratic Expertise versus Legislative Authority: A Model of Deception and Monitoring in Budgeting," *American Political Science Review* (December 1985), pp. 1041–60.

Congressional hearing on NASA astronauts' program. (*K. Jewell*)

control. Members of Congress, so this reasoning goes, profit from the growth and complexity of the bureaucracy. It is to their state and district members of Congress that most constituents, especially business people, turn for help as they battle federal red tape and complications. Hence, as the federal bureaucracy and its programs grow, so too does the influence of members of Congress. Members of Congress, in fact, get big political mileage by interceding in federal agencies on behalf of their constituents.

> The brutal fact is that only a small minority of our 535 congressmen would trade the present bureaucratic structure for one which was an efficient, effective agent of the general interest—the political payoffs of the latter are lower than those of the former. Congressional talk of inefficient, irresponsible, out-of-control bureaucracy is typically just that—talk—and when it is not, it usually refers to agencies under the jurisdiction of other congressmen's committees. Why do reformers continually ignore the fact that Congress has all the power necessary to enforce the "people's will" on the bureaucracy? The Congress can abolish or reorganize an agency. The Congress can limit or expand an agency's jurisdiction, or allow its authority to lapse entirely. The Congress can slash an agency's appropriations. The Congress can investigate. The Congress can do all these things, but individual congressmen generally find reasons not to do so.[35]

Basic to this point of view is the complaint that Congress does not pay enough attention to how its laws are administered, and that it delegates too much authority to bureaucrats. Congress, it is charged, anxious whenever possible to avoid conflict, adopts such sweeping legislation and delegates so much authority to the bureaucracy that bureaucrats, in effect, have become the nation's lawgivers.

But could Congress pass laws with very precise wording all the time? It would get too bogged down in the necessary details to complete its work. For example, imagine Congress is concerned that there be enough truck lines in operation to ensure prompt transportation service for shippers, but not so many as to lead to ruinous competition. If it should attempt to specify the exact circumstances under which a new truck route should be licensed, the statute would have to read as follows:

> Keokuk, Iowa, needs four truck lines unless the new superhighway that they have been talking about for ten years gets built. Then they will need five unless, of course, Uncle Charlie's Speedy Express gets rid of its Model T and gets two tractors and vans. Then they will only need three as long as two freight trains a day also stop there.
> On the other hand, Smithville, Tennessee, needs eight truck lines unless. . . .[36]

Of course, Congress seldom writes laws like these. Instead, it declares its policy in general terms and empowers the Interstate Commerce Commission to license new

YOU DECIDE !

Testing Civil Servants for Drugs?

Some 50 million Americans have tried marijuana, and 20 million are reputed to use it regularly. About six million use cocaine and about 500,000 are heroin addicts. The rise of "crack" is rapidly destroying lives and neighborhoods. Drug use and abuse costs the economy tens of billions in health and criminal justice expenses and lost productivity. Drug trade puts at risk everyone, not just those who use drugs. Drug use by federal employees can be especially hazardous, especially on the part of criminal investigators, air-traffic controllers, rangers, policy makers, and reduces the effectiveness of all of them.

Does this justify across-the-board urinalysis tests for major policy makers, senior civil servants, for all civil servants, as a condition of employment?

(Answer/Discussion on next page.)

[35] Morris P. Fiorina, "Flagellating the Federal Bureaucracy," *Society* (March/April 1983), p. 73.
[36] Martin Shapiro, *The Supreme Court and Administrative Agencies* (Free Press, 1968), p. 4.

truck lines when such action would be warranted by "public convenience and necessity." The regulatory commissioners then judge the situation in Keokuk and Smithville and make specific rules.

But how can we get rid of wasteful and obsolete programs? Many people agree that too many federal programs are allowed to continue indefinitely, whether or not they are accomplishing what they were meant to do. If the country's needs and priorities change, programs should be adjusted or abolished accordingly. One attempted reform, adopted in most state governments, is a **sunset process.** Sunset laws place government agencies or programs on limited life cycles, and force them to justify their existence every six or seven years. Sunset review processes have been set up in more than two-thirds of the states. Their chief purpose is to weed out ineffective programs and make room for new ones. The technique gets its name from a group in Colorado that proposed that "the sun should set" on programs that have outlived their original purpose or whose benefits are outweighed by other considerations. The burden would be on the bureaucrats to perform well, so that in six or seven years they can prove themselves worthy of staying in business.

Sunset legislation is opposed by those who say it is too simple for the complicated and subtle evaluation work that needs to be done. Still others argue that sunset laws require enormous amounts of time and paperwork for bureaucrats to justify their existence every few years. The state experience with sunset procedures has not led to major reductions in large, costly programs.

Remember that it is not Congress as a whole that shares the direction over the bureaucracy with the president. More accurately, it is individual members to whom Congress has delegated its authority. These people, primarily committee and subcommittee chairs, usually specialize in the appropriations and policies of a particular cluster of agencies—often the agencies serving constituents in their own districts. Some legislators stake out a claim over more general policies. Members of Congress, who see presidents come and go, come to think they know more about agencies than the president does (and sometimes this is the case). Although Congress as an institution may prefer to have presidents in charge of the executive branch, so that it can hold them responsible for its operation, some congressional leaders prefer to seal off "their" agencies from presidential direction in order to maintain their own influence over public policy.[37] Sometimes this is institutionalized—the Army chief of engineers, for example, is given authority by law to plan public works and report to Congress without going through the president.

Another factor works in favor of the Congress. Every day thousands of bureaucrats are involved in making thousands of decisions. A president has limited time, limited resources, and limited political influence over many of these agencies. Presidents and their staffs can become involved only in matters of significant political interest. Members of Congress, with staffs of over 30,000, however, can operate in areas far from the presidential spotlight.[38]

So who controls the bureaucrats? Presidents and members of Congress strive to do so, each in their own way. Interest groups also influence the way the bureaucracy operates. For their part career bureaucrats say they are responsive to the laws and statutes they work under and to their own standards of professionalism and responsibility. Plainly, there is no one answer to the question of who or what controls the bureaucracy. And because of this, there is a never-ending search for improved means of ensuring bureaucratic accountability. This search, and experiments with countless instruments—such as reorganizations, civil service reforms, sunset practices, budgetary planning, and oversight hearings—will always be with us—as they should.

[37] See R. Douglas Arnold, *Congress and the Bureaucracy: A Theory of Influence* (Yale University Press, 1979). See in general Morris B. Ogul, *Congress Oversees the Bureaucracy* (University of Pittsburgh Press, 1976).

[38] Herbert Kaufman, *The Administrative Behavior of Federal Bureau Chiefs* (Brookings Institution, 1981).

Answer/Discussion

Not too many years ago civil servants were required to prove their loyalty to the United States by taking oaths that they were not Communists. Such oaths raise serious First amendment questions. Compulsory drug testing raises serious Fourth amendment questions. The idea that a group of people should be subjected to random searches without reasonable individual cause was resisted at the outset of our life as a nation.

If Congress, or the president or head of a federal agency, should require drug testing as a condition of employment, even if evidence of drug use would not be used to dismiss employees, they would need to persuade skeptical judges that this was not an "unreasonable" search and seizure. Remember the case of *Winston* v. *Lee*, discussed in Chapter 6.

SUMMARY

1. We regularly condemn our bureaucracy and our bureaucrats, but we continue to turn to them to solve our toughest problems and to render more and better services. A survey of our bureaucratic agencies, then, is also a survey of how our political system has tried to identify many of our most important national goals.

2. The American bureaucracy does not strictly adhere to the textbook model of management organization. This is because our bureaucracy is not fully subordinate to any branch of government. It has at least two immediate bosses: Congress and the president. It must pay considerable attention as well to the courts and their rulings, and, of course, to well-organized interest groups. In many ways the bureaucracy is a semi-independent force—a fourth branch of government—in Washington politics.

3. Debates and controversy over big government and big bureaucracy, and over how to reorganize them and how

to eliminate waste in them, will continue. Meanwhile, most experts agree that the range and importance of the bureaucracy will expand in the years ahead. However, compared with many other nations and their centralized bureaucracies, the hand of the bureaucracy probably rests more gently and less oppressively on Americans than on other peoples.

4. Who and how the government hires and what discretion or powers it grants its employees will always be controversial topics. Still, to work in the career public service is often to have the opportunity to serve people, to solve problems, and to try to bring about a better society. Efforts to make the bureaucracy more responsive and more accountable are enduring struggles, and they are issues raised in every presidential election. But there are never any final answers or quick fixes.

FURTHER READING

LAWRENCE DODD and RICHARD SCHOTT. *Congress and the Administrative State* (Wiley, 1979).

ANTHONY DOWNS. *Inside Bureaucracy* (Little, Brown, 1967).

JAMES ECCLES. *The Hatch Act and the American Bureaucracy* (Vantage Press, 1981).

CHARLES T. GOODSELL. *The Case for Bureaucracy*, 2nd ed. (Chatham House, 1985).

J. PETER GRACE. *War on Waste: President's Private Sector Survey on Cost Control* (Macmillan, 1984).

HUGH HECLO. *A Government of Strangers* (Brookings Institution, 1977).

HERBERT KAUFMAN. *The Administrative Behavior of Federal Bureau Chiefs* (Brookings Institution, 1981).

HERBERT KAUFMAN. *Time, Chance and Organizations* (Chatham House, 1986).

CHARLES H. LEVINE, ed. *The Unfinished Agenda for Civil Service Reform* (Brookings Institution, 1985).

JOHN A. ROHR. *To Run a Constitution: The Legitimacy of the Administrative State* (University Press of Kansas, 1986).

FRANCIS E. ROURKE. *Bureaucracy, Politics and Public Policy* (Little, Brown, 1983).

HAROLD SEIDMAN and ROBERT GILMOUR. *Politics, Position, and Power*, 4th ed. (Oxford University Press, 1986).

STEPHEN SKOWRONEK. *Building a New American State: The Expansion of National Administrative Capacities, 1877–1920* (Cambridge University Press, 1982).

BRUCE SMITH and JAMES CARROLL, eds. *Improving the Accountability and Performance of Government* (Brookings Institution, 1982).

Two useful journals are *Journal of Policy Analysis and Management* and the *Public Administration Review*.

CHAPTER 18

Making Public Policy

The playwright George Bernard Shaw suggested that progress comes about because of unreasonable people. Reasonable people, he said, adjust themselves to reality and cope with what they find. Unreasonable people dream of a different and better place and try to adapt the world to these ideals. Discontent or unreasonableness is often the first step in the progress of a person, as well as in that of a nation. George Washington and his friends were decidedly unreasonable—from the British point of view—in the 1770s. Women suffragists, civil rights advocates, and social-issue activists often seem unreasonable—troublemakers or incurable idealists.

Many major policy changes in the United States have originated with those impatient with the old ways of doing things. These are often the catalysts, and actual policy change is frequently carried through and enacted into laws or court decisions by gifted coalition-building politicians, and by reasonable policy entrepreneurs.

Still, changes come mainly from the grass roots, and not primarily from Washington, D.C. The capital is more the terminating than the germinating stage for policy change. Ideologues, business leaders, labor unionists, state and local officials, farmers, ethnic advocates, consumer spokespersons, religious leaders, scholars, representatives of foreign nations, pundits, and just plain citizens either want policy changes from government, or they want to prevent things from changing.

Public policy is the substance of what government does. More specifically, it is the set of declared intentions and follow-up actions our elected officials take to meet human needs and to resolve conflict within society. This chapter examines some distinctive features and models of the national policy-making process. The five chapters that follow examine the most important policy functions of the national government: foreign, defense, economic, regulatory, and domestic public policy.

NATIONAL POLICY AGENDA SETTING

Have you ever wondered why one subject seems to be in the headlines for weeks, or why all of a sudden something that has been talked about for decades gets enacted into law? Why do we seem to be a nation with one or two issues dominating all the discussions and then all of sudden they disappear? Sometimes the answer is obvious. A catastrophic event—the Challenger tragedy that caused the death of seven astronauts will obviously trigger congressional hearings, presidential commission proceedings, investigative news stories, and books about our space program; or the destruction of a Soviet nuclear plant will lead to new safety regulations. But then there are other events—why after years of discussion did tax reform in 1986 become a reality or a Civil Rights Act in 1964?

If we look closely, we find that a variety of factors and people are involved— events, changes in expert opinion, changes in mass opinion, interest group agitation, and greater involvement by elected officials and their staffs. In recent years, political scientists have focused more attention on the agenda-setting or idea-generation part of the policy-making process.

Who sets the agenda? According to classical representation theory, our elected representatives should exercise the most influence in the making of laws and policies. Elected officials obviously do play major roles in raising, debating, and acting upon issues in ways that are meant to solve problems and improve the nation.[1] Yet both politicians and the media have so much else to do and are by definition generalists that in practice the agenda-setting function is often performed by other participants in the policy process.

Other people perform a role in calling attention to national policy deficiencies. They point to problems and perhaps write about them and organize groups to petition for change. It may be a scientist who has come up with a better way to prevent heart disease or cancer or AIDS; it may be an inventor who has better ideas about a weapon or transportation system; it may be a professor who has suggestions for better ways to encourage competition and deregulation. A close examination of the policy agenda-setting process suggests that a considerable amount of work is often needed before elected officials will get involved in a policy question. Somebody first has to clarify the problem and offer options, choices, and alternatives—or merely call attention to the problem as a problem in the first place.

No matter how meritorious an idea may be, our political system, prizing as it does gradualism and incrementalism, deliberation, and coalition-building, requires that various elites be persuaded and involved in the development of ideas for policy change. Policy innovation, especially new approaches to existing norms, must almost always win acceptance among certain professionals before the public-at-large is likely to consent or acquiesce in the proposed change. Such approval can take many forms, but ordinarily appropriate scientists, for example, will have to agree about the fact that smoking causes cancer, or that protectionist tariffs are really an undesirable tax on consumers, or that we can verify a particular Soviet weapons-testing process before the media and elected officials will have the courage to consider new initiatives in a policy area. Professional and scientific elites, in and out of government, play a subtle yet important role in initiating and specifying the kinds of policy changes desired in our political system.[2]

(The Economist, July 18–25, 1986)

(National Journal, Jan. 4, 1986/No. 1)

GETTING THINGS DONE IN WASHINGTON

If we follow national policy making as it is reported on television or in the newspapers, we rarely see behind bill-signing ceremonies, press conferences, or formal speeches. And we mainly hear about conflicts between the branches, or disarray within a

[1] John Kingdon, *Agendas, Alternatives, and Public Policies* (Little, Brown, 1984), and the special issue on "How Washington Works," *The National Journal* (June 14, 1986).

[2] See Nelson Polsby, *Political Innovation in America: The Politics of Policy Innovation* (Yale University Press, 1984). A prize-winning Ph.D. dissertation by John Zaller, "The Role of Elites in Shaping Public Opinion" (University of California, Berkeley, 1984) is especially helpful in making this case.

branch. Congress, we may be told, refuses to go along with the president on some foreign-aid package, or the Supreme Court overrules a provision of the Gramm-Rudman-Hollings Budget Balancing Act of 1986. Or the president vetoes a bill passed by Congress. These contests capture our interest much like sporting events do.

Washington journalism feeds on such contests because they make for more interesting copy than the numerous small cooperative and collaborative efforts to make policy. But box scores indicating how many of the president's legislative measures pass Congress often conceal as much as they reveal. They do not really tell us why a president has or has not been successful. Nor do they tell us much about the quality of measures proposed, passed, and rejected. A president with an eye solely on the box score, for example, can avoid endorsing measures that are unlikely to pass. Moreover, a higher success rate may be due more to rapidly increasing federal revenues than to presidential leadership.

Beneath and behind "the governing class," thousands of individuals are at work in the Washington policy-making process. They help resolve conflicts and facilitate cooperation across institutions. Only by understanding these people can we appreciate the patterns of national policy making.

Sometimes just being in the right place at the right time enables an individual to contribute to policy decisions. Usually, however, people who make a difference have formal positions or needed knowledge, or both. Specialists from various professional communities are often looked to for advice in the early stages, when policy makers are assigning relative importance to various competing issues. Of course, one must also be familiar with the rules of the Washington public-policy process.

Senior congressional committee staff positions, once a patronage payoff to campaign aides, are increasingly filled by highly qualified policy entrepreneurs. The ability of these professional staffs to analyze information for hearings and legislation gives them influence on policy making. They often become a kind of "shadow government" linking Congress, the executive branch, interest groups, and different constituencies around the nation. Federal biomedical policy has often been made by a small group of medical researchers, philanthropists, and members of Congress assisted by staffers in Congress and the White House.

Then, of course, come the lobbyists. There have been lobbyists in Washington for as long as there have been lobbies—but never so many as today. Although about 5000 lobbyists are formally registered with Congress, it is widely estimated that about 30,000 to 40,000 people in Washington (or people who frequent Washington on a regular basis) do some sort of lobbying at any given time. "Washington is rife with institutions whose leaders are ushered through decision makers' doors and taken seriously not because of who they are but because of the multitudes they speak for or the respected institutions they represent," reports the *National Journal*.[3] The margin box lists some institutions such lobbyists deem "influential."

Representatives of state and local governments are increasingly present in Washington to get hearings for their points of view. These governments send an official or hire consultants to represent their interests and to ensure that issues of great concern to them are not ignored. The number of offices representing individual governors or state legislatures in Washington has grown to at least three dozen; in addition, lobbying officials work for the National Governors Association and the National Conference of State Legislators.

Washington is full of unelected policy politicians who have served long periods within a given policy area and in a variety of governmental as well as nongovernmental positions. The career ladders of these specialists are neither tidy nor predictable. An economist at the OMB may move to the nongovernmental Brookings Institution and a few years later go back to government service within the Congressional Research Service. An aide to a senator may go to HUD and then back to an elective state

[3] Burt Solomon, "How Washington Works," *National Journal* (June 6, 1986), p. 1428.

government position. Later the aide may return to cabinet posts at HUD, Defense, and Justice, then become ambassador to Great Britain, again become a cabinet officer, and then once again become an ambassador. A young lawyer may work in the office of the secretary at the Department of Defense, then join the White House National Security Council Staff, leave to become counsel for the Senate Armed Services Committee, three years later enter private practice in Washington, D.C., three years later become undersecretary of the navy, and then return to private practice.

These illustrations are by no means unusual. Mobility in Washington is extensive, and career ladders diverse. As a result, complex networks of friendships, influence, and loyalties characterize the policy-making process.[4] One of the more fascinating aspects of Washington politics is the way in which policy activists in different branches of government, or associated with various nongovernmental organizations (such as research institutes, foundations, lobbyist units, or media), join forces in working alliances. Policy subsystems grow up around a set of interrelated issues— as much a response to the process of getting things done as to the issues themselves. Age and formal position are less important than information, imagination, energy, and persistence. Policy activists learn how to capture support from members of Congress and senior White House aides. This is easy sometimes, for certain members of Congress, as well as White House aides, are always looking for new ideas with which to promote their careers.

Then, too, some newspaper or journal is usually willing to provide a forum for debate on a new issue. Countless opportunities arise for testifying at hearings, bringing suits in court, or convincing staff people who serve cabinet or high executive office officials.

"Please understand. I don't sell access to the government. I merely sell access to the guys who do sell access to the government." (Drawing by Ed Fisher; © 1986 The New Yorker Magazine, Inc.)

POLICY-MAKING MODELS

There are almost as many approaches to studying public policy making as there are persons who study the policy processes. Much of choosing an approach depends on which policies are being considered and on what are the observer's political values. Differences may also reflect the particular stage of the policy process on which the researcher has chosen to focus. There is a certain amount of agreement, however, about how an issue gets attention and later becomes the subject of deliberation and action:

1. *Problem identification*: What is the problem? How does the problem fit with existing policy categories and rankings of goals? Does the government need to help out, intervene, regulate, or make some kind of decision? Should the issue or problem be placed on the agenda of government? For example, if air pollution is making people sick somewhere, is this a matter for governmental attention?

2. *Policy formulation*: What should be done? How can we best assess the alternatives, including benefits, costs, and equity? Who should be involved in the planning and design of the policy? For example, if air pollution requires government action, what action is preferable? Policy analysts need to consider all the alternatives, but they always have to remember that alternatives must realistically be able to be implemented in our country.

3. *Policy adoption*: Who needs to act? What branch of government should get involved? What constitutional, legal, or political requirements must be

[4] See Hugh Heclo, "Issue Networks and the Executive Establishment," in Anthony King, ed., *The New American Political System* (American Enterprise Institute, 1978), chap. 3.

met? How specific or how general must the decision be? For example, should Congress pass a clean air act, or should some regulatory body like the Environmental Protection Agency be asked to hold hearings on the matter and come up with recommendations? Or should this matter be one for presidential leadership—requiring an executive order and major addresses to the public?

4. *Policy implementation*: Once it is adopted, how should the policy be carried out? How much should be spent where, and how? How will the process of administration affect the policy?

5. *Policy evaluation*: Is the policy working? How is the effectiveness or impact of the policy measured? Who evaluates the policy? What are the consequences of policy evaluation and congressional oversight? For example, are antipollution laws really improving air quality?

Policy making can occur in any branch of government, and it can be carried out by a series of political participants, not just lawmakers. Note, too, that policy making cannot be separated entirely from administration, and, as we saw in Chapter 17, that appointed public officials often have as much influence as elected officials. Policy making is influenced by the political, economic, and social values of the people participating in each of the policy stages just listed. Also, it is clearly influenced by interest groups of all kinds, especially by highly organized and well-financed groups and associations that can afford to maintain lobbyists in Washington, D.C.

Among the variety of approaches used to study policy making in the United States are the rational person model, the power elite model, the bureaucratic politics model, the policy systems model, and the incremental, or gradualist model. Although these are not the only explanations of how the system operates, examining them gives a useful perspective on how policy is shaped and made in the United States.

The Rational Person Model

Even though the rational person model is primarily a textbook abstraction, it is still a helpful model to analyze public policy. The rational person model is sometimes called public-choice theory, deductive theory, rational choice theory, or even an economic approach to policy decision making. Rational policy makers try to protect or maximize their own personal interests or what they think is in the public or collective interest. They may be trying to make a welfare program more efficient or to improve a military procurement process, for example. This could also be said of a rational group. Groups are out to protect their interests and advance those policies from which they think they or society will profit. The rational choice approach suggests a calculating strategy: Participants constantly ask how much they or their values will gain or lose from government action or inaction, and how much effort and time they should spend lobbying and building a constituency.

Faced with an issue, rational participants will first clarify their goals or objectives and rank them. They will then list all the important possible solutions and investigate the likely results of each. After considering each likely outcome, they then choose the policy whose consequences most closely match their goals.[5]

Rational decision making in the policy process often fails or achieves only moderate success—due to the inevitability of incomplete information and uncertainty in the process.

The Power Elite Model

The power elite approach generally interprets what happens in the policy arena as the product of the political influence of powerful economic interests. The idea is that we have a government of the rich, by the friends of the rich, and for the

[5] For a general introductory example, see Peter H. Aranson, *American Government: Strategy and Choice* (Winthrop, 1981). See also the journal *Public Choice*.

rich. If 5 percent of U.S. families control 30 percent of the wealth, it is because our public policies favor the wealthy. If poverty programs seldom succeed in achieving their objectives, it is because the wealthy interests in the nation prefer these programs to be more symbolic than real.

The power elite school holds that we should study government *inaction* as much as government action, because powerful business interests are often able to keep certain issues *off* the agenda of government. And these powerful interests generally do not want any kind of governmental interference in the economy unless they stand to gain from it. In short, the power elite school believes there is a "ruling class" in America and that its influence and power are based upon the national corporate economy and the institutions that economy nourishes. Congress, presidents, and regulatory agencies are generally viewed as serving the interests of the powerful, monied class.[6]

The power elite model, although often described as one that visualizes the rich being the powerful, is somewhat compatible with the concept that many conservatives have of the way things get done in the United States. They sometimes think of the power elite as being the big unions, the big media, the big bureaucracy, and others who, in alliance with the "Eastern Establishment," force upon common people programs and goals contrary to what the majority wish. This might be called a "populist-conservative" school; it has been represented in part by the telepreacher Reverend Pat Robertson of Virginia, and Paul Gann and the late Howard Jarvis of California, and others who are also persuaded that a "ruling class" determines how policies get made and administered.

Another analysis, sometimes confused with the power elite approach, is a Marxist model. Marxists argue that policy development and outcomes, especially for the working and poor classes, occur only as placating devices to lessen the likelihood of unrest and preserve the stability of a basically unfair system.[7]

Critics of the power elite approach say if researchers start with the assumption that elites account for policy change or lack of change, they are likely to find evidence to support it. But if they start with the assumption that the policy process is more complicated, they will find evidence of a more complicated and subtle set of influences.[8]

The Bureaucratic Politics Model

An older theory of American politics holds that our politics and public policies are the product of the struggle among competing interest groups. As groups gain and lose power, public policy changes in favor of those who are on top at the moment. But more recent scholars have concluded that this theory overstates the role of outside interest groups and underestimates the role of public bureaucracies. They now suggest that what needs to be studied is the relative power and political strategies of the large bureaucracies in Washington: What bureaucracy one belongs to will determine one's policy views. This approach contends that concern for larger budgets and expanding mission all affect the information a bureaucracy will present to a president and to Congress. These same factors will also affect the way policies are implemented.

[6] C. Wright Mills made the classic statement of this view in *The Power Elite* (Oxford University Press, 1956). For another look at elite influence, see Thomas R. Dye, *Who's Running America? The Conservative Years* (Prentice-Hall, 1986). See also John Manley, "Neo-Pluralism: A Class Analysis of Pluralism I and Pluralism II," *American Political Science Review* (June 1983), pp. 368–83.

[7] See, for example, some of the interpretation in Edward S. Greenberg, *The American Political System: A Radical Approach*, 4th ed. (Little, Brown, 1986), and Robert Heilbroner, *Marxism: For and Against* (Norton, 1980).

[8] A study that skillfully examines a range of complicated questions about power relationships is John Gavanta, *Power and Powerlessness* (University of Illinois Press, 1980).

Adherents of this view recommend that students of public policy pay close attention to the way the bureaucracy functions and the way bureaucrats become involved in the various stages of the policy-making process.

The Policy Systems Model

A more ambitious yet more general approach is offered by those who want to place all the factors and all the stages of the process into a systems framework. They claim that everything is interrelated and that a full understanding of how policies are made or changed can come only from a comprehensive look at these relationships. Borrowing from engineering and biological models, these researchers examine the inputs of the policy system and stress the way the process translates inputs into outputs, and then how the outputs—laws—get converted into policy outcomes, or improvements in people's lives. The diagram on page 429 conveys much of the policy systems model. Note that the feedback loop that links policy outcomes with the other aspects of the system implies that policy results, and how the public reacts to the results, will in turn affect other policies.

The Incrementalist Model

Incrementalism is an approach suggesting that problems can be solved only, or best, through small changes or adjustments. Does incrementalism mean there is no single, right, comprehensive answer to a problem? No. The incrementalist system can sometimes allow for a single answer, but it does require that that answer be arrived at gradually.

Unlike the rational person model, the incrementalist model suggests that only some alternatives are examined. More attention is devoted to seeking mutual agreement about what small steps can be taken than to finding a single, comprehensive answer. Our system of separation of powers and dispersed authority promotes piecemeal policy change. Planning comprehensively is difficult in a system such as ours, which is glued together with alliance politics, majorities of the moment, and constant compromising.

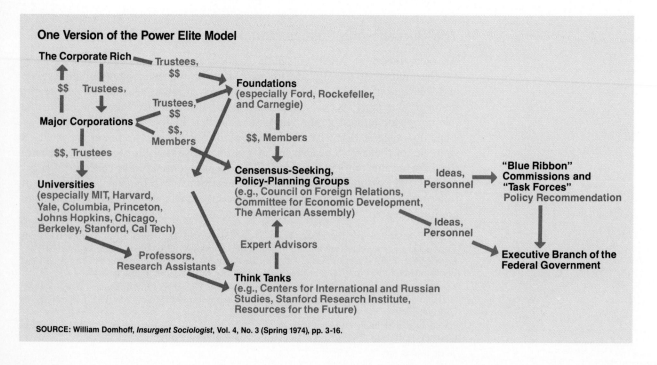

One Version of the Power Elite Model

SOURCE: William Domhoff, *Insurgent Sociologist*, Vol. 4, No. 3 (Spring 1974), pp. 3-16.

One Version of the Policy Systems Model

Inputs	Political Process	Policy Outputs	Policy Outcomes
Economic Resources Public Opinion Crises	Legislative Hearings and Debates Presidential Study Groups Court Deliberations Party Conventions Elections Interest Groups' Lobbying	Laws Passed Court Decisions Appropriations Regulations Issued Tax-Code Changes Troops Deployed	More Employment Better Education Cleaner Air Safer Cars A Fairer Justice System More Security

Feedback and Interaction Loop

(How people evaluate policy outcomes continues to affect other policies and the political process. Reactions to policy outcomes become inputs about whether the policy should be revised, extended, retained, or discontinued.)

Thinking comprehensively, however, is not impossible in our system. The problem is that in order to get something done and enforced, many different and often differing people must reach a consensus—with much compromising and bargaining. We have to get by so many potential veto groups that the resulting policy proposals are almost always different from what the sponsors desired.

Policy makers bend over backward to design programs that cultivate interest-group support and neutralize possible opponents. This results, not surprisingly, in watered-down objectives and laws that are extremely general and vague. To be sure, laws are often complex and detailed; yet they are deliberately written to permit a diversity of interpretations.

Defenders of the incrementalist model suggest that participants backing a new policy innovation commonly give up on it too soon, measure gains only in the short run, or become discouraged prematurely. They caution: Do not be tempted by tactics that are only momentarily gratifying, but are self-destructive in the longer run. With a more gradualist perspective about how the policy-change process works, we should "come to value not only those persons and events that rock the boat, that increase the pressures upon decision-makers to act, but also those persons who think deeply about problems, who search for and invent alternatives, and who keep alternative solutions alive and available to decision-makers."[9] So, in addition to the impatient and sometimes unreasonable cranks *who call attention* to the need for change, it is these policy brokers, adaptors, incubators, and issue entrepreneurs whose energy and ingenuity lay the groundwork for elected officials to bring about needed policy change.

In a democracy political leaders are not likely to be big risk takers, or to call on the people to sacrifice today in order to avoid some problem that may arise decades from now. We often do not do much about a trade-deficit crisis until millions of Americans have lost their jobs; nor do we do much about air pollution until people start coughing, choking, and dying of cancer.

In recent years we have begun to recognize that direct governmental intervention in the form of a command and control approach is not always the only or

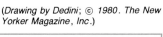

(*Drawing by Dedini*; © 1980. The New Yorker Magazine, Inc.)

[9] Nelson W. Polsby, *Political Innovation in America: The Politics of Policy Initiation* (Yale University Press, 1984), p. 174.

429

"Should we live miserably or die comfortably?" (*By permission of Bill Mauldin and Wil-Jo Associates, Inc.*)

best way to intervene, and that the market approach may often be more effective. To control pollution, for example, either the Environmental Protection Agency can enforce regulations for hundreds of thousands of different businesses, or we can make adjustments in the tax system to give industries an economic incentive to avoid pollution.

Transferring authority to states and localities also encourages incrementalism. With such strategies Washington officials are in effect saying: "Let local elites decide what is proper policy in their locality. Let us not interfere." Some people argue, and they are partly correct, that efficiency and a smaller federal bureaucracy should be a prime concern. But decentralization and "disaggregation" (dividing up policy making into fragmented, functional units) are also a means of getting Congress and federal bureaucrats to give up their power over federal funds. Thus, local policy making is still another way for Washington officials to make people happy. Yet it is often at the expense of national objectives, comprehensive planning, and swift action.

Policy-making processes in democratic countries are, except in some matters of foreign relations, rarely insulated from local politics. Our party system and popular values concentrate power at the state and local levels. Numerous case studies document how the structural arrangements of our government are better suited to protect the local status quo than to force unpopular controls on local governments. Even when the national government is unified in its views, localities are often able to delay or modify federal policies by local administrative manipulations.

Most of the models just outlined have some evidence to back them up, but it seems obvious that no single approach will explain everything. By and large, policies are shaped by a combination of events, the availability of resources, past experience, and the ideas of concerned public officials and activist citizens. Elections, public opinion, and competition among groups and bureaucracies, as well as struggles among the branches of government, all influence the way policies are defined and settled. We now turn to a more detailed examination of what takes place in some of the key stages of the policy-making process.

POLICY FORMULATION

Policy is certainly not formed in a vacuum. Organized interests representing varied points of view press claims and counterclaims. Some groups and persons clearly enjoy more access, more opportunities to get their cases heard, and more possibilities for vetoing measures than others. Still, we cannot explain with certainty why some issues become national controversies and others do not.[10]

According to some critics: "The most significant fact about the distribution of power in America is not who makes such decisions as are made, but rather how many matters of the greatest social importance are not the objects of anyone's decision at all."[11] Matters of great importance to some people sometimes do not even get on the public agenda.

However, government inactivity in some area does not mean the government is without a policy in that area: *Inaction is still a policy*. Inattention to an issue can be as important as decisive action. Indifference to racial or sexual discrimination clearly was policy—very important policy for those affected by it. A former White

[10] See, for example, T. R. Reid, *Congressional Odyssey: The Saga of a Senate Bill* (W. H. Freeman, 1980).

[11] Robert Paul Wolff, *The Poverty of Liberalism* (Beacon Press, 1968), p. 118. See also M. A. Crensen, *The Un-Politics of Air Pollution* (Johns Hopkins Press, 1971), and Peter Bachrach and Morton S. Baratz, "Decisions and Nondecisions: An Analytical Framework," *American Political Science Review* (September 1963), pp. 632–42.

House domestic adviser (currently a U.S. senator from New York), Daniel P. Moynihan, once called for a policy of "benign neglect" toward minority problems, not, presumably, because he was indifferent to racial discrimination but because he thought less governmental assertiveness was a better way to handle discrimination. In short, everything has political consequences—including doing nothing.

Shared Leadership

Inaction by some policy makers often forces an issue to another part of the political system. All branches of the national government—as well as the bureaucracy, media, and interest groups—seem to take turns initiating policy changes: The Supreme Court's holding in *Brown* v. *Board of Education* (1954) is a classic example of a landmark civil rights policy decision with implications for the other components of the political system. This court decision, itself the result of a variety of economic, social, and political changes in the country, in turn triggered actions and reactions that ricocheted back on the Court.

Separation of powers usually ensures that when things get clogged in one part of the system, a safety valve can be found elsewhere—sometimes in the courts, sometimes in a president, sometimes in regulatory agencies. Groups pressing for policy changes will seek to exert influence where they are most likely to succeed. People with large sums of money to contribute to political campaigns are more likely to have influence with Congress and the presidency than with the courts. Those lacking substantial funds and a political base may find it more effective to resort to litigation. The Legal Defense and Education Fund, Inc., for example, has won numerous cases in its long-term efforts to improve the legal protection of blacks. Litigation is also a weapon in the arsenal of consumer and community groups working for reform today. It does, however, require at least some money.

Just as Congress delegates extensive legislative power to the president, the chief executive delegates policy-making power to administrators. Obviously, a secretary of state can have a distinct influence on policy, as can other department heads and bureau, division, and section chiefs. In a sense, there is no level in the administrative hierarchy at which discretion ends. At any time the most routine matter may be called to the public's attention by a newspaper columnist or a member of Congress. The matter will then be given consideration by a bureau or department chief—perhaps even by the White House. In short, thousands of people throughout the government (and millions more outside, such as editors, lobbyists, and activist citizens) exert direct pressure on legislators, legislation, and policy.

The extent to which presidents wield legislative power turns not only on their formal constitutional powers but also on their political powers. How good is their timing? How active and articulate are their lieutenants—their cabinet members and key agency heads? How close are their relations with congressional leaders? Can they mobilize public opinion? Does their influence reach into states and districts throughout the country? Do their parties control Congress? Presidents' effectiveness turns also on their professional reputations as politicians. Their words and actions are closely watched. Do they reward those who help them and punish those who do not? How well do they bargain with other power centers? Are they on top of the struggle for power, submerged in it, or remote from it? Presidents' political skill and political power are interrelated. Their influence over others derives from what the latter think of them and their power.[12]

The Issue-Attention Cycle

The public's policy problem attention span is short. Shifting public moods and the need for publicity encourage elected officials to adopt new policies rather than

Understanding AIDS

A Message From The Surgeon General

This brochure has been sent to you by the Government of the United States. In preparing it, we have consulted with the top health experts in the country.

I feel it is important that you have the best information now available for fighting the AIDS virus, a health problem that the President has called "Public Enemy Number One."

Stopping AIDS is up to you, your family and your loved ones.

Some of the issues involved in this brochure may not be things you are used to discussing openly. I can easily understand that. But now you must discuss them. We all must know about AIDS. Read this brochure and talk about it with those you love. Get involved. Many schools, churches, synagogues, and community groups offer AIDS education activities.

I encourage you to practice responsible behavior based on understanding and strong personal values. This is what you can do to stop AIDS.

C. Everett Koop, M.D., Sc.D.
Surgeon General

Este folleto sobre el SIDA se publica en Español.
Para solicitar una copia, llame al 1-800-344-SIDA.

U.S. Department of Health
& Human Services
Public Health Service
Centers for Disease Control
P.O. Box 6003
Rockville, MD 20850

Official Business

BULK RATE
CARRIER ROUTE PRESORT
POSTAGE & FEES PAID
PHS/CDC
Permit No. G-284

POSTAL CUSTOMER

HHS Publication No. (CDC) HHS-88-8404. Reproduction of the contents of this brochure is encouraged.

Daniel P. Moynihan, former adviser to Presidents Kennedy, Johnson, and Nixon, is now a U.S. senator from New York. (*Owen Franken/Sygma*)

---

[12] Richard E. Neustadt, *Presidential Power*, rev. ed. (Wiley, 1980), chap. 3. See also Bert Rockman, *The Leadership Question* (Praeger, 1984).

restructure old ones. Rallying support for a new program is easier than cutting back ongoing programs. Too many beneficiaries—those who receive money from the programs and those who administer the programs—will fight any changes in programs already on the books. Thus, reworking or even rethinking old programs becomes subordinate to taking what might be called an "add-on" approach to policy making. In other words: "Each of these new problems suddenly leaps into prominence, remains there for a short time, and then—though still largely unresolved—generally fades from the center of public attention."[13] Public boredom often sets in when large numbers of people realize the cost of solving a particular problem would be high indeed. (Boredom may be the most underrated force in history.)

Policy makers, especially those in a democracy, do not like to make anybody mad if they can help it. They would rather enlarge the size of the national economic pie and give new groups funds than redistribute what is currently there.[14] Like fathers and mothers—and university administrators—anybody who has the responsibility for allocating scarce resources would rather make everybody happy than take an allowance back from one child and give it to another, or take funds from one university department and redistribute them to another. If a group that is presently getting "the short end of the stick" lacks political clout, it is likely *not* to get its fair share of the economic goods of the society.

POLICY IMPLEMENTATION

Once a policy is adopted, how should it be carried out? Even if we know what to do, can get political leaders to agree that it must be done, and can devise an appropriate strategy for doing it, we may still not be able to ensure that the strategy is implemented.[15] After the president has signed a bill into law or a regulatory agency has made its rules, the government must act. Money must be spent and rules enforced if goals are to be met.

Although the other parts of the policy process are well publicized, implementation is often hidden within the vast bureaucracy. A great number of federal programs fail to accomplish their desired goals because of problems that show up during the implementation phase. Kennedy economic-reform programs in Latin America, Johnson's Model Cities program, Nixon's and Ford's crime-control programs, Carter's human-rights initiatives in foreign policy, and Reagan's tax cuts, which were supposed to have the effect eventually of balancing the budget, all involved problems that were not fully understood until well after the programs had been put into operation. When such failures occur, it is relatively easy to blame the original legislation rather than examine what happened after the bill became law. Of course, poorly written legislation and badly conceived policy yield poor results. But policy analysts have begun to realize that even the best legislation can fail because of problems encountered during implementation.[16] Sometimes these problems lead to the outright failure

U.S. Senate committee hearing.
(*Ellis Herwig/Taurus*)

[13] Anthony Downs, "Up and Down with Ecology—The Issue-Attention Cycle," *The Public Interest* (Summer 1972), p. 38. But see also B. Guy Peters and Brian W. Hogwood, "In Search of the Issue-Attention Cycle," *Journal of Politics* (February 1985), pp. 238–53, which clarifies and expands on Downs's classic essay.

[14] For a discussion of some of the implications of interest-group and logrolling special claims, see Mancur Olson, *The Rise and Decline of Nations* (Yale University Press, 1982).

[15] See Eugene Bardach, *The Implementation Game: What Happens after a Bill Becomes a Law* (MIT Press, 1977).

[16] Many political scientists and economists who study policy implementation publish their articles and findings in the following quarterly publications: *The Public Interest*, *Policy Sciences*, and *The Journal of Policy Analysis and Management*. The Brookings Institution and the American Enterprise Institute for Public Policy Research, nonprofit, nongovernmental research organizations located in Washington, D.C., publish books and reports on policy. See also Malcolm L. Goggin, "The 'Too Few Costs/Too Many Variables' Problem in Implementation Research," *Western Political Quarterly* (June 1986), pp. 328–43.

of a program, but more often they mean excessive delay, watered down goals, or costs far above those originally expected.

The Difficulty with Implementing Federal Policies

The coalition of supporters that comes together to get a bill through Congress often does not stay together after the bill has been enacted. Further, Congress often passes ambiguous legislation that conceals serious policy differences. Rather than set clear goals, Congress—reflecting differences among the supporters of the policies—sets general or vague goals, and then passes on the responsibility for interpretation to the bureaucrats. Bureaucrats get the blame, but they are merely trying to carry out deliberately unclear policies, and they must act in a political atmosphere of conflict and competing groups.

Consider civil rights legislation, for example. Often the differences among women's groups, black groups, Hispanic groups, employer groups, and trade unions are momentarily resolved and a bill becomes law. But after the bill has been enacted, the coalition falls apart, and the resulting pressures are felt on the agencies trying to implement the policies. Conflicts arise and increase. Employers insist, for example, that the agencies' regulations are unrealistic and interfere with their rights; women's groups argue that the agencies are failing to enforce the law vigorously; black groups claim that the agencies favor the women's groups but ignore the wishes of the blacks, and so on. The more controversial the issue, the greater the chance of delay, as powerful interest groups clash over a program and force bureaucrats charged with implementation to move cautiously.

The implementation process involves a long chain of decision points that must be cleared before a program can be successfully carried out. At each decision point is a public official or community leader who has the power to advance—or delay—the program. The more decision points a program needs to clear, the greater the chance of failure or delay.[17] Special problems result if the successful implementation of a national program depends on the cooperation of state and local officials. One state or community may be eager to help; another may be opposed to a program and try to stop it.

Clearly, policy makers should consider the problems of implementation when they propose legislative solutions to national problems. One technique is to design policies and programs that can withstand buffeting by a constantly shifting set of political and social pressures. Another is to have public officials or consultants of some kind ready to serve as "fixers" to repair damage as it is detected. Still another plan is to write legislation that does not depend for its success on persuading people to help with it. For example, changes in the tax code are sometimes favored over complex public jobs programs by those seeking to stimulate the economy. In one case the apparatus for accomplishing a goal is already in place (the tax structure); in the other a large new administrative structure would have to be established, staffed, and supervised.

Policy Evaluation

Is the policy working? As noted, the adoption of a policy is only the beginning of the process. After Congress passes a law and the president signs it, implementation takes place. But what happens next? Who decides whether it is working or not? The answer—or so it often seems—is everybody and nobody.

Program supporters and administrators tend to exaggerate the success of their

(*Drawing by Richter*; © 1988. *The New Yorker Magazine, Inc.*)

Ralph Nader, the noted consumer advocate in America. His testimony before Congress, books and study reports have often influenced the debate on consumer and environmental protection issues. (*Rick Bloom*)

---

[17] Jeffrey Pressman and Aaron Wildavsky, *Implementation* (University of California Press, 1973). Other studies of policy execution include George C. Edwards, III, *Implementing Public Policy* (Congressional Quarterly Press, 1980), and Robert T. Nakamura and Frank Smallwood, *The Politics of Policy Implementation* (St. Martin's Press, 1980).

favorite programs in order to justify the funds allocated to them. Bureaus and agencies often cast their proposals so as to persuade, not to evaluate. Program "evaluation" reports coming into the White House or Congress from the bureaucracy have long been suspect. In this sense, evaluation is never entirely nonpolitical: It will be used by one party or branch of government against another. Evaluation will also be used by one department or agency against another.[18] Some bureaus become so involved with activities that enhance their prestige that they neglect the work for which they were created. Also, delays and deficiencies in evaluation may occur because an agency wants to hide the real cost of its operations. Still, it is difficult and expensive to develop outcome or impact measures. It is hard to relate expenditures to outcomes, or to be precise about what has caused social change, even if change can be noticed or measured. The problem is one of social measurement.

Political and social scientists have turned their attention to the product side of public policy. Instead of being concerned only with what affects government, or with what goes on inside government, they are paying attention to what social or economic change comes out of a policy. The test of a program is not input but *outcome*: "It is interesting, and at times important, to know how much money is spent on schools in a particular neighborhood or city. But the crucial question is how much do the children learn. Programs are for people, not for bureaucracies."[19]

Why have Congress and the White House not insisted on more systematic planning and evaluation? Short-term political incentives seem to propel their energies in the opposite direction: *Pass now, plan later!* Presidents, especially, are always eager for fast results. They say they were elected not to study policies but to get things done and to put ideas into operation. Analysis, testing, small-scale experiments, and systematic reappraisal of ongoing programs are sometimes shoved aside. As Congress has been eclipsed by the executive in more and more policy-formulation areas, there has been a move to strengthen it as a focus for **program oversight**. However, even its staunchest defenders readily admit Congress performs this responsibility with only modest success.

The Legislative Reorganization Act of 1946 assigned to each standing committee of Congress the responsibility to "exercise continuous watchfulness" over how agencies administer laws. Oversight is neither constant nor systematic, however. Comprehensive oversight of all federal programs would demand all the time of the staff and members of Congress. Members of Congress exercise the oversight function when they are particularly upset with the way they are being treated by executive branch officials and when it serves their constituents in a direct way. Certain standing committees have created specific oversight subcommittees, but it is unclear whether such subcommittees make any difference in the quality of policy making.

Another way in which evaluation takes place is through presidential commissions. Cabinet member appointed commissions are also common. Such diverse issues and problems as the NASA Challenger explosion, pornography, educational excellence, trade imbalances, social security, government waste, and Pentagon procurement methods have all been the subject of national commissions in recent years. The Presidential Commission on the Space Shuttle Challenger Accident and the Grace Commission on government waste, whose official title was the President's Private Sector Survey on Cost Control, are two of the better known such evaluation panels.

Evaluating programs, however, is not primarily a technical problem, but a political one. Of course, everyone will agree that something is wrong with Defense Department procurement when the cost of buying a weapons system is much more than Congress anticipated. But many evaluations involve choices between costs and benefits, a problem for which there is no expert answer. Is the welfare program

"Remember, son, if at first you don't succeed, re-evaluate the situation, draw up various hypotheses for your failure, choose reasonable corrective measures, and try, try again." (Copyright © 1974. Saturday Review Magazine Co. Reprinted by permission)

William Rogers headed NASA shuttle commission investigating the Challenger disaster. (G. Mathieson/ Sygma)

[18] Aaron Wildavsky, *Speaking Truth to Power: The Art and Craft of Policy Analysis* (Little, Brown, 1979), chap. 9.

[19] Daniel P. Moynihan, "Policy vs. Program in the '70s," *The Public Interest* (Summer 1970), p. 100.

worth the expenditure? Should we abolish subsidies to farmers? Has the auto emission-control program produced good or bad results in the nation? Are grants for students to attend medical schools worthwhile? No experts can tell us whether or not these programs are "successful," because the answers depend, in part, on political values. This is why we rely on the democratic system, on politicians chosen by popular vote, and why policy making and implementation are so complex and frustrating.

IDEOLOGY AND PUBLIC POLICY

Debates over what is "right" public policy seldom occur in a completely value-free context. Such debates are at least partially shaped by a person's **ideology**—that is, a person's set of attitudes and beliefs about freedom and equality, humankind, and the desired role of the state and government. An ideology is a simplified picture of the world. Phrased yet another way, an ideology refers to a somewhat integrated belief system that has a "world view," an image of the relationship of people to their government and of how power should be used in society.

Some students of American politics say most of us cannot be classified as ideologues. Our attitudes about politicians and public policies are not held in a highly systematic fashion. A voter may want increased spending for defense, but vote for the party that is for reducing defense spending, because he or she has always voted for that party. Or a person may be for the adoption of the **Equal Rights Amendment** and in favor of government-financed abortions but still vote for Ronald Reagan. Most people's consistency among various attitudes and opinions is relatively low: Most people, most of the time view political issues as isolated matters and do not apply a general standard of performance in evaluating parties and candidates. Indeed, most citizens have difficulty relating what happens in one policy situation to what happens in another. This problem becomes worse as government gets into more and more policy areas. Hence, people, not surprisingly, have difficulty finding candidates who reflect their preferences across a range of issues.

The absence of widespread, hardened ideologies in the United States makes for markedly different kinds of politics and policy-making processes than in many European or third-world nations. Our policy making is characterized more by coalitions of the moment than by fixed alignments pitting one set of warring ideologues against another. And our politics are more a politics of moderation and accommodation than a prolonged and strained battle between two, three, or more competing philosophies of government. Elsewhere—as in countries where a strong communist or Christian-Democratic party exists—things are different.

By no means, however, does this mean that policies or ideas are not taken into account in our politics. As a result of better and more education and better and more sources of information about political activities, we have witnessed a slight increase in ideological thinking and issue voting. Such issues as affirmative action, welfare assistance programs, the Supreme Court's abortion rulings, and the Strategic Defense Initiation (Star Wars) have aroused countless persons who previously were relatively passive about politics and political ideas. Evidently, a certain kind of modified ideology is playing an important role in our system.

Two major—but rather broad and hazy—schools of political thinking dominate American politics: *liberalism* and *conservatism*. However, two lesser—but more defined—schools of thought, *socialism* and *libertarianism*, also help define the spectrum of ideology in America.

Liberalism

In the seventeenth and eighteenth centuries, classical liberals fought to minimize the role of government. They were stressing individual rights and perceived govern-

---

Political Labels: Do They Help or Hurt?

Politicians are always concerned about being labeled. Sometimes they joke about being "pragmatic idealists." Humorists suggest we may be in need of a "Truth in Political Labeling Act."

A national survey asked whether a given label would make a person think better or worse of a public figure. The poll showed that "liberal" is one of the least helpful labels, whereas "conservative" or "progressive" would help. Here are the results of the poll:

Liberal:
    Better 15%
    Worse 17

Moderate:
    Better 21%
    Worse 13

Conservative:
    Better 27%
    Worse 13

Populist:
    Better   6%
    Worse 21

Progressive:
    Better 37%
    Worse   7

N = 1659 adults.

Source: The New York Times/CBS Poll (November, 1985).

ments as the primary threat to these rights and liberties. Thus, they favored a small government and sought ample guarantees of protection from governmental harrassment.

The emphasis on individualism has remained constant; it is the perception of government that has changed. Nowadays, proponents of **liberalism** view government as protecting individuals from being abused by a variety of nongovernmental forces (market vagaries, business decisions, and so on).

In its modern American usage, liberalism also refers to a belief in the positive uses of government to bring about justice and equality of opportunity. Modern-day liberals wish to preserve the rights of the individual and the right to own private property, but they are very willing to have the government intervene in the economy to remedy the defects of capitalism and a market economy. Contemporary American liberalism has its roots in Franklin Roosevelt's New Deal programs, designed to aid the poor and to protect people against the possibilities of unemployment, inadequate or deficient medical assistance, and inadequate or deficient housing and education. Liberals believe in affirmative action programs and in progressive taxation measures and regulatory efforts that help protect the average worker's health and safety. American liberals have also favored the right of unions to organize as well as to strike.

On a more philosophical level, liberals generally believe in the near-perfectability of humans, the possibility of progress. They believe things can be made to work, that the future will be better, that obstacles can be overcome. This positive set of beliefs may explain some of their willingness to also believe in the potential benefits of governmental action, a willingness to alter or even to negate the old Jeffersonian notion that "government governs best when it governs least." Liberals contend that the character of modern technology and the side effects of industrialization cry out for at least limited governmental programs to offset the loss of liberties suffered by the less well-to-do and the weak. Liberals frequently stress the need for a politics of compassion, a politics of affirmative government.

During the revival of conservative thought and electoral success in the 1980s, some moderate liberals, sometimes called "neoliberals," acknowledged they needed not only to come up with some new ideas but perhaps also to abandon some old prejudices. Charles Peters, a self-proclaimed neoliberal who is editor of the *Washington Monthly*, said he and his friends had taken a hard look at traditional liberalism and had founded it wanting: "We still believe in liberty and justice and a fair chance for all, in mercy for the afflicted and help for the down and out. But we no longer automatically favor unions and big government or oppose the military and big business. Indeed, in our search for solutions that work, we have come to distrust all automatic responses, liberal or conservative."[20]

Although Senator Gary Hart has perhaps been the most published neoliberal in the late 1980s, Senator Bill Bradley, Representative Richard Gephardt, and former Governors Charles Robb and Bruce Babbitt also frequently spoke out on such issues as tax reform, military preparedness, increasing reliance on the market system, and improving leadership at the state and local levels of government.[21]

Critics of liberalism, both old and new, say it still places too much reliance on government bureaucrats. They say liberalism may sound good, but its costs are greater than its benefits. Liberalism taken too far leads to a welfare state and a

"Someone once labelled me a reactionary, and it stuck." (*Drawing by Weber;* © *The New Yorker Magazine, Inc.*)

Congressional leaders answer questions about tax reform proposals. (*UPI/Bettmann Newsphotos*)

[20] Charles Peters and Philip Keisling, eds., *A New Road for America: The Neoliberal Movement* (University Press of America, 1984), p. 189. See also the favorable portrait of neoliberals by Randall Rothenberg, *The Neoliberals: Creating the New American Politics* (Simon and Schuster, 1984). For a review essay on these books and neoliberal thinking, see Victor Ferkiss, "Neoliberalism: How New? How Liberal? How Significant?" *Western Political Quarterly* (March 1986), pp. 165–79.

[21] See Gary Hart, *The New Democracy* (Quill, 1984); Bill Bradley, *The Fair Tax* (Pocket, 1984); and Gary Hart and William Lind, *American Can Win: The Case for Military Reform* (Adler and Adler, 1986).

Another Way of Looking at Ideology and Public Policy

		Extent of Policy Change	
		Incremental*	Major
Nature of Policy Change	**Progressive Redistribution****	Liberalism	Socialism
	Nonredistributive	Conservativism	Libertarianism

*Incremental here refers to small steps in policy change.
**Redistribution refers to altering opportunities and wealth in a society from the advantaged to the disadvantaged.

Neoconservatives: Who Are They and What Do They Favor?

Those who call themselves neoconservatives often prefer to be called pragmatic conservatives. They say they want to keep or enact programs that work or are truly necessary, and reject the rest. Neoconservatives have given up on New Deal and Great Society liberalism, which might lead to a paternalistic state. Though willing to interfere with the market for overriding social purposes, neoconservatives prefer to do so by "rigging" the market, or even creating new markets, rather than by increasing bureaucratic and central government controls.

Critics of neoconservatism view it as essentially a revitalization of anti-communist and anti-populist sentiments. They say the neoconservative strategy calls for: the restoration of governmental authority to protect us from threats to national security, increased reliance on tradition and religion as part of our culture, and a willingness to live with social injustice if necessary to foster economic growth.

Plainly, the use of this label raises as many questions as it solves. Writings with a neoconservative viewpoint can be found in *Commentary*, *The Public Interest*, and also often on the editorial page of the *Wall Street Journal*. For a general discussion of this new mood, see Peter Steinfels, *The Neoconservatives* (Simon and Schuster, 1979). For a general text from this perspective, see Richard T. Saeger, *American Government and Politics: A Neoconservative Approach* (Scott, Foresman, 1982).

dependence on a paternalistic government that is against American notions of efficiency and productivity. When we get too much government, government tends to start dictating to us, and then our rights and liberties are jeopardized. Moreover, too many governmental controls or regulations and too much taxation undermine the self-help or self-reliance ethic in our society. Critics of traditional liberalism, including the "neoliberals," favor doing things as much as possible in the private sector and according to the market economy. And they would revitalize wherever possible our nongovernmental and volunteer sectors. Critics of the neoliberals from the left accuse them of merely talking and acting like Republicans.

Conservatism

In America **conservatism** has its roots in the political thinking of John Adams and many of his contemporaries. They believed in limited government and encouraged individual excellence and personal achievement. Private property rights and belief in free enterprise have been cardinal attributes of contemporary conservatism. In contrast to liberals, conservatives want to do as much as possible to keep government small, except in the area of national defense.[22]

Most conservatives opposed New Deal programs and the War on Poverty in the 1960s, and they have seldom favored aggressive civil rights and affirmative action programs. Much of this, they say, could be done by charities or by encouraging citizens to be more tolerant. Conservatives place substantial faith in the private sector, and they consider social justice to be essentially an economic question. Conservatives dislike the tendency to turn to the national government for solutions to societal problems. Government social activism, they say, has been highly inflationary and counterproductive. Conservatives also prize stability: stability of the dollar, stability in international affairs, and political and economic stability.

Critics of conservatism from the left say it ignores the hardships of those not born into wealth or with considerable talents. Critics on the right say that conservatives have too often gone along with the liberals and have allowed government to grow too much. Critics on the right also attack the contradiction in conservatism that encourages the buildup of huge defense budgets and the CIA. The so-called "New Right" conservatives, especially concerned with abortion, prayer in schools, and lifestyle matters, put intense pressure on Reagan on such social issues.

Socialism

Socialism is an economic and governmental system based on public ownership of the means of production and exchange. Karl Marx once described socialism as a

[22] For discussions of some of these ideals and of how they are often compromised by their own political spokespersons, see David Stockman, *The Triumph of Politics* (Harper & Row, 1986).

A person can hold a number of views that are not necessarily ideologically consistent. For example, a person may favor gun control, a position held by many liberals. The same person might also favor a strong military and occasional military intervention abroad, a position held by conservatives who believe in a strong nation-state and a strengthened U.S. role in world affairs. Authoritarianism implies a belief in hierarchy and in strong central leadership by the government. The other terms used here are discussed in the text. Can some people be so highly consistent that all, or nearly all, of their views and policy preferences are located in one quadrant? Yes, but these people are probably the exception. Most Americans have no difficulty holding a variety of views that are seemingly contradictory—along the dimensions indicated in this diagram. Examine your own views and try to locate yourself ideologically.

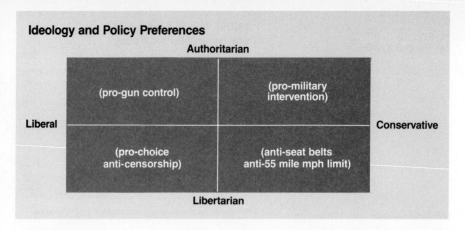

Ideology and Policy Preferences

transitional stage of society between capitalism and communism. In a capitalist system the means of production and most of the property are privately owned, whereas in a communist or socialist system the property is "owned" by the state in common for all the people. In the ultimate socialist country justice is achieved by having participants determine their own needs and take what is appropriate from the common product of society. Marx's dictum was: "From each according to his ability, to each according to his needs."

American socialists—of whom there are probably a few million—favor a greatly expanded role for the government. They would nationalize certain industries. They would institute a public jobs program so that all who want work would be put to work. They would change the tax system to place a much steeper tax burden on the wealthy and eliminate all tax preferences for the rich. In short, American socialists favor policies to help the underdog and the common person by means of government redistribution programs. They also favor economic justice and stepped-up efforts toward greater equality over property rights. American socialists would drastically cut defense spending as well.[23]

Critics of socialism here say the last thing we need is more governmental interference in the economy. Do we want more operations like the U.S. Postal Service? They complain that there are already few incentives for efficiency in our bureaucracies. Further, socialism places too much faith in the state at the expense of individual rights and liberties. They generally add that the right to own private property and skepticism toward centralized government are key factors that have made America great—factors that would be vastly less important in a socialist scheme of things.

Libertarianism

Libertarianism is an ideology that cherishes individual liberty and insists on a sharply limited state and government. It carries some overtones of anarchism, of the English liberalism of the past, and of a 1930-style conservatism. A Libertarian party has gained a following in recent years, especially among those who feel that both liberals and conservatives lack consistency in their attitude toward the power of the national government. The libertarians preach opposition to government and just about all its programs. They favor massive cuts in government spending, an end to the FBI and CIA and most regulatory commissions, a minimal defense establishment (one that would defend America only if we were directly attacked), and complete disengagement of American troops from overseas missions. Libertarians favor eliminating not only welfare programs, but also programs that subsidize business, farmers, and

[23] Irving Howe, *Socialism and America* (Harcourt, 1985); and Michael Harrington, *Taking Sides* (Holt, Rinehart & Winston, 1985).

the rich. They opposed government-backed guaranteed loans for Chrysler and would turn the functions of the Postal Service over to private companies. Unlike most conservatives, libertarians would repeal laws regulating personal morality, such as antiprostitution or antimarijuana laws.

In 1980 and again in 1984 a Libertarian party candidate for president was on the ballot in all fifty states (he won about 1 percent of the vote in 1980). A few books on libertarianism have become best sellers.[24] But critics dismiss libertarianism as hopelessly naive, and as ignoring the failure of the market and the at least occasional need for certain public goods and services. Critics on the left say advocates of libertarianism would indeed return us to the good old days—but it would be more like the days of serfdom.

[24] See, for example, Robert Ringer, *Restoring the American Dream* (QED, 1979), and Ed Clark, *A New Beginning* (Caroline House, 1980).

SUMMARY

1. Public policy is the *substance* of what government does. It is a process. Public policy is never made in any fixed or final way, but is always in the process of being made. Public policy is often expressed only in part by a law, then by a court decision interpreting that law, then by a law modifying the court decision, then by an agency regulation implementing that law, then by a presidential executive order, and then by another law of Congress, and so on.

2. Policy making in the United States is neither simple nor tidy. There is not a "top down" structure of authority, so policy is not made "on high." Rather, policy takes form gradually, and large numbers of persons help to formulate a new response to a public problem. Policies change slowly, reflecting gradual changes in public opinion. Mass public-opinion change is often the consequence of campaigns by political, professional, and scientific elites to alter the ways in which people define problems and policy options. Each shift in policy is a conscious action, as reflected in a new election, law, or court decision.

3. Policy outcomes are the consequences for society, the "so-what" or "bottom line" of what the government is doing

and how it affects citizens. Policy making can be studied through five stages—the identification of a problem, the formulation of solutions, the adoption or enactment of a new policy response, the implementation or application of the policy, and the evaluation of the policy.

4. Our policy-making processes permit large numbers of groups and individuals to battle both to protect their own private interests and to enhance the public interest. Our political system, like all large systems, is weighted in favor of the status quo and against swift or sweeping change. But those who know better ways of doing things and are willing to take part in the pulling and hauling of the policy-making process can make a difference. Knowledge, political skills, and the ability to build coalitions of like-minded supporters and to attract extensive press coverage are preconditions for changing public policy.

5. Making public policy cannot be easily described in the abstract. How policies change depends very much on what kinds of policies are being discussed and who and how many persons they affect. The five chapters that follow describe and analyze foreign, military, economic, regulatory, and subsidy and entitlements policies.

FURTHER READING

CARL P. CHELF. *Public Policymaking in America* (Scott, Foresman, 1982).

GEORGE C. EDWARDS, III. *Implementing Public Policy* (Congressional Quarterly Press, 1980).

LARRY GERSTON. *Making Public Policy: From Conflict to Resolution* (Scott, Foresman, 1983).

JOHN W. KINGDON. *Agendas, Alternatives and Public Policies* (Little, Brown, 1984).

CHARLES E. LINDBLOM. *The Policy-Making Process*, 2nd ed. (Prentice-Hall, 1980).

ROBERT T. NAKAMURA and FRANK SMALLWOOD. *The Politics of Policy Implementation* (St. Martin's Press, 1980).

RICHARD E. NEUSTADT and ERNEST R. MAY. *Thinking In Time: The Uses of History for Decision Makers* (Free Press, 1987).

MANCUR OLSON. *The Rise and Decline of Nations* (Yale University Press, 1982).

GUY PETERS. *American Public Policy*, 2nd ed. (Chatham House, 1986).

NELSON W. POLSBY. *Political Innovation in America* (Yale University Press, 1984).

KAY LEHMAN SCHLOZMAN and JOHN T. TIERNEY. *Organized Interests and American Democracy* (Harper & Row, 1986).

LEONARD SILK and MARK SILK. *The American Establishment* (Basic Books, 1980).

ALLAN P. SINDLER, ed. *American Politics and Public Policy* (Congressional Quarterly Press, 1982).

CARL VAN HORN, DONALD BAUMER, and WILLIAM GORMLEY. *Politics and Public Policy* (Congressional Quarterly Press, 1988).

AARON WILDAVSKY. *Speaking Truth to Power: The Art and Craft of Policy Analysis* (Little, Brown, 1979).

CHAPTER 19

Making Foreign Policy

Since World War II the United States has become involved in world affairs in a way and to a degree unprecedented in our history. Whether we like it or not, that involvement is increasing, primarily because we must pursue our security interests in an increasingly interlocked "global" world. Further, as the world's principal economic trader, we need markets for our products. We also depend on imported raw materials.

Our political values and interests are also a factor: We want to encourage peace and human rights, and to prevent terrorism, anarchy, and repression. We have a special relationship with those nations that share our commitment to representative democracy, or at least our common Western heritage of liberty and equality.

Our foreign policy leaders, whether Democratic or Republican, see American power as a vital means of shaping not only a more decent but also a more secure world. At the heart of our national security policy has been a recognition of the reality of Soviet power, and of the fact that the Soviets view the world differently than we do. But relationships with China, Japan, Europe and the **third world** (developing nations outside the traditional influence of the super powers—for example, in Africa and Latin America) hold a central place on our foreign policy agenda.

DEFINING AND DEFENDING OUR VITAL INTERESTS

The chief objective of American foreign policy has been to protect and promote the national security and economic well-being of the United States. But promoting our vital interests provides only hazy guidelines for those who must make foreign policy on a day-to-day basis. Further, Americans differ on what constitutes our national interest (note the differing views in Table 19–1).

Few would question the need to defend our country, to survive, to protect our institutions and our values. Controversy arises, however, in determining the means to these ends. For example, to what extent should we intervene in the affairs of other nations in order to maintain international stability or the flow of resources to our economy? Also, we are deeply concerned about the status of human

19–1 Survey Results About Foreign Policy Goals

	PERCENT SAYING "VERY IMPORTANT"	
	Public*	Leaders*
1. Protecting American jobs	77%	43%
2. Keeping up the value of the dollar	71	38
3. Securing adequate energy	70	72
4. Controlling arms worldwide	64	86
5. Containing communism	59	44
6. Combating world hunger	58	64
7. Defending our allies	50	82
8. Matching Soviet military power	49	52
9. Strengthening the United Nations	48	25
10. Protecting our business interests abroad	44	25
11. Promoting human rights abroad	43	41
12. Helping to improve standards of living abroad	35	55
13. Protecting weaker nations from foreign aggression	34	43
14. Promoting democratic forms of government	29	23

Public = national sample of 1546; Leaders = 341 officials or business and professional executives.

Source: Gallup poll. Table adapted from John E. Rielly, ed., *American Public Opinion and U.S. Foreign Policy 1983* (Chicago Council on Foreign Relations, 1983), p. 13.

rights and democratic institutions in foreign lands. This concern enhances both the challenge and complexities facing our foreign policy makers.

In the early nineteenth century, the Monroe Doctrine defined the western hemisphere as an area of vital interest to our country, and we have often used force to prevent any perceived threats to our security in this hemisphere.[1] Beginning with the Spanish-American War we began to be involved elsewhere. President Woodrow Wilson wanted the United States to take a more active role in the world in order to champion the cause of freedom and to encourage the rise of democratic nations. Wilsonian "internationalism"—sometimes also called idealism, globalism, or moralism—has been a powerful recurring strain in our foreign policy ever since. Jimmy Carter's human rights initiatives were in this tradition.[2] President Harry Truman's **Truman Doctrine** was more of a blend of idealism and realism, yet it clearly required international involvement. It promised our support to all free peoples who faced totalitarian aggression. Truman doubtless had Europe in mind, but some supporters of this *internationalist* brand of foreign policy were willing to intervene

[1] Cecil V. Crabb, Jr., *The Doctrines of American Foreign Policy* (Louisiana State University Press, 1982).

[2] Gaddis Smith, *Morality, Reason and Power: American Diplomacy in the Carter Years* (Hill & Wang, 1986).

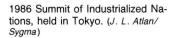
1986 Summit of Industrialized Nations, held in Tokyo. (*J. L. Atlan/Sygma*)

nearly anywhere in the world in order to create an international order congruent with American values.

Pragmatists contend that it is just such broad, sweeping definitions of our vital interests that lead us to overextend ourselves and involve us in conflicts such as Korea, Vietnam, and Lebanon. Policy makers, they say, should disregard ideology and shape foreign policy on rational, "realistic" calculations: What are our national interests? And are we able to defend them? The realists say we should intervene in world affairs *only* if *our* vital interests are at stake, and if the other country is the victim of overt, outside aggression, not just an internal rebellion. Still, realists would generally have the U.S. work with any ally, regardless of that country's internal politics, whereas idealists prefer that we work only with "good" governments.[3]

The limits of a unilateral American role in reforming the world and defending freedom against aggressors are plain: A single country can or should do only so much. The efforts of the United States in Lebanon taught us this lesson anew. But old questions remain and new ones arise. Is the Persian Gulf, for example, vital to our national interests? And if it is, can we effectively intervene to ensure its stability? Do the political conditions of Central America affect the United States? Should the Monroe Doctrine be applied to oppose the intervention by foreign nations into the internal affairs of these countries? How does the Cold War influence our options? What are our foreign policy strategies? What are the politics and options that shape foreign policy making in the United States?

THE COLD WAR AND ITS LEGACY

Basic to any understanding of our contemporary foreign and defense policies is a recognition of the impact of the Cold War. For a time in the 1970s the policy of **detente**—an easing of strained relations between nations—between the U.S. and the USSR was seen as heralding the beginning of a new era of Soviet-American relations. But, in fact, the Cold War left a legacy that continues to be the dominant factor in our foreign policy making.[4]

Although many people think the Cold War began after World War II, some scholars believe its roots lie in the troubled course of Soviet-American relations after the Russian Revolution of 1917. Americans considered the Bolsheviks to be immoral revolutionaries and believed communism threatened both democracy and the world order envisioned by Woodrow Wilson. Great Britain and France joined the United States in open hostility to the new Soviet leaders; they even intervened briefly in that country's affairs. (The United States sent 5000 troops into Russia in 1918 soon after the revolution—a fact most Americans forget, but Soviet officials never do.) American leaders followed a policy of diplomatic nonrecognition toward the Soviet government.

Although relations between the East and the West warmed slightly by the 1930s, the Soviet Union still felt isolated. The Soviets worried especially about Germany; they could not forget the 20 million casualties of World War I. Moscow's warnings about the dangers of Hitler's Germany went mostly unheeded by Western leaders. The inaction, and even appeasement, by some Western nations further isolated the Soviet Union, leaving it once again feeling vulnerable to German attack. The term **appeasement** describes concessions made to a potential enemy in the hope of preventing aggression. Britain's 1938 Munich agreement with Adolf Hitler

[3] For a discussion of crusaders (idealists) and pragmatists (realists), see John Stoessinger, *Crusaders and Pragmatists*, 2nd ed. (Norton, 1985).

[4] Useful treatments of the Cold War and its legacy are Daniel Yergin, *Shattered Peace: The Origins of the Cold War and the National Security State* (Houghton Mifflin, 1978), and Robert Dallek, *The American Style of Foreign Policy* (Alfred A. Knopf, 1983), especially chaps. 6–9.

to accept the partition of Czechoslovakia in exchange for a vague guarantee of peace was an example. Soviet leader Joseph Stalin, fearing his nation would be unable to repulse a Nazi attack, knowing he would have little assistance from the West, and not caring what happened to other countries, signed a nonaggression pact with Hitler in August 1939. But the Nazis soon attacked Poland, and World War II erupted in full force.

The West was outraged, and with reason, by this Soviet sellout. But in less than two years, Hitler also turned his military machine against the Russians, and the West and the Soviets faced Hitler as a common enemy. The wartime alliance between the United States and the USSR was an uneasy one. Although Stalin had advocated a European invasion by the Allies in 1941, this second front did not begin until 1944, after the Russians had sustained tremendous losses and had become bitter toward the West. To understand the origins of the Cold War, we must understand the aims of the United States and the Soviet Union as they emerged as superpowers at the end of World War II. Europe's economies had been crushed, and a power vacuum had to be filled. President Franklin D. Roosevelt saw a world based on the dominance of these two great nations, and therefore realized the necessity of maintaining an uneasy alliance with Stalin. Stalin's postwar priorities were to establish several pro-Soviet nations along its borders and to keep Germany divided and weak.

Joseph Stalin, Nikita Khrushchev, and Leonid Brezhnev. (UPI/Bettmann Newsphotos)

After World War II

In early 1945, with Hitler's defeat inevitable, Roosevelt, Stalin, and Winston Churchill met at Yalta (a port city in the southern Crimea, on the Black Sea) to decide on Europe's future. The agreement that emerged from these meetings has aroused controversy to this day. On the surface it appeared the three powers had agreed on a set of democratic principles that would govern Europe's recovery. Many analysts now think, however, that the Yalta meetings simply allowed a Soviet sphere of influence in eastern Europe in exchange for Soviet cooperation in pursuing the war against Japan and in furthering Roosevelt's vision of the postwar world. Roosevelt's death two months after Yalta signaled as well the death of cordial relations between the U.S. and the USSR. His successor, Harry Truman, soon embarked on a different path. Distrusting Soviet intentions, Truman and his advisers increasingly came to see Soviet-American competition as a conflict between two diametrically opposed ways of life. Possibilities for cooperation diminished.

Soviet intervention in eastern Europe, Iran, and Turkey reinforced U.S. views. Truman and his advisers developed the Truman Doctrine, mentioned earlier. The **Marshall Plan,** named after Secretary of State George C. Marshall, sought to rebuild Europe's economics with American economic assistance. NATO—the North Atlantic Treaty Organization—was created as a military alliance between the United States and western Europe. This was the strategy of **containment,** aimed at maintaining the international status quo and preventing any further Soviet territorial gains. Some of Truman's policies have been criticized as overextending the United States and as portraying Soviet-American relations as a simplistic struggle between good and evil rather than as traditional superpower competition. On the other hand, remember that the appeasement of Hitler remained fresh in policy makers' minds— "No More Munich!" was a fashionable saying—and that they did not want to make the same mistakes with Stalin. The result of Truman's policies was a military buildup and a state of constant readiness for war, coupled with a strong commitment to use American military force almost anywhere in the world. This was a notable departure from previous foreign policy.

Soon the United States was involved in the Korean War, and our overall foreign policy was set for the next twenty years. We believed we had no choice but to respond: Not to respond in Korea would have meant that our will and our commitments could be doubted, and that we might be challenged anywhere—or so our chief policy makers believed. With Eisenhower in the White House in the 1950s, our foreign policy changed somewhat, but the basic idea of containment remained. Eisenhower relied extensively on economic and military assistance and on covert operations by an expanded CIA to help overthrow unwanted governments, such as in Guatemala.[5] World order was still defined by the status quo and the **domino theory,** the idea that if one of our allies falls, a series of others may soon fall as well.

President John F. Kennedy, elected in late 1960, brought a fresh and youthful spirit to the country. He extended aid to newly independent nations and spoke boldly of a new and different world. Still, he was sharply anticommunist, so he built up nuclear weapons and military forces. He confronted the Soviets and their extending influence in Cuba (1961), Berlin (1961), and Vietnam.[6] He also acted decisively to oppose the Russians during the October 1962 Cuban Missile Crisis. Only in his third and last year did he hint at a possible detente with the Soviets.

Franklin Delano Roosevelt, Harry S Truman, and John F. Kennedy. (*Library of Congress*)

Vietnam

Lyndon Johnson's foreign policy became dominated by the Vietnam War, a conflict that must be viewed as a logical outgrowth of Cold War containment policy. Many American policy makers considered Vietnam to be a case of Soviet-controlled communist aggression. Critics charge it was primarily a revolutionary war deeply rooted in Vietnamese history.[7] Democratic institutions had few if any roots in Vietnam, and yet we became enmeshed in a war to prevent aggression and make the country safe for democracy. According to the domino theory, if Vietnam fell, so would the rest of Indo-China, Thailand, and then maybe the Philippines, and so on. Hence the United States had to make a stand in Vietnam so that it need not fight communists closer to home. President Johnson—in the Truman tradition—said in 1965 that if we failed to come to the aid of the South Vietnamese, we would be saying to the world that we "don't live up to our treaties and don't stand by our friends." No matter that South Vietnamese leaders might be corrupt, they were still our allies. Thus began our ever-escalating involvement in a war we hardly understood.

This is not the place to retell the story of the Vietnam War. It is enough to state that Vietnam, an undeclared war, was also our longest, and, next to the Civil War, it was our most controversial as well. As the war grew more costly and the chances for victory grew more remote, the American people began to express growing discontent with inflation, the draft that accompanied the war, and the rising number of American deaths. The average age of our combat soldiers was 19. More than 58,000 Americans died, 300,000 others suffered serious wounds. Massive bombing of North Vietnam failed to contain the opposition forces. The war divided the government, the Democratic party, the whole nation. It became a central issue in the 1968 election, as Nixon promised to end the war—but refused to say how.

Nixon and Detente

Once in office, Nixon continued to act on the same assumptions as his predecessors. He and his chief national security adviser, Henry Kissinger, believed the way to

[5] He also permitted the CIA to fly U-2 planes over the Soviet Union to gather intelligence—until one such flight was shot down with major consequences for U.S.-USSR relations. See Michael Beschloss, *MAYDAY: Eisenhower and Khrushchev, and the U-2 Affair* (Harper & Row, 1986).

[6] See R. B. Smith, *An International History of the Vietnam War: The Kennedy Strategy* (St. Martin's Press, 1986); George McT. Kahin, *Intervention* (Knopf, 1986).

[7] See especially Frances Fitzgerald, *Fire in the Lake* (Atlantic-Little, Brown, 1972), and Gabriel Kolko, *Anatomy of War: Vietnam, the United States, and the Modern Historical Experience* (Pantheon, 1986).

end the war was to increase the costs of the war to the Soviets and Chinese. But they also realized Americans would not continue to back further escalation. Thus were born the two principles of the Nixon-Kissinger foreign policy: *Vietnamization*, which sought to let the South Vietnamese shoulder more and more of the fighting while the American troops disengaged; and *detente* with the Soviet Union, a down-playing of the threat of force and a new emphasis on cooperation, trade, and mutual arms limitations. The first principle (letting others fight in order to prevent the spread of communism) became known as the **Nixon Doctrine.**

The Nixon Doctrine specifically held that the United States would keep its treaty commitments. Moreover, we would provide a shield if a nuclear power threatened the freedom of a nation allied with us, or a nation whose survival we considered vital to our security and the security of the region as a whole. Finally, in cases involving other types of aggression, the United States would furnish military and economic assistance when requested and as appropriate. But the nation directly threatened must assume the primary responsibility of providing the labor power for its own defense.[8]

Nixon presided over our exit from Vietnam; not long afterward, our former allies there fell to the opposition forces. Despite the reevaluation of our commitment to Vietnam, foreign policy makers in the 1970s still considered our role in the international system to be primarily in the context of Soviet-American competition. Nationalist movements in the third world were largely discounted as Soviet-inspired revolutionaries.

The Reagan Doctrines

Ronald Reagan came to the White House as a hawkish, anti-Soviet crusader. For more than a decade he had made campaign pledges to counter the massive Soviet military buildup and to take a much harder line in negotiations with the Soviets. He had disapproved of the Kennedy, Nixon, Ford, and Carter test ban and arms negotiations and the SALT agreements. He was convinced—and frequently used the bully pulpit of the White House to try to convince the American public—that the United States should never trust the Soviet leaders. They would do anything, he said, to achieve their objectives, including deception, intensive spying, aggression, and massive nuclear and conventional military buildups. He accused the Soviet leaders of failing to abide by the SALT II agreements of the late 1970s. He called the Soviet Union the focus of evil in the world and an "evil empire." Critics said Reagan was in effect describing the Soviet leaders, if not their people, as diabolical, and that this was highly unlikely to create a mood conducive to negotiations on arms production.

Such criticism rarely bothered Reagan. He apparently believed, even after his several summit meetings with Soviet leader Gorbachev, that the best way to deal with the Soviets was by publicly lashing out at them while also sending occasional signals that he was willing to negotiate. Reagan's longstanding views about the Soviet leaders and their goals modified somewhat. Yet Reagan the politician doubtless sensed, despite his comfortable election victory in 1984, that both the American people and people around the world yearned for a rollback of nuclear arms. U.S.-USSR relations had also sunk to their lowest point since the Cuban Missile Crisis in 1962.[9] Even losing badly in 1984, the Democrats had been able to portray Ronald

The Vietnam War Memorial in Washington, D.C., is engraved with the names of U.S. service men and service women killed in Vietnam. A statue of Vietnam soldiers is adjacent to the Memorial.

(*T. Cronin*)

(*Alex Cronin*)

[8] For Nixon's and Kissinger's own views, see Richard Nixon, *RN: The Memoirs of Richard Nixon* (Grosset and Dunlap, 1978), and Henry Kissinger, *The White House Years* (Little, Brown, 1979), pp. 223–25. See also Seymour M. Hersh, *The Price of Power: Kissinger in the Nixon White House* (Summit Books, 1983).

[9] Richard W. Stevenson, *The Rise and Fall of Détente* (University of Illinois Press, 1985); Sanford J. Ungar, ed., *Estrangement: America and the World* (Oxford University Press, 1985); and Raymond L. Garthoff, *Détente and Confrontation: American-Soviet Relations from Nixon to Reagan* (Brookings Institution, 1985).

Reagan and Gorbachev after signing the INF treaty at the 1988 summit meeting in Moscow. (*Tass/Sovfoto*)

American Foreign Policy Attitudes During the Reagan Era

Q. Should the U.S. support a right wing dictatorship which is friendly to us, or should the U.S. urge free elections even if that might lead to a communist government?

Yes, support	33%
No, urge elections	40
Depends	5
Stay out	3
Don't know/no answer	19

Q. Should the U.S. criticize governments that deny human rights to their citizens, even if those governments support us on important foreign policy issues?

Yes	54%
No	31
Depends	3
DK, NA	11

Q. Should the U.S. try to change a dictatorship to a democracy where it can, or should the U.S. stay out of other countries' affairs?

Change	28%
Stay out	62
DK, NA	10

Q. Does the Reagan administration try hard enough to reach diplomatic solutions, or is it too quick to get American military forces involved?

Too quick with military	42%
Tries diplomacy	39
Both	2
Neither	2
DK, NA	16

Reagan as a man who did not care about stopping the nuclear arms race. Reagan responded in two ways: He pushed even harder for his **Strategic Defense Initiative** (Star Wars program, discussed in the next chapter), and he told friends he really wanted to do something, before he left the White House, to quiet people's fears about the world's blowing up. His summit meetings with Gorbachev and the INF treaty of 1988 were the result.

Reagan himself avoided talking about a Reagan Doctrine, yet much of his foreign policy could simply be called: protect our values by fighting communism. In a more extended form, Reagan's aides often phrased his philosophy as follows: Where genuine national liberation movements seek to recapture their countries from communist tyranny imposed from without, America reserves the right, and may even have the duty, to support those people.[10] Reagan administration efforts in Grenada (1983), Nicaragua, and Angola illustrate this kind of intervention. Reagan also, of course, supported the Afghan "freedom fighters," following this same reasoning.

Elsewhere in its foreign policy dealings, the Reagan administration supported insurrectionist or opposition movements that sought to topple (or, in some cases, to regain their political rights from) authoritarian governments. Making its foreign policy fit a changing world, the Reagan administration, for example, eventually, if sometimes haltingly, supported moves to oust the leadership in Haiti and the Philippines and to put some pressure on the governments of Chile, South Korea, and South Africa. Too little, too late—critics often said. Still, the Reagan foreign policy team was often able to react more flexibly than most people expected. Reagan ended up putting pressure for democracy on governments of the right as well as the left. This emphasis on promoting democracy as the best ultimate guarantee of human rights rather than attacking specific human rights abuses became a feature of the Reagan doctrine or doctrines, especially in his second term.

Perhaps it was in everyone's best interest that there was no one Reagan doctrine. Doctrines not only simplify the complex, but are often used to rally the public, or to embarrass the namesake administration. Indeed, Reagan did have to shape and conduct his foreign policy in a climate of public opinion that often was opposed to what he may have preferred. Public opinion and Congress, in fact, restrained some of his more strident foreign policy views.

Despite these contraints, Reagan was a popular president in his second term— a time when most presidents witness a major decline in their public approval. And whenever he took vigorous action, such as the invasion of Grenada or the antiterrorist raids on Libya, he enjoyed impressive public support—at least after the fact: If

---

[10] See, for example, Jeane Kirkpatrick, *The Reagan Doctrine* (The Heritage Foundation, 1984). But see the critique by Robert W. Tucker, *Intervention and the Reagan Doctrine* (Council on Religion and Foreign Affairs, 1985).

Reagan Era Foreign
Policy Attitudes cont.

Q. Do you think the U.S. government should provide military
assistance to the people trying to overthrow the government of Nicargua, or not?

No, do not help	44%
Yes, help	30
DK, NA	26

Q. Do you think the U.S. has
done everything reasonable
to try to reach agreement
with the Soviet Union about
controlling nuclear weapons,
or should the U.S. do more?

Should do more	60%
Has done everything	31
DK, NA	9

Source: For first three questions,
The New York Times/CBS News Poll
(April, 1986). N = 1601. For second
three questions, The New York
Times/CBS News Poll (October
1984). N = 1463.

public attitudes in general constrained Reagan, public opinion nonetheless rallied to him when he did take action—even if it might not have sanctioned his action ahead of time.

The United States in a Changing World

The world continues to grow smaller. Technology alone makes this inevitable, with its introduction of nuclear weapons, long-range delivery missiles, and virtually instant communications. Common interests and mutual problems are forcing some traditional conflicts and rivalries aside, and resource scarcities are creating new ties.

In the nineteenth century stability was maintained by a balance of power, characterized by shifting alliances among five relatively equal countries: Great Britain, France, Austria, Prussia, and Russia. By the middle of the twentieth century, the international system was characterized by a balance of power—or a "balance of terror" as Winston Churchill once called it—between the two superpowers, the USSR and the U.S. The dominance of the international system by these two countries has been referred to as a condition of bipolar world politics, or **bipolarity**. There is growing evidence, however, that this concept no longer defines the international system, although militarily the USSR and the U.S. are still the dominant forces. Other powerful forces have emerged: Japan, China, the Common Market (officially called the European Economic Community), and OPEC (officially the Organization of Petroleum Exporting Countries). Nations such as Brazil and India are also becoming increasingly important in their regions of the world. The rise of these regional and transnational powers has resulted in a more diffuse distribution of power, especially economic power, in the last ten to fifteen years.

Another important feature in the international system has been the growing demands of the third-world nations for a greater say in their own development and in world affairs. These nations, mostly found in the southern hemisphere, feel they have been exploited in the past by the industrialized countries. Their problems, especially population growth and food and fuel shortages, threaten to grow worse. Third world indebtedness to northern nations like the U.S. has grown as have pleas from these countries for assistance from the developed world. Yet another problem is in the **fourth world** (or least-developed nations), countries so poor they cannot provide for themselves and must live off the charity of other nations.

Still another crisis that faces the world is nuclear arms proliferation. Competition for military superiority over one's enemies is no longer confined to the superpowers. By the year 2000 many nuclear powers will probably emerge, some of them in the third world. The rise in military power and the spread of nuclear weapons is almost sure to contribute to instability in the world.

Although it would be in the best interests of both the U.S. and the USSR to cooperate to face these problems, the legacy of the Cold War often prevents this. At least thus far it has limited the number of cooperative ventures. Further, solutions to our global problems would require many nations to redefine rather radically their traditional views of national security and perhaps also their ways of life. All this suggests that the world will become increasingly **multipolar** in the future, and increasingly interdependent. An optimist these days, said one wag, is someone who thinks the future is uncertain.

FOREIGN POLICY STRATEGIES

How is a foreign policy objective actually implemented? As a major power the United States can choose between varieties of options it can use, but it usually employs the following six, or some combination of them.

Conventional Diplomacy

Much of our day-to-day foreign policy is done through the Foreign Service and through our ambassadors in face-to-face discussions in Washington and other capitals, at the United Nations, in Geneva (at arms talks), and elsewhere around the world (in regional or international organizations and world conferences). Even though such traditional diplomacy has acquired a less-than-shining image in this era of telecommunications and jet travel, it is still a vital, if slow, process by which nations can gain information, talk about mutual interests, and try to resolve bilateral and multilateral disputes.

Patience and incrementalism are the secret weapons of diplomacy. Reagan's Secretary of State George Shultz liked to refer to his own work as that of a "gardener" of diplomacy who persistently cultivated the soil of relations for some future bounty or breakthrough. "To a certain extent what you do all day is cope. A tremendous amount of policy comes about through the way little things you do all day long add up. . . ."[11]

Much of the conventional diplomacy that goes on through the work of our State Department and its $1.5 billion budget may not add up to important break-throughs. Yet it is difficult to measure the value of diplomatic representation—for example, by placing a price tag on close personal relations with foreign officials, or on information gathered and arguments made to promote our interests around the world. Surely the closing of one embassy or the curtailment of our participation in one or even several international organizations is unlikely to cause major setbacks for our republic. "But less active diplomacy could mean less effective foreign policy or the 'loss' of a friendly nation—" warns Senator Charles McC. Mathias, Jr. (R-Maryland), "all for want of a cabled message containing a sound analysis of a crisis in one nation, or for want of timely meetings to cultivate contacts with future leaders of another."[12] Summit diplomacy is another form of conventional diplomacy.

Foreign Aid

The United States regularly grants economic and military assistance to foreign countries—in part for humanitarian reasons and in part to further good relations with other nations. We have offered aid to over 100 countries directly and to a number of other nations through our contributions to various United Nations development funds. Since 1945 we have provided over $300 billion in aid to foreign countries—a figure that looks and sounds impressive. Yet, these days, America devotes less of its gross national product to foreign aid and development than any other industrialized democracy. Most foreign aid goes to a few countries we deem to be of strategic importance—Israel, Eygpt, Turkey, Pakistan, India, and El Salvador, for examples. And most of the nearly $15 billion spent annually is actually spent in the United States, where it must be used to pay for the purchases of American services and products. It thus constitutes a hefty subsidy for American companies and their employees.

Ever since we began giving serious amounts of foreign aid after World War II, many Americans and many members of Congress have vigorously opposed it. Save for aid for Israel, no powerful interest groups or constituencies back foreign aid initiatives. Still, Republican and Democratic presidents alike keep asking Congress for increased funds for foreign aid. Successive presidents, despite differences of ideology and domestic priorities, have all wanted to maintain the leverage with

[11] Don Oberdorfer, "The Mind of George Shultz," *The Washington Post National Weekly Edition* (February 17, 1986), p. 6.
[12] Charles McC. Mathias, Jr., "Don't Straitjacket U.S. Diplomacy," *The New York Times* (June 26, 1986), p. 23.

key countries that economic and military assistance aid provides. Congress invariably trims these requests by between 15 and 40 percent. In recent years members of Congress have pointed to reports of waste and fraud in past foreign aid programs. Moreover, some Democrats adopted a strategy of challenging the Reagan administration for refusing to consider new taxes to pay for its priorities. "I will not fight for foreign aid paid for with borrowed money," says Representative David Obey (D-Wisc.)[13]

Economic Sanctions

The United States has frequently practiced the art of economic pressure in response to a nation's unwillingness to abide by what we perceive to be international law or proper relations. The United States grain embargo against the Soviet Union in the wake of the Soviet Union's invasion of Afghanistan is a classic instance of our use of economic sanctions. The Reagan administration waged economic warfare against Nicaragua, and, pushed by Congress and public opinion, it also agreed to certain sanctions against South Africa. Tariffs and protectionism are yet another form of economic sanctions; we treat them as subsidies to United States companies and unions in Chapter 23.

The popularity of economic sanctions has waxed and waned over the years, but they are still a potentially important weapon in the arsenal of diplomatic and foreign policy strategies. "Economic sanctions often emerge as the centerpiece when a balance is needed between actions that seem too soft or too strident. In these situations, sanctions are seldom regarded as the 'ideal' weapon; rather they are seen as the 'least bad' alternative."[14] Such sanctions are obviously not popular among the farmers or corporations who have to sacrifice part of their overseas economic markets to comply with government sanctions or controls. Nevertheless, the United States has employed this strategy at least seventy times since World War I.

Political Coercion

Occasionally our foreign policy officials decide that it is expedient to break diplomatic relations with, or otherwise isolate, a hostile country. This was our strategy toward the People's Republic of China during the 1950s and 1960s. Our relations with Iran and Libya have been of this kind in recent years. Our boycott of the 1980 Olympics was another illustration of this strategy.

This approach is, however, a next to last resort (force is the last), because a complete break in diplomatic relations obviously establishes a hostile atmosphere and undermines our ability to reason with the nation in question or to use other diplomatic strategies to resolve conflicts.

Covert Action

President Eisenhower often used the CIA to engage in covert or quasimilitary ventures both to avoid deploying the military and also to advance our foreign policy interests. Every recent president has employed covert action to gain support and encourage our friends abroad.

Covert action is distasteful to many Americans, who see it as incompatible with our basic principles of democracy. In the post-Vietnam years, Congress has insisted on being informed about such actions and has sought to retain a role in overseeing the goals and methods used in various CIA covert operations.

Iran-contra hearings—Congress investigates a celebrated White House misadventure. (*J.L. Atlan/ Sygma*)

[13] Quoted in David Rogers, "Foreign Aid, Pressured by Gramm-Rudman Cuts, Also Faces Erosion of Traditional Liberal Support," *The Wall Street Journal* (May 22, 1986), p. 64.

[14] Gary Clyde Hufbauer and Jeffrey J. Schott, "Economic Sanctions and Foreign Policy," *PS* (Fall 1985), p. 727. See also their longer study, *Economic Sanctions Reconsidered: History and Current Policy* (Institute for International Economics, 1985).

Military Intervention

War, it is often said, is merely an extension of diplomacy. The United States has intervened with military action in other nations on the average of almost once a year since 1789, although usually in relatively minor or short-term events, such as Reagan's use of troops in Grenada and of Navy and Air Force fighter planes over Libya. (Of course, these may not be considered minor events by the target nations!)

Intervention with force is plainly the ultimate response in trying to resolve a conflict. Its success or failure depends on a number of factors. Two observers note, "Military intervention may work against certain small and even medium-sized countries (Grenada and Argentina), but it often seems too dangerous in instances where the threat of big-power confrontation lurks (Poland and Afghanistan), and military intervention often proves ineffective in the context of national civil wars (the United States in Vietnam; Israel in Lebanon)."[15]

Although these are the options available, their use is often conditioned by the character of both the politics of foreign policy making and our processes for deciding and implementing national security decisions.

THE POLITICS OF MAKING FOREIGN POLICY

Foreign policy flows through much the same institutional and constitutional structures as domestic policy. Public opinion, interest groups, members of Congress, elections, separation of powers, and federalism all affect the politics of making foreign policy. Yet they operate somewhat differently from the way they do in internal affairs. And, of course, foreign governments and international organizations also play an important role.

Public Opinion and Foreign Policy

Different foreign policy issues evoke different degrees of public interest and involvement. In crisis situations—such as the Cuban Missile Crisis or the U.S. raids on

[15] Ibid., p. 728.

American Public Ratings of Foreign Ties

		Strengthen ties	Continue as now	Lessen ties	Don't know
The United States has formed ties of varying degrees with different nations in the world. For each of the countries listed below, would it be best in the long run for us to strengthen our ties with them, continue things about as they are or lessen our commitments to them?	Canada	54%	37%	1%	8%
	Russia	47	20	23	11
	England	45	43	3	8
	West Germany	42	39	6	13
	Mainland China	39	32	12	17
	Japan	36	37	17	10
	Israel	34	35	18	13
	New Zealand	31	38	6	25
	South Africa	28	22	34	17
	Vietnam	21	26	35	18
	Libya	11	14	58	17

Source: The Roper Organization, Inc. (February 1986).

Libya in 1986—decisions are made by a small group of persons. Yet even in these situations presidents and their advisers know that what they decide will ultimately require support from the public and from Congress.

In noncrisis situations the public appears to consist of three subcategories. The largest, comprising perhaps as much as 75 percent of the adult population, is the **mass public.** This groups knows little about foreign affairs, despite the importance of the subject. The mass public concerns itself with foreign affairs mainly in conflict situations, especially those involving the actual or possible use of American troops abroad. The second public is the **attentive public.** Comprising perhaps 15 to 20 percent of the population, it maintains an active interest in foreign policy. The **opinion makers** are the third and smallest public. They transmit information and judgments on foreign affairs and mobilize support in the other two publics. To illustrate the relationship between these three publics, one analyst has developed the analogy of a huge theater with a tense drama being played out on the stage:

> The *mass public*, occupying the many seats in the balcony, is so far removed from the scene of action that its members can hardly grasp the plot, much less hear all the lines or distinguish between the actors. Thus, they may sit in stony silence or applaud impetuously, if not so vigorously as to shake the foundations of the theater. Usually, however, they get thoroughly bored and leave. . . . The *attentive public*, on the other hand, is located in the few choice orchestra seats. Its members can not only hear every line clearly, but can also see the facial expressions of the actors. Thus they become absorbed in the drama, applauding its high spots and disparaging its flaws. Indeed, their involvement is such that during the intermission they make their views known to any occupants of the balcony who may have wandered into the lobby. As for the members of the *opinion-making public*, they are the actors on the stage, performing their parts with gusto and intensity, not infrequently in an effort to upstage each other. Many are directing their performance at some specific portion of the orchestra audience. Others, those with especially strong vocal cords, try to make themselves heard as far as the balcony. All are keenly aware that the quality of their performance will greatly affect their bargaining power when they seek higher salaries or better parts in future productions.[16]

Why are so many people indifferent or uninformed? First, foreign affairs are usually more remote than domestic issues. People have more firsthand information about unemployment or inflation than about Zimbabwean land reform or Turkish political problems. The worker in the factory and the boss in the front office know what labor-management relations are about, and they have strong opinions on the subject. They are likely to be less concerned about the internal struggles for power within Ethiopia or our policy on Cambodia—and probably feel that they could not do much about it anyway. Only when American soldiers, especially drafted soldiers, are being killed does the mass public become directly concerned with foreign affairs.

Lack of widespread concern, knowledge, and involvement in the politics of foreign policy should not be confused with lack of intense feelings about aspects of the international scene. Since World War II questions about our relations with other nations have been high on the list of public concerns. And when such issues as the Vietnam conflict or El Salvador and Nicaragua become domesticated—that is, when they visibly, directly, and immediately affect the people of the United States—the debate over them produces demonstrations, campaigns, and hearings: in other words, all the trappings of the ordinary political process.

---

[16] James N. Rosenau, ed., *Public Opinion and Foreign Policy* (Random House, 1961), pp. 34–35 italics added. See also Bernard C. Cohen, *The Public's Impact on Foreign Policy* (Little, Brown, 1973); and Ole Holsti and James Rosenau, *American Leadership in World Affairs* (Allen and Unwin, 1984).

Public Moods: An Unstable Base?

Fluctuating from no interest at all to intense feeling, the public reaction to foreign policy is sometimes based on moods. It is said the mass public oversimplifies the problems of foreign politics. It tends to reduce all issues to the one that is most urgent at the moment. It often thinks of the participants in terms of heroes and villains. It favors quick and easy remedies: Fire the secretary of state, or raise trade barriers, and all will be well. Although this "mood" theory has been challenged, it is conceded that Americans are extremely permissive with American foreign policy makers on international issues. However, even though members of the attentive public and the decision makers are also subject to mood responses and oversimplification, their responses tend to be more sophisticated.

Popular indifference means that policy makers often have to dramatize issues in order to arouse support. On the other hand, in periods of public excitement, fear of rash public opinion causes policy makers to be overcautious. To secure American participation in the United Nations, for example, the State Department carried on an intensive publicity campaign. But in so doing, it gave many people the impression that the United Nations would ensure peace and order in the world.

Too much has been made, however, of the American people's ignorance about foreign policy contrasted to their knowledge of domestic issues. The instability of public moods, to the extent that it does exist, probably does not affect policy makers all that much. Issues are usually defined by policy makers; the public generally reacts to them. Policy makers, and events, shape the agenda. Still, public opinion determines the broad limits within which others make decisions.

The State Department makes an effort to keep people informed about those areas of policy it thinks should be talked about publicly, and makes an effort to keep itself informed about public opinion. Nevertheless, almost all negotiations in which our government has a major role are conducted in secret, and both the public and Congress are frequently kept at a distance.

Special Interests and Foreign Policy

Interest groups and opinion leaders throughout society form an attentive public whose support is actively sought by official policy makers. They often have an influential voice in shaping foreign policy and serve as a national pulse for our decision makers.

The mass media are sometimes powerful in shaping public opinion, a fact reflected in frequent disputes between the media and government. Tension between the press and the State Department is an issue of long standing. The press gets especially upset when the government uses classification or secrecy to bury its mistakes. Press coverage of events in the Philippines and in South Africa put pressure on the Reagan administration to act differently than it might have otherwise acted.

Another segment of the attentive public consists of citizens' organizations dedicated to increasing public awareness of foreign policy. The Foreign Policy Association designs community and media programs to encourage citizens to study and discuss major controversies. The Council on Foreign Relations, sometimes called the cornerstone of the Eastern Establishment, publishes *Foreign Affairs* magazine and several books a year; it also provides a forum for bringing business leaders and government elites together for talks on new directions in foreign policy. Groups like the World Federalists argue for world government. Defense contractors also sometimes try to promote certain kinds of foreign policies. Religious and ethnic groups are particularly interested in certain phases of foreign policy. Antinuclear war activists and those opposed to our involvement in Central America have been active in 1980s. These groups sometimes have intense feelings about issues, and they are often strategically located to affect the outcomes of elections.

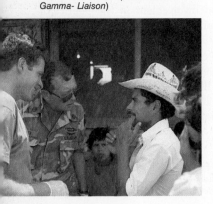

Former President Reagan stated that "defense of the Caribbean and Central America against Marxist-Leninist takeovers is vital to our national security." U.S. Military advisers in Honduras. (*Paolo Bosio/ Gamma- Liaison*)

It is difficult to generalize about the impact of special-interest groups on American foreign policies. At moments of international crisis a president is usually able to mobilize so much public support that special groups find it difficult to exert much influence. Investigations into such areas of policy as trade, outside the crisis areas, find that special groups rarely have a decisive role in the formulation of foreign policy. Of course, what is more difficult to determine is the impact on policy caused by policy makers' *anticipations* of group reactions.

Ethnic interest groups sometimes play a role in foreign policy making. For example, Greece might sometimes be favored over Turkey in part because of the number of Greek-Americans and the strategic location in Congress of legislators especially attuned to them—as well as because of the strategic location of Greece. The same is sometimes true for Israel and Jewish-Americans.

Foreign Countries and Foreign Companies

Most countries, large and small, have long had embassies lobbying for their interests in Washington, D.C. Nowadays, however, some countries, like Japan, have built up a powerful network of lawyers, lobbyists, and Washington-based publicists who are retained by Japanese companies and trade associations, as well as by the Japanese government, to defend their extensive economic interests in the United States. Lobbyists representing six newly industrial countries (South Korea, Taiwan, Hong Kong, Singapore, Brazil, and Mexico) have also beefed up their Washington representational efforts to fight U.S. protectionist and import quotas on textiles, shoes, and other of their exports. These countries have learned "to tap as legal counsel and lobbyists a reservoir of former top U.S. government trade officials. And, these nations are mastering the art of mobilizing U.S. companies and investors who have a stake in trade with the Third World to work on their behalf in key congressional districts."[17] These and other nations have also learned to hire former congressional staffers, and former White House staffers, to help them make their cases before congressional committees and among administration decision makers. Former White House aide Michael Deaver was criticized for his publicized and highly paid "influence efforts" on behalf of Canada, South Korea, and Singapore, made the year after he had left Reagan to start a public relations firm. In 1988, he was convicted of perjury.

Parties and Foreign Policy

Political parties do not usually play a major role in shaping foreign policy, for two reasons: First, many Americans would still prefer to keep foreign policy out of politics. Second, parties usually take less clear and candid stands on foreign policy than they do on domestic policy. All the party weaknesses discussed in Chapter 9 operate in full measure in foreign policy. Party platforms often obscure the issues instead of highlighting them, and many members of Congress fail to follow even a very general party line.

Should parties be concerned with foreign policy? At the end of World War II, sentiment grew stronger for a bipartisan approach to foreign policy. An ambiguous term, **bipartisanship** seems to mean (1) collaboration between the executive and the congressional foreign policy leaders of both parties; (2) support of presidential foreign policies by both parties in Congress; and (3) downplaying of foreign policy issues in national elections and especially in presidential debates. In general, bipartisanship is an attempt to remove the issues of foreign policy from partisan politics.

Bipartisanship has appeal. In this era of chronic crisis, it seems to symbolize people's standing shoulder to shoulder as they face an uncertain and potentially

[17] Bruce Stokes, "Developing Countries Join the Big Leagues in Washington Trade Lobbying," *National Journal* (January 25, 1986), p. 202.

hostile world. It provides more continuity of policy, and it ensures that a wider variety of leaders and interests are consulted in policy making. Psychologically, it helps to satisfy people's instincts to turn to one another for reassurance. Its motto—partisan politics stops at the water's edge—is comforting to the many Americans worried about disunity.

But the idea of bipartisanship sometimes comes under sharp attack. Some believe bipartisanship is merely a smokescreen for presidential domination of foreign policy. They suggest it obscures the fact that foreign policy is made by a relatively small, self-perpetuating elite of national security managers who are essentially nonpartisan *and* unelected. Other critics charge that it denies a basic tenet of democracy: the right of a people to choose between alternative lines of action. According to this argument, people in a free society should be allowed and even encouraged to differ. The need in a democracy is not to stifle differences or to ignore them. The need is to express the differences in a meaningful way, to find the will of the majority, and to permit the government to act and the opposition to oppose.

Major divisions have also developed *within* the parties. Debates over our role in Vietnam, when they finally did take place, occurred primarily within the Democratic party, not between Democrats and Republicans.

Congress and Foreign Policy

It may seem strange to discuss our national legislative body as part of the attentive public rather than as part of the formal foreign policy establishment. But despite the importance of foreign policy, and even though Congress can block the president's policy and undermine the chief executive's decisions, Congress as an institution seldom directly makes foreign policy. The power of Congress is mainly consultative, although the legislature has taken the initiative in some trade and foreign economic and military assistance questions. As we discussed in Chapter 15, Congress has attempted to curb presidential war-making powers. It is also a link between the policy makers and the public. Congress wants a meaningful relationship—especially "meaningful consultation" with the president in matters of foreign relations.

Individual members of Congress are sometimes included within the circle of those who make the decisions. For example, the leaders of the Senate Committee

---

19–2 Who Shapes U.S. Foreign Policy?

"How important a role do you think the following currently play in determining the foreign policy of the United States—a very important role, a somewhat important role, or hardly an important role at all?"

PERCENT ANSWERING
"VERY IMPORTANT"

	Public 1982	Leaders 1982
The President	70%	91%
Secretary of State	64	83
State Department	47	38
Congress	46	34
National Security Adviser	35	46
American Business	35	22
The Military	40	36
United Nations	29	2
The CIA	28	20
Public Opinion	23	15
Labor Unions	17	3

Source: John E. Rielly, ed., *American Public Opinion 1983* (Chicago Council on Foreign Relations, 1983), p. 33.

19–3 Who Should Shape U.S. Foreign Policy?

"Do you feel the roles of the following should be more important than they are now, should be less important than they are now, or should be about as important as they are now?"

PERCENT ANSWERING
"MORE IMPORTANT"

	Public 1982	Leaders 1982
The President	39%	17%
Secretary of State	33	22
State Department	34	34
Congress	44	34
National Security Adviser	31	13
American Business	23	22
The Military	26	3
United Nations	37	33
The CIA	16	9
Public Opinion	54	36
Labor Unions	17	14

Source: Reilly, *American Public Opinion*, p. 340.

on Foreign Relations have been involved at times, although their main role is usually helping to educate the public, or educating the president on what will, or will not, run into congressional opposition. When out of sympathy with the policies of the president, key senators sometimes use this committee to focus attention on their differences.

During the 1930s and after World War II, the almost unanimous opinion of academics and the attentive public favored strengthening the hand of the president and limiting the role of Congress in the foreign policy area. It was generally believed that only the president had the knowledge, the political base, and the broad, global perspective from which to develop coherent foreign policies. Congress was thought to be too responsive to the parochial and uninformed attitudes of the public. When conservative leaders tried to alter constitutional arrangements in order to limit the president's power to make executive agreements and to implement treaties, they ran into solid opposition from the intellectual and academic elites. In 1964, Congress, by means of the Gulf of Tonkin Resolution, virtually relinquished war-making decision making in Vietnam to the president.

This sentiment was challenged in the 1970s, when there was so much opposition to the Vietnam policies of Presidents Johnson and Nixon that Congress, especially the Senate, became more assertive: The 1973 vote to cut off funds for bombing Cambodia, the War Powers Resolution of 1973, and countless amendments restricting arms sales and economic and military aid in the late 1970s were signs of a growing restiveness over presidential supremacy. By the 1980s, the public again yearned for strong presidential leadership; it also wanted Congress and even public opinion to be consulted (see Tables 19–2 and 19–3).[18]

Can We Have a Democratic Foreign Policy?

A great paradox exists in conducting the foreign relations of a modern democracy. In the last century Tocqueville wrote that foreign relations "demand scarcely any of the qualities which are peculiar to a democracy; they require, on the contrary, the perfect use of all those in which it is deficient."[19] One leading scholar observed

[18] See Thomas E. Cronin, "President, Congress, and Foreign Policy" in Charles Kegley and Eugene Witkopf, eds. *The Domestic Sources of American Foreign Policy* (St. Martin's Press, 1988), pp. 149–65.
[19] Alexis de Tocqueville, *Democracy in America*, vol. I (Knopf, 1945), pp. 224–35.

more directly that policy makers in our democracy "either . . . must sacrifice what they consider good policy upon the altar of public opinion, or they must by devious means gain support for policies whose true nature is concealed from the public."[20] Critics have charged our leaders with misleading the people, the experts with misleading our leaders, and ideologies with blinding all of us, especially in Vietnam.

Where shall we draw the line? How *do* our policy makers reconcile public rights with political realities? A democratic foreign policy is one in which policy makers are known and held accountable to the people. That is a tough test for any policy, but there are special liabilities in foreign policy: secrecy, the need to act with speed, a generally lower level of information among the general public, and, of course, the complexity of issues and options. Still, the American public wants to be consulted and informed—and ultimately it wants its leaders to be accountable to it.

In Vietnam our apparent policy was to stop communist expansion. Our policy makers guessed wrong in thinking gradual military pressure would deter the North. They miscalculated the character of the war as well as the commitment of those who opposed the Saigon government.[21] Finally, they tried to get out with some face-saving gestures. And because they recognized mistakes, or believed the American people and Congress might not support them in what they thought necessary, they sought to conceal difficulties.

Perhaps our biggest disappointment in Vietnam was that our institutions did not make up for these failings, or at least did not warn us of them sooner. Students of government must ask themselves: How can we organize our institutions and processes to prevent these human failings from exacting such a large toll again?

If we believe we were kept in the dark, then we ignore the fact that no group of citizens has ever had access to more information about a war than the American people had about Vietnam. We did not have all the information, and we surely had some misinformation, but—because of a free press and independent judiciary—more was shown, written, and said about Vietnam than about any other war.

THE POLICY MACHINERY

It is the responsibility of those who formulate our foreign policies to determine the objectives vital to national interests and to devise programs to achieve those objectives. To the best of their ability and resources, these people must decide how to use (or not use) the instruments available to them: bargaining or negotiation, persuasion or propaganda, economic assistance or pressures, and the threat or actual use of armed force.

The responsibility for foreign policy was fixed in the Constitution at the national level. However, the powers over foreign relations are not divided cleanly or evenly. In England control over foreign relations had been given to the king and his ministers. Our framers tried to redress the balance a bit. Many of the powers given to Congress by the Constitution reflect the decision to take them away from the executive branch; the framers wanted to make what had been a prerogative of the executive into a more shared relationship with the legislature. Congress was given the power to declare war, to appropriate funds, and to make rules for the

President Roosevelt at the Yalta Conference in 1945, with Winston Churchill (l) and Joseph Stalin (r). (UPI/Bettmann Newsphotos)

[20] Hans Morgenthau, "The Conduct of American Foreign Policy," *Parliamentary Affairs* (Winter 1949), p. 147.

[21] For an excellent on-the-scene account of this miscalculation by a young Marine officer who fought there, see Philip Caputo, *A Rumor of War* (Holt, Rinehart & Winston, 1977). See also Leslie Gelb and Richard K. Betts, *The Irony of Vietnam: The System Worked* (Brookings Institution, 1979), and Harry G. Summers, Jr., *On Strategy: A Critical Analysis of the Vietnam War* (Presidio Press, 1983).

armed forces. But the president was left as commander in chief of the armed forces and was expected to negotiate treaties and receive and send ambassadors—that is, to recognize or refuse to recognize other governments. The courts have the power to interpret treaties, but by and large they have ruled that our relations with other nations are matters for the executive to negotiate. Executive domination of foreign policy is a fact of the political life of all nations, including democratic ones. To appreciate this phenomenon, let us look at the people within the executive departments who make up the foreign policy establishment.

Presidential Decision Making and Foreign Policy

The president's chief foreign policy adviser, according to what presidents say and according to formal statutes, is supposed to be the secretary of state. In recent administrations, however, the secretary of state has often had to compete with the president's national security adviser. Just how much influence the secretary of state has depends largely on the president's personal desires. Presidents Harding, Coolidge, Hoover, Eisenhower, and Ford turned over to their secretaries of state almost full responsibility for making important decisions. Other presidents—for example, Wilson, both Roosevelts, Kennedy, Nixon, and Carter—took a more active part themselves. Indeed, at times they were their own secretaries of state. Even so, important decisions on foreign policy are so numerous that both president and secretary of state play important roles.

Secretaries of state administer the State Department and fill multiple roles. They receive visits from foreign diplomats, attend international conferences, and usually head our delegation in the General Assembly of the United Nations. They also attempt to serve as the administration's chief coordinator of all governmental actions that affect our relations with foreign nations. Twice in this century secretaries of state have resigned because of policy differences with the presidents they served: William Jennings Bryan quit the Wilson administration, and Cyrus Vance resigned in mid-1980 over differences with Jimmy Carter. In 1982 Reagan requested that Secretary of State Alexander Haig resign, due to policy and style differences with the White House.

At one time *only* the secretary of state was called upon for advice in formulating and implementing foreign policies. Today, because of the interdependence of foreign, economic, and domestic policies, a president calls on an increasing number of civilian and economic advisers. The day-to-day conduct of foreign affairs is now the business of several major departments and agencies: State, Defense, Treasury, Agriculture, Commerce, Labor, Energy, the Central Intelligence Agency, and others. The need for immediate reaction and preparedness has transferred more responsibilities directly to the president—and to a great extent to the senior White House aides who assist in coordinating information and advice.

In recent years the national security adviser to the president has become a key—and often the most important—adviser. John Kennedy had McGeorge Bundy, Richard Nixon had Henry Kissinger, Jimmy Carter had Zbigniew Brzezinski, and Ronald Reagan had a series of White House assistants for national security, and all of them became powerful—the more so the longer they held office. Presidents grow to rely on these White House aides because of the latter's proximity and because—or at least so presidents believe—these aides owe their prime loyalties to the president, and not to any department or program.

International communications now makes it possible for presidents and their national security advisers to communicate directly with foreign ministers and heads of state all around the globe. No longer do they have to conduct diplomacy through the Foreign Service or be dependent on overseas ambassadors. This reality has transformed the way in which foreign policy is conducted and has undercut and sometimes even threatened the prime role and mission of the State Department.

Secretary of State, James Baker. (*Michael Evans/Sygma*)

The President's Foreign Policy Staff

Secretaries, agency chiefs, and their senior subordinates are chosen by the president and are expected to support and carry out the latter's decisions. Yet at the same time they retain a measure of independence; they naturally tend to reflect and defend the views of the departments and agencies they head. As a result, our presidents have found a need to appoint personal advisers whose loyalties lie solely with the chief executive. Because presidents view responsibility in a personal way, the special adviser has played a loosely defined role.

The key coordinating agency for the president is the National Security Council (NSC). Created by Congress in 1947, it is supposed to help presidents integrate foreign, military, and economic policies that affect national security.

The Iran-contra Affair—1985–1986

Each president has shaped the NSC structure and adapted its staff procedures to suit personal preferences. In Reagan's second term a small group of senior NSC aides believed that they alone knew what should be the law. Their undeclared and unauthorized policy initiatives with Iran and the Nicaraguan "contras" were contrary to laws passed by Congress. These NSC aides apparently viewed knowledge of their actions by others in the U.S. government as a threat to their objectives. They told neither Congress nor the secretary of state about their activities. When exposure was threatened, they destroyed official documents and lied to cabinet officials, the public, and Congress. They testified, too, that they withheld key facts from President Reagan.

Reagan fired NSC advisors John Poindexter and Oliver North and both were indicted, along with several others, for their failure to abide by the law and the Constitution. Their abuse of the National Security Council caused a major public outcry, yet Reagan did little to criticize them or their activities. However, both a Reagan appointed board of inquiry and congressional hearings roundly condemned both the flawed policies and flawed NSC procedures used by the Reagan White House in this affair.[22]

Intelligence and the CIA

Policy makers must have some idea of the direction in which other nations are going to move in order to be able to assess and, if necessary, to counter those moves. In other words, they need high-level foreign policy intelligence. Therefore, those who gather and analyze material are among the most important assistants to the policy makers. They often become policy makers themselves.

What is the balance of power between government and rebel forces in El Salvador or Nicaragua? How many trained infantrymen are there in Czechoslovakia? What are the weapons and air strength of the North Korean military? Before policy makers can act on important issues, they have to know a great deal about other countries—their probable reactions to a particular policy, their strengths and weaknesses, and, if possible, their strategic plans and intentions.

Although most of the information comes from open sources, the term *intelligence work* conjures up visions of spies and undercover agents. Secret intelligence occasionally does supply crucial data. Intelligence work involves three operations: reporting, research, and transmission. *Reporting* is based on the close and systematic observation of developments the world over; *research* is the attempt "to establish

[22] See Lee H. Hamilton and Daniel K. Inouye, *Iran-contra Affair,* Report of the Congressional Committees (U.S. Government Printing Office, 1987); and John Tower et al., *The Tower Commission Report* (Times Books, 1987).

National Security Council

Origin:

Established by an act of Congress under President Truman in 1947.

Duties:

To coordinate the policies of the Department of State, the Department of Defense, and the Central Intelligence Agency; to assess national security needs; and to make recommendations to the president.

Members:

The president, vice-president, secretary of state and the secretary of defense are the statutory members. Recent presidents have sometimes included as ex-officio members of the NSC the CIA Director, the White House chief of staff, the Attorney General and the national security adviser.

Staff:

About 80 persons, including thirty professionals with a variety of geographic and policy specialties.

CIA Director William H. Webster. Webster replaced the controversial William Casey, who died in 1987. (*Courtesy of Central Intellegence Agency*)

meaningful patterns out of what was observed in the past and to get meaning out of what appears to be going on now,"[23] and *transmission* is getting the right information to the right people at the right time.

Many agencies engage in intelligence work, among them the State Department's Bureau of Intelligence and Research, the Defense Intelligence Agency, the supersecret National Security Agency (which works on code breaking and electronic communications systems), the FBI, and the Central Intelligence Agency. These agencies form the United States Intelligence Board, which prepares intelligence surveys on most countries of the world.

The CIA was created in 1947 to coordinate the gathering and analysis of information that flows into the various parts of our government from all over the world. Yet organization alone cannot ensure that our policy makers will know all they need to know. As an expert on intelligence operations has pointed out:

> In both the Pearl Harbor and Cuban crises there was plenty of information. But in both cases, regardless of what the Monday morning quarterbacks have to say, the data was ambiguous and incomplete. There was never a single, definitive signal that said, "Get ready, get set, go!" but rather, a number of signals that, when put together, tended to crystallize suspicion. The true signals were always embedded in the noise or irrelevance of the false ones.[24]

Employing more than 16,000 persons, the CIA spends at least $3 billion annually. The CIA director, as head of our foreign intelligence community, oversees research, military intelligence operations, spy satellites, and U-2 and SR-71 exercises that may cost an additional $9 billion annually. (Another $12 billion is spent by the Defense Department in its intelligence needs.) Critics charge, with reason, that CIA operations amount to a secret foreign policy insulated from public control and public scrutiny. In a few nations the local CIA station chief has more staff, more agents, a larger budget, and more influence than the U.S. ambassador.

Since its creation in 1947, the CIA has left a trail of covert activities and deposed governments, such as those in Iran (1953) and Guatemala (1954). The ill-fated 1961 Bay of Pigs invasion of Cuba was directed by the CIA. Later the CIA organized and trained anticommunist forces in Laos, and contributed considerable support to the anti-Allende forces in Chile. Because of its past record and because it must act when our government cannot officially intervene in another nation's affairs, there has been a growing tendency to credit (or blame) the CIA for all coups, purges, and revolts, whether or not it was actually involved.

In 1967 several CIA "front groups" were discovered supporting a variety of research and political-action programs, both domestic and foreign. In the mid-1970s it was revealed that the CIA had kept illegal files on 10,000 domestic dissidents within the United States. In the 1980s the CIA played an important role in U.S. involvement in Central American nations. Some observers think these activities represent an integral part of our diplomacy and preparedness. Others have denounced them as jeopardizing the values we are dedicated to defending.

The CIA's political leverage, its information, its secrecy, its speed in communication, its ability to act, and its enormous size make it a potent force.[25] Congress has resolved that this power will be used only by publicly accountable decision makers. There are now committees in both the Senate and the House whose primary purpose is to hold the CIA accountable to Congress, although earlier versions of these committees seldom did their job well.

---

[23] Sherman Kent, *Strategic Intelligence for American Policy* (Princeton University Press, 1949), especially p. 4. On the limits of intelligence activities, see Richard K. Betts, "Analysis, War, and Decision: Why Intelligence Failures Are Inevitable," *World Politics* (October 1978).

[24] Roberta Wohlstetter, *Cuba and Pearl Harbor: Hindsight and Foresight* (Rand, 1965), p. 36.

[25] For differing accounts of the CIA's influence and effectiveness, see John Ranelagh, *The Agency* (Simon & Schuster, 1986), and Peter Maas, *Manhunt* (Random House, 1986).

United States Information Agency

The United States Information Agency (USIA), established in 1953, has general responsibility for administering foreign information and cultural exchange programs. It administers the Fulbright scholars exchange program, the Voice of America, Radio Free Europe, and similar programs. In the mid-1980s, it launched a worldwide satellite television network called WORLDNET, which permitted the USIA to "tell the message of American democracy to the world." In its first few years WORLDNET enabled the USIA to sponsor news conferences via satellite in about thirty countries. Through this videoconferencing technology foreign news journalists could meet and discuss issues with United States cabinet members, congressional leaders, scholars, and scientists.

The USIA is sometimes called the most technologically adroit propaganda machine in the world. It is also praised by officials in both political parties for its public diplomacy efforts and for its effective telling of the American story abroad. While most government programs were being cut back in the 1980s, the USIA, had its budget doubled to $1 billion in the late 1980s.

The Role of the State Department

The U.S. State Department has been variously called "a fudge factory," a "machine that fails," and "a bowl of jelly." The prime duty of the State Department has always been the security of the nation. Although our armed forces remain the ultimate line of defense, the State Department is our first line. It is dedicated to a round-the-clock, world-wide effort to see that our troops and weapons do not need to be used except in genuine emergencies. It is also the central agency in the day-to-day management of foreign affairs. This executive department has six duties:

1. To negotiate with other nations and international organizations.
2. To protect American citizens and interests abroad.
3. To promote American commercial interests and enterprises.
4. To collect and interpret intelligence.
5. To represent an American "presence" abroad.
6. To promote peace and human rights.

As the diplomatic arm of a superpower, the State Department has responded to our new global concerns with continuous reorganization. Some critics insist, however, that the more it changes, the more it stays the same. Among the cabinet departments, State's annual budget is the lowest—less than 2 percent of that of the Department of Defense. Considering the State Department's role and prestige, its staff of 23,000 worldwide is small, especially compared with the nearly 3 million civilian and military officers in the Department of Defense. IBM employs about as many people abroad as the State Department has overseas.

But even though the State Department is relatively small, critics allege it is oversized. According to one former State Department employee: "There are too many people chasing too few jobs in a system where there is no job tenure. The result is massive insecurity and an attempt to define even the most pathetic job as earthshakingly important as well as finding meaningful work for high level people where none really exists."

The Role of the Foreign Service

The American Foreign Service is the eyes and ears of the United States in other countries. Although part of the State Department, the service represents the entire government and performs jobs for many other agencies. Its main duties are to

(Drawing by Engleman, August 16, 1976. Federal Times)

U.S. President Reagan and Secretary of State George Shultz meet with Soviet Leader Mikhail Gorbachev and Foreign Minister Eduard Shevardnadze at the Geneva Summit, 1985. (J. T. Atlin/Sygma)

carry out foreign policy as expressed in the directives of the secretary of state, gather data for American policy makers, protect Americans and American interests in foreign countries, and cultivate friendly relations with host governments and foreign peoples.

The Foreign Service is composed of Foreign Service officers, Foreign Service reserve officers, and Foreign Service staff officers. At the core of the service are the Foreign Service officers, comparable to the officers of the regular army in the military services.[26] They are a select, specially trained body who are expected to take assignments any place in the world on short notice. There are approximately 4000 such officers; in recent years less than 250 junior officers won appointment.[27]

The Foreign Service is one of the most prestigious, and most criticized, career services of the national government. In the 1950s criticism seemed to outweigh respect, and morale suffered accordingly. Critics accused the service of being infiltrated by communist sympathizers; others charged that it was dominated by a high-society elite still under the impression that diplomacy was the near monopoly of "gentlemen." The charges about communist infiltration were obviously exaggerated.

In more recent years criticism of the Foreign Service has come as much from within as from outside. Most of the criticism claims the Foreign Service (1) stifles creativity; (2) attracts officers who are, or at least become, concerned more about *being* or *becoming* somebody than *doing* something; and (3) requires new recruits to wait fifteen to twenty years before being considered for positions of responsibility. The problems are recognized in Washington, and the task of improving the service continues. More women and minorities have been recruited in recent years. Certain managerial innovations have been tried. But the career service features of the Foreign Service—entry at the bottom, rank in the person rather than in the position, resistance to lateral entry, advancement through grades as determined by senior officers' evaluations, and the tendency toward self-government—make it resistant to change.

Criticism of the Foreign Service because of social-class homogeneity is probably overstated. More likely the structural characteristics of the State Department prevent independent reporting and creativity. There is an old saying in the Foreign Service that there are old Foreign Service officers and there are bold Foreign Service officers, but there are no old bold Foreign Service officers. So we can expect the Foreign Service exposés to keep coming. Its problems of overstaffing, empty jobs, and tedious apprenticeships are in fact common in most bureaucracies.

NATO Member Nations

Belgium
Canada
Denmark
France*
Great Britain
Greece
Iceland
Italy
Luxembourg
The Netherlands
Norway
Portugal
Spain
Turkey
United States
West Germany

* Although France withdrew from NATO's military committee in the mid-1960s, it is otherwise an active member of NATO.

INTERNATIONAL ORGANIZATIONS AND THE UN

The United States belongs to most important world organizations, and its representatives attend most major international conferences. These organizations and conferences are forums for American diplomacy. In addition to the United Nations and its related agencies, the United States is a member of more than 200 international organizations of various types. For example, in its own hemisphere the United States is a member of the Organization of American States (OAS), a regional agency of western hemisphere republics. We also belong to the sixteen-nation North Atlantic Treaty Organization (NATO).

The United Nations was set up by the victorious superpowers immediately after World War II in an effort to shape the postwar world and to promote peace.

---

[26] For a favorable treatment of the Foreign Service, see Andrew L. Steigman, *The Foreign Service of the United States* (Westview Press, 1985).

[27] See the assessments by James Fallows, "The Foreign Service as Mirror of America," *Washington Monthly* (April 1973), pp. 5–14, and by John M. Goshko, "Up or Out in the Foreign Service," *The Washington Post* (March 20, 1986) p. A13.

But when the superpowers, which of course included both the U.S. and the USSR, ceased to be friendly, the UN was doomed to political impotence. The liberal or idealist school of international relations believed the United Nations was destined to bring nations together, to maintain international peace and security, to achieve international cooperation in solving world problems, and to promote and encourage respect for human rights.

When it was founded the UN called for establishing conditions under which justice and respect for obligations arising from treaties and other sources of international law could be maintained. In the UN's first forty years, and directly against the provisions of Article 1 of the UN Charter, over 300 regional and civil wars throughout the world claimed up to 20 million lives. And, as wars continue in Africa, Central America, and Southeast Asia, the UN stands by, almost always helpless. Only occasionally does the UN play a constructive role in ceasefire or peace-keeping missions (as after Arab-Israeli wars, or during India-Pakistan clashes, and in Cyprus).

Public esteem for the UN, was very low until the UN was awarded a Nobel Peace Prize in 1988. It was viewed as drowning in a sea of words and suffocating under a rigid international civil service system. Even though it comprises three times as many countries today as when it was founded in 1945, the UN is characterized by timidity, bureaucracy, and "geographical" appeasement. Even friendly critics say it has become an assembly line of mass produced resolutions that have little relevance to the substance of the problems under discussion.[28]

The UN, like every other agency of international politics, is dominated by the fact the world is divided into separate nations acting in their own self-interests as they define it. The United States, like most nations, cites the UN Charter when it suits its short-term interest and ignores it when it does not. We grew impatient with the anti-U.S. propaganda occasioned by our involvement in Vietnam and by the UN condemnations of our involvement in Grenada and Nicaragua. Moreover, the Soviet Union's ability to line up nonaligned votes in the UN is greater today than ever. Probably the key element in the loss of faith in the UN by the United States is simply that the UN no longer so easily serves the interests of the U.S. foreign policy as it did in the 1950s and 1960s.

One U.S. response has been to cut back our financial contributions to the UN. A legislative measure sponsored by Senator Nancy Kassenbaum (R.-Kans), and signed into law by President Reagan, effectively reduced by one-fifth our UN dues in 1987. That legislation also advised the UN to replace its principle of one nation, one vote on budgetary matters. We want the world body to introduce weighted voting, with power accorded to each nation on the basis of its financial contribution to the UN. Secretary of State George Shultz called the existing system "taxation without representation" because it gives each of the 159 nations an equal say in determining the budget regardless of its contributions. Other cutbacks in the U.S. budget, brought about because of the Gramm-Rudman-Hollings budget balancing legislation will cause still further cuts in our UN contributions.

Some conservatives have long opposed our involvement in the UN, fearing we risk being trapped or outvoted by the communists or by nit-picking third-world nations. Critics across the political spectrum question whether it makes sense to give every UN member an equal vote in the UN's General Assembly regardless of its size, population, and contribution to the UN budget. (Britain, China, France, the Soviet Union, and the United States hold permanent seats in the UN's once-important Security Council, a fifteen-seat body.) Americans are plainly annoyed too by the increasing anti-U.S. rhetoric heard in the General Assembly.

[28] See Peter R. Baehr and Leon Gordenker, *The United Nations: Reality and Ideal* (Praeger,1984), and Shirley Hazzard, *Defeat of an Ideal: A Study of the Self Destruction of the United Nations* (Little, Brown, 1973).

The Nobel UN

The 1988 Nobel Peace Prize was awarded, as had four earlier ones, to a group related to the UN. This time the award recognized the UN's peacekeeping forces. The UN peacekeeping effort consists of some 11,000 troops and roughly 2,000 support personnel. In recent years they have sought to end or reduce conflicts between Iran and Iraq, between Israel and Syria, between Israel and Lebanon, and between Greece and Turkey, among other conflicts. In many respects, the 1988 award honored Secretary General Javier Perez de Cuellar who proved to be a masterful negotiator. "The most important role of the secretary general is to help the parties in a dispute save face," Perez de Cuellar said. "When someone has to make a concession, it is easier to do it through the secretary general than directly to one's adversary." This Nobel Peace Prize helped, at least for awhile, to enhance worldwide esteem for the UN and its delicate missions.

Idealists believe the UN fails because we have had so little faith in it. They counsel us to expect more of it: *Stick with it and try to make it work.* Make it the world switchboard, whose job is to alert the world to our common problems long before they get out of control. Use its peace-keeping forces and its forums for conflict reduction, to make the world a safer place.

If the UN did not exist, something else like it would no doubt be devised to curb quarrels among independent sovereign nations. Even though only about half of the American public says the UN is doing a good job, about 80 percent believe we should remain in it—because we are better with it than without it. Although it is improbable that the UN will soon recapture the optimistic vision and spirit with which it was founded, it is impossible for most of us to imagine not trying.

SUMMARY

1. American foreign policy during the past fifty years or more has been greatly influenced, and at times completely shaped, by our relations with the Soviet Union. To understand our foreign policy, we must first understand the continuing competition between these two major powers. Also, other economic and nuclear powers have emerged over the past twenty years thus complicating even more the challenge of formulating wise and effective foreign policies.

2. Foreign policy is not made according to any set formula, but represents various traditions, organized interests, and constitutional processes. Our democracy has given the primary responsibility for making foreign policy to the chief executive. But presidents in turn are dependent on accidents of history, on advisers, and, in the long run, on the American people. When there are no obvious solutions to international problems, our decision makers must predict, act, and wait—sometimes successfully, but sometimes with unforeseeable and catastrophic consequences.

3. Our foreign policy interests are advanced by one or a combination of the following strategies or means: diplomacy, foreign aid, economic sanctions, political coercion (including breaking off of diplomatic relations), covert action, and military intervention.

4. Presidents can act swiftly and decisively. They are often in a good position to see the nation's long-run interests above the tugging of bureaucratic and special interests. They must face the people in elections, but not so often that they must slavishly follow public opinion. Yet the desired presidential accountability between elections can only be achieved if the people are willing to inform themselves and demand answers, explanations, and honest reporting from their leaders.

5. War is merely an extension of diplomacy. Perhaps future generations will be able to eliminate this alternative entirely, but in our own time leaders must deal with realities, not dreams; with the world as they see it, not as they wish it. Greater restraints upon decision makers might undermine our security, and fewer restraints might endanger our freedom. In the end, we have to be aware of the limits of our power to assist nations threatened by totalitarian systems and of the need to reappraise the balance of power among our institutions.

FURTHER READING

Stephen E. Ambrose. *Rise to Globalism: American Foreign Policy, 1938–1980,* 2nd ed. (Penguin, 1980).

David A. Baldwin. *Economic Statecraft* (Princeton University Press, 1985).

Zbigniew Brzezinski. *Game Plan: A Geostrategic Framework for the Conduct of the U.S.-Soviet Contest* (Atlantic Monthly Press, 1986).

Cecil V. Crabb, Jr. *The Doctrines of American Foreign Policy* (Louisiana State University Press, 1982).

Chicago Council on Foreign Relations, *Gorbachev and Glasnost* (Chicago Council on Foreign Relations, 1987).

Gordon A. Craig and Alexander L. George. *Force and Statecraft: Diplomatic Problems of Our Time* (Oxford University Press, 1983).

I. M. Destler. *Making Foreign Economic Policy* (Brookings Institution, 1980).

Alexander L. George. *Presidential Decision Making in Foreign Policy: The Effective Use of Information and Advice* (Westview, 1980).

Lee H. Hamilton and Daniel K. Inouye et al., *Iran-contra Affair,* Report of the Congressional Committees Investigating the Iran-contra Affair, H. Rpt. 100–433 U.S. Government Printing Office, 1987).

Daniel J. Kaufman and Jeffrey S. McKitrick, eds. *U.S. National Security: A Framework for Analysis* (Lexington Books, 1985).

William B. Quandt. *Camp David: Peacemaking and Politics* (Brookings Institution, 1986).

Richard Rosencrance. *The Rise of the Trading State: Commerce and the Quest in the Modern World* (Basic Books, 1986).

Aaron Wildavsky. *Beyond Containment: Alternative American Policies toward the Soviet Union* (Institute for Contemporary Studies, 1983).

See also *Foreign Affairs* and *Foreign Policy*, two excellent journals published quarterly.

20

Providing for the Common Defense

The Constitution of 1787 was written, ratified, and put into effect in good part because the framers and their friends feared for the security and survival of the new nation. They knew that action, unity, and sure leadership would be needed for future military emergencies. Today, presidents, Congress, and the public alike hope, work, and pray for a world in which our weapons and military forces may no longer be necessary, but our policy makers must deal with the world as it is.

Our security rests on several factors: an overall military balance with the Soviet Union, arms control negotiations, our economic strength, as well as our heritage of human rights and justice.

Both Congress and the president are responsible for the common defense, and both have constitutional authority to discharge that responsibility. Congress appropriates the money and determines the size, structure, and organization of the fighting forces. The president is the commander in chief of these forces and initially determines how military power will be deployed. The president and Congress are jointly responsible for defining our defense objectives and ensuring that our deterrence and overall defense strategies are equal to the challenges from hostile nations. In defense, as in foreign policy, the president is often the key decision maker in emergencies.

Heated debates have taken place recently over what constitutes an effective national defense, especially over the controversial Strategic Defense Initiative (often called Star Wars). Other problems being debated by national defense policy makers are:

Are the Defense Department and the Joint Chiefs of Staff properly organized to provide the strategic direction needed to link long-range policies and military resources?

How can the procurement process deficiencies, such as cost overruns, stretched-out development and delivery schedules, and unsatisfactory weapons performance be remedied?

How can the poor inter-Service coordination during the Vietnam conflict, the Iranian hostage rescue mission, and even the intervention in Grenada be improved?

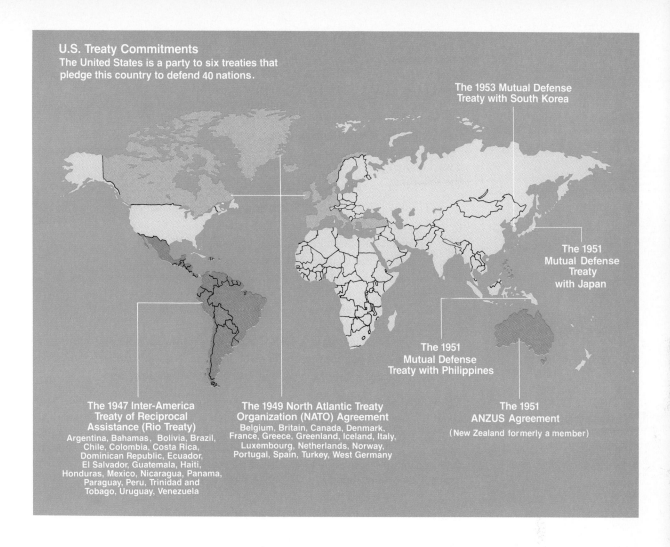

U.S. Treaty Commitments
The United States is a party to six treaties that pledge this country to defend 40 nations.

The 1953 Mutual Defense Treaty with South Korea

The 1951 Mutual Defense Treaty with Japan

The 1951 Mutual Defense Treaty with Philippines

The 1947 Inter-America Treaty of Reciprocal Assistance (Rio Treaty)
Argentina, Bahamas, Bolivia, Brazil, Chile, Colombia, Costa Rica, Dominican Republic, Ecuador, El Salvador, Guatemala, Haiti, Honduras, Mexico, Nicaragua, Panama, Paraguay, Peru, Trinidad and Tobago, Uruguay, Venezuela

The 1949 North Atlantic Treaty Organization (NATO) Agreement
Belgium, Britain, Canada, Denmark, France, Greece, Greenland, Iceland, Italy, Luxembourg, Netherlands, Norway, Portugal, Spain, Turkey, West Germany

The 1951 ANZUS Agreement
(New Zealand formerly a member)

How best can we prevent nuclear war: through further efforts on our current deterrence theories, reliance on the Strategic Defense Initiative, better conventional forces, more carriers and submarines, new technologies such as the cruise and stealth, through arms control, negotiations, and diplomacy?

What our national security goals are and how much money, personnel, and weapons are needed to provide for an effective national defense system are continually debated questions. Too often, however, most Americans leave this debate to a small number of informed officials, scientists, scholars, and the military. But the basic issues of defense policy are extremely important to every one of us: (1) What should be our national defense objectives? (2) How much should we spend on defense and how should that money be allocated? (3) How can we minimize the possibility of nuclear war? (4) Can we maximize our safety by threatening other nations, or is our security based on the principle of common security?

THE NATION'S DEFENSE OBJECTIVES

The overriding mission of America's defense program is to deter a nuclear attack against the United States. We seek a peaceful world. We are also committed to defend western Europe, Japan, and several other nations and to protect our vital other nations and to protect our vital interests. Americans expect the president, Congress, and the military to do everything in their power to prevent war and to protect the United States and its allies from attack.

Our defense programs also enable us to conduct our routine diplomatic activities and allow us to have a presence around the world. Because we are a major military power, more attention is paid to our positions and interests.

Our military and defense policies are intertwined with our foreign policy goals. Two hundred years after the beginning of the republic, these objectives include the following:

1. To preserve the United States as an independent nation.
2. To safeguard our institutions and values.
3. To maintain our ability to deter aggression.
4. To reduce the chances of nuclear war.
5. To protect as best we can our supplies of strategic resources, energy, and food.
6. To help resolve regional conflicts and prevent the terrorism that threatens global peace.
7. To defend allied nations with whom we have mutual defense pacts.

   To revitalize our bond with allies who share our traditions, values, and interests.

   To build more rational relationships with potential adversaries.

The United States has been involved in military interventions of one kind or another about 170 times, although only five of these occasions have been declared wars. Our last declaration of war was in 1941. American leaders sometimes use military forces for ends other than war. Since World War II alone we have alerted or deployed military units on more than 200 occasions to achieve specific goals that seemed important enough to warrant a show of military power.[1]

U.S. Defense Systems and the Strategic Debate

Since the advent of nuclear weapons after World War II, America's primary defense against a Soviet attack has been the strategy of **deterrence** based on the threat of a massive retaliation. Effective deterrence is commonly measured by the usable strength of a survivable second-strike force. This means the United States wants such a large, diversified, and well-protected defense system that a Soviet first strike would not cripple our ability to retaliate decisively. We seek to prevent war by maintaining military forces and demonstrating the determination to use them, if needed, in ways that will persuade opponents that the cost of any attack on our interests will exceed the benefits they could hope to gain.

This strategy of mutual assured destruction is the core of American policy, and has been for a generation or more. Pentagon officials claim it has worked reasonably well. At least, they point out, it has succeeded in winning for the United States and our allies more than four decades of peace with our primary adversary—a period twice as long as the time span between World Wars I and II.

To be effective, deterrence must meet four tests:

Survivability: Our forces must be able to survive a preemptive attack with sufficient retaliatory strength to threaten losses that outweigh gains.

Credibility: Our threatened response to an attack must be of a form that the potential aggressor believes we could and would carry out.

[1] Barry M. Blechman and Stephen S. Kaplan, *Force without War: U.S. Armed Forces as a Political Instrument* (Brookings Institution, 1978).

U.S. Active Duty Military Personnel Abroad

Total for All Locations	503,793
Ashore	447,998
Afloat	55,795
Major Locations Abroad	
Europe	344,120
Afloat	20,589
West Germany	249,753
United Kingdom	28,964
Italy	14,653
Spain	9,418
Turkey	5,174
Greece	3,746
Other	11,823
East Asia and Pacific	122,886
Afloat	19,197
Japan	46,663
South Korea	41,392
Philippines	14,534
Other	1,100
Western Hemisphere	21,848
Afloat	5,696
Panama	9,774
Guantanamo	2,274
Honduras	1,224
Other	2,880

Source: Department of Defense.

Clarity: The action to be deterred must be sufficiently clear to our adversaries that the potential aggressor knows what is prohibited.

Safety: The risk of failure through accident, unauthorized use, or miscalculation must be minimized.[2]

This strategy of mutual assured destruction means that the only deterrent we have to keep an adversary from using nuclear weapons on us is our commitment to kill as many or more of them as they kill of us. This, for obvious reasons, has never been a wholly pleasing strategy. Many Americans, including most of our recent presidents, have been fundamentally dissatisfied with this defense strategy. Groups such as the Catholic bishops and other religious peace activists have condemned this posture and challenged the morality of relying on nuclear weapons to deter, much less to fight, a nuclear war. Advocates of the nuclear freeze, including many members in Congress and millions of citizens who voted for the freeze in state referendums in the early 1980s, called on both the United States and the Soviet Union to halt production, testing, and deployment of nuclear weapons.

The most important challenge to the traditional deterrence strategies came from President Reagan. In a now famous address, Reagan called on American science to create a total defense against ballistic missiles, a defense of such qualitative difference that it could permit, he argued, a major shift in our defense systems. Nuclear strategy would no longer be based on offense, but rather on defense, no longer on assured destruction, but on assured survival. He put it this way:

> Up until now we have increasingly based our strategy of deterrence upon the threat of retaliation. But what if free people could live secure in the knowledge that their security did not rest on the threat of instant U.S. retaliation to deter a Soviet attack; that we could intercept and destroy strategic ballistic missiles before they reached our soil or that of our allies. I know this is a formidable task . . . but isn't it worth every investment necessary to free the world from the threat of nuclear war?[3]

Officially called the Strategic Defense Initiative, this proposal became popularly known as the "Star Wars" program. In the months that followed its announcement, "Star Wars" began to be envisioned as one of the biggest research projects in American history, a five year $26 billion undertaking. Its long-range objective is the erection of a space "shield" to destroy enemy warheads after they are launched, while they are in space flight, or as they reenter the atmosphere. The "shield" would not actually be a shield but rather a complex network of laser beams, particle beams, electromagnetic "slingshot" rail guns, and sensing, tracking, and aiming devices, all requiring highly sophisticated computer and satellite coordination at many different stages and levels.

Reagan was essentially saying that deterrence through the threat of mutual assured destruction should not be the basis for an enduring peace and that the threat to kill hundreds of millions of civilians as punishment for some unacceptable acts by a few government leaders was wrong. He was not the first American president to think this way. Every president going back to Harry Truman has sought an alternative to our primary defense strategy—yet no viable alternative has ever been developed.

What was the reaction to Reagan's initiative? Although it was not entirely a new idea, the boldness and size of his project aroused the nation and triggered a national debate about defense strategy that is still going on. Conservative Reagan supporters hailed it as a means of taking advantage of American scientific and economic superiority to render Soviet nuclear weapons obsolete. Critics argued that the Star Wars program will cause the Soviet Union to increase its offensive nuclear

[2] Caspar W. Weinberger, "U.S. Defense Strategy," *Foreign Affairs* (Spring 1986), p. 677.
[3] Ronald Reagan, March 23, 1983, address.

attack forces to overcome this defense, to devise countermeasures to defeat it, and to perceive preemptive first strike as its best course of action. Critics also say that the technological inventions SDI would require are highly unlikely to work and would cost too much. They propose that the events surrounding the Challenger and Chernobyl disasters should caution us against grand wishful thinking—and about relying on technology.

Following is a summary of the principal points made by supporters and opponents of the SDI proposal:

Supporters say:

1. The U.S. should move away from deterrence based on the threat of nuclear retaliation and toward protection by complete, nationwide defense.

2. Even if a complete defense against nuclear weapons were unattainable, partial defenses are feasible and would reinforce deterrence by retaliation.

3. The U.S. enjoys both technological and economic advantages over the Soviets and ought to exploit these strengths.

4. At least while the SDI is in the research stage, it is essential that the U.S. not be constrained by arms control agreements that might limit research into the development and utility of strategic defenses.

5. Major new space-based technologies for defense appear to be possible and must be studied, if for no other reason than that the Soviets might develop them first. Even though some of the technologies may not work out, research can discover others that will. SDI is merely a research program; development decisions can be made later, after the technologies and their effectiveness have been established.

Opponents say:

1. The goal of a sure-proof defense is an illusion that cannot be achieved because the task is too difficult, it requires too many technological breakthroughs, and it will not be cost effective, especially if we strive for a near-perfect system. In addition, the Soviets will devise countermeasures that undermine deployment.

2. Although limited defenses, especially those of hardened military targets, are possible, they are enormously expensive. There are other ways of protecting these targets, such as mobility and redundancy, but they do not eliminate dependence on deterrence by second-strike nuclear retaliation.

"Before we talk about my daughter—where do you stand on STAR WARS?" (© *Drawing by Berry,* © 1985. *NEA, Inc.*)

3. The Soviets can, and are likely to, respond to an American defense shield against their nuclear weapons with a variety of relatively low-cost measures including shortened launch times for missiles; increased numbers of missiles; increased numbers of warheads, decoys, and other penetration aids.

4. The cost of a multitiered space shield system will be enormous: $60 billion for research alone in the first decade, and estimates ranging from several hundred to $1000 billion for a final deployment of the full system.

5. A major U.S. program to develop SDI will only succeed if offensive forces are greatly reduced and constrained. Yet the SDI, if pursued unilaterally, could foreclose the possibility of negotiating joint reductions in nuclear arms.

6. The projected SDI is an attempt to apply military-technical solutions to what is basically a political problem between the U.S. and the USSR.[4]

7. SDI might encourage first strike by the country possessing "Star Wars", or may lead opposition nation into so thinking.

What is the status of the Star Wars program? It is still just a starry vision rather than an actual defense system. Congress went along with Reagan and funded, although somewhat scaled back from Reagan's requests, the early years of research. Whatever else, the concept of a space-based defensive shield system may have prompted the Soviet leaders to return to the bargaining table. The Soviets make it plain that they would like to see the United States abandon the goal of a space-based defensive system. Though they deny they used the SDI program as a bargaining chip, U.S. officials nonetheless did effectively use the program to gain certain other concessions from the Soviets.

We will be debating U.S. defense strategies and alternative offensive and defensive systems well into the 1990s. Meanwhile, research will continue. Critics worry that this whole research program may ultimately block negotiations of major reductions in offensive weapons. They also see it is a further step in the militarization of space. Optimists hope that it can be a turning in the nuclear age and that the mutual suicide pacts of the current era can be replaced by a lasting promise of peace based on the dignity of life. Pragmatic observers hope that if it does get developed, it will bring about the first genuine reversal in the nuclear arms race since it began in 1946.

HOW MUCH IS ENOUGH?

Americans of every political view want a strong and effective defense. But considerable controversy arises about whether the Defense Department spends too much and about whether its weapons systems are reliable. Recent critics from both the right and the left say the Pentagon is a bureaucracy run wild and that its monies are not as wisely or effectively spent as they should be.[5] The Defense Department itself has charged many of the nation's biggest weapons contractors with poor design, inadequate quality controls, and excessive costs. In one recent year, forty-five of the top 100 defense contractors were under criminal investigation.[6]

[4] This summary of points is adapted from Jeffrey Boutwell and F. A. Long, "The SDI and U.S. Security," in Franklin A. Long et al., eds., *Weapons in Space* (Norton, 1986), pp. 297–99. For other appraisals of the SDI-Star Wars proposal, see Keith B. Payne, *Strategic Defense: "Star Wars" in Perspective* (Hamilton Press, 1986); Gary L. Guertner and Donald M. Snow, *The Last Frontier: An Analysis of the Strategic Defense Initiative* (Lexington Books, 1986); and Union of Concerned Scientists, ed. *The Fallacy of Star Wars* (Vintage, 1984).

[5] See, for example, Edward N. Luttwak, *The Pentagon and the Art of War* (Simon & Schuster, 1985); Gary Hart and William Lind, *America Can Win* (Adler and Adler, 1986); and Arthur T. Hadley, *The Straw Giant* (Random House, 1986).

[6] Richard Halloran, "Making Arms Makers Do It Right," *The New York Times* (June 15, 1986), section F, p. 4.

20–1 Public Opinion and Defense Spending

Is the U.S. spending too much, about right, or too little on defense?
DEFENSE SPENDING

Year	Too Much	About Right	Too Little	No Opinion
1986	47%	36%	13%	4%
1980	14	24	49	13
1976	36	32	22	10
1974	44	32	12	12
1971	49	31	11	9
1969	52	31	8	9

Source: Gallup poll index.

Controlling the Defense Budget

During the peak of the Vietnam War effort, almost half the American people thought we were spending too much on defense. By 1980 many thought we were spending too little (Table 20–1). After Vietnam, expenditures for health, welfare, and education went way up. Those for national defense—at least as a proportion of the budget—went down. After defense spending had doubled in the 1981–86 period, these trends were reversed, and once again many people began to think we were spending too much on defense.

President Reagan dramatically increased defense spending even as he slowed increases in other areas and cut the federal budget in still others. But public concern over waste and purchasing practices in the Defense Department sharply increased. Critics of the approach pointed out that our investments must be carefully targeted to those areas most vital to national security—especially in strengthening our conventional forces, improving troop readiness, and upgrading the recruiting and training of military personnel.

Critics of the increases doubted the wisdom of funding every new system on the Pentagon's shopping list. They noted that historically the most important factor in winning wars has been people; strategy and tactics come second, and expensive equipment often comes third.

Constant Pressures to Increase Defense Spending

One of the chief reasons presidents and Congress have such difficulty controlling the defense budget is that many people oppose any bold program of closing military bases or consolidating military operations. Base closings anger politicians, as well as local constituents and economic interests; and the Defense Department must hold extensive hearings before it can actually close a base. Further, weapons are a major American industry—and the industry and the members of Congress from their areas work hard to promote their products. Representatives from shipyard districts push for more submarines; those from Texas, St. Louis, or Seattle push for new planes. Then too, the logrolling arrangements that operate in other pork-barrel areas work here as well: You fatten my district, and I'll fatten yours. Even the fiercest antiwar doves in Congress can shout the loudest when a base closing or contract termination is suggested for their districts or states.

Government is usually the sole purchaser of most military hardware. The high technological levels of defense weaponry create high research and development costs, sometimes strung out over several years or a decade, that often cause high initial capital investments. The arms industry has the appearance of private enterprise operating in the commercial marketplace. But this is misleading, "for most of the big contractors operate as monopolies while the Pentagon is a monopsony, the

The Top Defense Contractors

McDonnell
  Douglas
General
  Dynamics
Rockwell
  International
General Electric
Boeing
Lockheed
United
  Technologies
Hughes Aircraft
Raytheon
Grumman
Martin Marietta

Source: Department of Defense.

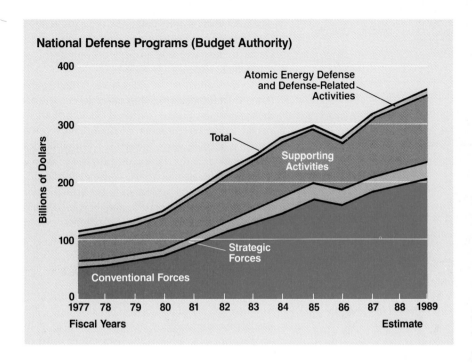

National Defense Programs (Budget Authority)

Atomic Energy Defense
and Defense-Related
Activities

Total

Supporting
Activities

Strategic
Forces

Conventional Forces

Billions of Dollars

400

300

200

100

0

1977 78 79 80 81 82 83 84 85 86 87 88 1989

Fiscal Years **Estimate**

sole customer. Competition is often artificial and does little to encourage quality, efficiency, or economy. For instance, the Navy can buy the F-18 only from McDonnall-Douglas—or threaten, as it once did, to buy a different airplane from another company."[7] Pentagon officials say they occasionally find themselves with no place to turn.

Tensions also arise because military contractors must serve two contending masters: the Pentagon and taxpayers who want effective arms made at the lowest possible cost, and corporate shareholders who obviously want to make profits. Critics say that when these contending interests conflict, profits appear to take priority and the quality of arms suffers. All of this has led to a burgeoning staff of government inspectors who attempt to audit and measure manufacturers' efficiency and arms effectiveness.

How much defense spending is enough? A nation can never tell if defense expenditures are adequate until they are not—and then it is too late. Hence, when in doubt, the tendency is to spend more. Further, some of the best technical minds in the nation have been enticed into defense research and development work, and good minds can almost always come up with better, more expensive systems. The contracting structure of defense projects further escalates costs. It used to be that defense contracts operated on a cost-plus basis: A percentage of costs was designated as profits, to provide a direct incentive to decrease costs. Today (sometimes, but not always) contracts involve all costs plus a fixed fee, which provides little incentive to hold defense costs down.

The Defense Department spends well over $350 billion a year. More than half the people employed by the national government work in the Defense Department. Nearly three-quarters of federal purchases of goods and services originate in the defense budget. Moreover, about 4000 defense installations are scattered across the country. Contracts in excess of $100 billion result in defense-related nongovern-

[7] Richard Halloran, Ibid., p. 4.

mental civilian employment of over 2 million. More than 1.5 million retired Defense Department personnel draw pensions and other fringe benefits. Clearly, the Defense Department's size and impact on our society raise questions about how it can be controlled.

According to the venerable foreign policy expert George Kennan, this vast flow of "military spending comes to constitute a vested interest on the part of all those who participate in it and benefit from it." The number of people who have a stake in the continuation of high defense spending is enormous, and their political punch is usually very powerful. "This includes not just the industrialists who get the money and the Pentagon purchasers who get the hardware and services," says Kennan, "but also all those who benefit from the arrangement in other ways: not only the uniformed personnel of the armed services but those who serve the Pentagon directly as civilian workers, and beyond them the many more who, as workers in defense plants or in other capacities, share in the spin-off from these vast expenditures."[8]

The Military-Industrial Complex

By its nature the defense industry is different from most other large industries in America. National defense is what economists call a "public good"—there is no way to exclude citizens from "consuming" national defense, whether they wish to pay for it or not. Thus, the government must provide for defense by taxing citizens. If it did not, most people would not pay, because they would figure they would receive the benefits anyway. Because the government is really the sole purchaser of defense, the defense industries—aerospace, electronics, and shipbuilding—rely heavily on government contracts for a large part of their business. In turn, the localities in which these industries are located, especially in the Sunbelt areas (Charleston, San Antonio, Colorado Springs, and San Diego, for example), rely heavily on defense spending for economic growth and stability. The defense industry is intertwined in the American economy; yet it responds to a different set of demands than other industries, and remains largely independent of private consumption and investment trends.

However, what some defense budget analysts are calling the "Reagan Revolution" has sharply increased federal defense spending in the 1980s. In recent years, for example, national defense outlays were at their highest levels since 1969 (the second most costly year of the Vietnam War) and higher than at any other time in peacetime history. National defense spending increased from 5.5 percent of the gross national product in the early 1980s to over 6.6 in the late 1980s. Real authority for defense procurement jumped by more than 100 percent in Reagan's first six years in office; procurement for strategic nuclear forces rose by 182 percent, and for conventional forces by 87 percent in that same period.[9]

Critics sometimes charge that the military conspires with defense contractors and other strategic elites to maintain a vast network of bases and fleets around the world. They contend that the **military-industrial complex** has a life of its own, is too big to be managed or controlled, spends too large a share of our national wealth, and is dedicated to exaggerating the "Soviet menace."

President Eisenhower once asked Soviet leader Nikita Khrushchev how he decided the question of funds for military expenses in his nation. Eisenhower began by saying:

Perhaps first I should tell you how it is with us. It's like this: My military leaders say, "Mr. President, we need such and such a sum for such and such a program." I

Answer/Discussion

A widespread perception that the defense budget is riddled with waste is reflected not only in media "horror stories" but in congressional hearings and even Pentagon acknowledgment of overcharges for weapons and spare parts and of rifles and tanks that do not meet specifications. Defenders of the Pentagon and contractors say these charges are overblown and that the worst way to improve things would be to impose more audits and intrusive inspections: These merely add to costs and weaken morale, they say. Senator William Proxmire of Wisconsin, on the other hand, urges the following steps: Take the profits out of the revolving door. Nothing erodes the credibility of defense contracting more than the public perception that high military and civilian Pentagon officials are feathering their nests by doing favors for contractors—and then joining those firms after they retire. Defense officials need to have "the strength of character to tell defense contractors when to get off and where to go." They need to end contracts, shift work to others, and maintain a tough policy with those who do not live up to their contracts. Finally, Proxmire urges prosecution and jail. "Nothing deters misconduct as much as the prospects of jail. Fines, temporary suspensions and resignations are not enough."*

* William Proxmire, "Why Military Contracting is Corrupt," *The New York Times* (December 15, 1985), section F, p. 3.

---

[8] George F. Kennan, *The Cloud of Danger* (Atlantic-Little, Brown, 1977), p. 13. See also Adam Yarmolinsky, *The Military Establishment* (Harper & Row, 1971).

[9] William W. Kaufman, *A Reasonable Defense* (Brookings Institution, 1986), chap. 3.

say, "Sorry, we don't have the funds." They say, "We have reliable information that the Soviet Union has already allocated funds for their own such program." So I give in. That's how they wring the money out of me. Now tell me, how is it with you?

Khrushchev responded:

It's just the same. They say, "Comrade Khrushchev, look at this! The Americans are developing such and such a system." I tell them there's no money. So we discuss it some more, and I end up giving them the money they asked for.[10]

Military leaders and many others generally deny the existence of a military-industrial complex. They point to the reduced size of the military and note that since its wartime peak in 1968, the number of military personnel has dropped from 3.5 million to about 2.2 million. Fewer people are in uniform now, they add, than at any time since 1950, and fewer U.S. troops are abroad than at any time since 1940. Further, our active fleet has dropped by nearly half.

Even though we hear much about the military-industrial complex, it is not all-powerful, and it is not the only elite that operates in our democracy. There is also a scientific-intellectual elite, an agribusiness elite, a public employees elite, a trade union elite, and a number of other interest-group coalitions, all seeking to define the public interest.

WILL U.S. CONVENTIONAL FORCES BE STRONG ENOUGH TO WIN?

Much of the debate over defense spending revolves around the question of *people* versus *weapons*. And central to this question is that of military personnel and their preparedness. We have to ask: If the country's army of volunteers has to go to war, could it fight and win, or would it be outnumbered and outfought?

The All-Volunteer Force

The means of maintaining our military forces have been debated since the beginning of the republic. As early as 1814 Daniel Webster asked his colleagues in Congress: "Where is it written in the Constitution . . . that you may take children from their parents, and parents from their children, and compel them to fight battles of any war in which the folly or the wickedness of government may engage it[self]?" The Constitution authorizes Congress to do what is "necessary and proper" in order to "raise and support armies," "to provide and maintain a navy," and "to provide for calling forth the militia." The problem is that America's role in the world has changed dramatically since 1789, as have our military needs. Although our boundaries once defined our national interest, that interest now reaches around the globe.

Military conscription, or draft, was first instituted in 1862, during the Civil War. It was next used during World War I, when Congress passed the Selective Service Act. This act called for a draft of males between the ages of 21 and 30, although exemptions were allowed for certain public officials and for clergy. In both instances conscription ended when the conflicts ended. The first peacetime draft began in 1940, with the Selective Service and Training Act. By the time of Pearl Harbor in late 1941, men between the ages of 18 and 35 were eligible for the draft. When World War II ended, however, the draft continued, in various forms, for almost three decades. Soon after Vietnam, the all-volunteer force (AVF)

---

[10] Quoted by Clayton Fritchey, June 16, 1973, in a syndicated column, cited in Robert Sherrill, *Why They Call It Politics*, 2nd ed. (Harcourt Brace Jovanovich, 1974), pp. 58–59.

SELECTIVE SERVICE SYSTEM
Registration Form
READ PRIVACY ACT STATEMENT ON REVERSE
PLEASE PRINT CLEARLY

—DO NOT WRITE IN THE ABOVE SPACE—

1 DATE OF BIRTH

_____ Name of Month _____ Day _____ Year

2 SEX
☐ MALE
☐ FEMALE

3 SOCIAL SECURITY NUMBER
___ ___ ___ | ___ ___ | ___ ___ ___ ___

4 PRINT FULL NAME

_____ Last _____ First _____ Middle

5 CURRENT MAILING ADDRESS

_____ Number and Street _____ City _____ State or Foreign Country _____ Zip Code

6 PERMANENT RESIDENCE

_____ Number and Street _____ City _____ State or Foreign Country _____ Zip Code

7 CURRENT PHONE NUMBER

_____ Area Code _____ Number

Postal Date Stamp & Clerk Initials
☐ ID

8 ☐ Check here if we may give your name, address and telephone number to Armed Forces recruiters.

☐ NO ID

9 I AFFIRM THE FOREGOING STATEMENTS ARE TRUE

_____ Today's Date _____ Signature of Registrant

☐ OTHER

SSS Form 1 (Feb 80) ☐ (Previous Editions Will Not Be Used) OMB Approval 194-R0002

---

was established by Congress. This force is to provide for our peacetime military personnel needs, although a draft is to be reinstituted in time of war. Draft registration ended in 1975—to the delight of most young men—making the United States the first and only world power to maintain large-scale armed forces without some form of conscription.

Since its beginning, the all-volunteer force has been the center of controversy. Some experts contend the AVF has worked, that the quality and quantity of recruits are as good or better than under the draft, and that the social costs are much lower. Other experts say quantity and quality have dropped; that the force is more and more made up of minoritites or the disadvantaged, and that the AVF would be largely unable to defend our vital interests abroad.

In the early 1980s, the military had problems attracting the desired number of recruits. All four services reported serious shortfalls; and active reserves were at only 80 percent strength. Further, experienced personnel, physicians, technicians, and even pilots were in short supply in certain areas of the military. Later in the 1980s the nation was running short of 18 year olds: The World War II baby boom was over; potential recruits in proportion to the total population were fewer than ever.

Total personnel in all services is over 2.2 million. Reserve enlistments are up. Today minorities are overrepresented in the armed services, notably in the Army, where blacks comprise over 30 percent of the enlisted ranks (this sometimes gives rise to the contention that the all-volunteer force is becoming a mercenary army).[11] Women are underrepresented, although the proportion of women to men in the armed forces is growing.

The combat readiness of the AVF is the subject, understandably, of heated

[11] But see Charles C. Moskos, "Success Story: Blacks in the Army," *The Atlantic Monthly* (May 1986), pp. 64–72.

debate. Preparedness may be judged in part by the educational level of new recruits. About 85 percent of all new enlisted troops have graduated from high school, a much higher level than the eligible pool. But maintaining this level requires extensive recruiting, and higher pay and fringe benefits. Another barometer of overall troop quality, reenlistment, is also increasing. Trends like these are often affected by economic conditions. High unemployment makes military service more attractive as compared to civilian employment; for many individuals it may actually be the only economically viable alternative. Long-term improvements such as higher pay and increased educational benefits are necessary to ensure the general strength and quality of the AVF.

Perhaps the most serious concern about the all-volunteer force is whether or not it is prepared for military combat. If there were a conflict requiring call-up of reserves and conscription, would we be able to produce enough combat-ready forces in time? Although some observers contend that conventional forces are obsolete in any large-scale conflict, such as a Soviet invasion of Europe, most insist we need conventional forces as a deterrent. The danger lies in becoming too reliant on "massive retaliation" and missiles, so that we would be forced to respond with nuclear weapons.[12]

The Politics of Draft Registration

The all-volunteer force was set up as a peacetime measure: If emergencies came, so would the draft. However, President Jimmy Carter won approval for the resumption of draft registration. Carter's original plan called for the registration of men and women born in 1960 and 1961. Thereafter individuals would be required to

Active Military Personnel*	
Army	780,000
Air Force	635,000
Navy	615,000
Marines	205,000
Total	**2,235,000**

Nonactive Reserve Forces	
Army	1,300,000
Navy	305,000
Air Force	250,000
Marines	130,000
Total	**1,985,000**

* Defense Department projections for 1990, figures rounded off.

[12] William Bowman et al., eds., *The All-Volunteer Force After a Decade* (Pergamon Press, 1985).

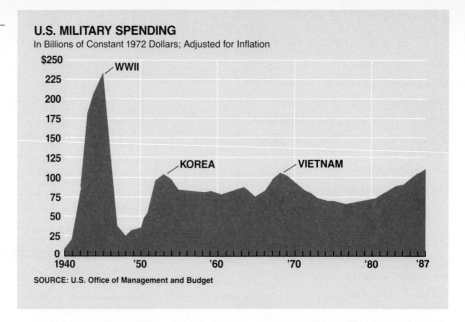

U.S. MILITARY SPENDING
In Billions of Constant 1972 Dollars; Adjusted for Inflation

WWII

KOREA   VIETNAM

SOURCE: U.S. Office of Management and Budget

Women take an increasingly active role in the armed services. (*U.S. Air Force Photo*)

register within thirty days of their 18th birthdays. However, Congress refused to appropriate funds for the registration of women. Later the Supreme Court ruled Congress could, if it wished, call for the registration of men and not of women (this is the practice now).

Carter based his advocacy for registration on two grounds. First, in the wake of the Soviet invasion of Afghanistan, registration would send a message to the Soviet Union demonstrating our resolve to resist Soviet aggression. Second, this new process would enable us to mobilize more quickly in wartime emergencies, by shortening the time period between initiation of conscription and full mobilization by as many as ninety days.

Some Americans oppose the draft registration process, because they believe it will inevitably lead to a draft. A report by a former director of the Selective Service suggests that registration would save less than two weeks in the event of mobilization. One political figure who spoke out against Carter's draft registration effort said it "destroys the very values that our society is committed to defending"— namely our freedom.[13] That critic, Ronald Reagan, changed his mind once he got to the White House. The Supreme Court has also upheld a law passed by Congress that makes male college students ineligible for federal scholarship aid if they have not registered for the draft.

The Case for Reviving the Draft

Some Americans favor substituting a draft for the present combination of volunteer enlistments and draft registration. Supporters of the draft generally include some conservatives, some members of the military establishment, such defense-conscious Democratic senators as Sam Nunn and Ernest Hollings, and presidential candidate Gary Hart, among others.[14] They claim the armed services have not been able to attract an adequate number of recruits; those who do enlist, critics charge, are not sufficiently qualified to handle the modern, highly sophisticated weapons systems of today's armed forces. Further, supporters add, a draft would be much more equitable than the present system, correcting the disproportionately large minority

[13] Ronald Reagan, quoted in Stuart Taylor, Jr., "Draft Registration: Snags Emerge in Prosecutions," *The New York Times* (December 8, 1982), p. 10.

[14] Some liberals and progressives also favor the draft. See, for example, James Fallows, *National Defense* (Random House, 1981), chap. 5.

membership in the services. Some draft advocates think the privilege of being an American justifies compulsory national service.

Another reason for returning to the draft is to lower defense spending: One of the largest single defense costs is for personnel. Also, as noted earlier, the declining number of teens in this era's pool of draftable males is another factor. But many Americans dispute the need for a draft—particularly the younger people most likely to be conscripted. Those opposed to the draft claim the all-volunteer force is working well: Not only can it fill its quotas, but the overall mental capability of its personnel is higher than that of conscripts. Also, draft opponents believe a peacetime draft contradicts the basic principles of liberty upon which America was founded.[15]

The Role of Women in the Military

One of the more controversial questions today is whether women should join men in military combat. Women now comprise nearly 12 percent of the total enlistment in the armed forces. They are now regularly admitted to, and graduated from, military academies; they have also moved into many military jobs once reserved for men. And as the military becomes more mechanized and technical, the role of women will increase. As one woman member of Congress put it, it doesn't take much muscle to launch an ICBM.

The rise of women in the military has not occurred without some problems. Some males have refused to take orders from women officers. Some have refused to assign females to certain hazardous duties. In addition, at any given time about 5 percent of women in the military are pregnant. However, by far the biggest problem is the question of women's role in combat. Women are currently excluded by law from combat duty in the Navy and Air Force. The Army and Marine Corps forbid the use of women in combat as a matter of established policy. Despite the legal and traditional barriers to the use of women in combat, some analysts say their large numbers and their increasing role in filling important positions make them destined to fight in any future war involving our military forces.

Women are destined to remain an integral part of our country's national defense. Each of the four armed services currently has women serving in "Flag" ranks as admirals and generals. And as long as the armed services continue to rely on volunteers to fill their personnel needs, they cannot afford to overlook such a major—indeed majority—demographic group. Women may face combat simply because it will be inescapable in wartime situations. Still, the country will have to undergo major changes in attitudes before large numbers of women are routinely used in combat situations. Meanwhile, the key to determining a proper role for women in the armed forces, a former secretary of defense has written, "is to move gradually toward expansion of the number of functions available to women, on a voluntary basis, and to insist that women accepted for such positions meet the same standards as the men who serve in them.[16]

REORGANIZING FOR A MORE EFFECTIVE DEFENSE

Another major issue in recent years has been how to organize the Defense Department to ensure that it can provide both the strategic vision and the practical coordination between the military services that is necessary for maximum effectiveness. Con-

[15] The issues concerning the draft and the all-volunteer force are discussed in Brent Scowcroft, ed., *Military Service in the United States* (Spectrum, 1982) and Martin Binkin, *America's Volunteer Military: Progress and Prospect* (Brookings Institution, 1984). See also an evaluation of a proposed compulsory national service requirement, Richard Danzig and Peter Szanton, *National Service: What Would It Mean?* (Lexington, 1986).

[16] Harold Brown, *Thinking About National Security* (Westview, 1983), p. 253.

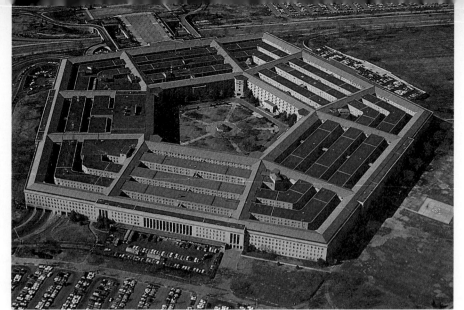

The Pentagon—headquarters for the Department of Defense and the Joint Chiefs of Staff. Built during World War II, the Pentagon is the world's largest office building. Constructed on swamps and landfill on the west bank of the Potomac River in northern Virginia, it has 20 miles of corridors. The Pentagon houses nearly 24,000 workers who tell time by 4200 clocks, drink water from 685 fountains, consume 30,000 cups of coffee daily, and place 200,000 phone calls a day on 87,000 phones connected by 100,000 miles of cable. (*UPI/Bettmann Newsphotos*)

gressional hearings, a presidential commission, and a shelf of books focused on this problem during recent years. This has led to reorganization and new staffing patterns, especially in the Joint Chiefs of Staff.

To understand the current arrangements calls for a look at the organizational apparatus of defense policy making. The president, Congress, the National Security Council, and the State Department make overall policy and attempt to integrate our national security programs. But the day-to-day work of organizing for defense is the job of the Defense Department. The Pentagon, its headquarters, houses within its miles of corridors nearly 24,000 top military and civilian personnel. The offices of several hundred generals and admirals are there, as is the office of the secretary of defense, symbolizing civilian control of the armed services.

Prior to 1947 there were two separate military departments, War and Navy. The difficulty of coordinating them during World War II led to demands for unification. In 1947 the Air Force, already an autonomous unit within the War Department, was made an independent unit. The three military departments—Army, Navy, and Air Force—were placed under the general supervision of the secretary of defense. The Unification Act of 1947 was a bundle of compromises between the Army, which favored a tightly integrated department, and the Navy, which wanted a loosely federated structure. It also reflected compromises between members of Congress who felt that disunity and interservice rivalries were undermining our defense efforts, and those who feared that a unified defense establishment would defy civilian control and smother dissenting views. Unfortunately, all the act really accomplished was to bring the military services under a common organizational chart. Instead of moving from two military departments to one, we ended up with three.

President Eisenhower felt strongly about the need to strengthen and centralize the Defense Department. Using his prestige as the victorious commander of the Allied Forces in World War II, he secured from Congress the Defense Department Reorganization Act. The act gave additional authority to the secretary of defense and the Joint Chiefs of Staff, especially its chair. But Congress continued to insist (and still does) that the appropriation of funds be made directly to the specific services, and funnelled to them through the office of the secretary of defense. Congress also insisted that the secretary of defense notify the House and Senate armed services committees when contemplating any major changes in combat functions. Congress also refused to repeal a provision, which Eisenhower called legalized insubordination, authorizing secretaries of a military department or members of the Joint Chiefs to make any recommendations they wish to Congress about Defense Department matters, even if their recommendations are contrary to department policy.

Procurement Fraud Scandal—1988

The great growth of defense spending in the 1980s may have fostered a get-rich-quick attitude among defense contractors and defense consultants. At the heart of a 1988 government probe were "allegations that defense contractors spied on the Pentagon, on one another and even on other countries. They allegedly paid consultants to get classified information on program objectives, contract specifications, and their competitors' secret bids. Investigators say the consultants, often ex-Pentagon officials, sold access and brokered information to the highest bidder."[17]

The Pentagon probe of the cozy relationships between defense contractors and top Pentagon officials was quickly dubbed "Pentagate." Critics say that as military contracts became more lucrative some contractors began to do anything to win these contracts. The Defense Department awards at least $150 billion worth of contracts each year. It is also said the Defense Department's management was inefficient and the Justice Department's efforts to combat procurement abuses were similarly mismanaged.

The scandals became a campaign issue in the 1988 elections and numerous proposals for reorganizing the Pentagon and its procurement processes will be debated on into the 1990s. Some members of Congress favor creating a "procurement czar" for all Pentagon acquisitions. Others urge stiff fines, long jail terms, and debarment from government contracts for those who violate existing bribery and bid-rigging laws.[18]

The Confederational Nature of the Defense Bureaucracy

It is common to hear criticisms of the "Pentagon machine," the "national military establishment," or the "military mind." The defense bureaucracy is, however, best understood—as is any bureaucracy—as something less than a monolith. In practice, the Defense Department is comprised of four major components: (1) the Office of the Secretary of Defense and the civilians in the Department of Defense; (2) the organization of the Joint Chiefs of Staff; (3) the individual armed services (Army, Navy, Air Force, Marines); and (4) the intelligence community (Defense Intelligence Agency and National Security Agency).

Reflecting the fragmented nature of the larger American political system, defense policy is thrashed out in a day-to-day process of give and take among these constituent units in the Defense Department along with officials in the State Department, CIA, and the National Security Council at the White House. Insiders often stress that this policy-making structure is best thought of as a confederation or bargaining arena as opposed to a tight chain-of-command hierarchy. In fact, in the late 1980s, a major issue has been the desirability of more centralized control and direction of the nation's defense bureaucracy.

Military Chief of Staff: Essential Reform or Too Much Centralization?

For decades there has been concern that the Joint Chiefs of Staff serve not to focus military planning but as an agency in which each military service chief defends his own service with the chair being so weak that little real leadership exists.

The Joint Chiefs of Staff (JCS) serve as the principal military advisers to the president, the National Security Council, and the secretary of defense. They include the military heads of the three armed services, the commandant of the

(Cartoon by Herblock, © 1988. The Washington Post)

---

[17] "We've Got Some of These Guys Dead to Rights," *Business Week*, July 4, 1988, p. 31.
[18] Elizabeth Tucker and Anne Swardson, "The Muddy 'Buddy System'," *The Washington Post* Weekly Edition, June 27–July 3, 1988, p. 8.

Marine Corps, and a chair. The service chiefs are all appointed by the president with the consent of the Senate for four-year, nonrenewable terms. The chair of the JCS is appointed by the president with the consent of the Senate for a two-year term that may be renewed once.

The joint chiefs shape strategic plans, work out supply programs, review major supply and personnel requirements, formulate programs for training, make recommendations to the secretary of defense on the establishment of unified commands in strategic areas, and provide American representation on the military commissions of the United Nations, NATO, and the OAS.

The chair of the joint chiefs takes precedence over all other military officers. The chair presides over the meetings of the joint chiefs, prepares the agenda, directs the staff of some 400 officers in an overall JCS organization of about 2000 people, and informs the secretary of defense and the president of issues on which the joint chiefs have been unable to reach agreement.[19]

Disputes among military services involve more than professional jealousies. The technological revolution in warfare has rendered obsolete existing concepts about military missions. In the past it made sense to divide command among land, sea, and air forces. Today technology makes a mockery of such distinctions. Defense research and development are constantly altering formerly established roles and missions. Yet the individual services are reluctant to give up their traditional functions, or to serve each others' crucial needs. The Navy, for example, is interested in waging sea warfare, not in running a freight service for the Army. Each branch supports weapons that bring it prestige. This often leads to such interservice rivalries as the Army and Air Force quarrel over who should provide air support for ground troops, and the Air Force and Navy dispute over land- versus sea-based missiles.[20]

Sometimes interservice rivalries break out in Congress and the press. Organizations such as the Association of the United States Army, the Navy League, and the Air Force Association lobby openly in behalf of their particular services. Behind the scenes the military themselves are active. The president tries to keep interservice disputes inside the administration, but military commanders who believe administration policy threatens the national security have a problem. They are taught to respect civilian supremacy and to obey civilian superiors. But which civilian superiors? The president as commander in chief? Or should they report to Congress, which is also a civilian superior? A few officers resolve the dilemma of conflicting loyalties by resigning, so that they can be free to carry their views to the nation. Sometimes military personnel who wish to dissent from official policy get their views to Congress by resorting to the Washington practice of "leaking" information to the press. And when testifying before congressional committees, officers can easily allow their views to come across.

The continuation of interservice differences led people to advocate the complete replacement of the joint chiefs by a single chief of staff, the complete integration of the military into a single branch, and the reassignment of forces in terms of strategic missions. Although such a system has had the support of some high-ranking Army and Air Force officers, it is opposed by most Navy officers, members of Congress, and respected students of the joint chiefs structure.

In 1982 former chair of the joint chiefs, General David Jones, called for strengthening the role of the chair of the JCS and increasing the organization's staff capability, and correspondingly reducing service involvement in joint actions. He also urged broadened training, experience, and rewards for officers assigned to

"No, no. When I say this new secret weapon can slip past their defenses undetected, I'm not referring to the Russians, I'm referring to Congress." (Drawing by Stevenson; © 1986 The New Yorker Magazine, Inc.)

---

[19] A dated but still useful study of the operations of the JCS is Lawrence J. Korb, *The Joint Chiefs of Staff: The First Twenty-five Years* (Indiana University Press, 1976).

[20] Bruce M. Russett, *What Price Vigilance? The Burdens of National Defense* (Yale University Press, 1970). A study of interservice rivalries as well as of bureaucratic caution is Edmund Beard, *Developing the ICBM: A Study of Bureaucratic Politics* (Columbia University Press, 1976).

JCS staff. He said service chairs are too often immobilized by their statesman-spokesman dilemma—that is, they are expected both to take the overall national view and also to remain advocates of their respective services. Jones believed the service chiefs were just too imbued with their services' traditions, doctrines, and disciplines, to be objective about innovative proposals and needed military change.

In 1984, the U.S. House of Representatives passed a bill strengthening the role of the JSC chair. A year later, due in part to the leadership of Senator Barry Goldwater, who believed the time had come to reduce service parochialism and to better unify the defense bureaucracy, the Senate issued a major report calling for Defense Department reorganization. This report highlighted the shortcomings of current decentralized management: operational deficiencies, insufficient weapons system acquisition, lack of strategic direction, and inadequate interservice coordination.[21]

Although the Secretary of Defense balked at some of these proposed changes in the defense structure, President Reagan eventually endorsed many of them, as did his presidential commission on defense management (the Packard Commission). Some changes were achieved by executive order, others by legislation in 1986. The net effect of these changes was to reinvigorate the JCS as a source of professional military advice to civilian decision makers. The JCS chair will serve as principal military adviser to the president, the National Security Council, and the secretary of defense. The chair is now required to develop a joint military doctrine and to see whether our personnel, equipment, and budgetary resources are sufficient to meet that task. These changes also stress the importance of joint operations from the JCS on down. In a separate move, Reagan called on Congress to provide for a new position, an undersecretary of defense, to establish and oversee policies for procurement, research, and development of weapons.

Strategic defense policy, much like policy in any other area, is the result not of a collective process of rational inquiry but of a mutual process of give and take. Whether strategic policies are worked out within the Defense Department, the White House, or Congress, the decisions result from a political process in which some measure of consensus is essential. And some conflict among the participants is not necessarily evil. The joint chiefs engage in the same type of logrolling tactics used in Congress. On budget issues they tend to endorse all the programs desired by each service. When forced to choose on an issue of policy, the chiefs have traditionally compromised among the different service positions rather than attempt to develop a position based on a unified military point of view. The challenge for the JCS chair now is to make and enforce critical decisions that impinge on service interests, yet do not prevent useful competition among the services. The goal is to overcome their most wasteful collusions and to provide the reasonable integration that is needed for truly joint operations in military emergencies.

ARMS BUILD UP AND ARMS CONTROL

People have dreamed for centuries of a world in which conflicts could be resolved without force. However, as long as the United States exists in a world of sovereign, independent nations, it will look to its own defenses. Few Americans pay much attention to Soviet proposals to eliminate all nuclear weapons, even though many Americans wish that this could be achieved. The reason is simple: Few Americans trust the Soviets to eliminate their weapons and to curb their overseas adventures in Syria, Libya, Angola, and elsewhere.

For the foreseeable future, as in the recent past, a reliance on the policy of

[21] *Defense Organization: The Need for Change* (Staff Report to the Committee on Armed Services, United States Senate, October 16, 1985), p. 15.

deterrence (mutual assured destruction), despite its unappealing aspects, appears to be the policy America will employ. The Strategic Defense Initiative will take at least ten or fifteen years to develop an effective population defense, if one can be developed at all. The program will end long before though if Reagan's successors or Congress do not share this vision. A more limited missile defense system intended to protect our retaliatory forces might have more support. Whatever the developments in the controversial Star Wars program, current deterrence programs would appear to be the future policy as well.

The buildup in the U.S. arsenal of weapons has been impressive in recent years. The Army has 5000 M-1 tanks; a major new armored personnel carrier, the M-2 Bradley infantry vehicle; a new rocket artillery system; new helicopters, and air defense missiles. The Air Force, after years of on-again, off-again politics, has finally got 100 B-1 bombers, more than 300 new F-15 fighter planes, and 1000 additional F-16 planes. Now it has the long-awaited, highly secret STEALTH aircraft that experts claim will make both our B-1 and Russian defenses for missiles obsolete. The STEALTH bomber is shaped like a sting ray; it has a flying wing without the usual tubelike fuselage, to present minimal reflecting surfaces to seaching radars. The Navy has sixty-five or more new combat surface vessels, about twenty-five new attack submarines, and more on the way. At this rate the notion of a 600-ship Navy is a distinct possibility by the early 1990s.

The history of the MX missile illustrates how weapons policy is made these days. Domestic, political, and technical considerations are often as much a factor as national security needs, as the following suggests:

An MX missile is a large, multiple-warhead, extremely accurate nuclear weapon. The idea for an MX-type ICBM (Inter-Continental Ballistic Missile) arose in the 1960s. The original purpose of the MX was to fill a perceived need on the part of the United States to maintain a land-based missile capable of surviving an attack by the Soviet Union. In addition, the MX was meant to give the United States, for the first time, the ability to threaten large numbers of Soviet land-based missiles. The combination of these two factors, it was expected, would deter the USSR from launching a nuclear attack.

President Carter's MX plan called for deployment of the missiles on a so-called "race track" in Utah and Nevada. Each missile was to have its own fifteen-mile roadway loop connecting twenty-three separate concrete launching points. The missiles were to be intermittently shuffled from one launching point to another in order to keep the Soviets guessing as to their whereabouts. The plan was later abandoned by the Reagan administration, in part because of widespread political opposition in Utah and Nevada. (One wag suggested that we merely put the MX on Amtrak trains. That way neither the USSR nor the U.S. would know where the MX missiles were—even with a schedule!)

President Reagan proposed placing 100 missiles in rows of two and three stretching in a fourteen-mile column. The theory behind this "dense pack" proposal was that a Soviet weapon detonating above an MX silo would destroy other incoming nuclear weapons before they reached their targets. The United States would then be able to launch the remaining MX missiles in retaliation. The dense pack proposal was rejected by Congress.

Reagan then appointed a blue-ribbon panel to try to break the political deadlock caused by congressional opposition to the various MX plans. It recommended, among other things, that the United States temporarily deploy 100 MX missiles in currently existing Minutemen missile silos. The commission also advised that the United States develop an unspecified number of smaller, single-warhead missiles to anchor America's long-term land-based defense.

Many of these recommendations were far-reaching in their implications. For example, they meant the entire complexion of U.S.-USSR arms control talks would

President John F. Kennedy once said: "We have the power to make this the best generation in the history of mankind, or to make it the last." (*United Nations*)

have to be changed. Currently the two countries count missiles and missile launchers to determine each other's relative strength for arms control purposes. This system encourages both nations to build multiple-warhead missiles. Reagan's advisers also suggested the United States eventually abandon large, multiple-warhead weapons in favor of small-warhead weapons. This has led to a call for new arms control agreements to negotiate and redefine the acceptable strength of nuclear forces.

Predictably, the new MX plan generated opposition. Several senators and two former CIA directors said it would mean an escalation of the arms race. Former CIA director William Colby added that the MX would be considered by the Soviets as an offensive first-strike weapon, and hence it would send a dangerous message. Others claim that deploying the MX in existing Minutemen silos would render the missiles too vulnerable.

Although the MX won congressional approval, it did so by only slender majorities. And opponents of the MX did win commitments from Reagan to adjust his arms control negotiating strategy and to deploy a single-warhead missile system. Opposition to the costly MX program reappeared in the 1984 appropriations process, and the 1984 Democratic platform called for ending its production. But Reagan forged ahead, and the placing of MX missiles in silos began. Congress authorized fifty of them; Reagan pressed for yet another fifty.

Even in 1989 and 1990, Congress, the president, and the defense policy experts continue to debate how many and what kind of MX missiles to build. Some say we need bigger missiles with more warheads; others say it all costs too much. Others fear that all of the systems are less stabilizing and less mobile than once promised, and less and less able to sustain widespread congressional support.[22] Retired Air Force Lt. General Brent Scowcroft complained in 1986 that the MX had been decimated by compromises and budget cuts. "We have spent a lot of money, but haven't got a thing to show for it."

U.S.-Soviet Arms Negotiations

Proponents of arms control say the arms race itself is a fundamental cause of international tension. They warn of the immense risks of the deterrence system: human errors, failures in the warning network, growing risk of preemptive attack due to adoption of counterforce strategies, and breakdown of safeguards against nuclear proliferation. But they paint an even grimmer picture of a future without arms control: heightened tension as the result of the development of more devastating nuclear warheads and longer-ranged, more accurate delivery vehicles; threats of biological, chemical, and neutron-radiation weapons; constant surveillance by spy satellites; and ever-increasing defense budgets and commitments of human resources to weapons technology.

Some substantial arms control agreements already exist among the major world powers. As outlined in the following paragraphs, several treaties have been negotiated—some among several nations and a few between the U.S. and the USSR. *Disarmament* refers to actually reducing arms. *Arms control* refers to monitoring, mutually excluding certain weapons, requiring notification, imposing common ceilings that require no reduction, and similar agreements. Arms control strives to reduce the likelihood of war, to reduce the cost of defense, and to reduce the damage if war should occur.

A brief look at some past negotiations suggests the kinds of arms control efforts that may be possible in the future. In 1963 the United Kingdom, the Soviet Union, and the United States agreed on a treaty to ban nuclear explosions in the atmosphere or in any other place where there was danger of radioactive debris.

[22] David C. Morrison, "Missile Gridlock," *National Journal* (June 7, 1986), pp. 1366–70.

YOU DECIDE !

Offensive nuclear missile installations, plainly made in the Soviet Union, are spotted by U.S. intelligence planes flying over Nicaragua in Central America. Defense and State Department advisers quickly prepare several policy options for the president. These recommendations include:
(1) Send U.S. Air Force jets on a surprise mission to knock the missiles out of commission. (2) Initiate diplomatic negotiations with the Soviets and the government of Nicaragua. (3) Impose a naval blockade on both coasts of Nicaragua, preventing any further shipments of Soviet weapons. (4) Begin immediate, direct negotiations with the Soviet leaders to have these missiles dismantled. You are president. What is in the best interests of the United States? With whom should you consult? What will you decide and why?

(Answer/Discussion on the next page.)

President Jimmy Carter and Soviet leader Leonid Brezhnev exchange signed copies of the SALT II treaty in Vienna, June 18, 1979. (*UPI/Bettmann Newsphotos*)

The treaty permits nations to test underground and has an escape clause allowing any signer to withdraw on three months' notice. Its ratification by the United States and the Soviet Union, and the subsequent adherence to it by more than 100 nations, was viewed as a first step toward nuclear disarmament.

The test-ban treaty was followed in 1967 by the International Treaty on the Peaceful Uses of Outer Space, which bans the use of satellites as vehicles or platforms for launching nuclear weapons. In 1968 came the **Nonproliferation Treaty,** which pledges the nuclear powers not to disseminate nuclear devices to nonnuclear powers for at least twenty-five years, and the nonnuclear nations not to seek to acquire such devices.

The first **SALT (Strategic Arms Limitations Treaty)** agreement was signed by President Nixon and Leonid Brezhnev in May 1972. In this treaty the United States sought to place a freeze on the Soviets for five years, the time needed for the United States to catch up by developing the Trident submarine, MX missile, cruise missile, and B-1 bomber. SALT I was criticized by some people for giving the Soviets a considerable advantage both in numbers and megatonnage, but Henry Kissinger defended the treaty as freezing an inequality "we inherited" in order to gain time to reverse the situation.

In October 1974 President Gerald Ford met with Brezhnev in Vladivostok to decide in principle the general outline of SALT II accords. These accords set a limit on the number of offensive delivery vehicles (2400), and a sublimit on the number of launchers of strategic missiles equipped with multiple independently targetable reentry vehicles (MIRVs). No limits were to be placed on such other weapons as the cruise missiles, backfire planes, or strategic space defense systems. However, both sides soon decided that SALT II should place further limits on the other's new weapons, while not hindering their own weapons development. American cruise missiles and the Soviet backfire plane became the center of this controversy.

The Carter administration proposed that SALT II also put limits on "throw-weight" (the weight of the useful payload of the missile) and MIRVs, but this was met with strong Soviet opposition. As the SALT II agreements eventually took shape, it became apparent that they would have only a minimal effect on curbing the arms race. Carter was unsuccessful in winning Senate approval for SALT II. In any event, debate on SALT II was abruptly suspended in 1980 because of Soviet intervention in Afghanistan. Although the SALT II treaty was never ratified, both the United States and the Soviet Union agreed to stay within the limits spelled out in the treaty as long as the other side continued to so so. And to a large extent both sides did.

Ronald Reagan campaigned against the SALT II treaty in 1980, saying it did not achieve sufficient cuts in the size of either country's weapons arsenal and it did allow the Soviets to achieve superiority in large, land-based multiple warhead missiles. For its first several years the Reagan administration appeared locked in disagreement over what to do about SALT and further arms control efforts. Then in 1986 Reagan said he no longer felt bound by the second strategic arms limitation accord. Why? First, he pointed out that it was never ratified. Second, it would have expired, he said, by 1986 in any event. Further, he claimed that the Soviets had failed to abide by it in certain instances.

Democrats and liberal Republicans expressed strong disapproval of Reagan's anti-SALT decision, saying that even though SALT agreement was far from perfect, it had at least imposed some restraints on both superpowers.

Reagan and Bush said that because nuclear weapons will remain a key to American security until a missile defense system (SDI) can be achieved, nuclear devices will have to be tested to perfect new ones and to ensure the reliability of older ones.

In meetings with Soviet leader Mikhail S. Gorbachev, Reagan agreed to hold regular high-level meetings to resolve political issues and to continue talks in Vienna on reducing conventional forces in central Europe. Gorbachev and Reagan also agreed to work on joint projects to prevent the spread of nuclear weapons capability.

United States—USSR INF Treaty—1988

At their fourth summit meeting over a three-year period Ronald Reagan and Mikhail Gorbachev signed a special agreement reducing certain intermediate nuclear forces. The celebrated Intermediate Nuclear Forces (INF) treaty eliminated only a modest fraction of the world's nuclear stockpile, yet it sent an important signal to the world and perhaps has ushered in a new period of "realistic engagement" between the world's two superpowers. It represents the first time two superpowers have been able to agree on abolishing weapons rather than merely limiting their growth.

The INF treaty also provided for on-site inspection by the two military rivals. Both nations also agreed to scrap many of their medium- and shorter-range missiles. Reagan, Bush, and other administration officials hailed this as a breakthrough in Soviet-American relations and argued that their defense buildup in the mid-1980s had allowed this small step in the direction of arms reduction to take place.

Critics of the INF treaty worry that reducing American medium- and short-range missiles in Europe without substantially keeping up our conventional forces there will reduce the credibility of NATO as a deterrent. Critics in Germany worry too that we may be leaving them to have a war fought in their area:

> The reasoning is as simple as it is critical. A war that is confined to Europe is one that might just happen. A war that is global will not happen, since it would destroy the superpowers along with Europe. Safety, then, has always consisted in the assurance of a common fate. But the INF agreement raises the distinct possibility that Europe—and, above all, Germany—may now have a separate fate.[23]

Despite extensive debate in the U.S. Senate, the United States ratified the INF treaty and a new engagement was set in motion. Gorbachev and Reagan won widespread praise for this diplomatic achievement. Strategic Arms Reduction Talks (START) continue between the two nations, but there are sharp differences over how to restrict sea-launched cruise missiles, an area where the U.S. has a decided advantage it is unwilling to give up. Those talks are likely to go on for some time.

Ronald Reagan and Mikhail Gorbachev chat before session of the Geneva Summit Meeting in November 1985. (*AP/Wide World Photos*)

THE NUCLEAR FREEZE DEBATE

U.S. Senator Edward Kennedy (D-Mass.) and Senator Mark Hatfield (R-Oregon) in discussion. They were cosponsors of the Nuclear Freeze Resolution. (*UPI/Bettmann Newsphotos*)

A nuclear freeze is an immediate, mutual, verifiable halt to the development, production, and deployment of nuclear weapons. And the nuclear freeze movement was one of the most volatile issues in the early 1980s.

Of the nuclear freeze resolutions placed on the ballots in several states and the District of Columbia, only the one in Arizona did not pass. Gallup polls found that seven in ten Americans favored the general idea of a freeze. The House of Representatives passed a nuclear freeze resolution, and the Democratic platform endorsed the freeze approach.

Opponent and proponent freeze arguments can be divided into five categories: the prevention of nuclear war, the strategic balance, the economics of the nuclear freeze, the morality of the nuclear freeze, and the nuclear freeze and arms control. Following is an outline of the main arguments for and against a nuclear freeze.

[23] Robert W. Tucker, "The INF Debate: The NOs Have It," *The National Interest*, Winter 1987/88, p. 116.

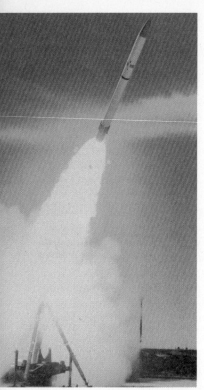

A 1986 testing flight of the Army's Flexible Lightweight Agile Guided Experiment vehicle (FLAGE). (*U.S. Army photo by Tom Moore, Courtesy Department of Defense*)

The Prevention of Nuclear War

Supporters of a nuclear freeze believe the continued development, production, and deployment of nuclear weapons greatly increases the likelihood of a nuclear holocaust. Ever-increasing numbers of nuclear weapons only serve to increase the odds of an accident involving nuclear weapons, terrorist acquisition of atomic weapons, or the unnecessary use of nukes by a trigger-happy government leader.

Opponents of a nuclear freeze directly refute this, saying a freeze would increase rather than decrease the likelihood of nuclear war. They claim the doctrine of deterrence has prevented nuclear war thus far, and a freeze would endanger this doctrine. The strategy of deterrence, remember, means that each side refrains from attacking the other because it fears retaliation in kind. Each side knows that nuclear aggression is tantamount to suicide.

The Strategic Balance

Freeze advocates believe a moratorium on nuclear weapons would enhance, not reduce, our overall national security. "It will halt the development of more powerful Soviet rockets and block their further deployment of existing weapons," according to Senator Edward Kennedy (D-Massachusetts), a leading freeze advocate and coauthor of the Senate version of the freeze resolution.[24] This argument assumes the United States and the Soviet Union are at "rough parity" in their nuclear arsenals. Each nation possesses relatively equal levels of destructive capability. Moreover, the arsenals of each nation are more than sufficient to achieve any deterrent, or first- or second-strike purpose. Each nation is unnecessarily and dangerously capable of overkill.

Detractors of a freeze say the Soviet Union currently enjoys strategic superiority over the United States. A freeze would lock the United States into this unequal position and provide an enticing target for Soviet aggression. The most prominent supporter of this viewpoint is President Reagan, who claims a freeze would preserve today's high, unequal, and unstable levels of nuclear forces.[25]

The Economics of the Nuclear Freeze

Continued production of nuclear weapons, freeze backers say, will increase inflation, produce fewer jobs, and force further cutbacks in services. They point to the futility of wasting vast sums of money on nonproductive goods such as nuclear weapons. Further, large savings would result from the reduction in arms that would immediately follow a freeze.

Opponents of a freeze hold that strategic nuclear weapons make up a relatively small share of the defense budget. Further, the protection provided by nuclear weapons is much cheaper than the same amount of protection provided by conventional forces. Opponents of a freeze argue that reliance on nuclear weapons results in large part from a desire to *reduce* government spending.[26]

The Morality of the Nuclear Freeze

Many religious leaders call for a freeze on moral grounds. The National Conference of Catholic Bishops issued a widely publicized position paper expressing its disapproval of nuclear weapons. The bishops question the morality of the indiscriminate

[24] Testimony of Senator Edward M. Kennedy before the U.S. Senate Foreign Relations Committee, May 11, 1982. See also Edward Kennedy and Mark Hatfield, *Freeze! How You Can Help Prevent Nuclear War* (Bantam Books, 1982).

[25] See also Patrick J. Garrity, "Why We Need Nuclear Weapons," *Policy Review* (Winter 1986), pp. 36–45.

[26] See, for example, Charles Krauthammer, "The Real Way to Prevent Nuclear War," *The New Republic* (April 28, 1982), p. 19.

Former Secretary of State Henry Kissinger (l), who served as a consultant to President Kennedy, as Secretary of State to Presidents Nixon and Ford, and as an occasional adviser to President Reagan on national security matters. (*U.S. State Department*)

Former UN Ambassador, Jeane Kirkpatrick (1981–85) (r). (*United Nations photo by Yutaka Nagata*)

killing of innocent civilians that would inevitably result from the use of nuclear weapons.

According to critics of the freeze, the moral questions raised by totalitarian communist regimes are more important than the moral questions raised by nuclear war and weapons. The deprivation of the human rights of hundreds of millions of people behind the Iron Curtain should be of primary concern, they say.

The Nuclear Freeze and Arms Control

Finally, supporters of a nuclear freeze claim that a halt to the development, production, and deployment of nuclear weapons is a necessary first step toward arms control and reduction. Senator Mark Hatfield (R-Oregon), coauthor of the Senate freeze resolution with Senator Kennedy, equates the arms race with a speeding locomotive. "You can't throw a freight train coming down the track into reverse," he says, "until you first stop it." Supporters of a comprehensive freeze claim it would facilitate verification of arms control agreements. *Any* testing or production activity would suggest a violation. Piecemeal arms control agreements are concerned with detecting subtle deviations in arms activity, verification of which is far more difficult.

Those opposed say it would eliminate the Soviet incentive to negotiate seriously in arms control talks. Soviet leaders participate in arms talks, they say, solely to stop the development, production, and deployment of new American weapons systems. A freeze would accomplish this for them, thereby ending all hope for future arms reductions. Those against a freeze claim a comprehensive freeze would be impossible to verify: The production, stockpiling, and qualitative upgrading of nuclear weapons cannot be detected by satellite, and the Soviets have always objected to on-site inspection.

The nuclear freeze issue is complex as well as controversial. Opposing sides in the debate interpret the same facts in different ways. Each side is committed to peace and genuinely believes its position represents the safest course. Although this debate has subsided somewhat in recent years, nearly everyone agrees we should do everything possible to reduce the risks of nuclear war in the short run and reduce our reliance on nuclear weapons over time.[27]

[27] See Joseph S. Nye, Jr., *Nuclear Ethics* (Free Press–Macmillan, 1986). See also Graham T. Allison et al., eds., *Hawks, Doves & Owls: An Agenda for Avoiding Nuclear War* (Norton, 1985).

SECURITY AND LIBERTY: NOT BY FORCE ALONE

What should be the role of the military in a democratic society? Although Americans have reasonably high confidence in the military, fear of the abuse of military force is deeply rooted in the American tradition. And the unpopularity of the Vietnam War, together with the belief that vast military expenditures are giving undue influence to the military and their allies in the industrial community, arouse concern about how to ensure civilian control over the so-called military-industrial complex.

The framers of 1787, recognizing that military domination is incompatible with free government, wove into the Constitution several precautions. The president, an elected official, is the commander in chief of the armed forces; with the Senate's consent the chief executive commissions all officers. No clear separation exists between military and civilian spheres of activity. In many cases the military decides what information must remain top secret. Members of Congress and the general public are thus sometimes at a disadvantage. With a large standing army and complicated intelligence and weapons systems invariably also comes increased centralization of power and responsibility in the executive. A nation preoccupied with defense is sometimes tempted to suppress dissent and to label critics as unpatriotic or subversive. Further, even though Congress formally has the power to control defense policy and defense spending, it has encouraged tremendous growth in military responsibilities. For most of the past fifty years members of Congress have followed the line of reasoning of the military leaders.

In the late 1980s, however, many members of Congress have tried to carve out a more independent and thoughtful role in defense policy matters. Indicative is the Military Reform Caucus in the Congress, a bipartisan, bicameral, informal discussion forum that has brought together members and senators for the purpose of rethinking military budgets, programs, and priorities. Not so long ago it was said, only partly with tongue in cheek, that most members of Congress couldn't care less about weapons systems and that most viewed the defense budget in terms of real estate and porkbarrel considerations that affected their home districts. Today this view is less persuasive. The new military reformers in Congress, who number nearly a fourth of the membership, stress the need for alternative defense priorities and programs and for a more generalist and less service (e.g., Army, Navy) perspective in defense management.[28]

This group in Congress enthusiastically endorses the changes in the Joint Chiefs of Staff discussed above. They urged reforming officer education so it might emphasize military theory or bureaucratic management. They also urge review of military doctrines, tactics, and force structures. Many of them call for a Navy rebuilt around the submarine rather than the aircraft carrier. They suggest that the Air Force's primary purpose should be shifted from its preoccupation with winning through air power to much greater support for the ground troops.

These members of Congress are often willing to get more specific than were their predecessors. "Reforms in personnel policy and training are equally important," wrote Gary Hart, one of the group's founders. "In all services, training must come to reflect the chaos and uncertainty that characterize combat, rather than following elaborate scripts. Because we have found that soldiers fight more for their buddies than for 'God and country,' we should reform troop rotation policies to build a greater stability and cohesion within fighting units."[29] Much of the impetus for the military "reformers" in Congress came from staff aides and "think tank" military experts who worked closely with these members.

[28] David C. Morrison, "Caucusing for Reform," *National Journal* (June 28, 1986), pp. 1596–1602.

[29] Gary Hart, "An Agenda for More Military Reform," *The New York Times* (May 13, 1986), section A, p. 13.

Defenders of the defense budget, like George Bush, say those who want to reduce it are naive. They point out that with the help of more analytical audits, military procurement has been improved. They argue that defense programs until the mid-1980s had exacted the smallest percentage of the gross national product and the smallest percentage of the federal budget since 1950. They explain that the military budget must include the increasing expenditures necessary to maintain an all-volunteer army and to match the major Soviet buildup of the past decade.

National debates about the military budget, deterrence strategies, and missile defense systems, weapons systems, arms control, and force levels are commonplace in American politics, as they should be. The objectives of an ever more effective, yet ever more efficient, military-preparedness effort will guide these debates. Everyone recognizes, however, that true national security lies in something considerably more than troops and weapons. Still, providing for the nation's defense is recognized by almost everyone as a basic condition or first requirement that must be satisfied before the nation can go about its other business or begin to achieve its other aspirations.

SUMMARY

1. Providing for the nation's defense is one of the fundamental functions of the national government. Yet it is also one of the most costly and controversial functions. Nearly everything the nation's military does becomes enmeshed in politics—as it should.

2. Americans are often bewildered by the complicated weapons systems and the almost foreign language of U.S. defense strategies and military appropriations debates. The prevailing attitude of Americans toward defense spending and the military establishment is one of modified support. But we want to prevent war. We want military strength that will help achieve our foreign policy objectives. We are also concerned about the high cost of arms and the possibility of either a nuclear war or nuclear proliferation that some day will lead to war.

3. Our system is designed to provide our civilian control over the military. This is always a challenge; presidents,

Congress, and the secretaries of defense must weigh national security against competing claims. This inevitably causes a certain amount of strain. Although the military in any society has enormous potential for direct political involvement, this has not occurred in the United States.

4. Americans today are concerned about military preparedness and strength. Yet they are equally concerned with arms control and reducing the threat of a nuclear war. We have had extensive debates about the draft, Reagan's Strategic Defense Initiative (Star Wars), SALT II, and a nuclear freeze. We know we are now more dependent on the outside world than ever. The capacity for conflict and violence in the Middle East, Korea, Cuba, Central America, and elsewhere is well recognized. Even though military power alone may not guarantee international stability, it is generally viewed as a necessary condition for it.

FURTHER READING

GRAHAM T. ALLISON et al., eds. *Hawks, Doves & Owls: An Agenda for Avoiding Nuclear War* (Norton, 1985).

ROBERT J. ART et al., eds. *Reorganizing America's Defense* (Pergamon Press, 1985).

HAROLD BROWN. *Thinking about National Security* (Westview Press, 1983).

PAUL M. COLE and WILLIAM J. TAYLOR, JR., eds. *The Nuclear Freeze Debate* (Westview Press, 1983).

Defense Organization: The Need for Change (Staff Report of the Committee on Armed Services, United States Senate, 1985).

JAMES FALLOWS. *National Defense* (Random House, 1981).

ARTHUR T. HADLEY. *The Straw Giant. Triumph and Failure: America's Armed Services* (Random House, 1986).

GARY HART and WILLIAM LIND. *America Can Win: The Case for Military Reform* (Adler and Adler, 1986).

ROBERT JERVIS. *The Illogic of American Nuclear Strategy* (Cornell University Press, 1984).

WILLIAM W. KAUFMAN. *A Reasonable Defense* (Brookings Institution, 1986).

EDWARD N. LUTTWAK. *The Pentagon and the Art of War* (Simon & Schuster, 1985).

JEFFREY RECORD. *Revising U.S. Military Strategy: Tailoring Means to Ends* (Pergamon, 1984).

R. JAMES WOOLSEY, eds. *Nuclear Arms: Ethics, Strategy and Politics* (Institute for Contemporary Studies, 1984).

21

The Politics
of Taxing
and Spending

The budget is the nation's number one priorities document, its chief political document, and its most important economic document. With tax collections of $1000 billion and a national budget of well over $1000 billion for 1989, our national government spends 24 percent of the **gross national product (GNP),** or nearly one dollar out of every four. We now have a national debt of over $2.5 trillion, and we must pay more than $150 billion just for the interest payments on that debt. Government has come to intervene in the economy in so many ways that political leaders are to a very real extent economic leaders as well. Tax and spending decisions are especially important because they determine the division of resources between public and private goods and the distribution of private resources among different families and individuals. Tax and budget choices determine the government's priorities. The politics of taxing and spending centers on the questions of what we want to accomplish as a nation and who will actually pay for it.

RAISING MONEY

Big government is expensive. Federal, state, and local governments spend money equal to about a third of the income of all Americans. The national government is the biggest spender of all. In recent years Washington has disbursed more than all state and local governments combined.

Where does all this money come from? The federal government gets most of its funds from taxes. Other monies come from loans, from special fees and fines, and from grants and gifts. A third source of federal funds is administrative and commercial revenues. Fees paid to the State Department for passports and the fines paid by criminals are administrative revenues that account for a small portion of federal income. More important are the funds paid to the federal government in exchange for direct services—payments to the Post Office for stamps, to the Park Service for recreation, and to the Government Printing Office for pamphlets.

U.S. Tax Milestones

1989	Tax receipts expected to total over $1 trillion.
1986	Tax reform enacted.
1983	Collection reaches about $600 billion.
1981	Inflation boosts collections to $407 billion; tax per capita $2687.
1950	Collections at $28 billion; tax per capita at $256.
1945	Wartime collections passed $43 billion.
1943	Withholding introduced.
1918	First $1 billion income tax collection.
1913	Income tax legalized by the Sixteenth amendment.
1895	Income tax declared unconstitutional.
1894	Income tax revived.
1872	Tax discontinued. Most revenue raised by taxing liquor and tobacco.
1862	First income tax to support Civil War.
Prior to 1862	The government only taxed imports, slaves, and certain manufactured goods.

Source: Adapted from © InfoGraphics 1983.

Levying Taxes

"In this world," Benjamin Franklin once said, "nothing is certain but death and taxes." Tax collecting is one of the oldest activities of government. Putting power over taxation into the hands of the people was a landmark in the rise of self-government. "No taxation without representation" has been the war cry of people the world over.

The Constitution clearly provides that Congress "shall have power to lay and collect taxes, duties, imposts, and excises." But duties and excise taxes have to be levied *uniformly* throughout the United States; direct taxes have to *be apportioned among the states* according to population; and no tax can be levied on articles exported from any state. Except during the Civil War, for a century the federal government relied on the tariff for most of its revenue. This hidden tax (see box on page 492)—which many people mistakenly thought to be a tax on foreigners—fluctuated with the rise and fall of trade and tariff levels. Congress supplemented these taxes with excise taxes on the manufacture or sale of certain goods. In 1894 an income tax law was enacted (such a tax had been used during the Civil War but was given up shortly afterward). The 1894 tax was not drastic—only 2 percent on all income over $4000. One opponent of the bill scorned it on the floor of the Senate as "an attempt to array the rich against the poor, the poor against the rich . . . Socialism, communism, *devilism.*" The next year, the Supreme Court declared the tax unconstitutional on the grounds that it was a direct tax and therefore had to be apportioned among the states according to population.[1] About twenty years later, in 1913, the Sixteenth amendment was adopted. It authorized Congress "to lay and collect taxes on incomes, from whatever source derived, without apportionment among the several States, and without regard to any census or enumeration."[2]

Raising money is only one important objective of taxation. Regulating and, more recently, promoting economic growth are others. (We discuss taxation as a device to promote economic growth later.) In a broad sense all taxation regulates human behavior. A graduated income tax, for example, has a leveling tendency on incomes, and a tariff act affects foreign trade. Congress has used its taxing power to prevent or regulate certain practices. Years ago Congress, for instance, laid a 10 percent tax on the circulation of notes by state banks, which put an immediate end to such issues. Today federal taxes include the following:

1. *Income taxes on individuals.* Taxes on individuals' incomes account for about 46 percent of the federal government's tax revenue. Originally set at a low rate, the income tax was greatly increased during World War I, and it went to new heights during World War II and the Korean conflict. Over the years the income tax has grown increasingly complex, as Congress has responded to claims for differing kinds of exemptions and rates. But the tax is believed to be modestly flexible: The schedule of rates can be raised or lowered in order to stimulate or restrain economic activity. The income tax is moderately progressive. People with high incomes generally pay larger fractions of their income than people with lower incomes, though many of the wealthy benefit from tax loopholes.[3]

2. *Income taxes on corporations.* These account for 12 percent of the national government's tax revenues. As late as 1942 corporate income taxes amounted to more than individual income taxes, but returns from the latter increased more rapidly during World War II.

[1] *Pollock* v. *Farmer's Loan and Trust Co.*, 158 U.S. 601 (1895).

[2] For studies on the origins of the income tax, see John F. Witte, *The Politics and Development of the Federal Income Tax* (University of Wisconsin Press, 1985), and Jerold L. Waltman, *Political Origins of the U.S. Income Tax* (University Press of Mississippi, 1985).

[3] See Joseph A. Pechman, *Who Paid The Taxes, 1965–1985* (Brookings Institution, 1985).

3. *Social insurance or payroll taxes.* This is the second largest and most rapidly rising source of federal revenue. From a mere $4 billion in 1950, this tax will raise over $350 billion in fiscal year 1989. These monies are collected mainly from payroll deductions to finance social security and other insurance programs. They are, economists point out, highly regressive (see next section). Low-income people generally pay larger fractions of their income than do high-income people.

4. *Excise taxes.* Federal taxes on liquor, tobacco, gasoline, telephones, air travel, and other so-called luxury items will total about $35 billion in 1989.

5. *Customs duties.* Though no longer the main source of federal income, in recent years these taxes provided an annual yield of more than $17 billion.

The Politics of Taxation

Most of us complain that our tax load is too heavy and that someone else is not carrying a fair share. People with high incomes who are in the highest tax brackets naturally grumble. Low-income people point out that even a low tax may deprive them of the necessities of life. People in the middle-income brackets feel their situation is the worst of all—their incomes are not high, but their taxes are.

What is the best type of tax? Some say the *graduated income tax*: It is relatively easy to collect, hits hardest those who are most able to pay, and hardly touches those at the bottom of the income ladder. Others argue that **excise taxes** are the fairest, because they are paid by people who are spending money for liquor, cigarettes, and gasoline, and who thus have money to spare. Further, by discouraging people from buying expensive goods, excise taxes sometimes have a deflationary effect in times of rising prices. On the other hand, excise taxes are more expensive to collect than income taxes. In some cases, moreover, such as the tax on tobacco, they may hit the poor the hardest. Excise taxes also face strong resistance from affected industries: tobacco, liquor, and airlines, for example.

Most controversial is the general **sales tax,** which is levied against the sales of all goods. Labor and liberal organizations call this form of tax **regressive** because lower-income citizens pay a higher proportion of their income in tax revenues than higher-income citizens. The sales tax is regressive because the poor spend a larger proportion of their income than do the wealthy. Proponents of the sales tax stress its potential antiinflationary effect and point to its successful use in a number of states.

Tax Reform, 1986

Talk of tax reform takes place every few years as people complain, usually with justification, that our tax system is unfair and confusing and that it is not doing what it is supposed to do. One of those years was 1986. After some major political battles Congress, as a result, enacted, and the president signed into law, a new tax system that brought more changes to the tax code than any in seventy years.

The function of tax legislation, at least ideally, is to decide who shall pay how much to finance government spending. In practice, however, tax legislation over the years has also sought to promote economic growth of various kinds and to reward certain types of behavior—such as owning a home, contributing to charities, and investing in high-risk but desirable (from a national standpoint) energy or housing ventures. Cynics suggest too that from a member of Congress's point of view, tax legislation has the additional and important function of raising campaign funds. As long as tax legislation is under consideration in Congress, swarms of lobbyists are eager to attend expensive campaign dinners and to contribute generously to campaign coffers.

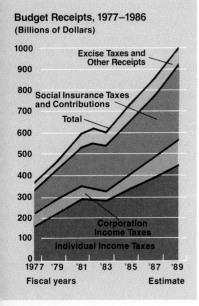

Budget Receipts, 1977–1986
(Billions of Dollars)

Excise Taxes and Other Receipts
Social Insurance Taxes and Contributions
Total
Corporation Income Taxes
Individual Income Taxes

1977 '79 '81 '83 '85 '87 '89
Fiscal years   Estimate

Tariffs as Taxes

Much debate exists over whether we should impose or raise tariffs on imported products such as steel and automobiles. Sometimes people say we should impose a tariff because a foreign government is subsidizing the industry that is exporting.

It is important to realize that a tariff is a tax on U.S. consumers. It is an additional cost to foreign producers of goods consumed in this nation. The additional cost is almost always passed on to consumers in the form of higher prices for both imported and domestically produced products. By imposing a tariff on imported goods, the U.S. is merely raising the prices on these goods.

CHAPTER 21
THE POLITICS OF TAXING
AND SPENDING

How to Raise Revenue

Would you favor one of the following revenue hikes or would you rather consider some other way to raise money for the government instead?

	Favor
Higher taxes on liquor and cigarettes	81%
A national lottery	65
Charging user fees	51
Higher tariffs on oil imports	45
A higher gasoline tax	36
A national sales tax	31
Higher costs for federally assisted home mortgages	31
Increasing income taxes	24
Charging more for Medicare	10

Source: © *Los Angeles Times* poll (1986) Reprinted by permission.

Senator Bill Bradley (D-New Jersey) was an early champion of the tax reform that eventually won passage in 1986. (*AP/Wide World Photos*)

Senator Bill Bradley (D-New Jersey) first learned about the complexity of and deficiencies in our tax system when, as a professional, high-bonus, highly-paid basketball star, he was told of the array of tax dodges available to him. He was told by tax advisers that, given the system, he could pay as much or as little in taxes as he wanted. Ronald Reagan developed a distaste for the tax system when he was a Hollywood movie actor and his paycheck got cut in half (until he learned about tax shelters and other ways to beat the system). Reagan and some of his movie friends even stopped making movies in some years to avoid paying higher taxes.

Both Bradley and Reagan were among those who encouraged Congress to take on both the tax code and the vast number of interests who benefit from the scores of loopholes and tax preferences that were built into the pre-1987 tax system. In the early 1980s Senator Bradley began to build support in Congress and across the country for changes in the tax code that included lowering rates and eliminating most itemized tax deductions. Bradley had learned from his contacts with voters that a growing number of Americans were upset by their lack of faith in and their inability to any longer understand the United States tax process. He learned, for example, that most middle-income people believed they paid more in taxes than many of their wealthy neighbors. He learned that citizens resented the thick hard-to-read book of tax instructions that arrives at tax time each year. "It's unfair. It's overly complex. It's distorting investment decisions," wrote Bradley, "encouraging people to put money into schemes to reduce their tax bills instead of enterprises to create jobs and to help our economy grow."[4]

Bradley and other supporters of tax reform urged that we should drop the tax rates from about fifteen categories to two or three. Even though the overall tax rates would come down, the taxable income base could be increased by the elimination of most existing tax deductions, or what is technically called **tax expenditures**. Tax expenditures are government revenue losses due to provisions of the federal tax laws that provide special tax incentives or benefits to individuals and businesses. These benefits, which totaled over $400 billion in the mid-1980s, arose from special exclusions, exemptions, or reductions from gross income, or from special credits, preferential tax rates, or deferrals of tax liability. Tax expenditures are so designated because they are one means by which the national government carries out public policy objectives. In most cases, they can be considered as an alternative to a direct-spending program. For example, investment in research and development is encouraged by allowing such costs to be deducted from a company's taxes. A program of direct federal grants could also achieve this objective.

Critics have often said that the rich often got their welfare through these tax loopholes or tax expenditure schemes and that these get placed in the tax code more easily by members of Congress because they are not officially expenditures. In effect, however meritorious the objective they are encouraging, these tax benefits are a cost to government and cause a shortfall in revenues. They also have the effect of providing benefits to the already financially advantaged. In many instances, they have also caused investors to waste resources on low-yield investments that carry large tax benefits; high-yield investments without such benefits, meanwhile, go unfunded. "The result is reduced national output, lower productivity, and sluggish economic growth."[5]

Tax reformers who advocated the flat tax or lower tax rates, or mere simplification of the tax code, came from all political persuasions. They believed the tax code of the recent past was no longer a *progressive tax* in that people of wealth could and did (with the help of their accountants and tax lawyers) significantly lower their tax brackets by taking advantage of many tax-expenditure or tax-shelter

[4] Bill Bradley, *The Fair Tax* (Pocket Books, 1984), p. 11.

[5] Henry J. Aaron and Harvey Galper, *Assessing Tax Reform* (Brookings Institution, 1985), p. 2.

programs. Most tax reformers also believed that tax rates were just too high and that they were encouraging widespread tax cheating. According to even the Internal Revenue Service, nearly 19 percent of all taxes owed on legitimate earnings go uncollected.

The 1986 tax-reform package, though spurred on by Bradley's long-term advocacy and by Reagan's general endorsement, became a bipartisan effort in both houses of Congress. Tax "reformers" eventually agreed on the following principles: Simplify the tax process; make it more fair; lower the marginal tax rates for individuals; slightly increase the tax burden on corporations; and encourage productive investments while discouraging wasteful investments in the economy.

In the end, Congress reduced the number of tax brackets from fifteen to two, slightly raised personal and standard deductions, repealed scores of previously existing deductions, and limited certain other tax breaks. For example, in the past, when a businessperson took a customer to lunch, the entire expense used to be deductible. After the tax reform only 80 percent of the cost is deductible. State and local sales taxes that were once deductible are no longer deductible in the current tax code.

Many business groups fought vigorously to stop the shift from business deductions, especially on investment credits, they had grown to enjoy under the previous tax code. Although they were successful in fighting off some of the proposed changes, businesses were defeated on many of the tax expenditures provided earlier. Their consolation was significantly lowered rates for individuals.[6]

Will the new tax system make much of a difference? Most observers hailed the legislation as a notable improvement over the old system. Most taxpayers will pay lower income taxes. And millions of lower-income taxpayers will be taken off the tax rolls altogether. Most upper-middle-income people will, in contrast, pay more. Most corporations will pay more, as their minimum tax is raised to 25 percent. Some close watchers of tax politics warned, however, that the improvement might be temporary. Nothing has changed to prevent the political process that produced the earlier tax system from starting over again. "When lobbyists get back to action, and as members of Congress try to raise campaign funds, old loopholes may be reintroduced and new ones invented. When this happens tax rates may start creeping up to offset the resulting loss of revenue."

"How do I spell 'relief'? T-A-X-C-U-T!" (*Reprinted by permission.* © *1979 NEA, Inc.*)

Congressman Dan Rostenkowski and Senator Bob Packwood, two of the congressional leaders who helped push tax reform through passage in 1986. (*Terry Ashe/Time Magazine*)

Levying and Collecting Taxes

Although the Constitution provides that all revenue bills must be initiated in the House of Representatives, usually the president "requests" tax legislation. With the help of tax experts at the White House and in the Treasury Department, a president draws up a tax program designed to meet the government's revenue needs. The program also takes into consideration the current and projected state of the economy. Often representatives of interest groups are consulted while the bill is being drawn up. Then the president submits the tax program to Congress, frequently along with the budget message. Next the House Ways and Means Committee holds hearings on the bill. Administration representatives, headed by the secretary of the treasury, usually lead the parade of witnesses, followed by representatives of interested groups, tax experts, and others. Then tax measures go through Congress in much the same way as other bills. Although the Senate cannot initiate tax legislation, it is active in tax matters. It often differs with the House and forces extensive changes in bills. Sometimes Congress refuses to follow the president's recommendations and works out a tax measure largely on its own.

[6]The best analysis of this legislative struggle is found in Jeffrey H. Birnbaum and Alan S. Murray, *Showdown at Gucci Gulch: Lawmakers, Lobbyists, and the Unlikely Triumph of Tax Reform* (Vintage, 1988).

A recent tax bill illustrates the impact of taxes on a variety of individuals and groups. Testifying on proposed tax changes before a congressional committee, 138 witnesses expressed their views. The printed testimony covered more than 1600 pages. Business representatives opposed new taxes on corporations. Small businesspeople complained that existing taxes favored big business. Representatives of tobacco growers, transportation interests, the wine and spirits industry, movies and legitimate theater, candymakers, telephone companies, and bowling alleys argued that the proposed tax would discriminate against them. Labor demanded a lighter burden for low-income groups and higher taxes on business. Unorganized workers and consumers, however, were seldom represented.

The Treasury Department, which employs more than 130,000 people, collects the taxes. The actual tax-collecting job falls mainly to the Department's Internal Revenue Service, which employs about 85,000 people. Fifty-eight district directors are located throughout the country, and taxes are paid into district offices rather than directly to Washington. Customs duties are collected by the Treasury Department's Bureau of Customs, which maintains ports of entry, inspects cargo, assesses the value of merchandise, and—with the United States Coast Guard—attempts to prevent smuggling.

Uncle Sam, Borrower

When individuals are suddenly faced with emergency expenses too heavy to meet out of their regular incomes, they often have to borrow money. The same used to be true of government. During military and economic crises the federal government has gone heavily into debt. But lately we have also gone into great debt during a period of peace with a relatively healthy economy. We borrowed $23 billion during World War I, about $13 billion more during the 1930s, and $200 billion more during World War II. By 1989 the gross federal debt will be more than $2.7 trillion.

Borrowing costs money. The federal government can borrow at a relatively low rate. Nevertheless the interest on the federal debt is over $150 billion a year. The size of the debt and the interest payments alarms many Americans. How long can we allow the debt to grow at this rate? Two considerations must be kept in mind: The government owes most of the money to its own people rather than to foreign governments or persons (see accompanying box). Also, the economic strength and resources of the country are more significant than the size of the public debt. Still, the interest we pay to service the debt is a real cause for concern.

Why do we have such huge deficits? These deficits are not the result of a weak economy, and they apparently cannot be cured simply by economic growth. The fact is that the United States is committed to spending more for defense and domestic programs than current tax revenues can afford, even though the economy is running at relatively full capacity. By tolerating unprecedented deficits in recent years, the Reagan administration has been able to "create an austere political climate in which proposed cuts, not expected increments, focus the discussions of federal domestic programs."[7] But this is also creating a precarious political and economic situation that could put the nation in great jeopardy if and when we face another recession.

High deficits are objectionable for a variety of reasons. Together with huge national debt interest payments they put a damper on economic growth. It works this way: The annual deficit is now absorbing about 30 percent of all capital raised in the United States. For every dollar Uncle Sam borrows another dollar cannot

Who Owns the Federal Debt?

	Share of Total
U.S. government accounts (such as trust funds)	17%
Foreign owners	11
Federal Reserve banks	9
Commercial banks	11
State and local governments	10
Individuals, including savings-bond holders	9
Money market funds	2
Insurance companies	5
Corporations	3
Others, including S & Ls, pension funds, brokers, and nonprofit groups	24

Source: U.S. Department of the Treasury, 1985.

[7] Paul E. Peterson, "The New Politics of Deficits," in John Chubb and Paul E. Peterson, eds., *New Directions in American Politics* (Brookings Institution, 1985), p. 365. But see a somewhat different view in Robert Eisner, *How Real Is the Federal Deficit?* (Free Press, 1986).

be channeled into productive resources by corporations, small business operators, and home buyers. When interest rates are kept artificially high, many companies and would-be investors just will not borrow money they need to modernize factories, create jobs, buy new homes.[8]

Our huge deficits in a time of relative economic prosperity also lessen our ability to rely on traditional economic remedies to revive the economy should the nation fall into another recession. Typically, during economic downturns the government has tried to increase demand for the goods and services that the nation has the capacity to produce. It does this by cutting taxes, stepping up government spending, and enlarging the budget deficit. This prescription helped us out of the depression of the 1930s, and many economists still view it as a plausible way to revive an ailing economy today. "But the huge buildup of deficits and debt, combined with the growing weight of foreign trade and fluctuating exchange rates in a closely knit world economy, makes it difficult and even dangerous, perhaps impossible, for the United States to escape its burdens simply by increasing demand through still greater public or private borrowing," writes economist Leonard Silk. "The harvest would likely include greater inflation, a further loss of international competitiveness, more people out of work, and a worsening of protectionism, with dangerous implications for the world economy and polity."[9]

How, then, does the government borrow money? The Constitution says Congress may "borrow money on the credit of the United States"; it puts no limit on the extent or method of borrowing. Under congressional authorization the Treasury Department sells securities to banks, corporations, and individuals. Usually these securities take the form of long-term bonds or short-term Treasury notes. Some bonds may be cashed in at any time, others not until maturity. Because the United States government guarantees these bonds, they are in demand, especially by banks and investment companies.

SPENDING THE MONEY

Nothing reflects the rise of big government more clearly than the change in the amounts and methods of its spending. As recently as 1933 the federal government spent only $4 billion, about $30 per capita. In 1989 the respective figures will be almost $1100 billion and about $4500. The machinery for spending has changed, too. At one time spending was loosely administered. Records show, for example, that in the early republic Nicholas Johnson, a Navy agent of Newburyport, Massachusetts, was handed several thousands dollars to supply "Cpt. Brown for recruiting his Crew."[10] Today Mr. Johnson would have to make out detailed forms and wait for a check.

Where does the money go? Much of it, of course, goes for national defense. In recent years nearly 30 percent has gone to national security; 15 percent to interest on the national debt; and more than 40 percent to social insurance, education, and other major social programs. Some of the federal debt is for payments for past wars. Defense-related expenditures, such as veterans' pensions and benefits, are often buried in categories other than national security.

Years ago federal revenues and outlays were so small that national taxing

YOU DECIDE

In 1985 the United States became the world's number one debtor nation. What does this mean and why is this the case? What can be done about it, in your judgment?

(Answer/Discussion on page 499.)

---

[8] Aaron and Galper, *Assessing Tax Reform*, p. 8.

[9] Leonard Silk, "Ailing Economy: Debt Buildup Called Cause," *The New York Times* (July 29, 1986), p. 34.

[10] L. D. White, *The Federalists* (Macmillan, 1948), p. 341.

and spending had little impact on the overall economy. Today the federal government cannot drain billions of dollars from certain areas of the economy and pump them back into others without profoundly effecting the economy of the nation and of the world. We consider this problem later in the chapter; first we must see how the federal budget is drawn up and made into law.

Formulating the Budget

As we have seen, Congress must authorize the spending of funds, but presidents now routinely propose or request funds. The first step in preparing a federal budget is for the various departments and agencies to estimate their needs.[11] This process starts early. While Congress is debating the budget for the fiscal year immediately ahead, the agencies are making estimates for the year following. The estimating job is handled largely by officers under the direction of agency chiefs. Agency officials must take into account not only their needs as they see them but also the overall presidential program and the probable reactions of Congress. Departmental budgets are detailed; they include estimates on expected needs for personnel, supplies, office space, and the like.

The Office of Management and Budget (OMB), a staff agency of the president, handles the next phase. Budget examiners in the OMB examine each agency budget to see if it is in accord with the president's plans. Hearings are then held to give agency people a chance to clarify and defend their estimates. The OMB director and OMB aides, who make the final decision, sometimes prune the agencies' requests rather severely.

Finally, the director goes to the White House with a single consolidated set of estimates of both revenue and expenditures, the product of perhaps a year's work. The president takes a few days to review these figures. The budget director also helps the president prepare a budget message that will stress key aspects of the budget and tie it in with broad national plans. But in January, soon after Congress convenes, the budget and the message are ready for the legislature and the public.

Processing Budget Proposals

Under the Constitution only Congress can appropriate funds. Yet, nowadays Congress essentially follows the lead of the president in making national budget decisions. In 1974 Congress adopted the Budget Reform Act, which was (as we discussed in Chapter 15) intended to give it a more effective role in the budget process. That act specifies that when submitting proposals, the president must include proposed changes in tax laws, estimates of amounts of revenue lost through existing preferential tax treatments, and five-year estimates of the costs of new and continuing federal programs. The act also calls on the president to seek authorizing legislation for a program a year before asking Congress to fund it. Preparing budget proposals is only the beginning: As we discussed earlier, the new Gramm–Rudman–Hollings budget procedures require Congress to make important changes in the way it participates in the budget process. According to that legislation, federal deficits must shrink by several billion dollars each year until they reach zero in 1993. Failure to hit the deficit targets will trigger automatic spending cuts in federal programs. No automatic cuts are permitted in social security, interest on the national debt, or such aid to low-income persons as medicaid, Aid to Families with Dependent Children, veterans' compensation, and veterans' pensions. A few other programs, such as unemployment assistance and student loans, will be subject to some but not

Presidents and Total Deficits, 1934–1989

Roosevelt	$197 billion
Truman	4.4
Eisenhower	15.8
Kennedy	11.9
Johnson	42.0
Nixon	68.7
Ford	124.6
Carter	181.0
Reagan	1,300 (est.)

Source: U.S. Department of Commerce, and Office of Management and Budget.

[11] For a discussion of the budgetary cycle, see Aaron Wildavsky, *The New Politics of the Budgetary Process*, (Scott, Foresman, 1988). See also Howard Shuman, *Politics and the Budget*, 2nd ed. (Prentice Hall, 1988).

sweeping across-the-board cuts. But most nondefense federal spending programs will be cut across the board. And defense programs will also be cut an equal amount. These automatic cuts will have to be made in March of each year, depending on how close the estimated deficit targets match the desired levels as of the previous October. Congress, however, is authorized to suspend the balanced-budget requirements if the economy dips into recession.

Checking Expenditures

After Congress has appropriated money, it reserves the right to check the way the money is being spent. The General Accounting Office (GAO) is headed by a comptroller general, who is appointed by the president with the approval of the Senate for a fifteen-year term. The comptroller general was originally intended to be an independent auditor serving as an arm of Congress to guard against improper and unauthorized expenditures. But as time went on the office was swamped by a gigantic accounting job that forced the auditor to evaluate administrative matters in the executive branch even though the office is not responsible to the chief executive. At the same time, overall management in the executive branch suffered, because daily accounting, an important instrument of administrative control, had been placed in a separate agency.

The GAO, with over 5400 employees, now uses spot sampling methods to check vouchers, and makes its audits in the field rather than in Washington. Although the comptroller general still has the authority to disallow expenditures, approval is no longer needed for the disbursement of funds. In the past twenty years, the GAO has taken on broader responsibilities in investigating and even evaluating programs. It is increasingly checking up on the adequacy and effectiveness, as well as the honesty, of a program's performance.[12]

"Remember, son, we are a government of loopholes, and not of men!"
(*Drawing by Dana Fradon,* © *1976. The New Yorker Magazine, Inc.*)

MANAGING THE MONEY

Today's economy is a money economy: We exchange commodities through a vast system of money and credit. Aside from its role as the biggest buyer and seller of goods and services, the national government has a more direct impact on our money economy. It regulates the value of money; it controls the nation's credit system.

Manufacturing money is relatively easy. The Bureau of Engraving and Printing in the Treasury Department turns out millions of dollars in the form of bills, bonds, and postage stamps every week. This money is fed into general circulation through the Treasury and the Federal Reserve banks. But in itself, this money is only so much paper. How does the government maintain its value?

(*T. Cronin*)

The Currency System

The Constitution gives the national government the right to manage the nation's monetary system. When the Articles of Confederation were in effect, the national currency consisted mainly of almost worthless paper money, and the individual states maintained separate currencies. To correct this, the Constitution gave Congress authority to coin money and to regulate its value, and carefully withheld this power from the states. Thanks partly to Alexander Hamilton, our first secretary of the

[12] For a study of changes in the GAO and its operations see Wallace Earl Walker, *Changing Organizational Culture: Strategy, Structure, and Professionalism in the U.S. General Accounting Office* (University of Tennessee Press, 1986).

treasury, Americans scrapped the confusing British system of guineas, pounds, shillings, and pence and adopted a decimal system.

In the early 1970s, the United States ended the gold exchange standard system by terminating the arrangement whereby foreign governments could exchange dollars for gold at a fixed price. Since the 1970s the major currencies in the industrialized capitalist countries have been adjusted largely by market conditions of supply and demand in a flexible exchange rate system. A few critics would like us to return to using the gold dollar coin as this country's monetary standard.[13] But it is highly unlikely that we will do so. The money of the United States is and will be redeemable only for other money of the United States.

Money, however, makes up only a part of the circulating medium; it is, in fact, less important to our economy than credit. The most important institutions in the expansion and contraction of credit are the banks and the Federal Reserve System.

The Federal Reserve System

In many nations a central bank owned and operated by the national government makes monetary policy. The Constitution does not specifically authorize the national government to create such a bank—indeed, it says nothing about banking. But Alexander Hamilton believed that some such institution was necessary. In 1791 the United States Bank was incorporated by the national government. This bank was partly private and partly public; the national government owned a minority of the shares and had only a minority voice in its management. Jefferson and his supporters opposed the bank and refused to renew the charter in 1812. But in 1816 Madison found it necessary to have the bank rechartered for another twenty years. In 1819, in *McCulloch* v. *Maryland*[14] (see Chapter 3), the Supreme Court upheld the constitutionality of the legislation that created the bank as a necessary and proper way for the national government to establish a uniform currency and to care for the property of the United States.

After the United States Bank closed in 1836, state banks, which had previously been restrained by the federal bank, began issuing notes that often could not be redeemed. A military crisis forced a housecleaning. To stabilize a war economy, in 1863 Congress authorized the chartering of national banks. (These are privately owned corporations, not central banks or an institution like the United States Bank.) State banks were permitted to continue in business, but a 10 percent federal tax on their notes quickly drove these notes out of existence.

The national bank system created during the Civil War was stable—so stable that it was inflexible. Financial crises during the late nineteenth century and in 1907 revealed a tendency to restrict loans and to contract the issuance of notes just when an expansion of money was needed. In order to furnish an elastic currency, and for other reasons, Congress established the Federal Reserve System in 1913.

The Federal Reserve Act of 1913 was a compromise. Whereas some wanted a strong central bank, others feared this would centralize control over currency in too few hands. Thus, a mechanism was established combining a modified central banking system with considerable decentralization.

A seven-member Board of Governors sits atop the **Federal Reserve System** (the Fed). The president appoints, but the Senate must confirm, these governors to fourteen-year nonrenewable terms. From these seven governors the president appoints a chair and a vice-chair, who must also be confirmed by the Senate. The chair and vice-chair serve for four years and may be reappointed. The chair of

---

[13] Lewis E. Lehrman, "To Move Forward, Go Back to Gold," *The New York Times* (February 9, 1986), section E, p. 23.

[14] Wheaton 316 (1819).

The Governors of the Federal Reserve Board in Washington in session. (*Rick Bloom*)

Federal Reserve Banks

Twelve banks represent the nation's 12 Federal Reserve districts. The 12 manage the day-to-day needs of the banking system by maintaining a stable flow of money.

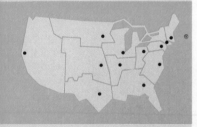

What they do

□ Act as lender of last resort to banks, savings associations, and credit unions in trouble

□ Keep reserves deposited by depository institutions

□ Supply currency and coins to banks

□ Destroy worn-out bills, coins

□ Operate clearinghouses for checks

□ Serve as fiscal agent for the U.S. Treasury

□ Conduct domestic and foreign monetary operations through the New York Federal Reserve Bank as agent for the Federal Open Market Committee

the Board of Governors of the Federal Reserve System is a highly visible member of the financial community. Fed chairmen Paul Volcker and Alan Greenspan have enjoyed as much visibility and notoriety as a leading member of the cabinet or United States Senate.

The chair, vice-chair, and remaining members of the Board of Governors oversee the Federal Reserve System, which is divided into twelve Federal Reserve districts, each containing a Federal Reserve bank. Most Federal Reserve banks have branches. Each Federal Reserve bank is owned by banks that are members of the Federal Reserve System. Membership in the Federal Reserve System is mandatory for national banks but voluntary for state banks that meet certain standards. The Depository Institutions Deregulation and Monetary Control Act of 1980 has considerably reduced the distinction between member and nonmember banks. Among other provisions, the act extended the Fed's power over reserves in nonmember banks. Today more than 6100 of the 15,000 banks in the United States are members of the system; these are the nation's largest banks and hold over 80 percent of total deposits.

Each Federal Reserve district is headed by a nineteen-member board of directors. The Federal Reserve Act of 1913 intended that the district bank directors have considerable autonomy. Over time, however, their power has eroded. Most of the major policy decisions are made by the Board of Governors in Washington, D.C. Although some district bank directors sit on important Federal Reserve committees, most notably the Federal Open Market Committee, the district banks are now primarily responsible only for carrying out the day-to-day operations of the Federal Reserve System. The district banks keep in close contact with member banks in order to implement the policies of the board of governors.

The Federal Reserve System's Board of Governors uses four major devices to control economic activity:

1. *Reserve requirements:* It can increase or decrease, within legal limits, the reserves member banks must maintain against their deposits in Federal Reserve banks.

2. *Discount rates:* It can raise or lower the discount rate charged by Federal Reserve banks to member banks. The discount rate is the price member banks must pay to get cash from the Federal Reserve banks for acceptable commercial notes the banks hold.

3. *Open market operations:* Through its federal open market committee, it can buy and sell government securities and certain other bills of exchange, bank acceptances, and so on.

4. *Margin requirements:* It can exercise direct control over credit extended in order to purchase securities. From time to time Congress has given the board of governors temporary authority to fix terms of consumer credit.

Of these four tools, open market operations is most commonly used. The purpose of the first three of these four devices is to increase or decrease the money supply. However, all four can obviously have a direct effect on the economy.

If inflation is threatening, for example, the Board of Governors can raise reserve requirements. Such a move cuts down on the cash banks have to lend, takes money out of circulation, and reduces inflation by making dollars already in circulation more valuable relative to goods. Or the Fed can raise the discount rate, making it expensive for member banks to borrow money. This encourages banks to reduce their lending. This also takes money out of circulation and thereby reduces inflation. The Fed can also take money out of circulation by selling government securities. Banks pay for these securities out of their reserves, thereby reducing the money supply. Finally, the Fed might raise margin requirements. This would reduce the credit available to bid up the prices of stocks and bonds.

Still, due to certain irregularities in financial markets, external factors beyond the control of the Fed, and the unpredictability of human behavior, the Fed has difficulty exerting rigorous control over the money supply. Moreover, the money supply itself is difficult to define precisely, due to the advent of new and different types of accounts in banks and savings institutions.

In addition to its money-management duties, the Federal Reserve System also performs other functions. Federal Reserve banks serve as depositories for government funds, clear checks, and transfer funds among member banks; they may, in case of economic emergency, lend money directly to businesses.

The Federal Reserve System is not under the control of the Treasury Department or any other executive agency. It finances its activities through internally generated funds and fees, so it is not subject to the customary congressional appropriations process. By statute the Fed is independent of the president. Devised as a service agency for banking and commerce—to achieve a semiautomatic adjustment of the money supply—today the Fed is also an influential policy-making institution with major responsibility for national economic stabilization.

Many observers think it is somehow improper to give this important responsibility to an agency seemingly so divorced from public accountability. The Board of Governors often has to choose between inflation that may cause unemployment and employment at the expense of inflation. Chair Paul Volcker, for example, was accused of being responsible for the 1982 recession precisely because he chose to tighten money supplies to fight inflation. Still, most bankers and political leaders want to preserve the system's relative independence. Only an agency insulated from political pressures, they believe, can take the unpopular steps needed to prevent severe inflation.[15]

In practice, the Fed is not entirely independent. The Federal Reserve is a political institution, directed by policy makers who live and work in a highly charged and highly constrained political environment.[16] In addition to the intangible political pressures from within and without government, the Fed is responsive in a variety of ways to both the executive and legislative branches. Members of the Board of Governors are appointed by a president (with the approval of the Senate) and are thus encouraged to lean somewhat toward the administration's beliefs. Most Board members have served in the executive branch at one time or another. The Fed's chair regularly meets with the president's top economic and financial advisers. Also, the chair must give an annual report to Congress and occasionally testifies before key congressional committees.

Under recent chairs, the Fed has grown both in power and independence. Almost all recent leaders of the Federal Reserve have made a strong case that a major source of high interest rates or sluggishness in the economy is government deficits. Although to some degree the Fed has the ability to aid or counter any attempts by a president or Congress to stimulate the economy, what are called the Fed's **monetary policy** strategies are only one weapon to combat depression, control inflation, foster full employment, and encourage economic growth.

Fed Board of Governors

Seven members appointed by the president and confirmed by the Senate. Terms are 14 years. The president names one member as chairman for a four-year term.

What it does

- Helps carry out policy for regulating the supply of money and credit by—
- Sets reserve requirements for the depository institutions
- Sets the discount rate on the Fed's loans to banks
- Makes margin rules for purchases of securities on credit
- Oversees major banks by regulating the nation's 6,146 bank holding companies
- Inspects and regulates 1,052 state-chartered banks that are members of the reserve system
- Monitors the economy
- Deals with international monetary problems
- Enforces consumer-credit laws
- Supervises Federal Reserve banks

Source: *U.S. News & World Report* (January 27, 1986), p. 49.

---

[15] For a detailed analysis of the present structure and policy implications of the Federal Reserve System, see *The Federal Reserve System: Purpose and Functions* (U.S. Government Printing Office, 1979). For a critical view of the Federal Reserve System and some of its myths, see John Kenneth Galbraith, *Money* (Houghton Mifflin, 1975), chap. 10. For a critical view from the right, see Maxwell Newton, *The Fed* (Times Books, 1983). See also William C. Melton, *Inside the Fed: Making Monetary Policy* (Dow Jones-Irwin, 1985), and Thibaut de Saint Phalle, *The Federal Reserve: An Intentional Mystery* (Praeger, 1985).

[16] Peter Quick and Robert Shapiro, "The Myth of the Fed," *The New York Times* (March 17, 1982), p. 27.

Does the government have the same direct control over the national economy that it has, say, over the military or national forests? No. Only if we had a socialized economy administered from Washington would we have a managed economy in that sense. In our economy a great deal of power is left to private individuals and enterprises. Yet the government keeps a firm hand on many of the gears and levers that control the economy's general direction and the rate at which it moves. These gears and levers are taxes, spending, and credit.

Lessons of the Great Depression

Depression is a hard teacher, and the 1930s had a tremendous impact on American thinking about the role of government in the economy. Although we had had long, severe depressions before—for example, in the 1870s and 1890s—the Great Depression of 1929 brought mass misery. "One vivid, gruesome moment of those dark days we shall never forget," wrote one observer. "We saw a crowd of some fifty men fighting over a barrel of garbage which had been set outside the back door of a restaurant. American citizens fighting for scraps of food like animals!"[17]

Despite the efforts of the Roosevelt administration to cope with the Depression, it hung on. Faint signs of recovery could be seen in the mid-1930s; but the recession of 1937 to 1938 indicated that we were by no means out of the woods. Eight or 9 million people were jobless in 1939. Then came the war, and unemployment seemed cured. Millions of people had more income, more security, and higher standards of living. Lord Beveridge in England posed a question that bothered many thoughtful Americans: "Unemployment has been practically abolished twice in the lives of most of us—in the last war and in this war. Why does war solve the problem of unemployment which is so insoluble in peace?"[18] Worried that the economy might collapse after the war, thousands of people came up with plans to ensure jobs for all.

Some people think the Great Depression was caused by the Federal Reserve and its mismanagement of the money supply. These people claim that had the Fed expanded the money supply in the early 1930s instead of keeping it constant and even reducing it, many of the bank failures and much of the misery of the Depression could have been avoided.

Others think the Depression lasted so long because the New Deal was hostile to business. Government intruded too long and too much into the economic life of the nation. Proponents of this theory urged the government to reduce spending, lower taxes, curb the power of labor, and generally leave business and the economy alone. Another large group said that the trouble with the New Deal was not that it had done too much but that it had done too little. The thinking of this group was deeply influenced by the work of English economist **John Maynard Keynes.**[19] In visits to the United States during the 1930s, Keynes warned that if people did not consume enough or invest enough, national income would fall. The way to increase national income is to spend money on consumption goods (such as clothes or food or automobiles), or on investment goods (electronic chips and dock facilities), or on both. Finally, *in a recession government must do the spending and investing*

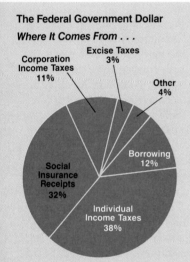

The Federal Government Dollar

Where It Comes From . . .

Corporation Income Taxes 11%

Excise Taxes 3%

Other 4%

Borrowing 12%

Social Insurance Receipts 32%

Individual Income Taxes 38%

Where It Goes . . .

National Defense 27%

Direct Benefit Payments for Individuals 43%

Net Interest 14%

Grants to States and Localities 11%

Other Federal Operations 5%

SOURCE: Fiscal Year 1989 Estimate, U.S. Office of Management and Budget

[17] Quoted in F. L. Allen, *Since Yesterday* (Harper, 1940), p. 64.

[18] W. H. Beveridge, *The Pillars of Security* (Macmillan, 1943), p. 51.

[19] The debate over Keynes and his economic theories still takes place in the United States. See, for example, the special issue on Keynes in *The Economist* (American Enterprise Institute, June 1983), and Robert Eisner, *How Real Is the Federal Deficit?* (Free Press, 1986).

if private enterprise by itself will not or cannot. Through the passage of the Employment Act of 1946, Congress accepted the Keynesian approach.

The Employment Act of 1946

Passing a law specifically recognizing the major role of the national government in maintaining full employment was bound to be difficult.[20] Major business groups strongly opposed it. Enacted in February 1946, however, the act declared:

> It is the continuing policy and responsibility of the Federal Government to use all practicable means consistent with its needs and obligations and other essential considerations of national policy, with the assistance and cooperation of industry, agriculture, labor, and state and local governments, to coordinate and utilize all its plans, functions, and resources for the purpose of creating and maintaining, in a manner calculated to foster and promote free competitive enterprise and the general welfare, conditions under which there will be afforded useful employment, for those able, willing, and seeking to work, and to promote maximum employment, production, and purchasing power.

If this sounds like double talk, it is because the bill was a medley of compromises. In effect, the bill made the government responsible for maintaining high employment. Equally important, the act established machinery to carry out that responsibility:

1. *The Council of Economic Advisers (CEA)*. This body of three members appointed by the president with the consent of the Senate is located in the executive office of the president. It studies and forecasts economic trends, assesses the contribution of federal programs to maximum employment, and recommends to the president "national economic policies to foster and promote free competition, to avoid economic fluctuations or to diminish the effects thereof, and to maintain employment, production, and purchasing power."
2. *The Economic Report of the President*. Every January the president must submit to Congress an economic report based on the data and forecasts of the council. The report must include a program for carrying out the policy of the act; it can also include recommendations for legislation.
3. *Joint Economic Committee (JEC)*. This committee of Congress composed of senators and representatives reports its findings and proposals in response to annual presidential recommendations. Aside from publishing various reports, the JEC tries to give Congress an overview of the economy. In this sense it is a planning and theory group in a legislature otherwise fiercely devoted to short-term, practical matters. The Senate and House Budget Committees also try to provide this kind of overview.

How has the Employment Act worked in practice? The CEA has emerged as a high-level presidential advisory body. Its chair serves both as an adviser to the president and as a spokesperson for the president before Congress and the country. The annual economic report and the budget message are major presidential statements on the role governmental fiscal policies will play in the economy. The JEC has usually played a useful role in developing information on important economic problems.[21] The various mechanisms of the act work reasonably well, but concern over trade imbalances and budget deficits have prompted recent presidents to set up an economic policy cabinet council in addition to the CEA. These cabinet-level coordinating units seek to provide policy options to the president and to coordi-

---

[20] For the full history of the bill, see Stephen K. Bailey, *Congress Makes a Law* (Columbia University Press, 1950). For a history of national efforts at economic planning since the 1930s, see Otis L. Graham, *Toward a Planned Society* (Oxford University Press, 1976).

[21] Herbert Stein, *Presidential Economics* (Simon & Schuster, 1985).

nate the actions that result from economic decisions.[22] Most of these mechanisms work reasonably well, but good processes themselves are no guarantee that the policies they generate will work well, if at all.

FISCAL POLICY

YOU DECIDE

Here is the actual wording of a proposed amendment to the U.S. Constitution that has the backing of several senators and members of Congress. Would you support it? If so, why? If not, why not? And what do you think are some of the reasons why people favor it or oppose it?

Text of a Proposed Amendment

Article

Resolved by the Senate and House of Representatives of the United States of America in Congress assembled (two-thirds of each House concurring therein), that the following article is proposed as an amendment to the Constitution of the United States, which shall be valid to all intents and purposes as part of the Constitution if ratified by the legislatures of three-fourths of the several states within seven years after its submission to the states for ratification:

Section 1. Prior to each fiscal year, the Congress shall adopt a statement of receipts and outlays for that year in which total outlays are not greater than total receipts. The Congress may amend such statement provided revised outlays are no greater than revised receipts. Whenever three-fifths of the whole number of both Houses shall deem it necessary, Congress in such statement may provide for a specific excess of outlays over receipts by a vote directed solely

Nowadays the national government unquestionably has tremendous economic power. But soaring government spending and soaring deficits have raised a number of questions about how effectively the government is doing its job. Through two types of policy—*monetary* (control of the money supply) and *fiscal* (taxing and spending)—the government attempts to manage the economy's ups and downs, moderating both while allowing steady economic growth. This management power emerged with such developments as the Federal Reserve System, the income tax, the great growth of government spending, and the Budget and Accounting Act of 1921.

Government management of the economy is still based to a degree on the theories of John Maynard Keynes—increasing aggregate demand by government spending during business slumps and curbing spending during booms. Politically, however, there is a problem: It is much easier to increase spending and government programs than it is to curb them. As a result, deficit spending is common. To stimulate demand, the government spends more money than it takes in. For many years this policy was thought to be beneficial to the economy—and it was convenient politically. As noted earlier, however, deficits have soared in recent years, and there have been no surpluses, even during economic upswings. In fact, there has been only one year of surpluses in over twenty-five years. Economists found that such policies, when accompanied by a loose-money policy by the Federal Reserve, resulted in a hidden cost: inflation. Even though taxpayers did not pay the entire cost of national programs, consumers did, as the pumped-up economy had too many dollars chasing too few goods. Although government spending is not responsible for all inflation, it has been a major contributor; as a result, more and more people have begun to look for new economic remedies.

Supply-Side Economics

Ronald Reagan came to the White House preaching an alternative to Keynesian economics (but in fact he relied on Keynesian strategies more than any other president). He pledged to balance the budget by cutting both taxes and government spending. He advocated **supply-side economics.** In simple terms, supply-side economics holds that large cuts in taxes will inspire productive investment so that the initial loss of federal revenues will be offset by the taxes generated from expanded private economic activity. Reagan maintained that by creating favorable conditions for businesses, investments would increase, companies would expand their operations, and more jobs would be created.

Once in office, President Reagan discovered that it was easier to cut taxes than federal spending and, in 1981, he pushed through Congress the largest tax cuts in our history. Critics of supply-side economics, including most economists, doubted that tax cuts alone would result in the economic expansion necessary to generate more tax revenues.

The extraordinary revenue growth forecast by supply-side economists in the early 1980s simply did not materialize. According to the supply siders, the implemen-

[22] See Roger B. Porter, *Presidential Decision-Making: The Economic Policy Board* (Cambridge University Press, 1980). See also Ronald Brownstein and Dick Kirschten, "Cabinet Power," *The National Journal* (June 28, 1986), pp. 1582–89.

Proposed Amendment *cont.*

to the subject. The Congress and the President shall, pursuant to legislation or through the exercise of their powers under the first and second articles, ensure that actual outlays do not exceed the outlays set forth in such statement.

Section 2. Total receipts for any fiscal year set forth in the statement adopted pursuant to this article shall not increase by a rate greater than the rate of increase in national income in the year or years ending not less than six months nor more than twelve months before such fiscal year, unless a majority of the whole number of both Houses of Congress have passed a bill directed solely to approving specific additional receipts and such bill has become law.

Section 3. The Congress may waive the provisions of this article for any fiscal year in which a declaration of war is in effect.

Section 4. Total receipts shall include all receipts of the United States except those derived from borrowing and total outlays shall include all outlays of the United States except those for repayment of debt principal.

Section 5. The Congress shall enforce and implement this article by appropriate legislation.

Section 6. On and after the day this article takes effect, the amount of federal public limit as of such date shall become permanent and there shall be no increase in such amount unless three-fifths of the whole number of both Houses of Congress shall have passed a bill approving such increase and such bill has become law.

Section 7. This article shall take effect for the second fiscal year beginning after its ratification.

(Answer/Discussion on next page.)

tation of major tax cuts would allow Americans to save more and to go to work in greater numbers. It would also encourage the economy to expand and more tax revenues to flow into the Treasury Department. But no extra savings were realized. And no significant increase in revenues resulted. "Although it was never publicly admitted, the Reagan Administration had become 'born again Keynesians,' converted to easy money, large tax cuts, big increases in government spending, and huge deficits," writes economist Lester Thurow. "Midway through his first term of office President Reagan had adopted precisely the policies which he had spent a lifetime denouncing."[23]

Monetarism

More significant than the supply-side approach in the Reagan years was the acceptance of the theory of *monetarism.* The core element of monetarism is the idea that prices, income, and economic stability are primarily the function of growth in the money supply. Monetarists contend the money supply is the key factor in affecting the economy's performance. Further, they argue that there should be restrained yet steady growth in the money supply, enough to encourage solid economic growth, but not inflation.

During the early 1980s the Federal Reserve Board, with the Reagan administration's encouragement, induced the longest and most severe post World War II recession. This seemed to succeed, at least temporarily, at reducing inflationary pressures. But unemployment soon reached 9 and 10 percent levels. The monetarist policy raised as many questions as it solved; it also divided many monetarists on such key questions as how long it should take to get from a position of high inflation to one with reasonable price stability: "It didn't say whether that reduction should occur in one year or in three or in five. It didn't say whether that reduction should be at a steady pace or should be faster at first or slower at first."[24]

The Balanced Budget Amendment

The apparent inability of the federal government to balance its budget has led some politicians and economists to propose that it be constitutionally required to do so. The proposed balanced budget amendment would require Congress to adopt a budget in which projected spending is no larger than projected tax receipts. In addition, the amendment would limit the increase in taxes (and/or spending) in any fiscal year to the percentage increase in the gross national product (GNP) during the previous calendar year. The amendment has two escape clauses. Congress could waive the requirements of the amendment by a vote of two-thirds of all members of both houses. Also, the provisions of the amendment would not apply in any year in which a war had been declared.

Advocates of a balanced budget amendment (among them Ronald Reagan and George Bush) claim that such an amendment is necessary to correct what they call the "spending bias" that currently exists in government decision making. Senators such as Orrin Hatch (R-Utah), Strom Thurmond (R-South Carolina), and Dennis DeConcini (D-Arizona) claim there is a structural deficiency within our political system that causes higher levels of spending than is desired by the citizenry. Well-organized, powerful, and heavily financed special-interest groups sometimes overwhelm relatively weak taxpayer lobbies and regularly win on spending measures in Congress.[25]

[23] Lester C. Thurow, *The Zero-Sum Solution* (Simon & Schuster, 1985), p. 30. See also Herbert Stein, *Presidential Economics* (Simon & Schuster, 1984).

[24] Herbert Stein, *Presidential Economics* (Simon & Schuster, 1984), p. 305.

[25] See the debate on the amendment in *Congressional Digest* (October 1982).

Representative Jack Kemp (R-New York) was a major influence on the tax cuts in Reagan's first term. He is also a key leader of the conservative wing of the Republican party. (*Twin Lens Photo/Courtesy Jack Kemp*)

Opponents of a balanced budget amendment say that such an amendment would reduce the flexibility of economic policy makers. It would virtually eliminate fiscal policy as a tool for managing the economy. Political leaders such as Senators Alan Cranston (D-California) and Daniel Patrick Moynihan (D-New York) say that often a federal budget deficit is an effective means of boosting the economy. In times of economic downturn, they say, government spending in excess of revenues can increase employment, generate investment, stimulate demand, and prevent a recession from deepening into a depression.

Opponents also say it is unwise to place an economic theory into the Constitution. The Constitution, they contend, should be a broad charter dealing with fundamental principles of governance, not a document that gets specific about theories of economic management. Further, they contend, balancing the budget is a legislative—not a constitutional—matter.

The balanced budget amendment is either a "fraud" or a "disaster," argue many opponents. It is a fraud in the sense that countless variables affect how much it will cost to run our national government and how much it will collect. Such changes as a drought in the south or a flood in California affect both sides of the budget—so much so it would be only an educated guess as to what federal revenues would be. If the balanced budget is adopted, Congress may very well have to resort to subterfuges to "pretend" it has balanced the books.

If the just described twisting of the intent is not accurate, and the amendment is actually used to cut back on federal expenditures to a level at which we can be sure that tax revenues will cover them, it will force alterations that themselves cause major social upheavals: social security entitlements, military pay, veterans' benefits, and a host of federal aid and educational benefits would have to be reduced, for instance.

Perhaps more likely, the balanced budget amendment would change the "rules of the game" and would make it easier for social and economic conservatives to win more legislative battles. More votes would be required to adopt new programs, and some of these would require a two-thirds vote to appropriate money.

A Constitutional Amendment to Limit Government Spending

A similar measure—also often supported by majorities in public-opinion surveys—would tie the percentage of increased annual government spending to increases in the nation's economic growth. Backed primarily by conservatives, this measure has won support from some moderates as well. Advocates of this amendment do not want to tamper with the Constitution—except, they say, when all else fails—and attempts to curb spending have so far failed. Government is growing so fast and becoming such a dominant force in so many aspects of the economy that we risk crushing what is left of the so-called private sector.

With a mandatory spending limitation, supporters say, perhaps the incentive to improve internal efficiency will be greatly increased. Writes one close student of the budgetary process:

> Knowing that they [government bureaucrats] are unlikely to get more and may well get less (depending on the state of the economy . . .), agencies will try to get the most out of what they have. Efficiency will no longer be a secondary consideration, to be satisfied if nothing else is pressing, or be no consideration at all if evidence that they can do less would reduce their future income: efficiency will be the primary path of the steady state in which they find themselves.[26]

[26] Aaron Wildavsky, *How to Limit Government Spending* (University of California Press, 1980), p. 36. See also Robert Lubar, "Making Democracy Less Inflation-Prone," *Fortune* (September 22, 1980), pp. 78–85. For somewhat different views on the same topic, see Lester Thurow, *The Zero-Sun Society: Distribution and the Possibilities for Economic Change* (Basic Books, 1980).

Critics of this proposed amendment say it is too drastic a step: They would prefer to make the budget processes work more effectively. They say too that a spending limitation would be a vote of no confidence in Congress—it would signify that Congress cannot handle its taxing and spending and power of the purse responsibilities. Further, critics contend the losers under such a new scheme would surely be the poor and less well-organized people, who cannot afford wealthy lobbyists to protect their interests in Congress. Besides, if we really need a spending limitation to discipline Congress and help bring some rationality to spending levels, why not do it by law rather than by constitutional amendment? This is, in fact, what Congress is currently trying to do.

The problem of trying to curb government spending and trying to avoid deficits is not unique to the United States; it remains a serious issue for all market-oriented democratic economies. In the old days factions were pitted against factions. Separation of powers and federalism were supposed to work against organized narrow interests. Later, parties sometimes played the mediating role. But modern technology has undermined many of the old premises. Groups now form more easily than ever, and they have previously unheard of means to press their cases and punish uncooperative legislators or public officials. We live in an interest-group state. The challenge today is to revitalize processes that can help discipline the natural selfish instincts of individuals and groups and to fashion macroeconomic policies that encourage economic growth and a competitive economy that must increasingly work within the global economy.

SUMMARY

1. The once easily defined boundaries between private and public life are now irretrievably blurred. A few still insist that government and the economy must be strictly separated. Whatever its theoretical merits, this view is unrealistic. In modern American society we have a political economy in which a decision in one area inevitably affects decisions in others. The political economy is a mixed economy: It blends private and public enterprise, individual initiative and government promotion, personal responsibility and public regulation, and federal and state governments.

2. During the past few years major efforts have been undertaken to reform the tax code (lowering tax rates and simplifying the tax system) and to devise economic policies (both fiscal and monetary) that would encourage economic growth but prevent inflation, high interest rates, and increased unemployment. Few policies have succeeded, but economists and political leaders continue to grope for a mix of the right economic strategies. Meanwhile, virtually everyone agrees that annual budgetary deficits and the soaring national debt are monumental problems that have been ignored for too long.

3. A central concern of the past few presidential elections, and one that will be with us throughout the 1990s, is how to limit government spending, keep interest rates and inflation low, avoid unreasonable unemployment, balance the budget, and keep our economy productive and competitive—all at the same time. Strategies to achieve these purposes are now being widely debated. But there are limits to all these strategies, and everything we do has consequences we never intend. Moreover, we are often limited in what we can do, because we must develop new policies by democratic procedures.

4. One of the greatest challenges in a democracy is mobilizing the government so that it can respond to changing economic conditions, but in a way that keeps government accountable to the people. The problem in part is whether a system such as ours can act effectively when action is needed. But the problem is also knowing what to do and when to do it. Further, we no longer have a domestic economy autonomous from an international economy. We have only just begun to understand the ramifications of this reality.

FURTHER READING

HENRY AARON and HARVEY GALPER. *Assessing Tax Reform* (Brookings Institution, 1985).

JEFFREY BIRNBAUM and ALAN MURRAY. *Showdown at Gucci Gulch: Lawmakers, Lobbyists, and the Unlikely Triumph of Tax Reform* (Vintage, 1988).

BILL BRADLEY. *The Fair Tax* (Pocket Books, 1984).

PHILIP CAGAN, ed. *Essays in Contemporary Economic Problems* (American Enterprise Institute, 1986).

HOWARD SHUMAN. *Politics and the Budget*, 2nd. ed. (Prentice Hall, 1988).

LESTER C. THUROW. *The Zero-Sum Solution* (Simon & Schuster, 1985).

WALLACE EARL WALKER. *Changing Organizational Culture: Strategy, Structure, and Professionalism in the U.S. General Accounting Office* (University of Tennessee Press, 1986).

JOHN F. WITTE. *The Politics and Development of the Federal Income Tax* (University of Wisconsin Press, 1985).

CHAPTER 22

The Politics
of Regulation

What do lawn mowers, automobiles, telephones, smoke detectors, cereal ads, pornography, banks, natural gas companies, nuclear power plants, and workers' wages all have in common? They are all regulated in some way by the federal government. Because virtually every activity in the United States is regulated in one form or another, regulation today is a vast enterprise. And any activity as pervasive as regulation is bound to generate controversy.

Even though there are no explicit references to regulation in the original Constitution, our regulatory arrangements were not arbitrarily created. They came into existence to clean up meatpacking conditions such as those exposed in Upton Sinclair's *The Jungle*, to prevent the kind of pesticide contamination described in Rachel Carson's *Silent Spring*, and to respond to the lack of auto safety concern documented in Ralph Nader's *Unsafe at Any Speed*. Regulations exist both to encourage competition and to achieve valued social objectives. More recently regulations have been enacted to protect us from raw sewage in rivers; lead in paint and gasoline; toxic wastes in the air; and asbestos, cotton dust, and hazardous substances in toys and furniture.

Many regulations have generated fierce resentment. Can we afford all these regulations? Are they driving people out of business? Do the costs outweigh the benefits? And many political and business leaders have been saying for a decade that the United States is overregulated. Labor, consumers, and environmentalists often disagree and say that in certain areas we need more—not less—regulation. Who is right? This chapter analyzes the goals of regulation, discusses some of the costs and consequences, and provides some examples of government regulation and the more recent efforts to undo or modify some regulatory programs.

WHAT IS REGULATION?

Regulation occurs when the government steps in and alters the natural procedures of the open market to achieve some desired goal. The main regulatory role of government is to improve or supplant markets when they do not or cannot function effectively. In this sense regulation is a middle ground between socialism, or government ownership, and a "laissez faire," or "hands off," policy. The open market is characterized by self-adjustment, or natural regulation. Regulation by government interjects political goals and values into the economy in the form of rules that direct behavior in the marketplace.

All economies are sets of rules and regulations; there simply are no unregulated economies. The United States operates with a competitive market economy: Wages, prices, the allocation of goods and services, and the employment of resources are generally regulated by the laws of supply and demand. Put another way, we rely on private enterprise and market incentives to carry out most of our production and distribution.

A government regulation is a limitation imposed on the discretion of a person or an organization—and it is backed up by government's use of police power. It means setting restraints on persons or groups, directly compelling them to take, or not take, certain actions.

Types of Regulation

Regulation is often broken down into two general categoreis or types: *economic* or traditional regulation and *social* or new regulation. *Economic regulation* generally refers to controlling the entry of individual firms into particular lines of business and setting the prices that firms in a particular industry may charge. Sometimes, too, it can refer to specifying the standards of service firms can offer. Such regulation began in the nineteenth century, when the Interstate Commerce Commission was established, and it has continued with the Federal Communications Commission and the Commodity Futures Trading Commission. It has usually been justified to correct inefficient markets and to limit one or a few firms who have been able to use their market power to discourage competition. Several of these regulatory agencies, and this type of regulation in general, have come under criticism in recent years; economic studies suggest that, because economic regulation has sometimes encouraged artificially high prices and barriers to entry in the industries it regulates, it is costly to consumers and to the economy as a whole.

Social regulation generally refers to government efforts to correct a wide variety of side effects, usually unintended, brought about by certain economic activity. Health, safety, and environmental hazards are often the target of social regulation. This type of regulation cuts across industry lines and aims at providing such goods as cleaner air and improved worker and consumer safety. In economic terms, producers regulated by social regulation must now pay for the "external costs" that once were free, such as using the atmosphere for waste disposal. These costs, however, are often passed along to the consumer, and the true cost of the product is more accurately reflected in its price. Some goods become too costly, and demand drops. Others become more popular (for instance, safe toys). In the end the goal of such regulation is a socially more beneficial allocation of resources. The Environmental Protection Agency (EPA), the Consumer Product Safety Commission, and the Occupational Safety and Health Administration (OSHA) are engaged in social regulation. Social regulation has also been widely criticized, as we discuss later in this chapter.

Regulatory efforts of the federal government are basically a twentieth-century development, although certain efforts, such as the Steamboat Inspection Service of 1837, would qualify in a general sense as a regulatory endeavor. By 1900 there were about five regulatory agencies; by 1933 about a dozen. Today, depending on how they are counted, over eighty regulatory organizations at the federal level employ nearly 100,000 federal civil servants. Congress has created both *executive branch* and *independent regulatory agencies*. Members of executive branch agencies serve at the pleasure of the president. Members of independent regulatory agencies are appointed by the president, confirmed by the Senate, and removable only for some

Controlling monopoly and oligopoly   To achieve many economic goals, including the best allocation of resources, government must encourage competition. In a monopoly or oligopoly (discussed later) power is concentrated in the hands of only one or a few firms, and there is no competition. The government works to ensure competition through antitrust regulation. When monopoly and oligopoly exist, as in the case of power companies, for example, government regulation prevents these industries from taking advantage of the consumer. In some markets, government regulates prices and sets standards of performance.

Another market imperfection involves **natural monopolies.** A natural monopoly exists when it would be grossly inefficient to have competition in a particular industry. If competition existed in electric utilities, the price of power might be higher to the public than if just one company supplied all the power: Because of the size of its operation, and the vast capital investment needed, one company can be more efficient, and thus more economical, than many. When such a natural monopoly exists, the government regulates it.

Compensating for market imperfections   The market does not always work to solve every problem, especially the problem of *externalities*, or side effects. Consider the example of pollution. For a long time no price was imposed on a business for using air and water to store or discharge toxic wastes. Therefore, market forces did not consider what it cost society to have its air and water polluted. Or take the case of commuters who use their cars to go to work. The more who do so, the more difficult it is for commuters to get to work. (That is why commuters frequently favor mass transportation—so that *other* people will use it and thus open the roadways for *them*.) Still, present market forces do not encourage taking a bus instead of a car to work.

When the market fails to set appropriate costs and benefits, pressures develop for the government to step in. The government can, for example, pass regulations that impose costs on air pollution.

Defending the economically weak   The government has involved itself directly in the economy to protect those who lack economic power. It has, for instance, worked to establish a minimum wage and to prevent such abuses as child labor. The government has also sought to control the conflict between labor and management and to protect workers' right to organize. In its role as protector of the weak, the government has sought to ensure equal opportunity (which we discussed in Chapter 5), and to protect the investor or consumer from fraud and unsafe products.

Government Regulation: A Finger in Every Pie?

Although regulation has traditionally been defended as intervention to ensure more socially beneficial outcomes, it is sometimes criticized as imposing more costs on society than its benefits warrant. Even though we have many desired objectives—economic, social, and political—our resources are limited. A critical task of modern democratic government is to make wise, balanced choices among courses of action and competing objectives. Increasingly regulation is coming into conflict with other economic objectives: Critics charge that it is contributing to higher inflation, lower productivity, and economic stagnation.[1] Proponents argue that government regula-

(T. Cronin)

---

[1] See, for example, Milton Friedman and Rose Friedman, *Free to Choose* (Harcourt Brace Jovanovich, 1980); Murray L. Weidenbaum, *Business, Government and the Public* (Prentice-Hall, 1977); and Murray L. Weidenbaum and Robert DeFina, *The Cost of Federal Regulation of Economic Activity* (American Enterprise Institute Reprint, May 1978).

tion, though not perfect, has brought improvements in the areas of environmental quality, worker safety, and consumer protection.[2]

How desirable is it to have considerably cleaner air or considerably safer workplaces? Although it is relatively inexpensive to remove a large amount of air pollution, and therefore socially desirable, it becomes increasingly expensive to remove all or even almost all of it. To do so would require an allocation of resources that, from a taxpayer's point of view, might be better used for something else—whether new missiles or schools. Is there a socially optimal point of pollution control or worker safety beyond which it is too costly to go? The challenge for policy makers is to determine what this point is. In our political system, with its many competing interest groups, there is much difference of opinion on this matter

Faced with this problem, Congress often legislates broad objectives for the regulatory agencies, which then set specific rules for meeting these goals. Thus far agency regulations have been largely in the form of specific rules that a firm may not violate without being punished. Usually of the "command-control" type, they have been criticized as being arbitrary, costly, and inflexible. The Carter administration cut back some of these unnecessary regulations; the Reagan administration went even further: OSHA has trimmed over 1000 "nitpicking" regulations that governed such things as the shape of toilet seats.

Economists have proposed various regulations that would make it less expensive for industries to meet requirements. The concept behind such ideas as performance standards or effluent fees is that the government should set requirements for pollution control or worker safety but that the means of reaching these goals should be left to the firms. For example, rather than factories being required to install expensive noise control facilities, workers could be required to wear hearing protectors.

The new regulatory techniques can be classified into four categories: (1) *market approaches*—reliance on the economic incentives of the free market to nudge industry in the direction of the public interest; (2) *performance standards*—replacement of regulations that spell out exactly how industry must meet a particular goal with broader statements that allow industry to choose the means; (3) *informational approaches*—requirements that manufacturers disclose complete information about their products, on the theory that consumers can then make intelligent choices; and (4) *self-regulation*—a government decision to do little more than help industry set its own voluntary standards.[3]

The Costs of Regulation

Although it is difficult to measure the costs and benefits of regulation, both the costs and benefits are to be measured in the billions of dollars.[4] It is generally agreed that regulation could be less costly to society by using more market incentives and streamlining rules, without a decrease in benefits.[5] The costs of traditional economic regulation has begun to decline because of various deregulation efforts, especially in the transportation industry. The demise of the Civil Aeronautics Board and the efforts to kill off the Interstate Commerce Commission are recent examples.

The Rise of Regulatory Agencies

	Number of agencies created
Before 1900	
1900–09	
1910–19	
1920–29	
1930–39	
1940–49	
1950–59	
1960–69	
1970–79	
1980–87	

0   4   8   12   16   20
Number of agencies created

DATA: Center for the Study of American Business

[2] See, for example, *Benefits of Environmental, Health and Safety Regulation* (Committee on Governmental Affairs, U.S. Senate, 1980); Steven Kelman, "Regulation that Works," *The New Republic* (November 25, 1978), pp. 16–19; and Timothy B. Clark, "The Costs and Benefits of Regulation," *National Journal* (December 1, 1979), pp. 2023–27.

[3] Timothy Clark, "New Approaches to Regulatory Reform—Letting the Market Do the Job," *National Journal* (August 11, 1979), p. 1316.

[4] See Arthur Andersen & Co., *Cost of Government Regulation Study* (Business Roundtable, 1979); and Murray L. Weidenbaum, *The Future of Business Regulation* (AMACON, 1979).

[5] See Robert E. Litan and William D. Nordhaus, *Reforming Federal Regulation* (Yale University Press, 1983).

REGULATING BUSINESS

Pat Boone with one of his daughters. (*UPI/Bettmann Newsphotos*)

Business has never been free of restrictive legislation, but during much of the latter part of the nineteenth century, our national policy was to leave business pretty much alone. With considerable freedom business leaders set about developing (as well as exploiting) a nation that was enormously rich in natural resources. The heroes of the 1870s and 1880s were not politicians but business magnates—the Rockefellers, Morgans, Carnegies, and Fricks. "From rags to riches" became the nation's motto.

Yet many businesspeople in the late nineteenth century were not just given freedom; they often were given prime sections of land to subsidize expansion of rail systems, tariffs to protect infant industries, and implicit—if not explicit—police assistance to prevent rapid unionization. Government actually helped to *promote* many of these businesses.

Toward the end of the century sharp depressions rocked the economy and threw people out of work. Millions labored long hours in factories and fields for meager wages. Muckrakers revealed that some of the most famous business leaders had indulged in shoddy practices and corrupt deals. A demand for government regulation sprang up, and a series of national and state laws were passed in an attempt to correct the worst abuses. Such laws were adopted on the pragmatic assumption that each problem could be handled as it arose. On balance, however, these laws still reflected a commitment to competitive markets. The government intervened only for the purpose of remedying the defects of the marketplace.

Antitrust Policy

Social critics and populist reformers in the late nineteenth century believed consumers were being cheated where monopolies controlled goods and services, especially in the oil, sugar, whiskey, and steel industries. At the same time people began to have mixed feelings about big business. Americans, who have always been impressed by bigness—the tallest skyscraper, the largest football stadium, the biggest steel mill—and the efficiency that often goes with it, have also been skeptical about the power and side effects of giant enterprises. We believe our economic system functions best under conditions of fair competition among many businesses. We would like to believe, too, that enterprising individuals can set themselves up in virtually any business. These mixed views have long been reflected in our attempts to prevent monopoly and the restraint of competition through **antitrust policy**. ("Trusts" are collusions or arrangements to reduce competition.)

In 1890 Congress responded to this new mood by passing the Sherman Antitrust Act. Designed to foster competition and stop the growth of private monopolies, the act made clear its intention "to protect trade and commerce against unlawful restraints and monopolies." Henceforth, persons making contracts, combinations, or conspiracies in restraint of trade in interstate and foreign commerce could be sued for damages, required to stop their illegal practices, and subjected to criminal penalties. The Sherman Antitrust Act had little immediate impact. Presidents made little attempt to enforce it, and the Supreme Court's early construction of the act limited its scope.[6]

During the administration of Woodrow Wilson, Congress added the Clayton Act to the antitrust arsenal. This act outlawed such specific abuses as charging different prices to different buyers in order to destroy a weaker competitor, granting rebates, making false statements about competitors and their products, buying up

[6] On the historical development of, the purpose for, and the underlying reasoning behind antitrust, see George Thompson and Gerald Brady, *Antitrust Fundamentals* (West, 1979).

supplies to stifle competition, bribing competitors' employees, and so on. In addition, **interlocking directorates** (by which an officer or director in one corporation serves on the board of another, especially a competitor) in large corporations were banned, and corporations were prohibited from acquiring stock (amended in 1950 to include assets) in competing concerns if such acquisitions substantially lessened interstate competition. Also, in 1914, Congress established the Federal Trade Commission (FTC), run by a five-person board, to enforce the Clayton Act and to prevent unfair competitive practices. The FTC was to be the "traffic cop" for competition.[7]

Still, antitrust activity continued to be weak during the 1920s. Times were prosperous: Republican administrations were actively probusiness. The FTC consisted of men who opposed government regulation of business. The Department of Justice, charged with enforcing the Sherman Act, paid little attention to it. During the Depression abuses were revealed, and popular resentment mounted against big business. At first the Roosevelt administration tried to fight the Depression by setting aside the antitrust laws. But by the late 1930s a period of trustbusting began in earnest. Since then the Supreme Court has shown a more sympathetic attitude toward the purposes of the Sherman Act, and the FTC has sometimes acted with more vigor.

But how effective has all this activity been? Have antitrust suits, FTC proceedings, and the fear of such reprisals kept our system competitive? It is difficult to tell. Some people think antitrust laws are out of date, in part because they were written when the major economic competitors in any industry were from this country alone. That has markedly changed in recent years.

Americans tend to think issues of domestic economic policy are solely within the jurisdiction of this government. But in recent years we have discovered that the economic fate of this nation and of its industries is tied closely to what happens elsewhere. For years we thought the automobile market in the United States was dominated by the Big Three (GM, Ford, and Chrysler), and that they could control the market and set the prices. But after they set the prices "too high," we discovered that firms located in Japan, Germany, and elsewhere can also make and sell cars: As a result, the Big Three look less Big. In fact, foreign corporations have captured increasing shares of our markets, and our corporations have moved more of their production facilities overseas. And more corporations have become multinational, seeking to benefit from the overlapping of national regulatory jurisdictions.

About one-third of our nation's manufacturing capacity is controlled by fifty companies, and well over two-thirds of all manufacturing assets are owned by only 500 corporations.[8] But monopolies as such have virtually disappeared from the economic arena. In place of monopolies two new threats to competition have emerged: the **oligopoly,** a situation in which a few firms dominate a market, such as in the automobile industry or the food processing industry; and the **conglomerate,** a situation in which a firm owns businesses in many unrelated industries, such as ITT.

Are the nation's antitrust laws, drawn up several decades ago, still practical for today's economy? This question evokes different responses. Some members of Congress and some former regulatory commissioners and Justice Department officials believe we need to design tighter penalties, impose more regulatory guidelines, and expand antitrust enforcement. But this was plainly a minority or nonexistent point of view in the Reagan administration. At the Justice Department's Antitrust Division, about 300 lawyers work on those cases brought to them in a general effort to protect the free enterprise system. Corporate conduct that may be illegal comes

"It so happens, Gregory, that your Grandfather Sloan was detained by an agency of our government over an honest misunderstanding concerning certain antitrust matters! He was not 'busted by the Feds'!"
(*Drawing by W. Miller;* © *1971 The New Yorker Magazine, Inc.*)

---

[7] On the origins of the FTC and the role of Louis B. Brandeis, see Thomas K. McCraw, *Prophets of Regulation* (Belknap, 1984), chap. 3.

[8] John Blair, *Economic Concentration: Structure, Behavior and Public Policy* (Harcourt Brace Jovanovich, 1972).

to their attention through complaints by competitors, customers, or suppliers. The Reagan enforcers took a dim view of firms that launched antitrust suits against rivals—such as the Chrysler Corporation, which unsuccessfully challenged General Motors Corporation's joint venture with Toyota Motor Corporation.

Many outside observers say the Antitrust Division has generally done a reasonably fair and adequate job in recent years. Most think that it is understaffed and, considering its responsibilities, that it must work with too small a budget. The Reagan White House liked it that way. The Federal Trade Commission, also influenced by the Reagan years and by substantive budget cutbacks, went about its work in a less aggressive and more probusiness manner than it had in previous years. Many of the FTC's important cases are settled during consent negotiations. **Consent decrees** are orders to cease anticompetitive conduct (although things other than anticompetitive conduct are sometimes specified in consent decrees).

The 1980s witnessed a wave of corporate *mergers* involving one company's buying out another or two companies' pooling assets to form a larger single company. General Motors bought Hughes Aircraft. R. J. Reynolds absorbed Nabisco. GE and RCA merged. ABC became part of Capital Cities Communications. And Philip Morris merged with General Foods. Several airlines have also merged. In many instances, these mergers occurred among competing companies. In one recent five-year period, more than 10,000 mergers took place. Invariably such mergers raise the question of whether a specific merger will increase or decrease competition.

The Reagan administration, ushering in a new attitude toward antitrust policy, generally adopted a permissive policy toward mergers. Its assumption has been that most mergers are inherently good—not, as the common wisdom had it in the 1960s, that such mergers were suspect. Reagan administration aides insisted that economic efficiency should be the main standard for judging mergers. Reagan's secretary of commerce even wanted to repeal the main sections of the Clayton Act, because, he claimed, American manufacturing firms are so battered by foreign competitors that we are light years away from the competitive scene of the early 1900s and the 1950s.

With few exceptions, the Reagan administration took a much more lenient attitude in antitrust matters than had its recent predecessors. Few mergers were prevented. It took an even more permissive attitude toward industries that were doing poorly because of foreign competition. It also urged Congress to dramatically reduce the penalty fines paid by companies convicted of competing too aggressively. In fact, the Reagan administration attempted the greatest overhaul of antitrust law the nation had seen in two generations. It failed to enact into law all it wanted, yet the way in which it enforced, or failed to enforce, existing laws and its general tone toward mergers reversed many of the trends of the 1960s and 1970s.[9]

Controlling Big Business

What should the government do about big business? Few policy makers agree on an answer. Some say we are doing too much—and even those who think we are doing too little do not agree on the solutions. Some economists, for example, see no need for new initiatives. They say the alleged damage done by big business is vastly overestimated, and that even the extent of concentration is exaggerated. They reject as pure myth the view that the United States has become a corporate state. They see the increasing size of business as an indication of increased economies of scale. Although the market is still as competitive as before, the companies are bigger. And we, as consumers, benefit from the technology provided by the large modern corporations.

[9] See Burt Solomon, "Administration Hopes to Extend the Reagan Revolution to Antitrust Laws," *National Journal* (January 19, 1986), pp. 144–46.

Economist John Kenneth Galbraith, among others, agrees that bigness contributes to efficiency, provides the capital necessary for innovation, and spurs economic growth. But he also recognizes that abuses can occur when economic power is concentrated in the hands of a few corporate managers. Galbraith suggests three new tasks for government:

1. Provide assistance to the segment of our economy that is still considered to be competitive—for example, the corner grocery store or the independent TV repair shop.
2. Manage the economy directly by implementing wage-price controls in all the industries that are dominated by big business and big unions.
3. Control the direction of big business by restricting the use of resources in areas that are already overdeveloped; by setting limits on the use of technology; and by establishing stringent standards on the byproducts of industry—for example, pollution—*and* enforcing the standards once set.[10]

"But this would be socialism!" exclaim many economists and policy makers. No, says Galbraith; government already plays a major role in the development of individual firms and in the distribution of economic rewards among different industries. All Galbraith calls for, or so he claims, is the *redirection* of government subsidies. "If these proposals are socialism," he would reply to his critics, "socialism already exists."

Still other reformers want to break up large corporations, not just regulate them. These individuals believe the market can work; all it needs is a chance. They are against bigness, charging that bigness leads to irresponsibility and misconduct.[11]

Antitrust Enforcement and the Phone Company

The Reagan administration maintained that bigness is not necessarily badness. Increased competition from foreign firms, rapid technological innovations, slow growth of the domestic economy, and stagnating productivity all combine to create a situation in which larger enterprises may be necessary to enable businesses to remain competitive. Although antitrust enforcement is sometimes necessary, it often loses sight of its major objective: making the United States a more efficient and productive economy. In this context bigness is not always something to be avoided.

Nonetheless, Justice Department officials in the Reagan administration did continue the government's antitrust case against American Telephone and Telegraph (AT&T). In 1975 the giant communications firm had been charged with monopolizing the telephone service and telephone equipment industry. The Justice Department claimed AT&T was using control of its twenty-two local phone companies to shut out competition in the long-distance and phone equipment sales markets. Antitrust laws were used in this instance by other business firms to break up AT&T. Pressures were not so much to protect consumers as to give other businesses an opportunity to sell telephones and long-distance services.

The huge antitrust case was settled in 1983, after costing AT&T over $360 million in legal fees over a seven-year period. Under the terms of the settlement, the twenty-two local phone companies owned by AT&T became reorganized into seven independent companies. AT&T was allowed to keep its long-distance operations, its equipment manufacturing and sales arms, and its research facilities. All other phone services, however, were divided among the local companies.

The long-term effects on telephone service and phone bills remain uncertain. Some analysts (including the president of AT&T) think rates for local service will

---

[10] John Kenneth Galbraith, *Economics and the Public Purpose* (Houghton Mifflin, 1973), pp. 221–22.
[11] See, for example, Ralph Nader et al., *Taming the Giant Corporation* (Norton, 1976).

increase as smaller phone companies are forced to pass on increased costs to consumers. Critics of the AT&T "break-up" think this is government regulation at its worst. Altering and weakening the world's best telephone service just doesn't make sense, they say. The only people who will profit, they added, will be lawyers, bankers, stock brokers, and those who print stock certificates. Others think increased competition in the long-distance market will result in savings that will more than offset local rate increases. Initial developments suggest that more competition and lower rates on long-distance service have, in fact, been achieved.

REGULATING LABOR-MANAGEMENT RELATIONS

Government regulation of business is essentially restrictive. Most governmental laws and rules have curbed certain business practices and steered private enterprise into socially useful channels. But regulation cuts two ways. In the case of American workers, most laws in recent decades have tended not to restrict but rather to confer rights and opportunities. Actually, many labor laws do not touch labor directly; instead, they regulate its relations with employers.

Labor and the Government

Labor leaders generally favor federal regulation. They fear labor would fare less well if regulation did not exist. Moreover, the federal government since FDR and prior to Reagan was usually a major ally in the campaign to improve job safety and working conditions.

During the first half of this century, governmental protection and promotion were gradually extended over the whole range of labor activity and organization. This was the result of two basic developments: labor's growing political power, and the awareness of millions of Americans that a healthy and secure nation depends in large measure on a healthy and secure labor force.

Labor's basic struggle was for the right to organize. For many decades trade unions had been held lawful by acts of state legislatures, but the courts had chipped away at their status by legalizing certain antiunion devices. The most notorious was the **yellow-dog contract,** by which employers made new workers promise not to join labor organizations. If labor organizers later tried to unionize the workers, the employers, on the basis of the yellow-dog contract, could apply for court orders to stop the organizers. In 1932 labor secured the passage of the Norris-La Guardia Act, which made yellow-dog contracts unenforceable and granted labor the right to organize. By 1932 unions had won other kinds of protection from the federal government, especially over conditions of labor. Yet progress was slow. With the New Deal, Congress began to enact a series of laws to protect workers and their right to form trade unions.

AFL/CIO Board Meeting. (*AFL/CIO News*)

Protecting Workers

Among the more important areas of federal regulation designed to protect workers are the following:

1. *Public contracts.* The Walsh-Healey Act of 1936, as amended, requires that no worker employed under contracts with the national government in excess of $10,000 be paid less than the prevailing wage; and that he or she be paid overtime for all work in excess of eight hours per day or forty hours per week. Two contested questions today are how to determine what the prevailing wage is and whether or not to retain this provision inserted in

(*T. Cronin*)

YOU
DECIDE
!

Since 1938 the federal government has maintained a floor on wages in order to achieve a minimal socially acceptable standard of living for all protected workers without eliminating too many jobs. The minimum wage is defended as the most direct, comprehensive means of increasing the earnings of the working poor. But several people have proposed that there should be a subminimum wage for youth—perhaps $2.50 or $3.00 an hour. What do you think about this proposal? What do you think the benefits and disadvantages would be?

(Answer/Discussion on page 521.)

the mid-1930s. Skilled craftworkers and union officials insist that the Davis-Bacon provision, as it is known, is still necessary to protect their standards of living and to ensure quality work on government projects. Others argue that in the present-day context the prevailing wage requirement makes public work unreasonably expensive and that the provision merely gives craftworkers a special privilege at the expense of the taxpayers.

2. *Wages and hours*. The Fair Labor Standards Act of 1938 set a maximum work week of forty hours for all employers engaged in interstate commerce or in the production of goods for interstate commerce (with certain exemptions). Work beyond that amount must be paid for at one and one-half times the regular rate. Minimum wages, first set at 25 cents an hour, were progressively increased; they reached $3.35 in recent years.

3. *Child labor*. The Federal Labor Standards Act prohibits child labor (under 16 years of age, or under 18 in hazardous occupations) in industries that engage in, or that produce goods for, interstate commerce.

4. *Industrial safety and occupational health*. The Occupational Safety and Health Act of 1970 created the first comprehensive federal industrial safety program. It gives the secretary of labor broad authority to set safety and health standards for workers of companies in interstate commerce.

Protecting Unions

Do unions need federal laws to protect their right to organize? The history of union efforts before 1933 suggests that organizing without federal protection was extremely difficult. Indeed, union membership and strength were waning fast until New Deal measures granted workers the right to organize and bargain collectively. The National Labor Relations Act of 1935 (usually called the Wagner Act) made these guarantees permanent. The preamble declared that workers in industries affecting interstate commerce (with certain exemptions) should have the right to organize and bargain collectively, and that inequality in bargaining power between employers and workers led to industrial strife and economic instability. The act made five types of action unfair for employers: (1) interfering with workers in their attempt to organize unions or bargain collectively; (2) supporting company unions (unions set up and dominated by the employer); (3) discriminating against members of unions; (4) firing or otherwise victimizing an employee for having taken action under the act; and (5) refusing to bargain with union representatives. The act was intended to prevent employers from using violence, espionage, propaganda, and community pressure to resist unionization.

To administer the act, a board of three (now five) members, holding overlapping terms of five years each, was set up. Under the act the National Labor Relations Board (NLRB), a regulatory commission, has the ticklish job of determining the appropriate bargaining unit—that is, whether the employees may organize by plant, by craft, or on some other basis. The board operates largely through regional officers, who investigate charges of unfair labor practices and issue formal complaints; and through trial examiners, who hold hearings and submit reports to the board in Washington.

Striking a Balance

From the start the Wagner Act was controversial. It strengthened the unions and helped them seize greater economic and political power. In 1936 a committee of noted attorneys declared it unconstitutional. But in 1937 the Supreme Court, by a vote of five to four, upheld the constitutionality of the act. The fight then shifted to Congress, where senators and representatives attacked the NLRB through denunciations, investigations, and slashes in appropriations.

What caused all this uproar? First, from the outset the board vigorously applied the prolabor provisions of the act. Second, the board got caught in the struggle between the AFL (American Federation of Labor) and the CIO (Congress of Industrial Organizations). Whichever way it decided certain cases, it was bound to antagonize one labor faction or the other. Third, the purpose of the act was widely misunderstood. Employers and editorial writers charged that the act was biased too much in favor of labor, and that it went well beyond merely improving the workers' bargaining power.

Most unions were run honestly and responsively. Nevertheless, public opinion seemed to swing against labor after World War II. Both labor excesses and a wave of great industrywide strikes intensified demands that Congress equalize the obligations of labor and management. In 1946 the Republicans won majorities in both the House and the Senate, paving the way for modification of the Wagner Act.

The Taft-Hartley Act

The result was the Labor-Management Relations Act of 1947, commonly called the **Taft-Hartley Act.** This act applies (with certain exceptions) to industries dealing in interstate commerce. The act:

1. Outlaws the **closed shop** and permits the **union shop** only under certain conditions. (A closed shop requires an employer to hire and retain only union members in good standing. A union shop is one in which new employees must join the union within a stated period of time.)
2. Outlaws jurisdictional strikes (strikes arising from disputes between unions over whose members should perform a particular task); **secondary boycotts** (efforts by unions involved in disputes with employers to encourage other unions to boycott a fourth party—usually the employers—who, in response to such pressure, might put pressure on the original offending employers); excessive union dues or fees; and strikes by federal employees.
3. Makes it an unfair labor practice for unions to refuse to bargain with employers.
4. Permits employers and unions to sue each other in federal court for violation of contracts.
5. Allows the use of the **labor injunction** on a limited scale. (Such an injunction is a court order forbidding specific individuals or groups to perform acts the court considers harmful to the rights or property of an employer or community.)
6. Permits states to outlaw union shops. **Right-to-work laws,** which states could now adopt, typically make it illegal for **collective bargaining** agreements to contain closed shop, union shop, preferential hiring, or any other clauses calling for compulsory union membership.

The Taft-Hartley Act also set up machinery for handling disputes affecting an entire industry or a major part of it, if a stoppage would threaten national health or safety. When such a strike breaks out, the following steps are authorized:

1. The president appoints a special board to investigate and report the facts.
2. The president may then instruct the attorney general to seek, in a federal court, an eighty-day injunction against the strike.
3. If the court agrees that national health or safety is endangered, it grants this injunction.
4. If the parties have not settled the strike within the eighty days, the board informs the president of the employer's last offer of settlement.
5. The NLRB takes a secret vote among the employees to see if they will accept the employer's last offer.

6. If no settlement is reached, the injunction expires, and the president reports to Congress with such recommendations as the chief executive may wish to make.

The Taft-Hartley Act has been invoked frequently against strikes in vital sectors of the economy, such as atomic energy, coal, shipping, steel, and telephone service. Sometimes a president and the secretary of labor attempt to mediate strikes without resorting to the act. The effectiveness of this act is difficult to assess because legislation is only one of the many factors that affect industrial peace. Still, the basic issue remains unresolved. Strikes are part of the price we pay for the system of **collective bargaining**. But under what conditions does the price become so high that the federal government should intervene, stop the strike, and force a settlement?

The policies of **collective bargaining** are part of a broader set of issues. Labor is deeply concerned with the traditional conditions of work—such as hours, wages, and pensions. But it must also deal with the issue of job security, which is now threatened by technological change and automation. Business faces not only rising costs but intense foreign competition. All this means labor leaders are having to deal as the best they can with such problems as the erosion of worker's wages, benefits, and even job security.

The 13 million member AFL-CIO is losing members, and, more important, it is losing its ability to influence how its members vote in federal elections. The AFL-CIO campaigned aggressively against Ronald Reagan in two elections, and it is already campaigning against the Republicans who will run in 1988. But polls reveal that the Republicans won major support from union members and their families—particularly among younger members. Although growth continues in public-sector unionization, membership in the United Auto Workers (UAW) and United Steelworkers of America—two of the hardest hit unions—has markedly declined.

One recent development in union-management relations is that labor in some areas is helping management raise productivity in exchange for lifetime jobs and institutional security for the union. The National Labor Relations Board has approved such arrangements between General Motors and the UAW. The UAW helps GM design work practices to use with new technology for producing the Saturn car, which will compete with low-priced imports. In return, GM pledges to hire UAW members from other plants to staff new plants, and thus ensures that the UAW will be the bargaining agent. In this particular instance GM and UAW employees jointly design the work systems and workers are given a greater voice in operations; certain traditional work rules and job classifications are thus relaxed. Critics on the right, such as the National Right to Work Committee, and critics on the left, such as old-line labor leaders, oppose these collaborative efforts. But such innovations, aimed at making companies more competitive, are part of a new trend. Moreover, in recent years, "federal judges have avoided a literal interpretation of decades-old labor laws which established rules for adversary relations, if that meant outlawing a cooperative venture."[12]

Answer/Discussion

Youth unemployment is a problem. It is usually at least double that of the adult population; for black teenagers, it is several times that of all adults. A sub-minimum wage would encourage some employers to put more younger people to work; it would probably also create some jobs.

But, if there were a subminimum wage, young people would often displace older workers because they would be cheaper to hire. Moreover, the minimum wage has been at $3.35 since 1981. And, after adjusting for inflation, the 8 million or more workers paid the current minimum wage in effect have had their income reduced nearly 30 percent in recent years. The debate over a subminimum wage for teenagers doubtless distracts attention from the more important issue of the substantial erosion in the minimum wage for all.

REGULATION TO PROTECT THE ENVIRONMENT

The issue of pollution vividly illustrates the regulatory dilemma. Critics of strict controls on air, water, and noise pollution say our pursuit of a clean environment has damaged our economy and will continue to cause unemployment. They call attention, for example, to the disastrous consequences of the shutdown of an industry

[12] "The NLRB Strikes a Blow for Worker Participation," *Business Week* (June 16, 1986), p. 36.

A Mayor's Revenge

Businessmen, local officials, and other victims seething over the burdens and insults of federal paperwork may find balm for their spirits in a nonfederal document that is floating around. It's a letter from Ernest Angelo Jr., mayor of Midland, Texas. Some time ago, Mayor Angelo went through the ordeal of applying for a grant from the U.S. Department of Housing and Urban Development, a process that lasted over ten months and turned into a red-tape nightmare. Not long afterward, he received from the Dallas regional office of HUD a request for a reserved parking space at Midland's municipal airport. Seizing the opportunity to give the feds a taste of their own medicine, he replied in a letter that read, in part, as follows:

1. You must obtain from the U.S. Government Printing Office, or the National Archives, or the Library of Congress, or someplace, a supply of application form COM-1975. You must submit three executed and fourteen conformed copies of this application . . .

2. With the application submit the make and model of the proposed vehicle together with certified assurances that everyone connected with the manufacture, servicing, and operation of same [was] paid according to a wage scale that complies with the requirements of the Davis-Bacon Act.

3. Submit a genealogical table for everyone who will operate said vehicle so that we can ascertain that there will be a precisely exact equal percentage of whites, blacks, and other minorities, as well as women and the elderly.

4. Submit certified assurances that this plan has been discussed at length with the EEOC and submit that commission's certification that requirement 3 above has been fully complied with.

5. Submit certified assurances that all operators of said vehicle and any filling station personnel that service same will be equipped with steel-toed boots, safety goggles, and crash helmets and that the vehicle will be equipped with at least safety belts and an air bag to show compliance with the Occupational Safety and Health Act.

6. Submit an Environmental Impact Statement . . . The statement should show the number of times the vehicle will be operated, times of day, the name of the operator of the vehicle, the number of other vehicles that might be coming into or leaving the parking lot at the same time, as well as the number and type of aircraft that might be landing or taking off at the airport at the same time and an exact conclusion as to the effect this will have on the atmosphere in West Texas.

7. In order to obtain approval of a negative Environmental Impact Statement, you will not be able to:

   (a) operate the car on gasoline produced from domestic oil because that would require that someone discover it, process it, and deliver it, and it is possible that some private person, firm or corporation might realize a profit as a result of such activities . . .
   (b) operate the car from energy produced by coal because this might require digging a hole in the ground . . .

8. Submit a certificate from the Attorney General of the United States that all of the certifiers of the above assurances are duly and legally authorized by Congress to make such certificates . . . and that the United States of America is a duly organized and legally existing independent nation with the full right, power, and authority to operate automobiles in the first place.

Upon receipt of the foregoing, rest assured that the application will be promptly referred to someone for approval. We cannot state at this time who that someone will be because whatever department he or she is in will be undergoing . . . reorganization. . . .

Source: Reprinted by permission of *Fortune* (November 1976).

(or even of one large company). Proponents of tough antipollution laws have argued that we must now pay the price for decades of environmental abuse. They further contend that the longer we delay, the greater the costs to society—both in dollars and in lives.

By its very nature the private sector of the economy tends to ignore pollution. If there is no cost attached to polluting the air or befouling a stream, firms will find it economically advantageous to do so. Because we all benefit from a pollution cleanup, whether we pay for it or not, it is not in any one party's interest to pay the cost. Consequently, the government must step in to control environmental damage. Although people usually agree that the government should do something about pollution, they agree far less about what it should do, how much it should do, to whom it should do it, and who should pay the cost. These questions take on increased importance because of the special nature of the pollution issue. Nowadays the immediate cost of pollution control tends to fall on the polluter, so we would expect opposition from industry. The benefits on the other hand, go to everyone. Thus, the issue evokes concentrated opposition but diffuse or weak support.

Historically environmental issues were discussed by local and state governments. In a study of the pollution question, one political scientist found that municipal *in*action had been a regular response to the air pollution problem in communities throughout the nation: "The federal government has taken on new responsibilities in the field of pollution abatement not so much because these local officials demand it, but because these lower levels of government have often failed to take action themselves."[13]

Using its power as a promoter, the federal government finances research into control devices and assists states both in maintaining their own pollution-control programs and in building waste-treatment facilities. The primary federal agencies concerned with the environment are the Council on Environmental Quality and the Environmental Protection Agency (EPA). Other federal agencies also regulate the environment, including the Interior Department, the Food and Drug Administration, and the Departments of Energy and Transportation. The Council on Environmental Quality, in the executive office of the president, develops and recommends policy options to the president and Congress. The Environmental Protection Agency is responsible for enforcing federal environmental laws and regulations.

The federal government today administers rules and regulations covering many forms of pollution—air, water, and noise—as well as dangers to the environment from harmful chemicals. Arguments about pollution control rarely concern whether to act or not; rather, they ask *what price* we are willing and able to pay for a clean environment and how best to achieve it.[14] Laws already on the books cost the average homeowner an extra $15 to $20 a month in electricity costs. Some private interests, including the automotive industry and the chemical industry, have been hit hard by pollution-control laws.[15]

Is pollution control too costly? Environmentalists point to the high costs of pollution itself. Dirty air and water and hazardous chemicals affect health care costs and worker productivity. It is estimated, for example, that one out of five workers in the asbestos industry may develop cancer; certain other job situations pose similar dangers.

Legislative action in environmental control has been extensive. The National Environmental Policy Act of 1969 set up the controversial requirement of **environmental impact statements.** The law requires the filing of statements assessing the potential effects of federal actions on the environment. This has been interpreted to require most projects utilizing federal funds to file such statements. Since 1970 thousands of statements have been filed. Critics claim environmental impact statements simply represent more government interference in the private sector. Supporters argue that the statements have pointed out major flaws in projects and have led to cost savings along with greater environmental awareness.

The Clean Air Act

One of the most significant pieces of environmental legislation is the 1970 amendment to the Air Quality Act of 1967.[16] The 1970 Clean Air Act establishes national quality standards for states, strict pollution guidelines for automobiles, and regulations

[13] Matthew A. Crenson, *The Un-Politics of Air Pollution* (Johns Hopkins University Press, 1971), p. 10.

[14] See John C. Whitaker, *Striking a Balance* (American Enterprise Institute/Hoover Institution, 1976), and Walter A. Rosenbaum, *Environmental Politics and Policy* (Congressional Quarterly Press, 1985).

[15] See, for example, Robert Crandall et al., *Regulating the Automobile* (Brookings Institution, 1986), chaps. 3 to 5.

[16] Charles O. Jones, *Clean Air: The Policies and Politics of Pollution* (University of Pittsburgh Press, 1975), offers a detailed analysis of national and local clean air legislation.

concerning stationary sources of pollution. It has been harshly criticized by business and industry, who contend that substantial changes are needed to ease its economic and regulatory burden. Environmentalists claim the act, even with its admitted weaknesses, has substantially improved the quality of the air. Further, the American public supports such a tough law; recent polls indicate that an overwhelming majority of Americans opposed changes that would make the antipollution law less strict.

The EPA: Agency in a Crossfire

The Environmental Protection Agency (EPA) is the primary center of federal environmental regulation. Its jurisdiction extends from agricultural pesticides to toxic waste. The Reagan administration, in keeping with its philosophy of cutting back on regulation, cut the EPA's budget and encouraged a more permissive approach to enforcement. Faced with reduction in revenue, the EPA was forced to cut back on its operations.

Corporations that produce dangerous chemicals as byproducts of manufacturing processes must follow strict guidelines concerning the disposal of these potentially hazardous wastes. The EPA is responsible for enforcing these guidelines. As a result of budget cutbacks and agency policy, the EPA reduced its activity in the area of toxic waste disposal supervision.

EPA directors chose to slow down utilization of a $1.6 billion "superfund" established by Congress in 1980 to finance cleanup of hazardous waste dumps. Critics charged that the EPA cleaned up dumps in selected states in order to help certain Republican candidates. More dangerously, according to critics, the EPA deliberately neglected to clean up many potentially hazardous dumps in order to avoid helping Democratic candidates.

EPA officials were also accused of conflicts of interest. One superfund administrator had been previously employed by a corporation that had polluted one of the toxic waste dumps the superfund was supposed to clean up. She and other EPA officials, counselors, and advisers were accused of providing their former employers and other business interests with favorable treatment in their dealings with the agency.

Several congressional committees and subcommittees began investigating these and other charges. The panels subpoenaed many EPA documents. The president ordered the director of the EPA, Anne Burford, to refuse the documents on the grounds that congressional access to them might jeopardize ongoing enforcement efforts. He claimed the documents were protected by executive privilege. Burford was cited for contempt of Congress for her lack of compliance. She later resigned under heavy pressure.[17]

The scandal at the EPA raised questions concerning the proper amount of direct political control over regulatory decisions. It also demonstrated the difficulty of implementing the Reagan administration's regulatory policies.

Disposing of Toxic Waste

The EPA "sewergate" scandal focused American attention on a uniquely modern problem: disposing of toxic waste. The United States produces more than 280 million metric tons of hazardous waste a year. Much of this waste is deposited in landfills, from where it seeps into and contaminates ground water. Toxic wastes create other types of health hazards as well: "Love Canal" and "Times Beach" have now joined Three Mile Island on the list of least desirable addresses in the United States.

EPA workers in protective suits pour a chemical absorbent on a toxic waste site, a former paint manufacturer, in Phoenixville, Pennsylvania. The site is being cleaned up as part of the federal superfund for toxic waste sites. (*UPI/Bettmann Newsphotos*)

Three Mile Island, Pennsylvania, site of a nuclear power plant accident. (*Jerry Irwin/Photo Researchers*)

---

[17] Her story can be found in Anne M. Burford with John Greenya, *Are You Tough Enough? An Insider's View of Washington Power Politics* (McGraw-Hill, 1985).

Love Canal, a residential community in Niagara Falls, New York, was evacuated about ten years ago, when health officials linked unusually high death rates and illness there to chemicals leaking from an old industrial dump. Times Beach, Missouri, suffered a similar fate. Officials discovered that unpaved roads there had been sprayed with Dioxin, which is not only one of the most toxic synthetic substances but also a suspected cause of cancer. The beleaguered EPA took the unprecedented move of buying the town of Times Beach. The agency paid out $36.7 million and evacuated the residents of the community.

Toxic waste disposal is rapidly replacing nuclear energy as the dominant environmental issue of the 1980s. The apparent move away from the construction of nuclear power plants—and increased public awareness—may help to solve the separate problem of disposal of nuclear wastes. For example, a referendum passed in Massachusetts in 1982 placed limitations on the establishment of nuclear waste dump sites in that state. The Nuclear Regulatory Commission (NRC) has also become more active in overseeing potential hazards of nuclear power plants.

The Acid Rain Debate

There now exist more than 50,000 synthetic chemicals, and 1000 new ones are created each year. Although most of them have beneficial effects, some are known to cause sickness and death to humans. Others are suspected of such effects. For years they have been used without much control, without regard for their effects on humans, and without regard for what they might do a few days or a few weeks later—as they infiltrate the atmosphere and rivers.

Until a few years ago the debate over "acid rain" focused on whether or not there was a problem. Today scientific consensus is that sulfur dioxide and other air pollutants belched from coal-burning utility boilers and other industries in the Midwest are damaging northeastern and Canadian lakes and water supplies, and are probably contributing to the damage of forests in the American South and elsewhere. Even President Reagan, who was not usually known as an environmentalist, acknowledged that acid rain is a serious environmental problem in both the United States and Canada, and he called for major study of the problem.

The challenge for policy makers is what to do and how to do it. Several measures proposed in Congress would mandate major power plants to install "scrubbers," complex equipment that removes sulfur dioxide from smokestacks. These measures usually direct states to develop their own strategies for meeting specified reductions. Industries and utilities have the option of switching to low sulfur coal, cleaning the coal before using it, or resorting to these scrubbers. Purchasing the scrubbers, however, is expensive. And switching to low sulfur coal means eliminating thousands of mining jobs in the East. Each of the options thus involves considerable costs and political liabilities. Regional politics are also involved, as one recent report describes:

> . . . the benefits of reducing acid rain would accrue primarily to the Northeast, while the billions of dollars in costs would land on the Midwest—from the loss of high-sulfur coal jobs and the considerable financial investment in pollution control. The West is somewhat sympathetic to control, which would benefit its low-sulfur coal industry, but not to a national subsidy program that would spread the cost burden beyond the Midwest.[18]

The political fights over approaches to solving the acid rain problem have divided the mining unions, the utilities, the Democratic and Republican parties, the coal associations, and the governors. Sharp differences of view also separate the United States and Canada. This problem will not be solved easily: It will be

(From HERBLOCK THROUGH THE LOOKING GLASS, W. W. Norton, 1984)

"WE'RE GOING TO GIVE IT MORE STUDY"

[18] Rochelle L. Stanfield, "The Acid Rainmakers," *National Journal* (June 14, 1986), p. 1500–03.

costly, it will take a long time, and it will require strict enforcement and regulation at the state, national, and international levels. Scientific and economic considerations will continue to be important, and political factors will continue to influence both the legislative and regulatory policies that are hammered out in this problem area.

The Reagan Impact on Environmental Regulation

Until the Reagan presidency, protection of the environment was not particularly a partisan issue. Both Democrats and Republicans had responded to the intense concern of the American people about pollution, carcinogens, and hazardous wastes that cause sickness, injury, and death. Reagan, however, appointed regulators who were hostile to the environmentalist agenda. Although they revised or changed few of the major environmental statutes, the different outlooks, combined with serious cutbacks, led to a marked change in how provisions of the law were applied and implemented. The Reagan administration tried to cut the toxic substances program, curbed the regulation of deadly air pollutants, and set a deliberate policy to proceed slowly with the cleanup of hazardous wastes. They cut the air quality and water quality programs and initially opposed all efforts to control acid rain. "Under-staffed, under-funded and under-Reagan" became the lament of those concerned with environmental regulation.[19]

No doubt, Reagan was acting in response to those, especially in the business community, who believed that during the previous fifteen years the government had gone overboard in its impulse to protect the environment. Reagan had campaigned on a series of pledges to cut back needless regulations and lessen the interference of the federal government in the private sector. His policies were consistent with his earlier stands. Reagan clearly achieved much of what he set out to do in this area, just as he succeeded in vastly increasing military spending and reducing federal income taxes, which he had also pledged to do. Yet his achievements in this area are less likely to enhance his reputation as a national leader—for the American people have been critical of Reagan's indifference to their concerns about the environment.

Each of the issues just discussed represents the fundamental problem at the heart of environmental regulation: the problem of priorities. In a system such as ours, one that aspires to ensure free enterprise, the government tries to balance economic and environmental concerns. It attempts to guarantee the health and safety of its citizens and preserve the natural beauty of America for future generations. At the same time it tries not to inhibit developments vital to improving the standard of living for all Americans.

REGULATING OCCUPATIONAL SAFETY AND HEALTH: A CASE STUDY

One of the most criticized federal regulatory agencies has been the Occupational Safety and Health Administration (OSHA), a unit in the Department of Labor. If you have read about the OSHA in the newspapers, you have doubtless come across some report of its endless rules or its allegedly arrogant or patronizing warnings to business operators. OSHA has thousands of rules that can be found in the Code of Federal Regulations. It employs some 2000 persons, about half of whom are safety and health inspectors.

OSHA was set up because the public perceived that too many people were

[19] Michael E. Kraft and Norman J. Vig, "Environmental Policy in the Reagan Presidency," *Political Science Quarterly* (Fall 1984), pp. 415–39.

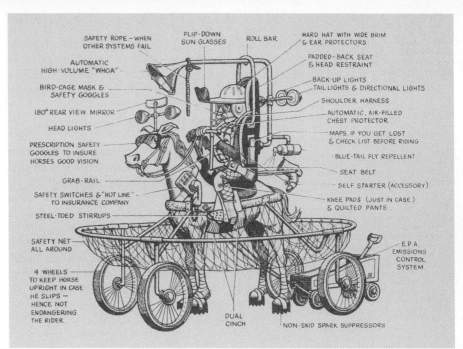

Cowboy after OSHA. Mythical supersafe cowboy illustrates what many businesspeople think of the practicality of federal health and safety rules. Union leaders, meanwhile, complain regulation is lax. (*J. N. Devin in National Safety News*)

Labels in the illustration:

SAFETY ROPE – WHEN OTHER SYSTEMS FAIL

FLIP-DOWN SUN GLASSES

ROLL BAR

HARD HAT WITH WIDE BRIM & EAR PROTECTORS

AUTOMATIC HIGH-VOLUME "WHOA"

PADDED–BACK SEAT & HEAD RESTRAINT

BIRD-CAGE MASK & SAFETY GOGGLES

BACK-UP LIGHTS TAIL LIGHTS & DIRECTIONAL LIGHTS

180° REAR VIEW MIRROR

SHOULDER HARNESS

HEAD LIGHTS

AUTOMATIC, AIR-FILLED CHEST PROTECTOR

PRESCRIPTION SAFETY GOGGLES TO INSURE HORSES GOOD VISION

MAPS, IF YOU GET LOST & CHECK LIST BEFORE RIDING

BLUE-TAIL FLY REPELLENT

GRAB-RAIL

SEAT BELT

SELF STARTER (ACCESSORY)

SAFETY SWITCHES & "HOT LINE" TO INSURANCE COMPANY

KNEE PADS (JUST IN CASE) & QUILTED PANTS

STEEL-TOED STIRRUPS

SAFETY NET ALL AROUND

E.P.A. EMISSIONS CONTROL SYSTEM

4 WHEELS TO KEEP HORSE UPRIGHT IN CASE HE SLIPS – HENCE NOT ENDANGERING THE RIDER

DUAL CINCH

NON-SKID SPARK SUPPRESSORS

becoming disabled, or were dying, from work-related accidents. As of 1970 over 14,000 people were dying each year in industrial accidents, and an estimated 100,000 a year were being permanently disabled in workplace injuries. The mandate of OSHA is nothing less than to protect the health and safety of more than 60 million workers in about 5 million workplaces. It is also asked to issue compulsory safety and health standards and to monitor compliance. To achieve these objectives, OSHA is empowered to inspect businesses and to issue notices of violation and fines.

Criticism of OSHA

In business circles OSHA quickly became a four-letter word. Many business executives criticize OSHA's standards as having only nuisance value. They also contend that inspectors are not familiar enough with their operations to make criticisms. Further, they believe many of the OSHA regulations do not protect the workers. They think, too, that the costs of many OSHA changes have had an inflationary effect. General Motors, for example, claims to have spent over $100 million to meet OSHA standards.

In the first years of OSHA, small businesses (55 percent of industrial fatalities occur in businesses employing twenty-five or fewer workers) complained that OSHA made rules that were too numerous, too complex, and too technical. Further, the costs of compliance are supposedly prohibitive for small business operators and raise the costs of production to unacceptable levels. Some businesses even said they had to close down; others said they might have to close down because of OSHA and similar governmental regulations.

Labor groups were OSHA's major source of support in its early years. But even labor officials criticized OSHA for being not strict enough with industry. Too much attention was given to trivial violations, and fines were too small. Still, labor believed workers could use OSHA to force an employer to correct unsafe conditions.

Nevertheless, the backlash from business interests was intense. Proposals sprang up in Congress to exempt small businesses from OSHA's provisions. President Ford repeatedly condemned OSHA, saying at one point he'd like to throw OSHA "into the ocean." Some of President Carter's economic advisers suggested abolishing it. President Reagan campaigned for office saying he would curb OSHA's tendency to harass businesses—and he did just that. He made it clear he wanted OSHA to be more conciliatory and to concentrate on major industries and major workplace hazards. After 1980 the whole tone of OSHA changed. It streamlined its restrictions, modified its enforcement policies, reduced its number of inspectors by a fourth, and nearly cut in half its dollar amount of penalties. Critics in the labor and environmental movements believe Reagan virtually dismantled the agency.[20] Even the Supreme Court worked to modify OSHA; it held that OSHA's practices of making unannounced inspections of all businesses for violations, even though authorized by Congress, violated the Constitution. Not surprisingly, the number of workplace injuries soon increased.

OSHA has not been as bad as its critics maintain, but neither has it been as effective as it should be. It deserves credit for its energetic action against polyvinyl chloride and other serious threats to workers' health. OSHA has tried to concentrate its limited energies on severe health hazards and make more use of an emergency power to restrict use of dangerous substances. It has dropped many trivial safety rules and focused on four major industries (construction, heavy manufacturing, transportation, and petrochemicals) that are considered especially hazardous. It also keeps pressure on a few industries it considers potentially dangerous, such as auto repair, dry cleaning, and building materials. Nowadays it uses more simply written guidelines, and simplified paperwork as well.

As the OSHA overhaul proceeds, more controversies are bound to arise. They cannot be avoided as the government faces up to some tough issues of industrial health in a world of complex technology. Workers are exposed to a host of substances whose effects on human health are not fully understood. Even when something is known to be toxic, the precise degree of risk—or an acceptable amount of exposure—is hard to calculate, and the costs of full protection can run very high. And the harmful effects of many substances (such as asbestos and cotton dust) do not appear until years later, making proof of causation more difficult and the establishment of regulations more tenuous.

OSHA's problems stem in part from the fact that it is an attempt by government to intervene in the private sector by using command-control types of devices (that is, by dictating do this, or don't do that) rather than economic incentives. Liberals as well as conservatives now hold that even though it should be costly for businesses not to adopt safety standards, the details of administration should usually be worked out by the businesses themselves rather than by a government agency.

REGULATORY OUTCOMES AND ISSUES

Positive accomplishments of regulation usually get overlooked. Considerable progress has been made in air pollution control. Lead paint poisonings and accidental aspirin poisonings have markedly decreased as a result of new regulatory efforts. Childproof bottle tops, automobile seat belts, and federally insured bank accounts are all byproducts of federal regulation. The prevention of thalidomide babies can be credited to regulatory activity, as can the banning of many cancer-producing pesticides.

Positive accomplishments are, of course, somewhat offset by the costs. Thus, there has been a lower rate of new drug development and introduction since the 1962 amendments to the Food and Drug Act were passed. There is also little doubt that get-tough pollution regulations have had an inflationary impact. Other

[20] See James Crawford, "The Dismantling of OSHA," *The Nation* (September 12, 1981). See also Richard Corrigan, "Rekindling OSHA," *National Journal* (May 3, 1986), pp. 1054–57.

studies argue that the Interstate Commerce Commission killed the railroad industry and that Federal Communications Commission regulations caused drab uniformity in television programming.

The major problems and criticisms of regulation are as follows:

1. *Regulation Distorts and Disrupts the Operation of the Market.* Sometimes governmental intervention upsets the normal adjustment processes of the market and thus encourages higher prices, misallocation of resources, and inefficiency.

2. *Regulation Can Discourage Competition.* Some forms of regulation (often the kind desired by industry) actually have the reverse of their desired effect. This is especially true where the government grants operating licenses and charters and seeks to maintain a certain level of quality or stability in the market. (This used to exist in trucking and air travel, where the federal government exerted control over entry into markets.) Regulatory red tape has also been charged with discouraging entry into industries and driving small businesses out.

3. *Regulation May Discourage Technological Development.* It is argued that if people perceive that the reward for an innovation is a new set of rules and a struggle for permission to use a new product, they may not find it worth the effort to innovate.

4. *Regulatory Agencies Are Often "Captured" by the Industries They Regulate.* It is suggested, especially by those on the political left, that some regulatory bodies are controlled by the big businesses they are supposed to be regulating. This is a popular view among those who consider big business to be a great power in our society. Although it may describe the view of a few of the older regulatory bodies, it has been downplayed by several scholars.[21]

The newer regulatory bodies are probably less "captured" because they deal with many industries and have intentionally been made harder to capture. Also public-interest groups are increasingly on the lookout for potential conflicts of interest in nominees to regulatory boards. A number of presidential nominees to regulatory positions have been defeated, or their names have been withdrawn, because of opposition of this kind. General standards have been suggested against which to measure these nominees. These include the following:

1. Nominees should be persons of integrity, whose past records demonstrate they have conducted their affairs honestly and have conscientiously complied with the law.

2. Nominees should be committed to basic principles of accountability in the executive branch, such as strong conflict of interest regulations, financial disclosure, open meetings, and checks on inordinate influence by regulated interests over agency policy.

3. Nominees should be knowledgeable about the industries they will regulate.

Still, some evidence of the capture thesis does exist in the "revolving door" situation, where federal regulators leave their jobs to take high-paying posts with the industries they previously regulated. There is evidence too that some people consider jobs in regulatory agencies as stepping stones to lucrative careers in private industry—and the industries obviously benefit in several ways from hiring some of the more able regulators.

Regulation increases costs to industry and to the consumer   Federal regulations, as noted earlier, are costly. Probusiness estimates claim that overall federal regulations cost well over $500 for every man, woman, and child in the United States. Such figures are disputed by many labor and consumer advocates who say health and safety standards are the best investment we can make. Every life and every limb

[21] James Q. Wilson, "The Dead Hand of Regulation," *The Public Interest* (Fall 1971), p. 47, and Paul Quirk, *Industry Influence in Federal Regulatory Agencies* (Princeton University Press, 1981).

we save, and every disease we prevent, represents not only a human achievement but also a reduction in the nation's enormous hospital and medical bills. The cost of neglecting health and safety requirements can be calculated in terms of loss of worker productivity and in such insurance costs as workers' compensation. Further, regulation provides new jobs in industry—perhaps as many as a million jobs in just the last few years. Plainly, however, the side you take in the debate over the costliness of federal regulations depends on where you sit—that is, on whether you favor labor or management, producer or consumer, energy developer or ecologist.

Regulation has often been introduced without cost-benefit analysis Many critics say too little attention is given to the questions of whether the benefits of a particular piece of regulation are great enough to justify its cost. Is it worth it to restrict new drugs if some who would benefit may die, even if the side effects are not yet well known? Is it worth it to clean up automobile emissions 95 percent if the cost is many times that of an 85 percent cleanup? The answers to these questions may be yes, but Congress and regulatory agencies are criticized for failing to ask, let alone to answer, various questions of this type.[22]

Regulatory agencies lack qualified personnel Critics of regulation and some heads of regulatory agencies themselves, say regulators lack the expertise to do their jobs properly. Regulatory agencies complain they need larger budgets to do their jobs properly. Regulatory agencies complain they need larger budgets to attract more qualified staff. Critics argue, too, that government should not meddle in complex chemical or technological industries about which it knows little.

THE DEREGULATION DEBATE

For the last thirty years every president has proposed a program for regulatory reform. Economists from the conservative "University of Chicago school," on the one side, to the most liberal pro-Ted Kennedy and pro-Mario Cuomo school, on the other, are all but unanimous in their view that much regulation is unnecessary and that some of it uses the wrong strategy. Although **deregulation** and regulatory reform have different meanings to different people, the terms are generally used to describe a cutback in the amount of regulation attempted by the federal government. Even if various parties agree that reform is needed, they find it more difficult to agree on what specific actions to take.

Deregulating Transporation

Airline investigators look over the burned cockpit section of an Air Canada DC-9 after flames forced an emergency landing at Greater Cincinnati Airport. A tarp covers the top of the burned out fuselage to protect it from a rain storm. (*UPI/Bettmann Newsphotos*)

No industry has undergone as extensive deregulation as has the transportation industry. Airlines, trucking, and railroads have all recently been granted more freedom in conducting their operations. Enough time has now elapsed so that we may analyze the reasons behind transportation deregulation, the key provisions of each particular deregulation act, and the effects on each specific industry.

Airline deregulation The Civil Aeronautics Board (CAB) was established by the federal government in 1938 to protect airlines from unreasonable competition by controlling rates and fares. Critics of CAB regulation charged that airlines were competing only in the frequency and convenience of flights and in the services they offered on flights. Because there was no competition over price, consumers were being forced to pay high rates for services they may not have desired. Others

[22] For some useful books on this, see Robert A. Leone, *Who Profits: Winners, Losers, and Government Regulation* (Basic Books, 1986), and Thomas C. Schelling, ed., *Incentives for Environmental Protection* (MIT Press, 1983).

Trucking is one of the industries deregulated. (*Pat & Tom Leeson/ Photo Researchers*)

claimed CAB regulation of fares may have been keeping them higher than they would have been under more competitive conditions. It was also charged that new routes were being opened up very slowly under CAB supervision.

In light of these and other considerations, Congress passed the Airline Deregulation Act in the fall of 1978.[23] The act sought to phase out the CAB (which was legislated out of existence in 1985), relax restrictions on airline fares and routes, and authorize federal subsidies to airlines serving certain unprofitable markets.

In the early years of airline deregulation, the industry faced difficult economic conditions. Also one of the first results of deregulation was that many medium-sized cities lost service as larger carriers found it more profitable to use their aircraft in other markets. In time many of these cities had service restored by smaller airlines using smaller planes. But in the meantime, this shift caused scheduling problems at major airports—problems that were compounded by the strike by and firing of the federal air traffic controllers in 1981. Also, airlines raised fares on routes over which they had monopolies in order to subsidize lower fares on more competitive routes. Finally, critics of airline deregulation charge that safety precautions and maintenance suffered as a result of cutthroat competition and the ease with which new airlines could enter the market.

Although there were some transitional problems as deregulation got underway, overall it has resulted in generally lower fares, greater choice of routes and fares in most markets, and more efficient use of assets by the industry.[24] It has also resulted in less good service and higher fares for many smaller or medium size cities.

The long-term effects of airline deregulation are likely to be positive. Eventually, analysts hope, the marketplace will determine the level of service. If an airline is overcharging passengers on a route, a competitor will eventually steal those travelers away by offering better or lower-priced service. In the long run, deregulation should strengthen the industry by forcing companies to streamline operations in order to survive in a competitive market.

Trucking and railroad deregulation   Deregulation of the trucking and railroad industries soon followed airline deregulation. In 1980 the railroad industry was in poor condition—as it had been for several decades, especially in the East. Many railroads were in serious financial trouble; two went bankrupt. In addition, many observers believed the Interstate Commerce Commission (ICC), which had regulated the railroads since 1887, was being too rigid in interpreting and enforcing federal regulations. Moreover, a growing body of economic evidence suggested that regulation was causing great inefficiencies and that market forces could generate better service to shippers and travelers at lower prices.[25]

The trucking industry was much healthier. In fact, many observers said the industry was too healthy. ICC regulations had limited the entry of new competitors into trucking and had kept rates high. Competition was generally low, allowing trucking companies to charge relatively high rates for hauling cargo. Both the trucking industry itself and the Teamsters Union opposed deregulation, fearing it would alter this mutually beneficial situation. Calls for deregulation came primarily from business leaders who were forced to pay high rates to have their goods transported.

In 1980 Congress passed the Staggers Rail Act to deregulate railroads and the Motor Carrier Act to relax supervision of trucking. Both acts loosened restrictions

[23] See the public document that helped pave the way for this act: *Civil Aeronautics Board Practices and Procedures*, Report of the Subcommittee on Administrative Practice and Procedure of the Committee on the Judiciary, U.S. Senate (U.S. Government Printing Office, 1975.)

[24] Steven Morrison and Clifford Winston, *The Economic Effects of Airline Deregulation* (Brookings Institution, 1986), and Martha Derthick and Paul J. Quirk, *The Politics of Deregulation* (Brookings Institution, 1985).

[25] See, for example, Theodore E. Keeler, *Railroads, Freight, and Public Policy* (Brookings Institution, 1983), p. 97.

531

on entry into their respective industries, made it easier for railroads and trucking companies to abandon unprofitable activities, and allowed each industry more freedom in setting rates.

The effects of deregulation on both industries have been broadly similar and, by most accounts, positive. In the case of trucking, the primary benefit of deregulation has been to increase profitability. In addition, new firms are entering the industry. Railroad deregulation has led to discounted rates, more competition, improved service, and service innovations.

The deregulation of the transportation industry illustrates the practical application of abstract economic theory. In the words of one observer:

> The airline, trucking and rail deregulation bills had several features in common. They represented attempts to eliminate what had come to be considered needless and damaging regulation. They signaled a return to relying on mechanisms of market competition to achieve what regulation was intended to do in the first place. They were designed to promote the well-being of the industry as a whole and to improve its services to the general public, the same goals that regulation initially was intended to achieve.[26]

Banking Deregulation

The relatively successful deregulation of airlines, railroads, and trucking has encouraged relaxing federal supervision over other industries as well. One such industry is banking. The banking industry has long been protected by the federal government. The trauma caused by the numerous bank failures during the Great Depression led to controls and regulations designed to ensure that such a shock would never recur. In addition, many economists point out the banking industry performs a special role in the economy and therefore warrants special treatment. Because banks and other financial institutions control the flow of money, the lifeblood of the economy, some observers believe the federal government must supervise the industry in order to guarantee that the flow is uninterrupted.[27]

Regulation of the banking industry has consisted mainly of protective devices. The federal government established the Federal Deposit Insurance Corporation (FDIC) to insure bank deposits up to a specified amount. (The FDIC had to assist over 100 banks that failed or required major assistance in 1986.) The Federal Savings and Loan Insurance Corporation (FSLIC) performs a similiar function for savings and loans institutions. In addition, financial institutions were barred from performing certain financial services. Banks and savings and loans institutions have been prevented from offering speculative investment services, for fear they would cover bad investments with the deposits of innocent third-party customers.

As a result of the deregulation movement, the directors of the FDIC and the FSLIC now seek to shift responsibility for insuring bank and savings and loan deposits to private companies. Also, the distinctions between financial institutions and securities firms are beginning to diminish. Investment firms such as Merrill Lynch now offer certain banking services. Even retailers such as Sears now compete with banks for deposits. Banking officials say deregulation is needed so that banks can compete with these new adversaries. And they are now allowed to compete in many areas.

Further banking deregulation is likely in the near future. Constant innovations in the now-crowded financial industry will increase pressure on federal regulators to allow banks and savings and loans institutions more freedom.[28] However, even the most ardent advocates of deregulation think we need to proceed carefully when

[26] Martha V. Gottron, ed., *Regulation: Process and Politics* (Congressional Quarterly Press, 1982), p. 90. Reprinted with the permission of Congressional Quarterly, Inc.

[27] Alan Stone, *Regulation and Its Alternatives* (Congressional Quarterly Press, 1982), p. 46.

[28] Leo Loevinger, "Antitrust and the Banking Revolution." *Regulation* (July/August 1985), pp. 19–24.

it comes to deregulation of financial institutions, especially banks. The effects of failure in the banking industry on the entire economy are such that the federal government will in all likelihood always play a greater role here than elsewhere. It is one thing for a railroad company to go bankrupt, but quite another for large financial institutions.

Evaluating Deregulation

Deregulation appears to be working better in some areas than in others. In the area of drug deregulation, the results are mixed. The Food and Drug Administration, especially under Reagan, relaxed the requirements for introducing new medicines. Those in the drug industry applaud these efforts. They urge that as a result of deregulation the public gets better medicines faster and cheaper. Opponents contend, however, and with some growing evidence, that the accelerated approval process is endangering public health by prematurely allowing potentially hazardous drugs on the market.[29]

Advocates of deregulation argue that consumers are capable of making intelligent choices and are profiting from the lower prices and expanded services brought about by deregulation. Opponents contend that deregulation results in such confusion in the marketplace that consumers cannot make sensible choices. In the airline business, they say, even experienced travel agents often cannot figure out the cheapest way to go "from here to there."

One other point: In our federal system the mere fact that the national government stops regulating an industry does not mean that that particular industry will be unregulated. On the contrary, when the national government ceases regulating it sometimes fifty different state regulations take over, making it even more difficult for that industry to operate on a large scale.[30] (This is why businesspeople themselves sometimes call for more, not less, national regulation. They often prefer one set of national regulations for auto safety to fifty different state ones.)

In the debate about deregulation it is desirable to separate those problems associated with transition from regulation to deregulation. There are always problems of getting adjusted to new ways. Every change hurts some and benefits others. The questions are whether in the long run deregulation benefits more people than does regulation, and which people it does benefit and which it does hurt.

The successes of deregulation in commercial air travel, freight trucking, and long-distance telephone service tell us a lot also about the political system. Powerful industries and much vaunted unions have only limited ability to protect their interests through political action when confronted with expert analysis and economic studies that point to broad conceptions of public-interest benefits. Initially the work of a small band of economists, the ideas about deregulation were soon embraced by thoughtful lawyers and eventually by politicians, including Presidents Ford, Carter, and Reagan. Members of Congress and interest-group leaders were soon enlisted; together they were able to take on the so-called "vested interests" who were fighting deregulation. Presidential leadership and influence over the regulatory commissions and their policies proved to be greater than was once supposed. This has led one team of investigators to conclude that whatever may have been true in the past, interests such as the airlines, truckers, AT&T, and the Teamsters today "derive much of their present apparent power merely from the absence of challenges— that is, from the inattentiveness of political leaders and allied forces that might

[29] See Martin Tolchin and Susan J. Tolchin, *Dismantling America: The Rush to Deregulate* (Houghton Mifflin, 1983).

[30] See, for example, Kenneth J. Meier, "The Politics of Consumer Protection." Paper delivered at the Western Political Science Association Meetings, March 28–30, 1985, Las Vegas, Nevada, and Martha M. Hamilton, "Just Because It Melts, That Doesn't Mean It's Cheese," *The Washington Post National Weekly Edition* (April 21, 1986), pp. 6–7.

launch an attack on broadly based grounds—and not from any reliable ability to defeat such challenges when they do occur."[31]

In general the overall effects of deregulation trends, especially as they affect traditional economic regulation, appear to be positive. Deregulation has forced some industries to become more efficient. Consumers have had better services at less cost. Also, and not insignificantly, in a democracy such as ours, deregulation has made transfers of wealth visible rather than hidden. Under government regulation, transfers of wealth (that is, benefits or profits from certain arrangements that get established and protected) are often the result of hidden subsidies. Prices of regulated goods are kept artificially high in order to finance losses on goods whose prices are kept artificially low due to government controls. Under deregulation, prices are more in accord with costs. Subsidies must be authorized by Congress and are therefore subject to public scrutiny. We examine subsidies in detail in the next chapter.

[31] Martha Derthick and Paul Quirk, *The Politics of Deregulation* (Brookings Institution, 1985), p. 258.

SUMMARY

1. Regulation in America is neither socialism nor laissez-faire policy but rather a kind of pervasive intervention into the private sector built upon a commitment to a market economy. Although we often think of politics as the pursuit of private power and private interests, it is plainly also an effort to define the public interest. We set up regulatory agencies in an effort to interpret the public interest and to achieve various goals.

2. Even though their members are nominated by the president, their powers derived from legislative delegation, and their decisions subject to review by the courts, independent regulatory agencies have a scope of responsibility in the American economy that sometimes exceeds that of the three regular branches of government.

3. Even though few people have kind words to say about regulation, we will doubtless have more of it in the future. Regulation is a means of controlling or eliminating some of the abuses and problems generated by the private economy while avoiding government ownership and the risks of too much centralization. Increasing regulation is an inevitable byproduct of a complex, industrialized, high-technology society.

4. A deregulation movement designed to get the government out of the regulation of certain businesses has achieved victories in recent years, especially in the transportation industries. Liberals generally favor deregulation to encourage more competition. Conservatives generally favor deregulation that will get federal regulators off their backs in areas such as affirmative action, safety and health, and environmental and consumer-protection standards. During the late 1980s and early 1990s even more pressure will come from both the left and the right to deregulate where possible. But deregulation efforts will have a tough time matching the constantly increasing number of federal regulations approved each year. Of one thing we can be sure: Controversies in regulatory politics will always be with us.

FURTHER READING

Benefits of Environmental, Health, and Safety Regulation. Report prepared for the Committee on Governmental Affairs, United States Senate, U.S. Government Document, 96th Congress, 2nd Session, 1980.

ANTHONY E. BROWN. The Politics of Airline Regulations (University of Tennessee Press, 1987).

MARTHA DERTHICK and PAUL J. QUIRK. *The Politics of Deregulation* (Brookings Institution, 1985).

ALFRED KAHN, *The Economics of Regulation* (MIT Press, 1988).

ROBERT A. KATZMANN. *Regulatory Bureaucracy: The Federal Trade Commission and Antitrust Policy* (MIT Press, 1980).

ROBERT A. LEONE. *Who Profits: Winners, Losers, and Government Regulation* (Basic Books, 1986).

ROBERT E. LITAN and WILLIAM D. NORDHAUS. *Reforming Federal Regulation* (Yale University Press, 1983).

KENNETH J. MEIER. *Regulation: Politics, Bureaucracy, and Economics* (St Martin's Press, 1985).

STEVEN MORRISON and CLIFFORD WINSTON. *The Economic Effects of Airline Deregulation* (Brookings Institution, 1986).

ALAN STONE. *Regulation and Its Alternatives* (Congressional Quarterly Press, 1982).

MARTIN TOLCHIN and SUSAN J. TOLCHIN. *Dismantling America: The Rush to Deregulate* (Houghton Mifflin, 1983).

NORMAN J. VIEG and MICHAEL E. KNOTT, eds. *Environmental Policy in the 1980s: Reagan's New Agenda* (Congressional Quarterly Press, 1984).

See also *Regulation*, a journal published every two months.

23

The Politics of Subsidies and Entitlements

Our economy is primarily based on the principle that businesses, farms, and individuals are better qualified than government to decide how to produce income and how to spend it. Yet the existence of a large array of government subsidies, tax incentives, and regulations (such as those discussed in the previous chapter) attests to the fact that the government too gets involved in a big way in decisions about the shape of our "free enterprise" system.

Indeed, it is no longer clear where the public sector ends and the private sector begins. Close to half the federal budget goes to what economists call transfer programs, or programs that provide direct support or subsidies to businesses, individuals, families, and households. Much of this money is explicitly directed toward people with low incomes, the disabled and handicapped, and persons who are not working because of unemployment or retirement. Transfer programs can provide cash payments, as in social security; in-kind benefits, as in hospital care through Medicare; vouchers, as in food payments; or various kinds of tax credits or tax deductions.

All kinds of individuals and corporations benefit from government subsidies. Welfare programs for the needy may be the most publicized government assistance efforts, but "it is probably safe to assume that the preponderance of the benefits of many programs is garnered by profitable corporations and citizens in the top half of the nation's income distribution."[1]

Subsidies and welfare assistance reflect the use of public funds to accomplish what are thought to be public purposes—but considerable disagreement exists as to what is in the public interest. Politics in a democracy is a continuous process of defining what is in the public interest. Conservatives say we need more economy in government and less government in the economy. Others say governmental "give-away" programs are undermining the values that made this nation great. Conservative economic advisers believe if we could only cut back drastically on the role of the government in the economy, we could make major strides in solving our inflation

[1] Robert D. Reischauer, "The Federal Budget: Subsidies for the Rich," in Michael J. Boskin and Aaron Wildavsky, eds., *The Federal Budget: Economics and Politics* (Institute for Contemporary Studies, 1982), p. 236.

and federal deficit problems. Critics on the left condemn subsidies to industry and tax shelters for the wealthy as "welfare for the rich." Critics on the far left charge that the so-called welfare state is merely a symbolic gesture by which the powerful hand out a few crumbs to keep the powerless quiet.

SUBSIDIES: WHY AND HOW

Government **subsidies** provide economic assistance to certain targeted producers or consumers at the expense of others in the economy. Magazine and book publishers enjoy reduced postal rates on the grounds that this will enhance public knowledge and democratic discussion. Oil companies get certain tax write-offs on the grounds that we vitally need more oil to free ourselves of dependence on imported foreign oil. Farmers and ranchers, much beloved as the contemporary examples of old-fashioned rugged individualism, are protected by a dizzying array of federal assistance programs. The Chrysler Corporation and the U.S. Postal Service have received special treatment as well, because we place special value on their services and continued existence. College students are the beneficiaries of subsidies both directly and indirectly because of the widespread conviction that all of us benefit from their education.

Government promotion, or subsidies, are not a new creation. In his first annual address to Congress, George Washington called for a **tariff** to protect business. Alexander Hamilton, Washington's secretary of the treasury, proposed that government give financial assistance to new business ventures. In the 1790s the new government promoted commerce in numerous ways: by establishing a money system and a postal service, granting charters, enforcing contracts in court, and subsidizing roads and waterways. Significant public purposes can be and are achieved—such as conserving and developing energy; preserving vital nongovernmental sectors that fund and operate private hospitals, colleges, and charitable institutions; encouraging small businesses, and so on.

Some subsidies have outlived their purpose and today create unnecessary costs for taxpayers and consumers. They benefit narrow, well-organized interests, even though their costs are spread out among unorganized taxpayers. Many subsidies are hard to see because they take the form of tax preferences, loans, or protective regulations. Subsidies that have outlived their usefulness are often continued because of effective lobbying. Beneficiaries make strategic campaign contributions during elections and fight ruthlessly in other ways to hold on to their special advantages.

Computing how much is spent on subsidy programs is difficult because many federal subsidy programs are called something else. They may be called grants-in-aid, price supports, tax incentives, import quotas, stabilization programs, and loan guarantees. Government subsidy programs include:

1. *Cash benefits.* The government pays sugar beet and cane growers to protect the welfare of the domestic sugar industry, and it pays sheep raisers to improve the quality of American wool. Cash payments also help to support artists as well as the privately owned U.S. merchant marine.

2. *Tax incentives.* The recipients of these subsidies receive no cash; they are permitted to pay lower taxes than would normally be required. Tax incentives to business to encourage oil exploration and production are examples. So too is the tax deductibility of interest on homes occupied by their owners. Although the government makes no expenditure, it still loses revenue.

3. *Credit subsidies.* These involve government participation in loan transactions that give lower rates of interest than prevailing market conditions would allow. Credit subsidies range from loans financing a student through college, to

those financing a major public works project at a fraction of prevailing interest rates, to those financing New York City.

4. *Benefit-in-kind subsidies.* Recipients receive a product or service paid for by the government. Food stamps for the poor or Medicare for the elderly are examples.

There are other ways in which the federal government has a direct impact on the economy. The government sometimes sets tariffs on imports that allow domestic producers to earn higher profits than free markets would bring. In fact, almost all groups at one time or another have benefited from government help. Many business officials have sought government aid—to bail out The Continental Bank of Illinois or Chrysler, to support government-backed loans to railroads, to subsidize the merchant marine industry, and so on. Similarly, spokespersons for the poor seek a larger government role in providing health services, establishing a floor below which incomes are not allowed to fall, and subsidizing improved housing and employment opportunities. Governmental promotion can be used to help any group. But who shall be aided in what way, and with what consequences, are the important questions.

HELPING BUSINESS

A government that protects and enforces contracts enables owners of businesses to operate in a stable situation. A government that promotes a prosperous economy enables businesses to enjoy a large volume of sales and good profits. The kind of monetary policy established by government—for example, tight or easy money—is of direct interest to business. But the national government also supplies a number of specific services and assists individual sectors of the business community.

The Department of Commerce

The Department of Commerce is sometimes known as the nation's "service center" for businesses. Its secretary, nearly always a person with an extensive business background, is a spokesperson for business interests. Historically, the department has been at the center of government's efforts to promote economic growth and encourage business research and development. Its Social and Economic Statistics Administration reports on business activity and prospects at home and around the world. Its Bureau of the Census has been called the greatest fact-finding and figure-counting agency in the world. The Constitution requires that a national census be taken every ten years; the results supply valuable information on business and agricultural activity, incomes, occupations, employment, housing and home ownership, and government finances.

Its National Bureau of Standards (NBS) provides highly valued technical assistance to corporations such as GE, DuPont, and IBM. The NBS has helped companies study the structures of enzymes, measure the trace elements in Teflo, look at submicroscopic flaws in jet-engine turbine blades, and probe the structure and properties of various materials used in biotechnology, electronics, fiber optics, and other fields.[2]

The Patent and Trademark Office (PTO) administers the patent system that Congress established to carry out its responsibilities "to promote the progress of . . . the useful arts . . ." under Article I of the Constitution. The PTO issues more than 72,000 patents each year to cover new and useful inventions which

[2] Nell Henderson, "It's Not a Subsidy, Exactly; It's Technical Assistance," *The Washington Post National Weekly Edition* (July 7, 1986), p. 33.

provide their owners certain exclusive rights for from 14 to 17 years. It also issues trademarks to protect distinctive names for commercial purposes.

The Department of Commerce also undertakes basic research in ocean science and engineering, meteorology, and weather forecasting. Its National Oceanic and Atmospheric Administration is currently operating research on hurricane predictions, acid rain, marine fisheries, and a wide assortment of undersea research activities.

The Department of the Interior

The Department of the Interior has long supported activities that assist mining and ranching interests, among others. Its Geological Survey undertakes research on the extent, distribution, and character of the nation's natural resources and on the geological processes, structures, and hazards that affect the development and use of virtually every aspect of the nation's physical lands. It appraises improved methods of miner extraction and preparing new technologies for energy development.

The Bureau of Mines subsidizes basic and applied research to improve understanding of mining and to reduce the hazards involved in the mining industries. These services assist private-sector firms even as they promote such national interests as productivity and mine disaster prevention.

The Department of Transportation

In a variety of ways, the Department of Transportation funds research that aids the airline, trucking, and highway construction industries. For example, the depart ment is currently developing and testing advanced automation equipment to improve air traffic control systems, studying motor vehicle and highway safety improvements, and supporting research in highway planning, design, construction, and maintenance to ensure an effective and efficient highway system. Beneficiaries of this research obviously include the airlines, the auto and trucking industries, and all those businesses who use these transportation systems.

Through the Department of Transportation's Maritime Administration the government subsidizes the American merchant marine by several hundred million dollars a year. For financial and security reasons Congress has determined we must have a domestic merchant marine capable of carrying a sizable part of our oceangoing trade. It is generally agreed that without these special arrangements there would be virtually *no* U.S. fleet and *no* U.S. shipbuilding industry. There are few industries in whose affairs the government has played so active a role.[3] The national government has, in fact, been paying operating subsidies to selected flag steamship companies since 1936. This program has cost well over $5 billion.

Critics say such subsidies discourage competition and raise the cost of ships to more than double the price of those built in foreign shipyards. They contend this government promotion causes more problems than it solves. The maritime industry, of course, denies these charges and maintains that we need these capabilities, especially during wartime. The maritime workers also fight, through their unions, to retain these subsidies. They, as much as the shippers and shipbuilders, are beneficiaries of this program.

Other Help for Business

The government also aids business through research and experimentation carried on by a variety of agencies. Examples include new commercial wood products resulting from work done in the laboratories of the U.S. Forest Service, and diversified

---

[3] This promotional program is explained in Gerald R. Jantscher, *Bread upon the Waters: Federal Aids to the Maritime Industries* (Brookings Institution, 1975), p. 10.

uses of bituminous coal arising from research in the Department of the Interior.

Through a range of tax benefits for certain segments of the population, government encourages various activities and investments. The money given up by the government through provisions in the tax code is called a **tax expenditure,** as was discussed in Chapter 21. The government defines a tax expenditure as a loss of tax revenue, attributable to provisions of the federal tax law that allow a special exclusion, exemption, or deduction from gross income or provide a special credit, preferential rate of tax, or a deferral of tax liability.

Tax expenditures, though reduced in number as a result of the tax reforms enacted in 1986, are a means by which the government pursues public policy objectives. Nearly all tax expenditures are meant to encourage certain economic activities—investment, exporting, petroleum exploration and development, spending by state and local governments, or support of charitable institutions. Every nation's tax laws are in part a reflection of economic and social policy. They create incentives and disincentives for the use of capital and for the allocation of wealth between current consumption and investment (future consumption).

Tax expenditures remain a form of subsidy, because Congress exercises little fiscal control over them. Indeed, many of these tax exemptions and exclusions get enacted without careful hearings and deliberations. And tax expenditures generally result in an upside-down welfare program: The richer the taxpayer, the greater the benefit.

The Chrysler Story—Free Enterprise with a Little Help from the Government

Should the federal government intervene in the economic system to save a failing and presumably mismanaged enterprise? If so, when? One of the fundamental precepts of our system is the freedom to succeed—but along with this comes the possibility of failure.

The Chrysler Corporation is about the tenth largest manufacturer in the United States. Between 1978 and 1981 Chrysler lost $3.5 billion. In 1979 its financial difficulties were so severe it was virtually bankrupt. It had not realized a profit since 1977, largely due to its failure to read market trends correctly. It was slow to respond to the demand for smaller, more fuel-efficient cars. It also continued operations that had become outdated and costly.

In 1979 the corporation appealed to the federal government for assistance. At first it merely asked the government to relax its regulations. But soon it was forced to ask for aid and for various kinds of loans. Chrysler and officials of the United Auto Workers (UAW) argued it was in the best interests of the government to "bail out" Chrysler. If Chrysler went under, they said, as many as 600,000 jobs would be lost. Chrysler workers, 4800 dealers, and about 20,000 Chrysler suppliers would be badly hurt, if not thrown out of business altogether. In addition, if Chrysler shut down, its employees would swell the welfare rolls, and national revenue would decrease. Cities in which Chrysler plants were located would be seriously injured.

Critics claimed bailing out Chrysler would set a bad precedent, and they questioned the propriety of government interference in a competitive market economy such as that of the United States. Opponents also said Chrysler's misfortunes were mainly due to its own lack of leadership and lack of management. Why should businesses that do not respond to the demands of consumers get protection? Thousands of companies fail every year, and the government does not ordinarily help them. Moreover, bailing out failed businesses as a matter of course would create an unworkable system, by effectively rewarding mismanagement and inefficiency.

YOU DECIDE

Chrysler Corporation was successfully rescued with federally guaranteed loans in 1979. Most people think the risk was well taken and that the results prove the government made a good investment. But some people still say it was a bad idea. What, in your view, is the best case against the Chrysler bailout and similar governmental loans or aid?

(Answer/Discussion on next page.)

Advocates of aiding Chrysler triumphed. The national government did not give Chrysler any money directly; instead, it guaranteed $1.2 billion in loans for the company. In order to receive aid, Chrysler was required to come up with an equivalent amount of unsupported loans from banks and elsewhere. The company was also required to sell off $300 million worth of its assets.

Management agreed to defer dividends, to issue $500 million worth of new stock, and to subject its operations to periodic government review. Chrysler was not alone in initiating austerity measures. The UAW had to swallow nearly $500 million worth of blue-collar employee wage concessions. White-collar workers suffered benefit cutbacks totaling $125 million. Chrysler suppliers were directed to pay $180 million. Finally, cities and states with Chrysler plants were required to supply $250 million in loan aid to the ailing firm.

With the aid of the federal government and other friendly interests, Chrysler survived. Many credited the spirited leadership and public relations efforts of Chrysler Chairman Lee Iacocca. Whatever the reasons, Chrysler streamlined its operations; it also paid back the government-backed loans seven years ahead of schedule.

The resurrection or rescue of the Chrysler Corporation is an intriguing example of governmental assistance or subsidy arrangements.[4] It is also in part a tale of the ideological conflict between economic "survival of the fittest" theories and government promotion and protection strategies. It suggests that some circumstances may justify modifying the rule that government should stay out of the economic system. Nevertheless, rigid adherents of a rugged free enterprise system are not persuaded by the Chrysler story. Others see a different lesson. Former U.S. Senator Paul Tsongas (D-Massachusetts) wrote that as a result of the Chrysler episode, he believed there may be circumstances when a bailout is in the national interest. "Chrysler is such a case. . . . The challenge is going beyond ideological posturing and looking at the particular situation. 'Will it work?' should be the test. Happily, in Chrysler's case, it did."[5]

[4] See Robert B. Reich and John D. Donahue, *New Deals: The Chrysler Revival and the American System* (Times Books, 1985).

[5] Paul E. Tsongas, "Did the Chrysler Bailout Work?" © 1983 by *The New York Times Company.* Reprinted by permission.

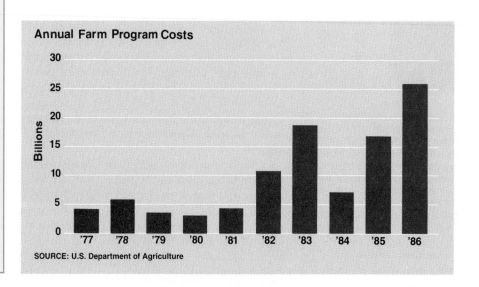

Annual Farm Program Costs

SOURCE: U.S. Department of Agriculture

The impressive success and competitiveness of American agriculture owes much to the federal government and its subsidies, almost as much as to fertile soil, hard work, and the technology revolution. Agriculture is our largest industry—bigger than computers and automobiles or the movie and record industries. Agriculture and food-related businesses generate nearly one out of every five jobs in our private sector and account for almost 20 percent of the GNP and 15 percent of our exports. It is also the industry with the highest rate of productivity. In the past fifty years, agricultural productivity, substantially due to federal support for research in land grant institutions, has increased at a rate of about 6 percent a year.

Although our great agricultural production is the result of many factors, it reflects one of the more successful partnerships between government and private enterprise. The federal government has invested major sums in basic and applied agricultural research as well as in ways to apply this research on our farms. Much of this work is done through so-called land grant state universities and colleges. What is learned in the laboratories is tested on experimental farms. New techniques and products are then brought to farmers, primarily through the Agricultural Extension Services of these schools. Local county agents, part of the Agricultural Extension Service, are supported by a combination of national, state and local funds.

The Depression of the 1930s ravaged virtually every farmer. The New Deal helped to get farmers back on their feet by means of credit support, loans, and crop price supports. Major federal initiatives in irrigation and rural electrification fostered significant strides in productivity. Numerous loans and credit programs were established to help the farmers purchase needed equipment. Some of these programs have become self-financing, even though they were begun with public money. Other federal initiatives have been enacted to stabilize incomes and output with price supports and acreage controls.

Aid to farmers continues. The Department of Agriculture spent more than $30 billion for farm aid in one recent year. A single California farming operation received $20 million that year, part of a bumper crop of multimillion-dollar payments that the government doled out. A number of federal programs pay farmers to reduce production. One program buys out dairy production operations for five years, and another crop-reduction program takes marginally productive land out of use for ten years. These voluntary programs are intended to reduce food surpluses. It is estimated that between 30 and 45 million acres will be taken out of production in these types of programs in the late 1980s.

Although the farm subsidy program includes separate benefits for growing, or not growing, everything from tobacco to mohair, most of the money is spent on grain. The government spends billions to buy up, at a guaranteed minimum price, any surplus grain that was produced. Most of the burden fell on consumers, in the form of higher prices at the supermarket. In 1985 Congress cut back on much of this price support, but it offers direct cash payments to help farmers make up some of their lost income. These payment programs are intended to give farmers a decent standard of living, but they are paid according to volume grown. The rich get richer this way. Many federal subsidy programs pay farmers for *not* planting crops. It is the biggest farmers who are able *not* to grow the greatest quantity of food, and who have lots of land *not* to grow it on. That they should get the lion's share of farm welfare should come as no surprise.

President Reagan and his political advisers took office pledging to reduce waste and unnecessary spending, but in the agricultural area they became the biggest spenders of all. Reagan's former budget director writes that the "worse nonsense of all in the budget . . . was farm subsidies. The nation's agriculturalists had never

(Paul Conklin/Monkmeyer Press)

been the same after the New Deal turned the wheat, corn, cotton, and dairy business into a way of life based on organized larceny."[6] But serious efforts to change the course failed.

The American farmers have had an enormously difficult time in recent years. Hundreds of thousands of farmers have simply closed their operations either because of bankruptcy or mortgage foreclosure. Meanwhile, as farmers pay more, the prices they receive are plummeting because the ballooning deficit distorts the value of the dollar worldwide. Yet the bleaker the farm situation becomes the greater the cry by farmers for more help: extensions on loans, bailouts of the farm credit system, and yet more subsidies or direct aid.

Plainly, the vast array of subsidies, loans, credits, and related programs of research and investment have helped successful American farmers increase productivity. Many economists point out, however, that not only do the big farmers gain the most from federal programs, but various federal government income transfers to farmers often hurt poor people by driving up the price of food. Thus, although helping farmers encourages productivity, it also increases poverty. Why do we do this? Farmers vote in large numbers. Further, not only are they organized, but, just like senior citizens and unions and Chrysler and its friends, the farmers know how to present their case to Congress.

Protectionism: Helping or Hurting?

America was once the dominant exporting nation, but our competitive edge eroded in the 1970s and 1980s. Today the U.S. must strive to be an equal among peers. America's biggest challenge is coming from Pacific rim nations such as Japan, Korea, Taiwan, and Singapore. How did this happen? Our wages became higher and higher. Other nations became more productive. We designed our products for the large home market and then tried to export the same products with the same standards abroad. Other nations designed their products specifically for our market. Management wages in this country are three and four times those in competing nations. Most of our business executives are lawyers and advertising or accounting specialists; most executives in Japan are scientists and engineers. Many foreign governments have worked closely with industries in planning competitive products and helping to maximize export possibilities.

The two areas in which we continued, until recently, to have a competitive trading edge have also come under attack. Both our leadership and research in technology and our vast agricultural industry are now threatened by other nations who are fast moving up and doing what we do at lower costs and with a fresh assertiveness.

The costs to Americans are staggering. Hundreds of thousands of plants have been closed. Hundreds of thousands of workers at steel mills, machine-tool factories, textile, and apparel manufacturing plants and in the computer, electronics, and communications industries have been laid off. In what is now becoming a familiar refrain, both industry and its unions blame their immediate problems on imports. Imports have doubled in recent years. In some clothing products, foreign competitors now enjoy more than half of our market.

The problem, in part, is not that we are importing too much, but that we are exporting too little. German cars, Japanese radios, and Indonesian textiles are fine products, provided we are productive enough to be able to pay for them. If other countries can produce better cars or shoes at a lower price, then we should deploy our labor and capital to do what we can do better. The question is whether there are still things we can do that will give us a competitive edge.

[6] David A. Stockman, *The Triumph of Politics* (Harper & Row, 1986), pp. 152–53.

A hundred years ago, U.S. policymakers worried that we might someday not have enough incentives to keep people on the farms, yet we are now getting along fine with most Americans *not* being farmers. Will the same thing be said fifty or one hundred years from now about people working in factories and in manufacturing?

In 1971 the United States experienced its first trade deficit in more than a century. By the late 1980s, our foreign trade imbalances grew to nearly $200 billion a year. Because the dollar was strong in the mid-1980s, foreign goods were less expensive to American buyers, causing an influx of imports, but American goods became prohibitively expensive in foreign markets. Another fact, not readily admitted by many Americans, is that the quality of American products left a lot to be desired, especially compared to available and cheaper imports.

Congress and the president come under continuing pressure from coalitions of industry, unions, and regional political leaders—trying to save jobs and companies and communities from foreign competition. These pressures come not only from the textile and auto industries, but from glass, steel, shoe, lumber, electronics, book publishing, aluminum, farming, and domestic wine and spirit coalitions, to name just a few.

Protectionists urge retaliation. They claim the United States' trade deficit justifies the imposition of tariffs and other trade sanctions. While urging Americans to "buy American" products, industries and unions regularly rushed to Washington, D.C., urging Congress to enact **tariffs** and import quotas.

Protectionism sounds easy and workable as a solution to the trade deficit, yet the deficit is only one of the many symptoms of more profound economic problems. Most economists almost always favor free trade and dislike protectionism. Protectionism, they say, prevents efficient use of resources. It merely postpones real solutions such as increased productivity and improved capital plant investments. It also inevitably invites retaliation from foreign countries.[7] Protectionism will only magnify most of the problems associated with America's trade problems.

All governments use tariffs on occasion to aid their businesses. Over the years, when our businesses have been threatened they and their employees have often successfully petitioned Congress to curb competitive imports. By imposing tariffs or negotiating trade agreements with other nations to restrict the quantities of cars, shoes, or motorcycles that are imported into the United States, the federal government maintains higher prices for these products—a situation that benefits (at least in the short run) domestic companies and their workers. The costs to American consumers, however, can be great. In recent years it has cost us between $25,000 and $1 million to produce a single job in certain industries.

Americans have usually favored free trade. Two hundred years ago Thomas Jefferson traveled to France to request that American whale oil, tobacco, and fish be allowed into that country without being subject to the intolerable tariff burdens the French had imposed. And over the years Americans have usually discovered that foreign trade is a two-way street: If we want people in a foreign market to buy our goods, we must be willing to buy theirs.

In the 1930s many nations experienced high unemployment, low production, and general economic misery. The United States was no exception. In an effort to aid ailing American industries, Congress passed the Smoot-Hawley tariff act. The act established the highest general tariff the United States had ever had. Supporters hoped high tariffs on imported goods would increase the demand for goods produced in the United States and thus help get the country out of the Depression. The exact opposite occurred. Other nations retaliated with high tariffs on American goods. Demand fell, heightening the Depression. In 1934 Congress gave the president

(T. Cronin)

---

[7] See the recent case against protectionism, for example, in Lester Thurow, *Zero Sum Solution: Building A World Class American Economy* (Simon & Schuster, 1985).

power to negotiate mutual tariff reductions with other nations, subject to certain restrictions. By the early 1970s tariffs on industrial products had been substantially reduced. But restrictions on agricultural commodities remain, along with nontariff limitations such as quotas, minimum import prices, and prohibitions on the sale of certain products.

There is a greater consensus to support the concerns of American industry and unions about "dumping." Certain nations have "dumped" products on our market (meaning they sell products here at below cost of manufacture) with the obvious intention of driving our producers out of the market and then later, after they dominate the market, raising their prices to profitable levels. Countries have also subsidized steel exported elsewhere in the world. Japan has protected several of its industries—producers of autos to baseball bats—by specifying standards that are virtually impossible for us to meet. Other nations have erected nontariff trade barriers, such as lengthy inspection procedures for imported goods.

The United States, of course, often reciprocates. In recent years we have imposed "voluntary" limits on Japanese automobiles and European steel imports. Further, as already indicated, the federal government has long subsidized agricultural exports in the form of price supports and inexpensive credit.

Opponents of these protectionist policies say that in the long run they cost us jobs rather than save them, and lead to higher prices. Protected American firms facing reduced competition from foreign firms are free to raise their prices. As demand falls, American manufacturers sell fewer products and are forced to lay off workers. Contrived protection of our industries also may lull an industry into complacent practices rather than encourage investment, renewal, and retooling that will lead to qualitative improvements necessary to remain competitive. Artificial protections also may mask the fact that we need to revitalize our educational system and merely postpone our recognition of the increasingly noncompetitive aspect of the American economy.

In short, protectionist measures are often merely another kind of subsidy—and often a subsidy that protects one industry at the expense of another. Protectionism is more expensive than taxpayers realize. Protectionism will rarely be the appropriate answer. Instead, the United States must: continue, through hard negotiations with our trading partners, to remove unfair trade practices; encourage greater investments in what we have traditionally done well (science, technology, medical, and agricultural research, etc.); educate workers with better skills and executives with greater leadership abilities; and encourage labor-management experiments that can maximize productivity with an eye on higher quality products that will be highly prized abroad. Policy makers in the United States have sought to devalue the dollar and thereby make our products more accessible in foreign markets.

'Buy American' rally in New York City. (*Martin A. Levick/Black Star*)

The U.S. Postal Service: Subsidizing a Government Monopoly?

The case of the U.S. Postal Service does not quite fit the description of a traditional subsidy program. Yet the government continues to operate the postal service because of the presumed benefits it brings to business and society. Ninety-four percent of the business of the postal service is business mail. Only 6 percent is personal mail. And publications, advertising, and books all have special rates. When the postal service runs deficits, as it has in some recent years, who bails it out? The taxpayers.

The government assumed the responsibility for delivering the mail even before the American Revolution. For many years postmasters general were more important for their political than for their administrative responsibilities. Presidents often ap-

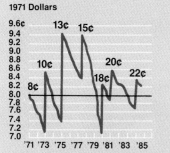

Real Price of a First-Class Stamp

1971 Dollars

SOURCE: *National Journal*, (April 5, 1986) p. 844. Data for chart from *U.S. Postal Service*.

pointed to this post the national chair of their own party or one of their key campaign managers. The reason was obvious: The U.S. Post Office Department had thousands of patronage jobs to give to local party workers. Over the years postal employees were gradually brought under the civil service, and there have been continuing efforts to restructure the Post Office as a self-supporting business enterprise. Yet the Post Office is still subsidized, and many people believe it always will be.

In 1970, in response to the recommendations of a presidential commission, and after two years of debate in Congress in which postal workers and their unions bargained hard to protect their positions, Congress abolished the Post Office Department and created a new independent agency, the United States Postal Service.

The Postal Service is governed by an eleven-member board of governors, nine of whom are appointed by the president with the consent of the Senate. No more than five may be from the same political party. These nine members in turn appoint a postmaster general, who joins them in selecting a deputy postmaster general.

Although postal employees retain their civil service status, the board has authority to set salaries and determine fringe benefits. Employees are permitted to engage in collective bargaining, but they may not legally strike. In the event of a deadlock between the board and its employees, there is to be compulsory arbitration. The Postal Service spends about 83 percent of its expenses for wages and benefits for its employees who, by law, must be paid comparably to what they would earn in the private sector.

The United States Postal Service is the biggest nonmilitary department of the national government. It handles over 150 billion pieces of mail every year, and has about 770,000 permanent employees, 38,000 offices, and 168,000 routes.

In recent years the Postal Service is becoming more self-supporting, sometimes even turning a slight profit. Like a business, the Postal Service is permitted to sell bonds to purchase capital equipment. Unlike a business, however, it may set its charges only after a recommendation from the presidentially appointed, five-member Postal Rate Commission. But the Postal Service still gets a "revenue foregone" subsidy of nearly $800 million for services it performs below cost. Congress explicitly intends this subsidy to provide free mailing for the blind and the handicapped, to provide lower rates for nonprofit organizations, and so on. However, this subsidy makes up only 3 percent of the Postal Service's more than $25 billion budget.

The new business organization reflects the fact that the decisions made by the Postal Service have a major impact on our economy and our political system. Its structure is designed to promote proper consideration of these political factors, and to avoid decisions made solely for profit. Has the experiment worked? Some say it works well. They point to the fact that the U.S. Postal Service provides the cheapest first-class rate of any nation in the world. It handles more pieces of mail per employee than any nation in the world. Moreover, it has made substantial cost savings through employee cutbacks and has eliminated patronage in the appointment of postmasters and carriers. The purpose of the Post Office is not to make money but to perform a service, and the U.S. Postal Service is doing that more efficiently than ever before.

Others disagree—and usually with fervor. Since its creation, they complain, costs of providing mail service have soared. Labor costs have risen greatly. Critics also say postal workers are sometimes rude, and lines at the post office grow longer every year. Could it be, they ask, that public enterprises such as the Postal Service do not have the incentives to innovate and please the consumer that private enterprises do?[8] The Postal Service is increasingly suffering from competition from private carriers of second- and third-class mail and parcel post. Some utilities are now

[8] For example, see Bill Green, "Competition and Monopoly in the Mails," *The Journal of the Institute for Socioeconomic Studies* (Summer 1986), pp. 74–85.

Postal workers processing and collecting the mail. (*Courtesy U.S. Postal Service*)

delivering their own bills to save postage costs; several newspapers and magazines are experimenting with private carriers. A major legal obstacle to private mail delivery is that only a uniformed U.S. postal carrier is allowed by law to open a private mailbox. One of President Reagan's budget directors once advocated abolishing the Postal Service's monopoly on delivering most kinds of mail, and opening up mail delivery to private competitors who might perform the job better. Reagan himself never went that far. Defenders of the Postal Service reject these "privatization" recommendations and point out that private outfits are mainly interested in the profitable services performed by the Postal Service. Without the Postal Service, who would deliver the mail in remote Alaska, in northwestern Colorado, and northern Maine?

Technological changes are also affecting the postal service. Instant communications via computers along with new competitors such as Federal Express, UPS, Purolator Courier, and others are a challenge to the traditional ways of doing business through the mail. UPS has bested the Postal Service in the parcel delivery area even though the Postal Service apparently subsidizes its parcel service from its more profitable activities. Some people think it is just a matter of years before most of us will be communicating and sending messages to one another via telex and other electronic devices. This is yet another example of how the world never stays the same and how technological developments alter the nature of the marketplace.

The major policy questions facing Congress are (1) Should the Postal Service continue to strive to break even at the expense of service? (2) Should federal subsidies be increased? (3) Should the Postal Service be abolished and responsibility for it returned to Congress or the president? Many believe the present system will work. They also suggest that small rural post offices be closed down, that postage rates be increased, and that Saturday service be dropped. Many members of Congress oppose these suggestions, for their constituents complain when services are curtailed.

Higher Postal Rates Really Aren't

For ordinary letter writers, postal rates go up mainly because of inflation. Since 1970, the price of a first-class stamp, then 8 cents, has gone up six times. But most of the increase was inflation: a 22-cent-stamp in 1984 was worth 8.2 cents in 1971 dollars.

U.S. postal rates are a bargain compared with those elsewhere in the industrial world. In Norway, which has the highest rates, a first-class letter cost the equivalent of 31.3 cents in 1985; in Japan, 27.7 cents.

Source: *National Journal* (April 5, 1986), p. 844. Data for chart from *U.S. Postal Service*.

HELPING RETIREES AND THE DISABLED

Social security, the world's largest "insurance" program for retirees, survivors, and the disabled, covers over 90 percent of the American workforce and will cost well over $225 billion by 1988. The program pays 36 million Americans every month,

Financing Social Security

The National Commission on Social Security Reform (1983) was created by President Reagan to recommend ways to save the social security system. Its suggestions, adopted by Congress, were the result of compromise among many political leaders. Among the most important of the commission's suggestions were the following:

A six-month delay in the cost-of-living adjustment from July 1983 to January 1984. This provision saved the social security system an estimated $40 billion.

A rescheduling of previously approved increases in social security payroll taxes. Increases will take place sooner than legislated in existing law. This provision will save the system an estimated $40 billion.

A gradual increase in the retirement age. An increase in the benefit bonus for early retirement will be phased in gradually until 2010.

An extension of coverage to all newly hired federal workers. New federal employees will contribute to the social security system rather than to their own pension plans. Also, all employees of nonprofit organizations not covered at present will come under the social security system. Further, state and local governments now in the system will be prohibited from withdrawing. These steps will save $23 billion.

Subjecting for the first time benefits to income tax. One-half of all social security benefits of individuals with other income over $20,000 and families with earnings over $25,000 will be taxed. The expected $30 billion yield will be credited to the social security system.

and 115 million people contribute to it. In the late 1980s social security provided an estimated average payment of over $500 per month to a retired worker without dependents. Full benefits are paid to those between the ages of 65 and 70 who are not presently earning wages of more than a certain amount. After age 70 people are entitled to retirement benefits regardless of wage earnings. Since the Social Security Act was passed in 1935, the history of social security programs has largely been one of steady growth. The purpose of the program is to provide support for the aged in American society, and it has grown to include disability payments and Medicare. It is financed through compulsory "contributions" by workers and employers in the form of a payroll tax.

The first social security check was paid to Ida Fuller of Brattleboro, Vermont, in 1940. She had contributed $22 in payroll taxes between the beginning of 1937, when the system began, and the end of 1939, when she retired. Ms. Fuller's first monthly check was for $22.54. She continued to receive checks for thirty-four years, until her death in late 1974 (shortly after her 100th birthday). All told, Ida collected almost $21,000.

> For proponents and critics alike Ida Fuller's story captures much of the essence of the social security system. Critics can point out that Ida joined late, paid almost nothing, and received benefits nearly a thousand times as large as the taxes she paid in. Proponents can point with pride to a system providing a reliable stream of benefits to someone lucky enough to live as long as Ida did, and to the comfort and peace of mind social security gave her. They can also observe that though she received a high return on her contributions, the system was only a small cushion for her. History does not record Ida's other sources of support, but she could not have lived thirty-four years sustained only by her social security checks.[9]

Until the 1970s growth was relatively noncontroversial, largely because "the costs were initially deceptively low," while benefits were steadily increasing, making the system politically painless.[10] The liberalization and expansion of benefits were made possible by the steady economic growth of the 1950s and 1960s. "The nature of the program in the short run has been such as to disguise the true cost of it, the true relation between costs and benefits, and the true principles by which benefits and costs have been distributed. The nature of policy making did little to correct, but instead reinforced, a complacent, poorly informed acceptance of the program."[11]

Few people really understand how the social security system works. Most Americans, for example, believe their payroll taxes go into some type of insurance investment pool to be held and invested until the day they retire and benefits begin. Many people believe the social security system accumulates a large trust fund filled with reserves in order to pay out benefits according to the contributions.

The reality is different. Payroll taxes are not calculated to cover the costs of future pensions for today's wage earners. Rather, current benefits are paid out of current receipts. In addition, a large percentage of social security benefits are disproportionate to contributions. The working poor, for example, receive a larger portion of their contributions in the form of benefits than does the working middle class. The social security system is so structured that almost all retirees can expect to receive more in benefits than they and their employers ever paid into the system.

In the 1930s, when the system was created, the life expectancy of Americans was about fifty-nine years. That figure has since risen to seventy-four. Most Americans

[9] Herman B. Leonard, *Checks Unbalanced: The Quiet Side of Public Spending* (Basic Books, 1986), p. 51.

[10] Martha Derthick, "No More Easy Votes for Social Security," *The Brookings Bulletin* (Fall 1979), p. 2.

[11] Martha Derthick, *Policymaking for Social Security* (Brookings Institution, 1979), p. 413.

now live longer and hence collect significantly more in social security benefits. Most Americans also face expensive medical costs in the later years of retirement. A steadily declining birthrate has placed the burden of supporting the social security system on fewer and fewer workers. Currently, for every three beneficiaries, ten employees contribute to the system. But by the year 2030 or so, the same ten employees will have to support about five social security recipients.

By the early 1980s this pay-as-you-go structure had plunged the system into a state of considerable financial uncertainty. Benefits, and especially the annual cost-of-living increases, were rapidly outstripping its reserves. Politicians in both parties skirted the issue of cutbacks or modifications in the system—fearing the wrath of the 36 million or more social security recipients. Meanwhile senior Americans were growing very anxious about the system.

In 1983 the system was said to be losing $20,000 every minute—and estimates of projected shortages ranged as high as $1.5 trillion. The pending crisis forced President Reagan and Congress to take action. Reagan created the bipartisan National Commission on Social Security Reform. This fifteen-member group was charged with suggesting ways to solve and improve the system's financial problems.

Among the commission's proposals were recommendations to delay for six months a cost-of-living benefit increase, increase payroll taxes, and gradually raise the retirement age. (See box page 547.) The commission also suggested (and Congress approved) that new federal employees be required to join the social security system and that benefits of some higher-income retired people be subject to federal income taxes. The commission's recommendations were quickly acted upon by Congress and signed into law by Reagan. Though these changes will mean more taxes and more money withheld from our monthly paychecks, they reassured most people that the financial solvency of this highly visible federal program would be guaranteed for at least the next decade. This bipartisan national commission truly helped to point the way to a sensible policy solution. And Congress responded to it in a timely fashion to solve a problem before the crisis came crashing down.[12]

HELPING THE NEEDY

Until the Great Depression the national government had no responsibility for taking care of persons in need, except for veterans and a few special groups. America was thought to be a land of unlimited opportunities. When persons failed to get ahead, people said, it was their own fault. The "worthy poor," widows and orphans, were taken care of through private or county relief. During the early twentieth century state governments extended relief to needy old people, the blind, and orphans, but the programs were limited. No work, no food was the ruling ethic.

Then came the Great Depression. In the early 1930s nearly 15 million people were without jobs. Breadlines, soup kitchens, private charity, and meager state and local programs were pitifully inadequate gestures. The Roosevelt administration created an elaborate series of emergency relief programs. But what started as an emergency response to a temporary condition has become a permanent feature of our system. During the past fifty years the national government has become progressively and deeply involved in welfare activities. Most programs are administered by state and local governments but funded by the national government and thus subject

[12] Paul Light, *Artful Work: The Politics of Social Security Reform* (Random House, 1985).

to Washington's control. The complex tangle of programs has produced an administrative maze.

Today, federal **entitlement programs**—programs that provide a specified set of benefits as a matter of right to all individuals who meet statutory criteria—have become a significant provider to millions of Americans, perhaps as many as a third of American households. In one recent year, "more than 32 million individuals received payments under the old age and survivors insurance component of the social security program, almost 3 million received unemployment compensation in an average week, and 21.6 million received food stamps. In the health sector, 30 million people were enrolled in medicare and 21.5 million in medicaid. And many more Americans will receive additional entitlements benefits at some time in their lives, notably through social security and medicare."[13]

Though most people believe the national government should do something about poverty, few agree on *what* it should do. There is not even agreement about the dimensions of the problem—how many poor exist, who they are, and why they are poor. But it is clear that a substantial number of Americans, perhaps 40 million, do not have access to a "comfortable" lifestyle. These are often the hidden poor. They remain invisible to the majority of Americans because they exist in the dark slums of the city and in the mountains and valleys of rural America.

A third of the poor are from families in which the breadwinner has been without a job for a long time. (At least 10 million people were unemployed in 1987.) Some of these are headed by a father or a mother whose skills are so meager that he or she cannot support the family. A large portion of the poor live in families headed by a person at least 65 years of age or someone with little or no education. Because black Americans have been subject to discrimination and denied opportunities for education, a greater percentage of blacks than whites are poor. Nevertheless, 70 percent of the poor are white.

Almost everybody is unhappy about the present state of national welfare policies, especially the largest of the so-called categorical relief programs, Aid to Families with Dependent Children. (There is little criticism of programs providing help for the aged, the blind, or the disabled.) Conservatives argue that the drain on the taxpayer is beyond endurance, and that welfare creates and perpetuates dependency.[14] Liberals argue that it is immoral for a rich nation to spend billions for defense, to subsidize wealthy farmers, and to assist business when millions are in want.[15] Liberals argue too that welfare will in many cases improve opportunities for the poor and compensate for disadvantages imposed by society. Radicals argue that the poor are in poverty because of the deliberate design of the powerful or the natural workings of capitalism.

The famous exchange between F. Scott Fitzgerald and Ernest Hemingway continues to set the framework within which we debate welfare policies. Fitzgerald is reported to have said: "The rich are different from the poor." Hemingway responded: "Yes, they have more money." On the Fitzgerald side of the argument are some social scientists who believe we must make a distinction between those without money and the poor. A college student from a middleclass background, or a space scientist out of work, may be without much money, but he or she is not poor. To be poor is to be part of the "culture of poverty." This subculture, with its own system of values and behaviors, makes it possible for those living in poverty to exist but difficult for them to succeed in the larger society. "There is . . . a language of the poor, a psychology of the poor, a world view of the poor.

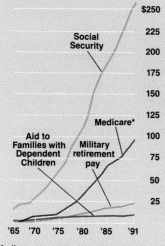

Growing Entitlement Spending

Benefits paid in four federal entitlement programs

(in billions of dollars by fiscal year figures for 1986 through 1991 are estimates from President Reagan's budget proposal)

Social Security

Medicare*

Aid to Families with Dependent Children

Military retirement pay

$250
225
200
175
150
125
100
75
50
25

'65 '70 '75 '80 '85 '91

*Medicare payments began in 1966
SOURCE: Office of Management and Budget

[13] R. Kent Weaver, "Controlling Entitlements," in John Chubb and Paul Peterson, eds., *The New American Politics* (Brookings Institution, 1985), p. 307.

[14] Michael Harrington, *The Other America* (Penguin, 1963), pp. 23–24.

[15] Charles Murray, *Losing Ground* (Basic Books, 1985).

(*By Wright for The Miami News*)

To be impoverished is to be an internal alien, to grow up in a culture that is radically different from one that dominates the society."[16] Although modern-day Fitzgeralds vary in their political views, they tend to emphasize that poverty is unlikely to be reduced unless people are given the education, training, and skill they need to break out of the culture of poverty. They also tend to favor measures to increase the political power of the poor so that they can secure their share of society's resources. Those who take the Hemingway position say what the poor need most is money. With more money they will be able to provide decent housing, secure education for their children, and in time become capable of taking care of themselves.

During the last several decades we have had several waves of welfare reform. In broad terms, these reforms have had the following purposes:

1. *Trying to substitute work for welfare.* In November 1934 President Roosevelt wrote: "What I am seeking is the abolition of relief altogether. I cannot say so out loud yet but I hope to be able to substitute work for relief." He hoped that with economic recovery and full employment, people would move from relief to employment—and many did. But five presidents later, Richard Nixon announced: "What America needs now is not more welfare but more workfare."[17] Recent administrations also tried this. More jobs would benefit the temporarily unemployed. But the problem is that many of those on welfare are unemployable or unskilled.

2. *Trying to substitute social services.* In the early 1960s the major aim of reform was to provide professional help for those on welfare. It was believed that with this kind of assistance, those in need could learn to take care of themselves.

[16] See, for example, Michael Harrington, *Taking Sides* (Holt, Rinehart, Winston, 1985), and Kenneth Dolbeare, *Democracy at Risk* (Chatham House, 1984).

[17] Quoted in Daniel P. Moynihan, *The Politics of a Guaranteed Income: The Nixon Administration and the Family Assistance Plan* (Random House, 1973), p. 225.

Thus, if the problem appeared to be illness, a social worker or caseworker was to see to it that adequate health care was provided. If a family was about to lose its breadwinner because of a marital dispute, a caseworker would be assigned to see if the family could be kept together. The difficulty, however, is that there are not enough trained caseworkers to provide help for all those on welfare. In any event, experiments in which one group received services and another group merely received welfare payments demonstrated that the former group was not any less dependent on welfare than the latter.

3. *Trying to increase the political influence of the poor.* Some aims of President Johnson's War on Poverty were to mobilize the poor for political action, to involve the poor in community-action programs, and to create structures outside the regular channels the poor could use to claim a more adequate share of services.

4. *Trying to increase the cash income available to the very poor.* These reforms, the most recent, involve some kind of income maintenance program such as a family allowance, a negative income tax, or a guaranteed minimum annual income. Here the emphasis is on providing those in need with more dollars.

5. *Trying to produce more jobs and get lower income people off the tax rolls.* Ronald Reagan and his supporters in Congress argued that a rising tide lifts all boats and that their policies of stimulating private enterprise would, after a while, do more to help the poor than most of the social strategies programs promoted by liberals or Democrats. Thus the Reagan program cut food stamps and similar programs and emphasized tax cuts that would, they hoped, stimulate investment and business expansion—which, in turn, would produce a healthy economy, lower inflation, lower interest rates, and more jobs. When these programs failed to affect poverty, the Reagan administration, with Congress's approval, moved to get several million low-income citizens removed from tax-paying responsibility, which, in effect, was a subsidy approach.[18]

Fifty years of experimentation, tinkering, and development have resulted in a system that reflects all these approaches and more. Outlined next are some of the continuing programs and controversies.

Unemployment Insurance

This income maintenance system is operated jointly by the national and the state governments. All employers pay a payroll tax. These funds are paid out to the states for workers who are not covered by other unemployment compensation programs. It is estimated that an average 3 million persons received benefits each week in the late 1980s. No one, however, receives funds indefinitely.

Aid to families with dependent children   The most costly, and most controversial, public assistance program is Aid to Families with Dependent Children (AFDC). A dependent child is one under 18 who has been deprived of parental support but who is living with a parent or with a close relative. AFDC helps over 10 million persons, most of whom are children. The program's aim is to keep families with children together. Some states have tried to deny assistance to families whose mothers are unwed, who have men living in the house, who have just moved to the state, or who are headed by aliens. But Congress and the Supreme Court have ruled against such restrictions. The Court has even ruled that a recipient may not have welfare taken away without first being provided with a hearing. The state must show why the recipient is ineligible and give him or her an opportunity to confront any adverse witnesses.

[18] See Gregory A. Fossedal, "Reagan's War on Poverty," *The New York Times* (May 28, 1986) section A, p. 23.

A welfare line in New York City.
(*J. P. Laffont/Sygma*)

Congress requires mothers of children over 6 years old to participate in job-training or work programs to qualify for federally assisted welfare. It has exempted from taxation a certain percentage of a mother's income so that she is not penalized because of earning a salary. The trouble is that nearly half of AFDC mothers have gone no further than the eighth grade. Even if AFDC children under 6 years of age were given a place in every licensed day-care facility in the country, there would still be 1 million such children left over.

A minimum income   The federal government guarantees a minimum income to Americans at least 65 years old, and to the blind and disabled of any age. This guarantee is an "absolute right." The program replaces state-administered programs of assistance to the aged, blind, and disabled. This program, called the Supplemental Security Income Program, is administered by the Social Security Administration. Its money, however, comes not from the Social Security Trust Fund but from general funds of the U.S. Treasury.

Is this income guarantee a step toward a universal cash income guarantee? Some people think so. Supplemental Security Income makes the cash income of millions of Americans—the aged, the blind, the disabled—a legal obligation of the federal government. For a bewildering and unfair variety of state rules to decide who is "needy" enough to be helped, SSI substitutes national standards of income and resources.

The War on Poverty

Welfare politics and welfare policies have been heatedly debated for the past three decades. Some improvements have been realized. The number of substandard housing units has been lowered. More minority persons have entered and graduated from colleges. But welfare and antipoverty offensives have always been controversial. Many measures once proposed have been allowed to die, or were later scuttled, or are still under consideration. The beleaguered war on poverty of the 1960s, the unsuccessful battle to pass a family assistance program, and the campaign for national health insurance are illustrative. Further, declining dollar value and a shrinking gross national product make upward mobility for all an almost impossible goal.[19]

One of the most heated arguments of the 1980s centered on whether the war on poverty and various welfare and affirmative action programs of the 1960s and 1970s helped or hurt the poor.[20] In *Losing Ground* Charles Murray suggests

[19] See Paul Blumberg, *Inequality in an Age of Decline* (Oxford University Press, 1980).

[20] For one view, see Sar A. Levitan and Robert Taggart, *The Promise of Greatness: The Social Programs of the Last Decade and their Major Achievements* (Harvard University Press, 1976), and Sar Levitan and Clifford Johnson, *Beyond the Safety Net* (Ballinger, 1984).

that helping the poor is really bad for them. He contends that many of the policies designed by Washington policy makers to help citizens, especially the poor, have had the opposite effect. They foster dependence and sap personal initiative. In Murray's view, poverty is like any other economic good; subsidize it and you merely get more of it. Trying to provide more for the poor merely produced more poor instead, according to Murray. He contends that poverty actually fell in the 1950s and early 1960s when there were few if any poverty programs, while poverty rose in the 1970s when such programs were in place. Based on these findings, Murray would strip away most welfare programs and end affirmative action programs as well.[21]

Murray's critics question his analysis and find it flawed on several grounds. Some pointed to the changing nature of the economy during this period as an alternative explanation for the persistence of poverty. Others pointed out that the welfare assistance programs have in most cases actually permitted people to improve their lot and break out of the poverty zone. Still others believed that welfare and job training programs never have been a match for the eroding manufacturing sector and the increasingly noncompetitive status of America in the global economy. Structural shifts in the economy are perhaps a better explanation of why many of the poor have been unable to break out of poverty in the recent past.[22]

Murray stirred up a debate that has been heard before and will be heard again. The critical question is whether the government can devise sensible programs to help the needy to become more self-reliant and play a role in the free enterprise system. Although Murray and certain libertarians to the right of Reagan want to end most federal welfare and entitlement programs, most Americans see a role for government programs to improve the condition of the poor. In fact, as the accompanying chart suggests, twice as many Americans believe the war on poverty in the past generation was a positive effort and two-thirds of Americans think the federal government should make a serious commitment to assisting the poor and trying to free them from the harsh cycle of poverty and dependence.

President Reagan's opposition to the Great Society's war on poverty programs was a rallying point for those who believed Reagan favored the rich over the poor. Reagan's critics said his reductions in social service programs and his emphasis on tighter definitions of need demonstrate his indifference to the needy in America. On the other side, Reagan and his supporters argue that too many federal programs have become entitlement programs—programs such as Social Security, Aid to Families with Dependent Children, Medicare, and unemployment insurance—to which qualified citizens are "entitled" by law. The problem raised by all these programs is that our federal budget is now set up so that certain subsidies are built into the system. Once Congress defines who gets benefits, these benefits get passed out no matter what. Moreover, it is increasingly difficult for Congress to reduce or redirect these entitlements for senior citizens, for students, or for government employees because of the political pressures raised by these groups.

Many of the entitlement programs benefit middle income groups. And these groups are politically alert and organized. A growing number of analysts of several different political persuasions are now worried that the federal budget is "out of control." Congress finds it difficult to curtail entitlement programs. The federal deficit continues to grow, and the debate over providing assistance to the poor intensifies.[23]

Public Opinion and Government Antipoverty Efforts

Q. There were many government programs in the 1960s to try to improve the condition of poor people. Do you think these programs generally made things better, worse, or do you think they didn't have much impact?

Made better	39%
Not much impact	38
Made worse	18

Q. Do you think the federal government should spend money now on a similar effort to try to improve the condition of poor people in this country?

Should	66%
Other/No opinion	12
Should not	22

Source: *CBS News-The New York Times* poll (1986).

[21] Charles Murray, *Losing Ground* (Basic Books, 1984), and Charles Murray "Have the Poor Been 'Losing Ground,'" *Political Science Quarterly* (Fall 1985), pp. 427–45.

[22] See Christopher Jencks, "How Poor Are the Poor?" *The New York Review of Books* (May 9, 1985), pp. 41–55; and Sam Levitan, "How the Welfare System Promotes Economic Security," *Political Science Quarterly* (Fall 1985), pp. 447–59.

[23] R. Kent Weaver, "Controlling Entitlements," in John E. Chubb and Paul E. Peterson, eds., *The New Direction in American Politics* (Brookings Institution, 1985), pp. 307–41.

SUMMARY

1. An entire book would be necessary just to describe all the subsidy and welfare efforts now being run by the federal government. We do not have space to talk about the complex ways government aids hospitals, homeowners, higher-education institutions, the airline industry, and others.

2. The role of government as promoter is not new. It is as old as the republic itself. We have witnessed intense governmental concern with energy development, support of businesses such as Chrysler, and the Continental Bank of Illinois and human resource assistance programs.

3. Many disagree with efforts by the national government to improve the quality of life, to focus resources and attention on the problems of the poor, and to improve the cities. They view with distaste the bureaucracy required for these programs, allege that the programs cost far more than they might cost if administered at the local level, and claim that many of these programs create a dependency that undermines our traditional ethic of self-reliance. On the other hand, most of these problems developed because local, private, and voluntary sectors were overwhelmed by them and were unable to respond in a meaningful way.

4. The pressures are usually for more, not less, involvement by the national government. In one way or another the government subsidizes nearly every segment of our population. Which of these programs are justified and which are not is the very heart of American politics. One person's subsidy is often viewed as the next person's boondoggle. Once a subsidy or entitlement program is established, it is hard to get rid of it.

FURTHER READING

CLAUDE E. BARFIELD and WILLIAM SCHAMBRA, eds. *The Politics of Industrial Policy* (American Enterprise Institute, 1986).

PAUL BLUMBERG. *Inequality in an Age of Decline* (Oxford University Press, 1980).

MARTIN CARNOY and DEREK SHEARER. *Economic Democracy: The Challenge of the 1980s* (M. E. Sharpe, 1980).

MARTHA DERTHICK. *Policymaking for Social Security* (Brookings Institution, 1979).

HERMAN B. LEONARD. *Checks Unbalanced: The Quiet Side of Public Spending* (Basic Books, 1986).

PAUL LIGHT. *Artful Work: The Politics of Social Security Reform* (Random House, 1985).

AMORY and HUNTER LOVINS. *Brittle Power: Energy Strategy for National Security* (Brick House, 1982).

DANIEL P. MOYNIHAN. *Family and Nation* (Harcourt, Brace, Jovanovich, 1986).

CHARLES MURRAY. *Losing Ground: American Social Policy, 1950–1980* (Basic Books, 1984).

BENJAMIN PAGE. *Who Gets What From Government* (University of California Press, 1983).

CLYDE V. PRESTOWITZ, JR. *Trading Places: How We Allowed Japan To Take the Lead* (Basic Books, 1988).

LESTER THUROW. *The Zero-Sum Society: Building a World Class American Economy* (Simon & Schuster, 1985).

JOHN T. TIERNEY. *The U. S. Postal Service: Status and Prospects of a Public Enterprise* (Auburn House, 1988).

The Democratic Faith and the Necessity of Politics

More than any other form of government, the kind of democracy that has emerged under our Constitution requires a certain kind of faith—and a certain kind of skepticism. It requires faith concerning the common human enterprise; a belief that if the people are informed and caring, they can be trusted with their own self-government; and an optimism that when things begin to go wrong, the people may be relied upon to set them right.

A healthy skepticism is needed as well. Democracy requires us to be questioning of our leaders and never too trusting of any group with too much power. Although we prize majority rule, we are skeptical enough to ask whether a majority is always right. Democracy requires us to be constantly concerned about whether we really tolerate and protect the rights and opinions of others, and about whether democratic processes are in fact serving the principles of liberty, equality, and justice. In short, the democratic faith rests upon a peculiar blend of faith in the people and skepticism of them.

Thomas Jefferson, our best-known champion of the democratic faith, believed in the common sense of humankind and in the flowering of the human spirit. Jefferson believed deeply that every government degenerates when it is trusted to rulers alone. The people themselves, he wrote, are the only safe depositories of government. His was a robust commitment to popular control, to representative processes, and to accountable leadership. But he was no believer in the simple participatory democratic system of ancient Greece or revolutionary France: The people, too, must have their power checked and balanced.

The customary government of humankind has been authoritarian, or tyrannical. Throughout history, including the present, most people have lived in societies in which a small group at the top imposed their will on the others. Today some authoritarian governments justify their actions by saying people are too weak to govern themselves; they need to be ruled. Others claim to be true representatives of all the people. But neither in Castro's Cuba nor in the military regime of Chile, neither in the People's Republic of China nor in South Africa, do ordinary people have a voice in the types of decisions Americans routinely make: Who should go to college, or work in the fields, or serve in the army? How much money should be spent for schools, stealth fighter planes, or environmental protection?

It is only by intense thought, great commitment, countless sacrifices, and an enduring faith in democracy that liberty and equality have prevailed—at least to the extent they have—in the United States. The celebrated efforts and faith that were necessary to create this democratic republic are fully as necessary to sustain it in our own time.

THE AMERICAN DREAM

"It's about the American Dream . . ." (© 1979. NEA Inc.)

Thomas Jefferson. As chief author of the Declaration of Independence, and as one of the major philosophers of the early Republic, Jefferson inspired dreams and an optimism about the promise of America. (*The Granger Collection*)

The beliefs people hold most dear are often called myths or dreams. These help hold societies together, and they can be powerful. Sometimes they are more powerful than logic, because usually they cannot be refuted. Is it any wonder that shrewd political leaders have seen the importance of myths and dreams and have often used them to acquire power? Plato argued that rulers should invent myths even when they know them to be wrong. Machiavelli, the brilliant observer of politics in Renaissance Italy, advised princes to use religion and myth as an aid to power. Dreams and myths have a different look today than in former times, but they are no less important.

The official philosophy in America, of course, is that America has no official philosophy. We do have a rather general body of ideas and values that serves as a rough but persisting guide to our civic and political actions and helps to define us as a people and as a nation. But we have no unified, consistent, and well-defined ideology. Indeed, many of the myths and dreams by which Americans live contradict one another. In part, this is because values from one era have been carried over uncritically into new situations. Also, it is part of American pragmatism to hold contradictory beliefs simultaneously without bothering to resolve the potential conflicts between them.

We do not mean to stress the uniqueness of the American people, as if America were isolated from the rest of the world. The American dream has much in common with the aspirations of most peoples: peace, prosperity, personal ownership of property, personal liberty, and the belief that individuals are free to achieve any goals, to accumulate material wealth, to live any lifestyle. Ralph Waldo Emerson wrote: "The office of America is to liberate, to abolish kingcraft, priestcraft, castle, monopoly, to pull down the gallows, to burn up the bloody statute-book, to take in the immigrant, to open the doors of the sea and the fields of the earth." All should have the chance to chart their own courses, to become rich, to be elected president, to mold their own destinies—to go as far as their abilities permit.

Some consider the "American Dream" to be a misleading term used by the middle and upper classes to fool the poor and unemployed into thinking their lives can be improved. Others point out that even though the dream has become a reality for some white Anglo-Saxon males, it has not been fulfilled for millions of others who suffer discrimination, unemployment, and substandard housing and medical care. For the latter the dream has often been a nightmare: Equality of opportunity is a bitter myth for those who cannot get decent educations, who are generally unorganized and unrepresented politically, and who do not know how to make the system work for them. These people have understandably become disillusioned and embittered. But however contradictory and paradoxical our dream may be, it nonetheless exists, and it helps to shape how most Americans conduct their lives and respond to government and its policies.

Central to the American Dream is the notion that this is the land of opportunity for the enterprising. Here, the competitive, practical go-getter can make a fortune,

Lincoln Memorial. (*Alex Cronin*)

The Statue of Liberty. (*N.Y. Convention & Visitor Bureau*)

or build a dream home. The achievement, self-help, or success ethic is so strong here—and always has been—that some people believe the prime function of the state is to assist private individuals in the production of wealth and the protection of property.

This part of the American Dream has doubtless shaped the American national character in several ways. Its focus is primarily self-centered, materialistic, pragmatic, and individualistic; rugged individualism and resourcefulness are celebrated in our folklore and ballads. One byproduct of this aspect of the American Dream has been the continuous quest for liberty and freedom. Often the hero is the lone cowboy—unrestrained, unregulated, and self-reliant. Often the villain is the bureaucrat—the government regulator, the tax collector, or (indeed) any restrictions.

Still another element of the American Dream is faith in the common sense of the ordinary person. The tradition of Abraham Lincoln and Harry Truman, that anyone can become president, has been a bold one. We prefer action to reflection; we are antitheoretical, antiexpert, and indeed antiintellectual. Stressing practicality and immediacy, the ethic of the marketplace—the notion of "street sense"—has become part of our image. Such poets as Walt Whitman, Stephen Vincent Benet, and Carl Sandburg, and such storytellers as Mark Twain and Will Rogers, helped make this idea into tradition. This reverence for the common person helps in part to explain Americans' ambivalence toward power, politics, and government authority. In America government has always been viewed as a necessary *evil* (with a certain stress on evil).

Paradoxically, however, even as we criticize our government as inept and corrupt, and as something to be feared, we are also deeply convinced that ours is the best system in the world. Some of us would even like to impose our political theories and practices on everyone else. Understanding this paradox is basic to understanding the most confusing aspect of our national character: Americans seem to live and breathe and function by paradox. We cherish our pragmatic, experimental, predominantly individualistic tradition, and yet we have always had a sense of moral superiority, manifest destiny, and collective nationalism in America.

We are told that great nations often identify their missions with divine purposes. Perhaps, then, it is not surprising that a streak of **messianic spirit** runs through our history: America as the symbol of the future, as a quasisacred mission. Even a Herman Melville could write that "we Americans are the peculiar chosen people . . . the Israel of our time." Woodrow Wilson claimed that "the heart of the people is pure" and talked often of the spiritual energy in this nation. Wilson rallied the nation by stressing that America came into existence not to vindicate the rights of property or of wealth but to vindicate the rights of people, "to show the way to mankind in every part of the world to justice and freedom and liberty." "America must be ready," Wilson insisted, "to exert her whole force, moral and physical, to the assertion of those rights throughout the round globe."

There remains a remarkable belief that America is better, stronger, and more virtuous than other nations. Doubtless this sense of mission is a source of discipline, an obvious builder of morale and fortifier of nationalism. But an excessive or wrongheaded sense of mission can also cause problems. The Wilsonian notion that "America is the most unselfish of nations" is an example of a romanticized and inflated sense of mission. Our dealings with native Americans, our compromises over slavery in order to get the Constitution ratified, our era of Manifest Destiny, and our intrusion into the affairs of others in the post World War II period are all illustrative.

Some of us, of course, deride this righteousness, this false purity, this notion of the United States as an elect or redeemer nation. Critics say this messianism or providential destiny is an illusion. No nation is sacred. America, like every country, has interests and motives that are generous as well as selfish; we have motives that are idealistic as well as squalid. We, too, are part of human history.

Still, a persistent idealism and moralism at times looms large as part of the promise of America. Our efforts in the human rights area today, our food relief, financial support for the International Red Cross and the United Nations, and other humanitarian contributions provide some evidence. America may not be the only hope for the world—but it is still one of the prime hopes.

CHALLENGING THE AMERICAN DREAM

In a commencement speech at Harvard University, Alexander Solzhenitsyn posed a number of sharp challenges to the American Dream. The famed Soviet exile soundly criticized America's unchecked materialism, timid leadership, irresponsible press, and legalism in the face of a spiritual and moral vacuum. Further, he said Americans have taken freedom too far, which has led to a permissiveness that in turn encourages crime, violence, pornography, and a tasteless, third-rate culture. He plainly thinks we have lost our way—that we need some kind of moral revitalization and more central direction to overcome our softness, our decadence, our drift.[1]

Solzhenitsyn is not alone in questioning the health and viability of the American ideology. Critics from all quarters attack American beliefs as inconsistent, contradictory, or purely illusory. The most fundamental dispute concerns our most strongly held values—namely, the principles of *liberty and equality* set forth in the Declaration of Independence.

These two principles, largely complementary at the time of our nation's founding, are often in conflict today. In the late eighteenth century, equality of an individ-

[1] Alexander Solzhenitsyn, "The West Has Lost Its Courage," *The Washington Post* (June 11, 1978), p. Cl.

Contending American Dreams

THE AMERICAN WAY	THE AMERICAN TESTAMENT
Liberty	Equality
Freedom	Liberation from discrimination
Rugged individualism	*E pluribus unum*—commonwealth
Private property rights	Community
Survival of the fittest	Pro underdog, pro yeoman farmer
Success to the best	Affirmative action
Achievement, merit, excellence	Help for those who can't help themselves
Leave me alone	Generosity
Don't fence me in	Fairness
"Life is unfair"	"We can do better"
People are not angels—government by the best	Government by the people
Emphasis on our republic	Emphasis on participatory democracy and the common sense of the common person
"This land became great not by what government did for the people but what the people did for themselves."	"America must educate every individual to his or her capacity, eliminate ignorance, prejudice, hate, and the squalor in which crime is bred. We must also protect against the economic catastrophies of illness, disability, and unemployment."

Note: Both lists of values are part of the American Dream. Most of us have grown up somewhat conditioned by both American Dreams. The list on the left has doubtless been the primary American Dream for most Americans—as most of it was for the founders of this nation in the 1770s and 1780s. Over the years, however, elements of the list on the right have evolved to take an important place in our lives. Many of our major national public documents, and the most memorable addresses of various American leaders, are associated with the list on the right: Jefferson,

Lincoln, Susan B. Anthony, Franklin and Eleanor Roosevelt, Martin Luther King, Jr., John F. Kennedy. On the other hand, many of our distinguished leaders and politicians are plainly associated with the list on the left: John Adams, Madison, Hamilton, Teddy Roosevelt, and Ronald Reagan, to name just a few. How about you? Which set of values and aspirations most define your views? Are you a partisan of one list to the exclusion of the other—or do you, like most modern Americans, subscribe to a mixture of the two?

Alexander Solzhenitsyn, the Russian Nobel Prize-winning novelist and political dissident, now lives in the United States. (*AFL-CIO News*)

ual before the law and personal liberty served as twin battle cries of the revolution. Government was viewed as the primary threat to these values, and restraining government served to enhance both. But with the concentration of vast wealth in a few hands, especially around 1900, individuals or giant corporations became threats to liberty as well; equality of opportunity became an empty promise when individuals were denied the education, political power, and economic security necessary to succeed in American society.

How do we choose when a supreme value like liberty clashes with a supreme value like equality? Part of the answer is to ask ourselves *whose* liberty or equality, how defined, in what circumstances? We might wish to give equality—or at least equality of opportunity—precedence during a period of reform like the New Deal. We might wish to put security—"freedom from fear"—first during a war. We might wish to give top priority to liberty—liberty from governmental regulation, for example—during a conservative era.

But it is not enough to answer the question of the priority of values by saying: It depends. Ultimately the thoughtful citizen must make such a choice. There are conflicts among values, and one may have to yield to another. The authors of this book urge that you, students of government, sort out your values and establish priorities among them.

We, of course, must practice what we preach. The three authors agree that freedom of speech in particular and the Bill of Rights in general stand at the very pinnacle of our hierarchy of values. Thus we would defend the principle of liberty against all comers—against forces of aggression from abroad that might threaten all our freedoms, against would-be censors at home who would deprive us of the right to read and speak and even think as we wish, against those who would prevent our fellow-citizens—even Nazis or Stalinists—from the right to stand up on soapboxes and preach their outrageous doctrines.

So if we had to choose between the values of liberty and equality, we put the former first. But much depends on how we define these values. If we define equality as equality of *condition*, as the idea of leveling everyone's income and living conditions, equality might mean taking **personal property** from some to redistribute to others who need it in a manner that might jeopardize individual liberties of the former. But if we define equality as equality of *opportunity*, it would mean providing youngsters, for example, with the kind of housing, home life, medical care, and schooling they need to expand their actual liberties, and thus give them a truly equal start. No one is more denied *all* freedoms than persons who are imprisoned in a poverty of ignorance, illness, low self-esteem, and other deprivations.

Some writers talk about this same clash of dreams or values in the context of a fundamental antagonism between liberty and equality. They note that even though most Americans favor a competitive, private economy in which the most industrious and enterprising individuals receive the greatest economic rewards, most Americans also yearn for a society in which all citizens can earn decent livings and have equal chances to realize their full human potentials. "Since these two sets of values often conflict with each other in practice, the mood of the country may shift from one era to another as the values of one tradition or the other predominate," write Herbert McClosky and John Zaller. They add:

> In one period the nation may be shocked by society's failure to fulfill the democratic promise of American life for the poor, the unemployed, and other disadvantaged groups, and may accelerate its efforts to rectify this failure; in the next period, however, many people may complain that the nation has gone too far in pursuing these goals and may advocate a shift back toward a more conservative, laissez-faire procapitalist course.[2]

[2] Herbert McClosky and John Zaller, *The American Ethos: Public Attitudes toward Capitalism and Democracy* (Harvard University Press, 1984), p. 292. See also Arthur M. Schlesinger, Jr., *The Cycles of American History* (Houghton Mifflin, 1986).

Because change is scary, and uncharted change frightening, people with certain fixed values or ideologies often cling tenaciously to simple definitions of reality. These in turn define their view of the American Dream and the kind of politics they want to encourage. Libertarian critics today, for example, argue that democracy, specifically majority rule, has gone too far in imposing the values of one group, due simply to their larger numbers, upon the values of others. The welfare state has gone too far, they argue, and it has undermined the American Dream and basic personal freedoms.

Critics on the left produce a different set of charges. They say the rich get richer, the poor get poorer. The rich are better treated before the law than the poor. Further, our tax system is regressive and most federal laws and regulations actually benefit the more prosperous in the nation.[3] The rich are also better represented in political decision-making bodies, such as legislatures or courts. Money alone may not buy elections, they say, but it buys just about all the political resources needed to gain information, influence voters, and shape the outcomes of public policy. Like money, freedom of expression is available to all, but in widely varying quantities. The rich have the time, the organizational knowhow, and the ability to hire experts (lobbyists, speechwriters, public relations firms), all of which allow them more access, more say, and hence more influence. The rich are more represented than the poor. A true democracy, say some of these critics, would necessitate a more equal distribution of the basic resources needed for real participation and valid representation.

Other, usually more moderate, voices have warned that the governability of America is threatened these days because of intense commitment to democratic and egalitarian ideals. They say, for example, that the effective operation of our political system requires some measure of apathy and noninvolvement. They point out that government needs to operate with a measure of secrecy, deception, and even manipulation, for in times of crisis government must have the political authority to impose upon its peoples certain necessary sacrifices. They quote John Adams, who said a democracy never lasts long: "It soon wastes, exhausts, and murders itself. There never was a democracy yet that did not commit suicide." In short, we must beware of the excesses of democracy. Just as we have come to recognize that there are potentially desirable limits to economic growth, we must realize "there are also potentially desirable limits to the indefinite extension of political democracy."[4]

We must nonetheless recognize certain realities. Many millions are still denied opportunity because of their race, ethnic background, and sex. An underclass persists in the form of impoverished families, ill-nourished and ill-educated children, and people living in the streets.[5] Many cities are actually "two cities"—thousands live in luxury, tens of thousands live in squalor. The gap between rich and poor has grown in recent years. The gap between rich farms and marginal farms has deepened. And a sharp difference between white and black income tenaciously persists. One's chances to succeed still depend, far more than we want to admit, on what block one grew up in.

To the extent we have failed to live up to our principles and the American Dream, can we identify the causes? Some may consider that the problem is the *values* themselves—their vagueness, superficiality, lack of popular support. Others might blame our *political system*—its built-in fragmentation and friction, its over-representation of the "haves" against the "have-nots," its domination by quarreling

"At the root of our disagreement, as I see it, is this: I hear America singing, and you *don't* hear America singing." (*Drawing by D. Reilly;* © *1985 The New Yorker Magazine, Inc.*)

[3] See Benjamin Page, *Who Gets What from Government* (University of California Press, 1983).

[4] Samuel Huntington, in Michel J. Crozier, Samuel P. Huntington, and Joji Wantanuki, *The Crisis of Democracy* (New York University Press, 1975), p. 115.

[5] For an analysis of one aspect of this, see Paul M. Sniderman and Michael Hagen, *Race and Inequality: A Study in American Values* (Chatham House, 1985).

politicians rather than far-seeing leaders. Still others might point to our *leadership* as lacking the concern, the skill, and the commitment necessary to convert our principles into down-to-earth performance.

All this has important implications for one other test of values: Can they be converted into clear guidelines for politicians in turn to convert them into policy and performance? Surely, the more we think through our values, define them, and rank them, the more effective such conversion will be. But even if our values are clear and explicit, are our politicians skillful enough to put them into practice? Are our leaders bold and creative enough? Our political system effective enough?

THE CASE FOR GOVERNMENT BY THE PEOPLE

The issues raised here are not frivolous. They pose fundamental questions about the health and direction of our political system. How faithfully does our democratic republic reflect the American Dream? Is that Dream still appropriate to the modern world? Is government of, by, and for the people a reality—or just another part of the myth? Following are some summary considerations, as well as some of our personal views.

The essence of our Constitution is that it both grants power to and withholds power from the national government. Fearing national weakness and popular disorder, the framers wanted to grant the government enough power to do its basic jobs, such as maintaining national defense and financial stability. Yet, valuing above all the principle of individual liberty, the framers also wanted to protect the people from too much government. They wanted a limited government—but one that would work. The solution was to make government responsive to the people—but not too responsive.

The first step was to distribute power among the three branches of government: legislative, executive, and judicial. The second was to leave extensive authority with state and local governments. Then the framers took a third step, the most brilliant and successful of all. Public officials were provided with different and competing constituencies to satisfy. The framers also assumed that the constituents themselves would be divided: Northerners versus Southerners, rich versus poor, city people versus country people. By their arrangement of offices, powers, and elections, the framers guaranteed that officials would compete and conflict with one another as they sought to please the voters.

The Liberty Bell. (*Independence National Historical Park Collection*)

This is not, of course, a very efficient system. But efficiency was not the main goal; the framers wanted a government that was safe. As the decades passed, the national government came under greater and greater pressure to perform effectively. The twentieth century in particular brought American involvement in vast global wars, depressions, and huge migrations of Europeans from abroad. There were also migrations of blacks and other rural people into northern cities, industrialization, and technological changes in transportation, communications, medicine, and education. Divided governments always have trouble pulling themselves together, but the American experiment had even more trouble. It is easy for leaders to "pass the buck." Certain arrangements also increased the power of political minorities: the filibuster in the Senate, for example, or the Supreme Court's power to declare national or state laws unconstitutional. The power of organized minorities to obstruct sharpened the whole question of a representative republic. If leaders acting for a majority of the people could not act—could not pass a gun-control law, for example, or obtain a constitutional amendment protecting the rights of women—was this really government by the people?

Most Americans now want a government that is efficient and effective—that gets things done. We want to maintain our commitment to liberty and freedom.

We want a government that acts for the majority but also protects minorities. We want to safeguard our nation in a world full of change and violence. We live in an era of rising demands on resources and declining supply, of widening concepts of the rights of the poor, the elderly, and others. Do we expect too much from government? Of course we do!

Democracy is a system of checks and balances. It continually balances values and competing dreams. We have to balance all individual liberties against the collective security and needs of society; we must also balance certain individual liberties against other individual liberties. The question is always which rights of which people are to be protected by what means and at what price.

PARTICIPATION AND REPRESENTATION

In essence, the challenge to the future of democracy is whether we can make our representative process work. No political problem is more complicated than this. For one thing, exact representation is impossible in the literal sense. Every man and woman has a host of conflicting desires, fears, hopes, and expectations; and no government can represent them all. Moreover, even if millions of voters could be represented in their billions of interests, the question would remain as to how they were to be represented. Through direct representation, such as a New England town meeting? Through economic or professional associations, such as labor unions or political-action committees? Through a coalition of minority groups? Through a direct popular majority? All these, and other alternatives can be defended as proper forms of representation in a pluralist democracy.

Some propose to bypass this thorny problem of representation by vastly increasing the role of direct popular participation in decision making. What many people would regard as the most perfect form of democracy exists when every person within a given group has a full and equal opportunity to participate in all decisions and in all the processes of influence, persuasion, and discussion that bear on that decision. Direct participation in decision making, its advocates contend, will serve two major purposes. It will enhance the dignity, self-respect, and understanding of individuals by giving them responsibility for the decisions that shape their lives. And it will act as a safeguard against antidemocratic and undemocratic forms of government and prevent the replacement of democracy by dictatorship or tyranny.[6] This idea rests on a theory of self-protection that says interests can be represented, furthered, and defended best by those whom they concern directly.

Experience with many forms of participatory democracy, however, suggests that it has limitations as a form of decision making. In an age of burgeoning population, increasingly complex economic and social systems, and enormously wide-ranging decision-making units of government, direct participation can work only in smaller communities or at the neighborhood level. As a practical matter, people simply cannot put in endless hours taking part in every decision that affects their lives.

Participatory democracy still has a great role in smaller units—in the running of colleges, communes, poverty organizations, local party committees, and the like. And perhaps the idea of participation should be greatly extended—for example, to greater control by workers over the running of factories. But we must distinguish between democracy as participation and a greater role for participation in a democracy. One course of action is to enlarge the role of participation in representation—that is, to broaden the power of all people to take part in local decision making and in choosing their representatives in larger units of government. And this brings us back to the hard questions of indirect representation.

[6] See Benjamin Barber, *Strong Democracy* (University of California Press, 1984).

To Protect the Dissenter

When one element in a pluralistic system becomes very powerful in relation to the others, the pluralism of the system itself is in danger. Even with the best of intentions, the dominant element is likely to squeeze out the other elements or render them impotent. . . .

So we have devised a variety of ways to protect the dissenter. Our civil liberties are a part of that system, and so are Robert's Rules of Order, and grievance procedures and the commonly held view that we should hear both sides of an argument. In short, we have a tradition, a set of attitudes and specific social arrangements designed to ensure that points of view at odds with prevailing doctrine will not be rejected out of hand.

But why be so considerate of dissent and criticism? To answer this question is to state one of the strongest tenets of our political philosophy. We do not expect organizations or societies to be above criticism nor do we trust the men who run them to be adequately self-critical. We believe that even those aspects of society that are healthy today may deteriorate tomorrow. We believe that power wielded justly today may be wielded corruptly tomorrow. We know that from the ranks of the critics come cranks and troublemakers, but from the same ranks come the saviors and innovators. And since the spirit that welcomes nonconformity is a fragile thing, we have not depended on that spirit alone. We have devised explicit legal and constitutional arrangements to protect the dissenter.

Source: John W. Gardner, *Self-Renewal* (Perennial Library edition, 1971), pp. 88–89.

If we must have representatives, who shall represent whom? Although this question can be answered in countless ways, in practice there are two basic ways to organize representation. By electing representatives in a multitude of local districts, it is possible to build into representative institutions—the American Congress, for example—most minority interests and attitudes found throughout the nation. The other way is through an election system that emphasizes majority representation. This can be achieved by creating a nationwide electorate that elects one representative (the American president, for example) or by developing a strong two-party system that knits all the local constituencies into coalitions that can elect and sustain national majorities. A nation does not have to choose between these alternatives. It can have both, as does the United States.

Which is better: a government that represents coalitions of minorities, or a government that represents a relatively clear-cut majority and has no obligation to the minority? The answer depends on what one expects from government. A system that represents coalitions of minorities usually reflects the trading, competition, and compromising that must take place in order to reach agreement among the various groups. Such a government has been called "broker rule"; the government acts essentially as a go-between, as a mediator among organized groups that have definite policy goals. Under broker rule leaders cannot get too far ahead of the groups; they must tack back and forth, shifting in response to changing group pressures. Instead of acting for a united popular majority with a fairly definite program, either liberal or conservative, the government tries to satisfy all major interests by giving them a voice in decisions and sometimes a veto over actions. In the pushing and hauling of political groups, the government is continually involved in delicate balancing acts.

Some critics believe in full representation of minority groups—in broker rule—but point out that fair representation has not been achieved in the American system. They point to the extent of nonvoting and other forms of nonparticipation in politics; the fact that low-income persons are less well organized in groups than upper-income persons; the bias of the stronger organized groups toward the status quo; the lack of competition among much of the news and opinion media, combined with the domination of television and the press by a few corporations; and the virtual monopoly of party politics by the two major parties, which do not always offer the voters meaningful alternatives. In the governmental system itself, critics note the devices in Congress that block majority will and overrepresent certain minorities; the distortion of representation embodied in the electoral college; and the power of the Supreme Court to invalidate laws demanded by popular majorities acting through the legislative and executive branches.

These charges may be exaggerated, but they cannot be denied, as the material in this book shows. Those who believe in fairer representation, however, can point to fairly steady improvement in recent years—for example, changes in election laws to simplify and extend voting, to enforce one-person–one-vote standards, and to renew political parties, especially in the conduct of presidential nominating conventions; efforts to regulate campaign finance; and some progress in Congress to strengthen majority rule.

By this point in the book you undoubtedly appreciate that democracy has to mean much more than popular government and unchecked majority rule. A democracy needs competing politicians with competing conceptions of the public interest. A vital democracy, living and growing, places its faith in the voters, faith that they will not just elect people who will mirror their views, but that they will elect leaders who will exercise their best judgment—"faith that the people will not condemn those whose devotion to principle leads them to unpopular courses, but will reward courage, respect honor, and ultimately recognize right."[7]

[7] John F. Kennedy, *Profiles in Courage* (Pocket Books, 1956), p. 108.

Americans have mixed views about their elected officials. We realize they are skillful at compromising, mediating, negotiating, "brokering"—and that governing often requires these qualities. But can there be too much of a good thing? Americans suspect politicians of being ambitious, conniving, unprincipled, opportunistic, and even corrupt—"just into politics for what they can get out of it for themselves." Not long ago a board game similar to *Monopoly* was invented and marketed with the cynical title *Lie, Cheat and Steal: The Game of Political Power*.

Yet we often find individual office holders to be responsive, bright, hardworking, and friendly (even though we may suspect they are simply trying to get out the vote). And our liking often turns into reverence after these same politicians depart or die. Surely Washington, Lincoln, Eisenhower, and John F. Kennedy are acclaimed today. Harry Truman liked to say that a statesman is merely a politician who has been dead for about ten years.

Of course, we must put the problem in perspective. In all democracies (perhaps even more in democracies) the public may expect too much from politicians. Further, people naturally dislike those who wield power. Public office holders, after all, tax us, regulate us, and conscript us. We dislike political compromisers, bargainers, and ambitious opportunists—even though we may need such people to get things done.

One of us has been conducting surveys in recent years on what people think of *the typical American politician*. Eighty percent of the responses are negative. Consider these responses: The typical American politician is "male, middle-aged, and usually a lawyer," authoritarian, power hungry, on an ego trip, slick, two-faced, outgoing, glib-talkative, superficial, evasive, self-serving, an opportunist, manipulative, preoccupied with getting elected, "listens to voters when he thinks they might be angry enough to vote him out of office," and promises too much.

When asked to describe *the ideal American politician*, people responded very differently. Common responses were as follows: The ideal American politician is honest, humble, patriotic, compassionate, sensitive to the needs of others, well-informed/competent, fair-minded, objective, intellectually honest, a good listener, candid, a good mediator, self-confident, inspiring, "a candidate of the people, not of the money," courageous enough to stand up to special interests, "someone who doesn't want power but leads because he is called upon to exercise his talents for the public good," and "does the job and gets out when finished."

Why the gap between our expectations about the typical and the ideal politician? The gap exists in part because we have overly high expectations. We want politicians to be perfect, to have all the answers, and to have all the right (in our minds) opinions. It is impossible for anyone to live up to these ideals. Politicians, like all individuals, live in a real world in which perfection may be a goal—but compromises, ambition, fund-raising, and self-promotion are necessary. Our "ideal leaders" are usually dead: Time makes myths and irons out the wrinkles. We want politicians to solve our worst problems, but we also want them to be the scapegoats for all the things we dislike about government: taxes, regulations, and any limitations on our freedom.

Politicians are absolutely necessary to run a democracy—certainly the American republic whose fragmented powers require politicians to mediate among factions, build coalitions, and compromise among and within branches of government to produce policy. But are such politicians adequate? Do we not also need *leaders* who can rise above everyday "wheeling and dealing" and lead the nation through great crises—or, better yet, plan ahead to avert such crises?

Assessments of Various Professions' Honesty and Ethical Standards

	Percent Answering High
Clergymen	67%
Druggists, pharmacists	65
Medical doctors	58
Dentists	56
College teachers	54
Engineers	53
Policemen	47
Bankers	37
TV reporters, commentators	33
Funeral directors	31
Journalists	31
Newspaper reporters	29
Lawyers	27
Business executives	23
U.S. Senators	23
Stockbrokers	20
Building contractors	20
Congressmen	20
Local political officeholders	18
Realtors	15
State political officeholders	15
Labor union leaders	13
Advertising practitioners	12
Insurance salesmen	10
Car salesmen	5

Source: *Gallup Report* 1985 nationwide survey of adults.

WHAT KIND OF POLITICAL LEADERSHIP?

"They're all out taking polls to see which way you want to be led." (*Drawing by Tom Engelhardt, May 14, 1978, The St. Louis Post-Dispatch*)

Can we generalize about the leadership abilities of those who are elected today? Although the concept of leadership—like many other concepts in political science—is broad and hazy, we can break it down to distinguish among *agitators*, *coalition builders*, and *office holders*.

Types of Leaders

Agitators or people who instigate movements, as noted in Chapter 8, arouse people's consciousness of their needs and problems, raise their hopes and expectations, organize or take leadership of political and social movements, and mobilize grass-roots pressure on government from the outside. Movement leaders are often considered crusaders or even prophets, whether they are abolitionists, women's suffrage leaders, antislavery leaders such as William Lloyd Garrison, or conservatives such as California's crusading tax cutter the late Howard Jarvis.[8]

Coalition builders are usually intent on winning elections, whereas agitators are more concerned with mobilizing groups of people who may or may not take part in elections. Coalition builders must knit together a variety of groups inside the process and movements in order to build a majority that can carry elections. Hence, such leaders tend to be power brokers, widening their political appeals as broadly as possible without becoming *too* thin or flabby, accommodating single-interest or single-cause groups or movements with intense concerns, and building compromise party platforms.

Office holders are in a mixed position to exercise leadership: They have the authority that goes with their offices, but they must try not to alienate elements of the electoral majority they will need at the next election. They dare not be too far in advance of their times. Their behavior under these circumstances may be closely affected by the political system. Presidents, for example, may wish not to worry about their electoral majorities until the last years of their terms, but they have to consider the midterm elections for senators and representatives. Because the latter too have to think about winning the next election in a year or two, most almost constantly refurbish their electoral majorities. Senators, with their six-year tenures, can think in somewhat longer terms.

The relationship between John F. Kennedy, office holder, and Martin Luther King, Jr., movement leader, exemplifies the diversity of leadership. Even though Kennedy raised civil rights issues during his campaign for the presidency in 1960, he never accorded them top priority in his program; rather, he held off making major civil rights proposals until he could get his economic program through Congress. In the meantime King and other black leaders were protesting, demonstrating, encountering violence, appealing to northern and southern public opinion, and putting intense pressure on Kennedy and other federal officials to protect their civil rights and especially to put through legislation that would protect their right to vote. As a result of this kind of *movement* pressure, by 1963 Kennedy was appealing to Congress for civil rights legislation. He worked closely with King and other civil rights leaders through his brother Robert, the attorney general, and at the same time tried to maintain old-time Democratic party coalitions of northerners and white southerners. Movement leaders like King put pressure on the government

---

[8] See, for example, Charles Madison, *Critics and Crusaders* (Holt, 1947); Saul Alinsky, *Rules for Radicals* (Random House, 1972); and Harvey Goldberg, ed., *American Radicals: Some Problems and Personalities* (Monthly Review Press, 1957). On Howard Jarvis, see Jarvis, *Mad as Hell!* (Times Books, 1979). See also Edward N. Kearney, *Mavericks in American Politics* (MIMIR Publishers, 1976).

from the outside—while also working with Attorney General Robert Kennedy and others from the inside. After JFK's assassination, office holders like President Lyndon B. Johnson, together with congressional leaders, built a broad coalition of blacks, liberals, and moderate whites that helped to put the Civil Rights Act of 1964 and the Voting Rights Act of 1965 into law.[9]

Politicians as Brokers

Most American politicians hardly aspire to such grand leadership roles as movement founders or coalition builders. They work at the grass roots as city council members, sheriffs, state legislators, district attorneys, and county commissioners. As such they are popular targets for cartoonists and others who picture them as ridiculous, confused, and addled—and above all as ignorant and incompetent. Most of these portraits, especially the last two, are caricatures. The average politician in office has an alert, shrewd, calculating mind.

THINKING ABOUT LEADERSHIP

An adequate democratic theory recognizes that democracy is not self-executing. A democracy needs leaders who have a sense of the past and who are willing to share their competing conceptions of the public interest.

Even though one of the most universal cravings of our time is a hunger for creative and compelling leadership, defining creative leadership is a challenge in itself. Leadership can be understood only in the context of both leaders and followers—a leader without followers is a contradiction in terms. Leadership is also situational and contextual. A person is often effective in only one kind of situation. Leadership is not necessarily transferable. James Madison, for example, was a brilliant political and constitutional theorist. He was also a superb founding politician. Still, he was not a particularly able presidential leader. The leadership required to lead a marine platoon up a hill in battle is different from the leadership needed to change racist, sexist attitudes in city or community governments. The leadership required of a campaign manager differs from that required of a candidate. Leaders of thought are not always effective as leaders of action.

Although leaders are often skilled managers, they often need more than just managerial skills. Managers do things *the right way*, whereas leaders are more concerned, or perhaps more preoccupied, with doing *the right thing*—that is, they are more concerned with the longer range, with the purposes and ends of a society or an organization. Put another way, managers are concerned with efficiency, and with keeping things going, especially routines and standard operating procedures. Leaders, on the other hand—in addition to having certain managerial skills—also are inventors, risk takers, and entrepreneurs. Further, they are morale builders who can infuse values and purpose into the mission of their community or nation.

Leaders have those indispensable qualities of contagious self-confidence, unwarranted optimism, and incurable idealism that attract others, and mobilize them to undertake tasks they never dreamed they could accomplish. In short, transcending or **transforming leaders** empower others, and enable many of their followers to become leaders in their own right. Most of the significant breakthroughs in our nation (as well as in our communities) have been made (or shaped) by people who, while seeing all the complexities and obstacles ahead of them, believed in

What Are the Most Important Qualities of a Leader?

No one knows—so much depends on the context, the challenge, and the need. Still, the following qualities or skills are often cited as critically important. (But none of these guarantees leadership effectiveness.)

Self-knowledge
Self-confidence
Optimism/hope
Sensitivity/empathy
Stamina/energy
Tenacity/persistence
Integrity
Vision
Imagination
Judgment
Risk taking
Morale building
Coalition building
Negotiating/mediating
Communicating
Breadth/creativity
Concern for results
Sense of humor
Enjoyment of people

[9] See Herbert S. Parmet, *The Presidency of John F. Kennedy* (Dial Press, 1983). See also Stephen B. Oates, *Let the Trumpets Sound! The Life of Martin Luther King, Jr.* (Harper & Row, 1982); and Harris Wofford, *Of Kennedys & Kings* (Farrar, Straus & Giroux, 1980).

Two of America's effective politicians, President Eisenhower and his successor, John F. Kennedy, shown in high hats as they leave the White House for the Capitol, where Kennedy was to take his oath of office on January 20, 1961. (*UPI/ Bettmann Newsphotos*)

themselves and in their purposes so much that they refused to be overwhelmed and paralyzed by self-doubts. They were willing to gamble, to take risks, to look at things in a fresh way, and often to invent new rules.[10]

Leaders must recognize the fundamental—unexpressed as well as felt—wants and needs of potential followers. By bringing followers to a fuller consciousness of their needs, they help convert the resulting hopes and aspirations into practical demands on other leaders (especially leaders in government). Leaders must also sense when people are ready for action. A leader in a democracy consults and listens while educating followers and attempting to renew the goals of an organization.

Leaders must also be sensitive to the distinctions between *power* and *authority*. Power is the strength or raw force to exercise control or coerce someone to do something. Authority is power that is accepted as legitimate by subordinates or constituents. The whole issue of leadership raises countless questions about participation in and acceptance of power in superior-subordinate, or leader-led, relationships. How best can leaders earn and sustain moral and social acceptance for their authority? Americans generally prize participation in all kinds of organizations, especially in civic and political life. Yet a part of us yearns for charismatic leaders—decisive, attractive leaders who will simplify problems and relieve us of the burdens of leadership. Ironically, however, savior figures and charismatic leaders often—indeed almost always—create distance, not participation.

Ultimately two overriding kinds of political leadership exist: *transactional leadership* and *transformational leadership*. The transactional leader engages in an exchange, usually a short-term bargain: "I'll vote for your bill if you'll vote for mine." Or "You raise money for my campaign and I'll help get your daughter a state job after I'm elected." Most political office holders practice transactional leadership as a practical necessity. It is the common means of doing business. The transforming leader is the person who, as we discussed earlier, so engages with followers as to bring them to heightened political consciousness and activity, and in the process converts many of them into leaders in their own right.[11]

The transforming leader is usually preoccupied with the longer term and is, as a rule, less interested in selfish gains than in community or societal improvements. The transforming leader is also in many ways an educator or teacher who points out the possibilities and the hopes and dreams of a people. Is it possible for most elected political officials to exercise transforming leadership? Does transforming leadership require a special set of circumstances, or a special set of personal qualities, or possibly certain kinds of constitutional and structural arrangements?

Politicians As Leaders

One reason we are often so skeptical or even cynical toward politicians is that we fail to appreciate the importance of politics and the limits or constraints within which politicians must work. Office holding politicians are in many ways **Act III leaders**. Most plays have three acts. In politics, different tasks or different periods often seem to require different kinds of political leaders.

Act I leaders are the *crowd gatherers* or *agitators*. They stir things up and thus are often viewed as cranks and troublemakers—Patrick Henry, Sam Adams, and Tom Paine, for example. Also in this category are John Brown (in the pre-Civil War days), Rap Brown (in the early civil rights protests of the 1960s), and Saul Alinsky (in urban protests).

Act II leaders are *coalition builders*. Often unelected and even unelectable,

Observations on John F. Kennedy by Martin Luther King, Jr.

"The basic thing about him—he had the ability to respond to creative pressure."

"I never wanted—and I told him this—to be in the position that I couldn't criticize him if I thought he was wrong."

"And Kennedy said, 'it often helps me to be pushed.'"

"When he saw the power of the movement, he didn't stand there arguing about it. He had the vision and wisdom to see the problem in all of its dimensions and the courage to do something about it."

Source: T. George Harris, "The Competent American," *Look* (November 17, 1964).

[10] See Thomas E. Cronin, "Thinking and Learning About Leadership," *Presidential Studies Quarterly* (Winter 1984), pp. 22–34.

[11] These distinctions are outlined in detail in James MacGregor Burns, *Leadership* (Harper & Row, 1978), chaps. 1 and 2.

One of the few photographs that show four presidents of the United States. From the left, John F. Kennedy, Lyndon B. Johnson, Dwight D. Eisenhower, and Harry S Truman. (*UPI/Bettmann Newsphotos*)

they galvanize movements and coalitions in such a way that politicians heed their messages. Martin Luther King, Jr., Susan B. Anthony, and the leaders of the contemporary balanced-budget amendment and nuclear freeze movements are examples.

Act III leaders typically are *the elected officials*. Some have highly publicized and sometimes even glamorous careers; but theirs are also often the hardest, least secure, and least rewarding careers. They have to be ambitious, and willing to assume frantic lifestyles. Yet they also have to be brokers, ever-sensitive to the policy views of pluralities and majorities. As elected representatives they cannot be too innovative. They usually have to be balancers and bargainers, and to reconcile competing claims of what is in "the public interest." Act III types have to follow public opinion as well as mold or shape it. They are usually more constrained than other kinds of political leaders. They depend on Act I and II leaders for fresh ideas and novel approaches to public problems.

Our elected officials are bold enough to step forward in the midst of endless controversies and give it a try. This requires ambition—a trait often not much admired. Politicians are usually self-selected. Ambition, however, lies at the heart of politics. One widely held ethical position is that politics ought not to revolve around personal ambition. Intellectuals insistently demand that political leaders be motivated by high principles or ideology. Shame to those who might run and win office to satisfy personal ambitions! But we ought to take another look at the important role of ambition. Personal ambition sparks just about any person's efforts to excel. It motivates the great problem solvers just as it motivates the great runners and the great composers.

Saul Alinsky (right) organized the poor and dispossessed for more than twenty years before he turned his attention to the middle class a few years ago. Here he shakes hands with black power advocate Stokely Carmichael after both shared the same platform in Detroit on January 18, 1967. (*UPI/Bettmann Newsphotos*)

If elected politicians often seem bewildered in dealing with controversial issues in these confusing times, so are the rest of us. If elected officials sometimes make mistakes, so do the rest of us. If they sometimes postpone things rather than directly confront them, so do we all. The late Senator Everett Dirksen of Illinois offered a helpful perspective on politicians:

> Politics is not something you can afford to leave to 'other people.' Since politics is the art of ordering the affairs of men through government, it should be the vocation of the very best in this Republic and the avocation of all.
>
> There have been many who seem to equate politics with that which is bad, that which is corrupt, that which is venal, and that which is corrosive of our moral fiber. I find that throughout history most such disparaging remarks are made by those who never dared seek elective office.
>
> To scorn all politicians and to decry their actions is to scorn those who elect them and support them—namely the citizen-elector.[12]

[12] Quoted in Conrad Joyner, *The American Politician* (University of Arizona Press, 1971). See also many of the essays in Paul Tillett, ed., *The Political Vocation* (Basic Books, 1965).

The American people will never be completely satisfied with their politicians, nor should they be. The ideal politician is truly a fictional character, for the ideal politician would be able to please absolutely everyone and to make conflicts absolutely disappear. Such a person could exist only in an extremely small community in which all the people shared the same ideas, ideals, and interests. But American liberties invite diversity and, therefore, conflict. Politicians as well as the people they represent have different ideas about what is best for the nation. After all, who is really to say what is good for anyone else—let alone for *everyone* else? That's why we have politicians and politics. To understand this is to better appreciate the delicate and crucial responsibilities entrusted to our elected Act III politicians.[13]

DEMOCRATIC LEADERSHIP

Our challenge of reconciling democracy and leadership is part definitional and part attitudinal. Too often in the past we have held a view of leaders as hierarchical, male, and upon whom followers are overly dependent. That conception is antithetical to our democratic aspirations. A nation of subservient followers can never be a democratic one. A democratic nation requires educated, skeptical, caring, engaged, and contentious citizen-leaders.

Such a democratic citizen-leader appreciates that power wielded justly today may be wielded corruptly tomorrow. The democratic citizen-leader is moved to protest when he or she knows a policy is wrong or when other citizens find their rights diminished. This leader appreciates that criticism of official error is not criticism of our country. Citizen-leaders recognize as well that democracy rests solidly upon a mixed view of human nature. Man's capacity for justice, as Reinhold Niebuhr observed, makes democracy possible. But man's inclination to injustice makes democracy necessary.

Democratic politics is the forum or arena for excellence and responsibility, where—by acting together—citizens become free. In this sense, politics is not a necessary evil, it is a realistic goal. It is the preoccupation of free people, and its existence is a test of freedom.

Thus democratic leadership can be enabling and facilitating. Leadership, thought of as an engagement among equals, a collegial collaboration, can empower

Leadership for a Change

[13] See Bernard Crick, *In Defense of Politics*, rev. ed. (Pelican Books, 1983), and Stimson Bullitt, *To Be a Politician*, rev. ed. (Yale University Press, 1977).

- To solve problems and promote the "American Dream"—enhancing liberty and justice
- To advance fresh ideas and approaches
- To "throw some rascal out" whose views you dislike
- To gain a voice in policy making

- To serve as a party spokesperson
- To acquire political influence and a platform from which to influence public opinion
- To gain prominence and power
- To satisfy ego needs

- To gain the opportunity to learn, grow, travel, and meet all kinds of people
- To be where the "action is"—involved in the thick of government and political life—campaigning, debating, drafting laws, reconciling diverse views, and making the system responsive.

and liberate people, and enlarge their options, choices, and freedoms. The answer for our republic lies not in producing a handful of great, charismatic, Mt. Rushmore leaders, but in educating a citizenship who can boast that we are no longer in need of great leaders, because we have become a nation of citizens who believe that one person can make a difference, and that every person should endeavor to do so.

THE DEMOCRATIC FAITH

Susan B. Anthony. (*UPI/Bettmann Newsphotos*)

The ultimate test of a democratic system is the legal existence of an *officially recognized opposition*. A cardinal characteristic of a democracy is that it not only recognizes the need for the free organization of opposing views but even positively encourages this organization. Freedom for political expression and dissent is basic—even freedom for nonsense to be spoken so that good sense not yet recognized gets a chance to be heard.

Crucial to the democratic faith is the belief that a democracy cherishes the free play of ideas. Only where the safety valve of public discussion is available and where almost any policy is subject to perpetual questioning and challenge can there be the assurance that both minority and majority rights will be served. To be afraid of public debate is to be afraid of self-government.

"Rulers always have and always will find it dangerous to their security to permit people to think, believe, talk, write, assemble, and particularly to criticize the government as they please," says Supreme Court Justice William J. Brennan, "but the language of the First amendment indicates the framers weighed the risk

- Loss of privacy for you and your family
- Less time to spend with families or favorite pastimes
- Less income than in many business or professional occupations
- Exposure to partisan and media criticism
- Campaigning involves many things most people would

rather not do—like marching in countless parades, attending county fairs, going to endless political dinners, banquets, service club meetings, and so on
- Rewards of serving in office appear meager
- Fear that one may have to compromise one's principles because of the complexity of our adversarial system

- Campaigning can often be expensive
- Some people don't want to show their ambitions, and they don't like conflict and divisiveness
- Some people think the constitutional structure and the party systems we now have make it nearly impossible to exercise meaningful leadership

James Madison. Madison is famous for his noted role at the Constitutional Convention and served as our fourth president. He also served effectively in Congress and as a party leader, and is remembered for his practical contributions to representative government. Read his brilliant *Federalist* essays Nos. 10 and 51, found in the Appendix to this book. (*New York Public Library Picture Collection*)

"The Athenians are here, Sire, with an offer to back us with ships, money, arms, and men—and, of course, their usual lectures about democracy." (*Drawing by Ed Fisher; © 1983 The New Yorker Magazine, Inc.*)

involved in such freedoms and deliberately chose to stake this government's security and life upon preserving liberty to discuss public affairs intact and untouched by government."[14]

We hold with Jefferson that there is nothing in the country so radically wrong that it cannot be cured by good newspapers and sound schoolmasters. Inform and educate the citizenry, and a major hurdle is overcome. Jefferson had boundless faith in education. He believed that people are rationally endowed by nature with an innate sense of justice; the average person has only to be informed to act wisely. In the long run, said Jefferson, only an educated and enlightened democracy can hope to endure.

James Bryce, an English citizen who visited our nation 100 years ago, observed that America represents an experiment in the rule of the multitude, tried on a vast scale. Yet, he added, it is something more than just an American experiment, for the rest of the world is watching.

Yet America is nonetheless an experiment. Every institution and policy is at best a reasonable approximation of what might work. Americans must constantly check their experiences to see how well or how badly our experiment is working. Experience, said James Madison, is the guide that ought always to be followed whenever it can be found. We must stand ready to preserve what is working and change what is not.

The American Dream that lured so many millions to our shores is not just a dream of material plenty. It is a dream of self-government, of tolerance of diverse races and ethnic backgrounds, and of individual freedom and opportunity. The framers embarked upon a great gamble—whether a more perfect union of peoples could develop trusting relations and institutions of governance they could hold to account. The American Dream welcomed diversity and encouraged inclusiveness. The triumph of America is the triumph of a coalescing federal system. Unity and disunity, uniformity and diversity, cooperation and conflict, these are basic elements in American society. The democratic faith cherishes the diversity in unity; it looks for the unity in diversity.

We are a restless, dissatisfied, and searching people. We are our own toughest critics. Our political system is far from perfect, but it still is an open system. People can fight city hall. People who disagree with policies in the nation can band together and be heard. We know only too well that the American Dream is never something fully attained, and it is certainly not something inherited: It is always something to be achieved. Ultimately, we the people will determine whether we can make a government by the people work. We need enormous stamina and democratic faith to do so.

Our future will be shaped by those who care about making and preserving our political rights and freedoms. Our individual liberties will never be assured unless there are people willing to take considerable personal responsibility for the progress of the whole community, and people willing to exercise their determination and democratic faith. Carved in granite on one of the long corridors in a building on the Harvard College campus are these words of American poet Archibald MacLeish: "How shall freedom be defended? By arms when it is attacked by arms; by truth when it is attacked by lies, by democratic faith when it is attacked by authoritarian dogma. Always, in the final act, by determination and faith."

Millions of Americans tour through the great monuments in our nation's capital each year. They admire the beauty and are always impressed by the memorials to Washington, Jefferson, Lincoln, and the Vietnam veterans, the Capitol, the Supreme Court, and the White House. The strength of the nation, however, resides not in these official buildings but in the hearts, minds, and behavior of citizens.

[14] William J. Brennan, Commencement Address, Brandeis University (May 18, 1986).

Independence Hall, Philadelphia. (*Philadelphia Convention & Visitors' Bureau*)

Walt Whitman, poet (1819–1892). Known for his free verse and his often mystical celebration of America, democracy, and the common person. (*UPI/Bettmann Newsphotos*)

If they lose faith, stop caring, stop participating, and stop believing in the possibilities of self-government, the monuments "will be meaningless piles of stone, and the venture that began with the Declaration of Independence, the venture familiarly known as America will be as lifeless as the stone."[15]

One thing is certain amid all the murk. The celebrations and the traumas, the advances and failures, the processes and institutions of "a government by the people"—as contrasted with something called "the state" in other lands—are inseparable from the daily lives and hopes and needs of 250 million Americans. No one has made this argument more eloquently than Walt Whitman, in his "By Blue Ontario's Shore":

O I see flashing that this America is only you and me,
Its power, weapons, testimony, are you and me.
Its crimes, lies, thefts, defections, are you and me,
Its Congress is you and me, the officers, capitols, armies, ships are you and me.
Its endless gestation of new states are you and me,
The war (that war so bloody and grim, the war I will henceforth forget),
    was you and me,
Freedom, language, poems, employments, are you and me,
Past, present, future, are you and me,
I dare not shirk any part of myself,
Nor any part of America good or bad. . . .

[15] John W. Gardner, *Self-Renewal* (Norton, 1981), Preface, p. xiv.

Getting Involved

Government by the people is just about the most exacting venture any nation can undertake. Washington, Adams, Jefferson, Hamilton, and Franklin, and their compatriots, surely knew this. Exhilarating, demanding, and frustrating, the burden falls on a large number of us if we would make constitutional democracy work.

Two hundred years ago, in simpler times, people in politics (mostly white, well-to-do males) could see the results of their participation, especially in small communities and even in their states. Today we have sixty-five times as many people, political participation has been opened to all citizens 18 or older, and the issues are complex and interrelated. It is more difficult to see the consequences of what one does. Yet we need, perhaps more than ever, large numbers of citizen-politicians to help make government and political processes work. Those who want to help can find plenty of opportunities. Here are a few suggestions and strategies.

RUNNING FOR OFFICE

The United States has several hundred thousand elective offices. One of the difficulties in our democracy is finding talented people of integrity to run for office. Most Americans have little or no interest in running for any elective post. Some are willing to serve but not to run. The personal sacrifices political life demands—less privacy, less time for families or for relaxation, more dangers to health, and often lower income—are more than most people are willing to make.

What makes for success? Certainly, luck plays a role in determining one's success in a political career. Optimists define luck as "when preparation meets opportunity," suggesting that luck may not be wholly random; some people make themselves luckier than others. This element of chance, along with the obvious lack of job security, often stops able people from even considering electoral politics. People who enter politics must realize they will have to live dangerously. In business the line between the red and the black divides anxiety and comfort, yet a businessperson can survive a bad year; in politics 0.1 percent of one's gross vote can mean the difference between success and ruin. Before entering politics, you would be wise to reflect on your personal strengths and weaknesses. If you are sensitive to criticism, shy, and short-tempered, and if you prefer to lead a quiet, peaceful life, the chances are strong you will neither be happy in politics nor able to develop the kind of temperament essential for elective public service today.

What can you do if you choose to seek political office? You can work actively in the campaigns of others to see at first hand the challenge of winning a nomination and then an election. You should also read widely in history, politics, economics, and philosophy, know how to use parables, develop an excellent memory, study the major issues of the day, cultivate the leadership of major organizations in your region, and develop as fully as possible the capacity to listen and to learn.

Former political leaders advise the following for those who would like to be active in politics and public affairs:

1. Become informed about the issues and the values and aspirations of the people in your area.

2. Always be honest. Integrity is probably the most important asset for a public servant.

3. Be patient but also persistent.

4. Exhibit and nurture self-confidence and a healthy self-esteem.

5. Always be tolerant and civil, even to your opponents. Today's foe may be tomorrow's ally.

6. Be able to show that you sincerely like and enjoy people.

7. Take your work and responsibilities seriously, but do not take yourself too seriously. Arrogance and overbearing pride undermine your ability to be effective in politics.

8. Be courageous and willing to take a stand and do what you believe is right, even if it is not the trendy or popular sentiment. Leadership involves educating and shaping public opinion in addition to being responsive.

9. Begin by helping people in your own community. Some say that "all politics is local." That is an overstatement, but you should settle down somewhere and work in local campaigns. Develop an understanding of the people, the problems, the issues, and the politics of your home region.

An important lesson learned time and again is that by finding out the rules and simply getting enough people to the right caucuses, preconvention meetings, party gatherings, and the polls, newcomers to politics can get themselves elected to important posts. Yet the rules are often difficult to figure out. Rarely is a candidacy successfully launched and brought to fruition in a few weeks. There is a long list of celebrated, successful politicians who won office only after losing election bids one or several times.

As a candidate for office you should also learn how to use several different advisers, and you should know the danger of listening to only one set of counselors. Many younger politicians find themselves surrounded by people who act more like cheerleaders than candid advisers.

Candidates these days are more and more dependent on campaign consultants, fundraisers, and media advisers. A whole new profession of people who help get individuals elected to office has emerged with the developing technologies of polling, television, VCRs, and direct-mail solicitations. Good political strategists can also make important contributions to the quality of our politics and parties.

ADVISING ON PUBLIC POLICIES

For many, elective politics is not the best way to contribute to government by the people. If you have specialized knowledge, you may prefer other alternatives.

Public officials and career public servants at all levels of government usually welcome advice on public policy. In practice, most officials conduct hearings, appoint study groups, and establish advisory committees; they frequently have small sums of money available for consultant studies as well. For the citizen-activist who wants to change existing policies or help pass and establish new policies, there are many opportunities to obtain a hearing and press his or her arguments.

It is important to remember, however, that especially in a democracy the well-researched argument may carry less weight than the political one. Whether an adviser believes a policy is "right" may be less important to many officials than how the policy will affect career or reelection chances. Politicians properly fear being too much out in front or out of line with those who elect them.

Every community needs a loose coalition of people willing to work together, often on a nonpartisan basis, to examine and offer policy advice on urgent local problems. What is needed are citizen-advisers who will apply their professional skills as well as their common sense to such issues. Help is also needed in assisting those in office to promote equitable and effective programs in areas such as tax reform, consumer protection, jobs, and so on.

Citizen-advisers, to be sure, will often be disillusioned by the clumsiness with which politicians and bureaucrats use advice; yet the adviser will also learn that knowledge is power. Most people in public office are receptive to constructive ideas. Anyone who is willing to undertake systematic policy and program evaluations and who can present convincing rationales for dealing with the realities will find a ready audience. If you can design cars that will cause less smog, invent more efficient ways

to produce energy and conserve natural resources, or formulate better foreign policies, you will find politicians knocking at your door.

You will learn too that once you have gained recognition and visibility in your field, your ability to influence officials is that much greater. You can help organize coalitions of experts. You can use your acknowledged expertise to educate other citizens to support or oppose government programs. You should also be concerned with the often inadequate means of putting programs into action. In the best of situations you will not only come up with new ideas but also develop new ways of turning these ideas into successful programs.

PRESSURE OR PROTEST POLITICS

The best insurance system for honest government is an alert citizenry, watchful of its leaders and increasingly imaginative in developing new means to keep public officials and party leaders accountable and within the Constitution. Government by the people need not be a utopia unrelated to present-day processes and politics.

The American political system is often biased in favor of producer interests and against the concerns of consumers. It often favors the wealthy and educated against the poor and ignorant. This has become well recognized, but it does not have to be accepted.

To choose pressure politics means to try to influence those who already hold power, who sit in official seats. Here again there are few established rules. Tactics differ markedly—from the nuclear freeze sit-ins and Saul Alinsky kind of militance on the one hand, to the less militant techniques of a Ralph Nader study report and of the League of Women Voters on the other. Certain general strategies are similar. Do not assume that all officials, media people, and outsiders will be hostile. Explore alliances and coalitions with other related groups. Make every effort to increase the membership's understanding of how government works and what the issues are.

PARTY POLITICS

Though you may have little interest in seeking a political or career job in government, you should consider taking an

active role in a political party. Parties need strengthening at every level. The country needs party politicians to hunt out good candidates, help elect them, and then to remind those elected of their responsibilities to those who elected them.

Jeffersonian Republicans and Democrats dreamed a great dream—that a party system could be effective, could raise issues for rational deliberation, and could build coalitions to achieve a more just and decent society. Seldom have our parties lived up to the Jeffersonian dream. Seldom have they served to discipline the whims of those in public office who have lost touch with the people. But if we have not lived up to the Jeffersonian hopes, this does not mean that parties are unimportant. We can still build a healthy, competitive party system that will recruit able public servants, spur provocative debate over national priorities, and inspire honesty in government.

The first step for citizen-activists is to call local party officials and find out their views, objectives, and organizational routines. If you disagree with their views, your initial work is clear. If you agree, they will probably welcome you and sign you up for some subcommittee or future campaign assignment.

One important job in party politics is enlarging the number of the party faithful. Getting people out to vote is equally important. Identification systems have to be devised. Names and addresses of those not registered must be obtained. Records of those who have moved away from and into the community must be continually updated. Registration laws vary from state to state. The unregistered voter is sometimes apathetic, yet in most states our complex system of registration also discourages many people who are interested in voting. They often do not know when or where they can register, what the registration deadlines are, and when and how they must affiliate with a particular party in order to participate directly in party caucuses and primaries. The shrewd party activist will know the answers to these questions.

The heart of registration and voting drives lies in approaching the voters in person, but the approach is much more effective if it comes as part of a general effort. Often the best procedure is a nonpartisan communitywide program. Much of this work would be simple drudgery under any other circumstances. In the heat of a campaign, however, it often takes on an aura of drama. Volunteers are part of a team engaged in a struggle. Party headquarters are always crowded; the phones seem always to be ringing. Crisis follows crisis. Candidates dash in to make arrangements for television spots and rush out to speak at the Kiwanis Club's annual barbecue. Rumors flow thick and fast.

Taking part in party politics can be a rewarding business, especially if, ideally, you have helped to nominate and elect the names on the ballot. However, new activists should go into party politics with a realistic view of how parties operate. On the local level organizations are often stagnant. Committees sometimes meet irregularly, and attendance is typically low. By and large, the parties are run by small groups of people. Often the power over such crucial matters as candidate selection, allocation of convention delegates, and campaign finances becomes centralized in the hands of a few state and county party insiders.

Party veterans often try to run campaigns by offering something for everyone, while at the same time saying nothing that will offend anyone. Typically they attempt to capture as many differing viewpoints and fence-sitting independents as they can. If parties today are often not as democratic as they could be in their internal activities, this can be changed. If corruption and the influence of wealthy individuals or organized groups are excessive, this too can be changed.

Old-line leaders may try to close out newcomers to keep the organization a kind of private preserve. Yet turnover in local and state party posts is higher than most people think. Affirmative action rules are helping to open the parties up. And many states have a variety of factions within the two major parties. If necessary, you can often work with another part of the organization or join or form a reform group.

VOLUNTEER SERVICE OPPORTUNITIES

The Peace Corps recruits from a wide range of skilled Americans for overseas work. "What in the world are you doing?" asks an effective Peace Corps recruiting poster. Think about it. After screening and training, volunteers are assigned to countries that request Peace Corps services. Applicants must be 18 years of age or older. Volunteers receive no salaries but get allowances to cover the cost of clothing, housing, food, and incidental expenses. Upon completion of service, Peace Corps volunteers receive a separation allotment based on time spent overseas. Further information and applications can be obtained by writing, Peace Corps, Washington, D.C. 20526.

Volunteers in Service to America (VISTA) is the domestic counterpart of the Peace Corps. Volunteers lend their talents for a year to communities that are striving to solve pressing economic and social problems. After a training period that stresses supervised field experience, volunteers are sent to work in communities of migrant workers, Indian reservations, rural and urban community-action programs, hospitals, schools, and mental health facilities. In short, workers may be sent wherever poverty exists. VISTA volunteers are paid only subsistence expenses and modest monthly stipends and personal allowances.

The several federal volunteer programs are consolidated in a national agency called ACTION. ACTION administers, VISTA, the National Student Volunteer Program, Foster Grandparents, the Retired Senior Volunteer Program, the Service Corps of Retired Executives, and the Action Drug Prevention Program. Address inquiries about these programs to ACTION Recruiting Office, Washington, D.C. 20525.

CAREERS IN PUBLIC SERVICE

Public employment involves a major segment of the American workforce. More than one out of every seven people in the workforce serve as employees of the 83,000 governmental agencies at the national, state, county, or municipal level. Most positions in government service are open to qualified people regardless of political persuasion. Career services at every level constantly need to recruit able newcomers.

At least 92 percent of the positions in the federal executive branch are open to qualified citizens by appointment. Most of these positions are filled through civil service examinations. Additional positions calling for extensive professional training are filled through interviews and questionnaires that enable the U.S. Office of Personnel Management and the appointing agencies to examine the competence and experience of the individuals.

Several federal agencies have their own personnel systems and are not covered by regular civil service rules. The TVA, FBI, National Security Agency, International Communications Agency, CIA, and Foreign Service Officer Corps, for example, recruit and hire their own employees.

The Foreign Service Officer Corps deserves special mention because of its more specialized testing and its important diplomatic responsibilities. Written, oral, and language tests are required, and intensive interviews are used. If you wish to take the examinations, you may receive application forms from the Board of Examiners for the Foreign Service, Department of State, Washington, D.C. 20520.

If you seek work in the federal career services, do so without illusions. Despite valiant efforts to make the merit system work, a seniority system often takes root. Departments and bureaus do develop political life of their own—as well as a passion for size, growth, and an independent mission.

State governments offer countless challenging jobs, from budget and finance director positions to the tasks of running state correctional and state highway departments. The positions of city manager and city planning director are especially challenging and demand talented executives with well-developed political and managerial skills.

Young people interested in sampling public service may participate in a variety of government internship programs. Such programs provide short-term experience and a firsthand look at the process. Many members of Congress take on college students as summer interns. Most states and many cities operate intern programs. You can usually obtain information about intern opportunities from your department of political science or from local student government officers.

LAST WORD

Citizen-activists can have an impact on governmental and political processes. To have impact, however, people must be willing to concentrate their energies, enlarge the number of those sharing their views, and work hard to channel their activities into effective political action.

The essence of democracy is participatory and advocacy politics. Politics without debate and parties, and without partisanship, is really not democratic and open politics at all. Beware of those who try to remove critical policy issues from politics.

Active involvement in politics is not for everyone. Yet the system will not work without creative participation by people like you. Politics is a tough profession and it requires professionals. If you want to have an impact, be prepared to get in there and learn what needs to be done, and do not assume that all the good guys are on one side.

Politics in the best sense is the arena of responsibility and excellence where, by acting together, people can become truly free. At its best, democratic politics enables us to transcend the domains of power and material interests by providing us with the opportunity of achieving enduring greatness and nobility.

For those who believe that the common human enterprise can best progress under a government of, by, and for the people, there is plenty to be done. For those who would make democracy work, the late 1980s cry out for better ways to keep the peace, manage our economy, and revitalize our productivity while protecting our liberties and enhancing our human rights. We must also provide better ways to

□ Allow the individual to participate in government and see that participation counts

□ Make government open, responsive, and effective

□ Make government serve our long-range common interests rather than the narrow, immediate interests of the few.

FURTHER READING

Saul D. Alinsky. *Rules for Radicals: A Pragmatic Primer for Realistic Radicals* (Vintage, 1972).

Ann Beaudry and Bob Schaeffer. *Winning Local and State Elections* (Free Press, 1986).

Warren Bennis and Burt Nanus. *Leaders: The Strategies of Taking Charge* (Harper & Row, 1985).

Stimson Bullitt. *To Be a Politician*, rev. ed. (Yale University Press, 1977).

Jeff Greenfield. *Playing to Win: An Insider's Guide to Politics* (Simon & Schuster, 1980).

Stuart Langton, ed. *Citizen Participation in America* (Lexington Books, 1978).

Louis Sandy Maisel. *From Obscurity to Oblivion: Running in the Congressional Primary*, 2nd ed. (University of Tennessee Press, 1986).

Richard E. Neustadt and Ernest R. May. *Thinking in Time: The Uses of History for Decision Makers* (Free Press, 1986).

Larry J. Sabato. *The Rise of Political Consultants: New Ways of Winning Elections* (Basic Books, 1981).

Michael Walzer. *Political Action: A Practical Guide to Movement Politics* (Quadrangle Books, 1971).

For Further Research: Sources and Resources

Newspaper, radio, and television are important sources of information, yet the person who depends solely on these sources will have an imperfect picture of the world. They provide only part of the story, usually the sensational—newsworthy—events. They tell little of the whys and wherefores.

Magazines of general circulation contain useful material but do not go deeply into particular questions. Where do you find a law? How do you look up a court decision? Where can you find information on the United Nations? How do you find out how your representative in Congress has voted? What are some good books on the USSR? Many aids and services have been designed to make such information readily available. An excellent place to begin is Clement Vose, *A Guide to Library Sources in Political Science: American Government* (1975), published by the American Political Science Association.

Among the important information-dispensing centers are the more than 7500 public libraries and the many hundreds of private libraries that are open to the public. These libraries contain, in addition to general-interest magazines, many specialized journals, such as *The American Political Science Review*, *The Journal of Politics*, *The Journal of American Politics*, *Political Science Quarterly*, and *American Politics Quarterly*. There are also a number of periodical indexes, of which the *Public Affairs Information Service* is particularly useful because it indexes books, pamphlets, and reports—as well as articles from hundreds of periodicals—for a broad range of current public-interest topics. Major political science journals are included in the *Social Sciences Index*. The *International Political Science Abstracts*, edited by the International Political Science Association, provides summaries of articles from major political science journals throughout the world. The *Reader's Guide to Periodical Literature* includes mainly popular magazines with mass or family circulation. The *Index to Legal Periodicals*, *Busi-*

ness *Periodicals Index*, the *Index of Economic Articles*, *Index to U.S. Government Periodicals*, *Urban Affairs Abstracts*, and *Energy Abstracts for Policy Analysis* are also useful.

The *Universal Reference System* is the most comprehensive reference to books, papers, journals, and reviews. Most of these indexes are published monthly and indexed cumulatively at the end of the year. They can help you locate materials on most subjects. Beginning in 1980 this system published an annual supplement, *Political Science Abstracts*. In addition, see Robert Harmon, *Political Science: A Bibliographical Guide to the Literature* (1965): no. 2 (1972), no. 3 (1974). See also, by the same author, *Political Science Bibliographies*, (Scarecrow Press): vol. 1 (1973), vol. 2 (1976).

Other bibliographies you might consult are Frederick Holler's five-volume *The Information Sources of Political Science*, 4th ed. (1986), and *ABC Pol Sci; A Bibliography of Contents: Political Science and Government*, a monthly service which reproduces the tables of contents of periodicals in the field of political science. The card catalog in the library lists the books available there. You may be able to learn about an author's reputation or a particular book in the *Book Review Digest*, but keep in mind that reviews in this digest are taken from a limited group of publications. You will also find the *Current Book Review Index* helpful; it complements the *Book Review Digest* but is more current and complete. It lists sources of all reviews in the periodicals indexed, and it is issued monthly and quarterly, with annual cumulations. Most larger libraries also subscribe to *Perspective*, a monthly journal that carries reviews of new books on government, politics, and international affairs.

Useful for foreign policy research are Richard D. Burns, *Guide to American Foreign Relations Since 1700* (ABC-CLIO Press, 1983), and Alexander DeConde, ed., *Encyclopedia of American Foreign Policy*, 3 vols. (Scribners, 1978). Students of foreign and defense policy may also wish to consult J. L. Black et al., *Origins, Evolution, and Nature of the Cold War: An Annotated Bibliography* (ABC-CLIO, 1985); Maya Chadda, *Paradox of Power The US in Southwest Asia, 1973–1984* (ABC-CLIO, 1986); and Richard Dean Burns and Milton Leitenberg, *The Wars in Vietnam, Cambodia and Laos, 1945–1982* (ABC-CLIO, 1984).

One of the most useful volumes is the *United States Government Manual*, an annual publication. This manual, which can be obtained from the Superintendent of Documents, U.S. Government Printing Office, Washington, D.C. 20402, covers the authority, organization and functions of all branches of the government. Up-to-date organizational charts tell who holds the higher executive positions, and brief descriptions of the work of each unit of government are given. The *Congressional Directory*, published every two years at the beginning of each Congress, has some of the materials found in the *Manual*, and it includes autobiographical sketches of members of Congress, lists of congressional committees and committee assignments, election statistics for the last several congressional elections, and maps of congressional districts. The *Directory* is the place to find out the name of your representative, a short sketch of his or her life, on which committees he or she serves, and his or her district boundaries. The *Almanac of American Politics*, published by *The National Journal*, contains current biographies, voting records, and lobbying interests, as well as political and economic profiles of a member's district. See also Congressional Quarterly's *Politics in America: Members of Congress in Washington and at Home*, first published in 1986.

Of special interest to persons interested in social sciences is the *Encyclopedia of the Social Sciences*, published in 1930 under the editorship of Edwin Seligman and Alvin Johnson. It contains articles on various topics—for example, political parties, sovereignty, representation, John Locke—that are among the best short treatments to be found. The *International Encyclopedia of the Social Sciences*, edited by David Sills and published in 1968, complements its predecessor and brings the information up to the date of its publication. Valuable review and survey articles can be found in the eight-volume series *Handbook of Political Science* (Addison-Wesley, 1975, 1976), edited by Fred Greenstein and Nelson Polsby. For historical perspective, see Frank Freidel, *Harvard Guide to American History* (Harvard University Press, 1974).

The *Dictionary of American Biography* is a prime source for biographical data. Included are some outstanding articles—one by Carl Becker on Benjamin Franklin, for example. In *Current Biography* you can find materials and background information on people in the news; a companion set, *Biography Index*, fills in specific information in case *Current Biography* has not been written up fully for ten years or so. Also of help will be *Who's Who in American Politics* and *Biographical Directory of the American Congress, 1774–1971* (U.S. Government Printing Office). See also John F. Bibby et al., *Vital Statistics on Congress* (American Enterprise Institute, 1980).

You will also find the following valuable for researching American politics: Congressional Quarterly's *Guide to U.S. Elections*, 2nd ed. (1985); *The American Electorate: A Historical Bibliography* (ABC-CLIO, 1984); *The Democratic and Republican Parties: A Historical Bibliography* (ABC-CLIO, 1984); Marvin Weinberger and David Greevy, *The PAC Directory: A Complete Guide to Political Action Committees* (Ballinger, 1982); and Edward Roeder, *PAC's Americana: A Dictionary of Political Action Committees and Their Interests* (Sunshine Services Corp., 1982). Because of the great growth of and interest in political action committees, these and similar collections will be republished every few years.

If you are studying legislatures, especially Congress, you should definitely consult Gerhard Loewenberg, Samuel C. Patterson, and Malcolm E. Jewell, eds., *Handbook of Legislative Research* (Harvard University Press, 1985). Congressional Quarterly's *Guide to Congress* is another valuable source, as is its *Congress and the Nation*, issued every few years. For materials on state legislatures, see Robert Goehlert and Frederick Musto, *State Legislatures* (ABC-CLIO Information Services, 1985). For general information about state government and politics, see Congressional Quarterly's annual *State Government: Guide to Current Issues and Activities*, edited by Thad Beyle. *Legislative Studies Quarterly* contains important articles on both state and national legislatures. *Congress and the Presidency*, a journal published twice a year, contains excellent essays on Congress and presidential-congressional relations.

Presidential Studies Quarterly prints useful articles on the executive branch and presidential politics. *Judica-*

577

ture, published six times a year, is a forum for articles on all aspects of the administration of justice and its improvement. *The Journal of Law and Politics*, founded in the mid-1980s and published at the University of Virginia, examines the politics of election law and its processes. *This Constitution*, a journal published by Project '87—a joint venture of the American Historical Association and the American Political Science Association—features general essays highlighting important historical and political issues raised by our bicentennial rethinking of the drafting, ratification, and early implementation of the U.S. Constitution.

To research public policy, use Stuart S. Nagel's *Basic Literature in Policy Studies: A Comprehensive Bibliography* (JAI Press, 1984). To study public law, consult Kermit L. Hall's exhaustive *Comprehensive Bibliography of American Constitutional and Legal History, 1896–1979* (Kraus International Publications, 1984); and J. Myron Jacobstein and Roy M. Mersky, *Fundamentals of Legal Research* (Foundation Press, 1985).

A quarterly journal of research, *Women and Politics*, offers an interdisciplinary approach to the growing field of women in politics and the political behavior of women.

Certain important tools are available for quick reference to current events, such as *Facts on File*, *The New York Times Index*, the *Wall Street Journal Index*, and *Keesing's Contemporary Archives*.

For raw figures, consult the *Statistical Abstract of the United States*, another yearly publication of the Government Printing Office. A reference librarian can point out other useful tools of this nature, such as the *Historical Statistics of the United States*, the *Congressional District Data Book*, and the many publications from the Bureau of the Census. The *American Statistics Index*, a comprehensive guide to the statistical publications of the U.S. government, can help you locate particular statistical publications issued by the government. Phyllis Carter's *U.S. Census Data for Political and Social Research: A Resource Guide*, published in 1976 by the American Political Science Association, is also helpful.

Where can you find the actual text of a law? The laws of the United States as passed by Congress are first printed individually and are known as slip laws. Each law has a number; in recent years public laws have been numbered according to the term of Congress in which they were enacted. At the end of each year, the laws are collected and published by the Government Printing Office under the title *United States Statutes at Large*. Each year's collection is separately numbered, and each number has two separate parts. Part one contains *public laws*—laws affecting the people generally or having to do with governmental organization. Part two contains *private laws*—those having to do with particular groups or individuals. The laws in the *Statutes at Large* are listed chronologically, and each constitutes a separate chapter. The Taft–Hartley Act, for example, is chapter 120 of volume 61, on page 136; it is cited as 61 Stat. 136.

Although the volumes of *Statutes at Large* are useful for research, they include many laws of only specialized interest. Further, many of the measures modify earlier legislation and are themselves modified by later legislation. To find current laws on a topic, it is best to refer to the *United States Code*, which contains the public laws of the United States that are currently in force. The official edition of the *United States Code* is published every six years. Supplements are issued annually between editions. The laws are arranged according to fifty titles; each title is divided into sections, and each section is broken down into paragraphs that are consecutively numbered for each title. The fifty titles cover such subjects as Congress, Title 2; Armed Forces, Title 10; Bankruptcy, Title 11; Labor, Title 29; and so on. The Code is cited by title and paragraph. The citation of the Taft–Hartley Act, for example, is 29 U.S.C. 141 ff.

The *Code*, like the *Statutes at Large*, is printed by the Government Printing Office, but a commercially published edition, known as *United States Code Annotated* (*USCA*), also exists.

The series *Treaties in Force* is the best source of information about treaties and executive agreements. These volumes are published annually and are organized chronologically. See also Peter H. Rohn, *World Treaty Index* (ABC-CLIO, 1984), 5 vol., 2nd ed.

Where can you find the rules and regulations issued by the president and the executive agencies? Every day except for the weekends the government publishes the *Federal Register*, which contains the executive orders, regulations, and proclamations issued by the president, as well as the orders and regulations promulgated by the executive agencies (including the independent regulatory commissions). These administrative rules and regulations are collected, codified, and kept up to date in the *Code of Federal Regulations*. The *Code of Federal Regulations*, the *Federal Register*, along with the *United States Government Manual* previously mentioned and the annual publication *Public Papers of the Presidents*, are part of what is known as the Federal Register System. See *The Federal Register: What It Is and How to Use It* (U.S. Office of the Federal Register, 1985).

The *Weekly Compilation of Presidential Documents*, which contains public messages, speeches, and statements of the president, is published every Monday. For research work on the presidency you should definitely consult Fred Greenstein et al., *Evolution of the Modern Presidency: A Bibliographical Survey* (American Enterprise Institute, 1977); George Edwards and Stephen Wayne, eds., *Studying the Presidency* (University of Tennessee Press, 1983); Kenneth Davison, *The American Presidency: A Guide to Information Sources* (Gale Research Company, 1983); and Robert Goehlert, *The Presidency: A Research Guide* (ABC-CLIO, 1984).

Still, the laws as they finally appear on the statute books give only part of the story. Where do you find out what went on before the laws were passed or why certain laws were not passed? This information can, in part, be found in one of the most interesting items of American letters—the *Congressional Record*. The *Record* is issued every day Congress is in session and is bound and indexed at the end of each session. It contains everything that is said on the floors of the two chambers, plus a lot that is not said. Congress freely allows its members "to revise and extend their remarks," which is a polite way of saying that members are permitted to include in the *Record* statements they did not make before Congress. Each day's *Record* is now accompanied by a *Daily Digest* that highlights the events both on the floor of Congress and in committees. Action on specific items can be traced by searching through the index.

An easier method is to use the *Digest of Public General Bills and Resolutions*, which gives a brief summary of all the public bills and traces their progress. *Major Legislation of the Congress*, issued by the Congressional Research Service (The Library of Congress) four or five times per year, gives a broad overview of legislation in various subject areas. It includes background information on topics as well as a survey of current bills under consideration.

General guides to help you study the congressional process are Robert Goehlert, *Congress and Law-Making: Researching the Legislative Process* (Clio Books, 1979); and Robert Goehlert and John Sayre, *The United States Congress: A Bibliography* (Free Press, 1982). Another reference work is Jerrold Zwirn, *Congressional Publications: A Research Guide to Legislation, Budgets, and Treaties* (Libraries Unlimited, 1983).

Several commercial services provide convenient references to congressional activities. The *Congressional Quarterly Weekly Report* contains voting records, legislative action, reports on lobbying, and other materials about Congress in action. This is the best source on lobbying activity. The materials are indexed and collected in the *Congressional Quarterly Almanac*, an annual publication. The *United States Code: Congressional and Administrative News* and the *Congressional Index* also provide ready reference to congressional activity. Another way to monitor congressional activity is through the *CIS/Index*, an index to publications of Congress that is issued monthly with annual compilations by the Congressional Information Service. It indexes and abstracts committee hearings, prints chamber reports and other congressional documents, and contains a brief summary of the statement of each witness in a hearing, including page numbers on which particular testimonies appear.

Because most of the real work of Congress is done in committees, the reports of these committees and the printed records of hearings are important sources of information. The hearings and reports may be found in any of the more than 1000 depository libraries in the United States. (A depository library receives regular publications issued by the Government Printing Office.)

Congress is not the only branch of the federal government that keeps a record of its work. All the other agencies have their own publications, which describe their work and supply citizens with general and specialized information. These publications can be obtained from the Superintendent of Documents, Government Printing Office, Washington, D.C. 20402, for a nominal price. They are indexed in the *Monthly Catalog of United States Government Publications*. One of the several general guides to government publications is Joe Morehead, *Introduction to United States Public Documents*, 3rd ed. (Libraries Unlimited, 1983).

Activities of the executive branch of the federal government as well as those of Congress and the courts are analyzed in the *National Journal*, a weekly publication. This is the best single source on developments within the federal executive branch. Congressional Quarterly, Inc., publishes two excellent annual sources, the *Federal Regulatory Directory* and the *Washington Information Directory*. *The Washington Monthly* and *The Public Interest* provide critical essays on policy politics and bureaucracy in Washington. Two publications, *Public Opinion* and *Regulation*, published by the American Enterprise Institute, are also helpful in following national politics and policy developments.

Where can you find the reports and rulings of the federal judiciary? The decisions of the Supreme Court are published by the government in numbered volumes known as the *United States Reports*. Cases are cited by volume and page number: *Regents of the University of California* v. *Bakke*, 438 U.S. 265 (1979) means that this case can be found in the 438th volume of the *United States Reports*, on page 265, and that the opinion was handed down in 1979. Decisions of the Court prior to 1875 are cited by the name of the Supreme Court reporter. Thus, *Marbury* v. *Madison*, 1 Cranch 137 (1803) can be found in the first volume of Cranch's Supreme Court reports, on page 137; the opinion was announced in 1803.

It now takes months before the official Supreme Court reports are available, so to review recent opinions you must consult *United States Law Week*—a comprehensive and promptly published review. Also available are the

Supreme Court Reporter, published by West Publishing Company, and *United States Supreme Court Reports*, *Lawyers Edition*, published by the Lawyers Cooperative Publishing Company. A general survey of the history, decisions, and procedures of the Supreme Court is the *Guide to the U.S. Supreme Court* (Congressional Quarterly, Inc., 1979). *The National Law Journal* and *The Legal Times* are two other weeklies that might be helpful.

To do research on the United Nations and its politics and policies, start with *Basic Facts about the United Nations* (1983, and regularly revised), published by the UN Office of Public Information, and with *Reference Guide to the United Nations* (1978), published by the UN Association of the United States of America. Also important for UN research are: *U.N. Chronicle*, a monthly (except August) published by the UN Department of Public Information, and, by that same department, *Yearbook of the United Nations*, an annual. See too Edmund Jan Osmanczyk, *The Encyclopedia of the United Nations and International Agreements* (Taylor and Francis, 1985). More specialized research guides are Peter Hajnal, *Guide to United Nations Organization, Documentation and Publishing for Students, Researchers and Librarians* (Oceana Publishers, 1978); and Mary K. Fetzer, *United Nations Documents and Publications: A Research Guide* (Rutgers University Graduate School of Library Service, 1978). Since 1979 many libraries have had the *UNDOC* guide, an up-to-date, comprehensive description of all United Nations documents, with subject, author, and title indexes.

Finally, a few additional general reference services that may be of help are: *Government Publications Index* (Information Access Corporation); and *Information Sources in Politics and Political Science Worldwide* (Butterworths, 1984). See also Diane L. Garner and Diane H. Smith, *The Complete Guide to Citing Government Documents: A Manual for Writers and Librarians* (Congressional Information Services, 1984). You can also get excellent assistance from your college and university reference-section librarians, who will gladly direct you to the newest reference and document sources.

The Declaration of Independence

IN CONGRESS, JULY 4, 1776
(The unanimous Declaration of the Thirteen United States of America)

PREAMBLE

When, in the course of human events, it becomes necessary for one people to dissolve the political bands which have connected them with another, and to assume, among the powers of the earth, the separate and equal station to which the laws of nature and of nature's God entitle them, a decent respect to the opinions of mankind requires that they should declare the causes which impel them to the separation.

NEW PRINCIPLES OF GOVERNMENT

We hold these truths to be self-evident; that all men are created equal, that they are endowed by their Creator with certain unalienable rights, that among these are life, liberty, and the pursuit of happiness.

That, to secure these rights, governments are instituted among men, deriving their just powers from the consent of the governed;

That whenever any form of government becomes destructive of these ends, it is the right of the people to alter or to abolish it, and to institute new government, laying its foundation on such principles, and organizing its powers in such form, as to them shall seem most likely to effect their safety and happiness. Prudence, indeed, will dictate that governments long established should not be changed for light and transient causes; and accordingly all experience hath shown that mankind are more disposed to suffer while evils are sufferable, than to right themselves by abolishing the forms to which they are accustomed. But when a long train of abuses and usurpations, pursuing invariably the same object, evinces a design to reduce them under absolute despostism, it is their right, it is their duty, to throw off such government, and to

provide new guards for their future security.

REASONS FOR SEPARATION

Such has been the patient sufference of these colonies; and such is now the necessity which constrains them to alter their former systems of government. The history of the present king of Great Britain is a history of repeated injuries and usurpations, all having in direct object the establishment of an absolute tyranny over these states. To prove this, let facts be submitted to a candid world.

He has refused his assent to laws, the most wholesome and necessary for the public good.

He has forbidden his governors to pass laws of immediate and pressing importance unless suspended in their operation till his assent should be obtained; and when so suspended, he has utterly neglected to attend to them.

He has refused to pass other laws for the accommodation of large districts of people, unless those people would relinquish the right of representation in the legislature, a right inestimable to them, and formidable to tyrants only.

He has called together legislative bodies at places unusual, uncomfortable, and distant from the depository of their public records, for the sole purpose of fatiguing them into compliance with his measures.

He has dissolved representative houses repeatedly, for opposing, with manly firmness, his invasions on the rights of people.

He has refused, for a long time after such dissolutions, to cause others to be elected; whereby the legislative powers, incapable of annihilation, have returned to the people at large for their exercise; the state remaining, in the mean time, exposed to all the dangers of invasion from without and convulsions within.

He has endeavored to prevent the population of these states; for that purpose obstructing the laws of naturaliza-

tion of foreigners, refusing to pass others to encourage their migration hither, and raising the conditions of new appropriations of lands.

He has obstructed the administration of justice, by refusing his assent to laws for establishing judiciary powers.

He has made judges dependent on his will alone for the tenure of their offices, and the amount and payment of their salaries.

He has erected a multitude of new offices, and sent hither swarms of officers to harass our people and eat out their substance.

He has kept among us, in times of peace, standing armies, without the consent of our legislature.

He has affected to render the military independent of, and superior to, the civil power.

He has combined with others to subject us to a jurisdiction foreign to our constitution and unacknowledged by our laws, giving his assent to their acts of pretended legislation:

For quartering large bodies of armed troops among us;

For protecting them, by a mock trial, from punishment for any murders which they should commit on the inhabitants of these states;

For cutting off our trade with all parts of the world;

For imposing taxes on us without our consent;

For depriving us, in many cases, of the benefits of trial by jury;

For transporting us beyond seas, to be tried for pretended offenses;

For abolishing the free system of English laws in a neighboring province, establishing therein an arbitrary government, and enlarging its boundaries, so as to render it at once an example and fit instrument for introducing the same absolute rule into these colonies;

For taking away our charters, abolishing our most valuable laws, and altering, fundamentally, the forms of our governments;

For suspending our own legislatures, and declaring themselves invested with power to legislate for us in all cases whatsoever.

He has abdicated government here, by declaring us out of his protection and waging war against us.

He has plundered our seas, ravaged our coasts, burned our towns, and destroyed the lives of our people.

He is at this time transporting large armies of foreign mercenaries to complete the works of death, desolation, and tyranny already begun with circumstances of cruelty and perfidy scarcely paralleled in the most barbarous ages and totally unworthy of the head of a civilized nation.

He has constrained our fellow-citizens, taken captive on the high seas, to bear arms against their country, to become the executioners of their friends and brethren, or to fall themselves by their hands.

He has excited domestic insurrections among us, and has endeavored to bring on the inhabitants of our frontiers the merciless Indian savages, whose known rule of warfare is an undistinguished destruction of all ages, sexes, and conditions.

In every stage of these oppressions we have petitioned for redress in the most humble terms; our repeated petitions have been answered only by repeated injury. A prince whose character is thus marked by every act which may define a tyrant is unfit to be the ruler of a free people.

Nor have we been wanting in attention to our British brethren. We have warned them, from time to time, of attempts by their legislature to extend an unwarrantable jurisdiction over us. We have reminded them of the circumstances of our emigration and settlement here. We have appealed to their native justice and magnanimity; and we have conjured them, by the ties of our common kindred, to disavow these usurpations, which would inevitably interrupt our connections and correspondence. They, too, have been deaf to the voice of justice and of consanguinity. We must, therefore, acquiesce in the necessity which denounces our separation, and hold them, as we hold the rest of mankind, enemies in war, in peace, friends.

We, therefore, the representatives of the United States of America, in General Congress assembled, appealing to the Supreme Judge of the world for the rectitude of our intentions, do, in the name and by authority of the good people of these colonies, solemnly publish and declare, that these united colonies are, and of right ought to be, free and independent states; that they are absolved from all allegiance to the British crown, and that all political connection between them and the state of Great Britain is, and ought to be, totally dissolved; and that, as free and independent states, they have full power to levy war, conclude peace, contract alliances, establish commerce, and do all other acts and things which independent states may of a right do. And, for the support of this declaration, with a firm reliance on the protection of Divine Providence, we mutually pledge to each other our lives, our fortunes, and our sacred honor.

Note: Drafted mainly by Thomas Jefferson, this document adopted by the Second Continental Congress, and signed by John Hancock and fifty-five others, outlines the rights of man and the rights to rebellion and self-government. It declared the independence of the colonies from Great Britain, justified rebellion, and listed the grievances against George the III and his government. What is memorable about this famous document is not only that it declared the birth of a new nation, but that it set forth, with eloquence, our basic philosophy of liberty and representative democracy.

The Federalist, No. 10, James Madison

To the People of the State of New York: Among the numerous advantages promised by a well-constructed union, none deserves to be more accurately developed than its tendency to break and control the violence of faction. The friend of popular governments, never finds himself so much alarmed for their character and fate, as when he contemplates their propensity to this dangerous vice. He will not fail, therefore, to set a due value on any plan which, without violating the principles to which he is attached, provides a proper cure for it. The instability, injustice, and confusion introduced into the public councils, have, in truth, been the mortal diseases under which popular governments have everywhere perished; as they continue to be the favourite and fruitful topics from which the adversaries to liberty derive their most specious declamations. The valuable improvements made by the American constitutions on the popular models, both ancient and modern, cannot certainly be too much admired; but it would be an unwarrantable partiality, to contend that they have as effectually obviated the danger on this side, as was wished and expected. Complaints are everywhere heard from our most considerate and virtuous citizens, equally the friends of public and private faith, and of public and personal liberty, that our governments are too unstable; that the public good is disregarded in the conflicts of rival parties; and that measures are too often decided, not according to the rules of justice, and the rights of the minor party, but by the superior force of an interested and overbearing majority. However anxiously we may wish that these complaints had no foundation, the evidence of known facts will not permit us to deny that they are in some degree true. It will be found, indeed, on a candid review of our situation, that some of the distresses under which we labour have been erroneously charged on the operation of our governments; but it will be found, at the same time, that other causes will not alone account for many of our heaviest misfortunes; and, particularly, for that prevailing and increasing distrust of public engagements, and alarm for private rights, which are echoed from one end of the continent to the other. These must be chiefly, if not wholly, effects of the unsteadiness and injustice, with which a factious spirit has tainted our public administrations.

By a faction, I understand a number of citizens, whether amounting to a majority or minority of the whole, who are united and actuated by some common impulse of passion, or of interest, adverse to the rights of other citizens, or to the permanent and aggregate interests of the community.

There are two methods of curing the mischiefs of faction: the one, by removing its causes; the other, by controlling its effects.

There are again two methods of removing the causes of faction: the one, by destroying the liberty which is essential to its existence; the other, by giving to every citizen the same opinions, the same passions, and the same interests.

It could never be more truly said, than of the first remedy, that it was worse than the disease. Liberty is to faction what air is to fire, an aliment without which it instantly expires. But it could not be a less folly to abolish liberty, which is essential to political life, because it nourishes faction, than it would be to wish the annihilation of air, which is essential to animal life, because it imparts to fire its destructive agency.

The second expedient is as impracticable, as the first would be unwise. As long as the reason of man continues fallible, and he is at liberty to exercise it, different opinions will be formed. As long as the connection subsists between his reason and his self-love, his opinions and his passions will have a reciprocal

influence on each other; and the former will be objects to which the latter will attach themselves. The diversity in the faculties of men, from which the rights of property originate, is not less an insuperable obstacle to an uniformity of interests. The protection of these faculties is the first object of government. From the protection of different and unequal faculties of acquiring property, the possession of different degrees and kinds of property immediately results; and from the influence of these on the sentiments and views of the respective proprietors, ensues a division of the society into different interests and parties.

The latent causes of faction are thus sown in the nature of man; and we see them everywhere brought into different degrees of activity, according to the different circumstances of civil society. A zeal for different opinions concerning religion, concerning government, and many other points, as well of speculation as of practice; an attachment to different leaders ambitiously contending for preeminence and power; or to persons of other descriptions whose fortunes have been interesting to the human passions, have, in turn, divided mankind into parties, inflamed them with mutual animosity, and rendered them much more disposed to vex and oppress each other, than to cooperate for their common good. So strong is this propensity of mankind, to fall into mutual animosities, that where no substantial occasion presents itself, the most frivolous and fanciful distinctions have been sufficient to kindle their unfriendly passions and excite their most violent conflicts. But the most common and durable source of factions, has been the various and unequal distribution of property. Those who hold, and those who are without property, have ever formed distinct interests in society. Those who are creditors, and those who are debtors, fall under a like discrimination. A landed interest, a manufacturing interest, a mercantile interest, a moneyed interest, with many lesser interests, grow up of necessity in civilized nations, and divide them into different classes, actuated by different sentiments and views. The regulation of these various and interfering interests forms the principal task of modern legislation, and involves the spirit of the party and faction in the necessary and ordinary operations of the government.

No man is allowed to be a judge

in his own cause; because his interest will certainly bias his judgment, and, not improbably, corrupt his integrity. With equal, nay, with greater reason, a body of men are unfit to be both judges and parties at the same time; yet what are many of the most important acts of legislation, but so many judicial determinations, not indeed concerning the right of single persons, but concerning the rights of large bodies of citizens? And what are the different classes of legislators, but advocates and parties to the causes which they determine? Is a law proposed concerning private debts? It is a question to which the creditors are parties on one side, and the debtors on the other. Justice ought to hold the balance between them. Yet the parties are, and must be, themselves the judges; and the most numerous party, or, in other words, the most powerful faction, must be expected to prevail. Shall domestic manufactures be encouraged, and in what degree, by restrictions on foreign manufactures? are questions which would be differently decided by the landed and the manufacturing classes; and probably by neither with a sole regard to justice and the public good. The apportionment of taxes, on the various descriptions of property, is an act which seems to require the most exact impartiality; yet there is, perhaps, no legislative act, in which greater opportunity and temptation are given to a predominant party to trample on the rules of justice. Every shilling, with which they overburden the inferior number, is a shilling saved to their own pockets.

It is in vain to say, that enlightened statesmen will be able to adjust these clashing interests, and render them all subservient to the public good. Enlightened statesmen will not always be at the helm; nor, in many cases, can such an adjustment be made at all, without taking into view indirect and remote considerations, which will rarely prevail over the immediate interest which one party may find in disregarding the rights of another, or the good of the whole.

The inference to which we are brought is, that the *causes* of faction cannot be removed; and that relief is only to be sought in the means of controlling its *effects*.

If a faction consists of less than a majority, relief is supplied by the republican principle, which enables the majority to defeat its sinister views, by regular vote. It may clog the administration, it may convulse the society; but it will be unable to execute and mask its violence under the forms of the Constitution. When a majority is included in a faction, the form of popular government, on the other hand, enables it to sacrifice to its ruling passion or interest, both the public good and the rights of other citizens. To secure the public good, and private rights, against the danger of such a faction, and at the same time to preserve the spirit and the form of popular government, is then the great object to which our inquiries are directed. Let me add, that it is the great desideratum, by which alone this form of government can be rescued from the opprobrium under which it has so long laboured, and be recommended to the esteem and adoption of mankind.

By what means is this object attainable? Evidently by one of two only. Either the existence of the same passion or interest in a majority, at the same time, must be prevented; or the majority, having such coexistent passion or interest, must be rendered, by their number and local situation, unable to concert and carry into effect schemes of oppression. If the impulse and the opportunity be suffered to coincide, we well know that neither moral nor religious motives can be relied on as an adequate control. They are not found to be such on the injustice and violence of individuals, and lose their efficacy in proportion to the number combined together; that is, in proportion as their efficacy becomes needful.

From this view of the subject, it may be concluded, that a pure democracy, by which I mean a society consisting of a small number of citizens, who assemble and administer the government in person, can admit of no cure for the mischiefs of faction. A common passion or interest will, in almost every case, be felt by a majority of the whole; a communication and concert, results from the form of government itself; and there is nothing to check the inducements to sacrifice the weaker party, or an obnoxious individual. Hence, it is, that such democracies have ever been spectacles of turbulence and contention; have ever been found incompatible with personal security, or the rights of property; and have in general been as short in their lives, as they have been violent in their deaths. Theoretic politi-

cians, who have patronized this species of government, have erroneously supposed, that by reducing mankind to a perfect equality in their political rights, they would, at the same time, be perfectly equalized and assimilated in their possessions, their opinions, and their passions.

A republic, by which I mean a government in which the scheme of representation takes place, opens a different prospect, and promises the cure for which we are seeking. Let us examine the points in which it varies from pure democracy, and we shall comprehend both the nature of the cure and the efficacy which it must derive from the union.

The two great points of difference, between a democracy and a republic, are, first, the delegation of the government, in the latter, to a small number of citizens, elected by the rest; secondly, the greater number of citizens, and greater sphere of country, over which the latter may be extended.

The effect of the first difference is, on the one hand, to refine and enlarge the public views, by passing them through the medium of a chosen body of citizens, whose wisdom may best discern the true interest of their country, and whose patriotism and love of justice, will be least likely to sacrifice it to temporary or partial considerations. Under such a regulation, it may well happen, that the public voice, pronounced by the representatives of the people, will be more consonant to the public good, than if pronounced by the people themselves, convened for the purpose. On the other hand the effect may be inverted. Men of factious tempers, of local prejudices, or of sinister designs, may by intrigue, by corruption, or by other means, first obtain the suffrages, and then betray the interest of the people. The question resulting is, whether small or extensive republics are most favourable to the election of proper guardians of the public weal; and it is clearly decided in favour of the latter by two obvious considerations.

In the first place, it is to be remarked that, however small the republic may be, the representatives must be raised to a certain number, in order to guard against the cabals of a few; and that however large it may be, they must be limited to a certain number, in order to guard against the confusion of a multitude. Hence, the number of represen-

tatives in the two cases not being in proportion to that of the constituents, and being proportionally greatest in the small republic, it follows, that if the proportion of fit characters be not less in the large than in the small republic, the former will present a greater option, and consequently a greater probability of a fit choice.

In the next place, as each representative will be chosen by a greater number of citizens in the large than in the small republic, it will be more difficult for unworthy candidates to practise with success the vicious arts, by which elections are too often carried; and the suffrages of the people being more free, will be more likely to centre in men who possess the most attractive merit, and the most diffusive and established characters.

It must be confessed, that in this, as in most other cases, there is a mean, on both sides of which inconveniences will be found to lie. By enlarging too much the number of electors, you render the representatives too little acquainted with all their local circumstances and lesser interests; as by reducing it too much, you render him unduly attached to these, and too little fit to comprehend and pursue great and national objects. The federal constitution forms a happy combination in this respect; the great and aggregate interests being referred to the national, the local and particular to the state legislatures.

The other point of difference is, the greater number of citizens, and extent of territory, which may be brought within the compass of republican, than of democratic government; and it is this circumstance principally which renders factious combinations less to be dreaded in the former, than in the latter. The smaller the society, the fewer probably will be the distinct parties and interests composing it; the fewer the distinct parties and interests, the more frequently will a majority be found of the same party; and the smaller the number of individuals composing a majority, and the smaller the compass within which they are placed, the more easily will they concert and execute their plans of oppression. Extend the sphere, and you take in a greater variety of parties and interests; you make it less probable that a majority of the whole will have a common motive to invade the rights of other citizens; or if such a common motive exists, it will be more difficult for all who feel it to discover their own strength, and to act in unison with each other. Besides other impediments, it may be remarked, that where there is a consciousness of unjust or dishonourable purposes, communication is always checked by distrust, in proportion to the number whose concurrence is necessary.

Hence, it clearly appears, that the same advantage, which a republic has over a democracy, in controlling the effects of faction, is enjoyed by a large over a small republic—is enjoyed by the union over the states composing it. Does this advantage consist in the substitution of representatives, whose enlightened views and virtuous sentiments render them superior to local prejudices, and to schemes of injustice? It will not be denied that the representation of the union will be most likely to possess these requisite endowments. Does it consist in the greater security afforded by a greater variety of parties, against the event of any one party being able to outnumber and oppress the rest? In an equal degree does the increased variety of parties, comprised within the union, increase the security? Does it, in fine, consist in the greater obstacles opposed to the concert and accomplishment of the secret wishes of an unjust and interested majority? Here, again, the extent of the union gives it the most palpable advantage.

The influence of factious leaders may kindle a flame within their particular states, but will be unable to spread a general conflagration through the other states; a religious sect may degenerate into a political faction in a part of the confederacy; but the variety of sects dispersed over the entire face of it, must secure the national councils against any danger from that source: a rage for paper money, for an abolition of debts, for an equal division of property, or for any other improper or wicked project, will be less apt to pervade the whole body of the union than a particular member of it; in the same proportion as such a malady is more likely to taint a particular county or district, than an entire state.

In the extent and proper structure of the union, therefore, we behold a republican remedy for the diseases most incident to republican government. And according to the degree of pleasure and pride we feel in being republicans, ought to be our zeal in cherishing the spirit, and supporting the character of federalists.

Note: *The Federalist*, No. 10, written by James Madison soon after the Constitutional Convention, was prepared as one of several dozen newspaper essays aimed at persuading New Yorkers to ratify the proposed constitution. One of the most important basic documents in American political history, it outlines the need for and the general principles of a democratic republic. It also provides a political and economic analysis of the realities of interest group or faction politics.

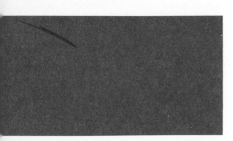

The Federalist, No. 51, James Madison

To what expedient, then, shall we finally resort, for maintaining in practice the necessary partition of power among the several departments as laid down in the Constitution? The only answer that can be given is that as all these exterior provisions are found to be inadequate the defect must be supplied, by so contriving the interior structure of the government as that its several constituent parts may, by their mutual relations, be the means of keeping each other in their proper places. Without presuming to undertake a full development of this important idea I will hazard a few general observations which may perhaps place it in a clearer light, and enable us to form a more correct judgment of the principles and structure of the government planned by the convention.

In order to lay a due foundation for that separate and distinct exercise of the different powers of government, which to a certain extent is admitted on all hands to be essential to the preservation of liberty, it is evident that each department should have a will of its own; and consequently should be so constituted that the members of each should have as little agency as possible in the appointment of the members of the others. Were this principle rigorously adhered to, it would require that all the appointments for the supreme executive, legislative, and judiciary magistracies should be drawn from the same fountain of authority, the people, through channels having no communication whatever with one another. Perhaps such a plan of constructing the several departments would be less difficult in practice than it may in contemplation appear. Some difficulties, however, and some additional expense would attend the execution of it. Some deviations, therefore, from the principle must be admitted. In the constitution of the judiciary department in particular, it might be inexpedient to insist rigorously on the principle: first, because peculiar qualifications being essential in the members, the primary consideration ought to be to select that mode of choice which best secures these qualifications; second, because the permanent tenure by which the appointments are held in that department must soon destroy all sense of dependence on the authority conferring them.

It is equally evident that the members of each department should be as little dependent as possible on those of the others for the emoluments annexed to their offices. Were the executive magistrate, or the judges, not independent of the legislature in this particular, their independence in every other would be merely nominal.

But the great security against a gradual concentration of the several powers in the same department consists in giving to those who administer each department the necessary constitutional means and personal motives to resist encroachments of the others. The provision for defense must in this, as in all other cases, be made commensurate to the danger of attack. Ambition must be made to counteract ambition. The interest of the man must be connected with the constitutional rights of the place. It may be a reflection on human nature that such devices should be necessary to control the abuses of government. But what is government itself but the greatest of all reflections on human nature? If men were angels, no government would be necessary. If angels were to govern men, neither external nor internal controls on government would be necessary. In framing a government which is to be administered by men over men, the great difficulty lies in this: you must first enable the government to control the governed; and in the next place oblige it to control itself. A dependence on the people is, no doubt, the primary control on the government; but experience has taught mankind the necessity of auxiliary precautions.

This policy of supplying, by opposite and rival interests, the defect of better motives, might be traced through the whole system of human affairs, private as well as public. We see it particularly displayed in all the subordinate distributions of power, where the constant aim is to divide and arrange the several offices in such a manner as that each may be a check on the other—that the private interest of every individual may be a sentinel over the public rights. These inventions of prudence cannot be less requisite in the distribution of the supreme powers of the State.

But it is not possible to give to each department an equal power of self-defense. In republican government, the legislative authority necessarily predominates. The remedy for this inconveniency is to divide the legislature into different branches; and to render them, by different modes of election and different principles of action, as little connected with each other as the nature

of their common functions and their common dependence on the society will admit. It may even be necessary to guard against dangerous encroachments by still further precautions. As the weight of the legislative authority requires that it should be thus divided, the weakness of the executive may require, on the other hand, that it should be fortified. An absolute negative on the legislature appears, at first view, to be the natural defense with which the executive magistrate should be armed. But perhaps it would be neither altogether safe nor alone sufficient. On ordinary occasions it might not be exerted with the requisite firmness, and on extraordinary occasions it might be perfidiously abused. May not this defect of an absolute negative be supplied by some qualified connection between this weaker department and the weaker branch of the stronger department, by which the latter may be led to support the constitutional rights of the former, without being too much detached from the rights of its own department?

If the principles on which these observations are founded be just, as I persuade myself they are, and they be applied as a criterion to the several State constitutions, and to the federal Constitution, it will be found that if the latter does not perfectly correspond with them, the former are infinitely less able to bear such a test.

There are, moreover, two considerations particularly applicable to the federal system of America, which place that system in a very interesting point of view.

First. In a single republic, all the power surrendered by the people is submitted to the administration of a single government; and the usurpations are guarded against by a division of the government into distinct and separate departments. In the compound republic of America, the power surrendered by the people is first divided between two distinct governments, and then the portion allotted to each subdivided among distinct and separate departments. Hence a double security arises to the rights of the people. The different governments will control each other, at the same time that each will be controlled by itself.

Second. It is of great importance in a republic not only to guard the society against the oppression of its rulers, but to guard one part of the society

against the injustice of the other part. Different interests necessarily exist in different classes of citizens. If a majority be united by a common interest, the rights of the minority will be insecure. There are but two methods of providing against this evil: the one by creating a will in the community independent of the majority—that is, of the society itself; the other, by comprehending in the society so many separate descriptions of citizens as will render an unjust combination of a majority of the whole very improbable, if not impracticable. The first method prevails in all governments possessing an hereditary or self-appointed authority. This, at best, is but a precarious security; because a power independent of the society may as well espouse the unjust views of the major as the rightful interests of the minor party, and may possibly be turned against both parties. The second method will be exemplified in the federal republic of the United States. Whilst all authority in it will be derived from and dependent on the society, the society itself will be broken into so many parts, interests and classes of citizens, that the rights of individuals, or of the minority, will be in little danger from interested combinations of the majority. In a free government the security for civil rights must be the same as that for religious rights. It consists in the one case in the multiplicity of interests, and in the other in the multiplicity of sects. The degree of security in both cases will depend on the number of interests and sects; and this may be presumed to depend on the extent of country and number of people comprehended under the same government. This view of the subject must particularly recommend a proper federal system to all the sincere and considerate friends of republican government, since it shows that in exact proportion as the territory of the Union may be formed into more circumscribed Confederacies, or States, oppressive combinations of a majority will be facilitated; the best security, under the republican forms, for the rights of every class of citizen, will be diminished; and consequently the stability and independence of some member of the government, the only other security, must be proportionally increased. Justice is the end of government. It is the end of civil society. It ever has been and ever will be pursued until it be obtained, or until liberty be lost in the pursuit. In a society under the forms of which the stronger faction can readily unite and oppress the weaker, anarchy may as truly be said to reign as in a state of nature, where the weaker individual is not secured against the violence of the stronger; and as, in the latter state, even the stronger individuals are prompted, by the uncertainty of their condition, to submit to a government which may protect the weak as well as themselves; so, in the former state, will the more powerful factions or parties be gradually induced, by a like motive, to wish for a government which will protect all parties, the weaker as well as the more powerful. It can be little doubted that if the State of Rhode Island was separated from the Confederacy and left to itself, the insecurity of rights under the popular form of government within such narrow limits would be displayed by such reiterated oppressions of factious majorities that some power altogether independent of the people would soon be called for by the voice of the very factions whose misrule had proved the necessity of it. In the extended republic of the United States, and among the great variety of interests, parties, and sects which it embraces, a coalition of a majority of the whole society could seldom take place on any other principles than those of justice and the general good; whilst there being thus less danger to a minor from the will of a major party, there must be less pretext, also, to provide for the security of the former, by introducing into the government a will not dependent on the latter, or, in other words, a will independent of the society itself. It is no less certain that it is important, notwithstanding the contrary opinions which have been entertained, that the larger the society, provided it lie within a practicable sphere, the more duly capable it will be of self-government. And happily for the *republican cause*, the practicable sphere may be carried to a very great extent by a judicious modification and mixture of the *federal principle*.

Note: *The Federalist*, No. 51, also written by Madison, is a classic statement in defense of separation of powers and republican processes. Its fourth paragraph is especially famous and is frequently quoted by students of government.

The Federalist, No. 78, Alexander Hamilton

We proceed now to an examination of the judiciary department of the proposed government.

In unfolding the defects of the existing Confederation, the utility and necessity of a federal judicature have been clearly pointed out. It is the less necessary to recapitulate the considerations there urged as the propriety of the institution in the abstract is not disputed; the only questions which have been raised being relative to the manner of constituting it, and to its extent. To these points, therefore, our observations shall be confined.

The manner of constituting it seems to embrace these several objects: 1st. The mode of appointing the judges. 2nd. The tenure by which they are to hold their places. 3rd. The partition of the judiciary authority between different courts and their relations to each other.

First. As to the mode of appointing the judges: this is the same with that of appointing the officers of the Union in general and has been so fully discussed in the two last numbers that nothing can be said here which would not be useless repetition.

Second. As to the tenure by which the judges are to hold their places: this chiefly concerns their duration in office, the provisions for their support, the precautions for their responsibility.

According to the plan of the convention, all judges who may be appointed by the United States are to hold their offices *during good behavior*; which is conformable to the most approved of the State constitutions, and among the rest, to that of this State. Its propriety having been drawn into question by the adversaries of that plan is no light symptom of the rage for objection which disorders their imaginations and judgments. The standard of good behavior for the continuance in office of the judicial magistracy is certainly one of the most valuable of the modern improvements in the practice of government. In a monarchy it is an excellent barrier to the despotism of the prince; in a republic it is a no less excellent barrier to the encroachments and oppressions of the representative body. And it is the best expedient which can be devised in any government to secure a steady, upright, and impartial administration of the laws.

Whoever attentively considers the different departments of power must perceive that, in a government in which they are separated from each other, the judiciary, from the nature of its functions, will always be the least dangerous to the political rights of the Constitution; because it will be least in a capacity to annoy or injure them. The executive not only dispenses the honors but holds the sword of the community. The legislature not only commands the purse but prescribes the rules by which the duties and rights of every citizen are to be regulated. The judiciary, on the contrary, has no influence over either the sword or the purse; no direction either of the strength or of the wealth of the society, and can take no active resoluton whatever. It may truly be said to have neither FORCE nor WILL but merely judgment; and must ultimately depend upon the aid of the executive arm even for the efficacy of its judgments.

This simple view of the matter suggests several important consequences. It proves incontestably that the judiciary is beyond comparison the weakest of the three departments of power; that it can never attack with success either of the other two; and that all possible care is requisite to enable it to defend itself against their attacks. It equally proves that though individual oppression may now and then proceed from the courts of justice, the general liberty of the people can never be endangered from that quarter; I mean so long as the judiciary remains truly distinct from both the legislature and the executive. For I agree that "there is no liberty if the power of judging be not separated from the legislative and executive powers." And it proves, in the last place, that as liberty can have nothing to fear from the judiciary alone, but would have everything to fear from its union with either of the other departments; that as all the effects of such a union must ensue from a dependence of the former on the latter, notwithstanding a nominal and apparent separation; that as, from the natural feebleness of the judiciary, it is in continual jeopardy of being overpowered, awed, or influenced by its co-ordinate branches; and that as nothing can contribute so much to its firmness and independence as permanency in office, this quality may therefore be justly regarded as an indispensable ingredient in its constitution, and, in a great measure, as the citadel of the public justice and the public security.

The complete independence of the courts of justice is peculiarly essential in a limited Constitution. By a limited Constitution, I understand one which contains certain specified exceptions to the legislative authority; such, for instance, as that it shall pass no bills of attainder, no *ex post facto* laws, and the like. Limitations of this kind can be preserved in practice no other way than through the medium of courts of justice, whose duty it must be to declare all acts contrary to the manifest tenor of the Constitution void. Without this, all the reservations of particular rights or privileges would amount to nothing.

Some perplexity respecting the rights of the courts to pronounce legislative acts void, because contrary to the Constitution, has arisen from an imagination that the doctrine would imply a superiority of the judiciary to the legislative power. It is urged that the authority which can declare the acts of another void must necessarily be superior to the one whose acts may be declared void. As this doctrine is of great importance in all the American constitutions, a brief discussion of the grounds on which it rests cannot be unacceptable.

There is no position which depends on clearer principles than that every act of a delegated authority, contrary to the tenor of the commission under which it is exercised, is void. No legislative act, therefore, contrary to the Constitution, can be valid. To deny this would be to affirm that the deputy is greater than his principal; that the servant is above his master; that the representatives of the people are superior to the people themselves; that men acting by virtue of powers may do not only what their powers do not authorize, but what they forbid.

If it be said that the legislative body are themselves the constitutional judges of their own powers and that the construction they put upon them is conclusive upon the other departments it may be answered that this cannot be the natural presumption where it is not to be collected from any particular provisions in the Constitution. It is not otherwise to be supposed that the Constitution could intend to enable the representatives of the people to substitute their *will* to that of their constituents. It is far more rational to suppose that the courts were designed to be an intermediate body between the people and the legislature in order, among other things, to keep the latter within the limits assigned to their authority. The interpretation of the laws is the proper and peculiar province of the courts. A constitution is, in fact, and must be regarded by the judges as, a fundamental law. It therefore belongs to them to ascertain its meaning as well as the meaning of any particular act proceeding from the legislative body. If there should happen to be an irreconcilable variance between the two, that which has the superior obligation and validity ought, of course, to be preferred; or, in other words, the Constitu-

tion ought to be preferred to the statute, the intention of the people to the intention of their agents.

Nor does this conclusion by any means suppose a superiority of the judicial to the legislative power. It only supposes that the power of the people is superior to both, and that where the will of the legislature, declared in its statutes, stands in opposition to that of the people, declared in the Constitution, the judges ought to be governed by the latter rather than the former. They ought to regulate their decisions by the fundamental laws rather than by those which are not fundamental.

This exercise of judicial discretion in determining between two contradictory laws is exemplified in a familiar instance. It not uncommonly happens that there are two statutes existing at one time, clashing in whole or in part with each other and neither of them containing any repealing clause or expression. In such a case, it is the province of the courts to liquidate and fix their meaning and operation. So far as they can, by any fair construction, be reconciled to each other, reason and law conspire to dictate that this should be done; where this is impracticable, it becomes a matter of necessity to give effect to one in exclusion of the other. The rule which has obtained in the courts for determining their relative validity is that the last in order of time shall be preferred to the first. But this is a mere rule of construction, not derived from any positive law but from the nature and reason of the thing. It is a rule not enjoined upon the courts by legislative provision but adopted by themselves, as consonant to truth and propriety, for the direction of their conduct as interpreters of the law. They thought it reasonable that between the interfering acts of an *equal* authority that which was the last indication of its will should have the preference.

But in regard to the interfering acts of a superior and subordinate authority of an original and derivative power, the nature and reason of the thing indicate the converse of that rule as proper to be followed. They teach us that the prior act of a superior ought to be preferred to the subsequent act of an inferior and subordinate authority; and that accordingly, whenever a particular statue contravenes the Constitution, it will be the duty of the judicial tribunals to adhere to the latter and disregard the former.

It can be of no weight to say that the courts, on the pretense of a repugnancy, may substitute their own pleasure to the constitutional intentions of the legislature. This might as well happen in the case of two contradictory statutes; or it might as well happen in every adjudication upon any single statute. The courts must declare the sense of the law; and if they should be disposed to exercise WILL instead of JUDGMENT, the consequence would equally be the substitution of their pleasure to that of the legislative body. The observation, if it prove anything, would prove that there ought to be no judges distinct from that body.

If, then, the courts of justice are to be considered as the bulwarks of a limited Constitution against legislative encroachments, this consideration will afford a strong argument for the permanent tenure of judicial offices, since nothing will contribute so much as this to that independent spirit in the judges which must be essential to the faithful performance of so arduous a duty.

This independence of the judges is equally requisite to guard the Constitution and the rights of individuals from the effects of those ill humors which the arts of designing men, or the influence of particular conjunctures, sometimes disseminate among the people themselves, and which, though they speedily give place to better information, and more deliberate reflection, have a tendency, in the meantime, to occasion dangerous innovations in the government, and serious oppressions of the minor party in the community. Though I trust the friends of the proposed Constitution will never concur with its enemies in questioning that fundamental principle of Republican government which admits the right of the people to alter or abolish the established Constitution whenever they find it inconsistent with their happiness; yet it is not to be inferred from this principle that the representatives of the people, whenever a momentary inclination happens to lay hold of a majority of their constituents incompatible with the provisions in the existing Constitution would, on that account, be justifiable in a violation of those provisions; or that the courts would be under a greater obligation to connive at infractions in this shape than when they had

proceeded wholly from the cabals of the representative body. Until the people have, by some solemn and authoritative act, annulled or changed the established form, it is binding upon themselves collectively, as well as individually; and no presumption, or even knowledge of their sentiments, can warrant their representatives in a departure from it prior to such an act. But it is easy to see that it would require an uncommon portion of fortitude in the judges to do their duty as faithful guardians of the Constitution, where legislative invasions of it had been instigated by the major voice of the community.

But it is not with a view to infractions of the Constitution only that the independence of the judges may be an essential safeguard against the effects of occasional ill humors in the society. These sometimes extend no farther than to the injury of the private rights of particular classes of citizens, by unjust and partial laws. Here also the firmness of the judicial magistracy is of vast importance in mitigating the severity and confining the operation of such laws. It not only serves to moderate the immediate mischiefs of those which may have been passed but it operates as a check upon the legislative body in passing them; who, perceiving that obstacles to the success of iniquitous intention are to be expected from the scruples of the courts, are in a manner compelled, by the very motives of the injustice they mediate, to qualify their attempts. This is a circumstance calculated to have more influence upon the character of our governments than but few may be aware of. The benefits of the integrity and moderation of the judiciary have already been felt in more States than one; and though they may have displeased those whose sinister expectations they may have disappointed, they must have commanded the esteem and applause of all the virtuous and disinterested. Considerate men of every description ought to prize whatever will tend to beget or fortify that temper in the courts; as no man can be sure that he may not be tomorrow the victim of a spirit of injustice, by which he may be a gainer today. And every man must now feel that the inevitable tendency of such a spirit is to sap the foundations of public and private confidence and to introduce in its stead universal distrust and distress.

That inflexible and uniform adher-

ence to the rights of the Constitution, and of individuals, which we perceive to be indispensable in the courts of justice, can certainly not be expected from judges who hold their offices by a temporary commission. Periodical appointments, however regulated, or by whomsoever made, would, in some way or other, be fatal to their necessary independence. If the power of making them was committed either to the executive or legislature there would be danger of an improper complaisance to the branch which possessed it; if to both, there would be an unwillingness to hazard the displeasure of either; if to the people, or to persons chosen by them for the special purpose, there would be too great a disposition to consult popularity to justify a reliance that nothing would be consulted but the Constitution and the laws.

There is yet a further and a weighty reason for the permanency of the judicial offices which is deducible from the nature of the qualifications they require. It has been frequently remarked with great propriety that a voluminous code of laws is one of the inconveniences necessarily connected with the advantages of a free government. To avoid an arbitrary discretion in the courts, it is indispensable that they should be bound down by strict rules and precedents which serve to define and point out their duty in every particular case that comes before them; and it will readily be conceived from the variety of controversies which grow out of the folly and wickedness of mankind that the records of those precedents must unavoidably swell to a very considerable bulk and must demand long and laborious study to acquire a competent knowledge of them. Hence it is that there can be but few men in the society who will have sufficient skill in the laws to qualify them for the stations of judges. And making the proper deductions for the ordinary depravity of human nature, the number must be still smaller of those who unite the requisite integrity with the requisite knowledge. These considerations apprise us that the government can have no great option between fit characters; and that a temporary duration in office which would naturally discourage such characters from quitting a lucrative line of practice to accept a seat on the bench would have a tendency to throw the administration of justice into hands less able and less well qualified to conduct it with utility and dignity. In the present circumstances of this country and in those in which it is likely to be for a long time to come, the disadvantages on this score would be greater than they may at first sight appear; but it must be confessed that they are far inferior to those which present themselves under the other aspects of the subject.

Upon the whole, there can be no room to doubt that the convention acted wisely in copying from the models of those constitutions which have established *good behavior* as the tenure of their judicial offices, in point of dura-tion; and that so far from being blamable on this account, their plan would have been inexcusably defective if it had wanted this important feature of good government. The experience of Great Britain affords an illustrious comment on the excellence of the institution.

Note: The Federalist, No. 78, written by Alexander Hamilton, explains and praises the provisions for the judiciary in the newly drafted Constitution. Notice especially how Hamilton asserts that the courts have a key responsibility in determining the meaning of the Constitution as fundamental law. Hamilton is outlining here the doctrine of *judicial review* as we now know it.

Presidential Election Results 1789–1988

Year	Candidates	Party	Popular Vote	Electoral Vote
1789	**George Washington**			69
	John Adams			34
	Others			35
1792	**George Washington**			132
	John Adams			77
	George Clinton			50
	Others			5
1796	**John Adams**	Federalist		71
	Thomas Jefferson	Democratic-Republican		68
	Thomas Pinckney	Federalist		59
	Aaron Burr	Democratic-Republican		30
	Others			48
1800	**Thomas Jefferson**	Democratic-Republican		73
	Aaron Burr	Democratic-Republican		73
	John Adams	Federalist		65
	Charles C. Pinckney	Federalist		64
1804	**Thomas Jefferson**	Democratic-Republican		162
	Charles C. Pinckney	Federalist		14
1808	**James Madison**	Democratic-Republican		122
	Charles C. Pinckney	Federalist		47
	George Clinton	Independent-Republican		6
1812	**James Madison**	Democratic-Republican		128
	DeWitt Clinton	Federalist		89
1816	**James Monroe**	Democratic-Republican		183
	Rufus King	Federalist		34
1820	**James Monroe**	Democratic-Republican		231
	John Quincy Adams	Independent-Republican		1
1824	**John Quincy Adams**	Democratic-Republican	108,740 (30.5%)	84
	Andrew Jackson	Democratic-Republican	153,544 (43.1%)	99
	Henry Clay	Democratic-Republican	47,136 (13.2%)	37
	William H. Crawford	Democratic-Republican	46,618 (13.1%)	41
1828	**Andrew Jackson**	Democratic	647,231 (56.0%)	178
	John Quincy Adams	National Republican	509,097 (44.0%)	83
1832	**Andrew Jackson**	Democratic	687,502 (55.0%)	219
	Henry Clay	National Republican	530,189 (42.4%)	49
	William Wirt	Anti-Masonic		7
	John Floyd	National Republican	33,108 (2.6%)	11
1836	**Martin Van Buren**	Democratic	761,549 (50.9%)	170
	William H. Harrison	Whig	549,567 (36.7%)	73
	Hugh L. White	Whig	145,396 (9.7%)	26
	Daniel Webster	Whig	41,287 (2.7%)	14
1840	**William H. Harrison**	Whig	1,275,017 (53.1%)	234
	Martin Van Buren	Democratic	1,128,702 (46.9%)	60
1844	**James K. Polk**	Democratic	1,337,243 (49.6%)	170
	Henry Clay	Whig	1,299,068 (48.1%)	105
	James G. Birney	Liberty	63,300 (2.3%)	

Year	Candidates	Party	Popular Vote	Electoral Vote
1848	**Zachary Taylor**	Whig	1,360,101 (47.4%)	163
	Lewis Cass	Democratic	1,220,544 (42.5%)	127
	Martin Van Buren	Free Soil	291,163 (10.1%)	
1852	**Franklin Pierce**	Democratic	1,601,474 (50.9%)	254
	Winfield Scott	Whig	1,386,578 (44.1%)	42
1856	**James Buchanan**	Democratic	1,838,169 (45.4%)	174
	John C. Fremont	Republican	1,335,264 (33.0%)	114
	Millard Fillmore	American	874,534 (21.6%)	8
1860	**Abraham Lincoln**	Republican	1,865,593 (39.8%)	180
	Stephen A. Douglas	Democratic	1,381,713 (29.5%)	12
	John C. Breckinridge	Democratic	848,356 (18.1%)	72
	John Bell	Constitutional Union	592,906 (12.6%)	79
1864	**Abraham Lincoln**	Republican	2,206,938 (55.0%)	212
	George B. McClellan	Democratic	1,803,787 (45.0%)	21
1868	**Ulysses S. Grant**	Republican	3,013,421 (52.7%)	214
	Horatio Seymour	Democratic	2,706,829 (47.3%)	80
1872	**Ulysses S. Grant**	Republican	3,596,745 (55.6%)	286
	Horace Greeley	Democratic	2,843,446 (43.9%)	66
1876	**Rutherford B. Hayes**	Republican	4,036,571 (48.0%)	185
	Samuel J. Tilden	Democratic	4,284,020 (51.0%)	184
1880	**James A. Garfield**	Republican	4,449,053 (48.3%)	214
	Winfield S. Hancock	Democratic	4,442,035 (48.2%)	155
	James B. Weaver	Greenback-Labor	308,578 (3.4%)	
1884	**Grover Cleveland**	Democratic	4,874,986 (48.5%)	219
	James G. Blaine	Republican	4,851,931 (48.2%)	182
	Benjamin F. Butler	Greenback-Labor	175,370 (1.8%)	
1888	**Benjamin Harrison**	Republican	5,444,337 (47.8%)	233
	Grover Cleveland	Democratic	5,540,050 (48.6%)	168
1892	**Grover Cleveland**	Democratic	5,554,414 (46.0%)	277
	Benjamin Harrison	Republican	5,190,802 (43.0%)	145
	James B. Weaver	People's	1,027,329 (8.5%)	22
1896	**William McKinley**	Republican	7,035,638 (50.8%)	271
	William J. Bryan	Democratic; Populist	6,467,946 (46.7%)	176
1900	**William McKinley**	Republican	7,219,530 (51.7%)	292
	William J. Bryan	Democratic; Populist	6,356,734 (45.5%)	155
1904	**Theodore Roosevelt**	Republican	7,628,834 (56.4%)	336
	Alton B. Parker	Democratic	5,084,401 (37.6%)	140
	Eugene V. Debs	Socialist	402,460 (3.0%)	
1908	**William H. Taft**	Republican	7,679,006 (51.6%)	321
	William J. Bryan	Democratic	6,409,106 (43.1%)	162
	Eugene V. Debs	Socialist	420,820 (2.8%)	
1912	**Woodrow Wilson**	Democratic	6,286,820 (41.8%)	435
	Theodore Roosevelt	Progressive	4,126,020 (27.4%)	88
	William H. Taft	Republican	3,483,922 (23.2%)	8
	Eugene V. Debs	Socialist	897,011 (6.0%)	
1916	**Woodrow Wilson**	Democratic	9,129,606 (49.3%)	277
	Charles E. Hughes	Republican	8,538,211 (46.1%)	254
1920	**Warren G. Harding**	Republican	16,152,200 (61.0%)	404
	James M. Cox	Democratic	9,147,353 (34.6%)	127
	Eugene V. Debs	Socialist	919,799 (3.5%)	
1924	**Calvin Coolidge**	Republican	15,725,016 (54.1%)	382
	John W. Davis	Democratic	8,385,586 (28.8%)	136
	Robert M. La Follette	Progressive	4,822,856 (16.6%)	13
1928	**Herbert C. Hoover**	Republican	21,392,190 (58.2%)	444
	Alfred E. Smith	Democratic	15,016,443 (40.8%)	87
1932	**Franklin D. Roosevelt**	Democratic	22,809,638 (57.3%)	472
	Herbert C. Hoover	Republican	15,758,901 (39.6%)	59
	Norman Thomas	Socialist	881,951 (2.2%)	
1936	**Franklin D. Roosevelt**	Democratic	27,751,612 (60.7%)	523
	Alfred M. Landon	Republican	16,681,913 (36.4%)	8
	William Lemke	Union	891,858 (1.9%)	

Presidential Election Results 1789–1988 (*Continued*)

Year	Candidates	Party	Popular Vote	Electoral Vote
1940	**Franklin D. Roosevelt**	Democratic	27,243,466 (54.7%)	449
	Wendell L. Willkie	Republican	22,304,755 (44.8%)	82
1944	**Franklin D. Roosevelt**	Democratic	25,602,505 (52.8%)	432
	Thomas E. Dewey	Republican	22,006,278 (44.5%)	99
1948	**Harry S Truman**	Democratic	24,105,812 (49.5%)	303
	Thomas E. Dewey	Republican	21,970,065 (45.1%)	189
	J. Strom Thurmond	States' Rights	1,169,063 (2.4%)	39
	Henry A. Wallace	Progressive	1,157,172 (2.4%)	
1952	**Dwight D. Eisenhower**	Republican	33,936,234 (55.2%)	442
	Adlai E. Stevenson	Democratic	27,314,992 (44.5%)	89
1956	**Dwight D. Eisenhower**	Republican	35,590,472 (57.4%)	457
	Adlai E. Stevenson	Democratic	26,022,752 (42.0%)	73
1960	**John F. Kennedy**	Democratic	34,227,096 (49.9%)	303
	Richard M. Nixon	Republican	34,108,546 (49.6%)	219
1964	**Lyndon B. Johnson**	Democratic	43,126,233 (61.1%)	486
	Barry M. Goldwater	Republican	27,174,989 (38.5%)	52
1968	**Richard M. Nixon**	Republican	31,783,783 (43.4%)	301
	Hubert H. Humphrey	Democratic	31,271,839 (42.7%)	191
	George C. Wallace	American Independent	9,899,557 (13.5%)	46
1972	**Richard M. Nixon**	Republican	46,632,189 (61.3%)	521
	George McGovern	Democratic	28,422,015 (37.3%)	17
1976	**Jimmy Carter**	Democratic	40,828,587 (50.1%)	297
	Gerald R. Ford	Republican	39,147,613 (48.0%)	240
1980	**Ronald Reagan**	Republican	42,951,145 (51.0%)	489
	Jimmy Carter	Democratic	34,663,037 (41.0%)	49
	John B. Anderson	Independent	5,551,551 (6.6%)	
1984	**Ronald Reagan**	Republican	53,428,357 (59%)	525
	Walter F. Mondale	Democratic	36,930,923 (41%)	13
1988	**George Bush**	Republican	47,900,000 (54%)	426
	Michael Dukakis	Democratic	41,000,000 (46%)	112

Glossary of Key Terms

We have tried to write a readable book about American politics and government. We realize, however, that certain legal terms and political science phrases may not be familiar to some readers. To make such words or phrases, which appear in the text in boldface, more understandable, we have compiled this glossary to define them. We welcome suggestions for additions.

Act III leaders Typically, office holders and elected politicians who are skilled in bargaining and brokerage politics—in reconciling competing conceptions of the public interest and making the necessary compromises so that government can work. The notion of Act III implies that these leaders often depend on other kinds of leaders to set the agenda, to mobilize public opinion, and to begin the movements and even the early stages of coalition building that precede law making and policy making.

Administrative law Law relating to the authority and procedures of administrative agencies, as well as to the rules and regulations issued by those agencies.

Admiralty and maritime law Law derived from the general maritime law of nations, modified by Congress. Applicable not only on the high seas but also on all navigable waterways in the United States.

Advisory Commission on Intergovernmental Relations A permanent national bipartisan board created by Congress in 1959 to monitor the operation of and to recommend improvements for the U.S. federal system. ACIR is composed of representatives from the executive and legislative branches of the federal, state, and local governments, as well as members from the general public.

Amendment Addition to or deletion from a constitution or law.

Amicus curiae (friend of the court) brief A brief filed by an individual or organization with the permission of the court. It provides arguments in addition to those presented by the immediate parties to the case.

Annapolis convention A convention held in August 1786 that issued the call to Congress and the states for what became the Constitutional Convention. The Annapolis Convention itself, attended by delegates from five states, was called to consider problems of trade and navigation.

Anti-Federalists Persons opposed to more nationally centralized government in general, and to the 1787 Philadelphia Constitution in particular.

Antitrust policy The several federal laws (of which the Sherman Antitrust Act of 1890 is most prominent), supplemented by state laws, that try to prevent one or a few business firms from dominating a particular market.

Appeasement Term used to describe concessions made to a potential military opponent.

Appellate jurisdiction Authority to review decisions of lower courts and administrative tribunals.

Articles of Confederation The first constitution of the newly independent American states. It was drafted in 1777, ratified in 1781, and replaced by the present Constitution in 1789.

Assigned counsel system Arrangement whereby attorneys are provided for persons accused of crime who are unable to hire their own lawyers. The judge assigns a member of the bar to provide counsel to a particular defendant.

Attentive public Those who follow public affairs fairly carefully; those who read newspapers and magazines to keep informed.

Autocracy Government in which all power is concentrated in one person.

Bad tendency doctrine Interpretation of the First amendment that would permit legislatures to make illegal speech that can reasonably be said to have a tendency to cause people to engage in illegal action.

Baker v. Carr A 1962 Supreme Court ruling that legislative apportionment could be challenged and reviewed by federal courts.

Bicameralism The principle of the two-house legislature.

Bicameral legislature Two-house legislature; form for forty-nine of the states, as well as for the U.S. Congress.

Bill of attainder Legislative act that inflicts punishment on either named individuals or on a readily identifiable group.

Binding arbitration See *Compulsory (and binding) arbitration.*

Bipartisanship Policy that emphasizes cooperation and a united front between the major political parties.

Bipolarity A world situation in which two major superpowers dominate world politics.

Block grant Broad grant of funds made by one level of government to another for specific program areas—for example, health programs or crime prevention.

Bureau Generally, the largest subunit of a government department or agency.

Bureaucrat Government official; normally, one who gains office by appointment rather than election.

Categorical formula grant Grant of funds made by one level of government to another, to be used for specified purposes and in specified ways.

Caucus (local party)   Meeting of party members in a ward or town to choose party officials and/or candidates for public office and to decide questions of policy (e.g., platforms).

Caucus (legislative) or conference   Meeting of the members of a party in a chamber of legislature to select the party leadership in that chamber and to take party positions on pending legislative issues.

Checks and balances   Constitutional grant of powers that ensures each of the three branches of government a sufficient role in the actions of the others so that no one branch may dominate the others: The branches must work together if governmental business is to be performed.

City-manager plan   Same as council-manager plan. A city hires a professional manager to administer city departments and agencies. In most cities, the city manager reports directly to the city council.

Civil law   The legal code regulating conduct between private persons. Under civil law, governments provide the forum for the settlement of disputes between private parties in such matters as contracts and business relations.

Class action suit   Lawsuit brought by a person or group of persons in behalf of all persons similarly situated. The class may consist of a few persons or of thousands of persons. An example of a class action would be a suit by one person against an airline, alleging overcharges in behalf of that person and all other persons charged the same price for the same flight.

Clear and present danger doctrine   Interpretation of the First amendment first announced by Justice Holmes. This doctrine would not let laws that directly or indirectly restrict freedom of speech be applied unless the particular speech, article, or book in question is made or published such that there is a clear and present danger that the speech will lead to acts that the government may make illegal.

Closed shop   Labor arrangement in which an employer must hire only those people who are continuing union members.

Cloture   Procedure for terminating debate (especially filibusters) in the U.S. Senate.

Coattail effect   Influence a popular or unpopular candidate has on the electoral success or failure of other candidates on the same party ticket.

Collective bargaining   Method whereby representatives of the union and the employer determine wages, hours, and other conditions of employment through direct negotiation.

Commerce clause   The clause of the Constitution giving Congress the power to regulate all business activities that affect more states than one and also prohibiting states from unduly burdening or discriminating against business activities of other nations or states.

Commission charter   Form of city government in which a group of commissioners (usually five) serve as the city council and act as heads of departments in the municipal administration.

Common law   Body of judge-made law developed as judges decided cases; part of the English and American systems of justice.

Comparable worth   The idea that jobs should be paid at the same rate if they require comparable skills and contributions, even if market considerations make it possible to secure employees for one job at a lower rate than for another. The notion of comparable worth is advocated by those who believe jobs traditionally dominated by women—as nurses,

secretaries, and elementary school teachers, for example—are held down in wage rates compared to equivalent type jobs traditionally dominated by men—as plumbers and janitors, for example—because of discrimination and role stereotyping.

Compulsory (and binding) arbitration   Process whereby a dispute between management and union is settled by an impartial third party. When the law dictates that a stalemated labor dispute must be turned over to an outside arbitrator, the process is called *compulsory arbitration*. When union and management are required by law to accept the decision of the arbitrator, it is called *binding arbitration*.

Concurrent powers   Powers the Constitution gives to both the national and state governments.

Concurring opinion   An opinion in which a Supreme Court justice agrees with the decision of the majority or plurality, but for reasons different from those of the majority or plurality.

Confederation   Government created when nation-states, by compact, create a new government and delegate certain powers to it. In contrast to a federation, a confederation does not have power to regulate the conduct of individuals directly.

Conference committee   Committee appointed by the presiding officers of each house of the legislature to adjust differences on a particular bill. The report of the conference committee back to each chamber cannot be amended but must be accepted or rejected as it stands.

Conglomerate   Firm that owns businesses in many unrelated industries.

Connecticut Compromise   Agreement by delegates to the Constitutional Convention to give each state two senators, regardless of population. This would offset the decision to allocate representatives in the House of Representatives among the states according to population. This compromise between the less and more populous states was the price required by the less populous states for agreeing to the new Constitution.

Consent decree   Order issued by either a regulatory commission or a court in which a party, though not conceding guilt, agrees to modify future behavior. It is often used by the Federal Trade Commission to require business firms to cease alleged anticompetitive or illegal practices.

Conservatism   Philosophical approach to the role of government that generally opposes governmental regulation of the economy and favors local or state governmental action over federal governmental action. Both Barry Goldwater in 1964 and Ronald Reagan in the 1980s were major proponents of this approach.

Conspiracy   Combination between two or more persons for the purpose of committing an unlawful act or an act that is lawful by itself but unlawful when done by the concerted action of two or more persons.

Constitution   The fundamental rules that determine how those who govern are selected, the procedures by which they operate, and the limits to their powers.

Constitutional convention   The convention in Philadelphia in 1787 (May 25 to September 17) that framed the Constitution of the United States. It invented the presidency and electoral college, and the federalism and separation of powers features that are still the central elements of American government. This convention's draft then had to be ratified by nine states before it was adopted in 1788.

Constitutional government Government that enforces recognized and regularly applied limits on the powers of those who govern.

Constitutional home rule State constitutional authorization for local governmental units to conduct their own affairs.

Constitutional law In an American context, the authoritative interpretations of the meaning of the Constitution of the United States; such interpretations are chiefly found in the opinions of the U.S. Supreme Court.

Containment Foreign policy strategy pursued to some extent by all post-World War II presidential administrations—but especially by the Truman administration. Its basic aim was to prevent the industrial or emerging powers of Europe or the Middle East from falling under the control of the Soviet Union.

Convention See party convention.

Council–manager plan Form of city government in which the city council hires a professional administrator to manage city affairs; also known as the city-manager plan.

Curtiss-Wright case (*U.S.* v. *Curtiss-Wright*, 1936) Supreme Court case upholding the sovereignty of the national government in foreign affairs and declaring the president to be its prime agent.

Dealignment Refers to the decline in attachment and loyalty to the two major political parties, and is an alternative to party realignment, which refers to shifting loyalties from one of the political parties to another.

De facto segregation Racial segregation that results from nongovernmental practices.

Defendant In a civil action, the party defending himself or herself against charges brought by the plaintiff. In a criminal action, the person charged with the offense.

De jure segregation Racial segregation that results from governmental actions. See also *Jim Crow laws*.

Delegate One view of the role of a member of a legislature. It holds that, as delegates, legislators should represent the views of constituents even when the legislators may personally hold different views.

Demagogue Leader who gains power by means of impassioned appeals to the prejudices and emotions of the masses.

Democracy Government by the people, either directly or indirectly, with free and frequent elections.

Deregulation Efforts to reduce or eliminate governmental controls, rules, or regulation of economic activity. Typically, deregulation implies allowing more of a market or "hands off" approach as opposed to detailing federal rules or specifications to guide some industrial operations.

Detente Relaxation of tension with another nation; conciliation or settlement with another nation.

Deterrence The U.S. defense policy of taking steps to prevent a nuclear attack by an adversary, commonly measured by the U.S. capacity to survive a first strike by the Soviets and still respond with a massive retaliation that would impose such costs on the Soviets that they would not consider the first strike. This capacity has to be effective enough to discourage any initial attack.

Deviating election Election in which the party out of power wins, but underlying voting patterns remain unchanged.

Direct primary Election, open to all members of the party,

in which voters choose the persons who will be the party's nominees in the general election.

Direct transmission satellite Communications satellite that transmits messages to individual receiving sets in homes or offices.

Discharge petition Petition that, if signed by a majority of the members of the House of Representatives, will pry a bill from committee and bring it to the floor for consideration.

Doctrine of Dual Federalism View that national and state governments are equal sovereigns, each granted certain powers by the Constitution with the Supreme Court to serve as arbitrator in case of conflicts between them.

Domino theory Doctrine that assumes if some key nation or region falls into Communist control, a string of other nations will subsequently fall. President Eisenhower and later presidents used this theory to describe the situation in Indochina.

Double jeopardy Trial for the *same* crime by the *same* government. Such a practice is forbidden by the Constitution.

Due process clauses Clauses in the Fifth and Fourteenth amendments that state that the national (Fifth) and the state (Fourteenth) governments shall not deprive any person of life, liberty, or property without due process of law.

Economies of scale The assumption that larger size makes possible lower per unit costs and thus more efficiency.

Electoral college In general, the procedures established by the Constitution for the election of the president and vice-president. More specifically, the gathering in each state of electors from that state who formally cast their ballots for their parties' candidates for president and vice-president. Largely a formality.

Eminent domain Power of governments to take private property for public use. The Constitution requires governments to provide just compensation for property so taken.

Entitlement programs Programs such as Social Security, Aid to Families with Dependent Children, Medicare, and unemployment insurance to which qualified citizens are "entitled" by definitions in national legislation.

Environmental impact statement A statement required by federal law from all agencies for any project using federal funds that assesses the potential effect of a federal action on the environment.

Equal protection clause Clause in the Fourteenth amendment that forbids any state (by interpretation, the Fifth amendment imposes the same limitation on the national government) to deny to any person within its jurisdiction the equal protection of the laws. This is the major constitutional restraint on the power of governments to discriminate against persons because of race, national origin, or sex.

Equal Rights Amendment (ERA) Constitutional amendment proposed by Congress in 1972, designed to guarantee women equality of rights under the law. Although ratified by thirty-five states, the additional three states necessary for ratification failed to approve the amendment by the June 30, 1982, deadline. An ERA-type amendment is likely to be proposed again by Congress.

Equal-time requirement Requirement of Congress and Federal Communications Commission that radio and television licencees must give opposing candidates for public office equal free air time.

Equity   Judicial remedy used whenever suits for money damages do not provide adequate justice.

Establishment clause   Clause in the First amendment that states that Congress (by interpretation, the Fourteenth amendment imposes the same limitation on state legislatures) shall make no law respecting an establishment of religion. It has been interpreted by the Supreme Court to forbid governmental support to any or all religions.

Ethnocentrism   Belief in the superiority of one's nation or ethnic society; an overriding concern or preoccupation with one's own group.

Excise tax   Consumer tax on a specific kind of merchandise, such as tobacco.

Executive agreement   International agreement made by a president that has the force of a treaty. It does not need the approval of the Senate.

Executive Office of the President   Cluster of staff agencies created by the Reorganization Act of 1939 to help the president. Currently the Executive Office includes an Office of Management and Budget, the Council of Economic Advisers, the National Security Council, and a number of specialized offices.

Executive privilege   The claim by presidents that they have the discretion to decide that the national interest will be better served if certain information in the custody of the executive departments is withheld from the public, including the courts and Congress. In *United States* v. *Nixon* the Supreme Court ruled that even though presidents are entitled to the privilege, the privilege is not unlimited, and its extent is subject to judicial determination.

Ex post facto law   Retroactive criminal law.

Express powers   Powers specifically granted to one of the branches of the national government by the Constitution.

Extradition   Legal process whereby an alleged criminal offender is surrendered by the officials of one state to officials of the state in which the crime is alleged to have been committed.

Faction   Organized group of politically active persons, usually less than a majority, seeking to realize group goals in competition with other groups.

Fairness doctrine   Doctrine, written into law and interpreted by the Federal Communications Commission, that imposes on radio and television licensees an obligation to ensure that differing viewpoints are presented about controversial issues or persons.

Federal Reserve System   The private-public banking regulatory system, created by Congress in 1913, to establish banking practices and regulate currency in circulation and the amount of credit available. It is comprised of twelve regional banks, and its major responsibilities are supervised by a seven-member presidentially appointed Federal Reserve Board of Governors in Washington, D.C.

Federalism   Governmental arrangement whereby power is divided by a constitution between a national government and constituent governments, called states in the U.S. The national and the constituent governments both exercise direct authority over individuals.

The Federalist   Series of essays favoring the new Constitution. Written by Alexander Hamilton, John Jay, and James Madison in 1787 and 1788, during the debate over ratification.

Federalists   Persons who supported the Constitution before its ratification in 1787 to 1788. After ratification a Federalist party developed under the leadership of Alexander Hamilton, Washington's first secretary of the treasury. Federalists like John Adams and John Marshall generally favored a strong central government and a fiscal policy of assuming state debts and establishing a national bank.

Fighting words   Words that by their very nature inflict injury upon those to whom they are addressed.

Filibuster   Holding the floor of the U.S. Senate to delay proceedings and thereby prevent a vote on a controversial issue.

Floating debt   Short-term government loans, in the form of bank notes or tax-anticipation warrants, that are paid out of current revenues.

Four Freedoms   American goals proclaimed by Franklin D. Roosevelt in his annual message to Congress, January 6, 1941: freedom of speech and expression, freedom of worship, freedom from want, and freedom from fear.

Fourth world   Those nations that are among the poorest in the world and whose per capita standard of living are among the lowest of any nations.

Franchise   The right to vote.

Full faith and credit clause   Clause in the Constitution requiring each state to recognize the civil judgments rendered by the courts of the other states.

General property tax   Tax levied by local (and some state) governments on real or personal, tangible property—the major portion of which is on the estimated value of one's home and land.

Gerrymandering   Drawing an election district in such a way that one party or group has a distinct advantage. The strategy is to provide a close but safe margin in numerous districts while concentrating (and hence wasting) the opposition's vote in a few districts.

Government corporation   Cross between a business corporation and a government agency, created to secure greater freedom of action for a particular program.

Grand jury   A jury comprising twelve to twenty-three persons who, in private, hear evidence presented by the government to determine whether persons shall be required to stand trial.

Gross national product (GNP)   The monetary value of all goods and services produced in the nation in a given year.

Habeas corpus   See *Writ of habeas corpus*.

Hatch Act   Federal statute barring federal employees from active participation in certain kinds of politics and protecting them from being fired on partisan grounds.

Ideology   Interrelated or integrated set of attitudes and beliefs about political values and the role of power and government.

Ideologue   Person who has a relatively fixed and highly integrated set of attitudes and beliefs about the role of government as it affects individuals and public policy.

Immunity   Exemption from prosecution based on evidence secured as the result of testimony compelled by a government agency.

Implied limitations   Doctrine regarding constitutional construction of state constitutions. It holds that powers not granted to municipal corporations are denied to such corporations.

Implied powers   Powers given to Congress, by the Constitution, that allow Congress to do whatever is necessary and proper in order to carry out one of the express powers or any combination of them.

Impoundment   Presidential refusal to allow an agency to spend funds authorized and appropriated by Congress.

Incrementalism   Theory of public policy and public administration that deemphasizes comprehensiveness and insists that administrative decisions are and should be made piecemeal.

Independent agency   Sometimes used interchangeably with "independent regulatory agency" to refer to an agency that is not part of the legislative, executive, or judicial branch, such as the Interstate Commerce Commission. The term also refers to an agency that is not part of a cabinet department, such as the Veterans Administration.

Indiana ballot   See *Party column ballot*.

Inflation   Rise in the general level of prices, which is the same thing as a fall in the value of money.

Information affidavit   Certification by a public prosecutor that there is evidence to justify bringing named individuals to trial.

Inherent powers   Those powers of the national government in the field of foreign affairs that the Supreme Court has declared do not depend upon constitutional grants but rather grow out of the very existence of the national government.

Initiative petition   Procedure whereby a certain number of voters may, by petition, propose a law and get it submitted to the people for a vote. Initiative may be direct (if the proposed law is voted on directly by the people) or indirect (if the proposal is submitted first to the legislature and then to the people, if the legislature rejects it).

Intangible property   Wealth indicated by cash, stocks, bonds, savings accounts, partnerships, money funds, and so on, in contrast to wealth in the form of such physical objects as land, houses, automobiles, and jewels.

Interest groups   Collections of persons who share some common interest or attitude, who interact with one another directly or indirectly, and who ordinarily make demands on other groups.

Interlocking directorate   Situation in which the same persons serve as members of the boards of directors of competing companies.

Interstate compacts   Agreements among the states. The Constitution requires that most such agreements be approved by Congress.

Isolationism   The attitude (somewhat in fashion in the 1930s) that the U.S. should retreat from world affairs and curb the tendency to intervene abroad—especially in military conflicts.

Item veto   Authority of the executive (usually the governor of a state) to veto parts of a legislative bill without having to veto the entire bill. Presidents do not have the power of the item veto.

Jim Crow laws   Laws that require public facilities and places of public accommodation, including those privately owned and operated, to be segregated by race.

Joint committee   Committee composed of members of both houses of a legislature. Such committees are intended to speed up legislative action.

Judicial activism   Variously defined. One definition is the philosophy proposing that judges cannot decide cases merely by applying the literal words of the Constitution or by discerning the intention of the framers, but that they must and should openly recognize that judicial decision making is choosing among conflicting values. Judges should so interpret the Constitution as to keep it reflecting the current values of the American people. Judicial activism is used in contrast with judicial restraint.

Judicial restraint   Variously defined. One definition is the philosophy proposing that, in deciding cases, judges should declare unconstitutional only those legislative actions and executive actions that clearly violate the words of the Constitution or the intent of the framers, and that constitutional changes should be left to the formal amendatory process.

Judicial review   The authority, spelled out by Chief Justice Marshall in *Marbury* v. *Madison* (1803), of judges when deciding cases to examine statutes and the actions of executive officials in order to determine their validity, according to the judges' interpretation of the Constitution.

Jus sanguinis   Citizenship acquired through citizenship of parents.

Jus soli   Citizenship acquired through place of birth.

Justiciable disputes   Disputes that, in contrast to political questions, raise questions about legality and that are appropriate for resolution before a court of law.

Keynes, John Maynard   English economist whose views have dominated economic thinking in recent decades.

Labor injunction   Court order forbidding specific individuals or groups from performing certain acts, such as striking, that the court considers harmful to the rights and property of others.

Lame duck   Official serving out a term of office after defeat for reelection and before the inauguration of a successor.

Legislative home rule   Power given by the legislature to local governments that eliminates the need for local governments to go back to the legislature for additional grants of power. However, state law still takes precedence over local ordinances, and powers given to the local governments by the legislature may be rescinded.

Legislative veto   Until it was declared unconstitutional by the Supreme Court in 1983, a provision in a law reserving to Congress, or to a chamber or committee of Congress, the power to reject by majority vote an act or regulation of a department or agency of the national government.

Libel   Written defamation of another person. Especially in the case of public officials and public figures, the constitutional tests designed to restrict libel actions are very rigid.

Liberalism   Philosophical approach to the role of government that generally favors governmental action, especially to help the underdog and achieve equal opportunity for all.

Libertarianism   Philosophical approach to the role of government that favors as limited a government as possible and believes in free-market economics and a noninterventionist foreign policy.

Lobby/lobbying   To conduct activities aimed at influencing public officials and the policies they enact. This is, of course, part of the citizen's right to petition the government.

Lobbyist   Person who acts for an organized interest group or association or corporation to try to influence policy decisions and positions in the executive and—especially—legislative branches.

Long ballot Ballot that came into general use in the late 1820s. Based on the belief that voters should elect all, or nearly all, the people who governed them. It is criticized as being unwieldy and confusing because it contains too many offices and candidates.

Lottery A form of voluntary taxation used by at least half of the states and the District of Columbia; it involves distributing prizes by lot or random chance to the buyers of winning tickets. The bulk of the profits go to the State Department of Revenue or its equivalent. State income from lotteries typically amounts to less than 3 or 4 percent of state revenue; lotteries do, however, generate income without raising taxes. They are also sometimes defended as means of reducing the amount of illegal gambling and of minimizing the influence of organized crime.

Maintaining election Election that shows a continuation of a pattern of partisan support.

Majority floor leader Legislature position held by an important party member selected by the majority party in caucus or conference. The majority floor leader helps frame party strategy and tries to keep the membership in line. In the U.S. Senate the majority leader (in consultation with the minority floor leader) determines the agenda and has strong influence in committee selection.

Marshall Plan The American program to assist European economic recovery following World War II.

Massachusetts ballot See *Office group ballot*.

Mass public The general public, including a large segment of the population that is often uninformed about the details of political controversy and policy debates.

Mayor-council charter The oldest and most common form of city government, consisting of either a weak mayor and city council or a strong mayor and council.

McCulloch v. *Maryland* (1819) Celebrated Supreme Court decision that established the doctrine of national supremacy and the principle that the implied powers of the national government are to be generously interpreted.

Medicaid A joint state and federal assistance program for impoverished individuals who do not qualify for the national medicare program. Medicaid ensures that the federal government pays up to 80 percent of the cost of medical care for those (often the elderly) whose nursing home and hospital costs readily exceed their social security and meager pension incomes.

Messianic spirit Belief in the future deliverance or saving of a people or a nation. The notion that a people are select, singled out for a special destiny.

Metropolis City regarded as the center or central community of a particular area. The city is generally an important one with a population of over 500,000.

Midterm party conference National meeting, formerly of Democratic party members, held halfway through a presidential term, designed to activate the party and bring its platform up to date.

Military-industrial complex Alleged alliance between top military and industrial leaders, who have a common interest in arms production and utilization.

Minority floor leader Party leader in each house of a legislature, elected by the minority party as spokesperson for the opposition.

Misdemeanor Offense of lesser gravity than a felony, for which punishment may be a fine or imprisonment for a relatively brief time, usually less than a year.

Missouri Plan System for selecting judges that combines features of the appointive and elective methods. The governor makes an initial appointment from a list of persons—usually three—presented by a panel of lawyers and laypersons (the panel is usually appointed by the chief judge of the state court of last resort). After the judge has served for a year, the electorate is asked at the next general election whether or not the judge should be retained in office. If a majority vote yes, the judge serves the rest of the term. At the end of the term, if a judge wishes to serve again, his or her name is once again presented to the electorate.

Monetary policy National government policy that seeks to change the interest, credit, or stock market rates. The Federal Reserve Board, for example, uses "tight money" policies to restrain and prolong boom periods and to fight inflation. "Loose money" policies—making credit and money more freely—are used to fight recessions or a depression.

Multipolar Refers to a world in which many nations shape world political developments and influence world affairs.

National Security Council Planning and advisory board that confers with the president on matters relating to national security. Permanent members include the president, vice-president, secretary of state, secretary of defense, and the chair of the joint chiefs of staff.

National supremacy Constitutional doctrine that whenever conflict occurs between the constitutionally authorized actions of the national government and those of a state or local government, the actions of the national government take priority.

Naturalization Process by which persons acquire citizenship in a country other than the nation of their birth.

National monopoly Condition that exists when it would be inefficient to have competition in a particular industry, as in the case of a power company.

Necessary and proper clause Clause of the Constitution setting forth the implied powers of Congress. It states that Congress, in addition to its enumerated powers, has the power to make all laws necessary and proper for carrying out all powers vested by the Constitution in the national government.

New Jersey Plan Plan presented by Paterson of New Jersey at the Constitutional Convention as a counterproposal to the Virginia Plan. The New Jersey Plan proposed only modifications in the Articles of Confederation and provided for a confederation built around powerful state governments.

Nixon Doctrine Policy suggested by President Nixon in the early 1970s that would have the U.S. come to the assistance of allies and friendly nations, but only if they themselves would do the main fighting.

Nonproliferation Treaty International agreement under which nuclear powers pledge not to distribute nuclear devices to nonnuclear powers.

Obscenity Work that taken as a whole appeals to a prurient interest in sex by depicting sexual conduct as specifically defined by legislation or judicial interpretation in a patently offensive way, and that lacks serious literary, artistic, political, or scientific value.

Office group ballot Method of voting in which all candidates are listed under the office for which they are running. Sometimes called the Massachusetts ballot or the office-block ballot.

Office of Management and Budget (OMB) Presidential staff agency that serves as a clearinghouse for budgetary requests and management improvements.

Oligarchy Government controlled by a small segment of the people, who are chosen on the basis of wealth or power.

Oligopoly Situation in which a few firms dominate an industry.

Ombudsman Office in Sweden and elsewhere that handles citizen complaints against the government.

On appeal Order issued by the Supreme Court to review those decisions of the lower courts, federal and state, that Congress has stipulated the Supreme Court is required to review.

Opinion maker Person who influences how the general public views policy problems—for example, an elected official, editor, writer, and teacher.

Override An action by Congress to try to reverse a presidential veto (a veto by the president of legislation) by means of a two-thirds vote in both chambers of the Congress. Veto overrides are rare; they are successful only about 3 percent of the time.

Palko Test A test established by the Supreme Court in the case of *Palko* v. *Connecticut* (1937). The test determines which provisions of the Bill of Rights should be "incorporated" into the Fourteenth amendment as a limitation on state and local governments: namely, those provisions that relate to rights that are so important that neither "liberty nor justice would exist if they were sacrificed."

Party column ballot Method of voting in which all candidates are listed under their party designations, which makes it easy for the voters to cast votes for all the candidates of one party. Sometimes called the Indiana ballot.

Party convention A meeting of party delegates to pass on matters of policy and in some cases to select party candidates for public office. Conventions are held on county, state, and national levels.

Party primary Election for choosing party nominees that is open to members and supporters of the party making the nomination.

Party realignment Fundamental change in the economic, racial, social, sectional, and other electoral foundations of a party as it seeks to maintain its competitive position in elections.

Patronage Dispensing government jobs to persons who belong to the winning political party.

Personal property As opposed to real estate—houses and land—this refers to household goods, jewelry, stocks, and bonds.

Petit jury The ordinary jury for the trial of a civil or criminal action. So called to distinguish it from the grand jury.

Plaintiff Party who brings a civil action or sues to obtain a legal remedy from a court for injury to his or her rights.

Plea bargaining Negotiations between prosecutor and defendant aimed at getting the defendant to plead guilty in return for prosecutor's agreeing to reduce the seriousness of the crime for which the defendant will be convicted.

Pluralistic power structure The notion that even though some people do have more influence than others, that influ-

ence is shared among many people and tends to be limited to particular issues and policy areas.

Pocket veto Special veto power exercised by a chief executive after a legislative body has adjourned. Bills that a chief executive refuses to sign at this time do not become law. In effect, by such an action, a governor or president "puts the bill in his or her pocket," and the bill thus dies.

Police powers Powers of a government to regulate persons and property in order to promote the public health, welfare, and safety. In the U.S., the states, but not the national government, have such general police power.

Political Action Committee (PAC) The political arms of organized interests. PACs have become major agencies through which to finance congressional campaigns.

Political machine Organized subgroup within a party, consisting of a political boss and supporting ward and precinct workers who get out the vote and perform a variety of "services" for local constituents between elections.

Political questions Constitutional questions that judges refuse to answer because to do so would involve judicial encroachment upon the authority of Congress or the president. For example: Congress determines if a sufficient number of states have ratified a constitutional amendment within a reasonable time; Congress determines which states have the required republican form of government; and the president determines which foreign governments are to be recognized by the U.S. Because the Supreme Court determines which constitutional questions are political and which are justiciable, this limitation on the authority of the courts is self-defined.

Political socialization Processes by which we develop our political attitudes, values, and behavior.

Poll tax Payment by a person, formerly required in some states, as a condition for voting.

Populists Adherents of a movement and political party of the 1880s and 1890s. Their geographical base was rural—in the Midwest, South, and Southwest especially. Waging "reformist" efforts against the banks, railroads, and other establishments, Populists raised issues that influenced the Progressive movement and the Democratic party after 1892.

Power elite Term originally used by sociologist C. Wright Mills to describe the small group of people he believed rule the country because of their socioeconomic status.

Preferred position doctrine Interpretation of the First amendment that holds that no law restricting expression is constitutional unless the government can demonstrate convincingly to a court that the law is absolutely necessary to prevent serious injury to the public well-being.

Presidential primaries Statewide primaries in which rank-and-file party members choose the delegates to the national party convention and may indicate their choice for the party's presidential nominee.

President pro tempore Officer of the U.S. Senate chosen from the ranks—usually the senior member of the majority party. Serves as president of the Senate in the absence of the vice-president.

Principle democrats Persons more concerned with the goals and values of "government by the people" than with the procedures used to reach those goals.

Prior restraint Restraint imposed prior to a speech's being made, a newspaper's being published, or a motion picture's being shown. The restraint may be of various kinds—for example, a requirement that a license be granted or that the approval of a censorship board be given.

Privatization   The contracting out to the "for profit" private sector "public services" that are typically provided by public organizations. Trash collection, ambulance, and fire protection services have been the most common privatizations of public services. The objectives are to obtain the public services at lower costs, and sometimes to shrink the public bureaucracy to encourage additional efficiencies.

Pro bono   Term used to refer to the work lawyers (or other professionals) do to serve the public good and for which they either receive no fees or decline fees.

Procedural due process   Constitutional requirement that governments proceed by proper means.

Process democrats   Persons who believe that if proper procedures are followed in running the government, the more likely it is that sound and democratic policy will result. (All democrats believe in both good processes and principles, they differ over the balance between the two.)

Program oversight   Process of monitoring and evaluating the details of how a program is being, or has been, carried out.

Progressives   Adherents of a "good government" movement in the first two decades of this century that advocated measures that would open up the system and weaken party bosses. They favored nonpartisan elections, participatory primaries, and direct elections of senators. The Progressive party, especially active from 1912 through the mid-1920s, emerged as a visible part of the Progressive movement.

Progressive tax   A tax whereby upper-income citizens pay a higher proportion of their incomes in tax revenues than do lower-income citizens.

Project grant   Federal funds given for specified purposes and based on the merits of applications.

Public defender   Public officer whose job is to provide legal assistance to those persons accused of crimes who are unable to hire their own attorneys.

Public opinion   Cluster of views and attitudes held by people on a significant issue. Because any complex society has many groups, it is more precise to talk about publics, subpublics, and public opinions than about a single public opinion.

Public policy   The substance of what government does. More generally, the intentions of a government and the subsequent follow-up actions to implement laws and other decisions of governmental bodies.

Public/special authority   Special government agencies frequently found in metropolitan areas, set up to undertake such highly specialized functions as overseeing mass transit, an interstate harbor complex, or a regional airport.

Quasilegislative and quasijudicial   Phrase coined by the Supreme Court to permit noncourt and nonlegislative bodies to decide disputes and make rules. Decisions must, however, be subject to court review and rules must be within the general guidelines established by the legislature.

Quota sampling   Accounting for the variables in the population and assigning a quota for each variable to produce a representative cross section.

Random sampling   Creating a representative sample through random selection—for example, by shuffling housing tracts and interviewing individuals in every fifth, tenth, or fifteenth house.

Rational basis test   Test used to measure laws for compliance with the requirements of the equal protection clause. This test is applied to laws that do *not* affect a suspect classification of fundamental rights. Such laws need only a rational basis in fact.

Realigning election   Election in which the basis partisan commitments of a significant segment of the electorate change, as in 1932.

Real property   Land and buildings.

Reapportionment   Redrawing of legislative district lines to recognize the existing population distribution.

Recall   Election held to determine whether or not an official should be removed from office before the end of his or her term. A certain number of voters must petition to hold a recall election.

Recidivists   One who habitually relapses into crime.

Redistributive policy   Governmental policy that seeks to use tax revenues in such a way as to help those who have less. In effect, tax monies from the upper and middle classes are channeled into programs that assist lower income or truly needy people by redistributing some of society's wealth.

Red tape   Procedures and forms used to carry out policies and governmental functions. The term often expresses dissatisfaction with especially slow and formal rules and procedures.

Reduction veto   The power of a governor in a few states to reduce a particular money-providing measure approved by the state legislature.

Referendum   Practice of submitting to popular vote measures passed by the legislature or proposed by initiative. Use of the referendum may be required or optional.

Regressive tax   Tax that weighs most heavily on those least able to pay.

Regulation   Governmental order having the force of law and designed to control or govern the behavior of a business, union, or similar organizations and individuals.

Regulatory board or commission   Agency responsible for enforcing particular statutes. Generally such an agency has quasilegislative and quasijudicial functions as well as executive powers.

Representative democracy   See *Republic*.

Republic   Form of government that derives its powers directly or indirectly from the people. Those chosen to govern are accountable, directly or indirectly, to those whom they govern. In contrast to a direct democracy, in which the people make rules directly, in a republic the people select representatives who make the rules.

Republican form of government   See *Republic*.

Revenue sharing   Program whereby federal funds are provided to state and local governments to be spent largely at the discretion of the receiving governments.

Right-to-work law   Provision in state laws that prohibits arrangements between a union and an employer requiring membership in a union as a condition for getting or keeping a job.

Runoff election   Election held when no candidate receives a required percentage of the vote in an earlier election. Usually held between the two candidates who received the most votes in the first election.

Safe seat   Electoral office, usually in legislature, for which the party or the incumbent is so strong that reelection is almost taken for granted.

Sales tax General tax on sales transactions.

Salience Significance of an event or issue.

SALT (Strategic Arms Limitation Treaty) An agreement between the U.S. and Soviet governments to limit both defensive and offensive weapons systems.

Sampling error The degree to which a sample is distorted and does not represent the "polling universe" to be measured.

Secondary boycott Concerted effort by a union involved in a dispute with an employer to place pressure on a third party, who—in response to such pressure—might put pressure on the workers' employer. Such boycotts are forbidden by the 1947 Taft-Hartley Act.

Sedition Attempting to overthrow the government by force or to interrupt its activities by violence.

Seditious Term used to describe speech that advocates the forceful overthrow of the government. The Supreme Court has ruled that Congress may make seditious speech a crime, but no one may be punished for seditious speech unless it can be shown that he or she specifically urged people to engage in concrete acts of violence.

Senate majority leader Elected leader of the majority party in the U.S. Senate. This person functions as the chief agenda setter and usually as the most important power broker in the U.S. Senate. Robert Dole, Robert Byrd, Mike Mansfield, and Lyndon Johnson have served in this influential position in the past thirty years.

Senatorial courtesy Custom in the U.S. Senate of (1) referring the names of prospective appointees, especially federal judges, to senators from the states in which the appointees reside; and (2) withdrawing any nominees these senators deem objectionable, especially if senators are from the same party as the nominating president.

Separation of powers Constitutional division of power among legislative, executive, and judicial branches. The legislative branch is assigned the power to make laws; the executive is charged with the power to apply the laws; and the judiciary receives the power to interpret laws.

Severance tax Tax on the privilege of "severing" natural resources such as coal, oil, and timber, charged to the companies doing the extracting or severing.

Shays's Rebellion Rural rebellion of 1786 to 1787 protesting mortgage foreclosures in western Massachusetts. Led by Daniel Shays, it brought conservative support for a stronger national government.

Shield law Law establishing a legal right for reporters and other representatives of the media to refuse, under certain circumstances, to respond to orders of legislative committees or court subpoenas to reveal sources of information.

Socialism Philosophical approach to the role of government that favors national planning and public ownership of business.

Social stratification Sociological theory suggesting that the upper class, or the wealthy, wield extensive influence over the decisions and policies made by governments at all levels.

Speaker Presiding officer in the House of Representatives, formally elected by the House but actually selected by the majority party. The Speaker's powers include referring legislation to committees, making appointments to the House Rules Committee, recognizing members who wish to speak, ruling on questions of parliamentary procedure, and appointing special conference committees.

Standard Metropolitan Statistical Area (SMSA) A central city—or twin cities—of at least 50,000 people, along with those surrounding counties that are economically and socially dependent on the city.

Stare decisis The rule of precedent, whereby a rule of law contained in a judicial decision is commonly viewed as binding on judges whenever the same question is presented.

Star Wars See *Strategic Defense Initiative*.

Statism Belief in the rights of the state over those of the individual—the opposite of the American tradition that the individual is exalted above the state.

Statutory law Law enacted by a legislature.

Strategic Defense Initiative (SDI) *Also known as Star Wars*. Proposed in 1983 by President Ronald Reagan, this system seeks to discover and construct a defensive "shield" against incoming nuclear missiles. The shield would be made of laser and electronic devices that would destroy such missiles launched to attack the U.S. The system figured prominently in the Reagan-Gorbachev Iceland Summit meeting of 1986.

Strong mayor–council Form of local government in which the public directly elects the mayor as well as the city council. However, the mayor appoints the department heads, with the approval of the council, and in effect serves as the chief executive officer for the city and its administration.

Subsidy Governmental support that can take many forms—reduction of taxes, government loans, special protections, outright cash, or credit assistance. Subsidies are designed to encourage a particular type of private-sector action.

Substantive due process Constitutional requirement that governments act reasonably and that the substance of the laws themselves be reasonable.

Subpoena Court order to present oneself before an official agency. A subpoena duces tecum is a court order to present specific documents.

Suburbs Residential areas or communities in the outlying regions around a city.

Sunset process Legislative review process that calls for the termination of a program after a certain number of years, often six or seven, unless it is carefully examined, certified to be doing what it was intended to do, and repassed by the legislature. Many states have adopted this practice. The word comes from the expression that "the sun should set" on programs that have outlived their usefulness.

Sunshine law Law requiring governmental agencies, under certain circumstances and usually subject to certain exceptions, to operate in public.

Supply-side economics Economic strategy of stimulating production through tax cuts or reduced governmental regulation.

Suspect classifications Racial or national origin classifications created by law and subject to careful judicial scrutiny. Likely to be declared unconstitutional unless they can be justified by overwhelmingly desirable state purposes that can be achieved in no other way.

Taft-Hartley Act Passed by Congress in 1947, an act that elaborates the terms of labor-management bargaining, the conditions under which strikes can occur, and related aspects of union organization.

Tariff Tax levied on imports in order to help protect a nation's industries, labor, or farmers from foreign competition. It can also be used merely to raise additional revenue.

Tax expenditure Loss of tax revenue due to provisions of the federal tax laws that allow special exclusions, exemptions, or deductions, or that provide special credit, preferential rates of tax, or deferrals of tax liability.

Third world Those nations that are relatively poor but that are seeking to modernize and develop.

Three-Fifths Compromise North-South agreement at the Constitutional Convention of 1787 to count only three-fifths of the slave population in determining representation in the House of Representatives.

Ticket splitting Practice of voting for candidates at the ballot box with little or no regard to their parties, with the result that one voter may vote for a Democrat for governor and a Republican for Congress, or vice versa.

Titular leader Nominal leader; leader by title only. The defeated presidential nominee is referred to as the titular leader of the party out of power, but the role is more honorary than it is a realistic power base.

Transactional leader A leader who deals in the short term and, generally, for self-interest. One who engages in exchanges and bargains as in a quid pro quo fashion.

Transforming leader A leader who helps liberate followers so they can achieve higher aspirations and longer range goals. A leader who so engages with followers as to heighten their political awareness and their own abilities for leadership.

Treason Carefully defined for the U.S. by the Constitution to consist *only* of levying war against the U.S., adhering to its enemies, or giving the latter aid and comfort. Moreover, no person can be convicted of treason unless the accused confesses in open court or unless two witnesses testify in court that they saw the acts of treason being committed.

Truman Doctrine Policy, sponsored by President Harry Truman in 1947, aimed at halting Communist expansion in southeastern Europe. It called for American support and funds for all free peoples so that they might resist being taken over by outside forces of repression.

Trustee One view of the function of a member of a legislature. It holds that, as trustees, legislators may believe that they were sent to Washington or the state capitals to think and vote independently for the general welfare—and not as their constituents determine.

Unicameral legislature One-house legislature, Nebraska and almost all cities use this form.

Union shop "Union-security" provision found in some collective bargaining agreements requiring all employees to become members of the union within a short period—usually thirty days after being hired—and to remain members as a condition of employment.

Unitary system Government with power concentrated by the constitution in the central government.

Unitary tax A state tax on a company's worldwide profits, typically based on a formula that takes into account payroll, property, and sales in the state as well as some percentage of out-of-state or worldwide receipts and profits. It is a controversial tax that is heatedly debated around the country: Some states view it as a legitimate means to secure added revenue, whereas other states avoid or repeal it as a means of luring companies to relocate into their states.

Unit rule Requirement that the whole delegation to a party convention cast its vote as the majority decides.

Universe The entire population of a group about which information is sought.

User charges Fees charged directly to individuals who use certain public services on the basis of service consumed. Sometimes called a user fee or user tax.

Virginia Plan Proposal at the Constitutional Convention that provided for a strong legislature with representation in each house determined by population. It thus favored the large states.

Watergate The general name given to a set of both major and minor violations of the law committed by Nixon administration officials and their "friends" in 1972—including obstruction of justice or covering up of crimes that took place when the National Democratic Committee headquarters was broken into in 1972. The Committee was then located in the Watergate Office Building adjacent to the fashionable Watergate Hotel in Washington, D.C. Other incidents involved misusing the Internal Revenue Service, the Central Intelligence Agency, and the FBI; the breaking in and entering of a psychiatrist's office; and perpetrating various "dirty tricks" on some of President Nixon's election opponents in the 1972 presidential election. Nixon was eventually forced out of office because of these events, and several of his advisers were indicted and served jail sentences.

Weak mayor–council Form of local government in which the mayor must share most of the executive powers of a city with other elected or appointed boards and commissions. The mayor in weak-mayor cities is often mainly a ceremonial leader.

Whip Party leader who is the liaison between the leadership and the rank and file in the legislature.

White primary Under the pretense that it was not governmental action, officials of the Democratic party in the South used to admit to its primaries only white persons. In the South in those days candidates of the Democratic party were the only ones with any chance of winning in the following general election; blacks were thus excluded from the only election that counted. The white primary in all its various forms was declared unconstitutional by the Supreme Court in *Smith* v. *Allwright* (1944).

Workfare A program at the state, and sometimes also local, level that either mandates or strongly encourages able-bodied welfare recipients to accept public-service jobs or similar low-paying private-sector jobs that would help free them of their dependency on welfare subsidies.

Writ of certiorari Writ used by the Supreme Court to review decisions of lower courts, federal and state, that are within the discretionary appellate jurisdiction of the Supreme Court. It is a formal device regularly used to bring a case up to the Court.

Writ of habeas corpus Court order requiring jailers to explain to a judge why they are holding a prisoner in custody.

Writ of mandamus Court order directing an official to perform a nondiscretionary, or ministerial, act as required by law.

Yellow-dog contract Contract by an antiunion employer that forces prospective workers to promise they will not join a union after employment.

Zero-based budgeting (ZBB) A budgeting procedure popularized by former President Carter that forces an agency or department to reevaluate its existing programs and performance. According to this procedure, agencies must specify alternative levels of service and rank their highest priorities.

Zoning The use of city laws to classify land uses and assign land to certain uses—for example, residential, commercial, or industrial.

About the Authors

James MacGregor Burns

James MacGregor Burns, a native and lifelong resident of Massachusetts, is Woodrow Wilson Professor of Political Science at Williams College, where he has taught for the past forty years. He has written several books, including *The Power to Lead* (1984); *The Vineyard of Liberty* (1982); *Leadership* (1979); *The Deadlock of Democracy: Four Party Politics in America* (1963); *Roosevelt: The Lion and The Fox* (1956); and *Roosevelt: The Soldier of Freedom* (1970). His most recent book is *The Workshop of Democracy* (1985). Active in professional and civic life, Burns is a past president of the American Political Science Association and a former congressional candidate. He is currently serving as cochair of Project '87, a scholarly effort to promote a serious commemoration of the Constitutional Bicentennial. Although his major love is writing (for which he has won numerous prizes, including the Pulitizer Prize and the National Book Award), he can sometimes be found chopping wood, running, skiing, or playing tennis in his own cherished Berkshire community of Williamstown.

J. W. Peltason

J. W. Peltason is one of the country's leading scholars on courts, judicial process and public law. Educated at the University of Missouri and Princeton University, he has taught political science at Princeton, Midwestern University, Smith College, and the University of Illinois. He is at present Chancellor and Professor of Political Science at University of California, Irvine; he is Chancellor Emeritus of the University of Illinois, Urbana-Champaign, and was president of the American Council on Education in Washington, D.C. He has represented higher education before Congress and state legislatures, and his writings include *Federal Courts in the Political Process* (1955); *Fifty-Eight Lonely Men: Southern Federal Judges and School Desegregation* (1961); and *Understanding the Constitution* (1985). Among his awards are the James Madison Medal from Princeton University (1982) and the American Political Science Association's Charles E. Merriam award in 1983 to "the person whose published work and career represents a significant contribution to the art of government. . . ." He is a member of the American Academy of Arts and Sciences.

Thomas E. Cronin

Tom Cronin is a leading student of the American presidency and national leadership and policymaking processes. He earned his PhD from Stanford University and served as a White House Fellow and White House staff aide. Cronin was the 1986 recipient of the American Political Science Association's Charles E. Merriam Award for "significant contribution to the art of government." Cronin's writings include *The State of the Presidency* (1980); *U.S. v. Crime-in-the-Streets* (1981); *Rethinking the Presidency* (1982) and he is contributing author to a score of books including *Election '84; Classic Readings in American Government; Classics of the American Presidency;* and *This Constitution.* Cronin has served on the staff of The Brookings Institution and was Visiting Professor of Politics at Princeton University (1985–86). He is currently the McHugh Distinguished Professor of American Institutions and Leadership at The Colorado College. A former candidate for the U.S. Congress and President of the Presidency Research Group, Cronin has lectured at over 200 colleges and universities. He has appeared as a political analyst on *Nightline, Late Night America, The Today Show,* C-SPAN, CNN and several PBS and network documentaries.

Index

WASHINGTON
Centers of Decision and Landmarks

Massachusetts Ave.

F St.

Embassy
Row Area

← Vice President's
Residence
(About 2 miles)

Home of many of the major Washington law firms
and interest group national headquarters

Pennsylvania Ave.

18th St.

Virginia Ave.

Seventeenth St.

Constitution Ave.

Fifteenth St.

← Dulles Airport
(About 25 miles)

Theodore Roosevelt
Memorial Bridge

Arlington Memorial
Bridge

1 Congress	12 Dept. of Health & Human Services	21 Republican National Committee	33 Internal Revenue Service
2 The White House		22 Congressional Budget Office	34 Museum of History and Tech
3 Supreme Court	13 Dept. of Housing and Urban Development	23 Food and Drug Administration	35 Washington Monument
4 Dept. of State		24 National Air and Space Museum	36 Interstate Commerce Commis
5 Dept. of Treasury	14 Dept. of Transportation	25 Smithsonian Institute	37 U.S. Postal Service
6 Dept. of Defense	15 Dept. of Energy	26 GSA Regional Office	38 FBI—Hoover Building
7 Dept. of Interior	16 Dept. of Education	27 Bureau of Engraving & Printing	39 General Accounting Office
8 Dept. of Justice	17 Senate Office Buildings	28 Jefferson Memorial	40 National Press Club
9 Dept. of Agriculture	18 Hall of States	29 Union Station (Railroad)	41 The Ellipse
10 Dept. of Commerce	19 Library of Congress Congressional Research Service	30 National Art Gallery Bldgs.	42 Executive Office of the Presi
11 Dept. of Labor		31 Federal Trade Commission	Office of Management and Budget
	20 House Office Buildings	32 Museum of Natural History	Council of Economic Advisers National Security Council